Creditors' Rights and Bankruptcy

CHAPTER 29

Creditors' Rights and Remedies

Normally, creditors have no problem collecting the debts owed to them. When disputes arise over the amount owed, however, or when the debtor simply cannot or will not pay, what happens? What remedies are available to creditors when a debtor **defaults** (fails to pay as promised)? In this chapter, we focus on some basic laws that assist the debtor and creditor in resolving their dispute without resorting to bankruptcy.

The remedies we discuss in this chapter are available regardless of whether a creditor is secured or unsecured. *Secured creditors* are those whose loans are backed by *collateral,* which is specific property (such as a car or a house) pledged by a borrower to ensure repayment. The loans made by *unsecured creditors,* such as companies that provide credit cards, are not backed by collateral. Under Article 9 of the Uniform Commercial Code (UCC), certain remedies are available only to secured creditors.

29–1 Laws Assisting Creditors

Both the common law and statutory laws other than Article 9 of the UCC create various rights and remedies for creditors. Next, we discuss some of these rights and remedies, including liens, garnishment, and creditors' composition agreements.

29–1a Liens

A **lien** is an encumbrance on (claim against) property to satisfy a debt or protect a claim for the payment of a debt. Liens may arise under the common law (usually by possession of the property) or under statutory law. *Mechanic's liens* are statutory liens, whereas *artisan's liens* were recognized at common law. *Judicial liens* may be used by a creditor to collect on a debt before or after a judgment is entered by a court. Liens are a very important tool for creditors because they generally take priority over other claims against the same property.

Mechanic's Liens Sometimes, a person who has contracted for labor, services, or materials to be furnished for making improvements on real property does not immediately pay for the improvements. When that happens, the creditor can place a **mechanic's lien** on the property.

Real Property Secures the Debt. A mechanic's lien creates a special type of debtor-creditor relationship in which the real estate itself becomes security for the debt. ■ **EXAMPLE 29.1** Kirk contracts to paint Tanya's house for an agreed-on price to cover labor and materials. If Tanya refuses to pay or pays only a portion of the charges after the work is completed, a mechanic's lien against the property can be created. Kirk is then a lienholder, and the real property is encumbered (burdened) with the mechanic's lien for the amount owed. ■

If the property owner fails to pay the debt, the lienholder is technically entitled to foreclose on the real estate and sell it. (*Foreclosure* is the process by which a creditor legally takes a debtor's property to satisfy a debt.) The sale proceeds are then used to pay the debt and the costs of the legal proceedings. The surplus, if any, is paid to the former owner.

In the real world, however, small-amount mechanic's liens are rarely the basis of foreclosure. Rather, these liens simply remain on the books of the state until the house is sold. At closing (when the sale is finalized), the seller agrees to pay any mechanic's liens out of the proceeds of the sale before the seller receives any of the funds.

Governed by State Law. State law governs the procedures that must be followed to create a mechanic's (or other statutory) lien. Generally, the lienholder must file a written notice of lien within a specific time period (usually within 60 to 120 days) from the last date that material or labor was provided.

In the following case, the state mechanic's lien statute required the lien to be filed no more than 90 days after "the completion of the work." The contractor that filed the lien and the owner of the project against which the lien was filed disputed the meaning of the term "completion."

Case Analysis 29.1

Picerne Construction Corp. v. Villas

California Court of Appeal, Third District, 244 Cal.App.4th 1201, 199 Cal.Rptr.3d 257 (2016).

In the Language of the Court
MAURO, J. [Judge]

* * * *

Castellino [Villas, LLC] and Picerne [Construction Corporation] entered into an agreement in which Picerne would build an apartment complex called Castellino Villas at Laguna West (project or property) in the City of Elk Grove [California] (the City). The project consisted of 11 apartment buildings, separate garages, a clubhouse, and other facilities.

* * * *

The City issued certificates of occupancy for the 11 buildings within the project * * * after a city inspector conducted a final inspection of each building. The first certificates of occupancy were issued on May 3, 2006. The final certificate of occupancy was issued on July 25, 2006.

Picerne employees and subcontractors continued to perform work at the project after July 25, 2006.

* * * *

[John] Olsen [Castellino's representative for the project] signed a document titled "Owner's Acceptance of Site" for Castellino on September 8, 2006.

* * * *

Castellino began renting apartments at the property in October 2006.

Picerne recorded a claim of mechanic's lien on November 28, 2006.

Picerne filed a complaint [in a California state court] to foreclose its mechanic's lien on December 29, 2006.

* * * *

* * * The trial court * * * determined * * * Picerne is entitled to foreclose its lien.

* * * *

[On appeal to this court] Castellino * * * contends Picerne does not have a valid mechanic's lien because Picerne did not record a claim of mechanic's lien within 90 days after substantial completion of the project.

* * * *

In order to have a valid mechanic's lien, a claimant must record a claim of lien within a prescribed period of time after completion of the work of improvement * * *. *The failure of a claimant to timely record a claim of lien precludes the enforcement of a mechanic's lien.* [Emphasis added.]

[When Picerne filed its lien, mechanic's liens were governed by California Civil Code Section 3115, which] provided, "Each original contractor [a contractor who has a direct contractual relationship with the owner for the work], in order to enforce a lien, must record his claim of lien after he completes his contract and before the expiration of 90 days after the completion of the work of improvement." [According to Section 3116, the term "work of improvement" means the entire structure or scheme of improvement as a whole.]

* * * The [California State] Legislature defined the term completion as "actual completion of the work of improvement." In addition, * * * deemed to be equivalent to a completion [was] the acceptance by the owner or his agent of the work of improvement.

Substantial evidence supports the trial court's finding that the owner accepted the project as of September 8, 2006. * * * Picerne timely recorded its claim of mechanic's lien within 90 days after September 8, 2006.

* * * *

Castellino * * * nevertheless claims that the time for Picerne to record its claim of mechanic's lien began to run before September 8, 2006. [Castellino] asserts the phrase "completion of the work of improvement" in Section 3115 means substantial completion of the work of improvement, and the project was substantially completed by July 25, 2006, when the City issued the final certificate of occupancy.

There are cases construing the * * * mechanic's lien statute which interpreted "completion" as substantial completion.

* * * *

[But these cases were decided before the Legislature amended Section 3115 to define] completion of the work of improvement as actual completion of the work of improvement * * *. The Legislature did not define "completion of the work of improvement" as substantial completion. Courts have looked at whether the work at issue was required under the claimant's contract in determining whether a work of improvement was completed.

Castellino argues that interpreting the term "completion" * * * to mean substantial completion would be sound

Case 29.1 Continues

Case 29.1 Continued

public policy because it would ensure transparency, visibility, objectivity, and certainty in the relationship between the contractor and the owner in the filing of mechanic's liens. However, following the language of the statute by construing "completion" as "actual completion" does not create uncertainty when reference can be made to the parties' agreement and the labor and materials furnished. Moreover, * * * deemed equivalent to completion [is] acceptance of the work of improvement.

In addition, contrary to Castellino's argument, public policy supports the interpretation of completion as actual completion in this specific context. *The mechanic's lien statute is intended [primarily to benefit] persons who perform labor or furnish materials for works of improvement, and it is to be liberally construed for the protection of laborers and material suppliers, with doubts concerning the meaning of the statute generally resolved in favor of the lien claimant.* Interpreting completion as actual completion gives lien claimants the maximum amount of time

to assert their rights before such rights are cut off, whereas interpreting completion as substantial completion could cut off mechanic's lien rights much earlier. The interpretation espoused by Castellino would contravene the purpose of California's mechanic's lien law to protect the right to payment of those who have furnished labor or materials to works of improvement. Our construction of the term "completion" * * * effectuates the intent of the mechanic's lien law. [Emphasis added.]

Substantial evidence supports the trial court's findings that even though the City had issued certificates of occupancy for the 11 buildings within the project, roof and stairway work required under the general contract continued between July 25, 2006 and September 19, 2006. Elizar Ortiz [an installer employed by Picerne's stairway subcontractor] testified he worked 22½ hours on September 15, 18, and 19, 2006, installing grip tape on all of the stairs at the project. The general contract called for the installation of anti-slip grip tape

on all concrete stair treads. Ortiz's testimony established the work he performed on September 15, 18, and 19, 2006 was not corrective or repair work.

The president of Picerne's roofing subcontractor testified his company performed roofing work at the project after July 25, 2006. He said such work included straightening out some of the valleys in the roofs, installing nailers and hips on the roof ridges, and nailing trim. * * * The roof and stairway work performed after July 25, 2006, is not comparable to adding a few strokes of paint or turning a screw.

Picerne recorded a claim of mechanic's lien * * * within 90 days of the date Castellino accepted the project and when the stairway and roofing subcontractors performed work required under their contracts. Accordingly, the trial court did not err in concluding Picerne timely recorded its claim of mechanic's lien.

* * * *

* * * The judgment is affirmed.

Legal Reasoning Questions

1. How did the California legislature define the term "completion"? Was this definition clear? Discuss.

2. How did the owner of the project at the center of this case want the court to interpret "completion"? What arguments support this contention?

3. Ultimately, how did the court define "completion"? Why?

Artisan's Liens When a debtor fails to pay for labor and materials furnished for the repair or improvement of *personal* property, a creditor can recover payment through an **artisan's lien.** As mentioned, artisan's liens usually take priority over other creditors' claims to the same property.[1]

Lienholder Must Retain Possession. In contrast to a mechanic's lien, an artisan's lien is *possessory.* That is, the lienholder ordinarily must have retained possession of the property and have expressly or impliedly agreed to provide the services on a cash, not a credit, basis. The lien remains

in existence as long as the lienholder maintains possession, and the lien is terminated once possession is *voluntarily* surrendered, unless the surrender is only temporary.[2]

■ **CASE IN POINT 29.2** Carrollton Exempted Village School District (in Ohio) hired Clean Vehicle Solutions America, LLC (CVSA, based in New York) to convert ten school buses from diesel to compressed natural gas. The contract price was $660,000. The district paid a $400,000 deposit and agreed to pay installments of $26,000 to CVSA after the delivery of each converted bus. After the first two buses were delivered, the district

---

1. An artisan's lien has priority over a filed statutory lien (such as a title lien on an automobile or a lien filed under Article 9 of the UCC) and a bailee's lien (such as a storage lien).

2. Involuntary surrender of possession by a lienholder, such as when a police officer seizes goods from a lienholder, does not terminate the lien.

refused to continue the contract, claiming that the conversion made the two buses unsafe to drive.

Both parties filed breach of contract lawsuits. CVSA also asserted an artisan's lien over two other buses that it still had in its possession because it had started converting them to natural gas and spent $65,000 doing so. Regardless of the outcome in the parties' lawsuits, CVSA has an artisan's lien that gives it a priority claim to those two buses so long as they remain in its possession. The buses will act as security for the district's payment of at least the amount CVSA has spent converting them to natural gas.[3] ∎

Foreclosure on Personal Property. Modern statutes permit the holder of an artisan's lien to foreclose and sell the property subject to the lien to satisfy the debt. As with a mechanic's lien, the lienholder is required to give notice to the owner of the property before the foreclosure and sale. The sale proceeds are used to pay the debt and the costs of the legal proceedings, and the surplus, if any, is paid to the former owner.

Judicial Liens When a debt is past due, a creditor can bring a legal action against the debtor to collect the debt. If the action is successful, the court awards the creditor a judgment against the debtor (usually for the amount of the debt plus any interest and legal costs incurred). Frequently, however, the creditor is unable to collect the awarded amount.

To ensure that a judgment in the creditor's favor will be collectible, the creditor may request that certain property of the debtor be seized to satisfy the debt. (As will be discussed, under state or federal statutes, some kinds of property are exempt from attachment by creditors.) A court's order to seize the debtor's property is known as a *writ of attachment* if it is issued before a judgment. If the order is issued after a judgment, it is referred to as a *writ of execution.*

Writ of Attachment. In the context of judicial liens, **attachment** refers to a court-ordered seizure and taking into custody of property before a judgment is obtained on a past-due debt. (Attachment has a different meaning in the context of secured transactions.[4]) Because attachment is a *prejudgment* remedy, it occurs either at the time a lawsuit is filed or immediately afterward.

A creditor must comply with the specific state's statutory restrictions and requirements. The due process clause of the Fourteenth Amendment to the U.S. Constitution requires that the debtor be given notice and an opportunity to be heard. The creditor must have an enforceable right to payment of the debt under law and must follow certain procedures. Otherwise, the creditor can be liable for damages for wrongful attachment.

The typical procedure for attachment is as follows:

1. The creditor files with the court an *affidavit* (a written statement, made under oath). The affidavit states that the debtor has failed to pay and indicates the statutory grounds under which attachment is sought.
2. The creditor must post a bond to cover at least the court costs, the value of the property attached, and the value of the loss of use of that property suffered by the debtor.
3. When the court is satisfied that all the requirements have been met, it issues a **writ of attachment.** The writ directs the sheriff or other officer to seize the debtor's nonexempt property. If the creditor prevails at trial, the seized property can be sold to satisfy the judgment.

Writ of Execution. If a creditor wins a judgment against a debtor and the debtor will not or cannot pay the amount due, the creditor can request a **writ of execution** from the court. A writ of execution is an order that directs the sheriff to seize (levy) and sell any of the debtor's nonexempt real or personal property. The writ applies only to property that is within the court's geographic jurisdiction (usually the county in which the courthouse is located).

The proceeds of the sale are used to pay the judgment, accrued interest, and costs of the sale. Any excess is paid to the debtor. The debtor can pay the judgment and redeem the nonexempt property at any time before the sale takes place. (Because of exemption laws and bankruptcy laws, however, many judgments are practically uncollectible.)

29–1b Garnishment

An order for **garnishment** permits a creditor to collect a debt by seizing property of the debtor that is being held by a third party. As a result of a garnishment proceeding, for instance, the debtor's employer may be ordered by the court to turn over a portion of the debtor's wages to pay the debt. Many other types of property can be garnished as well, including funds in a bank account, tax refunds, pensions, and trust funds. It is only necessary that the property is not exempt from garnishment and is in the possession of a third party.

---

3. *Clean Vehicle Solutions America, LLC v. Carrollton Exempted Village School District Board of Education*, 2015 WL 5459852 (S.D.N.Y. 2015).
4. In secured transactions, *attachment* refers to the process through which a security interest becomes effective and enforceable against a debtor with respect to the debtor's collateral [UCC 9–203].

■ **CASE IN POINT 29.3**   When Edward G. Tinsley divorced Michelle Townsend, they entered into a marital settlement contract. They agreed to sell the marital home and split the proceeds evenly. But Tinsley refused to cooperate with the sale. A court therefore appointed a trustee to sell the house for them and ordered the sheriff to evict Tinsley. Tinsley then conveyed the house to a trust established in his name. Even after the sheriff evicted Tinsley from the house and changed the locks, Tinsley managed to move back in and change the locks again.

Tinsley was arrested for trespassing and charged with contempt of court (for disobeying court orders). In the meantime, Tinsley secretly sold the home for $150,000 and deposited the proceeds into a bank account held in the name of Edward G. Tinsley Living Trust at SunTrust Bank. After learning of the sale, the court-appointed trustee obtained a writ of garnishment on all of Tinsley's and his trust's bank accounts at SunTrust Bank. Despite numerous objections from Tinsley (and a trial and appeal), Sun Trust eventually complied with the garnishment order and sent all the funds to the trustee.[5] ■

Procedures   Garnishment can be a prejudgment remedy, requiring a hearing before a court, but it is most often a postjudgment remedy. State law governs garnishment actions, so the specific procedures vary from state to state.

In some states, the judgment creditor needs to obtain only one order of garnishment, which will then apply continuously to the judgment debtor's wages until the entire debt is paid. In other states, the judgment creditor must go back to court for a separate order of garnishment for each pay period.

See this chapter's *Ethics Today* feature for a discussion of how creditors can obtain garnishment even when a debtor crosses state lines in an attempt to avoid paying the debt.

Laws Limiting the Amount of Wages Subject to Garnishment   Both federal and state laws limit the amount that can be taken from a debtor's weekly take-home pay through garnishment proceedings.[6] Federal law provides a minimal framework to protect debtors from losing all their income to pay judgment debts.[7] State laws also provide dollar exemptions, and these amounts are often larger than those provided by federal law.

Under federal law, an employer cannot dismiss an employee because his or her wages are being garnished.

29–1c Creditors' Composition Agreements

Creditors may contract with the debtor for discharge of the debtor's liquidated debts (debts that are definite, or fixed, in amount) on payment of a sum less than that owed. These agreements are referred to as **creditors' composition agreements** (or *composition agreements*) and usually are held to be enforceable unless they are formed under duress.

29–2 Mortgages

When individuals purchase real property, they typically make a **down payment** in cash and borrow the remaining funds from a financial institution. The borrowed funds are secured by a **mortgage**—a written instrument that gives the creditor a lien on the debtor's real property as security for payment of a debt. The creditor is the *mortgagee,* and the debtor is the *mortgagor.*

29–2a Fixed-Rate versus Adjustable-Rate Mortgages

Lenders offer various types of mortgages to meet the needs of different borrowers, but a basic distinction is whether the interest rate is fixed or variable. A *fixed-rate mortgage* has a fixed, or unchanging, rate of interest, so the payments remain the same for the duration of the loan. Lenders determine the interest rate for a standard fixed-rate mortgage loan based on a variety of factors, including the borrower's credit history, credit score, income, and debts.

With an *adjustable-rate mortgage (ARM),* the rate of interest paid by the borrower changes periodically. Typically, the initial interest rate for an ARM is set at a relatively low fixed rate for a specified period, such as a year or three years. After that time, the interest rate adjusts annually or by some other period, such as biannually or monthly. The interest rate adjustment is calculated by adding a certain number of percentage points (called the margin) to an index rate (one of various government interest rates).

ARMs contractually shift the risk that the interest rate will change from the lender to the borrower. Borrowers will have lower initial payments if they are willing to assume the risk of interest rate increases.

---

5. *Tinsley v. SunTrust Bank*, 2016 WL 687545 (Md.App. 2016).

6. A few states (such as Texas) do not permit garnishment of wages by private parties except under a child-support order.

7. For instance, the federal Consumer Credit Protection Act, 15 U.S.C. Sections 1601–1693r, provides that a debtor can retain either 75 percent of his or her disposable earnings per week or an amount equivalent to thirty hours of work paid at federal minimum wage rates, whichever is greater.

ETHICS TODAY   Creditors' Rights When Debtors Move to Another State

Creditors have rights when debtors default. The former often go to court and win judgments against the latter. But what can creditors do when judgment debtors simply "pack up and leave"? That is to say, when debtors engage in the ethically suspect action of crossing state lines to avoid judgments, is there recourse for creditors?

order affirming that the foreign judgment has been domesticated.

The equivalent at the federal level involves registering judgments between federal courts.[d] Unlike state court domestication procedures, federal court domestication procedures do not require that notice be given to the judgment debtor.

Full Faith and Credit

The Constitution of the United States provides that full faith and credit shall be given in each state to the public acts, records, and judicial proceedings of every other state.[a] Among other things, this means that judgments made in one state will be honored in other states. Fortunately for creditors, there is a long judicial history of the application of judgments to debtors who have moved to another state.[b]

The Uniform Enforcement of Foreign Judgments Act

Most states have adopted the Uniform Enforcement of Foreign Judgments Act.[c] The act allows judgments obtained in one jurisdiction (such as a state) to be "domesticated" (recognized and enforced) in a different jurisdiction (such as another state). One goal is to prevent judgment debtors from evading payment of their obligations by relocating to another state.

In most states, domestication of a foreign judgment can be accomplished rapidly. The judgment creditor files an authenticated copy of the judgment in the "foreign" state, along with an affidavit and a notice of foreign judgment. The notice of domestication action then is provided to the debtor. A local court enters an

Time Is of the Essence

Once domestication of a foreign judgment has occurred, judgment creditors must record the domestication order with the proper authorities within the jurisdiction to put others on notice. Thus, if real property is involved, a title search will show the foreign judgment against the debtor who has an ownership interest in the real property.

All states have specific lifespans (statutes of limitations) for foreign judgments. Often, a judgment debtor will attempt to counter a foreign judgment by claiming that the lifespan of the foreign judgment had lapsed.[e] Domestications of foreign judgments can be renewed, however.

Garnishment Actions

When a judgment debtor moves to another state, one method of obtaining repayment for debts owed is through the process of garnishment. The benefit for the creditor in such cases is that judgment debtors are often surprised when their bank accounts are frozen or their regular salaries are reduced. Garnishments are typically served against a bank, which then has to freeze any accounts belonging the debtor.

Critical Thinking *Is it fair that property or wage garnishments may "surprise" a judgment debtor?*

a. U.S. Const., Art. IV, Section 1.
b. See, for example, *Aultman, Miller & Co. v. Mills*, 9 Wash. 68, 36 P.1046 (Wash. S. Ct. 1894).
c. Originally issued by the National Conference of Commissioners on Uniform State Laws (NCCUSL) in 1948. Revised in 1964.

d. 28 U.S.C. Section 1963.
e. See, for instance, *Independent Bank v. Pandy*, __ P.3d __, 2015 WL 188988 (Colo.App. 2015).

29–2b Mortgage Provisions

Because a mortgage involves a transfer of real property, it must be in writing to comply with the Statute of Frauds. Mortgages normally are lengthy and formal documents containing many provisions, including the following:

1. *The terms of the underlying loan.* These include the loan amount, the interest rate, the period of repayment, and other important financial terms, such as the margin and index rate for an ARM.

2. *A prepayment penalty clause.* A **prepayment penalty clause** requires the borrower to pay a penalty if the mortgage is repaid in full within a certain period. A prepayment penalty helps to protect the lender should the borrower refinance within a short time after obtaining a mortgage.

3. *Provisions relating to the maintenance of the property.* Because the mortgage conveys an interest in the property to the lender, the lender often requires the

borrower to maintain the property to protect the lender's investment.

4. *A statement obligating the borrower to maintain homeowner's insurance on the property.* **Homeowner's insurance** protects the lender's interest in the event of a loss due to certain hazards, such as fire or storm damage.

5. *A list of the non-loan financial obligations to be borne by the borrower.* For instance, the borrower typically is required to pay all property taxes, assessments, and other claims against the property.

6. *Creditor protections.* When creditors extend mortgages, they are advancing a significant amount of funds for a number of years. Consequently, creditors usually require debtors to obtain **mortgage insurance** if they do not make a down payment of at least 20 percent of the purchase price.

Creditors record the mortgage with the appropriate office in the county where the property is located, so that their interest in the property is officially on record.

29–2c Mortgage Foreclosure

If the homeowner *defaults,* or fails to make the mortgage payments, the lender has the right to foreclose on the mortgaged property. **Foreclosure** is the legal process by which the lender repossesses and auctions off the property that has secured the loan.

Foreclosure is expensive and time consuming. It generally benefits neither the borrowers, who lose their homes, nor the lenders, which face the prospect of losses on their loans. Therefore, both lenders and borrowers are motivated to avoid foreclosure proceedings if possible.

Ways to Avoid Foreclosure Possible methods of avoiding foreclosure include forbearance, workout agreements, and short sales (see Exhibit 29–1).

A **forbearance** is a postponement of part or all of the payments on a loan for a limited time. This option works well when the debtor can solve the problem by securing a new job, selling the property, or finding another acceptable solution.

EXHIBIT 29–1 Methods of Avoiding Foreclosure

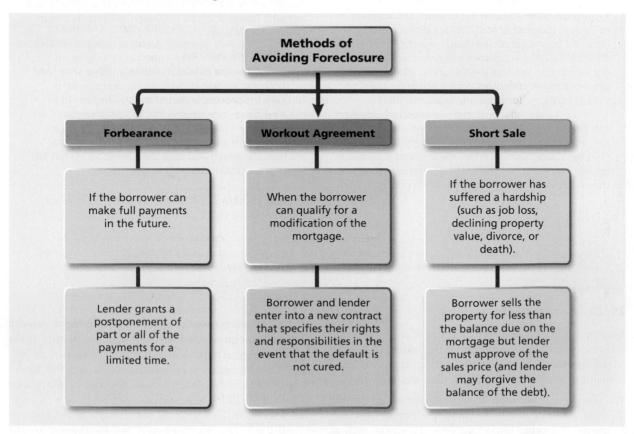

A **workout agreement** is a contract that describes the respective rights and responsibilities of the borrower and the lender as they try to resolve the default. Usually, the lender agrees to delay seeking foreclosure. In exchange, the borrower provides additional financial information that might be used to modify the mortgage.

A lender may sometimes agree to a **short sale,** which is a sale of the property for less than the balance due on the mortgage loan. Typically, the borrower has to show some hardship, such as the loss of a job, a decline in the value of the home, a divorce, or a death in the household. The lender often has approval rights in a short sale, so the sale process may take much longer than an ordinary real estate transaction.

Foreclosure Procedure If all efforts to find another solution fail, the lender will proceed to foreclosure. The lender must strictly comply with the state statute governing foreclosures. Many problems arose in the last ten years because lenders, facing a record number of foreclosures during the recent recession, had difficulty complying with the required statutory formalities.

To bring a foreclosure action, a bank must have standing to sue. In the following case, the court had to decide whether a bank could foreclose a mortgage even though the bank could not prove when it became the owner of the borrower's promissory note.

Spotlight on Foreclosures

Case 29.2 McLean v. JPMorgan Chase Bank, N.A.

District Court of Appeal of Florida, Fourth District, 79 So.3d 170 (2012).

Background and Facts On May 11, 2009, JPMorgan Chase Bank (Chase) filed a foreclosure action against Robert McLean. The complaint alleged that Chase was entitled to enforce the mortgage and promissory note on which McLean had defaulted. Nevertheless, the attached mortgage identified a different mortgagee and lender, and Chase claimed that the note had been "lost, stolen, or destroyed." When McLean filed a motion to dismiss, Chase produced a mortgage assignment dated May 14, 2009, which was three days after it had filed the lawsuit. Eventually, Chase also filed the original note. Although the indorsement to Chase was undated, Chase then filed a motion for summary judgment. The trial court granted Chase's motion even though the accompanying affidavit failed to show that Chase had owned the mortgage or note when it filed the complaint. McLean appealed.

In the Language of the Court

PER CURIAM [By the Whole Court].

* * * *

A crucial element in any mortgage foreclosure proceeding is that the party seeking foreclosure must demonstrate that it has standing to foreclose.

* * * *

* * * A party's standing is determined at the time the lawsuit was filed. Stated another way, *"the plaintiff's lack of standing at the inception of the case is not a defect that may be cured by the acquisition of standing after the case is filed." Thus, a party is not permitted to establish the right to maintain an action retroactively by acquiring standing to file a lawsuit after the fact.* [Emphasis added.]

* * * *

In the present case, as is common in recent foreclosure cases, Chase did not attach a copy of the original note to its complaint, but instead [filed a claim] to re-establish a lost note. Later, however, Chase filed * * * the original promissory note, which bore a special endorsement in favor of Chase. [Thus,] * * * it obtained standing to foreclose, at least at some point.

Nonetheless, the record evidence is insufficient to demonstrate that Chase had standing to foreclose *at the time the lawsuit was filed.* [Emphasis in original.] The mortgage was assigned to Chase three days after Chase filed the instant foreclosure complaint. While the original note contained an undated special endorsement in Chase's favor, the affidavit filed in support of summary judgment did not state when the endorsement was made to Chase. Furthermore, the affidavit, which was dated after the

Case 29.2 Continues

Case 29.2 Continued lawsuit was filed, did not specifically state when Chase became the owner of the note, nor did the affidavit indicate that Chase was the owner of the note before suit was filed.

We therefore reverse the summary judgment and corresponding final judgment of foreclosure. On remand, in order for Chase to be entitled to summary judgment, it must show * * * that it was the holder of the note on the date the complaint was filed (that the note was endorsed to Chase on or before the date the lawsuit was filed). By contrast, if the evidence shows that the note was endorsed to Chase after the lawsuit was filed, then Chase had no standing at the time the complaint was filed, in which case the trial court should dismiss the instant lawsuit and Chase must file a new complaint.

Decision and Remedy *The Florida appellate court held that Chase had not proved that it had standing to foreclose against McLean. The court therefore reversed the trial court's grant of summary judgment.*

Critical Thinking

- **Legal Environment** *If Chase cannot prove that it owned the note at the time of its complaint, what will happen next? Will Chase prevail? Why or why not?*

Redemption Rights Every state allows a defaulting borrower to redeem the property before the foreclosure sale by paying the full amount of the debt, plus any interest and costs that have accrued. This **equitable right of redemption** gives the defaulting buyer a chance to regain title and possession after default.

The *statutory right of redemption,* in contrast, entitles the borrower to repurchase property *after* a judicial foreclosure. In other words, in states that provide for statutory redemption, the homeowner has a right to buy the property back from a third party who bought it at a foreclosure sale. Generally, the borrower may exercise this right for up to one year from the time the house is sold at a foreclosure sale.[8] The borrower may retain possession of the property after the foreclosure sale until the statutory redemption period ends. If the borrower does not exercise the right of redemption, the new buyer receives title to and possession of the property.

Concept Summary 29.1 provides a synopsis of the remedies available to creditors.

29–3 Suretyship and Guaranty

When a third person promises to pay a debt owed by another in the event that the debtor does not pay, either a *suretyship* or a *guaranty* relationship is created. Exhibit 29–2 illustrates these relationships. The third person's creditworthiness becomes the security for the debt owed.

Suretyship and guaranty provide creditors with the right to seek payment from the third party if the primary debtor, or *principal,* defaults on her or his obligations. Normally a guaranty must be in writing to be enforceable under the Statute of Frauds, unless its main purpose is to benefit the guarantor. Traditionally, a suretyship agreement did not require a writing to be enforceable, and oral surety agreements were sufficient. Today, however, some states require a writing to enforce a suretyship.

At common law, there were significant differences in the liability of a surety and a guarantor. Today, however, the distinctions outlined here have been abolished in some states.

29–3a Suretyship

A contract of strict **suretyship** is a promise made by a third person to be responsible for the debtor's obligation. It is an express contract between the **surety** (the third party) and the creditor.

In the strictest sense, the surety is primarily liable for the debt of the principal. The creditor can demand payment from the surety from the moment the debt is due. The creditor need not exhaust all legal remedies against the principal debtor before holding the surety responsible for payment.

■ **EXAMPLE 29.4** Roberto Delmar wants to borrow from the bank to buy a used car. Because Roberto is still in college, the bank will not lend him the funds without a cosigner. Roberto's father, José Delmar, who has dealt with the bank before, agrees to cosign the note, thereby becoming a surety who is jointly liable for payment of the debt. When José Delmar cosigns the note, he becomes primarily liable to the bank. On the note's due

---

8. Some states do not allow a borrower to waive the statutory right of redemption. This means that a buyer at auction must wait one year to obtain title to, and possession of, a foreclosed property.

Concept Summary 29.1

Remedies Available to Creditors

Liens
- *Mechanic's lien*—A lien placed on an owner's real estate for labor, services, or materials furnished for improvements made to the realty (real property).
- *Artisan's lien*—A lien placed on an owner's personal property for labor performed or value added to that property.
- *Judicial liens*—Including the following:
  a. Writ of attachment: A court-ordered seizure of property prior to a court's final determination of the creditor's rights to the property. Creditors must strictly comply with applicable state statutes to obtain a writ of attachment.
  b. Writ of execution: A court order directing the sheriff to seize (levy) and sell a debtor's nonexempt real or personal property to satisfy a court's judgment in the creditor's favor.

Garnishment
- A collection remedy that allows the creditor to attach a debtor's funds—such as wages owed or bank accounts—and property that are held by a third person.

Creditors' Composition Agreement
- A contract between a debtor and her or his creditors by which the debtor's debts are discharged by payment of a sum less than the amount that is actually owed.

Mortgage Foreclosure
- On the debtor's default, the entire mortgage debt is due and payable, allowing the creditor to foreclose on the realty by selling it to satisfy the debt.

EXHIBIT 29–2 Suretyship and Guaranty Parties

In a suretyship or guaranty arrangement, a third party promises to be responsible for a debtor's obligations. A third party who agrees to be responsible for the debt even if the primary debtor does not default is known as a *surety*. A third party who agrees to be *secondarily* responsible for the debt—that is, responsible only if the primary debtor defaults—is known as a *guarantor*. Normally, a promise of guaranty (a collateral, or secondary, promise) must be in writing to be enforceable.

Principal Debtor

Creditor

Surety (Primary Liability to Creditor) or **Guarantor** (Secondary Liability to Creditor) date, the bank can seek payment from either Roberto or José Delmar, or both jointly. ■

29–3b Guaranty

With a suretyship arrangement, the surety is *primarily* liable for the debtor's obligation. With a guaranty arrangement, the **guarantor**—the third person making the guaranty—is *secondarily* liable.

The guarantor can be required to pay the obligation *only after the principal debtor defaults,* and usually only after the creditor has made an attempt to collect from the debtor. The guaranty contract terms determine the extent and time of the guarantor's liability.

■ **EXAMPLE 29.5**   BX Enterprises, a small corporation, needs to borrow funds to meet its payroll. BX's president is Dawson, a wealthy businessperson who owns 70 percent of the company. The bank is skeptical about the creditworthiness of BX and requires Dawson to sign an agreement making herself personally liable for payment if BX does not pay off the loan. As a guarantor of the loan, Dawson cannot be held liable until BX is in default. ■

The following case concerned a lender's attempt to recover on a loan guaranty.

Case 29.3

HSBC Realty Credit Corp. (USA) v. O'Neill

United States Court of Appeals, First Circuit, 745 F.3d 564 (2014).

Background and Facts   To finance a development project in Delaware, Brandywine Partners, LLC, borrowed $15.9 million from HSBC Realty Credit Corp. (USA). As part of the deal, Brian O'Neill, principal for Brandywine, signed a guaranty that designated him the "primary obligor" for $8.1 million of the loan. Brandywine defaulted, and HSBC filed a suit in a federal district court against O'Neill to recover on the guaranty. O'Neill filed a counterclaim, alleging fraud.

O'Neill based his fraud claim on two provisions in the loan agreement. The first provision expressed the loan-to-value ratio. O'Neill alleged that this clause valued the property at $26.5 million and that HSBC knew this was not the property's real value. The second provision stated that if Brandywine defaulted, HSBC could recover its loan by selling the property. According to O'Neill, this clause represented that HSBC would try to recover by selling the property before trying to collect from the guaranty.

The court granted HSBC's motion to dismiss O'Neill's counterclaim and issued a judgment in HSBC's favor. O'Neill appealed, still arguing that HSBC had fraudulently induced him to sign the guaranty.

In the Language of the Court

THOMPSON, Circuit Judge.
* * * *

O'Neill loudly protests that his fraudulent-inducement claim should have been enough to defeat HSBC's dismissal efforts. His theory rises or falls on his belief that two provisions in the project-loan agreement constitute false statements of material fact made to induce him to sign the guaranty and that he reasonably relied on those false statements to his detriment.

The first provision he points to involves the * * * loan-to-value ratio, which he alleges put the collateral property's value at $26.5 million and is an HSBC representation that the chance of its having to call the $8.1 million guaranty was basically zero. HSBC made that representation, he adds, even though HSBC—and not he—knew that this was not the property's real value.

The second project-loan-agreement provision he harps on provides that if Brandywine defaults, HSBC "can recover the obligations" by selling the property. He reads this contract language as an HSBC representation that it would move against the property before turning to his guaranty * * * . [But] we are unmoved. Merely to state the obvious, that proviso says that HSBC "can" proceed first against the property, not that it must do so.

Ultimately—and unhappily for O'Neill—we must enforce the guaranty according to its terms, with the parties' rights ascertained [determined] from the written text. * * * *Reliance on supposed misrepresentations that contradict the terms of the parties' agreement is unreasonable as a matter of law and so cannot support a fraudulent-inducement claim.* * * * The contract-inducing misrepresentations that O'Neill trumpets

Case 29.3 Continued are irreconcilably at odds with the guaranty's express terms. * * * O'Neill specifically warranted in the guaranty that he was familiar with the collateral property's value, that the property did not operate as an inducement for him to make the guaranty, and that HSBC said nothing to induce him to execute the guaranty—all of which destroys his fraudulent-inducement thesis centered on the project-loan agreement's loan-to-value-ratio provision. He also agreed with the guaranty's tagging him as the primary obligor and with its allowing HSBC to go after him first to recoup the debt—provisions that put the kibosh on [put an end to] his other suggestion that HSBC must first seek recourse against the property. [Emphasis added.]

* * * *

The net result of all this is that O'Neill's inducement-based arguments fail.

Decision and Remedy *The U.S. Court of Appeals for the First Circuit affirmed the lower court's judgment in favor of HSBC. The guaranty stated that O'Neill was familiar with the value of the property, that he was not relying on it as an inducement to sign the guaranty, and that HSBC made no representations to induce him to sign. The guaranty also provided that HSBC could enforce its rights against him without trying to recover on the property first.*

Critical Thinking

- **E-Commerce** *Do the principles applied to a written guaranty in this case also govern electronically recorded agreements and contracts entered into online? Why or why not?*
- **What If the Facts Were Different?** *Suppose that O'Neill had alleged a history of performance with HSBC that would have made his reliance on the complained-of representations reasonable. Could this have changed the result? Explain.*

29–3c Actions That Release the Surety and the Guarantor

Basically, the same actions will release either a surety or a guarantor from an obligation. For simplicity, this subsection and the following subsections will refer just to sureties, but remember that the same rules generally apply to guarantors.

1. *Material modification.* Making any material modification to the terms of the original contract without the surety's consent will discharge the surety's obligation. (The extent to which the surety is discharged depends on whether he or she was compensated and the amount of loss suffered from the modification. For instance, a father who receives no consideration for acting as a surety on his daughter's loan will be completely discharged if the loan contract is modified without his consent.)

2. *Surrender of property.* If a creditor surrenders the collateral to the debtor or impairs the collateral without the surety's consent, these acts can reduce the obligation of the surety. If the creditor's actions reduce the value of the property used as collateral, the surety is released to the extent of any loss suffered.

3. *Payment or tender of payment.* Naturally, any payment of the principal obligation by the debtor or by another person on the debtor's behalf will discharge the surety from the obligation. Even if the creditor refused to accept the payment when it was tendered, if the creditor knew about the suretyship, the obligation of the surety can be discharged.

29–3d Defenses of the Surety and the Guarantor

Generally, the surety or guarantor can also assert any of the defenses available to the principal debtor to avoid liability on the obligation to the creditor. A few exceptions do exist, however. They apply to both sureties and guarantors, but again, for simplicity, we refer just to sureties.

1. *Incapacity and bankruptcy.* Incapacity and bankruptcy are personal defenses, which can be asserted only by the person who is affected. Therefore, the surety cannot assert the principal debtor's incapacity or bankruptcy as a defense. (A surety may assert his or her own incapacity or bankruptcy as a defense, of course.)

2. *Statute of limitations.* The surety cannot assert the statute of limitations as a defense. (In contrast, the principal debtor can claim the statute of limitations as a defense to payment.)
3. *Fraud.* If the creditor fraudulently induced the person to act as a surety on the debt, the surety or guarantor can assert fraud as a defense. In most states, the creditor must inform the surety, before the formation of the suretyship contract, of material facts known by the creditor that would substantially increase the surety's risk. Failure to so inform may constitute fraud and render the suretyship obligation voidable.

29–3e Rights of the Surety and the Guarantor

When the surety or guarantor pays the debt owed to the creditor, he or she acquires certain rights, as discussed next. Again, for simplicity, the discussion refers just to sureties.

The Right of Subrogation The surety has the legal **right of subrogation.** Simply stated, this means that any right that the creditor had against the debtor now becomes the right of the surety. Included are creditor rights in bankruptcy, rights to collateral possessed by the creditor, and rights to judgments obtained by the creditor. In short, the surety now stands in the shoes of the creditor and may pursue any remedies that were available to the creditor against the debtor.

■ **CASE IN POINT 29.6** Guerrero Brothers, Inc. (GBI), contracted with the Public School System (PSS) to build a high school. Century Insurance Company (CIC) agreed to provide GBI with the required payment and performance bonds on the project. Thus, CIC acted as a surety of GBI's performance and promised to finish the project if GBI defaulted.

Four years after construction began, PSS canceled GBI's contract, and CIC fulfilled GBI's obligations by finishing construction of the school. Numerous disputes arose, and litigation ensued. Ultimately, PSS agreed to pay GBI $500,000 in contract funds. CIC then filed an action against GBI and PSS to recover the $867,000 it claimed PSS owed it for finishing the school. The court found that CIC, as a performing surety, was entitled to the remaining contract funds through the right of subrogation. It had performed GBI's obligations and therefore stepped into GBI's shoes and had the right to obtain payment from PSS.[9] ■

---

9. *Century Insurance Co. v. Guerrero Brothers, Inc.,* 2010 WL 997112 (N.Mariana Islands 2010).

The Right of Reimbursement The surety has a **right of reimbursement** from the debtor. Basically, the surety is entitled to receive from the debtor all outlays made on behalf of the suretyship arrangement. Such outlays can include expenses incurred as well as the actual amount of the debt paid to the creditor.

The Right of Contribution Two or more sureties are called **co-sureties.** When a co-surety pays more than her or his proportionate share on a debtor's default, she or he has a **right of contribution.** That means the co-surety is entitled to recover from the other co-sureties the amount paid above the surety's obligation. Generally, a co-surety's liability either is determined by agreement or, in the absence of agreement, is set at the maximum liability under the suretyship contract.

■ **EXAMPLE 29.7** Yasser and Itzhak, two co-sureties, are obligated under a suretyship contract to guarantee Jules's debt. Itzhak's maximum liability is $15,000, and Yasser's is $10,000. Jules owes $10,000 and is in default. Itzhak pays the creditor the entire $10,000.

In the absence of an agreement to the contrary, Itzhak can recover $4,000 from Yasser. The amount of the debt that Yasser agreed to cover ($10,000) is divided by the total amount that he and Itzhak together agreed to cover ($25,000). The result is multiplied by the amount of the default, yielding the amount that Yasser owes—($10,000 ÷ $25,000) × $10,000 = $4,000. ■

29–4 Protection for Debtors

The law protects debtors as well as creditors. Consumer protection statutes protect debtors' rights, for instance, and bankruptcy laws are designed specifically to assist debtors in need of help. In addition, in most states, certain types of real and personal property are exempt from execution or attachment. State exemption statutes usually include both real and personal property.

29–4a Exempted Real Property

Probably the most familiar exemption is the **homestead exemption.** The purpose of the homestead exemption is to ensure that the debtor will retain some form of shelter.

The General Rule Each state permits the debtor to retain the family home, either in its entirety or up to a specified dollar amount, free from the claims of unsecured creditors or trustees in bankruptcy. (Note that federal bankruptcy law places a cap on the amount that debtors filing bankruptcy can claim is exempt under their states' homestead exemption.)

■ **EXAMPLE 29.8** Vince Beere owes Chris Veltman $40,000. The debt is the subject of a lawsuit, and the court awards Veltman a judgment of $40,000 against Beere. Beere's homestead is valued at $50,000, and the homestead exemption is $25,000. There are no outstanding mortgages or other liens on his homestead. To satisfy the judgment debt, Beere's family home is sold at public auction for $45,000. The proceeds of the sale are distributed as follows:

1. Beere is given $25,000 as his homestead exemption.
2. Veltman is paid $20,000 toward the judgment debt, leaving a $20,000 deficiency judgment (that is, "leftover debt"). The deficiency judgment can be satisfied from any other nonexempt property (personal or real) that Beere may own, if permitted by state law. ■

Limitations In a few states, statutes allow the homestead exemption only if the judgment debtor has a family.

If a judgment debtor does not have a family, a creditor may be entitled to collect the full amount realized from the sale of the debtor's home. In addition, the homestead exemption interacts with other areas of law and can sometimes operate to cancel out a portion of a lien on a debtor's real property.

29–4b Exempted Personal Property

Personal property that is most often exempt from satisfaction of judgment debts includes the following:

1. Household furniture up to a specified dollar amount.
2. Clothing and certain personal possessions, such as family pictures or a Bible.
3. A vehicle (or vehicles) for transportation (at least up to a specified dollar amount).
4. Certain classified animals, usually livestock but including pets.
5. Equipment that the debtor uses in a business or trade, such as tools or professional instruments, up to a specified dollar amount.

Reviewing: Creditors' Rights and Remedies

Air Ruidoso, Ltd., operated a commuter airline and air charter service between Ruidoso, New Mexico, and airports in Albuquerque and El Paso. Executive Aviation Center, Inc., provided services for airlines at the Albuquerque International Airport. Air Ruidoso failed to pay more than $10,000 that it owed Executive Aviation on its account for fuel, oil, and oxygen. Executive Aviation then took possession of Air Ruidoso's plane, claiming that it had a lien on the plane. Using the information presented in the chapter, answer the following questions.

1. Can Executive Aviation establish an artisan's lien on the plane? Why or why not?
2. Suppose that Executive Aviation files a lawsuit in court against Air Ruidoso for the $10,000 past-due debt. What two methods discussed in this chapter would allow the court to order the seizure of Air Ruidoso's plane to satisfy the debt?
3. Suppose that Executive Aviation discovers that Air Ruidoso has sufficient assets in one of its bank accounts to pay the past-due amount. How might Executive Aviation attempt to obtain access to these funds?
4. Suppose that the contract between the companies provides that "if the airline becomes insolvent, Braden Fasco, the chief executive officer of Air Ruidoso, agrees to cover its outstanding debts." Is this a suretyship or a guaranty agreement?

Debate This . . . *Because writs of attachment are a prejudgment remedy for nonpayment of a debt, they are unfair and should be abolished.*

Terms and Concepts

artisan's lien 542	creditors' composition	down payment 544
attachment 543	agreement 544	equitable right of redemption 548
co-surety 552	default 540	forbearance 546

Continues

Issue Spotters

1. Jorge contracts with Larry of Midwest Roofing to fix Jorge's roof. Jorge pays half of the contract price in advance. Larry and Midwest complete the job, but Jorge refuses to pay the rest of the price. What can Larry and Midwest do? (See *Laws Assisting Creditors*.)

2. Alyssa owes Don $5,000 and refuses to pay. Don obtains a garnishment order and serves it on Alyssa's employer. If the employer complies with the order and Alyssa stays on the job, is one order enough to garnish Alyssa's wages for each pay period until the debt is paid? Explain. (See *Laws Assisting Creditors*.)

• **Check your answers to the Issue Spotters against the answers provided in Appendix D at the end of this text.**

Business Scenarios

29–1. Liens. Kanahara is employed part-time by the Cross-Bar Packing Corp. and earns take-home pay of $400 per week. He is $2,000 in debt to the Holiday Department Store for goods purchased on credit over the past eight months. Most of this property is nonexempt and is now in Kanahara's apartment. Kanahara is in default on his payments to Holiday. Holiday learns that Kanahara has a girlfriend in another state and that he plans to give her most of this property for Christmas. Discuss what actions can be taken by Holiday to collect the debt owed by Kanahara. (See *Laws Assisting Creditors*.)

29–2. Liens. Nabil is the owner of a relatively old home valued at $105,000. The home's electrical system is failing, and the wiring needs to be replaced. Nabil contracts with Kandhari Electrical to replace the electrical system. Kandhari performs the repairs, and on June 1 submits a bill of $10,000 to Nabil. Because of financial difficulties, Nabil does not pay the bill. Nabil's only asset is his home, but his state's homestead exemption is $60,000. Discuss fully Kandhari's remedies in this situation. (See *Laws Assisting Creditors*.)

Business Case Problems

29–3. Foreclosure on Mortgages and Liens. LaSalle Bank loaned $8 million to Cypress Creek 1, LP, to build an apartment complex. The loan was secured by a mortgage. Cypress Creek hired contractors to provide concrete work, plumbing, carpentry, and other construction services. Cypress Creek later went bankrupt owing LaSalle $3 million. The contractors recorded mechanic's liens when they were not paid for their work. The property was sold to LaSalle at a sheriff's sale for $1.3 million. The contractors claimed that their mechanic's liens should be satisfied out of the $1.3 million before any funds were distributed to LaSalle for its mortgage. The trial court distributed the $1.3 million primarily to LaSalle, with only a small fraction going to the contractors. Do the liens come before the mortgage in priority of payment? Discuss. [*LaSalle Bank National Association v. Cypress Creek 1, LP,* 242 Ill.2d 231, 950 N.E.2d 1109 (2011)] (See *Mortgages*.)

29–4. Guaranty. Timothy Martinez, owner of Koenig & Vits, Inc. (K&V), guaranteed K&V's debt to Community Bank & Trust. The guaranty stated that the bank was not required to seek payment of the debt from any other source before enforcing the guaranty. K&V defaulted. Through a Wisconsin state court, the bank sought payment of $536,739.40, plus interest at the contract rate of 7.5 percent, from Martinez. Martinez argued that the bank could not enforce his guaranty while other funds were available to satisfy K&V's debt. For example, the debt might be paid out of the proceeds of a sale of corporate assets. Is this an effective defense to a guaranty? Why or why not? [*Community Bank & Trust v. Koenig & Vits, Inc.,* 346 Wis.2d 279 (Wis.App. 2013)] (See *Suretyship and Guaranty*.)

29–5. Business Case Problem with Sample Answer— Liens. Daniel and Katherine Balk asked Jirak Construction, LLC, to remodel their farmhouse in Lawler, Iowa. Jirak provided the Balks with an initial estimate of $45,975 for the cost. Over the course of the work, the Balks made significant changes to the plan. Jirak agreed to the changes and regularly advised the Balks about the increasing costs. In mid-project, Jirak provided an itemized breakdown at their request. The Balks paid Jirak $67,000, but refused to pay more. Jirak claimed that they still owed $55,000 in labor and materials. Jirak filed a suit in an Iowa state court against the Balks to collect. Which of the liens discussed in this chapter would be most effective to Jirak in its attempt to collect? How does that type of lien work? Is the court likely to enforce it in this case? Explain. [*Jirak Construction, LLC v. Balk*, 863 N.W.2d 35 (Iowa App. 2015)] (See *Laws Assisting Creditors.*)

- **For a sample answer to Problem 29–5, go to Appendix E at the end of this text.**

29–6. Laws Assisting Creditors. Grand Harbour Condominium Owners Association, Inc., obtained a judgment in an Ohio state court against Gene and Nancy Grogg for $45,458.86. To satisfy the judgment, Grand Harbour filed a notice of garnishment with the court, seeking funds held by the Groggs in various banks. The Groggs disputed Grand Harbour's right to garnish the funds. They claimed that the funds were exempt Social Security and pension proceeds, but they offered no proof of this claim. The banks responded by depositing $23,911.97 with the court. These funds were delivered to Grand Harbour. Later, the Groggs filed a petition for bankruptcy in a federal bankruptcy court. After they were granted a discharge, they filed a "motion to return funds to debtors" but provided no evidence that their debt to Grand Harbour had been included in the discharge. What is Grand Harbour's best argument in response to the Groggs' motion? [*Grand Harbour Condominium Owners Association, Inc. v. Grogg*, 2016-Ohio-1386, __ Ohio App.3d __, __ N.E.2d __ (2016)] (See *Laws Assisting Creditors.*)

29–7. A Question of Ethics: Guaranty. *73-75 Main Avenue, LLC, agreed to lease a portion of the commercial property at 73 Main Avenue, Norwalk, Connecticut, to PP Door Enterprise, Inc. Nan Zhang, as manager of PP Door, signed the lease agreement. The lessor required the principal officers of PP Door to execute personal*

guaranties. In addition, the principal officers agreed to provide the lessor with credit information. Apparently, both the lessor and the principals of PP Door signed the lease and guaranty agreements that were sent to PP Door's office. When PP Door failed to make monthly payments, 73-75 Main Avenue filed a suit against PP Door and its owner, Ping Ying Li. At trial, Li testified that she was the sole owner of PP Door but denied that Zhang was its manager. She also denied signing the guaranty agreement. She claimed that she had signed the credit authorization form because Zhang had told her he was too young to have good credit. Li claimed to have no knowledge of the lease agreement. She did admit, however, that she had paid the rent. She claimed that Zhang had been in a car accident and had asked her to help pay his bills, including the rent at 73 Main Avenue. Li further testified that she did not see the name PP Door on the storefront of the leased location. [73-75 Main Avenue, LLC v. PP Door Enterprise Inc., 120 Conn.App. 150, 991 A.2d 650 (2010)] (See Suretyship and Guaranty.)

(a) Li argued that she was not liable on the lease agreement because Zhang was not authorized to bind her to the lease. Do the facts support Li? Why or why not?

(b) Li claimed that the guaranty for rent was not enforceable against her. Why might the court agree?

29–8. Special Case Analysis—Liens. Go to Case 29.1, *Picerne Construction Corp. v. Villas.* Read the excerpt and answer the following questions.

(a) Issue: What statutory term was the focus of the dispute in this case? Why?

(b) Rule of Law: Under the state statute that applied in this case, what must a party show to enforce a lien?

(c) Applying the Rule of Law: What proof supported the plaintiff's attempt to enforce its lien? What did the defendant argue in opposition?

(d) Conclusion: How did the court resolve the dispute between the creditor and debtor here? Who benefited from this decision?

Legal Reasoning Group Activity

29–9. Attachment. Brent Avery, on behalf of his law firm—The Law Office of Brent Avery—contracted with Marlin Broadcasting to air commercials on KRTV, a local radio station. Avery, who was the sole member of his firm, helped to create the commercials. The ads featured his voice, focused on his name and experience, and solicited direct contact with "defense attorney Brent Avery." When KRTV was not paid for the broadcasts, Marlin filed a lawsuit against Avery and his firm, alleging an outstanding balance of $35,250.

Pending the court's hearing of the suit, Marlin filed a request for a writ of attachment. Marlin offered in evidence

the parties' contracts, the ads' transcripts, and KRTV's invoices. Avery contended that he could not be held personally liable for the cost of the ads. Marlin countered that the ads unjustly enriched Avery by conferring a personal benefit on him to Marlin's detriment. (See *Laws Assisting Creditors.*)

(a) The first group will explain the purpose of attachment.

(b) The second group will outline what a creditor must prove to obtain a writ of attachment.

(c) The third group will determine whether Marlin Broadcasting is entitled to attachment in this scenario.

CHAPTER 30

BUSINESS LAW

CLARKSON · MILLER · CROSS

Secured Transactions

Whenever the payment of a debt is guaranteed, or *secured,* by personal property owned or held by the debtor, the transaction becomes known as a **secured transaction.** The concept of the secured transaction is as basic to modern business practice as the concept of credit. Logically, sellers and lenders do not want to risk nonpayment, so they usually will not sell goods or lend funds unless the promise of payment is somehow guaranteed. Indeed, business as we know it could not exist without laws permitting and governing secured transactions.

Article 9 of the Uniform Commercial Code (UCC) governs secured transactions in personal property. Personal property includes accounts, agricultural liens, and *chattel paper* (any documents or records evidencing a debt secured by personal property). It also includes commercial assignments of $1,000 or more, *fixtures* (certain property that is attached to land), instruments, and other types of intangible property, such as patents. Article 9 does not cover creditor-collection devices such as liens and mortgages on real property.

30–1 The Terminology of Secured Transactions

In every state, the UCC's terminology is now uniformly used in all documents that involve secured transactions. The following is a brief summary of the UCC's definitions of terms relating to secured transactions:

1. A **secured party** is any creditor who has a *security interest* in the debtor's *collateral.* This creditor can be a seller, a lender, a cosigner, or even a buyer of accounts or chattel paper [UCC 9–102(a)(72)].
2. A **debtor** is the party who *owes payment* or other performance of a secured obligation [UCC 9–102(a)(28)].
3. A **security interest** is the interest in the collateral (such as personal property, fixtures, or accounts) that *secures payment or performance* of an obligation [UCC 1–201(37)].
4. A **security agreement** is an *agreement* that creates or provides for a security interest [UCC 9–102(a)(73)].
5. **Collateral** is the *subject* of the *security interest* [UCC 9–102(a)(12)].
6. A **financing statement**—referred to as the UCC-1 form—is the *instrument normally filed to give public notice to third parties* of the secured party's security interest [UCC 9–102(a)(39)].

Together, these basic definitions form the concept under which a debtor-creditor relationship becomes a secured transaction relationship (see Exhibit 30–1).

30–2 Creation of a Security Interest

A creditor has two main concerns if the debtor defaults: (1) Can the debt be satisfied through the possession and (usually) sale of the collateral? (2) Will the creditor have priority over any other creditors or buyers who may have rights in the same collateral? These two concerns are met through the creation and perfection of a security interest. We begin by examining how a security interest is created.

30–2a Basic Requirements

To become a secured party, the creditor must obtain a security interest in the collateral of the debtor. Three requirements must be met for a creditor to have an enforceable security interest:

1. Unless the creditor has possession of the collateral, there must be a written or authenticated security agreement that clearly describes the collateral subject

EXHIBIT 30–1 Secured Transactions—Concept and Terminology

In a security agreement, a debtor and a creditor agree that the creditor will have a security interest in collateral in which the debtor has rights. In essence, the collateral secures the loan and ensures the creditor of payment should the debtor default.

to the security interest. This agreement must be signed or authenticated by the debtor.

2. The secured party must give the debtor something of value.

3. The debtor must have rights in the collateral.

Once these requirements have been met, the creditor's rights are said to *attach* to the collateral. **Attachment** gives the creditor an enforceable security interest in the collateral [UCC 9–203].[1]

■ **EXAMPLE 30.1** To furnish his new office suite, Abdul applies for a credit card at an office supply store. The application contains a clause stating that the store will retain a security interest in the goods purchased with the card until the goods have been paid for in full. This application is considered a *written security agreement*, which is the first requirement for an enforceable security interest. The goods that Abdul buys with the card are the *something of value* from the secured party (the second requirement). Abdul's ownership interest in those goods is the *right* that he has in them (the third requirement). Thus, the requirements for an enforceable security

interest are met. When Abdul buys something with the card, the store's rights attach to the purchased goods. ■

30–2b Written or Authenticated Security Agreement

When the collateral is not in the possession of the secured party, the security agreement must be either written or authenticated. Here, **authenticate** means to sign or, on an electronic record, to adopt any symbol that verifies the intent to adopt or accept the record [UCC 9–102(a)(7)]. Authentication thus provides for electronic filing (the filing process will be discussed later). See this chapter's *Digital Update* feature for a discussion of a type of secured transaction that is performed online.

A security agreement must also contain a description of the collateral that reasonably identifies it. Generally, such phrases as "all the debtor's personal property" or "all the debtor's assets" would *not* constitute a sufficient description [UCC 9–108(c)].

If the debtor signs, or otherwise authenticates, a security agreement, does he or she also have to sign an attached list of the collateral to create a valid security interest? That was the question before the court in the following case.

---

1. The term *attachment* has a different meaning in secured transactions than in the context of judicial liens, where it refers to a court-ordered seizure of property.

Case **30.1**

Royal Jewelers, Inc. v. Light

Supreme Court of North Dakota, 2015 ND 44, 859 N.W.2d 921 (2015).

Background and Facts Steven Light bought a $55,050 wedding ring for his wife, Sherri Light, on credit from Royal Jewelers, Inc., a store in Fargo, North Dakota. The receipt granted Royal a security interest in the ring. Later, Royal assigned its interest to GRB Financial Corp. Steven and GRB signed a

Case 30.1 Continues

Case 30.1 Continued

modification agreement changing the repayment terms. An attached exhibit listed the items pledged as security for the modification, including the ring. Steven did not separately sign the exhibit.

A year later, Steven died. Royal and GRB filed a suit in a North Dakota state court against Sherri, alleging that GRB had a valid security interest in the ring. Sherri cited UCC 9–203, under which there is an enforceable interest only if "the debtor has authenticated a security agreement that provides a description of the collateral." Sherri argued that the modification agreement did not "properly authenticate" the description of the collateral, including the ring, because Steven had not signed the attached exhibit. The court issued a judgment in GRB's favor. Sherri appealed.

In the Language of the Court

CROTHERS, Justice.

* * * *

Sherri Light * * * claims the * * * modification agreement signed by Steven Light * * * did not properly authenticate the agreement describing the collateral under [North Dakota Commercial Code (NDCC)] Section 41–09–13(2)(c)(1) [North Dakota's version of UCC 9–203] because he did not separately sign the exhibit identifying secured collateral, including the ring.

Section 41–09–13(2)(c)(1) provides:

2. * * * A security interest is enforceable against the debtor and third parties with respect to the collateral only if:

* * * *

c. One of the following conditions is met:
(1) The debtor has authenticated a security agreement that provides a description of the collateral * * *.

The plain language of that statute requires a debtor to authenticate a security agreement providing a description of the collateral. [Under NDCC Section 41–09–02(1)(g) [North Dakota's version of UCC 9–102(1)(g),] "authenticate" means "to sign" or "to execute or otherwise adopt a symbol, or encrypt or similarly process a record in whole or in part, with the present intent of the authenticating person to identify the person and adopt or accept a record." NDCC Section 41–09–08(2) [North Dakota's version of UCC 9–108(2)] says a description of collateral is sufficient if it reasonably identifies the collateral and may include a specific listing or any other method by which the collateral is objectively determinable.

* * * No authority [requires] a debtor to separately sign an exhibit attached to and referenced in a signed security agreement * * *. *A security agreement is not unenforceable merely because a description of collateral in an exhibit was attached to the security agreement * * *. Several documents may be considered together as a security agreement * * *.* [Emphasis added.]

Steven Light signed the * * * modification agreement which referenced an attached exhibit listing assets pledged as security for the note. * * * The attached exhibit listing the ring was part of the * * * agreement signed by Steven Light, and the [lower] court determined the modification agreement was properly executed by Steven Light. Evidence establishes Steven Light initially granted a valid security interest in the ring and the ring had not been fully paid for * * *. GRB Financial received an assignment of the security interest from Royal Jewelers * * *, and the court did not err in finding GRB Financial had a valid and enforceable security interest in the ring.

Decision and Remedy *The North Dakota Supreme Court affirmed the lower court's judgment. The court stated, "No authority [requires] a debtor to separately sign an exhibit attached to and referenced in a signed security agreement."*

Critical Thinking
- **Ethical** *Under the circumstances, is it ethical for GRB to enforce its security interest in the ring to recover the unpaid amount of the price? Discuss.*

30–2c Secured Party Must Give Value

The secured party must give something of value to the debtor. Under the UCC, value can include a binding commitment to extend credit and, in general, any consideration sufficient to support a simple contract [UCC 1–204]. Normally, the value given by a secured party involves a direct loan or a commitment to sell goods on credit.

DIGITAL UPDATE — Secured Transactions—Escrow Services Online

When you buy something online, you typically must use your credit card, make an electronic fund transfer, or send a check before the goods you bought are sent to you. If you are buying an expensive item, such as a car, you are not likely to send funds without being assured that you will receive the item in the condition promised. Enter the concept of escrow.

Escrow Accounts

Escrow accounts are commonly used in real estate transactions, but they are also useful for smaller transactions, particularly those done on the Internet. An escrow account involves three parties—the buyer, the seller, and a trusted third party that collects, holds, and disperses funds according to instructions from the buyer and seller.

Escrow services are provided by licensed and regulated escrow companies. For example, if you buy a car on the Internet, you and the seller will agree on an escrow company to which you send the funds. When you receive the car and are satisfied with it, the escrow company will release the funds to the seller. This is a type of secured transaction.

Escrow.com

One of the best-known online escrow firms is Escrow.com, which had processed more than $2.7 billion in secured transactions by 2017. All of its escrow services are offered via its Web site and provided independently by Internet Escrow Services, one of its operating subsidiaries. Escrow.com is particularly useful for transactions that involve an international buyer or seller. It has become the recommended transaction settlement service for AutoTrader, Resale Weekly, Cars.com, eBay Motors, and Flippa.com.

Critical Thinking *How could online escrow services reduce Internet fraud?*

30–2d Debtor Must Have Rights in the Collateral

The debtor must have rights in the collateral. That is, the debtor must have some ownership interest or right to obtain possession of that collateral. The debtor's rights can represent either a current or a future legal interest in the collateral. For instance, a retailer-debtor can give a secured party a security interest not only in existing inventory owned by the retailer but also in *future* inventory that the retailer will acquire. (A common misconception is that the debtor must have title to the collateral to have rights in it, but this is not a requirement.)

For a synopsis of the rules for creating a security interest, see Concept Summary 30.1.

30–3 Perfection of a Security Interest

Perfection is the legal process by which secured parties protect themselves against the claims of third parties who may wish to have their debts satisfied out of the same collateral. Whether a secured party's security interest is

Concept Summary 30.1

Creating a Security Interest

Requirements for Creating a Security Interest	1. Unless the creditor has possession of the collateral, there must be a written or authenticated security agreement signed or authenticated by the debtor that describes the collateral subject to the security interest. 2. The secured party must give value to the debtor. 3. The debtor must have rights in the collateral—that is, some ownership interest or right to obtain possession of the specified collateral.

perfected or unperfected can have serious consequences for the secured party.

What if a debtor has borrowed from two different creditors and used the same property as collateral for both loans? If the debtor defaults on both loans, which of the two creditors has first rights to the collateral? In this situation, the creditor with a perfected security interest will prevail.

Perfection usually is accomplished by filing a financing statement. In some circumstances, however, a security interest becomes perfected even though no financing statement is filed.

30–3a Perfection by Filing

The most common means of perfection is by filing a *financing statement* with the office of the appropriate government official. A financing statement gives public notice to third parties of the secured party's security interest. The security agreement itself can also be filed to perfect the security interest. The financing statement must provide the names of the debtor and the secured party, and it must indicate the collateral covered by the financing statement.

A uniform financing statement form (see Exhibit 30–2) is used in all states [UCC 9–521]. It must be filed in the appropriate office, together with payment of the correct

EXHIBIT 30–2 A Uniform Financing Statement Sample

UCC FINANCING STATEMENT
FOLLOW INSTRUCTIONS

A. NAME & PHONE OF CONTACT AT FILER (optional)

B. E-MAIL CONTACT AT FILER (optional)

C. SEND ACKNOWLEDGMENT TO: (Name and Address)

THE ABOVE SPACE IS FOR FILING OFFICE USE ONLY

1. DEBTOR'S NAME: Provide only <u>one</u> Debtor name (1a or 1b) (use exact, full name; do not omit, modify, or abbreviate any part of the Debtor's name); if any part of the Individual Debtor's name will not fit in line 1b, leave all of item 1 blank, check here ☐ and provide the Individual Debtor information in item 10 of the Financing Statement Addendum (Form UCC1Ad)

	1a. ORGANIZATION'S NAME			
OR	1b. INDIVIDUAL'S SURNAME	FIRST PERSONAL NAME	ADDITIONAL NAME(S)/INITIAL(S)	SUFFIX
	1c. MAILING ADDRESS	CITY	STATE	POSTAL CODE	COUNTRY

2. DEBTOR'S NAME: Provide only <u>one</u> Debtor name (2a or 2b) (use exact, full name; do not omit, modify, or abbreviate any part of the Debtor's name); if any part of the Individual Debtor's name will not fit in line 2b, leave all of item 2 blank, check her ☐ and provide the Individual Debtor information in item 10 of the Financing Statement Addendum (Form UCC1Ad)

	2a. ORGANIZATION'S NAME			
OR	2b. INDIVIDUAL'S SURNAME	FIRST PERSONAL NAME	ADDITIONAL NAME(S)/INITIAL(S)	SUFFIX
	2c. MAILING ADDRESS	CITY	STATE	POSTAL CODE	COUNTRY

3. SECURED PARTY'S NAME (or NAME of ASSIGNEE of ASSIGNOR SECURED PARTY): Provide only <u>one</u> Secured Party name (3a or 3b)

	3a. ORGANIZATION'S NAME			
OR	3b. INDIVIDUAL'S SURNAME	FIRST PERSONAL NAME	ADDITIONAL NAME(S)/INITIAL(S)	SUFFIX
	3c. MAILING ADDRESS	CITY	STATE	POSTAL CODE	COUNTRY

4. COLLATERAL: This financing statement covers the following collateral:

filing fee [UCC 9–516(a)]. The filing can be accomplished electronically [UCC 9–102(a)(18)]. Once completed, filings are indexed by the name of the debtor so that they can be located by subsequent searches. A financing statement may be filed even before a security agreement is made or a security interest attaches [UCC 9–502(d)].

The Debtor's Name The UCC requires that a financing statement be filed under the name of the debtor [UCC 9–502(a)(1)]. Slight variations in names normally will not be considered misleading if a search of the filing office's records, using a standard search engine routinely used by that office, would find the filings [UCC 9–506(c)].[2] If the debtor is identified by the correct name at the time the financing statement is filed, the secured party's interest retains its priority even if the debtor's name later changes.

Because most states use electronic filing systems, UCC 9–503 sets out detailed rules for determining when the debtor's name as it appears on a financing statement is sufficient.

1. *Corporations.* For corporations, which are organizations that have registered with the state, the debtor's name on the financing statement must be "the name of the debtor indicated on the public record of the debtor's jurisdiction of organization" [UCC 9–503(a)(1)].
2. *Trusts.* If the debtor is a trust or a trustee for property held in trust, the financing statement must disclose this information and provide the trust's name as specified in its official documents [UCC 9–503(a)(3)].
3. *Individuals and organizations.* For all others, the financing statement must disclose "the individual or organizational name of the debtor" [UCC 9–503(a)(4)(A)]. The word *organization* includes unincorporated associations, such as clubs and some churches, as well as joint ventures and general partnerships. If an organizational debtor does not have a group name, the names of the individuals in the group must be listed.
4. *Trade names.* Providing only the debtor's trade name (or a fictitious name) in a financing statement is *not* sufficient for perfection [UCC 9–503(c)]. Thus, the name Pete's Plumbing (if Pete's Plumbing is not a distinct legal entity) is not sufficient. The financing statement must also include the owner-debtor's actual name—Pete Hanson.

Changes in the Debtor's Name What if the debtor's name changes, and the financing statement becomes seriously misleading because of the name change? In this situation, the financing statement remains effective only for collateral the debtor acquired before or within four months after the name change. Unless an amendment to the financing statement is filed, the secured party's interest in goods that the debtor acquired after the four-month period is unperfected [UCC 9–507(b) and (c)].

A one-page uniform financing statement amendment form is available for filing name changes and for other purposes [UCC 9–521]. (See the discussion of amendments later in this chapter.)

Description of the Collateral Both the security agreement and the financing statement must describe the collateral in which the secured party has a security interest. (For land-related security interests, a legal description of the realty is also required [UCC 9–502(b)].)

The security agreement must describe the collateral because no security interest in goods can exist unless the parties agree on which goods are subject to the security interest. The financing statement must describe the collateral to provide public notice of the fact that certain goods of the debtor are subject to a security interest.

Sometimes, the descriptions in the two documents vary. The description in the security agreement must be more precise than the description in the financing statement. The UCC permits broad, general descriptions in the financing statement, such as "all assets" or "all personal property." Usually, if a financing statement accurately describes the agreement between the secured party and the debtor, the description is sufficient [UCC 9–504].

■ **EXAMPLE 30.2** A security agreement for a commercial loan to a manufacturer of automotive parts may list all of the manufacturer's equipment subject to the loan by serial number. The financing statement, in contrast, may simply state "all equipment owned or hereafter acquired." ■

Where to File In most states, a financing statement must be filed centrally in the appropriate state office in the state where the debtor is located. An exception occurs when the collateral consists of timber to be cut, fixtures, or items to be extracted—such as oil, coal, gas, and minerals [UCC 9–301(3) and (4), 9–502(b)]. In those

---

2. If the name listed in the financing statement is so inaccurate that a search using the standard search engine will not find the debtor's name, the financing statement is deemed seriously misleading under UCC 9–506. See also UCC 9–507, which governs the effectiveness of financing statements found to be seriously misleading.

circumstances, the financing statement is filed in the county where the collateral is located.

Note that the state in which a financing statement should be filed depends on the debtor's location, not the location of the collateral (with the exception of the collateral just mentioned) [UCC 9–301]. The debtor's location is determined as follows [UCC 9–307]:

1. For an *individual debtor,* it is the state of the debtor's principal residence.
2. For an organization registered with the state, such as a corporation, it is the state in which the organization is registered. Thus, if a debtor is incorporated in Delaware and has its chief executive office in New York, a secured party would file the financing statement in Delaware.
3. For *all other entities,* it is the state in which the business is located or, if the debtor has more than one office, the place from which the debtor manages its business operations and affairs.

Consequences of an Improper Filing Any improper filing renders the secured party's interest unperfected and reduces the secured party's claim to that of an unsecured creditor. For instance, if the debtor's name is incorrect or if the collateral is not sufficiently described on the financing statement, the filing may not be effective.

■ **EXAMPLE 30.3** Arthur Mendez Juarez, a strawberry farmer, leased farmland from Glendale Fruits, Inc., and borrowed funds from Glendale for payroll and production expenses. The sublease and other documents set out Juarez's full name, but Juarez generally went by the name "Mendez," and he signed the sublease "Arthur Mendez." To perfect its interests, Glendale filed financing statements that identified the debtor as "Arthur Mendez."

Some time later, Juarez contracted to sell strawberries to Frozun Fruits, LLC, which also advanced him funds secured by a financing statement. This statement identified the debtor as "Arthur Juarez." By the following year, Juarez was unable to pay his debts. He owed Glendale more than $200,000 and Frozun nearly $50,000. Both Glendale and Frozun filed suits against Juarez claiming to have priority under a perfected security interest.

In this situation, a properly filed financing statement would identify the debtor's true name (Arthur Juarez). Because a debtor name search for "Arthur Juarez" would not disclose a financing statement in the name of "Arthur Mendez," Glendale's financing statement was seriously misleading. Therefore, Frozun's security interest

would have priority because its financing statement was recorded properly. ■

30–3b Perfection without Filing

In two types of situations, security interests can be perfected without filing a financing statement. The first occurs when the collateral is transferred into the possession of the secured party. The second occurs when the security interest is one of a limited number under the UCC that can be perfected on attachment [UCC 9–309].

The phrase *perfected on attachment* means that these security interests are automatically perfected at the time of their creation, without a filing and without possession of the goods. Two of the most common security interests that are perfected on attachment are a *purchase-money security interest* in consumer goods (explained shortly) and an assignment of a beneficial interest in an estate of a deceased person [UCC 9–309(1), (13)].

Perfection by Possession In the past, one of the most frequently used means of obtaining financing under the common law was to pledge certain collateral as security for the debt. The collateral was then transferred into the creditor's possession. When the debt was paid, the collateral was returned to the debtor. Although the debtor usually entered into a written security agreement, oral security agreements were also enforceable as long as the secured party possessed the collateral.

The UCC retained the common law pledge and the principle that the security agreement need not be in writing if the collateral is transferred to the secured party [UCC 9–310, 9–312(b), 9–313]. ■ **EXAMPLE 30.4** Sheila needs cash to pay for a medical procedure. She obtains a loan for $4,000 from Trent. As security on the loan, she gives him a promissory note on which she is the payee. Even though the agreement to hold the note as collateral was oral, Trent has a perfected security interest. He does not need to file a financing statement, because he has possession of the note. No other creditor of Sheila's can attempt to recover the note from Trent in payment for other debts. ■

Certain items—such as stocks, bonds, negotiable instruments, and jewelry—are commonly transferred into the creditor's possession when they are used as collateral for loans. For most collateral, however, possession by the secured party is impractical because it would prevent the debtor from using or deriving income from the property to pay off the debt. ■ **EXAMPLE 30.5** Jeb, a farmer, takes out a loan to finance the purchase of a corn harvester and uses the equipment as collateral. Clearly, the purpose of the purchase would be defeated if Jeb transferred the collateral into the creditor's possession. ■

Perfection by Attachment—The Purchase-Money Security Interest in Consumer Goods

Under the UCC, fourteen types of security interests are perfected automatically at the time they are created [UCC 9–309]. The most common is the **purchase-money security interest (PMSI)** in *consumer goods* (items bought primarily for personal, family, or household purposes).

A PMSI in consumer goods is created when a seller or lender agrees to extend credit to a buyer for part or all of the purchase price of the goods in a sales transaction. The entity that extends the credit can be either the seller (a store, for instance) or a financial institution that lends the buyer the funds with which to purchase the goods [UCC 9–102(a)(2)].

Automatic Perfection. A PMSI in consumer goods is perfected automatically at the time of a credit sale—that is, at the time the PMSI is created. The seller in this situation does not need to do anything more to perfect her or his interest.

■ **EXAMPLE 30.6** Jami purchases a Whirlpool washer and dryer from West Coast Appliance for $2,500. Unable to pay the entire amount in cash, Jami signs a purchase agreement to pay $1,000 down and $100 per month until the balance, plus interest, is fully paid. West Coast Appliance is to retain a security interest in the appliances until full payment has been made. Because the security interest was created as part of the purchase agreement with a consumer, it is a PMSI, and West Coast Appliance's security interest is automatically perfected. ■

Exceptions to Automatic Perfection. There are two exceptions to the rule of automatic perfection for PMSIs:

1. Certain types of security interests that are subject to other federal or state laws may require additional steps to be perfected [UCC 9–311]. Many jurisdictions, for instance, have certificate-of-title statutes that establish perfection requirements for security interests in certain goods, including automobiles, trailers, boats, mobile homes, and farm tractors.
   ■ **EXAMPLE 30.7** Martin Sedek purchases a boat at a Florida dealership. Florida has a certificate-of-title

statute. Sedek obtains financing for his purchase through General Credit Corporation. General Credit Corporation will need to file a certificate of title with the appropriate state official to perfect the PMSI. ■

2. PMSIs in nonconsumer goods, such as a business's inventory or livestock, are not automatically perfected [UCC 9–324]. These types of PMSIs will be discussed later in this chapter in the context of priorities.

30–3c Perfection and the Classification of Collateral

Where or how to perfect a security interest sometimes depends on the classification or definition of the collateral. Collateral is generally divided into two classifications: *tangible collateral* (collateral that can be seen, felt, and touched) and *intangible collateral* (collateral that consists of or generates rights). Exhibit 30–3 summarizes various classifications of collateral and the methods of perfecting a security interest in collateral falling within each of those classifications.[3]

30–3d Effective Time Duration of Perfection

A financing statement is effective for five years from the date of filing [UCC 9–515]. If a **continuation statement** is filed *within six months prior to the expiration date,* the effectiveness of the original statement is continued for another five years. The continuation period starts with the expiration date of the first five-year period [UCC 9–515(d), (e)]. The effectiveness of the statement can be continued in the same manner indefinitely. Any attempt to file a continuation statement outside the six-month window will render the continuation ineffective, and the perfection will lapse at the end of the five-year period.

If a financing statement lapses, the security interest that had been perfected by the filing now becomes unperfected. A purchaser for value can take the property that was used as collateral as if the security interest had never been perfected [UCC 9–515(c)].

To review the ways of perfecting a security interest, see Concept Summary 30.2.

---

3. There are additional classifications, such as agricultural liens, commercial tort claims, and investment property. For definitions of these types of collateral, see UCC 9–102(a)(5), (a)(13), and (a)(49).

EXHIBIT 30–3 Selected Types of Collateral and Methods of Perfection

TANGIBLE COLLATERAL		METHOD OF PERFECTION
All things that are movable at the time the security interest attaches or that are attached to land, including timber and crops.		
Consumer Goods	Items bought primarily for personal, family, or household purposes, such as a home theatre system.	A purchase-money security interest (PMSI) in consumer goods is automatically perfected at the time it is created (except for certain vehicles that also must comply with certificate-of-title statutes). For other consumer goods, general rules of filing or possession apply.
Equipment	Goods bought for or used primarily in business (and not part of inventory or farm products)—for example, a delivery truck.	Filing or (rarely) possession by secured party.
Farm Products	Crops (including aquatic goods), livestock, or supplies produced in a farming operation —for example, ginned cotton, milk, eggs, and maple syrup.	Filing or (rarely) possession by secured party.
Inventory	Goods held by a person for sale or under a contract of service or lease; raw materials held for production and work in progress.	Filing or (rarely) possession by secured party.
INTANGIBLE COLLATERAL		METHOD OF PERFECTION
Nonphysical property that exists only in connection with something else.		
Chattel Paper	A writing or electronic record that evidences both a monetary obligation and a security interest in goods and software used in goods—for example, a security agreement.	Filing or possession or control by secured party.
Instruments	A negotiable instrument—such as a check, note, certificate of deposit, draft, or other writing—that evidences a right to the payment of money and is not a security agreement or lease, but rather a type that can ordinarily be transferred (after indorsement, if necessary) by delivery.	Normally, filing or possession. For the sale of promissory notes, perfection can be by attachment (automatically on the creation of the security interest).
Accounts	Any right to receive payment for property (real or personal), including intellectual licensed property, services, insurance policies, and certain other receivables.	Filing required except for certain assignments that can be perfected by attachment (automatically on the creation of the security interest).
Deposit Accounts	Any demand, time, savings, passbook, or similar account maintained with a bank.	Perfection by control, such as when the secured party is the bank in which the account is maintained or when the parties have agreed that the secured party can direct the disposition of funds in a particular account.

Concept Summary 30.2

Perfecting a Security Interest

Perfecting a Security Interest by Filing	The most common method of perfection is *by filing* a financing statement containing the names of the secured party and the debtor and indicating the collateral covered by the financing statement. • Communication of the financing statement to the appropriate filing office, together with the correct filing fee, constitutes a filing. • The financing statement must be filed under the name of the debtor. Fictitious (trade) names normally are not sufficient.
Perfecting a Security Interest without Filing	Two common methods to perfect a security interest *without filing* include the following: 1. *By transfer of collateral*—The debtor can transfer possession of the collateral to the secured party. For example, a *pledge* is this type of transfer. 2. *By attachment*—A limited number of security interests are perfected by attachment, such as a purchase-money security interest (PMSI) in consumer goods. If the secured party has a PMSI in consumer goods (for personal or household purposes, for example), the secured party's security interest is perfected automatically.

30–4 The Scope of a Security Interest

A security interest can cover property in which the debtor has either present or future ownership or possessory rights. Therefore, security agreements can cover the proceeds of the sale of collateral, after-acquired property, and future advances, as discussed next.

30–4a Proceeds

Proceeds are the cash or property received when collateral is sold or disposed of in some other way [UCC 9–102(a)(64)]. A security interest in the collateral gives the secured party a security interest in the proceeds acquired from the sale of that collateral.

■ **EXAMPLE 30.8** People's Bank has a perfected security interest in the inventory of a retail seller of heavy farm machinery. The retailer sells a tractor out of this inventory to Jacob Lamensdorf. Lamensdorf agrees, in a security agreement, to make monthly payments to the retailer for a period of twenty-four months. If the retailer goes into default on the loan from the bank, the bank is entitled to the remaining payments Lamensdorf owes to the retailer as proceeds. ■

A security interest in proceeds is automatically perfected at the same time as the secured party perfected its security interest in the original collateral. It remains perfected for twenty days after the debtor receives the proceeds from the sale of the collateral.

The parties can agree to extend the twenty-day automatic perfection period in the original security agreement [UCC 9–315(c), (d)]. Extensions are typically done when the collateral is the type that is likely to be sold, such as a retailer's inventory of tablets or smartphones. The UCC also permits a security interest in identifiable cash proceeds to remain perfected after twenty days [UCC 9–315(d)(2)].

The dispute in the following case focused on proceeds. The court was asked to decide whether the actions taken by the debtor and another creditor had stripped a secured creditor of its interest in certain proceeds.

Case 30.2

In re Tusa–Expo Holdings, Inc.
United States Court of Appeals, Fifth Circuit, 811 F.3d 786 (2016).

Background and Facts Tusa Office Solutions, Inc., a subsidiary of Tusa–Expo Holdings, Inc., was the largest retail dealer in new furniture made by Knoll, Inc. A customer ordered Knoll furniture from Tusa Office, which ordered it from Knoll and delivered it to the customer. The customer paid Tusa Office, which then paid Knoll. Knoll set a limit on the amount of the payments that could be outstanding before it would stop filling new orders. As part of the deal, Tusa Office granted Knoll a first-priority security interest in specified accounts receivable.

Meanwhile, Tusa Office obtained a loan from Textron Financial, Inc. Knoll and Textron agreed separately that Textron would have a first-priority security interest in all of Tusa Office's assets except Knoll's collateral.

The terms of the loan required Tusa Office to establish a bank account—called the lockbox—into which its customers made payments directly. Textron could withdraw funds from the lockbox and use them to increase the credit available to Tusa Office on its loan. Tusa Office used the increased credit to pay Knoll. By paying Knoll, Tusa Office kept its debt to Knoll below the furniture maker's limit, which enabled Tusa Office to fill new orders for its customers.

Ultimately, Tusa Office filed a bankruptcy petition in a federal bankruptcy court. Marilyn Garner, the bankruptcy trustee, sought to recapture some of the funds that Knoll had received through the lockbox.[a] To do this, Garner had to establish that Knoll had received more by these transfers than it would receive on Tusa Office's bankruptcy. The court issued a ruling against the trustee, who appealed.

In the Language of the Court
WIENER, Circuit Judge:
* * * *

* * * *A creditor who merely recovers its own collateral receives no more* * * * *than it would have received anyway.* [Emphasis added.]

The Trustee asserts that the transfers from Tusa Office to Knoll were not made from the proceeds of Knoll's collateral.
* * * *

The Trustee does not dispute that the payments Tusa Office's customers deposited into the lockbox were proceeds of Tusa Office's accounts receivable. She argues * * * that * * * Knoll's first-priority security interest in the payments was stripped by operation of [Texas Business and Commerce Code] Section 9.332(a) [Texas's version of UCC 9–332(a)]: "A transferee of money takes the money free of a security interest * * * ." Section 9.332(a) does not apply if such a transfer of money was made to the debtor. The Trustee therefore insists that Textron, not Tusa Office, was the transferee. In so doing, the Trustee contends that the lockbox was "owned * * * by Textron."
* * * *

* * * The Loan Agreement is clear. It specifies that * * * "Tusa Office shall have established a * * * lockbox * * * for its collections and the transfer thereof to Textron * * * ." The Loan Agreement also states that "Tusa Office shall have possession of Textron's Collateral."

Because Tusa Office, not Textron, owned the lockbox, Section 9.332(a) does not apply. Therefore, Knoll's first-priority security interest in the proceeds of Tusa Office's accounts receivable survived the deposit into the lockbox.
* * * *

The Trustee next contends that Section 9.332(b) [Texas's version of UCC 9–332(b)] stripped Knoll's first-priority security interest when they were transferred from the lockbox to Textron.
* * * *

---

a. A debtor files a petition in a federal bankruptcy court to liquidate its assets, pay its creditors with the proceeds, and obtain a discharge of any remaining debt. It is the job of the bankruptcy trustee to collect those assets and distribute them fairly among the debtor's creditors.

Case 30.2 Continued

The plain language of Section 9.332(b) states that a "transferee of funds from a deposit account takes the funds free of a security interest in the deposit account."

* * * *

The plain language of Section 9.332(b) is unambiguous. Knoll's first-priority security interest in the proceeds of Tusa Office's accounts receivable survived the transfer from the lockbox to Textron. Not only is this consistent with Section 9.332(b), but it is also consistent with the * * * Agreement between Knoll and Textron.

Decision and Remedy *The U.S. Court of Appeals for the Fifth Circuit affirmed the ruling of the lower court. The trustee could not recover the funds that were transferred to Knoll from Tusa Office through the lockbox because those funds were the proceeds of Knoll's own collateral.*

Critical Thinking

- **Legal Environment** *Why does UCC 9–332 permit transferees to take funds "free of a security interest"? How did this provision work to protect the parties in this case?*
- **Ethical** *Office Expo, Inc., a dealer in used furniture, was, like Tusa Office, a subsidiary of Tusa–Expo Holdings. Tusa Office operated profitably, but Office Expo did not. To bolster Office Expo, funds were transferred from Tusa Office to Office Expo on a regular basis, which caused problems for Tusa Office. Were these transfers unethical? Discuss.*

30–4b After-Acquired Property

After-acquired property is property that the debtor acquired after the execution of the security agreement. The security agreement may provide for a security interest in after-acquired property, such as a debtor's inventory [UCC 9–204(1)].

Generally, the debtor will purchase new inventory to replace the inventory sold. The secured party wants this newly acquired inventory to be subject to the original security interest. Thus, the after-acquired property clause continues the secured party's claim to any inventory acquired thereafter. (This is not to say that the original security interest will take priority over the rights of all other creditors with regard to this after-acquired inventory, as will be discussed later.)

■ **EXAMPLE 30.9** Amato buys factory equipment from Bronson on credit, giving as security an interest in all of her equipment—both what she is buying and what she already owns. The security agreement with Bronson contains an after-acquired property clause. Six months later, Amato pays cash to another seller of factory equipment for additional equipment. Six months after that, Amato goes out of business before she has paid off her debt to Bronson. Bronson has a security interest in all of Amato's equipment, even the equipment bought from the other seller. ■

30–4c Future Advances

Often, a debtor will arrange with a bank to have a *continuing line of credit* under which the debtor can borrow funds intermittently. Advances against lines of credit can be subject to a properly perfected security interest in certain collateral.

The security agreement may provide that any future advances made against that line of credit are also subject to the security interest in the same collateral [UCC 9–204(c)]. Future advances need not be of the same type or otherwise related to the original advance to benefit from this type of **cross-collateralization**.[4] Cross-collateralization occurs when an asset that is not the subject of a loan is used to collateralize that loan.

■ **EXAMPLE 30.10** Stroh is the owner of a small manufacturing plant with equipment valued at $1 million. He has an immediate need for $40,000 of working capital. He obtains a loan from Midwestern Bank and signs a security agreement, putting up all of his equipment as security. The bank properly perfects its security interest. The security agreement provides that Stroh can borrow up to $500,000 in the future, using the same equipment as collateral for any future advances. Midwestern Bank does not have to execute a new security agreement and perfect a security interest each time an advance is made, up to a cumulative total of $500,000. For priority purposes, each advance is perfected as of the date of the *original* perfection. ■

30–4d The Floating-Lien Concept

A security agreement that provides for a security interest in proceeds, in after-acquired property, or in collateral subject

---

4. See Official Comment 5 to UCC 9–204.

to future advances by the secured party is often characterized as a **floating lien.** This type of security interest continues in the collateral or proceeds even if the collateral is sold, exchanged, or disposed of in some other way.

A Floating Lien in Inventory Floating liens commonly arise in the financing of inventories. A creditor is not interested in specific pieces of inventory, which are constantly changing, so the lien "floats" from one item to another as the inventory changes.

■ **EXAMPLE 30.11** Cascade Sports, Inc., an Oregon corporation, operates as a cross-country ski dealer. The company has a line of credit with Portland First Bank to finance its inventory of cross-country skis. Cascade and Portland First enter into a security agreement that provides for coverage of proceeds, after-acquired inventory, present inventory, and future advances. Portland First perfects its security interest in the inventory by filing centrally with the office of the secretary of state in Oregon. One day, Cascade sells a new pair of the latest cross-country skis and receives a used pair in trade. That same day, Cascade purchases two new pairs of cross-country skis from a local manufacturer for cash. Later that day, to meet its payroll, Cascade borrows $8,000 from Portland First Bank under the security agreement.

Portland First has a perfected security interest in the used pair of skis under the proceeds clause. It also has a perfected security interest in the two new pairs of skis purchased from the local manufacturer under the after-acquired property clause. The new amount of funds advanced to Cascade is secured on all of the above-mentioned collateral by the future-advances clause. All of this is accomplished under the original perfected security interest. The various items in the inventory have changed, but Portland First still has a perfected security interest in Cascade's inventory. Hence, it has a floating lien in the inventory. ■

A Floating Lien in a Shifting Stock of Goods
The concept of the floating lien can also apply to a shifting stock of goods. The lien can start with raw materials, follow them as they become finished goods and inventories, and continue as the goods are sold and are turned into accounts receivable, chattel paper, or cash.

30–5 Priorities

When more than one party claims an interest in the same collateral, which has priority? The UCC sets out detailed rules to answer this question. In many situations the party who has a perfected security interest will have priority. There are, however, exceptions that give priority rights to another party, such as a buyer in the ordinary course of business.

30–5a General Rules of Priority

The basic rule is that when more than one security interest has been perfected in the same collateral, the first to be perfected (or filed) has priority over any perfected later. If only one of the conflicting security interests has been perfected, then that security interest has priority. If none of the security interests have been perfected, then the first security interest that attaches has priority.

The UCC's rules of priority can be summarized as follows:

1. *Perfected security interest versus unsecured creditors and unperfected security interests.* When two or more parties have claims to the same collateral, a perfected secured party's interest has priority over the interests of most other parties [UCC 9–322(a)(2)]. This includes priority to the proceeds from a sale of collateral resulting from a bankruptcy (giving the perfected secured party rights superior to those of the bankruptcy trustee).

2. *Conflicting perfected security interests.* When two or more secured parties have perfected security interests in the same collateral, generally the first to perfect (by filing or taking possession of the collateral) has priority [UCC 9–322(a)(1)].

3. *Conflicting unperfected security interests.* When two conflicting security interests are unperfected, the first to attach (be created) has priority [UCC 9–322(a)(3)]. This is sometimes called the "first-in-time" rule.

■ **EXAMPLE 30.12** Rick Morales and his wife and son own a dairy farm called Lost Creek Heifers (LCH) that has received multiple loans through Ag Services, Inc. Morales executes a promissory note and security agreement in favor of Ag Services. The note lists all of LCH's accounts, equipment, farm products, inventory, livestock, and proceeds as collateral. A year later, Morales and his wife separate, and he signs a separation agreement giving her some cash and land.

The following year, Morales buys out his son's interest in LCH by giving him a promissory note for $100,000. The note lists all of LCH's equipment, inventory, livestock, and proceeds as collateral. Morales also sells a herd of dairy cows for $500,000 and gives his former wife a check for $240,000. LCH files for bankruptcy shortly thereafter. A dispute arises over which party (Ag Services, Morales's son, or Morales's former wife) is entitled to the proceeds from the sale of the cows. In this situation, a court will likely find that because Ag Services' security interest in the proceeds was the first in time to *attach*, Ag Services has first priority to the proceeds. ■

30–5b Exceptions to the General Priority Rules

In some situations, on the debtor's default, the perfection of a security interest will not protect a secured party against certain other third parties having claims to the collateral. For instance, the UCC provides that in certain circumstances a PMSI, properly perfected,[5] will prevail over another security interest in after-acquired collateral, even though the other was perfected first.

Buyers in the Ordinary Course of Business
A major exception to the priority rules exists for a buyer in the ordinary course of business. A *buyer in the ordinary course of business* is a person who, in good faith, buys goods from a party in the business of selling such goods [UCC 1–201(9)].

A buyer in the ordinary course takes the goods free from any security interest created by the seller *even if the security interest is perfected and the buyer knows of its existence* [UCC 9–320(a)]. In other words, a buyer in the ordinary course will have priority even if a previously perfected security interest exists as to the goods. The rationale for this rule is obvious. If buyers could not obtain the goods free and clear of any security interest the merchant had created, the free flow of goods in the marketplace would be hindered.

■ **EXAMPLE 30.13** Dubbs Auto grants a security interest in its inventory to Heartland Bank for a $300,000 line of credit. Heartland perfects its security interest by filing financing statements with the appropriate state offices. Dubbs uses $9,000 of its credit to buy two used trucks and delivers the certificates of title, which designate Dubbs as the owner, to Heartland.

Later, Dubbs sells one of the trucks to Samuel Murdoch and another to Michael Laxton. National City Bank finances both purchases. New certificates of title designate the buyers as the owners and Heartland as the "first lienholder," but Heartland receives none of the funds from the sales. If Heartland sues National City, claiming that its security interest in the vehicles takes priority, it

will lose. Because Murdoch and Laxton are buyers in the ordinary course of business, Heartland's security interest in the motor vehicles was extinguished when the vehicles were sold to them. ■

PMSI in Goods Other than Inventory and Livestock
An important exception to the first-in-time rule involves a perfected PMSI in certain types of collateral, such as equipment, that is not inventory or livestock [UCC 9–324(a)]. (Remember that a PMSI that is *not* in consumer goods must still be perfected.) ■ **EXAMPLE 30.14** Piper Sandoval borrows funds from West Bank, signing a security agreement in which she puts up all of her present and after-acquired equipment as security. On May 1, West Bank perfects this security interest (which is not a PMSI). On July 1, Sandoval purchases a new piece of equipment from Zylex Company on credit, signing a security agreement. The delivery date for the new equipment is August 1.

Zylex thus has a PMSI in the new equipment (which is not part of its inventory), but the PMSI is not in consumer goods and thus is not automatically perfected. If Sandoval defaults on her payments to both West Bank and Zylex, which of them has priority with regard to the new piece of equipment? Generally, West Bank would have priority because its interest perfected first in time. In this situation, however, as long as Zylex perfected its PMSI in the new equipment within twenty days after Sandoval took possession on August 1, Zylex has priority. ■

PMSI in Inventory
Another important exception to the first-in-time rule has to do with security interests in inventory. A perfected PMSI in inventory has priority over a conflicting security interest in the same inventory. To maintain this priority, the holder of the PMSI must notify the holder of the conflicting security interest on or before the time the debtor takes possession of the inventory [UCC 9–324(b)].

■ **EXAMPLE 30.15** On May 1, SNS Electronics borrows funds from Key Bank. SNS signs a security agreement that puts up all of its present inventory and any after-acquired inventory as collateral. Key Bank perfects its interest (not a PMSI) on that date. On June 10, SNS buys new inventory from Martin, Inc., a manufacturer, to use for its Fourth of July sale. SNS makes a down payment for the new inventory and signs a security agreement giving Martin a PMSI in the new inventory as collateral for the remaining debt. Martin delivers the inventory to SNS on June 28, but SNS's Fourth of July sale is a disaster, and most of its inventory remains unsold. In August, SNS defaults on its payments to both Key Bank and Martin.

---

5. Recall that, with some exceptions (such as motor vehicles), a PMSI in *consumer goods* is automatically perfected—no filing is necessary. A PMSI that is *not* in consumer goods must still be perfected, however.

Does Key Bank or Martin have priority with respect to the new inventory delivered to SNS on June 28? If Martin has not perfected its security interest by June 28, Key Bank's after-acquired collateral clause has priority because it was the first to be perfected (on May 1). If, however, Martin has perfected *and* gives proper notice of its security interest to Key Bank before SNS takes possession of the goods on June 28, Martin has priority. ■

Buyers of the Collateral The UCC recognizes that there are certain types of buyers whose interest in purchased goods could conflict with those of a perfected secured party on the debtor's default. These include buyers in the ordinary course of business (as discussed), as well as buyers of farm products, instruments, documents, or securities. The UCC sets down special rules of priority for these types of buyers.

Exhibit 30–4 describes the various rules regarding the priority of claims to a debtor's collateral.

30–6 Rights and Duties of Debtors and Creditors

The security agreement itself determines most of the rights and duties of the debtor and the secured party. The UCC, however, imposes some rights and duties that apply unless the security agreement states otherwise.

30–6a Information Requests

At the time of filing a financing statement, a secured party can also furnish a *copy* of the financing statement to the filing officer. The secured party can request that the officer note the file number, date, and hour of the original filing on the copy [UCC 9–523(a)]. The filing officer must send this copy to the person designated by the secured party or to the debtor, if the debtor makes the request.

The filing officer must also give information to a person who is contemplating obtaining a security interest from a prospective debtor [UCC 9–523(c), (d)]. If requested, the filing officer must issue a certificate (for a fee) that provides information on possible perfected financing statements with respect to the named debtor.

30–6b Release, Assignment, and Amendment

A secured party can release all or part of any collateral described in the financing statement, thereby terminating its security interest in that collateral. The release is recorded by filing a uniform amendment form [UCC 9–512, 9–521(b)].

A secured party can also assign all or part of the security interest to a third party (the assignee). The assignee becomes the secured party of record if the assignment is filed by use of a uniform amendment form [UCC 9–514, 9–521(a)].

If the debtor and the secured party agree, they can amend the information in the filed financing statement and can add or substitute new collateral. They do so by filing a uniform amendment form that indicates the file number of the initial financing statement [UCC 9–512(a)]. An amendment does not extend the time period of perfection. If new collateral is added, however, the perfection date (for priority purposes) for the new collateral begins on the date the amendment is filed [UCC 9–512(b), (c)].

30–6c Confirmation or Accounting Request by Debtor

The debtor may believe that the amount of the unpaid debt or the list of the collateral subject to the security interest is inaccurate. The debtor has the right to request a confirmation of the unpaid debt or list of collateral [UCC 9–210]. The debtor is entitled to one request without charge every six months.

The secured party must comply with the debtor's confirmation request by authenticating and sending to the debtor an accounting within fourteen days after the request is received. Otherwise, the secured party can be held liable for any loss suffered by the debtor, plus $500 [UCC 9–210, 9–625(f)].

30–6d Termination Statement

When the debtor has fully paid the debt, if the secured party perfected the security interest by filing, the debtor is entitled to have a termination statement filed. Such a statement demonstrates to the public that the filed perfected security interest has been terminated [UCC 9–513].

Whenever consumer goods are involved, the secured party *must* file a termination statement (or, alternatively,

EXHIBIT 30–4 Priority of Claims to a Debtor's Collateral

PARTIES	PRIORITY
Perfected Secured Party versus **Unsecured Parties and Creditors**	A perfected secured party's interest has priority over the interests of most other parties, including unsecured creditors, unperfected secured parties, subsequent lien creditors, trustees in bankruptcy, and buyers who do not purchase the collateral in the ordinary course of business.
Perfected Secured Party versus **Perfected Secured Party**	Between two perfected secured parties in the same collateral, the general rule is that the first in time of perfection is the first in right to the collateral [UCC 9–322(a)(1)].
Perfected Secured Party versus **Perfected PMSI**	A PMSI, even if second in time of perfection, has priority providing that the following conditions are met: 1. *Other collateral*—A PMSI has priority, providing it is perfected within twenty days after the debtor takes possession [UCC 9–324(a)]. 2. *Inventory*—A PMSI has priority if it is perfected and proper written or authenticated notice is given to the other security-interest holder on or before the time the debtor takes possession [UCC 9–324(b)]. 3. *Software*—Applies to a PMSI in software only if used in goods subject to a PMSI. If the goods are inventory, priority is determined the same as for inventory. If they are not, priority is determined as for goods other than inventory [UCC 9–103(c), 9–324(f)].
Perfected Secured Party versus **Purchaser of Debtor's Collateral**	1. *Buyer of goods in the ordinary course of the seller's business*—Buyer prevails over a secured party's security interest, even if perfected and even if the buyer knows of the security interest [UCC 9–320(a)]. 2. *Buyer of consumer goods purchased outside the ordinary course of business*—Buyer prevails over a secured party's interest, even if perfected by attachment, providing the buyer purchased as follows: a. For value. b. Without actual knowledge of the security interest. c. For use as a consumer good. d. Prior to the secured party's perfection by filing [UCC 9–320(b)]. 3. *Buyer of chattel paper*—Buyer prevails if the buyer: a. Gave new value in making the purchase. b. Took possession in the ordinary course of the buyer's business. c. Took without knowledge of the security interest [UCC 9–330]. 4. *Buyer of instruments, documents, or securities*—Buyer who is a holder in due course, a holder to whom negotiable documents have been duly negotiated, or a bona fide purchaser of securities has priority over a previously perfected security interest [UCC 9–330(d), 9–331(a)]. 5. *Buyer of farm products*—Buyer from a farmer takes free and clear of perfected security interests unless, where permitted, a secured party files centrally an effective financing statement (EFS) or the buyer receives proper notice of the security interest before the sale.
Unperfected Secured Party versus **Unsecured Creditor**	An unperfected secured party prevails over unsecured creditors and creditors who have obtained judgments against the debtor but who have not begun the legal process to collect on those judgments [UCC 9–201(a)].

a release). The statement must be filed within one month of the final payment or within twenty days of receiving the debtor's authenticated demand, whichever is earlier [UCC 9–513(b)].

When the collateral is not consumer goods, the secured party is not required to file or to send a termination statement unless the debtor demands one [UCC 9–513(c)]. Whenever a secured party fails to file or send the termination statement as requested, the debtor can recover $500 plus any additional loss suffered [UCC 9–625(e)(4), (f)].

30–7 Default

Article 9 defines the rights, duties, and remedies of the secured party and of the debtor on the debtor's default. If the secured party fails to comply with his or her duties, the debtor is afforded particular rights and remedies under the UCC.

30–7a What Constitutes Default

What constitutes *default* is not always clear. In fact, Article 9 does not define the term. Instead, the UCC encourages the parties to include in their security agreements the standards under which their rights and duties will be measured [UCC 9–601, 9–603]. In so doing, parties can stipulate the conditions that will constitute a default. Often, these critical terms are shaped by creditors themselves in an attempt to provide the maximum protection possible.

The UCC does impose some requirements, however. The parties cannot agree to waive or alter certain UCC provisions, such as those involving the debtor's right to an accounting or disposition of collateral [UCC 9–602]. In addition, the terms may not run counter to the UCC's provisions regarding good faith and unconscionability.

Any breach of the terms of the security agreement can constitute default. Nevertheless, default occurs most commonly when the debtor fails to meet the scheduled payments that the parties have agreed on or when the debtor becomes bankrupt.

30–7b Basic Remedies

The rights and remedies of secured parties under Article 9 are *cumulative* [UCC 9–601(c)]. Therefore, if a creditor is unsuccessful in enforcing rights by one method, she

or he can pursue another method. Generally, a secured party's remedies can be divided into two basic categories: repossession and litigation.

Repossession of the Collateral—The Self-Help Remedy On the debtor's default, a secured party can take peaceful possession of the collateral covered by the security agreement without the use of the judicial process [UCC 9–609(b)]. This provision is referred to as the "self-help" provision of Article 9.

The UCC does not define what constitutes *peaceful possession*. The general rule is that the secured party must repossess the collateral without any breach of the peace (without trespassing or breaking and entering, for instance).

Judicial Remedies Alternatively, a secured party can relinquish the security interest and use any judicial remedy available, such as obtaining a judgment on the underlying debt, followed by execution and levy [UCC 9–601(a)]. **Execution** is the implementation of a court's decree or judgment. **Levy** is the legal process of obtaining of funds through the seizure and sale of nonexempt property, usually done after a writ of execution has been issued.

30–7c Disposition of Collateral

Once default has occurred and the secured party has obtained possession of the collateral, the secured party can:

1. Retain the collateral in full or partial satisfaction of the debt (subject to limitations, discussed next).
2. Sell, lease, license, or otherwise dispose of the collateral in any commercially reasonable manner and apply the proceeds toward satisfaction of the debt [UCC 9–602(7), 9–603, 9–610(a), 9–613, 9–620]. Any sale is always subject to procedures established by state law.

Retention of Collateral by the Secured Party Parties are sometimes better off if they do not sell the collateral. Therefore, the UCC generally allows secured parties to choose not to sell. A secured party may retain the collateral unless it consists of consumer goods and the debtor has paid 60 percent or more of the purchase price in a PMSI or debt in a non-PMSI [UCC 9–620(e)]. This general right to retain the collateral is subject to several limitations.

Notice Requirements. The secured party must notify the debtor of its proposal to retain the collateral. Notice is required unless the debtor has signed a statement renouncing or modifying her or his rights *after default* [UCC 9–620(a), 9–621].

If the collateral is consumer goods, the secured party does not need to give any other notice. In all other situations, the secured party must also send notice to any other secured party from whom the secured party has received notice of a claim of interest in the collateral. The secured party must also send notice to any *junior lien-holder* who held a security interest (or statutory lien) in the collateral ten days before the debtor consented to the retention [UCC 9–621]. (A **junior lienholder** is a party holding a lien that is subordinate to one or more other liens on the same property.)

Objections. The debtor or other party notified of the retention has the right to object. If, within twenty days after the notice is sent, the secured party receives a written objection, the secured party must sell or otherwise dispose of the collateral. If no written objection is received, the secured party may retain the collateral in full or partial satisfaction of the debtor's obligation [UCC 9–620(a), 9–621].

Consumer Goods When the collateral is consumer goods and the debtor has paid 60 percent of the purchase price on a PMSI or loan amount, the secured party must sell or otherwise dispose of the repossessed collateral within ninety days [UCC 9–620(e), (f)]. Failure to comply opens the secured party to an action for conversion or other liability under UCC 9–625(b) and (c). A secured party will not be liable, however, if the consumer-debtor signed a written statement *after default* renouncing or modifying the right to demand the sale of the goods [UCC 9–624].

Disposition of Collateral by the Secured Party
A secured party who does not choose to retain the collateral or who is required to sell it must dispose of it in a *commercially reasonable* manner. The secured party must notify the debtor and other specified parties in writing ahead of time about the sale or disposition of the collateral. Notification is not required if the collateral is perishable, will decline rapidly in value, or is of a type customarily sold on a recognized market [UCC 9–611(b), (c)].[6]

Sale Can Be Public or Private. The UCC allows substantial flexibility with regard to disposition. The sale can be public or private. The collateral can be disposed of in its present condition or following any commercially reasonable preparation or processing [UCC 9–610(a)]. The secured party may purchase the collateral at a public sale, but normally not at a private sale [UCC 9–610(c)].

Must Be Commercially Reasonable. Every aspect of the disposition's method, manner, time, and place must be commercially reasonable [UCC 9–610(b)]. If the secured party does not dispose of the collateral in a commercially reasonable manner, the price paid for the collateral at the sale may be negatively affected. In that situation, a court can reduce the amount of any deficiency that the debtor owes to the secured party [UCC 9–626(a)(3)].

Although the purpose of requiring a commercially reasonable disposition is to obtain a satisfactory price, the courts look at many factors to determine reasonableness. ■ **CASE IN POINT 30.16** Shannon Hicklin bought a used Ford Explorer under an installment sales contract. When she fell three payments behind—still owing $5,741.65—Onyx Acceptance Corporation repossessed the car and sold it for $1,500 at a private auction. After deducting the costs of repossession and sale, there was a deficiency under the contract of $5,018.88. Onyx filed a suit to collect this amount from Hicklin.

Onyx claimed that the sale was commercially reasonable because the auction price ($1,500) was more than 50 percent of the estimated market value ($2,335). The court, however, found that the price alone was not enough to prove reasonableness. Onyx needed to show that every aspect of the sale was conducted in a commercially reasonable manner. Alternatively, under UCC 9–627(b)(3), Onyx could show that the sale conformed with the reasonable commercial practices among dealers in that type of property. Because Onyx did not do either, it could not collect any deficiency from Hicklin.[7] ■

In the following case, two defaulting debtors alleged that their creditor's sale of the debtors' shares of stock was commercially unreasonable. The debtors contended that a different type of sale or a different "inducement" might have attracted a higher price.

---

6. The debtor may waive the right to receive a notice of disposition, but only after default [UCC 9–624(a)].

7. *Hicklin v. Onyx Corp.*, 970 A.2d 244 (Del.Sup.Ct. 2009).

Case Analysis 30.3

Smith v. Firstbank Corp.

Court of Appeals of Michigan, 2013 WL 951377 (2013).

In the Language of the Court

PER CURIAM.

* * * *

The facts in this secured transactions case are not in dispute. Plaintiffs [Bradley Smith, on his own behalf and on behalf of the John J. Smith Revocable Living Trust] borrowed funds from [defendant Firstbank Corporation] in 2002; the notes to defendant were secured with pledges of Sparton Corporation stock as well as other collateral. Plaintiffs defaulted on these loans. Eventually, after many modifications and extensions, defendant took possession of the pledged shares of Sparton stock. Shortly thereafter, defendant sold the stock in two private transactions: on January 12, 2010, it sold 602,170 shares to a brokerage firm at $4.84 per share, and on February 19, 2010, it sold 450,000 shares to a brokerage firm at $5.05 per share. The parties agree that the closing price for Sparton stock on the New York Stock Exchange on both sale dates was $6.05 per share. Defendant then released the remaining collateral to plaintiffs and remitted to plaintiffs by cashier's check the excess funds collected in the private sales. The value of the collateral retained by plaintiffs was over five million dollars.

Plaintiffs filed suit [in a Michigan state court] against defendant, alleging that the sales violated defendant's contractual duties to plaintiffs because they were "commercially unreasonable" * * *. Defendant moved the trial court for summary disposition [judgment]. * * * The trial court issued an Opinion and Order granting defendant's motion * * *. This appeal followed.

* * * *

At issue in the instant case is the secured party's disposition of collateral after the debtors' default. Defendant, the secured party, was authorized by MCL [Michigan Compiled Laws] 440.9609 [Michigan's version of UCC 9–609] to take possession of the collateral following plaintiffs' default. The parties agree that plaintiffs defaulted in the instant case, and that defendant was within its rights to take possession of the pledged shares.

MCL 440.9610 [Michigan's version of UCC 9–610] governs the disposition of collateral after default, and provides in relevant part: * * *

> Every aspect of a disposition of collateral, including the method, manner, time, place, and other terms, must be commercially reasonable.

Further, MCL 440.9627 [Michigan's version of UCC 9–627] provides guidance for determination of whether the disposition of collateral was commercially reasonable, and provides in relevant part: * * *

> The fact that a greater amount could have been obtained by a collection, enforcement, disposition, or acceptance at a different time or in a different method from that selected by the secured party is not of itself sufficient to preclude the secured party from establishing that the collection, enforcement, disposition, or acceptance was made in a commercially reasonable manner.

* * * *

* * * *The circumstances surrounding previous sales of Sparton stock on the public market, and concerns about what public sales would do to the share price, rendered defendant's choice to sell in private transactions reasonable.* * * * In 2008, Wachovia [Bank] sold approximately 400,000 shares of Sparton to satisfy plaintiff Smith's debts. The sale required 18 separate transactions over a two-month period; during that period the share price declined by almost 50 percent. * * * *It was not commercially unreasonable for defendant to seek a private sale to avoid this risk.* [Emphasis added.]

Plaintiffs further argue, however, that even if defendant's choice to conduct a private, bulk sale was reasonable, the manner in which it conducted the private sale was not. * * * The record does not support this contention. An e-mail from Rick Barratt, agent of defendant, to Oberon Securities indicated that, in addition to requesting that Oberon bring them a buyer, defendant * * * "directed [our investment banker] to bring similar type offers to us as well." In addition, defendant's Chief Executive Officer testified * * * that "discounts in large transactions, in thinly traded stocks, were common" and that he was advised by employees of Oberon Securities that selling a "block this large would require a discount of 15 to 20 percent."

The evidence thus does not support the contention that defendant did not seek multiple offers or seek to get the best price for the stock. Rather, the evidence shows that defendant * * * received one offer for Smith's stock, at a discount. Rather than risk public sales and a repeat of what happened in 2008, defendant made the sale. In fact, plaintiffs' contention that defendant did not attempt to garner the best sale price it could is contradicted by the fact that defendant was able to sell the second block of shares (the shares pledged by the trust) for 21 cents more per share, notwithstanding that the closing price for Sparton was exactly the same on the day of both the first and second sales.

* * * *

* * * Although plaintiffs speculate that public sales would have resulted in a higher price, or that the private buyer could have been induced to pay a higher price, speculation and conjecture are insufficient to allow an opposing party to survive a motion for summary disposition.

Affirmed.

Case 30.3 Continued

Legal Reasoning Questions

1. What type of property was at the center of the dispute in this case? How did that property become involved in the dispute?

2. On what ground did the plaintiffs argue that the bank should not have been granted a summary judgment?

3. Why does collateral have to be disposed of in a commercially reasonable manner? Is price alone enough to prove reasonableness? Why or why not?

Proceeds from Disposition Proceeds from the disposition of collateral after default on the underlying debt are distributed in the following order:

1. Reasonable expenses incurred by the secured party in repossessing, storing, and reselling the collateral.

2. Balance of the debt owed to the secured party.

3. Junior lienholders who have made written or authenticated demands.

4. Any surplus to the debtor, unless the collateral consists of accounts, payment intangibles, promissory notes, or chattel paper [UCC 9–608(a); 9–615(a), (e)].

Noncash Proceeds Sometimes, the secured party receives noncash proceeds from the disposition of collateral after default. Whenever that occurs, the secured party must make a value determination and apply this value in a commercially reasonable manner [UCC 9–608(a)(3), 9–615(c)].

Deficiency Judgment Often, after proper disposition of the collateral, the secured party still has not collected all that the debtor owes. Unless otherwise agreed, the debtor normally is liable for any deficiency, and the creditor can obtain a **deficiency judgment** from a court to collect the deficiency. Practically speaking, though, debtors who have defaulted on a loan rarely have the cash to pay any deficiency.

Note that if the underlying transaction is a sale of accounts, chattel paper, or promissory notes, the debtor is *not* liable for any deficiency. The debtor is also not entitled to any surplus from the disposition of these types of collateral, unless that right is granted by the security agreement [UCC 9–615(e)].

Redemption Rights The debtor or any other secured party can exercise the right of *redemption* of the collateral. Redemption may occur at any time before the secured party disposes of the collateral, enters into a contract for its disposition, or discharges the debtor's obligation by retaining the collateral. To redeem the collateral, the debtor or other secured party must tender the entire obligation that is owed, plus any reasonable expenses and attorneys' fees incurred by the secured party in retaking and maintaining the collateral [UCC 9–623].

Concept Summary 30.3 provides a review of the secured party's remedies on the debtor's default.

Concept Summary 30.3

Remedies of the Secured Party on the Debtor's Default

Repossession of the Collateral	The secured party may take possession (peacefully or by court order) of the collateral covered by the security agreement and then pursue one of two alternatives:
	1. *Retain the collateral*—unless the collateral is consumer goods and the debtor has paid 60 percent of the selling price on a PMSI or 60 percent of the debt on a non-PMSI. To retain the collateral, the secured party must—
	   a. Give notice to the debtor if the debtor has not signed a statement renouncing or modifying his or her rights after default. With consumer goods, no other notice is necessary.
	   b. Send notice to any other secured party who has given written or authenticated notice of a claim to the same collateral or who has filed a security interest or a statutory lien ten days before the debtor consented to the retention. If an objection is received within twenty days from the debtor or any other secured party given notice, the creditor must dispose of the collateral according to the requirements of UCC 9–602, 9–603, 9–610, and 9–613. Otherwise, the creditor may retain the collateral in full or partial satisfaction of the debt.
	2. *Dispose of the collateral*—in accordance with the requirements of UCC 9–602(7), 9–603, 9–610(a), and 9–613. To do so, the secured party must—
	   a. Dispose of (sell, lease, or license) the goods in a commercially reasonable manner.
	   b. Notify the debtor and (except in sales of consumer goods) other identified persons, including those who have given notice of claims to the collateral to be sold (unless the collateral is perishable or will decline rapidly in value).
	   c. Apply the proceeds in the following order:
	     i. Expenses incurred by the secured party in repossessing, storing, and reselling the collateral.
	     ii. The balance of the debt owed to the secured party.
	     iii. Junior lienholders who have made written or authenticated demands.
	     iv. Surplus to the debtor (unless the collateral consists of accounts, payment intangibles, promissory notes, or chattel paper).

Judicial Remedies	The secured party may relinquish the security interest and proceed with any judicial remedy available, such as obtaining a judgment on the underlying debt, followed by execution and levy on the nonexempt assets of the debtor.

Reviewing: Secured Transactions

Paul Barton owned a small property-management company, doing business as Brighton Homes. In October, Barton went on a spending spree. First, he bought a Bose surround-sound system for his home from KDM Electronics. The next day, he purchased a Wilderness Systems kayak and roof rack from Outdoor Outfitters, and the day after that he bought a new Toyota 4-Runner financed through Bridgeport Auto. Two weeks later, Barton purchased six new iMac computers for his office, also from KDM Electronics. Barton bought each of these items under an installment sales contract. Six months later, Barton's property-management business was failing. He could not make the payments due on any of these purchases and thus defaulted on the loans. Using the information presented in the chapter, answer the following questions.

1. For which of Barton's purchases (the surround-sound system, the kayak, the 4-Runner, and the iMacs) would the creditor need to file a financing statement to perfect its security interest?
2. Suppose that Barton's contract for the office computers mentioned only the name *Brighton Homes*. What would be the consequences if KDM Electronics filed a financing statement that listed only Brighton Homes as the debtor's name?
3. Which of these purchases would qualify as a PMSI in consumer goods?
4. Suppose that after KDM Electronics repossesses the surround-sound system, it decides to keep the system rather than sell it. Can KDM do this under Article 9? Why or why not?

Debate This . . .   *A financing statement that does not have the debtor's exact name should still be effective because creditors should always be protected when debtors default.*

Terms and Concepts

after-acquired property 567	deficiency judgment 575	proceeds 565
attachment 557	execution 572	purchase-money security
authenticate 557	financing statement 556	interest (PMSI) 563
collateral 556	floating lien 568	secured party 556
continuation statement 563	junior lienholder 573	secured transaction 556
cross-collateralization 567	levy 572	security agreement 556
debtor 556	perfection 559	security interest 556

Issue Spotters

1. Nero needs $500 to buy textbooks and other supplies. Olivia agrees to loan Nero $500, accepting Nero's computer as collateral. They put their agreement in writing. How can Olivia let other creditors know of her interest in the computer? (See *Creation of a Security Interest*.)
2. Liberty Bank loans Michelle $5,000 to buy a car, which is used as collateral to secure the loan. After repaying less than 50 percent of the loan, Michelle defaults. Liberty could repossess and keep the car, but the bank does not want it. What are the alternatives? (See *Default*.)

• **Check your answers to the Issue Spotters against the answers provided in Appendix D at the end of this text.**

Business Scenarios

30–1. Priorities. Redford is a seller of electric generators. He purchases a large quantity of generators from a manufacturer, Mallon Corp., by making a down payment and signing an agreement to make the balance of payments over a period of time. The agreement gives Mallon Corp. a security interest in the generators and the proceeds. Mallon Corp. properly files a financing statement on its security interest. Redford receives the generators and immediately sells one of them to Garfield on an installment contract, with payment to be made in twelve equal installments. At the time of the sale, Garfield knows of Mallon's security interest. Two months later, Redford goes into default on his payments to Mallon. Discuss Mallon's rights against Garfield in this situation. (See *Priorities.*)

30–2. Perfection of a Security Interest. Marsh has a prize horse named Arabian Knight. Marsh is in need of working capital. She borrows $50,000 from Mendez, who takes possession of Arabian Knight as security for the loan. No written agreement is signed. Discuss whether, in the absence of a written agreement, Mendez has a security interest in Arabian Knight. If Mendez does have a security interest, is it a perfected security interest? Explain. (See *Perfection of a Security Interest.*)

30–3. The Scope of a Security Interest. Edward owned a retail sporting goods shop. A new ski resort was being constructed in his area, and to take advantage of the potential business, Edward decided to expand his operations. He borrowed a large sum from his bank, which took a security interest in his present inventory and any after-acquired inventory as collateral for the loan. The bank properly perfected the security interest by filing a financing statement. Edward's business was profitable, so he doubled his inventory. A year later, just a few months after the ski resort had opened, an avalanche destroyed the ski slope and lodge. Edward's business consequently took a turn for the worse, and he defaulted on his debt to the bank. The bank then sought possession of his entire inventory, even though the inventory was now twice as large as it had been when the loan was made. Edward claimed that the bank had rights to only half of his inventory. Was Edward correct? Explain. (See *The Scope of a Security Interest.*)

Business Case Problems

30–4. Spotlight on Radio Shack—Priorities. In June 1995, Michael and Debra Boudreaux, doing business as D&J Enterprises, Inc., bought a retail electronics store operated under a franchise from Radio Shack. They borrowed from Cabool State Bank to pay for the business and signed loan documents and a financing statement, which identified them as "Debtors." Elsewhere on the financing statement, the bank identified "D&J Enterprises, Inc., Radio Shack, Dealer, Debra K. Boudreaux, Michael C. Boudreaux" as "Debtors." The statement covered, in part, the store inventory.

Before the end of the year, Michael and Debra changed the name of their business to Tri-B Enterprises, Inc. In January 1998, the store closed. The next month, Radio Shack terminated the franchise. Despite the lack of a security interest, Radio Shack took possession of the inventory, claiming that the couple and Tri-B owed the company $6,394.73. The bank filed a suit in a Missouri state court against Radio Shack, claiming a perfected security interest in the inventory with priority over Radio Shack's claim. Did the bank's security interest take priority over Radio Shack's claim? Why or why not? [*Cabool State Bank v. Radio Shack,* 65 S.W.3d 613 (Mo. App. 2002)] (See *Priorities.*)

30–5. Default. Primesouth Bank issued a loan to Okefenokee Aircraft, Inc. (OAI), to buy a plane. OAI executed a note in favor of Primesouth in the amount of $161,306.25 plus interest. The plane secured the note. When OAI defaulted, Primesouth repossessed the plane. Instead of disposing of the collateral and seeking a deficiency judgment, however, the bank retained possession of the plane and filed a suit in

a Georgia state court against OAI to enforce the note. OAI did not deny that it had defaulted on the note or dispute the amount due. Instead, OAI argued that Primesouth Bank was not acting in a commercially reasonable manner. According to OAI, the creditor must sell the collateral and apply the proceeds against the debt. What is a secured creditor's obligation in these circumstances? Can the creditor retain the collateral and seek a judgment for the amount of the underlying debt, or is a sale required? Discuss. [*Okefenokee Aircraft, Inc. v. Primesouth Bank,* 296 Ga.App. 782, 676 S.E.2d 394 (2009)] (See *Default.*)

30–6. Disposition of Collateral. PRA Aviation, LLC, borrowed $3 million from Center Capital Corp. to buy a Gates Learjet 55B. Center perfected a security interest in the plane. Later, PRA defaulted on the loan, and Center obtained possession of the jet. The market, design, and mechanical condition of similar aircraft were reviewed to estimate the jet's value at $1.45 million. The jet was marketed in trade publications, on the Internet, and by direct advertising to select customers for $1.595 million. There were three offers. Center sold the jet to the high bidder for $1.3 million. Was the sale commercially reasonable? Explain. [*Center Capital Corp. v. PRA Aviation, LLC,* 2011 WL 867516 (E.D.Pa. 2011)] (See *Default.*)

30–7. Business Case Problem with Sample Answer— Perfecting a Security Interest. Thomas Tille owned M.A.T.T. Equipment Co. To operate the business, Tille borrowed funds from Union Bank. For each loan, Union filed a financing statement that included Tille's signature and address, the bank's address, and a description of the collateral. The first loan covered all of Tille's equipment, including "any after-acquired property." The second loan covered a truck crane "whether owned now or acquired later." The third loan covered a "Bobcat mini-excavator." Did these financing statements perfect Union's security interests? Explain. [*Union Bank Co. v. Heban,* 2012-Ohio-30 (Ohio App. 2012)] (See *Perfection of a Security Interest.*)

• For a sample answer for Problem 30–7, go to Appendix E at the end of this text.

30–8. Disposition of Collateral. With a loan of 1.4 million euros from Barclays Bank, PLC, Thomas Poynter bought a yacht. The loan agreement gave Barclays multiple stand-alone options on default. One option required the lender to give ten days' advance notice of a sale. A different option permitted the lender to avoid this requirement. When Poynter did not repay the loan, Barclays repossessed the yacht and notified Poynter that it would be sold—but did not specify a date, time, or place. Two months later, the yacht was sold. The sale price was less than Poynter owed, and Barclays filed a suit in a federal district court for the deficiency. Is Barclays entitled to collect even though it did not give Poynter ten days' advance notice of the sale? Explain. [*Barclays Bank PLC v. Poynter,* 710 F.3d 16 (1st Cir. 2013)] (See *Default.*)

30–9. Perfection of a Security Interest. G&K Farms, a North Dakota partnership, operated a farm in Texas. G&K was insured under the Supplemental Revenue Assistance Payments Program (SURE), through which the federal government provides financial assistance for crop losses caused by natural disasters. PHI Financial Services, Inc., loaned G&K $6.6 million. PHI filed a financing statement that described the collateral as the debtor's interest in "Government Payments." The document did not refer to the farm's crops. G&K defaulted on the loan. Later, G&K received a SURE payment for crop losses and transferred some of the funds to its law firm, Johnston Law Office, P.C., in payment for services. PHI brought an action against Johnston to recover those funds as partial payment on its loan to G&K. Johnston argued that PHI did not have a perfected security interest in the SURE payment because the financing statement did not identify the crops. Was the description of the collateral in the financing statement sufficient? Why or why not? [*PHI Financial Services, Inc. v. Johnston Law Office, P.C.,* 2016 ND 20, 874 N.W.2d 910 (2016)] (See *Perfection of a Security Interest.*)

30–10. A Question of Ethics—Priorities. *Mark Denton cosigned a $101,250 loan issued by the First Interstate Bank (FIB) in Missoula, Montana, to Denton's friend Eric Anderson. Denton's business assets—a mini-warehouse operation—secured the loan. On his own, Anderson obtained a $260,000 U.S. Small Business Administration (SBA) loan from FIB at the same time. The purpose of both loans was to buy logging equipment so that Anderson could start a business. Two years after the loan was made, the business failed. As a consequence, FIB repossessed and sold the equipment and applied the proceeds to the SBA loan. FIB then asked Denton to pay the other loan's outstanding balance ($98,460), plus interest. When Denton refused, FIB initiated proceedings to obtain his business assets. Denton filed a suit in a Montana state court against FIB. He claimed, in part, that Anderson's equipment was the collateral for the loan that FIB was attempting to collect from Denton. [Denton v. First Interstate Bank of Commerce, 2006 MT 193, 333 Mont. 169, 142 P.3d 797 (2006)] (See Priorities.)*

(a) Denton's assets served as the security for Anderson's loan because Anderson had nothing to offer. When the loan was obtained, Dean Gillmore, FIB's loan officer, explained to them that if Anderson defaulted, the proceeds from the sale of the logging equipment would be applied to the SBA loan first. Under these circumstances, is it fair to hold Denton liable for the unpaid balance of Anderson's loan? Why or why not?

(b) Denton argued that the loan contract was unconscionable and constituted a "contract of adhesion." What makes a contract unconscionable? Did the transaction between the parties in this case qualify? What is a "contract of adhesion"? Was this deal unenforceable on that basis? Explain.

Legal Reasoning Group Activity

30–11. Security Interests. Nick Sabol, doing business in the recording industry as Sound Farm Productions, applied to Morton Community Bank for a $58,000 loan to expand his business. Besides the loan application, Sabol signed a promissory note that referred to the bank's rights in "any collateral." Sabol also signed a letter authorizing Morton Community Bank to execute, file, and record all financing statements, amendments, and other documents required by Article 9 to establish a security interest. Sabol did not sign any other documents, including the financing statement, which contained a description of the collateral. Two years later, without having repaid the loan, Sabol filed for bankruptcy. The bank claimed a security interest in Sabol's sound equipment. (See *Creation of a Security Interest.*)

(a) The first group will list all the requirements of an enforceable security interest and explain why each of these elements is necessary.

(b) The second group will determine if Morton Community Bank had a valid security interest.

(c) The third group will discuss whether a bank should be able to execute financing statements on a debtor's behalf without the debtor being present or signing them. Are there are any drawbacks to this practice? Explain.

CHAPTER 31

Bankruptcy Law

Many people in today's economy are struggling to pay their debts. Although in the old days, debtors were punished and sometimes even sent to prison for failing to pay what they owed, debtors today rarely go to jail. They have many other options, including *bankruptcy*—the last resort in resolving debtor-creditor problems.

The right to petition for bankruptcy relief under federal law is an essential aspect of our capitalistic society, in which we have great opportunities for financial success but may also encounter financial difficulties. Therefore, every businessperson should have some understanding of this topic.

31–1 The Bankruptcy Code

Bankruptcy relief is provided under federal law. Although state laws may play a role in bankruptcy proceedings, particularly state laws governing property, the governing law is based on federal legislation.

Article I, Section 8, of the U.S. Constitution gave Congress the power to establish "uniform laws on the subject of bankruptcies throughout the United States." Federal bankruptcy legislation was first enacted in 1898 and since then has undergone several modifications, most recently in the 2005 Bankruptcy Reform Act.[1] Federal bankruptcy laws (as amended) are called the Bankruptcy Code or, more simply, the Code.

31–1a Goals of Bankruptcy Law

Bankruptcy law in the United States has two main goals:

1. To protect a debtor by giving him or her a fresh start without creditors' claims.
2. To ensure equitable treatment of creditors who are competing for a debtor's assets.

Thus, the law attempts to balance the rights of the debtor and of the creditors.

Although the twin goals of bankruptcy remain the same, the balance between them shifted somewhat after the 2005 reform legislation. That law was enacted, in part, because of the growing concern that the law allowed too many debtors to avoid paying their debts. Thus, a major goal of the reforms was to require more consumers to pay as many of their debts as possible instead of having those debts fully extinguished in bankruptcy.

31–1b Bankruptcy Courts

Bankruptcy proceedings are held in federal bankruptcy courts, which are under the authority of U.S. district courts. Rulings from bankruptcy courts can be appealed to the district courts.

A bankruptcy court can conduct a jury trial if the appropriate district court has authorized it and the parties to the bankruptcy consent. Bankruptcy courts follow the Federal Rules of Bankruptcy Procedure rather than the Federal Rules of Civil Procedure. Bankruptcy court judges are appointed for terms of fourteen years.

31–1c Types of Bankruptcy Relief

The Bankruptcy Code is contained in Title 11 of the *United States Code* and has eight chapters. Chapters 1, 3, and 5 of the Code contain general definitional provisions, as well as provisions governing case administration, creditors, the debtor, and the estate. These three chapters normally apply to all kinds of bankruptcies.

Four chapters of the Code set forth the most important types of relief that debtors can seek:

1. Chapter 7 provides for **liquidation** proceedings (the selling of all nonexempt assets and the distribution of the proceeds to the debtor's creditors).

---

1. The full title of the act was the Bankruptcy Abuse Prevention and Consumer Protection Act, Pub. L. No. 109-8, 119 Stat. 23 (April 20, 2005).

2. Chapter 11 governs reorganizations.

3. Chapter 12 (for family farmers and family fishermen) and 13 (for individuals) provide for the adjustment of debts by persons with regular incomes.[2]

Note that a debtor (except for a municipality) need not be insolvent[3] to file for bankruptcy relief under the Bankruptcy Code. Anyone obligated to a creditor can declare bankruptcy.

31–1d Special Requirements for Consumer-Debtors

A **consumer-debtor** is a debtor whose debts result primarily from the purchase of goods for personal, family, or household use. The Bankruptcy Code requires that the clerk of the court give all consumer-debtors written notice of the general purpose, benefits, and costs of each chapter under which they might proceed. In addition, the clerk must provide consumer-debtors with information on the types of services available from credit counseling agencies.

31–2 Liquidation Proceedings

Liquidation under Chapter 7 of the Bankruptcy Code is probably the most familiar type of bankruptcy proceeding and is often referred to as an *ordinary,* or *straight, bankruptcy.* Put simply, a debtor in a liquidation bankruptcy turns all assets over to a **bankruptcy trustee,** a person appointed by the court to manage the debtor's funds. The trustee sells the nonexempt assets and distributes the proceeds to creditors. With certain exceptions, the remaining debts are then **discharged** (extinguished), and the debtor is relieved of the obligation to pay the debts.

Any "person"—defined as including individuals, partnerships, and corporations[4]—may be a debtor in a liquidation proceeding. A husband and wife may file jointly for bankruptcy under a single petition. Railroads, insurance companies, banks, savings and loan associations, investment companies licensed by the Small Business Administration, and credit unions *cannot* be debtors in a liquidation bankruptcy, however. Other chapters of the Bankruptcy Code or other federal or state statutes apply to them.

A straight bankruptcy can be commenced by the filing of either a voluntary or an involuntary **petition in bankruptcy**—the document that is filed with a bankruptcy court to initiate bankruptcy proceedings. If a debtor files the petition, the bankruptcy is voluntary. If one or more creditors file a petition to force the debtor into bankruptcy, the bankruptcy is involuntary. We discuss both voluntary and involuntary bankruptcy proceedings under Chapter 7 in the following subsections.

31–2a Voluntary Bankruptcy

To bring a voluntary petition in bankruptcy, the debtor files official forms designated for that purpose in the bankruptcy court. The law now requires that *before* debtors can file a petition, they must receive credit counseling from an approved nonprofit agency within the 180-day period preceding the date of filing. Debtors filing a Chapter 7 petition must include a certificate proving that they have received individual or group counseling from an approved agency within the last 180 days.

A consumer-debtor who is filing for liquidation bankruptcy must confirm the accuracy of the petition's contents. The debtor must also state in the petition, at the time of filing, that he or she understands the relief available under other chapters of the Code and has chosen to proceed under Chapter 7.

Attorneys representing the consumer-debtors must file an affidavit stating that they have informed the debtors of the relief available under each chapter of the Bankruptcy Code. In addition, the attorneys must reasonably attempt to verify the accuracy of the consumer-debtors' petitions and schedules (described next). Failure to do so is considered perjury.

Chapter 7 Schedules The voluntary petition must contain the following schedules:

1. A list of both secured and unsecured creditors, their addresses, and the amount of debt owed to each.

2. A statement of the financial affairs of the debtor.

3. A list of all property owned by the debtor, including property that the debtor claims is exempt.

4. A list of current income and expenses.

---

2. There are no Chapters 2, 4, 6, 8, or 10 in Title 11. Such "gaps" are not uncommon in the *United States Code.* They occur because chapter numbers (or other subdivisional unit numbers) are sometimes reserved for future use when a statute is enacted. (A gap may also appear if a law has been repealed.)

3. The inability to pay debts as they become due is known as *equitable* insolvency. *Balance sheet* insolvency, which exists when a debtor's liabilities exceed assets, is not the test. Thus, debtors whose cash-flow problems become severe may petition for bankruptcy voluntarily or be forced into involuntary bankruptcy even though their assets far exceed their liabilities.

4. The definition of *corporation* includes unincorporated companies and associations. It also covers labor unions.

5. A certificate of credit counseling (as mentioned previously).

6. Proof of payments received from employers within sixty days prior to the filing of the petition.

7. A statement of the amount of monthly income, itemized to show how the amount is calculated.

8. A copy of the debtor's federal income tax return for the most recent year ending immediately before the filing of the petition.

The official forms must be completed accurately, sworn to under oath, and signed by the debtor. To conceal assets or knowingly supply false information on these schedules is a crime under the bankruptcy laws.

With the exception of tax returns, failure to file the required schedules within forty-five days after the filing of the petition will result in an automatic dismissal of the petition. (An extension may be granted, however.) The debtor has up to seven days before the date of the first creditors' meeting to provide a copy of the most recent tax returns to the trustee.

Tax Returns during Bankruptcy In addition, a debtor may be required to file a tax return at the end of each tax year while the case is pending and to provide a copy to the court. This may be done at the request of the court or the **U.S. trustee**—a government official who performs administrative tasks that a bankruptcy judge would otherwise have to perform. Any *party in interest* (a party, such as a creditor, who has a valid interest in the outcome of the proceedings) may make this request as well. Debtors may also be required to file tax returns during Chapter 11 and 13 bankruptcies.

Substantial Abuse—Means Test In the past, a bankruptcy court could dismiss a Chapter 7 petition if the use of Chapter 7 would constitute a "substantial abuse" of bankruptcy law. Today, the law provides a *means test* to determine a debtor's eligibility for Chapter 7.

The purpose of the test is to keep upper-income people from abusing the bankruptcy process by filing for Chapter 7, as was thought to have happened in the past. The test forces more people to file for Chapter 13 bankruptcy rather than have their debts discharged under Chapter 7.

The Basic Formula. A debtor wishing to file for bankruptcy must complete the means test to determine whether she or he qualifies for Chapter 7. The debtor's average monthly income in recent months is compared with the median income in the geographic area in which the person lives. (The U.S. Trustee Program provides these data at its Web site.) If the debtor's income is below

the median income, the debtor usually is allowed to file for Chapter 7 bankruptcy, as there is no presumption of bankruptcy abuse.

Applying the Means Test to Future Disposable Income. If the debtor's income is above the median income, then further calculations must be made. The calculations are meant to determine whether the person will have sufficient disposable income in the future to repay at least some of his or her unsecured debts.

As a basis for the calculations, it is presumed that the debtor's recent monthly income will continue for the next sixty months. *Disposable income* is then calculated by subtracting living expenses and secured debt payments, such as mortgage payments, from monthly income.

Living expenses are amounts allowed under formulas used by the Internal Revenue Service (IRS). The IRS allowances include modest allocations for food, clothing, housing, utilities, transportation (including a car payment), health care, and other necessities. (The U.S. Trustee Program's Web site also provides these amounts.) The allowances do not include expenditures for items such as cell phones and cable television service.

Can the Debtor Afford to Pay Unsecured Debts? Once future disposable income has been estimated, that amount is used to determine whether the debtor will have income that could be applied to unsecured debts. The courts may also consider the debtor's bad faith or other circumstances indicating abuse.

■ **CASE IN POINT 31.1** Christopher Dean Ng and his wife filed for Chapter 7 bankruptcy, hoping primarily to discharge their mortgage debt of $464,830. At the time the petition was filed, Ng was forty-three years old and worked as an electronic technician. He earned a monthly salary of $7,439.47, as well as a military pension of $1,439.88 a month. His wife was not employed. From Ng's monthly salary, he made a voluntary contribution of $520 to an employer 401(k) plan and a $343 payment on a pension loan. In calculating his disposable income, Ng excluded these amounts.

The U.S. trustee filed a motion to dismiss Ng's petition due to substantial abuse, claiming that the retirement contributions should be disallowed. The court agreed and dismissed the Chapter 7 petition. The Ngs appealed, and the appellate court affirmed. Ng's retirement contributions were not reasonably necessary based on his age, his financial circumstances, and his testimony that he was not planning to retire for at least twenty years. The Ngs could afford to repay some of their debts before they made monthly contributions toward retirement.[5] ■

5. *In re Ng*, 422 Bankr. 118 (9th Cir. 2012).

Additional Grounds for Dismissal As already noted, a court can dismiss a debtor's voluntary petition for Chapter 7 relief for substantial abuse or for failure to provide the necessary documents within the specified time.

In addition, a court might dismiss a Chapter 7 in two other situations. First, if the debtor has been convicted of a violent crime or a drug-trafficking offense, the victim can file a motion to dismiss the voluntary petition.[6] Second, if the debtor fails to pay postpetition domestic-support obligations (which include child and spousal support), the court may dismiss the debtor's petition.

Order for Relief If the voluntary petition for bankruptcy is found to be proper, the filing of the petition will itself constitute an **order for relief.** (An order for relief is a court's grant of assistance to a petitioner.) Once a consumer-debtor's voluntary petition has been filed, the trustee and creditors must be given notice of the order for relief by mail not more than twenty days after entry of the order.

31–2b Involuntary Bankruptcy

An involuntary bankruptcy occurs when the debtor's creditors force the debtor into bankruptcy proceedings. An involuntary case cannot be filed against a charitable institution or a farmer (an individual or business that receives more than 50 percent of gross income from farming operations).

An involuntary petition should not be used as an everyday debt-collection device, and the Code provides penalties for the filing of frivolous petitions against debtors. If the court dismisses an involuntary petition, the petitioning creditors may be required to pay the costs and attorneys' fees incurred by the debtor in defending against the petition. If the petition was filed in bad faith, damages can be awarded for injury to the debtor's reputation. Punitive damages may also be awarded.

Requirements For an involuntary action to be filed, the following requirements must be met:

1. If the debtor has twelve or more creditors, three or more of these creditors having unsecured claims totaling at least $15,325 must join in the petition.
2. If a debtor has fewer than twelve creditors, one or more creditors having a claim totaling $15,325 or more may file.[7]

Order for Relief If the debtor challenges the involuntary petition, a hearing will be held, and the bankruptcy court will enter an order for relief if it finds either of the following:

1. The debtor is not paying debts as they come due.
2. A general receiver, assignee, or custodian took possession of, or was appointed to take charge of, substantially all of the debtor's property within 120 days before the filing of the petition.

If the court grants an order for relief, the debtor will be required to supply the same information in the bankruptcy schedules as in a voluntary bankruptcy.

31–2c Automatic Stay

The moment a petition, either voluntary or involuntary, is filed, an **automatic stay,** or suspension, of all actions by creditors against the debtor or the debtor's property normally goes into effect. The automatic stay prohibits creditors from taking any act to collect, assess, or recover a claim against the debtor that arose before the filing of the petition. The stay normally continues until the bankruptcy proceeding is closed or dismissed. (In some circumstances, it is possible to petition the bankruptcy court for relief from the automatic stay, as will be discussed shortly.)

If a creditor *knowingly* violates the automatic stay (a willful violation), any injured party, including the debtor, is entitled to recover actual damages, costs, and attorneys' fees. Punitive damages may be awarded as well.

■ **CASE IN POINT 31.2** Stefanie Kuehn filed for bankruptcy. When she requested a transcript from the university at which she had obtained her master's degree, the university refused because she owed more than $6,000 in tuition. Kuehn complained to the court. The court ruled that the university had violated the automatic stay by refusing to provide a transcript because it was attempting to collect an unpaid tuition debt.[8] ■

The Adequate Protection Doctrine Underlying the Code's automatic-stay provision for a secured creditor is a concept known as *adequate protection.* The **adequate protection doctrine,** among other things, protects secured creditors from losing their security as a result of the automatic stay.

The bankruptcy court can provide adequate protection by requiring the debtor or trustee to make periodic cash payments or a one-time cash payment. The court can also require the debtor or trustee to provide additional collateral or replacement liens to the extent that

---

6. Note that the court may not dismiss a case on this ground if the debtor's bankruptcy is necessary to satisfy a claim for a domestic-support obligation.
7. 11 U.S.C. Section 303. The amounts stated in this chapter are in accordance with those computed on April 1, 2016.

8. *In re Kuehn,* 563 F.3d 289 (7th Cir. 2009).

the stay may actually cause the value of the property to decrease.

Exceptions to the Automatic Stay

The Code provides the following exceptions to the automatic stay:

1. Collection efforts can continue for domestic-support obligations. These obligations include any debt owed to or recoverable by a spouse, a former spouse, a child of the debtor, that child's parent or guardian, or a governmental unit.
2. Proceedings against the debtor related to divorce, child custody or visitation, domestic violence, and support enforcement are not stayed.
3. Investigations by a securities regulatory agency (such as an investigation into insider trading) can continue.
4. Certain statutory liens for property taxes are not stayed.

Requests for Relief from the Automatic Stay

A secured creditor or other party in interest can petition the bankruptcy court for relief from the automatic stay. If a creditor or other party requests relief from the stay, the stay will automatically terminate sixty days after the request, unless the court grants an extension[9] or the parties agree otherwise.

Secured Property   The automatic stay on secured property terminates forty-five days after the creditors' meeting unless the debtor redeems or reaffirms certain debts. (Creditors' meetings and reaffirmation will be discussed later in this chapter.) In other words, the debtor cannot keep the secured property (such as a financed automobile), even if she or he continues to make payments on it, without reinstating the rights of the secured party to collect on the debt.

Bad Faith   If the debtor had two or more bankruptcy petitions dismissed during the prior year, the Code presumes bad faith. In such a situation, the automatic stay does *not* go into effect until the court determines that the petition was filed in good faith.

In addition, the automatic stay on secured debts will terminate thirty days after the petition is filed if the debtor filed a bankruptcy petition that was dismissed within the prior year. Any party in interest can request that the court extend the stay by showing that the filing is in good faith.

31–2d Estate in Bankruptcy

On the commencement of a liquidation proceeding under Chapter 7, an *estate in bankruptcy* (sometimes called an *estate in property*) is created. The estate consists of all the debtor's interests in property currently held, wherever located. The estate in bankruptcy includes all of the following:

1. *Community property* (property jointly owned by married persons in certain states).
2. Property transferred in a transaction voidable by the trustee.
3. Proceeds and profits from the property of the estate.

Certain after-acquired property to which the debtor becomes entitled *within 180 days after filing* may also become part of the estate. Such after-acquired property includes gifts, inheritances, property settlements (from divorce), and life insurance death proceeds.

Generally, though, the filing of a bankruptcy petition fixes a dividing line. Property acquired prior to the filing of the petition becomes property of the estate, and property acquired after the filing of the petition, except as just noted, remains the debtor's.

31–2e The Bankruptcy Trustee

Promptly after the order for relief in the liquidation proceeding has been entered, a trustee is appointed. The basic duty of the trustee is to collect the debtor's available estate and reduce it to cash for distribution, preserving the interests of both the debtor and the unsecured creditors. The trustee is held accountable for administering the debtor's estate.

To enable the trustee to accomplish this duty, the Code gives the trustee certain powers, stated in both general and specific terms. These powers must be exercised within two years of the order for relief.

Duties for Means Testing   The trustee is required to promptly review all materials filed by the debtor to determine if there is substantial abuse. Within ten days after the first meeting of the creditors (discussed shortly), the trustee must file a statement indicating whether the case is presumed to be an abuse under the means test. The trustee must provide a copy of this statement to all creditors within five days.

When there is a presumption of abuse, the trustee must either file a motion to dismiss the petition (or convert it to a Chapter 13 petition) or file a statement explaining why a motion would not be appropriate. If the debtor owes a domestic-support obligation (such as

---

9. The court might grant an extension, for example, on a motion by the trustee that the property is of value to the estate.

child support), the trustee must provide written notice of the bankruptcy to the claim holder (a former spouse, for instance).

The Trustee's Powers The trustee has the power to require persons holding the debtor's property at the time the petition is filed to deliver the property to the trustee.[10] To enable the trustee to implement this power, the Code provides that the trustee has rights *equivalent* to those of certain other parties, such as a creditor who has a judicial lien. This power of a trustee, which is equivalent to that of a lien creditor, is known as *strong-arm power.*

In addition, the trustee has specific *powers of avoidance.* They enable the trustee to set aside (avoid) a sale or other transfer of the debtor's property and take the property back for the debtor's estate. These powers apply to voidable rights available to the debtor, preferences, and fraudulent transfers by the debtor. Each power is discussed in more detail next. In addition, a trustee can avoid certain statutory liens (creditors' claims against the debtor's property).

The debtor shares most of the trustee's avoidance powers. Thus, if the trustee does not take action to enforce one of the rights just mentioned, the debtor in a liquidation bankruptcy can enforce that right.[11]

Voidable Rights A trustee steps into the shoes of the debtor. Thus, any reason that a debtor can use to obtain the return of her or his property can be used by the trustee as well. These grounds include fraud, duress, incapacity, and mutual mistake.

■ **EXAMPLE 31.3** Ben sells his boat to Tara. Tara gives Ben a check, knowing that she has insufficient funds in her bank account to cover the check. Tara has committed fraud. Ben has the right to avoid that transfer and recover the boat from Tara. If Ben files for bankruptcy relief under Chapter 7, the trustee can exercise the same right to recover the boat from Tara, and the boat becomes a part of the debtor's estate. ■

Preferences A debtor is not permitted to transfer property or to make a payment that favors—or gives a **preference** to—one creditor over others. The trustee is allowed to recover payments made both voluntarily and involuntarily to one creditor in preference over another.

To have made a recoverable preferential payment, an *insolvent* debtor must have transferred property, for a *preexisting* debt, within *ninety days* before the filing of the bankruptcy petition. The transfer must have given the creditor more than the creditor would have received as a result of the bankruptcy proceedings. The Code presumes that a debtor is insolvent during the ninety-day period before filing a petition.

If a **preferred creditor** (one who has received a preferential transfer) has sold the property to an innocent third party, the trustee cannot recover the property from the innocent party. The preferred creditor, however, generally can be held liable for the value of the property.

Preferences to Insiders. Sometimes, the creditor receiving the preference is an insider. An **insider** is an individual, partner, partnership, corporation, or officer or director of a corporation (or a relative of one of these) who has a close relationship with the debtor. In this situation, the avoidance power of the trustee extends to transfers made within *one year* before filing. (If the transfer was fraudulent, as will be discussed shortly, the trustee can avoid transfers made within *two years* before filing.) The trustee must, however, prove that the debtor was insolvent when the transfer occurred and that it was made to or for the benefit of an insider.

Transfers That Do Not Constitute Preferences. Not all transfers are preferences. Most courts generally assume that payment for services rendered *within fifteen days* before the payment is not a preference. If a creditor receives payment in the ordinary course of business from a debtor, such as payment of last month's cell phone bill, the bankruptcy trustee cannot recover the payment.

To be recoverable, a preference must be a transfer for an antecedent (preexisting) debt, such as a year-old landscaping bill. In addition, the Code permits a consumer-debtor to transfer any property to a creditor up to a total value of $6,225 without the transfer's constituting a preference. Payment of domestic-support debts does not constitute a preference.

Fraudulent Transfers The trustee may avoid fraudulent transfers or obligations if they (1) were made within two years prior to the filing of the petition or (2) were made with actual intent to hinder, delay, or defraud a creditor. ■ **EXAMPLE 31.4** Amy is planning to petition for bankruptcy, so she sells her gold jewelry, worth $10,000, to a friend for $500. The friend agrees that in

---

10. Usually, though, the trustee takes constructive, rather than actual, possession of the debtor's property. For instance, to obtain control of a debtor's business inventory, a trustee might change the locks on the doors to the business and hire a security guard.

11. Under a Chapter 11 bankruptcy, for which no trustee other than the debtor generally exists, the debtor has the same avoidance powers as a trustee under Chapter 7. Under Chapters 12 and 13, a trustee must be appointed.

the future he will "sell" the jewelry back to Amy for the same amount. This is a fraudulent transfer that the trustee can undo. ∎

Transfers made for less than reasonably equivalent consideration are also vulnerable if the debtor thereby became insolvent or was left engaged in business with an unreasonably small amount of capital. When a fraudulent transfer is made outside the Code's two-year limit, creditors may seek alternative relief under state laws. Some state laws may allow creditors to recover transfers made up to three years before the filing of a petition.

31–2f Exemptions

As just described, the trustee takes control of the debtor's property in a Chapter 7 bankruptcy, but an individual debtor is entitled to exempt (exclude) certain property from the bankruptcy.

Federal Exemptions The Bankruptcy Code exempts the following property, up to a specified dollar amount that changes every three years:[12]

1. A portion of equity in the debtor's home (the homestead exemption).
2. Motor vehicles, up to a certain value (usually just one vehicle).
3. Reasonably necessary clothing, household goods and furnishings, and household appliances (the aggregate value not to exceed a certain amount).
4. Jewelry, up to a certain value.
5. Tools of the debtor's trade or profession, up to a certain value.
6. A portion of unpaid but earned wages.
7. Pensions.
8. Public benefits, including public assistance (welfare), Social Security, and unemployment compensation, accumulated in a bank account.
9. Damages awarded for personal injury up to a certain amount.

Property that is *not* exempt under federal law includes bank accounts, cash, family heirlooms, collections of stamps and coins, second cars, and vacation homes.

State Exemptions Individual states have the power to pass legislation precluding debtors from using the federal exemptions within the state. A majority of the states have done this. In those states, debtors may use only state,

not federal, exemptions. In the rest of the states, debtors may choose either the exemptions provided under state law or the federal exemptions.

Limitations on the Homestead Exemption The Bankruptcy Code limits the amount of equity that can be claimed under the homestead exemption. In general, if the debtor acquired the homestead within three and a half years preceding the date of filing, the maximum equity exempted is $155,675, even if state law would permit a higher amount.

In addition, the state homestead exemption is available only if the debtor has lived in a state for two years before filing the bankruptcy petition. Furthermore, a debtor who has violated securities laws, been convicted of a felony, or engaged in certain other intentional misconduct may not be permitted to claim the homestead exemption.

31–2g Creditors' Meeting

Within a reasonable time after the order for relief has been granted (not more than forty days), the trustee must call a meeting of the creditors listed in the schedules filed by the debtor. The bankruptcy judge does not attend this meeting. The debtor is required to attend (unless excused by the court) and to submit to examination under oath by the creditors and the trustee. At the meeting, the trustee ensures that the debtor is aware of the potential consequences of bankruptcy and of the possibility of filing under a different chapter of the Code.

31–2h Creditors' Claims

To be entitled to receive a portion of the debtor's estate, each creditor normally files a *proof of claim* with the bankruptcy court within ninety days of the creditors' meeting. A proof of claim is necessary if there is any dispute concerning the claim. The proof of claim lists the creditor's name and address, as well as the amount that the creditor asserts is owed to the creditor by the debtor.

When the debtor has no assets—called a "no-asset case"—creditors are notified of the debtor's petition for bankruptcy but are instructed not to file a claim. In no-asset cases, the unsecured creditors will receive no payment, and most, if not all, of these debts will be discharged.

31–2i Distribution of Property

The Code provides specific rules for the distribution of the debtor's property to secured and unsecured creditors.

---

12. The dollar amounts stated in the Bankruptcy Code are adjusted automatically every three years on April 1 based on changes in the Consumer Price Index. The adjusted amounts are rounded to the nearest $25.

If any amount remains after the priority classes of creditors have been satisfied, it is turned over to the debtor.

Distribution to Secured Creditors The Code requires that consumer-debtors file a statement of intention with respect to secured collateral. They can choose to pay off the debt and redeem the collateral, claim it is exempt, reaffirm the debt and continue making payments, or surrender the property to the secured party.

If the collateral is surrendered to the secured party, the secured creditor can enforce the security interest. The secured party can either (1) accept the property in full satisfaction of the debt or (2) sell the collateral and use the proceeds to pay off the debt. Thus, the secured party has priority over unsecured parties as to the proceeds from the disposition of the collateral. Should the collateral be insufficient to cover the secured debt owed, the secured creditor becomes an unsecured creditor for the difference (deficiency).

There are limited exceptions to these rules. For instance, certain unsecured creditors can sometimes step into the shoes of secured tax creditors in Chapter 7 liquidation proceedings. In such situations, when the collateral securing the tax claims is sold, the unsecured creditors are paid first. This exception does not include holders of unsecured claims for administrative expenses incurred in Chapter 11 cases that are converted to Chapter 7 liquidations. In the following case, the plaintiff argued that it should.

Case 31.1

In re Anderson
United States Court of Appeals, Fourth Circuit, 811 F.3d 166 (2016).

Background and Facts Henry Anderson filed a voluntary petition in a federal bankruptcy court for relief under Chapter 11 of the Bankruptcy Code. The U.S. Department of the Treasury, through the Internal Revenue Service (IRS), filed a proof of claim against the bankruptcy estate for $997,551.80, of which $987,082.88 was secured by the debtor's property. Stubbs & Perdue, P.A., served as Anderson's counsel. During the proceedings, the court approved compensation of $200,000 to Stubbs for its services. These fees constituted an unsecured claim against the estate for administrative expenses. Later, Anderson's case was converted to a Chapter 7 liquidation. The trustee accumulated $702,630.25 for distribution to the estate's creditors—not enough to pay the claims of both the IRS and Stubbs. The trustee excluded Stubbs's claim. Stubbs objected. The court dismissed Stubbs's objection. A federal district court upheld the dismissal. Stubbs appealed, arguing that the IRS's claim should be subordinated to Stubbs's claim for fees.

In the Language of the Court
Pamela *HARRIS,* Circuit Judge:
* * * *

* * * Before any of the events at issue here, Section 724(b)(2) * * * provided all holders of administrative expense claims, like Stubbs, with the right to subordinate secured tax creditors in Chapter 7 liquidations. But that statutory scheme was criticized on the ground that it created perverse incentives, encouraging Chapter 11 debtors and their representatives to incur administrative expenses even where there was no real hope for a successful reorganization, to the detriment of secured tax creditors when Chapter 7 liquidation ultimately proved necessary.

* * * Congress responded with a fix * * * to limit the class of administrative expenses covered by Section 724(b)(2) * * *. *In order to provide greater protection for holders of tax liens * * * , unsecured Chapter 11 administrative expense claims would no longer take priority over secured tax claims in Chapter 7 liquidations.* [Emphasis added.]
* * * *

* * * The Bankruptcy Technical Corrections Act [BTCA] * * * clarified that Chapter 11 administrative expense claimants do not hold subordination rights under Section 724(b)(2).

* * * Eleven months later, the Debtor's bankruptcy case converted from Chapter 11 to Chapter 7, implicating Section 724(b)(2) for the first time.
* * * *

* * * *As a general rule, a court is to apply the law in effect at the time it renders its decision.* [Emphasis added.]

Case 31.1 Continues

Case 31.1 Continued   * * * *

Stubbs argues, however, that it would be unjust to apply the BTCA version of Section 724(b)(2) * * * to disallow payment on its unsecured claim for Chapter 11 fees. Prior to the BTCA, Stubbs contends, it was entitled to subordinate the IRS's secured claim.

The problem with Stubbs's argument is its premise: that Stubbs held subordination rights under Section 724(b)(2) before the BTCA was enacted * * * . Before the BTCA was enacted, Section 724(b)(2) had no application to the Debtor's case at all. It afforded Stubbs no entitlement to subordinate the IRS's secured tax claim for the threshold reason that it simply did not apply in the Chapter 11 proceedings that began in this case * * * and did not end until * * * eleven months *after* the BTCA's passage. The pre-BTCA version of Section 724(b)(2) that Stubbs invokes, in other words, never controlled this case.

Decision and Remedy *The U.S. Court of Appeals for the Fourth Circuit affirmed the dismissal of Stubbs's claim. Under Section 724(b)(2), "it is clear that Stubbs is not entitled to subordinate the IRS's secured tax claim in favor of its unsecured claim to Chapter 11 administrative expenses."*

Critical Thinking

- **Legal Environment** *Why, as a general rule, should a court apply the law that is in effect at the time the court renders its decision?*
- **What If the Facts Were Different?** *Suppose that Anderson had filed his initial bankruptcy petition under Chapter 7, not under Chapter 11. Would the result have been different? Discuss.*

Distribution to Unsecured Creditors Bankruptcy law establishes an order of priority for debts owed to *unsecured* creditors, and they are paid in the order of their priority. Claims for domestic-support obligations, such as child support and alimony, have the highest priority among unsecured creditors, so these claims must be paid first. Each class, or group, must be fully paid before the next class is entitled to any of the remaining proceeds.

If there are insufficient proceeds to fully pay all the creditors in a class, the proceeds are distributed *proportionately* to the creditors in that class. Classes lower in priority receive nothing. In almost all Chapter 7 bankruptcies, the funds will be insufficient to pay all creditors.

Exhibit 31–1 illustrates the collection and distribution of property in most voluntary bankruptcies. The exhibit includes a listing of the classes of unsecured creditors.

31–2j Discharge

From the debtor's point of view, the primary purpose of liquidation is to obtain a fresh start through a discharge of debts. A discharge voids, or sets aside, any judgment on a discharged debt and prevents any action to collect it. Certain debts, however, are not dischargeable in bankruptcy. Also, certain debtors may not qualify to have all debts discharged in bankruptcy. These situations are discussed next.

Exceptions to Discharge Claims that are not dischargeable in bankruptcy include the following:

1. Claims for back taxes accruing within two years prior to bankruptcy.
2. Claims for amounts borrowed by the debtor to pay federal taxes or any nondischargeable taxes.[13]
3. Claims against property or funds obtained by the debtor under false pretenses or by false representations.
4. Claims by creditors who were not notified of the bankruptcy. These claims did not appear on the schedules the debtor was required to file.
5. Claims based on fraud[14] or misuse of funds by the debtor while acting in a fiduciary capacity or claims involving the debtor's embezzlement or larceny.
6. Domestic-support obligations and property settlements as provided for in a separation agreement or divorce decree.
7. Claims for amounts due on a retirement account loan.
8. Claims based on willful or malicious conduct by the debtor toward another or the property of another. ■ **CASE IN POINT 31.5** Anthony Mickletz owned a pizza restaurant that employed John Carmello.

---

13. Taxes accruing within three years prior to bankruptcy are nondischargeable, including federal and state income taxes, employment taxes, taxes on gross receipts, property taxes, excise taxes, customs duties, and any other taxes for which the government claims the debtor is liable in some capacity. See 11 U.S.C. Sections 507(a)(8) and 523(a)(1).

14. Even if a debtor who is sued for fraud settles the lawsuit, the settlement agreement may not be discharged in bankruptcy because of the underlying fraud. See *Archer v. Warner*, 538 U.S. 314, 123 S.Ct. 1462, 155 L.Ed.2d 454 (2003); and *In re Sager*, ___ Bankr. ___, 2015 WL 1650654 (E.D. Pa. 2015).

EXHIBIT 31–1 Collection and Distribution of Property in Most Voluntary Bankruptcies

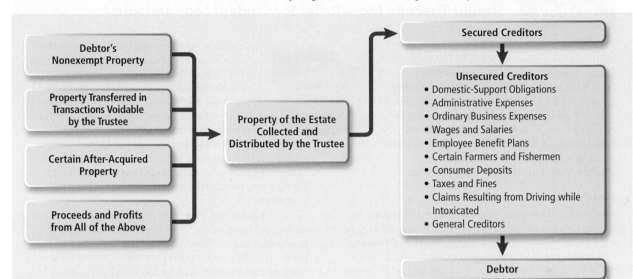

One night after Carmello had finished his shift, Mickletz called him back into the restaurant and accused him of stealing. An argument ensued, and Mickletz shoved Carmello, causing him to fall and injure his back. Because Mickletz did not provide workers' compensation coverage as required by law, the state prosecuted him criminally. He was ordered to pay more than $45,000 in restitution to Carmello for his injuries. Carmello also filed a civil suit against Mickletz, which the parties agreed to settle for $175,000. Later, Mickletz filed a petition for bankruptcy. Carmello argued that these debts were nondischargeable, and the court agreed. The exception from discharge includes any debts for willful (deliberate or intentional) injury, and Mickletz's actions were deliberate.[15] ∎

9. Certain government fines and penalties.
10. Student loans, unless payment of the loans imposes an undue hardship on the debtor and the debtor's dependents. (For an example of what constitutes undue hardship, see *Case in Point 31.6,* which follows this list.)
11. Consumer debts of more than $650 for luxury goods or services owed to a single creditor incurred within ninety days of the order for relief.
12. Cash advances totaling more than $925 that are extensions of open-end consumer credit obtained by the debtor within seventy days of the order for relief.
13. Judgments against a debtor as a result of the debtor's operation of a motor vehicle while intoxicated.

14. Fees or assessments arising from property in a homeowners' association, as long as the debtor retained an interest in the property.
15. Taxes with respect to which the debtor failed to provide required or requested tax documents.

∎ **CASE IN POINT 31.6** At the time he filed for Chapter 7 bankruptcy, Terence Wolfe had not been consistently employed for twenty years. He had been fired from numerous positions for behavioral issues and had difficulty finding and holding a job. Wolfe had been diagnosed with personality disorders and ultimately was granted disability status by the U.S. government. He was living on disability payments of $1,126 per month at the time he filed for Chapter 7 bankruptcy.

Among Wolfe's debts were more than $131,000 in student loan debts. Wolfe sought to have these debts discharged because repaying them would constitute undue hardship. The court agreed and granted a discharge. According to the court, although Wolfe is intelligent, "he has been unable, for more than two decades, to maintain full-time employment for any meaningful length of time. He is living at a minimal standard of living and it is unlikely that he will ever be able to repay these loans."[16] ∎ See this chapter's *Ethics Today* feature for a discussion of whether the law should make it easier to obtain a discharge of student loan debts.

---

15. *In re Mickletz,* 544 Bankr. 804 (E.D. Pa. 2016).

16. *In re Wolfe,* 501 Bankr. 426, 24 Fla.L.WeeklyFed. B235 (M.D.Fla. 2011).

ETHICS TODAY

Should There Be More Relief for Student Loan Defaults?

According to many observers, student loan debt has reached crisis levels in the United States. Outstanding student loan balances total $1.2 *trillion* nationally and are growing by around $3,000 *per second*. About 20 percent are ninety or more days' delinquent or are in default. That is the highest delinquency rate among all forms of debt, including credit cards, automobile loans, and mortgages. The average student loan debt is more than $30,000.

Consequences of Default

Any student borrower who has not made regular payments for nine months is in default. If you are in default on a student loan, the U.S. Department of Education can do any of the following to collect:

1. Keep your tax refund if you were supposed to receive one.
2. Garnish your paycheck without obtaining a court judgment.
3. Take your federal benefits, such as Social Security retirement payments or disability payments.

In addition, in some states any professional license that you have can be revoked. The Department of Education can also bring a lawsuit against you. If it wins, it can collect the judgment from your bank accounts or place a lien on any real property that you own.

Caps on Interest Rates, Forgiveness, and Income-Based Plans

Recently, Congress attempted to ease the burden on student loan debtors by reducing the interest rates they can be charged. In addition, President Barack Obama signed an executive order putting into place an income-based repayment plan. This plan caps payments at no more than 10 percent of disposable income. Any balance not paid off after twenty years will be forgiven.

Should the federal government go further? Yes, at least according to President Obama. In 2015, Obama signed a presidential memorandum titled "Student Aid Bill of Rights." The memorandum directs the Department of Education to implement actions to ensure that the debt collection process for defaulted student loans "is fair, transparent, [and] charges reasonable fees to defaulted borrowers."

Critics point out that such student loan debt forgiveness could have a cost. They claim that colleges and universities might "hint" to potential students that they need not worry about taking on higher student loans because some portion will be forgiven by the federal government.

Political Impetus

Politicians are increasingly discussing student loan debt and the costs of higher education. Some are asking Congress to allow federal student loans to be discharged in most bankruptcy proceedings. Others advocate making college education free or at least reducing the costs charged to certain students. One plan calls for allowing students to refinance their loans at very low interest rates. Another proposal is to prohibit the federal government from profiting from student loan debt (the government brings in more than $41 billion a year from student loans).

Critical Thinking *Why does the Bankruptcy Code provide that student loans should not be dischargeable unless there is undue hardship? What argument can be made in favor of allowing student loans to be dischargeable?*

Today, however, the federal government guarantees many student loans (similar to the way the government backs certain mortgages). When student loans are guaranteed, the lenders are not affected by default in the same way and have no reason to refuse to finance education. This bolsters the argument that student loan debts should be dischargeable in the same way as other types of debts.

Objections to Discharge In addition to the exceptions to discharge previously discussed, a bankruptcy court may also deny discharge based on the debtor's *conduct*. Grounds for denial of discharge of the debtor include the following:

1. The debtor's concealment or destruction of property with the intent to hinder, delay, or defraud a creditor.
2. The debtor's fraudulent concealment or destruction of financial records.
3. The grant of a discharge to the debtor within eight years before the petition was filed.
4. The debtor's failure to complete the required consumer education course.
5. The debtor's involvement in proceedings in which the debtor could be found guilty of a felony. (Basically, a court may not discharge any debt until the completion of felony proceedings against the debtor.)

When a discharge is denied under any of these circumstances, the debtor's assets are still distributed to the creditors. After the bankruptcy proceeding, however, the debtor remains liable for the unpaid portion of all claims.

In addition, a discharge may be revoked (taken back) within one year if it is discovered that the debtor acted fraudulently or dishonestly during the bankruptcy proceeding. If that occurs, a creditor whose claim was not satisfied in the distribution of the debtor's property can proceed with his or her claim against the debtor.

Whether a bankruptcy court properly denied a discharge based on the debtors' conduct was the issue in the following case.

Case 31.2

In re Cummings

United States Court of Appeals, Ninth Circuit, 595 Fed.Appx. 707 (2015).

Background and Facts Clarence and Pamela Cummings filed a petition for a Chapter 7 bankruptcy in a federal bankruptcy court. After the debtors filed two amended versions of the required schedules, the trustee asked for additional time to investigate. The court granted the request. The debtors then filed a third amended schedule. In it, they disclosed for the first time the existence of First Beacon Management Company, a corporation that they planned to use as part of their postbankruptcy "fresh start."

The trustee claimed that the Cummingses' failure to disclose their interest in First Beacon was a "false oath relating to a material fact made knowingly and fraudulently" in violation of the Bankruptcy Code. The court agreed and denied the debtors a discharge. The Bankruptcy Appellate Panel (BAP) affirmed the court's decision. The Cummingses appealed.

In the Language of the Court
MEMORANDUM.
* * * *

Chapter 7 debtors Clarence Thomas Cummings and Pamela K. Cummings appeal the judgment of the Bankruptcy Appellate Panel ("BAP") affirming * * * the bankruptcy court's order denying discharge on the ground that the debtors made false oaths * * * . The bankruptcy court rejected the explanatory testimony of Mr. Cummings as "not credible" and "beyond not credible" and the BAP found that "there is ample evidence to support the bankruptcy court's findings."
* * * *

* * * Debtors claim that the bankruptcy court failed to consider other "voluminous independent and undisputed documentary evidence" introduced at trial that, they assert, "completely obliterated any suggestion of fraudulent intent."

* * * These materials do not advance debtors' claim of inadvertence [lack of intent] or otherwise suggest bankruptcy court error. To the contrary, *the documents corroborate the obviousness of debtors' fraud and the objective it advanced, [namely], to insulate First Beacon Management Co., * * * the new corporate anchor of their post-petition fresh start, from the stigma of bankruptcy.* [Emphasis added.]

Debtors' eventual disclosure of their interest in First Beacon on their third amended Schedule * * * does not negate their initial fraud. To the contrary, the sequence of debtors' filings substantiates the presence of fraud: they elected, twice, to amend their Schedule * * * without adding First Beacon, and disclosed First Beacon only after the issuance of an order granting the Trustee additional time to investigate.
* * * *

The Trustee fully carried its burden of proving by a preponderance of the evidence * * * that under the circumstances, debtors' failure to disclose their interest in First Beacon as debtor property was a "false oath" relating to a material fact made knowingly and fraudulently.

Decision and Remedy *The U.S. Court of Appeals for the Ninth Circuit affirmed the ruling of the Bankruptcy Appellate Panel. The Cummingses' bankruptcy filings revealed the presence of fraud. Thus, their Chapter 7 petition for discharge of their debts was denied.*

Critical Thinking
- **Economic** *Why would a debtor risk the denial of a discharge to conceal assets? Discuss.*

31–2k Reaffirmation of Debt

An agreement to pay a debt dischargeable in bankruptcy is called a **reaffirmation agreement.** A debtor may wish to pay a debt—such as a debt owed to a family member, physician, bank, or some other creditor—even though the debt could be discharged in bankruptcy. Also, as noted previously, a debtor cannot retain secured property while continuing to pay without entering into a reaffirmation agreement.

Procedures To be enforceable, reaffirmation agreements must be made before the debtor is granted a discharge. The agreement must be signed and filed with the court. Court approval is required unless the debtor is represented by an attorney during the negotiation of the reaffirmation and submits the proper documents and certifications. Even when the debtor is represented by an attorney, court approval may be required if it appears that the reaffirmation will result in undue hardship to the debtor.

When court approval is required, a separate hearing will take place. The court will approve the reaffirmation only if it finds that the agreement will not result in undue hardship to the debtor and that the reaffirmation is consistent with the debtor's best interests.

Required Disclosures To discourage creditors from engaging in abusive reaffirmation practices, the law provides specific language for disclosures that must be given to debtors entering into reaffirmation agreements. Among other things, these disclosures explain that the debtor is not required to reaffirm any debt. They also inform the debtor that liens on secured property, such as mortgages and cars, will remain in effect even if the debt is not reaffirmed.

The reaffirmation agreement must disclose the amount of the debt reaffirmed, the rate of interest, the date payments begin, and the right to rescind. The disclosures also caution the debtor: "Only agree to reaffirm a debt if it is in your best interest. Be sure you can afford the payments you agree to make."

The original disclosure documents must be signed by the debtor, certified by the debtor's attorney, and filed with the court at the same time as the reaffirmation agreement. A reaffirmation agreement that is not accompanied by the original signed disclosures will not be effective.

■ **CASE IN POINT 31.7** Howard Lapides, who owned a seafood import business, signed a secured promissory note for $400,000 with Venture Bank for a revolving line-of-credit loan. Part of the collateral for that loan was a third mortgage on the Lapideses' home (two other banks held prior mortgages). Eventually, Howard and his wife filed for Chapter 7 bankruptcy protection, and their personal debts were discharged. Afterward, Venture Bank convinced the Lapideses to sign a reaffirmation agreement by telling them that it would refinance all three mortgages so that they could keep their house.

The Lapideses made twelve $3,500 payments to Venture Bank, but when the bank did not refinance the other mortgages, they stopped making payments. Venture Bank filed suit, but a court refused to enforce the reaffirmation agreement because it violated the Bankruptcy Code. The agreement had never been signed by Lapideses' attorney or filed with the bankruptcy court.[17] ■

31–3 Reorganizations

The type of bankruptcy proceeding most commonly used by corporate debtors is the Chapter 11 *reorganization.* In a reorganization, the creditors and the debtor formulate a plan under which the debtor pays a portion of the debts and is discharged of the remainder. The debtor is allowed to continue in business.

As noted, this type of bankruptcy generally involves a corporate reorganization. Nevertheless, any debtor (except a stockbroker or a commodities broker) who is eligible for Chapter 7 relief is eligible for relief under Chapter 11. Railroads are also eligible.

Congress has established a "fast-track" Chapter 11 procedure for small-business debtors whose liabilities do not exceed $2.49 million and who do not own or manage real estate. The fast track enables a debtor to avoid the appointment of a creditors' committee and also shortens the filing periods and relaxes certain other requirements. Because the process is shorter and simpler, it is less costly.

The same principles that govern the filing of a liquidation (Chapter 7) petition apply to reorganization (Chapter 11) proceedings. The case may be brought either voluntarily or involuntarily. The automatic-stay provision and its exceptions (such as substantial abuse), as well as the adequate protection doctrine, apply in reorganizations.

31–3a Workouts

In some instances, to avoid bankruptcy proceedings, creditors may prefer private, negotiated adjustments of creditor-debtor relations, also known as **workouts.** Often, these out-of-court workouts are much more

---

17. *Venture Bank v. Lapides,* 800 F.3d 442 (8th Cir. 2015).

flexible and thus more conducive to a speedy settlement. Speed is critical because delay is one of the most costly elements in any bankruptcy proceeding. Another advantage of workouts is that they avoid the various administrative costs of bankruptcy proceedings.

31–3b Best Interests of the Creditors

Once a Chapter 11 petition has been filed, a bankruptcy court can dismiss or suspend proceedings at any time if dismissal or suspension would better serve the interests of the creditors. Before taking such an action, the court must give notice and conduct a hearing. The Code also allows a court, after notice and a hearing, to dismiss a case under reorganization "for cause" when there is no reasonable likelihood of rehabilitation. Similarly, a court can dismiss when there is an inability to effect a plan or an unreasonable delay by the debtor that may harm the interests of creditors. A debtor whose petition is dismissed for these reasons can file a subsequent Chapter 11 petition in the future.[18]

31–3c Debtor in Possession

On entry of the order for relief, the debtor generally continues to operate the business as a **debtor in possession (DIP).** The court, however, may appoint a trustee (often referred to as a *receiver*) to operate the debtor's business. The court will choose this action if gross mismanagement of the business is shown or if appointing a trustee is in the best interests of the estate.

The DIP's role is similar to that of a trustee in a liquidation bankruptcy.[19] The DIP is entitled to avoid preferential payments made to creditors and fraudulent transfers of assets. The DIP can also exercise a trustee's strong-arm powers. The DIP has the power to decide whether to cancel or assume prepetition executory contracts (contracts that are not yet performed) or unexpired leases.

Cancellation of executory contracts or unexpired leases can be of substantial benefit to a Chapter 11 debtor. ■ **EXAMPLE 31.8** Five years ago, APT Corporation leased an office building for a twenty-year term. Now, APT can no longer pay the rent due under the lease and has filed for Chapter 11 reorganization. In this situation, the debtor in possession can cancel the lease, and APT will not be required to continue paying the substantial rent due for fifteen more years. ■

31–3d Creditors' Committees

As soon as practicable after the entry of the order for relief, a creditors' committee of unsecured creditors is appointed.[20] The business's suppliers may serve on the committee. The committee can consult with the trustee or the DIP concerning the administration of the case or the formulation of the plan. Additional creditors' committees may be appointed to represent special interest creditors.

Generally, no orders affecting the estate will be entered without the consent of the committee or after a hearing in which the judge is informed of the committee's position. As mentioned earlier, businesses with debts of less than $2.49 million that do not own or manage real estate can avoid creditors' committees. In these fast-track proceedings, orders can be entered without a committee's consent.

31–3e The Reorganization Plan

A reorganization plan to rehabilitate the debtor is a plan to conserve and administer the debtor's assets in the hope of an eventual return to successful operation and solvency. The plan must be fair and equitable and must do the following:

1. Designate classes of claims and interests.
2. Specify the treatment to be afforded to the classes of creditors. (The plan must provide the same treatment for all claims in a particular class.)
3. Provide an adequate means for the plan's execution. (Individual debtors are required to utilize postpetition assets as necessary to execute the plan.)
4. Provide for payment of tax claims over a five-year period.

The plan need not provide for full repayment to unsecured creditors. Instead, creditors receive a percentage of each dollar owed to them by the debtor.

Filing the Plan Only the debtor may file a plan within the first 120 days after the date of the order for relief. This period may be extended, but not beyond eighteen months from the date of the order for relief. If the debtor does not meet the 120-day deadline or obtain an extension, any party may propose a plan. If a small-business debtor chooses to avoid a creditors' committee, the time for the debtor's filing is 180 days.

Acceptance of the Plan Once the plan has been developed, it is submitted to each class of creditors for

---

18. See 11 U.S.C. Section 1112(b).
19. 11 U.S.C. Section 544(a).

20. If the debtor has filed a reorganization plan accepted by the creditors, the trustee may decide not to call a meeting of the creditors.

594 UNIT SIX Creditors' Rights and Bankruptcy

acceptance. For the plan to be adopted, each class must accept it. A class has accepted the plan when a majority of the creditors in the class, representing two-thirds of the amount of the total claim, vote to approve it. If the debtor fails to procure creditor consent of the plan within 180 days, any party may propose a plan.

Confirmation of the Plan Confirmation is conditioned on the debtor's certifying that all postpetition domestic-support obligations have been paid in full. In addition, even when all classes of creditors accept the plan, the court may refuse to confirm it if it is not "in the best interests of the creditors." For small-business debtors, if the plan meets the listed requirements, the court must confirm the plan within forty-five days (unless this period is extended).

The plan can be modified on the request of the debtor, the DIP, the trustee, the U.S. trustee, or a holder of an unsecured claim. If an unsecured creditor objects to the plan, specific rules apply to the value of property to be distributed under the plan. Tax claims must be paid over a five-year period.

Even if only one class of creditors has accepted the plan, the court may still confirm the plan under the Code's so-called **cram-down provision.** In other words, the court may confirm the plan over the objections of a class of creditors. Before the court can exercise the right of cram-down confirmation, it must be demonstrated that the plan does not discriminate unfairly against any creditors and is fair and equitable.

Discharge The plan is binding on confirmation. Nevertheless, the law provides that confirmation of a plan does not discharge an individual debtor. *For individual debtors, the plan must be completed before discharge will be granted,* unless the court orders otherwise. For all other debtors, the court may order discharge at any time after the plan is confirmed.

On discharge, the debtor is given a reorganization discharge from all claims not protected under the plan. This discharge does not apply to any claims that would be denied discharge under liquidation.

31–4 Bankruptcy Relief under Chapter 12 and Chapter 13

In addition to bankruptcy relief through liquidation and reorganization, the Code also provides for family-farmer and family-fisherman debt adjustments (Chapter 12) and

individuals' repayment plans (Chapter 13). The procedures for filing Chapter 12 and Chapter 13 plans are very similar. Because Chapter 13 plans are the more commonly used of the two types, we discuss Chapter 13 first.

31–4a Individuals' Repayment Plans—Chapter 13

Chapter 13 of the Bankruptcy Code provides for "Adjustment of Debts of an Individual with Regular Income." Individuals with regular income who owe fixed (liquidated) unsecured debts of less than $383,175 or fixed secured debts of less than $1,149,525 may take advantage of bankruptcy repayment plans. Partnerships and corporations are excluded.

Among those eligible are salaried employees and sole proprietors, as well as individuals who live on welfare, Social Security, fixed pensions, or investment income. Many small-business debtors have a choice of filing under either Chapter 11 or Chapter 13. Repayment plans offer some advantages because they are less expensive and less complicated than reorganization or liquidation proceedings.

Filing the Petition A Chapter 13 repayment plan case can be initiated only by the debtor's filing of a voluntary petition or by court conversion of a Chapter 7 petition. Recall that a court may convert a Chapter 7 petition because of a finding of substantial abuse under the means test. In addition, certain liquidation and reorganization cases may be converted to repayment plan cases with the consent of the debtor.[21]

A trustee, who will make payments under the plan, must be appointed. On the filing of a repayment plan petition, the automatic stay previously discussed takes effect. Although the stay applies to all or part of the debtor's consumer debt, it does not apply to any business debt incurred by the debtor or to any domestic-support obligations.

Good Faith Requirement The Bankruptcy Code imposes the requirement of good faith on a debtor at both the time of the filing of the petition and the time of the filing of the plan. The Code does not define good faith, but if the circumstances on the whole indicate bad faith, a court can dismiss a debtor's Chapter 13 petition.

---

21. A Chapter 13 repayment plan may be converted to a Chapter 7 liquidation at the request of the debtor or, under certain circumstances, by a creditor "for cause." A Chapter 13 case may be converted to a Chapter 11 case after a hearing.

In determining whether a Chapter 13 plan was proposed in good faith, should the bankruptcy court consider whether the debtor included his Social Security income in the amount of disposable income available for payment of unsecured creditors? That was the issue in the following case.

Case Analysis 31.3

In re Welsh
United States Court of Appeals, Ninth Circuit, 711 F.3d 1120 (2013).

In the Language of the Court
RIPPLE, Senior Circuit Judge:
* * * *

[David and Sharon Welsh] filed a voluntary Chapter 13 petition [in a federal bankruptcy court]. Their required schedules revealed the following assets: a home in Missoula, Montana, valued at $400,000, encumbered by a secured claim of $330,593.66; a Ford F-250 valued at $10,000, encumbered by a secured claim of $18,959; a 2006 Subaru Outback valued at of $9,500, encumbered by a secured claim of $12,211; a 2005 Toyota Matrix valued at $2,200, encumbered by a secured claim of $1,996; a 2005 Airstream trailer valued at $23,000, encumbered by a secured claim of $39,000; and two 2007 Honda ATVs each valued at $2,700, encumbered by secured claims of $3,065 and $4,500. In addition to their secured debts, the schedules revealed unsecured claims totaling approximately $180,500, the largest of which were their daughter's student loan debt in the amount of $60,000 and a joint debt owed to Bank of America on a line of credit in the amount of $50,000.

Mrs. Welsh is employed as a nurse and reported on Schedule I a monthly income of $6,975.40. She also draws a pension of $1,100 per month. Mr. Welsh is retired, but listed a monthly income of $358.03 from wages, salary and commissions, as well as Social Security income in the amount of $1,165.

Because their income exceeds the median for the state of Montana, the debtors calculated their disposable income according to the means test. * * * They listed their current monthly income as $8,116.31; their current monthly income did not include Mr.

Welsh's Social Security income of $1,165 because Social Security income is excluded from the current monthly income calculation. After deducting future payments on secured claims, the debtors were left with a disposable income of $218.12 per month.

The Welshes proposed a plan that provided for payments of $125 per month to unsecured creditors for the first thirty months of the plan. After their vehicle loans were paid, the payments would increase to $500 per month for the last thirty months of the plan. The proposed plan would pay off approximately $14,700 of the debtors' $180,500 unsecured debt.

The [Bankruptcy] Trustee objected on the ground that the debtors had not proposed their plan in good faith * * * because [they failed] to commit one hundred percent of their disposable income to the plan.
* * * *

The bankruptcy court * * * rejected the Trustee's argument.

[On the Trustee's appeal] the [Bankruptcy Appellate Panel (BAP) for the Ninth Circuit] affirmed the bankruptcy court's judgment.
* * * *

In this appeal, the Trustee * * * maintains that, in determining whether the Welshes proposed their Chapter 13 plan in good faith, the bankruptcy court * * * should have considered Mr. Welsh's Social Security income.
* * * *

In 2005, Congress * * * enacted the Bankruptcy Abuse Prevention and Consumer Protection Act ("BAPCPA"). The good faith requirement * * * remained the same, but there were significant changes with respect to the calculation

of disposable income. Before the BAP-CPA, bankruptcy judges had authority to determine a debtor's ability to pay based on the individual circumstances of each case and each debtor. Congress replaced this discretion with a detailed, mechanical means test, which requires debtors with above-median income to calculate their "disposable income" by subtracting specific expenses from "current monthly income," as defined by the Bankruptcy Code. For our purposes, several elements of this calculation are important. *The debtor begins with his "current monthly income," which, by definition, explicitly "excludes benefits received under the Social Security Act."* The debtor then subtracts living expenses based on the Internal Revenue Service's "Collection Financial Standards," a detailed series of averages for living expenses that the Service uses to calculate necessary expenditures for delinquent taxpayers. The debtor also subtracts his averaged payments to secured creditors due during the following sixty months. [Emphasis added.]

As is the case here, the manner in which the means test calculates "disposable income" may underestimate the amount of actual funds that a taxpayer has available to pay unsecured creditors. A debtor who receives Social Security income * * * does not have to account for that income when calculating "disposable income" according to the means test. * * * The result may be that * * * little "disposable income," as that figure is calculated, remains to pay unsecured creditors.
* * * *

Here, the Trustee does not contend, of course, that the calculation of

Case 31.3 Continues

Case 31.3 Continued

disposable income should have incorporated Social Security income; the statutory language is clearly to the contrary. Instead, he concedes that disposable income was calculated correctly under the BAPCPA, but nevertheless maintains that the Welshes' failure to dedicate Mr. Welsh's Social Security income to the payment of unsecured creditors requires a conclusion that the plan was not proposed in good faith * * * . We cannot conclude, however, that a plan

prepared completely in accordance with the very detailed calculations that Congress set forth is not proposed in good faith. To hold otherwise would be to allow the bankruptcy court to substitute its judgment of how much and what kind of income should be dedicated to the payment of unsecured creditors for the judgment of Congress. Such an approach would not only flout the express language of Congress, but also one of Congress's purposes in enacting

the BAPCPA, namely to reduce the amount of discretion that bankruptcy courts previously had over the calculation of an above-median debtor's income and expenses.

* * * *

We conclude that Congress's adoption of the BAPCPA forecloses a court's consideration of a debtor's Social Security income * * * as part of the inquiry into good faith * * * . We therefore affirm the judgment of the BAP.

Legal Reasoning Questions

1. On what ground did the trustee contend that the debtors had not proposed their Chapter 13 plan in good faith?

2. How did the court rule with respect to the trustee's argument? Why?

3. In evaluating a debtor's petition, what factors should be part of a good faith analysis? Should consideration of the calculation of disposable income play a role? Why or why not?

The Repayment Plan A plan of rehabilitation by repayment must provide for the following:

1. The turning over to the trustee of such future earnings or income of the debtor as is necessary for execution of the plan.

2. Full payment through deferred cash payments of all claims entitled to priority, such as taxes.[22]

3. Identical treatment of all claims within a particular class. (The Code permits the debtor to list co-debtors, such as guarantors or sureties, as a separate class.)

The repayment plan may provide either for payment of all obligations in full or for payment of a lesser amount. The debtor must begin making payments under the proposed plan within thirty days after the plan has been filed and must continue to make "timely" payments.[23] If the debtor fails to make timely payments or to commence payments within the thirty-day period, the court can convert the case to a Chapter 7 bankruptcy or dismiss the petition.

Allowable Expenses. In putting together a repayment plan, a debtor must apply the means test to identify the

amount of disposable income that will be available to repay creditors. The debtor is allowed to deduct certain expenses from monthly income to arrive at this amount, but only if they are appropriate.

■ **CASE IN POINT 31.9** Jason Ransom filed a Chapter 13 bankruptcy petition. Among his assets, he listed a Toyota Camry that he owned free of any debt. In his monthly expenses, he claimed a car-ownership deduction of $471 and a separate $388 deduction for costs to operate the car. He proposed a five-year plan that would repay about 25 percent of his unsecured debt.

FIA Card Services, N.A., an unsecured creditor, objected to the plan. FIA argued that Ransom was not entitled to the car-ownership allowance because he did not owe money on the car. Ultimately, the United States Supreme Court ruled in FIA's favor. A deduction is appropriate only if the debtor will incur that expense during the life of the Chapter 13 plan. A debtor who does not make loan or lease payments may not take a car-ownership deduction.[24] ■

Length of the Plan. The length of the payment plan can be three or five years, depending on the debtor's family income. If the family income is greater than the median family income in the relevant geographic area under the

---

22. As with a Chapter 11 reorganization plan, full repayment of all claims is not always required.

23. The bankruptcy trustee holds on to these payments until the court either confirms or denies the debtor's plan. If the court confirms the plan, the trustee distributes the funds to creditors as stated in the plan. If the court denies the debtor's plan, the trustee returns the funds, minus administrative expenses, to the debtor.

24. *Ransom v. FIA Card Services, N.A.,* 562 U.S. 61, 131 S.Ct. 716, 178 L.Ed.2d 603 (2011).

means test, the term of the proposed plan must be three years.[25] The term may not exceed five years.

Confirmation of the Plan. After the plan is filed, the court holds a confirmation hearing, at which interested parties (such as creditors) may object to the plan. The hearing must be held at least twenty days, but no more than forty-five days, after the meeting of the creditors. The debtor must have filed all prepetition tax returns and paid all postpetition domestic-support obligations before a court will confirm any plan.

The court will confirm a plan with respect to each claim of a secured creditor under any of the following circumstances:

1. If the secured creditors have accepted the plan.
2. If the plan provides that secured creditors retain their liens until there is payment in full or until the debtor receives a discharge.
3. If the debtor surrenders the property securing the claims to the creditors.

In addition, for a motor vehicle purchased within 910 days before the petition is filed, the plan must provide that a creditor with a purchase-money security interest (PMSI) retains its lien until the entire debt is paid. For PMSIs on other personal property, the payment plan must cover debts incurred within a one-year period preceding the filing.

Discharge After the debtor has completed all payments, the court grants a discharge of all debts provided for by the repayment plan. Generally, all debts are dischargeable except the following:

1. Allowed claims not provided for by the plan.
2. Certain long-term debts provided for by the plan.
3. Certain tax claims and payments on retirement accounts.
4. Claims for domestic-support obligations.
5. Debts related to injury or property damage caused while driving under the influence of alcohol or drugs.

An order granting discharge is final as to the debts listed in the repayment plan. ■ **CASE IN POINT 31.10** Francisco Espinosa filed a petition for an individual repayment plan under Chapter 13 of the Bankruptcy Code. His plan proposed to pay only the principal on his student loan and to discharge the interest. United Student Aid Funds, Inc. (the creditor), had notice of the plan and did not object. The court confirmed the plan without finding that payment of the student loan

interest would cause undue hardship (as required under the Code).

Years later, United filed a motion asking the bankruptcy court to rule that its order confirming the plan was void because it was in violation of the rules governing bankruptcy. The court denied United's petition and ordered the creditor to cease its collection efforts. The case ultimately reached the United States Supreme Court, which affirmed the lower court's holding that the student loan debt was discharged.[26] ■

31–4b Family Farmers and Fishermen—Chapter 12

Congress created Chapter 12 of the Bankruptcy Code to help relieve economic pressure on small farmers. In 2005, Congress extended this protection to family fishermen, modified its provisions somewhat, and made it a permanent chapter in the Bankruptcy Code. (Previously, the statutes authorizing Chapter 12 had to be periodically renewed by Congress.)

Concept Summary 31.1 compares bankruptcy procedures under Chapters 7, 11, 12, and 13.

Definitions For purposes of Chapter 12, a *family farmer* is one whose gross income is at least 50 percent farm dependent and whose debts are at least 50 percent farm related. The total debt for a family farmer must not exceed $4,031,575. A partnership or close corporation that is at least 50 percent owned by the farm family can also qualify as a family farmer.[27]

A *family fisherman* is one whose gross income is at least 50 percent dependent on commercial fishing operations[28] and whose debts are at least 80 percent related to commercial fishing. The total debt for a family fisherman must not exceed $1,868,200. As with family farmers, a partnership or close corporation can also qualify.

Filing the Petition The procedure for filing a family-farmer or family-fisherman bankruptcy plan is similar to the procedure for filing a repayment plan under Chapter 13. The debtor must file a plan not later than ninety days after the order for relief has been entered. The filing of the

---

25. See 11 U.S.C. Section 1322(d) for details on when the court will find that the Chapter 13 plan should extend to a five-year period.

26. *United Student Aid Funds, Inc. v. Espinosa*, 559 U.S. 260, 130 S.Ct. 1367, 176 L.Ed.2d 158 (2010).

27. Note that for a corporation or partnership to qualify under Chapter 12, at least 80 percent of the value of the firm's assets must consist of assets related to the farming operation.

28. Commercial fishing operations include catching, harvesting, or raising fish, shrimp, lobsters, urchins, seaweed, shellfish, or other aquatic species or products.

Concept Summary 31.1

Forms of Bankruptcy Relief Compared

FORM	CHAPTER 7	CHAPTER 11	CHAPTERS 12 AND 13
Purpose	Liquidation.	Reorganization.	Adjustment.
Who Can Petition	Debtor (voluntary) or creditors (involuntary).	Debtor (voluntary) or creditors (involuntary).	Debtor (voluntary) only.
Who Can Be a Debtor	Any "person" (including partnerships, corporations, and municipalities) except railroads, insurance companies, banks, savings and loan institutions, investment companies licensed by the Small Business Administration, and credit unions. Farmers and charitable institutions cannot be involuntarily petitioned. If the court finds the petition to be a substantial abuse of the use of Chapter 7, the debtor may be required to convert to a Chapter 13 repayment plan.	Any debtor eligible for Chapter 7 relief. Railroads are also eligible. Individuals have specific rules and limitations.	**Chapter 12**—Any family farmer (one whose gross income is at least 50 percent farm dependent and whose debts are at least 50 percent farm related) or family fisherman (one whose gross income is at least 50 percent dependent on commercial fishing operations and whose debts are at least 80 percent related to commercial fishing) or any partnership or close corporation at least 50 percent owned by a family farmer or fisherman, when total debt does not exceed a specified amount ($4,031,575 for farmers and $1,868,200 for fishermen). **Chapter 13**—Any individual (not partnerships or corporations) with regular income who owes fixed (liquidated) unsecured debts of less than $383,175 or fixed secured debts of less than $1,149,525.
Procedure Leading to Discharge	Nonexempt property is sold, and the proceeds are distributed (in order) to priority groups. Dischargeable debts are terminated.	Plan is submitted. If the plan is approved and followed, debts are discharged.	Plan is submitted and must be approved if the value of the property to be distributed equals the amount of the claims or if the debtor turns over disposable income for a three-year or five-year period. If the plan is followed, debts are discharged.
Advantages	On liquidation and distribution, most or all debts are discharged, and the debtor has an opportunity for a fresh start.	Debtor continues in business. Creditors can either accept the plan, or it can be "crammed down" on them. The plan allows for the reorganization and liquidation of debts over the plan period.	Debtor continues in business or possession of assets. If the plan is approved, most debts are discharged after the plan period.

petition acts as an automatic stay against creditors' and co-obligors' actions against the estate.

A farmer or fisherman who has already filed a reorganization or repayment plan may convert it to a Chapter 12 plan. The debtor may also convert a Chapter 12 plan to a liquidation plan.

Content and Confirmation of the Plan The content of a plan under Chapter 12 is basically the same as that of a Chapter 13 repayment plan. Generally, the plan must be confirmed or denied within forty-five days of filing.

The plan must provide for payment of secured debts at the value of the collateral. If the secured debt exceeds the value of the collateral, the remaining debt is unsecured.

For unsecured debtors, the plan must be confirmed in either of the following circumstances: (1) the value of the property to be distributed under the plan equals the amount of the claim, or (2) the plan provides that all of the debtor's disposable income to be received in a three-year period (or longer, by court approval) will be applied to making payments. Disposable income is all income received less amounts needed to support the farmer or fisherman and his or her family and to continue the farming or commercial fishing operation. Completion of payments under the plan discharges all debts provided for by the plan.

Reviewing: Bankruptcy Law

Three months ago, Janet Hart's husband of twenty years died of cancer. Although he had medical insurance, he left Janet with outstanding medical bills of more than $50,000. Janet has two teenage daughters to support. She has worked at the local library for the past ten years, earning $1,500 per month. Since her husband's death, she has also received $1,500 in Social Security benefits and $1,100 in life insurance proceeds every month, for a total monthly income of $4,100. After making the mortgage payment of $1,500 and paying the amounts due on other debts, Janet has barely enough left to buy groceries for her family. She decides to file for Chapter 7 bankruptcy, hoping for a fresh start. Using the information presented in the chapter, answer the following questions.

1. What must Janet do *before* filing a petition for relief under Chapter 7?
2. How much time does Janet have after filing the bankruptcy petition to submit the required schedules? What happens if Janet does not meet the deadline?
3. Assume that Janet files a petition under Chapter 7. Further assume that the median family income in the geographic area in which Janet lives is $49,300. What steps would a court take to determine whether Janet's petition is presumed to be "substantial abuse" using the means test?
4. Suppose that the court determines that no *presumption* of substantial abuse applies in Janet's case. Nevertheless, the court finds that Janet does have the ability to pay at least a portion of the medical bills out of her disposable income. What would the court likely order in that situation?

Debate This . . . *Rather than being allowed to file Chapter 7 bankruptcy petitions, individuals and couples should always be forced to make an effort to pay off their debts through Chapter 13.*

Terms and Concepts

adequate protection doctrine 583	discharge 581	preference 585
automatic stay 583	insider 585	preferred creditor 585
bankruptcy trustee 581	liquidation 580	reaffirmation agreement 592
consumer-debtor 581	order for relief 583	U.S. trustee 582
cram-down provision 594	petition in bankruptcy 581	workout 592
debtor in possession (DIP) 593		

Issue Spotters

1. After graduating from college, Tina works briefly as a salesperson before filing for bankruptcy. Tina's petition states that her only debts are student loans, taxes accruing within the last year, and a claim against her based on her misuse of customers' funds during her employment. Are these debts dischargeable in bankruptcy? Explain. (See *Liquidation Proceedings.*)

2. Ogden is a vice president of Plumbing Service, Inc. (PSI). On May 1, Ogden loans PSI $10,000. On June 1, the firm repays the loan. On July 1, PSI files for bankruptcy. Quentin is appointed trustee. Can Quentin recover the $10,000 paid to Ogden on June 1? Why or why not? (See *Liquidation Proceedings.*)

• **Check your answers to the Issue Spotters against the answers provided in Appendix D at the end of this text.**

Business Scenarios

31–1. Voluntary versus Involuntary Bankruptcy. Burke has been a rancher all her life, raising cattle and crops. Her ranch is valued at $500,000, almost all of which is exempt under state law. Burke has eight creditors and a total indebtedness of $70,000. Two of her largest creditors are Oman ($30,000 owed) and Sneed ($25,000 owed). The other six creditors have claims of less than $5,000 each. A drought has ruined all of Burke's crops and forced her to sell many of her cattle at a loss. She cannot pay off her creditors. (See *Liquidation Proceedings.*)

(a) Under the Bankruptcy Code, can Burke, with a $500,000 ranch, voluntarily petition herself into bankruptcy? Explain.

(b) Could either Oman or Sneed force Burke into involuntary bankruptcy? Explain.

31–2. Distribution of Property. Montoro petitioned himself into voluntary bankruptcy. There were three major claims against his estate. One was made by Carlton, a friend who held Montoro's negotiable promissory note for $2,500. Another was made by Elmer, Montoro's employee, who claimed that Montoro owed him three months' back wages of $4,500. The last major claim was made by the United Bank of the Rockies on an unsecured loan of $5,000. In addition, Dietrich, an accountant retained by the trustee, was owed $500, and property taxes of $1,000 were owed to Rock County. Montoro's nonexempt property was liquidated, with proceeds of $5,000. Discuss fully what amount each party will receive, and why. (See *Liquidation Proceedings.*)

Business Case Problems

31–3. Discharge in Bankruptcy. Caroline McAfee loaned $400,000 to Carter Oaks Crossing. Joseph Harman, president of Carter Oaks Crossing, signed a promissory note providing that the company would repay the amount with interest in installments beginning in 1999 and ending by 2006. Harman signed a personal guaranty for the note. Carter Oaks Crossing defaulted on the note, so McAfee sued Harman for payment under the guaranty. Harman moved for summary judgment on the ground that McAfee's claim against him had been discharged in his Chapter 7 bankruptcy case. The case had been filed after 1999 but before the default on the note. The guaranty was not listed among Harman's debts in the bankruptcy filing. Would the obligation under the guaranty have been discharged in bankruptcy, as Harman claimed? Why or why not? [*Harman v. McAfee,* 302 Ga.App. 698, 691 S.E.2d 586 (2010)] (See *Liquidation Proceedings.*)

31–4. Automatic Stay. Michelle Gholston leased a Chevy Impala from EZ Auto Van Rentals. In November 2011, Gholston filed for bankruptcy. Around November 21, the bankruptcy court notified EZ Auto of Gholston's bankruptcy and the imposition of an automatic stay. Nevertheless, because Gholston had fallen behind on her payments, EZ Auto repossessed the vehicle on November 28. Gholston's attorney then

reminded EZ Auto about the automatic stay, but the company failed to return the car. As a result of the car's repossession, Gholston suffered damages that included emotional distress, lost wages, attorneys' fees, and car rental expenses. Can Gholston recover from EZ Auto? Why or why not? [*In re Gholston,* 2012 WL 639288 (M.D.Fla. 2012)] (See *Liquidation Proceedings.*)

31–5. Business Case Problem with Sample Answer— Discharge in Bankruptcy. Like many students, Barbara Hann financed her education partially through loans. These loans included three federally insured Stafford Loans of $7,500 each ($22,500 in total). Hann believed that she had repaid the loans, but when she filed a Chapter 13 petition, Educational Credit Management Corp. (ECMC) filed an unsecured proof of claim based on the loans. Hann objected. At a hearing at which ECMC failed to appear, Hann submitted correspondence from the lender that indicated the loans had been paid. The court entered an order sustaining Hann's objection. Despite the order, can ECMC resume its effort to collect on Hann's loans? Explain. [*In re Hann,* 711 F.3d 235 (1st Cir. 2013)] (See *Liquidation Proceedings.*)

• **For a sample answer to Problem 31–5, go to Appendix E at the end of this text.**

31–6. Discharge. Michael and Dianne Shankle divorced. An Arkansas state court ordered Michael to pay Dianne alimony and child support, as well as half of the $184,000 in their investment accounts. Instead, Michael withdrew more than half of the investment funds and spent them. Over the next several years, the court repeatedly held Michael in contempt for failing to pay Dianne. Six years later, Michael filed for Chapter 7 bankruptcy, including in the petition's schedule the debt to Dianne of unpaid alimony, child support, and investment funds. Is Michael entitled to a discharge of this debt, or does it qualify as an exception? Explain. [*In re Shankle,* 554 Fed.Appx. 264 (5th Cir. 2014)] (See *Liquidation Proceedings.*)

31–7. Discharge under Chapter 13. James Thomas and Jennifer Clark married and had two children. They bought a home in Ironton, Ohio, with a loan secured by a mortgage. Later, they took out a second mortgage. On their divorce, the court gave Clark custody of the children and required Clark to pay the first mortgage. The divorce decree also required Thomas and Clark to make equal payments on the second mortgage and provided that Clark would receive all proceeds on the sale of the home. Thomas failed to make any payments, and Clark sold the home. At that point, she learned that Auto Now had a lien on the home because Thomas had not made payments on his car. Clark used all the sale proceeds to pay off the lien and the mortgages. When Thomas filed a petition for a Chapter 13 bankruptcy in a federal bankruptcy court, Clark filed a proof of claim for the mortgage and lien debts. Clark claimed that Thomas should not be able to discharge these debts because they were part of his domestic-support obligations. Are these debts dischargeable? Explain. [*In re Thomas,* 591 Fed.Appx. 443 (6th Cir. 2015)] (See *Bankruptcy Relief under Chapter 12 and Chapter 13.*)

31–8. Liquidation Proceedings. Jeffrey Krueger and Michael Torres, shareholders of Cru Energy, Inc., were embroiled in litigation in a Texas state court. Both claimed to act on Cru's behalf, and each charged the other with attempting to obtain control of Cru through fraud and other misconduct.

Temporarily prohibited from participating in Cru's business, Krueger formed Kru, a company with the same business plan and many of the same shareholders as Cru. Meanwhile, to delay the state court proceedings, Krueger filed a petition for a Chapter 7 liquidation in a federal bankruptcy court. He did not reveal his interest in Kru to the bankruptcy court. Ownership of Krueger's Cru shares passed to the bankruptcy trustee, but Krueger ignored this. He called a meeting of Cru's shareholders—except Torres—and voted those shares to remove Torres from the board and elect himself chairman, president, chief executive officer, and treasurer. The Cru board then dismissed all of Cru's claims against Krueger in his suit with Torres. Are there sufficient grounds for the bankruptcy court to dismiss Krueger's bankruptcy petition? Discuss. [*In re Krueger,* 812 F.3d 365 (5th Cir. 2016)] (See *Liquidation Proceedings.*)

31–9. A Question of Ethics—Discharge in Bankruptcy. *Monica Sexton filed a petition for Chapter 13 reorganization. One of her creditors was Friedman's Jewelers. Her petition misclassified Friedman's claim as $800 of unsecured debt. Within days, Friedman's filed proof of a secured claim for $300 and an unsecured claim for $462. Eventually, Friedman's was sent payments of about $300 by check. None of the checks were cashed. By then, Friedman's had filed its own petition under Chapter 11, Bankruptcy Receivables Management (BRM) had bought Friedman's unpaid accounts, and the checks had not been forwarded. Sexton received a discharge on the completion of her plan. BRM was not notified. BRM wrote to Sexton's attorney to ask about the status of her case, but received no response. BRM demanded that Sexton surrender the collateral on its claim. Sexton asked the court to impose sanctions on BRM for violating the discharge order.* [*In re Sexton, 2011 WL 284180 (E.D.N.C. 2011)]* (See *Liquidation Proceedings.*)

(a) Was Sexton's debt to Friedman's dischargeable? Discuss.

(b) Should BRM be sanctioned for willfully violating the discharge order? Why or why not?

Legal Reasoning Group Activity

31–10. Discharge in Bankruptcy. Cathy Coleman took out loans to complete her college education. After graduation, Coleman was irregularly employed as a teacher before filing a petition in a federal bankruptcy court under Chapter 13. The court confirmed a five-year plan under which Coleman was required to commit all of her disposable income to paying the student loans. Less than a year later, when Coleman was laid off, she still owed more than $100,000 to Educational Credit Management Corp. Coleman asked the court to discharge the debt on the ground that it would be an undue hardship for her to pay it. (See *Liquidation Proceedings.*)

(a) The first group will determine when a debtor normally is entitled to a discharge under Chapter 13.

(b) The second group will discuss whether student loans are dischargeable and when "undue hardship" is a legitimate ground for an exception to the general rule.

(c) The third group will outline the goals of bankruptcy law and make an argument, based on these facts and principles, in support of Coleman's request.

Federal Student Loans—Default and Discharge

Ruby borrows $16,000 from the U.S. Department of Education (DOE) to help pay for her education at State University. To obtain the funds, she signs a note for the borrowed amount plus interest payable to DOE. She does not make payments on the loan when they come due.

Has Ruby defaulted on the loan? What will happen?

Federal Student Loan Programs

Federal government loans make up about 93 percent of the $1.2 trillion student loan market. Loans from private lenders make up the rest. It is important for borrowers to know which type of loan they owe. The collection methods available to private lenders are different from the methods available to federal lenders.

Federal student loan programs include the following.[1]

- *William D. Ford Federal Direct Loans*, which are made by the DOE.[2]
- *Federal Perkins Loans*, which are made by schools to students who demonstrate financial need.[3]
- *Federal Family Education Loans (FFEL)*, which were made by banks or other private lenders before July 1, 2010. The federal government guaranteed these loans. This program has been discontinued, but the outstanding amounts of any of the loans must still be paid.[4]

Default

A borrower is in default on a federal student loan if he or she fails to repay it according to the terms in the note. For most federal student loans, this occurs if a payment has not been made for more than 270 days (330 days for FFELs).[5]

Consequences of Default on a Federal Student Loan

If a borrower defaults on a federal student loan, the entire balance of the loan, including both principal and interest, can become due in a single payment.

Transfer of the Note to a Collection Agency Once default occurs, the holder of the note—which may be the DOE, the school that made the loan, a state agency, or a private nonprofit organization—can transfer the note to a collection agency to recover the unpaid debt.

Any additional costs to collect payment can then be added to the outstanding principal.[6] These expenses can be up to 18.5 percent of the defaulted amount of the principal and interest for Federal Direct Loans and FFELs, and more for Federal Perkins Loans.

---

1. Each program has eligibility requirements, interest rates, loan limits, and other stipulations that are subject to change. See U.S. Department of Education, *Loans* (Dec. 7, 2015) *available at* https://studentaid.ed.gov/sa/types/loans.
2. 20 U.S.C. Sections 1087a–1087j.
3. 20 U.S.C. Sections 1087aa–1087ii.
4. 20 U.S.C. Sections 1071–1087-4.
5. U.S. Department of Education, *Understanding Default* (Dec. 7, 2015) *available at* https://studentaid.ed.gov/sa/repay-loans/default.
6. *Marx v. General Revenue Corp.*, __ U.S. __, 133 S.Ct. 1166, 185 L.Ed.2d 242 (2013).

Treasury Offset There are other actions that the holder of the note might take. The DOE has the authority to collect the amount of the loan. This can be done by withholding funds from the defaulted borrower's sources of income. For instance, the DOE can ask the Department of the Treasury to withhold a defaulted debtor's federal income tax refund and other payments of federal funds, including Social Security payments.[7] This is known as a *Treasury offset.*

Garnishment The DOE or any other holder of the note can order the debtor's employer to withhold up to 15 percent of the debtor's disposable pay. No court order is necessary (unlike with a garnishment to recover the unpaid amount of a *private* student loan, which requires a court order). The withholding can continue until the debt is paid or otherwise taken out of default.[8] The DOE can arrange for a similar amount to be withheld from a federal employee's wages through the *federal salary offset program.*

Whether a debtor's employer is a private business or the federal government, the debtor has rights with regard to garnishment or offset. The debtor has a right to be notified of a proposed garnishment or offset, a right to object to it, and a right to a hearing on the objection.

Forgiveness, Cancellation, and Discharge

A federal student loan must be repaid. This is true even for borrowers who do not finish school, do not find a job related to their program of study, or are not satisfied with the education they received.

In certain circumstances, however, some or all of a loan may be forgiven, canceled, or discharged. For all federal student loans, these circumstances include the following.

- *Closed school*—A debtor may be entitled to a discharge if the school closes while the student is enrolled or within 120 days after he or she withdraws.
- *Total and permanent disability*—To prove total and permanent disability, the debtor must show that he or she is unable to engage in any substantial gainful activity due to a physical or mental impairment.
- *Death*—If a borrower dies, his or her federal student loan will be discharged.
- *Bankruptcy*—A loan may be discharged in bankruptcy if its repayment would cause undue hardship. Undue hardship requires that repaying the loan would prevent the debtor from maintaining a minimal standard of living, the situation would continue for a significant portion of the repayment period, and good faith efforts to repay the loan were made before the bankruptcy filing.

Federal Direct Loans and FFELs may be discharged or forgiven in the following additional circumstances.

- *False certification of student eligibility*—This can happen when a school falsely certifies a student's eligibility to benefit from its program. It can also happen when the student does not qualify for the occupation in which he or she paid to be educated (because of a health condition, for instance). Finally, it can result from forgery or identity theft.
- *Unauthorized payment*—A loan may be discharged if a school signed a student's name on the loan application or endorsed the loan check without the student's knowledge. An exception exists when the proceeds were paid to the student or applied against charges owed by the student to the school.

Continues

---

7. *Lockhart v. United States*, 548 U.S. 142, 126 S.Ct. 699, 163 L.Ed.2d 557 (2005).
8. *Sanon v. Department of Higher Education*, 453 Fed.Appx. 28 (2d Cir. 2011).

- *Unpaid refund*—An unpaid refund occurs when a student takes out a loan to attend a school and withdraws, but the school does not refund the appropriate amount to the DOE.
- *Full-time teacher*—A teacher who has been teaching full-time in a low-income school or educational service agency for five consecutive years may have some or all of a loan forgiven.

Some or all of a Federal Perkins Loan may be canceled for those who are employed in certain occupations. These include the following.

- Volunteers in the Peace Corps or VISTA.
- Military personnel (serving in areas of hostilities).
- Nurses and other medical technicians.
- Law enforcement and corrections officers.
- Workers for Head Start, and other child and family services.
- Professional providers of early intervention services for disabled persons.
- Teachers who have been teaching full-time in low-income schools or in certain subject areas.[9]

Finally, a Federal Direct Loan may be forgiven if the borrower is employed in a particular public service job and has made 120 payments on the loan.

Ethical Connection

Many of the ways to avoid paying a federal student loan without defaulting are ethical, and even laudable. For example, a loan may be forgiven for a debtor who is a teacher, a military serviceperson, a law enforcement officer, a nurse, or a child-care provider. Individuals who pursue these occupations are likely to have high ethical standards. Their contribution to the public good may exceed any amount that they borrowed to go to school. Ultimately, the public may accrue the greatest benefit from their service. Thus, it will be *us* who owe *them*—a debt of gratitude.

Ethics Question *In addition to the borrowers listed in this feature, who deserves to have their federal student loans forgiven? Why?*

Critical Thinking *What are the consequences in addition to those stated in this feature of failing to make timely payments on federal student loans? Discuss.*

---

9. For more information on these options, see U.S. Department of Education, *Forgiveness, Cancellation, and Discharge* (Dec. 7, 2015) *available at* https://studentaid.ed.gov/sa/repay-loans/forgiveness-cancellation.

Agency and Employment

CHAPTER 32

Agency Formation and Duties

One of the most common, important, and pervasive legal relationships is that of **agency.** In an agency relationship involving two parties, one of the parties, called the *agent,* agrees to represent or act for the other, called the *principal.* The principal has the right to control the agent's conduct in matters entrusted to the agent.

Agency relationships are crucial in the business world. By using agents, a principal can conduct multiple business operations at the same time in different locations. Indeed, the only way that certain business entities can function is through their agents. For instance, a corporate officer is an agent who serves in a representative capacity for the corporation. The officer has the authority to bind the corporation to a contract. Only through its officers can corporations enter into contracts.

Most employees are also considered to be agents of their employers.

Today, however, the United States is experiencing a trend toward a so-called *gig economy,* which centers on short-term, independent workers who are not employees. Companies like Uber and Lyft (discussed in this chapter's feature) provide evidence of this trend. This type of on-demand employment raises questions related to agency, making agency an increasingly important topic for students of business law and the legal environment to understand.

32–1 Agency Relationships

Section 1(1) of the *Restatement (Third) of Agency*[1] defines *agency* as "the fiduciary relation [that] results from the manifestation of consent by one person to another that the other shall act in his [or her] behalf and subject to his [or her] control, and consent by the other so to act." In other words, in a principal-agent relationship, the parties have agreed that the agent will act *on behalf and instead of* the principal in negotiating and transacting business with third parties.

The term **fiduciary** is at the heart of agency law. This term can be used both as a noun and as an adjective. When used as a noun, it refers to a person having a duty created by his or her undertaking to act primarily for another's benefit in matters connected with the undertaking. When used as an adjective, as in the phrase *fiduciary*

relationship, it means that the relationship involves trust and confidence.

Agency relationships commonly exist between employers and employees. Agency relationships may sometimes also exist between employers and independent contractors who are hired to perform special tasks or services.

32–1a Employer-Employee Relationships

Normally, all employees who deal with third parties are deemed to be agents. A salesperson in a department store, for instance, is an agent of the store's owner (the principal) and acts on the owner's behalf. Any sale of goods made by the salesperson to a customer is binding on the principal. Similarly, most representations of fact made by the salesperson with respect to the goods sold are binding on the principal.

Because employees who deal with third parties generally are deemed to be agents of their employers, agency law and employment law overlap considerably. Agency relationships, however, can exist outside

---

1. The *Restatement (Third) of Agency* is an authoritative summary of the law of agency and is often referred to by judges in their decisions and opinions.

an employer-employee relationship, so agency law has a broader reach than employment law. Additionally, agency law is based on the common law, whereas much employment law is statutory law.

Employment laws (state and federal) apply only to the employer-employee relationship. Statutes governing Social Security, withholding taxes, workers' compensation, unemployment compensation, workplace safety, and employment discrimination apply only if an employer-employee relationship exists. *These laws do not apply to independent contractors.*

32–1b Employer–Independent Contractor Relationships

Independent contractors are not employees because, by definition, those who hire them have no control over the details of their work performance. Section 2 of the *Restatement (Third) of Agency* defines an **independent contractor** as follows:

[An independent contractor is] a person who contracts with another to do something for him [or her] but who is not controlled by the other nor subject to the other's right to control with respect to his [or her] physical conduct in the performance of the undertaking. He [or she] may or may not be an agent.

Building contractors and subcontractors are independent contractors. A property owner who hires a contractor and subcontractors to complete a project does not control the details of the way they perform their work. Truck drivers who own their vehicles and hire out on a per-job basis are independent contractors, but truck drivers who drive company trucks on a regular basis usually are employees. See this chapter's *Ethics Today* feature for a discussion of disputes involving the classification of drivers working for Uber and Lyft.

The relationship between a principal and an independent contractor may or may not involve an agency relationship. To illustrate: A homeowner who hires a real estate broker to sell her house has contracted with an independent contractor (the broker). The homeowner has also established an agency relationship with the broker for the specific purpose of selling the property. Another example is an insurance agent, who is both an independent contractor and an agent of the insurance company for which he sells policies. (Note that an insurance *broker,* in contrast, normally is an agent of the person obtaining insurance and not of the insurance company.)

32–1c Determination of Employee Status

The courts are frequently asked to determine whether a particular worker is an employee or an independent contractor. How a court decides this issue can have a significant effect on the rights and liabilities of the parties. Employers are required to pay certain taxes, such as Social Security and unemployment taxes, for employees but not for independent contractors. Therefore, workers may benefit from obtaining employee status in some situations.

Criteria Used by the Courts In deciding whether a worker is categorized as an employee or an independent contractor, courts often consider the following questions:

1. *How much control does the employer exercise over the details of the work?* If the employer exercises considerable control over the details of the work and the day-to-day activities of the worker, this indicates employee status. This is perhaps the most important factor weighed by the courts in determining employee status.
2. *Is the worker engaged in an occupation or business distinct from that of the employer?* If so, this points to independent-contractor, not employee, status.
3. *Is the work usually done under the employer's direction or by a specialist without supervision?* If the work is usually done under the employer's direction, this indicates employee status.
4. *Does the employer supply the tools at the place of work?* If so, this indicates employee status.
5. *For how long is the person employed?* If the person is employed for a long period of time, this indicates employee status.
6. *What is the method of payment—by time period or at the completion of the job?* Payment by time period, such as once every two weeks or once a month, indicates employee status.
7. *What degree of skill is required of the worker?* If a great degree of skill is required, this may indicate that the person is an independent contractor hired for a specialized job and not an employee.

Whether a worker is an employee or an independent contractor can affect the employer's liability for the worker's actions. An employer normally is not responsible for the actions of an independent contractor. In the following case, the court had to determine the status of an auto service company and its tow truck driver who assaulted the passenger of a vehicle the company had been hired to tow.

Case 32.1

Coker v. Pershad

Superior Court of New Jersey, Appellate Division, 2013 WL 1296271 (2013).

Background and Facts AAA North Jersey, Inc., contracted with Five Star Auto Service to perform towing and auto repair services for AAA. Terence Pershad, the driver of a tow truck for Five Star, responded to a call to AAA for assistance by the driver of a car involved in an accident in Hoboken, New Jersey. Pershad got into a fight with Nicholas Coker, a passenger in the car, and assaulted Coker with a knife.

Coker filed a suit in a New Jersey state court against Pershad, Five Star, and AAA. The court determined that Pershad was Five Star's employee and that Five Star was an independent contractor, not AAA's employee. Thus, AAA was "not responsible for the alleged negligence of its independent contractor, defendant Five Star, in hiring Mr. Pershad." Five Star entered into a settlement with Coker. Coker appealed the ruling in AAA's favor.

In the Language of the Court
PER CURIAM.
   * * * *

The important difference between an employee and an independent contractor is that one who hires an independent contractor has no right of control over the manner in which the work is to be done. [Emphasis added.]
   * * * *

   * * * Plaintiff [Coker] argues AAA controlled the means and method of the work performed by Five Star. * * * Factors * * * [that] determine whether a principal maintains the right of control over an individual or a corporation claimed to be an independent contractor [include]:

   (a) the extent of control which, by the agreement, the master may exercise over the details of the work;
   (b) whether or not the one employed is engaged in a distinct occupation or business;
   (c) the kind of occupation, with reference to whether, in the locality, the work is usually done under the direction of the employer or by a specialist without supervision;
   (d) the skill required in the particular occupation;
   (e) whether the employer or the workman supplies the * * * tools * * * ;
   (f) the length of time for which the person is employed * * * .

   Applying these factors to the facts of this case, it is clear AAA did not control the manner and means of Five Star's work. The Agreement specifically stated Five Star was an independent contractor. Five Star purchased its own trucks and any other necessary equipment. AAA assigned jobs to Five Star and Five Star completed the work without any further supervision by AAA. Five Star chose the employees to send on towing calls and the trucks and equipment the employees would use.

   Five Star was also in business for itself and performed auto repair services for principals and customers other than AAA. Five Star hired and fired its own employees * * * .
   * * * *

   Plaintiff also argues Five Star should be considered to be controlled by AAA because "providing towing and other roadside assistance is arguably the focus of the regular business of AAA." * * * [But] AAA is an automobile club that provides a wide variety of services to its members. It contracts with numerous service providers, such as gas stations, motels and other businesses, to provide these services. Thus, AAA is not solely in the towing business.

   * * * AAA had used Five Star to provide towing services for approximately eight years and there is nothing in the record to demonstrate it lacked the skill needed to provide these services.

Decision and Remedy *A state intermediate appellate court affirmed the lower court's ruling. AAA could not be held liable for the actions of Five Star, its independent contractor, because "AAA did not control the manner and means of Five Star's work."*

Critical Thinking
- **Legal** *Five Star's contract with AAA required Five Star to be available to provide service for AAA members. Does this support Coker's argument that Five Star was AAA's employee? Why or why not?*

ETHICS TODAY

Is It Fair to Classify Uber and Lyft Drivers as Independent Contractors?

The transportation-for-hire world has changed dramatically since Uber, Lyft, and other transportation-sharing companies came onto the scene. Uber started in San Francisco in 2009. Today, its services are available in one form or another in about 60 countries and more than 300 cities worldwide. Its main competitor, Lyft, was launched in 2012 and operates in more than 200 U.S. cities. The growth in transportation sharing has not been without its setbacks, though. Most of them involve laws that have prohibited Uber and Lyft from operating in certain cities, as well as lawsuits by drivers claiming that they were misclassified.

Classification of Workers

Workers in the United States generally fall into two categories: employees and independent contractors. Employment laws, including minimum wage and anti-discrimination statutes, cover employees. Such laws do not cover most independent contractors. Enter the digital age of on-demand workers who obtain job assignments via apps.

Workers for Lyft, Uber, and similar companies choose when and where they will perform their duties. They do not choose how much they will be paid, however. For them, employment is a take-it-or-leave-it proposition. They electronically accept the platform terms of the apps, or they obtain no work assignments.

Some critics of this contractual system argue that there should be a new category of workers with "dependent-contractor" status who receive some of the protections traditionally given only to employees. Certain aspects of current labor law would be attached to the relationships between dependent contractors and their employers.

Worker Misclassification Lawsuits

A number of former or current Uber and Lyft drivers have pursued legal remedies to change their job classification and to obtain better benefits. In California, for instance, two federal court judges allowed separate lawsuits to go before juries on the question of whether on-demand drivers should be considered employees rather than independent contractors.[a]

In a similar case, rather than go to court, Lyft settled a worker misclassification lawsuit for $12.25 million. The suit, which was settled in 2016, had been brought in 2013. The settlement did not achieve a reclassification of Lyft drivers as employees. Basically, Lyft agreed to change its terms of service to conform to California's independent contractor status regulations. For instance, the company can no longer deactivate drivers' accounts without reason and without warning the drivers. Drivers have to be given a fair hearing first. Even though the lawsuit and the agreement were California based, the new terms of service will apply to all Lyft's drivers nationwide.

Competitors Sue Uber

In many cities, competitors, especially taxi drivers, have sued Uber. These lawsuits have involved claims of unfair competition, lack of minimum wages, and unsafe vehicles. A taxi driver sued Uber in northern California, for instance, but a federal district court ruled in favor of Uber's request for summary judgment.[b]

Another suit was brought in Pennsylvania. In this one, Checker Cab of Philadelphia claimed that Uber was violating Pennsylvania's unfair competition law. Checker Cab sought a preliminary injunction to prevent Uber from taking away its customers. The federal district court refused to grant an injunction, however, because Checker Cab failed to show irreparable harm. That decision was upheld on appeal.[c]

Critical Thinking *What choices do disgruntled Uber and Lyft drivers have?*

a. *Cotter v. Lyft, Inc.,* 60 F.Supp.3d 1067 (N.D.Cal. 2015); *O'Connor v. Uber Technologies, Inc., et al.,* Case No. C-13-3826 EMC (N.D.Cal. 2015).
b. *Rosen v. Uber Technologies, Inc.,* __ F.Supp.3d __, 2016 WL 704078 (N.D.Cal. 2016).
c. *Checker Cab of Philadelphia v. Uber Technologies, Inc.,* __ Fed.Appx. __, 2016 WL 929310 (3d Cir. 2016).

Criteria Used by the IRS The Internal Revenue Service (IRS) has established its own criteria for determining whether a worker is an independent contractor or an employee. The most important factor is the degree of control the business exercises over the worker.

The IRS tends to closely scrutinize a firm's classification of its workers because, as mentioned, employers can avoid certain tax liabilities by hiring independent contractors instead of employees. Even when a firm has classified a worker as an independent contractor, the IRS may decide that the worker is actually an employee. If the IRS decides that an employee is misclassified, the employer will be responsible for paying any applicable Social Security, withholding, and unemployment taxes due for that employee.

Employee Status and "Works for Hire"   Ordinarily, a person who creates a copyrighted work is the owner of it—unless it is a "work for hire." Under the Copyright Act, any copyrighted work created by an employee within the scope of her or his employment at the request of the employer is a "work for hire." The employer owns the copyright to the work.

In contrast, when an employer hires an independent contractor—such as a freelance artist, writer, or computer programmer—the independent contractor normally owns the copyright. An exception is made if the parties agree in writing that the work is a "work for hire" and the work falls into one of nine specific categories. The nine categories include audiovisual works, collective works (such as magazines), motion pictures, textbooks, tests, and translations.

■ **CASE IN POINT 32.1**   As a freelance contractor, Brian Cooley created two sculptures of dinosaur eggs for the National Geographic Society for use in connection with an article in its magazine, *National Geographic.* Cooley spent hundreds of hours researching, designing, and constructing the sculptures. National Geographic hired Louis Psihoyos to photograph Cooley's sculptures for the article. Cooley and Psihoyos had separate contracts with National Geographic in which each transferred the copyrights in their works to National Geographic for a limited time.

The rights to the works were returned to the artists at different times after publication. Psihoyos then began licensing his photographs of Cooley's sculptures to third parties in return for royalties. He digitized the photographs and licensed them to various online stock photography companies, and they appeared in several books published by Penguin Group. Cooley sued Psihoyos for copyright infringement.

Psihoyos argued that he owned the photos and could license them however he saw fit, but a federal district court disagreed. The court found that Psihoyos did not have an unrestricted right to use and license the photos. When Psihoyos reproduced an image of a Cooley sculpture, he reproduced the sculpture, which infringed on Cooley's copyright. Therefore, the court granted a summary judgment to Cooley.[2] ■

---

2. *Cooley v. Penguin Group (USA), Inc.*, 31 F.Supp.3d 599 (S.D.N.Y. 2014).

32–2 Formation of the Agency Relationship

Agency relationships normally are consensual. They come about by voluntary consent and agreement between the parties. Normally, the agreement need not be in writing, and consideration is not required.

A person must have contractual capacity to be a principal.[3] The idea is that those who cannot legally enter into contracts directly should not be allowed to do so indirectly through an agent. Any person can be an agent, however, regardless of whether he or she has the capacity to contract (including minors).

An agency relationship can be created for any legal purpose. An agency relationship created for a purpose that is illegal or contrary to public policy is unenforceable. ■ **EXAMPLE 32.2**   Archer (as principal) contracts with Burke (as agent) to sell illegal narcotics. The agency relationship is unenforceable because selling illegal narcotics is a felony and is contrary to public policy. If Burke sells the narcotics and keeps the profits, Archer cannot sue to enforce the agency agreement. ■

An agency relationship can arise in four ways: by agreement of the parties, by ratification, by estoppel, and by operation of law.

32–2a Agency by Agreement

Most agency relationships are based on an express or implied agreement that the agent will act for the principal and that the principal agrees to have the agent so act. An agency agreement can take the form of an express written contract or be created by an oral agreement. ■ **EXAMPLE 32.3**   Reese asks Grace, a gardener, to contract with others for the care of his lawn on a regular basis. If Grace agrees, an agency relationship exists between Reese and Grace for the lawn care. ■

An agency agreement can also be implied by conduct. ■ **CASE IN POINT 32.4**   Gilbert Bishop was admitted to a nursing home, Laurel Creek Health Care Center, suffering from various physical ailments. He was not able to use his hands well enough to write but was otherwise mentally competent. Bishop's sister offered to sign the admission papers for him, but it was Laurel Creek's

---

3. Note that some states allow a minor to be a principal. When a minor is permitted to be a principal, any resulting contracts will be voidable by the minor principal but *not* by the adult third party.

policy to have the patient's spouse sign the forms if the patient could not.

Bishop's sister then brought his wife, Anna, to the hospital to sign the paperwork, which included a mandatory arbitration clause. Later, when the family filed a lawsuit against Laurel Creek, the nursing home sought to enforce the arbitration clause. Ultimately, a Kentucky appellate court held that Bishop was bound by the contract and the arbitration clause his wife had signed. Bishop's conduct had indicated that he was giving his wife authority to act as his agent in signing the admission papers.[4] ■

32–2b Agency by Ratification

On occasion, a person who is in fact not an agent (or who is an agent acting outside the scope of her or his authority) makes a contract on behalf of another (a principal). If the principal approves or affirms that contract by word or by action, an agency relationship is created by *ratification*. Ratification involves a question of intent, and intent can be expressed by either words or conduct.

32–2c Agency by Estoppel

Sometimes, a principal causes a third person to believe that another person is the principal's agent, and the third person acts to his or her detriment in reasonable reliance on that belief. When this occurs, the principal is "estopped to deny" (prevented from denying) the agency relationship. The principal's actions have created the *appearance* of an agency that does not in fact exist, creating an agency by estoppel.

The Third Party's Reliance Must Be Reasonable
The third person must prove that he or she *reasonably* believed that an agency relationship existed.[5] Facts and circumstances must show that an ordinary, prudent person familiar with business practice and custom would have been justified in concluding that the agent had authority.

Created by the Principal's Conduct
Note that the acts or declarations of a purported *agent* in and of themselves do not create an agency by estoppel. Rather, it is the deeds or statements of the *principal* that create an agency by estoppel. ■ **CASE IN POINT 32.5** Francis Azur

was president and chief executive officer of ATM Corporation of America. Michelle Vanek was Azur's personal assistant. Among other duties, she reviewed his credit-card statements. For seven years, Vanek took unauthorized cash advances from Azur's credit-card account with Chase Bank. The charges appeared on at least sixty-five monthly statements.

When Azur discovered Vanek's fraud, he fired her and closed the account. He filed a suit against Chase, arguing that the bank should not have allowed Vanek to take cash advances. The court concluded that Azur (the principal) had given the bank reason to believe that Vanek (the agent) had authority. Therefore, Azur was estopped (prevented) from denying Vanek's authority.[6] ■

32–2d Agency by Operation of Law

The courts may find an agency relationship in the absence of a formal agreement in other situations as well. This may occur in family relationships, such as when one spouse purchases certain basic necessaries and charges them to the other spouse's account. The courts often rule that a spouse is liable for payment for the necessaries because of either a social policy or a legal duty to supply necessaries to family members.

Agency by operation of law may also occur in emergency situations. If an agent cannot contact the principal and failure to act would cause the principal substantial loss, the agent may take steps beyond the scope of her or his authority. For instance, a railroad engineer may contract on behalf of his or her employer for medical care for an injured motorist hit by the train.

Concept Summary 32.1 reviews the various ways in which agency relationships are formed.

32–3 Duties of Agents and Principals

Once the principal-agent relationship has been created, both parties have duties that govern their conduct. As discussed previously, the principal-agent relationship is *fiduciary*—based on trust. In a fiduciary relationship, each party owes the other the duty to act with the utmost good faith. In this section, we examine the various duties of agents and principals.

---

4. *Laurel Creek Health Care Center v. Bishop*, 2010 WL 985299 (Ky.App. 2010).

5. These concepts also apply when a person who is, in fact, an agent undertakes an action that is beyond the scope of her or his authority.

6. *Azur v. Chase Bank, USA, N.A.*, 601 F.3d 212 (3d Cir. 2010).

Concept Summary 32.1

Formation of the Agency Relationship

By Agreement	• The agency relationship is formed through express consent (oral or written) or implied by conduct.
By Ratification	• The principal either by act or by agreement ratifies the conduct of a person who is not, in fact, an agent.
By Estoppel	• The principal causes a third person to believe that another person is the principal's agent, and the third person acts to his or her detriment in reasonable reliance on that belief.
By Operation of Law	• The agency relationship is based on a social or legal duty—such as the need to support family members. Or, it is formed in emergency situations when the agent is unable to contact the principal and failure to act outside the scope of the agent's authority would cause the principal substantial loss.

32–3a Agent's Duties to the Principal

Generally, the agent owes the principal five duties—performance, notification, loyalty, obedience, and accounting (see Exhibit 32–1).

Performance An implied condition in every agency contract is the agent's agreement to use reasonable diligence and skill in performing the work. When an agent fails to perform his or her duties, liability for breach of contract may result.

Standard of Care. The degree of skill or care required of an agent is usually that expected of a reasonable person under similar circumstances. Generally, this is interpreted to mean ordinary care. If an agent has represented herself or himself as possessing special skills, however, the agent is expected to exercise the degree of skill claimed. Failure to do so constitutes a breach of the agent's duty.

Gratuitous Agents. Not all agency relationships are based on contract. In some situations, an agent acts gratuitously—that is, without payment. A gratuitous agent cannot be liable for breach of contract because there is no contract. He or she is subject only to tort liability. Once a gratuitous agent has begun to act in an agency capacity, he or she has the duty to continue to perform in that

capacity. A gratuitous agent must perform in an acceptable manner and is subject to the same standards of care and duty to perform as other agents.

■ **EXAMPLE 32.6** Bower's friend Alcott is a real estate broker. Alcott offers to sell Bower's vacation home at no charge. If Alcott never attempts to sell the home, Bower has no legal cause of action to force her to do so. If Alcott does attempt to sell the home to Friedman, but then performs so negligently that the sale falls through, Bower can sue Alcott for negligence. ■

Notification An agent is required to notify the principal of all matters that come to her or his attention concerning the subject matter of the agency. This is the *duty of notification,* or the duty to inform.

■ **EXAMPLE 32.7** Perez, an artist, is about to negotiate a contract to sell a series of paintings to Barber's Art Gallery for $25,000. Perez's agent learns that Barber is insolvent and will be unable to pay for the paintings. The agent has a duty to inform Perez of Barber's insolvency because it is relevant to the subject matter of the agency, which is the sale of Perez's paintings. ■

Generally, the law assumes that the principal is aware of any information acquired by the agent that is relevant to the agency—regardless of whether the agent actually passes on this information to the principal. It is a basic tenet of agency law that notice to the agent is notice to the principal.

EXHIBIT 32–1 Duties of the Agent

Loyalty Loyalty is one of the most fundamental duties in a fiduciary relationship. Basically, the agent has the duty to act *solely for the benefit of his or her principal* and not in the interest of the agent or a third party. For instance, an agent cannot represent two principals in the same transaction unless both know of the dual capacity and consent to it.

Maintain Confidentiality. The duty of loyalty also means that any information or knowledge acquired through the agency relationship is confidential. It is a breach of loyalty to disclose such information either during the agency relationship or after its termination. Typical examples of confidential information are trade secrets and customer lists compiled by the principal.

Actions Must Benefit the Principal. The agent's loyalty must be undivided. The agent's actions must be strictly for the benefit of the principal and must not result in any secret profit for the agent.

■ **EXAMPLE 32.8** Don contracts with Leo, a real estate agent, to negotiate the purchase of an office building. Leo discovers that the property owner will sell the building only as a package deal with another parcel. So Leo buys the two properties, intending to resell the building to Don. Leo has breached his fiduciary duty. As a real estate agent, Leo has a duty to communicate all offers to Don, his principal, and not to purchase the property secretly and then resell it to Don. Leo is required to act in Don's best interests and can become the purchaser in this situation only with Don's knowledge and approval. ■

In the following case, an employer alleged that a former employee had breached his duty of loyalty by planning a competing business while still working for the employer.

Spotlight on Taser International

Case 32.2 Taser International, Inc. v. Ward

Court of Appeals of Arizona, Division 1, 224 Ariz. 389, 231 P.3d 921 (2010).

Background and Facts Taser International, Inc., develops and makes electronic control devices, commonly called stun guns, as well as accessories for electronic control devices, including a personal video and audio recording device called the TASER CAM.

Steve Ward was Taser's vice president of marketing when he began to explore the possibility of developing and marketing devices of his own design, including a clip-on camera. Ward talked to

Case 32.2 Continues

Case 32.2 Continued

patent attorneys and a product development company and completed most of a business plan. After he resigned from Taser, he formed Vievu, LLC, to market his clip-on camera.

Ten months after Ward resigned, Taser announced the AXON, a product that provides an audio-video record of an incident from the visual perspective of the person involved. Taser then filed a suit in an Arizona state court against Ward, alleging that he had breached his duty of loyalty to Taser. The court granted Taser's motion for a summary judgment in the employer's favor. Ward appealed.

In the Language of the Court
PORTLEY, Judge.

* * * *

* * * An agent is under the duty to act with entire good faith and loyalty for the furtherance of the interests of his principal in all matters concerning or affecting the subject of his agency.

One aspect of this broad principle is that an employee is precluded from actively competing with his or her employer during the period of employment.

Although an employee may not compete prior to termination, the employee may take action during employment, not otherwise wrongful, to prepare for competition following termination of the agency relationship. Preparation cannot take the form of acts in direct competition with the employer's business. [Emphasis added.]

* * * *

It is undisputed that, prior to his resignation, Ward did not solicit or recruit any Taser employees, distributors, customers, or vendors; he did not buy, sell, or incorporate any business; he did not acquire office space or other general business services; he did not contact or enter into any agreements with suppliers or manufacturers for his proposed clip-on camera; and he did not sell any products. However, Ward did begin developing a business plan, counseled with several attorneys, explored and abandoned the concept of an eyeglass-mounted camera device, and engaged, to some extent, in the exploration and development of a clip-on camera device.

Ward argues that his pre-termination activities did not constitute active competition but were merely lawful preparation for a future business venture. Taser contends, however, that "this case is * * * about developing a rival design during employment, knowing full well TASER has sold such a device and continues to develop a second-generation product."

* * * *

* * * Assuming Taser was engaged in the research and development of a recording device during Ward's employment, assuming Ward knew or should have known of those efforts, and assuming Taser's device would compete with Ward's concept, substantial design and development efforts by Ward during his employment would constitute direct competition with the business activities of Taser and would violate his duty of loyalty. In the context of a business which engages in research, design, development, manufacture, and marketing of products, we cannot limit "competition" to just actual sales of competing products.

Decision and Remedy *A state intermediate appellate court agreed with Taser that an employee may not actively compete with his employer before his employment is terminated. But the parties disputed the extent of Ward's pre-termination efforts, creating a genuine issue of material fact that could not be resolved on a motion for summary judgment. The appellate court thus reversed the lower court's decision in Taser's favor and remanded the case for further proceedings.*

Critical Thinking

• **Legal Environment** *Did Ward breach any duties owed to his employer in addition to his alleged breach of the duty of loyalty? Discuss.*

• **What If the Facts Were Different?** *Suppose that Ward's pre-termination activities focused on a product that was not designed to compete with Taser's products. Would these efforts have breached the duty of loyalty? Why or why not?*

Obedience When acting on behalf of the principal, an agent has a duty to follow all lawful and clearly stated instructions of the principal. Any deviation from such instructions is a violation of this duty.

During emergency situations, however, when the principal cannot be consulted, the agent may deviate from the instructions without violating this duty. Whenever instructions are not clearly stated, the agent can fulfill the duty of obedience by acting in good faith and in a manner reasonable under the circumstances.

Accounting Unless the agent and principal agree otherwise, the agent must keep and make available to the principal an account of all property and funds received and paid out on the principal's behalf. This includes gifts from third parties in connection with the agency. ■ **EXAMPLE 32.9** Marla is a salesperson for Roadway Supplies. Knife River Construction gives Marla a new tablet as a gift for prompt deliveries of Roadway's paving materials. The tablet belongs to Roadway. ■

The agent has a duty to maintain a separate account for the principal's funds and must not intermingle these funds with the agent's personal funds. If a licensed professional (such as an attorney) violates this duty, he or she may be subject to disciplinary action by the licensing authority (such as the state bar association). Of course, the professional will also be liable to his or her client (the principal) for failure to account.

32–3b Principal's Duties to the Agent

The principal also has certain duties to the agent (as shown in Exhibit 32–2). These duties relate to compensation, reimbursement and indemnification, cooperation, and safe working conditions.

Compensation In general, when a principal requests certain services from an agent, the agent reasonably expects payment. For instance, when an accountant or an attorney is asked to act as an agent, an agreement to compensate the

agent for this service is implied. The principal therefore has a duty to pay the agent for services rendered.

Unless the agency relationship is gratuitous and the agent does not act in exchange for payment, the principal must pay the agreed-on value for the agent's services. If no amount has been expressly agreed on, then the principal owes the agent the customary compensation for such services. The principal also has a duty to pay that compensation in a timely manner.

■ **CASE IN POINT 32.10** Keith Miller worked as a sales representative for Paul M. Wolff Company, a subcontractor specializing in concrete-finishing services. Sales representatives at Wolff are paid a 15 percent commission on projects that meet a 35 percent gross profit threshold. The commission is paid after the projects are completed. When Miller resigned, he asked for commissions on fourteen projects for which he had secured contracts but which had not yet been completed. Wolff refused, so Miller sued.

The court found that "an agent is entitled to receive commissions on sales that result from the agent's efforts," even after the employment or agency relationship ends. Miller had met the gross profit threshold on ten of the unfinished projects, and therefore, he was entitled to more than $21,000 in commissions.[7] ■

Reimbursement and Indemnification Whenever an agent disburses funds at the request of the principal, the principal has a duty to reimburse the agent. The principal must also reimburse the agent (even a gratuitous

---

7. *Miller v. Paul M. Wolff Co.*, 178 Wash.App. 957, 316 P.3d 1113 (2014).

EXHIBIT 32–2 Duties of the Principal

DUTIES OF THE PRINCIPAL			
Compensation	**Reimbursement and Indemnification**	**Cooperation**	**Safe Working Conditions**
Principal must pay the agreed-on (or reasonable) value for the agent's services.	Principal must reimburse the agent for any funds paid out at the principal's request, as well as for necessary expenses.	Principal must cooperate with and assist an agent in performing his or her duties.	Principal must provide a safe working environment for agents and employees.

agent) for any necessary expenses incurred in the course of the reasonable performance of her or his agency duties. Agents cannot recover for expenses incurred as a result of their own misconduct or negligence, though.

Subject to the terms of the agency agreement, the principal has the duty to *indemnify* (compensate) an agent for liabilities incurred because of authorized and lawful acts and transactions. For instance, if the agent, on the principal's behalf, forms a contract with a third party, and the principal fails to perform the contract, the third party may sue the agent for damages. In this situation, the principal is obligated to compensate the agent for any costs incurred by the agent as a result of the principal's failure to perform the contract.

Additionally, the principal must indemnify the agent for the value of benefits that the agent confers on the principal. The amount of indemnification usually is specified in the agency contract. If it is not, the courts will look to the nature of the business and the type of loss to determine the amount. Note that this rule applies to acts by gratuitous agents as well.

Cooperation A principal has a duty to cooperate with the agent and to assist the agent in performing his or her duties. The principal must do nothing to prevent that performance.

For instance, when a principal grants an agent an exclusive territory, the principal creates an **exclusive agency,** in which the principal cannot compete with the agent or appoint or allow another agent to compete. If the principal does so, he or she violates the exclusive agency and is exposed to liability for the agent's lost profits.

■ **EXAMPLE 32.11** Penny (the principal) creates an exclusive agency by granting Andrew (the agent) a territory within which only Andrew may sell Penny's organic skin care products. If Penny starts to sell the products herself within Andrew's territory—or permits another agent to do so—Penny has failed to cooperate with the agent. Because she has violated the exclusive agency, Penny can be held liable for Andrew's lost sales or profits. ■

In the following case, a pair of potential homebuyers entered into an agreement with a realtor to act as the buyers' exclusive agent in locating and purchasing property. Later, the buyers executed an exclusive agency agreement with a different realtor. Neither agent knew about the other until the buyers found a home that they liked and bought it.

NRT New England, LLC v. Jones

Appellate Court of Connecticut, 162 Conn.App. 840, 134 A.3d 632 (2016).

In the Language of the Court

HARPER, J. [Judge]

* * * *

The defendant [Christopher Jones] met Andrea Woolston, a licensed realtor working as an independent contractor [for NRT New England, LLC, doing business as Coldwell Banker Residential Brokerage], in October 2010. The defendant expressed to Woolston a desire to purchase a home for himself and his then fiancée, Katherine Wiltshire. One of the first things Woolston asked the defendant was whether he was represented by another agent. The defendant responded that he was not. After a number of conversations about the defendant's needs and wishes, the parties executed an exclusive right to represent buyer agreement (agreement), which established, among other things, that Woolston was the defendant's

exclusive agent for finding, negotiating, and purchasing property. Over the next several months, Woolston devoted a substantial amount of time searching for properties for the defendant to purchase. Specifically, Woolston researched available properties at six town halls in the communities in which the defendant was interested. She showcased a number of properties personally to the defendant and Wiltshire and introduced many more to them through e-mail. Woolston and the defendant had at least twenty appointments where they viewed multiple properties. Additionally, Woolston visited many properties alone to determine if they were suitable for the defendant. Altogether, Woolston spent hundreds of hours seeking a suitable home for the defendant.

The agreement was in effect from January 11, 2011 until July 11, 2011,

and set forth the geographical area that the defendant was interested in and the rate of compensation for the plaintiff's services. With respect to geographical area, the parties agreed that Woolston would seek properties in Killingworth, Guilford, Essex, Old Saybrook, Deep River, Lyme, and Old Lyme [Connecticut]. With respect to compensation, the defendant agreed to pay the plaintiff a commission equal to 2.5 percent of the purchase price of the property "if the [buyer] or any person or entity acting on the [buyer's] behalf purchases, options, exchanges, leases or trades any property, through the efforts of anyone, including the [buyer]." The agreement imposed the following duties on the defendant: "The [buyer] will not deal directly with any other broker, agent or licensee during the term of this agreement. The [buyer] will

Case 32.3 Continued

notify other brokers, agents or licensees at first contact that the [buyer] is being exclusively represented by [NRT]. The [buyer] will disclose to [NRT] any past and/or current contacts for any real property or with any other real estate broker or agent."

On May 10, 2011, the defendant informed Woolston via e-mail that he and Wiltshire purchased property at 300 Vineyard Point Road in Guilford for $1,375,000. The defendant learned of this property on May 4, 2011, from Mary Jane Burt, a realtor with H. Pearce Real Estate (H. Pearce), who previously had represented Wiltshire with the sale of her house in Hamden [Connecticut]. Woolston subsequently confronted the defendant and eventually learned that he and Wiltshire previously had executed an exclusive right to represent buyer agreement with Burt and H. Pearce. This agreement was in effect from August 1, 2010, until August 1, 2011, and contained a provision designating Burt as the exclusive agent for the defendant and Wiltshire. Thus, at the time the defendant purchased the property in Guilford, he was under contract for exclusive agency with both Woolston and Burt. The defendant never told Woolston or Burt that he had two agreements in effect at the same time. Woolston notified her superiors of what had transpired. * * * [NRT] filed a * * * complaint [in a Connecticut state court] against the

defendant [for] breach of contract * * * . After a trial * * * , the court * * * found that the plaintiff had proven * * * breach of contract * * * and damages. * * * The court awarded the plaintiff $34,375 in damages [which represented 2.5 percent of the purchase price for the Vineyard Point property] plus attorney's fees and costs. This appeal followed.

* * * *

The defendant * * * claims that the agreement was unenforceable. Specifically, he argues that the court improperly * * * found that it was inequitable to deny the plaintiff recovery.

* * * *

There is ample evidence in the record to support the court's conclusion that denying the plaintiff relief would be inequitable. Woolston testified, and the defendant himself conceded, that she rendered a significant amount of services to the defendant over several months. Specifically, Woolston researched properties at town halls for availability and encumbrances, contacted property owners, arranged personal visits, prepared and presented literature to the defendant on available properties, and attended appointments with the defendant and Wiltshire. Woolston spent hundreds of hours working for the defendant in total.

The defendant, on the other hand, accepted Woolston's services while under contract with another agent in violation of the agreement. Indeed, the defendant

acknowledged that he was untruthful with Woolston at the beginning of their relationship when he told her that he was not represented by another agent. In fact, he was scheduling appointments and viewing properties with both Woolston and Burt at approximately the same time in May 2011. For example, the defendant e-mailed Woolston on May 2, 2011, thanking her for showing him a property. Approximately one week later, the defendant e-mailed Woolston to inform her that he viewed 300 Vineyard Point Road with Burt and had "put in an all cash bid that has been accepted."

The defendant nevertheless argues that it would not be inequitable to deny recovery to the plaintiff because Woolston performed no services in connection with his purchase of 300 Vineyard Point Road. We are not persuaded. *The defendant agreed to pay a commission "equal to 2.5% of the purchase price if the [buyer] or any person or entity acting on the [buyer's] behalf purchases * * * any property, through the efforts of anyone, including the [buyer], where an agreement to purchase the property was entered into during the term of this agreement."* However unjust this result may seem to the defendant in hindsight, we cannot say it is inequitable because it is precisely what he agreed to. [Emphasis added.]

* * * *

The judgment is affirmed.

Legal Reasoning Questions

1. What is the advantage to a principal of an exclusive agency agreement? What was the advantage to Jones of his agreement with Woolston? Discuss.

2. Why, in addition to damages, was the plaintiff awarded attorneys' fees and costs?

3. Jones's agreement with Woolston provided that on the purchase of the property, NRT "will, whenever feasible, seek compensation from the seller or the seller's agent." The court determined that it was not feasible. Why would it not be reasonable in this situation to ask the seller of the property to pay part of Woolston's commission?

Safe Working Conditions The common law requires the principal to provide safe working premises, equipment, and conditions for all agents and employees. The principal has a duty to inspect working areas and to warn agents and employees about any

unsafe situations. When the agent is an employee, the employer's liability is frequently covered by state workers' compensation insurance. In addition, federal and state statutes often require the employer to meet certain safety standards.

32–4 Rights and Remedies of Agents and Principals

In general, for every duty of the principal, the agent has a corresponding right, and vice versa. When one party to the agency relationship violates his or her duty to the other party, the nonbreaching party is entitled to a remedy. The remedies available arise out of contract and tort law. These remedies include monetary damages, termination of the agency relationship, an injunction, and required accountings.

32–4a Agent's Rights and Remedies against the Principal

The agent has the right to be compensated, to be reimbursed and indemnified, and to have a safe working environment. An agent also has the right to perform agency duties without interference by the principal.

Tort and Contract Remedies Remedies of the agent for breach of duty by the principal follow normal contract and tort remedies. ■ **EXAMPLE 32.12** Aaron Hart, a builder who has just constructed a new house, contracts with a real estate agent, Fran Boller, to sell the house. The contract calls for the agent to have an exclusive ninety-day listing and to receive 6 percent of the selling price when the home is sold. Boller holds several open houses and shows the home to a number of potential buyers.

One month before the ninety-day listing terminates, Hart agrees to sell the house to another buyer—not one to whom Boller has shown the house—after the ninety-day listing expires. Hart and the buyer agree that Hart will reduce the price of the house by 3 percent because he will sell it directly and thus will not have to pay Boller's commission. If Boller learns of Hart's actions, she can terminate the agency relationship and sue Hart for the 6 percent commission she should have earned on the sale of the house. ■

Demand for an Accounting An agent can also withhold further performance and demand that the principal give an accounting. For instance, a sales agent may demand an accounting if the agent and principal disagree on the amount of commissions the agent should have received for sales made during a specific period.

No Right to Specific Performance When the principal-agent relationship is not contractual, the agent has no right to specific performance. An agent can

recover for past services and future damages but cannot force the principal to allow him or her to continue acting as an agent.

32–4b Principal's Rights and Remedies against the Agent

In general, a principal has contract remedies for an agent's breach of fiduciary duties. The principal also has tort remedies if the agent engages in misrepresentation, negligence, deceit, libel, slander, or trespass. In addition, any breach of a fiduciary duty by an agent may justify the principal's termination of the agency. The main actions available to the principal are constructive trust, avoidance, and indemnification.

Constructive Trust Anything that an agent obtains by virtue of the employment or agency relationship belongs to the principal. An agent commits a breach of fiduciary duty if he or she secretly retains benefits or profits that, by right, belong to the principal. Therefore, the agent holds such property in a *constructive trust* (an equitable trust imposed for reasons of fairness) for the principal. ■ **EXAMPLE 32.13** Lee, a purchasing agent for Metcalf, receives cash rebates from a customer. If Lee keeps the rebates for himself, he violates his fiduciary duty to his principal, Metcalf. On finding out about the cash rebates, Metcalf can sue Lee and recover them. ■

Avoidance When an agent breaches the agency agreement or agency duties under a contract, the principal has a right to avoid any contract entered into with the agent. This right of avoidance is at the election of the principal.

Indemnification In certain situations, when a principal is sued by a third party for an agent's negligent conduct, the principal can sue the agent for indemnification—that is, for an equal amount of damages. The same holds true if the agent violates the principal's instructions. ■ **EXAMPLE 32.14** Parker (the principal) owns a used-car lot where Moore (the agent) works as a salesperson. Parker tells Moore to make no warranties for the used cars. Moore is eager to make a sale to Walters, a customer, and adds a 50,000-mile warranty for the car's engine. Parker may be liable to Walters for engine failure, but if Walters sues Parker, Parker normally can then sue Moore for indemnification for violating his instructions. ■

Sometimes, though, it is difficult to distinguish between instructions of the principal that limit an agent's authority and those that are merely advice. ■ **EXAMPLE 32.15** Gutierrez (the principal) owns an office supply company, and Logan (the agent) is the manager. Gutierrez tells Logan, "Don't purchase any more inventory this month." Gutierrez goes on vacation. A large order comes in from a local business, and the inventory on hand is insufficient to meet it. What is Logan to do? In this situation, Logan probably has the inherent authority to purchase more inventory despite Gutierrez's command. It is unlikely that Logan would be required to indemnify Gutierrez in the event that the local business subsequently canceled the order. ■

Reviewing: Agency Formation and Duties

James Blatt hired Marilyn Scott to sell insurance for the Massachusetts Mutual Life Insurance Company. Their contract stated, "Nothing in this contract shall be construed as creating the relationship of employer and employee." The contract was terminable at will by either party. Scott financed her own office and staff, was paid according to performance, had no taxes withheld from her checks, and could legally sell products of Massachusetts Mutual's competitors. Blatt learned that Scott was simultaneously selling insurance for Perpetual Life Insurance Corporation, one of Massachusetts Mutual's fiercest competitors. Blatt therefore withheld client contact information from Scott. Scott complained to Blatt that he was inhibiting her ability to sell insurance for Massachusetts Mutual. Blatt subsequently terminated their contract. Scott filed a suit in a New York state court against Blatt and Massachusetts Mutual. Scott claimed that she had lost sales for Massachusetts Mutual—and commissions—as a result of Blatt's withholding contact information from her. Using the information presented in the chapter, answer the following questions.

1. Who is the principal and who is the agent in this scenario? By which method was an agency relationship formed between Scott and Blatt?
2. What facts would the court consider most important in determining whether Scott was an employee or an independent contractor?
3. How would the court most likely rule on Scott's employee status? Why?
4. Which of the four duties that Blatt owed Scott in their agency relationship has probably been breached?

Debate This . . .   *All works created by independent contractors should be considered works for hire under copyright law.*

Terms and Concepts

agency 606   fiduciary 606   independent contractor 607
exclusive agency 616

Issue Spotters

1. Winona contracted with XtremeCast, a broadcast media firm, to cohost an Internet-streaming sports program. Winona and XtremeCast signed a new contract for each episode. In each contract, Winona agreed to work for a certain number of days for a certain salary. During each broadcast, Winona was free to improvise her performance. She had no other obligation to work for XtremeCast. Was Winona an independent contractor? (See *Agency Relationships*.)

2. Dimka Corporation wants to build a new mall on a specific tract of land. Dimka contracts with Nadine to buy the property. There is a substantial difference between the price that Dimka is willing to pay and the price at which the owner is willing to sell. When Nadine learns of this, she wants to buy the land and sell it to Dimka herself. Can she do this? Discuss. (See *Duties of Agents and Principals*.)

• **Check your answers to the Issue Spotters against the answers provided in Appendix D at the end of this text.**

Business Scenarios

32–1. Agency Formation. Paul Gett is a well-known, wealthy financial expert living in the city of Torris. Adam Wade, Gett's friend, tells Timothy Brown that he is Gett's agent for the purchase of rare coins. Wade even shows Brown a local newspaper clipping mentioning Gett's interest in coin collecting. Brown, knowing of Wade's friendship with Gett, contracts with Wade to sell a rare coin valued at $25,000 to Gett. Wade takes the coin and disappears with it. On the payment due date, Brown seeks to collect from Gett, claiming that Wade's agency made Gett liable. Gett does not deny that Wade was a friend, but he claims that Wade was never his agent. Discuss fully whether an agency was in existence at the time the contract for the rare coin was made. (See *Formation of the Agency Relationship*.)

32–2. Duty of Loyalty. Peter hires Alice as an agent to sell a piece of property he owns. The price is to be at least $30,000. Alice discovers that the fair market value of Peter's property is actually at least $45,000 and could be higher because a shopping mall is going to be built nearby. Alice forms a real estate partnership with her cousin Carl. Then she prepares for Peter's signature a contract for the sale of the property to Carl for $32,000. Peter signs the contract. Just before closing and passage of title, Peter learns about the shopping mall and the increased fair market value of his property. Peter refuses to deed the property to Carl. Carl claims that Alice, as Peter's agent, solicited a price above that agreed on when the agency was created and that the contract is therefore binding and enforceable. Discuss fully whether Peter is bound to this contract. (See *Duties of Agents and Principals*.)

32–3. Employee versus Independent Contractor. Stephen Hemmerling was a driver for the Happy Cab Co. Hemmerling paid certain fixed expenses and followed various rules relating to the use of the cab, the hours that could be worked, and the solicitation of fares, among other things. Rates were set by the state. Happy Cab did not withhold taxes from Hemmerling's pay. While driving the cab, Hemmerling was injured in an accident and filed a claim for workers' compensation benefits in a state court. Such benefits are not available to independent contractors. On what basis might the court hold that Hemmerling was an employee? Explain. (See *Agency Relationships*.)

Business Case Problems

32–4. Agency by Ratification. Wesley Hall, an independent contractor managing property for Acree Investments, Ltd., lost control of a fire he had set to clear ten acres of Acree land. The runaway fire burned seventy-eight acres of Earl Barrs's property. Russell Acree, one of the owners of Acree Investments, had previously owned the ten acres, but he had put it into the company and was no longer the principal owner. Hall had worked for Russell Acree in the past and had told the state forestry department that he was burning the land for Acree. Barrs sued Russell Acree for the acts of his agent, Hall. In his suit, Barrs noted that Hall had been an employee of Russell Acree, Hall had talked about burning the land "for Acree," and Russell Acree had apologized to Barrs for the fire. Barrs also pointed out that Acree Investments had not been identified as the principal property owner until Barrs filed his lawsuit. Barrs argued that those facts were sufficient to create an agency by ratification to impose liability on Russell Acree. Was Barrs's agency by ratification claim valid? Why or why not? [*Barrs v. Acree,* 691 S.E.2d 575 (Ga.App. 2010)] (See *Formation of the Agency Relationship*.)

32–5. Employment Relationships. William Moore owned Moore Enterprises, a wholesale tire business. William's son, Jonathan, worked as a Moore Enterprises employee while he was in high school. Later, Jonathan started his own business, called Morecedes Tire. Morecedes regrooved tires and sold them to businesses, including Moore Enterprises. A decade after Jonathan started Morecedes, William offered him work with Moore Enterprises. On the first day, William told Jonathan to load certain tires on a trailer but did not tell him how to do it. Was Jonathan an independent contractor? Discuss. [*Moore v. Moore,* 152 Idaho 245, 269 P.3d 802 (2011)] (See *Agency Relationships*.)

32–6. Agent's Duties to Principal. William and Maxine Miller were shareholders of Claimsco International, Inc. They filed a suit against the other shareholders, Michael Harris and Kenneth Hoxie, and the accountant who worked for all of them—John Verchota. Among other things, the Millers alleged that Verchota had breached a duty that he owed them. They claimed that at Harris's instruction, Verchota had taken various actions that placed them at a disadvantage to the other shareholders. Verchota had allegedly adjusted Claimsco's books to maximize the Millers' financial liabilities, for instance, and had falsely reported distributions of income to them without actually transferring that income. Which duty are the Millers referring to? If the allegations can be proved, did Verchota breach this duty? Explain. [*Miller v. Harris,* 2013 IL App (2d) 120512, 985 N.E.2d 671 (2 Dist. 2013)] (See *Duties of Agents and Principals*.)

32–7. Business Case Problem with Sample Answer— Determining Employee Status. Nelson Ovalles worked as a cable installer for Cox Rhode Island Telecom, LLC, under an agreement with a third party, M&M Communications, Inc. The agreement stated that no employer-employee relationship existed between Cox and M&M's technicians, including Ovalles. Ovalles was required to designate his affiliation with Cox on his work van, clothing, and identification badge. Cox had minimal contact with him, however, and had limited power to control how he performed his duties. Cox supplied cable wire and similar items, but the equipment was delivered to M&M, not to Ovalles. On a workday, while Ovalles was fulfilling a work order, his van rear-ended a car driven by Barbara Cayer. Is Cox liable to Cayer? Explain. [*Cayer v. Cox*

Rhode Island Telecom, LLC, 85 A.3d 1140 (R.I. 2014)] (See *Agency Relationships.*)

- **For a sample answer to Problem 32–7, go to Appendix E at the end of this text.**

32–8. Agency Relationships. Standard Oil of Connecticut, Inc., sells home heating, cooling, and security systems. Standard schedules installation and service appointments with its customers and then contracts with installers and technicians to do the work. The company requires an installer or technician to complete a project by a certain time but to otherwise "exercise independent judgment and control in the execution of any work." The installers and technicians are licensed and certified by the state. Standard does not train them, provide instruction manuals, supervise them at customers' homes, or inspect their work. The installers and technicians use their own equipment and tools, and they can choose which days they work. Standard pays a set rate per project. According to criteria used by the courts, are these installers and technicians independent contractors or employees? Why? [*Standard Oil of Connecticut, Inc. v. Administrator, Unemployment Compensation Act,* 320 Conn. 611, __ A.3d __ (2016)] (See *Agency Relationships.*)

32–9. A Question of Ethics—Agency Formation and Duties. *Western Fire Truck, Inc., contracted with Emergency One, Inc. (EO), to be its exclusive dealer in Colorado and Wyoming through December 2003. James Costello, a Western salesperson, was authorized to order EO vehicles for his customers. Without informing Western, Costello e-mailed EO about Western's difficulties in obtaining cash to fund its operations. He asked about the viability of Western's contract and his possible employment with EO. On EO's request, and in disregard of Western's instructions, Costello sent some payments for EO vehicles directly to EO. In addition, Costello, with EO's help, sent a competing bid to a potential Western customer. EO's representative e-mailed Costello, "You have my permission to kick [Western's] ass." In April 2002, EO terminated its contract with Western. At about the same time, a Western manager discovered Costello's e-mails saying that he was dissatisfied with the company and fired Costello. Western filed a suit in a Colorado state court, alleging that Costello had breached his duty as an agent and that EO had aided and abetted the breach.* [Western Fire Truck, Inc. v. Emergency One, Inc., *134 P.3d 570 (Colo.App. 2006)]* (See *Formation of the Agency Relationship.*)

(a) Was there an agency relationship between Western and Costello? Western required monthly reports from its sales staff, but Costello did not report regularly. Does this indicate that Costello was not Western's agent? In determining whether an agency relationship exists, is the right to control or the fact of control more important? Explain.

(b) Did Costello owe Western a duty? If so, what was the duty? Did Costello breach it? If so, how?

(c) A Colorado state statute allows a court to award punitive damages in "circumstances of fraud, malice, or willful and wanton conduct." Did any of these circumstances exist in this case? Should punitive damages be assessed against either defendant? Why or why not?

Legal Reasoning Group Activity

32–10. Agent's Duties to Principal. John Warren wanted to buy a condominium in California. Hildegard Merrill was the agent for the seller. Because Warren's credit rating was poor, Merrill told him he needed a co-borrower to obtain a mortgage at a reasonable rate. Merrill said that her daughter Charmaine would "go on title" until the loan and sale were complete if Warren would pay her $10,000. Merrill also offered to defer her commission on the sale as a loan to Warren so that he could make a 20 percent down payment on the property. He agreed to both plans.

Merrill secured the mortgage in Charmaine's name alone by misrepresenting her daughter's address, business, and income.

To close the sale, Merrill had Warren remove his name from the title to the property. In October, Warren moved into the condominium, repaid Merrill the amount of her deferred commission, and began paying the mortgage. Within a few months, Merrill had Warren evicted. Warren subsequently filed a suit against Merrill and Charmaine. (See *Duties of Agents and Principals.*)

(a) The first group will determine who among these parties was in an agency relationship.

(b) The second group will discuss the basic duty that an agent owes a principal and decide whether that duty was breached here.

CHAPTER 33

Agency Liability and Termination

We have already discussed how agency relationships are formed and the duties of the principal and agent in that relationship. This chapter deals with another important aspect of agency law—the liability of principals and agents to third parties.

We look first at the liability of principals for contracts formed by agents with third parties. Generally, the liability of the principal will depend on whether the agent was authorized to form the contract. The second part of the chapter deals with an agent's liability to third parties in contract and

tort. It also discusses the principal's liability to third parties because of an agent's torts. The chapter concludes with a discussion of how agency relationships are terminated.

33–1 Scope of Agent's Authority

The liability of a principal to third parties with whom an agent contracts depends on whether the agent had the authority to enter into legally binding contracts on the principal's behalf. An agent's authority can be either *actual* (express or implied) or *apparent.* If an agent contracts outside the scope of his or her authority, the principal may still become liable by ratifying the contract.

33–1a Express Authority

Express authority is authority declared in clear, direct, and definite terms. Express authority can be given orally or in writing.

The Equal Dignity Rule In most states, the **equal dignity rule** requires that if the contract being executed is or must be in writing, then the agent's authority must also be in writing. (Recall that a writing includes an electronic record.) Failure to comply with the equal dignity rule can make a contract voidable *at the option of the principal.* The law regards the contract at that point as a mere offer. If the principal decides to accept the offer, the acceptance must be ratified, or affirmed, in writing.

■ **EXAMPLE 33.1** Paloma (the principal) orally asks Austin (the agent) to sell a ranch that Paloma owns. Austin finds a buyer and signs a sales contract on behalf of Paloma to sell the ranch. Because a contract for an interest in realty must be in writing, the equal dignity rule

applies. The buyer cannot enforce the contract unless Paloma subsequently ratifies Austin's agency status *in a writing.* Once the sales contract is ratified, either party can enforce rights under the contract. ■

Modern business practice allows several exceptions to the equal dignity rule:

1. An executive officer of a corporation normally can conduct *ordinary* business transactions without obtaining written authority from the corporation.
2. When the agent acts in the presence of the principal, the rule does not apply.
3. When the agent's act of signing is merely a formality, then the agent does not need written authority to sign. ■ **EXAMPLE 33.2** Sandra Healy (the principal) negotiates a contract but is called out of town the day it is to be signed. If Healy orally authorizes Derek Santini to sign, the oral authorization is sufficient. ■

Power of Attorney Giving an agent a **power of attorney** confers express authority.[1] The power of attorney is a written document and is usually notarized. (A document is notarized when a **notary public**—a person authorized to attest to the authenticity of signatures—signs, dates, and imprints the document with her or his seal of authority.) Most states have statutory provisions for creating a power of attorney.

---

1. An agent who holds a power of attorney is called an *attorney-in-fact* for the principal. The holder does not have to be an attorney-at-law (and often is not).

A power of attorney can be *special* (permitting the agent to perform specified acts only), or it can be *general* (permitting the agent to transact all business for the principal). Because a general power of attorney (see Exhibit 33–1) grants extensive authority to the agent, it should be used with great caution and usually only in exceptional circumstances. Ordinarily, a power of attorney terminates on the incapacity or death of the person giving the power.[2]

2. A *durable* power of attorney, however, continues to be effective despite the principal's incapacity or death. An elderly person, for instance, might grant a durable power of attorney to provide for the handling of property and investments or specific health-care needs should he or she become incompetent.

EXHIBIT 33–1 A Sample General Power of Attorney

GENERAL POWER OF ATTORNEY

Know All Men by These Presents:

That I, _____ , hereinafter referred to as PRINCIPAL, in the County of _____ State of _____ , do(es) appoint _____ as my true and lawful attorney.

In principal's name, and for principal's use and benefit, said attorney is authorized hereby;

(1) To demand, sue for, collect, and receive all money, debts, accounts, legacies, bequests, interest, dividends, annuities, and demands as are now or shall hereafter become due, payable, or belonging to principal, and take all lawful means, for the recovery thereof and to compromise the same and give discharges for the same;

(2) To buy and sell land, make contracts of every kind relative to land, any interest therein or the possession thereof, and to take possession and exercise control over the use thereof;

(3) To buy, sell, mortgage, hypothecate, assign, transfer, and in any manner deal with goods, wares and merchandise, choses in action, certificates or shares of capital stock, and other property in possession or in action, and to make, do, and transact all and every kind of business of whatever nature;

(4) To execute, acknowledge, and deliver contracts of sale, escrow instructions, deeds, leases including leases for minerals and hydrocarbon substances and assignments of leases, covenants, agreements and assignments of agreements, mortgages and assignments of mortgages, conveyances in trust, to secure indebtedness or other obligations, and assign the beneficial interest thereunder, subordinations of liens or encumbrances, bills of lading, receipts, evidences of debt, releases, bonds, notes, bills, requests to reconvey deeds of trust, partial or full judgments, satisfactions of mortgages, and other debts, and other written instruments of whatever kind and nature, all upon such terms and conditions as said attorney shall approve.

GIVING AND GRANTING to said attorney full power and authority to do all and every act and thing whatsoever requisite and necessary to be done relative to any of the foregoing as fully to all intents and purposes as principal might or could do if personally present.

All that said attorney shall lawfully do or cause to be done under the authority of this power of attorney is expressly approved.

Dated: _____ /s/_____

State of_____ } SS.
    County of_____
On _____ , before me, the undersigned, a Notary Public in and for said State, personally appeared_____

known to me to be the person _____ whose name _____ subscribed to the within instrument and acknowledged that_____ executed the same. Witness my hand and official seal. (Seal) _____
Notary Public in and for said State.

33–1b Implied Authority

An agent has the **implied authority** to do what is reasonably necessary to carry out express authority and accomplish the objectives of the agency. Authority can also be implied by custom or inferred from the position the agent occupies.

■ **EXAMPLE 33.3** Archer is employed by Packard Grocery to manage one of its stores. Packard has not expressly stated that Archer has authority to contract with third persons. Nevertheless, authority to manage a business implies authority to do what is reasonably required (as is customary or can be inferred from a manager's position) to operate the business. This includes forming contracts to hire employees, buying merchandise and equipment, and advertising the products sold in the store. ■

Note, however, that an agent's implied authority cannot contradict his or her express authority. Thus, if a principal has limited an agent's express authority, then the fact that the agent customarily would have such authority is irrelevant. ■ **EXAMPLE 33.4** Juanita Alvarez is the owner of six Baja Tacos restaurants. Alvarez (the principal) strictly forbids the managers (agents) of her taco shops from entering into contracts to hire additional workers. Therefore, the fact that managers customarily would have authority to hire employees is immaterial. ■

33–1c Apparent Authority

Actual authority (express or implied) arises from what the principal makes clear *to the agent.* Apparent authority, in contrast, arises from what the principal causes a third party to believe. An agent has **apparent authority** when the principal, by either word or action, causes a *third party* reasonably to believe that the agent has authority to act, even though the agent has no express or implied authority.

A Pattern of Conduct Apparent authority usually comes into existence through a principal's pattern of conduct over time. ■ **EXAMPLE 33.5** Bailey is a traveling salesperson. She solicits orders for goods but does not carry them with her. She normally would not have the implied authority to collect payments from customers on behalf of the principal. Suppose that she does accept payments from Corgley Enterprises, however, and submits them to the principal's accounting department for processing. If the principal does nothing to stop Bailey from continuing this practice, a pattern develops over time, and the principal confers apparent authority on Bailey to accept payments from Corgley. ■

At issue in the following *Spotlight Case* was whether the manager of a horse breeding operation had the authority to bind the farm's owner in a contract guaranteeing breeding rights.

Spotlight on Apparent Authority of Managers

Case 33.1 Lundberg v. Church Farm, Inc.
Court of Appeals of Illinois, 502 N.E.2d 806, 151 Ill.App.3d (1986).

Background and Facts Gilbert Church owned a horse breeding farm managed by Herb Bagley. Advertisements for the breeding rights to one of Church Farm's stallions, Imperial Guard, directed all inquiries to "Herb Bagley, Manager." Vern and Gail Lundberg bred Thoroughbred horses. The Lundbergs contacted Bagley and executed a preprinted contract giving them breeding rights to Imperial Guard "at Imperial Guard's location," subject to approval of the mares by Church. Bagley handwrote a statement on the contract that guaranteed the Lundbergs "six live foals in the first two years." He then signed it "Gilbert G. Church by H. Bagley."

The Lundbergs bred four mares, which resulted in one live foal. Church then moved Imperial Guard from Illinois to Oklahoma. The Lundbergs sued Church for breaching the contract by moving the horse. Church claimed that Bagley was not authorized to sign contracts for Church or to change or add terms, but only to present preprinted contracts to potential buyers. Church testified that although Bagley was his farm manager and the contact person for breeding rights, Bagley had never before modified the preprinted forms or signed Church's name on them. The jury found in favor of the Lundbergs and awarded $147,000 in damages. Church appealed.

In the Language of the Court
Justice *UNVERZAGT* delivered the opinion of the court.
    * * * *

    * * * *Defendant contends that plaintiffs have failed to establish that Bagley had apparent authority to negotiate and sign the Lundberg contract for Church Farm* * * *.

Case 33.1 Continued

*The party asserting an agency has the burden of proving its existence * * * but may do so by inference and circumstantial evidence. * * * Additionally, an agent may bind his principal by acts which the principal has not given him actual authority to perform, but which he appears authorized to perform. * * ** An agent's apparent authority is that authority which "the principal knowingly permits the agent to assume or which he holds his agent out as possessing. It is the authority that a reasonably prudent man, exercising diligence and discretion, in view of the principal's conduct, would naturally suppose the agent to possess." [Emphasis added.]

Plaintiffs produced evidence at trial that Gil Church approved the Imperial Guard advertisement listing Herb Bagley as Church Farm's manager, and directing all inquiries to him. Church also permitted Bagley to live on the farm and to handle its daily operations. Bagley was the only person available to visitors to the farm. Bagley answered Church Farm's phone calls, and there was a preprinted signature line for him on the breeding rights package.

The conclusion is inescapable that Gil Church affirmatively placed Bagley in a managerial position giving him complete control of Church Farm and its dealings with the public. We believe that this is just the sort of "holding out" of an agent by a principal that justifies a third person's reliance on the agent's authority.

We cannot accept defendant's contention that the Lundbergs were affirmatively obligated to seek out Church to ascertain the actual extent of Bagley's authority. Where an agent has apparent authority to act, the principal will be liable in spite of any undisclosed limitations the principal has placed on that authority.

Decision and Remedy *The state appellate court affirmed the lower court's judgment in favor of the Lundbergs for $147,000. Because Church allowed circumstances to lead the Lundbergs to believe Bagley had the authority to negotiate and sign the contract, Church was bound by Bagley's actions.*

Critical Thinking
- **Legal Environment** *The court held that Church had allowed the Lundbergs to believe that Bagley was his agent. What steps could Church have taken to protect himself against a finding of apparent authority?*
- **Ethical** *Does a principal have an ethical responsibility to inform an unaware third party that an apparent agent does not in fact have the authority to act on the principal's behalf? Explain.*

Apparent Authority and Estoppel A court can apply the doctrine of agency by estoppel when a principal has given a third party reason to believe that an agent has authority to act. If the third party honestly relies on the principal's representations to his or her detriment, the principal may be *estopped* (prevented) from denying that the agent had authority.

33–1d Emergency Powers

When an unforeseen emergency demands action by the agent to protect or preserve the property and rights of the principal, but the agent is unable to communicate with the principal, the agent has emergency power. ■ **EXAMPLE 33.6** Rob Fulsom is an engineer for Pacific Drilling Company. While Fulsom is acting within the scope of his employment, he is severely injured in an accident on an oil rig many miles from home. Acosta, the rig supervisor, directs Thompson, a physician, to give medical aid to Fulsom and to charge Pacific for the medical services.

Acosta, an agent, has no express or implied authority to bind the principal, Pacific Drilling, for Thompson's medical services. Because of the emergency situation, however, the law recognizes Acosta as having authority to act appropriately under the circumstances. ■

33–1e Ratification

Ratification occurs when the principal affirms, or accepts responsibility for, an agent's *unauthorized* act. When ratification occurs, the principal is bound to the agent's act, and the act is treated as if it had been authorized by the principal *from the outset*. Ratification can be either express or implied.

If the principal does not ratify the contract, the principal is not bound, and the third party's agreement with the agent is viewed as merely an unaccepted offer. Because the third party's agreement is an unaccepted offer, the third party can revoke it at any time, without liability, before the principal ratifies the contract. The agent, however, may be liable to the third party for misrepresenting her or his authority.

The requirements for ratification can be summarized as follows:

1. The agent must have acted on behalf of an identified principal who subsequently ratifies the action.
2. The principal must know all of the material facts involved in the transaction. If a principal ratifies a contract without knowing all of the facts, the principal can rescind (cancel) the contract.[3]
3. The principal must affirm the agent's act in its entirety.
4. The principal must have the legal capacity to authorize the transaction at the time the agent engages in the act and at the time the principal ratifies. The third party must also have the legal capacity to engage in the transaction.
5. The principal's affirmation (ratification) must occur before the third party withdraws from the transaction.

6. The principal must observe the same formalities when ratifying the act as would have been required to authorize it initially.

Concept Summary 33.1 summarizes the rules concerning an agent's authority to bind the principal and a third party.

33–2 Liability for Contracts

Liability for contracts formed by an agent depends on how the principal is classified and on whether the actions of the agent were authorized or unauthorized. Principals are classified as disclosed, partially disclosed, or undisclosed.[4]

1. A **disclosed principal** is a principal whose identity is known by the third party at the time the contract is made by the agent.

---

3. Note that if the third party has changed position in reliance on the apparent contract, the principal can still rescind the contract but must reimburse the third party for any costs.

4. *Restatement (Third) of Agency*, Section 1.04(2).

Concept Summary 33.1

Authority of an Agent to Bind the Principal and a Third Party

Express Authority	**Definition:** Authority expressly given by the principal to the agent.	**Effect:** Principal and third party are bound in contract.
Implied Authority	**Definition:** Authority implied (1) by custom, (2) from the position in which the principal has placed the agent, or (3) because such authority is necessary if the agent is to carry out expressly authorized duties and responsibilities.	**Effect:** Principal and third party are bound in contract.
Apparent Authority	**Definition:** Authority created when the conduct of the principal leads a third party to believe that the principal's agent has authority.	**Effect:** Principal and third party are bound in contract.
Unauthorized Acts	**Definition:** Acts committed by an agent that are outside the scope of his or her express, implied, or apparent authority.	**Effect:** Principal and third party are not bound in contract—*unless* the principal ratifies prior to the third party's withdrawal.

2. A **partially disclosed principal** is a principal whose identity is not known by the third party. Nevertheless, the third party knows that the agent is or *may* be acting for a principal at the time the contract is made. ■ **EXAMPLE 33.7** Eileen has contracted with a real estate agent to sell certain property. She wishes to keep her identity a secret, but the agent makes it clear to potential buyers of the property that he is acting in an agency capacity. In this situation, Eileen is a partially disclosed principal. ■

3. An **undisclosed principal** is a principal whose identity is totally unknown by the third party. In addition, the third party has no knowledge that the agent is acting in an agency capacity at the time the contract is made.

33–2a Authorized Acts

If an agent acts within the scope of her or his authority, normally the principal is obligated to perform the contract regardless of whether the principal was disclosed, partially disclosed, or undisclosed. Whether the *agent may also be held liable* under the contract, however, depends on the disclosed, partially disclosed, or undisclosed status of the principal.

Disclosed or Partially Disclosed Principal A disclosed or partially disclosed principal is liable to a third party for a contract made by the agent. If the principal is disclosed, the agent has no contractual liability for the nonperformance of the principal or the third party. If the principal is partially disclosed, in most states the agent is also treated as a party to the contract. Thus, the third party can hold the agent liable for contractual nonperformance.[5]

■ **CASE IN POINT 33.8** Stonhard, Inc., makes epoxy and urethane flooring and installs it in industrial and commercial buildings. Marvin Sussman contracted with Stonhard to install flooring at a Blue Ridge Farms food-manufacturing facility in Brooklyn, New York. Sussman did not disclose that he was acting as an agent for the facility's owner, Blue Ridge Foods, LLC, at the time of the contract.

When Stonhard was not paid for the flooring it installed, it filed a suit against the facility, its owner, and Sussman to recover damages for breach of contract. The lower court dismissed the complaint against Sussman personally, but on appeal a reviewing court reversed that decision. The contract had been signed by Sussman "of Blue Ridge Farms." That evidence indicated that

Sussman was acting as an agent for a partially disclosed principal, in that the agency relationship was known, but not the principal's identity. "As an agent for an undisclosed [or partially disclosed] principal, Sussman became personally liable under the contract."[6] ■

Undisclosed Principal When neither the fact of an agency relationship nor the identity of the principal is disclosed, the undisclosed principal is bound to perform just as if the principal had been fully disclosed at the time the contract was made.

■ **CASE IN POINT 33.9** Bobby Williams bought a car at Sherman Henderson's auto repair business in Louisiana for $3,000. Henderson (the agent) negotiated and made the sale for the car's owner, Joe Pike (the principal), whose name was not disclosed. Williams drove the car to Memphis, Tennessee, where his daughter was a student. Three days after the sale, the car's engine caught fire. Williams extinguished the blaze and contacted Henderson. The next day, the vehicle was stolen from a parking lot outside Williams's daughter's apartment.

Williams filed a suit in a Louisiana state court against Pike (the principal) and Henderson (the agent). The court awarded Williams $2,000, plus the costs of the suit, adding that if Williams had returned the car, it would have awarded him the entire price. A state appellate court affirmed. Both Pike and Henderson—the undisclosed principal and his agent—were liable to Williams.[7] ■

Indemnification. When a principal's identity is undisclosed and the agent is forced to pay the third party, the agent is entitled to be *indemnified* (compensated) by the principal. The principal had a duty to perform, even though his or her identity was undisclosed,[8] and failure to do so will make the principal ultimately liable.

Performance. Once the undisclosed principal's identity is revealed, the third party generally can elect to hold either the principal or the agent liable on the contract. Conversely, the undisclosed principal can require the third party to fulfill the contract, *unless* one of the following is true:

1. The undisclosed principal was expressly excluded as a party in the written contract.

---

5. *Restatement (Third) of Agency,* Section 6.02.

6. *Stonhard, Inc. v. Blue Ridge Farms, LLC,* 114 A.D.3d 757, 980 N.Y.S.2d 507 (2 Dept. 2014).
7. *Williams v. Pike,* 58 So.3d 525 (La.App. 2 Cir. 2011).
8. If the agent is a gratuitous agent, and the principal accepts the benefits of the agent's contract with a third party, then the principal will be liable to the agent on the theory of quasi contract.

2. The contract is a negotiable instrument signed by the agent with no indication of signing in a representative capacity.[9]

3. The performance of the agent is personal to the contract, thus allowing the third party to refuse the principal's performance.

33-2b Unauthorized Acts

If an agent has no authority but nevertheless contracts with a third party, the *principal* cannot be held liable on the contract. It does not matter whether the principal was disclosed, partially disclosed, or undisclosed. The *agent* is liable.

■ **EXAMPLE 33.10** Chu signs a contract for the purchase of a truck, purportedly acting as an agent under authority granted by Navarro. In fact, Navarro has not given Chu any such authority. Navarro refuses to pay for the truck, claiming that Chu had no authority to purchase it. The seller of the truck is entitled to hold Chu liable for payment. ■

Implied Warranty If the principal is disclosed or partially disclosed, and the agent contracts with a third party without authorization, the agent is liable to the third party. The agent's liability here is based on his or her breach of the *implied warranty of authority*, not on the breach of the contract itself.[10] An agent impliedly warrants that he or she has the authority to enter a contract on behalf of the principal.

■ **EXAMPLE 33.11** Pinnell, a reclusive artist, hires Auber to solicit offers for particular paintings from various galleries, but does not authorize her to enter into sales agreements. Olaf, a gallery owner, offers to buy two of Pinnell's paintings for an upcoming show. If Auber draws up a sales contract with Olaf, she impliedly warrants that she has the authority to enter into sales contracts on behalf of Pinnell. If Pinnell does not agree to ratify Auber's sales contract, Olaf cannot hold Pinnell liable, but he can hold Auber liable for breaching the implied warranty of authority. ■

Third Party's Knowledge Note that if the third party knows at the time the contract is made that the agent does not have authority, then the agent is not liable. Similarly, if the agent expresses to the third party *uncertainty* as to the extent of her or his authority, the agent is not personally liable.

33-2c Actions by E-Agents

Although in the past standard agency principles applied only to *human* agents, today these same agency principles also apply to e-agents. An electronic agent, or **e-agent,** is a semiautonomous software program that is capable of executing specific tasks, such as searching through many databases and retrieving relevant information for the user.

The Uniform Electronic Transactions Act (UETA), which was discussed previously, sets forth provisions relating to the principal's liability for the actions of e-agents. According to Section 15 of the UETA, e-agents can enter into binding agreements on behalf of their principals—at least, in those states that have adopted the act. Thus, if consumers place an order over the Internet, and the company (principal) takes the order via an e-agent, the company cannot later claim that it did not receive the order.

The UETA also stipulates that if an e-agent does not provide an opportunity to prevent errors at the time of the transaction, the other party to the transaction can avoid the transaction. Therefore, if an e-agent fails to provide an on-screen confirmation of a purchase or sale, the other party can avoid the effect of any errors. ■ **EXAMPLE 33.12** Bigelow wants to purchase three copies of three different books (a total of nine items). The e-agent mistakenly records an order for thirty-three of a single book and does not provide an on-screen verification of the order. If thirty-three books are then sent to Bigelow, he can avoid the contract to purchase them. ■

33-3 Liability for Torts and Crimes

Obviously, any person, including an agent, is liable for his or her own torts and crimes. Whether a principal can also be held liable for an agent's torts and crimes depends on several factors, which we examine here. In some situations, a principal may be held liable not only for the torts of an agent but also for torts committed by an independent contractor.

33-3a Principal's Tortious Conduct

A principal who acts through an agent may be liable for harm resulting from the principal's own negligence or recklessness. Thus, a principal may be liable if he or she gives improper instructions, authorizes the use of improper materials or tools, or establishes improper rules that result in the agent's committing a tort.

---

9. Under the Uniform Commercial Code (UCC), only the agent is liable if the instrument neither names the principal nor shows that the agent signed in a representative capacity [UCC 3–402(b)(2)].

10. The agent is not liable on the contract because the agent was never intended personally to be a party to the contract.

■ **EXAMPLE 33.13** Parker knows that Audrey's driver's license has been suspended but nevertheless tells her to use the company truck to deliver some equipment to a customer. If someone is injured as a result, Parker will be liable for his own negligence in instructing Audrey to drive without a valid license. ■

33–3b Principal's Authorization of Agent's Tortious Conduct

Similarly, a principal who authorizes an agent to commit a tort may be liable to persons or property injured thereby, because the act is considered to be the principal's. ■ **EXAMPLE 33.14** Pedro directs his agent, Andy, to cut the corn on specific acreage, which neither of them has the right to do. The harvest is therefore a trespass (a tort), and Pedro is liable to the owner of the corn. ■

Note that an agent acting at the principal's direction can be liable, along with the principal, for committing the tortious act even if the agent was unaware that the act was wrong. Assume in *Example 33.14* that Andy, the agent, did not know that Pedro lacked the right to harvest the corn. Andy can nonetheless be held liable to the owner of the field for damages, along with Pedro, the principal.

33–3c Liability for Agent's Misrepresentation

A principal is exposed to tort liability whenever a third person sustains a loss due to the agent's misrepresentation. The principal's liability depends on whether the agent was actually or apparently authorized to make representations and whether the representations were made within the scope of the agency. The principal is always directly responsible for an agent's misrepresentation made within the scope of the agent's authority. ■ **EXAMPLE 33.15** Ainsley is a demonstrator for Pavlovich's products. Pavlovich sends Ainsley to a home show to demonstrate the products and to answer questions from consumers. Pavlovich has given Ainsley authority to make statements about the products. If Ainsley makes only true representations, all is fine. But if he makes false claims, Pavlovich will be liable for any injuries or damages sustained by third parties in reliance on Ainsley's false representations. ■

Apparent Implied Authority When a principal has placed an agent in a position of apparent authority—making it possible for the agent to defraud a third party—the principal may also be liable for the agent's fraudulent acts. For instance, partners in a partnership generally have the apparent implied authority to act as agents of the firm. Thus, if one of the partners commits a tort or a crime, the partnership itself—and often the other partners personally—can be held liable for the loss.

■ **EXAMPLE 33.16** Saulheim & Company is a securities brokerage firm that operates as a partnership and provides various financial services. The firm's managing partner, Dan Saulheim, is caught embezzling funds that clients have turned over to the firm for investment. After he is convicted, other partners in the firm claim that they are not liable for losses resulting from his illegal activities. In this situation, other partners may be liable if a court finds that Saulheim had apparent implied authority to act in the ordinary course of the partnership's business. Thus, the firm, as principal, is liable, and the personal assets of the individual partners, as agents, can be used to pay the firm's liability. ■

Innocent Misrepresentation Tort liability based on fraud requires proof that a material misstatement was made knowingly and with the intent to deceive. An agent's *innocent* misstatements in a contract or warranty transaction can also provide grounds for the third party's rescission of the contract and the award of damages. Justice dictates that when a principal knows that an agent is not accurately advised of facts but does not correct either the agent's or the third party's impressions, the principal is responsible. The point is that the principal is always directly responsible for an agent's misrepresentation made within the scope of authority.

33–3d Liability for Agent's Negligence

An agent is liable for his or her own torts. A principal may also be liable for harm an agent causes to a third party under the doctrine of **respondeat superior**,[11] a Latin term meaning "let the master respond." Under the doctrine of *respondeat superior*, the principal-employer is liable for any harm caused to a third party by an agent-employee in the course or scope of employment. The doctrine imposes **vicarious liability,** or indirect liability, because the principal-employer is being held liable for torts committed by an agent-employee.

When an agent commits a negligent act in such a situation, *both* the agent and the principal are liable. ■ **EXAMPLE 33.17** Aegis hires SDI to provide landscaping services for its property. An herbicide sprayed by

---

11. Pronounced ree-*spahn*-dee-uht soo-*peer*-ee-your. The doctrine of *respondeat superior* applies not only to employer-employee relationships but also to other principal-agent relationships in which the principal has the right of control over the agent.

SDI employee David Hoggatt enters the Aegis building through the air-conditioning system and caused Catherine Warner, an Aegis employee, to suffer a heart attack. If Warner sues, both SDI (principal) and Hoggatt (agent) can be held liable for negligence. ■

The Doctrine of *Respondeat Superior* The doctrine of *respondeat superior* is similar to the theory of strict liability in that liability is imposed regardless of fault. At early common law, a servant (employee) was viewed as the master's (employer's) property. The master was deemed to have absolute control over the servant's acts and was held strictly liable for them, no matter how carefully the master supervised the servant. Although employers today are not masters of their employees, control is still a central concept to liability. This chapter's *Global Insight* feature discusses whether nations that follow Islamic law recognize the doctrine of *respondeat superior.*

Underlying Rationale. The rationale for the doctrine of *respondeat superior* is based on the social duty that requires every person to manage his or her affairs so as not to injure another. This duty applies even when a person acts through an agent (controls the conduct of another).

Public Policy. Generally, public policy requires that an injured person be afforded effective relief, and a business enterprise is usually better able to provide that relief than is an individual employee. Employers normally carry liability insurance to cover any damages awarded as a result of such lawsuits. They are also able to spread the cost of risk over the entire business enterprise.

Application Today. The courts have applied the doctrine of *respondeat superior* for nearly two centuries. It continues to have practical implications in all situations involving principal-agent (employer-employee) relationships. Today, the small-town store with one clerk and the multinational corporation with thousands of employees are equally subject to the doctrine.

Determining the Scope of Employment The key to determining whether a principal may be liable for the torts of an agent under the doctrine of *respondeat superior* is whether the torts are committed within the scope of the agency. Courts may consider the following factors in determining whether a particular act occurred within the course and scope of employment:

1. Whether the employee's act was authorized by the employer.
2. The time, place, and purpose of the act.
3. Whether the act was one commonly performed by employees on behalf of their employers.
4. The extent to which the employer's interest was advanced by the act.
5. The extent to which the private interests of the employee were involved.

GLOBAL INSIGHT — Islamic Law and *Respondeat Superior*

The doctrine of *respondeat superior* is well established in the legal systems of the United States and most Western countries. As you have already read, under this doctrine, employers can be held liable for the acts of their employees. The doctrine of *respondeat superior* is not universal, however. Most Middle Eastern countries, for example, do not follow this doctrine.

Codification of Islamic Law

Islamic law, as codified in the *sharia*, holds to a strict belief that responsibility for human actions lies with the individual and cannot be vicariously (indirectly) extended to others. This belief and other concepts of Islamic law are based on the writings of Muhammad, the seventh-century prophet whose revelations form the basis of the Islamic religion and, by extension, the

sharia. Muhammad's prophecies are documented in the Koran (Qur'an), which is the principal source of the *sharia.*

An Exception

Islamic law does allow for an employer to be responsible for an employee's actions when the actions result from a direct order given by the employer to the employee. This principle also applies to contractual obligations. Note that the master is responsible *only* if direct orders were given. Otherwise stated, unless an employee is obeying a direct order of the employer, liability for the employee's actions does not extend to the employer.

Critical Thinking *How would U.S. society be affected if employers could not be held vicariously liable for their employees' torts?*

6. Whether the employer furnished the means or instrumentality (such as a truck or a machine) by which an injury was inflicted.

7. Whether the employer had reason to know that the employee would perform the act in question and whether the employee had done it before.

8. Whether the act involved the commission of a serious crime.

In the following case, the court had to determine whether or not a dump truck operator was the employee of a concrete services contractor.

Case **33.2**

Asphalt & Concrete Services, Inc. v. Perry

Court of Special Appeals of Maryland, 221 Md.App. 235, 108 A.3d 558 (2015).

Background and Facts Asphalt & Concrete Services, Inc. (ACS), was working on a play pad at St. John Regional Catholic School in Frederick, Maryland. ACS project manager Blake Wood contacted William Johnson at Higher Power Trucking, LLC, to arrange for a dump truck to haul material from a quarry to the job site. One day, while Johnson was driving the dump truck between the job site and the quarry, the truck struck and injured Moran Perry, who was crossing an intersection.

To recover for his injuries, Perry filed a lawsuit in a Maryland state court against ACS. Perry alleged that Johnson's negligence in operating the dump truck was the proximate cause of his injuries and that Johnson was ACS's employee. ACS, however, claimed that Johnson was an independent contractor. A jury agreed with Perry and awarded him $529,500 in damages. The court issued a judgment in Perry's favor, and ACS appealed.

In the Language of the Court
GRAEFF, J. [Judge]
* * * *

* * * Pursuant to the doctrine of *respondeat superior,* an employer may be found liable for torts committed by its employee while acting in the scope of employment. ACS does not dispute this well-established rule, but it argues that the evidence showed that Mr. Johnson was not its employee.

* * * Maryland courts have traditionally considered five criteria in determining whether or not an employer/employee relationship exists between two parties. *These criteria, developed from the common law standard for determining the master/servant relationship, include (1) the power to select and hire the employee, (2) the payment of wages, (3) the power to discharge, (4) the power to control the employee's conduct, and (5) whether the work is part of the regular business of the employer.* [Emphasis added.]

Of the five factors, the factor of control stands out as the most important. * * * Whether the employer has the right to control and direct the employee in the performance of the work and in the manner in which the work is to be done is the decisive, or controlling, test.
* * * *

Here, * * * the evidence indicated as follows: (1) ACS called Mr. Johnson directly to reserve his trucking services; (2) Mr. Wood spoke only to Mr. Johnson when calling Higher Power; (3) ACS directed Mr. Johnson to go to the * * * quarry to pick up materials for the play pad project and gave him the time to be there for the pick-up; (4) Mr. Johnson was required to bring the materials directly to the job site after his truck was loaded, and if Mr. Johnson did not deliver the materials promptly, ACS had the right to dock his pay or to no longer employ him; (5) ACS paid Mr. Johnson on an hourly basis from the time he picked up his first load until ACS dismissed him from the job site; (6) after Mr. Johnson delivered his first load of materials, ACS directed him to return to the quarry to pick up and bring back additional materials; and (7) at the job site, Mr. Johnson was obligated to follow ACS's directions in terms of where to drop the materials, how much material to drop, and how many times he would need to return to the quarry. Based on that evidence, a jury could find that Mr. Johnson was subject to ACS's control, and ACS was liable for Mr. Johnson's negligence pursuant to the doctrine of *respondeat superior.*

Case 33.2 Continues

Case 33.2 Continued

Decision and Remedy *The state intermediate appellate court affirmed the jury's finding with respect to Johnson's status as ACS's employee. The court disagreed, however, with the lower court's admission of certain evidence that may have influenced the jury's finding of proximate cause for Perry's injuries. As a result, the court reversed the judgment on this ground and remanded the case for a new trial.*

Critical Thinking

• **Economic** *Why did ACS contend that Johnson was not its employee? Discuss.*

The Distinction between a "Detour" and a "Frolic"

A useful insight into the concept of "scope of employment" can be gained from Judge Baron Parke's classic distinction between a "detour" and a "frolic" in the case of *Joel v. Morison* (1834).[12] In this case, the English court held that if a servant merely took a detour from his master's business, the master will be responsible. If, however, the servant was on a "frolic of his own" and not in any way "on his master's business," the master will not be liable.

■ **EXAMPLE 33.18** While driving his employer's vehicle to call on a customer, Mandel decides to stop at a store—which is three blocks off his route—to take care of a personal matter. As Mandel approaches the store, he negligently runs into a parked vehicle owned by Chan. In this situation, because Mandel's detour from the employer's business is not substantial, he is still acting within the scope of employment, and the employer is liable.

But suppose instead that Mandel decides to pick up a few friends in another city for cocktails and in the process negligently runs his vehicle into Chan's. In this situation, the departure from the employer's business is substantial—Mandel is on a "frolic" of his own. Thus, the employer normally will not be liable to Chan for damages. ■

Employee Travel Time

An employee going to and from work or to and from meals usually is considered to be outside the scope of employment. If travel is part of a person's position, however, as it is for a traveling salesperson, then travel time is normally considered within the scope of employment. For such an employee, the entire business trip, including the return trip home, is within the scope of employment unless there is a significant departure from the employer's business.

Notice of Dangerous Conditions

The employer is charged with knowledge of any dangerous conditions discovered by an employee and pertinent to the employment situation.

■ **EXAMPLE 33.19** Brad, a maintenance employee in Martin's apartment building, notices a lead pipe protruding from the ground in the building's courtyard. Brad neglects either to fix the pipe or to inform Martin of the danger. John trips on the pipe and is injured. Martin is charged with knowledge of the dangerous condition regardless of whether Brad actually informed him. That knowledge is imputed to the employer by virtue of the employment relationship. ■

33–3e Liability for Agent's Intentional Torts

Most intentional torts that individuals commit have no relation to their employment, and their employers will not be held liable. Nevertheless, under the doctrine of *respondeat superior,* the employer can be liable for intentional torts that an employee commits within the course and scope of employment. For instance, a department store owner is liable when a security guard who is a store employee commits the tort of false imprisonment while acting within the scope of employment. Similarly, a nightclub owner is liable when a "bouncer" commits the tort of assault and battery while on the job.

In addition, an employer who knows or should know that an employee has a propensity for committing tortious acts is liable for the employee's acts even if they would not ordinarily be considered within the scope of employment. ■ **EXAMPLE 33.20** Chaz, the owner of the Comedy Club, hires Alec as a bouncer for the club even though he knows that Alec has a history of arrests for criminal assault and battery. In this situation, Chaz may be liable if Alec viciously attacks a customer in the parking lot after hours. ■

An employer is also liable for permitting an employee to engage in reckless actions that can injure others. ■ **EXAMPLE 33.21** The owner of Bates Trucking observes an employee smoking while filling containerized trucks with highly flammable liquids. Failure to stop the employee will cause the employer to be liable for

---

12. 6 Car. & P. 501, 172 Eng.Rep. 1338 (1834).

any injuries that result if a truck explodes. ■ Needless to say, most employers purchase liability insurance to cover their potential liability for employee conduct in many situations.

Whether an agent's allegedly tortious conduct fell within the scope of the agent's employment, making the principal vicariously liable, was at the heart of the dispute in the following case.

Case Analysis 33.3

M.J. v. Wisan

Utah Supreme Court, 2016 UT 13, __ P.3d __ (2016).

In the Language of the Court

Associate Chief Justice *LEE* * * * :

* * * *

[The United Effort Plan Trust ("UEP Trust" or the "Trust") was formed in Utah by members of the Fundamentalist Church of Jesus Christ of Latter-Day Saints ("FLDS Church"). The Trust] members deeded their property to the UEP Trust to be managed by Church leaders. Church leaders, who were also trustees, then used this property to minister to the needs of the members.

* * * *

[At the time of the events leading up to this case,] the Trust was operated for the express purpose of furthering the doctrines of the FLDS Church, including the practice of * * * marriage involving underage girls.

* * * *

[Later, as a result of unrelated litigation, a state court reformed the Trust] by excising the purpose of advancing the religious doctrines and goals of the FLDS Church to the degree that any of these were illegal, including * * * sexual activity between adults and minors. [The court appointed Bruce Wisan to head the Trust.]

* * * *

[Later] M.J., a former member of the FLDS Church and beneficiary of the UEP Trust, [filed this suit in a Utah state court against Wisan, as head of the Trust, alleging that] when she was fourteen years old, she was forced to marry Allen Steed, her first cousin. The wedding was performed by Warren Jeffs, who at the time was acting president of both the FLDS Church and * * * the Trust. * * * M.J. claims that Steed repeatedly sexually assaulted and raped her

* * * . She requested a divorce from Steed on multiple occasions, but Jeffs refused to allow it. He also refused to let M.J. live * * * separately from her husband.

* * * She seeks to hold * * * the Trust vicariously liable for intentional infliction of emotional distress.

* * * M.J. * * * claims that Jeffs and other trustees were acting "in furtherance of the trust administration and within the scope of their authority," and thus contends that the Trust should be liable under the doctrine of *respondeat superior.*

* * * *

The Trust filed a series of motions for summary judgment. All of those motions were denied. The Trust then filed [this] petition for review.

* * * *

* * * Under [Utah Code Section 75–7–1010, Utah's version of Section 1010 of the Uniform Trust Code,] a trust is liable for the trustee's acts performed "in the course of administering the trust."

* * * The terms of the statute, in context, are quite clear. "In the course of" *is the traditional formulation of the standard for vicarious liability under the doctrine of* respondeat superior. *We accordingly interpret the Uniform Trust Act as incorporating the established standard of* respondeat superior *liability.* Thus, under [Section 75–7–1010] a trust is liable for the acts of a trustee when the trustee was acting within the scope of his responsibility as a trustee. [Emphasis added.]

* * * *

The difficult question for the law in this field has been to define the line between a course of conduct subject to the employer's control and an

independent course of conduct not connected to the principal. *An independent course of conduct is a matter so removed from the agent's duties that the law, in fairness, eliminates the principal's vicarious liability.* Such a course of conduct is one that represents a departure from, not an escalation of, conduct involved in performing assigned work or other conduct that an employer permits or controls. [Emphasis added.]

Our cases have identified three factors of relevance to this inquiry: (1) whether the agent's conduct is of the general kind the agent is employed to perform; (2) whether the agent is acting within the hours of the agent's work and the ordinary spatial boundaries of the employment; and (3) whether the agent's acts were motivated, at least in part, by the purpose of serving the principal's interest.

* * * In the case law of a number of states, spatial and time boundaries are no longer essential hallmarks of an agency relationship. Instead, the law now recognizes that agents may interact on an employer's behalf with third parties although the employee is neither situated on the employer's premises nor continuously or exclusively engaged in performing assigned work.

A number of courts have also questioned the viability of the requirement that an agent's acts be motivated in some part by an intention to serve the principal's purposes.

* * * In [some] jurisdictions, * * * courts avoid the use of motive or intention to determine whether an employee's tortious conduct falls within the scope of employment and adopt a different

Case 33.3 Continues

Case 33.3 Continued

standard for identifying the tie between the tortfeasor's employment and the tort. One such standard is whether the tort is a generally foreseeable consequence of the enterprise undertaken by the employer or is incident to it—in other words, whether the agent's conduct is not so unusual or startling that it seems unfair to include the loss resulting from it in the employer's business costs, or whether the tort was engendered by the employment or an outgrowth of it. Another considers whether the employment furnished the specific impetus for a tort or increased the general risk that the tort would occur. These tests leave to the finder of fact the challenge of determining whether a tortfeasor's employment did more than create a happenstance opportunity to commit the tort.

* * * To resolve this case we need not choose * * * between the purpose or motive test * * * and the alternative formulations * * * because we find that the Trust's attempts to defeat its liability on summary judgment fail under any of the * * * formulations.

We do openly endorse one particular aspect of * * * the doctrine of *respondeat*

superior, however. Specifically * * * we hold that an agent need not be acting within the hours of the employee's work and the ordinary spatial boundaries of the employment in order to be acting within the course of his employment. * * * We acknowledge that in today's business world much work is performed for an employer away from a defined work space and outside of a limited work shift. And we accordingly reject the Trust's attempt to escape liability on the ground that Jeffs's acts as a trustee were not performed while he was on the Trust's clock or at a work space designated for his work for the Trust. Instead we hold that the key question is whether Jeffs was acting within the scope of employment when performing work assigned by the employer or engaging in a course of conduct subject to the employer's control.

[The Trust argues] that settled case-law establishes "as a matter of law that the sexual misconduct of an employee is outside the scope of employment." Granted, there are many cases that so conclude * * * and some of those cases * * * turn principally on the ground

that * * * an agent who commits a sexual assault * * * cannot be viewed as advancing, even in part, the purposes of his principal. Yet some of the cases in this field (particularly more recent ones) * * * adopt * * * a standard that turns not on motive or purpose but on foreseeability, or on whether the employee's acts were engendered by or an outgrowth of the employment, or the employment furnished the impetus for the tort.

* * * *

And we conclude that this is one of those cases. Given Jeffs's unique role as leader of the FLDS Church, and in light of the unusual, troubling function of * * * marriage involving young brides in the FLDS culture, we hold that a reasonable factfinder could conclude that Jeffs was acting within the scope of his role as a trustee in directing Steed to engage in sexual activity with M.J.

* * * *

* * * We affirm the denial of the Trust's motions for summary judgment on that basis.

Legal Reasoning Questions

1. Why do some courts apply a standard for imposing vicarious liability that does not rely on motive or purpose to determine whether an agent's tortious conduct falls within the scope of employment?

2. Why, in some states, are the boundaries of work time and space no longer essential factors in determining the scope of employment in an agency relationship?

3. Who does the result in this case benefit? Why?

33–3f Liability for Independent Contractor's Torts

Generally, an employer is not liable for physical harm caused to a third person by the negligent act of an independent contractor in the performance of the contract. This is because the employer does not have *the right to control* the details of an independent contractor's performance.

Courts make an exception to this rule when the contract involves unusually hazardous activities, such as

blasting operations, the transportation of highly volatile chemicals, or the use of poisonous gases. In these situations, strict liability is imposed, and an employer cannot be shielded from liability merely by using an independent contractor.

33–3g Liability for Agent's Crimes

An agent is liable for his or her own crimes. A principal or employer normally is *not* liable for an agent's crime even if the crime was committed within the scope of authority or employment. An exception to this rule is made when the principal or employer participated in the crime by conspiracy or other action.

In addition, in some jurisdictions, a principal may be liable under specific statutes if an agent, in the course and scope of employment, violates certain regulations. For instance, a principal might be liable for an agent's violation of sanitation rules or regulations governing prices, weights, or the sale of liquor.

33–4 Termination of an Agency

Agency law is similar to contract law in that both an agency and a contract may be terminated by an act of the parties or by operation of law. Once the relationship between the principal and the agent has ended, the agent no longer has the right (*actual* authority) to bind the principal. For an agent's *apparent* authority to be terminated, though, third persons may also need to be notified that the agency has been terminated.

33–4a Termination by Act of the Parties

An agency may be terminated by certain acts of the parties, which are listed and described in Exhibit 33–2. Bases for termination by act of the parties include lapse of time, achievement of purpose, occurrence of a specific event, mutual agreement, and at the option of one party.

When an agency agreement specifies the time period during which the agency relationship will exist, the agency ends when that time period expires. If no definite time is stated, then the agency continues for a reasonable time and can be terminated at will by either party. What constitutes a reasonable time depends on the circumstances and the nature of the agency relationship.

The parties can, of course, mutually agree to end their agency relationship. In addition, as a general rule, either party can terminate the agency relationship without the agreement of the other. The act of termination is called *revocation* if done by the principal and *renunciation* if done by the agent. Note, however, that the terminating party may face liability if the termination is wrongful.

EXHIBIT 33–2 Termination by Act of the Parties

METHOD	RULES	ILLUSTRATION
1. Lapse of Time.	Agency terminates automatically at the end of the stated time.	Page lists her property for sale with Alex, a real estate agent, for six months. The agency ends in six months.
2. Purpose Achieved.	Agency terminates automatically on the completion of the purpose for which it was formed.	Calvin, a cattle rancher, hires Abe as his agent in the purchase of fifty breeding stock. The agency ends when the cattle have been purchased.
3. Occurrence of a Specific Event.	Agency normally terminates automatically on the event's occurrence.	Meredith appoints Allen to handle her business affairs while she is away. The agency terminates when Meredith returns.
4. Mutual Agreement.	Agency terminates when both parties consent to end the agency relationship.	Linda and Greg agree that Greg will no longer be her agent in procuring business equipment.
5. At the Option of One Party (*revocation*, if by principal; *renunciation*, if by agent).	Either party normally has a right to terminate the agency relationship. Wrongful termination can lead to liability for breach of contract.	When Patrick becomes ill, he informs Alice that he is revoking her authority to be his agent.

Wrongful Termination Although both parties have the *power* to terminate the agency, they may not always possess the *right* to do so. Wrongful termination can subject the canceling party to a lawsuit for breach of contract. ■ **EXAMPLE 33.22** Rawlins has a one-year employment contract with Munro to act as agent in return for $65,000. Munro has the *power* to discharge Rawlins before the contract period expires. But if he does so, he can be sued for breaching the contract, because he had no *right* to terminate the agency. ■

Even in an agency at will—in which either party may terminate at any time—the principal who wishes to terminate must give the agent *reasonable* notice. The notice must be at least sufficient to allow the agent to recoup his or her expenses and, in some situations, to make a normal profit.

Agency Coupled with an Interest A special rule applies to an *agency coupled with an interest.* In an **agency coupled with an interest,** the agent has some legal right to (an interest in) the property that is the subject of the agency. This type of agency is not an agency in the usual sense because it is created for the agent's benefit instead of for the principal's benefit.

■ **EXAMPLE 33.23** Sylvia owns Harper Hills, a vacation home. She needs some cash right away, so she enters into an agreement with Rob under which Rob will lend her $10,000. In return, she will grant Rob a one-half interest in Harper Hills and "the exclusive right to sell" it. The loan is to be repaid out of the sale's proceeds. Rob is Sylvia's agent, and their relationship is an agency coupled with an interest. The agency was created when the loan agreement was made for the purpose of securing the loan. Therefore, Rob's agency power is irrevocable. ■

An agency coupled with an interest should not be confused with a situation in which the agent merely derives proceeds or profits from the sale of the subject matter. Many agents are paid a commission for their services, but the agency relationship involved does not constitute an agency coupled with an interest. For instance, a real estate agent who merely receives a commission from the sale of real property does not have a beneficial interest in the property itself.

Notice of Termination When the parties terminate an agency, it is the principal's duty to inform any third parties who know of the existence of the agency that it has been terminated. No particular form is required for notice of termination to be effective. The principal can personally notify the agent, or the agent can learn of the termination through some other means.

Although an agent's actual authority ends when the agency is terminated, an agent's *apparent authority* continues until the third party receives notice (from any source) that such authority has been terminated. ■ **EXAMPLE 33.24** Manning bids on a shipment of steel, and Stone is hired as an agent to arrange transportation for the shipment. When Stone learns that Manning has lost the bid, Stone's authority to make the transportation arrangement terminates. ■

If the principal knows that a third party has dealt with the agent, the principal is expected to notify that person *directly.* For third parties who have heard about the agency but have not yet dealt with the agent, *constructive notice* is sufficient.[13] If the agent's authority is written, however, normally it must be revoked in writing (unless the written document contains an expiration date).

33–4b Termination by Operation of Law

Certain events terminate agency authority automatically because their occurrence makes it impossible for the agent to perform or improbable that the principal would continue to want performance. We look at these events here. Note that when an agency terminates by operation of law, there is no duty to notify third persons—unless the agent's authority is coupled with an interest.

1. *Death or insanity.* The general rule is that the death or insanity of either the principal or the agent automatically and immediately terminates an ordinary agency relationship.[14] Knowledge of the death or insanity is not required. ■ **EXAMPLE 33.25** Grey sends Bosley to Japan to purchase a rare book. Before Bosley makes the purchase, Grey dies. Bosley's agent status is terminated at the moment of Grey's death, even though Bosley does not know that Grey has died. ■ (Some states, however, have enacted statutes that change the common law rule to require an agent's knowledge of the principal's death before termination.)

---

13. With *constructive notice* of a fact, knowledge of the fact is imputed by law to a person if he or she could have discovered the fact through proper diligence. Constructive notice is often accomplished by publication in a newspaper.
14. An exception to this rule exists in the bank-customer relationship. A bank, as agent, can continue to exercise specific types of authority after the customer's death or insanity and can continue to pay checks drawn by the customer for ten days after death.

2. *Impossibility.* When the specific subject matter of an agency is destroyed or lost, the agency terminates. ■ **EXAMPLE 33.26** Pedro employs Vasquez to sell Pedro's house. Prior to any sale, the house is destroyed by fire. Vasquez's agency and authority to sell the house terminate. ■ Similarly, when it is impossible for the agent to perform the agency lawfully because of a change in the law, the agency terminates.

3. *Changed circumstances.* Sometimes, an event occurs that has such an unusual effect on the subject matter of the agency that the agent can reasonably infer that the principal will not want the agency to continue. In such situations, the agency terminates. ■ **EXAMPLE 33.27** Baird hires Joslen to sell a tract of land for $40,000. Subsequently, Joslen learns that there is oil under the land and that the land is therefore worth $1 million. The agency and Joslen's authority to sell the land for $40,000 are terminated. ■

4. *Bankruptcy.* If either the principal or the agent petitions for bankruptcy, the agency is *usually* terminated. In certain circumstances, such as when the agent's financial status is irrelevant to the purpose of the agency, the agency relationship may continue. Insolvency, as distinct from bankruptcy, does not necessarily terminate the relationship. (An *insolvent* person is one who cannot pay debts as they come due or whose liabilities exceed his or her assets.)

5. *War.* When the principal's country and the agent's country are at war with each other, the agency is terminated. In this situation, the agency is automatically suspended or terminated because there is no way to enforce the legal rights and obligations of the parties.

See Concept Summary 33.2 for a synopsis of the rules governing the termination of an agency by operation of law.

Concept Summary 33.2

Agency Termination by Operation of Law

Death or Insanity — Termination of the agency is automatic on the death or insanity of either the principal or the agent—except when the agency is coupled with an interest.

Impossibility — Agency termination occurs any time the agency cannot be performed because of an event beyond the parties' control, such as the destruction of the specific subject matter.

Changed Circumstances — When events are so unusual that it would be inequitable to allow the agency to exist, the agency will terminate.

Bankruptcy — Bankruptcy petition—but not mere insolvency—usually terminates the agency.

War between Countries — War between the principal's country and the agent's country automatically suspends or terminates agency because there is no way to enforce legal rights.

Reviewing: Agency Liability and Termination

Lynne Meyer, on her way to a business meeting and in a hurry, stopped at a Buy-Mart store for a new car charger for her smartphone. There was a long line at one of the checkout counters, but a cashier, Valerie Watts, opened another counter and began loading the cash drawer. Meyer told Watts that she was in a hurry and asked Watts to work faster. Instead, Watts slowed her pace. At this point, Meyer hit Watts. It is not clear whether Meyer hit Watts intentionally or, in an attempt to retrieve the car charger, hit her inadvertently.

In response, Watts grabbed Meyer by the hair and hit her repeatedly in the back of the head, while Meyer screamed for help. Management personnel separated the two women and questioned them about the incident. Watts was immediately fired for violating the store's no-fighting policy. Meyer subsequently sued Buy-Mart, alleging that the store was liable for the tort (assault and battery) committed by its employee. Using the information presented in the chapter, answer the following questions.

1. Under what doctrine discussed in this chapter might Buy-Mart be held liable for the tort committed by Watts?
2. What is the key factor in determining whether Buy-Mart is liable under this doctrine?
3. How is Buy-Mart's potential liability affected by whether Watts's behavior constituted an intentional tort or a tort of negligence?
4. Suppose that when Watts applied for the job at Buy-Mart, she disclosed in her application that she had previously been convicted of felony assault and battery. Nevertheless, Buy-Mart hired Watts as a cashier. How might this fact affect Buy-Mart's liability for Watts's actions?

Debate This . . . *The doctrine of* respondeat superior *should be modified to make agents solely liable for their tortious (wrongful) acts committed within the scope of employment.*

Terms and Concepts

agency coupled with an interest 636	express authority 622	ratification 625
apparent authority 624	implied authority 624	*respondeat superior* 629
disclosed principal 626	notary public 622	undisclosed principal 627
e-agent 628	partially disclosed principal 627	vicarious liability 629
equal dignity rule 622	power of attorney 622	

Issue Spotters

1. Davis contracts with Estee to buy a certain horse on her behalf. Estee asks Davis not to reveal her identity. Davis makes a deal with Farmland Stables, the owner of the horse, and makes a down payment. Estee does not pay the rest of the price. Farmland Stables sues Davis for breach of contract. Can Davis hold Estee liable for whatever damages he has to pay? Why or why not? (See *Liability for Contracts*.)

2. Vivian, owner of Wonder Goods Company, employs Xena as an administrative assistant. In Vivian's absence, and without authority, Xena represents herself as Vivian and signs a promissory note in Vivian's name. In what circumstance is Vivian liable on the note? (See *Liability for Contracts*.)

• **Check your answers to the Issue Spotters against the answers provided in Appendix D at the end of this text.**

Business Scenarios

33–1. Unauthorized Acts. Janell Arden is a purchasing agent–employee for the A&B Coal Supply partnership. Arden has authority to purchase the coal needed by A&B to satisfy the needs of its customers. While Arden is leaving a coal mine from which she has just purchased a large quantity of coal, her car breaks down. She walks into a small roadside grocery store for help. While there, she encounters Will Wilson, who owns 360 acres back in the mountains with all mineral rights. Wilson, in need of cash, offers to sell Arden the property for $1,500 per acre.

On inspection of the property, Arden forms the opinion that the subsurface contains valuable coal deposits. Arden contracts to purchase the property for A&B Coal Supply, signing the contract "A&B Coal Supply, Janell Arden, agent." The closing date is August 1. Arden takes the contract to the partnership. The managing partner is furious, as A&B is not in the property business. Later, just before closing, both Wilson and the partnership learn that the value of the land is at least $15,000 per acre. Discuss the rights of A&B and Wilson concerning the land contract. (See *Liability for Contracts.*)

33–2. Respondeat Superior. ABC Tire Corp. hires Arnez as a traveling salesperson and assigns him a geographic area and time schedule in which to solicit orders and service customers. Arnez is given a company car to use in covering the territory. One day, Arnez decides to take his personal car to cover part of his territory. It is 11:00 A.M., and Arnez has just finished calling on all customers in the city of Tarrytown. His next appointment is at 2:00 P.M. in the city of Austex, twenty miles down the road. Arnez starts out for Austex, but halfway there he decides to visit a former college roommate who runs a farm ten miles off the main highway. Arnez is enjoying his visit with his former roommate when he realizes that it is 1:45 P.M. and that he will be late for the appointment in Austex. Driving at a high speed down the country road to reach the main highway, Arnez crashes his car into a tractor, severely injuring Thomas, the driver of the tractor. Thomas claims that he can hold ABC Tire Corp. liable for his injuries. Discuss fully ABC's liability in this situation. (See *Liability for Torts and Crimes.*)

Business Case Problems

33–3. Liability Based on Apparent Authority. Summerall Electric Co. and other subcontractors were hired by National Church Services, Inc. (NCS), which was the general contractor on a construction project for the Church of God at Southaven. As work progressed, payments from NCS to the subcontractors were late and eventually stopped altogether. The church had paid NCS in full for the entire project beforehand, but apparently NCS had mismanaged the project. When payments from NCS stopped, the subcontractors filed mechanic's liens for the value of the work they had performed but for which they had not been paid. The subcontractors sued the church, contending that it was liable for the payments because NCS was its agent on the basis of either actual or apparent authority. Was NCS an agent for the church, thereby making the church liable to the subcontractors? Explain your reasoning. [*Summerall Electric Co. v. Church of God at Southaven*, 25 So.3d 1090 (Miss.App. 2010)] (See *Scope of Agent's Authority.*)

33–4. Disclosed Principal. To display desserts in restaurants, Mario Sclafani ordered refrigeration units from Felix Storch, Inc. Felix faxed a credit application to Sclafani. The application was faxed back with a signature that appeared to be Sclafani's. Felix delivered the units. When they were not paid for, Felix filed a suit against Sclafani to collect. Sclafani denied that he had seen the application or signed it. He testified that he referred all credit questions to "the girl in the office." Who was the principal? Who was the agent? Who is liable on the contract? Explain. [*Felix Storch, Inc. v. Martinucci Desserts USA, Inc.*, 30 Misc.3d 1217, 924 N.Y.S.2d 308 (Suffolk Co. 2011)] (See *Liability for Contracts.*)

33–5. Liability for Contracts. Thomas Huskin and his wife entered into a contract to have their home remodeled by House Medic Handyman Service. Todd Hall signed the contract as an authorized representative of House Medic. It turned out that House Medic was a fictitious name for Hall Hauling, Ltd. The contract did not indicate this, however, and Hall did not inform the Huskins about Hall Hauling. When a contract dispute later arose, the Huskins sued Todd Hall personally for breach of contract. Can Hall be held personally liable? Why or why not? [*Huskin v. Hall*, 2012 WL 553136 (Ohio Ct.App. 2012)] (See *Liability for Contracts.*)

33–6. Business Case Problem with Sample Answer—Agent's Authority. Basic Research, L.L.C., advertised its products on television networks owned by Rainbow Media Holdings, Inc., through an ad agency, Icebox Advertising, Inc. As Basic's agent, Icebox had the express authority to buy ads from Rainbow on Basic's behalf, but the authority was limited to buying ads with cash in advance. Despite this limit, Rainbow sold ads to Basic through Icebox on credit. Basic paid Icebox for the ads, but Icebox did not pass all of the payments on to Rainbow. Icebox filed for bankruptcy. Can Rainbow recoup the unpaid amounts from Basic? Explain. [*American Movie Classics v. Rainbow Media Holdings*, 508 Fed.Appx. 826 (10th Cir. 2013)] (See *Scope of Agent's Authority.*)

- For a sample answer to Problem 33–6, go to Appendix E at the end of this text.

33–7. Agent's Authority. Terry Holden's stepmother, Rosie, was diagnosed with amyotrophic lateral sclerosis (ALS), and Terry's wife, Susan, became Rosie's primary caregiver. Rosie executed a durable power of attorney appointing Susan as her agent. Susan opened a joint bank account with Rosie at Bank of America, depositing $9,643.62 of Rosie's funds. Susan used some of the money to pay for "household expenses to keep us going while we were taking care of her." Rosie died three months later. Terry's father, Charles, as executor of Rosie's estate, filed a petition in a Texas state court against Susan for an accounting. What general duty did Susan owe Rosie as her agent? What does an agent's duty of accounting require? Did Susan breach either of these duties? Explain.

[*Holden v. Holden*, 456 S.W.3d 642 (Tex.App.—Tyler 2015)] (See *Scope of Agent's Authority*.)

33–8. Scope of Agent's Authority. Kindred Nursing Centers East, LLC, owns and operates Whitesburg Gardens, a long-term care and rehabilitation facility, in Huntsville, Alabama. Lorene Jones was admitted to the facility following knee-replacement surgery. Jones's daughter, Yvonne Barbour, signed the admission forms required by Whitesburg Gardens as her mother's representative in her presence. Jones did not object. The forms included an "Alternative Dispute Resolution Agreement," which provided for binding arbitration in the event of a dispute between "the Resident" (Jones) and "the Facility" (Whitesburg Gardens). Six days later, Jones was transferred to a different facility. After recovering from the surgery, she filed a suit in an Alabama state court against Kindred, alleging substandard care on a claim of negligence. Can Jones be compelled to submit her claim to arbitration? Explain. [*Kindred Nursing Centers East, LLC v. Jones*, __ So.3d __, 2016 WL 762450 (Ala. 2016)] (See *Scope of Agent's Authority*.)

33–9. A Question of Ethics—Vicarious Liability. *Jamie*

Paliath worked as a real estate agent for Home Town Realty of Vandalia, LLC (the principal, a real estate broker). Torri Auer, a California resident, relied on Paliath's advice and assistance to buy three rental properties in Ohio. Before the sales, Paliath had represented that each property was worth approximately twice as much as what Auer would pay and that there was a waiting list of prospective tenants. Paliath also stated that all of the property needed work

and agreed to do the work for a specified price. Nearly a year later, substantial work was still needed, and only a few of the units had been rented. Auer sued Paliath and Home Town Realty for fraudulent misrepresentation. [Auer v. Paliath, *140 Ohio St.3d 276, 17 N.E.3d 561, 2014-Ohio-3632 (2014)]* (See *Liability for Torts and Crimes*.)

(a) Were Paliath's representations to Auer within the scope of her employment? Explain. Will the court hold the principal (Home Town Realty) liable for the misrepresentations of the agent (Paliath)?

(b) What is the ethical basis for imposing vicarious liability on a principal for an agent's tort?

33–10. Special Case Analysis—Liability for Torts and Crimes. Go to Case Analysis 33.3, *M.J. v. Wisan*. Read the excerpt and answer the following questions.

(a) Issue: What conduct was at the center of the dispute in this case? Who did the plaintiff allege was liable for this conduct? Which of these parties was the principal, and which was the agent?

(b) Rule of Law: What rule applied to determine the liability of the parties for the conduct in dispute?

(c) Applying the Rule of Law: What factors did the court indicate could be considered in deciding whether to impose liability in this case?

(d) Conclusion: How did the court rule on the question of vicarious liability?

Legal Reasoning Group Activity

33–11. Liability for Independent Contractor's Torts. Dean Brothers Corp. owns and operates a steel drum manufacturing plant. Lowell Wyden, the plant superintendent, hired Best Security Patrol, Inc. (BSP), a security company, to guard Dean property and "deter thieves and vandals." Some BSP security guards, as Wyden knew, carried firearms. Pete Sidell, a BSP security guard, was not certified as an armed guard but nevertheless came to work with his gun (in a briefcase).

While working at the Dean plant on October 31, Sidell fired his gun at Tyrone Gaines, in the belief that Gaines was an intruder. The bullet struck and killed Gaines. Gaines's mother filed a lawsuit claiming that her son's death was the result of BSP's negligence, for which Dean was responsible. (See *Liability for Torts and Crimes*.)

(a) The first group will determine what the plaintiff's best argument is to establish that Dean is responsible for BSP's actions.

(b) The second group will discuss Dean's best defense and formulate arguments to support it.

CHAPTER 34

Employment, Immigration, and Labor Law

Until the early 1900s, most employer-employee relationships were governed by the common law. Even today, under the common law *employment-at-will doctrine*, private employers have considerable freedom to hire and fire workers at will, regardless of the employees' performance.

Numerous statutes and administrative agency regulations now also govern the workplace. Thus, to a large extent, statutory law has displaced common law doctrines. In this chapter and the next, we look at the most significant laws regulating employment relationships.

This chapter discusses federal statutes that regulate various aspects of the workplace, including employee wages, hours, medical leave, safety, and pension and health plans. It also examines immigration law, a topic of special importance to employers in our diverse society. The chapter concludes with coverage of labor laws, which continue to have an impact on the employment environment.

34–1 Employment at Will

Employment relationships have traditionally been governed by the common law doctrine of **employment at will.** Under this doctrine, either party may terminate the employment relationship at any time and for any reason, unless doing so violates an employee's statutory or contractual rights.

Today, the majority of U.S. workers continue to have the legal status of "employees at will." In other words, this common law doctrine is still in widespread use, and only one state (Montana) does not apply it.

Nonetheless, federal and state statutes governing employment relationships prevent the doctrine from being applied in a number of circumstances. An employer may not fire an employee if doing so would violate a federal or state statute, such as a law prohibiting employment discrimination.

Note that the distinction made under agency law between employee status and independent-contractor status is important here. The employment laws that will be discussed apply only to the employer-employee relationship. They do not apply to independent contractors.

34–1a Common Law Exceptions to the Employment-at-Will Doctrine

As noted, statutory law has affected the application of the employment-at-will doctrine. In addition, the courts have carved out various exceptions to the doctrine based on contract theory, tort theory, and public policy.

Exceptions Based on Contract Theory Some courts have held that an *implied* employment contract exists between the employer and the employee. If the employee is fired outside the terms of the implied contract, he or she may succeed in an action for breach of contract even though no written employment contract exists.

■ **EXAMPLE 34.1** BDI Enterprises' employment manual and personnel bulletin both state that, as a matter of policy, workers will be dismissed only for good cause. Jing Chin is an employee at BDI. If Chin reasonably expects BDI to follow this policy, a court may find that there is an implied contract based on the terms stated in the manual and bulletin. ■ Generally, the key consideration in determining whether an employment manual creates an implied contractual obligation is the employee's reasonable expectations.

An employer's oral promises to employees regarding discharge policy may also be considered part of an implied contract. If the employer fires a worker in a manner contrary to what was promised, a court may hold that the employer has violated the implied contract and is liable for damages.

Exceptions Based on Tort Theory In some situations, the discharge of an employee may give rise to an action for wrongful discharge (discussed shortly) under tort theories. Abusive discharge procedures may result in a lawsuit for intentional infliction of emotional distress or defamation. In addition, some courts have permitted workers to sue their employers under the tort theory of fraud. Fraud might be alleged when an employer made false promises to a prospective employee.

■ **EXAMPLE 34.2** Goldfinch Consulting, Inc., induces Brianna to leave a lucrative job and move to another state by offering her "a long-term job with a thriving business." In fact, Goldfinch is not only having significant financial problems but is also planning a merger that will result in the elimination of the position offered to Brianna. If she takes the job in reliance on Goldfinch's representations and is fired shortly thereafter, Brianna may be able to bring an action against the employer for fraud. ■

Exceptions Based on Public Policy The most common exception to the employment-at-will doctrine is made on the basis that the employer's reason for firing the employee violates a fundamental public policy of the jurisdiction. Generally, the courts require that the public policy involved be expressed clearly in the statutory law governing the jurisdiction.

The public-policy exception may apply to an employee discharged for **whistleblowing**—that is, telling government authorities, upper-level managers, or the media that the employer is engaged in some unsafe or illegal activity. Normally, however, whistleblowers seek protection from retaliatory discharge under federal and state statutes, such as the Whistleblower Protection Act.[1]

■ **CASE IN POINT 34.3** Donald Waddell worked for the Boyce Thompson Institute for Plant Research. Waddell did not have an employment contract for a fixed term, and the institute's employee manual said that his job was "terminable at will." Soon after he was hired, the institute implemented a whistleblower policy designed to encourage "the highest standards of financial reporting and lawful and ethical behavior."

Waddell repeatedly told his supervisor, Sophia Darling, that she needed to file certain financial documents more promptly. Darling fired Waddell, telling him that he was disrespectful and insubordinate. Waddell then sued the institute, contending that he should not have been fired because he was acting under the company's whistleblowing policy.

A New York appellate court, however, found that Waddell could be fired. Waddell was employed at will. In addition, he was not protected under the whistle-blower policy, which had been implemented after his employment. Thus, he could not have detrimentally relied on the policy in accepting the job.[2] ■

34–1b Wrongful Discharge

Whenever an employer discharges an employee in violation of an employment contract or a statutory law protecting employees, the employee may bring an action for **wrongful discharge.** For instance, an employee who is terminated in retaliation for some protected activity, such as whistleblowing or participating in an employment-discrimination investigation, can sue for wrongful discharge.

Even if an employer's actions do not violate any provisions in an employment contract or statute, the employer may still be subject to liability. An employee can sue for wrongful discharge under a common law doctrine, such as a tort theory or agency. For instance, if while firing a female employee, an employer publicly discloses private facts about her sex life, that employee could sue for wrongful discharge based on an invasion of privacy.

34–2 Wages, Hours, and Layoffs

In the 1930s, Congress enacted several laws to regulate the wages and working hours of employees, including the following:

1. The Davis-Bacon Act[3] requires contractors and subcontractors working on federal government construction projects to pay "prevailing wages" to their employees.
2. The Walsh-Healey Act[4] applies to U.S. government contracts. It requires that a minimum wage, as well as overtime pay at 1.5 times regular pay rates, be paid to employees of manufacturers or suppliers entering into contracts with agencies of the federal government.
3. The Fair Labor Standards Act (FLSA)[5] extended wage-hour requirements to cover all employers engaged in interstate commerce or in producing goods for interstate commerce. Certain other types of businesses were included as well. The FLSA, as amended, provides the most comprehensive federal regulation of wages and hours today.

---

1. 5 U.S.C. Section 1201.

2. *Waddell v. Boyce Thompson Institute for Plant Research, Inc.*, 92 A.D.3d 1172, 940 N.Y.S.2d 331 (2012).
3. 40 U.S.C. Sections 276a–276a-5.
4. 41 U.S.C. Sections 35–45.
5. 29 U.S.C. Sections 201–260.

34–2a Child Labor

The FLSA prohibits oppressive child labor. Restrictions on child labor differ by age group.

Children under fourteen years of age are allowed to do only certain types of work. They can deliver newspapers, work for their parents, and be employed in entertainment and (with some exceptions) agriculture. Children aged fourteen and fifteen are allowed to work, but not in hazardous occupations. There are also restrictions on how many hours per day and per week children in these age groups can work.

Working times and hours are not restricted for persons between the ages of sixteen and eighteen, but they cannot be employed in hazardous jobs. None of these restrictions apply to those over the age of eighteen.

34–2b Minimum Wages

The FLSA provides that a **minimum wage** of $7.25 per hour must be paid to covered nonexempt employees. Most states also have minimum wages. More than half of the states have set their minimum wages above the federal minimum wage. When the state minimum wage is greater than the federal minimum wage, the employee is entitled to the higher wage.

■ **EXAMPLE 34.4**   The Oakland Raiders paid $1.25 million in 2014 to settle wage claims made by the team's cheerleading squad (the Raiderettes) as a class action. The cheerleaders had complained that they were not being paid for hours that they spent attending other events and performing other tasks required of them by contract. After the time spent performing these other tasks was factored in, the cheerleaders were receiving wages that were well below California's minimum wage, persuading the Raiders to settle the dispute. ■

Are employees entitled to receive wages for all the time they spend at work, including times when they are taking a personal break? See this chapter's *Ethics Today* feature for a discussion of this issue.

34–2c Tipped Workers

When an employee receives tips while on the job, the FLSA gives employers a tip credit toward the minimum wage amount. The employer is required to pay only $2.13 an hour in direct wages—if that amount, plus the tips received, equals at least the federal minimum wage. If an employee's tips and direct wages do not equal the federal minimum wage, the employer must make up the difference. Note that some states have enacted laws to prevent employers from including tips in the minimum wage. In these states, tipped workers receive the regular minimum wage.

If employers pay at least the federal minimum wage, the FLSA allows them to take employee tips and make other arrangements for their distribution. ■ **CASE IN POINT 34.5** Misty Cumbie worked as a waitress at a café in Portland, Oregon, that was owned and operated by Woody Woo, Inc. Woody Woo paid its servers an hourly wage that was higher than the state's minimum wage, but the servers were required to contribute their tips to a "tip pool." Approximately one-third of the tip-pool funds went to the servers, and the rest was distributed to kitchen staff members, who otherwise rarely received tips for their services. When Cumbie filed a lawsuit against Woody Woo over her tips, the court held that the tip pool did not violate the FLSA.[6] ■

34–2d Overtime Provisions and Exemptions

Under the FLSA, any employee who works more than forty hours per week must be paid no less than 1.5 times her or his regular pay for all hours worked over forty. The FLSA overtime provisions apply only after an employee has worked more than forty hours per *week*. Therefore, employees who work ten hours a day, four days per week, are not entitled to overtime pay.

Certain employees are exempt from the FLSA's overtime provisions. These employees generally include executive, administrative, and professional employees, as well as outside salespersons and those who create computer code. Executive and administrative employees are those whose primary duty is management and who exercise discretion and independent judgment.

■ **CASE IN POINT 34.6** Patty Lee Smith was a pharmaceutical sales representative for Johnson and Johnson (J&J). She traveled to ten physicians' offices a day to promote the benefits of J&J's drug Concerta. Smith's work was unsupervised, she controlled her own schedule, and she received an annual salary of $66,000. When she filed a claim for overtime pay, the court held that she was an administrative employee and therefore exempt from the FLSA's overtime provisions.[7] ■

An employer can voluntarily pay overtime to ineligible employees but cannot waive or reduce the overtime requirements of the FLSA. In 2016, the Department of Labor updated its overtime regulations to allow millions more employees to receive overtime pay.[8]

---

6. *Cumbie v. Woody Woo, Inc.*, 596 F.3d 577 (9th Cir. 2010).
7. *Smith v. Johnson and Johnson*, 593 F.3d 280 (3d Cir. 2010).
8. 29 C.F.R. Part 541.

Is It Fair to Dock Employees' Pay for Bathroom Breaks?

For some employees, "punching a time clock" means accounting for *all* of the time that they are not working. These employees must "punch in" when they arrive and "punch out" when they leave for the day, of course, but they also must clock out when they take breaks. That includes bathroom breaks, coffee breaks, and smoking breaks.

What the Law Says

The Fair Labor Standards Act[a] does not require that an employer offer its employees personal breaks. If an employer does offer them, though, employees must be compensated during those breaks. Otherwise, the employer may effectively be in violation of federal minimum wage laws.

A Pennsylvania Publisher Faces Fines for Unpaid Bathroom Breaks

The issue of unpaid bathroom breaks came to the fore when the U.S. Department of Labor (DOL) filed a lawsuit against American Future Systems, Inc. (doing business as Progressive Business Publications). The DOL alleged that American Future Systems had created a compensation system in which none of its six thousand employees were compensated for bathroom breaks.[b]

The DOL argued that all workday breaks of twenty minutes or less are compensable time.[c] Because American Future Systems did not compensate its employees for such breaks, those employees were not properly credited for all compensable time. The result was that they had "been paid below the minimum wage established by the Fair Labor Standards Act (FLSA).[d]

U.S. district court judge L. Felipe Restrepo agreed, finding American Future Systems liable for unpaid wages under the FLSA, plus damages. The company will have to pay past and current employees almost $2 million, according to DOL estimates.

The Ethical Issue

Irrespective of the illegality of not paying for personal breaks, there is an ethical issue. Should workers have to face the choice of taking a bathroom break or getting paid? Adam Welsh, a senior trial attorney for the Department of Labor, argued that the answer was no. "I think it's the rare employer who doesn't allow its employees to go to the bathroom," Welsh said.

Critical Thinking *Consider a company whose employees include both smokers and nonsmokers. The smokers take numerous paid smoking breaks, while the nonsmokers do not. Is there an ethical issue here? Discuss.*

---

a. 29 U.S.C. Sections 201 *et seq.*

b. *U.S. Department of Labor v. American Future Systems, Inc.*, Memorandum, Case No. 12-6171 (E.D.Pa. 2015).

c. 29 C.F.R. Section 785.18.

d. 29 U.S.C. Section 206(a)(1)(c).

Whereas in the past, workers making more than $23,660 a year did not qualify for overtime pay, today, that threshold has been increased to $50,440 a year.

An employee's underreporting of hours worked can undercut his or her claim for overtime. But can an employee's underreporting *support* such a claim? That question was at the center of the following case.

Case 34.1

Bailey v. TitleMax of Georgia, Inc.

United States Court of Appeals, Eleventh Circuit, 776 F.3d 797 (2015).

Background and Facts Santonias Bailey was an employee of TitleMax of Georgia, Inc., in Jonesboro, Georgia. Bailey's supervisor told him that TitleMax did not pay overtime, so he regularly worked off the clock. For example, on some Saturdays, he would work from 8:30 A.M. to 5:30 P.M., but—as ordered by his supervisor—would log only seven hours despite having worked nine. His supervisor also

Case 34.1 Continued

edited Bailey's time records to report fewer hours than he actually worked by, for instance, subtracting a one-hour lunch break when there had been none.

Bailey resigned from TitleMax and filed a suit in a federal district court against the employer to recover for the unpaid overtime under the Fair Labor Standards Act (FLSA). TitleMax argued that Bailey was responsible for the unpaid time. According to TitleMax, he had never complained about his supervisor, and he had violated company policy with respect to keeping accurate time records. The court issued a judgment in the defendant's favor. Bailey appealed.

In the Language of the Court

MARTIN, Circuit Judge:

* * * *

* * * The goal of the FLSA is to counteract the inequality of bargaining power between employees and employers.

In the broadest sense, this principle * * * compels our holding here. If an employer knew or had reason to know that its employee underreported his hours, it cannot escape FLSA liability by asserting [a] defense based on that underreporting. To hold otherwise would allow an employer to wield its superior bargaining power to pressure or even compel its employees to underreport their work hours.

* * * *

If an employee has worked overtime without pay, he may bring a private FLSA action for damages. An unpaid-overtime claim has two elements: (1) an employee worked unpaid overtime, and (2) the employer knew or should have known of the overtime work. *Knowledge may be imputed [attributed] to the employer when its supervisors or management encourage artificially low reporting.* [Emphasis added.]

Mr. Bailey has shown both required elements. He worked overtime without pay. TitleMax knew or should have known he worked overtime, because Mr. Bailey's supervisor both encouraged artificially low reporting and squelched truthful timekeeping.

* * * *

* * * No one disputes that his supervisor knew he was working off the clock. *The supervisor's knowledge may be imputed to TitleMax, making it liable for the FLSA violation.* * * * TitleMax argues that * * * an employee [is] deprived of his FLSA claim because he underreported his time, even if knowledge of the underreporting is imputed to the employer. [Emphasis added.]

TitleMax has identified no case in which [any federal appellate court] approved the use of [this] defense as a total bar to an employee's FLSA claim when the employer knew the employee underreported his hours.

* * * The dearth [scarcity] of precedent supporting TitleMax's * * * argument is persuasive, if not conclusive, evidence that its argument is misguided.

Decision and Remedy *The U.S. Court of Appeals for the Eleventh Circuit reversed the judgment of the lower court and remanded the case for further proceedings. "Where, as here, an employer knew or had reason to know that its employee underreported his hours, it cannot invoke [a] defense based on that underreporting to bar the employee's FLSA claim."*

Critical Thinking

- **Legal Environment** *Congress enacted the FLSA in 1938. More than eight thousand FLSA suits are filed in federal district courts each year. How do these facts support the court's reasoning in this case?*

34–2e Layoffs

The Worker Adjustment and Retraining Notification (WARN) Act[9] applies to employers with at least one hundred full-time employees. The act requires these employ-ers to provide sixty days' notice before implementing a mass layoff or closing a plant that employs more than fifty full-time workers. A mass layoff is a layoff of at least one-third of the full-time employees at a particular job site.

The WARN Act is intended to give workers advance notice so that they can start looking for new jobs while they are still employed. It is also intended to alert state

---

9. 29 U.S.C. Sections 2101 *et seq.*

agencies so that they can provide training and other resources for displaced workers. Employers thus must provide advance notice of the layoff both to the affected workers and to state and local government authorities. (An employer may notify the workers' union representative, if the workers are members of a labor union.) Even companies that anticipate filing for bankruptcy normally must provide notice under the WARN Act.

An employer that violates the WARN Act can be fined up to $500 for each day of the violation. Employees can recover back pay for each day of the violation (up to sixty days), plus reasonable attorneys' fees.

34-3 Family and Medical Leave

The Family and Medical Leave Act (FMLA)[10] allows employees to take time off work for family or medical reasons or in certain situations that arise from military service. A majority of the states have similar legislation. The FMLA does not supersede any state or local law that provides more generous protection.

34-3a Coverage and Application

The FMLA requires employers that have fifty or more employees to provide *unpaid* leave for specified reasons. (Some employers voluntarily offer paid family leave, but this is not a requirement of the FMLA.) The

---

10. 29 U.S.C. Sections 2601, 2611–2619, 2651–2654.

FMLA expressly covers private and public (government) employees who have worked for their employers for at least a year.

An eligible employee may take up to *twelve weeks of leave* within a twelve-month period for any of the following reasons:

1. To care for a newborn baby within one year of birth.
2. To care for an adopted or foster child within one year of the time the child is placed with the employee.
3. To care for the employee's spouse, child, or parent who has a serious health condition.
4. If the employee suffers from a serious health condition and is unable to perform the essential functions of her or his job.
5. For any qualifying exigency (nonmedical emergency) arising out of the fact that the employee's spouse, son, daughter, or parent is a covered military member on active duty.[11] For instance, an employee can take leave to arrange for child care or to deal with financial or legal matters when a spouse is being deployed overseas.

In addition, an employee may take military caregiver leave to care for a family member with a serious injury or illness incurred as a result of military duty.[12] For military caregiver leave, the employee may take up to *twenty-six weeks* of leave within a twelve-month period.

In the following case, an employee asked for medical leave to care for her mother on a trip to Las Vegas, Nevada.

---

11. 29 C.F.R. Section 825.126.
12. 29 C.F.R. Section 825.200.

Case 34.2

Ballard v. Chicago Park District

United States Court of Appeals, Seventh Circuit, 741 F.3d 838 (2014).

Background and Facts Beverly Ballard worked for the Chicago Park District. She lived with her mother, Sarah, who suffered from end-stage congestive heart failure. Beverly served as Sarah's primary caregiver with support from Horizon Hospice & Palliative Care. The hospice helped Sarah plan and secure funds for an end-of-life goal, a "family trip" to Las Vegas. To accompany Sarah as her caretaker, Beverly asked the Park District for unpaid time off under the Family Medical and Leave Act (FMLA). The employer refused, but Beverly and Sarah took the trip as planned.

Later, the Park District terminated Beverly for "unauthorized absences." She filed a suit in a federal district court against the employer. The court issued a decision in Beverly's favor. The Park District appealed, arguing that Beverly had been absent from work on a "recreational trip."

In the Language of the Court
FLAUM, Circuit Judge.
＊ ＊ ＊ ＊

We begin with the text of the [FMLA]: an eligible employee is entitled to leave "in order to care for" a family member with a "serious health condition."

* * * *

* * * *The FMLA's text does not restrict care to a particular place or geographic location.* For instance, it does not say that an employee is entitled to time off "to care *at home* for" a family member. *The only limitation it places on care is that the family member must have a serious health condition.* We are reluctant, without good reason, to read in another limitation that Congress has not provided. [Emphasis added.]

* * * *

Sarah's basic medical, hygienic, and nutritional needs did not change while she was in Las Vegas, and Beverly continued to assist her with those needs during the trip. In fact, * * * Beverly's presence proved quite important indeed when a fire at the hotel made it impossible to reach their room, requiring Beverly to find another source of insulin and pain medicine. Thus, at the very least, [Beverly] requested leave in order to provide physical care.

* * * *

* * * The Park District describes [Beverly's] travel as a "recreational trip" or a "non-medically related pleasure trip." It also raises the specter that employees will help themselves to unpaid FMLA leave in order to take personal vacations, simply by bringing seriously ill family members along. So perhaps what the Park District means to argue is that the real reason Beverly requested leave was in order to take a free pleasure trip, and not in order to care for her mother. * * * However, * * * an employer concerned about the risk that employees will abuse the FMLA's leave provisions may of course require that requests be certified by the family member's health care provider. And any worries about opportunistic leave taking in this case should be tempered by the fact that this dispute arises out of the hospice and palliative care context.

If Beverly had sought leave to care for her mother in Chicago, her request would have fallen within the scope of the FMLA. So too if Sarah had lived in Las Vegas instead of with her daughter, and Beverly had requested leave to care for her mother there. Ultimately, other than a concern that our straightforward reading will "open the door to increased FMLA requests," the Park District gives us no reason to treat the current scenario any differently.

Decision and Remedy *The U.S. Court of Appeals for the Seventh Circuit affirmed the lower court's judgment. Under the FMLA, an eligible employee is entitled to take leave from work to care for a family member with a serious health condition. The care is not restricted to a particular place (such as "at home").*

Critical Thinking

- **What If the Facts Were Different?** *Suppose that Beverly had requested leave to make arrangements for a change in Sarah's care, such as a transfer to a nursing home. Is it likely that the result would have been different? Explain.*
- **Legal Environment** *Under the FMLA, an employee is eligible for leave when he or she is needed to care for a family member. Should "needed to care for" be interpreted to cover only ongoing physical care? Discuss.*

34–3b Benefits and Protections

When an employee takes FMLA leave, the employer must continue the worker's health-care coverage on the same terms as if the employee had continued to work. On returning from FMLA leave, most employees must be restored to their original position or to a comparable position (with nearly equivalent pay and benefits, for instance). An important exception allows the employer to avoid reinstating a *key employee*—defined as an employee whose pay falls within the top 10 percent of the firm's workforce.

34–3c Violations

An employer that violates the FMLA can be required to provide various remedies, including the following:

1. Damages to compensate the employee for lost wages and benefits, denied compensation, and actual monetary losses (such as the cost of providing care for a family member). Compensatory damages are available up to an amount equivalent to the employee's wages for twelve weeks.
2. Job reinstatement.
3. Promotion, if a promotion has been denied.

A successful plaintiff is also entitled to court costs and attorneys' fees. In addition, if the plaintiff shows that the employer acted in bad faith, the plaintiff can receive two times the amount of damages awarded by a judge or jury. Supervisors can also be held personally liable, as employers, for violations of the act.

Employers generally are required to notify employees when an absence will be counted against FMLA leave. If an employer fails to provide such notice, and that failure to notify causes harm to the employee, the employer can be sanctioned.[13]

34-4 Health, Safety, and Income Security

Under the common law, employees who were injured on the job had to file lawsuits against their employers to obtain recovery. Today, numerous state and federal statutes protect employees from the risk of accidental injury, death, or disease resulting from their employment. In addition, the government protects employees' income through Social Security, Medicare, unemployment insurance, and the regulation of pensions and health insurance plans.

34-4a The Occupational Safety and Health Act

At the federal level, the primary legislation protecting employees' health and safety is the Occupational Safety and Health Act,[14] which is administered by the Occupational Safety and Health Administration (OSHA). The act imposes on employers a general duty to keep the workplace safe.

To this end, OSHA has established specific safety standards that employers must follow, depending on the industry. For instance, OSHA regulations require the use of safety guards on certain mechanical equipment. It also sets maximum levels of exposure to substances in the workplace that may be harmful to workers' health.

Notices, Records, and Reports The act requires that employers post certain notices in the workplace, maintain specific records, and submit reports. Employers

with eleven or more employees are required to keep occupational injury and illness records for each employee. Each record must be made available for inspection when requested by an OSHA compliance officer.

Whenever a work-related injury or disease occurs, employers must make reports directly to OSHA. If an employee dies or three or more employees are hospitalized because of a work-related incident, the employer must notify OSHA within eight hours. A company that fails to do so will be fined. Following the incident, a complete inspection of the premises is mandatory.

Inspections OSHA compliance officers may enter and inspect the facilities of any establishment covered by the Occupational Safety and Health Act. Employees may also file complaints of violations. Under the act, an employer cannot discharge an employee who files a complaint or who, in good faith, refuses to work in a high-risk area if bodily harm or death might result.

34-4b State Workers' Compensation Laws

State **workers' compensation laws** establish an administrative procedure for compensating workers injured on the job. Instead of suing, an injured worker files a claim with the state agency or board that administers local workers' compensation claims.

All states require employers to provide workers' compensation insurance, but the specific rules vary by state. Most states have a state fund that employers pay into for workers' compensation coverage. Usually, employers can purchase insurance from a private insurer as an alternative to paying into the state fund. Most states also allow certain employers to be *self-insured*—that is, employers that show an ability to pay claims do not need to buy insurance.

No state covers all employees under its workers' compensation statute. Typically, domestic workers, agricultural workers, temporary employees, and employees of common carriers (companies that provide transportation services to the public) are excluded. Minors are covered.

Requirements for Receiving Workers' Compensation In general, the only requirements to recover benefits under state workers' compensation laws are:

1. The existence of an employment relationship.
2. An *accidental* injury that *occurred on the job or in the course of employment,* regardless of fault. (An injury that occurs while an employee is commuting to or from work usually is not covered because it did not occur on the job or in the course of employment.)

---

13. This was the United States Supreme Court's holding in *Ragsdale v. Wolverine World Wide, Inc.*, 535 U.S. 81, 122 S.Ct. 1155, 152 L.Ed.2d 167 (2002).
14. 29 U.S.C. Sections 553, 651–678.

An injured employee must notify her or his employer promptly (usually within thirty days of the accident). Generally, an employee must also file a workers' compensation claim within a certain period (sixty days to two years) from the time the injury is first noticed, rather than from the time of the accident.

Workers' Compensation versus Litigation If an employee accepts workers' compensation benefits, he or she may not sue for injuries caused by the employer's negligence. By barring lawsuits for negligence, workers' compensation laws also prevent employers from avoiding liability by using defenses, such as contributory negligence or assumption of risk. A worker may sue an employer who *intentionally* injures the worker, however.

34–4c Income Security

Federal and state governments participate in insurance programs designed to protect employees and their families from the financial impact of retirement, disability, death, hospitalization, and unemployment. The key federal law on this subject is the Social Security Act.[15]

Social Security The Social Security Act provides for old-age (retirement), survivors', and disability insurance. The act is therefore often referred to as OASDI. Retired workers who are covered by Social Security receive monthly payments from the Social Security Administration, which administers the Social Security Act. Social Security benefits are fixed by statute but increase automatically with increases in the cost of living.

Medicare Medicare is a federal government health-insurance program administered by the Social Security Administration for people sixty-five years of age and older and for some under age sixty-five who are disabled. It originally had two parts, one pertaining to hospital costs and the other to nonhospital medical costs, such as visits to physicians' offices. It now offers additional coverage options and a prescription-drug plan. People who have Medicare hospital insurance can obtain additional federal medical insurance if they pay monthly premiums.

Tax Contributions Under the Federal Insurance Contributions Act (FICA),[16] both employers and employees contribute to Social Security and Medicare, although the contributions are determined differently. The employer withholds the employee's FICA contributions from the employee's wages and ordinarily matches the contributions.

For Social Security, the basis for the contributions is the employee's annual wage base—the maximum amount of the employee's wages that is subject to the tax. As of 2016, the maximum amount subject to the tax was $118,500, and the tax rate was 12.4 percent.

The Medicare tax rate is 2.9 percent. Unlike Social Security, Medicare has no cap on the amount of wages subject to the tax. So even if an employee's salary is well above the cap for Social Security, he or she will still owe Medicare tax on the total earned income.

For Social Security and Medicare together, typically the employer and the employee each pay 7.65 percent. This is equivalent to 6.2 percent (half of 12.4 percent) for Social Security plus 1.45 percent (half of 2.9 percent) for Medicare up to the maximum wage base. Any earned income above that threshold is taxed only for Medicare. Self-employed persons pay both the employer's and the employee's portions of the Social Security and Medicare taxes.

Under the Affordable Care Act, high-income earners are subject to an additional Medicare tax of 3.8 percent on most investment income. This additional tax applies to single wage earners making more than $200,000 and married couples making more than $250,000.

Private Retirement Plans The major federal statute that regulates employee retirement plans is the Employee Retirement Income Security Act (ERISA).[17] This act empowers a branch of the U.S. Department of Labor to enforce its provisions governing employers that have private pension funds for their employees. ERISA does *not* require an employer to establish a pension plan. When a plan exists, however, ERISA provides standards for its management.

ERISA created the Pension Benefit Guaranty Corporation (PBGC), an independent federal agency, to provide timely and uninterrupted payment of voluntary private pension benefits. The pension plans pay annual insurance premiums (at set rates adjusted for inflation) to the PBGC, which then pays benefits to participants in the event that a plan is unable to do so.

A key provision of ERISA concerns vesting. **Vesting** gives an employee a legal right to receive pension benefits when she or he stops working. Before ERISA was enacted, some employees who had worked for companies for many years received no pension benefits when their employment terminated because those benefits had not vested. Under ERISA, generally all employee contributions to pension plans vest immediately. Employee

---

15. 42 U.S.C. Sections 301–1397e.
16. 26 U.S.C. Sections 3101–3125.

17. 29 U.S.C. Sections 1001 *et seq.*

rights to employer contributions vest after five years of employment.

Unemployment Insurance The Federal Unemployment Tax Act (FUTA)[18] created a state-administered system that provides unemployment compensation to eligible individuals who have lost their jobs. The FUTA and state laws require employers that fall under the provisions of the act to pay unemployment taxes at regular intervals. The proceeds from these taxes are then paid out to qualified unemployed workers.

To be eligible for unemployment compensation, a worker must be willing and able to work. Workers who have been fired for misconduct or who have voluntarily left their jobs are not eligible for benefits. Normally, workers must be actively seeking employment to continue receiving benefits.

■ **EXAMPLE 34.7** Martha works for Baily Snowboards in Vermont. One day at work, Martha receives a text from her son saying that he has been taken to the hospital. Martha rushes to the hospital and does not return to work for several days. Bailey hires someone else for Martha's position, and Martha files for unemployment benefits. Martha's claim will be denied because she left her job voluntarily and made no effort to maintain contact with her employer. ■

COBRA The Consolidated Omnibus Budget Reconciliation Act (COBRA)[19] enables employees to continue, for a limited time, their health-care coverage after they are no longer eligible for group health-insurance plans. The workers—not the employers—pay the premiums for the continued coverage.

COBRA prohibits an employer from eliminating a worker's medical, vision, or dental insurance when the worker's employment is terminated or when a reduction in the worker's hours would affect coverage. Termination of employment may be voluntary or involuntary. Only workers fired for gross misconduct are excluded from protection. Employers, with some exceptions, must inform employees of COBRA's provisions before the termination or reduction of work hours.

A worker has sixty days (from the date that the group coverage would stop) to decide whether to continue with the employer's group insurance plan. If the worker chooses to continue coverage, the employer is obligated to keep the policy active for up to eighteen months (twenty-nine months if the worker is disabled). The coverage must be the same as that provided to the worker

(and his or her family members) prior to the termination or reduction of work. An employer that does not comply with COBRA risks substantial penalties, including a tax of up to 10 percent of the annual cost of the group plan or $500,000, whichever is less.

Employer-Sponsored Group Health Plans The Health Insurance Portability and Accountability Act (HIPAA)[20] contains provisions that affect employer-sponsored group health plans. For instance, HIPAA restricts the manner in which employers collect, use, and disclose the health information of employees and their families. Employers must designate privacy officials, distribute privacy notices, and train employees to ensure that employees' health information is not disclosed to unauthorized parties.

Failure to comply with HIPAA regulations can result in civil penalties of up to $100 per person per violation (with a cap of $25,000 per year). Employers are also subject to criminal prosecution for certain types of HIPAA violations. An employer can face up to $250,000 in criminal fines and imprisonment for up to ten years if convicted.

Affordable Care Act The Affordable Care Act[21] (commonly referred to as Obamacare) requires most employers with fifty or more full-time employees to offer health-insurance benefits. Under the act, any business offering health benefits to its employees (even if not legally required to do so) may be eligible for tax credits of up to 35 percent to offset the costs.

An employer who fails to provide health benefits as required under the statute can be fined up to $2,000 for each employee after the first thirty people. (This is known as the 50/30 rule: employers with fifty employees must provide insurance, and those failing to do so will be fined for each employee after the first thirty.) An employer who offers a plan that costs an employee more than 9.5 percent of the employee's income may be assessed a penalty.

34–5 Employee Privacy Rights

Concerns about the privacy rights of employees have arisen as employers have purportedly used invasive tactics to monitor and screen workers. Perhaps the greatest privacy concern in employment today involves electronic monitoring of employees' activities.

---

18. 26 U.S.C. Sections 3301–3310.
19. 29 U.S.C. Sections 1161–1169.
20. 29 U.S.C. Sections 1181 *et seq.*
21. Pub. L. No. 111-148, 124 Stat. 119, March 23, 2010, codified in various sections of 42 U.S.C.

34–5a Electronic Monitoring

More than half of employers engage in some form of electronic monitoring of their employees. Many employers review employees' e-mail, as well as their social media posts and other Internet messages. Employers may also make video recordings of their employees at work, record their telephone conversations, and listen to their voice mail.

Employee Privacy Protection Employees of private (nongovernment) employers have some privacy protection under tort law and state constitutions. In addition, state and federal statutes may limit an employer's conduct in certain respects. For instance, the Electronic Communications Privacy Act prohibits employers from intercepting an employee's personal electronic communications unless they are made on devices and systems furnished by the employer.

Nonetheless, employers do have considerable leeway to monitor employees in the workplace. In addition, private employers generally are free to use filtering software to block access to certain Web sites, such as sites containing sexually explicit images. The First Amendment's protection of free speech prevents only *government employers* from restraining speech by blocking Web sites.

Reasonable Expectation of Privacy When determining whether an employer should be held liable for violating an employee's privacy rights, the courts generally weigh the employer's interests against the employee's reasonable expectation of privacy. Normally, if employees have been informed that their communications are being monitored, they cannot reasonably expect those interactions to be private. In addition, a court will typically hold that employees do not have a reasonable expectation of privacy when using a system (such as an e-mail system) provided by the employer.

If employees are *not* informed that certain communications are being monitored, the employer may be held liable for invading their privacy. Most employers that engage in electronic monitoring notify their employees about the monitoring. Nevertheless, a general policy may not sufficiently protect an employer monitoring forms of communications that the policy fails to mention. For instance, notifying employees that their e-mails and phone calls may be monitored does not necessarily protect an employer who monitors social media posts or text messages.

34–5b Other Types of Monitoring

In addition to monitoring their employees' online activities, employers also engage in other types of employee screening and monitoring. The practices discussed next have often been challenged as violations of employee privacy rights.

Lie-Detector Tests At one time, many employers required employees or job applicants to take polygraph examinations (lie-detector tests). Today, the Employee Polygraph Protection Act[22] generally prohibits employers from requiring employees or job applicants to take lie-detector tests or suggesting or requesting that they do so. The act also restricts employers' ability to use or ask about the results of any lie-detector test or to take any negative employment action based on the results.

Certain employers are exempt from these prohibitions. Federal, state, and local government employers, and certain security service firms, may conduct polygraph tests. In addition, companies that manufacture and distribute controlled substances may perform lie-detector tests. Other employers may use polygraph tests when investigating losses attributable to theft, including embezzlement and the theft of trade secrets.

Drug Testing In the interests of public safety and to reduce unnecessary costs, many employers, including the government, require their employees to submit to drug testing.

Public Employers. Government (public) employers are constrained in drug testing by the Fourth Amendment to the U.S. Constitution, which prohibits unreasonable searches and seizures. Drug testing of public employees is allowed by statute for transportation workers, however. Courts normally uphold drug testing of certain employees when drug use in a particular job may threaten public safety. Also, when there is a reasonable basis for suspecting public employees of drug use, courts often find that drug testing does not violate the Fourth Amendment.

Private Employers. The Fourth Amendment does not apply to drug testing conducted by private employers. Hence, the privacy rights and drug testing of private-sector employees are governed by state law. Many states have statutes that allow drug testing by private employers but restrict when and how the testing may be performed. A collective bargaining agreement (discussed later in this chapter) may also provide protection against drug testing (or may authorize drug testing in certain conditions).

The permissibility of testing a private employee for drugs often hinges on whether the employer's testing was reasonable. Random drug tests and even "zero-tolerance"

---

22. 29 U.S.C. Sections 2001 *et seq.*

policies (which deny a "second chance" to employees who test positive for drugs) have been held to be reasonable. It is also reasonable to require employees of private employers who are under contract with the federal government to undergo standard background investigations to disclose potential drug use.[23]

34–6 Immigration Law

The United States did not have any laws restricting immigration until the late nineteenth century. Immigration law has become increasingly important in recent years, however. An estimated 12 million undocumented immigrants now live in the United States, and many of them came to find jobs. Because U.S. employers face serious penalties if they hire undocumented workers, it is necessary for businesspersons to understand immigration laws. The most important laws affecting immigration in the context of employment are the Immigration Reform and Control Act (IRCA)[24] and the Immigration Act.[25]

34–6a The Immigration Reform and Control Act (IRCA)

When the IRCA was enacted in 1986, it provided amnesty to certain groups of aliens living illegally in the United States at the time. It also established a system that sanctions employers that hire immigrants who lack work authorization.

The IRCA makes it illegal to hire, recruit, or refer for a fee someone not authorized to work in this country. Through Immigration and Customs Enforcement officers, the federal government conducts random compliance audits and engages in enforcement actions against employers who hire undocumented workers.

I-9 Employment Verification To comply with IRCA requirements, an employer must perform **I-9 verifications** for new hires, including those hired as "contractors" or "day workers" if they work under the employer's direct supervision. Form I-9, Employment Eligibility Verification, which is available from U.S. Citizenship and Immigration Services,[26] must be completed *within three*

days of a worker's commencement of employment. The three-day period allows the employer to check the form's accuracy and to review and verify documents establishing the prospective worker's identity and eligibility for employment in the United States.

Documentation Requirements The employer must declare, under penalty of perjury, that an employee produced documents establishing his or her identity and legal employability. A U.S. passport establishing the person's citizenship is acceptable documentation. So is a document authorizing a foreign citizen to work in the United States, such as a permanent resident card or an *Alien Registration Receipt.*

Most legal actions alleging violations of I-9 rules are brought against employees who provide false information or documentation. If the employee enters false information on the I-9 form or presents false documentation, the employer can fire the worker, who then may be subject to deportation. Nevertheless, employers must be honest when verifying an employee's documentation. If an employer "should have known" that the worker was unauthorized, the employer has violated the rules.

Enforcement U.S. Immigration and Customs Enforcement (ICE) is the largest investigative arm of the U.S. Department of Homeland Security. ICE has a general inspection program that conducts random compliance audits. Other audits may occur if the agency receives a written complaint alleging that an employer has committed violations. Government inspections include a review of an employer's file of I-9 forms. The government does not need a subpoena or a warrant to conduct such an inspection.

If an investigation reveals a possible violation, ICE will bring an administrative action and issue a Notice of Intent to Fine, which sets out the charges against the employer. The employer has a right to a hearing on the enforcement action if it files a request within thirty days. This hearing is conducted before an administrative law judge, and the employer has a right to counsel and to discovery. The typical defense in such actions is good faith or substantial compliance with the documentation provisions.

Penalties An employer who violates the law by hiring an unauthorized worker is subject to substantial penalties. The employer can be fined up to $2,200 for each unauthorized employee for a first offense, $5,000 per employee for a second offense, and up to $11,000 for subsequent offenses. Employers who have engaged in a "pattern or

---

23. *See National Aeronautics and Space Administration v. Nelson,* 562 U.S. 134, 131 S.Ct. 746, 178 L.Ed.2d 667 (2011).
24. 29 U.S.C. Section 1802.
25. This act amended various provisions of the Immigration and Nationality Act of 1952, 8 U.S.C. Sections 1101 *et seq.*
26. U.S. Citizenship and Immigration Services is a federal agency that is part of the U.S. Department of Homeland Security.

practice of violations" are subject to criminal penalties, which include additional fines and imprisonment for up to ten years. A company can also be barred from future government contracts.

In determining the penalty, ICE considers the seriousness of the violation (such as intentional falsification of documents) and the employer's past compliance. ICE regulations also identify factors that will mitigate (lessen) or aggravate (increase) the penalty under certain circumstances. An employer that cooperates in the investigation, for instance, may receive a lesser penalty than an uncooperative employer.

34–6b The Immigration Act

Often, U.S. businesses find that they cannot hire enough domestic workers with specialized skills. For this reason, U.S. immigration laws have long made provisions for businesses to hire specially qualified foreign workers.

The Immigration Act of 1990 placed caps on the number of visas (entry permits) that can be issued to immigrants each year, including employment-based visas. Employment-based visas may be classified as permanent (immigrant) or temporary (nonimmigrant). Employers who wish to hire workers with either type of visa must comply with detailed government regulations.[27]

I-551 Alien Registration Receipts A company seeking to hire a noncitizen worker may do so if the worker is self-authorized. To be self-authorized, a worker must either be a lawful permanent resident or have a valid temporary Employment Authorization Document. A lawful permanent resident can prove his or her status to an employer by presenting an **I-551 Alien Registration Receipt,** known as a green card, or a properly stamped foreign passport.

Many immigrant workers are not already self-authorized, and an employer that wishes to hire them can attempt to obtain labor certification, or green cards, for them. A limited number of new green cards are issued each year. A green card can be obtained only for a person who is being hired for a permanent, full-time position. (A separate authorization system provides for the temporary entry and hiring of nonimmigrant visa workers.)

To gain authorization for hiring a foreign worker, an employer must show that no U.S. worker is qualified, willing, and able to take the job. The government has detailed regulations governing the advertising of positions as well as the certification process. Any U.S. applicants who meet the stated job qualifications must be interviewed for the position. The employer must also be able to show that the qualifications required for the job are a business necessity.

The H-1B Visa Program The most common and controversial visa program today is the H-1B visa system. To obtain an H1-B visa, the potential employee must be qualified in a "specialty occupation," meaning that the individual has highly specialized knowledge and has attained a bachelor's or higher degree or its equivalent. Individuals with H-1B visas can stay in the United States for three to six years and can work only for the sponsoring employer.

The recipients of these visas include numerous high-tech workers. A maximum of sixty-five thousand H-1B visas are set aside each year for new immigrants.[28] That limit is typically reached within the first few weeks of the year. Consequently, tech companies often complain that Congress needs to expand the number of H-1B visas available, to encourage the best and the brightest minds to work in the United States.

Critics of the H-1B visa program, however, believe that employers are sometimes using it to replace American workers with lower-paid foreign labor. For instance, Southern California Edison let go nearly five hundred workers from its information technology (IT) department in 2015. Shortly after that, allegations surfaced that the company had illegally replaced these employees with workers with H-1B visas, leading to a government investigation.

Labor Certification An employer who wishes to submit an H-1B application must first file a Labor Certification application on a form known as ETA 9035. The employer must agree to provide a wage level at least equal to the wages offered to other individuals with similar experience and qualifications. The employer must also show that the hiring will not adversely affect other workers similarly employed. The employer is required to inform U.S. workers of the intent to hire a foreign worker by posting the form. The U.S. Department of Labor reviews the applications and may reject them for omissions or inaccuracies.

H-2, O, L, and E Visas Other specialty temporary visas are available for other categories of employees. H-2 visas provide for workers performing agricultural labor of a seasonal nature. O visas provide entry for persons who

---

27. The most relevant regulations can be found at 20 C.F.R. Section 655 (for temporary employment) and 20 C.F.R. Section 656 (for permanent employment).

28. Immigration reform proposals generally raise this annual limit on H-1B visas to more than one hundred thousand.

have "extraordinary ability in the sciences, arts, education, business or athletics which has been demonstrated by sustained national or international acclaim." L visas allow a company's foreign managers or executives to work inside the United States. E visas permit the entry of certain foreign investors or entrepreneurs.

34–6c State Immigration Legislation

Until 2010, federal law exclusively governed immigration and the treatment of illegal immigrants. Then Arizona enacted a law that required Arizona law enforcement officials to identify and charge immigrants in Arizona who were there illegally, potentially leading to the immigrants' deportation. Among other things, that law required immigrants to carry their papers at all times and allowed police to check a person's immigration status during any law enforcement action.

Arizona's law was challenged in *Arizona v. United States,*[29] which reached the United States Supreme Court. The Court upheld the controversial "show-me-your-papers" provision, which requires police to check the immigration status of persons stopped for other violations. All other provisions of Arizona's law were struck down as unconstitutional violations of the supremacy clause.

The fact that the Supreme Court did not strike down all parts of Arizona's immigration law opened the door for other states to enact immigration legislation, and many states have done so. The Court's decision does set limits, however. Although states may require immigrants to show their papers if stopped by law enforcement for another reason, they may not make it a crime to fail to carry documentation. States also cannot authorize law enforcement to arrest anyone based solely on a reasonable suspicion that the person is in the country illegally.

34–7 Labor Unions

In the 1930s, in addition to wage and hour laws, Congress also enacted the first of several labor laws. These laws protect employees' rights to join labor unions, to bargain with management over the terms and conditions of employment, and to conduct strikes.

34–7a Federal Labor Laws

Federal labor laws governing union-employer relations have developed considerably since the first law was enacted in 1932. Initially, the laws were concerned with protecting the rights and interests of workers. Subsequent legislation placed some restraints on unions and granted rights to employers. We look here at four major federal statutes regulating union-employer relations.

Norris-LaGuardia Act Congress protected peaceful strikes, picketing, and boycotts in 1932 in the Norris-LaGuardia Act.[30] The statute restricted the power of federal courts to issue injunctions against unions engaged in peaceful strikes. In effect, this act declared a national policy permitting employees to organize.

National Labor Relations Act One of the foremost statutes regulating labor is the 1935 National Labor Relations Act (NLRA).[31] This act established the rights of employees to engage in collective bargaining and to strike.

Unfair Labor Practices. The NLRA specifically defined a number of employer practices as unfair to labor:

1. Interference with the efforts of employees to form, join, or assist labor organizations or to engage in concerted activities for their mutual aid or protection.
2. An employer's domination of a labor organization or contribution of financial or other support to it.
3. Discrimination in the hiring of or the awarding of tenure to employees for reason of union affiliation.
4. Discrimination against employees for filing charges under the act or giving testimony under the act.
5. Refusal to bargain collectively with the duly designated representative of the employees.

The National Labor Relations Board. The NLRA created the National Labor Relations Board (NLRB) to oversee union elections and to prevent employers from engaging in unfair and illegal union activities and unfair labor practices.

The NLRB has the authority to investigate employees' charges of unfair labor practices and to file complaints against employers in response to these charges. When violations are found, the NLRB may issue a **cease-and-desist order** compelling the employer to stop engaging in the unfair practices. Cease-and-desist orders can be enforced by a federal appellate court if necessary. After the NLRB rules on claims of unfair labor practices, its decision may be appealed to a federal court.

■ **CASE IN POINT 34.8** Roundy's, Inc., which operates a chain of stores in Wisconsin, became involved in a dispute with a local construction union. When union

---

29. ___ U.S. ___, 132 S.Ct. 2492, 183 L.Ed.2d 351 (2012).

30. 29 U.S.C. Sections 101–110, 113–115.
31. 20 U.S.C. Sections 151–169.

members started distributing "extremely unflattering" flyers outside the stores, Roundy's ejected them from the property. The NLRB filed a complaint against Roundy's for unfair labor practices. An administrative law judge ruled that Roundy's had violated the law by discriminating against the union, and a federal appellate court affirmed. It is an unfair labor practice for an employer to prohibit union members from distributing flyers outside a store when it allows nonunion members to do so.[32] ∎

Good Faith Bargaining. Under the NLRA, employers and unions have a duty to bargain in good faith. Bargaining over certain subjects is mandatory, and a party's refusal to bargain over these subjects is an unfair labor practice that can be reported to the NLRB. For instance, bargaining is mandatory for subjects relating to wages or working hours.

Workers Protected by the NLRA. To be protected under the NLRA, an individual must be an employee or a job applicant. (If job applicants were not covered, the NLRA's ban on discrimination in regard to hiring would mean little.) Additionally, individuals who are hired by a union to organize a company (union organizers) are to be considered employees of the company for NLRA purposes.[33]

Even a temporary worker hired through an employment agency might qualify for protection under the NLRA. ∎ **CASE IN POINT 34.9** Matthew Faush was an African American employee of Labor Ready, which provides temporary employees to businesses. Faush was assigned to a job stocking shelves at a Tuesday Morning store in Pennsylvania. After he was fired by Tuesday Morning, Faush filed a suit alleging discrimination. Tuesday Morning argued that Faush was not its employee. A federal court, however, found that the NLRA's protections may extend to temporary workers and that Faush was entitled to a trial.[34] ∎

Labor-Management Relations Act The Labor-Management Relations Act (LMRA or Taft-Hartley Act) of 1947[35] was passed to prohibit certain unfair union practices. For instance, the act outlawed the **closed shop**—a firm that requires union membership as a condition of employment. The act preserved the legality of the union shop, however. A **union shop** does not require union membership as a prerequisite for employment but can, and usually does, require that workers join the union after a specified time on the job.

The LMRA also prohibited unions from refusing to bargain with employers, engaging in certain types of picketing, and *featherbedding* (causing employers to hire more employees than necessary). In addition, the act allowed individual states to pass **right-to-work laws**—laws making it illegal for union membership to be required for *continued* employment in any establishment. Thus, union shops are technically illegal in the twenty-seven states that have right-to-work laws.

Labor-Management Reporting and Disclosure Act The Labor-Management Reporting and Disclosure Act (LMRDA)[36] established an employee bill of rights and reporting requirements for union activities. The act also outlawed **hot-cargo agreements,** in which employers voluntarily agree with unions not to handle, use, or deal in goods of other employers produced by nonunion employees.

The LMRDA strictly regulates unions' internal business procedures, including elections. For instance, it requires unions to hold regularly scheduled elections of officers using secret ballots. Former convicts are prohibited from holding union office. Moreover, union officials are accountable for union property and funds. Members have the right to attend and to participate in union meetings, to nominate officers, and to vote in most union proceedings.

34-7b Union Organization

Typically, the first step in organizing a union at a particular firm is to have the workers sign authorization cards. An **authorization card** usually states that the worker desires to have a certain union, such as the United Auto Workers, represent the workforce. If a majority of the workers sign authorization cards, the union organizers (unionizers) present the cards to the employer and ask for formal recognition of the union.

The employer is not required to recognize the union at this point in the process, but it may do so voluntarily on a showing of majority support. (Under pro-labor legislation proposed repeatedly, the employer would have to recognize the union as soon as a majority of the workers had signed authorization cards—without holding an election.)[37]

Union Elections If the employer refuses to voluntarily recognize the union—or if less than a majority of the workers sign authorization cards—the union organizers

---

32. *Roundy's, Inc. v. NLRB,* 647 F.3d 638 (7th Cir. 2012).
33. See the United States Supreme Court's landmark decision in *NLRB v. Town & Country Electric, Inc.,* 516 U.S. 85, 116 S.Ct. 450, 133 L.Ed.2d 371 (1995).
34. *Faush v. Tuesday Morning, Inc.,* 88 F.3d 208 (3d Cir. 2015).
35. 29 U.S.C. Sections 141 *et seq.*

36. 29 U.S.C. Sections 401 *et seq.*
37. The proposed legislation is the Employee Free Choice Act (or Card Check Bill).

can petition for an election. The organizers present the authorization cards to the NLRB with a petition to hold an election on unionization. For an election to be held, they must demonstrate that at least 30 percent of the workers to be represented support a union or an election.

Appropriate Bargaining Unit. Not every group of workers can form a single union. The proposed union must represent an *appropriate bargaining unit*. One key requirement is a *mutuality of interest* among all the workers to be represented by the union. Factors considered in determining whether there is a mutuality of interest include the similarity of the jobs of the workers to be unionized and their physical location.

New NLRB Rules Expedite Elections. New NLRB rules that took effect in 2015 significantly reduce the time between the filing of a petition and the ensuing election. As a result, the time before an election is held has changed from an average of thirty-eight days to as little as ten days after the filing. This change favors unions because it gives employers less time to respond to organizing campaigns, which unions often spend months preparing.

The NLRB now requires that a company hold a pre-election hearing within eight days after it receives a petition for an organizing election. On the day before the hearing, the company must also submit a "statement of position" laying out every argument it intends to make against the union. Any argument that the company does not include in its position paper can be excluded from evidence at the hearing. Once the hearing is held, an election can be scheduled right away.

Voting. If an election is held, the NLRB supervises the election and ensures secret voting and voter eligibility. If the proposed union receives majority support in a fair election, the NLRB certifies the union as the bargaining representative for the employees.

Union Election Campaigns   Many disputes between labor and management arise during union election campaigns. Generally, the employer has control over unionizing activities that take place on company property and during working hours. Thus, the employer may limit the campaign activities of union supporters as long as it has a legitimate business reason for doing so. The employer may also reasonably limit when and where union solicitation may occur in the workplace, provided that the employer is not discriminating against the union. (Can union organizers use company e-mail during campaigns? See this chapter's *Managerial Strategy* feature for a discussion of this topic.)

■ **EXAMPLE 34.10**   A union is seeking to organize clerks at a department store owned by Amanti Enterprises. Amanti can prohibit all union solicitation in areas of the store open to the public because the unionizing activities could interfere with the store's business. It can also restrict union-related activities to coffee breaks and lunch hours. If Amanti allows solicitation for charitable causes in the workplace, however, it may not prohibit union solicitation. ■

An employer may campaign among its workers against the union, but the NLRB carefully monitors and regulates the tactics used by management. If the employer issues threats ("If the union wins, you'll all be fired") or engages in other unfair labor practices, the NLRB may certify the union even though the union lost the election. Alternatively, the NLRB may ask a court to order a new election.

Whether an employer violated its employees' rights under the National Labor Relations Act during a union election campaign was at issue in the following case.

Case Analysis 34.3

Contemporary Cars, Inc. v. National Labor Relations Board

United States Court of Appeals, Seventh Circuit, 814 F.3d 859 (2016).

In the Language of the Court
HAMILTON, Circuit Judge.
  * * * *
    * * * Contemporary Cars, Inc., * * * sells and services cars in Maitland, Florida. Bob Berryhill, the dealership's general manager, is responsible for the dealership's overall operations. * * * AutoNation owns the dealership, as well

as over 200 other dealerships throughout the United States.
    This case focuses on the dealership's service department [which the dealership had previously split into three teams].
    * * * The International Association of Machinists began a campaign * * * to organize the service technicians.
    * * * The technicians talked among

themselves and held off-site meetings.
  * * * *
    * * * The union filed its representation petition. The [National Labor Relations Board] approved the proposed bargaining unit, and an election was scheduled.
    In the weeks before the election, Berryhill and AutoNation vice president

Case 34.3 Continued

* * * Brian Davis held group [and individual] meetings [with the technicians]. * * * One week before the election, * * * Berryhill * * * announced that the dealership was working on fixing problems the technicians had and that he was replacing two team leaders, [Andre] Grobler and Oudit Manbahal, with new team leaders.

* * * Technician Anthony Roberts * * * was then playing a leading role in the union organizing. * * * About a week before the union election, the dealership laid off Roberts, though Roberts had a higher skill rating, more hours, and more seniority than many other technicians.

* * * *

* * * The technicians voted in favor of unionizing.

* * * After the election, the dealership challenged the certification of the union as the exclusive representative of a bargaining unit consisting of service technicians. * * * The [National Labor Relations] Board affirmed the certification.

* * * The Board * * * filed a complaint alleging that the dealership and AutoNation had violated * * * the National Labor Relations Act. * * * An administrative law judge found * * * that the dealership and AutoNation had indeed violated the Act by interfering with their employees' protected rights to engage in concerted activity and to organize a union [and] by firing Anthony Roberts due to anti-union animus [hostility]. [The judge ordered the dealership to cease its interference with its employees' rights and to reinstate Roberts. The judge also ordered AutoNation to post a notice at all of its dealerships that it was rescinding the no-solicitation rule.] The Board affirmed the * * * order.

The dealership and AutoNation petitioned [the U.S. Court of Appeals for Seventh Circuit] for judicial review. [The NLRB cross-petitioned for enforcement of the order.]

* * * *

The administrative law judge found, and the Board affirmed, that the dealership and AutoNation in a number of

instances acted unlawfully to frustrate their employees' protected rights to engage in concerted activity and to organize a union.

* * * *

* * * The dealership violated [the Act] in the run-up to the election by coercively creating an impression of surveillance of union activity, interrogating employees about union activity, and soliciting and promising to remedy employee grievances.

* * * *

[Team Leader] Grobler created a coercive impression of surveillance when he commented on technician Juan Cazorla's attendance of union meetings. * * * Grobler asked [Cazorla] why he was in such a rush to leave work * * *, suggesting that Cazorla had "that meeting" to go to. Cazorla pretended not to know what Grobler was talking about, although he was in fact rushing to get to a union meeting. Again [on a different occasion] Grobler commented to Cazorla that he had "better rush" since he had a meeting * * *. It would have been reasonable for Cazorla to infer from Grobler's comments that his union activities were under management surveillance.

* * * *

* * * Berryhill coercively interrogated employees [when he] called them individually into his office and asked them about union activity. The dealership's service director was also present. * * * The setting of the meetings in Berryhill's office, Berryhill's and the director's positions of authority, and the fact that each technician was alone and outnumbered by managers all support the finding of coercion.

* * * *

* * * At the * * * meetings, Berryhill asked the technicians how the dealership could improve. * * * Berryhill [stated] that he was "working on" the problems and "in progress" on the solutions. * * * The * * * meetings also included inquiries about the union effort. * * * This was an effort to frustrate the union organizing drive by soliciting and at least implicitly promising to adjust grievances.

* * * *

* * * AutoNation vice president * * * Davis coercively interrogated a * * * technician, Tumeshwar Persaud * * *. Davis * * * asked him how he felt about the union election. * * * The question forced Persaud, who had not previously disclosed his union support, either to disclose his own union sympathies or to report on his perception of his fellow employees' union support.

* * * Davis held a meeting with employees at which he solicited employee complaints and, upon hearing that management had been unresponsive to employee complaints in the past, said that employees could call him or talk to him at any time. This meeting was part of a series of * * * meetings that management held in the run-up to the union election. * * * Davis was implicitly promising to remedy grievances with the goal of frustrating the union effort.

* * * *

* * * AutoNation * * * promulgated [publicized] an overly broad no-solicitation policy in the employee handbook used at all of its facilities. * * * AutoNation's policy prohibited any solicitation on AutoNation property at any time. * * * *The policy * * * amounted to an unfair labor practice because of the likelihood it would chill protected concerted activity.* [Emphasis added.]

* * * *

* * * The dealership's discharge of Anthony Roberts * * * a week before the election was motivated by anti-union animus.

* * * *

* * * Berryhill's identification of Roberts as a troublemaker and instigator of the organizational campaign established that anti-union animus was a substantial factor motivating Roberts's layoff. * * * The dealership's stated reason for firing Roberts—that he lacked sufficient electronic diagnostic skills—failed to establish that Roberts would have been laid off in the absence of anti-union animus. * * * Roberts was more productive and had a higher skill rating than many technicians who were retained.

Case 34.3 Continues

Case 34.3 Continued

* * * *

Substantial evidence and a reasonable basis in law support the Board's order and the administrative law judge's order to the extent affirmed by the Board. We DENY the dealership and AutoNation's petition for review and ENFORCE the Board's order in its entirety.

Legal Reasoning Questions

1. What might the dealership have asserted in defense to the charge that its actions violated its employees' rights?

2. After the election but before the union was certified, the dealership laid off four technicians and cut others' pay without bargaining with the union, claiming economic hard times. Did these steps constitute an unfair labor practice? Discuss.

3. What could the employer have done to avoid the charge in this case?

MANAGERIAL STRATEGY — Union Organizing Using a Company's E-Mail System

When union organizers start an organizing drive, there are certain restrictions on what they can do, particularly within the workplace. Both employers and employees must comply with Section 7 of the National Labor Relations Act (NLRA).

Protected Concerted Activities

Under Section 7, employees have certain rights to communicate among themselves. Section 7 states, "Employees shall have the right to self-organization, . . . and to engage in other concerted activities for the purpose of collective bargaining or other mutual aid or protection. . . ."

What about communication via e-mail? Can union organizers use a company-operated e-mail system for organizing purposes? Companies typically provide e-mail systems so that employees can communicate with outsiders and among themselves as part of their jobs. Generally, company policies have prohibited the use of company-owned and -operated e-mail systems for other than job-related communications. Starting in the early 2000s, some union organizers challenged this prohibition.

The NLRB's Perspective Evolves

The first major case concerning this issue was decided by the National Labor Relations Board (NLRB) in 2007.[a] The NLRB allowed an employer's written policy that prohibited the use of a company-provided e-mail system for non-job-related solicitations. This decision was affirmed in relevant part by a federal court two years later.[b]

In late 2014, the NLRB reversed its 2007 position. "We decide today that employee use of e-mail for statutorily protected communications on non-working time must presumptively be permitted by employers who have chosen to give employees access to their e-mail systems."[c] The NLRB argued that its 2007 decision had failed to adequately protect "employees' rights under the NLRA." The board also stated that it had a responsibility "to adapt the Act to the changing patterns of industrial life."

The new rules are clear. Once an organizing election is scheduled, a company must turn over all telephone numbers and home and e-mail addresses of the company's employees to union organizers within two days. The organizers can then communicate with employees via the company's e-mail system.

Business Questions

1. *Employees meeting around the water cooler or coffee machine have always had the right to discuss work-related matters. Is an employer-provided e-mail system or social media outlet simply a digital water cooler? Why or why not?*

2. *If your company instituted a policy stating that employees should "think carefully about 'friending' co-workers," would that policy be lawful? Why or why not?*

---

a. *Register Guard*, 351 NLRB 1110 (2007).
b. *Guard Publishing v. NLRB*, 571 F.3d 53 (D.C. Cir. 2009).

c. *Purple Communications, Inc. and Communication Workers of America, AFL-CIO*, Cases 21-CA-095151, 21-RC-091531, and 21-RC-091584, March 16, 2015.

34-7c Collective Bargaining

If the NLRB certifies the union, the union becomes the *exclusive bargaining representative* of the workers. The central legal right of a union is to engage in collective bargaining on the members' behalf. **Collective bargaining** is the process by which labor and management negotiate the terms and conditions of employment. Collective bargaining allows the representatives elected by union members to speak on behalf of the members at the bargaining table.

Terms and Conditions of Employment Wages, hours of work, and certain other conditions of employment may be discussed during collective bargaining sessions. For instance, subjects for negotiation may include workplace safety, employee discounts, health-care plans, pension funds, and apprentice and scholarship programs.

Good Faith Bargaining Once an employer and a union sit down at the conference table, they must negotiate in good faith and make a reasonable effort to come to an agreement. They are not obligated to reach an agreement. They must, however, approach the negotiations with the idea that an agreement is possible. Both parties may engage in hard bargaining, but the bargaining process itself must be geared to reaching a compromise—not avoiding a compromise.

Although good faith is a matter of subjective intent, a party's actions can be used to evaluate the party's good or bad faith. Excessive use of delaying tactics may be proof of bad faith, for instance, as is insistence on obviously unreasonable contract terms.

If an employer (or a union) refuses to bargain in good faith without justification, it has committed an unfair labor practice. Exhibit 34–1 illustrates some differences between good faith and bad faith bargaining.

34-7d Strikes

Even when labor and management have bargained in good faith, they may be unable to reach a final agreement. When extensive collective bargaining has been conducted and an impasse results, the union may call a strike against the employer to pressure it into making concessions.

In a **strike,** the unionized employees leave their jobs and refuse to work. The workers also typically picket the workplace, standing outside the facility with signs stating their complaints.

A strike is an extreme action. Striking workers lose their rights to be paid, and management loses production and may lose customers when orders cannot be filled. Labor law regulates the circumstances and conduct of strikes.

Most strikes take the form of "economic strikes," which are initiated because the union wants a better contract. ■ **EXAMPLE 34.11** Teachers in Eagle Point, Oregon, engage in an economic strike after contract

EXHIBIT 34–1 Good Faith versus Bad Faith in Collective Bargaining

GOOD FAITH BARGAINING	BAD FAITH BARGAINING
1. Negotiating with the belief that an agreement is possible	1. Excessive delaying tactics
2. Seriously considering the other side's positions	2. Insistence on unreasonable contract terms
3. Making reasonable proposals	3. Rejecting a proposal without offering a counterproposal
4. Being willing to compromise	4. Engaging in a campaign among workers to undermine the union
5. Sending bargainers who have the authority to enter into agreements for the company	5. Constantly shifting positions on disputed contract terms
	6. Sending bargainers who lack authority to commit the company to a contract

negotiations with the school district fail to bring an agreement on pay, working hours, and subcontracting jobs. The unionized teachers picket outside the school building. Classes are canceled for a few weeks until the district can find substitute teachers who will fill in during the strike. ■

The Right to Strike The right to strike is guaranteed by the NLRA, within limits. Strike activities, such as picketing, are protected by the free speech guarantee of the First Amendment to the U.S. Constitution. Persons who are not employees have a right to participate in picketing an employer. The NLRA also gives workers the right to refuse to cross a picket line of fellow workers engaged in a lawful strike. Employers are permitted to hire replacement workers to substitute for the striking workers.

Illegal Strikes In the following situations, the conduct of the strikers may cause the strikes to be illegal:

1. *Violent strikes.* The use of violence (including the threat of violence) against management employees or substitute workers is illegal.
2. *Massed picketing.* If the strikers form a barrier and deny management or other nonunion workers access to the plant, the strike is illegal.
3. *Sit-down strikes.* Strikes in which employees simply stay in the plant without working are illegal.
4. *No-strike clause.* A strike may be illegal if it contravenes a no-strike clause that was in the previous collective bargaining agreement between the employer and the union.
5. *Secondary boycotts.* A **secondary boycott** is an illegal strike that is directed against someone other than the strikers' employer, such as companies that sell materials to the employer. ■ **EXAMPLE 34.12** The unionized workers of SemiCo go out on strike. To increase their economic leverage, the workers picket the leading suppliers and customers of SemiCo in an attempt to hurt the company's business. SemiCo is considered the primary employer, and its suppliers and customers are considered secondary employers. Picketing of the suppliers or customers is a secondary boycott. ■
6. *Wildcat strikes.* A wildcat strike occurs when a small number of workers, perhaps dissatisfied with a union's representation, call their own strike. The union is the exclusive bargaining representative of a group of workers, and only the union can call a strike. Therefore, a wildcat strike, unauthorized by the certified union, is illegal.

After a Strike Ends In a typical strike, the employer has a right to hire permanent replacements during the strike. The employer need not terminate the replacement workers when the economic strikers seek to return to work. In other words, striking workers are not guaranteed the right to return to their jobs after the strike if satisfactory replacement workers have been found.

If the employer has not hired replacement workers to fill the strikers' positions, however, then the employer must rehire the economic strikers to fill any vacancies. Employers may not discriminate against former economic strikers, and those who are rehired retain their seniority rights.

34–7e Lockouts

Lockouts are the employer's counterpart to the workers' right to strike. A **lockout** occurs when the employer shuts down to prevent employees from working. Lockouts usually are used when the employer believes that a strike is imminent or the parties have reached a stalemate in collective bargaining.

■ **EXAMPLE 34.13** Owners of the teams in the National Football League (NFL) imposed a lockout on the NFL players' union in 2011 after negotiations on a new collective bargaining agreement broke down. The NFL owners had proposed to reduce players' salaries and extend the season by two games because of decreased profits due to the struggling economy. A settlement was reached before the start of the 2011 football season. The players accepted a somewhat smaller proportion of the revenue generated in exchange for better working conditions and more retirement benefits. The owners agreed to keep the same number of games per season.

The owners of the teams in the National Basketball Association (NBA) also locked out their players in 2011 after the two sides failed to reach a collective bargaining agreement. The dispute involved the division of revenue and a salary cap. During the lockout, the players could not access NBA facilities, trainers, or staff, and the owners could not trade, sign, or contract with players. The lockout lasted 161 days and resulted in the cancellation of all preseason games and several weeks of regular season games. ■

Some lockouts are illegal. An employer may not use a lockout as a tool to break the union and pressure employees into decertification, which occurs when union members vote to dissociate from the union. An employer must be able to show some economic justification for the lockout.

Reviewing: Employment, Immigration, and Labor Law

Rick Saldona began working as a traveling salesperson for Aimer Winery in 2008. Sales constituted 90 percent of Saldona's work time. Saldona worked an average of fifty hours per week but received no overtime pay. In June 2018, Saldona's new supervisor, Caesar Braxton, claimed that Saldona had been inflating his reported sales calls and required Saldona to submit to a polygraph test. Saldona reported Braxton to the U.S. Department of Labor, which prohibited Aimer from requiring Saldona to take a polygraph test for this purpose.

In August 2018, Saldona's wife, Venita, fell from a ladder and sustained a head injury while employed as a full-time agricultural harvester. Saldona presented Aimer's Human Resources Department with a letter from his wife's physician indicating that she would need daily care for several months, and Saldona took leave until December 2018. Aimer had sixty-three employees at that time. When Saldona returned to Aimer, he was informed that his position had been eliminated because his sales territory had been combined with an adjacent territory. Using the information presented in the chapter, answer the following questions.

1. Would Saldona have been legally entitled to receive overtime pay at a higher rate? Why or why not?
2. What is the maximum length of time Saldona would have been allowed to take leave to care for his injured spouse?
3. Under what circumstances would Aimer have been allowed to require an employee to take a polygraph test?
4. Would Aimer likely be able to avoid reinstating Saldona under the *key employee* exception? Why or why not?

Debate This . . .   *The U.S. labor market is highly competitive, so state and federal laws that require overtime pay are unnecessary and should be abolished.*

Terms and Concepts

authorization card 655	I-551 Alien Registration	strike 659
cease-and-desist order 654	Receipt 653	union shop 655
closed shop 655	lockout 660	vesting 649
collective bargaining 659	minimum wage 643	whistleblowing 642
employment at will 641	right-to-work law 655	workers' compensation law 648
hot-cargo agreement 655	secondary boycott 660	wrongful discharge 642
I-9 verification 652		

Issue Spotters

1. Erin, an employee of Fine Print Shop, is injured on the job. For Erin to obtain workers' compensation, must her injury have been caused by Fine Print's negligence? Does it matter whether the action causing the injury was intentional? Explain. (See *Health, Safety, and Income Security*.)

2. Onyx applies for work with Precision Design Company, which requires union membership as a condition of employment. She also applies for work with Quality

Engineering, Inc. That company does not require union membership as a condition of employment but requires employees to join a union after six months on the job. Are these conditions legal? Why or why not? (See *Labor Unions*.)

- **Check your answers to the Issue Spotters against the answers provided in Appendix D at the end of this text.**

Business Scenarios

34–1. Unfair Labor Practices. Consolidated Stores is undergoing a unionization campaign. Prior to the union election, management states that the union is unnecessary to protect workers. Management also provides bonuses and wage increases to the workers during this period. The employees reject the union. Union organizers protest that the wage increases during the election campaign unfairly prejudiced the vote. Should these wage increases be regarded as an unfair labor practice? Discuss. (See *Labor Unions.*)

34–2. Wrongful Discharge. Denton and Carlo were employed at an appliance plant. Their job required them to perform occasional maintenance work while standing on a wire mesh twenty feet above the plant floor. Other employees had fallen through the mesh, and one of them had been killed by the fall. When their supervisor told them to perform tasks that would likely involve walking on the mesh, Denton and Carlo refused because they feared they might suffer bodily injury or death. Because they refused to do the requested work, the two employees were fired from their jobs. Was their discharge wrongful? If so, under what federal employment law? To what federal agency or department should they turn for assistance? (See *Employment at Will.*)

Business Case Problems

34–3. Workers' Compensation. As a safety measure, Dynea USA, Inc., required an employee, Tony Fairbanks, to wear steel-toed boots. One of the boots caused a sore on Fairbanks's leg. The skin over the sore broke, and within a week, Fairbanks was hospitalized with a methicillin-resistant staphylococcus aureus (MRSA) infection. He filed a workers' compensation claim. Dynea argued that the MRSA bacteria that caused the infection had been on Fairbanks's skin before he came to work. What are the requirements to recover workers' compensation benefits? Does this claim qualify? Explain. [*Dynea USA, Inc. v. Fairbanks,* 241 Or.App. 311, 250 P.3d 389 (2011)] (See *Health, Safety, and Income Security.*)

34–4. Exceptions to the Employment-at-Will Doctrine. Li Li worked for Packard Bioscience, and Mark Schmeizl was her supervisor. In March 2000, Schmeizl told Li to call Packard's competitors, pretend to be a potential customer, and request "pricing information and literature." Li refused to perform the assignment. She told Schmeizl that she thought the work was illegal and recommended that he contact Packard's legal department. Although a lawyer recommended against the practice, Schmeizl insisted that Li perform the calls. Moreover, he later wrote negative performance reviews because she was unable to get the requested information when she called competitors and identified herself as a Packard employee. On June 1, 2000, Li was terminated on Schmeizl's recommendation. Can Li bring a claim for wrongful discharge? Why or why not? [*Li Li v. Canberra Industries,* 134 Conn.App. 448, 39 A.3d 789 (2012)] (See *Employment at Will.*)

34–5. Collective Bargaining. SDBC Holdings, Inc., acquired Stella D'oro Biscuit Co., a bakery in New York City. At the time, a collective bargaining agreement existed between Stella D'oro and Local 50, Bakery, Confectionary, Tobacco Workers and Grain Millers International Union. During negotiations to renew the agreement, Stella D'oro refused to give the union a copy of the company's financial statement. Stella D'oro did allow Local 50 to examine and take notes on the financial statement and offered the union an opportunity to make its own copy. Did Stella D'oro engage in an unfair labor practice? Discuss. [*SDBC Holdings, Inc. v. National Labor Relations Board,* 711 F.3d 281 (2d Cir. 2013)] (See *Labor Unions.*)

34–6. Business Case Problem with Sample Answer— Unemployment Compensation. Fior Ramirez worked as a housekeeper for Remington Lodging & Hospitality, a hotel in Atlantic Beach, Florida. After her father in the Dominican Republic suffered a stroke, she asked her employer for time off to be with him. Ramirez's manager, Katie Berkowski, refused the request. Two days later, Berkowski received a call from Ramirez to say that she was with her father. He died about a week later, and Ramirez returned to work, but Berkowski told her that she had abandoned her position. Ramirez applied for unemployment compensation. Under the applicable state statute, "an employee is disqualified from receiving benefits if he or she voluntarily left work without good cause." Does Ramirez qualify for benefits? Explain. [*Ramirez v. Reemployment Assistance Appeals Commission,* 39 Fla.L.Weekly D317, 135 So.3d 408 (1 Dist. 2014)] (See *Health, Safety, and Income Security.*)

• **For a sample answer to Problem 34–6, go to Appendix E at the end of this text.**

34–7. Labor Unions. Carol Garcia and Pedro Salgado were bus drivers for Latino Express, Inc., a transportation company. Garcia and Salgado began soliciting signatures from other drivers to certify the Teamsters Local Union No. 777 as the official representative of the employees. Latino Express fired Garcia and Salgado. The two drivers filed a claim with the National Labor Relations Board (NLRB), alleging that the employer had committed an unfair labor practice. Which employer practice defined by the National Labor Relations Act did the plaintiffs most likely charge Latino Express with committing? Is the employer's discharge of Garcia and Salgado likely to be construed as a legitimate act in opposition to union solicitation? If a violation is found, what can the NLRB do? Discuss. [*Ohr v. Latino Express, Inc.,* 776 F.3d 469 (7th Cir. 2015)] (See *Labor Unions.*)

34–8. Health, Safety, and Income Security. Jefferson Partners LP entered into a collective bargaining agreement (CBA) with the Amalgamated Transit Union. Under the CBA, drivers had to either join the union or pay a fair share—85 percent—of union dues, which were used to pay for administrative costs incurred by the union. An employee who refused to pay was subject to discharge. Jefferson hired Tiffany Thompson to work as a bus driver. When told of the CBA requirement, she said that she thought it was unfair. She asserted that it was illegal to compel her to join the union and that it would be illegal to discharge her for not complying. She refused either to join the union or to pay the dues. More than two years later, she was fired on the ground that her continued refusal constituted misconduct. Is Thompson eligible for unemployment compensation? Explain. [*Thompson v. Jefferson Partners LP,* 2016 WL 953038 (Minn.App. 2016)] (See *Health, Safety, and Income Security.*)

34–9. A Question of Ethics—Workers' Compensation Law.

In 1999, after working for Atchison Leather Products, Inc., for ten years, Beverly Tull began to complain of hand, wrist, and shoulder pain. Atchison recommended that she contact a certain physician, who in April 2000 diagnosed the condition as carpal tunnel syndrome "severe enough" for surgery. In August, Tull filed a claim with the state workers' compensation board. Because Atchison changed workers' compensation insurance companies every year, a dispute arose as to which company should pay Tull's claim. Fearing liability, no insurer would authorize treatment, and Tull was forced to delay surgery until December. The board granted her temporary total disability benefits for the subsequent six weeks that she missed work. On April 23, 2002, Berger Co. bought

Atchison. The new employer adjusted Tull's work so that it was less demanding and stressful, but she continued to suffer pain. In July, a physician diagnosed her condition as permanent. The board granted her permanent partial disability benefits. By May 2005, bickering over the financial responsibility for Tull's claim involved five insurers—four of which had each covered Atchison for a single year and one of which covered Berger. [Tull v. Atchison Leather Products, Inc., 37 Kan.App.2d 87, 150 P.3d 316 (2007)] (See *Health, Safety, and Income Security.*)

(a) When an injured employee files a claim for workers' compensation, a proceeding is held to assess the injury and determine the amount of compensation. Should a dispute between insurers over the payment of the claim be resolved in the same proceeding? Why or why not?

(b) The board designated April 23, 2002, as the date of Tull's injury. What is the reason for determining the date of a worker's injury? Should the board in this case have selected this date or a different date? Why?

(c) How should the board assess liability for the payment of Tull's medical expenses and disability benefits? Would it be appropriate to impose joint and several liability on the insurers (holding each of them responsible for the full amount of damages)? Or should the individual liability of each of the insurers be determined? Explain.

Legal Reasoning Group Activity

34–10. Immigration. Nicole Tipton and Sadik Seferi owned and operated a restaurant in Iowa. Acting on a tip from the local police, agents of Immigration and Customs Enforcement executed search warrants at the restaurant and at an apartment where some restaurant workers lived. The agents discovered six undocumented aliens who worked at the restaurant and lived together. When the I-9 forms for the restaurant's employees were reviewed, none were found for the six aliens. They were paid in cash while other employees were

paid by check. Tipton and Seferi were charged with hiring and harboring undocumented aliens. (See *Immigration Law.*)

(a) The first group will develop an argument that Tipton and Seferi were guilty of hiring and harboring illegal aliens.

(b) The second group will assess whether Tipton and Seferi can assert a defense by claiming that they did not know that the workers were unauthorized aliens.

CHAPTER 35

Employment Discrimination

Out of the 1960s civil rights movement to end racial and other forms of discrimination grew a body of law protecting employees against discrimination in the workplace. Legislation, judicial decisions, and administrative agency actions restrict employers from discriminating against workers on the basis of race, color, religion, national origin, gender, age, or disability. A class of persons defined by one or more of these criteria is known as a **protected class.**

Several federal statutes prohibit **employment discrimination** against members of protected classes. The most important is Title VII of the Civil Rights Act.[1] Title VII prohibits employment discrimination on the basis of race, color, religion, national origin, and gender. The Age Discrimination in Employment Act[2] and the Americans with Disabilities Act[3] pro-

hibit discrimination on the basis of age and disability, respectively. The protections afforded under these laws also extend to U.S. citizens who are working abroad for U.S. firms or for companies that are controlled by U.S. firms.

This chapter focuses on federal statutes, including the ones just mentioned. Many states have their own laws that protect employees against discrimination, however, and some provide more protection than federal laws do.

---

1. 42 U.S.C. Sections 2000e–2000e-17.
2. 29 U.S.C. Sections 621–634.
3. 42 U.S.C. Sections 12102–12118.

35–1 Title VII of the Civil Rights Act

Title VII of the Civil Rights Act prohibits job discrimination against employees, applicants, and union members on the basis of race, color, national origin, religion, and gender at any stage of employment. Title VII bans discrimination in the hiring process, discipline procedures, discharge, promotion, and benefits.

Title VII applies to employers with fifteen or more employees and labor unions with fifteen or more members. It also applies to labor unions that operate hiring halls (where members go regularly to be assigned jobs), employment agencies, and state and local governing units or agencies. The United States Supreme Court has ruled that an employer with fewer than fifteen employees is not automatically shielded from a lawsuit filed under Title VII.[4] In addition, the act prohibits discrimination in most federal government employment. When Title

---

4. *Arbaugh v. Y&H Corp.*, 546 U.S. 500, 126 S.Ct. 1235, 163 L.Ed.2d 1097 (2006).

VII applies to the employer, any employee—including an undocumented (alien) worker—can bring an action for employment discrimination.

35–1a The Equal Employment Opportunity Commission

The Equal Employment Opportunity Commission (EEOC) monitors compliance with Title VII. An employee alleging discrimination must file a claim with the EEOC before a lawsuit can be brought against the employer. The EEOC may investigate the dispute and attempt to obtain the parties' voluntary consent to an out-of-court settlement. If a voluntary agreement cannot be reached, the EEOC may file a suit against the employer on the employee's behalf.

■ **EXAMPLE 35.1** Jacqueline Cote met her wife, Diana Smithson, in Maine while they were both employees at Wal-Mart. They moved to Massachusetts and were married a few days after the state legalized same-sex marriage, and they continued working at a Wal-Mart there. Smithson eventually quit work to take care of Cote's elderly mother. Cote tried to enroll her partner in Wal-Mart's health plan, but coverage was denied. Five years later, Smithson was diagnosed with cancer.

Cote filed a claim with the EEOC arguing that Wal-Mart had intentionally discriminated against her on the basis of sex. In 2014, the commission agreed that Cote "was treated differently and denied benefits because of her sex." The EEOC ordered Wal-Mart to work with Cote to help pay Smithson's medical bills. ■

The EEOC does not investigate every claim of employment discrimination. Generally, it takes only "priority cases," such as claims that affect many workers and those involving retaliatory discharge (firing an employee in retaliation for submitting a claim to the EEOC). If the EEOC decides not to investigate a claim, the EEOC issues a "right to sue" that allows the employee to bring his or her own lawsuit against the employer.

35–1b Limitations on Class Actions

In an important decision, the United States Supreme Court limited the rights of employees to bring discrimination claims against their employer as a group, or class. The decision did not affect the rights of individual employees to sue under Title VII, however.

■ **CASE IN POINT 35.2** A group of female employees sued Wal-Mart, the nation's largest private employer. The employees alleged that store managers who had discretion over pay and promotions were biased against women and disproportionately favored men. The employees wished to bring a class action—a lawsuit in which a small number of plaintiffs sue on behalf of a larger group. Lower courts ruled that the employees' class-action suit could proceed, and Wal-Mart appealed. The Supreme Court ruled in favor of Wal-Mart, effectively blocking the class action. The Court held that the women had failed to prove a company-wide policy of discrimination that had a common effect on all women included in the class. Therefore, they could not maintain a class action.[5] ■

35–1c Intentional and Unintentional Discrimination

Title VII of the Civil Rights Act prohibits both intentional and unintentional discrimination.

---

5. *Wal-Mart Stores, Inc. v. Dukes,* 564 U.S. 338, 131 S.Ct. 2541, 180 L.Ed.2d 374 (2011).

Intentional Discrimination Intentional discrimination by an employer against an employee is known as **disparate-treatment discrimination.** Because intent may sometimes be difficult to prove, courts have established certain procedures for resolving disparate-treatment cases.

Prima Facie **Case.** A plaintiff who sues on the basis of disparate-treatment discrimination must first make out a *prima facie* **case.** *Prima facie* is Latin for "at first sight" or "on its face." Legally, it refers to a fact that is presumed to be true unless contradicted by evidence.

To establish a *prima facie* case of disparate-treatment discrimination in hiring, a plaintiff must show all of the following:

1. The plaintiff is a member of a protected class.
2. The plaintiff applied and was qualified for the job in question.
3. The plaintiff was rejected by the employer.
4. The employer continued to seek applicants for the position or filled the position with a person not in a protected class.

A plaintiff who can meet these relatively easy requirements has made out a *prima facie* case of illegal discrimination in hiring and will win in the absence of a legally acceptable employer defense.

Sometimes, current and former employees make a claim of discrimination. When the plaintiff alleges that the employer fired or took some other adverse employment action against him or her, the same basic requirements apply. To establish a *prima facie* case, the plaintiff must show that he or she was fired or treated adversely for discriminatory reasons.

Burden-Shifting Procedure. Once the *prima facie* case is established, the burden then shifts to the employer-defendant, who must articulate a legal reason for not hiring the plaintiff. (Again, this also applies to firing and other adverse employment actions.) If the employer did not have a legal reason for taking the adverse employment action, the plaintiff wins.

If the employer can articulate a legitimate reason for the action, the burden shifts back to the plaintiff. To prevail, the plaintiff must then show that the employer's reason is a *pretext* (not the true reason) and that the employer's decision was actually motivated by discriminatory intent.

Unintentional Discrimination Employers often use interviews and tests to choose from among a large number of applicants for job openings. Minimum educational requirements are also common. Some employer practices, such as those involving educational requirements, may have an unintended discriminatory impact on a protected class.

Disparate-impact discrimination occurs when a protected group of people is adversely affected by an employer's practices, procedures, or tests, even though they do not appear to be discriminatory. In a disparate-impact discrimination case, the complaining party must first show that the employer's practices, procedures, or tests are effectively discriminatory. Once the plaintiff has made out a *prima facie* case, the burden of proof shifts to the employer to show that the practices or procedures in question were justified.

There are two ways of showing that an employer's practices, procedures, or tests are effectively discriminatory—that is, that disparate-impact discrimination exists.

Pool of Applicants. A plaintiff can prove a disparate impact by comparing the employer's workforce to the pool of qualified individuals available in the local labor market. The plaintiff must show that (1) as a result of educational or other job requirements or hiring procedures, (2) the percentage of nonwhites, women, or members of other protected classes in the employer's workforce (3) does not reflect the percentage of that group in the pool of qualified applicants. If the plaintiff can show a connection between the practice and the disparity, he or she has made out a *prima facie* case and need not provide evidence of discriminatory intent.

Rate of Hiring. A plaintiff can also prove disparate-impact discrimination by comparing the employer's *selection rates* of members and nonmembers of a protected class (nonwhites and whites, for instance, or women and men). When an educational or other job requirement or hiring procedure excludes members of a protected class from an employer's workforce at a substantially higher rate than nonmembers, discrimination occurs.

Under EEOC guidelines, a selection rate for a protected class that is less than four-fifths, or 80 percent, of the rate for the group with the highest rate of hiring generally is regarded as evidence of disparate impact. ■ **EXAMPLE 35.3** Shady Cove District Fire Department administers an exam to applicants for the position of firefighter. At the exam session, one hundred white applicants take the test, and fifty pass and are hired. At the same exam session, sixty minority applicants take the test, but only twelve pass and are hired. Because twelve is only 20 percent of sixty, the test will be considered discriminatory under the EEOC guidelines. ■

35–1d Discrimination Based on Race, Color, and National Origin

Title VII prohibits employers from discriminating against employees or job applicants on the basis of race, color, or national origin. Race is interpreted broadly to apply to the ancestry or ethnic characteristics of a group of persons, such as Native Americans. National origin refers to discrimination based on a person's birth in another country or his or her ancestry or culture, such as Hispanic.

If an employer's standards or policies for selecting or promoting employees have a discriminatory effect on employees or job applicants in these protected classes, then a presumption of illegal discrimination arises. To avoid liability, the employer must show that its standards or policies have a substantial, demonstrable relationship to realistic qualifications for the job in question.

■ **CASE IN POINT 35.4** Jiann Min Chang was an instructor at Alabama Agricultural and Mechanical University (AAMU). When AAMU terminated his employment, Chang filed a lawsuit claiming discrimination based on national origin. Chang established a *prima facie* case because he (1) was a member of a protected class, (2) was qualified for the job, (3) suffered an adverse employment action, and (4) was replaced by someone outside his protected class (a non-Asian instructor).

When the burden of proof shifted to the employer, however, AAMU showed that Chang had argued with a vice president and refused to comply with her instructions. The court ruled that the university had not renewed Chang's contract for a legitimate reason—insubordination—and therefore was not liable for unlawful discrimination.[6] ■

Reverse Discrimination Title VII also protects against *reverse discrimination*—that is, discrimination against members of a majority group, such as white males. ■ **EXAMPLE 35.5** An African American woman fires four white men from their management positions at a school district. The men file a lawsuit for reverse discrimination. They argue that the woman was trying to eliminate white males from the district administration in violation of Title VII. The woman claims that the terminations were part of a reorganization plan to cut costs.

If the judge (or jury, in a jury trial) agrees with the men that they were fired for racially discriminatory reasons, then they will be entitled to damages. If, however, the school district can show that the real reason for the terminations was a legitimate attempt to cut costs, then normally their case will be dismissed. ■

---

6. *Jiann Min Chang v. Alabama Agricultural and Mechanical University,* 355 Fed.Appx. 250 (11th Cir. 2009).

Potential Section 1981 Claims Victims of racial or ethnic discrimination may also have a cause of action under 42 U.S.C. Section 1981. This section, which was enacted in 1866 to protect the rights of freed slaves, prohibits discrimination on the basis of race or ethnicity in the formation or enforcement of contracts. Because employment is often a contractual relationship, Section 1981 can provide an alternative basis for a plaintiff's action and is potentially advantageous because there is no limit on the damages that can be awarded.

35–1e Discrimination Based on Religion

Title VII of the Civil Rights Act also prohibits government employers, private employers, and unions from discriminating against persons because of their religion. (This chapter's *Digital Update* feature discusses how employers who examine prospective employees' social media posts, including posts concerning religion, might engage in unlawful discrimination.)

Employers cannot treat their employees more or less favorably based on their religious beliefs or practices. They also cannot require employees to participate in any religious activity or forbid them from participating in one. ■ **EXAMPLE 35.6** Jason Sewell claims that his employer, a car dealership, fired him for not attending the weekly prayer meetings of dealership employees. If the dealership does require its employees to attend prayer gatherings and fired Sewell for not attending, he has a valid claim of religious discrimination. ■

Reasonable Accommodation An employer must "reasonably accommodate" the religious practices and sincerely held religious beliefs of its employees, unless to do so would cause undue hardship to the employer's business. An employee's religion might prohibit her or him from working on a certain day of the week, for instance, or at a certain type of job. Reasonable accommodation is required even if the belief is not based on the doctrines of a traditionally recognized religion, such as Christianity or Judaism, or of a denomination, such as Baptist.

Undue Hardship A reasonable attempt to accommodate does not necessarily require the employer to make every change an employee requests or to make a permanent change for an employee's benefit. An employer is not required to make an accommodation that would cause the employer undue hardship. ■ **CASE IN POINT 35.7** Miguel Sánchez-Rodríguez sold cell phones at kiosks in shopping malls for AT&T in Puerto Rico. After six years, Sánchez informed his supervisors that he had become a Seventh Day Adventist and could no longer work on Saturdays for religious reasons. AT&T responded that his position required rotating Saturday shifts and that his inability to work on Saturdays would cause the company hardship.

As a reasonable accommodation, the company suggested that Sánchez swap schedules with others and offered him two alternative positions that would not require work on Saturdays. Sánchez was unable to find workers to swap shifts with him, however, and declined the other jobs because they would result in less income. He began missing work on Saturdays. After a time, AT&T indicated that it would discipline him for any additional Saturdays that he missed. Eventually, he was placed on active disciplinary status. Sánchez resigned and filed a religious discrimination lawsuit. The court found in favor of AT&T, and a federal appellate court affirmed. The company had made adequate efforts at accommodation by allowing Sánchez to swap shifts and offering him other positions that did not require work on Saturdays.[7] ■

35–1f Discrimination Based on Gender

Under Title VII and other federal acts, employers are forbidden from discriminating against employees on the basis of gender. Employers are prohibited from classifying or advertising jobs as male or female unless they can prove that the gender of the applicant is essential to the job. In addition, employers cannot have separate male and female seniority lists and cannot refuse to promote employees based on their gender.

Gender Must Be a Determining Factor Generally, to succeed in a suit for gender discrimination, a plaintiff must demonstrate that gender was a determining factor in the employer's decision to hire, fire, or promote him or her. Typically, this involves looking at all of the surrounding circumstances.

■ **CASE IN POINT 35.8** Wanda Collier worked for Turner Industries Group, LLC, in the maintenance department. She complained to her supervisor that Jack Daniell, the head of the department, treated her unfairly. Her supervisor told her that Daniell had a problem with her gender and was harder on women. The supervisor talked to Daniell about Collier's complaint but did not take any disciplinary action.

A month later, Daniell confronted Collier, pushing her up against a wall and berating her. After this incident, Collier filed a formal complaint and kept a male

---

7. *Sánchez-Rodríguez v. AT&T Mobility Puerto Rico, Inc.,* 673 F.3d 1 (1st Cir. 2012).

DIGITAL UPDATE   Hiring Discrimination Based on Social Media Posts

Human resource officers in most companies routinely check job candidates' social media posts when deciding whom to hire. Certainly, every young person is warned not to post photos that she or he might later regret having made available to potential employers. But a more serious issue involves standard reviewing of job candidates' social media information. Specifically, do employers discriminate based on such information?

An Experiment in Hiring Discrimination via Online Social Networks

Two researchers at Carnegie-Mellon University conducted an experiment to determine whether social media information posted by prospective employees influences employers' hiring decisions.[a] The researchers created false résumés and social media profiles. They submitted job applications on behalf of the fictional "candidates" to about four thousand U.S. employers. They then compared employers' responses to different groups—for example, to Muslim candidates versus Christian candidates.

The researchers found that candidates whose public profiles indicated that they were Muslim were less likely to be called for interviews than Christian applicants. The difference was particularly pronounced in parts of the country with more conservative residents. In those locations, Muslims received callbacks only 2 percent of the time, compared with 17 percent for Christian applicants. According to the authors of the study, "Hiring discrimination via online searches of candidates may not be widespread, but online disclosures of personal traits can significantly influence the hiring decisions of a self-selected set of employers."

a. A. Acquisti and C. N. Fong, "An Experiment in Hiring Discrimination via Online Social Networks," *Social Service Research Network*, October 26, 2014.

Job Candidates' Perception of the Hiring Process

In another study, researchers at North Carolina State University looked at how job applicants view prospective employers' use of their social media profiles during the hiring process.[b] Job candidates appear to view the hiring process as unfair when they know that their social media profiles have been used in the selection process. This perception, according to the researchers, makes litigation more likely.

The EEOC Speaks Up

Since 2014, the Equal Employment Opportunity Commission (EEOC) has investigated how prospective employers can use social media to engage in discrimination in the hiring process. Given that the Society for Human Resource Management estimates that more than three-fourths of its members use social media in employment screening, the EEOC is interested in regulating this procedure.

Social media sites, examined closely, can provide information to a prospective employer on the applicant's race, color, national origin, disability, religion, and other protected characteristics. The EEOC has reminded employers that such information—whether it comes from social media postings or other sources—may not legally be used to make employment decisions on prohibited bases, such as race, gender, and religion.

Critical Thinking *Can you think of a way a company could use information from an applicant's social media posts without running the risk of being accused of hiring discrimination?*

b. J. W. Stoughton, L. F. Thompson, and A. W. Meade, "Examining Applicant Reactions to the Use of Social Networking Websites in Pre-Employment Screening," *Journal of Business and Psychology*, November 2013, DOI: 10.1007/s10869-013-9333-6.

---

co-worker with her at all times. A month later, she was fired. She subsequently filed a lawsuit alleging gender discrimination. The court allowed Collier's claim to go to a jury because there was sufficient evidence that gender was a determining factor in Daniell's conduct.[8] ∎

8. *Collier v. Turner Industries Group, LLC*, 797 F.Supp.2d 1029 (D. Idaho 2011).

The Federal Bureau of Investigation (FBI) requires that its applicants meet certain physical fitness standards. For women, the standards include the ability to complete a minimum of fourteen push-ups. Men must be able to complete at least thirty. Whether this difference constitutes discrimination on the basis of gender was at issue in the following case.

Case Analysis 35.1

Bauer v. Lynch

United States Court of Appeals, Fourth Circuit, 812 F.3d 340 (2016).

In the Language of the Court

KING, Circuit Judge.

* * * *

The FBI trains its Special Agent recruits at the FBI Academy in Quantico, Virginia. * * * All Trainees must pass a physical fitness test (the "PFT").

* * * The FBI requires every Special Agent recruit to pass the PFT twice: once to gain admission to the Academy, and a second time to graduate.

* * * *

* * * Trainees * * * need to satisfy the following standards * * * :

Event	Men	Women
Sit-ups	38	35
300-meter sprint	52.4s	64.9s
Push-ups	30	14
1.5-mile run	12m, 42s	13m, 5s

* * * *

After the attacks of September 11, 2001, * * * Jay Bauer resolved to contribute to the defense of our country by becoming a Special Agent in the FBI. [At the time,] he * * * served as an assistant professor at the University of Wisconsin–Milwaukee.

* * * Bauer took the PFT for the first time and failed. Although he achieved sixteen points on the test, Bauer completed only twenty-five push-ups * * * . The FBI allowed Bauer to retest [three months later] and he passed, that time completing thirty-two push-ups. With his fitness screening complete, the FBI invited Bauer to report to the Academy.

Bauer's time at the Academy largely showed great potential for a career as a Special Agent. He passed all academic tests, demonstrated proficiency in his firearms and defensive tactics training, and met all expectations for the practical applications and skills components of the Academy. Bauer's classmates also selected him as the class leader and spokesperson for the Academy

graduation. Unfortunately, Bauer faced a dilemma: he was unable to pass the PFT at Quantico.

During his twenty-two weeks at the Academy, Bauer took the PFT five times. On each occasion, he would have passed but for his failure to achieve the minimum standard for push-ups. Bauer's results, and his corresponding point scores for each event, were as follows:

Week	Sit-ups	300-meter sprint	Push-ups	1.5-mile run	Total Points
Week 1	40 (2)	42.6 sec. (8)	26 (0)	10:49 (4)	14
Week 7	47 (4)	43.4 sec. (7)	25 (0)	10:24 (5)	16
Week 14	50 (6)	43.7 sec. (7)	28 (0)	10:45 (4)	17
Week 18	51 (6)	43.8 sec. (7)	27 (0)	11:09 (4)	17
Week 22	49 (5)	44.1 sec. (6)	29 (0)	10:57 (4)	15

Following his final failure of the PFT, Bauer * * * was [allowed to] resign with the possibility of future employment with the FBI * * * . Bauer * * * immediately signed a resignation letter. Two weeks later, the FBI offered Bauer a position as an Intelligence Analyst in its Chicago Field Office. He accepted and has been employed in that position since.

* * * *

* * * Bauer filed this Title VII action in [a federal district court] against [Loretta Lynch,] the Attorney General. According to the claims in Bauer's complaint, the FBI's use of the gender-normed PFT standards contravened * * * Title VII * * * which prohibits sex discrimination by federal employers.

* * * *

In his summary judgment motion, Bauer maintained that the FBI's use of the gender-normed PFT standards was facially discriminatory [involving explicit categorization, such as by sex or race].

* * * *

* * * The district court agreed with Bauer, granting his motion for summary judgment.

* * * *

The Attorney General * * * filed a timely * * * appeal.

* * * *

Title VII requires that any "personnel actions affecting employees or applicants for employment" taken by federal employers "shall be made free from any discrimination based on * * * sex." * * * *A plaintiff is entitled to demonstrate discrimination by showing that the employer uses a facially discriminatory employment practice. [The Supreme Court has outlined] a "simple test" for identifying facial sex discrimination: such discrimination appears "where the evidence shows treatment of a person in a manner which but for that person's sex would be different."* [Emphasis added.]

* * * The district court applied [this] test and concluded that, because Bauer would have been held to a lower minimum number of push-ups had he been a woman, the gender-normed PFT standards constitute facial sex discrimination. The Attorney General maintains on appeal, however, that because the PFT assesses an overall level of physical fitness, and equally fit men and women possess innate physiological differences that lead to different performance outcomes, the PFT's gender-normed standards actually require the same level of fitness for all Trainees. In that way, the Attorney General contends, the PFT standards do not treat the sexes differently and therefore do not contravene Title VII.

* * * *

* * * The Attorney General * * * maintains that * * * some differential treatment of men and women based upon inherent physiological differences is not only lawful but also potentially required.

* * * *

Men and women simply are not physiologically the same for the purposes

Case 35.1 Continues

Case 35.1 Continued

of physical fitness programs. * * * Physical fitness standards suitable for men may not always be suitable for women, and accommodations addressing physiological differences between the sexes are not necessarily unlawful.

* * * The physiological differences between men and women impact their relative abilities to demonstrate the same levels of physical fitness. In other words, equally fit men and women demonstrate their fitness differently. Whether physical fitness standards discriminate based on sex, therefore, depends on whether they require men and women to demonstrate different levels of fitness.

Put succinctly, *an employer does not contravene Title VII when it utilizes physical fitness standards that distinguish between the sexes on the basis of their physiological differences but impose an equal burden of compliance on both men and women, requiring the same level of physical fitness of each.* Because the FBI purports to assess physical fitness by imposing the same burden on both men and women, this rule applies to Bauer's Title VII claims. Accordingly, the district court erred in failing to apply the rule in its disposition of Bauer's motion for summary judgment. [Emphasis added.]
* * * *

Pursuant to the foregoing, we vacate the judgment of the district court and remand for * * * further proceedings.

Legal Reasoning Questions

1. According to the reasoning of the court in the *Bauer* case, when do different employment standards for men and women satisfy Title VII's requirement of equality?

2. In what other circumstances might the rule in this case apply?

3. If Bauer had ultimately succeeded in his claim, what might the remedy have been? What else might have resulted?

Pregnancy Discrimination The Pregnancy Discrimination Act[9] expanded Title VII's definition of gender discrimination to include discrimination based on pregnancy. Women affected by pregnancy, childbirth, or related medical conditions must be treated the same as other persons not so affected but similar in ability to work. For instance, an employer cannot discriminate against a pregnant woman by withholding benefits available to others under employee benefit programs.

In the following case, an employer accommodated many of its employees who had lifting restrictions due to disabilities. The employer refused to accommodate a pregnant employee with a similar restriction. Did this refusal constitute a violation of the Pregnancy Discrimination Act?

---

9. 42 U.S.C. Section 2000e(k).

Case 35.2

Young v. United Parcel Service, Inc.

Supreme Court of the United States, __ U.S. __, 135 S.Ct. 1338, 191 L.Ed.2d 279 (2015).

Background and Facts Peggy Young was a driver for United Parcel Service, Inc. (UPS). When she became pregnant, her doctor advised her not to lift more than twenty pounds. UPS required drivers to lift up to seventy pounds and told Young that she could not work under a lifting restriction. She filed a suit in a federal district court against UPS, claiming an unlawful refusal to accommodate her pregnancy-related lifting restriction. She alleged that UPS had multiple light-duty-for-injury categories to accommodate individuals whose non-pregnancy-related disabilities created work restrictions similar to hers.

UPS responded that, because Young did not fall into any of those categories, it had not discriminated against her. The court issued a summary judgment in UPS's favor. The U.S. Court of Appeals of the Fourth Circuit affirmed the judgment. Young appealed to the United States Supreme Court.

In the Language of the Court

Justice *BREYER* delivered the opinion of the Court.
* * * *

* * * A plaintiff alleging that the denial of an accommodation constituted disparate treatment under the Pregnancy Discrimination Act * * * may make out a *prima facie* case by showing that she belongs to

Case 35.2 Continued

the protected class, that she sought accommodation, that the employer did not accommodate her, and that the employer did accommodate others similar in their ability or inability to work.

The employer may then seek to justify its refusal to accommodate the plaintiff by relying on legitimate, non-discriminatory reasons for denying her accommodation. [Emphasis added.]

If the employer offers an apparently legitimate, nondiscriminatory reason for its actions, the plaintiff may in turn show that the employer's proffered reasons are in fact pretextual [contrived]. We believe that the plaintiff may reach a jury on this issue by providing sufficient evidence that the employer's policies impose a significant burden on pregnant workers, and that the employer's legitimate, nondiscriminatory reasons are not sufficiently strong to justify the burden, but rather—when considered along with the burden imposed—give rise to an inference of intentional discrimination.

The plaintiff can create a genuine issue of material fact as to whether a significant burden exists by providing evidence that the employer accommodates a large percentage of nonpregnant workers while failing to accommodate a large percentage of pregnant workers. Here, for example, if the facts are as Young says they are, she can show that UPS accommodates most nonpregnant employees with lifting limitations while categorically failing to accommodate pregnant employees with lifting limitations. Young might also add that the fact that UPS has multiple policies that accommodate nonpregnant employees with lifting restrictions suggests that its reasons for failing to accommodate pregnant employees with lifting restrictions are not sufficiently strong—to the point that a jury could find that its reasons for failing to accommodate pregnant employees give rise to an inference of intentional discrimination.

* * * *

* * * A party is entitled to summary judgment if there is no genuine dispute as to any material fact and the movant [that is, a person who applies to a court for a ruling in his or her favor] is entitled to judgment as a matter of law. * * * *Viewing the record in the light most favorable to Young, there is a genuine dispute as to whether UPS provided more favorable treatment to at least some employees whose situation cannot reasonably be distinguished from Young's.* [Emphasis added.]

Decision and Remedy *The United States Supreme Court vacated the judgment of the U.S. Court of Appeals for the Fourth Circuit and remanded the case for further proceedings. Young created a genuine dispute as to whether UPS had provided more favorable treatment to employees whose situation could not reasonably be distinguished from hers. On remand, the court must determine whether Young also created a genuine issue of material fact as to whether UPS's reasons for treating Young less favorably were a pretext.*

Critical Thinking
- **Legal Environment** *Could UPS have succeeded in this case if it had claimed simply that it would be more expensive or less convenient to include pregnant women among those whom it accommodates? Explain.*

Wage Discrimination The Equal Pay Act[10] requires equal pay for male and female employees working at the same establishment doing similar work. To determine whether the Equal Pay Act has been violated, a court looks to the primary duties of the two jobs—the job content rather than the job description controls. If a court finds that the wage differential is due to "any factor other than gender," such as a seniority or merit system, then it does not violate the Equal Pay Act.

The 2009 Lilly Ledbetter Fair Pay Act made discriminatory wages actionable under federal law regardless of when the discrimination began.[11] Previously, plaintiffs had to file a complaint within a limited time period. Today, if a plaintiff continues to work for the employer while receiving discriminatory wages, the time period for filing a complaint is practically unlimited.

Discrimination against Transgender Persons
In the past, most courts held that federal law (Title VII)

---

10. 29 U.S.C. Section 206(d).

11. Pub. L. No. 111-2, 123 Stat. 5 (January 5, 2009), amending 42 U.S.C. Section 2000e-5[e].

does not protect transgender persons from discrimination. The situation may be changing, however. A growing number of federal courts are interpreting Title VII's protections against gender discrimination to apply to transsexuals.

■ **CASE IN POINT 35.9** Dr. Deborah Fabian applied for a position as an on-call orthopedic surgeon at the Hospital of Central Connecticut. The hospital apparently declined to hire Fabian because she disclosed her identity as a transgender woman. Fabian sued the hospital alleging violations of Title VII of the Civil Rights Act and the Connecticut Fair Employment Practices Act (CFEPA).

The hospital filed a summary judgment motion, arguing that neither Title VII nor the Connecticut statute prohibits discrimination on the basis of transgender identity. The federal district court rejected this argument, however, finding that discrimination on the basis of transgender identity is discrimination on the basis of sex for Title VII purposes. Fabian was entitled to take her case to a jury and argue violations of Title VII and the CFEPA.[12] ■

35–1g Constructive Discharge

The majority of Title VII complaints involve unlawful discrimination in decisions to hire or fire employees. In some situations, however, employees who leave their jobs voluntarily can claim that they were "constructively discharged" by the employer. **Constructive discharge** occurs when the employer causes the employee's working conditions to be so intolerable that a reasonable person in the employee's position would feel compelled to quit.

When constructive discharge is claimed, the employee can pursue damages for loss of income, including back pay. These damages ordinarily are not available to an employee who left a job voluntarily.

Proving Constructive Discharge To prove constructive discharge, an employee must present objective proof of intolerable working conditions. The employee must also show that the employer knew or had reason to know about these conditions yet failed to correct them within a reasonable time period. In addition, courts generally require the employee to show causation—that the employer's unlawful discrimination caused the working conditions to be intolerable. Put in a different way, the employee's resignation must be a foreseeable result of the

employer's discriminatory action. Courts weigh the facts on a case-by-case basis.

Employee demotion is one of the most frequently cited reasons for a finding of constructive discharge, particularly when the employee was subjected to humiliation. ■ **EXAMPLE 35.10** Khalil's employer humiliates him by informing him in front of his co-workers that he is being demoted to an inferior position. Khalil's co-workers then continually insult him, harass him, and make derogatory remarks to him about his national origin (he is from Iran). The employer is aware of this discriminatory treatment but does nothing to remedy the situation, despite Khalil's repeated complaints. After several months, Khalil quits his job and files a Title VII claim. In this situation, Khalil will likely have sufficient evidence to maintain an action for constructive discharge in violation of Title VII. ■

Applies to All Title VII Discrimination Plaintiffs can use constructive discharge to establish any type of discrimination claim under Title VII, including race, color, national origin, religion, gender, and pregnancy. It is most commonly asserted in cases involving sexual harassment. Constructive discharge may also be used in cases involving discrimination based on age or disability (discussed later in this chapter).

35–1h Sexual Harassment

Title VII also protects employees against **sexual harassment** in the workplace. Sexual harassment can take two forms:

1. *Quid pro quo* harassment occurs when sexual favors are demanded in return for job opportunities, promotions, salary increases, or other benefits. *Quid pro quo* is a Latin phrase that is often translated as "something in exchange for something else."

2. *Hostile-environment* harassment occurs when a pattern of sexually offensive conduct runs throughout the workplace and the employer has not taken steps to prevent or discourage it. Such harassment exists when the workplace is permeated with discriminatory intimidation, ridicule, and insult, and this harassment is so severe or pervasive that it alters the conditions of employment.

A court considers a number of factors when determining whether the sexually offensive conduct was sufficiently severe or pervasive to create a hostile environment. As the following case shows, these factors include the nature and frequency of the conduct and whether it unreasonably interfered with the victim's work performance.

---

12. *Fabian v. Hospital of Central Connecticut,* ___ F.Supp.3d ___, 2016 WL 1089178 (D.Conn. 2016).

Roberts v. Mike's Trucking, Ltd.

Court of Appeals of Ohio, Twelfth District, 2014 -Ohio- 766, 9 N.E.3d 483 (2014).

Background and Facts Teresa Roberts worked for Mike's Trucking, Ltd., in Columbus, Ohio. Her supervisor was the company's owner, Mike Culbertson. According to Roberts, Culbertson called her his "sexretary" and constantly talked about his sex life. He often invited her to sit on "Big Daddy's" lap, rubbed against her, trapped her at the door and asked her for hugs or kisses, and inquired if she needed help in the restroom. Roberts asked him to stop this conduct, but he did not. She became less productive and began to suffer anxiety attacks and high blood pressure. Roberts filed a suit in an Ohio state court against Mike's, alleging a hostile work environment through sexual harassment in violation of Title VII. A jury decided in Roberts's favor, and Mike's appealed.

In the Language of the Court

HENDRICKSON, P.J. [Presiding Judge]
* * * *

* * * Conduct that is not severe or pervasive enough to create an objectively hostile or abusive work environment—an environment that a reasonable person would find hostile or abusive—is beyond Title VII's purview. Likewise, if the victim does not subjectively perceive the environment to be abusive, the conduct has not actually altered the conditions of the victim's employment, and there is no Title VII violation. Therefore, *the focus of this inquiry is: 1.) whether a reasonable person would find the environment objectively hostile; and 2.) whether the plaintiff subjectively found the conduct severe or pervasive.* [Emphasis added.]
* * * *

* * * Roberts' testimony was consistent with several witnesses affirming that Culbertson frequently engaged in a variety of conduct ranging from inappropriate discussions to groping women. The witnesses stated that Culbertson often discussed his sex life, asked Roberts and the women employees if they needed help in the bathroom * * * , referred to himself as "Big Daddy," asked Roberts and the women employees to sit in "Big Daddy's" lap, and asked them if they would give "Big Daddy" a hug.

The evidence established that the conduct occurred frequently. Roberts testified that throughout her employment, Culbertson's behavior became increasingly worse and that * * * he talked about sex hundreds of times, and attempted to corner her and hug and kiss her at least twice a week. [Former Mike's employees] testified that Culbertson talked about sex and asked the women if they needed help with the bathroom multiple times a week. The evidence also showed that the conduct became increasingly severe as Culbertson massaged Roberts [and] rubbed up against her * * * . Roberts testified that Culbertson's conduct was humiliating towards her as his remarks were in front of others and she often became "furious" with him. Other employees reported Roberts becoming angry towards Culbertson. Roberts also established that Culbertson's conduct unreasonably interfered with her work performance as she stated she did not want to go to work anymore, she became less productive, and she suffered anxiety attacks. Her fiancé testified that Roberts has lost confidence and that she is now prescribed anti-anxiety medication.

Consequently, there was sufficient and substantial evidence to support the jury's finding that a reasonable person would find Culbertson's conduct created a hostile environment and Roberts found the conduct to be sufficiently severe or pervasive to affect her employment.

Decision and Remedy *A state intermediate appellate court affirmed the lower court's judgment in Roberts's favor. During the trial, other Mike's employees and Roberts's fiancé testified to corroborate Roberts's account. The evidence sufficiently established that Culbertson's conduct was severe or pervasive enough to create a hostile work environment for Roberts.*

Critical Thinking

- **Ethical** *Was Culbertson's conduct at any point unethical? Discuss.*
- **Legal Environment** *Culbertson and some other witnesses testified that he did not engage in any sexually inappropriate behavior. Should an appellate court reverse a jury's decision simply due to contrary evidence? Why or why not?*

Harassment by Supervisors For an employer to be held liable for a supervisor's sexual harassment, the supervisor normally must have taken a *tangible employment action* against the employee. A **tangible employment action** is a significant change in employment status or benefits. Such an action occurs when an employee is fired, refused a promotion, demoted, or reassigned to a position with significantly different responsibilities, for instance. Only a supervisor, or another person acting with the authority of the employer, can cause this sort of harm. A constructive discharge also qualifies as a tangible employment action.

The United States Supreme Court issued several important rulings in cases alleging sexual harassment by supervisors that established what is known as the "*Ellerth/Faragher* affirmative defense."[13] The defense has two elements:

1. The employer must have taken reasonable care to prevent and promptly correct any sexually harassing behavior (by establishing effective harassment policies and complaint procedures, for instance).
2. The plaintiff-employee must have unreasonably failed to take advantage of preventive or corrective opportunities provided by the employer to avoid harm.

An employer that can prove both elements normally will not be liable for a supervisor's harassment.

Retaliation by Employers Employers sometimes retaliate against employees who complain about sexual harassment or other Title VII violations. Retaliation can take many forms. An employer might demote or fire the person, or otherwise change the terms, conditions, and benefits of employment.

Title VII prohibits retaliation, and employees can sue their employers when it occurs. In a *retaliation claim,* an individual asserts that she or he has suffered harm as a result of making a charge, testifying, or participating in a Title VII investigation or proceeding.

Requirements for Protection. To be protected under Title VII's retaliation provisions, the plaintiff must have opposed a practice prohibited by Title VII and suffered an adverse employment action as a result of that opposition. ■ **CASE IN POINT 35.11** Myrta Morales-Cruz had a tenure-track teaching position at the University of Puerto Rico School of Law. When her probationary period was almost over, Morales-Cruz asked the university's administrative committee to grant a one-year extension for her tenure review. The dean recommended that the extension be granted but also called her "insecure," "immature," and "fragile." Another professor commented that had she shown "poor judgment" and exhibited "personality flaws."

After Morales-Cruz complained about these comments in writing to the chancellor, the dean recommended denying the one-year extension, and the administrative committee did just that. Morales-Cruz later filed a retaliation lawsuit. She claimed that the dean had retaliated against her for complaining to the chancellor about the "discriminatory" comments made in the course of her request for an extension.

The court held that Morales-Cruz had not provided a reasonable foundation for a retaliation action. Under Title VII, an employer may not retaliate against an employee because he or she has opposed a practice prohibited by Title VII. But the court found that Morales-Cruz did not allege any facts that could be construed as gender-based discrimination. Although the comments she complained about were hardly flattering, they were entirely gender-neutral. Thus, she was not engaging in protected conduct when she opposed the remarks.[14] ■

Protection May Extend to Others. The Supreme Court has ruled that Title VII's retaliation protection extended to an employee who spoke out about discrimination against another employee during an employer's internal investigation.[15] The Court has also held that Title VII protected an employee who was fired after his fiancée filed a gender discrimination claim against their employer.[16]

Harassment by Co-Workers and Others When the harassment of co-workers, rather than supervisors, creates a hostile working environment, an employee may still have a cause of action against the employer. Normally, though, the employer will be held liable only if it knew or should have known about the harassment and failed to take immediate remedial action.

Occasionally, a court may also hold an employer liable for harassment by *nonemployees* if the employer knew about the harassment and failed to take corrective action. ■ **EXAMPLE 35.12** Jordan, who owns and manages a Great Bites restaurant, knows that one of his regular customers, Dean, repeatedly harasses Kaylia, a waitress. If Jordan does nothing and permits the harassment to continue, he may be liable under Title VII even though Dean is not an employee of the restaurant. ■

---

13. *Burlington Industries, Inc. v. Ellerth*, 524 U.S. 742, 118 S.Ct. 2257, 141 L.Ed.2d 633 (1998); and *Faragher v. City of Boca Raton*, 524 U.S. 775, 118 S.Ct. 2275, 141 L.Ed.2d 662 (1998).

14. *Morales-Cruz v. University of Puerto Rico*, 676 F.3d 220 (1st Cir. 2012).
15. *Crawford v. Metropolitan Government of Nashville and Davidson County, Tennessee*, 555 U.S. 271, 129 S.Ct. 846, 172 L.Ed.2d 650 (2009).
16. See *Thompson v. North American Stainless, LP*, 562 U.S. 170, 131 S.Ct. 863, 178 L.Ed.2d 694 (2011).

Same-Gender Harassment In *Oncale v. Sundowner Offshore Services, Inc.,*[17] the United States Supreme Court held that Title VII protection extends to individuals who are sexually harassed by members of the same gender. Proving that the harassment in same-gender cases is "based on sex" can be difficult, though. It is easier to establish a case of same-gender harassment when the harasser is homosexual.

Sexual-Orientation Harassment Federal law (Title VII) does not prohibit discrimination or harassment based on a person's sexual orientation. Nonetheless, a growing number of states have enacted laws that prohibit sexual-orientation discrimination in private employment.[18] Some states, such as Oregon, explicitly prohibit discrimination based on a person's gender identity or expression. Many companies have also voluntarily established nondiscrimination policies that include sexual orientation.

35–1i Online Harassment

Employees' online activities can create a hostile working environment in many ways. Racial jokes, ethnic slurs, or other comments contained in e-mail, texts, blogs, or social media can lead to claims of hostile-environment harassment or other forms of discrimination. A worker who regularly sees sexually explicit images on a co-worker's computer screen may find the images offensive and claim that they create a hostile working environment. Nevertheless, employers may be able to avoid liability for online harassment by taking prompt remedial action.

35–1j Remedies under Title VII

Employer liability under Title VII can be extensive. If the plaintiff successfully proves that unlawful discrimination occurred, he or she may be awarded reinstatement, back pay, retroactive promotions, and damages.

Several limits apply to damages. Compensatory damages are available only in cases of intentional discrimination. Punitive damages may be recovered against a private employer only if the employer acted with malice or reckless indifference to an individual's rights. The total amount of compensatory and punitive damages that plaintiffs can recover from specific employers depends on the size of the employer. For instance, there is a $50,000 cap on damages from employers with one hundred or fewer employees.

35–2 Discrimination Based on Age

Age discrimination is potentially the most widespread form of discrimination because anyone—regardless of race, color, national origin, or gender—could be a victim at some point in life. The Age Discrimination in Employment Act[19] (ADEA), as amended, prohibits employment discrimination on the basis of age against individuals forty years of age or older. The act also prohibits mandatory retirement for nonmanagerial workers. In addition, the ADEA protects federal and private-sector employees from retaliation based on age-related complaints.[20]

For the act to apply, an employer must have twenty or more employees, and the employer's business activities must affect interstate commerce. The EEOC administers the ADEA, but the act also permits private causes of action against employers for age discrimination.

35–2a Procedures under the ADEA

The burden-shifting procedure under the ADEA differs from the procedure under Title VII. This difference resulted from a United States Supreme Court decision that dramatically changed the burden of proof in age discrimination cases.[21]

As explained earlier, if the plaintiff in a Title VII case can show that the employer was motivated, at least in part, by unlawful discrimination, the burden of proof shifts to the employer. Thus, in cases in which the employer has a "mixed motive" for discharging an employee, the employer has the burden of proving that its reason was legitimate.

Under the ADEA, in contrast, a plaintiff must show that the unlawful discrimination was not just *a* reason but *the* reason for the adverse employment action. In other words, the employee has the burden of establishing *but for* causation—that is, "but for" the employee's age, the action would not have been taken.

***Prima Facie* Age Discrimination** To establish a *prima facie* case of age discrimination, the plaintiff must show that she or he was the following:

1. A member of the protected age group.
2. Qualified for the position from which she or he was discharged.
3. Discharged because of age discrimination.

---

17. 523 U.S. 75, 118 S.Ct. 998, 140 L.Ed.2d 207 (1998).
18. See, for instance, 775 Illinois Compiled Statutes 5/1–103.

19. 29 U.S.C. Sections 621–634.
20. *Gomez-Perez v. Potter,* 553 U.S. 474, 128 S.Ct. 1931, 170 L.Ed.2d 887 (2008).
21. *Gross v. FBL Financial Services, Inc.,* 557 U.S. 167, 129 S.Ct. 2343, 174 L.Ed.2d 119 (2009).

Then the burden shifts to the employer to give a legitimate nondiscriminatory reason for the adverse action.

Pretext   If the employer offers a legitimate reason for its action, then the plaintiff must show that the stated reason is only a pretext. The plaintiff is required to prove that the plaintiff's age was the real reason for the employer's decision.

■ **CASE IN POINT 35.13**   Josephine Mora, a fund-raiser for Jackson Memorial Foundation, Inc., was sixty-two years old when the foundation's chief executive officer (CEO) fired her. Mora filed an age discrimination suit against the foundation. She asserted that when she was fired, the CEO told her, "I need someone younger I can pay less." A witness heard that statement and also heard the CEO say that Mora was "too old to be working here anyway." The CEO denied making these statements, and the foundation claimed that Mora had been terminated for poor job performance.

A district court granted a summary judgment in the foundation's favor, and Mora appealed. A federal appellate court reversed, concluding that the lower court's analysis of causation was incorrect. The court held that a reasonable juror could have accepted that the CEO had made discriminatory remarks and could have found that these remarks were sufficient evidence of a discriminatory motive. If so, that could show that Mora was fired because of her age. The court therefore remanded the case to the lower court for a trial.[22] ■

35–2b Replacing Older Workers with Younger Workers

Numerous age discrimination cases have been brought against employers who, to cut costs, replaced older, higher-salaried employees with younger, lower-salaried workers. In such situations, whether a firing is discriminatory or simply part of a rational business decision to prune the company's ranks is not always clear.

The plaintiff must prove that the discharge was motivated by age bias. The plaintiff need not prove that she or he was replaced by a person "outside the protected class" (under the age of forty). The replacement worker need only be younger than the plaintiff. Nevertheless, the greater the age gap, the more likely the plaintiff will succeed in showing age discrimination.

35–2c State Employees Not Covered by the ADEA

Generally, the states are immune from lawsuits brought by private individuals in federal court (unless a state consents to such a suit). This immunity stems from the United States Supreme Court's interpretation of the Eleventh Amendment.

State immunity under the Eleventh Amendment is not absolute. In some situations, such as when fundamental rights are at stake, Congress has the power to abrogate (abolish) state immunity to private suits through legislation. Such legislation must unequivocally show Congress's intent to subject states to private suits.[23]

Generally, though, the Court has found that state employers are immune from private suits brought by employees under the ADEA. State employers are also immune from suits brought under the Americans with Disabilities Act[24] and the Fair Labor Standards Act.[25] They are *not* immune from the requirements of the Family and Medical Leave Act.[26]

35–3 Discrimination Based on Disability

The Americans with Disabilities Act (ADA)[27] prohibits disability-based discrimination in all workplaces with fifteen or more workers. An exception is state government employers, who are generally immune under the Eleventh Amendment, as just mentioned. Basically, the ADA requires that employers "reasonably accommodate" the needs of persons with disabilities unless to do so would cause the employer to suffer an "undue hardship." The ADA Amendments Act[28] broadened the coverage of the ADA's protections, as discussed shortly.

35–3a Procedures under the ADA

To prevail on a claim under the ADA, a plaintiff must show that he or she (1) has a disability, (2) is otherwise qualified for the employment in question, and (3) was

22. *Mora v. Jackson Memorial Foundation, Inc.*, 597 F.3d 1201 (11th Cir. 2010).

23. *Tennessee v. Lane*, 541 U.S. 509, 124 S.Ct. 1978, 158 L.Ed.2d 820 (2004).
24. *Board of Trustees of the University of Alabama v. Garrett*, 531 U.S. 356, 121 S.Ct. 955, 148 L.Ed.2d 866 (2001).
25. *Alden v. Maine*, 527 U.S. 706, 119 S.Ct. 2240, 144 L.Ed.2d 636 (1999).
26. *Nevada Department of Human Resources v. Hibbs*, 538 U.S. 721, 123 S.Ct. 1972, 155 L.Ed.2d 953 (2003).
27. 42 U.S.C. Sections 12103–12118.
28. 42 U.S.C. Sections 12103 and 12205a.

excluded from the employment solely because of the disability. As in Title VII cases, the plaintiff must pursue the claim through the EEOC before filing an action in court for a violation of the ADA.

The EEOC may decide to investigate and perhaps sue the employer on behalf of the employee. The EEOC can bring a suit even if the employee previously signed an agreement with the employer to submit job-related disputes to arbitration.[29] If the EEOC decides not to sue, then the employee may do so.

Plaintiffs in lawsuits brought under the ADA may seek many of the same remedies that are available under Title VII. These include reinstatement, back pay, a limited amount of compensatory and punitive damages (for intentional discrimination), and certain other forms of relief. Repeat violators may be ordered to pay fines of up to $100,000.

35–3b What Is a Disability?

The ADA is broadly drafted to cover persons with physical or mental impairments that "substantially limit" their everyday activities. Specifically, the ADA defines a *disability* as including any of the following:

1. A physical or mental impairment that substantially limits one or more of the major life activities of the affected individual.
2. A record of having such an impairment.
3. Being regarded as having such an impairment.

Health conditions that have been considered disabilities under federal law include alcoholism, acquired immune deficiency syndrome (AIDS), blindness, cancer, cerebral palsy, diabetes, heart disease, muscular dystrophy, and paraplegia. Testing positive for the human immunodeficiency virus (HIV) has qualified as a disability, as has morbid obesity. (A morbidly obese person weighs twice the normal weight for his or her height.)

Association with Disabled Persons A separate provision in the ADA prevents employers from taking adverse employment actions based on stereotypes or assumptions about individuals who associate with people who have disabilities.[30] An employer cannot, for instance, refuse to hire the parent of a child with a disability based on the assumption that the person will miss work too often or be unreliable.

■ **EXAMPLE 35.14** Joan, an employer, refuses to hire Edward, who has a daughter with a physical disability. She consciously bases her decision on the assumption that Edward will have to miss work frequently to care for his daughter. Edward can sue Joan for violating the ADA's provisions. ■

Mitigating Measures At one time, the courts focused on whether a person had a disability *after* the use of corrective devices or medication. Thus, a person with severe myopia (nearsightedness) whose eyesight could be corrected by wearing glasses did not qualify as having a disability. With the corrective lenses, the person's major life activities were not substantially impaired. Then Congress amended the ADA to strengthen its protections and prohibit employers from considering mitigating measures when determining if an individual has a disability.

Disability is now determined on a case-by-case basis. A condition may fit the definition of disability in one set of circumstances, but not in another. ■ **CASE IN POINT 35.15** Larry Rohr, a welding specialist for a power district in Arizona, was diagnosed with type 2 diabetes. To keep his condition under control, Rohr was required to follow a complex regimen of daily insulin injections and blood tests, as well as a strict diet. Therefore, his physician forbade him from taking work assignments that involved overnight, out-of-town travel, which were common in his job.

Because of these limitations, the power district asked him to transfer, apply for federal disability benefits, or take early retirement. Rohr sued for disability discrimination. The lower court granted summary judgment for the employer. Rohr appealed. A federal appellate court reversed. The court held that under the amended ADA, diabetes is a disability if it significantly restricts an individual's eating (a major life activity), as it did for Rohr. Therefore, Rohr was entitled to a trial on his discrimination claim.[31] ■

Disclosure of Confidential Medical Information ADA provisions also require employers to keep their employees' medical information confidential.[32] An employee who discovers that an employer has disclosed his or her confidential medical information has a right to sue the employer—even if the employee was not technically disabled. The prohibition against disclosure also applies to other employees acting on behalf of the employer.

---

29. This was the Supreme Court's ruling in *EEOC v. Waffle House, Inc.,* 534 U.S. 279, 122 S.Ct. 754, 151 L.Ed.2d 755 (2002).
30. 42 U.S.C. Section 12112(b)(4).

31. *Rohr v. Salt River Project Agricultural Improvement and Power District,* 555 F.3d 850 (9th Cir. 2009).
32. 42 U.S.C. Sections 12112(d)(3)(B), (C), and 12112(d)(4)(C).

■ **CASE IN POINT 35.16** George Shoun was working at his job at Best Formed Plastics, Inc., when he fell and injured his shoulder. Another Best Formed employee, Jane Stewart, prepared an accident report for the incident and processed Shoun's workers' compensation claim. As a result of the injury, Shoun had to take several months off work and received workers' compensation.

Stewart posted on her Facebook page a statement about how Shoun's shoulder injury "kept him away from work for 11 months and now he is trying to sue us." Shoun sued Best Formed under the ADA for wrongfully disclosing confidential information about his medical condition to other people via Facebook. He claimed that the action resulted in loss of employment and impairment of his earning capacity. The court allowed Shoun's claim to go forward to trial.[33] ■

35–3c Reasonable Accommodation

The ADA does not require that employers accommodate the needs of job applicants or employees with disabilities who are not otherwise qualified for the work. If a job applicant or an employee with a disability, with reasonable accommodation, can perform essential job functions, however, the employer must make the accommodation.

Required modifications may include installing ramps for a wheelchair, establishing flexible working hours, creating or modifying job assignments, and designing or improving training materials and procedures. Generally, employers should give primary consideration to employees' preferences in deciding what accommodations should be made.

Undue Hardship Employers who do not accommodate the needs of persons with disabilities must demonstrate that the accommodations would cause *undue hardship* in terms of being significantly difficult or expensive for the employer. Usually, the courts decide whether an accommodation constitutes an undue hardship on a case-by-case basis.

■ **EXAMPLE 35.17** Bryan Lockhart, who uses a wheelchair, works for a cell phone company that provides parking for its employees. Lockhart informs his supervisor that the parking spaces are so narrow that he is unable to extend the ramp on his van that allows him to get in and out of the vehicle. Lockhart therefore requests that the company reasonably accommodate his needs by paying a monthly fee for him to use a larger parking space in an adjacent lot. In this situation, a court will likely find that it is *not* an undue hardship for the employer to pay for additional parking for Lockhart. ■

Job Applications and Physical Exams Employers must modify their job-application and selection process so that those with disabilities can compete for jobs with those who do not have disabilities. For instance, a job announcement might be modified to allow applicants to respond by e-mail as well as by telephone, so that it does not discriminate against potential applicants with hearing impairments.

Employers are restricted in the kinds of questions they may ask on job-application forms and during pre-employment interviews. In addition, employers cannot require persons with disabilities to submit to preemployment physicals unless such exams are required of all other applicants. An employer can disqualify the applicant only if the medical problems discovered during a preemployment physical would make it impossible for the applicant to perform the job.

Health-Insurance Plans Workers with disabilities must be given equal access to any health insurance provided to other employees and cannot be excluded from coverage. An employer can put a limit, or cap, on health-care payments under its group health policy, but the cap must apply equally to all insured employees. Any group health-care plan that makes a disability-based distinction in its benefits violates the ADA (unless the employer can justify its actions under the business necessity defense, discussed shortly).

Substance Abusers Drug addiction is considered a disability under the ADA because it is a substantially limiting impairment. The act does not protect individuals who are actually using illegal drugs, however. Instead, the ADA protects only persons with *former* drug addictions—those who have completed or are now participating in a supervised drug-rehabilitation program. Individuals who have used drugs casually in the past also are not protected under the act. They are not considered addicts and therefore do not have a disability (addiction).

People suffering from alcoholism are also protected by the ADA. Employers cannot legally discriminate against employees simply because they suffer from alcoholism. Of course, employers can prohibit the use of alcohol in the workplace and require that employees not be under the influence of alcohol while working. Employers can also fire or refuse to hire a person who is an alcoholic if (1) the person poses a *substantial risk of harm* to himself or herself or to others, and (2) the risk cannot be reduced by reasonable accommodation.

---

33. *Shoun v. Best Formed Plastics, Inc.*, 28 F.Supp.3d 786 (N.D.Ind. 2014).

Exhibit 35–1 outlines the coverage of the employment discrimination laws discussed in this chapter.

35–4 Discrimination Based on Military Status

In 1994, Congress enacted the Uniformed Services Employment and Reemployment Rights Act (USERRA).[34] The USERRA protects civilian job rights and benefits for members of the military, former military personnel, and reservists. It also provides additional protections for veterans who are disabled. Most importantly, the USERRA prohibits discrimination against persons who have served in the military. In effect, it makes military service and status a protected class and gives members of this class a right to sue an employer for violations.

35–4a Broad Application and Provisions

The USERRA covers *all* employers, public and private, large and small. Even an employer with only one employee is subject to its provisions.[35] The act also applies to United States employers operating in foreign countries.

Under the USERRA, military plaintiffs can sue not only the employer but also individual employees who were

34. Pub. L. No. 103-353, codified at 38 U.S.C. Sections 4301-4335.
35. 20 C.F.R. Section 1002.34(a).

acting in an official capacity for the employer. In other words, these employees—supervisors, for instance—can be held personally liable for violations. Additionally, there is no statute of limitations for bringing a lawsuit. The cause of action could have arisen ten weeks or ten years before the suit was filed.

The USERRA specifies that veterans can be terminated from their employment only "for cause." The employer is obligated to give employees a list of all the behaviors that would trigger a for-cause termination.

35–4b *Prima Facie* Case of Discrimination under the USERRA

To establish a *prima facie* case of discrimination (and retaliation) under the USERRA, the plaintiff must establish that the employer took an adverse employment action based in part on the employee's connection with the military. The connection to the military may be through the plaintiff's membership, service, or application for service, or it may be through providing testimony or statements concerning the military service of another.[36] If another similarly situated person who did not serve in the military or engage in a protected activity was treated more favorably than the plaintiff, the employer has violated the USERRA.

■ **CASE IN POINT 35.18** Baldo Bello, a staff sergeant with the United States Marine Corps Reserve, was employed by the Village of Skokie as a police officer. Police officers

36. 38 U.S.C. Section 4311(c).

EXHIBIT 35–1 Coverage of Employment Discrimination Laws

Title VII of the Civil Rights Act	Age Discrimination in Employment Act	Americans with Disabilities Act (as Amended)
Prohibits discrimination based on race, color, national origin, religion, gender (including wage discrimination), and pregnancy; prohibits sexual harassment.	Prohibits discrimination against persons over forty years of age.	Prohibits discrimination against persons with a mental or physical impairment that substantially limits a major life activity now or in the past, or who are regarded as having such an impairment, or who are associated with a disabled person.
Applies to employers with fifteen or more employees.	Applies to employers with twenty or more employees.	Applies to employers with fifteen or more employees.

in Skokie normally have nine regular days off (RDO) per month and eight sick days per year. Skokie officers who are in the reserve receive two weeks of paid leave for annual training each summer, but they do not receive pay for the required weekend military training. During his first four years as an officer at Skokie, Bello always requested RDOs to cover his weekend training drills.

After that, Bello started requesting military leave for the two to four days of drills per month, in addition to his nine RDO days. Skokie at first granted Bello military leave for monthly drills but later began to deny the requests. When Skokie officials told Bello that he needed to schedule his RDOs to cover his weekend military training, Bello filed suit in a federal district court alleging violations of the USERRA. Skokie filed a motion for summary judgment, which the court denied. The court found that Bello was meeting his employer's legitimate expectations. Bello was therefore entitled to a trial on the issue of whether Skokie had treated his leave requests less favorably than requests from other employees.[37] ■

35–4c Plaintiffs May Be Entitled to Promotions

Under the USERRA, returning service members are to be reemployed in the jobs that they would have attained had they not been absent for military service. Reinstatement could affect their seniority, status, pay, and other rights and benefits (such as health and pension plans). In essence, this means that if a returning service member sues an employer for violations of the USERRA and is successful, she or he could receive not only damages and reinstatement but also a promotion.

35–5 Defenses to Employment Discrimination

The first line of defense for an employer charged with employment discrimination is to assert that the plaintiff has failed to meet his or her initial burden of proving that discrimination occurred. As noted, plaintiffs bringing age discrimination claims may find it difficult to meet this initial burden because they must prove that age discrimination was the reason for their employer's decision.

Once a plaintiff succeeds in proving that discrimination occurred, the burden shifts to the employer to justify the discriminatory practice. Possible justifications

---

37. *Bello v. Village of Skokie*, ___ F.Supp.3d ___, 2015 WL 9582986 (N.D. Ill. 2015).

include that the discrimination was the result of a business necessity, a bona fide occupational qualification, or a seniority system. In some situations, as noted earlier, an effective antiharassment policy and prompt remedial action when harassment occurs may shield employers from liability for sexual harassment under Title VII.

35–5a Business Necessity

An employer may defend against a claim of disparate-impact (unintentional) discrimination by asserting that a practice that has a discriminatory effect is a **business necessity.** ■ **EXAMPLE 35.19** EarthFix, Inc., an international consulting agency, requires its applicants to be fluent in at least one foreign language. If this requirement is shown to have a discriminatory effect, EarthFix can defend it based on business necessity. That is, the company can argue that its workers must speak more than one language to perform their jobs at the required level of competence. If EarthFix can demonstrate a definite connection between foreign language fluency and job performance, it normally will succeed in this business necessity defense. ■

35–5b Bona Fide Occupational Qualification

Another defense applies when discrimination against a protected class is essential to a job—that is, when a particular trait is a **bona fide occupational qualification (BFOQ).** Note that race, color, and national origin can never be BFOQs.

Generally, courts have restricted the BFOQ defense to situations in which the employee's gender or religion is essential to the job. For instance, a women's clothing store might legitimately hire only female sales attendants if part of an attendant's job involves assisting clients in the store's dressing rooms.

35–5c Seniority Systems

An employer with a history of discrimination may have no members of protected classes in upper-level positions. Nevertheless, the employer may have a defense against a discrimination suit if promotions or other job benefits have been distributed according to a fair *seniority system.* In a **seniority system,** workers with more years of service are promoted first or laid off last.

■ **CASE IN POINT 35.20** Cathalene Johnson, an African American woman, was a senior service agent for Federal Express Corporation (FedEx) for more than seventeen years. She resigned in 2014 and filed suit against FedEx for discrimination based on race and gender, as well as for violation of the Equal Pay Act. Johnson claimed that FedEx had paid a white male co-worker about two dollars more per hour than she had received for basically the same position. FedEx argued that the man had seniority. He had worked for FedEx for seven years longer, was the most senior employee at the station where Johnson worked, and had been a courier in addition to being a service agent. The court ruled that FedEx's seniority system was fair and provided a defense to Johnson's claims.[38] ■

35–5d After-Acquired Evidence of Employee Misconduct

In some situations, employers have attempted to avoid liability for employment discrimination on the basis of "after-acquired evidence" of an employee's misconduct. After-acquired evidence refers to evidence that the employer discovers after a lawsuit has been filed.

■ **EXAMPLE 35.21** Pratt Legal Services fires Lucy, who then sues Pratt for employment discrimination. During pretrial investigation, Pratt discovers that Lucy made material misrepresentations on her job application. Had Pratt known of these misrepresentations, it would have had grounds to fire Lucy. ■

After-acquired evidence of wrongdoing cannot shield an employer entirely from liability for employment discrimination. It may, however, be used to limit the amount of damages for which the employer is liable.

35–6 Affirmative Action

Federal statutes and regulations providing for equal opportunity in the workplace were designed to reduce or eliminate discriminatory practices with respect to hiring, retaining, and promoting employees. **Affirmative action** programs go a step further and attempt to "make up" for past patterns of discrimination by giving members of protected classes preferential treatment in hiring or promotion. During the 1960s, all federal and state government agencies, private companies that contracted to do business with the federal government, and institutions that received federal funding were required to implement affirmative action policies.

Title VII of the Civil Rights Act neither requires nor prohibits affirmative action. Thus, most private companies and organizations have not been required to implement affirmative action policies, though many have done so voluntarily. Affirmative action programs have been controversial, however, particularly when they have resulted in reverse discrimination against members of a majority group, such as white males.

35–6a Equal Protection Issues

Because of their inherently discriminatory nature, affirmative action programs may violate the equal protection clause of the Fourteenth Amendment to the U.S. Constitution. Any federal, state, or local government affirmative action program that uses racial or ethnic classifications as the basis for making decisions is subject to strict scrutiny (the highest standard to meet) by the courts.

Today, an affirmative action program normally is constitutional only if it attempts to remedy past discrimination and does not make use of quotas or preferences. Furthermore, once such a program has succeeded in the goal of remedying past discrimination, it must be changed or eliminated.

35–6b State Laws Prohibiting Affirmative Action Programs

Some states have enacted laws that prohibit affirmative action programs at public institutions (colleges, universities, and state agencies) within their borders. These states include California, Maryland, Michigan, New Hampshire, Oklahoma, Virginia, and Washington. The United States Supreme Court recognized that states have the power to enact such bans in 2014.

■ **CASE IN POINT 35.22** Michigan voters passed an initiative to amend the state's constitution to prohibit publicly funded colleges from granting preferential treatment to any group on the basis of race, sex, color, ethnicity, or national origin. The law also prohibited Michigan from considering race and gender in public hiring and contracting decisions.

A lawsuit was filed challenging the initiative as a violation of the equal protection clause in the U.S. Constitution. Although a federal appellate court held that the law violated the equal protection clause, the United States Supreme Court reversed. The Court ruled that a state has the inherent power to ban affirmative action within that state, but it did not rule on the constitutionality of any specific affirmative action program.[39] ■

---

38. *Johnson v. Federal Express Corp.*, 996 F.Supp.2d 302 (M.D.Pa. 2014).

39. *Schuette v. Coalition to Defend Affirmative Action, Integration and Immigrant Rights*, ___ U.S. ___, 134 S.Ct. 1623, 188 L.Ed.2d 613 (2014).

Reviewing: Employment Discrimination

Amaani Lyle, an African American woman, was hired by Warner Brothers Television Productions to be a scriptwriters' assistant for the writers of *Friends,* a popular adult-oriented television series. One of her essential job duties was to type detailed notes for the scriptwriters during brainstorming sessions in which they discussed jokes, dialogue, and story lines. The writers then combed through Lyle's notes after the meetings for script material. During these meetings, the three male scriptwriters told lewd and vulgar jokes and made sexually explicit comments and gestures. They often talked about their personal sexual experiences and fantasies, and some of these conversations were then used in episodes of *Friends.*

During the meetings, Lyle never complained that she found the writers' conduct offensive. After four months, Lyle was fired because she could not type fast enough to keep up with the writers' conversations during the meetings. She filed a suit against Warner Brothers, alleging sexual harassment and claiming that her termination was based on racial discrimination. Using the information presented in the chapter, answer the following questions.

1. Would Lyle's claim of racial discrimination be for intentional (disparate-treatment) or unintentional (disparate-impact) discrimination? Explain.
2. Can Lyle establish a *prima facie* case of racial discrimination? Why or why not?
3. When Lyle was hired, she was told that typing speed was extremely important to the position. At the time, she maintained that she could type eighty words per minute, so she was not given a typing test. It later turned out that Lyle could type only fifty words per minute. What impact might typing speed have on Lyle's lawsuit?
4. Lyle's sexual-harassment claim is based on the hostile working environment created by the writers' sexually offensive conduct at meetings that she was required to attend. The writers, however, argue that their behavior was essential to the "creative process" of writing for *Friends,* a show that routinely contained sexual innuendos and adult humor. Which defense discussed in the chapter might Warner Brothers assert using this argument?

> **Debate This** . . . *Members of minority groups and women have made enough economic progress in the last several decades that they no longer need special legislation to protect them.*

Terms and Concepts

affirmative action 681	disparate-impact	*prima facie* case 665
bona fide occupational qualification	discrimination 666	protected class 664
(BFOQ) 680	disparate-treatment	seniority system 680
business necessity 680	discrimination 665	sexual harassment 672
constructive discharge 672	employment discrimination 664	tangible employment action 674

Issue Spotters

1. Ruth is a supervisor for a *Subs & Suds* restaurant. Tim is a *Subs & Suds* employee. The owner announces that some employees will be discharged. Ruth tells Tim that if he has sex with her, he can keep his job. Is this sexual harassment? Why or why not? (See *Title VII of the Civil Rights Act.*)

2. Koko, a person with a disability, applies for a job at Lively Sales Corporation for which she is well qualified, but she is rejected. Lively continues to seek applicants and eventually fills the position with a person who does not have a disability. Could Koko succeed in a suit against Lively for discrimination? Explain. (See *Discrimination Based on Disability.*)

- **Check your answers to the Issue Spotters against the answers provided in Appendix D at the end of this text.**

Business Scenarios

35–1. Title VII Violations. Discuss fully whether either of the following actions would constitute a violation of Title VII of the 1964 Civil Rights Act, as amended: (*See Title VII of the Civil Rights Act.*)

(a) Tennington, Inc., is a consulting firm with ten employees. These employees travel on consulting jobs in seven states. Tennington has an employment record of hiring only white males.

(b) Novo Films is making a movie about Africa and needs to employ approximately one hundred extras for this picture. To hire these extras, Novo advertises in all major newspapers in Southern California. The ad states that only African Americans need apply.

35–2. Religious Discrimination. Gina Gomez, a devout Roman Catholic, worked for Sam's Department Stores, Inc.,

in Phoenix, Arizona. Sam's considered Gomez a productive employee because her sales exceeded $200,000 per year. At the time, the store gave its managers the discretion to grant unpaid leave to employees but prohibited vacations or leave during the holiday season—October through December. Gomez felt that she had a "calling" to go on a "pilgrimage" in October to a location in Bosnia where some persons claimed to have had visions of the Virgin Mary. The Catholic Church had not designated the site an official pilgrimage site, the visions were not expected to be stronger in October, and tours were available at other times. The store managers denied Gomez's request for leave, but she had a nonrefundable ticket and left anyway. Sam's terminated her employment, and she could not find another job. Can Gomez establish a *prima facie* case of religious discrimination? Explain. (*See Title VII of the Civil Rights Act.*)

Business Case Problems

35–3. Spotlight on Dress Code Policies—Discrimination Based on Gender. Burlington Coat Factory Warehouse, Inc., had a dress code that required male salesclerks to wear business attire consisting of slacks, shirt, and a necktie. Female salesclerks, by contrast, were required to wear a smock so that customers could readily identify them. Karen O'Donnell and other female employees refused to wear smocks. Instead they reported to work in business attire and were suspended. After numerous suspensions, the female employees were fired for violating Burlington's dress code policy. All other conditions of employment, including salary, hours, and benefits, were the same for female and male employees. Was the dress code policy discriminatory? Why or why not? [*O'Donnell v. Burlington Coat Factory Warehouse, Inc.,* 656 F.Supp. 263 (S.D. Ohio 1987)] (*See Title VII of the Civil Rights Act.*)

35–4. Sexual Harassment by Co-Worker. Billie Bradford worked for the Kentucky Department of Community Based Services (DCBS). One of Bradford's co-workers, Lisa Stander, routinely engaged in extreme sexual behavior (such as touching herself and making crude comments) in Bradford's presence. Bradford and others regularly complained about Stander's conduct to their supervisor, Angie Taylor. Rather than resolve the problem, Taylor nonchalantly told Stander to stop, encouraged Bradford to talk to Stander, and suggested that Stander was just having fun. Assuming that Bradford was subjected to a hostile work environment, could DCBS be liable? Why or why not? [*Bradford v. Department of Community Based Services,* 2012 WL 360032 (E.D.Ky. 2012)] (*See Title VII of the Civil Rights Act.*)

35–5. Business Case Problem with Sample Answer—Age Discrimination. Beginning in 1986, Paul Rangel was a sales professional for the pharmaceutical company sanofi-aventis U.S. LLC (S-A). Rangel had satisfactory performance reviews until 2006, when S-A issued new "Expectations" guidelines that included sales call quotas and other standards that he failed to meet. After two years of negative performance reviews, Rangel—who was then more than forty years old—was terminated. The termination was part of a nationwide reduction in force of all sales professionals who had not met the "Expectations" guidelines, including younger workers. Did S-A engage in age discrimination? Discuss. [*Rangel v. sanofi aventis U.S. LLC,* 2013 WL 142040 (10th Cir. 2013)] (*See Discrimination Based on Age.*)

• For a sample answer to Problem 35–5, go to Appendix E at the end of this text.

35–6. Discrimination Based on Disability. Cynthia Horn worked for Knight Facilities Management–GM, Inc., in Detroit, Michigan, as a janitor. When Horn developed a sensitivity to cleaning products, her physician gave her a "no exposure to cleaning solutions" restriction. Knight discussed possible accommodations with Horn. She suggested that restrooms be eliminated from her cleaning route or that she be provided with a respirator. Knight explained that she would be exposed to cleaning solutions in any situation and concluded that there was no work available within her physician's restriction. Has Knight violated the Americans with Disabilities Act by failing to provide Horn with the requested accommodations? Explain. [*Horn v. Knight Facilities Management–GM, Inc.,* 556 Fed.Appx. 452 (6th Cir. 2014)] (*See Discrimination Based on Disability.*)

35–7. Sexual Harassment. Jamel Blanton was a male employee at a Pizza Hut restaurant operated by Newton Associates, Inc., in San Antonio, Texas. Blanton was subjected to sexual and racial harassment by the general manager, who was female. Newton had a clear, straightforward antidiscrimination policy and complaint procedure. The policy provided that in such a situation, an employee should complain to the harasser's supervisor. Blanton alerted a shift leader and an assistant manager about the harassment, but they were subordinate to the general manager and did not report the harassment to higher-level management. When Blanton finally complained to a manager with authority over the general manager, the employer investigated and fired the general manager within four days. Blanton filed a suit in a federal district court against Newton, seeking to impose liability on the employer for the general manager's actions. What is Newton's best defense? Discuss. [*Blanton v. Newton Associates, Inc.,* 593 Fed.Appx. 389 (5th Cir. 2015)] (See *Title VII of the Civil Rights Act.*)

35–8. Discrimination Based on Disability. Dennis Wallace was a deputy sheriff for Stanislaus County, California, when he injured his left knee. After surgery, he was subject to limits on prolonged standing, walking, and running. The county assigned him to work as a bailiff. The sergeants who supervised him rated his performance above average. Less than a year later, without consulting those supervisors, the county placed him on an unpaid leave of absence, under the mistaken belief that he could not safely perform the essential functions of the job. Wallace filed an action in a California state court against the county, alleging discrimination based on disability. Under state law, discriminatory intent is shown by evidence that an actual or perceived disability was a "substantial motivating factor or reason" for an employer's adverse employment action. An employee is not required to show that the action was motivated by animosity or ill will. Could Wallace likely prove the "substantial motivating factor or reason" element? Explain. [*Wallace v. County of Stanislaus,* 245 Cal.App.4th 109, 199 Cal.Rptr.3d 462 (5 Dist. 2016)] (See *Discrimination Based on Disability.*)

35–9. A Question of Ethics—Retaliation by Employers. Shane Dawson, a male homosexual, worked for Entek International. Some of Dawson's co-workers, including his supervisor, made derogatory comments about his sexual orientation. Dawson's work deteriorated. He filed a complaint with Entek's human resources department. Two days later, he was fired. State law made it unlawful for an employer to discriminate against an individual based on sexual orientation. [Dawson v. Entek International, 630 F.3d 928 (9th Cir. 2011)] (See *Title VII of the Civil Rights Act.*)

(a) Could Dawson establish a claim for retaliation? Explain.

(b) Should homosexuals be a protected class under Title VII of the Civil Rights Act? Discuss the arguments for and against amending federal law to prohibit employment discrimination based on sexual orientation.

Legal Reasoning Group Activity

35–10. Racial Discrimination. Two African American plaintiffs sued the producers of the reality television series *The Bachelor* and *The Bachelorette* for racial discrimination. The plaintiffs claimed that the shows had never featured persons of color in the lead roles. The plaintiffs also alleged that the producers did not provide people of color who auditioned for the lead roles with the same opportunities to compete as white people who auditioned. (See *Title VII of the Civil Rights Act.*)

(a) The first group will assess whether the plaintiffs can establish a *prima facie* case of disparate-treatment discrimination.

(b) The second group will consider whether the plaintiffs can establish disparate-impact discrimination.

(c) The third group will assume that the plaintiffs established a *prima facie* case and that the burden has shifted to the employer to articulate a legal reason for not hiring the plaintiffs. What legitimate reasons might the employer assert for not hiring the plaintiffs in this situation? Should the law require television producers to hire persons of color for lead roles in reality television shows? Discuss.

Health Insurance and Small Business

Small businesses are the foundation of the U.S. economy. Increasing health-care costs and decreasing insurance coverage between 2000 and 2010 forced many small firms to stop offering health-care coverage to their employees.

Recent legislation put in place comprehensive health-insurance reforms intended to improve access, affordability, and quality in health care. An especially important law is the Patient Protection and Affordable Care Act (ACA) of 2010 (often referred to as Obamacare). The ACA sets forth responsibilities and benefits for businesses determined in part by the size of an employer's workforce.[1]

What Is a Small Business?

The ACA defines a *small business* as a firm with fewer than fifty full-time equivalent (FTE) employees. An FTE is an employee who works thirty or more hours per week. Two half-time employees count as one FTE.

This definition fits about 96 percent of all businesses (5.8 million out of 6 million firms). In fact, 90 percent of all U.S. firms have fewer than twenty FTEs.

What Responsibilities Does the ACA Impose on Small Businesses?

Large businesses—those with fifty or more FTEs—are required to offer health insurance to their employees or pay a penalty.[2] For a small business, there is no requirement to offer health insurance. For a small firm that chooses to do so, the ACA imposes minimum standards on health plans.

Summary of Benefits and Coverage All employers, including small businesses, are required to provide their employees with a "Summary of Benefits and Coverage" that includes an explanation of the costs. The summary should be in plain language. Employees can use this information to compare their employer's plan with private plans, which the employees may opt to buy instead. An employer is not required to contribute to the premium for an employee's private plan.

Waiting Period Employees who are eligible for employer-sponsored health insurance must not be made to wait more than ninety days for coverage.

Notice of Marketplace Coverage Options Small businesses that do not offer health insurance can provide their employees with a "Notice of Marketplace Coverage Options." The notice can inform employees about their options with respect to the health-insurance marketplace.

---

1. For the complete text of the ACA, see Pub. L. No. 111-148. Also significant are the health-care amendments of the Health Care and Education Reconciliation Act of 2010; see Pub. L. No. 111-152.
2. Before the ACA, more than 95 percent of these employers already offered health insurance to their employees.

Annual Returns All employers that provide self-insured health coverage are required to file annual information returns with the Internal Revenue Service for the individuals that are covered.[3]

What Benefits Does the ACA Offer Small Businesses?

The ACA provides benefits to small business by expanding insurance coverage options, reducing related costs, and giving employers and employees more control over their own health care.

Health-Insurance Marketplace A small business can buy health-insurance coverage for its employees through the ACA's Small Business Health Options Program (SHOP). Coverage can be offered to employees any time during the year.

The SHOP marketplace offers multiple plans from private insurance companies. An employer can choose which plans to make available to its employees, whether to cover the employees' dependents, how much of the premiums the employer will pay, and other options.[4]

Small Business Health-Care Tax Credit Employers with fewer than twenty-five FTEs, each of whom are paid an average annual wage of less than $50,000, may be eligible for a health-care tax credit. To be eligible, an employer must cover at least 50 percent of the cost of the premiums for its employees' health insurance and buy the coverage through SHOP. Dental and vision care coverage also qualifies. An employer does not need to offer coverage to part-time employees (those working fewer than thirty hours per week) or to employees' dependents to qualify for the credit.

The amount of the credit may be as much as 50 percent of an employer's contribution toward its employees' premium costs. The smaller the business, the higher the credit—the credit is highest for firms with fewer than ten employees paid an average of $25,000 or less. And eligible small businesses can claim a business expense deduction for the premiums in excess of the credit.[5]

Wellness Programs A wellness program requires individuals to meet a specific standard related to health, such as a lower blood cholesterol level, to obtain a reward. Employers that promote employee health through workplace wellness programs are eligible for a reward of up to 30 percent of the cost of health coverage. The reward for a program designed to prevent or reduce the use of tobacco can be as much as 50 percent. The cost of health coverage includes employer-paid premiums and benefits.

Rebates The ACA requires insurance companies to spend at least 80 percent of premiums on medical care, not administrative costs. Insurers who do not meet this goal must provide rebates to policyholders.[6] This includes employers that provide group health insurance for their employees.

---

3. 26 U.S.C. Section 6055.
4. See U.S. Department of Health and Human Services, *SHOP Marketplace How-To Guides, Fact Sheets, Tools, and Other Resources for Employers* (December 11, 2015), *available at* www.healthcare.gov/small-businesses/provide-shop-coverage/resources/.
5. See Internal Revenue Service, *Small Business Health Care Tax Credit and the SHOP Marketplace* (December 11, 2015), *available at* www.irs.gov/Affordable-Care-Act/Employers/Small-Business-Health-Care-Tax-Credit-and-the-SHOP-Marketplace.
6. See Internal Revenue Service, *Medical Loss Ration (MLR) FAQs* (December 11, 2015) at www.irs.gov/uac/Medical-Loss-Ratio-(MLR)-FAQs.

Standard Operating Rules The ACA accelerated the adoption of standard operating rules for health-insurance plan administration. Operating rules are the business rules and guidelines for health-insurance plans. The ACA requires one format and one set of codes for claims, remittance advice, service authorization, eligibility verification, and claims status inquiry.

Nondiscriminatory Pricing The ACA ended the discriminatory insurance industry practice of increasing premiums because an employee filed a claim or got older or because a business hired a woman. At one time, premiums could increase by up to 200 percent in these circumstances.

Ethical Connection

There has been considerable opposition to the ACA. For example, the mandate that large businesses offer health insurance to their employees or pay a penalty—called "the Obamacare effect"—has been much criticized. Detractors express concern that the mandate creates an incentive for large businesses to employ part-time workers instead of full-time employees. During the period preceding the start date of the ACA and the end of 2014, however, in the private sector the number of part-time jobs *decreased* and the number of full-time positions *increased*.

To date, there is controversial evidence that employers are reducing the hours of their employees to avoid the requirements of the ACA.[7] Many argue that the reduction in the percentage of Americans who could work but are choosing to remain out of the labor force is due to Obamacare. Why? Because good-paying full-time job opportunities have shrunk due to the higher employer cost of hiring.

Ethics Question *Are small businesses ethically obligated to offer their employees health insurance? Discuss.*

Critical Thinking *Should the mandate to offer employees health insurance be extended to include small businesses? Or should it be repealed altogether? Explain.*

---

7. Also, in separate legal challenges to the ACA, the United States Supreme Court has upheld key parts of the act. See *National Federation of Business v. Sebelius*, __ U.S. __, 132 S.Ct. 2566, 183 L.Ed.2d 450 (2012); and *King v. Burwell*, __ U.S. __, 135 S.Ct. 2480, 192 L.Ed.2d 483 (2015). The Court has held certain U.S. Department of Health and Human Services regulations issued under the act to be invalid, however. See *Burwell v. Hobby Lobby Stores, Inc.*, __ U.S. __, 134 S.Ct. 2751, 189 L.Ed.2d 675 (2014).

Business Organizations

CHAPTER 36

Small Businesses and Franchises

A goal of many business students is to become an **entrepreneur,** one who initiates and assumes the financial risk of a new business enterprise and undertakes to provide or control its management. One of the first decisions an entrepreneur must make is which form of business organization will be most appropriate for the new endeavor.

In selecting an organizational form, the entrepreneur will consider a number of factors. These include (1) ease of creation, (2) the liability of the owners, (3) tax considerations, and (4) the ability to raise capital. Keep these factors in mind as you read this unit and learn about the various forms of business organization. Remember, too, in considering these business forms that the primary motive of an entrepreneur is to make profits.

Traditionally, entrepreneurs have used three major business forms—the sole proprietorship, the partnership, and the corporation. In this chapter, we examine sole proprietorships and also look at franchises. Although the franchise is not strictly speaking a business organizational form, it is widely used today by entrepreneurs.

36–1 General Considerations for Small Businesses

Most small businesses begin as sole proprietorships. Once the business is under way, the sole proprietorship form may become too limited. The owner and any additional investors may then want to establish a more formal organization, such as a limited partnership (LP), a limited liability partnership (LLP), a limited liability company (LLC), or a corporation. These forms of business limit the owner's personal liability, or legal responsibility, for business debts and obligations. Each business form has its own advantages and disadvantages, but legal limited liability generally is necessary for those who wish to raise outside capital.

36–1a Requirements for All Business Forms

Any business, whatever its form, has to meet a variety of legal requirements, which typically relate to the following:

1. Business name registration.
2. Occupational licensing.
3. State tax registration (for instance, to obtain permits for collecting and remitting sales taxes).
4. Health and environmental permits.
5. Zoning and building codes.
6. Import/export regulations.

If the business has employees, the owner must also comply with a host of laws governing the workplace.

36–1b Protecting Intellectual Property

Protecting rights in intellectual property is a central concern for many small businesses. For instance, software companies and app developers depend on their copyrights and patents to protect their investments in the research and development required to create new programs. Without copyright or patent protection, a competitor or a customer could simply copy the software or app.

Trademarks Choosing a trademark or service mark and making sure that it is protected under trademark law can be crucial to the success of a new business venture. Indeed, a factor to consider in choosing a name for a business entity is whether the business name will be used as a trademark. The general rule is that a trademark cannot be the same as another's mark or so similar that confusion might result.

For the most protection, trademarks should be registered with the U.S. Patent and Trademark Office (PTO). If the mark is federally registered, the owner may use the symbol ® with the mark. This well-known symbol puts others on notice of the registration and helps to prevent trademark infringement. An owner who has not registered can use the symbol ™. Registration with the PTO should be renewed five years after the initial registration and at ten-year intervals thereafter.

Trade Secrets Much of the value of a small business may lie in its trade secrets, such as information about product development, production processes and techniques, and customer lists. Preserving the secrecy of the information is necessary for legal protection.

As a practical matter, trade secrets must be divulged to key employees. Thus, any business runs the risk that those employees might disclose the secrets to competitors—or even set up competing businesses themselves.

To protect their trade secrets, companies may require employees who have access to trade secrets to agree in their employment contracts never to divulge those secrets. A small business may also choose to include a covenant not to compete in an employment contract. A noncompete clause will help to protect against the possibility that a key employee will go to work for a competitor or set up a competing business.

36–1c Obtaining Loans

Raising capital is critical to the growth of most small businesses. In the early days of a business, the sole proprietor may be able to contribute sufficient capital, but as the business becomes successful, more funds may be needed. The owner may want to raise capital from external sources to expand the business. One way to do this is to borrow funds.

Obtaining a bank loan is beneficial for small businesses because it allows the owner to retain full ownership and control of the business. Note, though, that the bank may place some restrictions on future business decisions as a condition of granting the loan. In addition, bank loans may not be available for some businesses. Banks are usually reluctant to lend significant sums to businesses that are not yet established. Even if a bank is willing to make

such a loan, the bank may require personal guaranty contracts from the owner, putting the owner's personal assets at risk.

Loans with desirable terms may be available from the U.S. Small Business Administration (SBA). One SBA program provides loans of up to $25,000 to businesspersons who are women, low-income individuals, or members of minority groups. Be aware that the SBA requires business owners to put some of their own funds at risk in the business. In addition, many states offer small-business grants to individuals starting a business.

36–2 Sole Proprietorships

In the earliest stages, as mentioned, a small business may operate as a **sole proprietorship,** which is the simplest form of business. In this form, the owner is the business. Thus, anyone who does business without creating a separate business organization has a sole proprietorship. The law considers all new, single-owner businesses to be sole proprietorships unless the owner affirmatively adopts some other form.

More than two-thirds of all U.S. businesses are sole proprietorships. Sole proprietors can own and manage any type of business from an informal, home-office or Web-based undertaking to a large restaurant or construction firm. About 99 percent of the sole proprietorships in the United States have revenues of less than $1 million per year.

36–2a Advantages of the Sole Proprietorship

A major advantage of the sole proprietorship is that the proprietor owns the entire business and receives all of the profits (because she or he assumes all of the risk). In addition, starting a sole proprietorship is easier and less costly than starting any other kind of business because few legal formalities are required. Generally, no documents need to be filed with the government to start a sole proprietorship.[1]

---

1. Although starting a sole proprietorship involves fewer legal formalities than other business organizational forms, even a small sole proprietorship may need to comply with zoning requirements, obtain a state business license, and the like.

Taxes A sole proprietor pays only personal income taxes (including Social Security and Medicare taxes) on the business's profits. The profits are reported as personal income on the proprietor's personal income tax return. In other words, the business itself need not file an income tax return. Sole proprietors are allowed to establish retirement accounts that are tax-exempt until the funds are withdrawn.

Like any form of business enterprise, a sole proprietorship can be liable for other taxes, such as those collected and applied to the disbursement of unemployment compensation. Whether liability for the unpaid unemployment compensation taxes of a sole proprietorship remains with the seller or must be assumed by the buyer was at issue in the following case.

Case Analysis 36.1

A. Gadley Enterprises, Inc. v. Department of Labor and Industry Office of Unemployment Compensation Tax Services

Commonwealth Court of Pennsylvania, __ A.3d __, 2016 WL 55591 (2016).

In the Language of the Court
SIMPSON, Judge.
* * * *

[Julianne Gresh (Predecessor)] operated [Romper Room Day Care (Romper Room)], a childcare center, as a sole proprietorship for 12 years. Predecessor owed the [Pennsylvania Department of Labor and Industry Office of Unemployment Compensation Tax Services (Department)] substantial unpaid UC [unemployment compensation] contributions, interest and penalties. She admitted liability and entered payment plans with the Department * * * . Pursuant to these payment plans, she made monthly payments in the minimal amount of $50. Predecessor was on the verge of losing her license to operate, and sought another entity to operate the location as a childcare facility.

[A. Gadley Enterprises, Inc. (Purchaser)] operated a childcare center, Young Environment Learning Center, in Erie, Pennsylvania. Purchaser decided to purchase assets from Predecessor in order to open a satellite location of Young Environmental Learning Center at the prior location of Romper Room. Purchaser and Predecessor executed an asset purchase agreement (Agreement).

Through the Agreement, Purchaser paid a total of $37,000 for Predecessor's tangible and intangible assets. This total was comprised of $10,000 for the use of the name "Romper Room," $10,790 for a covenant not to compete, and $17,210 for tangible assets listed on [an attached] Inventory List.

* * * The Inventory List did not include any of Predecessor's personal assets other than those used in the operation of Romper Room.

* * * Four days *after* executing the Agreement, * * * Predecessor notified the Department of the sale.

* * * The Department issued Purchaser a Notice of Assessment (Notice) in the amount of $43,370.49 for UC contributions, interest and penalties owed by Predecessor. The Notice stated Purchaser was liable because it purchased 51% or more of Predecessor's assets.

In response, Purchaser filed a petition [with the Department] for reassessment.
* * * *

Based on the evidence presented at the hearing [held on the petition], the Department issued its decision and order denying the petition for reassessment.
* * * *

Purchaser then filed a petition to review to this Court.
* * * *

[43 Pennsylvania Statutes Section 788.3(a), part of the state's Unemployment Compensation Law] provides:

(a) Every employer * * * , who shall sell in bulk fifty-one percent or more of his assets, including but not limited to, any stock of goods, wares or merchandise of any kind, fixtures, machinery, equipment, building or real estate, shall give the department ten (10) days' notice of the sale prior to completion of the transfer * * * . The employer shall present to the purchaser of such property, a certificate * * * showing that all reports have been filed and contributions, interest and penalties paid to the date of the proposed transfer. The failure of the

purchaser to require such certificate shall render such purchaser liable to the department for the unpaid contributions, interest and penalties.

* * * *

There is no dispute that Purchaser did not obtain a clearance certificate reflecting Predecessor's payment of UC liability. There is also no dispute that Predecessor owed the Department for outstanding UC contributions, interest and penalties in the amount of $43,370.49 at the time of the sale.
* * * *

Purchaser argues substantial evidence does not support the Department's finding that it purchased more than 51% of the [Predecessor's] assets.
* * * *

The Agreement establishes that the Inventory List sets forth all business assets of Predecessor. Gresh confirmed the Inventory List was a complete list of assets used in the operation of her business.

The Inventory List reflects a total value of assets equaling $19,210. * * * The parties reduced the purchase price by $2,000 to account for the reduced value of the assets when Purchaser removed certain assets from the complete Inventory List. Purchaser acquired all the assets included in the Inventory List, other than those removed, for $17,210. The amount constitutes approximately 90% of the value of the complete list of assets ($19,210 × .9 = $17,289).

The Agreement, supplemented by corroborating [supporting] testimony,

Case 36.1 Continued

constitutes substantial evidence to support the Department's finding that the sale qualified as a bulk sale of more than 51% of Predecessor's assets.

* * * *

Purchaser also argues the Department erred in construing the term "assets" in the bulk sales provision to include only business assets when determining whether a sale met the 51% threshold. Purchaser asserts the provision does not differentiate between business and personal assets of an employer and there is no legal distinction when the employer is a sole proprietor.

* * * *

* * * The definition of "employer" [in the UC Law] includes a sole proprietor like Predecessor.

The word "assets" is not defined in the [UC] Law.

[In Section 788.3(a)] the term "assets" precedes a list of examples, followed by the phrase "including but not limited to."

* * * *

* * * The examples * * * indicate that the term "assets" refers to business assets. This conclusion is buttressed [reinforced] by the context of the statute as a whole, which pertains to employers operating businesses and paying employees as part of their business operations.

The factual circumstances surrounding the sale also indicate the term "assets" means "business assets." Here, the context is the sale of a business, in the childcare industry, to another business engaged in the same industry that intends to operate a childcare facility at the location of the former business. The Agreement reflects the intention of the parties that Purchaser would operate the childcare facility as a satellite location. [Emphasis added.]

* * * *

* * * The provision does not treat sole proprietors differently than other employers. The provision contains no exemption of liability for a purchaser when an employer operates as a sole proprietorship. Nor does it contain an exemption from liability when the former employer entered a repayment plan with the Department.

Moreover, Purchaser's interpretation does not consider *the purpose of the bulk sales provision. That purpose is to ensure an employer does not divest itself of assets without satisfying outstanding liabilities, either itself or by the purchaser.* This Court agrees with the Department that Gresh's repayment agreement in the minimal amount of $50 per month does not satisfy the UC liability. [Emphasis added.]

* * * *

In sum, the Department's construction of assets as business assets is reasonable and consistent with the context and purpose of [the] bulk sales provision. Purchaser's failure to obtain a clearance certificate rendered it liable for Predecessor's unpaid UC contributions, interest and penalties, regardless of Predecessor's repayment agreement. Therefore, this Court upholds the Department's interpretation of the bulk sales provision.

* * * *

* * * For the foregoing reasons, we affirm the Department.

Legal Reasoning Questions

1. As is clear from the law applied in this case, and the result, the liability of a business for unpaid taxes "follows the assets." Why?
2. What action can Gadley take now to avoid suffering the loss of the funds required to cover Gresh's unpaid taxes?
3. What action should a buyer take *before* purchasing the assets of a business to avoid liability for the seller's unpaid taxes?

Flexibility A sole proprietorship offers more flexibility than does a partnership or a corporation. The sole proprietor is free to make any decision she or he wishes concerning the business—including what kind of business to pursue, whom to hire, and when to take a vacation. The sole proprietor can sell or transfer all or part of the business to another party at any time without seeking approval from anyone else. In contrast, approval is typically required from partners in a partnership and from shareholders in a corporation.

36–2b Disadvantages of the Sole Proprietorship

The major disadvantage of the sole proprietorship is that the proprietor alone bears the burden of any losses or liabilities incurred by the business enterprise. In other words, the sole proprietor has unlimited liability for all obligations that arise in doing business. Any lawsuit against the business or its employees can lead to unlimited personal liability for the owner of a sole proprietorship.

■ **EXAMPLE 36.1** Aaron and Melissa Klein, owners of the Sweet Cakes by Melissa bakery, refused to bake a wedding cake for a same-sex couple's wedding. They claimed that their religious beliefs did not allow them to provide services for same-sex ceremonies. The Oregon State Bureau of Labor and Industries argued that their decision violated the law. In 2015, an administrative law judge ruled against the Kleins' motion to dismiss and ordered them to pay $135,000 in damages. As sole proprietors, the Kleins were personally responsible for paying the damages. ■

Personal Assets at Risk Creditors can pursue the owner's personal assets to satisfy any business debts. Although sole proprietors may obtain insurance to protect the business, liability can easily exceed policy limits. This unlimited liability is a major factor to be considered in choosing a business form.

■ **EXAMPLE 36.2** Sheila Fowler operates a golf shop near a world-class golf course as a sole proprietorship. One of Fowler's employees fails to secure a display of golf clubs. They fall on Dean Maheesh, a professional golfer, and seriously injure him. If Maheesh sues Fowler's shop and wins, Fowler's personal liability could easily exceed the limits of her insurance policy. Fowler could lose not only her business, but also her house, car, and any other personal assets that can be attached to pay the judgment. ■

Lack of Continuity and Limited Ability to Raise Capital The sole proprietorship also has the disadvantage of lacking continuity after the death of the proprietor. When the owner dies, so does the business—it is automatically dissolved.

Another disadvantage is that in raising capital, the proprietor is limited to his or her personal funds and any loans that he or she can obtain for the business. Lenders may be unwilling to make loans to sole proprietorships, particularly start-ups, because the sole proprietor risks unlimited personal liability and may not be able to pay. (See this chapter's *Digital Update* feature for a discussion of one court's refusal to discharge a loan made to a sole proprietor who had declared bankruptcy.)

DIGITAL UPDATE   A Sole Proprietorship, Facebook Poker, and Bankruptcy

One major downside of a sole proprietorship is that it is more difficult for a sole proprietor to obtain funding for start-up and expansion. Moreover, if funding is obtained through loans, the sole proprietor is exposed to personal liability.

Personal Liability Exposure for an Online Startup

A case in point went before the United States bankruptcy court in Massachusetts in 2015.[a] Michael Dewhurst, living in Raynham, Massachusetts, sometimes did computer work for Gerald Knappik. Dewhurst decided to start a new business venture—the commercial development of a Facebook poker–playing application. Dewhurst envisioned an application that would enable multiple individuals to play poker together over the Internet through Facebook. Dewhurst informed Knappik of his business plan and predicted that his Facebook poker application "was going to be something very big."

Knappik initially loaned $50,000 to Dewhurst for the project. The loan agreement stated, "The sole purpose of this loan agreement is to provide funds on a personal level for the startup of said business project, in conjunction with borrower's personal funds, not limited to startup costs, operating expenses, advertising costs."

That was the first of a series of personal loans that totaled $220,000.

Dewhurst had repaid only $9,000 on the total outstanding debt when he filed for bankruptcy. Ultimately, the bankruptcy court ascertained that at least $120,000 of the loans that were supposed to be used exclusively for the Facebook poker project had been used for other activities. Furthermore, Dewhurst kept "no contemporaneous records of his disbursements and uses of this cash, no cash journal, ledger, or disbursement slips of any kind."

The Lender Objects to a Bankruptcy Discharge of Monies Owed

During bankruptcy proceedings, Knappik requested that the bankruptcy court deny discharge of Dewhurst's debts to him. Upon review, the court stated that "Dewhurst's failure to keep and preserve adequate records makes it impossible to reconstruct an accurate and complete account of financial affairs and business transactions." The bankruptcy judge ultimately denied discharge of $120,000 of the debt owed to Knappik. Thus, a sole proprietor's failed attempt to create an online poker-playing application led to personal liability even after he had filed for bankruptcy.

Critical Thinking *Sole proprietorships, as well as other businesses, routinely seek funding for online projects. How can the individuals involved avoid personal liability?*

---

a. *In re Dewhurst*, 528 Bankr. 211 (D.Mass. 2015).

36–3 Franchises

Instead of setting up a sole proprietorship to market their own products or services, many entrepreneurs opt to purchase a franchise. A **franchise** is an arrangement in which the owner of intellectual property—such as a trademark, a trade name, or a copyright—licenses others to use it in the selling of goods or services. A **franchisee** (a purchaser of a franchise) is generally legally independent of the **franchisor** (the seller of the franchise). At the same time, the franchisee is economically dependent on the franchisor's integrated business system. In other words, a franchisee can operate as an independent businessperson but still obtain the advantages of a regional or national organization.

Today, franchising companies and their franchisees account for a significant portion of all retail sales in this country. Well-known franchises include McDonald's, 7-Eleven, and Holiday Inn. Franchising has also become a popular way for businesses to expand their operations internationally without violating the legal restrictions that many nations impose on foreign ownership of businesses.

36–3a Types of Franchises

Many different kinds of businesses sell franchises, and numerous types of franchises are available. Generally, though, franchises fall into one of three classifications: distributorships, chain-style business operations, and manufacturing arrangements.

Distributorship In a *distributorship,* a manufacturer (the franchisor) licenses a dealer (the franchisee) to sell its product. Often, a distributorship covers an exclusive territory. Automobile dealerships and beer distributorships are common examples.

■ **EXAMPLE 36.3** Black Bear Beer Company distributes its brands of beer through a network of authorized wholesale distributors, each with an assigned territory. Marik signs a distributorship contract for the area from Gainesville to Ocala, Florida. If the contract states that Marik is the exclusive distributor in that area, then no other franchisee may distribute Black Bear beer in that region. ■

Chain-Style Business Operation In a *chain-style business operation,* a franchise operates under a franchisor's trade name and is identified as a member of a select group of dealers that engage in the franchisor's business. The franchisee is generally required to follow standardized or prescribed methods of operation. Often, the franchisor insists that the franchisee maintain certain standards of performance.

In addition, the franchisee may be required to obtain materials and supplies exclusively from the franchisor. Chipotle Mexican Grill and most other fast-food chains are examples of this type of franchise. Chain-style franchises are also common in service-related businesses, including real estate brokerage firms, such as Century 21, and tax-preparing services, such as H&R Block, Inc.

Manufacturing Arrangement In a *manufacturing,* or *processing-plant, arrangement,* the franchisor transmits to the franchisee the essential ingredients or formula to make a particular product. The franchisee then markets the product either at wholesale or at retail in accordance with the franchisor's standards. Examples of this type of franchise include Pepsi-Cola and other soft-drink bottling companies.

36–3b Laws Governing Franchising

Because a franchise relationship is primarily a contractual relationship, it is governed by contract law. If the franchise exists primarily for the sale of products manufactured by the franchisor, the law governing sales contracts as expressed in Article 2 of the Uniform Commercial Code applies.

Additionally, the federal government and most states have enacted laws governing certain aspects of franchising. Generally, these laws are designed to protect prospective franchisees from dishonest franchisors and to prevent franchisors from terminating franchises without good cause.

Federal Regulation of Franchises The federal government regulates franchising through laws that apply to specific industries and through the Franchise Rule, created by the Federal Trade Commission (FTC).

Industry-Specific Standards. Congress has enacted laws that protect franchisees in certain industries, such as automobile dealerships and service stations. These laws protect the franchisee from unreasonable demands and bad faith terminations of the franchise by the franchisor.

An automobile manufacturer–franchisor cannot make unreasonable demands of dealer-franchisees or set unrealistically high sales quotas. If an automobile manufacturer–franchisor terminates a franchise because of a dealer-franchisee's failure to comply with unreasonable demands, the manufacturer may be liable for damages.[2]

---

2. Automobile Dealers' Franchise Act, also known as the Automobile Dealers' Day in Court Act, 15 U.S.C. Sections 1221 *et seq.*

Similarly, federal law prescribes the conditions under which a franchisor of service stations can terminate the franchise.[3] In addition, federal antitrust laws sometimes apply in specified circumstances to prohibit certain types of anticompetitive agreements.

The Franchise Rule. The FTC's Franchise Rule requires franchisors to disclose certain material facts that a prospective franchisee needs in order to make an informed decision concerning the purchase of a franchise.[4] Those who violate the Franchise Rule are subject to substantial civil penalties, and the FTC can sue on behalf of injured parties to recover damages.

The rule requires the franchisor to make numerous written disclosures to prospective franchisees (see Exhibit 36–1). All representations made to a prospective franchisee must have a reasonable basis. For instance, if a franchisor provides projected earnings figures, the franchisor must indicate whether the figures are based on actual data or hypothetical examples. If a franchisor makes sales or earnings projections based on actual data for a specific

franchise location, the franchisor must disclose the number and percentage of its existing franchises that have achieved this result.

State Regulation of Franchising State legislation varies but often is aimed at protecting franchisees from unfair practices and bad faith terminations by franchisors.

State Disclosures. A number of states have laws similar to the federal rules that require franchisors to provide presale disclosures to prospective franchisees.[5] Many state laws also require that a disclosure document (known as the Franchise Disclosure Document, or FDD) be registered or filed with a state official. State laws may also require that a franchisor submit advertising aimed at prospective franchisees to the state for approval.

To protect franchisees, a state law might require the disclosure of information such as the actual costs of operation, recurring expenses, and profits earned, along with facts substantiating these figures. State deceptive trade

---

3. Petroleum Marketing Practices Act (PMPA), 15 U.S.C. Sections 2801 *et seq.*
4. 16 C.F.R. Section 436.1.

5. These states include California, Florida, Hawaii, Illinois, Indiana, Maryland, Michigan, Minnesota, New York, North Dakota, Oregon, Rhode Island, South Dakota, Texas, Utah, Virginia, Washington, and Wisconsin.

EXHIBIT 36–1 The FTC's Franchise Rule Requirements

REQUIREMENT	EXPLANATION
Written (or Electronic) Disclosures	The franchisor must make numerous disclosures, such as the range of goods and services included and the value and estimated profitability of the franchise. Disclosures can be delivered on paper or electronically. Prospective franchisees must be able to download or save any electronic disclosure documents.
Reasonable Basis for Any Representations	To prevent deception, all representations made to a prospective franchisee must have a reasonable basis at the time they are made.
Projected Earnings Figures	If a franchisor provides projected earnings figures, the franchisor must indicate whether the figures are based on actual data or hypothetical examples. The Franchise Rule does not require franchisors to provide potential earnings figures, however.
Actual Data	If a franchisor makes sales or earnings projections based on actual data for a specific franchise location, the franchisor must disclose the number and percentage of its existing franchises that have achieved this result.
Explanation of Terms	Franchisors are required to explain termination, cancellation, and renewal provisions of the franchise contract to potential franchisees before the agreement is signed.

practices acts may also apply and prohibit certain types of actions by franchisors.

May Require Good Cause to Terminate the Franchise. To prevent arbitrary or bad faith terminations, a state law may prohibit termination without "good cause" or require that certain procedures be followed in terminating a franchise. ■ **CASE IN POINT 36.4** FMS, Inc., entered into a franchise agreement with Samsung Construction Equipment North America to become an authorized dealership selling Samsung construction equipment. Samsung then sold its equipment business to Volvo Construction Equipment North America, Inc., which was to continue selling Samsung brand equipment.

Later, Volvo rebranded the construction equipment under its own name and canceled FMS's franchise. FMS sued, claiming that Volvo had terminated the franchise without "good cause" in violation of state law. Because Volvo was no longer manufacturing the Samsung brand equipment, the court found that Volvo had good cause to terminate FMS's franchise. If Volvo had continued making the Samsung equipment, though, it could not have terminated the franchise.[6] ■

36–3c The Franchise Contract

The franchise relationship is defined by the contract between the franchisor and the franchisee. The franchise contract specifies the terms and conditions of the franchise and spells out the rights and duties of the franchisor and the franchisee. If either party fails to perform its contractual duties, that party may be subject to a lawsuit for breach of contract. Furthermore, if a franchisee is induced to enter into a franchise contract by the franchisor's fraudulent misrepresentation, the franchisor may be liable for damages. Generally, statutes and the case law governing franchising tend to emphasize the importance of good faith and fair dealing in franchise relationships.

Because each type of franchise relationship has its own characteristics, franchise contracts tend to differ. Nonetheless, certain major issues typically are addressed in a franchise contract. We look at some of them next.

Payment for the Franchise The franchisee ordinarily pays an initial fee or lump-sum price for the franchise license (the privilege of being granted a franchise). This fee is separate from the various products that the franchisee purchases from or through the franchisor. The franchise agreement may also require the franchisee to pay a

percentage of the franchisor's advertising costs and certain administrative expenses.

In some industries, the franchisor relies heavily on the initial sale of the franchise for realizing a profit. In other industries, the continued dealing between the parties brings profit to both. Generally, the franchisor receives a stated percentage of the annual (or monthly) sales or volume of business done by the franchisee.

Business Premises The franchise agreement may specify whether the premises for the business must be leased or purchased outright. Sometimes, a building must be constructed to meet the terms of the agreement. The agreement will specify whether the franchisor or the franchisee is responsible for supplying equipment and furnishings for the premises.

Location of the Franchise Typically, the franchisor determines the territory to be served. Some franchise contracts give the franchisee exclusive rights, or "territorial rights," to a certain geographic area. Other franchise contracts, while defining the territory allotted to a particular franchise, either specifically state that the franchise is nonexclusive or are silent on the issue of territorial rights.

Many franchise disputes arise over territorial rights, and the implied covenant of good faith and fair dealing often comes into play in this area of franchising. If the contract does not grant exclusive territorial rights to the franchisee and the franchisor allows a competing franchise to be established nearby, the franchisee may suffer significant lost profits. In this situation, a court may hold that the franchisor breached an implied covenant of good faith and fair dealing.

Business Organization The franchisor may require that the business use a particular organizational form and capital structure. The franchise agreement may also set out standards such as sales quotas and record-keeping requirements. Additionally, a franchisor may retain stringent control over the training of personnel involved in the operation and over administrative aspects of the business.

Quality Control by the Franchisor The day-to-day operation of the franchise business normally is left up to the franchisee. Nonetheless, the franchise agreement may specify that the franchisor will provide some degree of supervision and control so that it can protect the franchise's name and reputation.

Means of Control. When the franchise prepares a product, such as food, or provides a service, such as motel

---

6. *FMS, Inc. v. Volvo Construction Equipment North America, Inc.*, 557 F.3d 758 (7th Cir. 2009).

accommodations, the contract often states that the franchisor will establish certain standards for the facility. Typically, the contract will state that the franchisor is permitted to make periodic inspections to ensure that the standards are being maintained.

As a means of controlling quality, franchise agreements also typically limit the franchisee's ability to sell the franchise to another party. ■ **EXAMPLE 36.5** Mark Keller, Inc., an authorized Jaguar franchise, contracts to sell its dealership to Henrique Autos West. A Jaguar franchise generally cannot be sold without Jaguar Cars' permission. Prospective franchisees must meet Jaguar's customer satisfaction standards. If Henrique Autos fails to meet those standards, Jaguar can refuse to allow the sale and can terminate the franchise. ■

Degree of Control. As a general rule, the validity of a provision permitting the franchisor to establish and enforce certain quality standards is unquestioned. The franchisor has a legitimate interest in maintaining the quality of the product or service to protect its name and reputation.

If a franchisor exercises too much control over the operations of its franchisees, however, the franchisor risks potential liability. A franchisor may occasionally be held liable—under the doctrine of *respondeat superior*—for the tortious acts of the franchisees' employees. ■ **EXAMPLE 36.6** The National Labor Relations Board (NLRB) received 180 employee complaints that certain McDonald's restaurants had engaged in unfair labor practices. Employees alleged that the restaurants had fired or penalized workers for participating in protests over wages and working conditions. Investigators found that at least some of the complaints had merit. The NLRB ruled that McDonald's USA, LLC, could be held jointly liable along with several of its franchisees for labor and wage violations. The NLRB reasoned that McDonald's exerts sufficient control over its franchisees to be found liable for the franchisees' employment law violations. ■

Pricing Arrangements Franchises provide the franchisor with an outlet for the firm's goods and services. Depending on the nature of the business, the franchisor may require the franchisee to purchase certain supplies from the franchisor at an established price.[7] A franchisor cannot, however, set the prices at which the franchisee will resell the goods. Such price setting may be a violation of state or federal antitrust laws, or both. A franchisor can suggest retail prices but cannot mandate them.

36–4 Franchise Termination

The duration of the franchise is a matter to be determined between the parties. Sometimes, a franchise relationship starts with a short trial period, such as a year, so that the franchisee and the franchisor can determine whether they want to stay in business with one another. At other times, the duration of the franchise contract correlates with the term of the lease for the business premises, and both are renewable at the end of that period.

36–4a Grounds for Termination Set by Franchise Contract

Usually, the franchise agreement specifies that termination must be "for cause" and then defines the grounds for termination. Cause might include, for instance, the death or disability of the franchisee, insolvency of the franchisee, breach of the franchise agreement, or failure to meet specified sales quotas.

In the following case, franchise agreements provided that the franchisor could terminate a franchise for good cause.

---

7. Although a franchisor can require franchisees to purchase supplies from it, requiring a franchisee to purchase exclusively from the franchisor may violate federal antitrust laws.

Case 36.2

Century 21 Real Estate, LLC v. All Professional Realty, Inc.

United States Court of Appeals, Ninth Circuit, 600 Fed.Appx. 502 (2015).

Background and Facts Carol and Steve Wright owned All Professional Realty, Inc., and All Professional Hawaii Realty, Inc. The Wrights' companies signed four franchise agreements with Century 21 Real Estate, LLC, to operate offices in Sacramento and Folsom, California, and Honolulu, Hawaii, under the name "Century 21 All Professional." The agreements required All Professional to pay royalty and advertising fees. They also permitted Century 21 to terminate the agreements for good cause, including the franchisee's failure to operate at an approved location.

Case 36.2 Continued All Professional signed a note for $75,000 payable to Century 21 and agreed to make annual payments on the note. Four years later, All Professional stopped remitting the fees and making payments on the note, and it closed the Folsom office. Century 21 terminated the franchise agreements. The Wrights and All Professional filed a suit against Century 21, alleging breach of contract. Century 21 filed a counterclaim for breach. A federal district court issued a summary judgment in the franchisor's favor. All Professional appealed.

In the Language of the Court

MEMORANDUM.

* * * *

The district court did not err in granting summary judgment to Century 21 on the parties' cross-claims for breach of contract. *A * * * breach of contract claim requires a contract, breach of that contract, damages and that Century 21 performed its obligations under the contract.* [Emphasis added.]

The Wrights' companies breached the franchise agreements by not paying required fees, not paying principal due on the note and by abandoning the Folsom office.

* * * *

* * * It is undisputed that Century 21 provided the Wrights' companies with access to the Century 21 system defined in the franchise agreements [as "policies, procedures, and techniques designed to enable offices to compete more effectively in the real estate sales market" and "common use and promotion of certain Marks, copyrights, trade secrets, centralized advertising programs, recruiting programs, referral programs and sales management training programs."] Moreover, the franchise agreements specifically stated that the success of the franchise depended on the Wrights' efforts and that Century 21 made no guarantee or warranty that the Wrights would be successful. The Wrights have not created a triable issue [one necessitating a trial] that Century 21 failed to perform on the contract and that any such failure excused payment on the note.

Century 21 did not breach the agreements by preventing the Wrights from curing their defaults. Although the Wrights now claim they have the funds to pay Century 21, they testified repeatedly before the district court that they did not have the financial ability to cure their defaults.

Century 21 did not terminate the franchise agreements in bad faith. * * * Century 21 had a legal right to terminate all four franchise agreements.

Decision and Remedy *The U.S. Court of Appeals for the Ninth Circuit affirmed the lower court's judgment in Century 21's favor. Century 21 did not breach the franchise agreements. All Professional did. The Wrights' nonpayment of the fees and the note, and the abandonment of one of the franchisee's offices, constituted a material breach of the contract. These actions provided Century 21 with legitimate grounds for termination of the franchise agreement.*

Critical Thinking

- **Economic** *What is the most likely reason that All Professional stopped paying the franchise fees and making note payments, in addition to closing one of its offices? Why is this an insufficient justification for breach of the franchisee's agreements with Century 21?*

Notice Requirements Most franchise contracts provide that notice of termination must be given. If no set time for termination is specified, then a reasonable time, with notice, is implied. A franchisee must be given reasonable time to wind up the business—that is, to do the accounting and return the copyright or trademark or any other property of the franchisor.

Opportunity to Cure a Breach A franchise agreement may allow the franchisee to attempt to cure an ordinary, curable breach within a certain time after notice so as to postpone, or even avoid, termination. Even when a contract contains a notice-and-cure provision, however, a franchisee's breach of the duty of honesty and fidelity may be enough to allow the franchisor to terminate the franchise.

■ **CASE IN POINT 36.7** Milind and Minaxi Upadhyaya entered into a franchise contract with 7-Eleven, Inc., to operate a store in Pennsylvania. The contract included a notice-and-cure provision. Under 7-Eleven's usual contract, franchisees lease the store and equipment, and receive a license to use 7-Eleven's trademarks and other intellectual property. 7-Eleven receives a percentage of the store's gross profit (net sales less the cost of goods sold).

A 7-Eleven manager noticed a high rate of certain questionable transactions at the Upadhyayas' store and began investigating. The investigation continued for nearly two years and revealed that the store had been misreporting its sales so as to conceal sales proceeds from 7-Eleven. Evidence indicated that nearly one-third of the store's sales transactions had not been properly recorded. 7-Eleven sent a "non-curable" notice of material breach and termination of the franchise to the Upadhyayas. The franchisees argued that they had not been given an opportunity to cure the breach. The court found there was sufficient evidence of fraud to warrant immediate termination without an opportunity to cure.[8] ∎

36–4b Wrongful Termination

Because a franchisor's termination of a franchise often has adverse consequences for the franchisee, much franchise litigation involves claims of wrongful termination. Generally, the termination provisions of contracts are more favorable to the franchisor than to the franchisee. This means that the franchisee, who normally invests substantial time and financial resources in making the franchise operation successful, may receive little or nothing for the business on termination. The franchisor owns the trademark and hence the business.

It is in this area that statutory and case law become important. The federal and state laws discussed earlier

---

8. *7-Eleven, Inc. v. Upadhyaya,* 926 F.Supp.2d 614 (E.D.Penn. 2013).

attempt, among other things, to protect franchisees from the arbitrary or unfair termination of their franchises by the franchisors.

36–4c The Importance of Good Faith and Fair Dealing

Generally, both statutory law and case law emphasize the importance of good faith and fair dealing in terminating a franchise relationship. In determining whether a franchisor has acted in good faith when terminating a franchise agreement, the courts usually try to balance the rights of both parties.

■ **EXAMPLE 36.8** A car dealership enters into lending agreements, commonly known as floor plan financing, to enable it to buy new vehicles from General Motors Corporation (GM). At first, the dealership obtains floor plan financing from GM, but then it switches to Main Street Bank. Later, the bank declines to provide further financing, and the dealership is unable to obtain the financing from any other lender, including GM. The franchise contract gives GM a right to terminate a dealership for failure to maintain a line of credit. Therefore, GM can terminate the franchise because of the dealership's inability to obtain floor plan financing. ∎

If a court perceives that a franchisor has arbitrarily or unfairly terminated a franchise, the franchisee will be provided with a remedy for wrongful termination. A court will be less likely to consider a termination wrongful if the franchisor's decision was made in the normal course of business and reasonable notice was given.

The importance of good faith and fair dealing in a franchise relationship is underscored by the consequences of the franchisor's acts in the following case.

Spotlight on Holiday Inns

Case 36.3 Holiday Inn Franchising, Inc. v. Hotel Associates, Inc.

Court of Appeals of Arkansas, 2011 Ark.App. 147, 382 S.W.3d 6 (2011).

Background and Facts Buddy House was in the construction business in Arkansas and Texas. For decades, he collaborated on projects with Holiday Inn Franchising, Inc. Their relationship was characterized by good faith—many projects were undertaken without written contracts. At Holiday Inn's request, House inspected a hotel in Wichita Falls, Texas, to estimate the cost of getting it into shape. Holiday Inn wanted House to renovate the hotel and operate it as a Holiday Inn. House estimated that recovering the cost of renovation would take him more than ten years, so he asked for a franchise term longer than Holiday Inn's usual ten years. Holiday Inn refused, but said that if the hotel was run "appropriately," the term would be extended at the end of ten years. House bought the hotel, renovated it, and operated it as Hotel Associates, Inc. (HAI), generating substantial profits. He refused offers to sell it for as much as $15 million.

Case 36.3 Continued

Before the ten years had passed, Greg Aden, a Holiday Inn executive, developed a plan to license a different local hotel as a Holiday Inn instead of renewing House's franchise license. Aden stood to earn a commission from licensing the other hotel. No one informed House of Aden's plan. When the time came, HAI applied for an extension of its franchise, and Holiday Inn asked for major renovations. HAI spent $3 million to comply with this request. Holiday Inn did not renew HAI's license, however, but instead granted a franchise to the other hotel. HAI sold its hotel for $5 million and filed a suit in an Arkansas state court against Holiday Inn, asserting fraud. The court awarded HAI compensatory and punitive damages. Holiday Inn appealed.

In the Language of the Court

Raymond R. *ABRAMSON,* Judge.

* * * *

Generally, a mere failure to volunteer information does not constitute fraud. But *silence can amount to actionable fraud in some circumstances where the parties have a relation of trust or confidence, where there is inequality of condition and knowledge, or where there are other attendant circumstances.* [Emphasis added.]

In this case, substantial evidence supports the existence of a duty on Holiday Inn's part to disclose the Aden [plan] to HAI. Buddy House had a long-term relationship with Holiday Inn characterized by honesty, trust, and the free flow of pertinent information. He testified that [Holiday Inn's] assurances at the onset of licensure [the granting of the license] led him to believe that he would be relicensed after ten years if the hotel was operated appropriately. Yet, despite Holiday Inn's having provided such an assurance to House, it failed to apprise House of an internal business plan * * * that advocated licensure of another facility instead of the renewal of his license. *A duty of disclosure may exist where information is peculiarly within the knowledge of one party and is of such a nature that the other party is justified in assuming its nonexistence.* Given House's history with Holiday Inn and the assurance he received, we are convinced he was justified in assuming that no obstacles had arisen that jeopardized his relicensure. [Emphasis added.]

Holiday Inn asserts that it would have provided Buddy House with the Aden [plan] if he had asked for it. But, Holiday Inn cannot satisfactorily explain why House should have been charged with the responsibility of inquiring about a plan that he did not know existed. Moreover, several Holiday Inn personnel testified that Buddy House in fact should have been provided with the Aden plan. Aden himself stated that * * * House should have been given the plan. * * * In light of these circumstances, we see no ground for reversal on this aspect of HAI's cause of action for fraud.

Decision and Remedy *The state intermediate appellate court affirmed the lower court's judgment and its award of compensatory damages. The appellate court increased the amount of punitive damages, however, citing Holiday Inn's "degree of reprehensibility."*

Critical Thinking

- **Legal Environment** *Why should House and HAI have been advised of Holiday Inn's plan to grant a franchise to a different hotel in their territory?*
- **Economic** *A jury awarded HAI $12 million in punitive damages. The court reduced this award to $1 million, but the appellate court reinstated the original award. What is the purpose of punitive damages? Did Holiday Inn's conduct warrant this award? Explain.*

Reviewing: Small Businesses and Franchises

Carlos Del Rey decided to open a Mexican fast-food restaurant and signed a franchise contract with a national chain called La Grande Enchilada. The contract required the franchisee to strictly follow the franchisor's operating manual and stated that failure to do so would be grounds for terminating the franchise contract. The manual set forth detailed operating procedures and safety standards, and provided that a La Grande Enchilada representative would inspect the restaurant monthly to ensure compliance.

Nine months after Del Rey began operating his restaurant, a spark from the grill ignited an oily towel in the kitchen. No one was injured, but by the time firefighters were able to put out the fire, the kitchen had sustained extensive damage. The cook told the fire department that the towel was "about two feet from the grill" when it caught fire. This was in compliance with the franchisor's manual that required towels be placed at least one foot from the grills. Nevertheless, the next day La Grande Enchilada notified Del Rey that his franchise would terminate in thirty days for failure to follow the prescribed safety procedures. Using the information presented in the chapter, answer the following questions.

1. What type of franchise was Del Rey's La Grande Enchilada restaurant?
2. If Del Rey operates the restaurant as a sole proprietorship, who bears the loss for the damaged kitchen? Explain.
3. Assume that Del Rey files a lawsuit against La Grande Enchilada, claiming that his franchise was wrongfully terminated. What is the main factor that a court would consider in determining whether the franchise was wrongfully terminated?
4. Would a court be likely to rule that La Grande Enchilada had good cause to terminate Del Rey's franchise in this situation? Why or why not?

Debate This . . . *All franchisors should be required by law to provide a comprehensive estimate of the profitability of a prospective franchise based on the experiences of their existing franchisees.*

Terms and Concepts

entrepreneur 690	franchisee 695	sole proprietorship 691
franchise 695	franchisor 695	

Issue Spotters

1. Frank plans to open a sporting goods store and to hire Gogi and Hap. Frank will invest only his own funds. He expects that he will not make a profit for at least eighteen months and will make only a small profit in the three years after that. He hopes to expand eventually. Would a sole proprietorship be an appropriate form for Frank's business? Why or why not? (See *Sole Proprietorships*.)

2. Anchor Bottling Company and U.S. Beverages, Inc. (USB), enter into a franchise agreement that states the franchise may be terminated at any time "for cause." Anchor fails to meet USB's specified sales quota. Does this constitute "cause" for termination? Why or why not? (See *Franchise Termination*.)

• Check your answers to the Issue Spotters against the answers provided in Appendix D at the end of this text.

Business Scenarios

36–1. Franchising. Maria, Pablo, and Vicky are recent college graduates who would like to go into business for themselves. They are considering purchasing a franchise. If they enter into a franchising arrangement, they would have the support of a large company that could answer any questions they might have. Also, a firm that has been in business for many years would be experienced in dealing with some of the problems that novice businesspersons might encounter. These and other attributes of franchises can lessen some of the risks of the marketplace. What other aspects of franchising—positive and negative—should Maria, Pablo, and Vicky consider before committing themselves to a particular franchise? (See *Franchises*.)

36–2. Control of a Franchise. National Foods, Inc., sells franchises to its fast-food restaurants, known as Chicky-D's. Under the franchise agreement, franchisees agree to hire and train employees strictly according to Chicky-D's standards. Chicky-D's regional supervisors are required to approve all job candidates before they are hired and all general policies affecting those employees. Chicky-D's reserves the right to terminate a franchise for violating the franchisor's rules. In practice, however, Chicky-D's regional supervisors routinely approve new employees and individual franchisees' policies. After several incidents of racist comments and conduct by Tim, a recently hired assistant manager at a Chicky-D's, Sharon, a counterperson at the restaurant, resigns. Sharon files a suit in a federal district court against National. National files a motion for summary judgment, arguing that it is not liable for harassment by franchise employees. Will the court grant National's motion? Why or why not? (See *Franchises*.)

Business Case Problems

36–3. Spotlight on McDonald's—Franchise Termination.

J.C., Inc., had a franchise agreement with McDonald's Corp to operate McDonald's restaurants in Lancaster, Ohio. The agreement required J.C. to make monthly payments of certain percentages of gross sales to McDonald's. If any payment was more than thirty days late, McDonald's had the right to terminate the franchise. The agreement also stated that even if McDonald's accepted a late payment, that would not "constitute a waiver of any subsequent breach." McDonald's sometimes accepted J.C.'s late payments, but when J.C. defaulted on the payment for July 2010, McDonald's gave notice of thirty days to comply or surrender possession of the restaurants. J.C. missed the deadline. McDonald's demanded that J.C. vacate the restaurants, but J.C. refused. McDonald's alleged that J.C. had violated the franchise agreement. J.C. claimed that McDonald's had breached the implied covenant of good faith and fair dealing. Which party should prevail and why? [*McDonald's Corp. v. C.B. Management Co.,* 13 F.Supp.2d 705 (N.D.Ill. 1998)] (See *Franchise Termination*.)

36–4. Franchise Disclosure. Peaberry Coffee, Inc., owned and operated about twenty company stores in the Denver area. The company began a franchise program and prepared a disclosure document as required by the Federal Trade Commission (FTC). Peaberry sold ten franchises, and each franchisee received a disclosure document. Later, when the franchises did not do well, the franchisees sued Peaberry, claiming that its FTC disclosure document had been fraudulent. Specifically, the franchisees claimed that Peaberry had not disclosed that most of the company stores were unprofitable and that its parent company had suffered significant financial losses over the years. In addition, the franchisees stated that Peaberry had included in the franchisees' information packets an article from the *Denver Business Journal* in which an executive had said that Peaberry was profitable. That statement had proved to be false. The FTC disclosure document had also contained an exculpatory clause that said the buyers should not rely on any material that was not in the franchise contract itself. Can a franchisor disclaim the relevance of the information it provides to franchisees? Why or why not? [*Colorado Coffee Bean, LLC v. Peaberry Coffee, Inc.,* 251 P.3d 9 (Colo.App. 2010)] (See *Franchises*.)

36–5. The Franchise Contract. Kubota Tractor Corp. makes farm, industrial, and outdoor equipment. Its franchise contracts allow Kubota to enter into dealership agreements with "others at any location." Kejzar Motors, Inc., is a Kubota dealer in Nacogdoches and Jasper, Texas. These two Kejzar stores operate as one dealership with two locations. Kubota granted a dealership to Michael Hammer in Lufkin, Texas, which lies between Kejzar's two store locations. Kejzar filed a suit in a Texas state court against Kubota. Kejzar asked for an injunction to prevent Kubota from locating a dealership in the same market area. Kejzar argued that the new location would cause it to suffer a significant loss of profits. Which party in a franchise relationship typically determines the territory served by a franchisee? Which legal principles come into play in this area? How do these concepts most likely apply in this case? Discuss. [*Kejzar Motors, Inc. v. Kubota Tractor Corp.,* 334 S.W.3d 351 (Tex.App.—Tyler 2011)] (See *Franchises*.)

36–6. Business Case Problem with Sample Answer—Franchise Termination. George Oshana and GTO Invest-

ments, Inc., operated a Mobil gas station franchise in Itasca, Illinois. In 2010, Oshana and GTO became involved in a rental dispute with Buchanan Energy, to which Mobil had assigned the lease for the gas station facility. In November 2011, Buchanan terminated the franchise because Oshana and GTO had failed to pay the rent. Oshana and GTO, however, alleged that they had been "ready, willing, and able to pay the rent" but that Buchanan had failed to accept their electronic fund transfer. Have Oshana and GTO stated a claim for wrongful termination of their franchise? Why or why not? [*Oshana v. Buchanan Energy,* 2012 WL 426921 (N.D.Ill. 2012)] (See *Franchise Termination*.)

- **For a sample answer to Problem 36–6, go to Appendix E at the end of this text.**

36–7. Quality Control. JTH Tax, Inc., doing business as Liberty Tax Service, provides tax preparation and related loan services through company-owned and franchised stores. Liberty's agreement with its franchisees reserved the right to control their ads. In operations manuals, Liberty provided step-by-step instructions, directions, and limitations regarding the franchisees' ads and retained the right to unilaterally modify the steps at any time. The California attorney general filed a suit in a California state court against Liberty, alleging that its franchisees had used misleading or deceptive ads regarding refund anticipation loans and e-refund checks. Can Liberty be held liable? Discuss. [*People v. JTH Tax, Inc.,* 212 Cal.App.4th 1219, 151 Cal.Rptr.3d 728 (1 Dist. 2013)] (See *Franchises.*)

36–8. Quality Control. The franchise agreement of Domino's Pizza, L.L.C., sets out operational standards, including safety requirements, for a franchisee to follow but provides that the franchisee is an independent contractor. Each franchisee is free to use its own means and methods. For example, Domino's does not know whether a franchisee's delivery drivers are complying with vehicle safety requirements. MAC Pizza Management, Inc., operates a Domino's franchise. A vehicle driven by Joshua Balka, a MAC delivery driver, hydroplaned due to a bald tire and wet pavement. It struck the vehicle of Devavaram and Ruth Christopher, killing Ruth and injuring Devavaram. Is Domino's liable for negligence? Explain. [*Domino's Pizza, L.L.C. v. Reddy,* 2015 WL 1247349 (Tex.App.—Beaumont 2015)] (See *Franchises.*)

36–9. Franchise Termination. Executive Home Care Franchising, LLC, sells in-home health-care franchises. Clint, Massare, and Greer Marshall entered into a franchise agreement with Executive Home Care. The agreement provided that the franchisees' failure to comply with the agreement's terms would likely cause irreparable harm to the franchisor, entitling it to an injunction. About two years later, the Marshalls gave up their franchise. They returned thirteen boxes of documents, stationery, operating manuals, marketing materials, and other items—everything in their possession that featured Executive Home Care trademarks. They quit operating out of the franchised location. They transferred the phone number back to the franchisor and informed their clients that they were no longer associated with Executive Home Care. They continued to engage in the home health-care business, however, under the name "Well-Being Home Care Corp." Is Executive Home Care entitled to an injunction against the Marshalls and their new company? Discuss. [*Executive Home Care Franchising, LLC v. Marshall Health Corp.,* __ F.3d __, 2016 WL 703801 (3d Cir. 2016)] (See *Franchise Termination.*)

36–10. A Question of Ethics—Sole Proprietorship. *In* *August 2004, Ralph Vilardo contacted Travel Center, Inc., in Cincinnati, Ohio, to buy a trip to Florida in December for his family to celebrate his fiftieth wedding anniversary. Vilardo paid $6,900 to David Sheets, the sole proprietor of Travel Center. Vilardo also paid $195 to Sheets for a separate trip to Florida in February 2005. Sheets assured Vilardo that everything was set, but in fact no arrangements were made. Later, two unauthorized charges for travel services totaling $1,182.35 appeared on Vilardo's credit-card statement. Vilardo filed a suit in an Ohio state court against Sheets and his business, alleging, among other things, fraud and violations of the state consumer protection law. Vilardo served Sheets and Travel Center with copies of the complaint, the summons, a request for admissions, and other documents filed with the court, including a motion for summary judgment. Each of these filings asked for a response within a certain time period. Sheets responded once on his own behalf with a denial of all of Vilardo's claims. Travel Center did not respond. [Vilardo v. Sheets, 2006 -Ohio- 3473 (12 Dist. 2006)] (See Sole Proprietorships.)*

(a) Almost four months after Vilardo filed his complaint, Sheets decided that he was unable to adequately represent himself and retained an attorney, who asked the court for more time. Should the court grant this request? Why or why not? Ultimately, what should the court rule?

(b) Sheets admitted that Travel Center, Inc., was a sole proprietorship. He also argued that liability might be imposed on his business but not on himself. How would you rule with respect to this argument? Why? Would there be anything unethical about allowing Sheets to avoid liability on this basis? Explain.

Legal Reasoning Group Activity

36–11. Franchise Termination. Walid Elkhatib, an Arab American, bought a Dunkin' Donuts franchise in Illinois. Ten years later, Dunkin' Donuts began offering breakfast sandwiches with bacon, ham, or sausage through its franchises. Elkhatib refused to sell these items at his store on the ground that his religion forbade the handling of pork. Elkhatib then opened a second franchise, at which he also refused to sell pork products.

The next year, at both locations, Elkhatib began selling meatless sandwiches. He also opened a third franchise. When he proposed to relocate this franchise, Dunkin' Donuts refused to approve the new location. The company also informed him that it would not renew any of his franchise agreements because he did not carry the full sandwich line. Elkhatib filed a lawsuit against Dunkin' Donuts. (See *Franchise Termination.*)

(a) The first group will argue on behalf of Elkhatib that Dunkin' Donuts wrongfully terminated his franchises.

(b) The second group will take the side of Dunkin' Donuts and justify its decision to terminate the franchises.

(c) The third group will assess whether Dunkin' Donuts acted in good faith in its relationship with Elkhatib. Consider whether Dunkin' Donuts should be required to accommodate Elkhatib's religious beliefs and allow him not to serve pork in these three locations.

CHAPTER 37

All Forms of Partnerships

Historically, two or more persons entering into business together have most commonly organized their business as a partnership or a corporation. A *partnership* arises from an agreement, express or implied, between two or more persons to carry on a business for a profit. Partners are co-owners of the business and have joint control over its operation and the right to share in its profits.

In this chapter, we examine several forms of partnership. These include ordinary partnerships, or *general partnerships,* and special forms of partnerships known as *limited partnerships* and *limited liability partnerships*.

Although general partnerships are less common today than in the past, the limited liability forms of partnership are quite prevalent. Accountants, attorneys, and architects frequently organize as limited liability partnerships. DLA Piper, the second-largest U.S. law firm, for instance, is structured as two limited liability partnerships—DLA Piper U.S., LLP, and DLA Piper International, LLP.

37–1 Basic Partnership Concepts

Partnerships are governed both by common law concepts—in particular, those relating to agency—and by statutory law. As in so many other areas of business law, the National Conference of Commissioners on Uniform State Laws has drafted uniform laws for partnerships, and these have been widely adopted by the states.

37–1a Agency Concepts and Partnership Law

When two or more persons agree to do business as partners, they enter into a special relationship with one another. To an extent, their relationship is similar to an agency relationship because each partner is deemed to be the agent of the other partners and of the partnership. Thus, agency concepts apply—specifically, the imputation of knowledge of, and responsibility for, acts carried out within the scope of the partnership relationship. In their relationships with one another, partners, like agents, are bound by fiduciary ties.

In one important way, however, partnership law differs from agency law. The partners in a partnership agree to commit funds or other assets, labor, and skills to the business with the understanding that profits and losses will be shared. Thus, each partner has an *ownership interest* in the firm. In a nonpartnership agency relationship, the agent usually does not have an ownership interest in the business and is not obligated to bear a portion of ordinary business losses.

37–1b The Uniform Partnership Act

The Uniform Partnership Act (UPA) governs the operation of partnerships *in the absence of express agreement* and has done much to reduce controversies in the law relating to partnerships. A majority of the states have enacted the most recent version of the UPA (introduced in 1997 and last amended in 2013).

37–1c Definition of a Partnership

The UPA defines a **partnership** as "an association of two or more persons to carry on as co-owners a business for profit" [UPA 101(6)]. Note that the UPA's definition of *person* includes corporations, so a corporation can be a partner in a partnership [UPA 101(10)]. The *intent* to associate is a key element of a partnership, and one cannot join a partnership unless all other partners consent [UPA 401(i)].

37–1d Essential Elements of a Partnership

Conflicts sometimes arise over whether a business enterprise is a legal partnership, especially when there is no formal, written partnership agreement. To determine whether a partnership exists, courts usually look for the following three essential elements, which are implicit in the UPA's definition:

1. A sharing of profits or losses.
2. A joint ownership of the business.
3. An equal right to be involved in the management of the business.

If the evidence in a particular case is insufficient to establish all three factors, the UPA provides a set of guidelines to be used.

The Sharing of Profits and Losses The sharing of both profits and losses from a business creates a presumption that a partnership exists. ■ **EXAMPLE 37.1** Syd and Drake start a business that sells fruit smoothies near a college campus. They open a joint bank account, from which they pay for supplies and expenses, and they share the proceeds (and losses) that the smoothie stand generates. If a conflict arises as to their business relationship, a court will assume that a partnership exists unless the parties prove otherwise. ■

A court will not presume that a partnership exists, however, if shared profits were received as payment of any of the following [UPA 202(c)(3)]:

1. A debt by installments or interest on a loan.
2. Wages of an employee or for the services of an independent contractor.
3. Rent to a landlord.
4. An annuity to a surviving spouse or representative of a deceased partner.
5. A sale of the **goodwill** (the valuable reputation of a business viewed as an intangible asset) of a business or property.

■ **EXAMPLE 37.2** A debtor, Mason Snopel, owes a creditor, Alice Burns, $5,000 on an unsecured debt. They agree that Mason will pay 10 percent of his monthly business profits to Alice until the loan with interest has been repaid. Although Mason and Alice are sharing profits from the business, they are not presumed to be partners. ■

Joint Property Ownership Joint ownership of property does not in and of itself create a partnership [UPA 202(c)(1) and (2)]. The parties' intentions are key. ■ **EXAMPLE 37.3** Chiang and Burke jointly own farmland and lease it to a farmer for a share of the profits from the farming operation in lieu of fixed rental payments. This arrangement normally would not make Chiang, Burke, and the farmer partners. ■

37–1e Entity versus Aggregate

At common law, a partnership was treated only as an aggregate of individuals and never as a separate legal entity. Thus, at common law a lawsuit could never be brought by or against the firm in its own name. Each individual partner had to sue or be sued.

Today, in contrast, a majority of the states follow the UPA and treat a partnership as an entity for most purposes. For instance, a partnership usually can sue or be sued, collect judgments, and have all accounting performed in the name of the partnership entity [UPA 201, 307(a)].

As an entity, a partnership may hold the title to real or personal property in its name rather than in the names of the individual partners. Additionally, federal procedural laws permit the partnership to be treated as an entity in suits in federal courts and bankruptcy proceedings.

37–1f Tax Treatment of Partnerships

Modern law does treat a partnership as an aggregate of the individual partners rather than a separate legal entity in one situation—for federal income tax purposes. The partnership is a pass-through entity and not a taxpaying entity. A **pass-through entity** is a business entity that has no tax liability. The entity's income is passed through to the owners, who pay income taxes on it.

Thus, the income or losses the partnership incurs are "passed through" the entity framework and attributed to the partners on their individual tax returns. The partnership itself pays no taxes and is responsible only for filing an **information return** with the Internal Revenue Service.

A partner's profit from the partnership (whether distributed or not) is taxed as individual income to the individual partner. Similarly, partners can deduct a share of the partnership's losses on their individual tax returns (in proportion to their partnership interests).

37–2 Formation and Operation

A partnership is a voluntary association of individuals. As such, it is formed by the agreement of the partners.

37–2a The Partnership Agreement

As a general rule, agreements to form a partnership can be *oral, written,* or *implied by conduct.* Some partnership agreements, however, such as one authorizing partners to transfer interests in real property, must be in writing to be legally enforceable.

A partnership agreement, also known as **articles of partnership,** can include almost any terms that the parties wish, unless they are illegal or contrary to public policy or statute [UPA 103]. The provisions commonly included in a partnership agreement are listed in Exhibit 37–1.

The rights and duties of partners are governed largely by the specific terms of their partnership agreement. In the absence of provisions to the contrary in the partnership agreement, the law imposes certain rights and duties, as discussed in the following subsections. The character and nature of the partnership business generally influence the application of these rights and duties.

37–2b Duration of the Partnership

The partnership agreement can specify the duration of the partnership by stating that it will continue until a designated date or until the completion of a particular project. This is called a *partnership for a term.* Generally, withdrawing from a partnership for a term prematurely (before the expiration date) constitutes a breach of the agreement, and the responsible partner can be held liable for any resulting losses [UPA 602(b)(2)]. If no fixed duration is specified, the partnership is a *partnership at will.* A partnership at will can be dissolved at any time without liability.

37–2c Partnership by Estoppel

When a third person has reasonably and detrimentally relied on the representation that a nonpartner was part of a partnership, a court may conclude that a **partnership by estoppel** exists.

EXHIBIT 37–1 Provisions Commonly Included in a Partnership Agreement

Basic Structure	• Name of the partnership and the names of the partners. • Location of the business and the state law under which the partnership is organized. • Purpose and duration of the partnership.
Capital Contributions	• Amount of capital that each partner is contributing. • The agreed-on value of any real or personal property that is contributed instead of cash. • How losses and gains on contributed capital will be allocated, and whether contributions will earn interest.
Sharing of Profits and Losses	• Percentage of the profits and losses of the business that each partner will receive. • When distributions of profit will be made and how net profit will be calculated.
Management and Control	• How management responsibilities will be divided among the partners. • Name(s) of the managing partner or partners, and whether other partners have voting rights.
Dissociation and Dissolution	• Events that will cause the dissociation of a partner or dissolve the firm, such as the retirement, death, or incapacity of any partner. • How partnership property will be valued and apportioned on dissociation and dissolution. • Whether an arbitrator will determine the value of partnership property on dissociation and dissolution and whether that determination will be binding.

Liability Imposed A partnership by estoppel may arise when a person who is not a partner holds himself or herself out as a partner and makes representations that third parties rely on. In this situation, a court may impose liability—but not partnership rights—on the alleged partner.

Nonpartner as Agent A partnership by estoppel may also be imposed when a partner represents, expressly or impliedly, that a nonpartner is a member of the firm. In this situation, the nonpartner may be regarded as an agent whose acts are binding on the partnership [UPA 308].

■ **CASE IN POINT 37.4** Jackson Paper Manufacturing Company made paper used by Stonewall Packaging, LLC. Jackson and Stonewall had officers and directors in common, and they shared employees, property, and equipment. In reliance on Jackson's business reputation, Best Cartage, Inc., agreed to provide transportation services for Stonewall and bought thirty-seven tractor-trailers to use in fulfilling the contract. Best provided the services until Stonewall terminated the agreement.

Best filed a suit for breach of contract against Stonewall and Jackson, seeking $500,678 in unpaid invoices and consequential damages of $1,315,336 for the tractor-trailers it had purchased. Best argued that Stonewall and Jackson had a partnership by estoppel. The court agreed, finding that "defendants combined labor, skills, and property to advance their alleged business partnership." Jackson had negotiated the agreement on Stonewall's behalf. Jackson also had bought real estate, equipment, and general supplies for Stonewall with no expectation that Stonewall would repay these expenditures. This was sufficient to prove a partnership by estoppel.[1] ■

37–2d Rights of Partners

The rights of partners in a partnership relate to the following areas: management, interest in the partnership, compensation, inspection of books, accounting, and property.

Management Rights In a general partnership, all partners have equal rights in managing the partnership [UPA 401(f)]. Unless the partners agree otherwise, each partner has one vote in management matters *regardless of the proportional size of his or her interest in the firm*. In a large partnership, partners often agree to delegate daily management responsibilities to a management committee made up of one or more of the partners.

The majority rule controls decisions on ordinary matters connected with partnership business, unless otherwise specified in the agreement. Decisions that significantly change the nature of the partnership or that are outside the ordinary course of the partnership business, however, require the *unanimous* consent of the partners [UPA 301(2), 401(i), 401(j)]. For instance, unanimous consent is likely required for a partnership to admit new partners, to amend the partnership agreement, or to enter a new line of business.

Interest in the Partnership Each partner is entitled to the proportion of business profits and losses that is specified in the partnership agreement. If the agreement does not apportion profits (indicate how the profits will be shared), the UPA provides that profits will be shared equally. If the agreement does not apportion losses, losses will be shared in the same ratio as profits [UPA 401(b)].

■ **EXAMPLE 37.5** The partnership agreement between Rick and Brett provides for capital contributions of $60,000 from Rick and $40,000 from Brett. If the agreement is silent as to how Rick and Brett will share profits or losses, they will share both profits and losses equally.

In contrast, if the agreement provides for profits to be shared in the same ratio as capital contributions, 60 percent of the profits will go to Rick, and 40 percent will go to Brett. Unless the agreement provides otherwise, losses will be shared in the same ratio as profits. ■

Compensation Devoting time, skill, and energy to partnership business is a partner's duty and generally is not a compensable service. Rather, as mentioned, a partner's income from the partnership takes the form of a distribution of profits according to the partner's share in the business.

Partners can, of course, agree otherwise. For instance, the managing partner of a law firm often receives a salary—in addition to her or his share of profits—for performing special administrative or managerial duties.

Inspection of the Books Partnership books and records must be kept accessible to all partners. Each partner has the right to receive full and complete information concerning the conduct of all aspects of partnership business [UPA 403]. Partners have a duty to provide the information to the firm, which has a duty to preserve it and to keep accurate records.

The partnership books must be kept at the firm's principal business office (unless the partners agree otherwise). Every partner is entitled to inspect all books and records on demand and can make copies of the materials. The

---

1. *Best Cartage, Inc. v. Stonewall Packaging, LLC*, 727 S.E.2d 291 (N.C.App. 2012).

personal representative of a deceased partner's estate has the same right of access to partnership books and records that the decedent would have had [UPA 403].

Accounting of Partnership Assets or Profits

An accounting of partnership assets or profits is required to determine the value of each partner's share in the partnership. An accounting can be performed voluntarily, or it can be compelled by court order. Under UPA 405(b), a partner has the right to bring an action for an accounting during the term of the partnership, as well as on the partnership's dissolution.

Property Rights Property acquired *by* a partnership is the property of the partnership and not of the partners individually [UPA 203]. Partnership property includes all property that was originally contributed to the partnership and anything later purchased by the partnership or in the partnership's name (except in rare circumstances) [UPA 204].

A partner may use or possess partnership property only on behalf of the partnership [UPA 401(g)]. A partner is *not* a co-owner of partnership property and has no right to sell, mortgage, or transfer partnership property to another [UPA 501].[2]

Because partnership property is owned by the partnership and not by the individual partners, the property cannot be used to satisfy the personal debts of individual partners. A partner's creditor, however, can petition a court for a **charging order** to attach the partner's *interest* in the partnership to satisfy the partner's obligation [UPA 502]. A partner's interest in the partnership includes her or his proportionate share of any profits that are distributed. A partner can also assign her or his right to receive a share of the partnership profits to another to satisfy a debt.

---

2. Under the previous version of the UPA, partners were *tenants in partnership*. This meant that every partner was a co-owner with all other partners of the partnership property. The current UPA does not recognize this concept.

37–2e Duties and Liabilities of Partners

The duties and liabilities of partners are derived from agency law. Each partner is an agent of every other partner and acts as both a principal and an agent in any business transaction within the scope of the partnership agreement.

Each partner is also a general agent of the partnership in carrying out the usual business of the firm "or business of the kind carried on by the partnership" [UPA 301(1)]. Thus, every act of a partner concerning partnership business and "business of the kind" and every contract signed in the partnership's name bind the firm.

Fiduciary Duties The fiduciary duties that a partner owes to the partnership and to the other partners are the duty of care and the duty of loyalty [UPA 404(a)]. Under the UPA, a partner's *duty of care* is limited to refraining from "grossly negligent or reckless conduct, intentional misconduct, or a knowing violation of law" [UPA 404(c)].[3] A partner is not liable to the partnership for simple negligence or honest errors in judgment in conducting partnership business.

The *duty of loyalty* requires a partner to account to the partnership for "any property, profit, or benefit" derived by the partner in the conduct of the partnership's business or from the use of its property. A partner must also refrain from competing with the partnership in business or dealing with the firm as an adverse party [UPA 404(b)].

The duty of loyalty can be breached by self-dealing, misusing partnership property, disclosing trade secrets, or usurping a partnership business opportunity. The following case is a classic example.

---

3. The previous version of the UPA touched only briefly on the duty of loyalty and left the details of the partners' fiduciary duties to be developed under the law of agency.

Classic Case 37.1

Meinhard v. Salmon

Court of Appeals of New York, 249 N.Y. 458, 164 N.E. 545 (1928).

Background and Facts Walter Salmon negotiated a twenty-year lease for the Hotel Bristol in New York City. To pay for the conversion of the building into shops and offices, Salmon entered into an agreement with Morton Meinhard to assume half of the cost. They agreed to share the profits and losses from the joint venture. (A *joint venture* is similar to a partnership but typically is created for a single project.) Salmon was to have the sole power to manage the building, however.

Less than four months before the end of the lease term, the building's owner, Elbridge Gerry, approached Salmon about a project to raze the converted structure, clear five adjacent lots, and

Case 37.1 Continues

Case 37.1 Continued

construct a single building across the whole property. Salmon agreed and signed a new lease in the name of his own business, Midpoint Realty Company, without telling Meinhard. When Meinhard learned of the deal, he filed a suit in a New York state court against Salmon. The court ruled in Meinhard's favor, and Salmon appealed.

In the Language of the Court

CARDOZO, C.J. [Chief Justice]

* * * *

Joint adventurers, like copartners, owe to one another, while the enterprise continues, the duty of the finest loyalty. Many forms of conduct permissible in a work-a-day world for those acting at arm's length are forbidden to those bound by fiduciary ties. * * * Not honesty alone, but the punctilio [strictness in observance of details] of an honor the most sensitive, is then the standard of behavior. As to this there has developed a tradition that is unbending and inveterate [entrenched]. Uncompromising rigidity has been the attitude of courts * * * when petitioned to undermine the rule of undivided loyalty.

* * * The trouble about [Salmon's] conduct is that he excluded his coadventurer from any chance to compete, from any chance to enjoy the opportunity for benefit.

* * * The very fact that Salmon was in control with exclusive powers of direction charged him the more obviously with the duty of disclosure, [because] only through disclosure could opportunity be equalized.

* * * Authority is, of course, abundant that one partner may not appropriate to his own use a renewal of a lease, though its term is to begin at the expiration of the partnership. The lease at hand with its many changes is not strictly a renewal. Even so, the standard of loyalty for those in trust relations is without the fixed divisions of a graduated scale. * * * *A man obtaining [an]* * * * *opportunity* * * * *by the position he occupies as a partner is bound by his obligation to his copartners in such dealings not to separate his interest from theirs, but, if he acquires any benefit, to communicate it to them. Certain it is also that there may be no abuse of special opportunities growing out of a special trust as manager or agent.* [Emphasis added.]

* * * Very likely [Salmon] assumed in all good faith that with the approaching end of the venture he might ignore his coadventurer and take the extension for himself. He had given to the enterprise time and labor as well as money. He had made it a success. Meinhard, who had given money, but neither time nor labor, had already been richly paid. * * * [But] Salmon had put himself in a position in which thought of self was to be renounced, however hard the abnegation [self-denial]. He was much more than a coadventurer. He was a managing coadventurer. For him and for those like him the rule of undivided loyalty is relentless and supreme.

Decision and Remedy *The Court of Appeals of New York held that Salmon had breached his fiduciary duty by failing to inform Meinhard of the business opportunity and secretly taking advantage of it himself. The court granted Meinhard an interest "measured by the value of half of the entire lease."*

Impact of This Case on Today's Law *This classic case involved a joint venture, not a partnership. At the time, a member of a joint venture had only the duty to refrain from actively subverting the rights of the other members. The decision in this case imposed the highest standard of loyalty on joint-venture members. The duty is now the same in both joint ventures and partnerships. Courts today frequently quote the eloquent language used in this opinion when describing the standard of loyalty that applies to partnerships.*

Critical Thinking

• **What If the Facts Were Different?** *Suppose that Salmon had disclosed Gerry's proposal to Meinhard, who had said that he was not interested. Would the result in this case have been different? Explain.*

Waiver of Fiduciary Duties A partner's fiduciary duties may not be waived or eliminated in the partnership agreement. In fulfilling them, each partner must act consistently with the obligation of good faith and fair dealing [UPA 103(b), 404(d)]. The agreement can specify acts that the partners agree will violate a fiduciary duty.

Note that a partner may pursue his or her own interests without automatically violating these duties [UPA 404(e)]. The key is whether the partner has disclosed the interest to the other partners. ■ **EXAMPLE 37.6** Jayne Trell, a partner at Jacoby & Meyers, owns a shopping mall. Trell may vote against a partnership proposal to open a competing mall, provided that she has fully disclosed her interest in the existing shopping mall to the other partners at the firm. ∎ A partner cannot make secret profits or put self-interest before his or her duty to the interest of the partnership, however.

Authority of Partners The UPA affirms general principles of agency law that pertain to a partner's authority to bind a partnership in contract. If a partner acts within the scope of her or his authority, the partnership is legally bound to honor the partner's commitments to third parties.

A partner may also subject the partnership to tort liability under agency principles. When a partner is carrying on partnership business with third parties in the usual way, apparent authority exists, and both the partner and the firm share liability. The partnership will not be liable, however, if the third parties *know* that the partner has no such authority.

Limitations on Authority. A partnership may limit a partner's capacity to act as the firm's agent or transfer property on its behalf by filing a "statement of partnership authority" in a designated state office [UPA 105, 303]. Such limits on a partner's authority normally are effective only with respect to third parties who are notified of the limitation. (An exception is made in real estate transactions when the statement of authority has been recorded with the appropriate state office.)

The Scope of Implied Powers. The agency concepts relating to apparent authority, actual authority, and ratification apply to partnerships. The extent of implied authority generally is broader for partners than for ordinary agents, however.

In an ordinary partnership, the partners can exercise all implied powers reasonably necessary and customary to carry on that particular business. Some customarily implied powers include the authority to make warranties on goods in the sales business and the power to enter into contracts consistent with the firm's regular course of business.

∎ **EXAMPLE 37.7** Jamie Schwab is a partner in a firm that operates a retail tire store. He regularly promises that "each tire will be warranted for normal wear for 40,000 miles." Because Schwab has authority to make warranties, the partnership is bound to honor the warranty. Schwab would not, however, have the authority to sell the partnership's office equipment or other property without the consent of all of the other partners. ∎

Liability of Partners One significant disadvantage associated with a traditional partnership is that the partners are *personally* liable for the debts of the partnership. In most states, the liability is essentially unlimited, because the acts of one partner in the ordinary course of business subject the other partners to personal liability [UPA 305]. Note that normally the partnership's assets must be exhausted before creditors can reach the partners' individual assets, however.

Joint Liability. Each partner in a partnership generally is jointly liable for the partnership's obligations. **Joint liability** means that a third party must sue all of the partners as a group, but each partner can be held liable for the full amount.[4] If, for instance, a third party sues one partner on a partnership contract, that partner has the right to demand that the other partners be sued with her or him. In fact, if the third party does not name all of the partners in the lawsuit, the assets of the partnership cannot be used to satisfy the judgment.

Joint and Several Liability. In the majority of the states, under UPA 306(a), partners are both jointly and severally (separately, or individually) liable for all partnership obligations. **Joint and several liability** means that a third party has the option of suing all of the partners together (jointly) or one or more of the partners separately (severally). All partners in a partnership can be held liable even if a particular partner did not participate in, know about, or ratify the conduct that gave rise to the lawsuit.

A judgment against one partner severally (separately) does not extinguish the others' liability. (Similarly, a release of one partner does not discharge the partners' several liability.) Those not sued in the first action normally may be sued subsequently, unless the court in the first action held that the partnership was in no way liable. If a plaintiff is successful in a suit against a partner or partners, he or she may collect on the judgment only against the assets of those partners named as defendants.

Indemnification. With joint and several liability, a partner who commits a tort can be required to indemnify (reimburse) the partnership for any damages it pays. Indemnification will typically be granted *unless* the tort was committed in the ordinary course of the partnership's business.

∎ **EXAMPLE 37.8** Nicole Martin, a partner at Patti's Café, is working in the café's kitchen one day when her young son suffers serious injuries to his hands from a dough press. Her son, through his father, files a negligence

---

4. Under the prior version of the UPA, partners were subject to joint liability on partnership debts and contracts, but not on partnership debts arising from torts.

lawsuit against the partnership. Even if the suit is successful and the partnership pays damages to Martin's son, the firm is not entitled to indemnification. Martin would not be required to indemnify the partnership because her negligence occurred in the ordinary course of the partnership's business (making food for customers). ■

Liability of Incoming Partners. A partner newly admitted to an existing partnership is not personally liable for any partnership obligations incurred *before* the person became a partner [UPA 306(b)]. In other words, the new partner's liability to existing creditors of the partnership is limited to her or his capital contribution to the firm.

■ **EXAMPLE 37.9** Smartclub, an existing partnership with four members, admits a new partner, Alex Jaff. He contributes $100,000 to the partnership. Smartclub has debts amounting to $600,000 at the time Jaff joins the firm. Although Jaff's capital contribution of $100,000 can be used to satisfy Smartclub's obligations, Jaff is not personally liable for partnership debts incurred before he became a partner. If, however, the partnership incurs additional debts after Jaff becomes a partner, he will be personally liable for those amounts, along with all the other partners. ■

37–3 Dissociation and Termination

Dissociation occurs when a partner ceases to be associated in the carrying on of the partnership business. Dissociation normally entitles the partner to have his or her interest purchased by the partnership. It also terminates the partner's actual authority to act for the partnership and to participate in running its business.

Once dissociation occurs, the partnership may continue to do business without the dissociated partner.[5] If the partners no longer wish to (or are unable to) continue the business, the partnership may be terminated (dissolved).

37–3a Events That Cause Dissociation

Under UPA 601, a partner can be dissociated from a partnership in any of the following ways:

1. By the partner's voluntarily giving notice of an "express will to withdraw." (When a partner gives

notice of intent to withdraw, the remaining partners must decide whether to continue the partnership business. If they decide not to continue, the voluntary dissociation of a partner will dissolve the firm [UPA 801(1)].)

2. By the occurrence of an event specified in the partnership agreement.

3. By a unanimous vote of the other partners under certain circumstances, such as when a partner transfers substantially all of her or his interest in the partnership.

4. By order of a court or arbitrator if the partner has engaged in wrongful conduct that affects the partnership business. The court can order dissociation if a partner breached the partnership agreement or violated a duty owed to the partnership or to the other partners. Dissociation may also be ordered if the partner engaged in conduct that makes it "not reasonably practicable to carry on the business in partnership with the partner" [UPA 601(5)].

5. By the partner's declaring bankruptcy, assigning his or her interest in the partnership for the benefit of creditors, or becoming physically or mentally incapacitated, or by the partner's death.

37–3b Wrongful Dissociation

A partner has the *power* to dissociate from a partnership at any time, but she or he may not have the *right* to do so. If the partner lacks the right to dissociate, then the dissociation is considered wrongful under the law [UPA 602]. When a partner's dissociation breaches a partnership agreement, for instance, it is wrongful.

■ **EXAMPLE 37.10** Jenkins & Whalen's partnership agreement states that it is a breach of the agreement for any partner to assign partnership property to a creditor without the consent of the other partners. If Kenzie, a partner, makes such an assignment, she has not only breached the agreement but has also wrongfully dissociated from the partnership. ■

A partner who wrongfully dissociates is liable to the partnership and to the other partners for damages caused by the dissociation. This liability is in addition to any other obligation of the partner to the partnership or to the other partners.

37–3c Effects of Dissociation

Dissociation (rightful or wrongful) terminates some of the rights of the dissociated partner and requires that the partnership purchase his or her interest. It also alters the liability of the parties to third parties.

---

5. Under the previous version of the UPA, when a partner withdrew from a partnership, the partnership was considered dissolved, and the business had to end. The new UPA dramatically changed the law governing partnership breakups by no longer requiring that a partnership end if one partner dissociates.

Rights and Duties On a partner's dissociation, his or her right to participate in the management and conduct of the partnership business terminates [UPA 603]. The partner's duty of loyalty also ends. A partner's duty of care continues only with respect to events that occurred before dissociation, unless the partner participates in winding up the partnership's business (discussed shortly).

■ **EXAMPLE 37.11** Debbie Pearson is a partner at the accounting firm Bubb & Flint. If she leaves the partnership, she can immediately compete with the firm for new clients. She must exercise care in completing ongoing client transactions that involved the partnership, however. She must also account to Bubb & Flint for any fees received from the old clients based on those transactions. ■

Buyouts After a partner's dissociation, his or her interest in the partnership must be purchased according to the rules in UPA 701. The **buyout price** is based on the amount that would have been distributed to the partner if the partnership had been wound up on the date of dissociation. Offset against the price are amounts owed by the partner to the partnership, including damages for wrongful dissociation.

Liability to Third Parties For two years after a partner dissociates from a continuing partnership, the partnership may be bound by the acts of the dissociated partner based on apparent authority [UPA 702]. In other words, if a third party reasonably believed at the time of a transaction that the dissociated partner was still a partner, the partnership may be liable. Similarly, a dissociated partner may be liable for partnership obligations entered into during the two-year period following dissociation [UPA 703].

To avoid this possible liability, a partnership should notify its creditors, customers, and clients of a partner's dissociation. In addition, either the partnership or the dissociated partner can file a statement of dissociation in the appropriate state office to limit the dissociated partner's authority to ninety days after the filing [UPA 704]. Filing this statement helps to minimize the firm's potential liability for the former partner and vice versa.

37–3d Partnership Termination

The same events that cause dissociation can result in the end of the partnership if the remaining partners no longer wish to (or are unable to) continue the partnership business. A partner's departure will not necessarily end the partnership, though. Generally, the partnership can continue if the remaining partners consent [UPA 801].

The termination of a partnership is referred to as **dissolution,** which essentially means the commencement of the winding up process. **Winding up** is the actual process of collecting, liquidating, and distributing the partnership assets.

Dissolution Dissolution of a partnership generally can be brought about by acts of the partners, by operation of law, or by judicial decree [UPA 801]. Any partnership (including one for a fixed term) can be dissolved by the partners' agreement. If the partnership agreement states that it will dissolve on a certain event, such as a partner's death or bankruptcy, then the occurrence of that event will dissolve the partnership. A partnership for a fixed term or a particular undertaking is dissolved by operation of law at the expiration of the term or on the completion of the undertaking.

■ **CASE IN POINT 37.12** Clyde Webster, James Theis, and Larry Thomas formed T&T Agri-Partners Company to own and farm 180 acres in Christian County, Illinois. Under the partnership agreement, the firm was to continue until January 31, 2010, unless it was dissolved. The death of any partner would dissolve the partnership.

Webster died in 2002, but Theis and Thomas did not liquidate T&T and distribute its assets. Webster's estate, through its personal representative, Joseph Webster, filed a complaint in state court seeking to dissolve the partnership. The court ordered the partnership to be dissolved, but Theis and Thomas did not dissolve it.

In 2011, after a trial, the court found that the partnership had expired by its own terms on January 31, 2010, and again ordered the partnership dissolved. Theis and Thomas appealed, but the reviewing court affirmed. A partnership business cannot continue after one partner dies when the partnership agreement specified that the death of one partner would terminate the business.[6] ■

Illegality or Impracticality. Any event that makes it unlawful for the partnership to continue its business will result in dissolution [UPA 801(4)]. Under the UPA, a court may order dissolution when it becomes obviously impractical for the firm to continue—for instance, if the business can only be operated at a loss [UPA 801(5)]

■ **CASE IN POINT 37.13** Members of the Russell family began operating Russell Realty Associates (RRA) as a partnership. Eddie Russell had decision-making authority over the partnership's business, which involved buying, holding, leasing, and selling investment properties. After several years, Eddie and his sister, Nina Russell,

---

6. *Estate of Webster v. Thomas,* 2013 IL App (5th) 120121-U, 2013 WL 164041 (2013).

started having disputes, and Nina began to routinely question Eddie's business decisions. Because of their disagreements, RRA experienced two years of delays before it could sell one piece of property. Although the firm continued to profit, Eddie filed a complaint seeking a judicial dissolution of the partnership, which the court granted. Nina appealed.

The Virginia Supreme Court affirmed the lower court's decision that Russell Realty must be judicially dissolved. The partners' relationship had deteriorated to the point where the partnership was unable to function effectively. As a result, the firm had incurred substantial and unnecessary added costs, which frustrated the partnership's economic purpose and made it impracticable to continue.[7] ■

Good Faith. Each partner must exercise good faith when dissolving a partnership. Some state statutes allow partners injured by another partner's bad faith to file a tort claim for wrongful dissolution of a partnership.

■ **CASE IN POINT 37.14** Attorneys Randall Jordan and Mary Helen Moses formed a two-member partnership. Although the partnership was for an indefinite term, Jordan ended the partnership three years later and asked the court for declarations concerning the partners' financial obligations. Moses, who had objected to ending the partnership, filed a claim against Jordan for wrongful dissolution and for appropriating $180,000 in fees that should have gone to the partnership.

Ultimately, the court held in favor of Moses. A claim for wrongful dissolution of a partnership may be based on the excluded partner's loss of "an existing, or continuing, business opportunity" or of income and material assets. Because Jordan had attempted to appropriate partnership assets through dissolution, Moses could sue for wrongful dissolution.[8] ■

Winding Up and Distribution of Assets After dissolution, the partnership continues for the limited purpose of winding up the business. The partners cannot create new obligations on behalf of the partnership. They have authority only to complete transactions begun but not finished at the time of dissolution and to wind up the business of the partnership [UPA 803, 804(1)].

Duties and Compensation. Winding up includes collecting and preserving partnership assets, discharging liabilities (paying debts), and accounting to each partner for

the value of his or her interest in the partnership. Partners continue to have fiduciary duties to one another and to the firm during this process.

UPA 401(h) provides that a partner is entitled to compensation for services in winding up partnership affairs above and apart from his or her share in the partnership profits. A partner may also receive reimbursement for expenses incurred in the process.

Creditors' Claims. Both creditors of the partnership and creditors of the individual partners can make claims on the partnership's assets. In general, partnership creditors share proportionately with the partners' individual creditors in the partners' assets, which include their interests in the partnership.

A partnership's assets are distributed according to the following priorities [UPA 807]:

1. Payment of debts, including those owed to partner and nonpartner creditors.
2. Return of capital contributions and distribution of profits to partners.[9]

If the partnership's liabilities are greater than its assets, the partners bear the losses in the same proportion in which they shared the profits unless they have agreed otherwise.

Partnership Buy-Sell Agreements Before entering into a partnership, partners may agree on how the assets will be valued and divided in the event that the partnership dissolves. Such an agreement may eliminate costly negotiations or litigation later.

The agreement may provide for one or more partners to buy out the other or others, should the situation warrant. This is called a **buy-sell agreement**, or simply a *buyout agreement.* Alternatively, the agreement may specify that one or more partners will determine the value of the interest being sold and that the other or others will decide whether to buy or sell.

Under UPA 701(a), if a partner's dissociation does not result in a dissolution of the partnership, a buyout of the partner's interest is mandatory. The UPA contains an extensive set of buyout rules that apply when the partners do not have a buyout agreement. Basically, a withdrawing partner receives the same amount through a buyout that he or she would receive if the business were winding up [UPA 701(b)].

---

7. *Russell Realty Associates v. Russell,* 724 S.E.2d 690 (Va.Sup.Ct. 2012).
8. *Jordan v. Moses,* 291 Ga. 39, 727 S.E.2d 469 (2012).
9. Under the previous version of the UPA, creditors of the partnership had priority over creditors of the individual partners. Also, in distributing partnership assets, third party creditors were paid before partner creditors, and capital contributions were returned before profits.

Which of two buyout provisions in five partnership agreements applied to the sale of one partner's interest was the dispute in the following case. Although this case involved limited liability partnerships (discussed shortly) rather than traditional partnerships, it illustrates how the courts interpret buyout provisions.

Case Analysis 37.2

Shamburger v. Shamburger

Court of Appeals of Arkansas, Division I, 2016 Ark.App. 57, 481 S.W.3d 448 (2016).

In the Language of the Court

Cliff *HOOFMAN*, Judge

* * * *

There are five LLPs [limited liability partnerships] at issue in this case: (1) CMH Management, LLP; (2) S.E. Management, LLP; (3) Bryant Hospitality, LLP; (4) Winners Circle Hospitality, LLP; and (5) SJS Management, LLP. At the time these LLPs were created, they were each composed of six partners, or three married couples: Sarah Jane and Robert Shamburger, Karyn Ann and Ricky Alan Johnson, and Thresa Kay and James Shamburger, Jr. Each partner had a 16.667% interest in each of the five LLPs.

The partners executed partnership agreements in connection with each LLP, as well as separate buy-sell agreements setting forth the required procedure through which partners could transfer their interests. The buy-sell agreements * * * contained similar language regarding the transfer of a partner's interest. As an example, the relevant provisions of the buy-sell agreement for Bryant Hospitality, LLP, are set forth below:

1. * * * The parties agree that the only manner in which any of the partners may transfer a partnership interest * * * shall be in the manner set forth herein:
(a) Any couple may give notice * * * of an intent to either buy the others' entire company interests or to sell their entire company interest. Such notice shall contain one price at which such transaction shall occur. The offeree couples, or any single partner, shall, for sixty (60) days, have the option to either buy the offerors' entire interests for such price, or to sell their entire interest for such price.

* * * *

(c) If neither option is timely accepted by both individuals of the offeree couples, the offer shall be deemed an offer to purchase only, and acceptance of such offer shall be presumed.

* * * *

3. In the event of the death or divorce of a partner, the purchase price of such partner's interest, and the spouse's interest, or the interest of both in the event of common disaster, shall be the higher of the figures achieved in paragraphs (a) and (b) below:
(a) The aggregate * * * revenue * * * for the preceding thirty-six months (or so long as the partnership has been in business, if less than that time), as reflected on the books of the partnership, multiplied by the partner's percentage ownership.
(b) The applicable percentage of partnership interest of the value of the real property * * * as determined by the average of two appraisals.

* * * *

Appellant [Thresa Kay Shamburger] and her husband, James, divorced. [Two and a half years later] Sarah Jane and Robert Shamburger mailed a letter to appellant and James, stating that their divorce proceeding had "adversely affected the operation of all the family partnerships" and that, "in an effort to avoid continued disagreements and acrimony harmful to the businesses we propose to purchase your collective interest in all the partnerships, for a total price of $400,000, or $200,000 to each of you." The letter further referred appellant and James to the buy-sell agreements associated with each partnership and stated that they had sixty days from their receipt of the letter to make their election.

Appellant received the letter * * * but did not respond. Instead, she filed a complaint [in an Arkansas state court] against appellees [all of the partnerships and the other partners], alleging that her divorce from James had triggered the terms of the buy-sell agreements dealing with a divorced party's interest and that appellees were attempting to bypass that provision by attempting to invoke the transfer provision set forth in Paragraph 1 of the agreements. * * * Appellant requested an order from the * * * court * * * determining that the attempted buy-sell arrangement by Sarah Jane and Robert Shamburger was in violation of the buy-sell agreements.

* * * *

Separate appellees Sarah Jane and Robert Shamburger filed a counterclaim against appellant, alleging that appellant had failed to respond to their purchase offer within the sixty-day period required by the buy-sell agreements and that the offer should therefore be deemed an offer to purchase her interest for $200,000. Robert and Sarah Jane requested that the * * * court order specific performance of the terms of the buy-sell agreements.

* * * *

* * * The court granted appellees' motion for summary judgment * * * . In addition, the court granted the relief for specific performance requested in the counterclaim * * * . Appellant timely appealed.

* * * *

* * * *Where two provisions of a contract conflict, the specific provision controls over*

Case 37.2 Continues

Case 37.2 Continued

a more general provision, as it is assumed that the specific provision expresses the parties' intent. [Emphasis added.]

* * * *

* * * We agree with appellant that the specific provision governing transfers in the event of a divorce or death of a partner controls over the more general provision found in Paragraph 1. Appellees argue that Sarah Jane and Robert Shamburger's offer to purchase appellant's and her ex-husband's interest was not necessarily due to the divorce. However, this argument is belied by Sarah Jane and Robert Shamburger's statements in their offer letter * * * . Appellees also contend that the death-or-divorce provision is not more specific than the provision in Paragraph 1, and they compare the length and detail of the two provisions at issue. As appellant responds, however, it is the fact that the death-or-divorce provision applies only under specific and limited circumstances that renders it controlling over the more general provision in Paragraph 1, not the specificity of the language used to describe each method of purchase.

* * * *

In addition to the rule of construction discussed above, * * * the use of the word "shall" in each buy-sell agreement's death-or-divorce provision further supports [appellant's] claim that application of this provision was mandatory under the circumstances in this case. * * * *"Shall" is defined as "has a duty to" or "is required to." * * * "Shall," when used in a contract provision, means that compliance with that provision is mandatory.* [Emphasis added.]

* * * The combination of the specific nature of the death-or-divorce provision and its use of mandatory language such as "shall," indicates that compliance with this particular provision was required under the circumstances in this case. Appellees also contend that interpreting the death-or-divorce provision as mandatory supersedes the procedure set forth in Paragraph 1 of the agreements and "neutralizes" that provision in violation of our rule of construction that we will not adopt an interpretation neutralizing a provision if the various clauses of a contract can be reconciled. We disagree because interpreting the application of the death-or-divorce provision as mandatory in this case does not mean that the procedure set forth in Paragraph 1 of the agreements does not apply in all other situations that do not involve the death or divorce of a partner. Furthermore, as appellant argues, it is also possible to reconcile the two provisions in such a way that the general procedures set forth in Paragraph 1 apply, even in the event of a divorce or death of a partner, but the value of the partner's or couple's interest is determined pursuant to the formula set forth in the death-or-divorce provision.

Based on our rules of construction, we agree with appellant that the [lower] court erred in interpreting the buy-sell agreements in such a manner as to find that the death-or-divorce provisions did not apply to the offer to purchase appellant's interest in the LLPs. Accordingly, we reverse the * * * order granting summary judgment and remand for further proceedings.

Legal Reasoning Questions

1. Why would a partnership agreement contain one provision for a buyout on a partner's divorce or death and another for a partner's decision to quit the firm?

2. How did the court's interpretation of contract principles affect the result in this case?

3. The lower court awarded attorneys' fees to the defendants, who prevailed on their motion for summary judgment. By reversing the summary judgment, does the appellate court's decision also require a reversal of the award of attorneys' fees?

37–4 Limited Liability Partnerships

The **limited liability partnership (LLP)** is a hybrid form of business designed mostly for professionals who normally do business as partners in a partnership. Almost all of the states have enacted LLP statutes.

The major advantage of the LLP is that it allows a partnership to continue as a pass-through entity for tax purposes but limits the personal liability of the partners. The LLP is especially attractive for professional service firms and family businesses. All of the "Big Four" accounting firms—the four largest international accountancy and professional services firms—are organized as LLPs, including Ernst & Young, LLP, and PricewaterhouseCoopers, LLP.

37–4a Formation of an LLP

LLPs must be formed and operated in compliance with state statutes, which may include provisions of the UPA. The appropriate form must be filed with a central state agency, usually the secretary of state's office, and the business's name must include either "Limited Liability Partnership" or "LLP" [UPA 1001, 1002]. An LLP must file an annual report with the state to remain qualified as an LLP in that state [UPA 1003].

In most states, it is relatively easy to convert a traditional partnership into an LLP because the firm's basic organizational structure remains the same. Additionally, all of the statutory and common law rules governing partnerships still apply, apart from those modified by the LLP statute. Normally, LLP statutes are simply amendments to a state's already existing partnership law.

37–4b Liability in an LLP

An LLP allows professionals, such as attorneys and accountants, to avoid personal liability for the malpractice of other partners. Of course, a partner in an LLP is still liable for her or his own wrongful acts, such as negligence. Also liable is the partner who supervised the individual who committed a wrongful act. (This generally is true for all types of partners and partnerships, not just LLPs.)

■ **EXAMPLE 37.15** Five lawyers operate a law firm as an LLP. One of the attorneys, Dan Kolcher, is sued for malpractice and loses. The firm's malpractice insurance is insufficient to pay the judgment. If the firm had been organized as a traditional (general) partnership, the personal assets of the other attorneys could be used to satisfy the obligation. Because the firm is organized as an LLP, however, no other partner at the firm can be held *personally* liable for Kolcher's malpractice, unless she or he acted as Kolcher's supervisor. In the absence of a supervisor, only Kolcher's personal assets can be used to satisfy the judgment. ■

Although LLP statutes vary from state to state, generally each state statute limits the liability of partners in some way. For instance, Delaware law protects each innocent partner from the "debts and obligations of the partnership arising from negligence, wrongful acts, or misconduct." The UPA more broadly exempts partners in an LLP from personal liability for any partnership obligation, "whether arising in contract, in tort, or otherwise" [UPA 306(c)].

Liability outside the State of Formation When an LLP formed in one state wants to do business in another state, it may be required to file a statement of foreign qualification in the second state [UPA 1102]. Because state LLP statutes are not uniform, a question sometimes arises as to which law applies if the LLP statutes in the two states provide different liability protection. Most states apply the law of the state in which the LLP was formed, even when the firm does business in another state, which is also the rule under UPA 1101.

Sharing Liability among Partners When more than one partner in an LLP commits malpractice, there is a question as to how liability should be shared. Is each partner jointly and severally liable for the entire result, as a general partner would be in most states?

Some states provide instead for proportionate liability—that is, for separate determinations of the negligence of the partners. ■ **EXAMPLE 37.16** Accountants Zach and Lyla are partners in an LLP, with Zach supervising Lyla. Lyla negligently fails to file a tax return for a client, Centaur Tools. Centaur files a suit against Zach and Lyla. Under a proportionate liability statute, Zach will be liable for no more than his portion of the responsibility for the missed tax deadline. In a state that does not allow for proportionate liability, Zach can be held liable for the entire loss. ■

37–4c Family Limited Liability Partnerships

A **family limited liability partnership (FLLP)** is a limited liability partnership in which the partners are related to each other—for example, as spouses, parents and children, siblings, or cousins. A person acting in a fiduciary capacity for persons so related can also be a partner. All of the partners must be natural persons or be acting in a fiduciary capacity for the benefit of natural persons.

Probably the most significant use of the FLLP form of business organization is in agriculture. Family-owned farms sometimes find this form to their benefit. The FLLP offers the same advantages as other LLPs with certain additional advantages. For instance, in Iowa, FLLPs are exempt from real estate transfer taxes when partnership real estate is transferred among partners.[10]

37–5 Limited Partnerships

We now look at a business organizational form that limits the liability of *some* of its owners—the **limited partnership (LP)**. Limited partnerships originated in medieval Europe and have been in existence in the United States since the early 1800s. Today, most states and the District of Columbia have adopted laws based on the Revised Uniform Limited Partnership Act (RULPA).

Limited partnerships differ from traditional (general) partnerships in several ways. Exhibit 37–2 compares the characteristics of general and limited partnerships.[11]

---

10. Iowa Statutes Section 428A.2.
11. Under the UPA, a general partnership can be converted into a limited partnership and vice versa [UPA 902, 903]. The UPA also provides for the merger of a general partnership with one or more general or limited partnerships [UPA 905].

EXHIBIT 37–2 A Comparison of General Partnerships and Limited Partnerships

	GENERAL PARTNERSHIP (UPA)	**LIMITED PARTNERSHIP (RULPA)**
Creation	By agreement of two or more persons to carry on a business as co-owners for profit.	By agreement of two or more persons to carry on a business as co-owners for profit. Must include one or more general partners and one or more limited partners. Filing of a certificate with the secretary of state is required.
Sharing of Profits and Losses	By agreement. In the absence of agreement, profits are shared equally by the partners, and losses are shared in the same ratio as profits.	Profits are shared as required in the certificate agreement, and losses are shared likewise, up to the amount of the limited partners' capital contributions. In the absence of a provision in the certificate agreement, profits and losses are shared on the basis of percentages of capital contributions.
Liability	Unlimited personal liability of all partners.	Unlimited personal liability of all general partners; limited partners liable only to the extent of their capital contributions.
Capital Contribution	No minimum or mandatory amount; set by agreement.	Set by agreement.
Management	By agreement. In the absence of agreement, all partners have an equal voice.	Only the general partner (or the general partners). Limited partners have no voice or else are subject to liability as general partners (but only if a third party has reason to believe that the limited partner is a general partner). A limited partner may act as an agent or employee of the partnership and vote on amending the certificate or on the sale or dissolution of the partnership.
Duration	Terminated by agreement of the partners, but can continue to do business even when a partner dissociates from the partnership.	Terminated by agreement in the certificate or by retirement, death, or mental incompetence of a general partner in the absence of the right of the other general partners to continue the partnership. Death of a limited partner does not terminate the partnership, unless he or she is the only remaining limited partner.
Distribution of Assets on Liquidation— Order of Priorities	1. Payment of debts, including those owed to partner and nonpartner creditors. 2. Return of capital contributions and distribution of profit to partners.	1. Outside creditors and partner creditors. 2. Partners and former partners entitled to distributions of partnership assets. 3. Unless otherwise agreed, return of capital contributions and distribution of profit to partners.

A limited partnership consists of at least one **general partner** and one or more **limited partners**. A general partner assumes management responsibility for the partnership and has full responsibility for the partnership and for all its debts. A limited partner contributes cash or other property and owns an interest in the firm but is not involved in management responsibilities. A limited partner is not personally liable for partnership debts beyond the amount of his or her investment. If a limited partner takes part in the management of the business, however, she or he may forfeit that limited liability.

In the following case, two firms—a corporation and a limited partnership—were involved in the construction of a residential development. One individual served as the president of the corporation and the sole general partner of the partnership. In addition, he took charge of the activities at the construction site. How did this individual's status affect his responsibility for those activities?

Case 37.3

DeWine v. Valley View Enterprises, Inc.

Court of Appeals of Ohio, Eleventh District, Trumbull County, 2015 –Ohio– 1222 (2015).

Background and Facts Valley View Enterprises, Inc., built Pine Lakes Golf Club and Estates in Trumbull County, Ohio, in two phases—Phase I and Phase II. Valley View Properties, Ltd., a limited partnership, cut out the roadways and constructed sewer, water, and storm-water lines with water inlets for the development. Joseph Ferrara was the owner and the president of Valley View Enterprises and the sole general partner of Valley View Properties. Ferrara failed to obtain the proper permits for the development work in a timely manner and failed to comply with their requirements once they had been obtained.

Michael DeWine, the state's attorney general, filed a lawsuit in an Ohio court against the Valley View entities and Ferrara, alleging violations of the state's water pollution control laws and seeking civil penalties. The court entered a judgment in the defendants' favor, holding with respect to Ferrara that "a corporate officer cannot be held liable merely by virtue of his status as a corporate officer." DeWine appealed.

In the Language of the Court

Timothy J. *CANNON*, P.J. [Presiding Judge]

* * * *

Here, the state sought civil penalties from three entities: the property owner and Phase II permit holder, Valley View Properties, Ltd.; the Phase I permit holder, Valley View Enterprises, Inc.; and the sole general partner of the property owner, Mr. Ferrara.

* * * The state alleges the trial court erred in its finding that "Valley View Properties is the only party against whom civil penalties can be assessed." The trial court also found Mr. Ferrara was not liable based on his "good faith" actions and Valley View Enterprises, Inc. was not liable because it had no relationship to Pine Lakes Estates; [and] the state failed to present evidence that Mr. Ferrara ordered activities that caused pollution.

* * * Although the trial court found that Valley View Enterprises, Inc. had no relationship to Pine Lake Estates, the evidence establishes that Valley View Enterprises, Inc. applied for and was granted the [Phase I] Permit and, as the permittee, was required to ensure compliance with the permit. The [Phase I] Permit explicitly states, "the permittee must comply with all conditions of this permit, any permit noncompliance constitutes a violation of [state law]." Additionally, * * * *the evidence demonstrates that Mr. Ferrara personally was in charge of the activities performed at the sites; authorized the construction activities at the sites; and failed to obtain necessary certifications and permits.* [Emphasis added.]

Moreover, the trial court's finding that "a corporate officer cannot be held liable merely by virtue of his status as a corporate officer" is erroneous and not supported by the evidence. Admittedly, Mr. Ferrara is the sole general partner of Valley View Properties, Ltd., an Ohio limited partnership. He is not, in relation to Valley View Properties, Ltd., a "corporate officer." Therefore, he is not, in the course of his conduct as the general partner of that limited partnership, entitled to the insulation from liability of a corporate officer.

Case 37.3 Continues

Case 37.3 Continued

Decision and Remedy *A state intermediate appellate court reversed the lower court's judgment in favor of the defendants. With respect to Ferrara's status in relation to Valley View Properties, he was the general partner and therefore not "entitled to the insulation from liability of a corporate officer." On remand, the trial court was to determine the number of violations established by the state and to issue and apportion penalties among the liable parties.*

Critical Thinking
- **Legal Environment** *How are the penalties likely to be apportioned among the three defendants? Explain.*

37–5a Formation of an LP

In contrast to the private and informal agreement that usually suffices to form a general partnership, the formation of a limited partnership is a public and formal proceeding. The partners must strictly follow statutory requirements. Not only must a limited partnership have at least one general partner and one limited partner, but the partners must also sign a **certificate of limited partnership.**

The certificate of limited partnership must include certain information, including the name, mailing address, and capital contribution of each general and limited partner. The certificate must be filed with the designated state official—under the RULPA, the secretary of state. The certificate is usually open to public inspection.

37–5b Liabilities of Partners in an LP

General partners are personally liable to the partnership's creditors. Thus, at least one general partner is necessary in a limited partnership so that someone has personal liability. This policy can be circumvented in states that allow a corporation to be the general partner in a partnership. Because the corporation has limited liability by virtue of corporation statutes, if a corporation is the general partner, no one in the limited partnership has personal liability. (See this chapter's *Ethics Today* feature for a discussion of whether a general partner who is unaware of another general partner's wrongdoing should be held liable for it.)

The liability of a limited partner, as mentioned, is limited to the capital that she or he contributes or agrees to contribute to the partnership [RULPA 502]. Limited partners enjoy this limited liability only so long as they do not participate in management [RULPA 303].

A limited partner who participates in management will be just as liable as a general partner to any creditor who transacts business with the limited partnership.

Liability arises when the creditor believes, based on the limited partner's conduct, that the limited partner is a general partner [RULPA 303]. The extent to which a limited partner can engage in management before being exposed to liability is not always clear, however.

37–5c Rights and Duties in a Limited Partnership

With the exception of the right to participate in management, limited partners have essentially the same rights as general partners. Limited partners have a right of access to the partnership's books and to information regarding partnership business. On dissolution of the partnership, limited partners are entitled to a return of their contributions in accordance with the partnership certificate [RULPA 201(a)(10)]. They can also assign their interests subject to the certificate [RULPA 702, 704]. In addition, they can sue an outside party on behalf of the firm if the general partners with authority to do so have refused to file suit [RULPA 1001].

37–5d Dissociation and Dissolution

A general partner has the power to voluntarily dissociate, or withdraw, from a limited partnership unless the partnership agreement specifies otherwise. Under the RULPA, a limited partner can withdraw from the partnership by giving six months' notice, unless the partnership agreement specifies a term. In reality, though, most limited partnership agreements do specify a term, which eliminates the limited partner's right to withdraw. Also, some states have passed laws prohibiting the withdrawal of limited partners.

Events That Cause Dissociation In a limited partnership, a general partner's voluntary dissociation from the firm normally will lead to dissolution *unless* all partners

ETHICS TODAY

Should an Innocent General Partner Be Jointly Liable for Fraud?

When general partners in a limited partnership jointly engage in fraud, there is usually no question that they are jointly liable. But if one general partner engages in fraud and the other is unaware of the wrongdoing, is it fair to make the innocent partner share in the liability? Many states' limited partnership laws protect innocent general partners from suits for fraud brought by limited partners. The law is less clear, however, in some other situations.

A Developer's Misconduct

Robert Bisno and James Coxeter formed two limited partnerships to redevelop certain property in downtown Berkeley, California. Without Coxeter's knowledge, Bisno took almost $500,000 from one of the partnerships to buy a personal home. He also made material misrepresentations to potential investors.

One of those investors, George Miske—after purchasing an interest in the limited partnership—discovered the fraud and brought a lawsuit. Coxeter argued that he was an innocent general partner and should not be liable to Miske for Bisno's tortious conduct. Coxeter also claimed that Miske was a limited partner, not an innocent third party, and that the state's limited partnership law protected Coxeter from liability to a limited partner.

A California Court Finds the Innocent Co-Developer Liable

The court disagreed with Coxeter, however. The fraud at issue had induced Miske to purchase the limited partnership interest. Therefore, the court reasoned, at the time the fraud was perpetrated by Bisno, Miske was an innocent third party. As a result, the court held that Coxeter—even though he was innocent of any wrongdoing—was jointly liable to Miske.[a]

Critical Thinking *Why might it be fair for the court to hold Coxeter liable for his partner's fraud?*

a. *Miske v. Bisno*, 204 Cal.App.4th 1249, 139 Cal.Rptr.3d 626 (2012). See also *In re Barlaam*, 2014 WL 3398381 (9th Cir. 2014).

---

agree to continue the business. Similarly, the bankruptcy, retirement, death, or mental incompetence of a general partner will cause the dissociation of that partner and the dissolution of the limited partnership unless the other members agree to continue the firm [RULPA 801].

Bankruptcy of a limited partner, however, does not dissolve the partnership unless it causes the bankruptcy of the firm. In addition, death or an assignment of the interest (right to receive distributions) of a limited partner does not dissolve a limited partnership [RULPA 702, 704, 705]. A limited partnership can be dissolved by court decree [RULPA 802].

Distribution of Assets On dissolution, creditors' claims, including those of partners who are creditors, take first priority. After that, partners and former partners receive unpaid distributions of partnership assets. Unless otherwise agreed, they are also entitled to a return of their contributions in the proportions in which they share in distributions [RULPA 804].

Valuation of Assets Disputes commonly arise about how the partnership's assets should be valued and distributed and whether the business should be sold. ■ **CASE IN POINT 37.17** Actor Kevin Costner was a limited partner

in Midnight Star Enterprises, LP, which runs a casino, bar, and restaurant in South Dakota. There were two other limited partners, Carla and Francis Caneva, who owned a small percentage of the partnership (3.25 units each) and received salaries for managing its operations. Another company owned by Costner, Midnight Star Enterprises, Limited (MSEL), was the general partner. Costner thus controlled a majority of the partnership (93.5 units).

When communications broke down between the partners, MSEL asked a court to dissolve the partnership. MSEL's accountant determined that the firm's fair market value was $3.1 million. The Canevas presented evidence that a competitor would buy the business for $6.2 million. The Canevas wanted the court to force Costner to either buy the business for that price within ten days or sell it on the open market to the highest bidder. Ultimately, the state's highest court held in favor of Costner. A partner cannot force the sale of a limited partnership when the other partners want to continue the business. The court also accepted the $3.1 million buyout price of MSEL's accountant and ordered Costner to pay the Canevas the value of their 6.5 partnership units.[12] ■

---

12. *In re Dissolution of Midnight Star Enterprises, LP*, 2006 SD 98, 724 N.W.2d 334 (S.D.Sup.Ct. 2006).

Buy-Sell Agreements As mentioned earlier, partners can agree ahead of time on how the partnership's assets will be valued and divided if the partnership dissolves. This is true for limited partnerships as well as for general partnerships. Buy-sell agreements can help the partners avoid disputes. Nonetheless, buy-sell agreements do not eliminate all potential for litigation, especially if the terms are subject to more than one interpretation.

■ **CASE IN POINT 37.18** Natural Pork Production II, LLP (NPP), an Iowa limited liability partnership, raises hogs. Under a partnership buy-sell agreement, NPP was obligated to buy a dissociating partner's interests but could defer the purchase if it would adversely affect the firm's capital or cash flow. After these "impairment circumstances" changed, NPP was to make the purchase within thirty days. Two of NPP's limited partners, Craton Capital, LP, and Kruse Investment Company, notified NPP of their dissociation. A wave of similar notices from other limited partners followed.

NPP declared an impairment circumstance and refused to buy out the limited partners. Craton and Kruse filed a suit asking a state court to order NPP to buy their units. NPP claimed that it was not required to buy out the limited partners because of the impairment circumstance. The court ruled in the plaintiffs'

favor. The wording of the buyout provision stated the firm "shall" buy out the partners, which meant it was mandatory. The impairment circumstance only deferred the purchase, and thus NPP was required to buy out the limited partners.[13] ■

37–5e Limited Liability Limited Partnerships

A **limited liability limited partnership (LLLP)** is a type of limited partnership. An LLLP differs from a limited partnership in that a general partner in an LLLP has the same liability as a limited partner in a limited partnership. In other words, the liability of all partners is limited to the amount of their investments in the firm.

A few states provide expressly for LLLPs.[14] In states that do not provide for LLLPs but do allow for limited partnerships and limited liability partnerships, a limited partnership should probably still be able to register with the state as an LLLP.

---

13. *Craton Capital, LP v. Natural Pork Production II, LLP,* 797 N.W.2d 623 (Iowa App. 2011).
14. See, for example, Colorado Revised Statutes Annotated Section 7-62-109. Other states that provide for LLLPs include Delaware, Florida, Georgia, Kentucky, Maryland, Nevada, Texas, and Virginia.

Reviewing: All Forms of Partnerships

Grace Tarnavsky and her sons, Manny and Jason, bought a ranch known as the Cowboy Palace in March 2014, and the three verbally agreed to share the business for five years. Grace contributed 50 percent of the investment, and each son contributed 25 percent. Manny agreed to handle the livestock, and Jason agreed to handle the bookkeeping. The Tarnavskys took out joint loans and opened a joint bank account into which they deposited the ranch's proceeds and from which they made payments for property, cattle, equipment, and supplies.

In September 2017, Manny severely injured his back while baling hay and became permanently unable to handle livestock. Manny therefore hired additional laborers to tend the livestock, causing the Cowboy Palace to incur significant debt. In September 2018, Al's Feed Barn filed a lawsuit against Jason to collect $32,400 in unpaid debts. Using the information presented in the chapter, answer the following questions.

1. Was this relationship a partnership for a term or a partnership at will?
2. Did Manny have the authority to hire additional laborers to work at the ranch after his injury? Why or why not?
3. Under the current UPA, can Al's Feed Barn bring an action against Jason individually for the Cowboy Palace's debt? Why or why not?
4. Suppose that after his back injury in 2017, Manny sent his mother and brother a notice indicating his intent to withdraw from the partnership. Can he still be held liable for the debt to Al's Feed Barn? Why or why not?

Debate This . . . *A partnership should automatically end when one partner dissociates from the firm.*

Terms and Concepts

Issue Spotters

1. Darnell and Eliana are partners in D&E Designs, an architectural firm. When Darnell dies, his widow claims that as Darnell's heir, she is entitled to take his place as Eliana's partner or to receive a share of the firm's assets. Is she right? Why or why not? (See *Dissociation and Termination*.)

2. Finian and Gloria are partners in F&G Delivery Service. When business is slow, without Gloria's knowledge, Finian leases the delivery vehicles as moving vans. Because the vehicles would otherwise be sitting idle in a parking lot, can Finian keep the income resulting from the leasing of the delivery vehicles? Explain your answer. (See *Formation and Operation*.)

- **Check your answers to the Issue Spotters against the answers provided in Appendix D at the end of this text.**

Business Scenarios

37–1. Partnership Formation. Daniel is the owner of a chain of shoe stores. He hires Rubya to be the manager of a new store, which is to open in Grand Rapids, Michigan. Daniel, by written contract, agrees to pay Rubya a monthly salary and 20 percent of the profits. Without Daniel's knowledge, Rubya represents himself to Classen as Daniel's partner and shows Classen the agreement to share profits. Classen extends credit to Rubya. Rubya defaults. Discuss whether Classen can hold Daniel liable as a partner. (See *Formation and Operation*.)

37–2. Dissolution of a Limited Partnership. Dorinda, Luis, and Elizabeth form a limited partnership. Dorinda is a general partner, and Luis and Elizabeth are limited partners. Consider the separate events below, and discuss fully whether each event constitutes a dissolution of the limited partnership. (See *Limited Partnerships*.)
(a) Luis assigns his partnership interest to Ashley.
(b) Elizabeth is petitioned into involuntary bankruptcy.
(c) Dorinda dies.

Business Case Problems

37–3. Fiduciary Duties of Partners. Karl Horvath, Hein Rüsen, and Carl Thomas formed a partnership, HRT Enterprises, to buy a manufacturing plant. Rüsen and Thomas leased the plant to their own company, Merkur Steel. Merkur then sublet the premises to other companies owned by Rüsen and Thomas. The rent that these companies paid to Merkur was higher than the rent that Merkur paid to HRT. Rüsen and Thomas did not tell Horvath about the subleases. Did Rüsen and Thomas breach their fiduciary duties to HRT and Horvath? Discuss. [*Horvath v. HRT Enterprises*, 489 Mich.App. 992, 800 N.W.2d 595 (2011)] (See *Formation and Operation*.)

37–4. Partnership Formation. Patricia Garcia and Bernardo Lucero were in a romantic relationship. While they were seeing each other, Garcia and Lucero acquired an electronics service center, paying $30,000 apiece. Two years later, they purchased an apartment complex. The property was deeded to Lucero, but neither Garcia nor Lucero made a down payment. The couple considered both properties to be owned "50/50," and they agreed to share profits, losses, and management rights. When the couple's romantic relationship ended, Garcia asked a court to declare that she had a partnership with Lucero. In court, Lucero argued that the couple did not have a written partnership agreement. Did they have a partnership? Why or why not? [*Garcia v. Lucero*, 366 S.W.3d 275 (Tex. App. 2012)] (See *Formation and Operation*.)

37–5. Winding Up. Dan and Lori Cole operated a Curves franchise exercise facility in Angola, Indiana, as a partnership. The firm leased commercial space from Flying Cat, LLC, for a renewable three-year term and renewed the lease for a second three-year term. But two years after the renewal, the Coles divorced. By the end of the second term, Flying Cat was owed more than $21,000 on the lease. Without telling the landlord about the divorce, Lori signed another extension. More rent went unpaid. Flying Cat obtained a judgment in an Indiana state court against the partnership for almost $50,000. Can Dan be held liable? Why or why not? [*Curves for Women Angola v. Flying Cat, LLC,* 983 N.E.2d 629 (Ind.App. 2013)] (See *Dissociation and Termination.*)

37–6. Business Case Problem with Sample Answer—Partnerships.

 Karyl Paxton asked Christopher Sacco to work with her interior design business, Pierce Paxton Collections, in New Orleans. At the time, they were in a romantic relationship. Sacco was involved in every aspect of the business—bookkeeping, marketing, and design—but was not paid a salary. He was reimbursed, however, for expenses charged to his personal credit card, which Paxton also used. Sacco took no profits from the firm, saying that he wanted to "grow the business" and "build sweat equity." When Paxton and Sacco's personal relationship soured, she fired him. Sacco objected, claiming that they were partners. Is Sacco entitled to 50 percent of the profits of Pierce Paxton Collections? Explain. [*Sacco v. Paxton,* 133 So.3d 213 (La.App. 2014)] (See *Formation and Operation.*)

- **For a sample answer to Problem 37–6, go to Appendix E at the end of this text.**

37–7. Formation.
Leisa Reed and Randell Thurman lived together in Spring City, Tennessee. Randell and his father, Leroy, formed a cattle-raising operation and opened a bank account in the name of L&R Farm. Within a few years, Leroy quit the operation. Leisa and Randell each wrote a personal check for $5,000 to buy his cattle. Leisa picked up supplies, fed and administered medicine to cattle, collected hay, and participated in the bookkeeping for L&R. Later, checks drawn on her personal account for $12,000 to buy equipment and $35,000 to buy cattle were deposited into the L&R account. After several years, Leisa decided that she no longer wanted to associate with Randell, but they could not agree on a financial settlement. Was Leisa a partner in L&R? Is she entitled to half of the value of L&R's assets? Explain. [*Reed v. Thurman,* 2015 WL 1119449 (Tenn.App. 2015)] (See *Formation and Operation.*)

37–8. Formation and Operation.
FS Partners is a general partnership whose partners are Jerry Stahlman, a professional engineer, and Fitz & Smith, Inc., a corporation in the business of excavating and paving. Timothy Smith signed the partnership agreement on Fitz & Smith's behalf and deals with FS matters on Fitz & Smith's behalf. Stahlman handles the payment of FS's bills, including its tax bills, and is the designated partner on FS's federal tax return. FS was formed to buy and develop twenty acres of unoccupied, wooded land in York County, Pennsylvania. The deed to the property lists the owner as "FS Partners, a general partnership." When the taxes on the real estate were not paid, the York County Tax Claim Bureau published notice that the property would be sold at a tax sale. The bureau also mailed a notice to FS's address of record and posted a notice on the land. Is this sufficient notice of the tax sale? Discuss. [*FS Partners v. York County Tax Claim Bureau,* 132 A.3d 577 (Pa. 2016)] (See *Formation and Operation.*)

37–9. A Question of Ethics—Wrongful Dissociation.
 Elliot Willensky and Beverly Moran formed a partnership to buy, renovate, and sell a house. Moran agreed to finance the effort, which was to cost no more than $60,000. Willensky agreed to oversee the work, which was to be done in six months. Willensky lived in the house during the renovation. As the project progressed, Willensky incurred excessive and unnecessary expenses, misappropriated funds for his personal use, did not pay bills on time, and did not keep Moran informed of the costs. More than a year later, the renovation was still not completed, and Willensky walked off the project. Moran completed the renovation, which ultimately cost $311,222, and sold the house. Moran then sued to dissolve the partnership and recover damages from Willensky for breach of contract and wrongful dissociation. [Moran v. Willensky, 339 S.W.3d 651 (Tenn.App.Ct. 2010)] (See Dissociation and Termination.)

(a) Moran alleged that Willensky had wrongfully dissociated from the partnership. When did this dissociation occur? Why was his dissociation wrongful?

(b) Which of Willensky's actions simply represent unethical behavior or bad management, and which constitute a breach of the agreement?

Legal Reasoning Group Activity

37–10. Liability of Partners.
At least six months before the Summer Olympic Games in Atlanta, Georgia, Stafford Fontenot and four others agreed to sell Cajun food at the games and began making preparations. On May 19, the group (calling themselves "Prairie Cajun Seafood Catering of Louisiana") applied for a business license from the county health department. Later, Ted Norris sold a mobile kitchen to them for $40,000. They gave Norris an $8,000 check drawn on the "Prairie Cajun Seafood Catering of Louisiana" account and two promissory notes, one for $12,000 and the other for $20,000. The notes, which were dated June 12, listed only Fontenot "d/b/a Prairie Cajun Seafood" as the maker (*d/b/a* is an abbreviation for "doing business as").

On July 31, Fontenot and his friends signed a partnership agreement, which listed specific percentages of profits and losses. They drove the mobile kitchen to Atlanta, but business was "disastrous." When the notes were not paid, Norris filed a suit in a Louisiana state court against Fontenot, seeking payment. (See *Formation and Operation.*)

(a) The first group will discuss the elements of a partnership and determine whether a partnership exists among Fontenot and the others.

(b) The second group will determine who can be held liable on the notes and why.

CHAPTER 38

Limited Liability Companies and Special Business Forms

Our government allows entrepreneurs to choose from a variety of business organizational forms. In selecting among them, businesspersons are motivated to choose organizational forms that limit their liability. Limited liability may allow them to take more business risk, which is associated with the potential for higher profits.

A relatively new and increasingly common form of business organization is the *limited liability company (LLC)*. LLCs have become the organizational form of choice among many small businesses. Other special business forms include joint ventures, syndicates, joint stock companies, business trusts, and cooperatives.

38–1 The Limited Liability Company

A **limited liability company (LLC)** is a hybrid that combines the limited liability aspects of a corporation and the tax advantages of a partnership. The LLC has been available for only a few decades, but it has become the preferred structure for many small businesses.

LLCs are governed by state statutes, which vary from state to state. In an attempt to create more uniformity, the National Conference of Commissioners on Uniform State Laws issued the Uniform Limited Liability Company Act (ULLCA). Less than one-fifth of the states have adopted it, however. Thus, the law governing LLCs remains far from uniform.

Nevertheless, some provisions are common to most state statutes. We base our discussion of LLCs on these common elements.

38–1a The Nature of the LLC

LLCs share many characteristics with corporations. Like corporations, LLCs must be formed and operated in compliance with state law. Like the shareholders of a corporation, the owners of an LLC, who are called **members,** enjoy limited liability [ULLCA 303].[1]

Limited Liability of Members Members of LLCs are shielded from personal liability in most situations. In other words, the liability of members is normally limited to the amount of their investments.

An exception arises when a member has significantly contributed to the LLC's tortious conduct. ■ **CASE IN POINT 38.1** Randy Coley, the sole member and manager of East Coast Cablevision, LLC, installed cable television systems for many hotels and resorts. Coley established a DIRECTV Satellite Master Antenna Television (SMATV) account in the name of Massanutten Resort. The system provided programming to 168 timeshare units, as well as to the resort's bar, golf shop, lobbies, and waterpark. The bill for the resort's account was sent to (and paid by) East Coast Cablevision, which in turn billed the customers.

Over time, East Coast Cablevision began providing cable services to additional customers using the resort's SMATV account but did not pay DIRECTV for these other customers. Ultimately, another cable dealer affiliated with DIRECTV sued Coley for not paying for all of the DIRECTV programming transmissions that East Coast's customers had received. The court held that because Coley had played a direct role in the unauthorized transmissions, he could be held personally liable for them.[2] ■

When Liability May Be Imposed The members of an LLC, like the shareholders in a corporation, can lose their limited personal liability in certain circumstances. For instance, when an individual guarantees payment of

---

1. Members of an LLC can also bring derivative actions, which you will read about in regard to corporations, on behalf of the LLC [ULLCA 101]. As with a corporate shareholder's derivative suit, any damages recovered go to the LLC, not to the members personally.

2. *Sky Cable, LLC v. Coley*, ___ F.Supp.3d ___, 2013 WL 3517337 (W.D.Va. 2013).

a business loan to the LLC, that individual is personally liable for the business's obligation. In addition, if an LLC member fails to comply with certain formalities, such as by commingling personal and business funds, a court can impose personal liability.

Under various principles of corporate law, courts may hold the owners of a business liable for its debts. On rare occasions, for instance, courts ignore the corporate structure ("pierce the corporate veil") to expose the shareholders to personal liability when it is required to achieve justice.

Similarly, courts will sometimes pierce the veil of an LLC to hold its members personally liable. Note, however, that courts have reserved piercing the veil of an LLC for circumstances that are clearly extraordinary. There must normally be some flagrant disregard of the LLC formalities, as well as fraud or malfeasance on the part of the LLC member.

■ **CASE IN POINT 38.2** Tom and Shannon Brown purchased a new home in Hattiesburg, Mississippi, from Ray Richard and Nick Welch. Richard had hired Waldron Properties, LLC (WP), to build the home. Several years later, cracks began to develop in the walls of the Browns' home as a result of defects in the construction of the foundation. The Browns sued Murray Waldron, the sole member of WP, for breach of warranty under the state's New Home Warranty Act (NHWA). Because the required NHWA notice they had received when they bought the home was signed by Waldron personally, they claimed that Waldron was liable personally.

The trial court found that WP, not Waldron individually, was the builder of the Browns' home. The Browns appealed. They contended that even if WP was the builder, the court should pierce the veil of the LLC and hold Waldron personally liable. The state appellate court disagreed and affirmed the lower court's ruling. The Browns had not entered into a contract with either Waldron or WP. There was not sufficient evidence that Waldron had disregarded LLC formalities or had engaged in fraud or other misconduct to justify piercing the LLC's veil to hold him personally liable.[3] ■

Other Similarities to Corporations

Another similarity between corporations and LLCs is that LLCs are legal entities apart from their owners. As a legal person, the LLC can sue or be sued, enter into contracts, and hold title to property [ULLCA 201]. The terminology used to describe LLCs formed in other states or nations is also similar to that used in corporate law. For instance, an LLC formed in one state but doing business in another state is referred to in the second state as a *foreign LLC*.

38–1b The Formation of the LLC

LLCs are creatures of statute and thus must follow state statutory requirements.

Articles of Organization To form an LLC, **articles of organization** must be filed with a central state agency—usually the secretary of state's office [ULLCA 202].[4] Typically, the articles must include the name of the business, its principal address, the name and address of a registered agent, the members' names, and how the LLC will be managed [ULLCA 203]. The business's name must include the words *Limited Liability Company* or the initials *LLC* [ULLCA 105(a)]. Although a majority of the states permit one-member LLCs, some states require at least two members.

Preformation Contracts Businesspersons sometimes enter into contracts on behalf of a business organization that is not yet formed. Persons who are forming a corporation, for instance, may enter into contracts during the process of incorporation but before the corporation becomes a legal entity. These contracts are referred to as *preincorporation contracts*. The individual promoters who sign the contracts are bound to their terms. Once the corporation is formed and adopts the preincorporation contracts (by means of a *novation*, which substitutes a new contract for the old contract), it can enforce the contract terms.

In dealing with the preorganization contracts of LLCs, courts may apply the well-established principles of corporate law relating to preincorporation contracts. That is to say, when the promoters of an LLC enter preformation contracts, the LLC, once formed, can adopt the contracts by a novation and then enforce them.

■ **CASE IN POINT 38.3** 607 South Park, LLC, entered into an agreement to sell a hotel to 607 Park View Associates, Ltd., which then assigned the rights to the purchase to another company, 02 Development, LLC. At the time, 02 Development did not yet exist—it was legally created several months later. 607 South Park subsequently refused to sell the hotel to 02 Development, and 02 Development sued for breach of the purchase agreement.

A California appellate court ruled that LLCs should be treated the same as corporations with respect to preorganization contracts. Although 02 Development did not exist when the agreement was executed, once it came into existence, it could enforce any preorganization contract made on its behalf.[5] ■

---

3. *Brown v. Waldron*, 186 So.3d 955 (Miss.App. 2016).

4. In addition to requiring articles of organization to be filed, a few states require that a notice of the intention to form an LLC be published in a local newspaper.

5. *02 Development, LLC v. 607 South Park, LLC*, 159 Cal.App.4th 609, 71 Cal.Rptr.3d 608 (2008). See also, *Davis Wine Co. v. Vina Y Bodega Estampa, S.A.*, 823 F.Supp.2d 1159 (D.Or. 2011).

38–1c Jurisdictional Requirements

As we have seen, LLCs and corporations share several characteristics, but a significant difference between these organizational forms involves federal jurisdictional requirements. Under the federal jurisdiction statute, a corporation is deemed to be a citizen of the state where it is incorporated and maintains its principal place of business. The statute does not mention the state citizenship of partnerships, LLCs, and other unincorporated associations. The courts, however, have tended to regard these entities as citizens of every state of which their members are citizens.

The state citizenship of an LLC may come into play when a party sues the LLC based on diversity of citizenship. Remember that when parties to a lawsuit are from different states and the amount in controversy exceeds $75,000, a federal court can exercise diversity jurisdiction. *Total* diversity of citizenship must exist, however.

■ **EXAMPLE 38.4** Jen Fong, a citizen of New York, wishes to bring a suit against Skycel, an LLC formed under the laws of Connecticut. One of Skycel's members also lives in New York. Fong will not be able to bring a suit against Skycel in federal court on the basis of diversity jurisdiction because the defendant LLC is also a citizen of New York. The same would be true if Fong was bringing a suit against multiple defendants and one of the defendants lived in New York. ■

38–1d Advantages of the LLC

The LLC offers many advantages to businesspersons, which is why this form of business organization has become increasingly popular.

Limited Liability A key advantage of the LLC is the limited liability of its members. The LLC as an entity can be held liable for any loss or injury caused by the wrongful acts or omissions of its members. As we have seen, however, members themselves generally are not personally liable.

In the following case, a consumer died as a result of using an allegedly defective product made and sold by an LLC. The consumer's children sought to hold the LLC's sole member and manager personally liable for the firm's actions.

Case 38.1

Hodge v. Strong Built International, LLC

Court of Appeal of Louisiana, Third Circuit, 159 So.3d 1159 (2015).

Background and Facts   Donald Hodge was hunting in a deer stand when its straps—which held Hodge high up in a tree—failed. When the straps failed, Hodge and the deer stand fell to the ground, killing Hodge. Louisiana-based Strong Built International, LLC, was the maker and seller of the deer stand, and Ken Killen was Strong Built's sole member and manager.

Hodge's children, Donald and Rachel Hodge, filed a lawsuit in a Louisiana state court against Strong Built and Killen. They sought damages on a theory of product liability for the injury and death of their father caused by the allegedly defective deer stand. Killen filed a motion for summary judgment, asserting that he was not personally liable to the Hodges. The court granted the motion and issued a summary judgment in Killen's favor, dismissing the claims against him. The Hodges appealed.

In the Language of the Court
AMY, Judge.
* * * *

* * * An LLC member or manager's liability to third parties is delineated in [Louisiana Revised Statute (La.R.S.)] 12:1320, which states:
* * * *

* * * no member, manager, employee, or agent of a limited liability company is liable in such capacity for a debt, obligation, or liability of the limited liability company.
* * * *

* * * That protection is not unlimited. Pursuant to La.R.S. 12:1320(D), *a member or manager may be subjected to personal liability for claims involving* * * * *breach of a professional duty or other negligent or wrongful act.* [Emphasis added.]

* * * In an affidavit, Mr. Killen asserted that he is "not an engineer, nor a licensed professional in any profession in Louisiana or any other state." Mr. Killen also asserts that he:

Case 38.1 Continues

Case 38.1 Continued

was a participant in the creation of the deer stand which * * * Strong Built International, L.L.C. manufactured and sold, but he never personally dictated or participated in the design, selection of materials used in the manufacture, or the manufacture of, or the selection of any warnings to any deer stand for the use or consumption by any consumer beyond my input and work as a manager * * * and member of * * * Strong Built International, L.L.C.

The plaintiffs offered no evidence to contradict Mr. Killen's affidavit in this regard. Accordingly, we find no basis for Mr. Killen's personal liability under the "breach of professional duty" exception.

Neither do we find sufficient evidence in the record to create a genuine issue of material fact with regard to the "other negligent or wrongful act" exception.

* * * With regard to [this exception], the member (or manager) must have a duty of care to the plaintiff. * * * That duty must be "something more" than the duties arising out of the LLC's contract with the plaintiff.

* * * *

* * * Mr. Killen states in his affidavit that not only was he not personally responsible for the design and manufacture of the deer stands while involved with Strong Built International * * * but that any involvement that he may have had was in his capacity as a member and manager. *The plaintiffs have submitted nothing to show that Mr. Killen's actions are "something more" than his duties as a member/manager of the LLC.* [Emphasis added.]

Decision and Remedy *A state intermediate appellate court affirmed the judgment in Killen's favor. Under the applicable Louisiana state LLC statute, no member or manager of an LLC is liable in that capacity for the liability of the company. There are exceptions, but the Hodges failed to show that Killen's actions went beyond his duties as a member and manager of Strong Built.*

Critical Thinking
- **Economic** *Why does the law allow—and even encourage—limits to the liability of a business organization's owners and managers for the firm's actions? Discuss.*

Flexibility in Taxation Another advantage of the LLC is its flexibility in regard to taxation. An LLC that has *two or more members* can choose to be taxed as either a partnership or a corporation. A corporate entity normally must pay income taxes on its profits, and the shareholders must then pay personal income taxes on any of those profits that are distributed as dividends. An LLC that wants to distribute profits to its members almost always prefers to be taxed as a partnership to avoid the "double taxation" that is characteristic of the corporate entity.

Unless an LLC indicates that it wishes to be taxed as a corporation, the Internal Revenue Service (IRS) automatically taxes it as a partnership. This means that the LLC, as an entity, pays no taxes. Rather, as in a partnership, profits are "passed through" the LLC to the members, who then personally pay taxes on the profits. If an LLC's members want to reinvest profits in the business rather than distribute the profits to members, however, they may prefer to be taxed as a corporation. Corporate income tax rates may be lower than personal tax rates. Part of the attractiveness of the LLC is this flexibility with respect to taxation.

An LLC that has only *one member* cannot be taxed as a partnership. For federal income tax purposes, one-member LLCs are automatically taxed as sole proprietorships unless they indicate that they wish to be taxed as corporations. With respect to state taxes, most states follow the IRS rules.

Management and Foreign Investors Another advantage of the LLC for businesspersons is the flexibility it offers in terms of business operations and management, as will be discussed shortly. Foreign investors are allowed to become LLC members, so organizing as an LLC can enable a business to attract investors from other countries. (Many nations—including France, Germany, Japan and places in Latin America—have particular business forms that provide for limited liability much like an LLC.)

38–1e Disadvantages of the LLC

The main disadvantage of the LLC is that state LLC statutes are not uniform. Therefore, businesses that operate in more than one state may not receive consistent treatment in these states.

Generally, most states apply to a foreign LLC (an LLC formed in another state) the law of the state where the LLC was formed. Difficulties can arise, though, when one state's court must interpret and apply another state's laws.

38–2 LLC Management and Operation

The members of an LLC have considerable flexibility in managing and operating the business. Here, we discuss management options, fiduciary duties owed, and the operating agreement and general operating procedures of LLCs.

38–2a Management of an LLC

Basically, LLC members have two options for managing the firm, as shown in Exhibit 38–1. The firm can be either a "member-managed" LLC or a "manager-managed" LLC. Most state LLC statutes and the ULLCA

EXHIBIT 38–1 Management of an LLC

provide that unless the articles of organization specify otherwise, an LLC is assumed to be member managed [ULLCA 203(a)(6)].

In a *member-managed* LLC, all of the members participate in management, and decisions are made by majority vote [ULLCA 404(a)]. In a *manager-managed* LLC, the members designate a group of persons to manage the firm. The management group may consist of only members, both members and nonmembers, or only nonmembers.

However an LLC is managed, its managers need to be aware of the firm's potential liability under employment-discrimination laws. Those laws may sometimes extend to individuals who are not members of a protected class, as discussed in this chapter's *Managerial Strategy* feature.

38–2b Fiduciary Duties

Under the ULLCA, managers in a manager-managed LLC owe fiduciary duties (the duty of loyalty and the duty of care) to the LLC and its members [ULLCA 409(a), 409(h)]. (This same rule applies in corporate law—corporate directors and officers owe fiduciary duties to the corporation and its shareholders.) Because not all states have adopted the ULLCA, though, some state statutes provide that managers owe fiduciary duties only to the LLC and not to the LLC's members.

To whom the fiduciary duties are owed can affect the outcome of litigation. ■ **CASE IN POINT 38.5** Leslie Polk and his children, Yurii and Dusty Polk and Lezanne Proctor, formed Polk Plumbing, LLC, in Alabama. Dusty and Lezanne were managers of the LLC. Eventually, Yurii quit the firm. A year and a half later, Leslie "fired" Dusty and Lezanne and denied them access to the LLC's books and offices, but continued to operate the business.

Dusty and Lezanne filed a suit in an Alabama state court against Leslie, claiming breach of fiduciary duty. The trial court instructed the jury that it could not consider the plaintiffs' "firing" as part of their claim. Thus, although the jury found in their favor, it awarded only one dollar to each in damages. The plaintiffs appealed, and a state intermediate appellate court reversed and remanded the case for a new trial. Leslie did not have the authority under the terms of the LLC's operating agreement to fire two managers. The trial court had erred in not allowing the jury to consider the circumstances of Dusty and Lezanne's "firing" as part of their breach-of-fiduciary-duty claim.[6] ■

---

6. *Polk v. Polk*, 70 So.3d 363 (Ala.App. 2011).

Can a Person Who Is Not a Member of a Protected Class Sue for Discrimination?

Under federal law and the laws of most states, discrimination in employment based on race, color, religion, national origin, gender, age, or disability is prohibited. Persons who are members of these protected classes can sue if they are subjected to discrimination. But can a person subjected to discrimination bring a lawsuit if he is not a member of a protected class, even though managers and other employees believe that he is? This somewhat unusual situation occurred in New Jersey.

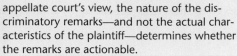

Courts in New Jersey

Myron Cowher worked at Carson & Roberts Site Construction & Engineering, Inc. For more than a year, at least two of his supervisors directed almost daily barrages of anti-Semitic remarks at him. They believed that he was Jewish, although his actual background was German-Irish and Lutheran.

Cowher brought a suit against the supervisors and the construction company, claiming a hostile work environment. The trial court, however, ruled that he did not have standing to sue under New Jersey law because he was not Jewish and, thus, was not a member of a protected class. Cowher appealed.

The appellate court disagreed with the trial court. The court ruled that if Cowher could prove that the discrimination "would not have occurred but for the perception that he was Jewish," his claim was covered by New Jersey's antidiscrimination law.[a] Thus, in the

appellate court's view, the nature of the discriminatory remarks—and not the actual characteristics of the plaintiff—determines whether the remarks are actionable.

Another New Jersey court followed the precedent set by the *Cowher* case to allow Shi-Juan Lin, a Chinese worker whose fiancé and child were black, to recover for racial discrimination. The employer created a hostile work environment by allowing Lin's supervisor to constantly use the "n" word at work. The employer knew that even though Lin was not black, she was hurt by the supervisor's remarks. Therefore, the court affirmed an administrative law judge's award of damages for pain and suffering, plus attorneys' fees.[b]

Business Questions

1. *Should a manager for an LLC respond to employee complaints of discrimination any differently than a manager at a corporation, a partnership, or a sole proprietorship? Why or why not?*

2. *How can a company, whether an LLC or some other business form, reduce the chances of discrimination lawsuits?*

---

a. *Cowher v. Carson & Roberts*, 425 N.J.Super. 285, 40 A.3d 1171 (2012). See also, *Sheridan v. Egg Harbor Township Board of Education*, 2015 WL 9694404 (N.J.Sup.Ct. 2016), involving a plaintiff who alleged discrimination based on obesity.

b. *Lin v. Dane Construction Co.*, 2014 WL 8131876 (N.J.Super.A.D. 2015).

38–2c The LLC Operating Agreement

The members of an LLC can decide how to operate the various aspects of the business by forming an **operating agreement** [ULLCA 103(a)]. In many states, an operating agreement is not required for an LLC to exist, and if there is one, it need not be in writing. Generally, though, LLC members should protect their interests by creating a written operating agreement.

Operating agreements typically contain provisions relating to the following areas:

1. Management and how future managers will be chosen or removed. (Although most LLC statutes are silent on this issue, the ULLCA provides that members

may choose and remove managers by majority vote [ULLCA 404(b)(3)].)

2. How profits will be divided.

3. How membership interests may be transferred.

4. Whether the dissociation of a member, such as by death or departure, will trigger dissolution of the LLC.

5. Whether formal members' meetings will be held.

6. How voting rights will be apportioned. (If the agreement does not cover voting, LLC statutes in most states provide that voting rights are apportioned according to each member's capital contributions.[7])

---

7. In contrast, partners in a partnership generally have equal rights in management and equal voting rights unless they specify otherwise in their partnership agreement.

EXHIBIT 38–2 Provisions Commonly Included in an LLC Operating Agreement

Management	Sets forth who will manage the LLC and how future managers will be chosen or removed. (The ULLCA provides that members may choose and remove managers by majority vote.)
Profits	Establishes how profits will be divided among members.
Membership	Specifies how membership interests may be transferred.
Dissociation and Dissolution	Clarifies which events cause the dissociation of a member—such as by death or retirement—and trigger the LLC's dissolution. Provides a method of calculating a buyout price for a member's dissociation.
Member Meetings	Determines whether or not formal members' meetings will be held.
Voting Rights	Details how voting rights will be apportioned, such as according to each member's capital contribution or by allowing one vote for each member.

Some states provide that, in the absence of an agreement to the contrary, each member has one vote.)

The provisions commonly included in operating agreements are also shown in Exhibit 38–2.

If a dispute arises and there is no agreement covering the topic under dispute, the state LLC statute will govern the outcome. For instance, most LLC statutes provide that if the members have not specified how profits will be divided, they will be divided equally among the members. When an issue is not covered by an operating agreement or by an LLC statute, the courts often apply principles of partnership law.

Of course, LLC members are bound by the operating agreement that they make, as the following case illustrates.

Case 38.2

Mekonen v. Zewdu
Court of Appeals of Washington, 179 Wash.App. 1042 (2014).

Background and Facts Green Cab Taxi and Disabled Service Association LLC ("Green Cab") is a taxi service company in King County, Washington. The operating agreement requires the members to pay weekly fees. Members who do not pay are in default and must return their taxi licenses to the company. In addition, a member in default cannot hold a seat on the board or withdraw from the company without the consent of all of the members.

Case 38.2 Continues

Case 38.2 Continued

A disagreement arose among the members concerning the company's management, and several members, including Shumet Mekonen, withdrew from the company without the consent of the other members. Both sides continued to drive under the Green Cab name.

Mekonen's group filed a suit in a Washington state court against a group of members who had not withdrawn, including Dessie Zewdu. In part, the Mekonen group sought the right to operate as Green Cab. The court held that the plaintiffs could not represent themselves as Green Cab and ordered them to return their taxi licenses to the company. The plaintiffs appealed the order to return their licenses.

In the Language of the Court

LAU, J. [Judge]

* * * *

* * * The [lower] court found in defendants' favor regarding * * * the right of management and control over Green Cab. It found plaintiffs had no right to represent themselves as part of Green Cab's management or to operate under Green Cab's name.

* * * *

* * * Plaintiffs seek to retain the taxicab licenses affixed to the cars they own. According to Paragraph 6.4 of the LLC Operating Agreement, "the Company shall hold all rights to any taxi and other licenses and permits necessary to operate its vehicles." *The Plaintiffs have no right to use the taxicab licenses unless they are members of Green Cab LLC in good standing and are making any contributions toward the company's operating expenses that the board of directors deems necessary.* Plaintiffs admit that they withdrew their membership from Green Cab LLC and that they have paid no weekly fees since [their withdrawal]. As a result, the Plaintiffs have no legal right to retain the King County taxicab licenses currently in their possession. [Emphasis added.]

* * * The [lower] court deemed the members "defaulting members."

* * * *

* * * Plaintiffs admitted to default both in failing to make weekly payments and in withdrawing from the company in violation of article 5.6 of the operating agreement. That article states, "A Member may not withdraw as a Member prior to dissolution and commencement of winding up of the Company * * * without the written consent of all the other Members." The trial court imposed relief that was reasonably calculated to install defendants as the proper group to manage Green Cab and to preserve their interests in operating the company * * * . Given the relative interests of the parties and the LLC, the trial court acted well within its discretion to order plaintiffs to return their taxi licenses.

Decision and Remedy *A state intermediate appellate court upheld the lower court's order to the plaintiffs to return their taxi licenses to Green Cab. Under the provisions of the company's operating agreement, the plaintiffs, as "defaulting members," had no right to retain and use the licenses.*

Critical Thinking

- **What If the Facts Were Different?** *Suppose that Green Cab had maintained a company Web site on which it posted its operating agreement, conducted all internal company business, and offered a forum where members could vent their complaints. How might the result have been different? Why?*
- **Legal Environment** *During discovery, the plaintiffs were asked to answer requests for admission, but they did not respond. Does it seem likely that their failure to answer affected the outcome? Why or why not?*

38–3 Dissociation and Dissolution of an LLC

Recall that in a partnership, *dissociation* occurs when a partner ceases to be associated in the carrying on of the partnership business. The same concept applies to LLCs. And like a partner in a partnership, a member of an LLC has the *power* to dissociate at any time but may not have the *right* to dissociate.

Under the ULLCA, the events that trigger a member's dissociation from an LLC are similar to the events causing a partner to be dissociated under the Uniform Partnership Act (UPA). These include voluntary withdrawal, expulsion by other members, court order, incompetence, bankruptcy, and death. Generally, if a member dies or otherwise dissociates from an LLC, the other members may continue to carry on the LLC business unless the operating agreement provides otherwise.

38–3a Effects of Dissociation

When a member dissociates from an LLC, he or she loses the right to participate in management and the right to act as an agent for the LLC. The member's duty of loyalty to the LLC also terminates, and the duty of care continues only with respect to events that occurred before dissociation.

Generally, the dissociated member also has a right to have his or her interest in the LLC bought out by the other members. The LLC's operating agreement may contain provisions establishing a buyout price. If it does not, the member's interest is usually purchased at fair value. In states that have adopted the ULLCA, the LLC must purchase the interest at fair value within 120 days after the dissociation.

If the member's dissociation violates the LLC's operating agreement, it is considered legally wrongful, and the dissociated member can be held liable for damages caused by the dissociation. ■ **EXAMPLE 38.6** Chadwick and Barrow are members in an LLC. Chadwick manages the accounts, and Barrow, who has many connections in the community and is a skilled investor, brings in the business. If Barrow wrongfully dissociates from the LLC, the LLC's business will suffer, and Chadwick can hold Barrow liable for the loss of business resulting from her withdrawal. ■

38–3b Dissolution

Regardless of whether a member's dissociation was wrongful or rightful, normally the dissociated member has no right to force the LLC to dissolve. The remaining members can opt either to continue or to dissolve the business.

Members can also stipulate in their operating agreement that certain events will cause dissolution, or they can agree that they have the power to dissolve the LLC by vote. As with partnerships, a court can order an LLC to be dissolved in certain circumstances. For instance, a court might order dissolution when the members have engaged in illegal or oppressive conduct, or when it is no longer feasible to carry on the business.

■ **CASE IN POINT 38.7** Three men—Walter Perkins, Gary Fordham, and David Thompson—formed Venture Sales, LLC, to develop a subdivision in Petal, Mississippi. Each of them contributed land and funds, resulting in total holdings of 466 acres of land and about $158,000 in cash.

Perkins, who was working as an assistant coach for the Cleveland Browns, trusted Fordham and Thompson to develop the property. More than ten years later, however, they still had not done so, although they had formed two other LLCs and developed two other subdivisions in the area.

Fordham and Thompson claimed that they did not know when they could develop Venture's property and suggested selling it at a discounted price, but Perkins disagreed. Perkins then sought a judicial dissolution of Venture Sales. The court ordered the dissolution. Because Venture Sales was not meeting the economic purpose for which it was established (developing a subdivision), continuing the business was impracticable.[8] ■

A judge's exercise of discretion to order the dissolution of an LLC was disputed in the following case.

---

8. *Venture Sales, LLC v. Perkins,* 86 So.3d 910 (Miss.Sup. 2012).

Case Analysis 38.3

Reese v. Newman

District of Columbia Court of Appeals, 131 A.3d 880 (2016).

In the Language of the Court

KING, Senior Judge:

* * * Allison Reese and * * * Nicole Newman were co-owners of ANR Construction Management, LLC * * *. Following disputes over management of the company, Newman notified Reese in writing that she intended to * * * dissolve and wind-up the LLC. Reese did not want to dissolve the LLC but preferred that Newman simply be dissociated so that Reese could continue the business herself. Newman filed an action

for judicial dissolution in [a District of Columbia court against Reese]. Reese filed a counterclaim for Newman's dissociation * * *. Following a jury trial, the jury * * * found grounds for both judicial dissolution and forced dissociation of Newman; the court, thereafter, ordered judicial dissolution of the LLC. * * * Reese appeals.

* * * *

Reese argues that the trial court erred when it purported to use discretion in choosing between dissolution of the

LLC, as proposed by Newman, and forcing dissociation of Newman from the LLC, as proposed by Reese. Reese argues that the [District of Columbia (D.C.)] statute [governing dissociation from an LLC] does not allow for any discretion by the court, and that, in fact, the statute mandates that the court order dissociation of Newman based on the jury's findings.

In matters of statutory interpretation, we review the trial court's decision

Case 38.3 Continues

de novo. Our analysis starts with the plain language of the statute, as the general rule of statutory interpretation is that the intent of the lawmaker is to be found in the language that he has used. To that end, *the words of the statute should be construed according to their ordinary sense and with the meaning commonly attributed to them.* [Emphasis added.]

Reese argues that the court was required to dissociate Newman from the LLC under [D.C. Code] Section 29–806.02(5) which reads:

> A person *shall* be dissociated as a member from a limited liability company when:
> * * * *
> (5) On application by the company, the person is expelled as a member by judicial order because the person has:
> (A) Engaged, or is engaging, in wrongful conduct that has adversely and materially affected, or will adversely and materially affect, the company's activities and affairs;
> (B) Willfully or persistently committed, or is willfully and persistently committing, a material breach of the operating agreement or the person's duties or obligations under Section 29–804.09; or
> (C) Engaged in, or is engaging, in conduct relating to the company's activities which makes it not reasonably practicable to carry on the activities with the person as a member.

Reese's interpretation of the statute is that, upon application to the court by a company, a judge shall dissociate a member of an LLC, when that member commits any one of the actions described in subsections (5)(A)-(C).

* * * While the introductory language of Section 29–806.02 does use the word "shall"—that command is in no way directed at the trial judge. It reads, "a person shall be dissociated * * * when," and then goes on to recite fifteen separate circumstances describing different occasions when a person shall be dissociated from an LLC. That is to say, when one of the events described in subparagraphs (1) through (15) occurs, the member shall be dissociated. Subparagraph (5), however, is merely one instance for which a person shall be dissociated; that is, when and if a judge has ordered a member expelled because she finds that any conditions under (5)(A)-(C) have been established. In other words, the command in the introductory language is not directed at the trial judge, it is directed at all the circumstances set forth in subparagraphs (1) through (15) * * * . There is nothing in the language of Section 29–806.02(5) that strips a judge of her discretion because it does not require the judge to expel the member if any of the enumerated conditions are established. In short, Section 29–806.02(5) means: *when a judge has used her discretion to expel a member of an LLC by judicial order, under any of the enumerated circumstances in (5)(A)-(C), that member shall be dissociated.*

* * * Although Reese argues that the language of the "dissociation" section of the District's code should be read as forcing the hand of a trial judge who finds grounds for dissociation, Reese attempts to read the "dissolution" section differently.

Reese differentiates the sections by pointing to the dissolution section's express authorization to order a remedy other than dissolution in Section 29–807.01(b) which provides: "in a proceeding brought under subsection (a)(5) of this section, the * * * Court may order a remedy other than dissolution."

While we are satisfied that judicial dissolution of an LLC is discretionary under this statute, Reese's attempt to buttress [reinforce] her argument that Section 29–806.02(5) is compulsory by pointing to this express provision in the dissolution section and the absence of a similar express provision in the dissociation section is unavailing. First, * * * the only "shall" in the dissociation section is in the introductory language, and the same "shall" can be found in the same place, in the dissolution section: "a limited liability company is dissolved, and its activities and affairs *shall be wound up,* upon the occurrence of any of the following." If that language does not make the rest of the section mandatory in the dissolution section, and we are persuaded that it does not, it cannot be said that the "shall" in the introduction of the dissociation section does the opposite.

* * * *

In sum, we hold that Section 29–806.02(5) can only be interpreted to mean: when a judge finds that any of the events in (5)(A)-(C) have taken place, she may (*i.e.,* has discretion to) expel by judicial order a member of an LLC, and when a judge has done so the member shall be dissociated. *Moreover, when both grounds for dissociation of a member and dissolution of the LLC exist, the trial judge has discretion to choose either alternative.* [Emphasis added.]

Here, the jury * * * found that grounds were present for either outcome. The trial judge acknowledged that both options were on the table and then exercised her discretion in ordering that dissolution take place. We find no reason to disturb that order.

* * * *

Accordingly, the judgment in this appeal is therefore affirmed.

Legal Reasoning Questions

1. What dispute gave rise to the action filed in the court in this case? How did that dispute lead to the issue on appeal?

2. What is the role of an appellate court when reviewing the exercise of discretion by a trial court?

3. Newman alleged that after she delivered her notice to dissolve ANR, Reese locked her out of the LLC's bank accounts, blocked her access to the LLC's files and e-mail, and ended her salary and health benefits. Did any of the jury's findings support these allegations? Explain.

38–3c Winding Up

When an LLC is dissolved, any members who did not wrongfully dissociate may participate in the winding up process. To wind up the business, members must collect, liquidate, and distribute the LLC's assets.

Members may preserve the assets for a reasonable time to optimize their return, and they continue to have the authority to perform reasonable acts in conjunction with winding up. In other words, the LLC will be bound by the reasonable acts of its members during the winding up process.

Once all of the LLC's assets have been sold, the proceeds are distributed. Debts to creditors are paid first (including debts owed to members who are creditors of the LLC). The members' capital contributions are returned next, and any remaining amounts are then distributed to members in equal shares or according to their operating agreement.

38–4 Special Business Forms

Besides the business forms already discussed in this unit, several other forms can be used to organize a business. For the most part, these special business forms are hybrid organizations—that is, they combine features of other organizational forms, such as partnerships and corporations. These forms include joint ventures, syndicates, joint stock companies, business trusts, and cooperatives.

38–4a Joint Venture

In a **joint venture,** two or more persons or business entities combine their efforts or their property for a single transaction or project or a related series of transactions or projects. For instance, when several contractors combine their resources to build and sell houses in a single development, their relationship is a joint venture. Unless otherwise agreed, joint venturers share profits and losses equally and have an equal voice in controlling the project.

Joint ventures range in size from very small activities to multimillion-dollar joint actions carried out by some of the world's largest corporations. Large organizations often form joint ventures with other enterprises to produce new products or services. ■ **EXAMPLE 38.8** Intel Corporation and Micron Technology, Inc., formed a joint venture to manufacture NAND flash memory. NAND is a data-storage chip widely used in digital cameras, cell phones, and portable music players. ■

Similarities to Partnerships A joint venture resembles a partnership and is taxed like a partnership. For this reason, most courts apply the same principles to joint ventures as they apply to partnerships. Joint venturers owe each other the same fiduciary duties, including the duty of loyalty, that partners owe each other. Thus, if one of the venturers secretly buys land that was to be acquired by the joint venture, the other joint venturers may be awarded damages for the breach of loyalty.

Liability and Management Rights. A joint venturer can be held personally liable for the venture's debts (because joint venturers share losses as well as profits). Like partners, joint venturers have equal rights to manage the activities of the enterprise, but they can agree to give control of the operation to one of the members.

Authority to Enter Contracts. Joint venturers have authority as agents to enter into contracts that will bind the joint venture. ■ **CASE IN POINT 38.9** Murdo Cameron developed components for replicas of vintage P-51 Mustang planes. Cameron and Douglas Anderson agreed in writing to collaborate on the design and manufacture of two P-51s, one for each of them.

Without Cameron's knowledge, Anderson borrowed funds from SPW Associates, LLP, to finance the construction, using the first plane as security for the loan. After Anderson built one plane, he defaulted on the loan. SPW filed a lawsuit to obtain possession of the aircraft.

The court ruled that Anderson and Cameron had entered into a joint venture and that the plane was the venture's property. Under partnership law, partners have the power as agents to bind the partnership. Because this principle applies to joint ventures, Anderson had the authority to grant SPW a security interest in the plane, and SPW was entitled to take possession of the plane.[9] ■

Differences from Partnerships Joint ventures differ from partnerships in several important ways. A joint venture is typically created for a single project or series of transactions, whereas a partnership usually (though not always) involves an ongoing business. Also, unlike most partnerships, a joint venture normally terminates when the project or the transaction for which it was formed has been completed.

Because the activities of a joint venture are more limited than the business of a partnership, the members of a joint venture are presumed to have less power to bind their co-venturers. Thus, the members of a joint venture have less implied and apparent authority than the

---

9. *SPW Associates, LLP v. Anderson,* 2006 ND 159, 718 N.W.2d 580 (N.D.Sup.Ct. 2006).

partners in a partnership (each of whom is treated as an agent of the other partners). In *Case in Point 38.9*, for instance, if Anderson's loan agreement with SPW had not been directly related to the business of building vintage planes, the court might have concluded that Anderson lacked the authority to bind the joint venture.

38–4b Syndicate

In a **syndicate,** or *investment group,* several individuals or firms join together to finance a particular project. Syndicates can finance projects such as the construction of a shopping center or the purchase of a professional basketball franchise. The form of such groups varies considerably.

A syndicate may be organized as a corporation or as a general or limited partnership. In some situations, the members do not have a legally recognized business arrangement but merely purchase and own property jointly.

38–4c Joint Stock Company

A **joint stock company** is a true hybrid of a partnership and a corporation. It has many characteristics of a corporation in that (1) its ownership is represented by transferable shares of stock, (2) it is managed by directors and officers of the company or association, and (3) it can have a perpetual existence.

Most of its other features, however, are more characteristic of a partnership, and it generally is treated as a partnership. Like a partnership, a joint stock company is formed by agreement (not statute). Property usually is held in the names of the owners, who are called shareholders, and they have personal liability. In a joint stock company, however, shareholders are not considered to be agents of each other, as they would be in a true partnership.

38–4d Business Trust

A **business trust** is created by a written trust agreement that sets forth the interests of the beneficiaries and the obligations and powers of the trustees. Legal ownership and management of the trust's property stay with one or more of the trustees, and the profits are distributed to the beneficiaries.

A business trust resembles a corporation in many respects. Beneficiaries of the trust, for instance, are not personally responsible for the trust's debts or obligations. In fact, in a number of states, business trusts must pay corporate taxes.

38–4e Cooperative

A **cooperative** is an association that is organized to provide an economic service to its members (or shareholders). It may or may not be incorporated. Most cooperatives are organized under state statutes for cooperatives, general business corporations, or LLCs. Co-ops range in size from small, local cooperatives to national businesses such as Ace Hardware and Land O'Lakes, a well-known producer of dairy products.

The cooperative form of business is generally adopted by groups of individuals who wish to pool their resources to gain some advantage in the marketplace. *Consumer purchasing co-ops,* for instance, are formed to obtain lower prices through quantity discounts. *Seller marketing co-ops* are formed to control the market and thereby enable members to sell their goods at higher prices.

Incorporated Co-ops Generally, an incorporated cooperative distributes dividends, or profits, to its owners on the basis of their transactions with the cooperative rather than on the basis of the amount of capital they contributed. Members of incorporated cooperatives have limited liability, as do shareholders of corporations and members of LLCs.

Unincorporated Co-ops Cooperatives that are not incorporated are often treated like partnerships. The members have joint liability for the cooperative's acts.

See Concept Summary 38.1 for a review of the types of special business forms discussed in this chapter.

Concept Summary 38.1

Special Business Forms

Joint Venture
An organization created by two or more persons in contemplation of a limited activity or a single transaction; similar to a partnership in many respects.

Syndicate
An investment group that undertakes to finance a particular project; may be organized as a corporation or as a general or limited partnership.

Joint Stock Company
A business form similar to a corporation in some respects (transferable shares of stock, management by directors and officers, perpetual existence) but otherwise resembling a partnership.

Business Trust
A business form created by a written trust agreement that sets forth the interests of the beneficiaries and the obligations and powers of the trustee(s). A business trust is similar to a corporation in many respects. Beneficiaries are not personally liable for the debts or obligations of the business trust.

Cooperative
An association organized to provide an economic service, without profit, to its members. A cooperative can take the form of a corporation or a partnership.

Reviewing: Limited Liability Companies and Special Business Forms

The city of Papagos, Arizona, had a deteriorating bridge in need of repair on a prominent public roadway. The city posted notices seeking proposals for an artistic bridge design and reconstruction. Davidson Masonry, LLC, which was owned and managed by Carl Davidson and his wife, Marilyn Rowe, decided to submit a bid to create a decorative concrete structure that incorporated artistic metalwork. They contacted Shana Lafayette, a local sculptor who specialized in large-scale metal creations, to help them design the bridge. The city selected their bridge design and awarded them the contract for a commission of $184,000.

Davidson Masonry and Lafayette then entered into an agreement to work together on the bridge project. Davidson Masonry agreed to install and pay for concrete and structural work, and Lafayette agreed to install the metalwork at her expense. They agreed that overall profits would be split, with 25 percent going to Lafayette and 75 percent going to Davidson Masonry. Lafayette designed numerous metal sculptures of trout that were incorporated into colorful decorative concrete forms designed by Rowe. Davidson performed the structural engineering. The group worked together successfully until the completion of the project. Using the information presented in the chapter, answer the following questions.

1. Would Davidson Masonry automatically be taxed as a partnership or a corporation?
2. Is Davidson Masonry member managed or manager managed?

Continues

3. When Davidson Masonry and Lafayette entered an agreement to work together, what kind of special business form was created? Explain.

4. Suppose that during construction, Lafayette entered into an agreement to rent space in a warehouse that was close to the bridge so that she could work on her sculptures near the site where they would eventually be installed. She entered into the contract without the knowledge or consent of Davidson Masonry. In this situation, would a court be likely to hold that Davidson Masonry was bound by the contract that Lafayette entered? Why or why not?

> **Debate This . . .** *Because LLCs are essentially just partnerships with limited liability for members, all partnership laws should apply.*

Terms and Concepts

articles of organization 726	joint venture 735	member 725
business trust 736	limited liability company	operating agreement 730
cooperative 736	(LLC) 725	syndicate 736
joint stock company 736		

Issue Spotters

1. Gabriel, Harris, and Ida are members of Jeweled Watches, LLC. What are their options with respect to the management of their firm? (See *LLC Management and Operation*.)

2. Greener Delivery Company and Hiway Trucking, Inc., form a business trust. Insta Equipment Company and Jiffy Supply Corporation form a joint stock company.

Kwik Mart, Inc., and Luscious Produce, Inc., form an incorporated cooperative. What do these forms of business organization have in common? (See *Special Business Forms*.)

• **Check your answers to the Issue Spotters against the answers provided in Appendix D at the end of this text.**

Business Scenarios

38–1. Limited Liability Companies. John, Lesa, and Tabir form a limited liability company. John contributes 60 percent of the capital, and Lesa and Tabir each contribute 20 percent. Nothing is decided about how profits will be divided. John assumes that he will be entitled to 60 percent of the profits, in accordance with his contribution. Lesa and Tabir, however, assume that the profits will be divided equally. A dispute over the profits arises, and ultimately a court has to decide the issue. What law will the court apply? In most states, what will result? How could this dispute have been avoided in the first place? Discuss fully. (See *The Limited Liability Company*.)

38–2. Special Business Forms. Bateson Corp. is considering entering into contracts with two organizations. One is a

joint stock company that distributes home products east of the Mississippi River. The other is a business trust formed by a number of sole proprietors who are sellers of home products on the West Coast. Both contracts will require Bateson to make large capital outlays in order to supply the businesses with restaurant equipment. In both business organizations, at least two shareholders or beneficiaries are personally wealthy, but the organizations themselves have limited financial resources. The owner-managers of Bateson are not familiar with either form of business organization. Because each form resembles a corporation, they are concerned about potential limits on liability in the event that either organization breaches the contract by failing to pay for the equipment. Discuss fully Bateson's concern. (See *Special Business Forms*.)

Business Case Problems

38–3. Joint Venture. Holiday Isle Resort & Marina, Inc., operated four restaurants, five bars, and various food kiosks at its resort in Islamorada, Florida. Holiday entered into a "joint-venture agreement" with Rip Tosun to operate a fifth

restaurant, called "Rip's—A Place for Ribs." The agreement gave Tosun authority over the employees and "full authority as to the conduct of the business." It also prohibited Tosun from competing with Rip's without Holiday's approval but did not prevent Holiday from competing. Later, Tosun sold half of his interest in Rip's to Thomas Hallock. Soon, Tosun and Holiday opened the Olde Florida Steakhouse next to Rip's. Holiday stopped serving breakfast at Rip's and diverted employees and equipment from Rip's to the steakhouse, which then started offering breakfast. Hallock filed a suit in a Florida state court against Holiday. Did Holiday breach the joint-venture agreement? Did it breach the duties that joint venturers owe each other? Explain. [*Hallock v. Holiday Isle Resort & Marina, Inc.,* 4 So.3d 17 (Fla.App. 3 Dist. 2009)] (See *Special Business Forms.*)

38–4. Limited Liability Companies.

Coco Investments, LLC, and other investors participated in a condominium conversion project to be managed by Zamir Manager River Terrace, LLC. The participants entered into a new LLC agreement for the project. The investors subsequently complained that Zamir had failed to disclose its plans for dramatic changes involving higher-than-expected construction costs and delays. They also claimed that Zamir had failed to provide financial information and had restructured loans in a manner that allowed Zamir representatives to avoid personal liability. The investors sued Zamir on various grounds, including breach of contract and breach of fiduciary duty. Zamir moved for summary judgment. How should the court rule? Explain. [*Coco Investments, LLC v. Zamir Manager River Terrace, LLC,* 26 Misc.3d 1231 (N.Y.Sup. 2010)] (See *The Limited Liability Company.*)

38–5. LLC Dissolution.

Walter Van Houten and John King formed 1545 Ocean Avenue, LLC, with each managing 50 percent of the business. Its purpose was to renovate an existing building and construct a new commercial building. Van Houten and King quarreled over many aspects of the work on the properties. King claimed that Van Houten paid the contractors too much for the work performed. As the projects neared completion, King demanded that the LLC be dissolved and that Van Houten agree to a buyout. Because the parties could not agree on a buyout, King sued for dissolution. The trial court enjoined (prevented) further work on the projects until the dispute was settled. As the ground for dissolution, King cited the fights over management decisions. There was no claim of fraud or frustration of purpose. The trial court ordered that the LLC be dissolved, and Van Houten appealed. Should either of the owners be forced to dissolve the LLC before the completion of its purpose—that is, before the building projects are finished? Explain. [*In re 1545 Ocean Avenue, LLC,* 893 N.Y.S.2d 590 (N.Y.A.D. 2 Dept. 2010)] (See *Dissociation and Dissolution of an LLC.*)

38–6. Business Case Problem with Sample Answer— LLC Operation.

 After Hurricane Katrina struck the Gulf Coast, James Williford, Patricia Mosser, Marquetta Smith, and Michael Floyd formed Bluewater Logistics, LLC, to bid on construction contracts. Under Mississippi law, every member of a member-managed LLC is entitled to participate in managing the business. The operating agreement provided for a "super majority" 75 percent vote to remove a member who

"has either committed a felony or under any other circumstances that would jeopardize the company status" as a contractor. After Bluewater had completed more than $5 million in contracts, Smith told Williford that she, Mosser, and Floyd were exercising their "super majority" vote to fire him. No reason was provided. Williford sued Bluewater and the other members. Did Smith, Mosser, and Floyd breach the state LLC statute, their fiduciary duties, or the Bluewater operating agreements? Discuss. [*Bluewater Logistics, LLC v. Williford,* 55 So.3d 148 (Miss. 2011)] (See *LLC Management and Operation.*)

- For a sample answer to Problem 38–6, go to Appendix E at the end of this text.

38–7. Jurisdictional Requirements.

Fadal Machining Centers, LLC, and MAG Industrial Automation Centers, LLC, sued a New Jersey–based corporation, Mid-Atlantic CNC, Inc., in federal district court. Ten percent of MAG was owned by SP MAG Holdings, a Delaware LLC. SP MAG had six members, including a Delaware limited partnership called Silver Point Capital Fund and a Delaware LLC called SPCP Group III. In turn, Silver Point and SPCP Group had a common member, Robert O'Shea, who was a New Jersey citizen. Assuming that the amount in controversy exceeds $75,000, does the district court have diversity jurisdiction? Why or why not? [*Fadal Machining Centers, LLC v. Mid-Atlantic CNC, Inc.,* 2012 WL 8669 (9th Cir. 2012)] (See *The Limited Liability Company.*)

38–8. Jurisdictional Requirements.

Siloam Springs Hotel, LLC, operates a Hampton Inn in Siloam Springs, Arkansas. Siloam bought insurance from Century Surety Co. to cover the hotel. When guests suffered injuries due to a leak of carbon monoxide from the heating element of an indoor swimming pool, Siloam filed a claim with Century. Century denied coverage, which Siloam disputed. Century asked a federal district court to resolve the dispute. In asserting that the federal court had jurisdiction, Century noted that the amount in controversy exceeded $75,000 and that the parties had complete diversity of citizenship. Century is "a corporation organized under the laws of Ohio, with its principal place of business in Michigan," and Siloam is "a corporation organized under the laws of Oklahoma, with its principal place of business in Arkansas." Can the court exercise diversity jurisdiction in this case? Discuss. [*Siloam Springs Hotel, L.L.C. v. Century Surety Co.,* 781 F.3d 1233 (10th Cir. 2015)] (See *The Limited Liability Company.*)

38–9. Special Business Forms.

Randall and Peggy Norman operated a dairy farm in Pine River, Minnesota. About ten years after the operation was begun, the cows started to experience health issues. Over the next eighteen years, the herd suffered many serious health problems. Eventually, stray electrical voltage—which can use cow hooves as an unintended pathway, causing health issues—was detected. By then, milk production in the Normans' herd had declined from 27 percent above the state average to 20 percent below it. The Normans filed a suit in a Minnesota state court against Crow Wing

Cooperative Power & Light Company, a member-owned electrical cooperative that provided electricity to the Normans' farm. If Crow Wing is found to have acted negligently, can its members be held jointly liable for the cooperative's acts? Explain. [*Norman v. Crow Wing Co-operative Power & Light Co.*, __ N.W.2d __, 2016 WL 687472 (Minn.App. 2016)] (See *Special Business Forms*.)

38–10. A Question of Ethics—Limited Liability Companies.

 Blushing Brides, LLC, a publisher of wedding planning magazines in Columbus, Ohio, opened an account with Gray Printing Co. in July 2000. On behalf of Blushing Brides, Louis Zacks, the firm's member-manager, signed a credit agreement that identified the firm as the "purchaser" and required payment within thirty days. Despite the agreement, Blushing Brides typically took up to six months to pay the full amount for its orders. Gray printed and shipped 10,000 copies of a fall/winter 2001 issue for Blushing Brides but had not been paid when the firm ordered 15,000 copies of a spring/summer 2002 issue. Gray refused to print the new order without an assurance of payment. On May 22, Zacks signed a promissory note payable to Gray within thirty days for $14,778, plus interest at 6 percent per year. Gray printed the new order but by October had been paid only $7,500. Gray filed a suit in an Ohio state court against Blushing Brides and Zacks to collect the balance. [Gray Printing Co. v. Blushing Brides, LLC, 2006 WL 832587 (Ohio App. 2006)] (See *The Limited Liability Company*.)

(a) Under what circumstances is a member of an LLC liable for the firm's debts? In this case, is Zacks personally liable under the credit agreement for the unpaid amount on Blushing Brides' account? Did Zacks's promissory note affect the parties' liability on the account? Explain.

(b) Should a member of an LLC assume an ethical responsibility to meet the obligations of the firm? Discuss.

(c) Gray shipped only 10,000 copies of the spring/summer 2002 issue of Blushing Brides' magazine, waiting for the publisher to identify a destination for the other 5,000 copies. The magazine had a retail price of $4.50 per copy. Did Gray have a legal or ethical duty to "mitigate the damages" by attempting to sell or otherwise distribute these copies itself? Why or why not?

38–11. Special Case Analysis—LLC Dissolution.
Go to Case Analysis 38.3, *Reese v. Newman*. Read the excerpt and answer the following questions.

(a) **Issue:** Which party's choice between two alternatives was at the heart of the issue on the appeal of the *Reese* case?

(b) **Rule of Law:** What rules of interpretation did the appellate court use to construe the language of the statutes that created those alternatives?

(c) **Applying the Rule of Law:** How did the court construe the language of those statutes?

(d) **Conclusion:** How did the court's construction of that language lead to the result?

Legal Reasoning Group Activity

38–12. Fiduciary Duties in LLCs. Newbury Properties Group owns, manages, and develops real property. Jerry Stoker and the Stoker Group, Inc. (the Stokers), also develop real property. Newbury entered into agreements with the Stokers concerning a large tract of property in Georgia. The parties formed Bellemare, LLC, to develop various parcels of the tract for residential purposes. The operating agreement of Bellemare indicated that "no Member shall be accountable to the LLC or to any other Member with respect to any other business or activity even if the business or activity competes with the LLC's business." Later, when the Newbury group contracted with other parties to develop parcels within the tract in competition with Bellemare, LLC, the Stokers sued, alleging breach of fiduciary duty. (See *LLC Management and Operation*.)

(a) The first group will discuss and outline the fiduciary duties that the members of an LLC owe to each other.

(b) The second group will determine whether the terms of an operating agreement can alter these fiduciary duties.

(c) The last group will decide in whose favor the court should rule in this situation.

CHAPTER 39

Corporate Formation and Financing

The corporation is a creature of statute. A corporation is an artificial being, existing only in law and being neither tangible nor visible. Its existence generally depends on state law, although some corporations, especially public organizations, are created under federal law. Each state has its own body of corporate law, and these laws are not entirely uniform.

The Model Business Corporation Act (MBCA) is a codification of modern corporation law that has been influential in shaping state corporation statutes. Today, the majority of state statutes are guided by the most recent version of the MBCA, often referred to as the Revised Model Business Corporation Act (RMBCA).

Keep in mind, however, that there is considerable variation among the laws of states that have used the MBCA or the RMBCA as a basis for their statutes. In addition, several states do not follow either act. Consequently, individual state corporation laws should be relied on to determine corporate law rather than the MBCA or RMBCA.

39-1 The Nature and Classification of Corporations

A corporation is a legal entity created and recognized by state law. This business entity can have one or more owners (called shareholders), and it operates under a name distinct from the names of its owners. Both individuals and other businesses can be shareholders. The corporation substitutes itself for its shareholders when conducting corporate business and incurring liability. Its authority to act and the liability for its actions, however, are separate and apart from the shareholders who own it.

A corporation is recognized under U.S. law as a person—an artificial *legal person,* as opposed to a *natural person.* As a "person," it enjoys many of the same rights and privileges under state and federal law that U.S. citizens enjoy. For instance, corporations possess the same right of access to the courts as citizens and can sue or be sued. The constitutional guarantees of due process, free speech, and freedom from unreasonable searches and seizures also apply to corporations.

39-1a Corporate Personnel

In a corporation, the responsibility for the overall management of the firm is entrusted to a *board of directors,* whose members are elected by the shareholders. The board of directors makes the policy decisions and hires *corporate officers* and other employees to run the daily business operations.

When an individual purchases a share of stock in a corporation, that person becomes a shareholder and an owner of the corporation. Unlike the partners in a partnership, the body of shareholders can change constantly without affecting the continued existence of the corporation. A shareholder can sue the corporation, and the corporation can sue a shareholder. Additionally, under certain circumstances, a shareholder can sue on behalf of a corporation.

39-1b The Limited Liability of Shareholders

One of the key advantages of the corporate form is the limited liability of its owners. Normally, corporate shareholders are not personally liable for the obligations of the corporation beyond the extent of their investments.

In certain limited situations, however, a court can *pierce the corporate veil* and impose liability on shareholders for the corporation's obligations. Additionally, creditors often will not extend credit to small companies unless the shareholders assume personal liability, as guarantors, for corporate obligations.

39–1c Corporate Earnings and Taxation

When a corporation earns profits, it can either pass them on to shareholders in the form of **dividends** or retain them as profits. These **retained earnings,** if invested properly, will yield higher corporate profits in the future. In theory, higher profits will cause the price of the company's stock to rise. Individual shareholders can then reap the benefits in the capital gains they receive when they sell their stock.

Corporate Taxation Whether a corporation retains its profits or passes them on to the shareholders as dividends, those profits are subject to income taxation by various levels of government. Failure to pay taxes can lead to severe consequences. The state can suspend the organization's corporate status until the taxes are paid and can even dissolve the corporation for failing to pay taxes.

Another important aspect of corporate taxation is that corporate profits can be subject to double taxation. The company pays tax on its profits. Then, if the profits are passed on to the shareholders as dividends, the shareholders must also pay income tax on them. (This is true unless the dividends represent distributions of capital, which are returns of holders' investments in the stock of the company.) The corporation normally does not receive a tax deduction for dividends it distributes. This double-taxation feature is one of the major disadvantages of the corporate form.

Holding Companies Some U.S. corporations use holding companies to reduce or defer their U.S. income taxes. At its simplest, a **holding company** (sometimes referred to as a *parent company*) is a company whose business activity consists of holding shares in another company. Typically, the holding company is established in a low-tax or no-tax offshore jurisdiction, such as the Cayman Islands, Dubai, Hong Kong, Luxembourg, Monaco, or Panama.

Sometimes, a U.S. corporation sets up a holding company in a low-tax offshore environment and then transfers its cash, bonds, stocks, and other investments to the holding company. In general, any profits received by the holding company on these investments are taxed at the rate of the offshore jurisdiction where the company is registered. Once the profits are brought "onshore," though, they are taxed at the federal corporate income tax rate. Any payments received by the shareholders are also taxable at the full U.S. rates.

39–1d Criminal Acts

Under modern criminal law, a corporation may be held liable for the criminal acts of its agents and employees.

Although corporations cannot be imprisoned, they can be fined. (Of course, corporate directors and officers can be imprisoned, and many have been in recent years.) In addition, under sentencing guidelines for crimes committed by corporate employees (white-collar crimes), corporations can face fines amounting to hundreds of millions of dollars.

39–1e Tort Liability

A corporation is liable for the torts committed by its agents or officers within the course and scope of their employment. The doctrine of *respondeat superior* applies to corporations in the same way as it does to other agency relationships.

■ **CASE IN POINT 39.1** Mark Bloom was an officer and a director of MB Investment Partners, Inc. (MB), at the time that he formed North Hills, LP, a stock investment fund. Bloom and other MB employees used MB's offices and equipment to administer investments in North Hills.

Later, investors in North Hills requested a full redemption of their investments. By that time, however, most of the funds that had been invested were gone. North Hills had, in fact, been a Ponzi scheme that Bloom had used to finance his lavish personal lifestyle, taking at least $20 million from North Hills for his personal use.

Barry Belmont and other North Hills investors filed a suit in a federal district court against MB, alleging fraud. The court held that MB was liable for Bloom's fraud. MB appealed, and the appellate court affirmed. Tort liability can be attributed to a corporation for the acts of its agent that were committed within the scope of the agent's employment.[1] ■

Because corporations can be liable for their employees' fraud and other misconduct, companies need to be careful about whom they hire and how much they monitor or supervise their employees. Some companies are using special software designed to predict employee misconduct before it occurs, as discussed in this chapter's *Digital Update* feature.

39–1f Classification of Corporations

Corporations can be classified in several ways. The classification of a corporation normally depends on its location, purpose, and ownership characteristics, as described in the following subsections.

Domestic, Foreign, and Alien Corporations A corporation is referred to as a **domestic corporation** by its

---

1. *Belmont v. MB Investment Partners, Inc.*, 708 F.3d 470 (3d Cir. 2013).

Programs That Predict Employee Misconduct

Monitoring employees' e-mails and phone conversations at work is generally legal.[a] But what about using software to analyze employee behavior with the goal of predicting, rather than observing, wrongdoing? Now we are entering into the digital realm of *predictive analytics*.

Spy agencies around the world today use analytic software to predict who will engage in a terrorist act, where it will happen, and when. Software applied to data mining of employee behavior (usually just online) actually has been around for several years as well. For example, Amazon started using employee-monitoring programs to predict who might quit. But only recently have such programs been used to predict misconduct.

JPMorgan Chase Attempts to Reduce Its Legal Bills

JPMorgan, the world's largest private financial institution, also is perhaps the world's largest purchaser of legal services in that sector. Its legal bills have exceeded $36 billion since the financial crisis of 2008. The company's management found that employees had

engaged in dubious mortgage bond sales and rigged foreign exchange and energy markets, among many other transgressions. The company hired an extra 2,500 compliance officers and spent almost $750 million on compliance operations during a recent three-year period.

Now JPMorgan is using new software to identify—in advance of any wrongdoing—"rogue" employees. The software analyzes a wide range of inputs on employees' behavior in an attempt to identify patterns that point to future misconduct. If successful, the program will certainly be copied by other financial institutions.

An Ethical Problem?

A former Federal Reserve Bank examiner, Mark Williams, has raised an important issue with respect to predictive analytics: "Policing intentions can be a slippery slope. Do people get a scarlet letter for something they have yet to do?" In other words, will employees be labeled as wrongdoers before they have actually done anything wrong?

Critical Thinking *Is thinking about committing a crime illegal?*

a. Electronic Communications Privacy Act, 18 U.S.C.A. Sec. 2511(2)(d).

home state (the state in which it incorporates). A corporation formed in one state but doing business in another is referred to in the second state as a **foreign corporation.** A corporation formed in another country (say, Mexico) but doing business in the United States is referred to in the United States as an **alien corporation.**

A corporation does not have an automatic right to do business in a state other than its state of incorporation. In some instances, it must obtain a *certificate of authority* in any state in which it plans to do business. Once the certificate has been issued, the corporation generally can exercise in that state all of the powers conferred on it by

its home state. If a foreign corporation does business in a state without obtaining a certificate of authority, the state can impose substantial fines and sanctions on that corporation.

Note that most state statutes specify certain activities, such as soliciting orders via the Internet, that are not considered "doing business" within the state. For instance, a foreign corporation normally does not need a certificate of authority to sell goods or services via the Internet or by mail.

What constitutes doing business within a state? In the following case, the court answered that question.

Case 39.1

Drake Manufacturing Co. v. Polyflow, Inc.

Superior Court of Pennsylvania, 2015 PA Super 16, 109 A.3d 250 (2015).

Background and Facts Drake Manufacturing Company, a Delaware corporation, entered into a contract to sell certain products to Polyflow, Inc., headquartered in Pennsylvania. Drake promised to ship the goods from Drake's plant in Sheffield, Pennsylvania, to Polyflow's place of business in Oaks, Pennsylvania, as well as to addresses in California, Canada, and Holland.

Case 39.1 Continues

When Polyflow withheld payment of about $300,000 for some of the goods, Drake filed a breach of contract suit in a Pennsylvania state court against Polyflow seeking to collect the unpaid amount. But Drake had failed to obtain a certificate of authority to do business in Pennsylvania as a foreign corporation. Polyflow asserted that this failure to register with the state deprived Drake of the capacity to bring an action against Polyflow in the state's courts. The court issued a judgment in Drake's favor. Polyflow appealed.

In the Language of the Court
Opinion by *JENKINS*, J. [Judge]:
* * * *

[15 Pennsylvania Consolidated Statutes (Pa.C.S.)] Section 4121 provides: "A foreign business corporation, before doing business in this Commonwealth, shall procure a certificate of authority to do so from the Department of State."

* * * Typical conduct requiring a certificate of authority includes maintaining an office to conduct local intrastate business [and] entering into contracts relating to local business or sales.

A corporation is not "doing business" solely because it resorts to the courts of this Commonwealth to recover an indebtedness. [Emphasis added.]
* * * *

[15 Pa.C.S.] Section 4141(a) provides in relevant part that "a nonqualified foreign business corporation doing business in this Commonwealth * * * shall not be permitted to maintain any action or proceeding in any court of this Commonwealth until the corporation has obtained a certificate of authority."
* * * *

* * * The evidence demonstrates that Drake failed to submit a certificate of authority into evidence prior to the verdict in violation of 15 Pa.C.S. Section 4121. Therefore, the trial court should not have permitted Drake to prosecute its action.

The trial court contends that Drake is exempt from the certificate of authority requirement because it merely commenced suit in Pennsylvania to collect a debt * * * . Drake did much more, however, than file suit or attempt to collect a debt. Drake maintains an office in Pennsylvania to conduct local business, conduct which typically requires a certificate of authority. Drake also entered into a contract with Polyflow, and * * * shipped couplings and portable swaging machines to Polyflow's place of business in Pennsylvania * * * . In short, *Drake's conduct was * * * regular, systematic, and extensive, * * * thus constituting the transaction of business and requiring Drake to obtain a certificate of authority.* [Emphasis added.]

We also hold that Drake needed a certificate of authority to sue Polyflow in Pennsylvania for Polyflow's failure to pay for out-of-state shipments in California, Canada and Holland. A foreign corporation that "does business" in Pennsylvania * * * must obtain a certificate in order to prosecute a lawsuit in this Commonwealth, regardless of whether the lawsuit itself concerns in-state conduct or out-of-state conduct.

Decision and Remedy *A state intermediate appellate court reversed the judgment in Drake's favor. Under Pennsylvania state statutes, Drake was required to obtain a certificate of authority to do business in that state. Drake failed to do so. The court should not have allowed Drake to prosecute its action against Polyflow.*

Critical Thinking
• **Legal Environment** *Why would the appellate court permit Polyflow to get away with not paying for delivered and presumably merchantable goods?*

Public and Private Corporations A **public corporation** is a corporation formed by the government to meet some political or governmental purpose. Cities and towns that incorporate are common examples. In addition, many federal government organizations, such as the U.S. Postal Service, the Tennessee Valley Authority, and AMTRAK, are public corporations.

Note that a public corporation is not the same as a **publicly held corporation**. A publicly held corporation (often called a *public company*) is any corporation whose shares are publicly traded in a securities market, such as the New York Stock Exchange or the NASDAQ.

Private corporations, in contrast, are created either wholly or in part for private benefit—that is, for profit. Most corporations are private. Although they may serve a public purpose, as a public electric or gas utility does, they are owned by private persons rather than by a government.[2]

***

2. The United States Supreme Court first recognized the property rights of private corporations and clarified the distinction between public and private corporations in the landmark case *Trustees of Dartmouth College v. Woodward*, 17 U.S. (4 Wheaton) 518, 4 L.Ed. 629 (1819).

Nonprofit Corporations Corporations formed for purposes other than making a profit are called *nonprofit* or *not-for-profit* corporations. Private hospitals, educational institutions, charities, and religious organizations, for instance, are frequently organized as nonprofit corporations. The nonprofit corporation is a convenient form of organization that allows various groups to own property and to form contracts without exposing the individual members to personal liability.

In some circumstances, a nonprofit corporation and its members may also be immune from liability for a personal injury caused by its negligence. Whether those circumstances were present in the following case was the question before the court.

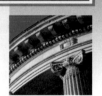

Case Analysis 39.2

Pantano v. Newark Museum

Superior Court of New Jersey, Appellate Division, __ A.3d __, 2016 WL 528771 (2016).

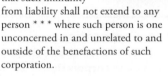

In the Language of the Court
PER CURIAM.
* * * *

* * * Plaintiff [Loredana Pantano] slipped and fell on icy steps at an entrance to the [Newark] Museum, suffering injuries to her back. At the time, plaintiff was employed as an immigration attorney by La Casa de Don Pedro (La Casa), a nonprofit organization located in Newark [New Jersey]. Upon arrival at her office that day, plaintiff was told by La Casa's Director of Personal Development to go to the Museum for an educational panel discussion being held as part of La Casa's fortieth anniversary celebration.

* * * The event was one of several organized to celebrate and commemorate the organization's history and role in the development of Newark. Staff members were not directly engaged in fundraising, but they were told to mingle with those attending the event, some of whom were contributors to La Casa. The Museum charged La Casa a fee for the use of the facility, specifically an auditorium to be used by the panel and those in attendance.

The Museum is a nonprofit association organized exclusively for charitable, artistic, scientific, educational, historical and cultural purposes * * * . It does, on occasion, rent its facilities to the public in order to generate income.

Plaintiff filed suit [in a New Jersey state court against the Museum] alleging the Museum was negligent in its maintenance of the premises. * * * The Museum moved for summary judgment, contending that plaintiff was a direct beneficiary of its charitable endeavors.
* * * *

* * * The judge granted the Museum's motion, and this appeal followed.

Plaintiff contends that she was not a beneficiary of the Museum's charitable purposes at the time of her fall because she was on the premises at the direction of her employer. We agree that pursuant to the [New Jersey Supreme] Court's holding in *Mayer v. Fairlawn Jewish Center*, 38 N.J. 549, 186 A.2d 274 (1962), plaintiff was not a direct recipient of the Museum's good works.
* * * *

In pertinent part, the [state Charitable Immunity Act (CIA)] provides:

No nonprofit corporation * * * shall * * * be liable to respond in damages to any person who shall suffer damage from the negligence * * * of such corporation * * * where such person is a beneficiary, to whatever degree, of the works of such nonprofit corporation * * * ; provided, however, that such immunity from liability shall not extend to any person * * * where such person is one unconcerned in and unrelated to and outside of the benefactions of such corporation.

The CIA serves two primary purposes. *First, immunity preserves a charity's assets. Second, immunity recognizes that a beneficiary of the services of a charitable organization has entered into a relationship that exempts the benefactor from liability.* [Emphasis added.]

* * * The established test for determining whether a party is a beneficiary of the works of a charity has two prongs. The first is that the institution pleading the immunity, at the time in question, was engaged in the performance of the charitable objectives it was organized to advance. The second is that the injured party must have been a direct recipient of those good works.
* * * *

As to the first prong, * * * a qualifying organization does not lose its statutory immunity merely because it charges money for its services, unless it makes a profit or collects fees for services totally unrelated to its organizational pursuits. * * * Hosting an educational panel

Case 39.2 Continues

Case 39.2 Continued

discussion in the auditorium was entirely consistent with the Museum's charitable endeavors.

The second prong of the test * * * distinguishes between persons benefiting from the charity, and persons who contribute to the charity by virtue of their attendance or participation.

* * * *

In *Mayer*, * * * an employee of the Development Corporation for Israel was promoting the sale of bonds at a dinner on the premises of [Fairlawn Jewish Center, the defendant, when he sustained an injury].

* * * *

* * * He was there in fulfillment of his function and obligation as an employee to engage in the employer's work at the direction of the employer, and not for the purpose of receiving personally the philanthropy of the Center. Under the circumstances present he was a stranger to the charity and the [CIA did] not stand in the way of recovery.

* * * *

* * * *[Thus, under the CIA,] to be a beneficiary under the second prong, the injured party must be a direct recipient of the Museum's good works. Only those*

unconcerned in and unrelated to the benefactions of the organization are not beneficiaries. [Emphasis added.]

* * * *

As an intermediate appellate court, we are bound to follow and enforce the decisions of the Supreme Court. Under [*Mayer*], plaintiff, as an employee of La Casa who was ordered on the day of her fall to attend the panel discussion at the Museum, was not a direct beneficiary of the Museum's charitable endeavors.

We therefore reverse the order granting summary judgment to the Museum and remand the matter.

Legal Reasoning Questions

1. How do the purposes of the CIA support each other?

2. Can a person be a direct beneficiary of a nonprofit's good works even though the person is on the nonprofit's premises under the direction of a third party? Explain.

3. Suppose that the museum had not been hosting an educational panel in its auditorium but instead had rented the facility to an organization for a sales conference. Would the result have been different? Discuss.

Close Corporations Most corporate enterprises in the United States fall into the category of close corporations. A **close corporation** is one whose shares are held by relatively few persons, often members of a family. Close corporations are also referred to as *closely held, family,* or *privately held* corporations.

Usually, the members of the small group constituting the shareholders of a close corporation are personally known to each other. Because the number of shareholders is so small, there is no trading market for the shares. In practice, a close corporation is often operated like a partnership.

The statutes in many states allow close corporations to depart significantly from certain formalities required by traditional corporation law.[3] Under the RMBCA, close corporations have considerable flexibility in determining their operating rules [RMBCA 7.32]. If all of a corporation's shareholders agree in writing, the corporation can operate without directors and bylaws. In addition, the corporation can operate without annual or special shareholders' or directors' meetings, stock

certificates, or formal records of shareholders' or directors' decisions.[4]

Management of Close Corporations. Management of a close corporation resembles that of a sole proprietorship or a partnership, in that control is held by a single shareholder or a tightly knit group of shareholders. As a corporation, however, the firm must meet all specific legal requirements set forth in state statutes.

To prevent a majority shareholder from dominating the company, a close corporation may require that more than a simple majority of the directors approve any action taken by the board. In a larger corporation, such a requirement would typically apply only to extraordinary actions (such as selling all the corporate assets) and not to ordinary business decisions.

Transfer of Shares in Close Corporations. By definition, a close corporation has a small number of shareholders. Thus, the transfer of one shareholder's shares to someone else can cause serious management problems. The other

---

3. In some states, such as Maryland, a close corporation need not have a board of directors.

4. Shareholders cannot agree, however, to eliminate certain rights of shareholders, such as the right to inspect corporate records or the right to bring *derivative actions* (lawsuits on behalf of the corporation).

shareholders may find themselves required to share control with someone they do not know or like. ■ **EXAMPLE 39.2** Three siblings, Sherry, Karen, and Henry Johnson, are the only shareholders of Johnson's Car Wash, Inc. Henry wants to sell his shares, but Sherry and Karen do not want him to sell the shares to a third person unknown to them. ■

To avoid this situation, a close corporation can restrict the transferability of shares to outside persons. Shareholders can be required to offer their shares to the corporation or to the other shareholders before selling them to an outside purchaser. In fact, in a few states close corporations must transfer shares in this manner under state statutes.

One way the close corporation can effect restrictions on transferability is by spelling them out in a **shareholder agreement.** A shareholder agreement can also provide for proportional control when one of the original shareholders dies. The decedent's shares of stock in the corporation can be divided in such a way that the proportionate holdings of the survivors, and thus their proportionate control, will be maintained.

Misappropriation of Close Corporation Funds. Sometimes, a majority shareholder in a close corporation takes advantage of his or her position and misappropriates company funds. In such situations, the normal remedy for the injured minority shareholders is to have their shares appraised and to be paid the fair market value for them. ■ **CASE IN POINT 39.3** John Murray, Stephen Hopkins, and Paul Ryan were officers, directors, employees, and majority shareholders of Olympic Adhesives, Inc. Merek Rubin was a minority shareholder. Murray, Hopkins, and Ryan were paid salaries. Twice a year, they paid themselves additional compensation—between 75 and 98 percent of Olympic's net profits, allocated according to their stock ownership. Rubin filed a suit against the majority shareholders, alleging that their compensation deprived him of his share of Olympic's profits.

The court explained that a salary should reasonably relate to a corporate officer's ability and the quantity and quality of his or her services. The court found that a reasonable amount of compensation would have been 10 percent of Olympic's average annual net sales. Therefore, the additional compensation the majority shareholders paid themselves—based on stock ownership and not on performance—was excessive. The court ordered the defendants to repay Olympic nearly $6 million to be distributed among its shareholders. On appeal, the reviewing court affirmed this decision.[5] ■

---

5. *Rubin v. Murray,* 79 Mass.App.Ct. 64, 943 N.E.2d 949 (2011).

S Corporations A close corporation that meets the qualifying requirements specified in Subchapter S of the Internal Revenue Code can choose to operate as an **S corporation.** (A corporation will automatically be taxed under Subchapter C unless it elects S corporation status.) If a corporation has S corporation status, it can avoid the imposition of income taxes at the corporate level while retaining many of the advantages of a corporation, particularly limited liability.

Important Requirements. Among the numerous requirements for S corporation status, the following are the most important:

1. The corporation must be a domestic corporation.
2. The corporation must not be a member of an affiliated group of corporations.
3. The shareholders must be individuals, estates, or certain trusts and tax-exempt organizations. Partnerships and nonqualifying trusts cannot be shareholders. Corporations can be shareholders under certain circumstances.
4. The corporation must have no more than one hundred shareholders.
5. The corporation must have only one class of stock, although it is not necessary that all shareholders have the same voting rights.
6. No shareholder of the corporation may be a nonresident alien.

Effect of S Election. An S corporation is treated differently than a regular corporation for tax purposes. An S corporation is taxed like a partnership, so the corporate income passes through to the shareholders, who pay personal income tax on it. This treatment enables the S corporation to avoid the double taxation imposed on regular corporations.

In addition, the shareholders' tax brackets may be lower than the tax bracket that the corporation would have been in if the tax had been imposed at the corporate level. The resulting tax saving is particularly attractive when the corporation wants to accumulate earnings for some future business purpose. If the corporation has losses, the S election allows the shareholders to use the losses to offset other income.

In spite of these benefits, the S corporation has lost much of its appeal. The newer limited liability business forms (such as LLCs, LPs, and LLPs) offer similar tax advantages and greater flexibility.

Professional Corporations Professionals such as physicians, lawyers, dentists, and accountants can incorporate. A professional corporation is typically identified by the letters *P.C.* (professional corporation), *S.C.* (service corporation), or *P.A.* (professional association).

In general, the laws governing the formation and operation of professional corporations are similar to those governing ordinary business corporations. There are some differences in terms of liability, however, because the shareholder-owners are professionals who are held to a higher standard of conduct.

For liability purposes, some courts treat professional corporations somewhat like partnerships and hold each professional liable for malpractice committed within the scope of the business by others in the firm. A shareholder in a professional corporation generally cannot be held liable for torts committed by other professionals at the firm except those related to malpractice or breach of duty to clients.

Benefit Corporations A growing number of states have enacted legislation that creates a relatively new corporate form called a *benefit corporation*. A **benefit corporation** is a for-profit corporation that seeks to have a material positive impact on society and the environment. Benefit corporations differ from traditional corporations in the following ways:

1. *Purpose.* Although the corporation is designed to make a profit, its purpose is to benefit the public as a whole. (In contrast, the purpose of an ordinary business corporation is to provide long-term shareholder value.) The directors of a benefit corporation must, during the decision-making process, consider the impact of their decisions on society and the environment.
2. *Accountability.* Shareholders of a benefit corporation determine whether the company has achieved a material positive impact. Shareholders also have a right of private action, called a *benefit enforcement proceeding,* enabling them to sue the corporation if it fails to pursue or create public benefit.
3. *Transparency.* A benefit corporation must issue an annual benefit report on its overall social and environmental performance that uses a recognized third-party standard to assess its performance. The report must be delivered to the shareholders and posted on a public Web site.

See Concept Summary 39.1 for a review of the ways in which corporations are classified.

39–2 Corporate Formation and Powers

Many of today's largest companies started as sole proprietorships or partnerships. They converted to corporate entities as they grew because they needed to obtain additional capital by issuing shares of stock. Incorporating a business is much simpler today than it was twenty years ago, and many states allow businesses to incorporate via the Internet. Here, we examine the process by which a corporation comes into existence.

39–2a Promotional Activities

In the past, preliminary steps were taken to organize and promote a business prior to incorporating. Contracts were made with investors and others on behalf of the future corporation. Today, due to the relative ease of forming a corporation in most states, persons incorporating their business rarely, if ever, engage in preliminary promotional activities.

Nevertheless, businesspersons should understand that they are personally liable for any preincorporation contracts made with investors, accountants, or others on behalf of the future corporation. Personal liability continues until the newly formed corporation assumes liability for the preincorporation contracts through a novation.

39–2b Incorporation Procedures

Each state has its own set of incorporation procedures. Most often, they are listed on the secretary of state's Web site. Generally, however, all incorporators follow several basic steps, discussed next.

Select the State of Incorporation Because state corporate laws differ, individuals seeking to incorporate a business may look for the states that offer the most advantageous tax or other provisions. Many corporations, for instance, have chosen to incorporate in Delaware because it has historically had the least restrictive laws, along with provisions that favor corporate management. For reasons of convenience and cost, though, businesses often choose to incorporate in the state in which the corporation's business will primarily be conducted.

Secure the Corporate Name The choice of a corporate name is subject to state approval to ensure against duplication or deception. Most state statutes require a search to confirm that the chosen corporate name is available. A

Concept Summary 39.1

Classification of Corporations

Domestic, Foreign, and Alien Corporations	• A corporation is referred to as a *domestic corporation* in its home state (the state in which it incorporates). • A corporation is referred to as a *foreign corporation* by any state that is not its home state. • A corporation is referred to as an *alien corporation* if it originates in another country but does business in the United States.
Public and Private Corporations	• A *public corporation* is formed by a government (for instance, a city, town, or public project). • A *private corporation* is formed wholly or in part for private benefit (profit). Most corporations are private corporations.
Nonprofit Corporation	• A *nonprofit corporation* is formed without a profit-making purpose (for example, charitable, educational, and religious organizations and hospitals).
Close Corporation	• A *close corporation* is owned by a family or a relatively small number of individuals. Because the number of shareholders is small and the transfer of shares is usually restricted, the shares are not traded in a public securities market.
S Corporation	• An *S corporation* is a small domestic corporation (must have no more than one hundred shareholders) that, under Subchapter S of the Internal Revenue Code, is given special tax treatment. An S corporation allows shareholders to enjoy the limited legal liability of the corporate form but avoid its double-taxation feature. (Shareholders pay taxes on the income at personal income tax rates, and the S corporation is not taxed separately.)
Professional Corporation	• A *professional corporation* is formed by professionals—such as physicians or lawyers—to obtain the advantages of incorporation. A professional corporation functions like an ordinary corporation but is treated differently in terms of liability. Courts may treat the shareholders like partners with regard to malpractice liability.
Benefit Corporation	• A *benefit corporation* is designed for businesses that want to consider society and the environment in addition to profit. Shareholders have a right to sue the corporation in enforcement proceedings if it fails to benefit the public.

new corporation's name cannot be the same as, or deceptively similar to, the name of an existing corporation doing business within the state. All states require the corporation's name to include the word *Corporation (Corp.), Incorporated (Inc.), Company (Co.),* or *Limited (Ltd.).*[6]

6. Failure to use one of these terms to disclose corporate status may be grounds for holding an individual incorporator liable for corporate contracts under agency law.

Prepare the Articles of Incorporation The primary document needed to incorporate a business is the **articles of incorporation** (for a sample, see Exhibit 39–1). The articles include basic information about the corporation and serve as a primary source of authority for its future organization and business functions. The person or persons who execute (sign) the articles are the *incorporators.*

EXHIBIT 39–1 Sample Articles of Incorporation

ARTICLE I. The name of the corporation is _____ .

ARTICLE II. The period of its duration is _____ (may be a number of years or until a certain date).

ARTICLE III. The purpose (or purposes) for which the corporation is organized is (are) _____

_____

_____ .

ARTICLE IV. The aggregate number of shares that the corporation shall have the authority to issue is _____ with

the par value of _____ dollar(s) each (or without par value).

ARTICLE V. The corporation will not commence business until it has received for the issuance of its shares

consideration of the value of $1,000 (can be any sum not less than $1,000).

ARTICLE VI. The address of the corporation's registered office is _____

and the name of its registered agent at such address is _____

_____ .

ARTICLE VII. The number of initial directors is _____ , and the names and addresses of the directors are

_____

_____

ARTICLE VIII. The names and addresses of the incorporators are

_____   _____   _____

(Name)   (Address)   (Signature)

_____   _____   _____

(Name)   (Address)   (Signature)

_____   _____   _____

(Name)   (Address)   (Signature)

Sworn to on _____ by the above-named incorporators.

       (Date)

_____

            Notary Public

(Notary Seal)

Articles of incorporation vary widely depending on the jurisdiction and the size and type of the corporation. Generally, though, the articles *must* include the following information [RMBCA 2.02]:

1. The name of the corporation.
2. The number of shares of stock the corporation is authorized to issue [RMBCA 2.02(a)]. (Large corporations often also state a par value for each share, such as $0.20 per share, and specify the various types or classes of stock authorized for issuance.)
3. The name and street address of the corporation's initial registered agent and registered office. The registered agent is the person who can receive legal documents (such as orders to appear in court) on behalf of the corporation. The registered office is usually the main corporate office.
4. The name and address of each incorporator.

In addition, the articles *may* set forth other information, such as the names and addresses of the initial members of the board of directors and the duration and purpose of the corporation. A corporation has perpetual existence unless the articles state otherwise. As to the corporation's purpose, a corporation can be formed for any lawful purpose, and the RMBCA does not require the articles to include a specific statement of purpose. Consequently, the articles often include only a general statement of purpose. By not mentioning specifics, the corporation avoids the need for future amendments to the corporate articles [RMBCA 2.02(b)(2)(i), 3.01]. Similarly, the articles do not provide much detail about the firm's operations, which are spelled out in the company's *bylaws* (discussed shortly).

File the Articles with the State Once the articles of incorporation have been prepared and signed, they are sent to the appropriate state official, usually the secretary of state, along with the required filing fee. In most states, the secretary of state then stamps the articles "Filed" and returns a copy of the articles to the incorporators. Once this occurs, the corporation officially exists.

39–2c First Organizational Meeting to Adopt Bylaws

After incorporation, the first organizational meeting must be held. If the articles of incorporation named the initial board of directors, then the directors, by majority vote, call the meeting. If the articles did not name the directors (as is typical), then the incorporators hold the meeting to elect the directors and complete any other business necessary.

Usually, the most important function of this meeting is the adoption of **bylaws,** which are the internal rules of management for the corporation. The bylaws cannot conflict with the state corporation statute or the articles of incorporation [RMBCA 2.06]. Under the RMBCA, the shareholders may amend or repeal the bylaws. The board of directors may also amend or repeal the bylaws, unless the articles of incorporation or provisions of the state corporation statute reserve this power to the shareholders [RMBCA 10.20].

The bylaws typically describe such matters as voting requirements for shareholders, the election of the board of directors, and the methods of replacing directors. Bylaws also frequently outline the manner and time of holding shareholders' and board meetings.

39–2d Improper Incorporation

The procedures for incorporation are very specific. If they are not followed precisely, others may be able to challenge the existence of the corporation. Errors in incorporation procedures can become important when, for instance, a third party who is attempting to enforce a contract or bring a suit for a tort injury learns of them.

De Jure Corporations If a corporation has substantially complied with all conditions precedent to incorporation, the corporation is said to have *de jure* (rightful and lawful) existence. In most states and under RMBCA 2.03(b), the secretary of state's filing of the articles of incorporation is conclusive proof that all mandatory statutory provisions have been met [RMBCA 2.03(b)].

Sometimes, the incorporators fail to comply with all statutory mandates. If the defect is minor, such as an incorrect address listed on the articles of incorporation, most courts will overlook the defect and find that a *de jure* corporation exists.

De Facto Corporations If the defect in formation is substantial, such as a corporation's failure to hold an organizational meeting to adopt bylaws, the outcome will vary depending on the jurisdiction. Some states, including Mississippi, New York, Ohio, and Oklahoma, recognize the common law doctrine of *de facto* corporation.[7] In those states, the courts will treat a corporation as a legal corporation despite a defect in its formation if the following three requirements are met:

1. A state statute exists under which the corporation can be validly incorporated.

---

7. See, for example, *In re Hausman.* 13 N.Y.3d 408. 921 N.E.2d 191. 893 N.Y.S.2d 499 (2009).

2. The parties have made a good faith attempt to comply with the statute.
3. The parties have already undertaken to do business as a corporation.

Many state courts, however, have interpreted their states' version of the RMBCA as abolishing the common law doctrine of *de facto* corporations. These states include Alaska, Arizona, Minnesota, New Mexico, Oregon, South Dakota, Tennessee, Utah, and Washington, as well as the District of Columbia. In those jurisdictions, if there is a substantial defect in complying with the incorporation statute, the corporation does not legally exist, and the incorporators are personally liable.

Corporation by Estoppel Sometimes, a business association holds itself out to others as being a corporation when it has made no attempt to incorporate. In those situations, the firm normally will be estopped (prevented) from denying corporate status in a lawsuit by a third party. The estoppel doctrine most commonly applies when a third party contracts with an entity that claims to be a corporation but has not filed articles of incorporation. It may also apply when a third party contracts with a person claiming to be an agent of a corporation that does not in fact exist.

When justice requires, courts in some states will treat an alleged corporation as if it were an actual corporation for the purpose of determining rights and liabilities in particular circumstances.[8] Recognition of corporate status does not extend beyond the resolution of the problem at hand.

■ **CASE IN POINT 39.4** W.P. Media, Inc., and Alabama MBA, Inc., agreed to form a wireless Internet services company. W.P. Media was to create a wireless network, and Alabama MBA was to contribute the capital. Hugh Brown signed the parties' contract on behalf of Alabama MBA as the chair of its board. At the time, however, Alabama MBA's articles of incorporation had not yet been filed. Brown filed the articles of incorporation the following year.

Later, Brown and Alabama MBA filed a suit alleging that W.P. Media had breached their contract by not building the wireless network. W.P. Media contended that Alabama MBA had not existed as a corporation when the agreement was signed and thus the agreement was void. The Supreme Court of Alabama held that because W.P. Media had treated Alabama MBA as a corporation, W.P. Media was estopped from denying Alabama MBA's corporate existence.[9] ■

39–2e Corporate Powers

When a corporation is created, the express and implied powers necessary to achieve its purpose also come into existence.

Express Powers The express powers of a corporation are found in its articles of incorporation, in the law of the state of incorporation, and in the state and federal constitutions. Corporate bylaws and the resolutions of the corporation's board of directors also establish express powers.

The following order of priority is used if a conflict arises among the various documents involving a corporation:

1. The U.S. Constitution.
2. State constitutions.
3. State statutes.
4. The articles of incorporation.
5. Bylaws.
6. Resolutions of the board of directors.

It is important that the bylaws set forth the specific operating rules of the corporation. State corporation statutes frequently provide default rules that apply if the company's bylaws are silent on an issue.

On occasion, the U.S. government steps in to challenge what a corporation may consider one of its express powers. This chapter's *Global Insight* discusses a dispute between the government and Microsoft Corporation over a demand that the company provide the government with access to e-mail stored in servers on foreign soil.

Implied Powers When a corporation is created, it acquires certain implied powers. Barring express constitutional, statutory, or other prohibitions, the corporation has the implied power to perform all acts reasonably necessary to accomplish its corporate purposes. For this reason, a corporation has the implied power to borrow and lend funds within certain limits and to extend credit to parties with whom it has contracts.

Most often, the president or chief executive officer of the corporation signs the necessary documents on behalf of the corporation. Corporate officers such as these have the implied power to bind the corporation in matters directly connected with the *ordinary* business affairs of the enterprise.

---

8. Some states have expressly rejected the common law theory of corporation by estoppel, finding that it is inconsistent with their statutory law. Other states have abolished only the doctrines of *de facto* and *de jure* corporations. See, for example, *Stone v. Jetmar Properties, LLC*, 733 N.W.2d 480 (Minn.App. 2007).

9. *Brown v. W.P. Media, Inc.*, 17 So.3d 1167 (2009).

GLOBAL INSIGHT — Does Cloud Computing Have a Nationality?

Everyone has heard of "the cloud," and most people use it for the storage of their digital data—photos, e-mails, music, documents, and just about anything else. Not surprisingly, major global digital players like Apple, Amazon, Google, and Microsoft have spent billions to create "clouds" of servers all over the world. In the clouds are stored confidential, organized, and secure data. The revenues generated by the U.S. cloud computing industry exceed $100 billion a year. But is the long-term picture for such revenues in doubt?

Microsoft Battles and the Global Cloud Industry Waits

The U.S. government issued a warrant to Microsoft to produce e-mails related to a narcotics case from a Hotmail account. That account was hosted in a Microsoft cloud location in Ireland. Microsoft refused, but a magistrate judge in the Southern District of New York confirmed the government's right to the Ireland-located e-mails.[a] On appeal to a U.S. district court, Microsoft again lost.[b] Microsoft appealed to the United States Court of Appeals for the Second Circuit and won in 2016.[c]

---

a. *In re Warrant to Search a Certain E-Mail Account Controlled and Maintained by Microsoft Corp.*, 15 F.Supp.3d 466 (S.D.N.Y. 2014).
b. *In re Warrant to Search a Certain E-Mail Account Controlled and Maintained by Microsoft Corp.*, 2014 WL 4629624 (S.D.N.Y. 2014).
c. *In Matter of Warrant to Search a Certain E-Mail Account Controlled and Maintained by Microsoft Corp.*, ___ F.3d ___, 2016 WL 3770056 (2d Cir. 2016).

Microsoft maintained that "the power to embark on unilateral law enforcement incursions into a foreign sovereign country—directly or indirectly—has profound policy consequences. Worse still, it threatens the privacy of U.S. citizens." According to Microsoft's deputy general counsel, David Howard, "The U.S. government doesn't have the power to search a home in another country, nor should it have the power search the content of e-mails stored overseas."

A number of organizations—including the ACLU, Apple, eBay, and Fox News—apparently agreed with Microsoft. The federal appellate court was persuaded that the warrant could not be enforced against Microsoft extraterritorially.

Impact on the Industry

More was at stake in this case than the issues Microsoft identified. If Microsoft had lost, some industry experts predicted that U.S. technology companies would lose up to $35 billion a year from their cloud storage business. Foreign corporations and individuals would no longer trust U.S. companies to keep their data secret.

Critical Thinking *The law underlying the case against Microsoft is the Electronic Communications Privacy Act, which was enacted three years before the invention of the World Wide Web. Should that law still apply today? Why or why not?*

There is a limit to what a corporate officer can do, though. A corporate officer does not have the authority to bind the corporation to an action that will greatly affect the corporate purpose or undertaking, such as the sale of substantial corporate assets.

Ultra Vires Doctrine The term *ultra vires* means "beyond the power." In corporate law, acts of a corporation that are beyond its express or implied powers are *ultra vires* acts. In the past, most cases dealing with *ultra vires* acts involved contracts made for unauthorized purposes. Now, because the articles of incorporation of most private corporations do not state a specific purpose, the *ultra vires* doctrine has declined in importance.

Today, cases that allege *ultra vires* acts usually involve nonprofit corporations or municipal (public) corporations. ■ **CASE IN POINT 39.5** Four men formed a nonprofit corporation to create the Armenian Genocide Museum

& Memorial (AGM&M). The bylaws appointed them as trustees (similar to corporate directors) for life. One of the trustees, Gerard L. Cafesjian, became the chair and president of AGM&M. Eventually, the relationship among the trustees deteriorated, and Cafesjian resigned.

The corporation then brought a suit claiming that Cafesjian had engaged in numerous *ultra vires* acts, self-dealing, and mismanagement. Although the bylaws required an 80 percent affirmative vote of the trustees to take action, Cafesjian had taken many actions without the board's approval. He had also entered into contracts for real estate transactions in which he had a personal interest. Because Cafesjian had taken actions that exceeded his authority and had failed to follow rules set forth in the bylaws, the court ruled that the corporation could go forward with its suit.[10] ■

---

10. *Armenian Assembly of America, Inc. v. Cafesjian*, 692 F.Supp.2d 20 (D.C. Cir. 2010).

Remedies for *Ultra Vires* Acts   Under Section 3.04 of the RMBCA, shareholders can seek an injunction from a court to prevent (or stop) the corporation from engaging in *ultra vires* acts. The attorney general in the state of incorporation can also bring an action to obtain an injunction against the *ultra vires* transactions or to seek dissolution of the corporation. The corporation or its shareholders (on behalf of the corporation) can seek damages from the officers and directors who were responsible for the *ultra vires* acts.

39–3 Piercing the Corporate Veil

Occasionally, the owners use a corporate entity to perpetrate a fraud, circumvent the law, or in some other way accomplish an illegitimate objective. In these situations, the courts will ignore the corporate structure by **piercing the corporate veil** and exposing the shareholders to personal liability [RMBCA 2.04].

Generally, courts pierce the veil when the corporate privilege is abused for personal benefit or when the corporate business is treated so carelessly that it is indistinguishable from that of a controlling shareholder. When the facts show that great injustice would result from a shareholder's use of a corporation to avoid individual responsibility, a court will look behind the corporate structure to the individual shareholders.

39–3a Factors That Lead Courts to Pierce the Corporate Veil

The following are some of the factors that frequently cause the courts to pierce the corporate veil:

1. A party is tricked or misled into dealing with the corporation rather than the individual.
2. The corporation is set up never to make a profit or always to be insolvent. Alternatively, it is too thinly capitalized—that is, it has insufficient capital at the time it is formed to meet its prospective debts or potential liabilities.
3. The corporation is formed to evade an existing legal obligation.
4. Statutory corporate formalities, such as holding required corporation meetings, are not followed.
5. Personal and corporate interests are mixed together, or **commingled,** to such an extent that the corporation has no separate identity.

State corporation codes usually do not prohibit a shareholder from lending funds to her or his corporation. Courts will scrutinize such a transaction closely if the loan comes from an officer, director, or majority shareholder, however. Loans from persons who control the corporation must be made in good faith and for fair value.

In the following case, the court looked at various factors in deciding whether to pierce the corporate veil.

Case 39.3

Dog House Investments, LLC v. Teal Properties, Inc.

Court of Appeals of Tennessee, 448 S.W.3d 905 (2014).

Background and Facts   Dog House Investments, LLC, operated a dog "camp" in Nashville, Tennessee. Dog House leased the property from Teal Properties, Inc., which was owned by Jerry Teal, its sole shareholder. Under the lease, the landlord promised to repair damage from fire or other causes that rendered the property "untenantable" (unusable). Following a flood, Dog House notified Jerry that the property was untenantable. Jerry assured Dog House that the flood damage was covered by insurance but took no steps to restore the property. The parties then agreed that Dog House would undertake the repairs and be reimbursed by Teal Properties.

Dog House spent $39,000 to repair the damage and submitted invoices for reimbursement. Teal Properties recovered $40,000 from its insurance company but did not pay Dog House. Close to bankruptcy, Dog House filed a suit in a Tennessee state court against Teal Properties and Jerry. The court held Jerry personally liable for the repair costs. Jerry appealed.

In the Language of the Court
David R. FARMER, J. [Judge]
   * * * *

It is well-settled that courts may pierce the corporate veil and attribute the actions of a corporation to its shareholders when appropriate. *A party seeking to pierce the corporate veil bears the burden of*

Case 39.3 Continued

demonstrating that the separate corporate entity is a sham or dummy or that disregarding the separate corporate entity is necessary to accomplish justice. [Emphasis added.] When determining whether piercing the corporate veil is appropriate, the court must consider whether the corporate entity has been used to work a fraud or injustice in contravention of public policy and also:

(1) whether there was a failure to collect paid-in capital; (2) whether the corporation was grossly undercapitalized; (3) the nonissuance of stock certificates; (4) the sole ownership of stock by one individual; (5) the use of the same office or business location; (6) the employment of the same employees or attorneys; (7) the use of the corporation as an instrumentality or business conduit for an individual or another corporation; (8) the diversion of corporate assets by or to a stockholder or other entity to the detriment of creditors, or the manipulation of assets and liabilities in another; (9) the use of the corporation as a subterfuge in illegal transactions; (10) the formation and use of the corporation to transfer to it the existing liability of another person or entity; and (11) the failure to maintain arms length relationships among related entities.

No single factor is conclusive and not every factor must exist to pierce the corporate veil. The question depends on the specific facts and circumstances of the case. The equities, however, must substantially favor the party requesting the court to disregard the corporate status. The presumption of the corporation's separate identity should be set aside only with great caution and not precipitately [hastily]. [Emphasis added.]

In this case, Mr. Teal denied personal liability but admitted * * * that he owned the property leased by Dog House in Nashville. The trial court found that Teal Properties owns no property, has no assets, and has no cash except that which is deposited by Mr. Jerry Teal when he has the opportunity to do so; that Teal Properties receives rents and immediately pays it out to pay Mr. Teal's financial obligations; that Mr. Teal is the sole stockholder of Teal Properties and owns the corporation; and that Teal Properties has no purpose other than to collect the rent on properties owned by Mr. Teal. The trial court also found that Mr. Teal does not receive a salary from Teal Properties but utilizes its assets, including the flood insurance proceeds at issue in this case, to pay Mr. Teal's personal expenses and his personal obligations. The trial court found that Mr. Teal did not maintain an arms-length relationship with the corporation, and that it was, in fact, his alter ego. Mr. Teal does not dispute these findings * * *, but asserts that "there is no proof that Teal Properties is a sham or dummy corporation * * *." We discern no error on the part of the trial court and affirm on this issue.

Decision and Remedy *A state intermediate appellate court affirmed the lower court's decision. Teal Properties owned no property and had no assets. It received rent, but paid it immediately to Jerry Teal. "Mr. Teal did not maintain an arms-length relationship with the corporation, and . . . it was, in fact, his alter ego."*

Critical Thinking
- **Ethical** *The failure of Teal Properties and Jerry to reimburse the tenant, Dog House, for the repair costs placed Dog House in a dire financial situation. Does this consequence make the landlord's conduct unethical? Discuss.*
- **Legal Environment** *The trial court also concluded, and the appellate court affirmed, that Teal Properties had breached its contract with Dog House. What was the contract? How was it breached?*

39–3b A Potential Problem for Close Corporations

The potential for corporate assets to be used for personal benefit is especially great in a close corporation. In such a corporation, the separate status of the corporate entity and the shareholders (often family members) must be carefully preserved. Practices that invite trouble for a close corporation include the commingling of corporate and personal funds and the shareholders' continuous personal use of corporate property (for instance, vehicles).

Typically, courts are reluctant to hold shareholders in close corporations personally liable for corporate obligations unless there is some evidence of fraud or wrongdoing. ■ **CASE IN POINT 39.6** Pip, Jimmy, and Theodore Brennan are brothers and shareholders of Brennan's, Inc., which owns and operates New Orleans's famous Brennan's Restaurant. As a close corporation, Brennan's, Inc., did not hold formal corporate meetings with agendas and minutes, but it did maintain corporate books, hold corporate bank accounts, and file corporate tax returns.

The Brennan brothers retained attorney Edward Colbert to represent them in a family matter, and the attorney's bills were sent to the restaurant and paid from the corporate account. Later, when Brennan's, Inc., sued Colbert for malpractice, Colbert argued that the court should pierce the corporate veil because the Brennan brothers did not observe corporate formalities. The court refused to do so, however, because there was no evidence of fraud, malfeasance, or other wrongdoing by the Brennan brothers. There is no requirement for small, close corporations to operate with the formality usually expected of larger corporations.[11] ∎

39–3c The Alter-Ego Theory

Sometimes, courts pierce the corporate veil under the theory that the corporation was not operated as a separate entity. Rather, it was just another side (the *alter ego*) of the individual or group that actually controlled the corporation. This is called the alter-ego theory.

The alter-ego theory is applied when a corporation is so dominated and controlled by an individual (or group) that the separate identities of the person (or group) and the corporation are no longer distinct. Courts use the alter-ego theory to avoid injustice or fraud that would result if wrongdoers were allowed to hide behind the protection of limited liability.

---

11. *Brennan's, Inc. v. Colbert,* 85 So.3d 787 (La.App.4th Cir. 2012).

■ **CASE IN POINT 39.7**   Steiner Electric Company (Steiner) is an Illinois corporation that sells electrical products. Steiner sold goods to Delta Equipment Company and Sackett Systems, Inc., on credit. Both Delta and Sackett were owned and controlled by a single shareholder—Leonard J. Maniscalco. Steiner was not fully paid for the products it sold on credit to Delta and Sackett. Eventually, Steiner sued Delta and won a default judgment, but by that time, Delta had been dissolved. Steiner then asked a state court to pierce the corporate veil and hold Maniscalco liable for the debts of the two companies, claiming the companies were merely Maniscalco's alter egos.

The court agreed and held Maniscalco liable. Delta and Sackett were inadequately capitalized, transactions were not properly documented, funds were commingled, and corporate formalities were not observed. Maniscalco had consistently treated both companies in such a manner that they were, in practice, his alter egos.[12] ∎

39–4 Corporate Financing

Part of the process of corporate formation involves financing. Corporations normally are financed by the issuance and sale of corporate securities. **Securities**—stocks and bonds—evidence an ownership interest in a corporation or a promise of repayment of debt by a corporation. The ways in which stocks and bonds differ are summarized in Exhibit 39–2.

---

12. *Steiner Electric Co. v. Maniscalco,* ___ N.E.3d ___, 2016 IL App (1st) 132023 (2016).

EXHIBIT 39–2   How Do Stocks and Bonds Differ?

STOCKS	BONDS
1. Stocks represent ownership.	1. Bonds represent debt.
2. Stocks (common) do not have a fixed dividend rate.	2. Interest on bonds must always be paid, whether or not any profit is earned.
3. Stockholders can elect the board of directors, which controls the corporation.	3. Bondholders usually have no voice in or control over management of the corporation.
4. Stocks do not have a maturity date. The corporation usually does not repay the stockholder.	4. Bonds have a maturity date, when the corporation is to repay the bondholder the face value of the bond.
5. All corporations issue or offer to sell stocks. This is the usual definition of a corporation.	5. Corporations do not necessarily issue bonds.
6. Stockholders have a claim against the property and income of the corporation after all creditors' claims have been met.	6. Bondholders have a claim against the property and income of the corporation that must be met before the claims of stockholders.

39–4a Bonds

Bonds are *debt securities*, which represent the borrowing of funds. Bonds are issued by business firms and by governments at all levels as evidence of funds they are borrowing from investors.

Bonds normally have a designated *maturity date*—the date when the principal, or face amount, of the bond is returned to the bondholder. Bondholders also receive fixed-dollar interest payments, usually semiannually, during the period of time prior to maturity. For that reason, they are sometimes referred to as *fixed-income securities*. Because debt financing represents a legal obligation of the corporation, various features and terms of a particular bond issue are specified in a lending agreement.

Of course, not all debt is in the form of bonds. For instance, some debt is in the form of accounts payable and notes payable, which typically are short-term debts. Bonds are simply a way for the corporation to split up its long-term debt so that it can be more easily marketed.

39–4b Stocks

Issuing stocks is another way for corporations to obtain financing [RMBCA 6.01]. **Stocks,** or *equity securities,* represent the purchase of ownership in the business firm. The two major types are *common stock* and *preferred stock.*

Common Stock The true ownership of a corporation is represented by **common stock.** Common stock provides an interest in the corporation with regard to (1) control, (2) earnings, and (3) net assets. A shareholder's interest is generally proportionate to the number of shares he or she owns out of the total number of shares issued. Any person who purchases common stock acquires voting rights—one vote per share held.

An issuing firm is not obligated to return a principal amount per share to each holder of its common stock, nor does the firm have to guarantee a dividend. Indeed, some corporations never pay dividends. Holders of common stock are investors who assume a *residual* position in the overall financial structure of a business. They benefit when the market price of the stock increases. In terms of receiving payment for their investments, they are last in line.

Preferred Stock **Preferred stock** is an equity security with *preferences*. Usually, this means that holders of preferred stock have priority over holders of common stock as to dividends and payment on dissolution of the

corporation. The preferences must be stated in the articles of incorporation. Holders of preferred stock may or may not have the right to vote.

Like other equity securities, preferred shares have no fixed maturity date on which the firm must pay them off. Although firms occasionally buy back preferred stock, they are not legally obligated to do so.

Holders of preferred stock have assumed a more cautious position than holders of common stock. They have a stronger position than common shareholders with respect to dividends and claims on assets, but they will not share in the full prosperity of the firm if it grows successfully over time. Preferred stockholders do receive fixed dividends periodically, however, and they may benefit to some extent from changes in the market price of the shares.

Exhibit 39–3 offers a summary of the types of stocks issued by corporations.

39–4c Venture Capital and Private Equity Capital

Corporations traditionally obtain financing by issuing and selling securities (stocks and bonds) in the capital market. Many investors do not want to purchase stock in a business that lacks a track record, however, and banks generally are reluctant to extend loans to high-risk enterprises. Therefore, to obtain funds, many entrepreneurs seek alternative financing.

Venture Capital Start-up businesses and high-risk enterprises often obtain venture capital financing. **Venture capital** is capital provided to new businesses by professional, outside investors (*venture capitalists,* usually groups of wealthy investors and securities firms). Venture capital investments are high risk—the investors must be willing to lose all of their invested funds—but offer the potential for well-above-average returns in the future.

To obtain venture capital financing, the start-up business typically gives up a share of its ownership to the venture capitalists. In addition to funding, venture capitalists may provide managerial and technical expertise, and they nearly always are given some control over the new company's decisions. Many Internet-based companies, such as Google and Amazon, were initially financed by venture capital.

Private Equity Capital Private equity firms pool funds from wealthy investors and use this **private equity capital** to invest in existing corporations. Usually, a

EXHIBIT 39–3 Common and Preferred Stocks

COMMON STOCK

Voting shares that represent ownership interest in a corporation.

Common stock has the lowest priority with respect to payment of dividends and distribution of assets on the corporation's dissolution.

PREFERRED STOCK

Stock that has priority over common stock shares as to payment of dividends and distribution of assets on dissolution.

Dividend payments are usually a fixed percentage of the face value of the share. Preferred shares may or may not be voting shares.

CUMULATIVE PREFERRED STOCK

Preferred shares on which required dividends not paid in a given year must be paid in a subsequent year before any common-stock dividends can be paid.

PARTICIPATING PREFERRED STOCK

Preferred shares entitling the owner to receive the preferred-stock dividend and additional dividends after the corporation has paid dividends on common stock.

CONVERTIBLE PREFERRED STOCK

Preferred shares that, under certain conditions, can be converted into a specified number of common shares either in the issuing corporation or, sometimes, in another corporation.

REDEEMABLE PREFERRED STOCK

Preferred shares issued with the express condition that the issuing corporation has the right to repurchase the shares as specified. (Sometimes referred to as callable preferred stock.)

private equity firm buys an entire corporation and then reorganizes it. Sometimes, divisions of the purchased company are sold off to pay down debt.

Ultimately, the private equity firm may sell shares in the reorganized (and perhaps more profitable) company to the public in an *initial public offering (IPO)*. Then the private equity firm can make profits by selling its shares in the company to the public.

39–4d Crowdfunding

Start-up businesses can also attempt to obtain financing through *crowdfunding*. **Crowdfunding** is a cooperative activity in which people network and pool funds and other resources via the Internet to assist a cause or invest in a venture. Sometimes, crowdfunding is used to raise funds for charitable purposes, such as disaster relief, but increasingly it is being used to finance budding entrepreneurs.

In 2016, new Securities and Exchange Commission (SEC) rules went into effect to allow companies to offer and sell securities through crowdfunding. The rules removed a decades-old ban on public solicitation for private investments, which means that companies can advertise investment opportunities to the general public. According to the SEC, the new rules are intended to help smaller companies raise capital while providing investors with additional protections. Companies are required to make specific disclosures and are limited to raising $1 million a year through crowdfunding.

Reviewing: Corporate Formation and Financing

William Sharp was the sole shareholder and manager of Chickasaw Club, Inc., an S corporation that operated a popular nightclub of the same name in Columbus, Georgia. Sharp maintained a corporate checking account but paid the club's employees, suppliers, and entertainers in cash out of the club's proceeds. Sharp owned the property on which the club was located. He rented it to the club but made mortgage payments out of the club's proceeds and often paid other personal expenses with Chickasaw corporate funds.

At 12:45 A.M. on July 31, eighteen-year-old Aubrey Lynn Pursley, who was already intoxicated, entered the Chickasaw Club. A city ordinance prohibited individuals under the age of twenty-one from entering nightclubs, but Chickasaw employees did not check Pursley's identification to verify her age. Pursley drank more alcohol at Chickasaw and was visibly intoxicated when she left the club at 3:00 A.M. with a beer in her hand. Shortly afterward, Pursley lost control of her car, struck a tree, and was killed. Joseph Dancause, Pursley's stepfather, filed a tort lawsuit in a Georgia state court against Chickasaw Club, Inc., and William Sharp, seeking damages. Using the information presented in the chapter, answer the following questions.

1. Under what theory might the court in this case make an exception to the limited liability of shareholders and hold Sharp personally liable for the damages? What factors would be relevant to the court's decision?
2. Suppose that Chickasaw's articles of incorporation failed to describe the corporation's purpose or management structure, as required by state law. Would the court be likely to rule that Sharp is personally liable to Dancause on that basis? Why or why not?
3. Suppose that the club extended credit to its regular patrons, although neither the articles of incorporation nor the corporate bylaws authorized this practice. Would the corporation likely have the power to engage in this activity? Explain.
4. How would the court classify the Chickasaw Club corporation—domestic or foreign, public or private? Why?

Debate This . . . *The sole shareholder of an S corporation should not be able to avoid liability for the torts of her or his employees.*

Terms and Concepts

alien corporation 743
articles of incorporation 750
benefit corporation 748
bond 757
bylaws 751
close corporation 746
commingle 754
common stock 757
crowdfunding 758

dividends 742
domestic corporation 742
foreign corporation 743
holding company 742
pierce the corporate veil 754
preferred stock 757
private equity capital 757
public corporation 744

publicly held corporation 745
retained earnings 742
S corporation 747
securities 756
shareholder agreement 747
stock 757
ultra vires 753
venture capital 757

Issue Spotters

1. Northwest Brands, Inc., is a small business incorporated in Minnesota. Its one class of stock is owned by twelve members of a single family. Ordinarily, corporate income is taxed at the corporate and shareholder levels. Is there a way for Northwest Brands to avoid this double taxation? Explain your answer. (See *The Nature and Classification of Corporations*.)

2. The incorporators of Consumer Investments, Inc., want their new corporation to have the authority to transact nearly any conceivable type of business. Can they grant this authority to their firm? If so, how? If not, why not? (See *Piercing the Corporate Veil.*)

• **Check your answers to the Issue Spotters against the answers provided in Appendix D at the end of this text.**

Business Scenarios

39–1. Preincorporation. Cummings, Okawa, and Taft are recent college graduates who want to form a corporation to manufacture and sell digital tablets. Peterson tells them he will set in motion the formation of their corporation. First, Peterson makes a contract with Owens for the purchase of a piece of land for $20,000. Owens does not know of the prospective corporate formation at the time the contract is signed. Second, Peterson makes a contract with Babcock to build a small plant on the property being purchased. Babcock's contract is conditional on the corporation's formation. Peterson secures all necessary subscription agreements and capitalization, and he files the articles of incorporation. (See *Corporate Formation.*)

(a) Discuss whether the newly formed corporation, Peterson, or both are liable on the contracts with Owens and Babcock.

(b) Discuss whether the corporation is automatically liable to Babcock on formation.

39–2. *Ultra Vires* Doctrine. Oya Paka and two business associates formed a corporation called Paka Corp. for the purpose of selling computer services. Oya, who owned 50 percent of the corporate shares, served as the corporation's president. Oya wished to obtain a personal loan from her bank for $250,000, but the bank required the note to be cosigned by a third party. Oya cosigned the note in the name of the corporation. Later, Oya defaulted on the note, and the bank sued the corporation for payment. The corporation asserted, as a defense, that Oya had exceeded her authority when she cosigned the note on behalf of the corporation. Had she? Explain. (See *Corporate Formation and Powers.*)

Business Case Problems

39–3. Spotlight on Smart Inventions—Piercing the Corporate Veil. Thomas Persson and Jon Nokes founded Smart Inventions, Inc., to market household consumer products. The success of their first product, the Smart Mop, continued with later products, which were sold through infomercials and other means. Persson and Nokes were the firm's officers and equal shareholders. Persson was responsible for product development, and Nokes was in charge of day-to-day operations. In time, they became dissatisfied with each other's efforts. Nokes represented the firm as financially "dying," "in a grim state, . . . worse than ever," and offered to buy all of Persson's shares for $1.6 million. Persson accepted.

On the day that they signed the agreement to transfer the shares, Smart Inventions began marketing a new product—the Tap Light. It was an instant success, generating millions of dollars in revenues. In negotiating with Persson, Nokes had intentionally kept the Tap Light a secret. Persson sued Smart Inventions, asserting fraud and other claims. Under what principle might Smart Inventions be liable for Nokes's fraud? Is Smart Inventions liable in this case? Explain. [*Persson v. Smart Inventions, Inc.,* 125 Cal.App.4th 1141, 23 Cal. Rptr.3d 335 (2 Dist. 2005)] (See *Piercing the Corporate Veil.*)

39–4. Piercing the Corporate Veil. Smith Services, Inc., a trucking business owned by Tony Smith, charged its fuel purchases to an account at Laker Express. When Smith Services was not paid on several contracts, it ceased doing business and was dissolved. Smith continued to provide trucking services, however, as a sole proprietor. Laker Express sought to recover Smith Services' unpaid fuel charges, which amounted to about $35,000, from Smith. He argued that he was not personally liable for a corporate debt. Should the court pierce the corporate veil? Explain. [*Bear, Inc. v. Smith,* 303 S.W.3d 137 (Ky.App. 2010)] (See *Piercing the Corporate Veil.*)

39–5. Close Corporations. Mark Burnett and Kamran Pourgol were the only shareholders in a corporation that built and sold a house. When the buyers discovered that the house exceeded the amount of square footage allowed by the building permit, Pourgol agreed to renovate the house to conform to the permit. No work was done, however, and Burnett filed a suit against Pourgol. Burnett claimed that, without his knowledge, Pourgol had submitted incorrect plans to obtain the building permit, misrepresented the extent of the renovation, and failed to fix the house. Was Pourgol guilty of misconduct? If so, how might it have been avoided? Discuss. [*Burnett v. Pourgol,* 83 A.D.3d 756, 921 N.Y.S.2d 280 (2 Dept. 2011)] (See *Piercing the Corporate Veil.*)

39–6. Piercing the Corporate Veil. In 1997, Leon Greenblatt, Andrew Jahelka, and Richard Nichols incorporated Loop Corp. with only $1,000 of capital. Three years later, Banco Panamericano, Inc., which was run entirely by Greenblatt and owned by a Greenblatt family trust, extended a large line of credit to Loop. Loop's subsidiaries participated in the credit, giving $3 million to Loop while acquiring a security interest in Loop itself. Loop then opened an account with Wachovia Securities, LLC, to buy stock shares using credit provided by Wachovia. When the stock values plummeted, Loop owed Wachovia $1.89 million. Loop also defaulted on its loan from Banco, but Banco agreed to lend Loop millions of dollars more.

Rather than repay Wachovia with the influx of funds, Loop gave the funds to closely related entities and "compensated" Nichols and Jahelka without issuing any W-2 forms (forms reporting compensation to the Internal Revenue Service). Loop made loans to other related entities and shared office space, equipment, and telephone and fax numbers with related entities. Loop also moved employees among related entities, failed to file its tax returns on time (and sometimes did not file them at all), and failed to follow its own bylaws. In a lawsuit brought by Wachovia, can the court hold Greenblatt, Jahelka, and Nichols personally liable by piercing the corporate veil? Why or why not? [*Wachovia Securities, LLC v. Banco Panamericano, Inc.,* 674 F.3d 743 (9th Cir. 2012)] (See *Piercing the Corporate Veil.*)

39–7. Business Case Problem with Sample Answer—Piercing the Corporate Veil.

 Scott Snapp contracted with Castlebrook Builders, Inc., which was owned by Stephen Kappeler, to remodel a house. Kappeler estimated that the remodeling would cost around $500,000. Eventually, however, Snapp paid Kappeler more than $1.3 million. Snapp filed a suit in an Ohio state court against Castlebrook, alleging breach of contract and fraud, among other things. During the trial, it was revealed that Castlebrook had issued no shares of stock and that personal and corporate funds had been commingled. The minutes of the corporate meetings all looked exactly the same. In addition, Kappeler could not provide an accounting for the Snapp project. In particular, he could not explain evidence of double and triple billing nor demonstrate that the amount Snapp paid had actually been spent on the remodeling project. Are these sufficient grounds to pierce the corporate veil? Explain. [*Snapp v. Castlebrook Builders, Inc.,* 2014 -Ohio- 163, 7 N.E.3d 574 (2014)] (See *Corporate Formation and Powers.*)

- **For a sample answer to Problem 39–7, go to Appendix E at the end of this text.**

39–8. Torts.

Jennifer Hoffman took her cell phone to a store owned by R&K Trading, Inc., for repairs. Later, Hoffman filed a suit in a New York state court against R&K, Verizon Wireless, Inc., and others. Hoffman sought to recover damages for a variety of torts, including infliction of emotional distress and negligent hiring and supervision. She alleged that an R&K employee, Keith Press, had examined her phone in a back room, accessed private photos of her stored on her phone, and disseminated the photos to the public. Hoffman testified that "after the incident, she learned from another R&K employee that personal information and pictures had been removed from the phones of other customers." Can R&K be held liable for the torts of its employees? Explain. [*Hoffman v. Verizon Wireless, Inc.,* 5 N.Y.S.3d 123, 125 A.D.3d 806 (2015)] (See *The Nature and Classification of Corporations.*)

39–9. A Question of Ethics—Piercing the Corporate Veil.

 In New York City, 2406-12 Amsterdam Associates LLC brought an action in a New York state court against Alianza Dominicana and Alianza LLC to recover unpaid rent. The plaintiff asserted cause to pierce the corporate veil, alleging that Alianza Dominicana had made promises to pay its rent while discreetly forming Alianza LLC to avoid liability for it. According to 2406-12, Alianza LLC was 90 percent owned by Alianza Dominicana, had no employees, and had no function but to hold Alianza Dominicana's assets away from its creditors. The defendants filed a motion to dismiss the plaintiff's claim. [2406-12 Amsterdam Associates, LLC v. Alianza, LLC, *136 A.D.3d 512, 25 N.Y.S.2d 167 (1 Dept. 2016)] (See *Piercing the Corporate Veil.*)

(a) Assuming that 2406-12's allegations are true, are there sufficient grounds to pierce Alianza LLC's corporate veil? Discuss.

(b) Suppose that the parties to this dispute were small, close corporations. How might that circumstance affect the result in this case?

Legal Reasoning Group Activity

39–10. Corporate versus LLC Form of Business.

The limited liability company (LLC) may be the best organizational form for most businesses. For a significant number of firms, however, the corporate form or some other form of organization may be better. (See *The Nature and Classification of Corporations.*)

(a) The first group will outline several reasons why a firm might be better off as a corporation than as an LLC.

(b) The second group will discuss the differences between corporations and LLCs in terms of their management structures.

CHAPTER 40

Corporate Directors, Officers, and Shareholders

A corporation joins together the efforts and resources of a large number of individuals for the purpose of producing greater returns than those persons could have obtained individually. Corporate directors, officers, and shareholders all play different roles within the corporate entity.

Sometimes, actions that may benefit the corporation as a whole do not coincide with the separate interests of the individuals making up the corporation. In such situations, it is important to know the rights and duties of all participants in the corporate enterprise. This chapter focuses on these rights and duties and the ways in which conflicts among corporate participants are resolved.

40–1 Role of Directors and Officers

The board of directors is the ultimate authority in every corporation. Directors have responsibility for all policy-making decisions necessary to the management of all corporate affairs. Additionally, the directors must act as a body in carrying out routine corporate business. The board selects and removes the corporate officers, determines the capital structure of the corporation, and declares dividends. Each director has one vote, and customarily the majority rules. The general areas of responsibility of the board of directors are shown in Exhibit 40–1.

Directors are sometimes inappropriately characterized as *agents* because they act on behalf of the corporation. No *individual* director, however, can act as an agent to bind the corporation. As a group, directors collectively control the corporation in a way that no agent is able to control a principal. In addition, although directors occupy positions of trust and control over the corporation, they are not *trustees*, because they do not hold title to property for the use and benefit of others.

Few qualifications are required for directors. Only a handful of states impose minimum age and residency requirements. A director may be a shareholder, but that is not necessary (unless the articles of incorporation or bylaws require ownership interest).

40–1a Election of Directors

Subject to statutory limitations, the number of directors is set forth in the corporation's articles or bylaws.

Historically, the minimum number of directors has been three, but today many states permit fewer. Normally, the incorporators appoint the first board of directors at the time the corporation is created, or the directors are named in the articles of incorporation. The initial board serves until the first annual shareholders' meeting. Subsequent directors are elected by a majority vote of the shareholders.

A director usually serves for a term of one year—from annual meeting to annual meeting. Most state statutes permit longer and staggered terms. A common practice is to elect one-third of the board members each year for a three-year term. In this way, there is greater management continuity.

Removal of Directors A director can be removed *for cause*—that is, for failing to perform a required duty—either as specified in the articles or bylaws or by shareholder action. The board of directors may also have the power to remove a director for cause, subject to shareholder review. In most states, a director cannot be removed without cause unless the shareholders reserved the right to do so at the time of election.

Vacancies on the Board Vacancies occur on the board if a director dies or resigns or when a new position is created through amendment of the articles or bylaws. In these situations, either the shareholders or the board itself can fill the vacant position, depending on state law or on the provisions of the bylaws. Often, for instance, an election is held and shareholders vote to fill the vacancy.

EXHIBIT 40–1 Directors' Management Responsibilities

Authorize Major Corporate Policy Decisions

Examples:
- Oversee major contract negotiations and management-labor negotiations.
- Initiate negotiations on the sale or lease of corporate assets outside the regular course of business.
- Decide whether to pursue new product lines or business opportunities.

Make Executive-Level Personnel Decisions

Examples:
- Engage in selection of officers and determine their appropriate total compensation, which may include stock options.
- Supervise managerial employees and make decisions regarding their termination.

Make Financial Decisions

Examples:
- Make decisions regarding the issuance of authorized shares and bonds.
- Decide when to declare dividends to be paid to shareholders.

Note that even when an election is authorized, a court can invalidate the results if the directors have attempted to manipulate the election in order to reduce the shareholders' influence.

40–1b Compensation of Directors

In the past, corporate directors were rarely compensated. Today, directors are often paid at least nominal sums. In large corporations, they may receive more substantial compensation because of the time, work, effort, and especially risk involved.

Most states permit the corporate articles or bylaws to authorize compensation for directors. In fact, the Revised Model Business Corporation Act (RMBCA) states that unless the articles or bylaws provide otherwise, the board itself may set the directors' compensation [RMBCA 8.11]. Directors also receive indirect benefits, such as business contacts and prestige, and other rewards, such as stock options.

In many corporations, directors are also chief corporate officers (such as president or chief executive officer) and receive compensation in their managerial positions. A director who is also an officer of the corporation is referred to as an **inside director,** whereas a director who does not hold a management position is an **outside director.** Typically, a corporation's board of directors includes both inside and outside directors.

40–1c Board of Directors' Meetings

The board of directors conducts business by holding formal meetings with recorded minutes. The dates of regular meetings are usually established in the articles or bylaws or by board resolution, and ordinarily no further notice is required. Special meetings can be called as well, with notice sent to all directors.

Most states allow directors to participate in board of directors' meetings from remote locations. Directors can participate via telephone, Web conferencing, or Skype, provided that all the directors can simultaneously hear each other during the meeting [RMBCA 8.20].

Quorum of Directors Unless the articles of incorporation or bylaws specify a greater number, a majority of the board of directors normally constitutes a *quorum* [RMBCA 8.24]. (A **quorum** is the minimum number of members of a body of officials or other group that must be present for business to be validly transacted.) Some state statutes specifically allow corporations to set a quorum at less than a majority but not less than one-third of the directors.[1]

Voting Once a quorum is present, the directors transact business and vote on issues affecting the corporation.

---

1. See, for example, Delaware Code Annotated Title 8, Section 141(b); and New York Business Corporation Law Section 707.

Each director present at the meeting has one vote.[2] Ordinary matters generally require a simple majority vote, but certain extraordinary issues may require a greater-than-majority vote.

40–1d Committees of the Board of Directors

When a board of directors has a large number of members and must deal with myriad complex business issues, meetings can become unwieldy. Therefore, the boards of large, publicly held corporations typically create committees of directors and delegate certain tasks to these committees. By focusing on specific subjects, committees can increase the efficiency of the board.

Two common types of committees are the *executive committee* and the *audit committee*. An executive committee handles interim management decisions between board meetings. It is limited to dealing with ordinary business matters and does not have the power to declare dividends, amend the bylaws, or authorize the issuance of stock. The audit committee is responsible for the selection, compensation, and oversight of the independent public accountants that audit the firm's financial records. *The Sarbanes-Oxley Act requires all publicly held corporations to have an audit committee.*

40–1e Rights of Directors

A corporate director must have certain rights to function properly in that position, including the rights of participation, inspection, and indemnification.

Right to Participation The *right to participation* means that directors are entitled to participate in all board of directors' meetings and have a right to be notified of these meetings. Because the dates of regular board meetings are usually specified in the bylaws, no notice of these meetings is required. If special meetings are called, however, notice is required unless waived by the director [RMBCA 8.23].

Right of Inspection A director also has a *right of inspection*, which means that each director can access the corporation's books and records, facilities, and premises. Inspection rights are essential for directors to make informed decisions and to exercise the necessary supervision over corporate officers and employees. This right of inspection is almost absolute and cannot be restricted (by the articles, bylaws, or any act of the board of directors).

■ **CASE IN POINT 40.1** NavLink, Inc., a Delaware corporation, provides high-end data management for customers and governments in Saudi Arabia, Qatar, Lebanon, and the United Arab Emirates. NavLink's co-founders, George Chammas and Laurent Delifer, served on its board of directors.

Chammas and Delifer were concerned about the company's 2015 annual budget and three-year operating plan. Despite repeated requests, Chammas was never given the meeting minutes from several board meetings in 2015. Chammas and Delifer believed that the other directors were withholding information and holding secret "pre-board meetings" at which plans and decisions were being made without them. They filed suit in a Delaware state court seeking inspection rights.

The court ordered NavLink to provide the plaintiffs with board meeting minutes and with communications from NavLink's secretary regarding the minutes. The plaintiffs were also entitled to inspect corporate documents and communications concerning NavLink's 2015 budget and three-year plan.[3] ■

Right to Indemnification When a director becomes involved in litigation by virtue of her or his position, the director may have a *right to indemnification* (reimbursement) for the legal costs, fees, and damages incurred. Most states allow corporations to indemnify and purchase liability insurance for corporate directors [RMBCA 8.51].

40–1f Corporate Officers and Executives

Corporate officers and other executive employees are hired by the board of directors. At a minimum, most corporations have a president, one or more vice presidents, a secretary, and a treasurer. In most states, an individual can hold more than one office, such as president and secretary, and can be both an officer and a director of the corporation.

In addition to carrying out the duties articulated in the bylaws, corporate and managerial officers act as agents of the corporation. Therefore, the ordinary rules of agency normally apply to their employment.

Corporate officers and other high-level managers are employees of the company, so their rights are defined by employment contracts. Nevertheless, the board of directors normally can remove a corporate officer at any

---

2. Except in Louisiana, which allows a director to vote by proxy under certain circumstances.

3. *Chammas v. NavLink, Inc.,* 2016 WL 767714 (Del.Ch.Ct. 2016).

time with or without cause. If the directors remove an officer in violation of the terms of an employment contract, however, the corporation may be liable for breach of contract.

For a synopsis of the roles of directors and officers, see Concept Summary 40.1.

40–2 Duties and Liabilities of Directors and Officers

The duties of corporate directors and officers are similar because both groups are involved in decision making and

---

Concept Summary 40.1

Roles of Directors and Officers

Election of Directors	• The incorporators usually appoint the first board of directors. Thereafter, shareholders elect the directors. • Directors usually serve a one-year term, although the term can be longer. Few qualifications are required. • A director can be a shareholder but is not required to be. • Compensation usually is specified in the corporate articles or bylaws.
Board of Directors' Meetings	• The board of directors conducts business by holding formal meetings with recorded minutes. • The dates of regular meetings are usually established in the corporate articles or bylaws. • Special meetings can be called, with notice sent to all directors. • Usually, a quorum is a majority of the corporate directors. Once a quorum is present, each director has one vote, and the majority normally rules in ordinary matters.
Rights of Directors	• Directors' rights include the rights of participation, inspection, compensation, and indemnification.
Board of Directors' Committees	• Directors may appoint committees and delegate some of their responsibilities to the committees and to corporate officers and executives. For instance, directors commonly appoint an *executive committee*, which handles ordinary, interim management decisions between board of directors' meetings. • Directors may also appoint an *audit committee* to hire and supervise the independent public accountants who audit the corporation's financial records.
Role of Corporate Officers and Executives	• The board of directors normally hires the corporate officers and other executive employees. • In most states, a person can hold more than one office and can be both an officer and a director of a corporation. • The rights of corporate officers and executives are defined by employment contracts.

are in positions of control. Directors and officers are considered to be fiduciaries of the corporation because their relationship with the corporation and its shareholders is one of trust and confidence. As fiduciaries, directors and officers owe ethical—and legal—duties to the corporation and to the shareholders as a group. These fiduciary duties include the duty of care and the duty of loyalty.

40–2a Duty of Care

Directors and officers must exercise due care in performing their duties. The standard of *due care* has been variously described in judicial decisions and codified in many state corporation codes. Generally, it requires a director or officer to:

1. Act in good faith (honestly).
2. Exercise the care that an ordinarily prudent (careful) person would exercise in similar circumstances.
3. Do what she or he believes is in the best interests of the corporation [RMBCA 8.30(a), 8.42(a)].

If directors or officers fail to exercise due care and the corporation or its shareholders suffer harm as a result, the directors or officers can be held liable for negligence. (An exception is made if the *business judgment rule* applies, as will be discussed shortly.)

Duty to Make Informed Decisions Directors and officers are expected to be informed on corporate matters and to conduct a reasonable investigation of the situation before making a decision. They must, for instance, attend meetings and presentations, ask for information from those who have it, read reports, and review other written materials. In other words, directors and officers must investigate, study, and discuss matters and evaluate alternatives before making a decision. They cannot decide on the spur of the moment without adequate research.

Although directors and officers are expected to act in accordance with their own knowledge and training, they are also normally entitled to rely on information given to them by certain other persons. Under the laws of most states and Section 8.30(b) of the RMBCA, such persons include competent officers or employees, professionals such as attorneys and accountants, and committees of the board of directors. (The committee must be one on which the director does not serve, however.) The reliance must be in good faith to insulate a director from liability if the information later proves to be inaccurate or unreliable.

Duty to Exercise Reasonable Supervision Directors are also expected to exercise a reasonable amount of supervision when they delegate work to corporate officers and employees. ■ **EXAMPLE 40.2** Dana, a corporate bank director, fails to attend any board of directors' meetings for five years. In addition, Dana never inspects any of the corporate books or records and generally fails to supervise the activities of the bank president and the loan committee. Meanwhile, Brennan, the bank president, who is a corporate officer, makes various improper loans and permits large overdrafts. In this situation, Dana (the corporate director) can be held liable to the corporation for losses resulting from the unsupervised actions of the bank president and the loan committee. ■

Dissenting Directors Directors' votes at board of directors' meetings should be entered into the minutes. Sometimes, an individual director disagrees with the majority's vote (which becomes an act of the board of directors). Unless a dissent is entered in the minutes, the director is presumed to have assented. If the directors are later held liable for mismanagement as a result of a decision, dissenting directors are rarely held individually liable to the corporation. For this reason, a director who is absent from a given meeting sometimes registers a dissent with the secretary of the board regarding actions taken at the meeting.

40–2b The Business Judgment Rule

Directors and officers are expected to exercise due care and to use their best judgment in guiding corporate management, but they are not insurers of business success. Under the **business judgment rule,** a corporate director or officer will not be liable to the corporation or to its shareholders for honest mistakes of judgment and bad business decisions.

Courts give significant deference to the decisions of corporate directors and officers, and consider the reasonableness of a decision at the time it was made, without the benefit of hindsight. Thus, corporate decision makers are not subjected to second-guessing by shareholders or others in the corporation.

When the Rule Applies The business judgment rule will apply as long as the director or officer:

1. Took reasonable steps to become informed about the matter.
2. Had a rational basis for her or his decision.
3. Did not have a conflict between her or his personal interest and the interest of the corporation.

Whether these conditions were met formed the basis for the court's decision in the following case.

Oliveira v. Sugarman

Court of Special Appeals of Maryland, 226 Md.App. 524, 130 A.3d 1085 (2016).

Background and Facts iStar, Inc., a Maryland corporation, promised to award shares of company stock to employees for their performance if the stock averaged a certain target price per share over a specific period. The stock price rose 300 percent, but the target was missed. The board changed the basis for an award from performance to service—an employee who had been with iStar for a certain period was entitled to an award. It then issued additional shares to pay the awards.

Albert and Lena Oliveira, iStar shareholders, demanded that the board rescind the awards. The Oliveiras alleged misconduct and demanded that the board file a suit on the company's behalf to seek damages or other relief. The board appointed Barry Ridings, an outside director, to investigate the allegation. Ridings recommended that the board refuse the demand. The board acted on his recommendation.

The Oliveiras filed a suit in a Maryland state court against Jay Sugarman, the board chairman, and the other directors, including Ridings, alleging a breach of fiduciary duty. The court dismissed the claim. The Oliveiras appealed.

In the Language of the Court

BURGER, J. [Judge]

* * * *

Judicial review of a demand refusal is subject to the business judgment rule, and the court * * * limits its review to whether the board acted independently, in good faith, and within the realm of sound business judgment. [Emphasis added.]

* * * *

* * * The Shareholders [the Oliveiras] assert that [Ridings's] investigation of the Shareholders' demand was rife with improper procedure. The Shareholders argue that * * * Ridings lacked sufficient corporate experience to make a proper recommendation to the Board and that Ridings was not sufficiently disinterested. Both contentions are baseless. Ridings has forty years of business experience, including service on the boards of several public companies, including the American Stock Exchange. Furthermore, Ridings hired highly respected and experienced legal counsel to assist him and conducted multiple interviews.

We further reject the Shareholders' contention that Ridings was interested or lacked independence. Ridings joined the Board after the challenged conduct and had no business, personal, social, or other relationships with any other member of the Board. Although Ridings's employer [Lazard Freres & Company, where Ridings was vice chairman of investment banking] performed banking services for iStar [for two years], Lazard has no ongoing business relationship with iStar. *Furthermore, allegations of mere personal friendship or a mere outside business relationship, standing alone, are insufficient to raise a reasonable doubt about a director's independence.* [Emphasis added.]

The Shareholders' contention that Ridings lacks independence because he is compensated for his service as a Director is similarly unfounded. The Shareholders further contend that Ridings lacks independence because he is a named defendant in this lawsuit. This assertion is contrary to established law. Accordingly, we reject the Shareholders' contentions that Ridings was interested or lacked independence.

* * * *

In conclusion, the Shareholders have failed to surmount the presumption of the business judgment rule. In failing to do so, they have failed to state a claim upon which relief may be granted.

Decision and Remedy *A state intermediate appellate court affirmed the lower court's dismissal of the Oliveiras' claim. "The Shareholders' bald allegations of impropriety are plainly insufficient to overcome the presumption of the business judgment rule."*

Critical Thinking

- **Legal Environment** *In a letter to the Oliveiras, the board explained that it saw "no upside—and much downside—to the action and lawsuit proposed in the Demand." What would the "downside" consist of?*
- **What If the Facts Were Different?** *Only one member of the iStar board—Sugarman—received an award as an employee. The others who made the decision to change the award were, like Ridings, outside directors. Suppose that the opposite had been true. Would the result have been the same?*

Provides Broad Protections The business judgment rule provides broad protections to corporate decision makers. In fact, most courts will apply the rule unless there is evidence of bad faith, fraud, or a clear breach of fiduciary duties.

■ **CASE IN POINT 40.3** The board of directors of the Chugach Alaska Corporation (CAC) voted to remove Sheri Buretta as the chair and install Robert Henrichs. During his term, Henrichs acted without board approval, made decisions with only his supporters present, retaliated against directors who challenged his decisions, and ignored board rules for conducting meetings. He refused to comply with bylaws that required a special shareholders' meeting in response to a shareholder petition and personally mistreated directors, shareholders, and employees. After six months, the board voted to reinstall Buretta.

CAC filed a suit in an Alaska state court against Henrichs, alleging a breach of fiduciary duty. A jury found Henrichs liable, and the court barred him from serving on CAC's board for five years. The appellate court affirmed. Given the nature and seriousness of Henrichs's misconduct, the business judgment rule did not protect him.[4] ■

---

4. *Henrichs v. Chugach Alaska Corp.*, 250 P.3d 531 (Alaska Sup.Ct. 2011).

40–2c Duty of Loyalty

Loyalty can be defined as faithfulness to one's obligations and duties. In the corporate context, the duty of loyalty requires directors and officers to subordinate their personal interests to the welfare of the corporation. For instance, a director should not oppose a transaction that is in the corporation's best interest simply because pursuing it may cost the director his or her position. Directors cannot use corporate funds or confidential corporate information for personal advantage and must refrain from self-dealing.

Cases dealing with the duty of loyalty typically involve one or more of the following:

1. Competing with the corporation.
2. Usurping (taking personal advantage of) a corporate opportunity.
3. Pursuing an interest that conflicts with that of the corporation.
4. Using information that is not available to the public to make a profit trading securities (insider trading).
5. Authorizing a corporate transaction that is detrimental to minority shareholders.
6. Selling control over the corporation.

The following *Classic Case* illustrates the conflict that can arise between a corporate officer's personal interest and his or her duty of loyalty.

Classic Case 40.2

Guth v. Loft, Inc.
Supreme Court of Delaware, 23 Del.Ch. 255, 5 A.2d 503 (1939).

Background and Facts In 1930, Charles Guth became the president of Loft, Inc., a candy-and-restaurant chain. Guth and his family also owned Grace Company, which made syrups for soft drinks. Coca-Cola Company supplied Loft with cola syrup. Unhappy with what he felt was Coca-Cola's high price, Guth entered into an agreement with Roy Megargel to acquire the trademark and formula for Pepsi-Cola and form Pepsi-Cola Corporation. Neither Guth nor Megargel could finance the new venture, however, and Grace Company was insolvent.

Without the knowledge of Loft's board, Guth used Loft's capital, credit, facilities, and employees to further the Pepsi enterprise. At Guth's direction, a Loft employee made the concentrate for the syrup, which was sent to Grace to add sugar and water. Loft charged Grace for the concentrate but allowed forty months' credit. Grace charged Pepsi for the syrup but also granted substantial credit. Grace sold the syrup to Pepsi's customers, including Loft, which paid on delivery or within thirty days. Loft also paid for Pepsi's advertising. Finally, with profits declining as a result of switching from Coca-Cola, Loft filed a suit in a Delaware state court against Guth, Grace, and Pepsi, seeking their Pepsi stock and an accounting. The court entered a judgment in the plaintiff's favor. The defendants appealed to the Delaware Supreme Court.

In the Language of the Court
LAYTON, Chief Justice, delivering the opinion of the court:
        * * * *

Corporate officers and directors are not permitted to use their position of trust and confidence to further their private interests. * * * They stand in a fiduciary relation to the corporation and its stockholders.

Case 40.2 Continued

A public policy, existing through the years, and derived from a profound knowledge of human characteristics and motives, has established *a rule that demands of a corporate officer or director, peremptorily [not open for debate] and inexorably [unavoidably], the most scrupulous observance of his duty, not only affirmatively to protect the interests of the corporation committed to his charge, but also to refrain from doing anything that would work injury to the corporation* * * * . The rule that requires an undivided and unselfish loyalty to the corporation demands that there shall be no conflict between duty and self-interest. [Emphasis added.]

* * * *

* * * *If there is presented to a corporate officer or director a business opportunity which the corporation is financially able to undertake [that] is * * * in the line of the corporation's business and is of practical advantage to it * * * and, by embracing the opportunity, the self-interest of the officer or director will be brought into conflict with that of his corporation, the law will not permit him to seize the opportunity for himself. * * * In such circumstances, * * * the corporation may elect to claim all of the benefits of the transaction for itself, and the law will impress a trust in favor of the corporation upon the property, interests and profits so acquired. [Emphasis added.]

* * * *

* * * The appellants contend that no conflict of interest between Guth and Loft resulted from his acquirement and exploitation of the Pepsi-Cola opportunity [and] that the acquisition did not place Guth in competition with Loft * * * . [In this case, however,] Guth was Loft, and Guth was Pepsi. He absolutely controlled Loft. His authority over Pepsi was supreme. As Pepsi, he created and controlled the supply of Pepsi-Cola syrup, and he determined the price and the terms. What he offered, as Pepsi, he had the power, as Loft, to accept. Upon any consideration of human characteristics and motives, he created a conflict between self-interest and duty. He made himself the judge in his own cause. * * * Moreover, a reasonable probability of injury to Loft resulted from the situation forced upon it. Guth was in the same position to impose his terms upon Loft as had been the Coca-Cola Company.

* * * The facts and circumstances demonstrate that Guth's appropriation of the Pepsi-Cola opportunity to himself placed him in a competitive position with Loft with respect to a commodity essential to it, thereby rendering his personal interests incompatible with the superior interests of his corporation; and this situation was accomplished, not openly and with his own resources, but secretly and with the money and facilities of the corporation which was committed to his protection.

Decision and Remedy   *The Delaware Supreme Court upheld the judgment of the lower court. The state supreme court was "convinced that the opportunity to acquire the Pepsi-Cola trademark and formula, goodwill and business belonged to [Loft], and that Guth, as its President, had no right to appropriate the opportunity to himself."*

Impact of This Case on Today's Law   *This early Delaware decision was one of the first to set forth a test for determining when a corporate officer or director has breached the duty of loyalty. The test has two basic parts: Was the opportunity reasonably related to the corporation's line of business, and was the corporation financially able to undertake the opportunity? The court also considered whether the corporation had an interest or expectancy in the opportunity. It recognized that when the corporation had "no interest or expectancy, the officer or director is entitled to treat the opportunity as his own."*

Critical Thinking
- **What If the Facts Were Different?**   *Suppose that Loft's board of directors had approved Pepsi-Cola's use of its personnel and equipment. Would the court's decision have been different? Discuss.*

40–2d Conflicts of Interest

Corporate directors often have many business affiliations, and a director may sit on the board of more than one corporation. Of course, directors are precluded from entering into or supporting businesses that operate in direct competition with corporations on whose boards they serve. Their fiduciary duty requires them to make a full disclosure of any potential conflicts of interest that might arise in any corporate transaction [RMBCA 8.60].

Sometimes, a corporation enters into a contract or engages in a transaction in which an officer or director has a personal interest. The director or officer must make a *full disclosure* of the nature of the conflicting interest and all facts pertinent to the transaction. He or she must also abstain from voting on the proposed transaction. When these rules are followed, the transaction can proceed. Otherwise, directors would be prevented from ever having financial dealings with the corporations they serve.

■ **EXAMPLE 40.4** Ballo Corporation needs office space. Stephanie Colson, one of its five directors, owns the building adjoining the corporation's headquarters. Colson can negotiate a lease for the space to Ballo if she fully discloses her conflicting interest and any facts known to her about the proposed transaction to Ballo and the other four directors. If the lease arrangement is fair and reasonable, Colson abstains from voting on

it, and the other members of the corporation's board of directors unanimously approve it, the contract is valid. ■

40–2e Liability of Directors and Officers

Directors and officers are exposed to liability on many fronts. They can be held liable for negligence in certain circumstances, as previously discussed. They may also be held liable for the crimes and torts committed by themselves or by corporate employees under their supervision. (See this chapter's *Global Insight* feature for a discussion of how the United States criminally prosecutes corporations and their managers for bribery.)

GLOBAL INSIGHT — Anti-Bribery Charges Take Their Toll on U.S. and Foreign Corporations

Hitachi, Ltd., was established in 1920 in Tokyo, Japan. Among other activities, it builds and operates electrical power systems throughout the world. Almost a hundred years after its founding, Hitachi agreed to a consent decree offered by the U.S. Securities and Exchange Commission (SEC).[a] (A consent decree is a means of resolving a dispute without going to trial or admitting guilt.) Part of that decree required Hitachi to pay a fine of $19 million for violating the Foreign Corrupt Practices Act (FCPA).[b]

Hitachi had admitted to creating a system to bribe South Africa's ruling political party to give Hitachi preference in awarding electrical power station contracts. The SEC claimed jurisdiction over Hitachi even though the company was no longer listed on the New York Stock Exchange (NYSE). While the bribery scheme was taking place, Hitachi was a company whose shares could be traded in the United States. The long arm of U.S. anti-bribery laws had struck again.

Anti-Bribery Lawsuits and Investigations Take Years

U.S.-owned and -based retailing giant Walmart was accused by the U.S. Department of Justice (DOJ) of bribing Mexican officials. By the time Walmart settles with the DOJ, it will have paid between $1 billion and $2 billion to forensic accountants and attorneys. Further, it will have to pay a fine. Finally, the company's managers will have spent thousands of hours conducting internal investigations.

Total U.S. fines for violations of the FCPA were estimated to be almost $2 billion in 2015 alone. Back in 2007, no fine under the FCPA exceeded $50 million. Today, accused firms pay ten to fifteen times that amount. And the United States is not the only country investigating and fining corporations for bribery. Britain, France, Germany, Italy, Norway, South Korea, and Switzerland assess bribery fines, as well.

The biggest bribery case during the decade 2000–2010 involved Siemens. That case took three years to resolve. Current cases, such as the one involving Walmart, could take up to ten years to resolve.

Costs Continue Even after a Settlement

In most anti-bribery settlements, the accused firms must also bear the cost of being overseen for a number of years by independent compliance monitors. In addition, firms that have been involved in bribery investigations often are excluded from bidding for new business in the countries in which they allegedly offered bribes. Some accused companies have also had to defend against shareholder lawsuits.

Not surprisingly, anti-bribery compliance departments within corporations have grown in size and therefore in cost. In Germany, Siemens has spent more than $3 billion on fines and costs since it was first accused of bribery in 2008. It now has a compliance department with about four hundred employees.

Critical Thinking *Why do you think officers and directors of accused companies accept consent decrees rather than contest accusations at trial?*

---

a. *Securities and Exchange Commission v. Hitachi, Ltd.*, 2015 WL 7566666 (D.D.C. 2015).
b. 15 U.S.C. Sections 78m(b)(2)(A) and (B).

Additionally, if shareholders perceive that the corporate directors are not acting in the best interests of the corporation, they may sue the directors on behalf of the corporation. (This is known as a *shareholder's derivative suit,* which will be discussed later in this chapter.) Directors and officers can also be held personally liable under a number of statutes, such as statutes enacted to protect consumers or the environment.

See Concept Summary 40.2 for a review of the duties and liabilities of directors and officers.

40–3 The Role of Shareholders

The acquisition of a share of stock makes a person an owner and a shareholder in a corporation. Shareholders thus own the corporation. Although they have no legal title to corporate property, such as buildings and equipment, they do have an equitable (ownership) interest in the firm.

As a general rule, shareholders have no responsibility for the daily management of the corporation, although they are ultimately responsible for choosing the board of directors, which does have such control. Ordinarily, corporate officers and other employees owe no direct duty to individual shareholders (unless some contract or special relationship exists between them in addition to the corporate relationship).

The duty of officers and directors is to act in the best interests of the corporation and its shareholder-owners *as a whole.* In turn, as you will read later in this chapter, controlling shareholders owe a fiduciary duty to minority shareholders.

40–3a Shareholders' Powers

Shareholders must approve fundamental changes affecting the corporation before the changes can be implemented. Hence, shareholder approval normally is required to amend the articles of incorporation or bylaws, to conduct a merger or dissolve the corporation, and

---

Concept Summary 40.2

Duties and Liabilities of Directors and Officers

Duties of Directors and Officers	1. *Duty of care*—Directors and officers are obligated to act in good faith, to use prudent business judgment in the conduct of corporate affairs, and to act in the corporation's best interests. If a director or officer fails to exercise this duty of care, he or she may be answerable to the corporation and to the shareholders for breaching the duty. The *business judgment rule* immunizes a director from liability for a corporate decision as long as it was within the power of the corporation and the authority of the director to make and was an informed, reasonable, and loyal decision. 2. *Duty of loyalty*—Directors and officers have a fiduciary duty to subordinate their own interests to those of the corporation in matters relating to the corporation. 3. *Conflicts of interest*—To fulfill their duty of loyalty, directors and officers must make a full disclosure of any potential conflicts between their personal interests and those of the corporation.
Liability of Directors and Officers	1. Corporate directors and officers are personally liable for their own torts and crimes (when not protected under the business judgment rule). Additionally, they may be held personally liable for the torts and crimes committed by corporate personnel under their direct supervision. 2. They may also be held personally liable for violating certain statutes, such as environmental and consumer protection laws, and can sometimes be sued by shareholders for mismanaging the corporation.

to sell all or substantially all of the corporation's assets. Some of these powers are subject to prior board approval. Shareholder approval may also be requested (though it is not required) for certain other actions, such as to approve an independent auditor.

Shareholders also have the power to vote to elect or remove members of the board of directors. As described earlier, the first board of directors is either named in the articles of incorporation or chosen by the incorporators to serve until the first shareholders' meeting. From that time on, selection and retention of directors are exclusively shareholder functions.

Directors usually serve their full terms. If the shareholders judge them unsatisfactory, they are simply not reelected. Shareholders have the inherent power, however, to remove a director from office *for cause* (breach of duty or misconduct) by a majority vote.[5] Some state statutes (and some articles of incorporation) permit removal of directors without cause by the vote of a majority of the shareholders entitled to vote.[6]

40–3b Shareholders' Meetings

Shareholders' meetings must occur at least annually. In addition, special meetings can be called to deal with urgent matters.

Notice of Meetings A corporation must notify its shareholders of the date, time, and place of an annual or special shareholders' meeting at least ten days, but not more than sixty days, before the meeting date [RMBCA 7.05].[7] (The date and time of the annual meeting can be specified in the bylaws.) Notice of a special meeting must include a statement of the purpose of the meeting, and business transacted at the meeting is limited to that purpose.

The RMBCA does not specify how the notice must be given. Most corporations do specify in their bylaws the acceptable methods of notifying shareholders about meetings. Also, some states' incorporation statutes outline the means of notice that a corporation can use in that jurisdiction. For instance, in Alaska, notice may be

given in person, by mail, or by fax, e-mail, blog, or Web post—as long as the shareholder has agreed to that electronic method.[8]

Proxies It usually is not practical for owners of only a few shares of stock of publicly traded corporations to attend a shareholders' meeting. Therefore, the law allows stockholders to appoint another person as their agent to vote their shares at the meeting. The agent's formal authorization to vote the shares is called a **proxy** (from the Latin *procurare,* meaning "to manage or take care of"). Proxy materials are sent to all shareholders before shareholders' meetings.

Management often solicits proxies, but any person can solicit proxies to concentrate voting power. Proxies have been used by groups of shareholders as a device for taking over a corporation. Proxies normally are revocable (can be withdrawn), unless they are specifically designated as irrevocable and coupled with an interest. A proxy is coupled with an interest when, for instance, the person receiving the proxies from shareholders has agreed to buy their shares. Under RMBCA 7.22(c), proxies are valid for eleven months, unless the proxy agreement mandates a longer period.

Shareholder Proposals When shareholders want to change a company policy, they can put their ideas up for a shareholder vote. They do this by submitting a shareholder proposal to the board of directors and asking the board to include the proposal in the proxy materials that are sent to all shareholders before meetings.

Rules for Proxies and Shareholder Proposals The Securities and Exchange Commission (SEC) regulates the purchase and sale of securities. The SEC has special provisions relating to proxies and shareholder proposals. SEC Rule 14a-8 provides that all shareholders who own stock worth at least $1,000 are eligible to submit proposals for inclusion in corporate proxy materials. The corporation is required to include information on whatever proposals will be considered at the shareholders' meeting along with proxy materials. Only those proposals that relate to significant policy considerations, not ordinary business operations, must be included.

Under the SEC's e-proxy rules,[9] all public companies must post their proxy materials on the Internet and notify shareholders how to find that information. Although the law requires proxy materials to be posted online, public companies may also send the materials to shareholders

---

5. A director can often demand court review of removal for cause, however.
6. Most states allow *cumulative voting* for directors (described later in the chapter). If cumulative voting is authorized, a director may not be removed if the number of votes against removal would be sufficient to elect a director under cumulative voting. See, for instance, California Corporations Code Section 303A. See also Section 8.08(c) of the RMBCA.
7. The shareholder can waive the requirement of notice by signing a waiver form [RMBCA 7.06]. A shareholder who does not receive notice but who learns of the meeting and attends without protesting the lack of notice is said to have waived notice by such conduct.

8. Alaska Statutes Section 10.06.410 Notice of Shareholders' Meetings.
9. 17 C.F.R. Parts 240, 249, and 274.

by other means, including paper documents and DVDs sent by mail.

40–3c Shareholder Voting

Shareholders exercise ownership control through the power of their votes. Corporate business matters are presented in the form of *resolutions,* which shareholders vote to approve or disapprove. Each common shareholder normally is entitled to one vote per share.

The articles of incorporation can exclude or limit voting rights, particularly for certain classes of shares. For instance, owners of preferred shares are usually denied the right to vote [RMBCA 7.21]. If a state statute requires specific voting procedures, the corporation's articles or bylaws must be consistent with the statute.

Quorum Requirements   For shareholders to act during a meeting, a quorum must be present. Generally, a quorum exists when shareholders holding more than 50 percent of the outstanding shares are present. State laws often permit the articles of incorporation to set higher or lower quorum requirements, however. In some states,

obtaining the unanimous written consent of shareholders is a permissible alternative to holding a shareholders' meeting [RMBCA 7.25].

Once a quorum is present, voting can proceed. If a state statute requires specific voting procedures, the corporation's articles or bylaws must be consistent with the statute. A majority vote of the shares represented at the meeting usually is required to pass resolutions. At times, more than a simple majority vote is required, either by a state statute or by the corporate articles. Extraordinary corporate matters, such as a merger, consolidation, or dissolution of the corporation, require approval by a higher percentage of all corporate shares entitled to vote [RMBCA 7.27].

The corporation in the following case had eighty-four shares of voting common stock outstanding. The shareholder-appellee owned twenty shares, he and his estranged wife jointly held another sixteen shares, and three different individuals owned sixteen shares each. At a shareholders' meeting, the appellee was the only shareholder present in person. Another shareholder (not the appellee's wife) was present by proxy. Could the shares held jointly by the appellee and his wife be counted for purposes of a quorum?

Case Analysis 40.3

Case v. Sink & Rise, Inc.

Supreme Court of Wyoming, 2013 WY 19, 297 P.3d 762 (2013).

In the Language of the Court
HILL, Justice.

This case involves a dispute over corporate action during a shareholder meeting of Appellee Sink & Rise, Inc., (Sink & Rise) a Wyoming corporation. Appellee James Caleb Case (Cale Case) was the only shareholder present at the meeting. He concluded that a quorum existed and thus voted on and passed several resolutions. Cale Case also elected himself and another shareholder as the directors of the corporation, and replaced his estranged wife, Appellant Shirley Case, as the corporation's secretary.

Shirley Case took issue with her estranged husband's actions during the shareholder meeting and filed a complaint in [a Wyoming state] district court to set aside the corporate action that occurred at the shareholder meeting. * * * The district court concluded that the resolutions were passed with requisite

authority and thus they were not set aside after trial. This appeal followed.

* * * *

* * * Shirley Case argues that because her estranged husband was not entitled to vote the jointly held shares, those same shares could not be counted for quorum purposes. She reasons that because she was absent from the meeting and because only shares "entitled to vote" are to be counted in establishing a quorum, the shares in question were essentially useless at the meeting.

* * * We find the answer in the Sink & Rise corporate documents, and within Wyoming law. First, we reiterate the [district court's] characterization of the stock as being owned by husband and wife with rights of survivorship. We agree with the district court's further classification of the stock as creating a presumption of tenancy by the entirety under Wyoming law. As tenants by the

entirety, each owns an undivided 100% interest in the 16 shares.

In an estate of the entirety, the husband and the wife during their joint lives each owns, not a part, or a separate or a separable interest, but the whole. [Emphasis added.]

To further help us in our consideration, we turn to the corporate documents.

* * * Sink & Rise's bylaws * * * define what constitutes a "quorum," and relate the corporation's rule on voting shares:

6. *Quorum.* A majority of the outstanding shares entitled to vote, represented in person or by proxy, shall constitute a quorum at a meeting of Shareholders. If a quorum is present, the affirmative vote of the majority of shares entitled to vote at the meeting shall be the act of the Shareholders. * * *

Case 40.3 Continues

Case 40.3 Continued

7. *Voting of Shares.* * * * Each outstanding share is entitled to vote the number of shares owned by him/her on each matter submitted to a vote at a meeting of Shareholders. * * *

According to the bylaws, for the corporation to count shares in determining a quorum, the shares must be (1) entitled to vote, and (2) represented in person or by proxy. From our reading of the corporate documents, and because the joint stock was held by husband and wife as tenants by the entirety, we conclude that the shares held jointly by Cale Case

and Shirley Case were "entitled to vote" at the meeting. Cale Case represented the stock in person, as required by the bylaws. [Emphasis added.]

As the district court noted, and the parties agree here, the joint stock in question cannot be, and was not, voted without agreement between Cale Case and Shirley Case. * * * [But] the fact that Cale Case and Shirley Case must agree on how to vote the stock before it can actually be voted does not strip it of its voting privileges. Cale Case did not attempt to vote the stock at the meeting,

but instead considered it only for quorum purposes.

Sink & Rise's bylaws do not prevent stock owned by a husband and wife as tenants by the entirety * * * from being counted for purposes of a quorum if represented in person. The stock in question was represented in person by Cale Case at the * * * shareholder meeting, and it was properly counted to establish a quorum.

* * * *

We affirm the district court's decision.

Legal Reasoning Questions

1. How many shareholders were present at the shareholders' meeting that gave rise to the dispute in this case?

2. How did the court "characterize" and "classify" the shares of stock that Cale and Shirley Case held jointly?

3. According to the court, how many shares were represented at the shareholders' meeting? Was a quorum present? Explain.

Voting Lists The corporation prepares a voting list before each shareholders' meeting. Ordinarily, only persons whose names appear on the corporation's stockholder records as owners are entitled to vote.[10]

The voting list contains the name and address of each shareholder as shown on the corporate records on a given cutoff date, or *record date*. (Under RMBCA 7.07, the bylaws or board of directors may fix a record date that is as much as seventy days before the meeting.) The voting list also includes the number of voting shares held by each owner. The list is usually kept at the corporate headquarters and must be made available for shareholder inspection [RMBCA 7.20].

Cumulative Voting Most states permit, and many require, shareholders to elect directors by *cumulative voting*, a voting method designed to allow minority shareholders to be represented on the board of directors.[11]

Formula. With cumulative voting, each shareholder is entitled to a total number of votes equal to the number of

board members to be elected multiplied by the number of voting shares that the shareholder owns. The shareholder can cast all of these votes for one candidate or split them among several nominees for director. All candidates stand for election at the same time.

How Cumulative Voting Works. Cumulative voting can best be understood by example. ■ **EXAMPLE 40.5** A corporation has 10,000 shares issued and outstanding. The minority shareholders hold 3,000 shares, and the majority shareholders hold the other 7,000 shares. Three members of the board are to be elected. The majority shareholders' nominees are Alvarez, Beasley, and Caravel. The minority shareholders' nominee is Dovrik. Can Dovrik be elected to the board by the minority shareholders?

If cumulative voting is allowed, the answer is yes. The minority shareholders have 9,000 votes among them (the number of directors to be elected times the number of shares, or 3 × 3,000 = 9,000 votes). All of these votes can be cast to elect Dovrik. The majority shareholders have 21,000 votes (3 × 7,000 = 21,000 votes), but these votes must be distributed among their three nominees.

The principle of cumulative voting is that no matter how the majority shareholders cast their 21,000 votes, they will not be able to elect all three directors if the minority shareholders cast all of their 9,000 votes for Dovrik, as illustrated in Exhibit 40–2. ■ In contrast, when cumulative voting is not required, the entire board can be elected by a majority of shares.

---

10. When the legal owner of shares is deceased, bankrupt, mentally incompetent, or in some other way under a legal disability, his or her vote can be cast by a person designated by law to control and manage that owner's property.

11. See, for instance, California Corporations Code Section 708. Some states, such as Nebraska, require cumulative voting in their state constitutions. Under RMBCA 7.28, no cumulative voting rights exist unless the articles of incorporation so provide.

EXHIBIT 40–2 Results of Cumulative Voting

Ballot	Majority Shareholder Votes			Minority Shareholder Votes	Directors Elected
	Alvarez	Beasley	Caravel	Dovrik	
1	10,000	10,000	1,000	9,000	Alvarez, Beasley, Dovrik
2	9,001	9,000	2,999	9,000	Alvarez, Beasley, Dovrik
3	6,000	7,000	8,000	9,000	Beasley, Caravel, Dovrik

Other Voting Techniques Before a shareholders' meeting, a group of shareholders can agree in writing to vote their shares together in a specified manner. Such agreements, called *shareholder voting agreements,* usually are held to be valid and enforceable. A shareholder can also vote by proxy, as noted earlier.

Another technique is for shareholders to enter into a *voting trust.* A **voting trust** is an agreement (a trust contract) under which a shareholder assigns the right to vote his or her shares to a trustee, usually for a specified period of time. The trustee is then responsible for voting the shares on behalf of all the shareholders in the trust. The shareholder retains all rights of ownership (for instance, the right to receive dividend payments) except the power to vote the shares [RMBCA 7.30].

40–4 Rights of Shareholders

Shareholders possess numerous rights in addition to the right to vote their shares, and we examine several here.

40–4a Stock Certificates

In the past, corporations commonly issued **stock certificates** that evidenced ownership of a specified number of shares in the corporation. Only a few jurisdictions still require physical stock certificates, and shareholders there have the right to demand that the corporation issue certificates (or replace those that were lost or destroyed). Stock is intangible personal property, however, and the ownership right exists independently of the certificate itself.

In most states and under RMBCA 6.26, a board of directors may provide that shares of stock will be uncertificated, or "paperless"—that is, no actual, physical stock certificates will be issued. Notice of shareholders' meetings, dividends, and operational and financial reports are distributed according to the ownership lists recorded in the corporation's books.

40–4b Preemptive Rights

Sometimes, the articles of incorporation grant preemptive rights to shareholders [RMBCA 6.30]. With **preemptive rights,** a shareholder receives a preference over all other purchasers to subscribe to or purchase a prorated share of a new issue of stock. Generally, preemptive rights must be exercised within a specific time period (usually thirty days).

A shareholder who is given preemptive rights can purchase a percentage of the new shares being issued that is equal to the percentage of shares she or he already holds in the company. This allows each shareholder to maintain her or his proportionate control, voting power, and financial interest in the corporation. ■ **EXAMPLE 40.6** Katlin is a shareholder who owns 10 percent of a company. Because she also has preemptive rights, she can buy 10 percent of any new issue (to maintain her 10 percent position). Thus, if the corporation issues 1,000 more shares, Katlin can buy 100 of the new shares. ■

Preemptive rights are most important in close corporations because each shareholder owns a relatively small number of shares but controls a substantial interest in the corporation. Without preemptive rights, it would be possible for a shareholder to lose his or her proportionate control over the firm. Nevertheless, preemptive rights do not exist unless provided for in the articles of incorporation.

40–4c Stock Warrants

Stock warrants are rights given by a company to buy stock at a stated price by a specified date. Usually, when preemptive rights exist and a corporation is issuing additional shares, it gives its shareholders stock warrants. Warrants are often publicly traded on securities exchanges.

40–4d Dividends

As mentioned, a **dividend** is a distribution of corporate profits or income *ordered by the directors* and paid to the shareholders in proportion to their shares in the corporation. Dividends can be paid in cash, property, stock of the corporation that is paying the dividends, or stock of other corporations.[12]

State laws vary, but each state determines the general circumstances and legal requirements under which dividends are paid. State laws also control the sources of revenue to be used. All states allow dividends to be paid from the undistributed net profits earned by the corporation, for instance. A number of states allow dividends to be paid out of any surplus.

Illegal Dividends Dividends are illegal if they are improperly paid from an unauthorized account or if their payment causes the corporation to become insolvent. Generally, shareholders must return illegal dividends only if they knew that the dividends were illegal when the payment was received (or if the dividends were paid when the corporation was insolvent). Whenever dividends are illegal or improper, the board of directors can be held personally liable for the amount of the payment.

The Directors' Failure to Declare a Dividend When directors fail to declare a dividend, shareholders can ask a court to compel the directors to do so. To succeed, the shareholders must show that the directors have acted so unreasonably in withholding the dividend that their conduct is an abuse of their discretion.

Often, a corporation accumulates large cash reserves for a legitimate corporate purpose, such as expansion or research. The mere fact that the firm has sufficient earnings or surplus available to pay a dividend normally is not enough to compel the directors to declare a dividend. The courts are reluctant to interfere with corporate operations and will not compel directors to declare dividends unless abuse of discretion is clearly shown.

40–4e Inspection Rights

Shareholders in a corporation enjoy both common law and statutory inspection rights. The RMBCA provides that every shareholder is entitled to examine specified corporate records, including voting lists [RMBCA 7.20, 16.02]. The shareholder may inspect in person, or an attorney, accountant, or other authorized assistant can do so as the shareholder's agent. In some states, a shareholder must have held her or his shares for a minimum period of time immediately preceding the demand to inspect or must hold a certain percentage of outstanding shares.

Proper Purpose A shareholder has a right to inspect and copy corporate books and records only for a *proper purpose,* and the request to inspect must be made in advance. A shareholder who is denied the right of inspection can seek a court order to compel the inspection.

■ **CASE IN POINT 40.7** Trading Block Holdings, Inc., offers online brokerage services. On April 1, 2013, some shareholders of Trading Block, through an attorney, sent a letter asking to inspect specific items in the corporation's books and records. The letter indicated that the purpose was to determine the financial condition of the company, how it was being managed, and whether the company's financial practices were appropriate. It also stated that the shareholders wanted to know whether Trading Block's management had engaged in any self-dealing that had negatively impacted the company as a whole.

On April 30, Trading Block responded with a letter stating that the plaintiffs were on a "fishing expedition" and did not have a proper purpose for inspecting the corporate records. Eventually, the shareholders filed a motion to compel inspection in an Illinois state court. The trial court denied the plaintiffs' motion. On appeal, the reviewing court held that the plaintiffs' allegations of self-dealing by directors and officers constituted a proper purpose for their inspection request. The trial court's decision was reversed.[13] ■

Potential for Abuse The power of inspection is fraught with potential abuses, and the corporation is allowed to protect itself from them. For instance, a share-

---

12. On one occasion, a distillery declared and paid a dividend in bonded whiskey.

13. *Sunlitz Holding Co., W.L.L. v. Trading Block Holdings, Inc.,* 2014 IL App (1st) 133938, 17 N.E.3d 715, 384 Ill.Dec. 733 (4 Dist. 2014).

holder can properly be denied access to corporate records to prevent harassment or to protect trade secrets or other confidential corporate information.[14]

40–4f Transfer of Shares

Corporate stock represents an ownership right in intangible personal property. The law generally recognizes the owner's right to transfer stock to another person unless there are valid restrictions on its transferability, such as frequently occur with close corporation stock.

When shares are transferred, a new entry is made in the corporate stock book to indicate the new owner. Until the corporation is notified and the entry is complete, all rights—including voting rights, notice of shareholders' meetings, and the right to dividend distributions—remain with the current record owner.

40–4g The Shareholder's Derivative Suit

When the corporation is harmed by the actions of a third party, the directors can bring a lawsuit in the name of the corporation against that party. If the corporate directors fail to bring a lawsuit, shareholders can do so "derivatively" in what is known as a **shareholder's derivative suit.**

The right of shareholders to bring a derivative action is especially important when the wrong suffered by the corporation results from the actions of the corporate directors and officers. For obvious reasons, the directors and officers would probably be unwilling to take any action against themselves.

Written Demand Required Before shareholders can bring a derivative suit, they must submit a written demand to the corporation, asking the board of directors to take appropriate action [RMBCA 7.40]. The directors then have ninety days in which to act. Only if they refuse to do so can the derivative suit go forward. In addition, a court will dismiss a derivative suit if a majority of the directors or an independent panel determines in good faith that the lawsuit is not in the best interests of the corporation [RMBCA 7.44].

Any Damages Awarded Go to the Corporation When shareholders bring a derivative suit, they are not pursuing rights or benefits for themselves personally but are acting as guardians of the corporate entity. Therefore, if the suit is successful, any damages recovered normally

go into the corporation's treasury, not to the shareholders personally.[15]

40–5 Duties and Liabilities of Shareholders

One of the hallmarks of the corporate form of organization is that shareholders are not personally liable for the debts of the corporation. If the corporation fails, the shareholders can lose their investments, but that generally is the limit of their liability. As discussed previously, in certain instances, a court will pierce the corporate veil (disregard the corporate entity) and hold the shareholders individually liable. But these situations are the exception, not the rule.

A shareholder can also be personally liable in certain other rare instances. One relates to illegal dividends, which were mentioned previously. Another relates to *watered stock.* Finally, in certain instances, a majority shareholder who engages in oppressive conduct or attempts to exclude minority shareholders from receiving certain benefits can be held personally liable.

Concept Summary 40.3 reviews the role, rights, and liability of shareholders in a corporation.

40–5a Watered Stock

When a corporation issues shares for less than their fair market value, the shares are referred to as **watered stock.**[16] Usually, the shareholder who receives watered stock must pay the difference to the corporation (the shareholder is personally liable). In some states, the shareholder who receives watered stock may be liable to creditors of the corporation for unpaid corporate debts.

■ **EXAMPLE 40.8** During the formation of a corporation, Gomez, one of the incorporators, transfers his property, Sunset Beach, to the corporation for 10,000 shares of stock at a par value of $100 per share for a total price of $1 million. After the property is transferred and the shares are issued, Sunset Beach is carried on the corporate books at a value of $1 million.

On appraisal, it is discovered that the market value of the property at the time of transfer was only $500,000. The

---

14. See, for example, *United Technologies Corp. v. Treppel,* 109 A.3d 553 (Del.Ch. 2014).

15. The shareholders may be entitled to reimbursement for reasonable expenses of the derivative lawsuit, including attorneys' fees.

16. The phrase *watered stock* was originally used to describe cattle that were kept thirsty during a long drive and then were allowed to drink large quantities of water just before their sale. The increased weight of the watered stock allowed the seller to reap a higher profit.

Concept Summary 40.3

Role, Rights, and Liability of Shareholders

Shareholders' Powers	Shareholders' powers include approval of all fundamental changes affecting the corporation and election of the board of directors.
Shareholders' Meetings	Shareholders' meetings must occur at least annually, and special meetings can be called when necessary. Notice of the time and place of a meeting (and its purpose, if the meeting is specially called) must be sent to shareholders. A minimum number of shareholders (quorum) must be present to vote.
Shareholders' Rights	Shareholders have numerous rights, which may include the following: • Voting rights. • Preemptive rights (depending on the corporate articles). • The right to receive dividends (at the discretion of the directors). • The right to inspect the corporate records. • The right to transfer shares (this right may be restricted in close corporations). • The right to receive a share of corporate assets when the corporation is dissolved. • The right to sue on behalf of the corporation (bring a shareholder's derivative suit) when the directors fail to do so.
Shareholders' Liability	Shareholders may be liable for watered stock. In certain situations, majority shareholders may be regarded as having a fiduciary duty to minority shareholders and will be liable if that duty is breached.

---

shares issued to Gomez are therefore watered stock, and he is liable to the corporation for the difference between the value of the shares and the value of the property. ∎

40–5b Duties of Majority Shareholders

In some instances, a majority shareholder is regarded as having a fiduciary duty to the corporation and to the minority shareholders. This duty arises when a single shareholder (or a few shareholders acting in concert) owns a sufficient number of shares to exercise *de facto* control over the corporation. In these situations, the majority shareholder owes a fiduciary duty to the minority shareholders.

When a majority shareholder breaches her or his fiduciary duty to a minority shareholder, the minority shareholder can sue for damages. A breach of fiduciary duties by those who control a close corporation normally constitutes what is known as *oppressive conduct*. A common example of a breach of fiduciary duty occurs when the majority shareholders "freeze out" the minority shareholders and exclude them from certain benefits of participating in the firm.

∎ **EXAMPLE 40.9** Brodie, Jordan, and Barbara form a close corporation to operate a machine shop. Brodie and Jordan own 75 percent of the shares in the company, but all three are directors. After disagreements arise, Brodie asks the company to purchase his shares, but his requests are refused. A few years later, Brodie dies, and his wife, Ella, inherits his shares. Jordan and Barbara refuse to perform a valuation of the company, deny Ella access to corporate information, do not declare any dividends, and refuse to elect Ella as a director. In this situation, the majority shareholders have violated their fiduciary duty to Ella. ∎

Reviewing: Corporate Directors, Officers, and Shareholders

David Brock was on the board of directors of Firm Body Fitness, Inc., which owned a string of fitness clubs in New Mexico. Brock owned 15 percent of the Firm Body stock and was also employed as a tanning technician at one of the fitness clubs. After the January financial report showed that Firm Body's tanning division was operating at a substantial net loss, the board of directors, led by Marty Levinson, discussed terminating the tanning operations. Brock successfully convinced a majority of the board that the tanning division was necessary to market the clubs' overall fitness package. By April, the tanning division's financial losses had risen. The board hired a business analyst, who conducted surveys and determined that the tanning operations did not significantly increase membership.

A shareholder, Diego Peñada, discovered that Brock owned stock in Sunglow, Inc., the company from which Firm Body purchased its tanning equipment. Peñada notified Levinson, who privately reprimanded Brock. Shortly thereafter, Brock and Mandy Vail, who owned 37 percent of the Firm Body stock and also held shares of Sunglow, voted to replace Levinson on the board of directors. Using the information presented in the chapter, answer the following questions.

1. What duties did Brock, as a director, owe to Firm Body?
2. Does the fact that Brock owned shares in Sunglow establish a conflict of interest? Why or why not?
3. Suppose that Firm Body brought an action against Brock claiming that he had breached the duty of loyalty by not disclosing his interest in Sunglow to the other directors. What theory might Brock use in his defense?
4. Now suppose that Firm Body did not bring an action against Brock. What type of lawsuit might Peñada be able to bring based on these facts?

Debate This . . . *Because most shareholders never bother to vote for directors, shareholders have no real control over corporations.*

Terms and Concepts

business judgment rule 766	preemptive rights 775	stock certificate 775
dividend 776	proxy 772	stock warrant 776
inside director 763	quorum 763	voting trust 775
outside director 763	shareholder's derivative suit 777	watered stock 777

Issue Spotters

1. Wonder Corporation has an opportunity to buy stock in XL, Inc. The directors decide that instead of Wonder buying the stock, the directors will buy it. Yvon, a Wonder shareholder, learns of the purchase and wants to sue the directors on Wonder's behalf. Can she do it? Explain. (See *Rights of Shareholders*.)

2. Nico is Omega Corporation's majority shareholder. He owns enough stock in Omega that if he were to sell it,

the sale would be a transfer of control of the firm. Discuss whether Nico owes a duty to Omega or the minority shareholders in selling his shares. (See *Duties and Liabilities of Shareholders*.)

- **Check your answers to the Issue Spotters against the answers provided in Appendix D at the end of this text.**

Business Scenarios

40–1. Conflicts of Interest. Oxy Corp. is negotiating with Wick Construction Co. for the renovation of Oxy's corporate headquarters. Wick, the owner of Wick Construction Co., is also one of the five members of Oxy's board of directors. The

contract terms are standard for this type of contract. Wick has previously informed two of the other directors of his interest in the construction company. Oxy's board approves the contract by a three-to-two vote, with Wick voting with the majority. Discuss whether this contract is binding on the corporation. (See *Duties and Liabilities of Directors and Officers*.)

40–2. Liability of Directors. AstroStar, Inc., has approximately five hundred shareholders. Its board of directors consists of three members—Eckhart, Dolan, and Macero. At a regular board meeting, the board selects Galiard as president of the corporation by a two-to-one vote, with Eckhart dissenting. The minutes of the meeting do not register Eckhart's dissenting vote. Later, an audit reveals that Galiard is a former convict and has embezzled $500,000 from the corporation that is not covered by insurance. Can the corporation hold directors Eckhart, Dolan, and Macero personally liable? Discuss. (See *Duties and Liabilities of Directors and Officers*.)

Business Case Problems

40–3. Fiduciary Duty of Officers. Designer Surfaces, Inc., supplied countertops to homeowners who shopped at stores such as Lowe's and Costco. The homeowners paid the store, which then contracted with Designer to fabricate and install the countertops. Designer bought materials from Arizona Tile, LLC, on an open account. Designer's only known corporate officers were Howard Berger and John McCarthy. Designer became insolvent and could not pay Arizona Tile for all the materials it had purchased, including materials for which Designer had already received payment from the retail stores. Arizona Tile sued Designer and won a default judgment, but the company had no funds. Arizona Tile then sued Berger and McCarthy personally for diverting company funds that Designer had received in trust for payment to Arizona Tile. Arizona Tile argued that the use of the funds for other purposes was a breach of fiduciary duty. Berger and McCarthy argued that corporate law imposed neither a fiduciary duty on corporate officers nor personal liability for breach of a duty to suppliers of materials. Which argument is more credible, and why? [*Arizona Tile, LLC v. Berger*, 223 Ariz. 491, 224 P.3d 988 (Ariz.App. 2010)] (See *Role of Directors and Officers*.)

40–4. Business Case Problem with Sample Answer—Rights of Shareholders. Stanka Woods was the sole member of Hair Ventures, LLC. Hair Ventures owned 3 million shares of stock in Biolustré, Inc. For several years, Woods and other Biolustré shareholders did not receive notice of shareholders' meetings or financial reports. On learning that Biolustré planned to issue more stock, Woods, through Hair Ventures, demanded to see Biolustré's books and records. Biolustré asserted that the request was not for a proper purpose. Does Woods have a right to inspect Biolustré's books and records? If so, what are the limits? Do any of those limits apply in this case? Explain. [*Biolustré Inc. v. Hair Ventures, LLC*, 2011 WL 540574 (Tex.App.—San Antonio 2011)] (See *Rights of Shareholders*.)

- For a sample answer to Problem 40–4, go to Appendix E at the end of this text.

40–5. Duty of Loyalty. Kids International Corp. produced children's wear for Walmart and other retailers. Gila Dweck was a Kids director and its chief executive officer. Because she felt that she was not paid enough, she started Success Apparel to compete with Kids. Success operated out of Kids' premises, used its employees, borrowed on its credit, took advantage of its business opportunities, and capitalized on its customer relationships. As an "administrative fee," Dweck paid Kids 1 percent of Success's total sales. Did Dweck breach any fiduciary duties? Explain. [*Dweck v. Nasser*, 2012 WL 3194069 (Del.Ch. 2012)] (See *Duties and Liabilities of Directors and Officers*.)

40–6. Duties of Majority Shareholders. Bill McCann was the president and chief executive officer of McCann Ranch & Livestock Co. He and his brother Ron each owned 36.7 percent of the stock. Ron had been removed from the board of directors on their father's death, however, and was not authorized to work for the firm. Their mother, Gertrude, owned the rest of the stock, which was to pass to Bill on her death. The corporation paid Gertrude's personal expenses in an amount that represented about 75 percent of the net corporate income. Bill received regular salary increases. The corporation did not issue a dividend. Was Ron the victim of a freeze-out? Discuss. [*McCann v. McCann*, 152 Idaho 809, 275 P.3d 824 (2012)] (See *Duties and Liabilities of Shareholders*.)

40–7. Business Judgment Rule. Country Contractors, Inc., contracted to provide excavation services for A Westside Storage of Indianapolis, Inc., but did not complete the job and later filed for bankruptcy. Stephen Songer and Jahn Songer were Country's sole shareholders. The Songers had not misused the corporate form to engage in fraud. The firm had not been undercapitalized, personal and corporate funds had not been commingled, and Country had kept accounting records and minutes of its annual board meetings. Are the Songers personally liable for Country's failure to complete its contract? Explain. [*Country Contractors, Inc. v. A Westside Storage of Indianapolis, Inc.*, 4 N.E.3d 677 (Ind.App. 2014)] (See *Duties and Liabilities of Directors and Officers*.)

40–8. Rights of Shareholders. FCR Realty, LLC, and Clifford B. Green & Sons, Inc., were co-owned by three brothers—Frederick, Clifford Jr., and Richard Green. Each brother was a shareholder of the corporation. Frederick was a controlling shareholder, as well as president. Each brother owned a one-third interest in the LLC. Clifford believed that Frederick had misused LLC and corporate funds to pay nonexistent debts and liabilities and had diverted LLC assets to the corporation. He also contended that Frederick had disbursed about $1.8 million in corporate funds to Frederick's own separate business. Clifford hired an attorney and filed an action on behalf of the two companies against Frederick for breach of fiduciary duty. Frederick argued that Clifford lacked the knowledge necessary to adequately represent the companies' interest because he did not understand financial statements. Can Clifford maintain the action against Frederick? If so, and if the suit is successful, who recovers the damages? Explain. [*FCR Realty, LLC v. Green*, __ Conn.Supp. __, __ Conn.L.Rptr. __, 2016 WL 571449 (Super. 2016)] (See *Rights of Shareholders*.)

40–9. A Question of Ethics—Duties of Directors and Officers. *New Orleans Paddlewheels, Inc. (NOP), was a Louisiana corporation formed in 1982. James Smith, Sr., and Warren Reuther were its only shareholders, with each holding 50 percent of the stock. NOP was part of a sprawling enterprise of tourism and hospitality companies in New Orleans controlled by Smith and Reuther. The positions on the board of each company were split equally between the Smith and Reuther families.*

At Smith's request, his son James Smith, Jr. (JES), became involved in the businesses. In 1999, NOP's board elected JES as president, to be in charge of day-to-day operations, and Reuther as chief executive officer (CEO), to be in charge of marketing and development. Over the next few years, animosity developed between Reuther and JES. In October 2001, JES terminated Reuther as CEO and denied him access to the offices and books of NOP and the other companies, literally changing the locks on the doors. At the next meetings of the boards of NOP and the overall enterprise, deadlock ensued, with the directors voting along family lines on every issue.

Complaining that the meetings were a "waste of time," JES began to run the entire enterprise by taking advantage of an unequal balance of power on the companies' executive committees. In NOP's subsequent bankruptcy proceeding, Reuther filed a motion for the appointment of a trustee to formulate a plan for the firm's reorganization, alleging, among other things, misconduct by NOP's management. [In re New Orleans Paddlewheels, Inc., 350 Bankr. 667 (E.D.La. 2006)] (See *Duties and Liabilities of Directors and Officers*.)

(a) Was Reuther legally entitled to have access to the books and records of NOP and the other companies? JES maintained, among other things, that NOP's books were "a mess." Was JES's denial of that access unethical? Why or why not?

(b) How would you describe JES's attempt to gain control of NOP and the other companies? Were his actions devious and self-serving in the pursuit of personal gain or legitimate and reasonable in the pursuit of a business goal? Discuss.

Legal Reasoning Group Activity

40–10. Shareholders' Duties. Milena Weintraub and Larry Griffith were shareholders in Grand Casino, Inc., which operated a casino in South Dakota. Griffith owned 51 percent of the stock and Weintraub 49 percent. Weintraub managed the casino, which Griffith typically visited once a week. At the end of 2012, an accounting audit showed that the cash on hand was less than the amount posted in the casino's books. Later, more shortfalls were discovered. In October 2014, Griffith did a complete audit. Weintraub was unable to account for $200,500 in missing cash. Griffith then took all of the casino's most recent profits, including Weintraub's $90,447.20 share, and, without telling Weintraub, sold the casino for $400,000 and kept all of the proceeds. Weintraub filed a suit against Griffith, asserting a breach of fiduciary duty. Griffith countered with evidence of Weintraub's misappropriation of corporate cash. (See *Duties and Liabilities of Shareholders*.)

(a) The first group will discuss the duties that these parties owed to each other and determine whether Weintraub or Griffith, or both, breached those duties.

(b) The second group will decide how this dispute should be resolved and who should pay what to whom to reconcile the finances.

(c) A third group will discuss whether Weintraub or Griffith violated any ethical duties to each other or to the corporation.

CHAPTER 41

Mergers and Takeovers

A corporation may grow simply by reinvesting retained earnings in more equipment or by hiring more employees. A corporation may also extend its operations by combining with another corporation through a merger, a consolidation, or a share exchange. In addition, a corporation may purchase the assets of, or a controlling interest in, another corporation.

This chapter examines each of these types of corporate expansion. We also discuss dissolution and winding up—the processes by which a corporation terminates its existence. The chapter concludes with a brief comparison of the major forms of business organization discussed in this text.

41–1 Merger, Consolidation, and Share Exchange

The terms *merger* and *consolidation* traditionally referred to two legally distinct proceedings, but some people today use the term *consolidation* to refer to all types of combinations. Whether a combination is a merger, a consolidation, or a share exchange, the rights and liabilities of shareholders, the corporation, and the corporation's creditors are the same. Note that the power to merge, consolidate, and exchange shares is conferred by statute, and thus state law establishes the specific procedures.

41–1a Merger

A **merger** involves the legal combination of two or more corporations. After a merger, only one of the corporations continues to exist. ■ **EXAMPLE 41.1** Corporation A and Corporation B decide to merge. They agree that A will absorb B. Therefore, after the merger, B ceases to exist as a separate entity, and A continues as the **surviving corporation.** ■ Exhibit 41–1 graphically illustrates this process.

One of the Firms Survives Continuing with *Example 41.1,* after the merger, Corporation A—the surviving corporation—is recognized as a single corporation, and B no longer exists as an entity. A's articles of incorporation are deemed amended to include any changes stated in the **articles of merger** (a document setting forth the terms and conditions of the merger). Corporation A will issue shares or pay some fair consideration to the shareholders of B.

It Inherits All Legal Rights and Obligations of the Other Firm After the merger, Corporation A possesses all of the rights, privileges, and powers of itself and B. It automatically acquires all of B's property and assets without the necessity of a formal transfer. In addition, it becomes liable for all of B's debts and obligations, and it inherits B's preexisting legal rights. Thus, if Corporation B had a right of action against a third party under tort or property law, Corporation A can bring a suit after the merger to recover B's damages.

41–1b Consolidation

In a **consolidation,** two or more corporations combine in such a way that each corporation ceases to exist and a new one emerges. ■ **EXAMPLE 41.2** Corporation A and

EXHIBIT 41–1 Merger

Corporation A and Corporation B decide to merge. They agree that A will absorb B, so after the merger, B no longer exists as a separate entity, and A continues as the surviving corporation.

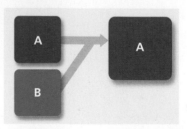

Corporation B consolidate to form an entirely new organization, Corporation C. In the process, A and B both terminate, and C comes into existence as a new entity. ∎ Exhibit 41–2 graphically illustrates this process.

A New Corporation Is Formed The results of a consolidation are similar to those of a merger—only one company remains—but it is a completely new entity (the *consolidated corporation*). In terms of *Example 41.2,* Corporation C is recognized as a new corporation, while A and B cease to exist. C's *articles of consolidation* take the place of A's and B's original corporate articles and are thereafter regarded as C's corporate articles. As with a merger, the newly formed corporation will issue shares or pay some fair consideration to the shareholders of the disappearing corporations.

It Inherits All Rights and Liabilities of Both Predecessors Corporation C inherits all of the rights, privileges, and powers previously held by A and B. Title to any property and assets owned by A and B passes to C without a formal transfer. C assumes liability for all debts and obligations owed by A and B.

True consolidations have become less common among for-profit corporations because it is often advantageous for one of the combining firms to survive. In contrast, nonprofit corporations and associations may prefer consolidation because it suggests a new beginning in which neither of the two initial entities is dominant.

41–1c Share Exchange

In a **share exchange,** some or all of the shares of one corporation are exchanged for some or all of the shares of another corporation, but both corporations continue

to exist. Share exchanges are often used to create *holding companies* (companies that own part or all of other companies' outstanding stock).

If one corporation owns *all* of the shares of another corporation, it is referred to as the **parent corporation,** and the wholly owned company is the **subsidiary corporation.** ∎ **EXAMPLE 41.3** United Continental Holdings, Inc. (UAL), is a large holding company that owns United Airlines. UAL is the parent corporation, and United Airlines is the subsidiary. ∎

41–1d Merger, Consolidation, and Share Exchange Procedures

All states have statutes authorizing mergers, consolidations, and share exchanges for domestic (in-state) and foreign (out-of-state) corporations. The procedures vary somewhat among jurisdictions. In some states, for instance, a consolidation resulting in an entirely new corporation simply follows the same incorporation procedures as any new corporation, and other rules apply to other combinations.

The Revised Model Business Corporation Act (RMBCA) does set forth the following basic requirements for mergers and share exchanges [RMBCA 11.01–11.07]:

1. The board of directors of *each* corporation involved must approve the merger or share exchange plan.
2. The plan must specify any terms and conditions of the merger. It also must state how the value of the shares of each merging corporation will be determined and how they will be converted into shares or other securities, cash, property, or additional interests in another corporation.
3. The majority of the shareholders of *each* corporation must vote to approve the plan at a shareholders' meeting. If any class of stock is entitled to vote as a separate group, the majority of each separate voting group must approve the plan. Frequently, a corporation's articles of incorporation or bylaws require approval by more than a majority once a quorum is present. In addition, some state statutes require the approval of two-thirds of the outstanding shares of voting stock (not just the shareholders present at the meeting), and others require a four-fifths approval.
4. Once the plan is approved by the directors and the shareholders of each corporation, the surviving corporation files the plan (articles of merger, consolidation, or share exchange) with the appropriate official. Usually the plan is filed with the appropriate secretary of state.

EXHIBIT 41–2 Consolidation

Corporation A and Corporation B consolidate to form an entirely new organization, Corporation C. In the process, A and B terminate, and C comes into existence.

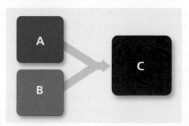

5. When state formalities are satisfied, the state issues a certificate of merger to the surviving corporation or a certificate of consolidation to the newly consolidated corporation.

In the following case, the attorneys for a group of shareholders argued that the shareholders had not been given enough information before they were asked to vote on a proposed merger.

Case Analysis 41.1

In re Trulia, Inc. Stockholder Litigation
Court of Chancery of Delaware, 129 A.3d 884 (2016).

In the Language of the Court
BOUCHARD, C. [Chancellor]

This opinion concerns the proposed settlement of a stockholder class action challenging Zillow, Inc.'s acquisition of Trulia, Inc. in a stock-for-stock merger * * * . Shortly after the public announcement of the proposed transaction, four Trulia stockholders filed essentially identical complaints alleging that Trulia's directors had breached their fiduciary duties in approving the proposed merger * * * . Less than four months later, * * * the parties reached an agreement-in-principle to settle.

* * * Trulia agreed to supplement the proxy materials disseminated to its stockholders before they voted on the proposed transaction to include some additional information that theoretically would allow the stockholders to be better informed in exercising their [voting] rights. In exchange, plaintiffs dropped their motion to preliminarily enjoin the transaction and agreed to provide a release of claims on behalf of a proposed class of Trulia's stockholders.

Because a class action impacts the legal rights of absent class members, it is the responsibility of [this] Court * * * to exercise independent judgment to determine whether a proposed class settlement is fair and reasonable to the affected class members.

* * * *

I. BACKGROUND
* * * *

Defendant Trulia, Inc., a Delaware corporation, is an online provider of information on homes for purchase or for rent in the United States.

Defendant Zillow, Inc., a Washington corporation, is a real estate marketplace that helps home buyers, sellers, landlords and others find and share information about homes. Defendant Zebra Holdco, Inc. ("Holdco"), now known as Zillow Group, Inc., is a Washington corporation that was formed to facilitate the merger at issue and is now the parent company of Zillow and Trulia.

* * * *

II. LEGAL ANALYSIS
* * * *

Under Delaware law, *when directors solicit stockholder action, they must disclose fully and fairly all material information within the board's control.* * * * *Information is material if there is a substantial likelihood that a reasonable shareholder would consider it important in deciding how to vote.* In other words, information is material if, from the perspective of a reasonable stockholder, there is a substantial likelihood that it significantly alters the total mix of information made available. [Emphasis added.]

Here, the * * * Proxy that Trulia and Zillow stockholders received in advance of their respective stockholders' meetings to consider whether to approve the proposed transaction ran 224 pages in length, excluding annexes. It contained extensive discussion concerning, among other things, the background of the mergers, each board's reasons for recommending approval of the proposed transaction, prospective financial information concerning the companies that had been reviewed by their respective boards and financial advisors, and explanations of the opinions of each company's financial advisor. In the case of Trulia, the opinion of J.P. Morgan [Securities LLC] was summarized in ten single-spaced pages.

The Supplemental Disclosures plaintiffs obtained in this case solely concern the section of the Proxy summarizing J.P. Morgan's financial analysis, which the Trulia board cited as one of the factors it considered in deciding to recommend approval of the proposed merger. Specifically, these disclosures provided additional details concerning * * * certain synergy [creation of a whole that is greater than the sum of its parts] numbers in J.P. Morgan's value creation analysis.

* * * Under Delaware law, when the board relies on the advice of a financial advisor in making a decision that requires stockholder action, those stockholders are entitled to receive in the proxy statement a fair summary of the substantive work performed by the investment bankers upon whose advice the recommendations of their board as to how to vote on a merger or tender rely.

A fair summary, however, is a *summary*. By definition, it need not contain all information underlying the financial advisor's opinion or contained in its report to the board. * * * *The summary does not need to provide sufficient data to allow the stockholders to perform their own independent valuation.* The essence of a fair summary is not a cornucopia [abundance] of financial data, but rather an accurate description of the advisor's methodology and key assumptions. * * * Disclosures that provide extraneous details do not contribute to a fair summary and do not add value for stockholders. [Emphasis added.]

* * * *

The Supplemental Disclosures provided some additional details in the

Case 41.1 Continued

sections of J.P. Morgan's analysis entitled "Value Creation Analysis—Intrinsic Value Approach" and "Value Creation Analysis—Market-Based Approach."

As supplemented, the disclosure concerning the Intrinsic Value Approach * * * added: * * *

> The present value of after-tax synergies was based on an estimate of $175.0 million in synergies * * * based on assumptions provided by Trulia's management.

Plaintiffs argue that the disclosure of the $175 million synergies figure * * * was important because it is substantially different from the $100 million in synergies that J.P. Morgan used in the Market-Based Approach * * * . There are three fundamental problems with this argument.

First, * * * plaintiffs question why J.P. Morgan used two different synergies figures in two different analyses * * * . [But] the Proxy accurately disclosed which synergies assumptions the financial advisor deemed appropriate to use in each analysis.

Second, the $175 million synergies figure that plaintiffs consider so important was not new information. It already was disclosed in the Proxy.

Third, * * * the Proxy indicates that the Market-Based Approach analysis was less important than the Intrinsic Value Approach analysis. Thus, the notion that the disclosure of the $175 million synergies figure used in one analysis * * * was significant because it was higher than the $100 million figure used in a second, different analysis is based on a false equivalence of the relative importance of the two analyses.

In sum, the disclosures in the original Proxy already provided a fair summary of J.P. Morgan's methodology and assumptions in its two "Value Creation" analyses. Inserting additional minutiae [details] underlying some of the assumptions could not reasonably have been expected to significantly alter the total mix of information and thus was not material. Indeed, * * * the supplemental information was not even helpful to stockholders.

* * * *

* * * As such, from the perspective of Trulia's stockholders, the "get" in the form of the Supplemental Disclosures does not provide adequate consideration to warrant the "give" of providing a release of claims to defendants and their affiliates * * * . Accordingly, * * * the proposed settlement is not fair or reasonable to Trulia's stockholders.

III. CONCLUSION

For the foregoing reasons, approval of the proposed settlement is DENIED.

Legal Reasoning Questions

1. The announcement of a proposed merger often triggers a shareholder action alleging that directors breached their fiduciary duty by agreeing to sell the corporation for an unfair price. When and how does such litigation benefit the shareholders?

2. In the *Trulia* case, the settlement, if approved, would not have yielded any genuine benefit for the shareholders. If the court had approved the settlement, however, who would have benefited?

3. When the parties to a dispute agree to a settlement, they share the same interest in obtaining the court's approval. What are the advantages and disadvantages of this situation?

41–1e Short-Form Mergers

RMBCA 11.04 provides a simplified procedure for the merger of a substantially owned subsidiary corporation into its parent corporation. Under these provisions, a **short-form merger**—also referred to as a *parent-subsidiary merger*—can be accomplished *without* the approval of the shareholders of either corporation.

The short-form merger can be used only when the parent corporation owns at least 90 percent of the outstanding shares of each class of stock of the subsidiary corporation. Once the board of directors of the parent corporation approves the plan, it is filed with the state, and copies are sent to each shareholder of record in the subsidiary corporation.

41–1f Shareholder Approval

As mentioned, except in a short-form merger, the shareholders of both corporations must approve a merger or other plan of consolidation. Shareholders invest in a corporation with the expectation that the board of directors will make decisions on *ordinary* business matters. For *extraordinary* matters, normally both the board of directors and the shareholders must approve the transaction.

Mergers and other combinations are extraordinary business matters, meaning that the board of directors must normally obtain the shareholders' approval and provide appraisal rights (discussed next). Amendments to the articles of incorporation and the dissolution of the corporation also generally require shareholder approval.

Sometimes, a transaction can be structured in such a way that shareholder approval is not required, but if the shareholders challenge the transaction, a court might require shareholder approval. For this reason, the board of directors may request shareholder approval even when it might not be legally required.

41–1g Appraisal Rights

What if a shareholder disapproves of a merger or a consolidation but is outvoted by the other shareholders? The law will not force a dissenting shareholder to become an unwilling shareholder in a corporation that is new or different from the one in which the shareholder originally invested.

Dissenting shareholders therefore have a statutory right to be paid the fair value of the shares they held on the date of the merger or consolidation. This right is referred to as the shareholder's **appraisal right.** The "fair value of the shares" normally is the value on the day prior to the date on which the vote was taken [RMBCA 13.21]. So long as the transaction does not involve fraud or other illegal conduct, appraisal rights are the exclusive remedy for a shareholder who is dissatisfied with the price received for the stock.

When Appraisal Rights Apply Appraisal rights normally extend to mergers, consolidations, share exchanges, and sales of substantially all of the corporate assets. Such rights can be particularly important in a short-form merger because the minority stockholders do not receive advance notice of the merger, the directors do not consider or approve it, and there is no vote. Appraisal rights are often the only recourse available to shareholders who object to short-form mergers.

Procedures Each state establishes the procedures for asserting appraisal rights in that jurisdiction. Shareholders may lose their appraisal rights if they do not adhere precisely to the procedures prescribed by statute. When they lose the right to an appraisal, dissenting shareholders must go along with the transaction despite their objections.

Concept Summary 41.1 reviews mergers, consolidations, and share exchanges.

41–2 Purchase of Assets

When a corporation acquires all or substantially all of the assets of another corporation by direct purchase, the *acquiring corporation* simply extends its ownership and control over more assets. Because no change in the legal entity occurs, the acquiring corporation usually does not need to obtain shareholder approval for the purchase.

In contrast, the corporation that is *selling* all of its assets is substantially changing its business position and perhaps its ability to carry out its corporate purposes. For that reason, the corporation whose assets are being sold must obtain approval from both its board of directors and its shareholders [RMBCA 12.02]. In most states and under RMBCA 13.02, dissenting shareholders of the selling corporation can demand appraisal rights.

Both the U.S. Department of Justice and the Federal Trade Commission have guidelines that significantly constrain and often prohibit mergers that could result from a purchase of assets. (These guidelines will be discussed in the materials covering federal antitrust laws.)

41–2a When Shareholder Approval May Be Required

Although shareholder approval is not typically required, it may be required in a few situations. If the acquiring corporation plans to pay for the assets with its stock but not enough authorized unissued shares are available, then the shareholders must approve the issuance of additional shares. Shareholder approval is also needed if the acquiring corporation's stock is traded on a national stock exchange and the corporation will be issuing a significant number of shares.

41–2b Successor Liability in Purchases of Assets

Generally, a corporation that purchases the assets of another corporation is *not automatically responsible for the liabilities of the selling corporation.* Exceptions are made in certain circumstances, however. In any of the following situations, the acquiring corporation will be held to have assumed *both* the assets and the liabilities of the selling corporation:

1. *Express or implicit agreement.* The purchasing corporation impliedly or expressly assumes the seller's liabilities.
2. De facto *merger.* The sale transaction amounts to a merger or consolidation of the two companies.
3. *Continuation.* The purchaser continues the seller's business and retains the same shareholders, directors, and officers.
4. *Fraud exception.* The sale is entered into fraudulently for the purpose of escaping liability.

Concept Summary 41.1

Merger, Consolidation, and Share Exchange

Merger	The legal combination of two or more corporations, with the result that the surviving corporation acquires all of the assets and obligations of the other corporation, which then ceases to exist.
Consolidation	The legal combination of two or more corporations, with the result that each corporation ceases to exist and a new one emerges. The new corporation assumes all of the assets and obligations of the former corporations.
Share Exchange	A form of business combination in which some or all of the shares of one corporation are exchanged for some or all of the shares of another corporation, but both firms continue to exist.
Procedure	Determined by state statutes. Basic requirements are the following: • The board of directors of each corporation involved must approve the plan of merger, consolidation, or share exchange. • The shareholders of each corporation must approve the merger or other consolidation plan at a shareholders' meeting. • Articles of merger or consolidation (the plan) must be filed, usually with the secretary of state. • The state issues a certificate of merger (or consolidation) to the surviving (or newly consolidated) corporation.
Short-Form Merger (Parent-Subsidiary Merger)	When the parent corporation owns at least 90 percent of the outstanding shares of each class of stock of the subsidiary corporation, shareholder approval is not required for the two firms to merge.
Appraisal Rights	Rights of dissenting shareholders (provided by state statute) to receive the fair value for their shares when a merger or consolidation takes place. If the shareholder and the corporation do not agree on the fair value, a court will determine it.

■ **CASE IN POINT 41.4** American Standard, Inc., sold its Kewanee Boiler division to OakFabco, Inc. The agreement stated that OakFabco would purchase Kewanee assets subject to Kewanee liabilities. "Kewanee liabilities" were defined as "all the debts, liabilities, obligations, and commitments (fixed or contingent) connected with or attributable to Kewanee existing and outstanding at the Closing Date."

Because the boilers manufactured by Kewanee had been insulated with asbestos, many tort claims arose in the years following the purchase of the business. Some of those claims were brought by plaintiffs who had suffered injuries after the closing of the transaction that were allegedly attributable to boilers manufactured and sold before the closing.

American Standard filed an action against OakFabco in New York, asking the court for a declaratory judgment on the issue of whether liabilities for such injuries were among the "Kewanee liabilities" that OakFabco had assumed. The court held that OakFabco had expressly assumed the liabilities of the selling corporation in the contract, including claims that arose after the closing date. A state appellate court affirmed that decision. According to the reviewing court, "nothing in the nature of the transaction suggested that the parties intended OakFabco, which got all the assets, to escape any of the related obligations."[1] ∎

41-3 Purchase of Stock

An alternative to the purchase of another corporation's assets is the purchase of a substantial number of the voting shares of its stock. This enables the acquiring corporation to control the **target corporation** (the corporation being acquired). The process of acquiring control over a corporation in this way is commonly referred to as a corporate **takeover.**

41-3a Tender Offers

The acquiring corporation deals directly with the target company's shareholders in seeking to purchase the shares they hold. It does this by making a **tender offer** to buy shares of stock from all of the target company's shareholders in exchange for cash or stock. The tender offer can be conditioned on the receipt of a specified number of outstanding shares by a certain date.

To induce shareholders to accept the offer, the tender price offered generally is higher than the market price of the target's stock before the tender offer was announced. ∎ **EXAMPLE 41.5** In a merger of two major pharmaceutical companies, Pfizer, Inc., paid $68 billion to acquire its rival, Wyeth. Wyeth shareholders received approximately $50.19 per share (part in cash and part in Pfizer stock), which amounted to a 15 percent premium over the market price of the stock. ∎

1. *American Standard, Inc. v. OakFabco, Inc.,* 14 N.Y.3d 399, 901 N.Y.S.2d 572 (2010).

41-3b Application of Securities Laws

Federal securities laws strictly control the terms, duration, and circumstances under which most tender offers are made. In addition, many states have passed antitakeover statutes.

Generally, the offering corporation does not need to notify the Securities and Exchange Commission (SEC) or the target corporation's management until after the tender offer is made. The offeror must then disclose to the SEC the source of the funds used in the offer, the purpose of the offer, and the acquiring corporation's plans for the firm if the takeover is successful.

41-3c Responses to Tender Offers

A firm may respond to a tender offer in numerous ways. If the target firm's board of directors views the tender offer as favorable, the board will recommend that the shareholders accept it. Frequently, though, the target corporation's management opposes the proposed takeover. This is referred to as a *hostile takeover.*

To resist a takeover, a target company may make a *self-tender,* in which it offers to acquire stock from its own shareholders and thereby retain corporate control. The target corporation may also engage in a media campaign to persuade its shareholders that the tender offer is not in their best interests. Another possible defense is for the target firm to issue additional stock, thereby increasing the number of shares that the acquiring corporation must purchase to gain control. Several other tactics to resist a takeover are described in Exhibit 41–3.

Concept Summary 41.2 reviews purchases of assets and purchases of stock.

41-3d Takeover Defenses and Directors' Fiduciary Duties

As mentioned, the board of directors of the target corporation often opposes the takeover. Clearly, board members have an interest in keeping their jobs and control, but they also have a fiduciary duty to the corporation and its shareholders to act in the best interests of the company.

In a hostile takeover attempt, sometimes directors' duties of care and loyalty collide with their self-interest. Then the shareholders, who would have received a premium for their shares as a result of the takeover, file lawsuits. Such lawsuits frequently allege that the directors breached their fiduciary duties in defending against the tender offer.

EXHIBIT 41–3 The Terminology of Takeover Defenses

Term	Definition
Crown Jewel	When threatened with a takeover, management makes the company less attractive to the raider by selling the company's most valuable asset (the "crown jewel") to a third party.
Golden Parachute	When a takeover is successful, top management usually is changed. With this in mind, a company may establish special termination or retirement benefits that must be paid to top managers if they are "retired." In other words, a departing high-level manager's parachute will be "golden" when he or she is forced to "bail out" of the company.
Greenmail	To regain control, a target company may pay a higher-than-market price to repurchase all of the stock that the acquiring corporation bought. When a takeover is attempted through a gradual accumulation of target stock rather than a tender offer, the intent may be to induce the target company to buy back the shares at a premium price—a concept similar to blackmail.
Pac-Man	Named after the Atari video game, this is an aggressive defense in which the target corporation attempts its own takeover of the acquiring corporation.
Poison Pill	The target corporation issues to its stockholders rights to purchase additional shares at low prices when there is a takeover attempt. This makes the takeover undesirably or even prohibitively expensive for the acquiring corporation.
White Knight	The target corporation solicits a merger with a third party, which then makes a better (often simply a higher) tender offer to the target's shareholders. The third party that "rescues" the target is the "white knight."

Business Judgment Rule Courts apply the *business judgment rule* when analyzing whether the directors acted reasonably in resisting the takeover attempt. The directors must show that they had reasonable grounds to believe that the tender offer posed a danger to the corporation's policies and effectiveness.

In addition, the board's response must have been rational in relation to the threat posed. Basically, the defensive tactics used must have been reasonable, and the board of directors must have been trying to protect the corporation and its shareholders from a perceived danger. If the directors' actions were reasonable under the circumstances, then they are not liable for breaching their fiduciary duties.

An Example: The Poison Pill Defense One technique to avoid takeovers is the poison pill defense (described in Exhibit 41–3). With this defensive measure, a board gives shareholders the right to buy new, additional shares at low prices. The right is triggered when a party

acquires a certain proportion of the target corporation's stock—often between 15 and 20 percent. (This party, of course, does not have the right to purchase shares at a discount.) With more shares outstanding, the acquiring party's interest is diluted. The tactic is meant to make a takeover too expensive for the acquiring party.

■ **EXAMPLE 41.6** In 2012, Netflix, Inc., used the poison pill defense to effectively block a takeover attempt by billionaire investor Carl Icahn. Netflix gave its shareholders the right to acquire newly issued stock if any individual acquired more than 10 percent of the company. At the time, Icahn held 9.98 percent of the shares. If his interest had risen to 10 percent, new shares would have flooded the market, and his interest in the corporation would have been immediately diluted. Consequently, he was effectively prevented from buying more shares. ■

In the following case, shareholders claimed that the directors had breached their fiduciary duties in their use of a poison pill defense.

Concept Summary 41.2

Purchases of Assets and Purchases of Stock

Purchase of Assets

A purchase of assets occurs when one corporation acquires all or substantially all of the assets of another corporation.

1. *Acquiring corporation*—The acquiring (purchasing) corporation is not required to obtain shareholder approval. The corporation is merely increasing its assets, and no fundamental business change occurs.
2. *Acquired corporation*—The acquired (purchased) corporation is required to obtain the approval of both its directors and its shareholders for the sale of its assets because the sale will substantially change the corporation's business position.

Purchase of Stock

A purchase of stock occurs when one corporation acquires a substantial number of the voting shares of the stock of another (target) corporation.

1. *Tender offer*—A public offer to all shareholders of the target corporation to purchase their stock at a price generally higher than the market price of the target stock prior to the announcement of the tender offer. Federal and state securities laws strictly control the terms, duration, and circumstances under which most tender offers are made.
2. *Target responses*—The ways in which target corporations respond to takeover bids include self-tender (the target firm's offer to acquire its own shareholders' stock) and numerous other strategies (see Exhibit 41–3).

Case 41.2

Air Products and Chemicals, Inc. v. Airgas, Inc.

Court of Chancery of Delaware, 16 A.3d 48 (2011).

Background and Facts Air Products and Chemicals, Inc., which provides gases and chemicals for industrial uses, made a tender offer of $70 per share for all of the shares of Airgas, Inc. The Airgas board of directors, which had expressed the view that the company's stock was worth at least $78 per share, rejected the offer as "clearly inadequate." The board took defensive measures to block the bid, including a poison pill that would be triggered if any party acquired 15 percent of the Airgas stock. Air Products and some Airgas shareholders filed a suit in a Delaware state court against Airgas. The plaintiffs sought to compel the board to remove the poison pill and allow the Airgas shareholders to decide whether to accept Air Products' offer. The shareholders alleged that the board had breached its fiduciary duties.

In the Language of the Court

CHANDLER, Chancellor
* * * *

Now, having thoroughly read, reviewed, and reflected upon all of the evidence presented to me, and having carefully considered the arguments made by counsel, I conclude that the Airgas board * * * has not breached its fiduciary duties owed to the Airgas stockholders. I find that the board has acted in good faith and in the honest belief that the Air Products offer, at $70 per share, is inadequate.

*Inadequate price has become a form of substantive coercion * * * . That is, the idea that Airgas's stockholders will disbelieve the board's views on value * * * and so they may mistakenly tender into an inadequately*

Case 41.2 Continued *priced offer. Substantive coercion has been clearly recognized by [the Delaware] Supreme Court as a valid threat.* [Emphasis added.]

* * * *

* * * *A board that has a good faith, reasonable basis to believe a bid is inadequate may block that bid using a poison pill, irrespective of stockholders' desire to accept it.* [Emphasis added.]

Here, * * * the Airgas board has demonstrated that it has a reasonable basis for sustaining its long-term corporate strategy—the Airgas board is independent, and has relied on the advice of three different outside independent financial advisors in concluding that Air Products' offer is inadequate. Air Products' own three nominees who were elected to the Airgas board have joined wholeheartedly in the Airgas board's determination, and when the Airgas board met to consider the $70 "best and final" offer, it was one of those Air Products Nominees who said, "We have to protect the pill." Indeed, one of Air Products' own directors conceded at trial that the Airgas board members had acted within their fiduciary duties in their desire to "hold out for the proper price," and that if an offer was made for Air Products that he considered to be unfair to the stockholders of Air Products * * * he would likewise use every legal mechanism available to hold out for the proper price as well. Under Delaware law, the Airgas directors have complied with their fiduciary duties.

Decision and Remedy *The court dismissed the shareholders' claims. The power to defeat an inadequate tender offer lies with the board of the target corporation. In this case, the Airgas board identified a valid threat—the allegedly inadequate price of Air Products' offer, coupled with the fact that a majority of Airgas's shareholders would likely accept it. The board responded reasonably and did not breach its fiduciary duties to shareholders.*

Critical Thinking

- **What If the Facts Were Different?** *Suppose that the Airgas board had opposed the takeover in order to perpetuate the directors' own corporate power, and not to preserve shareholder value. Would the result have been different? Explain.*
- **Social** *One reason for using a poison pill defense is to gain time for the shareholders of a target corporation to obtain the information they need to make an informed decision about a tender offer. How much time is enough?*

41–4 Termination

The termination of a corporation's existence has two phases—dissolution and winding up. **Dissolution** is the legal death of the artificial "person" of the corporation. Dissolution can be brought about by the following:

1. An act of the state.
2. An agreement of the shareholders and the board of directors.
3. The expiration of a time period stated in the certificate of incorporation.
4. A court order.

Winding up is the process by which corporate assets are *liquidated,* or converted into cash and distributed among creditors and shareholders according to specific rules of preference.[2]

---

2. Some prefer to call this phase *liquidation,* but we use the term *winding up* to mean all acts needed to bring the legal and financial affairs of the business to an end, including liquidating the assets and distributing them among creditors and shareholders. See RMBCA 14.05.

41–4a Voluntary Dissolution

Dissolution can be either voluntary or involuntary. State corporation statutes establish the procedures required for the voluntary dissolution of a corporation. Basically, there are two possible methods of voluntarily dissolving a corporation:

1. By the shareholders' unanimous vote to initiate dissolution proceedings (in some states).
2. By a proposal of the board of directors that is submitted to the shareholders at a shareholders' meeting.

Articles of Dissolution When a corporation is dissolved voluntarily, the corporation must file *articles of dissolution* with the state. The corporation must also establish a date (at least 120 days after the date of dissolution) by which all claims against the corporation must be received [RMBCA 14.06].

Notice to Creditors The corporation must notify its creditors of the dissolution. The creditors want to be notified so that they can file claims for payment. If a corporation's assets are liquidated without notice to a party who has a claim against the firm, shareholders of the former corporation can be held personally liable for the debt.

■ **CASE IN POINT 41.7** Richard and Kara Hartley were the sole shareholders of Hartley's Catering, Inc., a close corporation that operated Schlesinger's Deli Depot. Jennifer Esposito worked at the deli and was sexually harassed and physically assaulted by one of her co-workers. Esposito complained to Kara Hartley, who informed her husband, but the harassment continued and Esposito was fired.

Esposito sued Hartley's Catering (and the co-worker) for employment discrimination and won a $350,000 judgment. Soon afterwards, the Hartleys dissolved their close corporation, without notifying Esposito, and filed a petition for bankruptcy. The bankruptcy court found that because Hartley's Catering had not notified Esposito (a creditor) of the dissolution or bankruptcy, her claim against the corporation could not be discharged. Richard and Kara Hartley, as Hartley's shareholders, were held liable for paying the debt to Esposito.[3] ■

41–4b Involuntary Dissolution

Because corporations are creatures of statute, the state can also dissolve a corporation in certain circumstances. The secretary of state or the state attorney general can bring an action to dissolve a corporation that has failed to pay its annual taxes or submit required annual reports [RMBCA 14.20]. A state court can also dissolve a corporation for making fraudulent misrepresentations to the state during incorporation or for engaging in mismanagement [RMBCA 14.30].

In some circumstances, a shareholder or a group of shareholders may petition a court to have the corporation dissolved. The RMBCA permits any shareholder to initiate an action for dissolution in any of the following circumstances [RMBCA 14.30]:

1. The directors are deadlocked in the management of corporate affairs, and the shareholders are unable to break the deadlock. As a result, the corporation is suffering irreparable injury or is about to do so.
2. The acts of the directors or those in control of the corporation are illegal, oppressive, or fraudulent.
3. Corporate assets are being misapplied or wasted.
4. The shareholders are deadlocked in voting power and have failed, for a specified period (usually two annual meetings), to elect successors to directors whose terms have expired or would have expired with the election of successors.

■ **CASE IN POINT 41.8** Mt. Princeton Trout Club, Inc. (MPTC), was formed to own land in Colorado and to provide recreational benefits to its shareholders. The articles of incorporation prohibited MPTC from selling or leasing any of its property without the approval of a majority of the directors. Nevertheless, MPTC officers entered into leases and contracts to sell corporate property without even notifying the directors. When a shareholder petitioned for dissolution, the court dissolved MPTC based on a finding that its officers had engaged in illegal, oppressive, and fraudulent conduct.[4] ■

41–4c Winding Up

Winding up differs to some extent based on whether voluntary or involuntary dissolution has occurred. When dissolution takes place by voluntary action, the members of the board of directors act as trustees of the corporate assets. As trustees, they are responsible for winding up the affairs of the corporation for the benefit of corporate creditors and shareholders. This responsibility makes the board members personally liable for any breach of their fiduciary trustee duties.

When dissolution is involuntary—or if board members do not wish to act as trustees—the court will appoint a **receiver** to wind up corporate affairs and liquidate corporate assets. Courts may also appoint a receiver when shareholders or creditors can show that the board of directors should not be permitted to act as trustees of the corporate assets.

On dissolution, the liquidated assets are first used to pay creditors. Any remaining assets are distributed to shareholders according to their respective stock rights. Preferred stock has priority over common stock. Generally, the preferences are stated in the corporate articles.

41–5 Major Business Forms Compared

When deciding which form of business organization to choose, businesspersons normally consider several factors, including ease of creation, the liability of the owners, tax considerations, and the ability to raise capital. Each major form of business organization offers distinct advantages and disadvantages with respect to these and other factors.

Exhibit 41–4 summarizes the essential advantages and disadvantages of each of the forms of business organization discussed in this text.

---

3. *In re Hartley*, 479 Bankr. 635 (S.D.N.Y. 2012).

4. *Colt v. Mt. Princeton Trout Club, Inc.*, 78 P.3d 1115 (Colo.App. 2003).

EXHIBIT 41–4 Major Forms of Business Compared

	SOLE PROPRIETORSHIP	PARTNERSHIP	CORPORATION
Method of Creation	Created at will by owner.	Created by agreement of the parties.	Authorized by the state under the state's corporation law.
Legal Position	Not a separate entity; owner is the business.	A general partnership is a separate legal entity in most states.	Always a legal entity separate and distinct from its owners—a legal fiction for the purposes of owning property and being a party to litigation.
Liability	Unlimited liability.	Unlimited liability.	Limited liability of shareholders—shareholders are not liable for the debts of the corporation.
Duration	Determined by owner; automatically dissolved on owner's death.	Terminated by agreement of the partners, but can continue to do business even when a partner dissociates from the partnership.	Can have perpetual existence.
Transferability of Interest	Interest can be transferred, but individual's proprietorship then ends.	Although partnership interest can be assigned, assignee does not have full rights of a partner.	Shares of stock can be transferred.
Management	Completely at owner's discretion.	Each partner has a direct and equal voice in management unless expressly agreed otherwise in the partnership agreement.	Shareholders elect directors, who set policy and appoint officers.
Taxation	Owner pays personal taxes on business income.	Each partner pays pro rata share of income taxes on net profits, whether or not they are distributed.	Double taxation—corporation pays income tax on net profits, with no deduction for dividends, and shareholders pay income tax on disbursed dividends they receive.
Organizational Fees, Annual License Fees, and Annual Reports	None or minimal.	None or minimal.	All required.
Transaction of Business in Other States	Generally no limitation.	Generally no limitation.[a]	Normally must qualify to do business and obtain certificate of authority.

a. A few states have enacted statutes requiring that foreign partnerships qualify to do business there.

Continues

EXHIBIT 41–4 Major Forms of Business Compared *(Continued)*

	LIMITED PARTNERSHIP	LIMITED LIABILITY COMPANY	LIMITED LIABILITY PARTNERSHIP
Method of Creation	Created by agreement to carry on a business for profit. At least one party must be a general partner and the other(s) limited partner(s). Certificate of limited partnership is filed.	Created by an agreement of the member-owners of the company. Articles of organization are filed. Charter must be issued by the state.	Created by agreement of the partners. A statement of qualification for the limited liability partnership is filed.
Legal Position	Treated as a legal entity.	Treated as a legal entity.	Generally, treated same as a general partnership.
Liability	Unlimited liability of all general partners. Limited partners are liable only to the extent of capital contributions.	Member-owners' liability is limited to the amount of capital contributions or investments.	Varies, but under the Uniform Partnership Act, liability of a partner for acts committed by other partners is limited.
Duration	By agreement in certificate, or by termination of the last general partner (retirement, death, and the like) or last limited partner.	Unless a single-member LLC, can have perpetual existence (same as a corporation).	Remains in existence until cancellation or revocation.
Transferability of Interest	Interest can be assigned, but if assignee becomes a member with consent of other partners, certificate must be amended.	Member interests are freely transferable.	Interest can be assigned same as in a general partnership.
Management	General partners have equal voice or by agreement. Limited partners may not retain limited liability if they actively participate in management.	Member-owners can fully participate in management or can designate a group of persons to manage on behalf of the members.	Same as a general partnership.
Taxation	Generally taxed as a partnership.	LLC is not taxed, and members are taxed personally on profits "passed through" the LLC.	Same as a general partnership.
Organizational Fees, Annual License Fees, and Annual Reports	Organizational fee required; usually not others.	Organizational fee required. Others vary with states.	Fees are set by each state for filing statements of qualification, statements of foreign qualification, and annual reports.
Transaction of Business in Other States	Generally no limitations.	Generally no limitations, but may vary depending on state.	Must file a statement of foreign qualification before doing business in another state.

Reviewing: Mergers and Takeovers

Mario Bonsetti and Rico Sanchez incorporated Gnarly Vulcan Gear, Inc. (GVG), to manufacture windsurfing equipment. Bonsetti owned 60 percent and Sanchez owned 40 percent of the corporation's stock, and both men served on the board of directors. Hula Boards, Inc., owned solely by Mai Jin Li, made a public offer to buy GVG stock. Hula offered 30 percent more than the market price per share for the GVG stock, and Bonsetti and Sanchez each sold 20 percent of their stock to Hula. Jin Li became the third member of the GVG board of directors.

An irreconcilable dispute soon arose between Bonsetti and Sanchez over design modifications of their popular Baked Chameleon board. Sanchez and Jin Li voted to merge GVG with Hula Boards under the latter name, despite Bonsetti's dissent. GVG was dissolved, and production of the Baked Chameleon ceased. Using the information presented in the chapter, answer the following questions.

1. What rights does Bonsetti have (in most states) as a minority shareholder dissenting to the merger of GVG and Hula Boards?
2. Could the parties have used a short-form merger procedure in this situation? Why or why not?
3. What is the term used for Hula's offer to purchase GVG stock? By what method did Hula acquire control over GVG?
4. Suppose that after the merger, a person who was injured on a Baked Chameleon board sued Hula (the surviving corporation). Can Hula be held liable for an injury? Why or why not?

Debate This . . . *Corporate law should be altered to prohibit incumbent management from using most of the legal methods available for fighting takeovers.*

Terms and Concepts

appraisal right 786
articles of merger 782
consolidation 782
dissolution 791
merger 782

parent corporation 783
receiver 792
share exchange 783
short-form merger 785
subsidiary corporation 783

surviving corporation 782
takeover 788
target corporation 788
tender offer 788

Issue Spotters

1. Macro Corporation and Micro Company combine, and a new organization, MM, Inc., takes their place. What is the term for this type of combination? What happens to the assets, property, and liabilities of Micro? (See *Merger, Consolidation, and Share Exchange.*)
2. Peppertree, Inc., hired Robert McClellan, a licensed contractor, to repair a condominium complex that was damaged in an earthquake. McClellan completes the work, but Peppertree fails to pay. McClellan is awarded $181,000 in an arbitration proceeding. Peppertree then forms another corporation and transfers all of its assets to the new corporation without notifying McClellan. Can McClellan hold Peppertree's shareholders personally liable for the debt? Why or why not? (See *Purchase of Assets.*)

• **Check your answers to the Issue Spotters against the answers provided in Appendix D at the end of this text.**

Business Scenarios

41–1. Corporate Merger. Alir owns 10,000 shares of Ajax Corp. Her shares represent a 10 percent ownership interest in Ajax. Zeta Corp. is interested in acquiring Ajax in a merger, and the board of directors of each corporation has approved the merger. The shareholders of Zeta have already approved the acquisition, and Ajax has called for a shareholders' meeting to approve the merger. Alir disapproves of the merger and does not want to accept Zeta shares for the Ajax shares she holds. The market price of Ajax shares is $20 per share the day before the shareholder vote and drops to $16 on the day the shareholders of Ajax approve the merger. Discuss Alir's rights in this matter, beginning with the notice of the proposed merger. (See *Merger, Consolidation, and Share Exchange.*)

41–2. Purchase of Assets. Paradise Pools, Inc. (PPI) entered into a contract with Vittorio, LLP, to build a pool as part of a hotel being developed by Takahashi Development. PPI built the pool, but Vittorio, the general contractor, defaulted on other parts of the project. Takahashi completed the construction. Litigation followed, and Takahashi was awarded $18,656 against PPI. Meanwhile, Paradise Corp. (PC) was incorporated with the same management as PPI, but different shareholders. PC acquired PPI's assets, without assuming its liabilities, and soon became known as "Paradise Pools and Spas." Takahashi sought to obtain a writ of garnishment against PC to enforce the judgment against PPI. Is PC liable for PPI's obligation to Takahashi? Why or why not? (See *Purchase of Assets.*)

41–3. Corporate Takeover. Alitech Corp. is a small midwestern business that owns a valuable patent. Alitech has approximately a thousand shareholders with 100,000 authorized and outstanding shares. Block Corp. would like to have the use of the patent, but Alitech refuses to give Block a license. Block has tried to acquire Alitech by purchasing Alitech's assets, but Alitech's board of directors has refused to approve the acquisition. Alitech's shares are selling for $5 per share. Discuss how Block Corp. might proceed to gain the control and use of Alitech's patent. (See *Purchase of Stock.*)

Business Case Problems

41–4. Successor Liability. In 2004, the Watergate Hotel in Washington, D.C., obtained a loan from PB Capital. At this time, hotel employees were represented by a labor union, and under a collective bargaining agreement, the hotel agreed to make contributions to an employees' pension fund run by the union. In 2007, the hotel was closed due to poor business, although the owner stated that the hotel would reopen in 2010. Despite this expectation, PB Capital—which was still owed $40 million by the hotel owner—instituted foreclosure proceedings. At the foreclosure sale, PB Capital bought the hotel and reopened it under new management and with a new workforce. The union sued PB Capital, contending that it should pay $637,855 owed by the previous owner into the employees' pension fund. Should PB Capital, as the hotel's new owner, have to incur the previous owner's obligation to pay into the pension fund under the theory of successor liability? Why or why not? [*Board of Trustees of Unite Here Local 25 v. MR Watergate, LLC,* 677 F.Supp.2d 229 (D.D.C. 2010)] (See *Purchase of Assets.*)

41–5. Business Case Problem with Sample Answer— **Purchase of Assets.** Grand Adventures Tour & Travel Publishing Corp. (GATT) provided travel services. Duane Boyd, a former GATT director, incorporated Interline Travel & Tour, Inc. At a public sale, Interline bought GATT's assets. Interline moved into GATTs office building, hired former GATT employees, and began to serve GATT's customers. A GATT creditor, Call Center Technologies, Inc., filed an action to collect the unpaid amount on a contract with GATT from Interline. Is Interline liable? Why or why not? [*Call Center Technologies, Inc. v. Grand Adventures Tour & Travel Publishing Corp.,* 635 F.3d 48 (2d Cir. 2011)] (See *Purchase of Assets.*)

- **For a sample answer to Problem 41–5, go to Appendix E at the end of this text.**

41–6. Purchase of Assets. Lockheed Martin Corporation owned an aluminum refinery in St. Croix, Virgin Islands, that produced hazardous waste. Lockheed sold the refinery to Glencore Ltd. Their contract provided that Glencore would indemnify Lockheed for "pre-closing" environmental conditions. Alcoa World Alumina LLC bought the refinery from Glencore. Their contract stated that the buyer assumed only certain liabilities, including those relating to two specific contracts. Glencore's contract with Lockheed was not on the list. A decade later, the government of the Virgin Islands brought actions against the current and former owners of the refinery to recover for the environmental damage. In a settlement, Lockheed agreed to pay for certain remediation costs. Lockheed then filed a suit against Glencore to recover costs related to the settlement. Does Alcoa have to indemnify Glencore for costs related to Lockheed's suit? Why or why not? [*Alcoa World Alumina LLC v. Glencore Ltd.,* __ Conn.Supp. __, __ Conn.L.Rptr. __, 2016 WL 521193 (Super. 2016)] (See *Purchase of Assets.*)

41–7. Special Case Analysis—Dissolution. Go to Case Analysis 41.1 *In re Trulia, Inc. Stockholder Litigation.* Read the excerpt and answer the following questions.

(a) **Issue:** On what basis did the plaintiffs in this case seek to enjoin the proposed merger?

(b) **Rule of Law:** What is the standard for the disclosure of information by corporate directors in connection with any shareholder action?

(c) **Applying the Rule of Law:** How did the disclosure standard apply to the reliance of the directors on the advice of a financial advisor in making a decision on a proposed merger?

(d) **Conclusion:** How did the court's conclusion with respect to the information provided to the shareholders relate to the court's decision concerning the parties' proposed settlement?

41–8. A Question of Ethics—Purchase of Stock. *Topps Co. makes baseball and other trading cards, including the Pokemon collection, and distributes Bazooka bubble gum and other confections. One of the company's founders was Joseph Shorin, who was the inspiration for "Bazooka Joe" (a character in the comic strip wrapped around each piece of gum). As of 2007, Arthur Shorin, Joseph's son, had worked for Topps for fifty years and had served as its board chair and chief executive officer since 1980. Shorin's son-in-law, Scott Silverstein, served as Topps's president and chief operating officer.*

When Topps's financial performance began to lag, the board considered selling the company. Michael Eisner (formerly head of Disney Studios) offered to pay $9.75 per share and to retain Topps's management in a merger with his company. Upper Deck Co., Topps's chief competitor in the sports-card business, offered $10.75 per share but did not offer to retain the managers. Topps

demanded that Upper Deck not reveal its bid publicly. Topps publicized the offer, however, and did not accurately represent Upper Deck's interest or its seriousness. Upper Deck asked Topps to allow it to tell its side of events and to make a tender offer to Topps's shareholders. Topps refused and scheduled a shareholder vote on the Eisner offer. Topps's shareholders filed a suit in a Delaware state court against their firm, asking the court to prevent the vote. [In re Topps Co. Shareholders Litigation, 926 A.2d 58 (Del. Ch. 2007)] (See *Purchase of Stock.*)

(a) The shareholders contended that Topps's conduct had "tainted the vote." What factors support this contention? How might these factors affect the vote?

(b) Why might Topps's board and management be opposed to either of the offers for the company? Is this opposition ethical? Should the court prevent the scheduled vote? Explain.

Legal Reasoning Group Activity

41–9. Mergers and Acquisitions. Angie Jolson is the chair of the board of directors of Artel, Inc., and Sam Douglas is the chair of the board of directors of Fox Express, Inc. Jolson and Douglas meet to consider the possibility of combining their corporations into a single corporate entity. They consider two alternative courses of action: Artel could acquire all of the stock and assets of Fox Express, or the corporations could combine to form a new corporation. Both Jolson and Douglas are concerned about the necessity of a formal transfer of property, liability for existing debts, and the need to amend the articles of incorporation. (See *Merger, Consolidation, and Share Exchange.*)

(a) The first group will identify the first proposed combination and outline its legal effect on the transfer of property, the liabilities of the combined corporations, and the need to amend the articles of incorporation.

(b) The second group will do the same for the second proposed combination. That is, it will identify the combination and describe its legal effect on the transfer of property, the liabilities of the combined corporations, and the need to amend the articles of incorporation.

CHAPTER 42

Investor Protection, Insider Trading, and Corporate Governance

After the stock market crash of October 29, 1929, and the ensuing economic depression, Congress enacted legislation to regulate securities markets. The result was the Securities Act of 1933[1] and the Securities Exchange Act of 1934.[2] Both acts were designed to provide investors with more information to help them make buying and selling decisions about securities and to prohibit deceptive, unfair, and manipulative practices. **Securities** generally include any instruments evidencing corporate ownership (stock) or debt (bonds).

Today, the sale and transfer of securities are heavily regulated by federal and state statutes and by government agencies. The Securities and Exchange Commission (SEC) is the main independent regulatory agency that administers the 1933 and 1934 securities acts. The SEC also plays a key role in interpreting the provisions of these acts (and their amendments) and in creating regulations governing the purchase and sale of securities. The agency continually updates regulations in response to legislation, such as the Dodd-Frank Wall Street Reform and Consumer Protection Act,[3] and particular challenges, such as climate change.[4]

---

1. 15 U.S.C. Sections 77a-77aa.
2. 15 U.S.C. Sections 778a-78mm.

3. Pub. L. No. 111-203, July 21, 2010, 124 Stat. 1376; codified at 12 U.S.C. Sections 5301 *et seq.*
4. The SEC now requires companies to make disclosures about the potential impacts of climate change on their future profitability. See 17 C.F.R. Parts 211, 231, and 241.

42-1 The Securities Act of 1933

The Securities Act of 1933 governs initial sales of stock by businesses. The act was designed to prohibit various forms of fraud and to stabilize the securities industry by requiring that investors receive financial and other significant information concerning the securities being offered for public sale. Basically, the purpose of this act is to require disclosure. The 1933 act provides that all securities transactions must be registered with the SEC unless they are specifically exempt from the registration requirements.

42-1a What Is a Security?

Section 2(1) of the Securities Act contains a broad definition of securities, which generally include the following:[5]

1. Instruments and interests commonly known as securities, such as preferred and common stocks, bonds, debentures, and stock warrants.
2. Interests commonly known as securities, such as stock options, puts, and calls, that involve the right to purchase a security or a group of securities on a national security exchange.
3. Notes, instruments, or other evidence of indebtedness, including certificates of interest in a profit-sharing agreement and certificates of deposit.
4. Any fractional undivided interest in oil, gas, or other mineral rights.
5. Investment contracts, which include interests in limited partnerships and other investment schemes.

The *Howey* Test In interpreting the act, the United States Supreme Court has held that an **investment contract** is any transaction in which a person (1) invests (2) in a common enterprise (3) reasonably expecting profits (4) derived *primarily* or *substantially* from others' managerial or entrepreneurial efforts. Known as the *Howey* test, this definition continues to guide the determination of what types of contracts can be considered securities.[6]

■ **CASE IN POINT 42.1** James Nistler and his wife bought undeveloped land in Jackson County, Oregon, and created an LLC to develop it. The property, called Tennessee Acres, was divided into six lots. Nistler obtained investors for the development by telling them

---

5. 15 U.S.C. Section 77b(1). Amendments in 1982 added stock options.

6. *SEC v. W. J. Howey Co.*, 328 U.S. 293, 66 S.Ct. 1100, 90 L.Ed. 1244 (1946).

that they would earn 12 to 15 percent interest on their investment and be repaid in full within a specified time. The property was never developed, the investors were never paid, and a substantial part of the funds provided by investors were used to pay Nistler and his wife.

Nistler was convicted of securities fraud. He appealed, claiming that the investments at issue did not involve "securities," but a state appellate court affirmed his conviction. The court found that there had been a pooling of funds from a group of investors whose interests had been secured by the same land. The value of that land had been highly dependent on Nistler's use of the investors' funds to develop the land. In other words, the investors had engaged in a common enterprise from which they reasonably expected to profit, and that profit would be derived from the development efforts of Nistler.[7] ■

Many Types of Securities For our purposes, it is convenient to think of securities in their most common form—stocks and bonds issued by corporations. Bear in mind, though, that securities can take many forms, including interests in whiskey, cosmetics, worms, beavers, boats, vacuum cleaners, muskrats, and cemetery lots. Almost any stake in the ownership or debt of a company can be considered a security. Investment contracts in condominiums, franchises, limited partnerships in real estate, and oil or gas or other mineral rights have qualified as securities.

42–1b Registration Statement

Section 5 of the Securities Act of 1933 broadly provides that if a security does not qualify for an exemption, that security must be *registered* before it is offered to the public. Issuing corporations must file a *registration statement* with the SEC and must provide all investors with a *prospectus*.

A **prospectus** is a disclosure document that describes the security being sold, the financial operations of the issuing corporation, and the investment or risk attaching to the security. The prospectus also serves as a selling tool for the issuing corporation. The SEC now allows an issuer to deliver its prospectus to investors electronically via the Internet.[8]

In principle, the registration statement and the prospectus supply sufficient information to enable unsophisticated investors to evaluate the financial risk involved.

Contents of the Registration Statement The registration statement must be written in plain English and fully describe the following:

1. The securities being offered for sale, including their relationship to the registrant's other securities.
2. The corporation's properties and business (including a financial statement certified by an independent public accounting firm).
3. The management of the corporation, including managerial compensation, stock options, pensions, and other benefits. (See this chapter's *Managerial Strategy* for a discussion of a new SEC rule that imposes additional requirements on the disclosure of management compensation.) Any interests of directors or officers in any material transactions with the corporation must also be disclosed.
4. How the corporation intends to use the proceeds of the sale.
5. Any pending lawsuits or special risk factors.

All companies, both domestic and foreign, must file their registration statements electronically so that they can be posted on the SEC's online EDGAR (Electronic Data Gathering, Analysis, and Retrieval) database. Investors can then access the statements via the Internet. The EDGAR database includes material on initial public offerings (IPOs), proxy statements (concerning voting authority), annual reports, registration statements, and other documents that have been filed with the SEC.

Registration Process The registration statement does not become effective until it has been reviewed and approved by the SEC (unless it is filed by a *well-known seasoned issuer*, as discussed shortly). The 1933 act restricts the types of activities that an issuer can engage in at each stage of the registration process. If an issuer violates these restrictions, investors can rescind their contracts to purchase the securities.

Prefiling Period. During the *prefiling period* (before the registration statement is filed), the issuer normally cannot sell or offer to sell the securities. Once the registration statement has been filed, a waiting period begins while the SEC reviews the registration statement for completeness.[9]

Waiting Period. During the waiting period, the securities can be offered for sale but cannot be sold by the issuing corporation. Only certain types of offers are allowed at this time. All issuers can distribute a *preliminary*

---

7. *State of Oregon v. Nistler,* 286 Or.App. 470, 342 P.3d 1035 (2015).
8. Basically, an electronic prospectus must meet the same requirements as a printed prospectus. The SEC rules address situations in which the graphics, images, or audio files in or accompanying a printed prospectus cannot be reproduced in an electronic form. 17 C.F.R. Section 232.304.

9. The waiting period must last at least twenty days but always extends much longer because the SEC inevitably requires numerous changes and additions to the registration statement.

MANAGERIAL STRATEGY

The SEC's New Pay-Ratio Disclosure Rule

After the financial meltdown of recent years, Congress passed the Dodd-Frank Wall Street Reform and Consumer Protection Act.[a] One of the goals of the act was to improve accountability and transparency in the financial system. A brief section[b] in the lengthy bill requires a publicly held company to disclose the ratio of the total compensation of its chief executive officer (CEO) to the median compensation of its workers. For instance, if the annual pay of the median employee is $45,790 and the total compensation of the CEO is $12,260,000, then the pay ratio is 1 to 268. Otherwise stated, the CEO makes 268 times more than the median income for employees.

Five Years in the Making

For five years, the Securities and Exchange Commission (SEC) hesitated to adopt a disclosure rule as mandated by the Dodd-Frank act. The SEC received almost 300,000 comments and issued its own comments on the proposed rule.[c] The commissioners indicated that they were unsure what potential economic benefits, "if any," would be realized from making this information public. The SEC has estimated that the regulation will cause companies almost 550,000 annual paperwork hours, plus about $75 million per year to hire outside professionals.

---
a. Pub. L. No. 111-203, July 21, 2010, 124 Stat. 1376 (2010); codified at 12 U.S.C. Sections 5301 *et seq.*
b. *Ibid.*, Section 953(b).
c. 2013 WL 6503197 (2013, S.E.C. Release Nos. 33-9452 and 34-70443).

Dealing with the New Rule

The new rule is 1,800 words long, and managers initially may find it difficult to implement. Fortunately for them, the SEC realizes that it can only ask for "reasonable estimates" of the CEO-worker pay ratio.

The CEO's measured compensation includes salary, bonuses, stocks and options, incentive plans, and other compensation. In theory, calculating this amount is fairly straightforward.

Calculating the median income of the company's labor force is more difficult. Note that the median income is not the average income of employees. Rather, the rule requires the company to identify a "median" employee as the basis for comparison.

The rule does give companies flexibility in determining how to identify this median employee. Statistical sampling can be used, for instance. And the rule states, "Since identifying the median involves finding the employee in the middle, it may not be necessary to determine the exact compensation amounts for every employee paid more or less than that employee in the middle." The rule also permits companies to make the median employee determination only once every three years.

Business Questions

1. *Why might the new SEC pay-ratio disclosure rule cause certain businesses to eliminate low-wage workers?*
2. *How might the new SEC pay-ratio disclosure rule help shareholders?*

---

prospectus,[10] which contains most of the information that will be included in the final prospectus but often does not include a price.

Most issuers can use a *free-writing prospectus* during this period (although some inexperienced issuers will need to file a preliminary prospectus first).[11] A **free-writing prospectus** is any type of written, electronic, or graphic offer that describes the issuer or its securities and includes a legend indicating that the investor may obtain the prospectus at the SEC's Web site.

Posteffective Period. Once the SEC has reviewed and approved the registration statement and the waiting

period is over, the registration is effective, and the *posteffective period* begins. The issuer can now offer and sell the securities without restrictions.

If the company issued a preliminary or free-writing prospectus to investors, it must provide those investors with a final prospectus either before or at the time they purchase the securities. The issuer can make the final prospectus available to investors to download from a Web site if it notifies them of the appropriate Internet address.

42–1c Well-Known Seasoned Issuers

A *well-known seasoned issuer* (WKSI) is a firm that has issued at least $1 billion in securities in the last three years or has outstanding stock valued at $700 million or more in the hands of the public. WKSIs have greater flexibility than other issuers. They can file registration

---
10. A preliminary prospectus may also be called a *red herring prospectus*. The name comes from the legend printed in red across the prospectus stating that the registration has been filed but has not become effective.
11. See SEC Rules 164 and 433.

statements the day they announce a new offering and are not required to wait for SEC review and approval. They can also use a free-writing prospectus at any time, even during the prefiling period.

42–1d Exempt Securities and Transactions

Certain types of securities are exempt from the registration requirements of the Securities Act. These securities—which generally can also be resold without being registered—are summarized under the heading "Exempt Securities" in Exhibit 42–1.[12] The exhibit also lists and describes certain transactions that are exempt from registration requirements under various SEC regulations.

The transaction exemptions are important because they are very broad and can enable an issuer to avoid the high cost and complicated procedures associated with registration. Indeed, many sales occur without registration. Even when a transaction is exempt from the registration requirements, however, the offering is still subject to the antifraud provisions of the 1933 act (as well as those of the 1934 act, to be discussed later in this chapter).

Regulation A Offerings An exemption from registration is available for an issuer's security offerings that do not exceed $50 million during any twelve-month period.[13] Under Regulation A,[14] the issuer must file with the SEC a notice of the issue and an offering circular, which must also be provided to investors before the sale. Additional review requirements apply to issuers raising between $20 and $50 million. Overall, Regulation A provides a much less expensive process than the procedures associated with full registration.

Note that the cap for Regulation A was $5 million until 2015, when the SEC approved rule changes to make it easier for small and mid-sized businesses to raise capital. These changes were made in connection with the Jumpstart Our Business Startups, or JOBS, Act.[15] Expanding the issuers that qualify for exemption under Regulation A will likely decrease the significance of the other exemptions listed in Exhibit 42–1. In addition, the amended Regulation A—popularly known as Reg A+— has allowed for an increase in online crowdfunding.

Testing the Waters. Before preparing a Regulation A offering circular, companies are allowed to "test the waters" for potential interest. To *test the waters* means to determine potential interest without actually selling any securities or requiring any commitment from those who express interest. Small-business issuers can also use an integrated registration and reporting system that requires simpler forms than the full registration system.

Using the Internet. Some companies have sold their securities on the Internet using Regulation A. ■ **EXAMPLE 42.2** The Spring Street Brewing Company was the first company to sell securities via an online initial public offering (IPO). Spring Street raised about $1.6 million without incurring high expenses. ■ Online IPOs are particularly attractive to small companies and start-up ventures that may find it difficult to raise capital from institutional investors or through underwriters.

Small Offerings—Regulation D The SEC's Regulation D contains several exemptions from registration requirements (Rules 504, 505, and 506) for offers that either involve a small dollar amount or are made in a limited manner.

Rule 504. Rule 504 is the exemption used by most small businesses. It provides that noninvestment company offerings up to $1 million in any twelve-month period are exempt.[16] Noninvestment companies are firms that are not engaged primarily in the business of investing or trading in securities. (In contrast, an **investment company** is a firm that buys a large portfolio of securities and professionally manages it on behalf of many smaller shareholders/owners. A **mutual fund** is a well-known type of investment company.)

■ **EXAMPLE 42.3** Zeta Enterprises is a limited partnership that develops commercial property. Zeta intends to offer $600,000 of its limited partnership interests for sale between June 1 and next May 31. The buyers will become limited partners in Zeta. Because an interest in a limited partnership meets the definition of a security (discussed earlier), this offering would be subject to the registration and prospectus requirements of the Securities Act of 1933.

Under Rule 504, however, the sales of Zeta's interests are exempt from these requirements because Zeta is a noninvestment company making an offering of less than $1 million in a given twelve-month period. Therefore, Zeta can sell its interests without filing a registration statement with the SEC or issuing a prospectus to any investor. ■

---

12. 15 U.S.C. Section 77c.
13. 15 U.S.C. Section 77c(b).
14. 17 C.F.R. Sections 230.251–230.263.
15. Pub.L.No. 112-106 (June 19, 2012).

---

16. 17 C.F.R. Section 230.504. Small businesses in California may also be exempt under SEC Rule 1001. California's rule permits limited offerings of up to $5 million *per transaction*, if they satisfy certain conditions.

EXHIBIT 42–1 Exemptions for Securities Offerings under the 1933 Securities Act

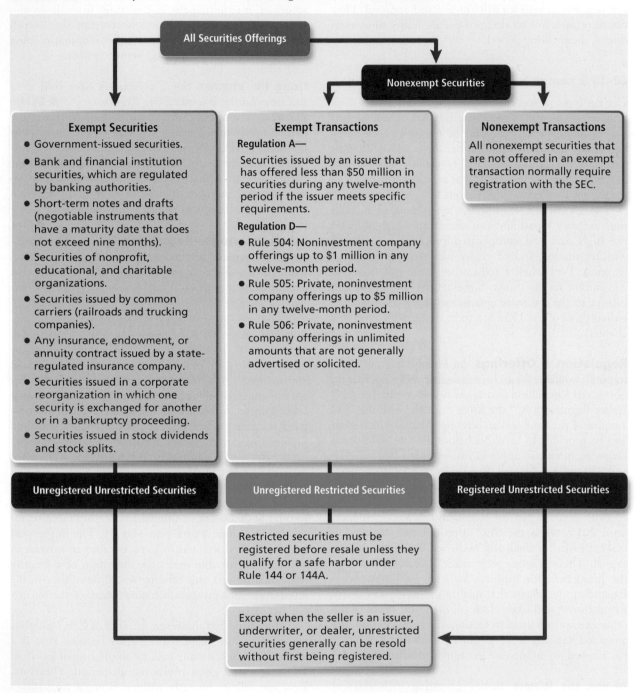

All Securities Offerings

Nonexempt Securities

Exempt Securities
- Government-issued securities.
- Bank and financial institution securities, which are regulated by banking authorities.
- Short-term notes and drafts (negotiable instruments that have a maturity date that does not exceed nine months).
- Securities of nonprofit, educational, and charitable organizations.
- Securities issued by common carriers (railroads and trucking companies).
- Any insurance, endowment, or annuity contract issued by a state-regulated insurance company.
- Securities issued in a corporate reorganization in which one security is exchanged for another or in a bankruptcy proceeding.
- Securities issued in stock dividends and stock splits.

Exempt Transactions
Regulation A—
Securities issued by an issuer that has offered less than $50 million in securities during any twelve-month period if the issuer meets specific requirements.

Regulation D—
- Rule 504: Noninvestment company offerings up to $1 million in any twelve-month period.
- Rule 505: Private, noninvestment company offerings up to $5 million in any twelve-month period.
- Rule 506: Private, noninvestment company offerings in unlimited amounts that are not generally advertised or solicited.

Nonexempt Transactions
All nonexempt securities that are not offered in an exempt transaction normally require registration with the SEC.

Unregistered Unrestricted Securities

Unregistered Restricted Securities

Registered Unrestricted Securities

Restricted securities must be registered before resale unless they qualify for a safe harbor under Rule 144 or 144A.

Except when the seller is an issuer, underwriter, or dealer, unrestricted securities generally can be resold without first being registered.

Rule 505. Another exemption is available under Rule 505 for private, noninvestment company offerings up to $5 million in any twelve-month period. The offer may be made to an unlimited number of *accredited investors* and up to thirty-five unaccredited investors.

Accredited investors include banks, insurance companies, investment companies, employee benefit plans, the issuer's executive officers and directors, and persons whose income or net worth exceeds a certain threshold.

The SEC must be notified of the sales, and precautions must be taken, because these *restricted securities* may be resold only by registration or in an exempt transaction. No general solicitation or advertising is allowed. The issuer must provide any unaccredited investors with disclosure documents, which generally are the same as those used in registered offerings.

Rule 506—Private Placement Exemption. Rule 506 exempts private, noninvestment company offerings in unlimited amounts that are not generally solicited or advertised. This exemption is often referred to as the *private placement exemption* because it exempts "transactions not involving any public offering."[17] There can be an unlimited number of accredited investors and up to thirty-five unaccredited investors. To qualify for the exemption, the issuer must believe that each unaccredited investor has sufficient knowledge or experience in financial matters to be capable of evaluating the investment's merits and risks.[18]

The private placement exemption is perhaps the most important exemption for firms that want to raise funds through the sale of securities without registering them. ■ **EXAMPLE 42.4** Citco Corporation needs to raise capital to expand its operations. Citco decides to make a private $10 million offering of its common stock directly to two hundred accredited investors and a group of thirty highly sophisticated, but unaccredited, investors. Citco provides all of these investors with a prospectus and material information about the firm, including its most recent financial statements.

As long as Citco notifies the SEC of the sale, this offering will likely qualify as an exempt transaction under Rule 506. The offering is nonpublic and not generally advertised. There are fewer than thirty-five unaccredited investors, and each of them possesses sufficient knowledge and experience to evaluate the risks involved. The issuer has provided all purchasers with the material information. Thus, Citco will likely *not* be required to comply with the registration requirements of the Securities Act of 1933. ■

Resales and Safe Harbor Rules Most securities can be resold without registration. The Securities Act provides exemptions for resales by most persons other than issuers or underwriters. The average investor who sells shares of stock need not file a registration statement with the SEC.

Resales of restricted securities acquired under Rule 505 or Rule 506, however, trigger the registration requirements *unless the party selling them complies with Rule 144 or Rule 144A.* These rules are sometimes referred to as safe harbors.

Rule 144. Rule 144 exempts restricted securities from registration on resale if all of the following conditions are met:

1. There is adequate current public information about the issuer. ("Adequate current public information" refers to the reports that certain companies are required to file under the 1934 Securities Exchange Act.)
2. The person selling the securities has owned them for at least six months if the issuer is subject to the reporting requirements of the 1934 act. If the issuer is not subject to the 1934 act's reporting requirements, the seller must have owned the securities for at least one year.
3. The securities are sold in certain limited amounts in unsolicited brokers' transactions.
4. The SEC is notified of the resale.[19]

Rule 144A. Securities that at the time of issue were not of the same class as securities listed on a national securities exchange or quoted in a U.S. automated interdealer quotation system may be resold under Rule 144A.[20] They may be sold only to a qualified institutional buyer (an institution, such as an insurance company or a bank, that owns and invests at least $100 million in securities). The seller must take reasonable steps to ensure that the buyer knows that the seller is relying on the exemption under Rule 144A.

42–1e Violations of the 1933 Act

It is a violation of the Securities Act to intentionally defraud investors by misrepresenting or omitting facts in a registration statement or prospectus. Liability may also be imposed on those who are negligent with respect to the preparation of these publications. Selling securities before the effective date of the registration statement or under an exemption for which the securities do not qualify also results in liability.

Can the omission of a material fact make a statement of opinion misleading to an ordinary investor? That was the question before the United States Supreme Court in the following case.

17. 15 U.S.C. Section 77d(2).
18. 17 C.F.R. Section 230.506.
19. 17 C.F.R. Section 230.144.
20. 17 C.F.R. Section 230.144A.

Omnicare, Inc. v. Laborers District Council Construction Industry Pension Fund

Supreme Court of the United States, __ U.S. __, 135 S.Ct. 1318, 191 L.Ed.2d 253 (2015).

Background and Facts Omnicare, Inc., a pharmacy services company, filed a registration statement in connection with a public offering. The statement expressed the company's opinion that it was in compliance with federal and state laws. Later, the federal government accused Omnicare of receiving kickbacks from pharmaceutical manufacturers. The Laborers District Council Construction Industry Pension Fund and others, which had bought the stock, filed a suit in a federal district court against Omnicare.

The plaintiffs alleged that Omnicare's legal-compliance opinion was "untrue" and that Omnicare had, in violation of the Securities Act, "omitted to state [material] facts necessary" to make that opinion not misleading. Omnicare argued that "no reasonable person, in any context, can understand a pure statement of opinion to convey anything more than the speaker's own mindset." The district court dismissed the pension funds' suit, but the U.S. Court of Appeals for the Sixth Circuit reversed the dismissal. Omnicare appealed to the United States Supreme Court.

In the Language of the Court

Justice *KAGAN* delivered the opinion of the Court.

* * * *

* * * Whether a statement is "misleading" depends on the perspective of a reasonable investor: The inquiry * * * is objective.

* * * *

* * * A reasonable person understands, and takes into account, the difference * * * between a statement of fact and one of opinion. She recognizes the import of words like "I think" or "I believe," and grasps that they convey some lack of certainty as to the statement's content.

But Omnicare takes its point too far, because a reasonable investor may, depending on the circumstances, understand an opinion statement to convey facts about how the speaker has formed the opinion—or, otherwise put, about the speaker's basis for holding that view. And if the real facts are otherwise, but not provided, the opinion statement will mislead its audience. Consider an unadorned statement of opinion about legal compliance: "We believe our conduct is lawful." * * * If the issuer made the statement in the face of its lawyers' contrary advice, or with knowledge that the Federal Government was taking the opposite view, the investor * * * has cause to complain: He expects not just that the issuer believes the opinion (however irrationally), but that it fairly aligns with the information in the issuer's possession at the time. Thus, *if a registration statement omits material facts about the issuer's inquiry into or knowledge concerning a statement of opinion, and if those facts conflict with what a reasonable investor would take from the statement itself, then [the Securities Act] creates liability.* [Emphasis added.]

An opinion statement, however, is not necessarily misleading when an issuer knows, but fails to disclose, some fact cutting the other way. * * * A reasonable investor does not expect that *every* fact known to an issuer supports its opinion statement. [Emphasis in the original.]

Moreover, *whether an omission makes an expression of opinion misleading always depends on context.* Registration statements as a class are formal documents, filed with the SEC as a legal prerequisite for selling securities to the public. Investors do not, and are right not to, expect opinions contained in those statements to reflect baseless, off-the-cuff judgments, of the kind that an individual might communicate in daily life. At the same time, an investor reads each statement within such a document, whether of fact or opinion, in light of all its surrounding text, including hedges, disclaimers, and apparently conflicting information. And the investor takes into account the customs and practices of the relevant industry. * * * The reasonable investor understands a statement of opinion in its full context, and [the Securities Act] creates liability only for the omission of material facts that cannot be squared with such a fair reading. [Emphasis added.]

Decision and Remedy The United States Supreme Court concluded that "neither [lower court] considered the Funds' omissions theory with the right standard in mind." The Court therefore vacated the decision

Case 42.1 Continued   *of the lower court and remanded the case "for a determination of whether the Funds have stated a viable omissions claim (or, if not, whether they should have a chance to replead)."*

Critical Thinking
- **Legal Environment**   *Would a reasonable investor have cause to complain if an issuer, without having consulted a lawyer, states, "We believe our conduct is lawful"? Explain.*

Remedies   Criminal violations are prosecuted by the U.S. Department of Justice. Violators may be fined up to $10,000, imprisoned for up to five years, or both.

The SEC is authorized to impose civil sanctions against those who willfully violate the 1933 act. It can request an injunction to prevent further sales of the securities involved or ask a court to grant other relief, such as ordering a violator to refund profits. Private parties who purchase securities and suffer harm as a result of false or omitted statements or other violations may bring a suit in a federal court to recover their losses and additional damages.

Defenses   There are three basic defenses to charges of violations under the 1933 act. A defendant can avoid liability by proving any of the following:

1. The statement or omission was not material.
2. The plaintiff knew about the misrepresentation at the time the stock was purchased.
3. The defendant exercised *due diligence* in preparing or reviewing the registration and reasonably believed at the time that the statements were true. This important defense is available to an underwriter or subsequent seller but not to the issuer.

■ **CASE IN POINT 42.5**   In preparation for an initial public offering (IPO), Blackstone Group, LP, filed a registration statement with the SEC. At the time, Blackstone's corporate private equity investments included FGIC Corporation (which insured investments in subprime mortgages) and Freescale Semiconductor, Inc. Before the IPO, FGIC's customers began to suffer large losses, and Freescale lost an exclusive contract to make wireless 3G chipsets for Motorola, Inc. (its largest customer). The losses suffered by these two companies would affect Blackstone. Nevertheless, Blackstone's registration statement did not mention the impact on its revenues of the investments in FGIC and Freescale.

Martin Litwin and others who had invested in Blackstone's IPO filed a suit in a federal district court against Blackstone and its officers, alleging material omissions from the statement. Blackstone argued as a defense that the omissions were not material, and the lower court dismissed the case. The plaintiffs appealed. A federal appellate court ruled that the alleged omissions were reasonably likely to be material, and remanded the case. The plaintiffs were entitled to the opportunity to prove at a trial that Blackstone had omitted material information that it was required to disclose.[21] ■

42–2 The Securities Exchange Act of 1934

The 1934 Securities Exchange Act provides for the regulation and registration of securities exchanges, brokers, dealers, and national securities associations, such as the National Association of Securities Dealers (NASD). Unlike the 1933 act, which is a one-time disclosure law, the 1934 act provides for continuous periodic disclosures by publicly held corporations to enable the SEC to regulate subsequent trading.

The Securities Exchange Act applies to companies that have assets in excess of $10 million and five hundred or more shareholders. These corporations are referred to as *Section 12 companies* because they are required to register their securities under Section 12 of the 1934 act. Section 12 companies are required to file reports with the SEC annually and quarterly, and sometimes even monthly if specified events occur (such as a merger).

The act also authorizes the SEC to engage in market surveillance to deter undesirable market practices such as fraud, market manipulation, and misrepresentation. In addition, the act provides for the SEC's regulation of proxy solicitations for voting.

42–2a Section 10(b), SEC Rule 10b-5, and Insider Trading

Section 10(b) is one of the more important sections of the Securities Exchange Act. This section prohibits the use of any manipulative or deceptive mechanism in violation of

---

21. *Litwin v. Blackstone Group, LP,* 634 F.3d 706 (2d Cir. 2011).

SEC rules and regulations. Among the rules that the SEC has promulgated pursuant to the 1934 act is **SEC Rule 10b-5,** which prohibits the commission of fraud in connection with the purchase or sale of any security.

SEC Rule 10b-5 applies to almost all cases concerning the trading of securities, whether on organized exchanges, in over-the-counter markets, or in private transactions. Generally, the rule covers just about any form of security. The securities need not be registered under the 1933 act for the 1934 act to apply.

Private parties can sue for securities fraud under Rule 10b-5. The basic elements of a securities fraud action are as follows:

1. A *material misrepresentation* (or omission) in connection with the purchase and sale of securities.
2. *Scienter* (a wrongful state of mind).
3. *Reliance* by the plaintiff on the material misrepresentation.
4. An *economic loss.*
5. *Causation,* meaning that there is a causal connection between the misrepresentation and the loss.

Insider Trading One of the major goals of Section 10(b) and SEC Rule 10b-5 is to prevent **insider trading,** which occurs when persons buy or sell securities on the basis of information that is not available to the public. Corporate directors, officers, and majority shareholders, among others, often have advance inside information that can affect the future market value of the corporate stock. Obviously, if they act on this information, their positions give them a trading advantage over the general public and other shareholders.

The 1934 act defines inside information. It also extends liability to those who take advantage of such information in their personal transactions when they know that the information is unavailable to those with whom they are dealing. Section 10(b) of the 1934 act and SEC Rule 10b-5 apply to anyone who has access to or receives information of a nonpublic nature on which trading is based—not just to corporate "insiders."

Disclosure under SEC Rule 10b-5 Any material omission or misrepresentation of material facts in connection with the purchase or sale of a security may violate Section 10(b) of the 1934 act and SEC Rule 10b-5. The key to liability (which can be civil or criminal) is whether the information omitted or misrepresented is *material.*

The following are some examples of material facts calling for disclosure under SEC Rule 10b-5:

1. Fraudulent trading in the company stock by a broker-dealer.
2. A dividend change (whether up or down).
3. A contract for the sale of corporate assets.
4. A new discovery, a new process, or a new product.
5. A significant change in the firm's financial condition.
6. Potential litigation against the company.

Note that any one of these facts, by itself, is not automatically considered material. It will be regarded as a material fact only if it is significant enough that it would likely affect an investor's decision as to whether to purchase or sell the company's securities.

■ **EXAMPLE 42.6** Zilotek, Inc., is the defendant in a class-action product liability suit that its attorney, Paula Frasier, believes the company will lose. Frasier has advised Zilotek's directors, officers, and accountants that the company will likely have to pay a substantial damages award. Zilotek plans to make a $5 million offering of newly issued stock before the date when the trial is expected to end. Zilotek's potential liability and the financial consequences to the firm are material facts that must be disclosed, because they are significant enough to affect an investor's decision to purchase the stock. ■

The case that follows is a *Classic Case* interpreting materiality under SEC Rule 10b-5.

Classic Case 42.2

SEC v. Texas Gulf Sulphur Co.
United States Court of Appeals, Second Circuit, 401 F.2d 833 (1968).

Background and Facts Texas Gulf Sulphur Company (TGS) conducted aerial geophysical surveys over more than 15,000 square miles of eastern Canada. The operations indicated concentrations of commercially exploitable minerals. At one site near Timmins, Ontario, TGS drilled a hole that appeared to yield a core with an exceedingly high mineral content. The company did not disclose the results of the core sample to the public.

After learning of the sample, TGS officers and employees made substantial purchases of TGS's stock or accepted stock options (rights to purchase stock). On April 11, 1964, an unauthorized report

Case 42.2 Continued

of the mineral find appeared in the newspapers. On the following day, TGS issued a press release that played down the discovery and stated that it was too early to tell whether the ore find would be significant.

Several months later, TGS announced that the strike was expected to yield at least 25 million tons of ore. Subsequently, the price of TGS stock rose substantially. The Securities and Exchange Commission (SEC) brought a suit against the officers and employees of TGS for violating SEC Rule 10b-5. The officers and employees argued that the information on which they had traded had not been material at the time of their trades because the mine had not then been commercially proved. The trial court held that most of the defendants had not violated SEC Rule 10b-5, and the SEC appealed.

In the Language of the Court

WATERMAN, Circuit Judge.

* * * *

* * * Whether facts are material within Rule 10b-5 when the facts relate to a particular event and are undisclosed by those persons who are knowledgeable thereof *will depend at any given time upon a balancing of both the indicated probability that the event will occur and the anticipated magnitude of the event in light of the totality of the company activity.* Here, * * * knowledge of the possibility, which surely was more than marginal, of the existence of a mine of the vast magnitude indicated by the remarkably rich drill core located rather close to the surface (suggesting mineability by the less expensive openpit method) within the confines of a large anomaly (suggesting an extensive region of mineralization) might well have affected the price of TGS stock and would certainly have been an important fact to a reasonable, if speculative, investor in deciding whether he should buy, sell, or hold. [Emphasis added.]

* * * *

* * * A major factor in determining whether the * * * discovery was a material fact is the importance attached to the drilling results by those who knew about it. * * * The timing by those who knew of it of their stock purchases * * *—purchases in some cases by individuals who had never before purchased * * * TGS stock—virtually compels the inference that the insiders were influenced by the drilling results.

Decision and Remedy *The appellate court ruled in favor of the SEC. All of the trading by insiders who knew of the mineral find before its true extent had been publicly announced had violated SEC Rule 10b-5.*

Impact of This Case on Today's Law *This landmark case affirmed the principle that the test of whether information is "material," for SEC Rule 10b-5 purposes, is whether it would affect the judgment of reasonable investors. The corporate insiders' purchases of stock and stock options indicated that they were influenced by the drilling results and that the information about the drilling results was material. The courts continue to cite this case when applying SEC Rule 10b-5 to cases of alleged insider trading.*

Critical Thinking

- **What If the Facts Were Different?** *Suppose that further drilling had revealed that there was not enough ore at this site for it to be mined commercially. Would the defendants still have been liable for violating SEC Rule 10b-5? Why or why not?*

Outsiders and SEC Rule 10b-5 The traditional insider-trading case involves true insiders—corporate officers, directors, and majority shareholders who have access to (and trade on) inside information. Increasingly, however, liability under Section 10(b) of the 1934 act and SEC Rule 10b-5 has been extended to include certain "outsiders"—those who trade on inside information acquired indirectly. Two theories have been developed under which outsiders may be held liable for insider

trading: the *tipper/tippee theory* and the *misappropriation theory.*

Tipper/Tippee Theory. Anyone who acquires inside information as a result of a corporate insider's breach of his or her fiduciary duty can be liable under SEC Rule 10b-5. This liability extends to **tippees** (those who receive "tips" from insiders) and even *remote tippees* (tippees of tippees).

The key to liability under this theory is that the inside information must be obtained as a result of someone's breach of a fiduciary duty to the corporation whose shares are traded. The tippee is liable only if the following requirements are met:

1. There is a breach of a duty not to disclose inside information.
2. The disclosure is made in exchange for personal benefit.
3. The tippee knows (or should know) of this breach and benefits from it.

■ **EXAMPLE 42.7** Eric McPhail was a member of the same country club as an executive at American Superconductor. While they were golfing, the executive shared information with McPhail about the company's expected earnings, contracts, and other major developments, trusting that McPhail would keep the information confidential. Instead, McPhail tipped six of his other golfing buddies at the country club, and they all used the nonpublic information to their advantage in trading. In this situation, the executive breached his duty not to disclose the information, which McPhail knew. McPhail (the tippee) is liable under SEC Rule 10b-5, and so are his other golfing buddies (remote tippees). All traded on inside information to their benefit.[22] ■

Misappropriation Theory. Liability for insider trading may also be established under the misappropriation theory. This theory holds liable an individual who wrongfully obtains (misappropriates) inside information and trades on it for her or his personal gain. Basically, this individual has stolen information rightfully belonging to another.

The misappropriation theory has been controversial because it significantly extends the reach of SEC Rule 10b-5 to outsiders who ordinarily would *not* be deemed fiduciaries of the corporations in whose stock they trade. It is not always wrong to disclose material, nonpublic information about a company to a person who would not otherwise be privy to it. Nevertheless, a person who obtains the information and trades securities on it can be held liable.[23]

Insider Reporting and Trading—Section 16(b)
Section 16(b) of the 1934 act provides for the recapture by the corporation of all profits realized by an insider on a purchase and sale, or sale and purchase, of the

corporation's stock within any six-month period.[24] It is irrelevant whether the insider actually uses inside information—all such **short-swing profits** must be returned to the corporation.

In the context of Section 16(b), insiders means officers, directors, and large stockholders of Section 12 corporations. (Large stockholders are those owning 10 percent of the class of equity securities registered under Section 12 of the 1934 act.) To discourage such insiders from using nonpublic information about their companies to their personal benefit in the stock market, the SEC requires them to file reports concerning their ownership and trading of the corporation's securities.

Section 16(b) applies not only to stock but also to warrants, options, and securities convertible into stock. In addition, the courts have fashioned complex rules for determining profits. Note, though, that the SEC exempts a number of transactions under Rule 16b-3.[25]

Exhibit 42–2 compares the effects of SEC Rule 10b-5 and Section 16(b). Because of the various ways in which insiders can incur liability under these provisions, corporate insiders should seek the advice of competent counsel before trading in the corporation's stock.

The Private Securities Litigation Reform Act
The disclosure requirements of SEC Rule 10b-5 had the unintended effect of deterring the disclosure of forward-looking information. To understand why, consider the following situation. ■ **EXAMPLE 42.8** XT Company announces that its projected earnings for a future time period will be a certain amount, but its forecast turns out to be wrong. The earnings are in fact much lower, and the price of XT's stock is affected negatively. The shareholders bring a class-action suit against XT, alleging that its directors violated SEC Rule 10b-5 by disclosing misleading financial information. ■

In an attempt to solve the problem and promote full disclosure, Congress passed the Private Securities Litigation Reform Act (PSLRA).[26] Among other things, the PSLRA provides a "safe harbor" for publicly held companies that make forward-looking statements, such as financial forecasts. Those who make such statements are protected against liability for securities fraud if they include "meaningful cautionary statements identifying important factors that could cause actual results to differ materially from those in the forward-looking statement."[27]

---

22. Three of the defendants in this case agreed to settle with the SEC and return the trading profits. See SEC press release 2014-134 "SEC Charges Group of Amateur Golfers in Insider Trading Ring."
23. See, for instance, *United States v. Gansman*, 657 F.3d 85 (2d Cir. 2011).
24. A person who expects the price of a particular stock to decline can realize profits by "selling short"—selling at a high price and repurchasing later at a lower price to cover the "short sale."
25. 17 C.F.R. Section 240.16b-3.
26. Pub.L.No. 104-67, 109 Stat. 737, codified in various sections of Title 15 of the *United States Code*.
27. 15 U.S.C. Sections 77z-2, 78u-5.

EXHIBIT 42–2 Comparison of Coverage, Application, and Liability under SEC Rule 10b-5 and Section 16(b)

AREA OF COMPARISON	SEC RULE 10b-5	SECTION 16(b)
What is the subject matter of the transaction?	Any security (does not have to be registered).	Any security (does not have to be registered).
What transactions are covered?	Purchase or sale.	Short-swing purchase and sale or short-swing sale and purchase.
Who is subject to liability?	Almost anyone with inside information under a duty to disclose—including officers, directors, controlling shareholders, and tippees.	Officers, directors, and certain shareholders who own 10 percent or more.
Is omission or misrepresentation necessary for liability?	Yes.	No.
Are there any exempt transactions?	No.	Yes, there are a number of exemptions.
Who may bring an action?	A person transacting with an insider, the SEC, or a purchaser or seller damaged by a wrongful act.	A corporation or a shareholder by derivative action.

The PSLRA also affected the level of detail required in securities fraud complaints. Plaintiffs must specify each misleading statement and say how it led them to a mistaken belief.

42–2b Regulation of Proxy Statements

Section 14(a) of the Securities Exchange Act regulates the solicitation of proxies from shareholders of Section 12 companies. The SEC regulates the content of proxy statements. Whoever solicits a proxy must fully and accurately disclose in the proxy statement all of the facts that are pertinent to the matter on which the shareholders are to vote. SEC Rule 14a-9 is similar to the antifraud provisions of SEC Rule 10b-5. Remedies for violations range from injunctions to prevent a vote from being taken to monetary damages.

42–2c Violations of the 1934 Act

As mentioned earlier, violations of Section 10(b) of the Securities Exchange Act and SEC Rule 10b-5, including insider trading, may lead to both criminal and civil liability.

Scienter Requirement For either criminal or civil sanctions to be imposed, _scienter_ must exist—that is, the violator must have had an intent to defraud or knowledge of his or her misconduct. _Scienter_ can be proved by showing that the defendant made false statements or wrongfully failed to disclose material facts. In some situations, it can even be proved by showing that the defendant was consciously reckless as to the truth or falsity of his or her statements.

■ **CASE IN POINT 42.9** Alvin Gebhart and Jack Archer started a business venture purchasing mobile home parks (MHPs) from owners and converting them to resident ownership. They formed MHP Conversions, LP, to facilitate the conversion process and issue promissory notes that were sold to investors to raise funds for the purchases. Archer ran the MHP program, and Gebhart sold the promissory notes. Gebhart sold nearly $2.4 million in MHP promissory notes to clients, who bought the notes based on Gebhart's positive statements about the investment.

During the time Gebhart was selling the notes, however, he never actually looked into the finances of the MHP program. He relied entirely on information that Archer gave him, some of which was not true. When

Gebhart was later sued for securities fraud, a federal appellate court concluded that there was sufficient evidence of *scienter*. Gebhart knew that he had no knowledge of the financial affairs of MHP, and he had been consciously reckless as to the truth or falsity of his statements about investing in MHP.[28] ■

Complaint Must Raise an Inference of *Scienter*. In a complaint alleging a violation, the plaintiff must state facts giving rise to an inference of *scienter*. ■ **CASE IN POINT 42.10** Between May 4 and June 22, Boeing Company made announcements that its new plane called the Dreamliner, which had not yet flown, was on track for its first flight on June 30. Meanwhile, however, the plane failed important stress tests before and after redesign. On June 23, Boeing canceled the scheduled debut flight and warned of a delay in the delivery of the Dreamliner to the commercial airlines. Boeing's stock price dropped more than 10 percent.

A group of investors filed a suit against Boeing for securities fraud. They claimed that Boeing and its officers had known about the likely postponement of the first flight when they made public statements to the contrary. The plaintiffs argued that Boeing's "internal e-mails" would confirm this theory but did not identify the source of these messages. A federal court dismissed the suit, and that dismissal was affirmed on appeal. Allegations "merely implying unnamed confidential sources" was not sufficient to give rise to an inference of *scienter*. *Scienter* can also be established by showing a defendant's motive to commit fraud, but Boeing had nothing to gain by delaying the postponement of the first flight.[29] ■

Whether the plaintiff alleged sufficient facts to give rise to an inference of *scienter* was the question in the following case.

---

28. *Gebhart v. SEC*, 595 F.3d 1034 (9th Cir. 2010).

29. *City of Livonia Employees' Retirement System and Local 295/Local 851 v. Boeing Co.*, 711 F.3d 754 (7th Cir. 2013).

Case Analysis 42.3

Rand-Heart of New York, Inc. v. Dolan

United States Court of Appeals, Eighth Circuit, 812 F.3d 1172 (2016).

In the Language of the Court

BENTON, Circuit Judge.

* * * *

I.

[Dolan Company specializes in professional services and business information from its base in Minneapolis, Minnesota.] DiscoverReady—a subsidiary of Dolan Company—performed litigation support [discovery management and document review services, including technology services related to processing and hosting discovery data], working mostly for Bank of America. In May or June 2013, Bank of America met with James Dolan (Chief Executive Officer of Dolan Company) and other DiscoverReady representatives. Bank of America noted concerns about Dolan Company's finances * * * and indicated it would send no new work to DiscoverReady until the financial concerns were resolved. * * * Dolan reported what transpired at the meeting to Dolan Company's Board of Directors, which

proceeded to authorize DiscoverReady for sale. Bank of America stopped sending new work to DiscoverReady in June.

On August 1, Dolan Company released a Form 10-Q [for the second quarter], which stated:

> * * * To operate profitably on a continuous basis in the future, the Company must increase revenue and eliminate costs * * * . These challenges make it probable that the Company will be unable to comply with certain of its financial covenants.

Also on August 1, Dolan spoke with stock analysts. [Dolan made] the [following] statements during the conference:

> For 2013, we expect * * * DiscoverReady * * * to grow at double-digit rates over the prior year * * *. However, we must point out that we expect DiscoverReady's third quarter revenues to be below last year's all time record revenue quarter. We make this comment not to dampen enthusiasm

about our growth prospects for DiscoverReady, but to set proper expectations for a business that may experience lumpiness on a quarter-to-quarter basis.

Asked to elaborate about "lumpiness," Dolan stated:

> Well, it's hard to be very specific about the lumpiness now without getting into details we normally do not disclose. * * * These things do come and they come sometimes unexpectedly, sometimes quickly. So * * * we have to be cautious in how we describe things.

On November 12, 2013, Dolan * * * filed its Form 10-Q ending September 30. [Form 10-Q is a quarterly report required by the Securities and Exchange Commission.] The 10-Q reported that the decline in revenue "exceeded our expectations," largely due to "a reduction in new work from DiscoverReady's largest customer, a reduction that we identified

Case 42.3 Continued

towards the end of the quarter. We believe this reduction resulted from the customer's evaluation of the Company's overall financial condition." The closing price for Dolan Company stock fell to $2.08 on November 11, to $1.05 on November 12, to $0.90 on November 13.

On January 2, 2014, Dolan Company issued a final press release announcing the appointment of a Chief Restructuring Officer * * * . Share prices then fell by $0.14. In March, Dolan Company filed a Chapter 11 bankruptcy.

II.
* * * *

Rand-Heart [of New York, Inc.] brought a class action suit [in a federal district court on behalf of purchasers of Dolan Company's securities between August 1, 2013, and January 2, 2014,] alleging Dolan made material misrepresentations and omissions about DiscoverReady's financial stability [in violation of Section 10(b) and Rule 10b–5]. The district court granted Dolan's motion to dismiss * * * . It found that Rand-Heart failed to allege *scienter*.

[Rand-Heart appealed the dismissal to the U.S. Court of Appeals for the Eighth Circuit.]

* * * *

A.

Rand-Heart argues the district court erred in finding inadequate allegations of *scienter*.
* * * *

Rand-Heart maintains it adequately pled *scienter* by alleging that Dolan had been severely reckless. *Severe recklessness is defined as highly unreasonable omissions or misrepresentations involving an extreme departure from the standards of ordinary care, and presenting the danger of misleading buyers or sellers which is either known to the defendant or is so obvious that the defendant must have been aware of it.* [Emphasis added.]

* * * *

Rand-Heart * * * argues that Dolan was reckless in failing to disclose that Bank of America had stopped sending new work to DiscoverReady in May or June 2013. Bank of America was DiscoverReady's biggest client, providing over 50% of DiscoverReady's work. In the second half of 2013, however, Bank of America work sharply declined. The complaint quoted DiscoverReady's Chief Operating Officer's acknowledgment: "We were, our work, our revenues

were dropping and our case origination had dropped, as I said earlier, to almost nothing from Bank of America." By May or June 2013, DiscoverReady had "completed a large document review project for Bank of America" immediately causing "great concerns." This decline prompted the Company's Board in June 2013 to "authorize the marketing of DiscoverReady for sale." Taking these allegations as true, DiscoverReady's financial instability caused by the decline in Bank of America work was, at the least, so obvious that Dolan must have been aware of it. The facts pled are sufficient to survive a motion to dismiss.

B.
* * * *

The district court erred in dismissing the Section 10(b) and Rule 10b–5 claims for failure to state a claim.

III.
* * * *

The district court's decision is * * * reversed * * * and remanded for proceedings consistent with this opinion.

Legal Reasoning Questions

1. *Scienter* can be established by showing a defendant's motive to commit fraud. In the context of the *Rand-Heart* case, what act might have established motive on Dolan's part?

2. When Bank of America met with Dolan to discuss his company's financial situation, it demanded that the company be restructured. Dolan did not disclose this fact in the Form 10-Q or in his conference with stock analysts. Was this omission misleading?

3. Suppose that Dolan had disclosed Bank of America's action with respect to DiscoverReady in the Form 10-Q and the conference. Would the result in this case have been different? Explain.

***

***Scienter* Not Required for Section 16(b) Violations** Violations of Section 16(b) include the sale by insiders of stock acquired less than six months before the sale (or, for a short sale, less than six months after the sale). (Recall that a short sale involves selling securities that one does not yet own.) These violations are subject to civil sanctions. Liability under Section 16(b) is strict liability. Neither *scienter* nor negligence is required.

Criminal Penalties For violations of Section 10(b) and Rule 10b-5, an individual may be fined up to $5 million, imprisoned for up to twenty years, or both. A partnership or a corporation may be fined up to $25 million. Under Section 807 of the Sarbanes-Oxley Act, for a *willful* violation of the 1934 act the violator can be imprisoned for up to twenty-five years (in addition to being subject to a fine).

For a defendant to be convicted in a criminal prosecution under the securities laws, there can be no reasonable doubt that the defendant knew he or she was acting wrongfully. In other words, a jury is not allowed merely to speculate that the defendant may have acted willfully.

■ **CASE IN POINT 42.11**   Douglas Newton was the president and sole director of Real American Brands, Inc. (RLAB). RLAB owned the Billy Martin's USA brand and operated a Billy Martin's retail boutique at the Trump Plaza in New York City. (Billy Martin's, a Western wear store, was co-founded by Billy Martin, the one-time manager of the New York Yankees.)

Newton agreed to pay kickbacks to Chris Russo, whom he believed to be the manager of a pension fund, to induce the fund to buy shares of RLAB stock. Newton later arranged for his friend Yan Skwara to pay similar kickbacks for the fund's purchase of stock in U.S. Farms, Inc. In reality, the pension fund was fictitious, and Newton and Skwara had been dealing with agents of the Federal Bureau of Investigation (FBI). Newton was charged with securities fraud and convicted by a jury (Skwara pled guilty). Newton appealed, but a federal appellate court upheld his conviction.

According to the court, the evidence established that in each transaction, the amount of the kickback was added to the price of the stock, which artificially increased the stock price. The evidence sufficiently proved that Newton had engaged in a scheme to defraud the supposed pension fund. His words and conduct, which were revealed on video at the trial, showed his intent to defraud the pension fund investors.[30] ■

Civil Sanctions   The SEC can also bring a civil action against anyone who purchases or sells a security while in possession of material nonpublic information in violation of the 1934 act or SEC rules.[31] The violation must occur through the use of a national securities exchange or a broker or dealer.[32] A court can assess a penalty amounting to as much as triple the profits gained or the loss avoided by the guilty party.[33]

The Insider Trading and Securities Fraud Enforcement Act enlarged the class of persons who may be subject to civil liability for insider trading. In addition, this act gave the SEC authority to offer monetary rewards to informants.[34]

Private parties may also sue violators of Section 10(b) and Rule 10b-5. A private party can obtain rescission (cancellation) of a contract to buy securities or damages to the extent of the violator's illegal profits. Those found liable have a right to seek contribution from those who share responsibility for the violations, including accountants, attorneys, and corporations. For violations of Section 16(b), a corporation can bring an action to recover the short-swing profits.

42–2d   Securities Fraud Online and Ponzi Schemes

A problem facing the SEC today is how to enforce the antifraud provisions of the securities laws in the online environment. Internet-related forms of securities fraud include many types of investment scams. Spam, online newsletters and bulletin boards, chat rooms, blogs, social media, and tweets can all be used to spread false information and perpetrate fraud. For a relatively small cost, fraudsters can even build sophisticated Web pages to facilitate their investment scams.

Investment Newsletters   Hundreds of online investment newsletters provide information on stocks. Legitimate online newsletters can help investors gather valuable information, but some e-newsletters are used for fraud. The law allows companies to pay these newsletters to tout their securities. The newsletters are required to disclose who paid for the advertising, but many newsletters do not follow that law. Thus, an investor reading an online newsletter may believe that the information is unbiased, when in fact the fraudsters will directly profit by convincing investors to buy or sell particular stocks.

Ponzi Schemes   Although much securities fraud occurs online, schemes conducted primarily offline have not disappeared. In recent years, the SEC has filed an increasing number of enforcement actions against perpetrators of *Ponzi schemes.* (Ponzi schemes are fraudulent investment operations that pay returns to investors from new capital paid to the fraudsters rather than from a legitimate investment.) Such schemes sometimes target U.S. residents and convince them to invest in offshore companies or banks.

---

30. *United States v. Newton,* 559 Fed.Appx. 902 (11th Cir. 2014).
31. 15 U.S.C. Section 78u(d)(2)(A).
32. Transactions pursuant to a public offering by an issuer of securities are exempted.
33. 15 U.S.C. Section 78u(d)(2)(C).

---

34. 15 U.S.C. Section 78u-1.

42–3 State Securities Laws

Today, every state has its own corporate securities laws, or **blue sky laws,** that regulate the offer and sale of securities within its borders. (The phrase *blue sky laws* comes from a 1917 United States Supreme Court decision. The Court stated that the purpose of such laws was to prevent "speculative schemes which have no more basis than so many feet of 'blue sky.'")[35] Article 8 of the Uniform Commercial Code, which has been adopted by all of the states, also imposes various requirements relating to the purchase and sale of securities.

42–3a Requirements under State Securities Laws

State securities laws apply mainly to intrastate transactions (transactions within one state). Typically, state laws have disclosure requirements and antifraud provisions, many of which are patterned after Section 10(b) of the Securities Exchange Act of 1934 and SEC Rule 10b-5. State laws also provide for the registration of securities offered or issued for sale within the state and impose disclosure requirements.

■ **CASE IN POINT 42.12** Randall Fincke was the founder, director, and officer of Access Cardiosystems, Inc., a small start-up company that sold portable automated external heart defibrillators. Fincke prepared a business plan stating that Access's "patent counsel" had advised the firm that "its product does not infringe any patents." This statement was false—patent counsel never offered Access any opinion on the question of infringement.

Fincke gave this plan to potential investors, including Joseph Zimmel, who bought $1.5 million in Access shares. When the company later filed for Chapter 11 bankruptcy protection, Zimmel filed a complaint with the federal bankruptcy court, alleging that Fincke had violated the Massachusetts blue sky law. The court awarded Zimmel $1.5 million in damages, and the award was affirmed on appeal. Fincke had solicited investors "by means of" a false statement of material fact, in violation of the fraud provisions in the state's securities laws.[36] ■

Methods of registration, required disclosures, and exemptions from registration vary among states. Unless an exemption from registration is applicable, issuers must register or qualify their stock with the appropriate state official, often called a *corporations commissioner.* Additionally, most state securities laws regulate securities brokers and dealers.

42–3b Concurrent Regulation

Since the adoption of the 1933 and 1934 federal securities acts, the state and federal governments have regulated securities concurrently. Issuers must comply with both federal and state securities laws, and exemptions from federal law are not exemptions from state laws.

The dual federal and state system has not always worked well, particularly during the early 1990s, when the securities markets underwent considerable expansion. Today, many of the duplicate regulations have been eliminated, and the SEC has exclusive power to regulate most national securities activities.

The National Conference of Commissioners on Uniform State Laws has substantially revised the Uniform Securities Act to coordinate state and federal securities regulation and enforcement efforts. Nineteen states have adopted the most recent version of the Uniform Securities Act.[37]

42–4 Corporate Governance

Corporate governance can be narrowly defined as the relationship between a corporation and its shareholders. Some argue for a broader definition—that corporate governance specifies the rights and responsibilities among different participants in the corporation, such as the board of directors, managers, shareholders, and other stakeholders, and spells out the rules and procedures for making decisions on corporate affairs. Regardless of the way it is defined, effective corporate governance requires more than just compliance with laws and regulations.

Effective corporate governance is essential in large corporations because corporate ownership (by shareholders)

---

35. *Hall v. Geiger-Jones Co.*, 242 U.S. 539, 37 S.Ct. 217, 61 L.Ed. 480 (1917).

36. *In re Access Cardiosystems, Inc.*, 776 F.3d 60 (1st Cir. 2015).

37. At the time this book went to press, the Uniform Securities Act had been adopted in Georgia, Hawaii, Idaho, Indiana, Iowa, Kansas, Maine, Michigan, Minnesota, Mississippi, Missouri, New Hampshire, New Mexico, Oklahoma, South Carolina, South Dakota, Vermont, Wisconsin, and Wyoming, as well as in the U.S. Virgin Islands.

is separated from corporate control (by officers and managers). Under these circumstances, officers and managers may attempt to advance their own interests at the expense of the shareholders. The well-publicized corporate scandals in the early 2000s clearly illustrated how the misconduct of corporate managers can cause harm to companies and to society. Indeed, with the globalization of business, corporate governance has become even more important because a corporation's bad acts (or lack of control systems) can have far-reaching consequences.

42–4a Aligning the Interests of Officers and Shareholders

Some corporations have sought to align the financial interests of their officers with those of the company's shareholders by providing the officers with **stock options.** These options enable holders to purchase shares of the corporation's stock at a set price. When the market price rises above that level, the officers can sell their shares for a profit. Because a stock's market price generally increases as the corporation prospers, the options give the officers a financial stake in the corporation's well-being and supposedly encourage them to work hard for the benefit of the shareholders.

Problems with Stock Options Options have turned out to be an imperfect device for encouraging effective governance. Executives in some companies have been tempted to "cook" the company's books in order to keep share prices higher so that they can sell their stock for a profit. Executives in other corporations have experienced no losses when share prices dropped because their options were "repriced" so that they did not suffer from the price decline. Thus, although stock options theoretically can motivate officers to protect shareholder interests, stock option plans have sometimes become a way for officers to take advantage of shareholders.

Outside Directors With stock options generally failing to work as planned, there has been an outcry for more outside directors (those with no formal employment affiliation with the company). The theory is that independent directors will more closely monitor the actions of corporate officers. Hence, today we see more boards with outside directors. Note, though, that outside directors may not be truly independent of corporate officers. They may be friends or business associates of the leading officers.

42–4b Promoting Accountability

Effective corporate governance standards are designed to address problems such as those briefly discussed earlier and to motivate officers to make decisions that promote the financial interests of the company's shareholders. Generally, corporate governance entails corporate decision-making structures that monitor employees (particularly officers) to ensure that they are acting for the benefit of the shareholders. Thus, corporate governance involves, at a minimum:

1. The audited reporting of financial conditions at the corporation so that managers can be evaluated.
2. Legal protections for shareholders so that violators of the law who attempt to take advantage of shareholders can be punished for misbehavior and victims can recover damages for any associated losses.

Governance and Corporate Law State corporation statutes set up the legal framework for corporate governance. Under the corporate law of Delaware, where most major companies incorporate, all corporations must have certain structures of corporate governance in place. The most important structure, of course, is the board of directors, because the board makes the major decisions about the future of the corporation.

The Board of Directors Under corporate law, a corporation must have a board of directors elected by the shareholders. Directors are responsible for ensuring that the corporation's officers are operating wisely and in the exclusive interest of shareholders. Directors receive reports from the officers and give them managerial direction. In reality, though, corporate directors devote a relatively small amount of time to monitoring officers.

Ideally, shareholders would monitor the directors' supervision of the officers. In practice, however, it can be difficult for shareholders to monitor directors and hold them responsible for corporate failings. Although the directors can be sued if they fail to do their jobs effectively, directors are rarely held personally liable.

The Audit Committee. A crucial committee of the board of directors is the *audit committee,* which oversees the corporation's accounting and financial reporting processes, including both internal and outside auditors. Unless the committee members have sufficient expertise and are willing to spend the time to carefully examine the corporation's bookkeeping methods, however, the audit committee may be ineffective.

The audit committee also oversees the corporation's "internal controls." These controls, carried out largely by the company's internal auditing staff, are measures taken to ensure that reported results are accurate. For instance, internal controls help to determine whether a corporation's debts are collectible. If the debts are not collectible, it is up to the audit committee to make sure that the corporation's financial officers do not simply pretend that payment will eventually be made.

The Compensation Committee. Another important committee of the board of directors is the *compensation committee,* which determines the compensation of the company's officers. As part of this process, the committee must assess the officers' performance and attempt to design a compensation system that will align the officers' interests with those of the shareholders.

42–4c The Sarbanes-Oxley Act

In 2002, following a series of corporate scandals, Congress passed the Sarbanes-Oxley Act,[38] which addresses certain issues relating to corporate governance. Generally, the act attempts to increase corporate accountability by imposing strict disclosure requirements and harsh penalties for violations of securities laws. Among other things, the act requires chief corporate executives to take personal responsibility for the accuracy of financial statements and reports that are filed with the SEC.

Additionally, the act requires that certain financial and stock-transaction reports be filed with the SEC earlier than was required under the previous rules. The act also created a new entity, called the Public Company Accounting Oversight Board, to regulate and oversee public accounting firms. Other provisions of the act established private civil actions and expanded the SEC's remedies in administrative and civil actions.

Because of the importance of this act for corporate leaders and for those dealing with securities transactions, we highlight some of its key provisions relating to corporate accountability in Exhibit 42–3.

More Internal Controls and Accountability

The Sarbanes-Oxley Act introduced direct *federal* corporate governance requirements for publicly traded companies. The law addressed many of the corporate governance procedures just discussed and created new requirements

in an attempt to make the system work more effectively. The requirements deal with independent monitoring of company officers by both the board of directors and auditors.

Sections 302 and 404 of the Sarbanes-Oxley Act require high-level managers (the most senior officers) to establish and maintain an effective system of internal controls. The system must include "disclosure controls and procedures" to ensure that company financial reports are accurate and timely and to document financial results prior to reporting.

Senior management must reassess the system's effectiveness annually. Some companies have had to take expensive steps to bring their internal controls up to the new federal standards. Hundreds of companies have reported that they identified and corrected shortcomings in their internal control systems as a result.

Exemptions for Smaller Companies

The act initially required all public companies to have an independent auditor file a report with the SEC on management's assessment of internal controls. Congress, however, enacted an exemption for smaller companies in 2010 in an effort to reduce compliance costs. Public companies with a market capitalization, or public float, of less than $75 million no longer need to have an auditor report on management's assessment of internal controls.

Certification and Monitoring Requirements

Section 906 of the Sarbanes-Oxley Act requires that chief executive officers and chief financial officers certify the accuracy of the information in the corporate financial statements. The statements must "fairly represent in all material respects, the financial conditions and results of operations of the issuer." This requirement makes the officers directly accountable for the accuracy of their financial reporting and precludes any "ignorance defense" if shortcomings are later discovered.

The act also includes requirements to improve directors' monitoring of officers' activities. All members of a publicly traded corporation's audit committee, which oversees the corporation's accounting and financial reporting processes, must be outside directors. The audit committee must have a written charter that sets out its duties and provides for performance appraisal. At least one "financial expert" must serve on the audit committee, which must hold executive meetings without company officers being present. In addition to reviewing the internal controls, the committee also monitors the actions of the outside auditor.

---

38. 15 U.S.C. Sections 7201 *et seq.*

EXHIBIT 42–3 Some Key Provisions of the Sarbanes-Oxley Act Relating to Corporate Accountability

CERTIFICATION REQUIREMENTS

Under *Section 906* of the Sarbanes-Oxley Act, the chief executive officers (CEOs) and chief financial officers (CFOs) of most major companies listed on public stock exchanges must certify financial statements that are filed with the SEC. CEOs and CFOs have to certify that filed financial reports "fully comply" with SEC requirements and that all of the information reported "fairly represents in all material respects, the financial conditions and results of operations of the issuer."

Under *Section 302* of the act, CEOs and CFOs of reporting companies are required to certify that a signing officer reviewed each quarterly and annual filing with the SEC and that none contained untrue statements of material fact. Also, the signing officer or officers must certify that they have established an internal control system to identify all material information and that any deficiencies in the system were disclosed to the auditors.

INTERNAL CONTROLS

Financial Controls—*Section 404(a)* regulates all public companies are required to assess the effectiveness of their internal control over financial reporting. *Section 404(b)* requires independent auditors to report on management's assessment of internal controls, but certain companies are exempted.

Loans to Directors and Officers—*Section 402* prohibits any reporting company—as well as any private company that is filing an initial public offering—from making personal loans to directors and executive officers are exempted.

Protection for Whistleblowers—*Section 806* protects "whistleblowers"—employees who "blow the whistle" on securities violations by their employers—from being fired or in any way discriminated against by their employers.

Blackout Periods—*Section 306* prohibits certain types of securities transactions during "blackout periods"—periods during which the issuer's ability to purchase, sell, or otherwise transfer funds in individual account plans (such as pension funds) is suspended.

ENHANCED PENALTIES

- *Violations of Section 906 Certification Requirements*—A CEO or CFO who certifies a financial report or statement filed with the SEC knowing that the report or statement does not fulfill all of the requirements of *Section 906* will be subject to criminal penalties of up to $1 million in fines, ten years in prison, or both. *Willful* violators of the certification requirements may be subject to $5 million in fines, twenty years in prison, or both.

- *Violations of the Securities Exchange Act of 1934*—Penalties for securities fraud under the 1934 act were also increased. Individual violators may be fined up to $5 million, imprisoned for up to twenty years, or both. *Willful* violators may be imprisoned for up to twenty-five years in addition to being fined.

- *Destruction or Alteration of Documents*—Anyone who alters, destroys, or conceals documents or otherwise obstructs any official proceeding will be subject to fines, imprisonment for up to twenty years, or both.

- *Other Forms of White-Collar Crime*—The act stiffened the penalties for certain criminal violations, such as federal mail and wire fraud, and ordered the U.S. Sentencing Commission to revise the sentencing guidelines for white-collar crimes.

STATUTE OF LIMITATIONS FOR SECURITIES FRAUD

Section 804 provides that a private right of action for securities fraud may be brought no later than two years after the discovery of the violation or five years after the violation, whichever is earlier.

Reviewing: Investor Protection, Insider Trading, and Corporate Governance

Dale Emerson served as the chief financial officer for Reliant Electric Company, a distributor of electricity serving portions of Montana and North Dakota. Reliant was in the final stages of planning a takeover of Dakota Gasworks, Inc., a natural gas distributor that operated solely within North Dakota. Emerson went on a weekend fishing trip with his uncle, Ernest Wallace. Emerson mentioned to Wallace that he had been putting in a lot of extra hours at the office planning a takeover of Dakota Gasworks. When he returned from the fishing trip, Wallace purchased $20,000 worth of Reliant stock. Three weeks later, Reliant made a tender offer to Dakota Gasworks stockholders and purchased 57 percent of Dakota Gasworks stock. Over the next two weeks, the price of Reliant stock rose 72 percent before leveling out. Wallace then sold his Reliant stock for a gross profit of $14,400. Using the information presented in the chapter, answer the following questions.

1. Would registration with the SEC be required for Dakota Gasworks securities? Why or why not?
2. Did Emerson violate Section 10(b) of the Securities Exchange Act of 1934 and SEC Rule 10b-5? Why or why not?
3. What theory or theories might a court use to hold Wallace liable for insider trading?
4. Under the Sarbanes-Oxley Act, who would be required to certify the accuracy of the financial statements Reliant filed with the SEC?

Debate This . . . *Insider trading should be legalized.*

Terms and Concepts

accredited investor 802
blue sky laws 813
corporate governance 813
free-writing prospectus 800
insider trading 806

investment company 801
investment contract 798
mutual fund 801
prospectus 799
SEC Rule 10b-5 806

securities 798
short-swing profits 808
stock option 814
tippee 807

Issue Spotters

1. When a corporation wishes to issue certain securities, it must provide sufficient information for an unsophisticated investor to evaluate the financial risk involved. Specifically, the law imposes liability for making a false statement or omission that is "material." What sort of information would an investor consider material? (See *The Securities Exchange Act of 1934.*)

2. Lee is an officer of Magma Oil, Inc. Lee knows that a Magma geologist has just discovered a new deposit of oil. Can Lee take advantage of this information to buy and sell Magma stock? Why or why not? (See *The Securities Exchange Act of 1934.*)

• **Check your answers to the Issue Spotters against the answers provided in Appendix D at the end of this text.**

Business Scenarios

42–1. Registration Requirements. Estrada Hermanos, Inc., a corporation incorporated and doing business in Florida, decides to sell $1 million worth of its common stock to the public. The stock will be sold only within the state of Florida. José Estrada, the chair of the board, says the offering need not be registered with the Securities and Exchange Commission. His brother, Gustavo, disagrees. Who is right? Explain. (See *The Securities Act of 1933.*)

42–2. Registration Requirements. Huron Corp. has 300,000 common shares outstanding. The owners of these

outstanding shares live in several different states. Huron has decided to split the 300,000 shares two for one. Will Huron Corp. have to file a registration statement and prospectus on the 300,000 new shares to be issued as a result of the split? Explain. (See *The Securities Act of 1933.*)

42–3. Insider Trading. David Gain was the chief executive officer (CEO) of Forest Media Corp., which became interested in acquiring RS Communications, Inc. To initiate negotiations, Gain met with RS's CEO, Gill Raz, on Friday,

July 12. Two days later, Gain phoned his brother Mark, who bought 3,800 shares of RS stock on the following Monday. Mark discussed the deal with their father, Jordan, who bought 20,000 RS shares on Thursday. On July 25, the day before the RS bid was due, Gain phoned his parents' home, and Mark bought another 3,200 RS shares. The same routine was followed over the next few days, with Gain periodically phoning Mark or Jordan, both of whom continued to buy RS shares.

Forest's bid was refused, but on August 5, RS announced its merger with another company. The price of RS stock rose 30 percent, increasing the value of Mark's and Jordan's shares by $664,024 and $412,875, respectively. Did Gain engage in insider trading? What is required to impose sanctions for this offense? Could a court hold Gain liable? Why or why not? (See *The Securities Exchange Act of 1934.*)

Business Case Problems

42–4. Business Case Problem with Sample Answer— Violations of the 1934 Act. Matrixx Initiatives, Inc., makes and sells over-the-counter pharmaceutical products. Its core brand is Zicam, which accounts for 70 percent of its sales. Matrixx received reports that some consumers had lost their sense of smell (a condition called anosmia) after using Zicam Cold Remedy. Four product liability suits were filed against Matrixx, seeking damages for anosmia. In public statements relating to revenues and product safety, however, Matrixx did not reveal this information.

James Siracusano and other Matrixx investors filed a suit in a federal district court against the company and its executives under Section 10(b) of the Securities Exchange Act of 1934 and SEC Rule 10b-5, claiming that the statements were misleading because they did not disclose information regarding the product liability suits. Matrixx argued that to be material, information must consist of a statistically significant number of adverse events that require disclosure. Because Siracusano's claim did not allege that Matrixx knew of a statistically significant number of adverse events, the company contended that the claim should be dismissed. What is the standard for materiality in this context? Should Siracusano's claim be dismissed? Explain. [*Matrixx Initiatives, Inc. v. Siracusano*, 563 U.S. 27, 131 S.Ct. 1309, 179 L.Ed.2d 398 (2011)] (See *The Securities Exchange Act of 1934.*)

- **For a sample answer to Problem 42–4, go to Appendix E at the end of this text.**

42–5. Disclosure under SEC Rule 10b-5. Dodona I, LLC, invested $4 million in two securities offerings from Goldman, Sachs & Co. The investments were in collateralized debt obligations (CDOs). Their value depended on residential mortgage-backed securities (RMBS), whose value in turn depended on the performance of subprime residential mortgages.

Before marketing the CDOs, Goldman had noticed several "red flags" relating to investments in the subprime market, in which it had invested heavily. To limit its risk, Goldman began betting against subprime mortgages, RMBS, and CDOs, including the CDOs it had sold to Dodona. In other words, Goldman made investments based on the assumption that subprime mortgages and the securities instruments built upon them would decrease in value. In an internal e-mail, one

Goldman official commented that the company had managed to "make some lemonade from some big old lemons." Nevertheless, Goldman's marketing materials provided only boilerplate statements about the risks of investing in the securities.

The CDOs were later downgraded to junk status, and Dodona suffered a major loss while Goldman profited. Assuming that Goldman did not affirmatively misrepresent any facts about the CDOs, can Dodona still recover under SEC Rule 10b-5? If so, how? [*Dodona I, LLC v. Goldman, Sachs & Co.*, 847 F.Supp.2d 624 (S.D.N.Y. 2012)] (See *The Securities Exchange Act of 1934.*)

42–6. Violations of the 1933 Act. Three shareholders of iStorage sought to sell their stock through World Trade Financial Corp. The shares were *restricted securities*—that is, securities acquired in an unregistered, private sale. Restricted securities typically bear a "restrictive" legend clearly stating that they cannot be resold in the public marketplace. This legend had been wrongly removed from the iStorage shares, however. Information about the company that was publicly available included the fact that, despite a ten-year life, it had no operating history or earnings. In addition, it had net losses of about $200,000, and its stock was thinly traded. Without investigating the company or the status of its stock, World Trade sold more than 2.3 million shares to the public on behalf of the three customers. Did World Trade violate the Securities Act of 1933? Discuss. [*World Trade Financial Corp. v. Securities and Exchange Commission*, 739 F.3d 1243 (9th Cir. 2014)] (See *The Securities Act of 1933.*)

42–7. Securities Act of 1933. Big Apple Consulting USA, Inc., provided small publicly traded companies with a variety of services, including marketing, business planning, and Web site development and maintenance. CyberKey Corp. sold customizable USB drives. CyberKey falsely informed Big Apple that CyberKey had been awarded a $25 million contract with the Department of Homeland Security. Big Apple used this information in aggressively promoting CyberKey's stock and was compensated for the effort in the form of CyberKey shares. When the Securities and Exchange Commission (SEC) began to investigate, Big Apple sold its shares for $7.8 million. The SEC filed an action in a federal district court against Big Apple, alleging a violation of the Securities Act of 1933. Can liability be imposed on a seller for a false statement that was made by someone else? Explain. [*U.S. Securities and Exchange*

Commission v. Big Apple Consulting USA, Inc., 783 F.3d 786 (11th Cir. 2015)] (See *The Securities Act of 1933*.)

42–8. The Securities Exchange Act of 1934. Dilean Reyes-Rivera was the president of Global Reach Trading (GRT), a corporation registered in Puerto Rico. His brother Jeffrey was the firm's accountant. Along with GRT sales agents and other promoters, the brothers solicited funds from individuals by promising to invest the funds in low-risk, short-term, high-yield securities. The investors were guaranteed a rate of return of up to 20 percent. Through this arrangement, more than 230 persons provided the brothers with about $22 million. This money was not actually invested. Instead, the funds received from later investors were used to pay "returns" to earlier investors. The Reyes-Riveras spent $4.6 million of the proceeds to buy luxury vehicles, houses, furniture, jewelry, and trips for themselves. What is this type of scheme called? What are the potential consequences? Discuss. [*United States v. Reyes-Rivera*, 812 F.3d 79 (1st Cir. 2016)] (See *The Securities Exchange Act of 1934*.)

42–9. A Question of Ethics—Violations of the 1934 Act. *Melvin Lyttle told John Montana and Paul Knight about a "Trading Program" that purportedly would buy and sell securities. Lyttle said the securities deals were fully insured, as well as monitored and controlled by the Federal Reserve. Without checking the details or even verifying whether the Program existed, Montana and Knight, with Lyttle's help, began to sell interests in the Program to investors. For a minimum investment of $1 million, the investors were* promised extraordinary rates of return—from 10 percent to as much as 100 percent per week—without risk. They were told, among other things, that the Program would "utilize banks that can ensure full bank integrity of The Transaction whose undertaking[s] are in complete harmony with international banking rules and protocol and who guarantee maximum security of a Funder's Capital Placement Amount." Nothing was required but the investors' funds and their silence—the Program was to be kept secret. Over a four-month period in 1999, Montana raised approximately $23 million from twenty-two investors. The promised gains did not accrue, however. Instead, Montana, Lyttle, and Knight depleted investors' funds in high-risk trades or spent the funds on themselves. [SEC v. Montana, 464 F.Supp.2d 772 (S.D.Ind. 2006)] (See The Securities Exchange Act of 1934.)*

(a) The Securities and Exchange Commission (SEC) filed a suit in a federal district court against Montana and the others, seeking an injunction, civil penalties, and refund of profits with interest. The SEC alleged, among other things, violations of Section 10(b) of the Securities Exchange Act of 1934 and SEC Rule 10b-5. What is required to establish such violations? Describe how and why the facts in this case meet, or fail to meet, these requirements.

(b) It is often remarked, "There's a sucker born every minute!" Does that phrase describe the Program's investors? Ultimately, about half of the investors recouped the amount they invested. Should the others be considered at least partly responsible for their own losses? Why or why not?

Legal Reasoning Group Activity

42–10. Violations of Securities Laws. Karel Svoboda, a credit officer for Rogue Bank, evaluated and approved his employer's extensions of credit to clients. These responsibilities gave Svoboda access to nonpublic information about the clients' earnings, performance, acquisitions, and business plans from confidential memos, e-mail, and other sources. Svoboda devised a scheme with Alena Robles, an independent accountant, to use this information to trade securities. Pursuant to their scheme, Robles traded in the securities of more than twenty different companies and profited by more than $2 million. Svoboda also executed trades for his own profit of more than $800,000, despite their agreement that Robles would do all of the trading. Aware that their scheme violated Rogue Bank's policy, they attempted to conduct their trades in such a way as to avoid suspicion. When the bank questioned Svoboda about his actions, he lied, refused to cooperate, and was fired. (See *The Securities Exchange Act of 1934*.)

(a) The first group will determine whether Svoboda or Robles committed any crimes.

(b) The second group will decide whether Svoboda or Robles is subject to civil liability. If so, who could file a suit, and on what ground? What are the possible sanctions?

(c) A third group will identify any defenses that Svoboda or Robles could raise and determine their likelihood of success.

Business Start-Ups Online

Hundreds of thousands of new businesses open each year in the United States. A large percentage of them fail within the first five years. But those that succeed more than offset the losses—the survivors are responsible for the creation of most new jobs.

Today, many new businesses—following in the footsteps of Facebook, Inc., Google, Inc., Twitter, Inc., and others—start online. Going into business online can be a good way to reach a wider market and experience higher sales. Generally, the steps for setting up an online business are the same as those for starting a brick-and-mortar operation. But there are added legal considerations.

Starting an Online Business

Starting a business requires taking certain preliminary steps—for example, finding a product niche, researching potential markets, and formulating a business plan. Actually setting up the business involves additional steps. As noted, these steps are similar for all new businesses, but here we focus on online startups.

Create a Legal Entity and Obtain a License Creating a legal entity, such as a corporation or a limited liability company, under which to do business online can insulate the owners from personal liability. It may also give the business a greater appearance of solidity. Considerations for starting a business as a corporation, a limited liability company, or another form of organization were discussed earlier in this unit.

In any business situation, federal and state licenses and permits must be obtained if required. A license or permit is often needed to engage in an activity supervised and regulated by a federal or state administrative agency. For instance, sales of alcoholic beverages require a permit from the U.S. Treasury Department's Alcohol and Tobacco Tax and Trade Bureau.

Select and Register a Domain Name A domain name is the address of an online business. Once a name is selected, the registration process is simple. The Internet Corporation for Assigned Names and Numbers (ICANN), a nonprofit corporation, is responsible for coordinating the maintenance and procedures of several databases related to the namespaces of the Internet. Among other things, ICANN oversees the distribution of domain names.[1]

Choose a Web Host and Design a Site The Web host of an online business stores all the pages of the business's Web site and makes them available on the Internet. The Web host should be reliable, secure, and suitable for the business. Some Web hosts will perform site development and maintenance, as well as search engine registration.

The design of a site should comply with intellectual property laws. For instance, any trademark used on a site should not infringe on another's mark. Images used as part of the design should not infringe on others' copyrights.

---

1. A directory of registrars is available at https://www.internic.net.

Managing an Online Business

Managing any business requires complying with federal, state, and local laws. When transacting business online in global markets, there are also international regulations to follow.

Comply with Advertising Rules Advertising online is subject to many of the same laws as advertising offline. Goods and services must be described truthfully, disclosures must be clear and conspicuous, and customers must understand what they are paying for. If customers must click on a link to get the information, the link must be obvious. The purpose is to provide a marketplace in which businesses can compete free of deceptive and unfair practices.

Among the regulations that apply to advertising is the Federal Trade Commission's Mail, Internet, or Telephone Order Merchandise rule, which governs representations with respect to shipping.[2] Generally, a business must ship ordered merchandise within thirty days, unless a customer agrees otherwise, or promptly refund the price of the unshipped goods.

Protect Users' Privacy Businesses typically collect and retain their customers' account numbers and other personal information. Keeping this data private can protect against liability for wrongful disclosure or misuse. An online business is subject to federal and state privacy laws that cover offline businesses. And wherever a firm does business, it must comply with the location's data protection laws—many foreign countries have privacy laws that apply to online businesses.

Offer Payment Options Online businesses generally accept credit or debit cards for payment. International sales can be increased by offering a variety of payment options, especially options that match customers' local business practices. In many European countries, for example, consumers often pay online merchants by wire transfer.

Another option is a service such as PayPal that processes payments between businesses and their customers and forwards the funds to the appropriate party. Some services specialize in processing payments from international customers. Of course, there is always some risk, but in general these services guarantee the payments.

Collect State and Local Taxes Federal, state, and local tax laws apply to online businesses. A tax permit must be obtained from the appropriate government agency when this is required. State and local sales taxes must be collected from customers in a state in which an online business has a *nexus*, or physical presence—a store, an office, or a warehouse, for instance.[3]

Follow International Guidelines An online business can make sales to, and engage in other transactions with, businesses and individuals in every continent on the globe. Even the smallest firm has the potential to reach more than a billion customers online.

The Organization for Economic Cooperation and Development, of which the United States is a member, issued a set of guidelines for doing business in international markets online. The principles expressed in the guidelines make up a voluntary code of conduct that encourages an online business to do the following:

- Use fair marketing practices.
- Offer accurate, clear information about the business's goods and services.

---

2. 16 C.F.R. Chapter I, Subchapter D, Part 435.
3. *Quill v. North Dakota*, 504 U.S. 298, 112 S.Ct. 1904, 119 L.Ed.2d 91 (1992).

- Disclose full information about the terms and costs of a transaction.
- Provide a secure method for online payment.
- Protect consumer privacy.[4]

Comply with International Trade Laws Doing business online in global markets requires compliance with international trade laws, including shipping and tariff and tax regulations. Customers should be informed that tariffs and taxes can significantly increase the final prices of goods and services.[5]

The United States imposes additional requirements on businesses that export products. All goods are subject to the regulations that cover economic and trade sanctions against foreign countries, companies, and individuals. Nearly every commercial transaction with any sanctioned party is prohibited.

Goods with both commercial and military applications are known as *dual-use products*. These items must be licensed by the U.S. Department of Commerce under its Export Administrative Regulations.[6] The International Traffic in Arms Regulations control sales of defense-related goods. Under these regulations, items on the U.S. Munitions List must be licensed for export.[7]

Ethical Connection

Dealing in good faith can be more important in doing business online than in a brick-and-mortar location because Internet customers are more reliant on a business's reputation. For an online business, this involves more than minimal compliance with the relevant laws of the targeted market.

In some industries, the law imposes a repair, replace, or refund policy on merchants for some types of defects in delivered goods. In any industry, to build and maintain a customer base requires an effective customer service program. This program should go beyond what is legally required. How customer complaints are resolved is important to building trust and confidence.

Ethics Question *To attain success in global commerce, an online business should design its Web site with what in mind?*

Critical Thinking *Between 2 and 4 percent of online orders involve fraud. What can an online business do to avoid being the victim?*

---

4. A checklist of practices that follow these guidelines is in Federal Trade Commission, *Electronic Commerce: Selling Internationally A Guide for Businesses available at* https://www.ftc.gov/tips-advice/business-center/guidance/electronic-commerce-selling-internationally-guide-businesses.
5. Information on conducting business online, particularly in international markets, is provided by a number of federal agencies through BusinessUSA.gov, *Conducting Business Online, available at* business.usa.gov/export/a-guide-to-exporting-basics/conducting-business-online.
6. 15 C.F.R. Subtitle B, Chapter VII, Subchapter C.
7. 22 C.F.R. Chapter I, Subchapter M.

Unit Nine

Government Regulation

43. Administrative Agencies

44. Consumer Law

45. Environmental Protection

46. Antitrust Law

47. Professional Liability and Accountability

CHAPTER 43

Administrative Agencies

Government agencies established to administer the law have a great impact on the day-to-day operations of businesses. In its early years, the United States had a simple, nonindustrial economy with little regulation. As the economy has grown and become more complex, the size of government has also increased, and so has the number, size, and power of administrative agencies.

In some instances, new agencies have been created in response to a crisis. In the wake of the financial crisis that led to the latest economic recession, for instance, Congress enacted the Dodd-Frank Wall Street Reform and Consumer Protection Act. Among other things, this statute created the Financial Stability Oversight Council to identify and respond to emerging risks in the financial system. It also created the Consumer Financial Protection Bureau (CFPB) to protect consumers from alleged abusive practices by financial institutions, mortgage lenders, and credit-card companies.

As the number of agencies has multiplied, so have the rules, orders, and decisions that they issue. Today, there are rules covering almost every aspect of a business's operations. These regulations make up the body of *administrative law.*

43–1 The Practical Significance of Administrative Law

Whereas statutory law is created by legislatures, administrative law is created by administrative agencies. When Congress—or a state legislature—enacts legislation, it typically adopts a rather general statute and leaves its implementation to an **administrative agency.** The agency then creates the detailed rules and regulations necessary to carry out the statute. The administrative agency, with its specialized personnel, has the time, resources, and expertise to make the detailed decisions required for regulation.

43–1a Administrative Agencies Exist at All Levels of Government

Administrative agencies are spread throughout the government. At the federal level, the Securities and Exchange Commission regulates a firm's capital structure and financing, as well as its financial reporting. The National Labor Relations Board oversees relations between a firm and any unions with which it may deal. The Equal Employment Opportunity Commission also regulates employer-employee relationships. The Environmental Protection Agency and the Occupational Safety and Health Administration affect the way a firm manufactures its products, and the Federal Trade Commission influences the way it markets those products.

There are administrative agencies at the state and local levels as well. Commonly, a state agency (such as a state pollution-control agency) is created as a parallel to a federal agency (such as the Environmental Protection Agency). Just as federal statutes take precedence over conflicting state statutes, so do federal agency regulations take precedence over conflicting state regulations. Because the rules of state and local agencies vary widely, we focus here exclusively on federal administrative law.

43–1b Agencies Provide a Comprehensive Regulatory Scheme

Often, administrative agencies at various levels of government work together and share the responsibility of creating and enforcing particular regulations. ■ **EXAMPLE 43.1** When Congress enacted the Clean Air Act, it provided only general directions for the prevention of air pollution. The specific pollution-control requirements imposed on businesses are almost entirely the product of decisions made by the Environmental Protection Agency (EPA). Moreover, the EPA works with parallel environmental agencies at the state level to analyze existing data and determine the appropriate pollution-control standards. ■

Legislation and regulations have significant benefits—in the example of the Clean Air Act, a cleaner environment than existed in decades past. At the same time, these benefits entail considerable costs for business. The EPA has estimated the costs of compliance with the Clean Air Act at many tens of billions of dollars yearly. Although the agency has calculated that the overall benefits of its regulations often exceed their costs, the burden on business is substantial. Business therefore has a strong incentive to try to influence the regulatory environment through lobbying.

43–2 Agency Creation and Powers

Congress creates federal administrative agencies. By delegating some of its authority to make and implement laws, Congress can indirectly monitor a particular area in which it has passed legislation. Delegation enables Congress to avoid becoming bogged down in the details relating to enforcement—details that are often best left to specialists.

To create an administrative agency, Congress passes **enabling legislation,** which specifies the name, purposes, functions, and powers of the agency being created. Federal administrative agencies can exercise only those powers that Congress has delegated to them in enabling legislation. Through similar enabling acts, state legislatures create state administrative agencies.

An agency's enabling statute defines its legal authority. An agency cannot regulate beyond the powers granted by the statute, and it may be required to take some regulatory action by the terms of that statute. When regulated groups oppose a rule adopted by an agency, they often bring a lawsuit arguing that the rule was not authorized by the enabling statute and is therefore void. Conversely, a group may file a suit claiming that an agency has illegally *failed* to pursue regulation required by the enabling statute.

43–2a Enabling Legislation—An Example

Congress created the Federal Trade Commission (FTC) in the Federal Trade Commission Act.[1] The act prohibits unfair methods of competition and deceptive trade practices. It also describes the procedures that the FTC must follow to charge persons or organizations with violations of the act, and it provides for judicial review of agency orders. The act grants the FTC the power to do the following:

---

1. 15 U.S.C. Sections 41–58.

1. Create "rules and regulations for the purpose of carrying out the Act."
2. Conduct investigations of business practices.
3. Obtain reports from interstate corporations concerning their business practices.
4. Investigate possible violations of federal antitrust statutes. (The FTC shares this task with the Antitrust Division of the U.S. Department of Justice.)
5. Publish findings of its investigations.
6. Recommend new legislation.
7. Hold trial-like hearings to resolve certain trade disputes that involve FTC regulations or federal antitrust laws.

The commission that heads the FTC is composed of five members. The president, with the advice and consent of the Senate, appoints each of the FTC commissioners for a term of seven years. The president also designates one of the commissioners to be the chair.

43–2b Types of Agencies

There are two basic types of administrative agencies: executive agencies and independent regulatory agencies. Federal *executive agencies* include the cabinet departments of the executive branch, which assist the president in carrying out executive functions, and the subagencies within the cabinet departments. The Occupational Safety and Health Administration, for instance, is a subagency within the U.S. Department of Labor.

Executive agencies usually have a single administrator, director, or secretary who is appointed by the president to oversee the agency and can be removed by the president at any time. Exhibit 43–1 lists the cabinet departments and some of their most important subagencies.

Independent regulatory agencies, such as the Federal Trade Commission and the Securities and Exchange Commission (SEC), are outside the federal executive departments (those headed by a cabinet secretary). The president's power is less pronounced in regard to independent agencies, whose officers serve for fixed terms and cannot be removed without just cause. See Exhibit 43–2 for a list of selected independent regulatory agencies and their principal functions.

43–2c Agency Powers and the Constitution

Administrative agencies occupy an unusual niche in the U.S. governmental structure, because they exercise powers that normally are divided among the three branches of government. Agencies' powers include functions

EXHIBIT 43–1   Executive Departments and Important Subagencies

DEPARTMENT	SELECTED SUBAGENCIES
State	Passport Office; Bureau of Diplomatic Security; Foreign Service; Bureau of Intelligence and Research
Treasury	Internal Revenue Service; U.S. Mint
Interior	U.S. Fish and Wildlife Service; National Park Service; Bureau of Indian Affairs; Bureau of Land Management
Justice[a]	Federal Bureau of Investigation; Drug Enforcement Administration; Bureau of Prisons; U.S. Marshals Service
Agriculture	Soil Conservation Service; Agricultural Research Service; Food Safety and Inspection Service
Commerce[b]	Bureau of the Census; Bureau of Economic Analysis; U.S. Patent and Trademark Office; National Oceanic and Atmospheric Administration
Labor[b]	Occupational Safety and Health Administration; Bureau of Labor Statistics; Employment Standards Administration; Office of Labor-Management Standards
Defense[c]	National Security Agency; Joint Chiefs of Staff; Departments of the Air Force, Navy, Army
Housing and Urban Development	Government National Mortgage Association; Office of Fair Housing and Equal Opportunity
Transportation	Federal Aviation Administration; Federal Highway Administration; National Highway Traffic Safety Administration
Energy	Office of Civilian Radioactive Waste Management; Office of Nuclear Energy; Energy Information Administration
Health and Human Services[d]	Food and Drug Administration; Centers for Medicare and Medicaid Services; Centers for Disease Control and Prevention; National Institutes of Health
Education[d]	Office of Elementary and Secondary Education; Office of Postsecondary Education; Office of Vocational and Adult Education
Veterans Affairs	Veterans Health Administration; Veterans Benefits Administration; National Cemetery Administration
Homeland Security	U.S. Citizenship and Immigration Services; Directorate of Border and Transportation Services; U.S. Coast Guard; Federal Emergency Management Agency

a. Formed from the Office of the Attorney General.
b. Formed from the Department of Commerce and Labor.
c. Formed from the Department of War and the Department of the Navy.
d. Formed from the Department of Health, Education, and Welfare.

associated with the legislature *(rulemaking)*, the executive branch *(enforcement)*, and the courts *(adjudication)*.

The constitutional principle of *checks and balances* allows each branch of government to act as a check on the actions of the other two branches. Furthermore, the U.S. Constitution authorizes only the legislative branch to create laws. Yet administrative agencies, to which the Constitution does not specifically refer, can make

legislative rules, or *substantive rules,* that are as legally binding as laws that Congress passes.

Administrative agencies also issue **interpretive rules,** which simply declare policy and do not affect legal rights or obligations. ■ **EXAMPLE 43.2** The Equal Employment Opportunity Commission periodically issues interpretive rules indicating how it plans to interpret the provisions of certain statutes, such as the Americans with

EXHIBIT 43–2   Selected Independent Regulatory Agencies

NAME OF AGENCY	PRINCIPAL DUTIES
Federal Reserve System (the Fed) Board of Governors	Determines policy with respect to interest rates, credit availability, and the money supply (including various "bailouts" in the financial sector).
Federal Trade Commission (FTC)	Prevents businesses from engaging in unfair trade practices; stops the formation of monopolies in the business sector.
Securities and Exchange Commission (SEC)	Regulates the nation's stock exchanges, in which shares of stock are bought and sold; enforces the securities laws.
Federal Communications Commission (FCC)	Regulates communications by telegraph, cable, telephone, radio, satellite, Internet, and television.
National Labor Relations Board (NLRB)	Protects employees' rights to join unions and bargain collectively with employers; attempts to prevent unfair labor practices by both employers and unions.
Equal Employment Opportunity Commission (EEOC)	Works to eliminate discrimination in employment based on religion, gender, race, color, disability, national origin, or age; investigates claims of discrimination.
Environmental Protection Agency (EPA)	Undertakes programs aimed at reducing air and water pollution; works with state and local agencies to help fight environmental hazards.
Nuclear Regulatory Commission (NRC)	Ensures that electricity-generating nuclear reactors in the United States are built and operated safely; regularly inspects operations of such reactors.

Disabilities Act. These informal rules provide enforcement guidelines for agency officials. ■

The Delegation Doctrine Courts generally hold that Article I of the U.S. Constitution is the basis for all administrative law. Section 1 of that article grants all legislative powers to Congress and requires Congress to oversee the implementation of all laws. Article I, Section 8, gives Congress the power to make all laws necessary for executing its specified powers. Under what is known as the **delegation doctrine,** courts interpret these passages as granting Congress the power to establish administrative agencies and delegate to them the power to create rules for implementing those laws.

The three branches of government exercise certain controls over agency powers and functions, as discussed next, but in many ways administrative agencies function independently. For this reason, administrative agencies, which constitute the **bureaucracy,** are sometimes referred to as the fourth branch of the U.S. government.

Executive Controls The executive branch of government exercises control over agencies both through the president's power to appoint federal officers and through the president's veto power. The president may veto enabling legislation passed by Congress or congressional attempts to modify an existing agency's authority.

Legislative Controls Congress exercises authority over agency powers through legislation. Congress gives power to an agency through enabling legislation and can take power away—or even abolish an agency altogether—through subsequent legislation. Legislative authority is required to fund an agency, and enabling legislation usually sets certain time and monetary limits on the funding of particular programs. Congress can always revise these limits.

In addition to its power to create and fund agencies, Congress has the authority to investigate the implementation of its laws and the agencies that it has created. Congress also has the power to "freeze" the enforcement of most federal regulations before the regulations take effect. (Another legislative check on agency actions is the Administrative Procedure Act, discussed shortly.)

The question that a court faces when confronted with an agency's interpretation of a statute it administers is always whether the agency has acted within its statutory authority. At issue in the following case was an agency's authority under a statute enacted in the nineteenth century.

Loving v. Internal Revenue Service

United States Court of Appeals, District of Columbia Circuit, 742 F.3d 1013 (2014).

Background and Facts The Internal Revenue Service (IRS) is a subagency of the U.S. Department of the Treasury. Responding to concerns about the performance of some paid tax-return preparers, the IRS issued a new rule. The rule required paid preparers to pass an initial certification exam, pay annual fees, and complete at least fifteen hours of continuing education courses each year. As authority for the rule, the IRS relied on a statute enacted in 1884 and recodified in 1982. The statute authorizes the agency to "regulate the practice of representatives of persons before the Department of the Treasury." Three independent preparers filed a suit in a federal district court against the IRS, contending that the rule exceeded the agency's authority. The court ruled in the plaintiffs' favor. The IRS appealed.

In the Language of the Court

KAVANAUGH, Circuit Judge.

* * * *

In our view, at least six considerations foreclose the IRS's interpretation of the statute.

First is the meaning of the key statutory term "representatives." * * * The term "representative" is traditionally and commonly defined as an agent with authority to bind others, a description that does not fit tax-return preparers.

Put simply, *tax-return preparers are not agents. They do not possess legal authority to act on the taxpayer's behalf. They cannot legally bind the taxpayer by acting on the taxpayer's behalf.* [Emphasis added.]

* * * *

Second is the meaning of the phrase "practice * * * before the Department of the Treasury."

* * * To "practice before" a court or agency ordinarily refers to practice during an investigation, adversarial hearing, or other adjudicative proceeding.

That is quite different from the process of filing a tax return. * * * *Tax-return preparers do not practice before the IRS when they simply assist in the preparation of someone else's tax return.* [Emphasis added.]

* * * *

Third is the history of [the statute]. The language [in the original statute included the phrase] "agents, attorneys, or other persons representing claimants."

That original language plainly would not encompass tax-return preparers. * * * When Congress re-codified the statute in 1982, Congress simplified the phrase * * * to the current "representatives of persons." But * * * Congress made clear in the statute itself that * * * the 1982 Act was designed "to revise, codify, and enact" the amended provisions "without substantive change."

* * * *

Fourth is the broader statutory framework.

* * * *

* * * [By enacting other statutes specific to tax-return preparers,] multiple Congresses have acted as if [the statute at the center of this case] did not extend so broadly as to cover tax-return preparers. * * * The meaning of one statute may be affected by other Acts, particularly where Congress has spoken * * * more specifically to the topic at hand. So it is here.

Fifth is the nature and scope of the authority being claimed by the IRS.

If we were to accept the IRS's interpretation of [the statute,] the IRS would be empowered for the first time to regulate hundreds of thousands of individuals in the multi-billion dollar tax-preparation industry. Yet nothing in the statute's text or the legislative record contemplates that vast expansion of the IRS's authority.

Sixth is the IRS's past approach to this statute. Until [now] the IRS never interpreted the statute to give it authority to regulate tax-return preparers.

* * * In light of the text, history, structure, and context of the statute, it becomes apparent that the IRS never before adopted its current interpretation for a reason: It is incorrect.

Case 43.1 Continued

Decision and Remedy *The U.S. Court of Appeals for the District of Columbia Circuit affirmed the lower court's ruling. Under the IRS's interpretation of the statute, the agency "would be empowered for the first time to regulate hundreds of thousands of individuals in the multi-billion dollar tax-preparation industry." Nothing in the statute's text, history, structure, or context "contemplates that vast expansion of the IRS's authority."*

Critical Thinking
- **Legal Environment** *As a policy matter, some observers might argue that the IRS should be allowed to regulate tax-return preparers more strictly. Under the reasoning of the court, who has the authority to give effect to such a policy, and how would it be accomplished?*

Judicial Controls The judicial branch exercises control over agency powers through the courts' review of agency actions. As you will read shortly, the Administrative Procedure Act provides for judicial review of most agency decisions. Agency actions are not automatically subject to judicial review, however. The party seeking court review must first exhaust all administrative remedies under what is called the **exhaustion doctrine.** In other words, the complaining party normally must have exhausted all available administrative remedies before seeking court review.[2]

■ **EXAMPLE 43.3** The Federal Trade Commission (FTC) claims that Sysco Industries used deceptive advertising and orders it to run new ads correcting the misstatements. Sysco contends that its ads were not deceptive. Under the exhaustion doctrine, Sysco must go through the entire FTC process before it can bring a suit against the FTC in court to challenge the order. ■

43–2d The Administrative Procedure Act

Sometimes, Congress specifies certain procedural requirements in an agency's enabling legislation. In the absence of any directives from Congress concerning a particular agency procedure, the Administrative Procedure Act (APA)[3] applies.

The Arbitrary and Capricious Test One of Congress's goals in enacting the APA was to provide for more judicial control over administrative agencies. To that end, the APA provides that courts should "hold unlawful and set aside" agency actions found to be "arbitrary, capricious, an abuse of discretion, or otherwise not in accordance with law."[4] Under this standard, parties can

challenge regulations as contrary to law or as so irrational that they are arbitrary and capricious.

There is no precise definition of what makes a rule arbitrary and capricious, but the standard includes factors such as whether the agency has done any of the following:

1. Failed to provide a rational explanation for its decision.
2. Changed its prior policy without justification.
3. Considered legally inappropriate factors.
4. Entirely failed to consider a relevant factor.
5. Rendered a decision plainly contrary to the evidence.

See this chapter's *Digital Update* feature for a discussion of administrative rules for broadband operators that have been challenged as arbitrary and capricious.

Fair Notice The APA also includes many requirements concerning the notice that regulatory agencies must give to those affected by its regulations. For instance, an agency may change the way it applies a certain regulatory principle. Before the change can be carried out, the agency must give fair notice of what conduct will be expected in the future.

■ **CASE IN POINT 43.4** The 1934 Communications Act established a system of limited-term broadcast licenses subject to various conditions. One condition was the indecency ban, which prohibited the uttering of "any obscene, indecent, or profane language by means of radio communication." For nearly thirty years, the Federal Communications Commission (FCC) invoked this ban only when the offensive language had been repeated, or "dwelled on," in the broadcast. It was not applied to "fleeting expletives" (offensive words used only briefly).

Then the FCC changed its policy, declaring that an offensive term, such as the F-word, was actionably indecent even if it was used only once. In 2006, the FCC applied this new rule to two Fox Television broadcasts, each of which

---

2. The plaintiff must also have *standing to sue* the agency.
3. 5 U.S.C. Sections 551–706.
4. 5 U.S.C. Section 706(2)(A).

DIGITAL UPDATE

Imposing a 1930s Regulatory Law on Broadband Operators

Since the advent of the Internet, it has remained largely unregulated. President Bill Clinton (1993–2001) said clearly and often that the Internet should remain lightly regulated, at most. During the Obama administration, however, pressure from the president himself applied to the Federal Communications Commission (FCC) started to change that thinking.

An Unsuccessful Attempt to Impose Regulation on Internet Service Providers

In 2010, under the authority of the Telecommunications Act of 1996,[a] the FCC attempted to regulate Internet service providers (ISPs) by enacting the "Open Internet Order." Under this order, the FCC would have required broadband ISPs to transfer data files equally, without consideration of the size or source of the files—so-called net neutrality. The policy prohibited providers from transmitting certain content at slower speeds or higher costs than other types of content. Challenged in court, the order was overturned.[b]

The Advent of "Obamanet"

In early 2015, the FCC commissioners voted to regulate ISPs as "common carriers" under Title II of the

a. 47 U.S.C. Sections 1302(a), (b).
b. *Verizon v. Federal Communications Commission,* 740 F.3d 623 (D.C. Cir. 2014).

Communications Act of 1934.[c] Normally, a common carrier is a business that transports items from one place to another, such as a trucking company. Under the 1934 act, this definition was widened to include telephone companies. Under the new FCC rules, the Internet would fall under the act as well. The new rules are still under discussion, and legal challenges have been filed.

What the New FCC Rules Mean

Here is a summary of the new rules:
- No Internet service provider can prevent a user from accessing "legal content, applications, services, or non-harmful devices" on the Internet. The goal to is prevent censorship and discrimination.
- No Internet service provider can deliberately reduce the speed of data from particular sites or applications.
- No Internet service provider can charge content providers more to provide them with faster service.

Critical Thinking *Some observers predict that numerous lawsuits will be filed against the FCC. Why would this be likely?*

c. 47 U.S.C. Sections 201 *et seq.*

---

contained a single use of the F-word. The broadcasts had aired before the FCC's change in policy. The FCC ruled that these two broadcasts were indecent, and Fox appealed the ruling. Ultimately, the case reached the United States Supreme Court, and the Court determined that the FCC's order should be set aside. Because the FCC did not provide fair notice prior to the broadcasts in question that fleeting expletives could constitute actionable indecency, the standards were unconstitutionally vague.[5] ∎

43–3 The Administrative Process

All federal agencies must follow specific procedural requirements as they go about fulfilling their three basic

functions: rulemaking, enforcement, and adjudication. These three functions make up what is known as the **administrative process.** As mentioned, the APA imposes requirements that all federal agencies must follow in the absence of contrary provisions in the enabling legislation. This act is an integral part of the administrative process.

43–3a Rulemaking

The major function of an administrative agency is **rulemaking**—the formulation of new regulations, or rules. The APA defines a *rule* as "an agency statement of general or particular applicability and future effect designed to implement, interpret, or prescribe law and policy."[6]

Regulations are sometimes said to be *legislative* because, like statutes, they have a binding effect. Thus, violators of agency rules may be punished. Because

5. *Federal Communications Commission v. Fox Television Stations, Inc.,* __ U.S. __, 132 S.Ct. 2307, 183 L.Ed.2d 234 (2012).

6. 5 U.S.C. Section 551(4).

agency rules have such significant legal force, the APA established procedures for agencies to follow in creating rules.

Many rules must be adopted using the APA's **notice-and-comment rulemaking,** which involves three basic steps:

1. Notice of the proposed rulemaking.
2. A comment period.
3. The final rule.

The APA recognizes some limited exceptions to its procedural requirements, but they are seldom invoked. ■ **EXAMPLE 43.5** The Occupational Safety and Health Act authorized the Occupational Safety and Health Administration (OSHA) to develop and issue rules governing safety in the workplace. When OSHA wants to formulate rules regarding safety in the steel industry, it has to follow the specific procedures outlined by the APA. ■

The impetus for rulemaking may come from various sources, including Congress and the agency itself. In addition, private parties may petition an agency to begin a rulemaking (or repeal a rule). For instance, environmental groups have petitioned for stricter air-pollution controls to combat emissions that may contribute to climate change.

Notice of the Proposed Rulemaking When a federal agency decides to create a new rule, the agency publishes a notice of the proposed rulemaking proceedings in the *Federal Register.* The *Federal Register* is a daily publication of the executive branch that prints government orders, rules, and regulations.

The agency's notice states where and when the proceedings will be held, the agency's legal authority for making the rule (usually its enabling legislation), and the terms or subject matter of the rule. The agency must also make available to the public certain other information, such as the key scientific data underlying the proposal. The proposed rule is often reported by the news media and published in the trade journals of the industries that will be affected.

Comment Period Following the publication of the notice of the proposed rulemaking proceedings, the agency must allow ample time for persons to comment in writing on the proposed rule. The purpose of this comment period is to give interested parties the opportunity to express their views on the proposed rule in an effort to influence agency policy. The comments can be made in writing or, if a hearing is held, orally. All comments become a public record that others can examine.

■ **EXAMPLE 43.6** Brown Trucking learns that the U.S. Department of Transportation is considering a new regulation that will have a negative impact on its ability to do business and on its profits. A notice of the rulemaking is published in the *Federal Register.* Later, a public hearing is held so that proponents and opponents can offer evidence and question witnesses. At this hearing, Brown's owner orally expresses his opinion about the pending rule. ■

The agency need not respond to all comments, but it must respond to any significant comments that bear directly on the proposed rule. The agency responds by either modifying its final rule or explaining, in a statement accompanying the final rule, why it did not make any changes. In some circumstances, particularly when less formal procedures are used, an agency may accept comments after the comment period is closed.

The Final Rule After the agency reviews the comments, it drafts the final rule and publishes it in the *Federal Register.* A final rule must contain a "concise general statement of . . . basis and purpose" that describes the reasoning behind the rule.[7] The final rule can include modifications based on the public comments. If substantial changes are made, however, a new proposal and a new opportunity for comment are required.

The final rule is later compiled along with the rules and regulations of other federal administrative agencies in the *Code of Federal Regulations.* Final rules have binding legal effect unless the courts later overturn them.

Failure to Follow Rulemaking Procedures If an agency fails to follow proper rulemaking procedures, the resulting rule may not be binding. ■ **EXAMPLE 43.7** Members of the Hemp Industries Association (HIA) manufacture and sell food products made from hemp seed and oil. These products may contain trace amounts of THC, a component of marijuana. Without following formal rulemaking procedures, the Drug Enforcement Administration (DEA) publishes rules that effectively ban the possession and sale of HIA's food products, treating them as controlled substances. A court will most likely overturn the rules because the DEA did not follow formal rulemaking procedures. ■

Informal Agency Actions Rather than take the time to conduct notice-and-comment rulemaking, agencies have increasingly been using more informal methods of policymaking, such as issuing interpretive rules and guidance documents. As mentioned earlier, unlike

---

7. 5 U.S.C. Section 555(c).

legislative rules, interpretive rules simply declare policy and do not affect legal rights or obligations. Guidance documents advise the public on the agencies' legal and policy positions.

Informal agency actions are exempt from the APA's requirements because they do not establish legal rights. A party cannot be directly prosecuted for violating an interpretive rule or a guidance document. Nevertheless, an informal action can be important because it warns regulated entities that the agency may engage in formal rulemaking if they ignore its informal policymaking.

43–3b Enforcement

Although rulemaking is the most prominent agency activity, rule enforcement is also critical. Often, an agency enforces its own rules. After a final rule is issued, agencies conduct investigations to monitor compliance with the rule or the terms of the enabling statute.

An agency investigation of this kind might begin when the agency receives a report of a possible violation. In addition, many agency rules require compliance reporting from regulated entities, and such a report may trigger an enforcement investigation.

Inspections and Tests In conducting investigations, many agencies gather information through on-site inspections. Sometimes, inspecting an office, a factory, or some other business facility is the only way to obtain the evidence needed to prove a regulatory violation. At other times, an inspection or test is used in place of a formal hearing to show the need to correct or prevent an undesirable condition.

Administrative inspections and tests cover a wide range of activities, including safety inspections of underground coal mines, safety tests of commercial equipment and automobiles, and environmental monitoring of factory emissions. An agency may also ask a firm or individual to submit certain documents or records to the agency for examination.

Normally, business firms comply with agency requests to inspect facilities or business records because it is in any firm's interest to maintain a good relationship with regulatory bodies. In some instances, however, such as when a firm thinks an agency's request is unreasonable and disruptive, the firm may refuse to comply with the request. In such situations, an agency may resort to the use of a subpoena or a search warrant.

Subpoenas There are two basic types of subpoenas. The subpoena *ad testificandum*[8] ("to testify") is an ordinary subpoena. It is a writ, or order, compelling a witness to appear at an agency hearing. The subpoena *duces tecum*[9] ("bring it with you") compels an individual or organization to hand over books, papers, records, or documents to the agency. An administrative agency may use either type of subpoena to obtain testimony or documents.

There are limits on what an agency can demand. To determine whether an agency is abusing its discretion in pursuing information as part of an investigation, a court may consider such factors as the following:

1. *The purpose of the investigation.* An investigation must have a legitimate purpose. Harassment is an example of an improper purpose. An agency may not issue an administrative subpoena to inspect business records if the motive is to harass or pressure the business into settling an unrelated matter.
2. *The relevance of the information being sought.* Information is relevant if it reveals that the law is being violated or if it assures the agency that the law is not being violated.
3. *The specificity of the demand for testimony or documents.* A subpoena must, for instance, adequately describe the material being sought.
4. *The burden of the demand on the party from whom the information is sought.* For instance, the cost to the company of copying requested documents or providing digital information may become burdensome. (Note that a business generally is protected from revealing information such as trade secrets.)

Search Warrants The Fourth Amendment protects against unreasonable searches and seizures by requiring that in most instances a physical search for evidence must be conducted under the authority of a search warrant. An agency's search warrant is an order directing law enforcement officials to search a specific place for a specific item and seize it for the agency. It was once thought that administrative inspections were exempt from the warrant requirement, but the United States Supreme Court has held that the requirement does apply to the administrative process.[10]

Nevertheless, agencies can conduct warrantless searches in several situations. Warrants are not required to conduct searches in highly regulated industries. Firms that sell firearms or liquor, for instance, are automatically subject to inspections without warrants. Sometimes, a statute permits warrantless searches of certain types of hazardous operations, such as coal mines. Also, a warrantless inspection in an emergency situation is normally considered reasonable.

---

8. Pronounced ad tes-te-fe-*kan*-dum.

9. Pronounced *doo*-suhs *tee*-kum.
10. *Marshall v. Barlow's, Inc.,* 436 U.S. 307, 98 S.Ct. 1816, 56 L.Ed.2d 305 (1978).

43-3c Adjudication

After conducting an investigation of a suspected rule violation, an agency may initiate an administrative action against an individual or organization. Most administrative actions are resolved through negotiated settlements at their initial stages. Sometimes, though, an action ends in formal **adjudication**—the resolution of the dispute through a hearing conducted by the agency.

Negotiated Settlements Depending on the agency, negotiations may involve a simple conversation or a series of informal conferences. Whatever form the negotiations take, their purpose is to rectify the problem to the agency's satisfaction and eliminate the need for additional proceedings.

Settlement is an appealing option to firms for two reasons: to avoid appearing uncooperative and to avoid the expense involved in formal adjudication proceedings and in possible later appeals. Settlement is also an attractive option for agencies. To conserve their resources and avoid formal actions, administrative agencies devote a great deal of effort to giving advice and negotiating solutions to problems.

Formal Complaints If a settlement cannot be reached, the agency may issue a formal complaint against the suspected violator. ■ **EXAMPLE 43.8** The Environmental Protection Agency (EPA) finds that Acme Manufacturing, Inc., is polluting groundwater in violation of federal pollution laws. The EPA issues a complaint against Acme in an effort to bring the plant into compliance with federal regulations. This complaint is a public document, and a press release may accompany it. Acme will respond by filing an answer to the EPA's allegations. If Acme and the EPA cannot agree on a settlement, the case will be adjudicated. ■

The Hearing Agency adjudication may involve a trial-like arbitration procedure before an **administrative law judge (ALJ).** The Administrative Procedure Act (APA) requires that before the hearing takes place, the agency must issue a notice that includes the facts and law on which the complaint is based, the legal authority for the hearing, and its time and place. The administrative agency adjudication process is described next and illustrated graphically in Exhibit 43–3.

The Role of the Administrative Law Judge An ALJ presides over the hearing and has the power to administer oaths, take testimony, rule on questions of evidence, and make determinations of fact. Technically, the ALJ, who works for the agency prosecuting the case, is not an

EXHIBIT 43–3 The Formal Administrative Agency Adjudication Process

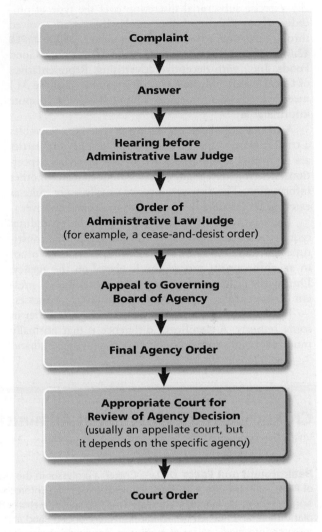

- Complaint
- Answer
- Hearing before Administrative Law Judge
- Order of Administrative Law Judge (for example, a cease-and-desist order)
- Appeal to Governing Board of Agency
- Final Agency Order
- Appropriate Court for Review of Agency Decision (usually an appellate court, but it depends on the specific agency)
- Court Order

independent judge. Nevertheless, the law requires an ALJ to be unbiased.

Certain safeguards prevent bias on the part of the ALJ and promote fairness in the proceedings. For instance, the APA requires that the ALJ be separate from an agency's investigative and prosecutorial staff. The APA also prohibits *ex parte* (private) communications between the ALJ and any party to an agency proceeding, including the agency and the company involved. Finally, provisions of the APA protect the ALJ from agency disciplinary actions unless the agency can show good cause for such an action.

Hearing Procedures Hearing procedures vary widely from agency to agency. Administrative agencies generally exercise substantial discretion over the type of procedure that will be used. Frequently, disputes are resolved through informal adjudication proceedings. ■ **EXAMPLE 43.9** The Federal Trade Commission (FTC) charges Good Foods, Inc., with deceptive advertising. Representatives of Good Foods and the FTC, their counsel, and the ALJ meet at a table in a conference room to resolve the dispute informally. ■

A formal adjudicatory hearing, in contrast, resembles a trial in many respects. Prior to the hearing, the parties are permitted to undertake discovery—involving depositions, interrogatories, and requests for documents or other information. The discovery process usually is not quite as extensive as it would be in a court proceeding, however.

The hearing itself must comply with the procedural requirements of the APA and must also meet the constitutional standards of due process. The burden of proof in an enforcement proceeding is placed on the agency. During the hearing, the parties may give testimony, present other evidence, and cross-examine adverse witnesses.

Trials and administrative agency hearings do differ in some respects. A significant difference is that normally much more information, including hearsay (secondhand information), can be introduced as evidence during an administrative hearing.

Agency Orders Following a hearing, the ALJ renders an **initial order,** or decision, on the case. Either party can appeal the ALJ's decision to the board or commission that governs the agency. If displeased with the result, the party can appeal that decision to a federal appellate court.

■ **EXAMPLE 43.10** The EPA issues a complaint against Acme Manufacturing, Inc., for polluting groundwater. The complaint results in a hearing before an ALJ, who rules in the EPA's favor. If Acme is dissatisfied with the decision, it can appeal to the EPA commission and then to a federal appellate court. ■

If no party appeals the case, the ALJ's decision becomes the **final order** of the agency. The ALJ's decision also becomes final if a party appeals and the commission and the court decline to review the case. If a party appeals and the case is reviewed, the final order comes from the commission's decision or (if that decision is appealed) the decision of the reviewing court.

In the following case, a federal appeals court reviewed the Drug Enforcement Administration's denial of a university professor's application to register to cultivate marijuana.

Case 43.2

Craker v. Drug Enforcement Administration

United States Court of Appeals, First Circuit, 714 F.3d 17 (2013).

Background and Facts Dr. Lyle Craker, a professor in the University of Massachusetts's Department of Plant, Soil and Insect Sciences, applied to the Drug Enforcement Administration (DEA) for permission to register to manufacture marijuana for clinical research. He stated that "a second source of plant material is needed to facilitate privately funded Food and Drug Administration (FDA)-approved research into medical uses of marijuana, ensuring a choice of sources and an adequate supply of quality, research-grade marijuana for medicinal applications."

An administrative law judge recommended that Craker's application be granted, but a DEA deputy administrator issued an order denying his application. Under the DEA's interpretation, the Controlled Substances Act (CSA) requires an applicant to prove both that effective controls against diversion of the marijuana for unapproved purposes are in place and that its supply and the competition to supply it are inadequate. The administrator determined that the professor had not proved that effective controls against the marijuana's diversion were in place or that supply and competition were inadequate. Craker petitioned the U.S. Court of Appeals for the First Circuit to review the order.

In the Language of the Court

HOWARD, Circuit Judge.

* * *

Since 1968, the National Center for Natural Products Research ("NCNPR") at the University of Mississippi has held the necessary registration and a government contract to grow marijuana for research purposes. The contract is administered by the National Institute on Drug Abuse ("NIDA"), a component of the National Institutes of Health ("NIH"), which, in turn, is a component of the [U.S.]

Case 43.2 Continued

Department of Health and Human Services ("HHS"). The contract is opened for competitive bidding every five years. The NCNPR is the only entity registered by the DEA to manufacture marijuana.

* * * *

Dr. Craker's argument with respect to competition is essentially that there cannot be "adequately competitive conditions" when there is only one manufacturer of marijuana.

The Administrator * * * observed that NIDA had provided marijuana manufactured by the University of Mississippi either at cost or free to researchers, and that Dr. Craker had made no showing of how he could provide it for less * * * . Additionally, the Administrator noted that Dr. Craker is free to bid on the contract when it comes up for renewal.

*We see nothing improper in the Administrator's approach. The [CSA's] term "adequately competitive conditions" is not necessarily as narrow as the petitioner suggests. * * * That the current regime may not be the most competitive situation possible does not render it "inadequate."* [Emphasis added.]

* * * *

In finding that Dr. Craker failed to demonstrate that the current supply of marijuana was not adequate and uninterrupted, the Administrator observed that there were over 1,000 kilograms of marijuana in NIDA possession, an amount which far exceeds present research demands and "any foreseeable" future demand. Dr. Craker does not dispute this finding, or that the current amount is more than ninety times the amount he proposes to supply. Instead, he argues that the adequacy of supply must not be measured against NIDA-approved research, but by whether the supply is adequate to supply projects approved by the FDA. But even if we were to accept his premise—which we don't—Dr. Craker fails to demonstrate that the supply is inadequate for those needs, either. He merely states that certain projects were rejected as "not bona-fide" by NIDA, a claim which does not address the adequacy of supply. The fact that Dr. Craker disagrees with the method by which marijuana research is approved does not undermine the substantial evidence that supports the Administrator's conclusion.

Decision and Remedy *The U.S. Court of Appeals for the First Circuit denied Craker's petition to review the agency's order "because the Administrator's interpretation of the CSA is permissible and her findings are reasonable and supported by the evidence."*

Critical Thinking

- **Economic** *Why should a court wait to review an agency's order until the order has gone through the entire procedural process and can be considered final?*
- **Legal Environment** *Under what standard does a court defer to an agency's interpretation of a statute? Did the court in this case appear to have applied that standard to the DEA's interpretation of the Controlled Substances Act? Discuss.*

43–4 Judicial Deference to Agency Decisions

When asked to review agency decisions, courts historically granted deference to the agency's judgment. In other words, the courts tended to accept the agency's judgment, often citing the agency's great expertise in the subject area of the regulation. This deference seems especially appropriate when applied to an agency's analysis of factual questions, but should it also extend to an agency's interpretation of its own legal authority? In *Chevron U.S.A., Inc. v. Natural Resources Defense Council, Inc.*,[11] the United States Supreme Court held that it should.

11. 467 U.S. 837, 104 S.Ct. 2778, 81 L.Ed.2d 694 (1984).

By so ruling, the Court created a standard of broadened deference to agencies on questions of legal interpretation.

43–4a The Holding of the *Chevron* Case

At issue in the *Chevron* case was whether the courts should defer to an agency's interpretation of a statute giving it authority to act. The Environmental Protection Agency (EPA) had interpreted the phrase "stationary source" in the Clean Air Act as referring to an entire manufacturing plant, and not to each facility within a plant. The agency's interpretation enabled it to adopt the so-called bubble policy, which allowed companies to offset increases in emissions in part of a plant with decreases elsewhere in the plant. This interpretation reduced pollution-control compliance costs to manufacturers. An environmental group challenged the legality of the EPA's interpretation.

The Supreme Court held that the courts should defer to an agency's interpretation of law as well as fact. The Court found that the agency's interpretation of the statute was reasonable. The Court's decision in the *Chevron* case created a new standard for courts to use when reviewing agency interpretations of law. This standard involves the following two questions:

1. Did Congress directly address the issue in dispute in the statute? If so, the statutory language prevails.
2. If the statute is silent or ambiguous, is the agency's interpretation "reasonable"? If it is, a court should uphold the agency's interpretation even if the court would have interpreted the law differently.

43–4b When Courts Will Give *Chevron* Deference to Agency Interpretation

The notion that courts should defer to agencies on matters of law was controversial. Under the holding of the *Chevron* case, when the meaning of a particular statute's language is unclear and an agency interprets it, the court must follow the agency's interpretation as long as it is reasonable. This led to considerable discussion and litigation to test the boundaries of the *Chevron* holding.

For instance, are courts required to give deference to all agency interpretations or only to those that result from adjudication or formal rulemaking procedures? The United States Supreme Court has held that in order for agency interpretations to be assured *Chevron* deference, they must meet the formal legal standards for notice-and-comment rulemaking. Nevertheless, there are still gray areas, and many agency interpretations are challenged in court.

■ **CASE IN POINT 43.11** The Federal Insurance Contributions Act (FICA) requires employees and employers to pay Social Security taxes on all wages. The FICA excludes wages paid for any service to a school "performed by a student who is enrolled and regularly attending classes." The Mayo Foundation for Medical Education and Research offers educational residency programs to physicians who seek instruction in a chosen specialty. In addition to receiving instruction, the physicians are paid to spend fifty to eighty hours a week caring for patients. The U.S. Treasury Department issued a rule providing that anyone who works forty or more hours per week is an employee, not a student. The Mayo Foundation asserted that the rule did not apply to its residents.

The United States Supreme Court upheld the rule. Congress gave the Treasury Department the authority to make rules to enforce the Internal Revenue Code. The employee rule was issued after notice-and-comment procedures, and it was based on a reasonable determination that imposing Social Security taxes on medical residents would further the purpose of the statute. The physicians were "the kind of workers that Congress intended to both contribute to and benefit from the Social Security system."[12] ■

The following case involves a federal agency's role in determining whether alien pilots may be certified to operate large, U.S.-registered aircraft.

---

12. *Mayo Foundation for Medical Education and Research v. United States,* 562 U.S. 44, 131 S.Ct. 704, 178 L.Ed.2d 588 (2011).

Case Analysis 43.3

Olivares v. Transportation Security Administration
United States Court of Appeals, District of Columbia Circuit, 819 F.3d 454 (2016).

In the Language of the Court
EDWARDS, Senior Circuit Judge:
* * * *

I. BACKGROUND
In the aftermath of the tragic terrorist attacks on September 11, 2001, Congress created the Transportation Security Administration [TSA] to shore up our nation's civil aviation security. [TSA is part of the U.S.] Department of Homeland Security under the direction of the Secretary of Homeland Security.

* * * No pilot may serve in any capacity as an airman with respect to a civil aircraft * * * without an airman certificate from FAA [Federal Aviation Administration]. For large aircraft, pilots must obtain additional certification known as a Type Rating. [Under the Aviation and Transportation Security Act of 2001,] aliens who seek training and certification to operate large, U.S.-registered aircraft must first secure clearance by TSA. If TSA determines that an alien applicant presents a risk to aviation or national security, then that applicant is ineligible to receive the training necessary to secure a large aircraft Type Rating from FAA.
* * * *

[Alberto Olivares (Petitioner), a citizen of Venezuela,] received [an] opportunity to pilot a large, U.S.-registered aircraft. * * * Petitioner applied to attend an FAA-certified flight school in France, and TSA conducted a background investigation.

Case 43.3 Continued

* * * *

* * * TSA concluded that Petitioner was a "Threat to Transportation/ National Security" [and] sent an email to Petitioner denying his application.

* * * Petitioner filed his petition for review with this court. * * * Andrea Vara executed a sworn declaration explaining TSA's grounds for denying Petitioner's application for training. Ms. Vara is employed by [TSA] as the Alien Flight Student Program Manager. She has been responsible for managing TSA's Alien Flight Student Program, which conducts security threat assessments on individuals who are not U.S. citizens or nationals who seek flight instruction or recurrent training from FAA-certified flight training providers.

The Vara Declaration makes it clear that Ms. Vara was the Government official who made the determination that Petitioner's application should be denied * * * . The Vara Declaration states:

* * * Petitioner submitted Training Request # 565192, seeking to train at FlightSafety International—Paris Learning Center.

* * * Petitioner was subject to an investigation, which revealed the following. In 2007, Petitioner pled guilty to conspiracy to possess with intent to distribute controlled substances and the U.S. District Court for the Northern District of Illinois sentenced him to eighty (80) months imprisonment. Petitioner's conviction made him inadmissible to the United States and led to the revocation of his FAA Airman's Certificate. Petitioner was deported to his home country of Venezuela in March 2010.

A public news article published after Petitioner was deported provided a U.S. address for Petitioner. Further, records indicated that Petitioner was a suspected international trafficker in firearms. There was evidence that Petitioner had previously been involved in the export of weapons and U.S. currency to Venezuela by private aircraft, was the second pilot of an aircraft from which several weapons and $500,000 was seized by local

authorities in Aruba, and that one of his associates was arrested in Aruba for smuggling firearms.

This information, viewed as a whole, demonstrated Petitioner's willingness to consistently disregard the law and to use an aircraft for criminal activity, in opposition to U.S. security interests. The information also raised concerns that Petitioner may use his flight training to advance the interests of a criminal enterprise, which could include an enterprise that seeks to do harm to the United States.

Based on all the foregoing information, I concluded Petitioner posed a threat to aviation and national security and * * * denied his training request.

* * * *

II. ANALYSIS

A. THE COURT'S JURISDICTION

* * * An action taken by TSA on behalf of the Secretary of Homeland Security is clearly subject to review.

* * * *

B. STANDARD OF REVIEW

Pursuant to the Administrative Procedure Act, we must uphold TSA's decisions unless they are arbitrary, capricious, an abuse of discretion, or otherwise not in accordance with law.

What is important here is that, because Congress has entrusted TSA with broad authority over civil aviation security, it is TSA's job—not * * * ours— to strike a balance between convenience and security. Therefore, *in cases of this sort, we must defer to TSA actions that reasonably interpret and enforce the safety and security obligations of the agency. * * * Courts do not second-guess expert agency judgments on potential risks to national security. Rather, we defer to the informed judgment of agency officials whose obligation it is to assess risks to national security.* [Emphasis added.]

* * * *

D. PETITIONER'S * * * CLAIM

* * * *

* * * Petitioner argues that TSA should not have used his suspected firearms trafficking or his Massachusetts

address to support its decision. [TSA had discovered that, even though Olivares had been deported with no right to return to the United States, he maintained a local address in Massachusetts.] Petitioner claims that the Massachusetts address actually belongs to his brother, and Petitioner insists that he has never illegally entered the United States. Petitioner also points out that the firearms incident occurred nearly two decades ago and that he was merely suspected of being involved. In light of the limited standard of review that controls the disposition of this case, these arguments are not persuasive. It was rational for TSA to find it suspicious and thus consider information indicating that a deported individual appeared to maintain a current U.S. address and had been suspected of involvement in firearms trafficking. The agency's weighing of this information, along with the information regarding Petitioner's known criminal history, was not inconsistent with reasoned decision making.

Given TSA's broad authority to assess potential risks to aviation and national security, the agency's clear and reasonable explanation offered in the Vara Declaration, and the limited standard of review [under the holding in the *Chevron* case], we are in no position to second-guess TSA's judgment in denying Petitioner's application. In assessing risks to national security, conclusions must often be based on informed judgment rather than concrete evidence, and that reality affects what we may reasonably insist on from the Government. When it comes to collecting evidence and drawing factual inferences in this area, the lack of competence on the part of the courts is marked, and respect for the Government's conclusions is appropriate. Where no factual certainties exist or where facts alone do not provide the answer * * * we require only that the agency so state and go on to identify the considerations it found persuasive.

It is self-evident that TSA's action against Petitioner was related to the agency's goals of improving the safety of air

Case 43.3 Continues

Case 43.3 Continued

travel. TSA was not required to show that Petitioner would engage in activities designed to compromise aviation or national security. Rather, the agency was merely required to give a reasonable explanation as to why it believed that Petitioner presented a risk to aviation or national security. The Vara Declaration satisfies this legal obligation. [Emphasis added.]

III. CONCLUSION

For the reasons set forth above, the petition for review is denied.

Legal Reasoning Questions

1. What impact did the Vara Declaration have on the court's ruling in this case?

2. Is a court's evaluation of an agency's assessment of a risk to national security different from a review of other agency determinations? Explain.

3. Should the agency at the center of this case have revealed the reasons for its decision before Olivares filed a suit challenging it? Explain.

43–5 Public Accountability

As a result of growing public concern over the powers exercised by administrative agencies, Congress passed several laws to make agencies more accountable through public scrutiny. Here, we discuss the most significant of these laws.

43–5a Freedom of Information Act

The Freedom of Information Act (FOIA)[13] requires the federal government to disclose certain records to any person or entity on written request, even if no reason is given for the request. All federal government agencies must make their records available electronically on the Internet and in other electronic formats.

The FOIA exempts certain types of records, such as those pertaining to national security and those containing information that is confidential or personal. ■ **EXAMPLE 43.12** Juanita, a reporter from an online health magazine, makes an FOIA request to the Centers for Disease Control and Prevention for a list of people who have contracted a highly contagious virus. The Centers for Disease Control and Prevention will not have to comply, because the requested information is confidential and personal. ■

For other records, a request that complies with the FOIA procedures need only contain a reasonable description of the information sought. An agency's failure to comply with an FOIA request can be challenged in a federal district court. The media, industry trade associations, public-interest groups, and even companies seeking information about competitors rely on these FOIA provisions to obtain information from government agencies.

43–5b Government in the Sunshine Act

The Government in the Sunshine Act,[14] or open meeting law, requires that "every portion of every meeting of an agency" be open to "public observation." The act also requires that the public be provided with adequate advance notice of scheduled meetings and agendas.

Like the FOIA, the Sunshine Act contains certain exceptions. Closed meetings are permitted in the following situations:

1. The subject of the meeting concerns accusing any person of a crime.
2. Open meetings would frustrate implementation of future agency actions.
3. The subject of the meeting involves matters relating to future litigation or rulemaking.

Courts interpret these exceptions to allow open access whenever possible.

43–5c Regulatory Flexibility Act

Concern over the effects of regulation on the efficiency of businesses, particularly smaller ones, led Congress to pass the Regulatory Flexibility Act[15] in 1980. Under this act, whenever a new regulation will have a "significant impact upon a substantial number of small entities," the

---

13. 5 U.S.C. Section 552.

14. 5 U.S.C. Section 552b.
15. 5 U.S.C. Sections 601–612.

agency must conduct a regulatory flexibility analysis. The analysis must measure the cost that the rule would impose on small businesses and consider less burdensome alternatives. The act also contains provisions to alert small businesses about forthcoming regulations. The act relieved small businesses of some record-keeping burdens, especially with regard to hazardous waste management.

43–5d Small Business Regulatory Enforcement Fairness Act

The Small Business Regulatory Enforcement Fairness Act[16] includes various provisions intended to ease the regulatory burden on small businesses:

---

16. 5 U.S.C. Sections 801 *et seq.*

1. Federal agencies must prepare guides that explain in plain English how small businesses can comply with federal regulations.
2. Congress may review new federal regulations for at least sixty days before they take effect, giving opponents of the rules time to present their arguments.
3. The courts may enforce the Regulatory Flexibility Act. This provision helps to ensure that federal agencies will consider ways to reduce the economic impact of new regulations on small businesses.
4. The Office of the National Ombudsman at the Small Business Administration was set up to receive comments from small businesses about their dealings with federal agencies. Based on these comments, Regional Small Business Fairness Boards rate the agencies and publicize their findings.

Reviewing: Administrative Agencies

Assume that the Securities and Exchange Commission (SEC) has a rule that it will enforce statutory provisions prohibiting insider trading only when the insiders make monetary profits for themselves. Then the SEC makes a new rule, declaring that it will now bring enforcement actions against individuals for insider trading even if the individuals did not personally profit from the transactions. In making the new rule, the SEC does not conduct a rulemaking procedure but simply announces its decision. A stockbrokerage firm objects that the new rule was unlawfully developed without opportunity for public comment. The brokerage firm challenges the rule in an action that ultimately is reviewed by a federal appellate court. Using the information presented in the chapter, answer the following questions.

1. Is the SEC an executive agency or an independent regulatory agency? Does it matter to the outcome of this dispute? Explain.
2. Suppose that the SEC asserts that it has always had the statutory authority to pursue persons for insider trading regardless of whether they personally profited from the transactions. This is the only argument the SEC makes to justify changing its enforcement rules. Would a court be likely to find that the SEC's action was arbitrary and capricious under the Administrative Procedure Act (APA)? Why or why not?
3. Would a court be likely to give *Chevron* deference to the SEC's interpretation of the law on insider trading? Why or why not?
4. Now assume that a court finds that the new rule is merely "interpretive." What effect would this determination have on whether the SEC had to follow the APA's rulemaking procedures?

Debate This . . .   *Because an administrative law judge (ALJ) acts as both judge and jury, there should always be at least three ALJs in each administrative hearing.*

Terms and Concepts

adjudication 833
administrative agency 824
administrative law judge (ALJ) 833
administrative process 830
bureaucracy 827

delegation doctrine 827
enabling legislation 825
exhaustion doctrine 829
final order 834
initial order 834

interpretive rule 826
legislative rule 826
notice-and-comment
   rulemaking 831
rulemaking 830

Issue Spotters

1. The U.S. Department of Transportation (DOT) sometimes hears an appeal from a party whose contract with the DOT has been canceled. An administrative law judge (ALJ) who works for the DOT hears this appeal. What safeguards promote the ALJ's fairness? (See *The Administrative Process*.)

2. Techplate Corporation learns that a federal administrative agency is considering a rule that will have a negative impact on the firm's ability to do business. Does the firm have any opportunity to express its opinion about the pending rule? Explain. (See *The Administrative Process*.)

- **Check your answers to the Issue Spotters against the answers provided in Appendix D at the end of this text.**

Business Scenarios

43–1. Rulemaking and Adjudication Powers. For decades, the Federal Trade Commission (FTC) resolved fair trade and advertising disputes through individual adjudications. In the 1960s, the FTC began promulgating rules that defined fair and unfair trade practices. In cases involving violations of these rules, the due process rights of participants were more limited and did not include cross-examination. Although anyone charged with violating a rule would receive a full adjudication, the legitimacy of the rule itself could not be challenged in the adjudication. Furthermore, a party charged with violating a rule was almost certain to lose the adjudication. Affected parties complained to a court, arguing that their rights before the FTC were unduly limited by the new rules. What would the court examine to determine whether to uphold the new rules? (See *The Administrative Process*.)

43–2. Informal Rulemaking. Assume that the Food and Drug Administration (FDA), using proper procedures, adopts a rule describing its future investigations. This new rule covers all future circumstances in which the FDA wants to regulate food additives. Under the new rule, the FDA is not to regulate food additives without giving food companies an opportunity to cross-examine witnesses. Later, the FDA wants to regulate methylisocyanate, a food additive. The FDA undertakes an informal rulemaking procedure, without cross-examination, and regulates methylisocyanate. Producers protest, saying that the FDA promised them the opportunity for cross-examination. The FDA responds that the Administrative Procedure Act does not require such cross-examination and that it is free to withdraw the promise made in its new rule. If the producers challenge the FDA in court, on what basis would the court rule in their favor? Explain. (See *The Administrative Process*.)

Business Case Problems

43–3. Rulemaking. The Investment Company Act prohibits a mutual fund from engaging in certain transactions when there may be a conflict of interest between the manager of the fund and its shareholders. Under rules issued by the Securities and Exchange Commission (SEC), however, a fund that meets certain conditions may engage in an otherwise prohibited transaction. In June 2004, the SEC added two new conditions. A year later, the SEC reconsidered the new conditions in terms of the costs that they would impose on the funds. Within eight days, and without asking for public input, the SEC readopted the conditions. The Chamber of Commerce of the United States asked a federal appellate court to review the new rules. The Chamber argued that in readopting the rules, the SEC relied on materials not in the "rulemaking record" without providing an opportunity for public comment. The SEC countered that the information was otherwise "publicly available." In adopting a rule, should an agency consider information that is not part of the rulemaking record? Why or why not? [*Chamber of Commerce of the United States v. Securities and Exchange Commission*, 443 F.3d 890 (D.C.Cir. 2006)] (See *The Administrative Process*.)

43–4. Business Case Problem with Sample Answer—Agency Powers. A well-documented rise in global temperatures has coincided with a significant increase in the concentration of carbon dioxide in the atmosphere. Many scientists believe that the two trends are related, because when carbon dioxide is released into the atmosphere, it produces a greenhouse effect, trapping solar heat. Under the Clean Air Act (CAA), the Environmental Protection Agency (EPA) is authorized to regulate "any" air pollutants "emitted into . . . the ambient air" that in its "judgment cause, or contribute to, air pollution."

A group of private organizations asked the EPA to regulate carbon dioxide and other "greenhouse gas" emissions from new motor vehicles. The EPA refused, stating, among other things, that Congress last amended the CAA in 1990 without authorizing new, binding auto emissions limits. Nineteen states, including Massachusetts, asked a district court to review the EPA's denial. Did the EPA have the authority to regulate greenhouse gas emissions from new motor vehicles? If so, was its stated reason for refusing to do so consistent with that authority? Discuss. [*Massachusetts v. Environmental*

Protection Agency, 549 U.S. 497, 127 S.Ct. 1438, 167 L.Ed.2d 248 (2007)] (See *Agency Creation and Powers.*)

- **For a sample answer to Problem 43–4, go to Appendix E at the end of this text.**

43–5. Judicial Deference. After Dave Conley died of lung cancer, his widow filed for benefits under the Black Lung Benefits Act. To qualify for benefits under the act, she had to show that exposure to coal dust was a substantial contributing factor to her husband's death. Conley had been a coal miner, but he had also been a longtime smoker. At the benefits hearing, a physician testified that coal dust was a substantial factor in Conley's death. No evidence was presented to support this conclusion, however. The administrative law judge awarded benefits. On appeal, should a court defer to this decision? Discuss. [*Conley v. National Mines Corp.,* 595 F.3d 297 (6th Cir. 2010)] (See *Judicial Deference to Agency Decisions.*)

43–6. Arbitrary and Capricious Test. Michael Manin, an airline pilot, was twice convicted of disorderly conduct, a minor misdemeanor. To renew his flight certification with the National Transportation Safety Board (NTSB), Manin filed an application that asked him about his criminal history. He did not disclose his two convictions. When these came to light more than ten years later, Manin argued that he had not known that he was required to report convictions for minor misdemeanors. The NTSB's policy was to consider an applicant's understanding of what information a question sought before determining whether an answer was false. But without explanation, the agency departed from this policy, refused to consider Manin's argument, and revoked his certification. Was this action arbitrary or capricious? Explain. [*Manin v. National Transportation Safety Board,* 627 F.3d 1239 (D.C.Cir. 2011)] (See *Agency Creation and Powers.*)

43–7. Adjudication. Mechanics replaced a brake assembly on the landing gear of a CRJ–700 plane operated by GoJet Airlines, LLC. The mechanics installed gear pins to lock the assembly in place during the repair but failed to remove one of the pins after they had finished. On the plane's next flight, a warning light alerted the pilots that the landing gear would not retract after takeoff. There was a potential for danger, but the pilots flew the CRJ–700 safely back to the departure airport. No one was injured, and no property was damaged. The Federal Aviation Administration (FAA) cited GoJet for violating FAA regulations by "carelessly or recklessly operating an unairworthy airplane." GoJet objected to the citation. To which court can GoJet appeal for review? On what ground might that court decline to review the case? [*GoJet Airlines, LLC v. F.A.A.,* 743 F.3d 1168 (8th Cir. 2014)] (See *The Administrative Process.*)

43–8. Judicial Deference to Agency Decisions. Knox Creek Coal Corporation operates coal mines in West Virginia. The U.S. Department of Labor charged Knox's Tiller No. 1 Mine with "significant and substantial" (S&S) violations of the Federal Mine Safety and Health Act. According to the charges, inadequately sealed enclosures of electrical equipment in the mine created the potential for an explosion. The Mine Act designates a violation as S&S when it "*could* significantly and substantially contribute to the cause and effect of a coal or other mine safety or health hazard." Challenging the S&S determination, Knox filed a suit against the secretary of labor. The secretary argued that "could" means "merely possible"—if there is a violation, the existence of a hazard is assumed. This position was consistent with agency and judicial precedent and the Mine Act's history and purpose. Knox argued that "could" requires proof of the likelihood of a hazard. When does a court defer to an agency's interpretation of law? Do those circumstances exist in this case? Discuss. [*Knox Creek Coal Corp v. Secretary of Labor,* 811 F.3d 148 (4th Cir. 2016)] (See *Judicial Deference to Agency Decisions.*)

43–9. A Question of Ethics—Rulemaking. *To ensure highway safety and protect driver health, Congress charged federal agencies with regulating the hours of service of commercial motor vehicle operators. Between 1940 and 2003, the regulations that applied to long-haul truck drivers were mostly unchanged. (Long-haul drivers are those who operate beyond a 150-mile radius of their base.) In 2003, the Federal Motor Carrier Safety Administration (FMCSA) revised the regulations significantly, increasing the number of daily and weekly hours that drivers could work. The agency had not considered the impact of the changes on the health of the drivers, however, and the revisions were overturned.*

The FMCSA then issued a notice that it would reconsider the revisions and opened them up for public comment. The agency analyzed the costs to the industry and the crash risks due to driver fatigue under different options. It concluded that the safety benefits of not increasing the hours were less than the economic costs. In 2005, the agency issued a rule that was nearly identical to the 2003 version. Public Citizen, Inc., and others, including the Owner-Operator Independent Drivers Association, asked the U.S. Court of Appeals for the District of Columbia Circuit to review the 2005 rule as it applied to long-haul drivers. [Owner-Operator Independent Drivers Association, Inc. v. Federal Motor Carrier Safety Administration, 494 F.3d 188 (D.C.Cir. 2007)] (See The Administrative Process.)

(a) The FMCSA's cost-benefit analysis included new methods that were not disclosed to the public in time for comments. Was this unethical? Should the agency have disclosed the new methodology sooner? Why or why not?

(b) The FMCSA created a graph to show the risk of a crash as a function of the time a driver spent on the job. The graph plotted the first twelve hours of a day individually, but the rest of the time was depicted with an aggregate figure at the seventeenth hour. This made the risk at those hours appear to be lower. Is it unethical for an agency to manipulate data? Explain.

Legal Reasoning Group Activity

43–10. Investigation. Maureen Droge was a flight attendant for United Air Lines, Inc. (UAL). After being assigned to work in Paris, France, she became pregnant. Because UAL does not allow its flight attendants to fly during their third trimester of pregnancy, Droge was placed on involuntary leave. She applied for temporary disability benefits through the French social security system. Her request was denied because UAL does not contribute to the French system on behalf of its U.S.-based flight attendants. Droge filed a charge of discrimination with the U.S. Equal Employment Opportunity Commission (EEOC), alleging that UAL had discriminated against her and other Americans. The EEOC issued a subpoena, asking UAL to detail all benefits received by all UAL employees living outside the United States. UAL refused to provide the information on the ground that it was irrelevant and compliance would be unduly burdensome. The EEOC filed a suit in a federal district court against UAL. (See *The Administrative Process.*)

(a) The first group will decide whether the court should enforce the subpoena and explain why.

(b) The second group will discuss whether the EEOC should be able to force a U.S. company operating overseas to provide the same disability benefits to employees located there as it does to employees in the United States. Should UAL be required to contribute to the French social security system for employees who reside in France?

CHAPTER 44

Consumer Law

All statutes, agency rules, and common law judicial decisions that serve to protect the interests of consumers are classified as **consumer law.** Traditionally, in disputes involving consumers, it was assumed that the freedom to contract carried with it the obligation to live by the deal made. Over time, this attitude has changed considerably.

Today, countless federal and state laws attempt to protect consumers

from unfair trade practices, unsafe products, discriminatory or unreasonable credit requirements, and other problems related to consumer transactions. Nearly every agency and department of the federal government has an office of consumer affairs, and most states have one or more such offices to help consumers. Also, typically the attorney general's office assists consumers at the state level.

In recent years, there has been a renewed interest in attempting to protect consumers in their dealings with credit-card companies, financial institutions, and insurance companies. Congress has enacted new credit-card regulations and financial reforms to regulate the nation's largest banks. It has also enacted health-care reforms and revised food safety laws.

44–1 Advertising, Marketing, and Sales

Numerous federal laws have been passed to define the duties of sellers and the rights of consumers. Exhibit 44–1 shows many of the areas of consumer law that are regulated by federal statutes. We begin our discussion of this legislation by examining some of the laws and regulations relating to advertising, marketing, and sales. Although we focus on federal law, realize that state consumer protection laws in these and other areas often provide more sweeping and significant protections than do federal laws.

44–1a Deceptive Advertising

One of the most important federal consumer protection laws is the Federal Trade Commission Act.[1] The act created the Federal Trade Commission (FTC) to carry out the broadly stated goal of preventing unfair and deceptive trade practices, including deceptive advertising.

Generally, **deceptive advertising** occurs if a reasonable consumer would be misled by the advertising claim. Vague generalities and obvious exaggerations are permissible. These claims are known as *puffery.* When a claim

takes on the appearance of authenticity, however, it may create problems.

Claims That Appear to Be Based on Factual Evidence Advertising that *appears* to be based on factual evidence but, in fact, is not reasonably supported by evidence will be deemed deceptive. ■ **CASE IN POINT 44.1** MedLab, Inc., advertised that its weight-loss supplement ("The New Skinny Pill") would cause users to lose substantial amounts of weight rapidly. The ads claimed that "clinical studies prove" that people who take the pill lose "as much as 15 to 18 pounds per week and as much as 50 percent of all excess weight in just 14 days, without dieting or exercising." The FTC sued MedLab for deceptive advertising.

An expert hired by the FTC to evaluate the claim testified that to lose this much weight, "a 200-pound individual would need to run between 57 and 68 miles every day"—the equivalent of more than two marathons per day. The court concluded that the advertisement was false and misleading, granted the FTC a summary judgment, and issued a permanent injunction to stop MedLab from running the ads.[2] ■

The following case involved an advertising claim based on limited scientific evidence.

---

1. 15 U.S.C. Sections 41–58.

2. *Federal Trade Commission v. MedLab, Inc,* 615 F.Supp.2d 1068 (N.D.Cal. 2009).

EXHIBIT 44–1 Selected Areas of Consumer Law Regulated by Statutes

Labeling and Packaging

Example—The Fair Packaging and Labeling Act

Advertising

Example—The Federal Trade Commission Act

Sales

Example—The FTC Mail-Order Rule

CONSUMER LAW

Food and Drugs

Example—The Federal Food, Drug, and Cosmetic Act

Product Safety

Example—The Consumer Product Safety Act

Credit Protection

Example—The Consumer Credit Protection Act

Case **44.1**

POM Wonderful, LLC v. Federal Trade Commission

United States Court of Appeals, District of Columbia Circuit, 777 F.3d 478 (2015).

Background and Facts POM Wonderful, LLC, makes and sells pomegranate-based products. In ads, POM touted medical studies claiming to show that daily consumption of its products could treat, prevent, or reduce the risk of heart disease, prostate cancer, and erectile dysfunction. These ads mischaracterized the scientific evidence.

The Federal Trade Commission (FTC) charged POM with, and held POM liable for, making false, misleading, and unsubstantiated representations in violation of the FTC Act. POM was barred from running future ads asserting that its products treat or prevent any disease unless "randomized, controlled, human clinical trials" (RCTs, for "randomized controlled trials") demonstrated statistically significant results. POM petitioned the U.S. Court of Appeals for the District of Columbia Circuit to review this injunctive order.

In the Language of the Court

SRINIVASAN, Circuit Judge:

* * * *

* * * POM's ads * * * convey the net impression that clinical studies or trials show that a causal relation has been established between the consumption of the challenged POM products and its efficacy to treat, prevent or reduce the risk of the serious diseases in question. The Commission found that experts in the relevant fields would require RCTs * * * to establish such a causal relationship.

The Commission examined each of the studies invoked by petitioners in their ads, concluding that the referenced studies fail to qualify as RCTs of the kind that could afford adequate substantiation. Petitioners' claims therefore were deceptive.

Case 44.1 Continued

* * * *

* * * The Commission's finding is supported by substantial record evidence. That evidence includes written reports and testimony from medical researchers stating that experts in the fields of cardiology and urology require randomized, double-blinded, placebo-controlled clinical trials to substantiate any claim that a product treats, prevents, or reduces the risk of disease.

The Commission drew on that expert testimony to explain why the attributes of well-designed RCTs are necessary to substantiate petitioners' claims. A control group, for example, allows investigators to distinguish between real effects from the intervention, and other changes, including those due to the mere act of being treated (placebo effect) and the passage of time. Random assignment of a study's subjects to treatment and control groups increases the likelihood that the treatment and control groups are similar in relevant characteristics, so that any difference in the outcome between the two groups can be attributed to the treatment. And when a study is double-blinded ([that is,] when neither the study participants nor the investigators know which patients are in the treatment group and which patients are in the control group), it is less likely that participants or investigators will consciously or unconsciously take actions potentially biasing the results.

* * * *

* * * The need for RCTs is driven by the claims petitioners have chosen to make. * * * *An advertiser * * * may assert a health-related claim backed by medical evidence falling short of an RCT if it includes an effective disclaimer disclosing the limitations of the supporting research.* Petitioners did not do so. [Emphasis added.]

Decision and Remedy *The U.S. Court of Appeals for the District of Columbia Circuit enforced the FTC's order with respect to POM's ads. The court pointed out that "An advertiser who makes express representations about the level of support for a particular claim must possess the level of proof claimed in the ad and must convey that information to consumers in a non-misleading way."*

Critical Thinking

- **Ethical** *POM claimed that it is unethical to require RCTs to substantiate disease-related claims about food products. It argued that, for instance, "doctors cannot . . . ethically deprive a control group of patients of all Vitamin C for a decade to determine whether Vitamin C helps prevent cancer." Is this a valid argument? Why or why not?*

Claims Based on Half-Truths Some advertisements contain "half-truths," meaning that the presented information is true but incomplete and may therefore lead consumers to a false conclusion. ■ **EXAMPLE 44.2** The maker of Campbell's soups advertised that "most" Campbell's soups are low in fat and cholesterol and thus helpful in fighting heart disease. What the ad did not say was that many Campbell's soups are high in sodium and that high-sodium diets may increase the risk of heart disease. Hence, the FTC ruled that Campbell's claims were deceptive. ■ In addition, advertising that contains an endorsement by a celebrity may be deemed deceptive if the celebrity does not actually use the product.

Bait-and-Switch Advertising The FTC has issued rules that govern specific advertising techniques. One of the most important rules is contained in the FTC's "Guides Against Bait Advertising."[3]

Some retailers systematically advertise merchandise at low prices to get customers into their stores. But when the customers arrive, they find that the merchandise is not in stock. Salespersons then encourage them to purchase more expensive items instead. This practice, known as **bait-and-switch advertising,** is a form of deceptive advertising. The low price is the "bait" to lure the consumer into the store. The salesperson is instructed to "switch" the consumer to a different, more expensive item.

Under the FTC guidelines, bait-and-switch advertising occurs if the seller does any of the following:

1. Refuses to show the advertised item.
2. Fails to have a reasonable quantity of the item in stock.
3. Fails to promise to deliver the advertised item within a reasonable time.
4. Discourages employees from selling the advertised item.

---

3. 16 C.F.R. Part 238.

Online Deceptive Advertising Deceptive advertising occurs in the online environment as well as offline. The FTC actively monitors online advertising. It has identified hundreds of Web sites that have made false or deceptive claims for products and services ranging from medical treatments to exercise equipment and weight-loss aids.

The FTC has issued guidelines to help online businesses comply with existing laws prohibiting deceptive advertising. These guidelines include the following requirements:

1. All ads—both online and offline—must be truthful and not misleading.
2. The claims made in an ad must be substantiated—that is, advertisers must have evidence to back up their claims.
3. Ads cannot be unfair, which the FTC defines as "likely to cause substantial consumer injury that consumers could not reasonably avoid and that is not outweighed by the benefit to consumers or competition."
4. Ads must disclose relevant limitations and qualifying information concerning the claims advertisers are making.
5. Required disclosures must be "clear and conspicuous." For instance, because consumers may not read an entire Web page, an online disclosure should be placed as close as possible to the claim being qualified. Generally, hyperlinks to a disclosure are recommended only for lengthy disclosures. If hyperlinks are used, they should be obvious and should be placed as close as possible to the relevant information it qualifies.

The FTC creates additional guidelines as needed to respond to new issues that arise with online advertising. One new issue involves so-called native ads, which are discussed in this chapter's *Digital Update* feature.

Federal Trade Commission Actions The FTC receives complaints from many sources, including competitors of alleged violators, consumers, trade associations, Better Business Bureaus, and government organizations and officials. When the agency receives numerous and widespread complaints about a particular problem, it will investigate.

Formal Complaint. If the FTC concludes that a given advertisement is unfair or deceptive, it drafts a formal complaint, which is sent to the alleged offender. The company may agree to settle the complaint without further proceedings. If not, the FTC can conduct a hearing in which the company can present its defense.

FTC Orders and Remedies. If the FTC succeeds in proving that an advertisement is unfair or deceptive, it usually issues a **cease-and-desist order** requiring the company to stop the challenged advertising. In some circumstances, it may also impose a sanction known as **counteradvertising.** This requires the company to advertise anew—in print, on the Internet, on radio, and on television—to inform the public about the earlier misinformation. The FTC sometimes institutes a **multiple product order,** which requires a firm to stop false advertising for all of its products, not just the product involved in the original action.

Damages When Consumers Are Injured. When a company's deceptive ad involves wrongful charges to consumers, the FTC may seek other remedies, including damages. ■ **CASE IN POINT 44.3** The FTC sued Bronson Partners, LLC, for deceptively advertising two products—Chinese Diet Tea and Bio-Slim Patch. Bronson's ads claimed that the diet tea "eliminates 91 percent of absorbed sugars," "prevents 83 percent of fat absorption," and "doubles your metabolic rate to burn calories fast." The Bio-Slim Patch ads promised "lasting weight loss" and claimed that "ugly fatty tissue will disappear at a spectacular rate" as product users wear the patch while carrying on their normal lifestyle.

Eventually, Bronson conceded that it had engaged in deceptive advertising, and the FTC sought damages. The court awarded the FTC $1,942,325, which was the amount of Bronson's revenues from the two products.[4] ■

Restitution Possible. When a company's deceptive ad leads to wrongful payments by consumers, the FTC may seek other remedies, including restitution. ■ **CASE IN POINT 44.4** Verity International, Ltd., billed phone-line subscribers who accessed certain online pornography sites at the rate for international calls to Madagascar. When consumers complained about the charges, Verity told them that the charges were valid and had to be paid, or the consumers would face further collection actions. A federal appellate court held that this representation of "uncontestability" was deceptive and a violation of the FTC act. The court ordered Verity to pay nearly $18 million in restitution to consumers.[5] ■

---

4. *Federal Trade Commission v. Bronson Partners, LLC,* 664 F.3d 359 (2d Cir. 2011).
5. *Federal Trade Commission v. Verity International, Ltd.,* 443 F.3d 48 (2d Cir. 2006).

DIGITAL UPDATE — Regulating "Native" Ads on the Internet

Sponsored content on the Internet—content that someone pays to put there—is everywhere. One particular type of sponsored content is the "native" ad. Here, *native* describes advertisements that follow the natural form and function of the user experience into which they are placed. Thus, such an ad matches the rest of a Web page's content, including the visual design, as if it were "native" to the page.

Native Ad Integration on Desktops and Mobile Devices

Perhaps the most obvious native ads are in search engine results. When you type "native ads" in a Google search box, you will find that the first several "hits" listed in the search results are actually sponsored ads. Yet they have the look and feel of the rest of the search results.

Additionally, native ads are often placed within stories in online publications. Suppose, for instance, that you are reading a story on new fashions on your smartphone. You will likely see a native ad that looks as if it is part of the story but that is actually sponsored and perhaps written by a clothing company.

Some native ads are delivered via "recommendation widgets." Usually, the widgets are integrated into a page but do not mimic the appearance of the page. Rather, they direct you to a different Web page—perhaps telling you that "you might like" that site. Clicking the widget takes you to the site.

Native ads have become increasingly popular because desktop, smartphone, and tablet users have figured out how to block traditional online ads. Moreover, native ads are less intrusive than traditional online ads—important because of the increasing number of consumers who most often access small screens, such as those on smartphones.

The Federal Trade Commission Takes Action

In response to the growth in native advertising, the Federal Trade Commission (FTC) has issued guidelines.[a] The FTC starts out with the basic question "[A]s native advertising evolves, are consumers able to differentiate advertising from other content?" In its guidance document,[b] the FTC suggests the following:

- Disclosures should be placed where consumers will notice them.
- Disclosures should be placed not after the native ad, but before or above it.
- Disclosures should remain with native ads if the ads are republished.
- Once consumers arrive on a click- or tap-into page where the complete native ad appears, disclosures should be placed as close as possible to where consumers will look first.
- Disclosures should stand out and should be understandable.

Critical Thinking *What is the equivalent of native advertising in commercially released movies?*

a. Federal Trade Commission, *Native Advertising: A Guide to Business,* December 2015.
b. Federal Trade Commission, *.com Disclosures: How to Make Effective Disclosures in Digital Advertising,* March 2013, available at www.ftc.gov/tips-advice/business-center/guidance/com-disclosures-how-make-effective-disclosures-digital.

False Advertising Claims under the Lanham Act The Lanham Act[6] protects trademarks, as discussed elsewhere. The act also covers false advertising claims. To state a successful claim for false advertising under this act, a business must establish each of the following elements:

1. An injury to a commercial interest in reputation or sales.

2. Direct causation of the injury by false or deceptive advertising.
3. A loss of business from buyers who were deceived by the advertising.

The dispute between the parties in the following case focused initially on a mimicked microchip. When the case reached the United States Supreme Court, the question was whether Static Control Components, Inc., could sue Lexmark International, Inc., for false advertising under the Lanham Act.

---

6. 15 U.S.C. Sections 1051–1128.

Case 44.2

Lexmark International, Inc. v. Static Control Components, Inc.

Supreme Court of the United States, __ U.S. __, 134 S.Ct. 1377, 188 L.Ed.2d 392 (2014).

Background and Facts Lexmark International, Inc., sells the only style of toner cartridges that work with the company's laser printers. Other businesses—known as remanufacturers—acquire and refurbish used Lexmark cartridges to sell in competition with the cartridges sold by Lexmark. To deter remanufacturing, Lexmark introduced a program that gave customers a 20 percent discount on new toner cartridges if they agreed to return the empty cartridges to Lexmark. Static Control Components, Inc., makes and sells components for the remanufactured cartridges, including microchips that mimic the chips in Lexmark's cartridges.

Lexmark released ads that claimed Static Control's microchips illegally infringed Lexmark's patents. Lexmark then filed a suit in a federal district court against Static Control, alleging violations of intellectual property law. Static Control counterclaimed, alleging that Lexmark had engaged in false advertising in violation of the Lanham Act. The court dismissed the counterclaim. It held that Static Control lacked standing to bring that claim. On Static Control's appeal, the U.S. Court of Appeals for the Sixth Circuit reversed the dismissal. Lexmark appealed to the United States Supreme Court.

In the Language of the Court

Justice *SCALIA* delivered the opinion of the Court.
* * * *

First, * * * a statutory cause of action extends only to plaintiffs whose interests fall within the zone of interests protected by the law invoked.
* * * *

* * * To come within the zone of interests in a suit for false advertising under [the Lanham Act,] a plaintiff must allege an injury to a commercial interest in reputation or sales.
* * * *

Second, * * * a statutory cause of action is limited to plaintiffs whose injuries are proximately caused by violations of the statute.
* * * *

* * * A plaintiff suing under [the Lanham Act] ordinarily must show economic or reputational injury flowing directly from the deception wrought by the defendant's advertising; and that occurs when deception of consumers causes them to withhold trade from the plaintiff.
* * * *

Applying those principles to Static Control's false-advertising claim, we conclude that Static Control comes within the class of plaintiffs whom Congress authorized to sue under [the Lanham Act].

To begin, Static Control's alleged injuries—lost sales and damage to its business reputation—are injuries to precisely the sorts of commercial interests the Act protects. *Static Control is suing not as a deceived consumer, but [in the words of the statute] as a "person engaged in * * * commerce within the control of Congress" whose position in the marketplace has been damaged by Lexmark's false advertising.* There is no doubt that it is within the zone of interests protected by the statute. [Emphasis added.]

Static Control also sufficiently alleged that its injuries were proximately caused by Lexmark's misrepresentations.

First, Static Control alleged that Lexmark disparaged its business and products by asserting that Static Control's business was illegal. *When a defendant harms a plaintiff's reputation by casting aspersions [abuse] on its business, the plaintiff's injury flows directly from the audience's belief in the disparaging statements.* [Emphasis added.]
* * * *

The District Court emphasized that Lexmark and Static Control are not direct competitors [since Static Control is not itself a remanufacturer]. But when a party claims reputational injury from disparagement, competition is not required for proximate cause; and that is true even if the defendant's aim was to harm its immediate competitors, and the plaintiff merely suffered collateral damage.

Case 44.2 Continued In addition, Static Control adequately alleged proximate causation by alleging that it designed, manufactured, and sold microchips that both (1) were necessary for, and (2) had no other use than, refurbishing Lexmark toner cartridges. It follows from that allegation that any false advertising that reduced the remanufacturers' business necessarily injured Static Control as well.

Decision and Remedy *The United States Supreme Court affirmed the lower court's ruling. Static Control had adequately pleaded the elements of a cause of action under the Lanham Act for false advertising. The Court's decision clarified that businesses do not need to be direct competitors to bring an action for false advertising under the act.*

Critical Thinking
- **What If the Facts Were Different?** *Suppose that Lexmark had issued a retraction of its advertising claims before this case reached the Supreme Court. Would the outcome have been different? Discuss.*
- **Legal Environment** *Under the Court's ruling in this case, is Static Control now entitled to relief? Explain your answer.*

44–1b Marketing

In addition to regulating advertising practices, Congress has passed several laws to protect consumers against other marketing practices.

Telephone Solicitation The Telephone Consumer Protection Act (TCPA)[7] prohibits telephone solicitation using an automatic telephone dialing system or a prerecorded voice. In addition, most states have statutes regulating telephone solicitation. The TCPA also makes it illegal to transmit ads via fax without first obtaining the recipient's permission. (Most states also have laws regulating telephone solicitation.)

The Federal Communications Commission (FCC) enforces the TCPA. The FCC imposes substantial fines ($11,000 each day) on companies that violate the junk fax provisions of the act.[8] The TCPA also gives consumers a right to sue for either $500 for each violation of the act or for the actual monetary losses resulting from a violation, whichever is greater. If a court finds that a defendant willfully or knowingly violated the act, the court has the discretion to treble (triple) the amount of damages awarded.

Fraudulent Telemarketing The Telemarketing and Consumer Fraud and Abuse Prevention Act[9] directed the FTC to establish rules governing telemarketing and to bring actions against fraudulent telemarketers.

The FTC's Telemarketing Sales Rule (TSR)[10] requires a telemarketer to identify the seller's name, describe the product being sold, and disclose all material facts related to the sale (such as the total cost). The TSR makes it illegal for telemarketers to misrepresent information or facts about their goods or services. A telemarketer must also remove a consumer's name from its list of potential contacts if the customer so requests.

An amendment to the TSR established the national Do Not Call Registry. Telemarketers must refrain from calling those consumers who have placed their names on the list. Significantly, the TSR applies to any offer made to consumers in the United States—even if the offer comes from a foreign firm. Thus, the TSR helps to protect consumers from illegal cross-border telemarketing operations.

44–1c Sales

A number of statutes protect consumers by requiring the disclosure of certain terms in sales transactions and providing rules governing unsolicited merchandise. The FTC has regulatory authority in this area, as do some other federal agencies.

Many states and the FTC have **"cooling-off" laws** that permit the buyers of goods sold door to door to cancel their contracts within three business days. The FTC rule also requires that consumers be notified in Spanish of this right if the oral negotiations for the sale were in that language.

The contracts that fall under these cancellation rules include trade show sales contracts, contracts for home

---

7. 47 U.S.C. Sections 227 *et seq.*
8. See, for instance, *Imhoff Investment, LLC v. Alfoccinio, Inc.,* 792 F.3d 627 (6th Cir. 2015).
9. 15 U.S.C. 6101–6108.

---

10. 16 C.F.R. Sections 310.1–310.8.

equity loans, Internet purchase contracts, and home (door-to-door) sales contracts. In addition, certain states have passed laws allowing consumers to cancel contracts for dating services, gym memberships, and weight loss programs.

The FTC Mail or Telephone Order Merchandise Rule[11] protects consumers who purchase goods via mail, Internet, phone, or fax. Merchants are required to ship orders within the time promised in their advertisements and to notify consumers when orders cannot be shipped on time. If the seller does not give an estimated shipping time, it must ship within thirty days. Merchants must also issue a refund within a specified period of time when a consumer cancels an order.

44-2 Labeling and Packaging Laws

A number of federal and state laws deal specifically with the information given on labels and packages. In general, labels must be accurate, and they must use words that are easily understood by the ordinary consumer. In some instances, labels must specify the raw materials used in the product, such as the percentage of cotton, nylon, or other fiber used in a garment. In other instances, the product must carry a warning, such as those required on cigarette packages and advertising.[12]

44-2a Automobile Fuel Economy Labels

The Energy Policy and Conservation Act (EPCA)[13] requires automakers to attach an information label to every new car. The label must include the Environmental Protection Agency's fuel economy estimate for the vehicle. ■ **CASE IN POINT 44.5** Gaetano Paduano bought a new Honda Civic Hybrid in California. The information label on the car included the fuel economy estimate from the Environmental Protection Agency (EPA). Honda's sales brochure added, "Just drive the Hybrid like you would a conventional car and save on fuel bills."

When Paduano discovered that the car's fuel economy was less than half of the EPA's estimate, he sued Honda for deceptive advertising under a California law. The automaker claimed that the federal law (the EPCA) preempted the state's deceptive advertising law. The court held in Paduano's favor, finding that the federal statute did not preempt a claim for deceptive advertising made under state law.[14] ■

44-2b Food Labeling

Because the quality and safety of food are so important to consumers, several statutes deal specifically with food labeling. The Fair Packaging and Labeling Act requires that food product labels identify (1) the product, (2) the net quantity of the contents (and, if the number of servings is stated, the size of a serving), (3) the manufacturer, and (4) the packager or distributor. The act includes additional requirements concerning descriptions on packages, savings claims, components of nonfood products, and standards for the partial filling of packages.

Nutritional Content of Food Products Food products must bear labels detailing the nutritional content, including the number of calories and the amounts of various nutrients that the food contains. The Nutrition Labeling and Education Act[15] requires food labels to provide standard nutrition facts and regulates the use of such terms as *fresh* and *low fat*.

The U.S. Food and Drug Administration (FDA) and the U.S. Department of Agriculture (USDA) are the primary agencies that issue regulations on food labeling. These rules are published in the *Federal Register* and updated annually.

Caloric Content of Restaurant Foods The health-care reforms enacted in 2010 (the Affordable Care Act, or Obamacare) included provisions aimed at combating the problem of obesity in the United States. All restaurant chains with twenty or more locations are now required to post the caloric content of the foods on their menus so that customers will know how many calories the foods contain.[16] Foods offered through vending machines must also be labeled so that their caloric content is visible to would-be purchasers.

In addition, restaurants must post guidelines on the number of calories that an average person requires daily so that customers can determine what portion of a day's calories a particular food will provide. The hope is that consumers, armed with this information, will consider the number of calories when they make their food choices. The federal law on menu labeling supersedes all previous state and local laws in this area.

---

11. 16 C.F.R. Sections 435.1–435.2.
12. 15 U.S.C. Sections 1331–1341.
13. 49 U.S.C. Section 32908(b)(1).

14. *Paduano v. American Honda Motor Co.*, 169 Cal.App.4th 1453, 88 Cal. Rptr.3d 90 (2009).
15. 21 U.S.C. Section 343.1.
16. See Section 4205 of the Patient Protection and Affordable Care Act, Pub. L. No. 111-148, 124 Stat. 119 (March 23, 2010).

44–3 Protection of Health and Safety

Although labeling and packaging laws promote consumer health and safety, there is a significant distinction between regulating the information dispensed about a product and regulating the actual content of the product. The classic example is tobacco products. Producers of tobacco products must use labels that warn consumers about the health hazards associated with their use, but the sale of tobacco products has not been subjected to significant restrictions. We now examine various laws that regulate the actual products made available to consumers.

44–3a The Federal Food, Drug, and Cosmetic Act

The most important federal legislation regulating food and drugs is the Federal Food, Drug, and Cosmetic Act (FDCA).[17] The act protects consumers against adulterated (contaminated) and misbranded foods and drugs. The FDCA establishes food standards, specifies safe levels of potentially hazardous food additives, and provides classifications of foods and food advertising. Most of these statutory requirements are monitored and enforced by the Food and Drug Administration (FDA).

Interestingly, the European Union and a number of other countries, such as Canada, have banned some foods that the FDA assumes to be safe. These foods include brominated vegetable oil (a common ingredient in sports drinks, such as Gatorade) and Olestra/Olean (a cholesterol-free fat substitute found in certain potato chips). Food products containing such substances may not be sold in the European Union. Similarly, certain food colorings found in processed foods in the United States (in M&Ms and Kraft macaroni and cheese, for instance) are not allowed in foods in some other countries.

Tainted Foods In the last twenty years or so, many people in the United States have contracted food poisoning from eating foods that were contaminated, often with salmonella or *E. coli* bacteria. ■ **EXAMPLE 44.6** During 2015 and 2016, hundreds of people across the United States were sickened by eating tainted food at the popular restaurant chain Chipotle Mexican Grill. Causes of illness in these outbreaks included *E-coli* and salmonella, as well as the highly contagious norovirus. ■

In response to the problem of food contamination, Congress enacted the Food Safety Modernization Act (FSMA)[18] to provide greater government control over the U.S. food safety system. The act gives the FDA authority to directly recall any food products that it suspects are tainted, rather than relying on the producers to recall items.

The FSMA requires anyone who manufactures, processes, packs, distributes, receives, holds, or imports food products to pay a fee and register with the U.S. Department of Health and Human Services. (There are some exceptions for small farmers.) Owners and operators of such facilities are required to analyze and identify food safety hazards, implement preventive controls, monitor effectiveness, and take corrective actions. The FSMA places additional restrictions on importers of food and requires them to verify that imported foods meet U.S. safety standards.

Drugs and Medical Devices The FDA is also responsible under the FDCA for ensuring that drugs are safe and effective before they are marketed to the public. Because the FDA must ensure the safety of new medications, there is always a delay before drugs are available to the public, and this sometimes leads to controversy.

■ **CASE IN POINT 44.7** A group of citizens petitioned the FDA to allow everyone access to "Plan B"—the morning-after birth control pill—without a prescription. The FDA denied the petition and continued to require women under the age of seventeen to obtain a prescription. The group appealed to a federal district court, claiming that the prescription requirement can delay access to the pill. The pill should be taken as soon as possible after sexual intercourse, preferably within twenty-four hours. The court ruled in favor of the plaintiffs and ordered the FDA to make the morning-after pill available to people of any age without a prescription.[19] ■

44–3b The Consumer Product Safety Act

The Consumer Product Safety Act[20] created a comprehensive regulatory scheme over consumer safety matters and established the Consumer Product Safety Commission (CPSC).

The CPSC's Authority The CPSC conducts research on the safety of individual consumer products and maintains a clearinghouse on the risks associated with various products. The Consumer Product Safety Act authorizes the CPSC to do the following:

---

17. 21 U.S.C. Sections 301–393.

18. Pub. L. No. 111-353, 124 Stat. 3885 (January 4, 2011). This statute affected numerous parts of Title 21 of the U.S.C.
19. *Tummino v. Hamburg,* 936 F.Supp.2d 162 (E.D.N.Y. 2013).
20. 15 U.S.C. Sections 2051–2083.

1. Set safety standards for consumer products.
2. Ban the manufacture and sale of any product that the commission believes poses an "unreasonable risk" to consumers. (Products banned by the CPSC have included various types of fireworks, cribs, and toys, as well as many products containing asbestos or vinyl chloride.)
3. Remove from the market any products it believes to be imminently hazardous. The CPSC frequently works in conjunction with manufacturers to conduct voluntary recalls of defective products from stores. ■ **EXAMPLE 44.8** In cooperation with the CPSC, the Scandinavian company IKEA recalled three million baby bed canopies and thirty million wall-mounted children's lamps because they posed a strangulation risk to children. ■
4. Require manufacturers to report on any products already sold or intended for sale if the products have proved to be hazardous.
5. Administer other product-safety legislation, including the Child Protection and Toy Safety Act[21] and the Federal Hazardous Substances Act.[22]

Notification Requirements The Consumer Product Safety Act requires the distributors of consumer products to notify the CPSC immediately if they receive information that a product "contains a defect which . . . creates a substantial risk to the public" or "an unreasonable risk of serious injury or death."

■ **EXAMPLE 44.9** A company that sells juicers receives twenty-three letters from customers complaining that during operation the juicer suddenly exploded, sending pieces of glass and razor-sharp metal across the room. The company must immediately notify the CPSC because the alleged defect creates a substantial risk to the public. ■

44–3c Health-Care Reforms

The health-care reforms enacted in 2010 gave Americans new rights and benefits with regard to health care.[23] The legislation also prohibited certain insurance company practices.

Expanded Coverage for Children and Seniors The reforms enabled more children to obtain health-insurance coverage and allowed young adults (under age twenty-six) to remain on their parents' health insurance policies. The legislation also ended lifetime limits and most annual limits on care, and gave insured persons access to recommended preventive services (such as cancer screening and vaccinations) without cost. People can no longer be denied insurance because of preexisting conditions. Medicare recipients now receive a 50 percent discount on name-brand drugs, and the reforms will eliminate a gap in Medicare's prescription drug coverage by 2020.

Controlling Costs of Health Insurance In an attempt to control the rising costs of health insurance, certain restrictions were placed on insurance companies. Insurance companies must spend at least 85 percent of all premium dollars collected from large employers (80 percent of the premiums collected from individuals and small employers) on benefits and quality improvement. If insurance companies do not meet these goals, they must provide rebates to consumers. Additionally, states can require insurance companies to justify any premium increases to be eligible to participate in the new health-insurance exchanges. In spite of the legislation, health insurance costs have continued to increase.

44–4 Credit Protection

Credit protection is one of the more important aspects of consumer protection legislation. Nearly 80 percent of U.S. consumers have credit cards, and most carry a balance on these cards—a total of about $2.5 trillion of debt nationwide. The Consumer Financial Protection Bureau (CFPB) is the agency that oversees the credit practices of banks, mortgage lenders, and credit-card companies.[24]

44–4a The Truth-in-Lending Act

A key statute regulating the credit and credit-card industries is the Truth-in-Lending Act (TILA), the name commonly given to Title I of the Consumer Credit Protection Act, as amended.[25] The TILA is basically a *disclosure law*. It is administered by the Federal Reserve Board and requires sellers and lenders to disclose credit terms and loan terms so that individuals can shop around for the best financing arrangements.

21. 15 U.S.C. Section 1262(e).
22. 15 U.S.C. Sections 1261–1273.
23. Patient Protection and Affordable Health Care Act of 2010, Pub. L. No.111-148, 124 Stat. 119 (March 23, 2010); and the Health Care and Education Reconciliation Act of 2010, Pub. L. No. 111-152, 124 Stat. 1029 (March 30, 2010).
24. Title 10 of the Restoring American Financial Stability Act of 2010, S.B. 3217, April 15, 2010.
25. 15 U.S.C. Sections 1601–1693r.

Application TILA requirements apply only to those who, in the ordinary course of business, lend funds, sell on credit, or arrange for the extension of credit. Thus, sales or loans made between two consumers do not come under the protection of the act. Additionally, this law protects only debtors who are natural persons (as opposed to the artificial "person" of a corporation). It does not extend to other legal entities.

Disclosure Requirements The TILA's disclosure requirements are contained in **Regulation Z,** issued by the Federal Reserve Board of Governors. If the contracting parties are subject to the TILA, the requirements of Regulation Z apply to any transaction involving an installment sales contract that calls for payment to be made in more than four installments. Transactions subject to Regulation Z typically include installment loans, retail and installment sales, car loans, home-improvement loans, and certain real estate loans if the amount of financing is less than $25,000.

Under the provisions of the TILA, all of the terms of a credit instrument must be clearly and conspicuously disclosed. A lender must disclose the annual percentage rate (APR), finance charge, amount financed, and total payments (the sum of the amount loaned, plus any fees, finance charges, and interest). If a creditor fails to follow the *exact* procedures required by the TILA, the creditor risks contract rescission (cancellation) under the act.

Equal Credit Opportunity Congress enacted the Equal Credit Opportunity Act (ECOA)[26] as an amendment to the TILA. The ECOA prohibits the denial of credit solely on the basis of race, religion, national origin, color, gender, marital status, or age. The act also prohibits credit discrimination on the basis of whether an individual receives certain forms of income, such as public-assistance benefits.

Under the ECOA, a creditor may not require a cosigner on a credit instrument if the applicant qualifies under the creditor's standards of creditworthiness for the amount and terms of the credit request. ■ **CASE IN POINT 44.10** T.R. Hughes, Inc., and Summit Pointe, LLC, obtained financing from Frontenac Bank to construct two real estate developments near St. Louis, Missouri. The bank also required the builder, Thomas R. Hughes, and his wife, Carolyn Hughes, to sign personal guaranty agreements for the loans.

When the borrowers failed to make the loan payments, the bank sued the two companies and Thomas and Carolyn Hughes personally, and foreclosed on the properties. Carolyn claimed that the personal guaranty contracts that she signed were obtained in violation of the ECOA. The court held that because the applicant, Thomas R. Hughes, was creditworthy, the personal guarantys of Carolyn Hughes were obtained in violation of the ECOA and therefore unenforceable.[27] ■

Credit-Card Rules The TILA also contains provisions regarding credit cards. One provision limits the liability of a cardholder to $50 per card for unauthorized charges made before the creditor is notified that the card has been lost. If a consumer receives an *unsolicited* credit card in the mail that is later stolen, the company that issued the card cannot charge the consumer for any unauthorized charges.

Another provision requires credit-card companies to disclose the balance computation method that is used to determine the outstanding balance and to state when finance charges begin to accrue. Other provisions set forth procedures for resolving billing disputes with the credit-card company. These procedures are used if, for instance, a cardholder thinks that an error has occurred in billing or wishes to withhold payment for a faulty product purchased by credit card.

Amendments to Credit-Card Rules Amendments to the TILA's credit-card rules added the following protections:

1. A company may not retroactively increase the interest rates on existing card balances unless the account is sixty days delinquent.
2. A company must provide forty-five days' advance notice to consumers before changing its credit-card terms.
3. Monthly bills must be sent to cardholders twenty-one days before the due date.
4. The interest rate charged on a customer's credit-card balance may not be increased except in specific situations, such as when a promotional rate ends.
5. A company may not charge over-limit fees except in specified situations.
6. When the customer has balances at different interest rates, payments in excess of the minimum amount due must be applied first to the balance with the highest rate. (For instance, a higher interest rate is commonly charged for cash advances.)
7. A company may not compute finance charges based on the previous billing cycle (a practice known as double-cycle billing). This practice hurts consumers because they are charged interest for the previous cycle even if they have paid the bill in full.

---

26. 15 U.S.C. Sections 1691–1691f.

27. *Frontenac Bank v. T.R. Hughes, Inc.,* 404 S.W.3d 272 (Mo.App. 2012).

44–4b The Fair Credit Reporting Act

The Fair Credit Reporting Act (FCRA)[28] protects consumers against inaccurate credit reporting and requires that lenders and other creditors report correct, relevant, and up-to-date information. The act provides that con-

28. 15 U.S.C. Sections 1681–1681t.

sumer credit reporting agencies may issue credit reports to users only for specified purposes. Legitimate purposes include the extension of credit, the issuance of insurance policies, and responding to the consumer's request.

Whether an Internet service provider had a legitimate purpose to pull a customer's credit report was at issue in the following case.

Case Analysis 44.3

Santangelo v. Comcast Corporation

United States District Court, Northern District of Illinois, Eastern Division, __ F.Supp.3d __, 2016 WL 464223 (2016).

In the Language of the Court
John Z. *LEE*, United States District Judge
* * * *

I. Factual and Procedural Background
[Keith Santangelo filed a complaint in a federal district court against Comcast Corporation, alleging a violation of the Fair Credit Reporting Act (FCRA).] Santangelo alleges * * * that he contacted Comcast through the company's online customer service "Chat" function * * * and requested Internet service for his new apartment. During the chat session, a Comcast representative asked Santangelo for permission to run a credit inquiry. Santangelo asked if any option was available to avoid the credit inquiry. The Comcast representative told him that the company would forgo the inquiry if he paid a $50 deposit.

The option to pay a $50 deposit in order to avoid a credit inquiry was an explicit part of Comcast's official Risk Management Policy * * * .The policy also required a $50 deposit from any prospective customer who agreed to a credit inquiry but whose credit score proved to be unsatisfactory. According to Santangelo, the deposit policy "reflects Comcast's calculated business decision and belief that the collection of a $50 deposit is sufficient to cover the risk presented by a person with bad credit and is sufficient to cover the risk presented by a person who refuses a credit pull."

Santangelo opted to pay the $50 deposit in lieu of a credit inquiry. * * * Nevertheless, Comcast, without Santangelo's authorization, pulled his credit

report * * * . This credit inquiry depleted [lowered] Santangelo's credit score.
* * * *

* * * Comcast now moves to dismiss the * * * complaint.
II. Analysis
* * * *

*FCRA prohibits the obtaining of a "consumer report," commonly known as a credit report, except for purposes authorized by that statute. The statute lists specific permissible purposes, such as * * * any * * * "legitimate business need * * * in connection with a business transaction that is initiated by the consumer."* These limitations are intended to produce a balance between consumer privacy and the needs of a modern, credit-driven economy. [Emphasis added.]

Santangelo contends that Comcast did not have a permissible purpose for obtaining his credit report after he paid the $50 deposit in exchange for the company's promise not to check his credit. If he is correct and the company's violation was willful, he would be entitled to recover attorney's fees and either actual damages or statutory damages between $100 and $1,000. If the company's violation was merely negligent, Santangelo would be permitted to recover only attorney's fees and actual damages.
1. Standing
Comcast first argues that Santangelo lacks standing to bring his FCRA claim. To establish standing * * * a plaintiff must show * * * the injury is fairly traceable to the challenged action of the defendant.

According to Comcast, Santangelo has not alleged an injury-in-fact that is fairly traceable to the FCRA violation he claims. Santangelo responds that he has sustained three injuries-in-fact: the loss of the $50 he paid as a deposit, the violation of his legal right not to have his credit report pulled without a permissible purpose, and the resulting depletion of his credit score.
* * * *

* * * It was the very fact that Comcast received the $50 from Santangelo before it performed the credit check that made it illegal. * * * And once Comcast checked Santangelo's credit, it should have refunded the deposit immediately, rather than keeping it. Comcast's receipt and withholding of the $50, therefore, is inextricable [inseparable] from the FCRA violation and can be said to be fairly traceable to the FCRA violation. * * * Even if the $50.00 deposit were fully refundable, Santangelo still has standing based on the lost time-value of the money.

* * * Santangelo also has sufficiently alleged an injury-in-fact by alleging that Comcast obtained his credit report without a permissible purpose in violation of the FCRA.

*Because the FCRA grants consumers a legally protected interest in limiting access to their credit reports and provides redress for violations, * * * Santangelo's allegations about Comcast's interference with that legally protected interest are sufficient*

Case 44.3 Continued

to establish * * * *standing.* [Emphasis added.]

* * * Santangelo also alleges that the FCRA violation in this case depleted his credit score. In response, Comcast contends that a reduced credit score, without resulting damages, does not constitute an injury.

* * * The Court agrees with Santangelo that a depleted credit score is sufficient to constitute an injury * * *. Credit scores are of great importance in our economy, and a depleted credit score could affect a consumer in numerous ways, inflicting harm that often may be difficult to prove or quantify. Congress has the power to discourage the needless depletion of consumers' credit scores even when the depleted score cannot be neatly tied to a financial harm.

2. Sufficiency of Santangelo's allegations

Comcast next argues that Santangelo's allegations do not state an FCRA claim.

* * * *

In his * * * complaint, Santangelo * * * alleges that Comcast's deposit policies demonstrate its lack of a legitimate need to run credit checks with respect

to consumers who paid a $50 deposit. According to the * * * complaint, Comcast's established policy is to forgo a credit check in exchange for a $50 deposit. The company also has a policy of accepting a $50 deposit from consumers who opt for a credit check but prove to have poor credit. Santangelo compares this situation to that of a car dealer who accepts a cash payment for the full purchase price of a car. * * * The car dealer * * * does not have a legitimate need to obtain the purchaser's credit report. Similarly, a landlord does not have a legitimate need to obtain a tenant's credit report if the tenant is entitled to a lease renewal without regard to creditworthiness.

In response, Comcast * * * argues that it had a legitimate business need to establish Santangelo's creditworthiness despite his deposit because—unlike in the car dealer example—his $50 deposit would cover less than two months of service in a long-term contract. * * * [Santangelo] contends that, under company policy, his creditworthiness was irrelevant to Comcast's determination of his eligibility for service once the deposit

was collected, much like the tenants in [the landlord example].

* * * *

* * * Comcast's mere violation of its alleged agreement not to pull Santangelo's credit report does not support an FCRA claim. But the possibility that the company itself believed that its customers' creditworthiness was irrelevant if they paid a deposit is enough.

Comcast's final argument for dismissing Santangelo's FCRA claim is that he neither explicitly alleges that the company's actions were willful, which is necessary to trigger statutory damages, nor identifies any actual damages that he could recover if Comcast acted only negligently. Although [Santangelo] does not use the word willful in his complaint, he alleges that the company obtained his credit report despite that it "knew that it did not have a legitimate business need." This allegation implies recklessness at the very least, and reckless conduct qualifies as willful conduct under the FCRA.

* * * *

III. Conclusion

* * * The Court denies Comcast's motion to dismiss.

Legal Reasoning Questions

1. Comcast argued that it had refunded Santangelo's $50, plus interest in the amount of $10, four months after pulling his credit report. Does this argument undercut the plaintiff's claim to have standing? Why or why not?
2. What might discovery reveal that would affect the outcome in this case? Explain.
3. What damages might Santangelo be able to prove based on the depletion of his credit score?

Consumer Notification and Inaccurate Information Any time a consumer is denied credit or insurance on the basis of her or his credit report, the consumer must be notified of that fact. The notice must include the name and address of the credit-reporting agency that issued the report. The same notice must be sent to consumers who are charged more than others ordinarily would be for credit or insurance because of their credit reports.

Under the FCRA, consumers may request the source of any information used by the credit agency, as well as the identity of anyone who has received an agency's report.

Consumers are also permitted to access the information about them contained in a credit reporting agency's files.

If a consumer discovers that an agency's files contain inaccurate information, he or she should report the problem to the agency. On the consumer's written (or electronic) request, the agency must conduct a systematic examination of its records. Any unverifiable or erroneous information must be deleted within a reasonable period of time.

Remedies for Violations A credit reporting agency that fails to comply with the act is liable for actual damages, plus additional damages not to exceed $1,000 and attorneys' fees.[29] Creditors and other companies that use information from credit reporting agencies may also be liable for violations of the FCRA. The United States Supreme Court has held that an insurance company's failure to notify new customers that they were paying higher insurance rates as a result of their credit scores was a *willful* violation of the FCRA.[30]

■ **CASE IN POINT 44.11** Branch Banking & Trust Company of Virginia (BB&T) gave Rex Saunders an auto loan but failed to give him a payment coupon book and refused his attempts to make payments on the loan. In fact, BB&T told him that it had not extended a loan to him. Eventually, BB&T discovered its mistake and demanded full payment, plus interest and penalties.

When payment was not immediately forthcoming, BB&T declared that Saunders was in default. It then repossessed the car and forwarded adverse credit information about Saunders to credit reporting agencies, without noting that Saunders disputed the information. Saunders filed a lawsuit alleging violations of the FCRA and was awarded $80,000 in punitive damages. An appellate court found that the damages award was reasonable, given BB&T's willful violation.[31] ■

44–4c The Fair and Accurate Credit Transactions Act

Congress passed the Fair and Accurate Credit Transactions (FACT) Act in an effort to combat identity theft.[32] The act established a national fraud alert system. Consumers who suspect that they have been or may be victimized by identity theft can place an alert on their credit files. When a consumer establishes that identify theft has occurred, the credit reporting agency must stop reporting allegedly fraudulent account information.

The act also requires the major credit reporting agencies to provide consumers with free copies of their own credit reports every twelve months. Another provision requires account numbers on credit-card receipts to be truncated (shortened). Merchants, employees, or others who may have access to the receipts can no longer obtain the consumers' names and full credit-card numbers. Financial institutions must work with the FTC to identify

"red flag" indicators of identity theft and to develop rules for the disposal of sensitive credit information.

44–4d The Fair Debt Collection Practices Act

The Fair Debt Collection Practices Act (FDCPA)[33] attempts to curb perceived abuses by collection agencies. The act applies only to specialized debt-collection agencies and attorneys who regularly attempt to collect debts on behalf of someone else, usually for a percentage of the amount owed. Creditors attempting to collect debts are not covered by the act unless, by misrepresenting themselves, they cause debtors to believe they are collection agencies.

Requirements of the Act Under the FDCPA, a collection agency may not do any of the following:

1. Contact the debtor at the debtor's place of employment if the debtor's employer objects.
2. Contact the debtor at inconvenient or unusual times (such as three o'clock in the morning), or at any time if the debtor is being represented by an attorney.
3. Contact third parties other than the debtor's parents, spouse, or financial adviser about payment of a debt unless a court authorizes such action.
4. Harass or intimidate the debtor (by using abusive language or threatening violence, for instance) or make false or misleading statements (such as posing as a police officer).
5. Communicate with the debtor at any time after receiving notice that the debtor is refusing to pay the debt, except to advise the debtor of further action to be taken by the collection agency.

The FDCPA also requires a collection agency to include a **validation notice** when it initially contacts a debtor for payment of a debt or within five days of that initial contact. The notice must state that the debtor has thirty days in which to dispute the debt and to request a written verification of the debt from the collection agency.

Enforcement of the Act The Federal Trade Commission is primarily responsible for enforcing the FDCPA. A debt collector who fails to comply with the act is liable for actual damages, plus additional damages not to exceed $1,000 and attorneys' fees.

---

29. 15 U.S.C. Section 1681n.
30. *Safeco Insurance. Co. of America v. Burr,* 551 U.S. 47, 127 S.Ct. 2201, 167 L.Ed.2d 1045 (2007).
31. *Saunders v. Branch Banking & Trust Co. of Virginia,* 526 F.3d 142 (4th Cir. 2008).
32. Pub. L. No. 108-159, 117 Stat. 1952.

33. 15 U.S.C. Section 1692.

Debt collectors who violate the act are exempt from liability if they can show that the violation was not intentional and resulted from a bona fide error. Furthermore, the error must have occurred in spite of procedures the company had already put in place to avoid such errors. The "bona fide error" defense typically has been applied to mistakes of fact or clerical errors. A few courts have gone further and allowed the good faith error defense in other circumstances.[34]

<hr/>

34. See, for instance, *Zortman v. J.C. Christensen & Associates, Inc.*, 2012 WL 1563918 (D.Minn. 2012); see also *Mbaku v. Bank of America, N.A.*, 2013 WL 425981 (D.Colo. 2013).

Reviewing: Consumer Law

Leota Sage saw a local motorcycle dealer's newspaper advertisement offering a MetroRider EZ electric scooter for $1,699. When she went to the dealership, however, she learned that the EZ model had been sold out. The salesperson told Sage that he still had the higher-end MetroRider FX model in stock for $2,199 and would sell her one for $1,999. Sage was disappointed but decided to purchase the FX model.

When Sage said that she wished to purchase the scooter on credit, she was directed to the dealer's credit department. As she filled out the credit forms, the clerk told Sage, who is an Asian American, that she would need a cosigner to obtain a loan. Sage could not understand why she would need a cosigner and asked to speak to the store manager. The manager apologized, told her that the clerk was mistaken, and said that he would "speak to" the clerk. The manager completed Sage's credit application, and Sage then rode the scooter home. Seven months later, Sage received a letter from the manufacturer informing her that a flaw had been discovered in the scooter's braking system and that the model had been recalled. Using the information presented in the chapter, answer the following questions.

1. Did the dealer engage in deceptive advertising? Why or why not?
2. Suppose that Sage had ordered the scooter through the dealer's Web site but the dealer was unable to deliver it by the date promised. What would the FTC have required the merchant to do in that situation?
3. Assuming that the clerk required a cosigner based on Sage's race or gender, what act prohibits such credit discrimination?
4. What organization has the authority to ban the sale of scooters based on safety concerns?

Debate This . . . *Laws against bait-and-switch advertising should be abolished because no consumer is ever forced to buy anything.*

Terms and Concepts

bait-and-switch advertising 845
cease-and-desist order 846
consumer law 843

"cooling-off" laws 849
counteradvertising 846
deceptive advertising 843

multiple product order 846
Regulation Z 853
validation notice 856

Issue Spotters

1. United Pharmaceuticals, Inc., believes that it has developed a new drug that will be effective in the treatment of patients with AIDS. The drug has had only limited testing, but United wants to make the drug widely available as soon as possible. To market the drug, what must United prove to the U.S. Food and Drug Administration? (See *Protection of Health and Safety*.)

2. Gert buys a notebook computer from EZ Electronics. She pays for it with her credit card. When the computer proves defective, she asks EZ to repair or replace it, but EZ refuses. What can Gert do? (See *Credit Protection*.)

• **Check your answers to the Issue Spotters against the answers provided in Appendix D at the end of this text.**

Business Scenarios

44–1. Unsolicited Merchandise. Andrew, a resident of California, received an advertising circular in the U.S. mail announcing a new line of regional cookbooks distributed by the Every-Kind Cookbook Co. Andrew didn't want any books and threw the circular away. Two days later, Andrew received in the mail an introductory cookbook entitled *Lower Mongolian Regional Cookbook*, as announced in the circular, on a "trial basis" from Every-Kind. Andrew was not interested but did not go to the trouble to return the cookbook. Every-Kind demanded payment of $20.95 for the *Lower Mongolian Regional Cookbook*. Discuss whether Andrew can be required to pay for the book. (See *Advertising, Marketing, and Sales.*)

44–2. Credit-Card Rules. Maria Ochoa receives two new credit cards on May 1. She has solicited one of them from Midtown Department Store, and the other arrives unsolicited from High-Flying Airlines. During the month of May, Ochoa makes numerous credit-card purchases from Midtown Department Store, but she does not use the High-Flying Airlines card. On May 31, a burglar breaks into Ochoa's home and steals both credit cards, along with other items. Ochoa notifies the Midtown Department Store of the theft on June 2, but she fails to notify High-Flying Airlines. Using the Midtown credit card, the burglar makes a $500 purchase on June 1 and a $200 purchase on June 3. The burglar then charges a vacation flight on the High-Flying Airlines card for $1,000 on June 5. Ochoa receives the bills for these charges and refuses to pay them. Discuss Ochoa's liability for the charges. (See *Credit Protection.*)

Business Case Problems

44–3. Spotlight on McDonald's—Food Labeling.

McDonald's Corp.'s Happy Meal® meal selection consists of an entrée, a small order of french fries, a small drink, and a toy. In the early 1990s, McDonald's began to aim its Happy Meal marketing at children aged one to three. In 1995, McDonald's began making nutritional information for its food products available in documents known as "McDonald's Nutrition Facts." Each document lists the food items that the restaurant serves and provides a nutritional breakdown, but the Happy Meal is not included.

Marc Cohen filed a suit against McDonald's in an Illinois state court. Among other things, Cohen alleged that McDonald's had violated a state law prohibiting consumer fraud and deceptive business practices by failing to adhere to the Nutrition Labeling and Education Act (NLEA). The NLEA sets out different requirements for products specifically intended for children under the age of four—for instance, the products' labels cannot declare the percent of daily value of nutritional components. Does it make sense to have different requirements for children of this age? Why or why not? Should a state court impose such regulations? Explain. [*Cohen v. McDonald's Corp.*, 347 Ill.App.3d 627, 808 N.E.2d 1, 283 Ill.Dec. 451 (1 Dist. 2004)] (See *Labeling and Packaging Laws.*)

44–4. Deceptive Advertising. Brian Cleary and Rita Burke filed a suit against cigarette maker Philip Morris USA, Inc., seeking class-action status for a claim of deceptive advertising. Cleary and Burke claimed that "light" cigarettes, such as Marlboro Lights, were advertised as safer than regular cigarettes, even though the health effects are the same. They contended that the tobacco companies concealed the true nature of light cigarettes. Philip Morris correctly claimed that it was authorized by the government to advertise cigarettes, including light cigarettes. Assuming that is true, should the plaintiffs still be able to bring a deceptive advertising claim against the tobacco company? Why or why not? [*Cleary v. Philip Morris USA, Inc.*, 683 F.Supp.2d 730 (N.D.Ill. 2010)] (See *Advertising, Marketing, and Sales.*)

44–5. Business Case Problem with Sample Answer—Fair Debt-Collection Practices. Bank of America hired

Atlantic Resource Management, LLC, to collect a debt from Michael E. Engler. Atlantic called Engler's employer and asked his supervisor about the company's policy concerning the execution of warrants. The caller then told the supervisor that, to stop process of the warrant, Engler needed to call Atlantic about "Case Number 37291 NY0969" during the first three hours of his next shift. When Engler's supervisor told him about the call, Engler feared that he might be arrested, and he experienced discomfort, embarrassment, and emotional distress at work. Can Engler recover under the Fair Debt Collection Practices Act? Why or why not? [*Engler v. Atlantic Resource Management, LLC*, 2012 WL 464728 (W.D.N.Y. 2012)] (See *Credit Protection.*)

- **For a sample answer to Problem 44–5, go to Appendix E at the end of this text.**

44–6. Deceptive Advertising. Innovative Marketing, Inc. (IMI), sold "scareware"—computer security software. IMI's Internet ads redirected consumers to sites where they were told that a scan of their computers had detected dangerous files—viruses, spyware, and "illegal" pornography. In fact, no scans were conducted. Kristy Ross, an IMI cofounder and vice president, reviewed and edited the ads, and was aware of the many complaints that consumers had made about them. An individual can be held liable under the Federal Trade Commission Act's prohibition of deceptive practices if the person (1) participated directly in the deceptive practices or had the authority to control them and (2) had or should have had knowledge of them. Were IMI's ads deceptive? If so, can Ross be held liable?

Explain. [*Federal Trade Commission v. Ross,* 743 F.3d 886 (4th Cir. 2014)] (See *Advertising, Marketing, and Sales.*)

44–7. A Question of Ethics—Fair Debt-Collection Practices. *Barry Sussman graduated from law school, but also served time in prison for attempting to collect debts by posing as an FBI agent. He theorized that if a debt-collection business collected only debts that it owned as a result of buying checks written on accounts with insufficient funds (NSF checks), it would not be subject to the Fair Debt Collection Practices Act (FDCPA). Sussman formed Check Investors, Inc., to act on his theory. Check Investors bought more than 2.2 million NSF checks, with an estimated face value of about $348 million, for pennies on the dollar. Check Investors added a fee of $125 or $130 (more than the legal limit in most states) to the face amount of each check and aggressively pursued its drawer to collect. The firm's employees were told to accuse drawers of being criminals and to threaten them with arrest and prosecution. The threats were false. Check Investors never took steps to initiate a prosecution. The employees contacted the drawers' family members and used "saturation phoning"—phoning a drawer numerous times in a short period. They used abusive language, referring to drawers as "deadbeats," "retards," "thieves," and "idiots." Between January 2000 and January 2003, Check Investors netted more than $10.2 million from its efforts. [Federal Trade Commission v. Check Investors, Inc., 502 F.3d 159 (3d Cir. 2007)]* (See *Credit Protection.*)

(a) The Federal Trade Commission filed a suit in a federal district court against Check Investors and others, alleging, in part, violations of the FDCPA. Was Check Investors a "debt collector," collecting "debts," within the meaning of the FDCPA? If so, did its methods violate the FDCPA? Were its practices unethical? What might Check Investors argue in its defense? Discuss.

(b) Are "deadbeats" the primary beneficiaries of laws such as the FDCPA? If not, how would you characterize debtors who default on their obligations?

Legal Reasoning Group Activity

44–8. Consumer Protections. Many states have enacted laws that go even further than federal law to protect consumers. These laws vary tremendously from state to state. (See *Advertising, Marketing, and Sales.*)

(a) The first group will decide whether having different laws is fair to sellers who may be prohibited from engaging in a practice in one state that is legal in another.

(b) The second group will consider how these different laws might affect a business.

(c) A third group will determine whether it is fair that residents of one state have more protection than residents of another.

CHAPTER 45

Environmental Protection

Concern over the degradation of the environment has increased over time in response to the environmental effects of population growth, urbanization, and industrialization. Environmental protection is not without a price, however. For many businesses, the costs of complying with environmental regulations are high, and for some they may seem too high. A constant tension exists between the desire to increase profits and productivity and the need to protect the environment.

To a great extent, environmental law consists of statutes passed by federal, state, or local governments and regulations issued by administrative agencies. Before examining statutory and regulatory environmental laws, however, we look at the remedies against environmental pollution that are available under the common law.

45–1 Common Law Actions

Common law remedies against environmental pollution originated centuries ago in England. Those responsible for operations that created dirt, smoke, noxious odors, noise, or toxic substances were sometimes held liable under common law theories of nuisance or negligence. Today, individuals who have suffered a harm from pollution continue to rely on the common law to obtain damages and injunctions against business polluters.

45–1a Nuisance

Under the common law doctrine of **nuisance,** persons may be held liable if they use their property in a manner that unreasonably interferes with others' rights to use or enjoy their own property. Courts typically balance the harm caused by the pollution against the costs of stopping it.

Courts have often denied injunctive relief on the ground that the hardships that would be imposed on the polluter and on the community are greater than the hardships suffered by the plaintiff. ■ **EXAMPLE 45.1** Hewitt's factory causes neighboring landowners to suffer from smoke, soot, and vibrations. But if the factory is the core of the local economy, a court may leave it in operation and award monetary damages to the injured parties. Damages can include compensation for any decline in the value of their property caused by Hewitt's operation. ■

To obtain relief from pollution under the nuisance doctrine, a property owner may have to identify a distinct harm separate from that affecting the general public. This harm is referred to as a "private" nuisance. Under the common law, individuals were denied standing (access to the courts) unless they suffered a harm distinct from that suffered by the public at large. Some states still require this. A public authority (such as a state's attorney general), however, can sue to stop a "public" nuisance.

45–1b Negligence and Strict Liability

An injured party may sue a business polluter in tort under negligence and strict liability theories. A negligence action is based on a business's alleged failure to use reasonable care toward a party whose injury was foreseeable and was caused by the lack of reasonable care. For instance, employees might sue an employer whose failure to use proper pollution controls has contaminated the air, causing the employees to suffer respiratory illnesses. Lawsuits for personal injuries caused by exposure to a toxic substance, such as asbestos, radiation, or hazardous waste, have given rise to a growing body of tort law known as **toxic torts.**

Businesses that engage in ultrahazardous activities—such as the transportation of radioactive materials—are strictly liable for any injuries the activities cause. In a strict liability action, the injured party does not have to prove that the business failed to exercise reasonable care.

45–2 Federal, State, and Local Regulations

All levels of government in the United States regulate some aspect of the environment. In this section, we look at some of the ways in which the federal, state, and local governments control business activities and land use in the interests of environmental preservation and protection.

45–2a State and Local Regulations

In addition to the federal regulations to be discussed shortly, many states have enacted laws to protect the environment. State laws may restrict a business's discharge of chemicals into the air or water or regulate its disposal of toxic wastes. States may also regulate the disposal or recycling of other wastes, including glass, metal, plastic containers, and paper. Additionally, states may restrict emissions from motor vehicles.

City, county, and other local governments also regulate some aspects of the environment. For instance, local zoning laws may be designed to inhibit or regulate the growth of cities and suburbs. In the interest of safeguarding the environment, such laws may prohibit certain land uses. Even when zoning laws permit a business's proposed development plan, the plan may have to be altered to lessen the development's environmental impact. In addition, cities and counties may impose rules regulating methods of waste removal, the appearance of buildings, the maximum noise level, and other aspects of the local environment.

State and local regulatory agencies also play a significant role in implementing federal environmental legislation. Typically, the federal government relies on state and local governments to enforce federal environmental statutes and regulations, such as those regulating air quality.

45–2b Federal Regulations

Congress has passed a number of statutes to control the impact of human activities on the environment. Exhibit 45–1 lists and summarizes the major federal environmental statutes discussed in this chapter. Most of these statutes are designed to address pollution in the air, water, or land. Some specifically regulate toxic chemicals, including pesticides, herbicides, and hazardous wastes.

Environmental Regulatory Agencies The primary federal agency regulating environmental law is the Environmental Protection Agency (EPA). Other federal agencies with authority to regulate specific environmental matters include the Department of the Interior, the Department of Defense, the Department of Labor, the Food and Drug Administration, and the Nuclear Regulatory Commission. In addition, as mentioned, state and local agencies play an important role in enforcing federal environmental legislation.

Most federal environmental laws provide that citizens can sue to enforce environmental regulations if government agencies fail to do so. Similarly, citizens can sue to limit enforcement actions if agencies go too far in their actions. Typically, a threshold hurdle in such suits is meeting the requirements for standing to sue.

In the following case, an animal advocacy organization brought a suit to stop the "taking" (killing or capture) of migratory birds at New York City's John F. Kennedy International Airport (JFK). Birds had been involved in several near-catastrophes at JFK. A collision between herring gulls and a passenger jet, for instance, had caused the jet's engine to explode and the aircraft to catch fire.

To reduce the risks, the Port Authority of New York and New Jersey—which operates JFK—obtained a permit from the U.S. Fish and Wildlife Service (FWS) to "take" certain birds that threatened to interfere with aircraft at JFK. The advocacy organization, Friends of Animals, challenged the issuance of this permit.

Case Analysis 45.1

Friends of Animals v. Clay
United States Court of Appeals, Second Circuit, 811 F.3d 94 (2016).

In the Language of the Court
José A. *CABRANES*, Circuit Judge.
    * * * *

BACKGROUND
    The taking of migratory birds is governed by the Migratory Bird Treaty Act ("MBTA"). The MBTA, which

implements a series of treaties as federal law, prohibits the taking of any bird protected by those treaties unless and except as permitted by regulations promulgated [declared] under the statute. * * * One such regulation is 50 C.F.R. [Code of Federal Regulations] Section

21.41. Under Section 21.41, FWS may issue "depredation permits" that authorize the taking (or possession or transport) of migratory birds that are causing injury to certain human interests.

Case 45.1 Continues

* * * *

[Friends of Animals (FOA) filed a suit in a federal district court against William Clay, Deputy Administrator in the U.S. Department of Agriculture and others, including the U.S. Fish and Wildlife Service (FWS), challenging the issuance of the permit. The court issued a summary judgment in favor of the defendants. FOA appealed to the U.S. Court of Appeals for the Second Circuit.]

The permit * * * identifies eighteen species of migratory birds that have, in the past, compromised public safety at JFK, and authorizes the Port Authority to take a quota of birds of each species.

In addition to setting out these species-specific quotas, the challenged permit contains an "emergency-take" provision. This provision empowers the Port Authority, "in emergency situations only," to take any migratory bird (except bald eagles, golden eagles, or endangered or threatened species) that poses a "direct threat to human safety"—defined as a "threat of serious bodily injury or a risk to human life"—even if it is of a species not listed on the permit. FWS rarely includes an emergency take provision in its migratory bird permits, but—mindful of the grave risks that arise when birds congregate near aircraft—it makes an exception for airports.

DISCUSSION

FOA directs its challenge at the * * * permit's emergency-take provision. According to FOA, Section 21.41 does not authorize FWS to issue a permit that allows the emergency take of a migratory bird irrespective of its species. Instead, FOA argues, permit applicants like the Port Authority must provide species-specific information to FWS, and FWS may authorize the taking of only those species specifically listed on the permit.

Contending that FWS's alleged failure to abide by the requirements of Section 21.41 has resulted in the Port Authority's unlawful taking of a number of migratory birds, * * * FOA asks us to invalidate the operative permit as the product of agency action that was arbitrary, capricious, an abuse of discretion, or otherwise not in accordance with law.

* * * *

FWS's authority to issue depredation permits under Section 21.41 is limited in certain respects by subsections (c) and (d) of that provision. Subsection (d) provides, for instance, that a permit's duration is limited to one year. Subsection (c) sets forth conditions common to all permits, such as the prohibition of certain hunting practices and mandatory steps for disposing of birds that have been killed; it also states that depredation permits are subject to the general conditions set forth in 50 C.F.R. Part 13. Various provisions in Part 13, in turn, further hem in the agency's permitting authority. *But among the express limitations on FWS's discretion imposed by Section 21.41(c)–(d) and Part 13, we find nothing to indicate that FWS may not issue a permit that contains an emergency-take provision. Accordingly, unless some other feature of the regulatory regime counsels otherwise, we must conclude that FWS has authority to issue permits of the type challenged here.* [Emphasis added.]

FOA argues that this other feature is found in Section 21.41(b). This provision states that an application for a depredation permit must [identify] * * * "the particular species of migratory birds committing [an] injury." According to FOA, that regulation, when read in connection with Section 21.41(c)(1)—which provides that "permittees may not kill migratory birds unless specifically authorized on the permit"—makes

clear that a depredation permit may not authorize the taking of bird species not listed on the permit's face.

We disagree. Section 21.41(b) by its terms governs the conduct of applicants, not FWS, and specifies what information must be included in the permit application, not the permit itself. Indeed, the provision is styled as a direct address to applicants, to whom it gives point-by-point instructions for seeking a permit. FOA identifies no particular reason why we should read this subsection, contrary to its plain language, as a limit on FWS's authority to issue permits rather than as a means to ensure that applicants provide FWS with information germane to the permitting determination. Section 21.41(b) is a hopelessly slender reed on which to rest the argument that FWS is powerless to authorize the Port Authority to take migratory birds that threaten air safety.

Nor does the language of Section 21.41(c)(1) alter this conclusion. True, this subsection provides that permittees must "not kill migratory birds unless specifically authorized on the permit." But this is in no way inconsistent with the * * * permit's emergency-take provision. *The permit authorizes the Port Authority, in emergency situations, to "take * * * any migratory birds * * * when the migratory birds * * * are posing a direct threat to human safety."* The permit thus specifically authorizes the taking of migratory birds if certain conditions are met—and one method of taking a bird is killing it. [Emphasis added.]

* * * *

CONCLUSION

In sum, we hold that FWS did not run afoul of Section 21.41 in issuing to the Port Authority the * * * depredation permit. The * * * order of the District Court is accordingly AFFIRMED.

Legal Reasoning Questions

1. In what circumstance might the Port Authority—or anyone else—take a migratory bird without a permit and *not* be sanctioned?

2. Under the plaintiff's suggested reading of the regulation at issue in this case, what difficult choice would the Port Authority face?

3. Why is the taking of birds, or any wildlife, protected by treaty and federal law? What should be the limit to this protection?

EXHIBIT 45–1 Major Federal Environmental Statutes

POPULAR NAME	PURPOSE	STATUTE REFERENCE
Rivers and Harbors Appropriations Act	To prohibit ships and manufacturers from discharging and depositing refuse in navigable waterways.	33 U.S.C. Sections 401–418.
Federal Insecticide, Fungicide, and Rodenticide Act	To control the use of pesticides and herbicides.	7 U.S.C. Sections 136–136y.
Federal Water Pollution Control Act	To eliminate the discharge of pollutants from major sources into navigable waters.	33 U.S.C. Sections 1251–1387.
Clean Air Act	To control air pollution from mobile and stationary sources.	42 U.S.C. Sections 7401–7671q.
National Environmental Policy Act	To limit environmental harm from federal government activities.	42 U.S.C. Sections 4321–4370d.
Ocean Dumping Act	To prohibit the dumping of radiological, chemical, and biological warfare agents and high-level radioactive waste into the ocean.	16 U.S.C. Sections 1401–1445.
Endangered Species Act	To protect species that are threatened with extinction.	16 U.S.C. Sections 1531–1544.
Safe Drinking Water Act	To regulate pollutants in public drinking water systems.	42 U.S.C. Sections 300f–300j-25.
Toxic Substances Control Act	To regulate toxic chemicals and chemical compounds.	15 U.S.C. Sections 2601–2692.
Comprehensive Environmental Response, Compensation, and Liability Act	To regulate the clean-up of hazardous waste–disposal sites.	42 U.S.C. Sections 9601–9675.
Small Business Liability Relief and Brownfields Revitalization Act	To allow developers who comply with state voluntary clean-up programs to avoid federal liability for the properties that they decontaminate and develop.	42 U.S.C. Section 9628.

Environmental Impact Statements All agencies of the federal government must take environmental factors into consideration when making significant decisions. The National Environmental Policy Act[1] requires that an **environmental impact statement (EIS)** be prepared for every major federal action that significantly affects the quality of the environment. (See Exhibit 45–2.) An EIS must analyze the following:

1. The impact that the action will have on the environment.
2. Any adverse effects on the environment and alternative actions that might be taken.
3. Any irreversible effects the action might generate.

An action qualifies as "major" if it involves a substantial commitment of resources (monetary or otherwise). An action is "federal" if a federal agency has the power to control it. ■ **EXAMPLE 45.2** Development of a ski resort by a private developer on federal land may require an EIS. Construction or operation of a nuclear plant, which requires a federal permit, necessitates an EIS, as does creation of a dam as part of a federal project. ■

If an agency decides that an EIS is unnecessary, it must issue a statement supporting this conclusion. Private individuals, consumer interest groups, businesses, and others who believe that a federal agency's activities threaten the environment often use EISs as a means to challenge those activities.

1. 42 U.S.C. Sections 4321–4370d.

EXHIBIT 45–2 Environmental Impact Statements

45–3 Air Pollution

Federal involvement with air pollution goes back to the 1950s and 1960s, when Congress authorized funds for air-pollution research and enacted the Clean Air Act.[2] The Clean Air Act provides the basis for issuing regulations to control multistate air pollution. It covers both mobile sources (such as automobiles and other vehicles) and stationary sources (such as electric utilities and industrial plants) of pollution.

45–3a Mobile Sources

Regulations governing air pollution from automobiles and other mobile sources specify pollution standards and establish time schedules for meeting the standards. The EPA periodically updates the pollution standards in light of new developments and data, usually reducing the amount of emissions allowed.

Reducing Emissions The Obama administration set a long-term goal of reducing emissions, including those from cars and sport utility vehicles, by 80 percent by 2050. The administration also ordered the EPA to develop national standards regulating fuel economy and

emissions for medium- and heavy-duty trucks starting with 2014 models.

Authority to Regulate Greenhouse Gases A growing concern among many scientists and others around the world is that greenhouse gases, such as carbon dioxide (CO_2), contribute to climate change. The Clean Air Act, as amended, however, does not specifically mention CO_2 emissions. Therefore, the EPA did not regulate CO_2 emissions from motor vehicles until 2009, after the Supreme Court ruled that it had the authority to do so.

■ **CASE IN POINT 45.3** Environmental groups and several states, including Massachusetts, sued the EPA in an effort to force the agency to regulate CO_2 emissions from motor vehicles. The case eventually reached the United States Supreme Court. The EPA argued that the plaintiffs lacked standing because global climate change has widespread effects, so the individual plaintiffs could not show particularized harm. Furthermore, the agency claimed that it did not have authority under the Clean Air Act to address global climate change and regulate CO_2.

The Court, however, ruled that Massachusetts had standing because its coastline, including state-owned lands, faced an imminent threat from rising sea levels purportedly caused by climate change. The Court also held that the Clean Air Act's broad definition of "air pollutant" gives the EPA authority to regulate CO_2. The Clean Air Act requires the EPA to regulate any air

---

2. 42 U.S.C. Sections 7401–7671q.

pollutants that might "endanger public health or welfare." Accordingly, the Court ordered the EPA to determine whether CO_2 was a pollutant that endangered public health.[3] ∎

The EPA later concluded that greenhouse gases, including CO_2 emissions, *do* constitute a public danger. In fact, in 2015, the EPA started regulating greenhouse gas emissions from airplanes.

Controlling Climate Change In 2016, a federal district court in Oregon allowed an unprecedented lawsuit to go forward against the U.S. government for doing too little to control climate change. ∎ **CASE IN POINT 45.4** A group of young people (aged eight to nineteen) filed a suit against the federal government, as well as the fossil fuel industry. The plaintiffs argued that the government has known for years that CO_2 pollution causes climate change and threatens catastrophic consequences. By failing to address the causes of this pollution, they claimed, the government has violated their constitutional rights.

The court found that the plaintiffs had alleged particular, concrete harms to young people and future generations sufficient to give them standing to pursue their claims in court. Of course, this ruling means only that the plaintiffs have met their threshold burden of establishing standing. The court simply denied the government's motion to dismiss—it did not decide the merits of the case or grant relief to the plaintiffs. Those issues have yet to be resolved.[4] ∎

45–3b Stationary Sources

The Clean Air Act also authorizes the EPA to establish air-quality standards for stationary sources (such as manufacturing plants). But the act recognizes that the primary responsibility for implementing these standards rests with state and local governments. The standards are aimed at controlling hazardous air pollutants—those likely to cause death or a serious, irreversible, or incapacitating condition, such as cancer or neurological or reproductive damage.

The EPA sets primary and secondary levels of ambient standards—that is, maximum permissible levels of certain pollutants—and the states formulate plans to achieve

those standards. Different standards apply depending on whether the sources of pollution are located in clean areas or polluted areas and whether they are existing sources or major new sources.

Hazardous Air Pollutants The Clean Air Act requires the EPA to list all hazardous air pollutants (HAPs) on a prioritized schedule. In all, nearly two hundred substances—including asbestos, benzene, beryllium, cadmium, mercury, and vinyl chloride—have been classified as hazardous. They are emitted from stationary sources by a variety of business activities, including smelting (melting ore to produce metal), dry cleaning, house painting, and commercial baking.

Maximum Achievable Control Technology Instead of establishing specific emissions standards for each hazardous air pollutant, the Clean Air Act requires major *new* sources[5] to use pollution-control equipment that represents the *maximum achievable control technology,* or MACT, to reduce emissions. The EPA issues guidelines as to what equipment meets this standard.[6]

45–3c Violations of the Clean Air Act

For violations of emission limits under the Clean Air Act, the EPA can assess civil penalties of up to $25,000 per day. Additional fines of up to $5,000 per day can be assessed for other violations, such as failure to maintain the required records. To penalize those who find it more cost-effective to violate the act than to comply with it, the EPA is authorized to impose a penalty equal to the violator's economic benefits from noncompliance. Persons who provide information about violators may be paid up to $10,000. Private citizens can also sue violators.

Those who knowingly violate the act, including corporate officers, may be subject to criminal penalties. For instance, knowingly making false statements or failing to report violations may be punishable by fines of up to $1 million and imprisonment for up to two years.

In the following case, the phrase "knowingly violate" was at the center of the dispute in an individual's appeal of his conviction for Clean Air Act violations.

---

3. *Massachusetts v. Environmental Protection Agency*, 549 U.S. 497, 127 S.Ct. 1438, 167 L.Ed.2d 248 (2007).

4. *Juliana v. United States,* ___ F.Supp.3d ___, 2016 WL 1442435 (D.Or. 2016).

5. The term *major new sources* includes existing sources modified by a change in a method of operation that increases emissions.

6. The EPA has also issued rules to regulate hazardous air pollutants emitted by landfills. See 40 C.F.R. Sections 60.750–60.759.

United States v. O'Malley

United States Court of Appeals, Seventh Circuit, 739 F.3d 1001 (2014).

Background and Facts   Duane O'Malley owned and operated Origin Fire Protection. Michael Pinski hired Origin to remove and dispose of 2,200 feet of insulation from a building Pinski owned in Kankakee, Illinois. The insulation contained asbestos, which Pinski, O'Malley, and O'Malley's employees recognized. O'Malley did not have a license to remove asbestos, and none of his employees were trained in complying with federal asbestos regulations. Nevertheless, Origin removed the debris and disposed of it at various sites, including a vacant lot where it spilled onto the soil, resulting in clean-up costs of nearly $50,000.

In a federal district court, a jury convicted O'Malley of removing, transporting, and dumping asbestos in violation of the Clean Air Act. The court sentenced him to 120 months of imprisonment, three years of supervised release, a fine of $15,000, and $47,085.70 in restitution to the Environmental Protection Agency (EPA). O'Malley appealed.

In the Language of the Court

TINDER, Circuit Judge.

* * * *

On appeal to this court, O'Malley * * * claims that because the [EPA's regulations] define "asbestos-containing material" as only six types of regulated asbestos, the government was required to prove that O'Malley knew that the asbestos in the building was one of the six forms of regulated asbestos. He asserts that the government did not present evidence to demonstrate O'Malley's knowledge of the type of asbestos in the building.

* * * *

O'Malley is correct that not all forms of asbestos are subject to regulation. The Clean Air Act [under Section 7412] authorizes the regulation of hazardous air pollutants, one of which is asbestos. "Because asbestos is not typically emitted through a conveyance designed and constructed to emit or capture it, such as a pipe or smokestack, but rather escapes from more diffuse sources such as open construction or demolition sites, EPA adopted a work-practice standard for the handling of asbestos in building demolition and renovation." * * * The work practice standard promulgated for the handling of asbestos applies only to the six types of "regulated asbestos-containing material (RACM)," [which includes "friable asbestos material"]. "Friable asbestos material" is defined as "any material containing more than 1 percent asbestos * * * that, when dry, can be crumbled, pulverized, or reduced to powder by hand pressure." Thus, there is no question that the material in [this case]—which was both friable and contained asbestos at concentrations ranging from four percent to forty-eight percent—was indeed "regulated asbestos-containing material."

* * * *

*The Clean Air Act makes it a crime for any person to "knowingly violate any * * * requirement or prohibition of * * * Section 7412, * * * including a requirement of any rule" promulgated under Section 7412.* * * * The district court instructed the jury on the knowledge elements as follows: "The government must prove * * * the defendant knew that asbestos-containing material was in the building." [Emphasis added.]

O'Malley argues that the knowledge element instruction should have required the government to prove that the defendant knew that regulated asbestos-containing material, not simply asbestos-containing material, was in the building. But this cannot be correct. * * * The phrase "knowingly violates" does not "carv[e] out an exception to the general rule that ignorance of the law is no excuse." The *mens rea* [criminal intent] required by the phrase is one that is higher than strict liability * * *. But it is certainly much lower than specific intent, especially when, as here, "dangerous * * * materials are involved," because "the probability of regulation is so great that anyone who is aware that he is in possession of them or dealing with them must be presumed to be aware of the regulation." The very fact that O'Malley was knowingly working with asbestos-containing material met the *mens rea* requirement.

Case 45.2 Continued

Decision and Remedy *The U.S. Court of Appeals for the Seventh Circuit affirmed the lower court's judgment. The appellate court disagreed with O'Malley's claim that the government was required to prove he knew the asbestos was one of the six types of regulated asbestos. "The very fact that O'Malley was knowingly working with asbestos-containing material met the* mens rea *requirement."*

Critical Thinking

• **What If the Facts Were Different?** *Suppose that O'Malley had been licensed to remove the asbestos. Would the result have been different? Why or why not?*

45–4 Water Pollution

Water pollution stems mostly from industrial, municipal, and agricultural sources. Pollutants entering streams, lakes, and oceans include organic wastes, heated water, sediments from soil runoff, nutrients (including fertilizers and human and animal wastes), and toxic chemicals and other hazardous substances.

Federal regulations governing water pollution can be traced back to the 1899 Rivers and Harbors Appropriations Act.[7] These regulations prohibited ships and manufacturers from discharging or depositing refuse in navigable waterways without a permit.[8] In 1948, Congress passed the Federal Water Pollution Control Act (FWPCA),[9] but its regulatory system and enforcement powers proved to be inadequate.

45–4a The Clean Water Act

In 1972, Congress passed amendments to the FWPCA, and the amended act became known as the Clean Water Act (CWA). The CWA established the following goals: (1) make waters safe for swimming, (2) protect fish and wildlife, and (3) eliminate the discharge of pollutants into the water. The CWA also set specific schedules, which were later extended by amendment and by the Water Quality Act.[10] Under these schedules, the EPA limits the discharge of various types of pollutants based on the technology available for controlling them.

Permit System for Point-Source Emissions The CWA established a permit system for regulating discharges from "point sources" of pollution, which include industrial, municipal (such as sewage pipes and treatment plants), and agricultural facilities.[11] Under this system, called the National Pollutant Discharge Elimination System (NPDES), any point source emitting pollutants into water must have a permit. Pollution not from point sources, such as runoff from small farms, is not subject to much regulation.

NPDES permits can be issued by the EPA and authorized state agencies and Indian tribes. The permits may be issued only if the discharge will not violate water-quality standards, and they must be reissued every five years. Although initially the NPDES system focused mainly on industrial wastewater, it was later expanded to cover stormwater discharges.

In practice, the NPDES system under the CWA includes the following elements:

1. National effluent (pollution) standards set by the EPA for each industry.
2. Water-quality standards set by the states under EPA supervision.
3. A discharge permit program that sets water-quality standards to limit pollution.
4. Special provisions for toxic chemicals and for oil spills.
5. Construction grants and loans from the federal government for publicly owned treatment works, primarily sewage treatment plants.

Standards for Equipment Regulations generally specify that the *best available control technology*, or BACT, be installed. The EPA issues guidelines as to what equipment meets this standard. Essentially, the guidelines require the most effective pollution-control equipment available.

New sources must install BACT equipment before beginning operations. Existing sources are subject to

---

7. 33 U.S.C. Sections 401–418.
8. The term *navigable waters* is interpreted today as including *intra*state lakes and streams used by interstate travelers and industries, as well as coastal and freshwater wetlands.
9. 33 U.S.C. Sections 1251–1387.
10. This act amended 33 U.S.C. Section 1251.

11. 33 U.S.C. Section 1342.

EXHIBIT 45–3 Pollution-Control Equipment Standards under the Clean Air Act and the Clean Water Act

THE CLEAN AIR ACT

• Major sources of pollution must use pollution-control equipment that represents the *maximum achievable control technology,* or MACT, to reduce emissions.

THE CLEAN WATER ACT

• New sources of pollution must install the *best available control technology,* or BACT, before beginning operations.
• Existing sources must immediately install equipment that utilizes the *best practical control technology,* or BPCT, and meet a timetable for installing BACT equipment.

timetables for the installation of BACT equipment and must immediately install equipment that utilizes the *best practical control technology,* or BPCT. The EPA also issues guidelines as to what equipment meets this standard.

Exhibit 45–3 graphically illustrates the pollution-control equipment standards required under the Clean Air Act and the Clean Water Act.

The EPA must take into account many factors when issuing and updating its rules. Some provisions of the CWA instruct the EPA to weigh the cost of the technology required relative to the benefits achieved. The provision that covers power plants, however, neither requires nor prohibits a cost-benefit analysis. The question in the following case was whether the EPA could base its decision on such an analysis.

Case 45.3

Entergy Corp. v. Riverkeeper, Inc.

Supreme Court of the United States, 556 U.S. 208, 129 S.Ct. 1498, 173 L.Ed.2d 369 (2009).

Background and Facts As part of its implementation of the Clean Water Act, the Environmental Protection Agency (EPA) developed two sets of rules that apply to the cooling systems of power plants. Phase I rules require new power plants to restrict their inflow of water "to a level commensurate with that which can be attained by a closed-cycle recirculating cooling water system." Phase II rules apply "national performance standards" to more than five hundred existing plants but do not require closed-cycle systems.

The EPA had found that converting these existing facilities to closed-cycle operations would cost $3.5 billion per year. The facilities would then produce less power while burning the same amount of coal. Moreover, other technologies can attain nearly the same results as closed-cycle systems. Phase II rules also allow a variance from the national performance standards if a facility's cost of compliance "would be significantly greater than the benefits."

Environmental organizations, including Riverkeeper, Inc., challenged the Phase II regulations, arguing that existing plants should be required to convert to closed-cycle systems. The U.S. Court of Appeals for the Second Circuit issued a ruling in the plaintiffs' favor. Power-generating companies, including Entergy Corporation, appealed to the United States Supreme Court.

In the Language of the Court
Justice *SCALIA* delivered the opinion of the Court.
 * * * *

In setting the Phase II national performance standards and providing for site-specific cost-benefit variances, the EPA relied on its view that [the] "best technology available" standard permits consideration of the technology's costs and of the relationship between those costs and the environmental benefits produced.

 * * * The "best" technology—that which is "most advantageous"—may well be the one that produces the most of some good, here a reduction in adverse environmental impact. But "best technology" may also describe the technology that most efficiently produces some good. *In common parlance one could*

Case 45.3 Continued

certainly use the phrase "best technology" to refer to that which produces a good at the lowest per-unit cost, even if it produces a lesser quantity of that good than other available technologies. [Emphasis added.]

* * * This latter reading is [not] precluded by the statute's use of the phrase "for minimizing adverse environmental impact." *Minimizing * * * is a term that admits of degree and is not necessarily used to refer exclusively to the "greatest possible reduction."* [Emphasis added.]

Other provisions in the Clean Water Act also suggest the agency's interpretation. When Congress wished to mandate the greatest feasible reduction in water pollution, it did so in plain language: The provision governing the discharge of toxic pollutants into the Nation's waters requires the EPA to set "effluent limitations which shall require the elimination of discharges of all pollutants * * * ." The less ambitious goal of "minimizing adverse environmental impact" suggests, we think, that the agency retains some discretion to determine the extent of reduction that is warranted under the circumstances. That determination could plausibly involve a consideration of the benefits derived from reductions and the costs of achieving them.

* * * [Under other Clean Water Act provisions that impose standards on sources of pollution,] the EPA is instructed to consider, among other factors, "the total cost of application of technology in relation to the * * * benefits to be achieved."

* * * *

This * * * comparison of * * * statutory factors * * * leads us to the conclusion that it was well within the bounds of reasonable interpretation for the EPA to conclude that cost-benefit analysis is not categorically forbidden.

* * * *

While not conclusive, it surely tends to show that the EPA's current practice is a reasonable and hence legitimate exercise of its discretion to weigh benefits against costs that the agency has been proceeding in essentially this fashion for over 30 years.

Decision and Remedy *The United States Supreme Court concluded that the EPA had permissibly relied on a cost-benefit analysis to set national performance standards and to allow for variances from those standards. The Court reversed the lower court's judgment and remanded the case.*

Critical Thinking

- **Ethical** *In this case, aquatic organisms were most directly at risk. Is it acceptable to apply cost-benefit analyses to situations in which the lives of people are directly affected? Explain.*
- **Global** *In analyzing the costs and benefits of an action that affects the environment, should a line be drawn at a nation's borders? Why or why not?*

Wetlands The CWA prohibits the filling or dredging of **wetlands** unless a permit is obtained from the Army Corps of Engineers. The EPA defines *wetlands* as "those areas that are inundated or saturated by surface or ground water at a frequency and duration sufficient to support . . . vegetation typically adapted for life in saturated soil conditions." Wetlands are thought to be vital to the ecosystem because they filter streams and rivers and provide habitat for wildlife.

■ **CASE IN POINT 45.5** To build a home in Idaho, Michael and Chantell Sackett filled part of their residential lot with dirt and rock. A few months later, they received a compliance order from the EPA that required them to restore their property immediately or face fines of $75,000 a day. The EPA order claimed that, because their property was near a major lake, the Sacketts had polluted wetlands in violation of the Clean Water Act.

The Sacketts requested a hearing with the EPA, but it was denied. They then sued the EPA in federal district court, asserting, among other things, that the compliance order was "arbitrary and capricious" under the Administrative Procedure Act. The district court held that it could not review the EPA's compliance order because it was not a final agency action. An appellate court affirmed, but the United States Supreme Court reversed. The Court held that the Sacketts could challenge the EPA's compliance order in federal court. The government could not force them to comply with the EPA order without providing an opportunity for judicial review.[12] ■

---

12. *Sackett v. Environmental Protection Agency*, ___ U.S. ___, 132 S.Ct. 1367, 182 L.Ed.2d 367 (2012).

Violations of the Clean Water Act Because point-source water pollution control is based on a permit system, the permits are the key to enforcement. States have primary responsibility for enforcing the permit system, subject to EPA monitoring.

Discharging emissions into navigable waters without a permit, or in violation of pollution limits under a permit, violates the CWA. Violators are subject to a variety of civil and criminal penalties. Depending on the violation, civil penalties range from $10,000 to $25,000 per day, but not more than $25,000 per violation. Lying about a violation is more serious than admitting the truth about improper discharges.

Criminal penalties apply only if a violation was intentional. Criminal penalties range from a fine of $2,500 per day and imprisonment for up to one year to a fine of $1 million and fifteen years' imprisonment. Injunctive relief and damages can also be imposed. The polluting party can be required to clean up the pollution or pay for the cost of doing so.

45–4b Drinking Water

The Safe Drinking Water Act[13] requires the EPA to set maximum levels for pollutants in public water systems. The operators of public water systems must come as close as possible to meeting the EPA's standards by using the best available technology that is economically and technologically feasible.

Under the act, each supplier of drinking water is required to send an annual statement describing the source of its water to every household it supplies. The statement must also disclose the level of any contaminants in the water and any possible health concerns associated with the contaminants.

■ **EXAMPLE 45.6** In 2014, Flint, Michigan, changed its source of drinking water from the Detroit water system to the Flint River. Detroit's water had been treated to prevent lead from leaching from aging lead pipes into the water. Flint River water was not treated, which allowed lead to leach into the water from the pipes. Flint's drinking water became contaminated with lead—a serious public health hazard. By the time Flint sent out the required EPA notices, thousands of children had been exposed to drinking water with high lead levels. Several civil lawsuits have been filed against government officials as a result of the incident, and three individuals face criminal prosecution. The city will end up paying millions to fix the problem. ■

45–4c Ocean Dumping

The Marine Protection, Research, and Sanctuaries Act[14] (popularly known as the Ocean Dumping Act) regulates the transportation and dumping of pollutants into ocean waters. It prohibits the ocean dumping of any radiological, chemical, and biological warfare agents and high-level radioactive waste.

The act also established a permit program for transporting and dumping other materials, and designated certain areas as marine sanctuaries. Each violation of any provision or permit requirement in the Ocean Dumping Act may result in a civil penalty of up to $50,000. A knowing violation is a criminal offense that may result in a $50,000 fine, imprisonment for not more than a year, or both. A court may also grant an injunction to prevent an imminent or continuing violation.

45–4d Oil Pollution

When more than 10 million gallons of oil leaked into Alaska's Prince William Sound from the *Exxon Valdez* supertanker in 1989, Congress responded by passing the Oil Pollution Act.[15] (At that time, the *Exxon Valdez* disaster was the worst oil spill in U.S. history, but the British Petroleum oil spill in the Gulf of Mexico in 2010 surpassed it.)

Under the Oil Pollution Act, any oil facility, oil shipper, vessel owner, or vessel operator that discharges oil into navigable waters or onto an adjoining shore may be liable for clean-up costs and damages. The polluter can also be ordered to pay for damage to natural resources, private property, and the local economy, including the increased cost of providing public services.

45–5 Toxic Chemicals and Hazardous Waste

Originally, most environmental clean-up efforts were directed toward reducing smog and making water safe for fishing and swimming. Today, control of toxic chemicals and hazardous waste has become increasingly important. If not properly disposed of, these substances may seriously endanger human health and the environment—for instance, by contaminating public drinking water.

---

13. 42 U.S.C. Sections 300f to 300j-25.

14. 16 U.S.C. Sections 1401–1445.
15. 33 U.S.C. Sections 2701–2761.

45–5a Pesticides and Herbicides

The Federal Insecticide, Fungicide, and Rodenticide Act (FIFRA)[16] regulates the use of pesticides and herbicides. These substances must be (1) registered before they can be sold, (2) certified and used only for approved applications, and (3) used in limited quantities when applied to food crops.

EPA Actions The EPA can cancel or suspend registration of substances that it has identified as harmful and can inspect the factories where the chemicals are made. A substance is deemed harmful if human exposure to the substance, including exposure through eating food, results in a risk of one in a million (or higher) of developing cancer.[17]

Violations and Penalties It is a violation of FIFRA to sell a pesticide or herbicide that is either unregistered or has had its registration canceled or suspended. It is also a violation to sell a pesticide or herbicide with a false or misleading label. For instance, it is an offense to sell a substance that has a chemical strength that is different from the concentration described on the label. It is also a violation to destroy or deface any labeling required under the act.

Penalties for commercial dealers include imprisonment for up to one year and a fine of up to $25,000 (producers can be fined up to $50,000). Farmers and other private users of pesticides or herbicides who violate the act are subject to a $1,000 fine and incarceration for up to thirty days.

Note that a state can also regulate the sale and use of federally registered pesticides. ■ **CASE IN POINT 45.7** The EPA conditionally registered Strongarm, a weed-killing pesticide made by Dow Agrosciences, LLC. Dow sold Strongarm to Texas peanut farmers. When the farmers applied it, Strongarm damaged their crops and failed to control the growth of weeds. The farmers sued Dow for violations of Texas law, but the lower courts ruled that FIFRA preempted their claims. The farmers appealed to the United States Supreme Court. The Court held that under a specific provision of FIFRA, a state can regulate the sale and use of federally registered pesticides so long as the regulation does not permit anything that FIFRA prohibits.[18] ■

45–5b Toxic Substances

The Toxic Substances Control Act[19] regulates chemicals and chemical compounds that are known to be toxic, such as asbestos and polychlorinated biphenyls (PCBs). The act also controls the introduction of new chemical compounds by requiring investigation of any possible harmful effects from these substances.

Under the act, the EPA can require that manufacturers, processors, and other entities planning to use chemicals first determine their effects on human health and the environment. The EPA can regulate substances that could pose an imminent hazard or an unreasonable risk of injury to health or the environment. The EPA can also require special labeling, limit the use of a substance, set production quotas, or prohibit the use of a substance altogether.

45–5c The Resource Conservation and Recovery Act

The Resource Conservation and Recovery Act (RCRA)[20] was Congress's response to growing concerns about the effects of hazardous waste materials on the environment. The RCRA required the EPA to determine which forms of solid waste should be considered hazardous and to establish regulations to monitor and control hazardous waste disposal.

Among other things, the act requires all producers of hazardous waste materials to label and package properly any hazardous waste to be transported. Amendments to the RCRA decrease the use of land containment in the disposal of hazardous waste and require smaller generators of hazardous waste to comply with the act.

Under the RCRA, a company may be assessed a civil penalty of up to $25,000 for each violation.[21] The penalty is based on the seriousness of the violation, the probability of harm, and the extent to which the violation deviates from RCRA requirements. Criminal penalties include fines of up to $50,000 for each day of violation, imprisonment for up to two years (in most instances), or both. Criminal fines and the time of imprisonment can be doubled for certain repeat offenders.

45–5d Superfund

The Comprehensive Environmental Response, Compensation, and Liability Act (CERCLA),[22] commonly known

---

16. 7 U.S.C. Sections 136–136y.
17. 21 U.S.C. Section 346a.
18. *Bates v. Dow Agrosciences, LLC*, 544 U.S. 431, 125 S.Ct. 1788, 161 L.Ed.2d 687 (2005).

19. 15 U.S.C. Sections 2601–2692.
20. 42 U.S.C. Sections 6901–6986.
21. 42 U.S.C. Section 6928(a).
22. 42 U.S.C. Sections 9601–9675.

as Superfund, regulates the clean-up of disposal sites in which hazardous waste is leaking into the environment. CERCLA, as amended, has four primary elements:

1. It established an information-gathering and analysis system that enables the government to identify chemical dump sites and determine the appropriate action.
2. It authorized the EPA to respond to emergencies and to arrange for the clean-up of a leaking site directly if the persons responsible fail to clean up the site.
3. It created a Hazardous Substance Response Trust Fund (also called *Superfund*) to pay for the clean-up of hazardous sites using funds obtained through taxes on certain businesses.
4. It allowed the government to recover the cost of clean-up from persons who were (even remotely) responsible for hazardous substance releases.

Potentially Responsible Parties Superfund provides that when a release or a potential release of hazardous chemicals from a site occurs, the following persons may be held responsible for cleaning up the site:

1. The person who generated the wastes disposed of at the site.
2. The person who transported the waste to the site.
3. The person who owned or operated the site at the time of the disposal.
4. The current owner or operator.

A person falling within one of these categories is referred to as a **potentially responsible party (PRP).** If the PRPs do not clean up the site, the EPA can clean up the site and recover the clean-up costs from the PRPs.

Strict Liability of PRPs. Superfund imposes strict liability on PRPs, and that liability cannot be avoided through transfer of ownership. Thus, selling a site where hazardous wastes were disposed of does not relieve the seller of liability, and the buyer also becomes liable for the clean-up.

Liability also extends to businesses that merge with or buy corporations that have violated CERCLA. A parent corporation is not automatically liable for the violations of its subsidiary. It can be held liable, however, if the subsidiary was merely a shell company or if the parent corporation participated in or controlled the facility.[23]

Joint and Several Liability of PRPs. Liability under Superfund is usually joint and several. In other words, a PRP who generated *only a fraction of the hazardous waste* disposed of at a site may nevertheless be liable for *all* of

the clean-up costs. CERCLA authorizes a party who has incurred clean-up costs to bring a "contribution action" against any other person who is liable or potentially liable for a percentage of the costs.

Minimizing Liability One way for a business to minimize its potential liability under Superfund is to conduct environmental compliance audits of its own operations regularly. That is, the business can investigate its own operations and property to determine whether any environmental hazards exist.

The EPA encourages companies to conduct self-audits and promptly detect, disclose, and correct wrongdoing. Companies that do so are subject to lighter penalties for violations of environmental laws. (Fines may be reduced as much as 75 percent.)

In addition, under EPA guidelines, the EPA will waive all fines if a small company corrects environmental violations within 180 days after being notified of the violations (or 360 days if pollution-prevention techniques are involved). The policy does not apply to criminal violations of environmental laws, though, or to violations that pose a significant threat to public health, safety, or the environment.

Defenses There are a few defenses to liability under CERCLA. The most important is the *innocent landowner defense*.[24] This defense may protect a landowner who acquired the property after it was used for hazardous waste disposal.

The landowner claiming the innocent landowner defense must not have had a contractual or employment relationship with the person (or other entity) who owned the land when the contamination occurred. Because land is often transferred by contract, it would seem that this defense would not normally be available. However, a landowner who can show that he or she had no knowledge of the hazardous waste disposal at the time of purchase can still assert the defense.

To succeed, the landowner must show that at the time the property was acquired, she or he had no reason to know that it had been used for hazardous waste disposal. The landowner must also show that at the time of the purchase, she or he undertook "all appropriate inquiries." That is, he or she investigated the previous ownership and uses of the property to determine whether there was reason for concern about hazardous substances. In effect, then, this defense protects only property owners who took precautions and investigated the possibility of environmental hazards before buying the property.

---

23. The landmark case establishing the liability of a parent corporation under CERCLA is *United States v. Bestfoods*, 524 U.S. 51, 118 S.Ct. 1876, 141 L.Ed.2d 43 (1998).

24. 42 U.S.C. Section 9601(35)(B).

Reviewing: Environmental Protection

Residents of Lake Caliopa, Minnesota, began noticing an unusually high number of lung ailments among the local population. Several concerned citizens pooled their resources and commissioned a study to compare the frequency of these health conditions in Lake Caliopa with national averages. The study concluded that residents of Lake Caliopa experienced four to seven times the rate of frequency of asthma, bronchitis, and emphysema as the population nationwide.

During the study period, citizens began expressing concerns about the large volume of smog emitted by the Cotton Design apparel manufacturing plant on the outskirts of town. The plant had a production facility two miles east of town beside the Tawakoni River and employed seventy full-time workers. Just downstream on the Tawakoni River, the city of Lake Caliopa operated a public water works facility, which supplied all city residents with water.

The Minnesota Pollution Control Agency required Cotton Design to install new equipment to control air and water pollution. Later, citizens sued Cotton Design for various respiratory ailments allegedly caused or compounded by smog from Cotton Design's factory. Using the information presented in the chapter, answer the following questions.

1. Under the common law, what would each plaintiff be required to identify in order to be given relief by the court?
2. What standard for limiting emissions into the air does Cotton Design's pollution-control equipment have to meet?
3. If Cotton Design's emissions violated the Clean Air Act, how much can the EPA assess in fines per day?
4. What information must the city send to every household that it supplies with water?

Debate This . . .   *The courts should reject all cases in which the wetlands in question do not consist of actual bodies of water that exist during the entire year.*

Terms and Concepts

environmental impact
  statement (EIS) 863
nuisance 860

potentially responsible
  party (PRP) 872
toxic tort 860

wetlands 869

Issue Spotters

1. Resource Refining Company's plant emits smoke and fumes. Resource's operation includes a short railway system, and trucks enter and exit the grounds continuously. Constant vibrations from the trains and trucks rattle nearby residential neighborhoods. The residents sue Resource. Are there any reasons why the court might refuse to issue an injunction against Resource's operation? Explain. (See *Common Law Actions*.)

2. ChemCorp generates hazardous wastes from its operations. Disposal Trucking Company transports those wastes to Eliminators, Inc., which owns a site for hazardous waste disposal. Eliminators sells the property on which the disposal site is located to Fluid Properties, Inc. If the Environmental Protection Agency cleans up the site, from whom can it recover the cost? (See *Toxic Chemicals and Hazardous Waste*.)

• **Check your answers to the Issue Spotters against the answers provided in Appendix D at the end of this text.**

Business Scenarios

45–1. The Clean Water Act. Fruitade, Inc., is a processor of a soft drink called Freshen Up. Fruitade uses returnable bottles, which it cleans with a special acid to allow for further beverage processing. The acid is diluted with water and then allowed to pass into a navigable stream. Fruitade crushes its broken bottles and throws the crushed glass into the stream. Discuss fully any environmental laws that Fruitade has violated. (See *Water Pollution*.)

45–2. Environmental Protection. Moonbay is a home-building corporation that primarily develops retirement communities. Farmtex owns a number of feedlots in Sunny Valley. Moonbay purchases 20,000 acres of farmland in the same area and begins building and selling homes on this acreage. In the meantime, Farmtex continues to expand its feedlot business, and eventually only 500 feet separate the two operations.

Because of the odor and flies from the feedlots, Moonbay finds it difficult to sell the homes in its development. Moonbay wants to enjoin (prevent) Farmtex from operating its feedlot in the vicinity of the retirement home development. Under what common law theory would Moonbay file this action? Has Farmtex violated any federal environmental laws? Discuss. (See *Common Law Actions.*)

Business Case Problems

45–3. Spotlight on the Grand Canyon—Environmental Impact Statement.

 The U.S. National Park Service (NPS) manages the Grand Canyon National Park in Arizona under a management plan that is subject to periodic review. In 2006, after nine years of background work and the completion of a comprehensive environmental impact statement, the NPS issued a new management plan for the park. The plan allowed for the continued use of rafts on the Colorado River, which runs through the Grand Canyon. The number of rafts was limited, however. Several environmental groups criticized the plan because they felt that it still allowed too many rafts on the river. The groups asked a federal appellate court to overturn the plan, claiming that it violated the wilderness status of the national park. When can a federal court overturn a determination by an agency such as the NPS? Explain. [*River Runners for Wilderness v. Martin,* 593 F.3d 1064 (9th Cir. 2010)] (See *Federal, State, and Local Regulations.*)

45–4. Superfund.

A by-product of phosphate fertilizer production is pyrite waste, which contains arsenic and lead. From 1884 to 1906, seven phosphate fertilizer plants operated on a forty-three-acre site in Charleston, South Carolina. Planters Fertilizer & Phosphate Co. bought the site in 1906 and continued to make fertilizer. In 1966, Planters sold the site to Columbia Nitrogen Corp. (CNC), which also operated the fertilizer plants. In 1985, CNC sold the site to James Holcombe and J. Henry Fair. Holcombe and Fair subdivided and sold the site to Allwaste Tank Cleaning Inc., Robin Hood Container Express, the city of Charleston, and Ashley II of Charleston, Inc. Ashley spent almost $200,000 cleaning up the contaminated soil. Who can be held liable for the cost? Why? [*PCS Nitrogen Inc. v. Ashley II of Charleston LLC,* 714 F.3d 161 (4th Cir. 2013)] (See *Toxic Chemicals and Hazardous Waste.*)

45–5. Business Case Problem with Sample Answer—Environmental Impact Statements.

 The U.S. Forest Service (USFS) proposed a travel management plan (TMP) for the Beartooth Ranger District in the Pryor and Absaroka Mountains in the Custer National Forest of southern Montana. The TMP would convert unauthorized user-created routes within the wilderness to routes authorized for motor vehicle use. It would also permit off-road "dispersed vehicle camping" within 300 feet of the routes, with some seasonal restrictions. The TMP would ban cross-country motorized travel outside the designated routes. Is an environmental impact statement required before

the USFS implements the TMP? If so, what aspects of the environment should the USFS consider in preparing it? Discuss. [*Pryors Coalition v. Weldon,* 551 Fed.Appx. 426 (9th Cir. 2014)] (See *Federal, State, and Local Regulations.*)

- For a sample answer to Problem 45–5, go to Appendix E at the end of this text.

45–6. The Clean Water Act.

ICG Hazard, LLC, operates the Thunder Ridge surface coal mine in Leslie County, Kentucky, under a National Pollutant Discharge Elimination System permit issued by the Kentucky Division of Water (KDOW). As part of the operation, ICG discharges selenium into the surrounding water. Selenium is a naturally occurring element that endangers aquatic life once it reaches a certain concentration. KDOW knew when it issued the permit that mines in the area could produce selenium but did not specify discharge limits for the element in ICG's permit. Instead, the agency imposed a one-time monitoring requirement, which ICG met. Does ICG's discharge of selenium violate the Clean Water Act? Explain. [*Sierra Club v. ICG Hazard, LLC,* 781 F.3d 281 (6th Cir. 2015)] (See *Water Pollution.*)

45–7. Special Case Analysis—Environmental Regulatory Agencies.

Go to Case Analysis 45.1, *Friends of Animals v. Clay.* Read the excerpt and answer the following questions.

(a) Issue: What regulation was at issue in this case? What activity does it regulate?

(b) Rule of Law: What rule of statutory interpretation did the court apply to construe this regulation?

(c) Applying the Rule of Law: How did the plaintiff want the regulation to be interpreted? What was the court's response?

(d) Conclusion: What were the results of the court's interpretation of the regulation?

45–8. A Question of Ethics—Clean Air Act.

 In the Clean Air Act, Congress allowed California, which has particular problems with clean air, to adopt its own standard for emissions from cars and trucks. California's standard is subject to the approval of the Environmental Protection Agency (EPA) based on certain criteria. Congress also allowed other states to adopt California's standard after the EPA's approval.

In 2004, in an effort to address climate change, the California Air Resources Board amended the state's standard to attain "the maximum feasible and cost-effective reduction of GHG

[greenhouse gas] emissions from motor vehicles." The regulation, which applies to new passenger vehicles and light-duty trucks for 2009 and later, imposes decreasing limits on emissions of carbon dioxide through 2016. While EPA approval was pending, Vermont and other states adopted similar standards.

Green Mountain Chrysler Plymouth Dodge Jeep and other auto dealers, automakers, and associations of automakers filed a suit in a federal district court against George Crombie (then the secretary of the Vermont Agency of Natural Resources) and others, seeking relief from the state regulations. [Green Mountain Chrysler Plymouth Dodge Jeep v. Crombie, 508 F.Supp.2d 295 (D.Vt. 2007)] (See *Air Pollution.*)

(a) Under the Environmental Policy and Conservation Act (EPCA) of 1975, the National Highway Traffic Safety Administration sets fuel economy standards for new cars. The plaintiffs argued, among other things, that the EPCA, which prohibits states from adopting separate fuel economy standards, preempts Vermont's GHG regulation. Do the GHG rules equate to the fuel economy standards? Discuss.

(b) Do Vermont's rules tread on the efforts of the federal government to address climate change internationally? Who should regulate GHG emissions? The federal government? The state governments? Both? Neither? Why?

(c) The plaintiffs claimed that they would go bankrupt if they were forced to adhere to the state's GHG standards. Should they be granted relief on this basis? Does history support their claim? Explain.

Legal Reasoning Group Activity

45–9. Clean-Up Costs. It has been estimated that for every dollar spent cleaning up hazardous waste sites, administrative agencies spend seven dollars in overhead. (See *Toxic Chemicals and Hazardous Waste.*)

(a) The first group will list and explain possible ways to trim these administrative costs.

(b) The second group will evaluate whether the laws pertaining to hazardous waste clean-up can or should be changed to reduce the costs to government.

CHAPTER 46

Antitrust Law

After the Civil War (1861–1865), the American public became increasingly concerned about declining competition in the marketplace. Large corporate enterprises were attempting to reduce or eliminate competition by legally tying themselves together in *business trusts*.

The most famous trust was the Standard Oil trust of the late 1800s. Participants in the trust transferred their stock to a trustee. The trustee then fixed prices, controlled production, and established exclusive geographic markets for all of the oil companies that were members of the trust. Some observers began to argue that the trust wielded so much economic power that corporations outside the trust could not compete effectively.

Eventually, legislators at both the state and the federal level began to enact laws to rein in the trusts. Hence, the laws regulating economic competition in the United States today are referred to as **antitrust laws.** At the national level, antitrust legislation began when Congress passed the Interstate Commerce Act[1] in 1887, followed by the Sherman Antitrust Act[2] in 1890. In 1914, Congress passed the Clayton Act[3] and the Federal Trade Commission Act.[4] We examine these major federal antitrust statutes in this chapter.

The purpose of antitrust legislation was—and still is—to foster competition. Behind these laws lies our society's belief that competition leads to lower prices, better products, a wider selection of goods, and more product information.

---

1. 49 U.S.C. Sections 501–526

2. 15 U.S.C. Sections 1–7.
3. 15 U.S.C. Sections 12–27.
4. 15 U.S.C. Sections 41–58a.

46–1 The Sherman Antitrust Act

The author of the Sherman Antitrust Act, Senator John Sherman, was the brother of the famed Civil War general William Tecumseh Sherman. He was also a recognized financial authority. He had been concerned for years about what he saw as diminishing competition within U.S. industry and the emergence of monopolies. He told Congress that the Sherman Act "does not announce a new principle of law, but applies old and well-recognized principles of the common law."[5]

Indeed, today's antitrust laws are the direct descendants of common law actions intended to limit **restraints of trade** (agreements between or among firms that have the effect of reducing competition in the marketplace). Such actions date to the fifteenth century in England. The common law was not always consistent, however, and had not been effective in curbing the trusts. That is why Sherman proposed the Sherman Antitrust Act, often simply called the Sherman Act.

---

5. 21 *Congressional Record* 2456 (1890).

46–1a Major Provisions of the Sherman Act

Sections 1 and 2 contain the main provisions of the Sherman Act:

1. Every contract, combination in the form of trust or otherwise, or conspiracy, in restraint of trade or commerce among the several States, or with foreign nations, is hereby declared to be illegal [and is a felony punishable by fine and/or imprisonment].
2. Every person who shall monopolize, or attempt to monopolize, or combine or conspire with any other person or persons, to monopolize any part of the trade or commerce among the several States, or with foreign nations, shall be deemed guilty of a felony [and is similarly punishable].

46–1b Differences between Section 1 and Section 2

The two sections of the Sherman Act are quite different. Section 1 requires two or more persons, because a person cannot contract, combine, or conspire alone. Thus, the essence of the illegal activity is *the act of joining together.* Section 2, though, can apply either to one person or to two or more persons because it refers to "every person." Thus, unilateral conduct can result in a violation of Section 2.

It follows that the cases brought to the courts under Section 1 of the Sherman Act differ from those brought under Section 2. Section 1 cases are often concerned with whether an agreement (written or oral) leads to a restraint of trade. Section 2 cases deal with the structure of a monopoly that exists in the marketplace.

The term **monopoly** generally is used to describe a market in which there is a single seller or a very limited number of sellers. Whereas Section 1 focuses on agreements that are restrictive—that is, agreements that have a wrongful purpose—Section 2 looks at the so-called misuse of **monopoly power** in the marketplace. Monopoly power exists when a firm has an extreme amount of **market power**—the ability to affect the market price of its product.

Both Section 1 and Section 2 seek to curtail market practices that result in undesired monopoly pricing and output behavior. For a case to be brought under Section 2, however, the "threshold" or "necessary" amount of monopoly power must already exist. We illustrate the different requirements for violating these two sections of the Sherman Act in Exhibit 46–1.

46–1c Jurisdictional Requirements

The Sherman Act applies only to restraints that have a significant impact on interstate commerce. Courts have generally held that any activity that substantially affects interstate commerce falls within the scope of the Sherman Act. As will be discussed later in this chapter, the Sherman Act also extends to U.S. nationals abroad who are engaged in activities that affect U.S. foreign commerce.

Federal courts have exclusive jurisdiction over antitrust cases brought under the Sherman Act. State laws regulate local restraints on competition, and state courts decide claims brought under those laws.

46–2 Section 1 of the Sherman Act

The underlying assumption of Section 1 of the Sherman Act is that society's welfare is harmed if rival firms are permitted to join in an agreement that consolidates their market power or otherwise restrains competition. The types of trade restraints that Section 1 of the Sherman Act prohibits generally fall into two broad categories: *horizontal restraints* and *vertical restraints,* both of which will be discussed shortly. First, though, we look at the rules that the courts may apply when assessing the anticompetitive impact of alleged restraints of trade.

46–2a *Per Se* Violations versus the Rule of Reason

Some restraints are so substantially anticompetitive that they are deemed ***per se* violations**—illegal *per se* (inherently)—under Section 1. Other agreements, however, even though they result in enhanced market power, do not *unreasonably* restrain trade and are therefore lawful. Using the **rule of reason,** the courts analyze anticompetitive agreements that allegedly violate Section 1 of the Sherman Act to determine whether they actually constitute reasonable restraints of trade.

Rationale for the Rule of Reason The need for a rule-of-reason analysis of some agreements in restraint of trade is obvious. If the rule of reason had not been

EXHIBIT 46–1 Required Elements of a Sherman Act Violation

SECTION 1 VIOLATION REQUIREMENTS	SECTION 2 VIOLATION REQUIREMENTS
1. An agreement between two or more parties that 2. Unreasonably restrains competition and 3. Affects interstate commerce.	1. The possession of monopoly power in the relevant market, and 2. The willful acquisition or maintenance of that power as distinguished from its growth or development as a consequence of a superior product, business acumen, or historic accident.

developed, almost any business agreement could conceivably be held to violate the Sherman Act. United States Supreme Court Justice Louis Brandeis effectively phrased this sentiment in *Chicago Board of Trade v. United States,* a case decided in 1918:

> Every agreement concerning trade, every regulation of trade, restrains. To bind, to restrain, is of their very essence. The true test of legality is whether the restraint imposed is such as merely regulates and perhaps thereby promotes competition or whether it is such as may suppress or even destroy competition.[6]

Factors That Courts Consider When analyzing an alleged Section 1 violation under the rule of reason, a court will consider the following factors:

1. The purpose of the agreement.
2. The parties' ability to implement the agreement to achieve that purpose.
3. The effect or potential effect of the agreement on competition.
4. Whether the parties could have relied on less restrictive means to achieve their purpose.

■ **CASE IN POINT 46.1** A group of consumers sued NBC Universal, the Walt Disney Company, and other broadcasters, as well as cable and satellite distributors. The consumers claimed that the bundling together of high-demand and low-demand television channels in cable and satellite programming packages violates the Sherman Act. Bundling forces consumers to pay for channels they do not watch to have access to channels they watch regularly.

The consumers argued that the defendants, through their control of high-demand programming, exercised market power that made it impossible for any distributor to offer unbundled programs. A federal appellate court ruled in favor of the defendants and dismissed the case. The court reasoned that the Sherman Act applies to actions that diminish competition and that the bundling of channels does not injure competition.[7] ■

46–2b Horizontal Restraints

The term **horizontal restraint** is encountered frequently in antitrust law. A horizontal restraint is any agreement that in some way restrains competition between rival firms competing in the same market. Horizontal restraints may include price-fixing, group boycotts, market divisions, and trade associations.

Price Fixing Any **price-fixing agreement**—an agreement among competitors to fix prices—constitutes a *per se* violation of Section 1. The agreement on price need not be explicit. As long as it restricts output or artificially fixes price, it violates the law.

The Reason Behind the Agreement Is Not a Defense. A price-fixing agreement is always a violation of Section 1, even if there are good reasons behind it. ■ **CASE IN POINT 46.2** In a classic price-fixing case, independent oil producers in Texas and Louisiana were caught between falling demand due to the Great Depression of the 1930s and increasing supply from newly discovered oil fields. A group of the major refining companies agreed to buy "distress" gasoline (excess supplies) from the independents so as to dispose of it in an "orderly manner." Although there was no explicit agreement as to price, it was clear that the purpose of the agreement was to limit the supply of gasoline on the market and thereby raise prices.

There may have been good reasons for the agreement. Nonetheless, the United States Supreme Court recognized the potentially adverse effects that such an agreement could have on open and free competition. The Court held that the reasonableness of a price-fixing agreement is never a defense. Any agreement that restricts output or artificially fixes price is a *per se* violation of Section 1.[8] ■

Price-Fixing Cartels Today. Price-fixing cartels (groups) are still commonplace in today's business world, particularly among global companies. The U.S. government actively pursues companies that it suspects of being involved in price-fixing cartels. International price-fixing cartels have been alleged in numerous industries, including air freight, auto parts, computer monitors, digital commerce, and drug manufacturers.

■ **CASE IN POINT 46.3** After Amazon.com released the Kindle e-book reader, it began selling e-book downloads at $9.99 (lower than the actual cost) and made up the difference by selling more Kindles. When the iPad entered the e-book scene, Apple and some book publishers agreed to use Apple's "agency" model, which Apple was already using for games and apps. The agency model allowed the book publishers to set their own prices while Apple kept 30 percent as a commission.

The U.S. government sued Apple and the publishers for price fixing. Because the publishers involved in the arrangement chose prices that were relatively similar, the government argued that price fixing was evident

---

6. 246 U.S. 231, 38 S.Ct. 242, 62 L.Ed. 683 (1918).
7. *Brantley v. NBC Universal, Inc.,* 675 F.3d 1192 (9th Cir. 2012).

8. *United States v. Socony-Vacuum Oil Co.,* 310 U.S. 150, 60 S.Ct. 811, 84 L.Ed. 1129 (1940).

and "would not have occurred without the conspiracy among the defendants." Ultimately, a federal appellate court held that Apple's agreement with publishers to raise e-book prices was a *per se* illegal price-fixing conspiracy. As a result, Apple was ordered to pay $400 million to consumers and $50 million in attorneys' fees.[9] ■

Group Boycotts A **group boycott** is an agreement by two or more sellers to refuse to deal with (that is, to boycott) a particular person or firm. Because they involve concerted action, group boycotts have been held to constitute *per se* violations of Section 1 of the Sherman Act.

To prove a violation of Section 1, the plaintiff must demonstrate that the boycott or joint refusal to deal was undertaken with the intention of eliminating competition or preventing entry into a given market. Although most boycotts are illegal, a few, such as group boycotts against a supplier for political reasons, may be protected under the First Amendment right to freedom of expression.

Horizontal Market Division It is a *per se* violation of Section 1 of the Sherman Act for competitors to divide up territories or customers. ■ **EXAMPLE 46.4** Axm Electronics Basics, Halprin Servo Supplies, and Aicarus Prime Electronics compete against each other in the states of Kansas, Nebraska, and Oklahoma. The three firms agree that Axm will sell products only in Kansas, Halprin will sell only in Nebraska, and Aicarus will sell only in Oklahoma.

This concerted action violates Section 1 of the Sherman Act. It reduces marketing costs and allows all three firms (assuming there is no other competition) to raise the price of the goods sold in their respective states. The same violation would take place if the three firms divided up their customers by class rather than region. They might agree that Axm would sell only to institutional purchasers (such as governments and schools) in all three states, Halprin only to wholesalers, and Aicarus only to retailers. The result would be the same. ■

Trade Associations Businesses in the same general industry or profession frequently organize trade associations to pursue common interests. A trade association may engage in various joint activities, such as exchanging information, representing the members' business interests before governmental bodies, and conducting advertising campaigns. Trade associations also frequently are involved in setting regulatory standards to govern the industry or profession.

Generally, the rule of reason is applied to many of these horizontal actions. If a court finds that a trade association practice or agreement that restrains trade is sufficiently beneficial both to the association and to the public, it may deem the restraint reasonable.

In *concentrated industries,* however, trade associations can be, and have been, used as a means to facilitate anticompetitive actions, such as fixing prices or allocating markets. A **concentrated industry** is one in which either a single firm or a small number of firms control a large percentage of market sales. When trade association agreements have substantially anticompetitive effects, a court will consider them to be in violation of Section 1 of the Sherman Act.

Joint Ventures Joint ventures undertaken by competitors are also subject to antitrust laws. If a joint venture does not involve price fixing or market divisions, the agreement will be analyzed under the rule of reason. Whether the joint undertaking violates Section 1 will then depend on the factors stated earlier in this chapter. A court will look at the venture's purpose, the potential benefits relative to the likely harms, and whether there are less restrictive alternatives for achieving the same goals.

46–2c Vertical Restraints

A **vertical restraint** of trade results from an agreement between firms at different levels in the manufacturing and distribution process. In contrast to horizontal relationships, which occur at the same level of operation, vertical relationships encompass the entire chain of production.

The chain of production normally includes the purchase of inventory, basic manufacturing, distribution to wholesalers, and eventual sale of a product at the retail level. For some products, these distinct phases are carried on by different firms. In other instances, a single firm carries out two or more of the separate functional phases. Such enterprises are said to be **vertically integrated firms.**

Even though firms operating at different functional levels are not in direct competition with one another, they are in competition with other firms. Thus, agreements between firms standing in a vertical relationship may affect competition. Some vertical restraints are *per se* violations of Section 1. Others are judged under the rule of reason.

Territorial or Customer Restrictions In arranging for the distribution of its products, a manufacturing firm often wishes to insulate dealers from direct

9. *United States v. Apple, Inc.,* 791 F.3d 290 (2d Cir. 2015). Apple had previously agreed to settle the case for these amounts if its appeal was unsuccessful.

competition with other dealers selling its products. To do so, the manufacturer may institute territorial restrictions or attempt to prohibit wholesalers or retailers from reselling the products to certain classes of buyers, such as competing retailers.

May Have Legitimate Purpose. A firm may have legitimate reasons for imposing territorial or customer restrictions. For instance, an electronics manufacturer may wish to prevent a dealer from reducing costs and undercutting rivals by offering its products without promotion or customer service. In this situation, the cost-cutting dealer reaps the benefits (sales of the product) paid for by other dealers who undertake promotion and arrange for customer service. By not providing customer service (and relying on a nearby dealer to provide these services), the cost-cutting dealer may also harm the manufacturer's reputation.

Judged under the Rule of Reason. Territorial and customer restrictions were once considered *per se* violations of Section 1.[10] In 1977, the United States Supreme Court held that they should be judged under the rule of reason. ■ **CASE IN POINT 46.5** The Supreme Court case involved GTE Sylvania, Inc., a manufacturer of television sets. Sylvania limited the number of retail franchises that it granted in any given geographic area. It also required each franchisee to sell only Sylvania products from the location at which it was franchised. Sylvania retained sole discretion to increase the number of retailers in an area.

When Sylvania decided to open a new franchise, it terminated the franchise of Continental T.V., Inc., an existing franchisee in that area that would have been in competition with the new franchise. Continental filed a lawsuit claiming that Sylvania's vertically restrictive franchise system violated Section 1 of the Sherman Act. The United States Supreme Court found that "vertical restrictions promote interbrand competition by allowing the manufacturer to achieve certain efficiencies in the distribution of his products." Therefore, Sylvania's vertical system, which was not price restrictive, did not constitute a *per se* violation of Section 1 of the Sherman Act.[11] ■

The decision in the *Continental* case marked a definite shift from rigid characterization of territorial and customer restrictions to a more flexible, economic analysis

of these vertical restraints under the rule of reason. This rule is still applied in most vertical restraint cases.

Resale Price Maintenance Agreements An agreement between a manufacturer and a distributor or retailer in which the manufacturer specifies what the retail prices of its products must be is known as a **resale price maintenance agreement.** Such agreements were once considered to be *per se* violations of Section 1 of the Sherman Act.

Today, however, both *maximum* resale price maintenance agreements and *minimum* resale price maintenance agreements are judged under the rule of reason.[12] The setting of a maximum price that retailers and distributors can charge for a manufacturer's products may sometimes increase competition and benefit consumers.

46–3 Section 2 of the Sherman Act

Section 1 of the Sherman Act proscribes certain concerted, or joint, activities that restrain trade. In contrast, Section 2 condemns "every person who shall monopolize, or attempt to monopolize." Thus, two distinct types of behavior are subject to sanction under Section 2: *monopolization* and *attempts to monopolize.*

One tactic that may be involved in either offense is predatory pricing. **Predatory pricing** occurs when one firm (the predator) attempts to drive its competitors from the market by selling its product at prices substantially *below* the normal costs of production. Once the competitors are eliminated, the predator presumably will raise its prices far above their competitive levels to recapture its losses and earn higher profits.

46–3a Monopolization

The United States Supreme Court has defined **monopolization** as involving the following two elements:

1. The possession of monopoly power in the relevant market.
2. "The willful acquisition or maintenance of the power as distinguished from growth or development as a

---

10. See *United States v. Arnold, Schwinn & Co.*, 388 U.S. 365, 87 S.Ct. 1856, 18 L.Ed.2d 1249 (1967).
11. *Continental T.V., Inc. v. GTE Sylvania, Inc.*, 433 U.S. 36, 97 S.Ct. 2549, 53 L.Ed.2d 568 (1977).

12. The United States Supreme Court ruled that maximum resale price agreements should be judged under the rule of reason in *State Oil Co. v. Khan*, 522 U.S. 3, 118 S.Ct. 275, 139 L.Ed.2d 199 (1997). In *Leegin Creative Leather Products, Inc. v. PSKS, Inc.*, 551 U.S. 877, 127 S.Ct. 2705, 168 L.Ed.2d 623 (2007), the Supreme Court found that the rule of reason also applies to minimum resale price agreements.

consequence of a superior product, business acumen, or historic accident."[13]

To establish a violation of Section 2, a plaintiff must prove both of these elements—monopoly power and an *intent* to monopolize.

Defining Monopoly Power The Sherman Act does not define *monopoly*. In economic theory, monopoly refers to control of a specific market by a single entity. It is well established in antitrust law, however, that a firm may be a monopolist even though it is not the sole seller in a market.

Additionally, size alone does not determine whether a firm is a monopoly. ■ **EXAMPLE 46.6** A "mom and pop" grocery located in the isolated town of Happy Camp, Idaho, is a monopolist if it is the only grocery serving that particular market. Size in relation to the market is what matters, because monopoly involves the power to affect prices. ■

Proving Monopoly Power Monopoly power can be proved by direct evidence that the firm used its power to control prices and restrict output.[14] Usually, though, there is not enough evidence to show that the firm intentionally controlled prices, so the plaintiff has to offer indirect, or circumstantial, evidence of monopoly power.

To prove monopoly power indirectly, the plaintiff must show that the firm has a dominant share of the relevant market and that there are significant barriers for new competitors entering that market. ■ **CASE IN POINT 46.7** DuPont manufactures and sells para-aramid fiber, a synthetic fiber used to make body armor, fiber-optic cables, and tires, among other things. Although several companies around the world manufacture this fiber, only three sell in the U.S. market—DuPont (based in the United States), Teijin (based in the Netherlands), and Kolon Industries, Inc. (based in Korea). DuPont is the industry leader, and at times has produced 60 percent of all para-aramid fibers purchased in the United States.

After DuPont brought suit against Kolon for theft and misappropriation of trade secrets, Kolon counterclaimed that DuPont had illegally monopolized and attempted to monopolize the U.S. para-aramid market in violation of Section 2. Kolon claimed that, to deter competition, DuPont had illegally used multiyear supply agreements for all of its high-volume para-aramid customers. A

federal appellate court, however, found that there was insufficient proof that DuPont had possessed monopoly power in the U.S. market during the relevant time period (between 2006 and 2009). Additionally, the court concluded that Kolon had not shown that the supply agreements foreclosed competition. Therefore, the court held in favor of DuPont on the antitrust claims.[15] ■

Relevant Market Before a court can determine whether a firm has a dominant market share, it must define the relevant market. The relevant market consists of two elements: (1) a relevant product market and (2) a relevant geographic market.

Relevant Product Market. The relevant product market includes all products that have identical attributes (all brands of tea, for instance), as well as products that are reasonably interchangeable with them. Products are considered reasonably interchangeable if consumers treat them as acceptable substitutes. For instance, tea and coffee are reasonably interchangeable, so they may be included in the same relevant product market.

Establishing the relevant product market is often the key issue in monopolization cases because the way the market is defined may determine whether a firm has monopoly power. When the product market is defined narrowly, the degree of a firm's market power appears greater.

■ **EXAMPLE 46.8** White Whale Apps acquires Springleaf Apps, its main competitor in nationwide Android-based mobile phone apps. White Whale maintains that the relevant product market consists of all online retailers of mobile phone apps. The Federal Trade Commission (FTC), however, argues that the relevant product market consists of retailers that sell only apps for Android mobile phones. Under the FTC's narrower definition, White Whale can be seen to have a dominant share of the relevant product market. Thus, the FTC can take appropriate actions against White Whale. ■

In the following case, the FTC alleged that the leading U.S. producer of domestic ductile iron pipe fittings sought to maintain monopoly power in violation of antitrust law. The FTC filed this action under Section 5 of the Federal Trade Commission Act. Section 5, like Section 2 of the Sherman Act, requires proof of both the possession of monopoly power in the relevant market and the willful acquisition or maintenance of that power.

---

13. *United States v. Grinnell Corp.*, 384 U.S. 563, 86 S.Ct. 1698, 16 L.Ed.2d 778 (1966).

14. See, for example, *Broadcom Corp. v. Qualcomm, Inc.*, 501 F.3d 297 (3d Cir. 2007).

15. *Kolon Industries, Inc. v. E.I. DuPont de Nemours & Co.*, 748 F.3d 160 (4th Cir. 2014).

McWane, Inc. v. Federal Trade Commission

United States Court of Appeals, Eleventh Circuit, 783 F.3d 814 (2015).

In the Language of the Court

MARCUS, Circuit Judge:

* * * *

* * * Pipe fittings join together pipes and help direct the flow of pressurized water in pipeline systems. They are sold primarily to municipal water authorities and their contractors. Although there are several thousand unique configurations of fittings (different shapes, sizes, coatings, etc.), approximately 80% of the demand is for about 100 commonly used fittings.

Fittings are commodity products produced to American Water Works Association ("AWWA") standards, and any fitting that meets AWWA specifications is interchangeable, regardless of the country of origin.

* * * Certain municipal, state, and federal laws require [government] waterworks projects to use domestic-only fittings. Domestic fittings sold for use in projects with domestic-only specifications command higher prices than imported fittings.

* * * *

* * * In late 2009, McWane [Inc., headquartered in Birmingham, Alabama,] was the only supplier of domestic fittings.

* * * Looking to take advantage of the increased demand for domestic fittings prompted by [the passage of the American Recovery and Reinvestment Act of 2009 (ARRA), which provided a large infusion of money for waterworks projects that required domestic pipe fittings, Star Pipe Products] decided to enter the market for domestic [fittings].

In response to Star's forthcoming entry into the * * * market, McWane implemented its "Full Support Program" in order "to protect its domestic brands and market position." * * * McWane informed customers that if they did not "fully support McWane branded

products for their domestic fitting and accessory requirements," they "may forgo participation in any unpaid rebates they had accrued for domestic fittings and accessories or shipment of their domestic fitting and accessory orders of McWane products for up to 12 weeks."

* * * *

* * * The FTC issued a * * * complaint charging * * * that McWane's * * * Full Support Program constituted unlawful maintenance of a monopoly over the domestic fittings market.

* * * *

* * * The Commission found that the relevant market was the supply of domestically manufactured fittings for use in domestic-only waterworks projects, because imported fittings are not a substitute for domestic fittings for such projects. The Commission noted that this conclusion was bolstered by the higher prices charged for domestic fittings used in domestic-only projects. The Commission also found that McWane had monopoly power in that market, with 90–95% market share * * * and [that there were] substantial barriers to entry in the form of major capital outlays required to produce domestic fittings.

The Commission [also found] that McWane's Full Support Program * * * foreclosed Star's access to distributors for domestic fittings and harmed competition, thereby contributing significantly to the maintenance of McWane's monopoly power in the market. It noted that * * * the country's two largest waterworks distributors (with a combined 60% market share), prohibited their branches from purchasing domestic fittings from Star after the Full Support Program was announced * * *. Unable to attract [customers], Star was prevented from generating the revenue needed to acquire its own foundry, a

more efficient means of producing domestic fittings; thus, its growth into a rival that could challenge McWane's monopoly power was artificially stunted.

Moreover, the Commission found that * * * McWane's * * * conduct had an impact on price: after the Full Support Program was implemented, McWane raised domestic fittings prices and increased its gross profits despite flat production costs, and it did so across states, regardless of whether Star had entered the market as a competitor.

* * * *

[The Commission issued an order directing McWane to stop requiring exclusivity from its customers.] McWane filed a timely petition in this Court seeking review of the Commissioner's order.

* * * *

* * * *Given the identification of persistent price differences between domestic fittings and imported fittings, the distinct customers, and the lack of reasonable substitutes in this case, there was sufficient evidence to support the Commission's market definition.* [Emphasis added.]

* * * *

* * * The evidence of McWane's overwhelming market share (90%), the large capital outlays required to enter the domestic fittings market, and McWane's undeniable continued power over domestic fittings prices amount to sufficient evidence that a reasonable mind might accept as adequate to support the Commission's conclusion [that McWane possessed monopoly power in the relevant market].

* * * *

* * * We agree that [McWane's] conduct amounts to a violation of Section 5 of the Federal Trade Commission Act.

Accordingly, we AFFIRM.

Case 46.1 Continued

Legal Reasoning Questions

1. How did McWane's Full Support Program harm competition? Explain.
2. What did the Federal Trade Commission conclude? What "factual and economic" evidence supported this conclusion?
3. Instead of imposing an exclusivity policy, what action might McWane have taken to benefit its customers and compete with Star?

Relevant Geographic Market. The second component of the relevant market is the geographic extent of the market in which the firm and its competitors sell the product or services. For products that are sold nationwide, the geographic boundaries of the market can encompass the entire United States.

If transportation costs are significant or a producer and its competitors sell in only a limited area (one in which customers have no access to other sources of the product), then the geographic market is limited to that area. A national firm may thus compete in several distinct areas and have monopoly power in one geographic area but not in another.

Generally, the geographic market is that section of the country within which a firm can increase its price a bit without attracting new sellers or losing many customers to alternative suppliers outside that area. Of course, the Internet is changing perceptions of the size and limits of a geographic market. It may become difficult to perceive any geographic market as local, except for products that are not easily transported, such as concrete.

The Intent Requirement Monopoly power, in and of itself, does not constitute the offense of monopolization under Section 2 of the Sherman Act. The offense also requires an *intent* to monopolize.

A dominant market share may be the result of good business judgment or the development of a superior product. It may simply be the result of a historical accident. In these situations, the acquisition of monopoly power is not an antitrust violation. Indeed, it would be contrary to society's interest to condemn every firm that acquired a position of power because it was well managed and efficient and marketed a product desired by consumers.

If a firm possesses market power as a result of carrying out some purposeful act to acquire or maintain that power through anticompetitive means, then it is in violation of Section 2. In most monopolization cases, intent may be inferred from evidence that the firm had monopoly power and engaged in anticompetitive behavior.

Unilateral Refusals to Deal As discussed previously, joint refusals to deal (group boycotts) are subject to close scrutiny under Section 1 of the Sherman Act. A single manufacturer acting unilaterally, though, normally is free to deal, or not to deal, with whomever it wishes.[16]

Nevertheless, in some instances, a unilateral refusal to deal will violate Section 2 of the Sherman Act. These instances occur only if (1) the firm refusing to deal has—or is likely to acquire—monopoly power and (2) the refusal is likely to have an anticompetitive effect on a particular market.

■ **EXAMPLE 46.9** Clark Industries owns three of the four major downhill ski areas in Blue Hills, Idaho. Clark refuses to continue participating in a jointly offered six-day "all Blue Hills" lift ticket. Clark's refusal to cooperate with its smaller competitor is a violation of Section 2 of the Sherman Act. Because Clark owns three-fourths of the local ski areas, it has monopoly power. Thus, its unilateral refusal to deal has an anticompetitive effect on the market. ■

46–3b Attempts to Monopolize

Section 2 also prohibits **attempted monopolization** of a market, which requires proof of the following three elements:

1. Anticompetitive conduct.
2. The specific intent to exclude competitors and garner monopoly power.

---

16. For a classic case in this area, see *United States v. Colgate & Co.*, 250 U.S. 300, 39 S.Ct. 465, 63 L.Ed. 992 (1919). See also *Pacific Bell Telephone Co. v. Linkline Communications, Inc.*, 555 U.S. 438, 129 S.Ct. 1109, 172 L.Ed.2d 836 (2009).

3. A "dangerous" probability of success in achieving monopoly power. The probability cannot be dangerous unless the alleged offender possesses some degree of market power. Only serious threats of monopolization are condemned as violations.

As mentioned earlier, predatory pricing is a form of anticompetitive conduct that, in theory, could be used by firms that are attempting to monopolize. Related to predatory pricing is *predatory bidding*. This practice involves the acquisition and use of *monopsony power*, which is market power on the *buy* side of a market. Predatory bidding occurs when a buyer bids up the price of an input too high for its competitors to pay, causing them to leave the market. The predatory bidder then attempts to drive down input prices to reap above-competitive profits and recoup any losses it suffered in bidding up the input prices.

The question in the following *Spotlight Case* was whether a claim of predatory bidding was sufficiently similar to a claim of predatory pricing that the same antitrust test should apply to both.

Spotlight on Weyerhaeuser

Case 46.2 Weyerhaeuser Co. v. Ross-Simmons Hardwood Lumber Co.
Supreme Court of the United States, 549 U.S. 312, 127 S.Ct. 1069, 166 L.Ed.2d 911 (2007).

Background and Facts Weyerhaeuser Company entered the Pacific Northwest's hardwood lumber market in 1980. By 2000, Weyerhaeuser owned six mills processing 65 percent of the red alder logs in the region. Meanwhile, Ross-Simmons Hardwood Lumber Company operated a single competing mill. When the prices of the logs rose and those for the lumber fell, Ross-Simmons suffered heavy losses. Several million dollars in debt, the mill closed in 2001.

Ross-Simmons filed a suit in a federal district court against Weyerhaeuser, alleging attempted monopolization under Section 2 of the Sherman Act. Ross-Simmons claimed that Weyerhaeuser used its dominant position in the market to bid up the prices of logs and prevent its competitors from being profitable. Weyerhaeuser argued that the antitrust test for predatory pricing applies to a claim of predatory bidding and that Ross-Simmons had not met this standard. The district court ruled in favor of the plaintiff, the U.S. Court of Appeals for the Ninth Circuit affirmed, and Weyerhaeuser appealed to the United States Supreme Court.

In the Language of the Court
Justice *THOMAS* delivered the opinion of the Court.
* * * *

Predatory-pricing and predatory-bidding claims are analytically similar. This similarity results from the close theoretical connection between monopoly and monopsony. The kinship between monopoly and monopsony suggests that similar legal standards should apply to claims of monopolization and to claims of monopsonization.

* * * Both claims involve the deliberate use of unilateral pricing measures for anticompetitive purposes. And both claims logically require firms to incur short-term losses on the chance that they might reap supracompetitive [above-competitive] profits in the future.
* * * *

* * * *Predatory pricing schemes are rarely tried, and even more rarely successful.*" Predatory pricing requires a firm to suffer certain losses in the short term on the chance of reaping supracompetitive profits in the future. A rational business will rarely make this sacrifice.* The same reasoning applies to predatory bidding. [Emphasis added.]
* * * *

* * * A failed predatory-pricing scheme may benefit consumers. * * * Failed predatory-bidding schemes can also * * * benefit consumers.

In addition, predatory bidding presents less of a direct threat of consumer harm than predatory pricing. A predatory-pricing scheme ultimately achieves success by charging higher prices to consumers. By

Case 46.2 Continued

contrast, a predatory-bidding scheme could succeed with little or no effect on consumer prices because a predatory bidder does not necessarily rely on raising prices in the output market to recoup its losses.

* * * *

* * * [Thus,] our two-pronged [predatory pricing] test should apply to predatory-bidding claims.

* * * A plaintiff must prove that the alleged predatory bidding led to below-cost pricing of the predator's outputs. That is, the predator's bidding on the buy side must have caused the cost of the relevant output to rise above the revenues generated in the sale of those outputs. * * * Given the multitude of procompetitive ends served by higher bidding for inputs, the risk of chilling procompetitive behavior with too lax a liability standard is * * * serious * * *. Consequently, only higher bidding that leads to below-cost pricing in the relevant output market will suffice as a basis for liability for predatory bidding.

A predatory-bidding plaintiff also must prove that the defendant has a dangerous probability of recouping the losses incurred in bidding up input prices through the exercise of monopsony power. Absent proof of likely recoupment, a strategy of predatory bidding makes no economic sense because it would involve short-term losses with no likelihood of offsetting long-term gains.

Ross-Simmons has conceded that it has not satisfied [this] standard. Therefore, its predatory-bidding theory of liability cannot support the jury's verdict.

Decision and Remedy *The United States Supreme Court held that the antitrust test that applies to claims of predatory pricing also applies to claims of predatory bidding. Because Ross-Simmons conceded that it had not met this standard, the Court vacated the lower court's judgment and remanded the case.*

Critical Thinking

- **Social** *Do predatory-bidding schemes ever benefit consumers? Explain your answer.*
- **Economic** *Why does a plaintiff alleging predatory bidding have to prove that the defendant's "bidding on the buy side caused the cost of the relevant output to rise above the revenues generated in the sale of those outputs"?*

46–4 The Clayton Act

Congress enacted the Clayton Act to strengthen federal antitrust laws. The act was aimed at specific anticompetitive or monopolistic practices that the Sherman Act did not cover. The substantive provisions of the act—set out in Sections 2, 3, 7, and 8—deal with four distinct forms of business behavior, which are declared illegal but not criminal. For each provision, the act states that the behavior is *illegal only if it tends to substantially lessen competition or to create monopoly power.*

46–4a Section 2—Price Discrimination

Section 2 of the Clayton Act prohibits **price discrimination,** which occurs when a seller charges different prices to competing buyers for identical goods or services. Congress strengthened this section by amending it with the passage of the Robinson-Patman Act in 1936. As amended, Section 2 prohibits price discrimination that cannot be justified by differences in production costs, transportation costs, or cost differences due to other

reasons. In short, a seller cannot charge one buyer a lower price than it charges that buyer's competitor.

Requirements To violate Section 2, the seller must be engaged in interstate commerce, the goods must be of like grade and quality, and the goods must have been sold to two or more purchasers. In addition, the effect of the price discrimination must be to substantially lessen competition, tend to create a monopoly, or otherwise injure competition. Without proof of an actual injury resulting from the price discrimination, the plaintiff cannot recover damages.

Note that price discrimination claims can arise from discounts, offsets, rebates, or allowances given to one buyer over another. Moreover, giving favorable credit terms, delivery, or freight charges to some buyers, but not others, can also lead to allegations of price discrimination. For instance, when a seller offers goods to different customers at the same price but includes free delivery for certain buyers, it may violate Section 2 in some circumstances.

Defenses There are several statutory defenses to liability for price discrimination.

1. *Cost justification.* If the seller can justify the price reduction by demonstrating that a particular buyer's purchases saved the seller costs in producing and selling the goods, the seller will not be liable for price discrimination.

2. *Meeting a competitor's prices.* If the seller charged the lower price in a good faith attempt to meet an equally low price of a competitor, the seller will not be liable for price discrimination. **■ EXAMPLE 46.10** Rogue, Inc., is a retail dealer of Mercury Marine outboard motors in Shady Cove, Oregon. Mercury Marine also sells its motors to other dealers in the Shady Cove area. When Rogue discovers that Mercury is selling its outboard motors at a substantial discount to Rogue's largest competitor, it files a price discrimination lawsuit. Mercury Marine can defend itself by showing that the discounts given to Rogue's competitor were made in good faith to meet the low price charged by another manufacturer of marine motors. ■

3. *Changing market conditions.* A seller may lower its price on an item in response to changing conditions affecting the market for or the marketability of the goods concerned. Sellers are allowed to readjust their prices to meet the realities of the market without liability for price discrimination. Thus, if an advance in technology makes a particular product less marketable than it was previously, a seller can lower the product's price.

46–4b Section 3—Exclusionary Practices

Under Section 3 of the Clayton Act, sellers or lessors cannot condition the sale or lease of goods on the buyer's or lessee's promise not to use or deal in the goods of the seller's competitor. In effect, this section prohibits two types of vertical agreements involving exclusionary practices— exclusive-dealing contracts and tying arrangements.

Exclusive-Dealing Contracts A contract under which a seller forbids a buyer to purchase products from the seller's competitors is called an **exclusive-dealing contract.** A seller is prohibited from making an exclusive-dealing contract under Section 3 if the effect of the contract is "to substantially lessen competition or tend to create a monopoly."

In the past, courts were more inclined to find that exclusive-dealing contracts substantially lessened competition. **■ CASE IN POINT 46.11** In one classic case, Standard Oil Company, the largest gasoline seller in the nation in the late 1940s, made exclusive-dealing contracts with independent stations in seven western states.

The contracts involved 16 percent of all retail outlets, whose sales were approximately 7 percent of all retail sales in that market. The United States Supreme Court ruled that the market was substantially concentrated because the seven largest gasoline suppliers all used exclusive-dealing contracts with their independent retailers and together controlled 65 percent of the market.

Looking at market conditions after the arrangements were instituted, the Court found that market shares were extremely stable and that entry into the market was apparently restricted. Thus, the Court held that the Clayton Act had been violated because competition was "foreclosed in a substantial share" of the relevant market.[17] ■ Note that since the Supreme Court's 1949 decision, a number of subsequent decisions have called the holding in this case into doubt.[18]

Today, it is clear that to violate antitrust law, an exclusive-dealing agreement (or a tying arrangement, discussed next) must qualitatively and substantially harm competition. To prevail, a plaintiff must present affirmative evidence that the performance of the agreement will foreclose competition and harm consumers.

Tying Arrangements When a seller conditions the sale of a product (the tying product) on the buyer's agreement to purchase another product (the tied product) produced or distributed by the same seller, a **tying arrangement** results. The legality of a tying arrangement (or *tie-in sales agreement*) depends on several factors, such as the purpose of the agreement. Courts also focus on the agreement's likely effect on competition in the relevant markets (the market for the tying product and the market for the tied product).

Section 3 of the Clayton Act has been held to apply only to commodities, not to services. Tying arrangements, however, can also be considered agreements that restrain trade in violation of Section 1 of the Sherman Act. Thus, cases involving tying arrangements of services have been brought under Section 1 of the Sherman Act. Although earlier cases condemned tying arrangements as illegal *per se,* courts now evaluate tying agreements under the rule of reason.[19]

---

17. *Standard Oil Co. of California v. United States,* 337 U.S. 293, 69 S.Ct. 1051, 93 L.Ed. 1371 (1949).

18. See, for example, *Illinois Tool Works, Inc. v. Independent Ink, Inc.,* 547 U.S. 28, 126 S.Ct. 1281, 164 L.Ed.2d 26 (2006); and *Stop & Shop Supermarket Co. v. Blue Cross & Blue Shield of Rhode Island,* 373 F.3d 57 (1st Cir. 2004).

19. *Illinois Tool Works, Inc. v. Independent Ink, Inc.,* 547 U.S. 28, 126 S.Ct. 1281, 164 L.Ed.2d 26 (2006). This decision was the first time the Supreme Court recognized that tying arrangements can have legitimate business justifications.

■ **CASE IN POINT 46.12** James Batson bought a nonrefundable ticket from Live Nation Entertainment, Inc., to attend a rock concert at the Charter One Pavilion in Chicago. The front of the ticket noted that the price included a nine-dollar parking fee. Batson did not have a car to park, however. In fact, he had walked to the concert venue and had bought the ticket just before the performance.

Frustrated at being charged for parking that he did not need, Batson filed a suit in a federal district court against Live Nation. He argued that the bundled parking fee was unfair because consumers were forced to pay it or forego the concert. He asserted that this was a tying arrangement in violation of Section 1 of the Sherman Act. The court dismissed the suit, and a federal appellate court affirmed. The court was unable to identify a product market in which Live Nation had sufficient power to force consumers who wanted to attend a concert (the tying product) to buy "useless parking rights" (the tied product). While such bundles may be annoying, there was no evidence that Live Nation's parking tie-in restrained competition for parking in Chicago.[20] ■

46–4c Section 7—Mergers

Under Section 7 of the Clayton Act, a person or business organization cannot hold stock or assets in more than one business when "the effect . . . may be to substantially lessen competition." Section 7 is the statutory authority for preventing mergers or acquisitions that could result in monopoly power or a substantial lessening of competition in the marketplace. Section 7 applies to both horizontal and vertical mergers, as discussed in the following subsections.

A crucial consideration in most merger cases is **market concentration.** Determining market concentration involves allocating percentage market shares among the various companies in the relevant market. When a small number of companies share a large part of the market, the market is concentrated. ■ **EXAMPLE 46.13** If the four largest grocery stores in Chicago account for 80 percent of all retail food sales, the market is concentrated in those four firms. If one of these stores absorbs the assets and liabilities of another, so that the other ceases to exist, the result is a merger that further concentrates the market and possibly diminishes competition. ■

Competition is not necessarily diminished solely as a result of market concentration, however. Courts will consider other factors in determining if a merger violates

Section 7. One factor of particular importance is whether the merger will make it more difficult for *potential* competitors to enter the relevant market.

Horizontal Mergers Mergers between firms that compete with each other in the same market are called **horizontal mergers.** If a horizontal merger creates an entity with a significant market share, the merger may be considered illegal because it increases market concentration. The Federal Trade Commission (FTC) and the U.S. Department of Justice (DOJ) have established guidelines for determining which mergers will be challenged.[21]

When analyzing the legality of a horizontal merger, the courts consider three additional factors. The first factor is the overall concentration of the relevant market. The second is the relevant market's history of tending toward concentration. The final factor is whether the merger is apparently designed to establish market power or restrict competition.

Vertical Mergers A **vertical merger** occurs when a company at one stage of production acquires a company at a higher or lower stage of production. An example of a vertical merger is a company merging with one of its suppliers or retailers.

Whether a vertical merger will be deemed illegal generally depends on several factors, such as whether the merger creates a single firm that controls an undue percentage share of the relevant market. The courts also analyze the concentration of firms in the market, barriers to entry into the market, and the apparent intent of the merging parties. If a merger does not prevent competitors of either of the merging firms from competing in a segment of the market, the merger will not be condemned as foreclosing competition and thus is legal.

46–4d Section 8— Interlocking Directorates

Section 8 of the Clayton Act deals with *interlocking directorates*—that is, the practice whereby individuals serve as directors on the boards of two or more competing companies simultaneously. Specifically, no person may be a director for two or more competing corporations at the same time if either of the corporations has capital, surplus, or undivided profits aggregating more than $31,841,000

---

20. *Batson v. Live Nation Entertainment, Inc.,* 746 F.3d 827 (7th Cir. 2014).

21. These guidelines include a formula for assessing the degree of concentration in the relevant market called the *Herfindahl-Hirschman Index* (HHI), which is available at **www.justice.gov/atr/public/guidelines/hmg-2010.html.**

or competitive sales of $3,184,100 or more. The Federal Trade Commission adjusts these threshold amounts each year. (The amounts given here are those announced by the commission in 2016.)

46–5 Enforcement and Exemptions

The federal agencies that enforce the federal antitrust laws are the U.S. Department of Justice (DOJ) and the Federal Trade Commission (FTC), which was established by the Federal Trade Commission Act. Section 5 of that act condemns all forms of anticompetitive behavior that are not covered under other federal antitrust laws.

46–5a Agency Actions

Only the DOJ can prosecute violations of the Sherman Act, which can be either criminal or civil offenses. Violations of the Clayton Act are not crimes, but the act can be enforced by either the DOJ or the FTC through civil proceedings.

The DOJ or the FTC may ask the courts to impose various remedies, including **divestiture** (making a company give up one or more of its operations) and dissolution. A meatpacking firm, for instance, might be forced to divest itself of control or ownership of butcher shops.

The FTC has sole authority to enforce violations of Section 5 of the Federal Trade Commission Act. FTC actions are effected through administrative orders, but if a firm violates an FTC order, the FTC can seek court sanctions for the violation.

46–5b Private Actions

A private party who has been injured as a result of a violation of the Sherman Act or the Clayton Act can sue for **treble damages** (three times the actual damages suffered) and attorneys' fees. In some instances, private parties may also seek injunctive relief to prevent antitrust violations. A party wishing to sue under the Sherman Act must prove that:

1. The antitrust violation either caused or was a substantial factor in causing the injury that was suffered.
2. The unlawful actions of the accused party affected business activities of the plaintiff that were protected by the antitrust laws.

Additionally, the United States Supreme Court has held that to pursue antitrust lawsuits, private parties must present some evidence suggesting that an illegal agreement was made.[22]

A private party can bring an action under Section 2 of the Sherman Act based on the attempted enforcement of a fraudulently obtained patent. This is called a *Walker Process* claim.[23] To prevail, the plaintiff must first show that the defendant obtained the patent by fraud on the U.S. Patent and Trademark Office and enforced the patent with knowledge of the fraud. The plaintiff must then establish all the other elements of a Sherman Act monopolization claim—anticompetitive conduct, an intent to monopolize, and a dangerous probability of achieving monopoly power.

In the following case, a respiratory filter maker was accused of patent infringement. The maker sought a declaratory judgment of non-infringement, asserting a *Walker Process* claim. One of the primary issues was whether attorney fees were an appropriate basis for damages.

---

22. *Bell Atlantic Corp. v. Twombly*, 550 U.S. 544, 127 S.Ct. 1955, 167 L.Ed.2d 929 (2007).
23. The name of the claim comes from the title of the case in which the claim originated—*Walker Process Equipment v. Food Machine and Chemical Corp.*, 382 U.S. 172, 86 S.Ct. 347, 15 L.Ed.2d 247 (1965).

Case 46.3

TransWeb, LLC v. 3M Innovative Properties Co.

United States Court of Appeals, Federal Circuit, 812 F.3d 1295 (2016).

Background and Facts TransWeb, LLC, makes respirator filters made of nonwoven fibrous material to be worn by workers at contaminated worksites. At a filtration industry exposition, TransWeb's founder, Kumar Ogale, handed out samples of TransWeb's filter material. At the time, 3M Innovative Products Company was experimenting with filter materials. At the expo, 3M employees obtained the TransWeb samples.

Case 46.3 Continued

More than a year later, 3M obtained patents for its filter products and filed a suit against TransWeb, claiming infringement. 3M asserted that it had not received the TransWeb samples until after its patent application had been filed. The suit was dismissed.

TransWeb then filed a suit in a federal district court, seeking a declaratory judgment of non-infringement and asserting a *Walker Process* claim. A jury found that 3M had obtained its patents through fraud, that its assertion of the patents against TransWeb violated antitrust law, and that TransWeb was entitled to attorney fees as damages. TransWeb had incurred $7.7 million defending against 3M's infringement suit. The court trebled this to $23 million. 3M appealed.

In the Language of the Court
HUGHES, Circuit Judge.
    * * * *

3M argues that the district court erred in awarding the $23 million of attorney-fees damages, because TransWeb failed to show any link between those attorney fees and an impact on competition. 3M argues that those attorney fees had no effect on competition because they did not force TransWeb out of the market or otherwise affect prices in the market.
    * * * *

3M's argument focuses on the fact that the harmful effect on competition proven by TransWeb at trial never actually came about. TransWeb proved at trial that increased prices for fluorinated filter * * * respirators would have resulted had 3M succeeded in its suit.
    * * * *

* * * 3M's unlawful act was * * * aimed at reducing competition and would have done so had the suit been successful. 3M's unlawful act was the bringing of suit based on a patent known to be fraudulently obtained. What made this act unlawful under the antitrust laws was its attempt to gain a monopoly based on this fraudulently obtained patent. TransWeb's attorney fees flow directly from this unlawful aspect of 3M's act. * * * The attorney fees are precisely the type of loss that the claimed violations would be likely to cause.
    * * * *

* * * *It is the abuse of the legal process by the antitrust-defendant that makes the attorney fees incurred by the antitrust-plaintiff during that legal process a relevant antitrust injury.* [Emphasis added.]

No assertion of a patent known to be fraudulently obtained can be a proper use of legal process. No successful outcome of that litigation, regardless of how much the patentee subjectively desires it, would save that suit from being improper due to its tainted origin.

* * * The antitrust laws exist to protect competition. If we were to hold that TransWeb can seek antitrust damages only [by] forfeiture of competition, but not [by] defending the anticompetitive suit, then we would be incentivizing the former over the latter. * * * This is not in accord with the purpose of those very same antitrust laws.

Furthermore, it furthers the purpose of the antitrust laws to encourage TransWeb to bring its antitrust suit * * * instead of waiting to be excluded from the market * * * . If TransWeb proceeds only after being excluded from the market * * * , then the [injury] will no longer be borne by TransWeb alone, but rather would be shared by all consumers in the relevant markets.

Decision and Remedy *The U.S. Court of Appeals for the Federal Circuit affirmed the lower court's judgment and award of trebled attorney fees. "TransWeb's attorney fees appropriately flow from the unlawful aspect of 3M's antitrust violation and thus are an antitrust injury that can properly serve as the basis for antitrust damages."*

Critical Thinking
- **Legal Environment** *How would TransWeb's injury have been "shared by all consumers in the relevant markets" if TransWeb had not sued until* after *it had been driven out of those markets by 3M's actions?*
- **Ethical** *What does 3M's conduct suggest about its corporate ethics?*

46–5c Exemptions from Antitrust Laws

There are many legislative and constitutional limitations on antitrust enforcement. Most of the statutory and judicially created exemptions to the antitrust laws apply only in certain areas (see Exhibit 46–2). One of the most significant exemptions covers joint efforts by businesspersons to obtain legislative, judicial, or executive action. Under this exemption, for example, DVD producers can jointly lobby Congress to change the copyright laws without being held liable for attempting to restrain trade. Another exemption covers professional baseball teams.

46–6 U.S. Antitrust Laws in the Global Context

U.S. antitrust laws have a broad application. Not only may persons in foreign nations be subject to their provisions, but the laws may also be applied to protect foreign consumers and competitors from violations committed by U.S. business firms. Consequently, *foreign persons,* a term that by definition includes foreign governments, may sue under U.S. antitrust laws in U.S. courts.

46–6a The Extraterritorial Application of U.S. Antitrust Laws

Section 1 of the Sherman Act provides for the extraterritorial effect of the U.S. antitrust laws. Any conspiracy that has a *substantial effect* on U.S. commerce is within the reach of the Sherman Act. The violation may even occur outside the United States, and foreign governments as well as individuals can be sued for violation of U.S. antitrust laws.

Before U.S. courts will exercise jurisdiction and apply antitrust laws, it must be shown that the alleged violation had a substantial effect on U.S. commerce. U.S. jurisdiction is automatically invoked, however, when a *per se* violation occurs.

If a domestic firm, for instance, joins a foreign cartel to control the production, price, or distribution of goods, and this cartel has a *substantial effect* on U.S. commerce, a *per se* violation may arise. Hence, both the domestic firm and the foreign cartel could be sued for violation of the U.S. antitrust laws.

Likewise, if a foreign firm doing business in the United States enters into a price-fixing or other anticompetitive agreement to control a portion of U.S. markets, a *per se* violation may exist. ■ **CASE IN POINT 46.14** Carrier Corporation is a U.S. firm that manufactures air-conditioning and refrigeration (ACR) equipment. To make these products, Carrier uses ACR copper tubing it buys from Outokumpu Oyj, a Finnish company. Carrier is one of the world's largest purchasers of ACR copper tubing.

After the Commission of the European Communities found that Outokumpu had conspired with other companies to fix ACR tubing prices in Europe, Carrier filed a suit in a U.S. court. Carrier alleged that the cartel had also conspired to fix prices in the United States by agreeing that only Outokumpu would sell ACR tubing in the U.S. market. The district court dismissed the case for lack of jurisdiction, but a federal appellate court reversed. The reviewing court found that the alleged anticompetitive conspiracy had a substantial effect on U.S. commerce. Therefore, the U.S. courts had jurisdiction over the Finnish defendant.[24] ■

46–6b The Application of Foreign Antitrust Laws

Large U.S. companies increasingly must be concerned about the application of foreign antitrust laws. The European Union (EU), in particular, has stepped up its enforcement actions against antitrust violators.

European Union Enforcement The EU's laws promoting competition are stricter in many respects than those of the United States and define more conduct as anticompetitive. The EU actively pursues antitrust violators, especially individual companies and cartels that allegedly engage in monopolistic conduct. EU investigations of possible antitrust violations often take years. See this chapter's *Digital Update* feature for a discussion of how the EU is pursuing Google, Inc., for antitrust violations.

Increased Enforcement in Asia and Latin America Many other nations also have laws that promote competition and prohibit trade restraints. Japanese antitrust laws forbid unfair trade practices, monopolization, and restrictions that unreasonably restrain trade. China's antitrust rules restrict monopolization and price fixing (except that the Chinese government can set prices on exported goods). Indonesia, Malaysia, South Korea, and Vietnam all have statutes protecting competition.

24. *Carrier Corp. v. Outokumpu Oyj,* 673 F.3d 430 (6th Cir. 2012).

EXHIBIT 46–2 Exemptions to Antitrust Enforcement

EXEMPTION	SOURCE AND SCOPE
Labor	The Clayton Act—Permits unions to organize and bargain without violating antitrust laws and specifies that strikes and other labor activities normally do not violate any federal law.
Agricultural Associations	The Clayton Act and the Capper-Volstead Act—Allow agricultural cooperatives to set prices.
Fisheries	The Fisheries Cooperative Marketing Act—Allows the fishing industry to set prices.
Insurance Companies	The McCarran-Ferguson Act—Exempts the insurance business in states in which the industry is regulated.
Exporters	The Webb-Pomerene Act—Allows U.S. exporters to engage in cooperative activity to compete with similar foreign associations. The Export Trading Company Act—Permits the U.S. Department of Justice to exempt certain exporters.
Professional Baseball	The United States Supreme Court—Has held that professional baseball is exempt because it is not "interstate commerce."[a]
Oil Marketing	The Interstate Oil Compact—Allows states to set quotas on oil to be marketed in interstate commerce.
Defense Activities	The Defense Production Act—Allows the president to approve, and thereby exempt, certain activities to further the military defense of the United States.
Small Businesses' Cooperative Research	The Small Business Administration Act—Allows small firms to undertake cooperative research.
State Actions	The United States Supreme Court—Has held that actions by a state are exempt if the state clearly articulates and actively supervises the policy behind its action.[b]
Regulated Industries	Federal Agencies—Industries (such as airlines) are exempt when a federal administrative agency (such as the Federal Aviation Administration) has primary regulatory authority.
Businesspersons' Joint Efforts to Seek Government Action	The United States Supreme Court—Cooperative efforts by businesspersons to obtain legislative, judicial, or executive action are exempt unless it is clear that an effort is "objectively baseless" and is an attempt to make anticompetitive use of government processes.[c]

a. *Federal Baseball Club of Baltimore, Inc. v. National League of Professional Baseball Clubs,* 259 U.S. 200, 42 S.Ct. 465, 66 L.Ed. 898 (1922). See *City of San Jose v. Office of the Commissioner of Baseball,* 776 F.3d 686 (9th Cir. 2015).
b. See *Parker v. Brown,* 317 U.S. 341, 63 S.Ct. 307, 87 L.Ed. 315 (1943).
c. *Eastern Railroad Presidents Conference v. Noerr Motor Freight, Inc.,* 365 U.S. 127, 81 S.Ct. 523, 5 L.Ed.2d 464 (1961); and *United Mine Workers of America v. Pennington,* 381 U.S. 657, 89 S.Ct. 1585, 14 L.Ed.2d 626 (1965). These two cases established the exception often referred to as the *Noerr-Pennington* doctrine.

Argentina, Brazil, Chile, Peru, and several other Latin American countries have adopted modern antitrust laws as well.

Most of the antitrust laws apply extraterritorially, as U.S. antitrust laws do. This means that a U.S. company may be subject to another nation's antitrust laws if the company's conduct has a substantial effect on that nation's commerce. For instance, in 2015, China fined the U.S. chipmaker Qualcomm, Inc., $975 million for violating antitrust laws. China has also targeted Microsoft, Inc., in its antitrust investigations and has searched Microsoft's company servers in China for evidence of violations.

DIGITAL UPDATE   Google Faces an Antitrust Complaint from the European Union

"Just google it." Google's search engine is so dominant that the company name has become a verb synonymous with conducting an Internet search. According to the European Commissioner for Competition, Margrethe Vestager, Google has become too dominant, at least with respect to comparison shopping and product search. For that reason, the European Union (EU) has formally charged Google with an antitrust violation. The charges relate specifically to Google operations in the EU.

The EU's Antitrust Objections

According to the EU, Google is abusing a dominant position—a breach of EU antitrust rules. The EU has alleged that Google promotes its own comparison shopping service at the expense of competitors. It does this by "positioning and prominently displaying its comparison shopping service in its general search result pages, irrespective of its merits." As a result, "users do not necessarily see the most relevant results in response to queries—to the detriment of consumers and rival comparison shopping services." Presumably, this conduct started in 2008.

What the EU Wants Google to Do and Google's Response

Now that the EU has established its complaint against Google, here is what it wants Google to do: change the way it displays search results in the EU. When Google shows comparison shopping services in response to a user's query, the search results should show the most relevant services first.

In response to both the complaint and the suggested remedy, Google offered a 130-page rebuttal. It contends that it cannot change its core software. It also claims that the results in its search algorithms are based on relevance. In addition, Google contends that it has actually boosted traffic to its Web competitors. Therein lies the major argument against the EU's antitrust complaint. Search engines have proliferated on the Web, suggesting that Google's success has not eliminated competition.

The Compartmentalization of Search on the Web

More and more frequently, Internet users do not engage in general searches. Rather, they know exactly where to go to obtain product information. When they want information on movies, for instance, they go to the Internet Movie Data Base (IMDB) rather than Google. When they want information on music, they go to iTunes. When they want to search for the cheapest airfares, they go to Kayak or similar sites. When they want to find the best rates on hotels, they go to sites such as hotels.com. And when they are interested in buying a product, they frequently go to Amazon or eBay. Amazon, in particular, has fine-tuned its ability to generate advertising revenues through its Amazon-sponsored links.

And, of course, social media must be considered. More people are on social media sites than ever before, particularly on their mobile devices. Users spend four times more time on Facebook than they do on Google. These users often "crowdsource"—that is, look for answers from Facebook friends rather than search on Google. Facebook is also becoming increasingly competitive with Google in the services it offers, including mobile payments and the Facebook Messenger instant messaging service.

Whether the European Antitrust Commission accepts Google's arguments will determine Google's fate. Will it pay billions of dollars in fines and be forced to make significant changes in how it does business? That probably will not be decided any time soon. Experts estimate that the case could go on for years.

Critical Thinking *Which companies in Europe do you think may have pressured the European Union to lodge its antitrust complaint against Google?*

Reviewing: Antitrust Law

The Internet Corporation for Assigned Names and Numbers (ICANN) is a nonprofit entity that organizes Internet domain names. It is governed by a board of directors elected by various groups with commercial interests in the Internet. One of ICANN's functions is to authorize an entity to serve as a registry for certain "Top Level Domains" (TLDs). ICANN and VeriSign entered into an agreement that authorized VeriSign to serve as a registry for the ".com" TLD and provide registry services in accordance with ICANN's specifications. VeriSign complained that ICANN was restricting the services that it could make available as a registrar, blocking new services, imposing unnecessary conditions on those services, and setting the prices at which the services were offered. VeriSign claimed that ICANN's control of the registry services for domain names violated Section 1 of the Sherman Act. Using the information presented in the chapter, answer the following questions.

1. Should ICANN's actions be judged under the rule of reason or be deemed *per se* violations of Section 1 of the Sherman Act? Why?
2. Should ICANN's actions be viewed as a horizontal or a vertical restraint of trade? Why?
3. Does it matter that ICANN's directors are chosen by groups with a commercial interest in the Internet? Explain.
4. If the dispute is judged under the rule of reason, what might be ICANN's defense for having a standardized set of registry services that must be used?

Debate This . . .   *The Internet and the rise of e-commerce have rendered our current antitrust concepts and laws obsolete.*

Terms and Concepts

antitrust law 876
attempted monopolization 883
concentrated industry 879
divestiture 888
exclusive-dealing contract 886
group boycott 879
horizontal merger 887
horizontal restraint 878
market concentration 887
market power 877

monopolization 880
monopoly 877
monopoly power 877
per se violation 877
predatory pricing 880
price discrimination 885
price-fixing agreement 878
resale price maintenance
 agreement 880

restraint of trade 876
rule of reason 877
treble damages 888
tying arrangement 886
vertical merger 887
vertical restraint 879
vertically integrated firm 879

Issue Spotters

1. Under what circumstances would Pop's Market, a small store in a small, isolated town, be considered a monopolist? If Pop's is a monopolist, is it in violation of Section 2 of the Sherman Act? Why or why not? (See *Section 2 of the Sherman Act.*)
2. Maple Corporation conditions the sale of its syrup on the buyer's agreement to buy Maple's pancake mix. What factors

would a court consider to decide whether this arrangement violates the Clayton Act? (See *The Clayton Act.*)

• **Check your answers to the Issue Spotters against the answers provided in Appendix D at the end of this text.**

Business Scenarios

46–1. Group Boycott. Jorge's Appliance Corp. was a new retail seller of appliances in Sunrise City. Because of its innovative sales techniques and financing, Jorge's attracted many customers. As a result, the appliance department of No-Glow Department Store, a large chain store with a great deal of buying power, lost a substantial number of sales. No-Glow told a number of appliance manufacturers from whom it made large-volume purchases that if they continued to sell to Jorge's, No-Glow would stop buying from them. The manufacturers immediately stopped selling appliances to Jorge's. Jorge's filed a suit against No-Glow and the manufacturers, claiming that their actions constituted an antitrust violation. No-Glow and the manufacturers were able to prove that Jorge's was a small retailer with a small market share. They claimed that because the relevant market was not substantially affected, they were not guilty of restraint of trade. Discuss fully whether there was an antitrust violation. (See *Section 1 of the Sherman Act.*)

46–2. Antitrust Laws. Allitron, Inc., and Donovan, Ltd., are interstate competitors selling similar appliances, principally in the states of Illinois, Indiana, Kentucky, and Ohio. Allitron and Donovan agree that Allitron will no longer sell in Indiana and Ohio and that Donovan will no longer sell in Illinois and Kentucky. Have Allitron and Donovan violated any antitrust laws? If so, which law? Explain. (See *Section 1 of The Sherman Act.*)

Business Case Problems

46–3. Section 2 of the Sherman Act. While Deer Valley Resort Co. (DVRC) was developing its ski resort in the Wasatch Mountains near Park City, Utah, it sold parcels of land in the resort village to third parties. Each sales contract reserved the right of approval over the conduct of certain businesses on the property, including ski rentals. For fifteen years, DVRC permitted Christy Sports, LLC, to rent skis in competition with DVRC's ski rental outlet. Then DVRC opened a new midmountain ski rental outlet and revoked Christy's permission to rent skis. This meant that most skiers who flew into Salt Lake City and shuttled to Deer Valley had few choices. They could carry their ski equipment with them on their flights, take a shuttle into Park City and look for cheaper ski rentals there, or rent from DVRC. Christy filed a suit in a federal district court against DVRC. Was DVRC's action an attempt to monopolize in violation of Section 2 of the Sherman Act? Why or why not? [*Christy Sports, LLC v. Deer Valley Resort Co.,* 555 F.3d 1188 (10th Cir. 2009)] (See *Section 2 of the Sherman Act.*)

46–4. Price Fixing. Together, EMI, Sony BMG Music Entertainment, Universal Music Group Recordings, Inc., and Warner Music Group Corp. produced, licensed, and distributed 80 percent of the digital music sold in the United States. The companies formed MusicNet to sell music to online services that sold the songs to consumers. MusicNet required all of the services to sell the songs at the same price and subject to the same restrictions. Digitization of music became cheaper, but MusicNet did not change its prices. Did MusicNet violate the antitrust laws? Explain. [*Starr v. Sony BMG Music Entertainment,* 592 F.3d 314 (2d Cir. 2010)] (See *Section 1 of the Sherman Act.*)

46–5. Business Case Problem with Sample Answer— Price Discrimination. Dayton Superior Corp. sells its

products in interstate commerce to several companies, including Spa Steel Products, Inc. The purchasers often compete directly with each other for customers. From 2005 to 2007, one of Spa Steel's customers purchased Dayton Superior's products from two of Spa Steel's competitors. According to the customer, Spa Steel's prices were always 10 to 15 percent higher for the same products. As a result, Spa Steel lost sales to at least that customer and perhaps others. Spa Steel wants to sue Dayton Superior for price discrimination. Which requirements for such a claim under Section 2 of the Clayton Act does Spa Steel satisfy? What additional facts will it need to prove? [*Dayton Superior Corp. v. Spa Steel Products, Inc.,* 2012 WL 113663 (N.D.N.Y. 2012)] (See *The Clayton Act.*)

- For a sample answer to Problem 46–5, go to Appendix E at the end of this text.

46–6. Section 1 of the Sherman Act. The National Collegiate Athletic Association (NCAA) and the National Federation of State High School Associations (NFHS) set a new standard for non-wood baseball bats. Their goal was to ensure that aluminum and composite bats performed like wood bats in order to enhance player safety and reduce technology-driven home runs and other big hits. Marucci Sports, LLC, makes non-wood bats. Under the new standard, four of Marucci's eleven products were decertified for use in high school and collegiate games. Marucci filed suit against the NCAA and the NFHS under Section 1 of the Sherman Act. At trial, Marucci's evidence focused on injury to its own business. Did the NCAA and NFHS's standard restrain trade in violation of the Sherman Act? Explain. [*Marucci Sports, L.L.C. v. National Collegiate Athletic Association,* 751 F.3d 368 (5th Cir. 2014)] (See *Section 1 of the Sherman Act.*)

46–7. Mergers. St. Luke's Health Systems, Ltd., operated an emergency clinic in Nampa, Idaho. Saltzer Medical Group, P.A., had thirty-four physicians practicing at its offices in Nampa. Saint Alphonsus Medical Center operated the only hospital in Nampa. St. Luke's acquired Saltzer's assets and entered into a five-year professional service agreement with the Saltzer physicians. This affiliation resulted in a combined share of two-thirds of the Nampa adult primary care provider market. Together, the two entities could impose a significant increase in the prices charged to patients and insurers, and correspondence between the parties indicated that they would. Saint Alphonsus filed a suit against St. Luke's to block the merger. Did this affiliation violate antitrust law? Explain. [*Saint Alphonsus Medical Center-Nampa, Inc. v. St. Luke's Health System, Ltd.*, 778 F.3d 775 (9th Cir. 2015)] (See *The Clayton Act.*)

46–8. Section 1 of the Sherman Act. Manitou North America, Inc., makes and distributes telehandlers (forklifts with extendable telescopic booms) to dealers throughout the United States. Manitou agreed to make McCormick International, LLC, its exclusive dealer in the state of Michigan. Later, Manitou entered into an agreement with Gehi Company, which also makes and sells telehandlers. The companies agreed to allocate territories within Michigan among certain dealers for each manufacturer, limiting the dealers' selection of competitive products to certain models. Under this agreement, McCormick was precluded from buying or selling Gehi telehandlers. What type of trade restraint did the agreement between Manitou and Gehi represent? Is this a violation of antitrust law? If so, who was injured, and how were they injured? Explain. [*Manitou North America, Inc. v. McCormick International, LLC*, __ N.W.2d __, 2016 WL 439354 (2016)] (See *Section 1 of the Sherman Act.*)

46–9. A Question of Ethics—Section 1 of the Sherman

 Act. In the 1990s, DuCoa, L.P., made choline chloride, a B-complex vitamin essential for the growth and development of animals. DuCoa, Bioproducts, Inc., and Chinook Group, Ltd., each had one-third of the U.S. market for choline chloride. To stabilize the market and keep the price of the vitamin higher than it would otherwise have been, the companies took action. They agreed to fix the price and allocate market share by deciding which of them would offer the lowest price to each customer. At times, however, the companies disregarded the agreement.

During an increase in competitive activity in August 1997, Daniel Rose became president of DuCoa. The next month, a subordinate advised him of the conspiracy. By February 1998, Rose had begun to implement a strategy to persuade DuCoa's competitors to rejoin the conspiracy. By April, the three companies had reallocated their market shares and increased their prices. In June, the U.S. Department of Justice began to investigate allegations of price fixing in the vitamin market. Ultimately, a federal district court convicted Rose of conspiracy to violate Section 1 of the Sherman Act. [United States v. Rose, *449 F.3d 627 (5th Cir. 2006)*] (See *Section 1 of the Sherman Act.*)

(a) The court "enhanced" Rose's sentence to thirty months' imprisonment, one year of supervised release, and a $20,000 fine. Among other things, the court based this enhancement on Rose's role as "a manager or supervisor" in the conspiracy. Rose appealed the enhancement to the U.S. Court of Appeals for the Fifth Circuit. Was it fair to increase Rose's sentence on this ground? Why or why not?

(b) Was Rose's participation in the conspiracy unethical? If so, how might Rose have behaved ethically instead? If not, could any of the participants' conduct be considered unethical? Explain.

Legal Reasoning Group Activity

46–10. Antitrust Violations. Residents of the city of Madison, Wisconsin, became concerned about overconsumption of liquor near the campus of the University of Wisconsin (UW). The city initiated a new policy, imposing conditions on area bars to discourage reduced-price "specials" that were believed to encourage high-volume and dangerous drinking. Later, the city began to draft an ordinance to ban all drink specials. Bar owners responded by announcing that they had "voluntarily" agreed to discontinue drink specials on Friday and Saturday nights after 8:00 P.M. The city put its ordinance on hold. Several UW students filed a lawsuit against the local bar owners' association, alleging violations of antitrust law. (See *Section 1 of the Sherman Act.*)

(a) The first group will identify the grounds on which the plaintiffs might base their claim for relief and formulate an argument on behalf of the plaintiffs.

(b) The second group will determine whether the defendants are exempt from the antitrust laws.

(c) The third group will decide how the court should rule in this dispute and provide reasons for the ruling.

CHAPTER 47

Professional Liability and Accountability

Professionals, such as accountants, attorneys, physicians, and architects, are increasingly faced with the threat of liability. In part, this is because the public has become more aware that professionals are required to deliver competent services and adhere to certain standards of performance within their professions.

The failure of several major companies and leading public accounting firms in the past twenty years has focused attention on the importance of abiding by professional accounting standards. Numerous corporations and former corporations have been accused of engaging in accounting fraud. These include American International Group (AIG, the world's largest insurance company), HealthSouth, Goldman Sachs, Lehman Brothers, Tyco International, and India-based Satyam Computer Services, to name a few. These companies may have reported fictitious revenues, concealed liabilities or debts, or artificially inflated their assets.

Considering the many potential sources of legal liability that they face, accountants, attorneys, and other professionals should be very aware of their legal obligations. In this chapter, we look at the potential liability of professionals under both the common law and statutory law. We conclude the chapter with a brief examination of the relationships of professionals, particularly accountants and attorneys, with their clients.

47–1 Potential Liability to Clients

Under the common law, professionals may be liable to clients for breach of contract, negligence, or fraud.

47–1a Liability for Breach of Contract

Accountants and other professionals face liability under the common law for any breach of contract. A professional owes a duty to her or his client to honor the terms of their contract and to perform the contract within the stated time period. If the professional fails to perform as agreed in the contract, then she or he has breached the contract, and the client has the right to seek to recover damages from the professional.

Damages can include expenses incurred by the client to hire another professional to provide the contracted-for services and any other reasonable and foreseeable losses that arise from the professional's breach. For instance, if the client had to pay liquidated damages or penalties for failing to meet deadlines, the court may order the professional to pay an equivalent amount in damages to the client.

47–1b Liability for Negligence

Accountants and other professionals may also be held liable under the common law for negligence in the performance of their services. Recall that to establish negligence, the plaintiff must prove four elements: duty, breach, causation, and damages.

Negligence cases against professionals often focus on the standard of care exercised by the professionals. All professionals are subject to the standards of conduct and the ethical codes established by their profession, by state statutes, and by judicial decisions. They are also governed by the contracts they enter into with their clients.

In performing their contracts, professionals must exercise the established standards of care, knowledge, and judgment generally accepted by members of their professional group. How do those standards apply when an attorney stores confidential client information and other data on the cloud? See this chapter's *Ethics Today* feature for a discussion of this issue.

Accountant's Duty of Care Accountants play a major role in a business's financial system. Accountants

ETHICS TODAY

What Are an Attorney's Responsibilities for Protecting Data Stored in the Cloud?

To achieve both cost savings and better security, more and more attorneys are storing their data, including confidential client information, on the cloud. Sometimes, professionals assume that once their data have migrated to the cloud, they no longer have to be concerned with keeping the information secure. But cloud computing is simply the virtualization of the computing process. In other words, the professional is still ultimately responsible for the information.

Rules of Professional Conduct and Stored Information

Attorneys' obligations for their clients' information are spelled out in the American Bar Association's Model Rules of Professional Conduct, which serve as the basis for the ethics rules for attorneys adopted by most states. Comment 17 to Model Rule 1.6 states, "The lawyer must take reasonable precautions to prevent the [client's] information from coming into the hands of unintended recipients." Thus, lawyers have an ethical duty to safeguard confidential client information. It makes no difference whether the information is stored as documents in a filing cabinet or as electromagnetic impulses on a server that might be located anywhere. (Note that Rule 1.6 does not require an attorney to guarantee that a breach of confidentiality will never occur.)

Certainly, it is harder to maintain control over information stored on the cloud. Although the attorney "owns" the data, he or she probably does not even know the location of the computer where the information is stored. Furthermore, a provider of cloud computing services may move data from one server to another. Attorneys should be aware of jurisdictional issues and make sure that their cloud computing provider is complying with data protection regulations and privacy notification requirements wherever the provider's servers are located.

Litigation Issues

The problems presented by e-discovery become even more complex when information is stored in the cloud. Not only will adequate data maps have to be readily available during discovery and subsequent litigation, but the attorney will have to ascertain who will have access to sensitive information.

Attorneys must be particularly careful to avoid spoliation, or the negligent altering or destruction of evidence relevant to the litigation. Preserving information in the cloud can be more difficult if the data are spread across multiple physical storage sites. Sometimes, attorneys can be required to isolate the relevant data within their cloud computing provider's cloud resources.

Critical Thinking *To what extent must attorneys reveal to their clients where confidential data are stored?*

---

have the expertise and experience necessary to establish and maintain accurate financial records, and to design, control, and audit record-keeping systems. They also prepare reliable statements reflecting an individual's or a business's financial status, give tax advice, and prepare tax returns.

Generally, an accountant is expected to possess the skills that an ordinarily prudent accountant would have and to exercise the degree of care that an ordinarily prudent accountant would exercise. The level of skill expected of accountants and the degree of care that they should exercise in performing their services are reflected in the standards discussed next.

GAAP and GAAS. When performing their services, accountants must comply with **generally accepted** **accounting principles (GAAP)** and **generally accepted auditing standards (GAAS).** The Financial Accounting Standards Board (FASB, usually pronounced "faz-bee") determines what accounting conventions, rules, and procedures constitute GAAP at a given point in time. Similarly, the American Institute of Certified Public Accountants established GAAS to identify the professional qualities and the judgment that an auditor should exercise in auditing financial records.

A violation of GAAP and GAAS is considered *prima facie* evidence of negligence on the part of the accountant. Compliance with GAAP and GAAS, however, does not *necessarily* relieve an accountant from potential legal liability. An accountant may be held to a higher standard of conduct established by state statutes or by judicial decisions.

Global Accounting Rules. Although the United States has used the GAAP standards for many years, they are being replaced by global accounting rules. The Securities and Exchange Commission (SEC) now requires U.S. companies to use global accounting rules for all financial reports filed with the SEC. These rules, known as **International Financial Reporting Standards (IFRS),** are established by the London-based International Accounting Standards Board.

The SEC decided to replace GAAP with IFRS for several reasons. GAAP are rule based, whereas IFRS focus more on general principles. As a result, GAAP are very detailed and fill nearly 25,000 pages. IFRS are simpler, more straightforward, and shorter, filling only 2,500 pages. Consequently, companies should find it less difficult to comply with IFRS.

Another benefit is that investors will find it easier to make cross-country comparisons between the financial statements of, say, a technology company in Silicon Valley and one in Japan. Furthermore, having uniform accounting rules that apply to all nations makes sense in a global economy. The members of the European Union and more than one hundred other nations—including nearly all of the trading partners of the United States—use IFRS.

Discovering Improprieties. An accountant is not required to discover every impropriety, **defalcation**[1] (embezzlement), or fraud in a client's books. If, however, an impropriety goes undiscovered because of the accountant's negligence or failure to perform a duty, the accountant will be liable for any resulting losses suffered by the client. Therefore, an accountant who uncovers suspicious financial transactions and fails to investigate the matter fully or to inform the client of the discovery can be held liable to the client for the resulting loss.

Audits. One of the more important tasks that an accountant may perform for a business is an audit. An *audit* is a systematic inspection, by analyses and tests, of a business's financial records. An accountant qualified to perform audits is often called an **auditor.** After performing an audit, the auditor issues an opinion letter stating whether, in his or her opinion, the financial statements fairly present the business's financial position.

The purpose of an audit is to provide the auditor with evidence to support an opinion on the reliability of the business's financial statements. A normal audit is not intended to uncover fraud or other misconduct.

Nevertheless, an accountant may be liable for failing to detect misconduct if a normal audit would have revealed it. Also, if the auditor agreed to examine the records for evidence of fraud or other obvious misconduct and then failed to detect it, he or she may be liable.

Qualified Opinions and Disclaimers. In issuing an opinion letter, an auditor may *qualify* the opinion or include a *disclaimer*. In a qualified opinion, the auditor approves the financial statements overall but identifies one or two issues that are still in question. In a disclaimer, the auditor basically states that she or he does not have sufficient information to issue an opinion. A qualified opinion or a disclaimer must be specific and identify the reason for the qualification or disclaimer.

■ **EXAMPLE 47.1** Richard Zehr performs an audit of Lacey Corporation's financial statements. In the opinion letter, Zehr qualifies his opinion by stating that there is uncertainty about how a lawsuit against the firm will be resolved. In this situation, Zehr will not be liable if the outcome of the suit is unfavorable for the firm. Zehr could still be liable, however, if he failed to discover other problems that an audit in compliance with GAAS and IFRS would have revealed. ■

Unaudited Financial Statements. Sometimes, accountants are hired to prepare unaudited financial statements. (A financial statement is considered unaudited if incomplete auditing procedures have been used in its preparation or if insufficient procedures have been used to justify an opinion.) Lesser standards of care are typically required in this situation.

Nevertheless, accountants may be liable for omissions from unaudited statements. Accountants may be subject to liability for failing, in accordance with standard accounting procedures, to designate a balance sheet as "unaudited." An accountant will also be held liable for failure to disclose to a client facts or circumstances suggesting that misstatements have been made or that fraud has been committed.

Defenses to Negligence. If an accountant is found guilty of negligence, the client can collect damages for losses that arose from the accountant's negligence. An accountant facing a negligence claim, however, has several possible defenses, including the following:

1. The accountant was not negligent.
2. If the accountant was negligent, this negligence was not the proximate cause of the client's losses.
3. The client was also negligent (depending on whether the state applies contributory negligence or comparative negligence).

---

1. This term, pronounced deh-ful-*kay*-shun, is derived from the Latin *de* ("off") and *falx* ("sickle"—a tool for cutting grain or tall grass). In law, the term refers to the act of a defaulter or of an embezzler. As used here, it means embezzlement.

■ **EXAMPLE 47.2** Coopers & Peterson, LLP, provide accounting services for Bandon Steel Mills, Inc. (BSM). Coopers advises BSM to report a certain transaction as a $12.3 million gain on its financial statements. Later, BSM plans to make a public offering of its stock. The SEC reviews its financial statements and determines that the accounting treatment of the transaction has to be corrected before the sale.

Because of the delay, the public offering does not occur as planned on May 2, when BSM's stock is selling for $16 per share. It takes place instead on June 13, when, due to unrelated factors, the price has fallen to $13.50. If BSM files a lawsuit against Coopers claiming that the negligent accounting resulted in the stock's being sold at a lower price, BSM is unlikely to prevail. Although the accountant's negligence may have delayed the stock offering, the negligence was not the proximate cause of the decline in the stock price. Coopers would not be liable for damages based on the price decline. ■

Attorney's Duty of Care The conduct of attorneys is governed by rules established by each state and by the American Bar Association's Model Rules of Professional Conduct. All attorneys owe a duty to provide competent and diligent representation. Attorneys are required to be familiar with well-settled principles of law applicable to a case and to find relevant law that can be discovered through a reasonable amount of research. They must also investigate and discover facts that could materially affect clients' legal rights.

Normally, an attorney's performance is expected to be that of a reasonably competent general practitioner of ordinary skill, experience, and capacity. Often, an attorney holds himself or herself out as having expertise in a particular area of law (such as intellectual property). In this instance, the attorney is held to a higher standard of care in that area of law than attorneys without such knowledge.

Misconduct. Typically, state rules of professional conduct for attorneys provide that committing a criminal act that reflects adversely on the attorney's "honesty or trustworthiness, or fitness as a lawyer" is professional misconduct. The rules often further provide that a lawyer should not engage in conduct involving "dishonesty, fraud, deceit, or misrepresentation." Under these rules, state authorities can discipline attorneys for many types of misconduct.

Note, though, that states do not frequently discipline attorneys if their misconduct does not reflect on their honesty and trustworthiness. ■ **CASE IN POINT 47.3** Daniel Johns, a Wisconsin attorney, was the driver in a one-vehicle drunk driving accident in which his brother was killed. He pleaded guilty to homicide by use of a vehicle while driving with a blood alcohol level over the legal limit. Johns served 120 days in jail and was released on five years' probation. The court terminated his probation early because of his good behavior, and he went back to practicing law.

The state's office of lawyer regulation (OLR) then initiated disciplinary proceedings seeking to suspend Johns's license to practice for sixty days for professional misconduct. The court, however, explained that the "commission of a criminal act by a Wisconsin licensed lawyer does not, *per se,* constitute professional misconduct." The OLR had not proved that Johns's crime reflected adversely on his honesty, trustworthiness, or fitness as a lawyer in other respects. In fact, except for this one tragic event, Johns had led an exemplary life without a hint of professional misconduct. The court therefore dismissed the disciplinary complaint.[2] ■

Liability for Malpractice. When an attorney fails to exercise reasonable care and professional judgment, she or he breaches the duty of care and can be held liable for *malpractice* (professional negligence). In malpractice cases—as in all cases involving allegations of negligence—the plaintiff must prove that the attorney's breach of the duty of care actually caused the plaintiff to suffer some injury.

■ **CASE IN POINT 47.4** The law firm of Husch Blackwell Sanders, LLP, represented Brian Nail in a dispute with his former employer over stock options. When Nail left the company, he acquired options to purchase his former employer's stock within eighteen months. But then the former employer merged with another company, and the stock was "locked up" for twelve months after the merger. The value of the stock declined significantly during this period. Husch Blackwell eventually negotiated a settlement that extended Nail's option period. When Nail attempted to exercise his options under the settlement agreement, however, complications arose that prevented him from immediately obtaining the stock.

Nail sued Husch Blackwell in a Missouri state court for malpractice, alleging that the firm had negligently drafted the settlement agreement and negligently delayed advising him to exercise the options. Nail sought to recover damages equal to the difference between the highest value of the stock during the lock-up period and his cost to acquire the stock. The trial court granted a summary judgment in favor of the law firm, and the Missouri Supreme Court affirmed. Nail had failed to prove that Husch Blackwell's alleged negligence was the proximate

---

2. *In re Disciplinary Proceedings against Johns,* 2014 WI 32, 353 Wis.2d 746, 847 N.W.2d 179 (2014).

cause of his damages. The decline in the stock price was unrelated to the law firm's alleged misconduct.[3] ∎

47-1c Liability for Fraud

Fraud, or misrepresentation, involves the following elements:

1. A misrepresentation of a material fact.
2. An intent to deceive.
3. Justifiable reliance by the innocent party on the misrepresentation.

In addition, to obtain damages, the innocent party must have been injured. Both actual and constructive fraud are potential sources of legal liability for an accountant or other professional.

Actual Fraud A professional may be held liable for *actual* fraud when (1) he or she intentionally misstates a material fact to mislead a client and (2) the client is injured as a result of justifiably relying on the misstated fact. A material fact is one that a reasonable person would consider important in deciding whether to act.

Among other penalties, an accountant guilty of fraudulent conduct may suffer penalties imposed by a state board of accountancy. ∎ **CASE IN POINT 47.5** Michael Walsh, a certified public accountant (CPA), impersonated his brother-in-law, Stephen Teiper, on the phone to obtain financial information from Teiper's insurance company. Teiper wrote a letter reporting Walsh's conduct to the Nebraska Board of Public Accountancy. After a hearing, the board reprimanded Walsh, placed him on probation for three months, and ordered him to attend four hours of ethics training. He also had to pay the costs of the hearing. The Nebraska Supreme Court affirmed the board's decision on appeal.[4] ∎

Constructive Fraud A professional may sometimes be held liable for **constructive fraud** whether or not he or she acted with fraudulent intent. Constructive fraud may be found when a professional is grossly negligent in performing his or her duties. ∎ **EXAMPLE 47.6** Paula, an accountant, is conducting an audit of ComCo, Inc. Paula accepts the explanations of Ron, a ComCo officer, regarding certain financial irregularities, despite evidence that contradicts those explanations and indicates that the irregularities may be illegal. Paula's conduct could be characterized as an intentional failure to perform a duty

in reckless disregard of the consequences of such failure. This would constitute gross negligence and could be held to be constructive fraud. ∎

47-2 Potential Liability to Third Parties

Traditionally, a professional owed a duty only to those with whom she or he had a direct contractual relationship—that is, those with whom she or he was in *privity of contract*. A professional's duty was only to her or his client. Violations of statutes, fraud, and other intentional or reckless acts of wrongdoing were the only exceptions to this general rule.

Today, this situation has changed, perhaps most noticeably with respect to accountants who conduct audits (auditors). Numerous third parties—including investors, shareholders, creditors, corporate managers and directors, and regulatory agencies—rely on the opinions of auditors when making decisions. In view of this extensive reliance, many courts have all but abandoned the privity requirement in regard to accountants' liability to third parties.

In this discussion, we focus primarily on the potential liability of auditors to third parties. Understanding an auditor's common law liability to third parties is critical. Often, when a business fails, its independent auditor may be one of the few defendants still *solvent*—that is, able to pay expenses and debts. The majority of courts now hold that auditors can be held liable to third parties for negligence, but the standard for the imposition of this liability varies.

47-2a The *Ultramares* Rule

The traditional rule regarding an accountant's liability to third parties based on privity of contract was enunciated by Chief Judge Benjamin Cardozo in 1931. ∎ **CASE IN POINT 47.7** Fred Stern & Company had hired the public accounting firm of Touche, Niven & Company to review Stern's financial records and prepare a balance sheet for the year ending December 31, 1923.[5] Touche prepared the balance sheet and supplied Stern with thirty-two certified copies. According to the certified balance sheet, Stern had a net worth (assets less liabilities) of $1,070,715.26.

---

3. *Nail v. Husch Blackwell Sanders, LLP*, 436 S.W.3d 556 (2014).
4. *Walsh v. State*, 276 Neb. 1034, 759 N.W.2d 100 (2009).

5. Banks, creditors, stockholders, purchasers, and sellers often rely on balance sheets when making decisions related to a company's business.

In reality, however, Stern's liabilities exceeded its assets—the company's records had been falsified by insiders at Stern to reflect a positive net worth. In reliance on the certified balance sheets, Ultramares Corporation loaned substantial amounts to Stern. After Stern was declared bankrupt, Ultramares brought an action against Touche for negligence in an attempt to recover damages.

The New York Court of Appeals (that state's highest court) refused to impose liability on Touche. The court concluded that Touche's accountants owed a duty of care only to those persons for whose "primary benefit" the statements were intended. In this case, the statements were intended only for the primary benefit of Stern. The court held that in the absence of privity or a relationship "so close as to approach that of privity," a party could not recover from an accountant.[6] ∎

The Requirement of Privity The requirement of privity has since been referred to as the *Ultramares* rule, or the New York rule. It continues to be used in some states. ∎ **CASE IN POINT 47.8** Toro Company supplied equipment and credit to Summit Power Equipment Distributors and required Summit to submit audited reports indicating its financial condition. Accountants at Krouse, Kern & Company prepared the reports, which allegedly contained mistakes and omissions regarding Summit's financial condition.

Toro extended large amounts of credit to Summit in reliance on the audited reports. When Summit was unable to repay these amounts, Toro brought a negligence action against Krouse and proved that the accountants knew the reports would be used by Summit to induce Toro to extend credit. Nevertheless, under the *Ultramares* rule, the court refused to hold the accounting firm liable because the firm was not in privity with Toro.[7] ∎

Modification to Allow "Near Privity" The *Ultramares* rule was restated and somewhat modified in a 1985 New York case, *Credit Alliance Corp. v. Arthur Andersen & Co.*[8] In that case, the court held that if a third party has a sufficiently close relationship or *nexus* (connection) with an accountant, then the *Ultramares* privity requirement may be satisfied without the establishment of an accountant-client relationship. The rule enunciated in the *Credit Alliance* case is often referred to as the "near privity"

rule. Only a minority of states have adopted this rule of accountants' liability to third parties.

47–2b The *Restatement* Rule

The *Ultramares* rule has been severely criticized. Much of the work performed by auditors is intended for use by persons who are not parties to the contract. Critics of the *Ultramares* rule assert that auditors should owe a duty to these third parties. As support for this position has grown, there has been an erosion of the *Ultramares* rule, and accountants may now be liable to third parties in some situations.

The majority of courts have adopted the position taken by the *Restatement (Third) of Torts*. This rule states that accountants are subject to liability for negligence not only to their clients but also to foreseen, or known, users of their reports or financial statements. Under the *Restatement (Third) of Torts*, an accountant's liability extends to:

1. Persons for whose benefit and guidance the accountant intends to supply the information or knows that the recipient intends to supply it.
2. Persons whom the accountant intends the information to influence or knows that the recipient so intends.

∎ **EXAMPLE 47.9** Steve, an accountant, prepares a financial statement for Tech Software, Inc., a client, knowing that Tech will submit that statement when it applies for a loan from First National Bank. If the statement includes negligent misstatements or omissions, the bank may hold Steve liable, because he knew that the bank would rely on his work when deciding whether to make the loan. ∎

47–2c The "Reasonably Foreseeable Users" Rule

A small minority of courts hold accountants liable to any users whose reliance on an accountant's statements or reports was *reasonably foreseeable*. This standard has been criticized as extending liability too far and exposing accountants to massive liability.

The majority of courts have concluded that the *Restatement's* approach is more reasonable because it allows accountants to control their exposure to liability. Liability is "fixed by the accountants' particular knowledge at the moment the audit is published," not by the foreseeability of the harm that might occur to a third party after the report is released.

Exhibit 47–1 summarizes the three different views of accountants' liability to third parties.

---

6. *Ultramares Corp. v. Touche*, 255 N.Y. 170, 174 N.E. 441 (1931).
7. *Toro Co. v. Krouse, Kern & Co.*, 827 F.2d 155 (7th Cir. 1987). See also *Citibank, F.S.B. v. McGladrey & Pullen, LLP*, 2007 WL 7134666 (Ill. 2007).
8. 65 N.Y.2d 536, 483 N.E.2d 110 (1985). A "relationship sufficiently intimate to be equated with privity" is enough for a third party to sue another's accountant for negligence.

EXHIBIT 47–1 Three Basic Rules of an Accountant's Liability to Third Parties

RULE	DESCRIPTION	APPLICATION
The *Ultramares* Rule	Liability will be imposed only if the accountant is in privity, or near privity, with the third party.	A minority of courts apply this rule.
The *Restatement* Rule	Liability will be imposed only if the third party's reliance is foreseen, or known, or if the third party is among a class of foreseen, or known, users.	The majority of courts have adopted this rule.
The "Reasonably Foreseeable Users" Rule	Liability will be imposed only if the third party's use was reasonably foreseeable.	A small minority of courts use this rule.

47–2d Liability of Attorneys to Third Parties

Like accountants, attorneys may be held liable under the common law to third parties who rely on legal opinions to their detriment. Generally, an attorney is not liable to a nonclient unless the attorney has committed fraud (or malicious conduct). The liability principles stated in the *Restatement (Third) of Torts,* however, may apply to attorneys as well as to accountants.

Should an attorney's duty of care extend to third party beneficiaries whose rights were harmed by the attorney's malpractice? That question was at issue in the following case.

Case Analysis 47.1

Perez[a] v. Stern

Nebraska Supreme Court, 279 Neb. 187, 777 N.W.2d 545 (2010).

In the Language of the Court
GERRARD, J. [Justice]
* * * *

[Reyna] Guido is the mother of two minor children. [Domingo] Martinez, the children's father, died after he was run over by a car on July 8, 2001. Martinez was the victim of a hit-and-run accident.

Guido, as personal representative of Martinez's estate, retained [Sandra] Stern to file a wrongful death lawsuit. On July 8, 2003, Stern filed a wrongful death complaint in the district court. But Stern admits that she never perfected service of the complaint, and because the complaint was not served within six months of filing, the case was dismissed by operation of law.

* * * On February 6, 2007, Guido filed these legal malpractice claims against Stern on behalf of herself, the children, and the estate. Guido alleged that the wrongful death claim expired as a result of Stern's failure to timely perfect service of the complaint. Stern moved for summary judgment on the ground that the malpractice claims were barred by the two-year statute of limitations for professional negligence. Before the court ruled on the motion, Guido voluntarily dismissed her individual claim, but maintained claims as personal representative of the estate and next friend of the children.

The district court found that the malpractice claims accrued on May 7, 2004, when the wrongful death claim was dismissed. The court found that the estate's claim against Stern was time barred. In response to Guido's argument that the children's minority tolled

[suspended] the statute of limitations with respect to them, the court found that because the children could not have brought the underlying wrongful death claim in their own names, the statute of limitations for the legal malpractice claims was not tolled by reason of the children's minority. The court granted summary judgment in favor of Stern and dismissed the complaint.

* * * *

Guido [appealed, claiming] that the district court erred in granting Stern's motion for summary judgment on her affirmative defense of the statute of limitations and, specifically, determining that the children had no independent standing to sue Stern and that Stern owed no independent duty to the minor children to protect their rights and interests.

---

a. Estaban Perez was one of the minor children of Domingo Martinez, the man killed in the accident.

Case 47.1 Continued

We note that neither Guido's assignments of error nor the argument in her appellate brief challenges the district court's dismissal of Guido's claims as an individual and as personal representative of Martinez's estate. Therefore, those aspects of the court's judgment will be affirmed.

* * * *

The issue in this case is whether Stern owed an independent duty to the children, as Martinez's next of kin, to timely prosecute the underlying wrongful death claim.

* * * *

In Nebraska, *a lawyer owes a duty to his or her client to use reasonable care and skill in the discharge of his or her duties, but ordinarily this duty does not extend to third parties, absent facts establishing a duty to them.* [Emphasis added.]

But that does not end our analysis. * * * We have never said that privity [of contract] is an absolute requirement of a legal malpractice claim. Instead, we have said that a lawyer's duty to use reasonable care and skill in the discharge of his or her duties *ordinarily* does not extend to third parties, *absent facts establishing a duty to them.* On the facts of this case, we conclude, as have other courts to have addressed this issue in the context of a wrongful death action, that the facts establish an independent legal duty from Stern to Martinez's statutory beneficiaries. [Emphasis in the original]

* * * Courts have repeatedly emphasized that *the starting point for analyzing an attorney's duty to a third party is determining whether the third party was a direct and intended beneficiary of the attorney's services.* [Emphasis added.]

* * * *

In this case, we conclude that Stern owed a duty to the children, as direct and intended beneficiaries of her services, to competently represent their interests. To hold otherwise would deny legal recourse to the children for whose benefit Stern was hired in the first place.

* * * Stern owed a legal duty to Martinez's minor children to exercise reasonable care in representing their interests. Therefore, they have standing to sue Stern for neglecting that duty, and their claims against Stern were tolled by their minority. The district court erred in concluding that their claims were time barred. We affirm the court's dismissal of Guido's individual claim and its determination that the estate's claim against Stern was time barred. But with respect to the children, this cause is reversed and remanded for further proceedings to fully adjudicate Guido's claims on behalf of the children * * * .

Affirmed in part, and in part reversed and remanded for further proceedings.

Legal Reasoning Questions

1. If the children had suffered no harm as a result of the attorney's malpractice, would the outcome of this case have been different? Why or why not?

2. Why did the court affirm the dismissal of Guido's individual claim but not the claims that she had brought on behalf of the children?

3. If one of the children had not been a minor at the time of the father's death, the court would have dismissed that child's claims against Stern, even though the child was an intended beneficiary. Is it fair for the law to treat minors differently from other children with regard to a statute of limitations? Why or why not?

Concept Summary 47.1 reviews the common law rules under which accountants, attorneys, and other professionals may be held liable.

47-3 The Sarbanes-Oxley Act

The Sarbanes-Oxley Act imposes a number of strict requirements on both domestic and foreign public accounting firms. These requirements apply to firms that provide auditing services to companies ("issuers") whose securities are sold to public investors. The act defines the term *issuer* as a company (1) that has securities registered under Section 12 of the Securities Exchange Act of 1934, (2) that is required to file reports under Section 15(d) of the 1934 act, or (3) that has filed a registration statement that has not yet become effective under the Securities Act of 1933.

47-3a The Public Company Accounting Oversight Board

The Sarbanes-Oxley Act increased government oversight of public accounting practices by creating the Public Company Accounting Oversight Board, which reports to the Securities and Exchange Commission. The board oversees the audit of public companies that are subject to securities laws. The goal is to protect public investors and to ensure that public accounting firms comply with the provisions of the act. The act defines *public accounting*

Concept Summary 47.1

Common Law Liability of Accountants and Other Professionals

Liability to Clients	• *Breach of contract*—A professional who fails to perform according to his or her contractual obligations can be held liable for breach of contract and resulting damages. • *Negligence*—An accountant, attorney, or other professional, in performing her or his duties, must use the care, knowledge, and judgment generally used by professionals in the same or similar circumstances. Failure to do so is negligence. An accountant's violation of generally accepted accounting principles and generally accepted auditing standards is *prima facie* evidence of negligence. • *Fraud*—Intentionally misrepresenting a material fact to a client, when the client relies on the misrepresentation, is actual fraud. Gross negligence in performance of duties is constructive fraud.
Liability to Third Parties	• *Liability of accountants*—An accountant may be liable for negligence to any third person the accountant knows or should have known will benefit from the accountant's work. The standard for imposing this liability varies, but generally courts follow the *Ultramares* rule, the *Restatement* rule, or the "Reasonably Foreseeable Users" rule. • *Liability of attorneys*—An attorney generally is not liable to a nonclient unless the attorney committed fraud or other malicious conduct. In some situations, an attorney may be liable to persons whose reliance is foreseen or known.

---

firms as firms "engaged in the practice of public accounting or preparing or issuing audit reports." Smaller companies—those with less than $75 million in publicly held shares—no longer need to file an auditor's report on management's assessment of internal controls under Section 404(b). The key provisions relating to the duties of the oversight board and the requirements relating to public accounting firms are summarized in Exhibit 47–2.

47–3b Requirements for Maintaining Working Papers

In performing an audit for a client, an accountant accumulates various **working papers**—the documents used and developed during the audit. These include notes, computations, memoranda, copies, and other papers that make up the work product of an accountant's services to a client.

Under the common law, which in this instance has been codified in a number of states, working papers remain the accountant's property. It is important for accountants to retain such records in the event that they need to defend against lawsuits for negligence or other actions in which their competence is challenged. The client also has a right to access an accountant's working papers because they reflect the client's financial situation. On a client's request, an accountant must return any of the client's records or journals to the client, and failure to do so may result in liability.

The Sarbanes-Oxley Act initially provided that accountants must maintain working papers relating to an audit or review for five years from the end of the fiscal period in which the audit or review was concluded. The period was subsequently increased to seven years. A knowing violation of this requirement will subject the accountant to a fine, imprisonment for up to ten years, or both.

EXHIBIT 47–2   Key Provisions of the Sarbanes-Oxley Act Relating to Public Accounting Firms

AUDITOR INDEPENDENCE

To help ensure that auditors remain independent of the firms that they audit, Title II of the Sarbanes-Oxley Act does the following:

1. Makes it unlawful for Registered Public Accounting Firms (RPAFs) to perform both audit and nonaudit services for the same company at the same time. Nonaudit services include the following:

   - Bookkeeping or other services related to the accounting records or financial statements of the audit client.
   - Financial information systems design and implementation.
   - Appraisal or valuation services.
   - Fairness opinions.
   - Management functions.
   - Broker or dealer, investment adviser, or investment banking services.

2. Requires preapproval for most auditing services from the issuer's (the corporation's) audit committee.

3. Requires audit partner rotation by prohibiting RPAFs from providing audit services to an issuer if either the lead audit partner or the audit partner responsible for reviewing the audit has provided such services to that corporation in each of the prior five years.

4. Requires RPAFs to make timely reports to the audit committees of the corporations. The report must indicate all critical accounting policies and practices to be used; all alternative treatments of financial information within generally accepted accounting principles that have been discussed with the corporation's management officials, the ramifications of the use of such alternative treatments, and the treatment preferred by the auditor; and other material written communications between the auditor and the corporation's management.

5. Makes it unlawful for an RPAF to provide auditing services to an issuer if the corporation's chief executive officer, chief financial officer, chief accounting officer, or controller was previously employed by the auditor and participated in any capacity in the audit of the corporation during the one-year period preceding the date when the audit began.

DOCUMENT DESTRUCTION

The Sarbanes-Oxley Act provides that anyone who destroys, alters, or falsifies records with the intent to obstruct or influence a federal investigation or in relation to bankruptcy proceedings can be criminally prosecuted and sentenced to a fine, imprisonment for up to twenty years, or both.

DOCUMENT RETENTION

The Sarbanes-Oxley Act also requires accountants who audit or review publicly traded companies to retain all working papers related to the audit or review for a period of five years (now amended to seven years). Violators can be sentenced to a fine, imprisonment for up to ten years, or both.

47–4 Potential Liability of Accountants under Securities Laws

Both civil and criminal liability may be imposed on accountants under the Securities Act of 1933, the Securities Exchange Act of 1934, and the Private Securities Litigation Reform Act of 1995.[9]

47–4a Liability under the Securities Act of 1933

The Securities Act of 1933 requires registration statements to be filed with the Securities and Exchange Commission (SEC) prior to an offering of securities.[10] Accountants frequently prepare and certify the issuer's financial statements that are included in the registration statement.

---

9. Civil and criminal liability may also be imposed on accountants and other professionals under other statutes, including the Racketeer Influenced and Corrupt Organizations Act (RICO).

---

10. Many securities and transactions are expressly exempted from the 1933 act.

Liability under Section 11 Section 11 of the Securities Act imposes civil liability on accountants for misstatements and omissions of material facts in registration statements. Accountants may be held liable if a financial statement they prepared for inclusion "contained an untrue statement of a material fact or omitted to state a material fact required to be stated therein or necessary to make the statements therein not misleading."[11]

An accountant may be liable to anyone who acquires a security covered by the registration statement. A purchaser of a security need only demonstrate that she or he has suffered a loss on the security. Proof of reliance on the materially false statement or misleading omission ordinarily is not required. Nor is there a requirement of privity between the accountant and the security purchaser.

The Due Diligence Standard. Section 11 imposes a duty on accountants to use **due diligence** in preparing financial statements included in the filed registration statements. Once a purchaser has proved a loss on a security, the accountant has the burden of showing that he or she exercised due diligence.

To prove due diligence, the accountant must demonstrate that she or he followed generally accepted standards and did not commit negligence or fraud. The accountant must show that he or she:

1. Conducted a reasonable investigation.
2. Had reasonable grounds to believe and did believe, at the time the registration statement became effective, that the statements therein were true and that there was no omission of a material fact that would be misleading.[12]

In particular, the due diligence standard places a burden on accountants to verify information furnished by a corporation's officers and directors. Merely asking questions is not always sufficient to satisfy the requirement of due diligence. Accountants may be held liable, for instance, for failing to detect danger signals in documents furnished by corporate officers that required further investigation.

Other Defenses to Liability. Besides proving that he or she has acted with due diligence, an accountant may raise the following defenses to Section 11 liability:

1. There were no misstatements or omissions.
2. The misstatements or omissions were not of material facts.

3. The misstatements or omissions had no causal connection to the plaintiff's loss.
4. The plaintiff-purchaser invested in the securities knowing of the misstatements or omissions.

Liability under Section 12(2) Section 12(2) of the 1933 Securities Act imposes civil liability for fraud in relation to offerings or sales of securities.[13] Liability arises when the offeror or seller makes an oral statement to an investor or provides a written prospectus[14] that includes an untrue statement or omits a material fact. Accountants may be liable under Section 12(2) if they participated in preparing materials in which the false misrepresentation or omission was made.

Those who purchase securities and suffer harm as a result of a false or omitted statement, or some other violation, may bring a suit in a federal court to recover their losses and other damages. The U.S. Department of Justice brings criminal actions against those who commit willful violations.

The penalties include fines up to $10,000, imprisonment up to five years, or both. The SEC is authorized to seek an injunction against a willful violator to prevent further violations. The SEC can also ask a court to grant other relief, such as an order to a violator to refund profits derived from an illegal transaction.

47–4b Liability under the Securities Exchange Act of 1934

Under Sections 18 and 10(b) of the 1934 Securities Exchange Act and SEC Rule 10b-5, an accountant may be found liable for fraud. A plaintiff has a substantially heavier burden of proof under the 1934 act than under the 1933 act because an accountant does not have to prove due diligence to escape liability under the 1934 act. The 1934 act relieves an accountant from liability if the accountant acted in "good faith."

Liability under Section 18 Section 18 of the 1934 act imposes civil liability on an accountant who makes or causes to be made in any application, report, or document a statement that at the time and in light of the circumstances was false or misleading with respect to any material fact.[15]

Section 18 liability is narrow in that it applies only to applications, reports, documents, and registration

---

11. 15 U.S.C. Section 77k(a).
12. 15 U.S.C. Section 77k(b)(3).

---

13. 15 U.S.C. Section 77*l*.
14. A *prospectus* contains financial disclosures about the corporation for the benefit of potential investors.
15. 15 U.S.C. Section 78r(a).

statements filed with the SEC. In addition, it applies only to sellers and purchasers. Under Section 18, a seller or purchaser must prove one of the following:

1. The false or misleading statement affected the price of the security.
2. The purchaser or seller relied on the false or misleading statement in making the purchase or sale and was not aware of the inaccuracy of the statement.

Sellers and purchasers must bring a cause of action "within one year after the discovery of the facts constituting the cause of action and within three years after such cause of action accrued."[16] A court has the discretion to assess reasonable costs, including attorneys' fees, against accountants who violate Section 18.

Good Faith Defense. An accountant will not be liable for violating Section 18 if he or she acted in good faith in preparing the financial statement. To demonstrate good faith, an accountant must show that he or she had no knowledge that the financial statement was false or misleading. Also, the accountant must have had no intent to deceive, manipulate, defraud, or seek unfair advantage over another party.

Other Defenses. In addition to the good faith defense, accountants can escape liability by proving that the buyer or seller of the security in question knew that the financial statement was false and misleading. Note, too, that "mere" negligence in preparing a financial statement does not lead to liability under the 1934 act. This differs from the 1933 act, under which an accountant is liable for all negligent acts.

Liability under Section 10(b) and SEC Rule 10b-5

Accountants additionally face potential legal liability under the antifraud provisions contained in the Securities Exchange Act and SEC Rule 10b-5. The scope of these antifraud provisions is very broad and allows private parties to bring civil actions against violators.

Prohibited Conduct. Section 10(b) makes it unlawful for any person, including an accountant, to use, in connection with the purchase or sale of any security, any manipulative or deceptive device or plan that is counter to SEC rules and regulations.[17] Rule 10b-5 further makes it unlawful for any person, by use of any means or instrumentality of interstate commerce, to do the following:

1. Employ any device, scheme, or strategy to defraud.
2. Make any untrue statement of a material fact or omit to state a material fact necessary to make the statements made, in light of the circumstances, not misleading.
3. Engage in any act, practice, or course of business that operates or would operate as a fraud or deceit on any person, in connection with the purchase or sale of any security.[18]

Extent of Liability. Accountants may be held liable only to sellers or purchasers of securities under Section 10(b) and Rule 10b-5. Privity is not necessary for a recovery. An accountant may be liable not only for fraudulent misstatements of material facts in written material filed with the SEC, but also for any fraudulent oral statements or omissions made in connection with the purchase or sale of any security.

For a plaintiff to succeed in recovering damages under these antifraud provisions, he or she must prove intent *(scienter)* to commit the fraudulent or deceptive act. Ordinary negligence is not enough.

Do accountants have a duty to correct misstatements that they discover in *previous* financial statements if they know that potential investors are relying on those statements? That was the question in the following case.

---

16. 15 U.S.C. Section 17r(c).

17. 15 U.S.C. Section 78j(b).
18. 17 C.F.R. Section 240.10b-5.

Spotlight on Accountant's Duty to Correct Mistakes

Case 47.2 Overton v. Todman & Co., CPAs
United States Court of Appeals, Second Circuit, 478 F.3d 479 (2007).

Background and Facts From 1999 through 2002, Todman & Company, CPAs, P.C., audited the financial statements of Direct Brokerage, Inc. (DBI), a broker-dealer in New York registered with the Securities and Exchange Commission (SEC). Each year, Todman issued an unqualified opinion that DBI's financial statements were accurate. DBI filed its statements and Todman's opinions with the SEC.

Case 47.2 Continues

Case 47.2 Continued

Despite the certifications of accuracy, Todman made significant errors that concealed DBI's largest liability—its payroll taxes—in the 1999 and 2000 audits. The errors came to light in 2003 when the New York State Division of Taxation subpoenaed DBI's payroll records. It became clear that the company had not filed or paid its payroll taxes for 1999 and 2000. This put DBI in a precarious financial position, owing the state more than $3 million in unpaid taxes, interest, and penalties.

To meet its needs, DBI sought outside investors, including David Overton, who relied on DBI's statements and Todman's opinion for 2002 to invest in DBI. When DBI collapsed under the weight of its liabilities in 2004, Overton and others filed a suit in a federal district court against Todman. Among other things, the plaintiffs asserted fraud under Section 10(b) and Rule 10b-5. The court dismissed the complaint. The plaintiffs appealed to the U.S. Court of Appeals for the Second Circuit.

In the Language of the Court
STRAUB, Circuit Judge.
* * * *

A fundamental principle of securities law is that before an individual becomes liable for his silence, he must have an underlying duty to speak. [Emphasis added.]
* * * *

* * * The Supreme Court [has] held that [Section] 10(b) does not authorize aiding and abetting liability. In order to be liable under [Section] 10(b), the Court held, an actor must himself "mak[e] * * * a material misstatement (or omission) or * * * commit * * * a manipulative act." The rationale underpinning this holding was that (1) by its terms, [Section] 10(b) requires the making of a statement or omission and (2) without such a statement or omission, the "critical" element of reliance would be absent.

Although the Court did not specifically discuss an auditor's duty to correct, it made clear that * * * secondary actors such as accountants may incur primary liability based on their omissions * * *.

* * * For many years we have recognized the existence of an accountant's duty to correct its certified opinions, but never squarely held that such a duty exists for the purposes of primary liability under [Section] 10(b) of the 1934 Act and Rule 10b-5. Presented with an opportunity to do so, we now so hold. *Specifically, we hold that an accountant violates the "duty to correct" and becomes primarily liable under [Section] 10(b) and Rule 10b-5 when it (1) makes a statement in its certified opinion that is false or misleading when made; (2) subsequently learns or was reckless in not learning that the earlier statement was false or misleading; (3) knows or should know that potential investors are relying on the opinion and financial statements; yet (4) fails to take reasonable steps to correct or withdraw its opinion and/or the financial statements; and (5) all the other requirements for liability are satisfied.* [Emphasis added.]
* * * *

In light of the above principles, we conclude that the District Court erred in dismissing the complaint. Plaintiffs pled that Todman's certified opinion and DBI's 2002 financial statements were misleading at the time they were issued, especially with respect to DBI's payroll tax liability; Todman * * * subsequently learned that its certified opinion was false; Todman also knew that DBI was soliciting outside investors based in part on its 2002 certified financial statements and Todman's accompanying opinion; and that despite this knowledge, Todman took no action to correct or withdraw its opinion and/or DBI's financial statements. These allegations adequately state a claim of primary accountant liability under [Section] 10(b) and Rule 10b-5.

Decision and Remedy *The U.S. Court of Appeals for the Second Circuit held that an accountant is liable in these circumstances under Section 10(b) and Rule 10b-5. The court vacated the lower court's dismissal and remanded the case.*

Critical Thinking
- **What If the Facts Were Different?** *If Todman had conducted an audit for DBI but had not issued a certified opinion about DBI's financial statements, would the result in this case have been the same? Explain.*
- **Legal Environment** *Did Overton have a valid reason to sue DBI's auditors? Why or why not?*

47–4c The Private Securities Litigation Reform Act of 1995

The Private Securities Litigation Reform Act made some changes to the potential liability of accountants and other professionals in securities fraud cases. Among other things, the act imposed a statutory obligation on accountants. An auditor must use adequate procedures in an audit to detect any illegal acts of the company being audited. If something illegal is detected, the auditor must disclose it to the company's board of directors, the audit committee, or the SEC, depending on the circumstances.[19]

Proportionate Liability The act provides that, in most situations, a party is liable only for the proportion of damages for which he or she is responsible.[20] In other words, the parties are subject to proportionate liability rather than joint and several liability. An accountant who participates in, but is unaware of, illegal conduct may not be liable for the entire amount of the loss caused by the illegality.

■ **EXAMPLE 47.10** Nina Chavez, an accountant, helped the president and owner of Midstate Trucking Company draft financial statements that misrepresented Midstate's financial condition. If Nina was not actually aware of the fraud, she can still be held liable, but the amount of her liability could be less than the entire loss. ■

Aiding and Abetting The act also made it a crime to aid and abet a violation of the 1934 Securities Exchange Act. Aiding and abetting might include knowingly participating or assisting in some improper activity or keeping quiet about it. If an accountant knowingly aids and abets a primary violator, the SEC can seek an injunction or monetary damages.

■ **EXAMPLE 47.11** Smith & Jones, an accounting firm, performs an audit for Belco Sales Company that is so inadequate as to constitute gross negligence. Belco uses the financial statements provided by Smith & Jones as part of a scheme to defraud investors. When the scheme is uncovered, the SEC can bring an action against Smith & Jones for aiding and abetting. The firm knew or should have known that its audited statements contained material misrepresentations on which investors were likely to rely. ■

47–4d Potential Criminal Liability of Accountants

An accountant may be found criminally liable for violations of securities laws and tax laws. In addition, most states make it a crime to (1) knowingly certify false reports, (2) falsify, alter, or destroy books of account, and (3) obtain property or credit through the use of false financial statements.

Criminal Violations of Securities Laws Accountants may be subject to criminal penalties for *willful* violations of the 1933 Securities Act and the 1934 Securities Exchange Act. If convicted, they face imprisonment for up to five years and/or a fine of up to $10,000 under the 1933 act and imprisonment for up to ten years and a fine of $100,000 under the 1934 act.

Under the Sarbanes-Oxley Act, if an accountant's false or misleading certified audit statement is used in a securities filing, the accountant may be held criminally liable. The accountant may be fined up to $5 million, imprisoned for up to twenty years, or both.

Criminal Violations of Tax Laws The Internal Revenue Code makes it a felony to aid or assist in the preparation of a false tax return. Violations are punishable by a fine of $100,000 ($500,000 for a corporation's return) and imprisonment for up to three years.[21] This provision applies to anyone who prepares tax returns for others for compensation, not just to accountants.[22]

A penalty of $250 per tax return is levied on tax preparers for negligent understatement of the client's tax liability. For willful understatement of tax liability or reckless or intentional disregard of rules or regulations, a penalty of $1,000 is imposed.[23]

A tax preparer may also be subject to penalties for failing to furnish the taxpayer with a copy of the return, failing to sign the return, or failing to furnish the appropriate tax identification numbers.[24] In addition, those who prepare tax returns for others may be fined $1,000 per document for aiding and abetting another's understatement of tax liability (the penalty is increased to $10,000 for corporate returns).[25] The tax preparer's liability is limited to one penalty per taxpayer per tax year.

Concept Summary 47.2 outlines the potential statutory liability of accountants and other professionals.

---

19. 15 U.S.C. Section 78j-1.
20. 15 U.S.C. Section 78u-4(g).

21. 26 U.S.C. Section 7206(2).
22. 26 U.S.C. Section 7701(a)(36).
23. 26 U.S.C. Section 6694.
24. 26 U.S.C. Section 6695.
25. 26 U.S.C. Section 6701.

Concept Summary 47.2

Statutory Law Liability of Accountants and Other Professionals

Sarbanes-Oxley Act	• See Exhibit 47–2 for key the provisions of the act.
Securities Act of 1933, Sections 11 and 12(2)	• Under Section 11 of the 1933 Securities Act, an accountant who makes a false statement or omits a material fact in audited financial statements required for registration of securities under the law may be liable to anyone who acquires securities covered by the registration statement. • The accountant's defense is basically the use of due diligence and the reasonable belief that the work was complete and correct. The burden of proof is on the accountant. • Willful violations of this act may be subject to criminal penalties. • Section 12(2) of the 1933 act imposes civil liability for fraud on anyone who makes an untrue statement or omits a material fact when offering or selling a security to any purchaser of the security.
Securities Exchange Act of 1934, Sections 10(b) and 18	• Under Sections 10(b) and 18 of the 1934 Securities Exchange Act, accountants are held liable for false and misleading applications, reports, and documents required under the act. • The burden is on the plaintiff, and the accountant has numerous defenses, including good faith and lack of knowledge that what was submitted was false. • Willful violations of this act may be subject to criminal penalties.
Internal Revenue Code	• Aiding or assisting in the preparation of a false tax return is a felony. Aiding and abetting an individual's understatement of tax liability is a separate crime. • Tax preparers who negligently or willfully understate a client's tax liability or who recklessly or intentionally disregard Internal Revenue Code rules or regulations are subject to penalties. • Tax preparers who fail to provide a taxpayer with a copy of the return, fail to sign the return, or fail to furnish the appropriate tax identification numbers may also be subject to penalties.

47–5 Confidentiality and Privilege

Professionals are restrained by the ethical tenets of their professions to keep all communications with their clients confidential.

47–5a Attorney-Client Relationships

The confidentiality of attorney-client communications is protected by law, which confers a *privilege* on such communications. This privilege exists because of the client's need to fully disclose the facts of his or her case to the attorney.

To encourage frankness, confidential attorney-client communications relating to representation are normally held in strictest confidence and protected by law. The attorney and her or his employees may not discuss the client's case with anyone—even under court order—without the client's permission. The client holds the privilege, and only the client may waive it—by disclosing privileged information to someone outside the privilege, for example.

Note, however, that the SEC has implemented rules requiring attorneys who become aware that a client has violated securities laws to report the violation to the SEC. Reporting a client's misconduct could be a breach of the attorney-client privilege, so these rules have created a potential conflict for some attorneys.

Once an attorney-client relationship arises, all communications between the parties are privileged. The question in the following case was whether communications between an attorney and an individual *before* that individual was informed that the attorney was *not* his counsel were privileged.

Case 47.3

Commonwealth of Pennsylvania v. Schultz

Superior Court of Pennsylvania, 133 A.3d 294 (2016).

Background and Facts An investigation into allegations of sexual misconduct involving minors and Jerry Sandusky, former defensive coordinator for the Pennsylvania State University football team, led a grand jury to subpoena Gary Schultz. Schultz, a retired vice president of the university, had overseen the campus police at the time of the alleged events.

Before testifying, Schultz met with Cynthia Baldwin, counsel for Penn State. He told her that he did not have any documents relating to the two incidents, believing this disclosure to be in the strictest confidence between attorney and client. Baldwin, however, saw her role as counsel only for Penn State, representing Schultz as an agent of the university, not personally. She did not explain this to him, and she appeared with him during his testimony.

Later, a file was found in Schultz's office containing notes pertaining to the two incidents. When Baldwin was called to testify, she revealed what he had told her at their meeting. On the basis of this testimony, the grand jury charged Schultz with the crimes of perjury, obstruction of justice, and conspiracy. Before a trial was held on these charges, Schultz filed a motion to preclude Baldwin's testimony and quash (suppress) the charges, arguing that her testimony violated the attorney-client privilege. The court denied the motion. Schulz appealed.

In the Language of the Court

Opinion by *BOWES*, J. [Judge]

* * * *

Communications between a putative [assumed] client and corporate counsel are generally privileged prior to counsel informing the individual of the distinction between representing the individual as an agent of the corporation and representing the person in his or her personal capacity. [Emphasis added.]

When corporate counsel clarifies the potential inherent conflict of interest in representing the corporation and an individual and explains that the attorney may divulge the communications between that person and the attorney because they do not represent the individual, the individual may then make a knowing, intelligent, and voluntary decision whether to continue communicating with corporate counsel.

* * * *

* * * Where an attorney purports to offer only limited representation before and at a grand jury proceeding, * * * a putative client must be made expressly aware of that fact.

As Schultz consulted with Ms. Baldwin for purposes of preparing for his grand jury testimony * * *, and reasonably believed she represented him, and Ms. Baldwin neglected to adequately explain the distinction between personal representation and agency representation * * *, we conclude that all the communications between Schultz and Ms. Baldwin were protected by the attorney-client privilege.

* * * Accordingly, we preclude Ms. Baldwin from testifying in future proceedings regarding privileged communications between her and Schultz, absent a waiver by Schultz.

* * * *

* * * Schultz * * * was not aware that Ms. Baldwin was not appearing with him [during his grand jury testimony] in order to protect his interests and therefore unable to provide advice concerning whether he should answer potentially incriminating questions or invoke his right against self-incrimination. Since Schultz was constructively without counsel during his grand jury testimony, and he did not provide

Case 47.3 Continues

Case 47.3 Continued

informed consent as to limited representation, * * * his right against self-incrimination was not protected by Ms. Baldwin's agency representation, and the appropriate remedy is to quash the perjury charge.
* * * *

[Finally] since the obstruction of justice and related conspiracy charges in this matter relied extensively on a presentment from an investigating grand jury privy to impermissible privileged communications, we quash the counts of obstruction of justice and the related conspiracy charge.

Decision and Remedy *A state intermediate appellate court reversed the order of the lower court regarding Schultz's pretrial motion. Baldwin was precluded from testifying about Schultz's privileged communications with her, and the charges of perjury, obstruction of justice, and conspiracy against Schultz were quashed.*

Critical Thinking

* **Legal Environment** *How does the result in this case further the purpose of the attorney-client privilege?*
* **What If the Facts Were Different?** *Suppose that a hearing had been held on the question of the attorney-client privilege before Baldwin testified. Would the result have been different?*

47–5b Accountant-Client Relationships

In a few states, accountant-client communications are privileged by state statute. In these states, accountant-client communications may not be revealed even in court or in court-sanctioned proceedings without the client's permission.

The majority of states, however, abide by the common law, which provides that, if a court so orders, an accountant must disclose information about his or her client to the court. Physicians and other professionals may similarly be compelled to disclose in court information given to them in confidence by patients or clients.

Communications between professionals and their clients—other than those between an attorney and her or his client—are not privileged under federal law. *In cases involving federal law, state-provided rights to confidentiality of accountant-client communications are not recognized.* Thus, in those cases, in response to a court order, an accountant must provide the information sought.

Reviewing: Professional Liability and Accountability

Superior Wholesale Corporation planned to purchase Regal Furniture, Inc., and wished to determine Regal's net worth. Superior hired Lynette Shuebke, of the accounting firm Shuebke Delgado, to review an audit that had been prepared by Norman Chase, the accountant for Regal. Shuebke advised Superior that Chase had performed a high-quality audit and that Regal's inventory on the audit dates was stated accurately on the general ledger. As a result of these representations, Superior went forward with its purchase of Regal.

After the purchase, Superior discovered that the audit by Chase had been materially inaccurate and misleading, primarily because the inventory had been grossly overstated on the balance sheet. Later, a former Regal employee who had begun working for Superior exposed an e-mail exchange between Chase and former Regal chief executive officer Buddy Gantry. The exchange revealed that Chase had cooperated in overstating the inventory and understating Regal's tax liability. Using the information presented in the chapter, answer the following questions.

1. If Shuebke's review was conducted in good faith and conformed to generally accepted accounting principles, can Superior hold Shuebke Delgado liable for negligently failing to detect material omissions in Chase's audit? Why or why not?
2. According to the rule adopted by the majority of courts to determine accountants' liability to third parties, could Chase be liable to Superior? Explain.
3. Generally, what requirements must be met before Superior can recover damages under Section 10(b) of the 1934 Securities Exchange Act and SEC Rule 10b-5? Can Superior meet these requirements? Why or why not?

4. Suppose that a court determined that Chase had aided Regal in willfully understating its tax liability. What is the maximum penalty that could be imposed on Chase?

Debate This . . . *Only the largest publicly held companies should be subject to the Sarbanes-Oxley Act.*

Terms and Concepts

auditor 898	generally accepted accounting	International Financial Reporting
constructive fraud 900	principles (GAAP) 897	Standards (IFRS) 898
defalcation 898	generally accepted auditing	working papers 904
due diligence 906	standards (GAAS) 897	

Issue Spotters

1. Dave, an accountant, prepares a financial statement for Excel Company, a client, knowing that Excel will use the statement to obtain a loan from First National Bank. Dave makes negligent omissions in the statement that result in a loss to the bank. Can the bank successfully sue Dave? Why or why not? (See *Potential Liability to Third Parties.*)

2. Nora, an accountant, prepares a financial statement as part of a registration statement that Omega, Inc., files with the Securities and Exchange Commission before making a public offering of securities. The statement contains a misstatement of material fact that is not attributable to Nora's fraud or negligence. Pat relies on the misstatement, buys some of the securities, and suffers a loss. Can Nora be held liable to Pat? Explain. (See *Potential Liability of Accountants under Securities Laws.*)

• **Check your answers to the Issue Spotters against the answers provided in Appendix D at the end of this text.**

Business Scenarios

47–1. The *Ultramares* Rule. Larkin, Inc., retains Howard Patterson to manage its books and prepare its financial statements. Patterson, a certified public accountant, lives in Indiana and practices there. After twenty years, Patterson has become a bit bored with generally accepted accounting principles (GAAP) and has adopted more creative accounting methods. Now, though, Patterson has a problem, as he is being sued by Molly Tucker, one of Larkin's creditors. Tucker alleges that Patterson either knew or should have known that Larkin's financial statements would be distributed to various individuals. Furthermore, she asserts that these financial statements were negligently prepared and seriously inaccurate. What are the consequences of Patterson's failure to follow GAAP? Under the traditional *Ultramares* rule, can Tucker recover damages from Patterson? Explain. (See *Potential Liability to Third Parties.*)

47–2. The *Restatement* Rule. The accounting firm of Goldman, Walters, Johnson & Co. prepared financial statements for Lucy's Fashions, Inc. After reviewing the various financial statements, Happydays State Bank agreed to loan Lucy's Fashions $35,000 for expansion. When Lucy's Fashions declared bankruptcy under Chapter 11 six months later, Happydays State Bank promptly filed an action against Goldman, Walters, Johnson & Co., alleging negligent preparation of financial statements. Assuming that the court has abandoned the *Ultramares* approach, what is the result? What are the policy reasons for holding accountants liable to third parties with whom they are not in privity? (See *Potential Liability to Third Parties.*)

47–3. Accountant's Liability under Rule 10b-5. In early 2014, Bennett, Inc., offered a substantial number of new common shares to the public. Harvey Helms had a long-standing interest in Bennett because his grandfather had once been president of the company. On receiving a prospectus prepared and distributed by Bennett, Helms was dismayed by the pessimism it embodied. Helms decided to delay purchasing stock in the company. Later, Helms asserted that the prospectus prepared by the accountants was overly pessimistic and contained materially misleading statements. Discuss fully how successful Helms would be in bringing a cause of action under Rule 10b-5 against the accountants of Bennett, Inc. (See *Potential Liability of Accountants under Securities Laws.*)

Business Case Problems

47–4. Accountant's Liability for Audit. A West Virginia bank ran its asset value from $100 million to $1 billion over seven years by aggressively marketing subprime loans. The Office of the Comptroller of the Currency, a federal regulator, audited the bank and discovered that the books had been falsified for several years and that the bank was insolvent. The Comptroller closed the bank and brought criminal charges against its managers.

The Comptroller fined Grant Thornton, the bank's accounting firm, $300,000 for recklessly failing to meet generally accepted auditing standards during the years it audited the bank. The Comptroller claimed Thornton violated federal law by "participating in . . . unsafe and unsound banking practice." Thornton appealed, contending that it was not involved in bank operations to that extent based on its audit function. What would be the key to determining if the accounting firm could be held liable for that violation of federal law? [*Grant Thornton, LLP v. Office of the Comptroller of the Currency,* 514 F.3d 1328 (D.C. Cir. 2008)] (See *Potential Liability to Clients.*)

47–5. Professional's Liability. Soon after Teresa DeYoung's husband died, her mother-in-law also died, leaving an inheritance of more than $400,000 for DeYoung's children. DeYoung hired John Ruggerio, an attorney, to ensure that her children would receive it. Ruggerio advised her to invest the funds in his real estate business. She declined. A few months later, $300,000 of the inheritance was sent to Ruggerio. Without telling DeYoung, he deposited the $300,000 in his account and began to use the funds in his real estate business. Nine months later, $109,000 of the inheritance was sent to Ruggerio. He paid this to DeYoung. She asked about the remaining amount. Ruggerio lied to hide his theft. Unable to access these funds, DeYoung's children changed their college plans to attend less expensive institutions. Nearly three years later, DeYoung learned the truth. Can she bring a suit against Ruggerio? If so, on what ground? If not, why not? Did Ruggerio violate any standard of professional ethics? Discuss. [*DeYoung v. Ruggerio,* 185 Vt. 267, 971 A.2d 627 (2009)] (See *Potential Liability to Clients.*)

47–6. Professional Malpractice. Jeffery Guerrero hired James McDonald, a certified public accountant, to represent him and his business in an appeal to the Internal Revenue Service. The appeal was about audits that showed Guerrero owed more taxes. When the appeal failed, McDonald helped Guerrero prepare materials for an appeal to the Tax Court, which was also unsuccessful. Guerrero then sued McDonald for professional negligence in the preparation of his evidence for the court. Guerrero claimed that McDonald had failed to adequately prepare witnesses and to present all the arguments that could have been made on his behalf so that he could have won the case. Guerrero contended that McDonald was liable for all of the additional taxes he was required to pay. Is Guerrero's claim likely to result in liability on McDonald's part? What factors would the court consider? [*Guerrero v. McDonald,* 302 Ga.App. 164, 690 S.E.2d 486 (2010)] (See *Potential Liability to Clients.*)

47–7. Business Case Problem with Sample Answer—Potential Liability to Third Parties. In 2006, twenty-seven entities became limited partners in two hedge funds that had invested with Bernard Madoff and his investment firm. The partners' investment adviser gave them various investment information, including a memorandum indicating that an independent certified public accountant, KPMG, LLP, had audited the hedge funds' annual reports. Since 2004, KPMG had also prepared annual reports addressed to the funds' "Partners." Each report stated that KPMG had investigated the funds' financial statements, had followed generally accepted auditing principles, and had concluded that the statements fairly summarized the funds' financial conditions. Moreover, KPMG used the information from its audits to prepare individual tax statements for each fund partner.

In 2008, Madoff was charged with securities fraud for running a massive Ponzi scheme. In a 2009 report, the Securities and Exchange Commission identified numerous "red flags" that should have been discovered by investment advisers and auditors. Unfortunately, the auditors did not find them, and the hedge funds' partners lost millions of dollars. Is KPMG potentially liable to the funds' partners under the *Restatement (Third) of Torts*? Why or why not? [*Askenazy v. Tremont Group Holdings, Inc.,* 2012 WL 440675 (Mass.Super. 2012)] (See *Potential Liability to Third Parties.*)

- **For a sample answer to Problem 47–7, go to Appendix E at the end of this text.**

47–8. Attorney's Duty of Care. Luis and Maria Rojas contracted to buy a house in Westchester County, New York, from Andrew and Karen Paine. The house was on property designated as "Lot No. 8" on a subdivision map filed in the county clerk's office. The Paines had acquired the property in two parts by the transfer of two separate deeds. At the closing, they delivered a deed stating that it covered "the same property." In fact, however, the legal description attached to the deed covered only the portion of Lot No. 8 described in one of the two previous deeds. Attorney Paul Herrick represented the Rojases in the deal with the Paines. When the Rojases sought to sell the property two years later, the title search revealed that they owned only part of Lot No. 8, and the buyer refused to go through with the sale. Is Herrick liable for malpractice? Explain. [*Rojas v. Paine,* 125 A.D.3d 745, 4 N.Y.S.3d 223 (2 Dept. 2015)] (See *Potential Liability to Clients.*)

47–9. A Question of Ethics—Liability for Negligence.

Portland Shellfish Co. processes live shellfish in Maine. As one of the firm's two owners, Frank Wetmore held 300 voting and 150 nonvoting shares of the stock. Donna Holden held the other 300 voting shares. Donna's husband, Jeff, managed the company's daily operations, including production, procurement, and sales. The board of directors consisted of Frank and Jeff. In 2001, disagreements

arose over the company's management. The Holdens invoked the "Shareholders' Agreement," which provided that "[i]n the event of a deadlock, the directors shall hire an accountant at [Macdonald, Page, Schatz, Fletcher & Co., LLC] to determine the value of the outstanding shares. . . . [E]ach shareholder shall have the right to buy out the other shareholder(s)' interest."

Macdonald Page estimated the stock's "fair market value" at $1.09 million. Donna offered to buy Frank's shares at a price equal to his proportionate share. Frank countered by offering $1.25 million for Donna's shares. Donna rejected Frank's offer and insisted that he sell his shares to her or she would sue. In the face of this threat, Frank sold his shares to Donna for $750,705. Believing the stock to be worth more than twice Macdonald Page's estimate, Frank filed a suit in a federal district court against the accounting firm. [Wetmore v. Macdonald, Page, Schatz, Fletcher & Co., LLC, 476 F.3d 1 (1st Cir. 2007)] (See Potential Liability to Clients.)

(a) Frank claimed that in valuing the stock, the accounting firm had disregarded "commonly accepted and reliable methods of valuation in favor of less reliable methods." He alleged negligence, among other things. Macdonald Page filed a motion to dismiss the complaint. What are the elements that establish negligence? Which is the most critical element in this case?

(b) Macdonald Page evaluated the company's stock by identifying its "fair market value," defined as "the price at which the property would change hands between a willing buyer and a willing seller, neither being under a compulsion to buy or sell and both having reasonable knowledge of relevant facts." The firm knew that the shareholders would use its estimate to determine the price that one would pay to the other. Under these circumstances, was Frank's injury foreseeable? Discuss.

(c) What factor might have influenced Frank to sell his shares to Donna even though he thought that Macdonald Page's "fair market value" figure was less than half of what it should have been? Does this factor represent an unfair, or unethical, advantage? Explain.

Legal Reasoning Group Activity

47–10. Attorney-Client Privilege. Napster, Inc., offered a service that allowed its users to browse digital music files on other users' computers and download selections for free. Music industry principals sued Napster for copyright infringement, and the court ordered Napster to remove from its service files that were identified as infringing. When Napster failed to comply, it was shut down.

A few months later, Bertelsmann, a German corporation, loaned Napster $85 million to fund its anticipated transition to a licensed digital music distribution system. The terms allowed Napster to spend the loan on "general, administrative and overhead expenses." In an e-mail, Napster's chief executive officer referred to a "side deal" under which Napster could use up to $10 million of the loan to pay litigation expenses. Napster failed to launch the new system before declaring bankruptcy. The plaintiffs filed a suit against Bertelsmann, alleging that its loan had prolonged Napster's infringement. The plaintiffs asked the court to order the disclosure of all attorney-client communications related to the loan. (See *Confidentiality and Privilege.*)

(a) The first group will identify the principle that Bertelsmann could assert to protect these communications and outline the purpose of this protection.

(b) The second group will decide whether this principle should protect a client who consults an attorney for advice that will help the client commit fraud.

(c) A third group will determine whether the court should grant the plaintiffs' request.

Application and Ethics

Climate Change

Our planet's average temperature has risen by 1.5 degrees Fahrenheit over the last hundred years. It is predicted that it will rise another 0.5 to 4.5 degrees over the next century. These seemingly small increases in the average temperature can result in significant change to our climate.

What Are the Causes?

Over the last century, our atmosphere experienced a large increase in carbon dioxide and other *greenhouse gases (GHGs)*. GHGs act like a blanket around our planet, absorbing radiation from the surface, trapping it as heat in the atmosphere, and reflecting it back to the surface.

This process, known as the *greenhouse effect*, is necessary to support life. The recent increase in GHGs, however, may be changing our climate. Deforestation, industrial processes, and agricultural practices emit these gases, but the majority of GHGs come from burning fossil fuels to produce energy.[1]

What Are the Effects?

The warmer it gets, the greater the risk for more change to the climate. Ultimately, the climate that we are used to may no longer be a guide for what to expect in the future.

Changes in Weather Rising global temperatures have sometimes coincided with changes in weather. Some locations have seen altered rainfall, resulting in heavier rains and more floods, or more frequent and intense heat waves and droughts. The rising temperatures may also be making our planet's oceans warmer and more acidic. Some glaciers and ice caps are melting, which may cause sea levels to rise.

Impacts on Society The warmer temperatures and changes in weather can affect society in many ways. Agricultural yields, human health, and the supply of energy are affected. More severe weather can lead to higher food and energy prices and increasing insurance costs. (Note, though, that higher average temperatures could lead to more agricultural output and hence lower food prices.) Of course, any impact in one area of human activity can have widespread and unforeseen effects throughout society.

What Can We Do about It?

The effects of climate change may be lessened by choices that reduce GHGs. About half of the states have set statewide GHG emission goals.[2] In the areas of transportation and power generation, two of the options for reducing emissions are the use of low-emission fuels and increased energy efficiency.

Reduce Emissions at the Pump and the Plant Motor vehicles and transportation fuels are sources for nearly a third of U.S. GHG emissions. To reduce these emissions, the federal

---

1. Fossil fuel-burning power plants are the largest single source of U.S. GHG emissions—33 percent.
2. California established the first statewide goals in 2006 in the Global Warming Solutions Act.

government and the states impose emission standards on cars and trucks, and encourage the use of fuel-efficient vehicles and alternative fuels.

The federal Environmental Protection Agency (EPA) and National Highway Transportation Safety Administration have established standards for GHG emissions and fuel economy for new light-duty cars and trucks through the model year 2025.[3] The standards are projected to save about 4 billion barrels of oil and avoid 2 billion metric tons of GHG emissions per year.

Some states have set low-emission fuel standards. More than a dozen states have set renewable fuel standards to encourage the use of low-emission fuels. Incentives to use alternative fuels include tax exemptions, tax credits, and grants.

To reduce GHG emissions from coal- and gas-fired power plants, the EPA issued the Clean Power Plan (CPP).[4] It is projected that, when the CPP is fully in place in 2030, carbon pollution from the power sector will be 32 percent below 2005 levels. Emissions of sulfur dioxide from power plants will be 90 percent lower than 2005 levels, and emissions of nitrogen oxides will be 72 percent lower.

About two-thirds of the states will require power companies to generate a certain percentage or amount of power from renewable energy sources by a specific date, which varies by state. These targets aim to reduce emissions and to improve air quality, diversify energy sources, and create jobs in the renewable energy industry.

Become More Energy Efficient More than half of the states have set standards requiring power companies to save specified amounts of energy. To attain these goals, the utilities must adopt more efficient technology in their operations and encourage their customers to become more energy efficient.

About half of the states dedicate funds to the support of renewable energy projects. More than a dozen of these states formed the Clean Energy States Alliance to coordinate their investments.

Nearly all states permit utility customers to sell electricity back to the grid. In most states, utilities offer their customers the opportunity to have a portion of their power provided from renewable sources.

Many states participate in regional climate initiatives. For example, nine states in the north-eastern United States formed the Regional Greenhouse Gas Initiative to implement a market-based program to reduce GHG emissions from power plants. The initiative sets an emissions budget, or cap, for each member state. Credits that exceed the actual emissions can be sold. The proceeds are generally invested in energy-efficient renewable energy programs.

Adapt to the Changes The EPA's State and Local Climate and Energy Program provides technical assistance, analytical tools, and outreach support on climate change issues to state, local, and tribal governments.[5] The program directs resource managers to set priorities and to design and implement climate and energy policies tailored to the particular circumstances of their locations.

Part of the process is to assess an area's vulnerability to the effects of climate change and to consider approaches for adapting to the effects. For example, a coastal estuary that is subject to

---

3. 40 C.F.R. Parts 85, 86, and 600, and 49 C.F.R. Parts 523, 531, 533, 600 *et al.* The United States Supreme Court has made clear that the Environmental Protection Agency can regulate GHGs under the Clean Air Act. See *Massachusetts v. E.P.A.*, 549 U.S. 497, 127 S.Ct. 1438, 167 L.Ed.2d 248 (2007).
4. 40 C.F.R. Part 60. This act is being challenged in court.
5. See Environmental Protection Agency, *State and Local Climate and Energy Program* (December 28, 2015) available at http://www3.epa.gov/statelocalclimate/index.html.

Continues

salt-water inundation as a consequence of rising sea levels might benefit from a coastal restoration project.

The U.S. Interagency Climate Change Adaptation Task Force coordinates the efforts for adaptation across government agencies.[6] The task force recommends actions that the federal government can take to respond to the needs of states and local communities. The top priority is to enhance the resilience of natural resources to absorb the impacts of climate change.

Agree to More Limits on Emissions The European Union and 195 nations, including the United States, participated in the 2015 United Nations Climate Change Conference in Paris, France. The parties negotiated the Paris Agreement to encourage the reduction of GHG emissions.[7] The agreement sets a goal of limiting the global temperature increase to less than 2 degrees Celsius. The parties agreed to make "nationally determined contributions" (NDCs) to this goal and to pursue domestic measures designed to achieve the NDCs.[8] None of these agreements are binding, however, and therefore rely on voluntary actions by governments throughout the world.

Ethical Connection

Have all these efforts had an effect? It seems that they have. The transition to clean energy is happening faster than anticipated, and GHG emissions and air pollution have decreased somewhat.

Furthermore, climate change could have some positive effects. For example, the goals to lessen the impact and adapt to the changes create economic opportunities. There are new markets for alternative sources of power and sales of GHG emission credits, for instance. Climate change also represents a political opportunity to improve air quality and develop domestic sources of clean energy.

A business that takes advantage of these opportunities is not acting unethically. Such a business is, in fact, acting in the best interest of all of us.

Ethics Question *Is it ethical to continue to use fossil fuels? Explain.*

Critical Thinking *What are the advantages of fossil fuels? What are the disadvantages? Discuss.*

---

6. Executive Order, *Preparing the United States for the Impacts of Climate Change* (November 11, 2013) available at https://www.whitehouse.gov/the-press-office/2013/11/01/executive-order-preparing-united-states-impacts-climate-change.

7. United Nations Framework Convention on Climate Change, Conference of the Parties, *Adoption of the Paris Agreement. Proposal by the President*, FCCC/CP/2015/L.9/Rev. 1 (December 12, 2015) available at http://unfccc.int/resource/docs/2015/cop21/eng/l09r01.pdf.

8. There are, however, no binding emission targets or financial commitments. And the agreement itself will not become binding until fifty-five of the participants who produce more than 55 percent of global GHGs have ratified it.

Property and Its Protection

CHAPTER 48

Personal Property and Bailments

Property consists of the legally protected rights and interests a person has in anything with an ascertainable value that is subject to ownership. For instance, virtual property has become quite valuable in today's world, as you will read later in this chapter. Property would have little value, however, if the law did not define the rights of owners to use, sell, dispose of, and control their property and prevent others from trespassing on it.

In the United States, a substantial body of law protects the rights of property owners, but that protection is not absolute. Property owners may have to prove that their ownership rights in a particular item of property are superior to the claims of others. In addition, through its police powers, the government can impose regulations and taxes on property, and can take or seize private property under certain circumstances.

In this chapter, we examine the differences between personal and real property and look at the methods of acquiring ownership of personal property. We also consider issues relating to mislaid, lost, and abandoned personal property. In the remainder of the chapter, we discuss bailment relationships. A *bailment* is created when personal property is temporarily delivered into the care of another without a transfer of title, such as when a person takes an item of clothing to the dry cleaners. The fact that there is no passage of title and no intent to transfer title is what distinguishes a bailment from a sale or a gift.

48–1 Personal Property versus Real Property

Property is divided into real property and personal property. **Real property** (sometimes called *realty* or *real estate*) means the land and everything permanently attached to it, including structures and anything permanently attached to the structures. Everything else is **personal property** (sometimes referred to as *personalty* or **chattel**). In essence, real property is immovable, whereas personal property is capable of being moved.

Personal property can be tangible or intangible. *Tangible* personal property, such as a flat-screen TV, heavy construction equipment, or a car, has physical substance.

Intangible personal property represents some set of rights and interests, but it has no physical existence. Stocks and bonds, patents, trademarks, and copyrights—as well as digital and virtual property—are examples of intangible personal property.

Both personal property and real property can be owned by an individual person or by some other entity. When two or more persons own real or personal property together, concurrent ownership exists. (The different types of joint or concurrent ownership will be discussed in the chapter on real property.)

In the following case, a concurrent owner of a copyright to an unpublished autobiography contended that she was entitled to an accounting for the use of the work to create a successful theatrical production.

Corbello v. DeVito

United States Court of Appeals, Ninth Circuit, 777 F.3d 1058 (2015).

Background and Facts Rex Woodward contracted with Thomas DeVito, one of the original members of The Four Seasons rock band, to ghostwrite DeVito's autobiography. Before it was published, Woodward died, and his interest in the manuscript's copyright passed to his widow, Donna Corbello. Later, DeVito agreed to grant former bandmates Frankie Valli and Bob Gaudio the right to use "aspects of his life related to The Four Seasons, including . . . his creative contributions, biographies, events in

Case 48.1 Continued

his life, name and likeness (the Materials)" to develop a musical about The Four Seasons. The result was a Broadway hit called *Jersey Boys*.

Actors and others involved in the show attributed their inspiration, in part, to DeVito's unpublished autobiography. Corbello filed a suit in a federal district court against DeVito and his bandmates for an accounting of the profits earned from this use of the work. The court issued a judgment in the defendants' favor. Corbello appealed.

In the Language of the Court

O'SCANNLAIN, Circuit Judge:
* * * *

A co-owner of a copyright must account to other co-owners for any profits he earns from * * * use of the copyright.
* * * *

Pursuant to [DeVito's agreement with former Four Seasons band members Frankie Valli and Bob Gaudio,] DeVito "granted to Valli and Gaudio the exclusive right to use and incorporate the Materials in one or more theatrical productions, and any and all ancillary and subsidiary exploitations thereof." As defined in the Agreement, "Materials" includes * * * DeVito's "biographies."
* * * *

In the context of the * * * Agreement, the term "biographies" is not ambiguous [confusing or uncertain]. [Under] standard dictionary definitions * * * a "biography" is a "history of a person's life" * * * that is "usually written" * * *. As an account of DeVito's life that has been reduced to writing, [Woodward's] Work, on its face, qualifies under these straightforward definitions as a "biography."
* * * *

* * * DeVito granted Valli and Gaudio the "exclusive right to use" his "biographies," unambiguously including [Woodward's] Work, to create a play. Such play constitutes a "derivative work," the right to create which resides in each copyright holder of the underlying work and may be transferred by that holder to a third party. Thus, in granting this exclusive right to create, * * * the * * * Agreement constitutes a transfer of ownership of DeVito's derivative-work right in the Work to Valli and Gaudio.
* * * *

* * * *A joint-owner cannot transfer more than he himself holds; thus, [a transfer] from one joint-owner to a third party cannot bind the other joint-owners or limit their rights in the copyright without their consent.* In other words, the third party's right is "exclusive" as to the [transferring] co-owner, but not as to the other co-owners. [Emphasis added.]
* * * *

* * * Because the Agreement unambiguously transfers DeVito's derivative-work right to Valli and Gaudio, and copyright co-owners must account to one another for any profits earned by exploiting that copyright, the district court erred in rejecting Corbello's claim for [an] accounting.

Decision and Remedy *The U.S. Court of Appeals for the Ninth Circuit reversed the lower court's judgment. Woodward's work qualified as a biography, the use of which DeVito granted to Valli and Gaudio to develop the Broadway play* Jersey Boys. *This grant constituted a transfer of DeVito's right in the work. As Woodward's widow and thus as a concurrent owner of the work's copyright, Corbello was entitled to an accounting of the profits from the play.*

Critical Thinking

- **Legal Environment** *Under what circumstances would Corbello* not *be entitled to an accounting? Why?*

48–1a Why Is the Distinction Important?

How property is taxed and what is required to transfer or acquire the property is determined by whether the property is classified as real or personal property.

Taxation The two types of property are usually subject to different types of taxes. Generally, each state assesses property taxes on real property. Typically, the tax rate is based on the market value of the real property and the services provided by the city, state, and county in which the property is located. For instance, higher taxes may be imposed on real property located within the city limits to pay for schools, roads, and libraries.

Businesses also often pay taxes on the personal property they own, use, or lease, including office or farm equipment and supplies. Individuals may pay sales tax when purchasing personal property, but generally they are not required to pay annual taxes on personal property that is not used for business.

Acquisition Another reason for distinguishing between real and personal property has to do with the way the property is acquired or transferred. Personal property can be transferred with a minimum of formality. In contrast, real property transfers generally involve a written sales contract and a *deed* that is recorded with the state.

Similarly, establishing ownership rights is simpler for personal property than for real property. ■ **EXAMPLE 48.1** If Mia gives Shawn an iPad Air as a gift, Shawn does not need to have any paperwork evidencing title, as he would if she had given him real property. (The ways to acquire ownership of personal property will be discussed shortly.) ■

48–1b Conversion of Real Property to Personal Property

Sometimes, real property can be turned into personal property by detaching it from the land. For instance, the trees, bushes, and plants growing on land are considered part of the real property (with the exception of crops that must be planted every year). If the property is sold, all the vegetation growing on the land normally is transferred to the new owner of the real property.

Once the items are severed (removed) from the land, however, they become personal property. If the trees are cut from the land, the timber is personal property. If apples, grapes, or raspberries are picked from trees or vines growing on real property, they become personal property. Similarly, if land contains minerals (including oil) or other natural resources (such as marble), the resources are part of the real property. But once removed, they become personal property.

Conversely, personal property may be converted into real property by permanently attaching it to the real property. When personal property is affixed to real property in a permanent way, as when tile is installed in a house, it is known as a *fixture*. (Fixtures will be discussed in the context of real property.)

48–2 Acquiring Ownership of Personal Property

The most common way of acquiring personal property is by purchasing it. (Today, even virtual property is often purchased, as discussed in this chapter's *Digital Update*

DIGITAL UPDATE   The Exploding World of Digital Property

Jon Jacobs took out a real mortgage on his real house so that he could pay $100,000 in real dollars for a virtual asteroid near the virtual Planet Calypso in the virtual world Entropia Universe. A few years later, he sold Club Neverdie, the virtual space resort he had constructed on the virtual asteroid, for more than $600,000. At the time, Jacobs was making $200,000 per year from players' purchases of virtual goods at the resort.

If the prospect of paying real funds for virtual property seems disconcerting, remember that property does not have to be tangible. Property consists of a bundle of rights in anything that has an ascertainable value and is subject to ownership—a definition that encompasses virtual property, including all the intangible objects used in virtual worlds like Entropia Universe and Second Life.

Digital Goods Have Value, Too

Digital goods include virtual goods, but more important, they include digital books, music libraries, and movie downloads, as well as domain names and expensively created Web sites. This digital property has real value. Some digital music libraries, for example, cost thousands of dollars.

Who Keeps the Digital Goods?

The growing value of digital goods raises some legal questions. For instance, what are the respective rights of the creator/owner of a virtual-world Web site and the players at that site? And what happens when a husband and wife decide to divorce after they have purchased virtual real estate or digital goods with real-world dollars? The couple—or a court—will have to figure out a way to divide the goods. Property and divorce laws will have to adapt to take into account this changing world.

Critical Thinking *How might a couple who enjoys purchasing digital goods together avoid property division issues in the event of a divorce?*

feature.) Another way in which personal property is often acquired is by will or inheritance. Here, we look at additional ways in which ownership of personal property can be acquired, including acquisition by possession, production, gift, accession, and confusion.

48–2a Possession

Sometimes, a person can become the owner of personal property merely by possessing it. For instance, one way to acquire ownership through possession is the capture of wild animals. Wild animals belong to no one in their natural state, and the first person to take possession of a wild animal normally owns it. A hunter who kills a deer, for instance, has assumed ownership of it (unless he or she acted in violation of the law). Those who find lost or abandoned property can also acquire ownership rights through mere possession of the property, as will be discussed later in this chapter.

48–2b Production

Production—the fruits of labor—is another means of acquiring ownership of personal property. For instance, writers, inventors, manufacturers, and others who produce personal property may thereby acquire title to it. (In some situations, though, as when a researcher is hired to invent a new product or technique, the researcher may not own what is produced.)

48–2c Gift

A **gift** is a fairly common means of acquiring or transferring ownership of property. A gift is essentially a *voluntary* transfer of property ownership for which no consideration is given. The presence of consideration is what distinguishes a contractual obligation to transfer ownership of property from a gift.

For a gift to be effective, the following three elements are required:

1. Donative intent on the part of the *donor* (the one giving the gift).
2. Delivery.
3. Acceptance by the *donee* (the one receiving the gift).

Until these three requirements are met, no effective gift has been made. ■ **EXAMPLE 48.2** Gary's Aunt Celia tells him that she is going to give him a new Mercedes-Benz for his next birthday. Aunt Celia has simply made a promise to make a gift. There is no gift until the Mercedes-Benz is delivered and accepted. ■

Donative Intent When a gift is challenged in court, the court will determine whether donative intent exists by looking at the language of the donor and the surrounding circumstances. A court may look at the relationship between the parties and the size of the gift in relation to the donor's other assets. When a person has given away a large portion of her or his assets, the court will scrutinize the transaction closely. The court will analyze the donor's mental capacity and look for indications of fraud or duress.

■ **CASE IN POINT 48.3** Over a period of three months, Jean Knowles Goodman, who was eighty-five years old, gave Steven Atwood several checks that totaled $56,100. Atwood was a veterinarian who had cared for Goodman's dogs for nearly twenty years, and he and Goodman had become friends. Shortly after writing the last check, Goodman was hospitalized and diagnosed with dementia (loss of brain function) and alcohol dependency.

The guardian who was appointed to represent Goodman filed a lawsuit to invalidate the gifts, claiming that Goodman had lacked mental capacity and donative intent. At trial, a psychiatrist who had examined Goodman testified on behalf of Atwood that while Goodman lacked the capacity to care for herself, she would have understood that she was giving away her funds. Therefore, the court concluded that Goodman had donative intent to make the gifts to Atwood.[1] ■

Delivery The gift must be delivered to the donee. Delivery may be accomplished by means of a third person who is the agent of either the donor or the donee. Naturally, no delivery is necessary if the gift is already in the hands of the donee (provided there is donative intent and acceptance). Delivery is obvious in most cases, but some objects cannot be relinquished physically. Then the question of delivery depends on the surrounding circumstances.

Constructive Delivery. When the object itself cannot be physically delivered, a symbolic, or constructive, delivery will be sufficient. **Constructive delivery** confers the right to take possession (rather than actual possession) of the object in question. It is a general term for all of those acts that the law holds to be equivalent to acts of real delivery.

■ **EXAMPLE 48.4** Teresa wants to make a gift of rare coins that she has stored in a safe-deposit box at her bank. Teresa certainly cannot deliver the box itself to the donee, and she does not want to take the coins out of the bank. In this situation, she can simply deliver the key to the box to the donee and authorize the donee's access to the box and its contents. This constitutes symbolic, or constructive, delivery of the contents of the box. ■

Constructive delivery is always necessary for gifts of intangible personal property—such as stocks, bonds,

---

1. *Goodman v. Atwood*, 78 Mass.App.Ct. 655, 940 N.E.2d 514 (2011).

insurance policies, and contracts. What will be delivered are documents that represent rights and are not, in themselves, the true property.

Relinquishing Dominion and Control. An effective delivery also requires that the donor give up complete control and **dominion** (power, ownership rights) over the subject matter of the gift. The outcome of disputes often turns on whether control has actually been relinquished. The Internal Revenue Service carefully examines transactions between relatives, especially when one has given income-producing property to another who is in a lower marginal tax bracket. Unless complete control over the property has been relinquished, the "donor"—not the family member who received the "gift"—will have to pay taxes on the income from that property.

In the following *Classic Case*, the court focused on the requirement that a donor must relinquish complete control and dominion over property before a gift can be effectively delivered.

In re Estate of Piper
Missouri Court of Appeals, 676 S.W.2d 897 (1984).

Background and Facts Gladys Piper died intestate (without a will). At the time of her death, she owned miscellaneous personal property worth $5,150 and had in her purse $206.75 in cash and two diamond rings. Wanda Brown, Piper's niece, took the contents of her purse, allegedly to preserve the items for the estate. Clara Kauffman, a friend of Gladys Piper, filed a claim against the estate for $4,800. For several years before Piper's death, Kauffman had taken Piper to the doctor, beauty salon, and grocery store. She had also written Piper's checks to pay her bills and helped her care for her home.

Kauffman maintained that Piper had promised to pay her for these services and that Piper had given her the diamond rings as a gift. The trial court denied Kauffman's request for payment of $4,800 on the basis that the services had been voluntary. Kauffman then filed a petition for delivery of personal property (the rings), which was granted by the trial court. The defendants—Piper's heirs and the administrator of Piper's estate—appealed.

In the Language of the Court
GREENE, Judge.
* * * *

While no particular form is necessary to effect a delivery, and while the delivery may be actual, constructive, or symbolical, there must be some evidence to support a delivery theory. What we have here, at best, * * * was an intention on the part of Gladys, at some future time, to make a gift of the rings to Clara. Such an intention, no matter how clearly expressed, which has not been carried into effect, confers no ownership rights in the property in the intended donee. *Language written or spoken, expressing an intention to give, does not constitute a gift, unless the intention is executed by a complete and unconditional delivery of the subject matter, or delivery of a proper written instrument evidencing the gift.* There is no evidence in this case to prove delivery, and, for such reason, the trial court's judgment is erroneous. [Emphasis added.]

Decision and Remedy *The judgment of the trial court was reversed. No effective gift of the rings had been made, because Piper had never delivered the rings to Kauffman.*

Impact of This Case on Today's Law *This classic case clearly illustrates the delivery requirement for making a gift. Assuming that Piper did, indeed, intend for Kauffman to have the rings, it was unfortunate that Kauffman had no right to receive them after Piper's death. Yet the alternative might lead to even more unfairness. The policy behind the delivery requirement is to protect alleged donors and their heirs from fraudulent claims based solely on parol evidence. If not for this policy, an alleged donee could easily claim that a gift had been made when, in fact, it had not.*

Case 48.2 Continued   **Critical Thinking**

• **What If the Facts Were Different?** *Suppose that Piper had told Kauffman that she was giving the rings to Kauffman but wished to keep them in her possession for a few more days. Would this have affected the court's decision in this case? Explain.*

Acceptance The final requirement of a valid gift is acceptance by the donee. This rarely presents any problems, because most donees readily accept their gifts. The courts generally assume acceptance unless the circumstances indicate otherwise.

Gifts *Inter Vivos* and Gifts *Causa Mortis* A gift made during the donor's lifetime is called a **gift *inter vivos.*** A gift made in contemplation of imminent death is a **gift *causa mortis*** (a so-called *deathbed gift*). To be effective, a gift *causa mortis* must meet the three requirements of intent, delivery, and acceptance.

In addition, a gift *causa mortis* does not become absolute until the donor dies from the contemplated illness or event, and it is automatically revoked if the donor survives.[2] ■ **EXAMPLE 48.5** Yang, who is about to undergo surgery to remove a cancerous tumor, delivers an envelope to Chao, a close business associate. The envelope contains a letter saying, "I want to give you $1 million in U.S. government bonds in the event of my death from this operation." Chao redeems (cashes in) the bonds. The surgeon performs the operation and removes the tumor. Yang recovers fully from the operation, but the day after he leaves the hospital, he is killed when his home is struck by a tornado.

If the administrator of Yang's estate tries to recover the $1 million, she will normally succeed. The gift *causa mortis* to Chao is automatically revoked if Yang survives the operation. The *specific event* that was contemplated in making the gift was death from a particular operation. Because Yang's death was not the result of this event, the gift is revoked, and the $1 million passes to Yang's estate. ■

A gift *causa mortis* may also be revoked if the prospective donee dies before the donor. Therefore, even if Yang in *Example 48.5* had died during the operation, the gift would have been revoked if Chao had died a few minutes earlier. In that event, the $1 million would have passed to Yang's estate, and not to Chao's heirs.

48–2d Accession

Accession means "something added." Accession occurs when someone adds value to an item of personal property by the use of either labor or materials.

Generally, there is no dispute about who owns the property after accession occurs, especially when the accession is accomplished with the owner's consent. ■ **EXAMPLE 48.6** Hays buys all the materials necessary to customize his Corvette. He hires Zach, a customizing specialist, to come his house to perform the work. Hays pays Zach for the value of the labor, obviously retaining title to the property. ■

If an improvement is made wrongfully—without the permission of the owner—the owner retains title to the property and normally does not have to pay for the improvement. This is true even if the accession increased the value of the property substantially. ■ **EXAMPLE 48.7** Colton steals a truck and puts expensive new tires on it. If the rightful owner later recovers the truck, the owner obviously will not be required to compensate Colton, a thief, for the value of the new tires. ■

48–2e Confusion

Confusion is the commingling (mixing together) of goods to such an extent that one person's personal property cannot be distinguished from another's. Confusion frequently occurs with *fungible goods,* such as grain or oil, which consist of identical units.[3]

If confusion occurs as a result of agreement, an honest mistake, or the act of some third party, the owners share ownership in the commingled goods in proportion to the amount each contributed. ■ **EXAMPLE 48.8** Five farmers in a small Iowa community enter into a cooperative arrangement. Each fall, the farmers harvest the same amount of number 2–grade yellow corn and store it in silos that are held by the cooperative. Each farmer thus owns one-fifth of the total corn in the silos. If a fire burns down one of the silos, each farmer will bear one-fifth of the loss. ■ If goods are confused due to an intentional

---

2. For a classic case on the requirement that the donor must die from the contemplated peril, see *Brind v. International Trust Co.*, 66 Colo. 60, 179 P. 148 (1919).

3. See Section 1–201(17) of the Uniform Commercial Code (UCC).

wrongful act, then the innocent party ordinarily acquires title to the whole.

Concept Summary 48.1 reviews various ways in which personal property can be acquired.

48-3 Mislaid, Lost, and Abandoned Property

As already noted, one of the methods of acquiring ownership of property is to possess it. Simply finding something and holding onto it, however, does not *necessarily* give the finder any legal rights in the property. Different rules apply, depending on whether the property was mislaid, lost, or abandoned.

48-3a Mislaid Property

Property that has been voluntarily placed somewhere by the owner and then inadvertently forgotten is **mislaid property.** A person who finds mislaid property does not obtain title to the goods. Instead, the owner of the place where the property was mislaid becomes the caretaker

---

Concept Summary 48.1

Acquisition of Personal Property

By Purchase or by Will	The most common means of acquiring ownership in personal property is by purchasing it. Another way in which personal property is often acquired is by will or inheritance.
Possession	Ownership may be acquired by possession if no other person has ownership title, such as capturing wild animals or finding abandoned property.
Production	Any product or item produced by an individual (with minor exceptions) becomes the property of that individual.
Gift	An effective gift is made when the following three requirements are met: • There is evidence of *intent* to make a gift of the property in question. • The gift is *delivered* (physically or constructively) to the donee or the donee's agent. • The gift is *accepted* by the donee.
Accession	When value is added to personal property by use of labor or materials, the owner of the original property generally retains title to the property and benefits from the added value.
Confusion	If confusion occurs as a result of agreement, an honest mistake, or the act of some third party, the owners share ownership in the commingled goods in proportion to the amount each contributed. If goods are confused due to an intentional wrongful act, the innocent party ordinarily acquires title to the whole.

of the property, because it is highly likely that the true owner will return.[4]

■ **EXAMPLE 48.9** Maya goes to a movie theater. While paying for popcorn at the concessions stand, she sets her smartphone on the counter and then leaves it there. The smartphone is mislaid property, and the theater owner is entrusted with the duty of reasonable care for it. ■

48–3b Lost Property

Property that is *involuntarily* left is **lost property.** A finder of lost property can claim title to the property against the whole world—*except the true owner.*[5] If the true owner is identified and demands that the lost property be returned, the finder must return it. In contrast, if a third party attempts to take possession of the lost property, the finder will have a better title than the third party.

■ **EXAMPLE 48.10** Kayla works in a large library at night. As she crosses the courtyard on her way home, she finds a gold bracelet set with what seem to be precious stones. She takes the bracelet to a jeweler to have it appraised. While pretending to weigh the bracelet, the jeweler's employee removes several of the stones. If Kayla brings an action to recover the stones from the jeweler, she normally will win, because she found lost property and holds title against everyone *except the true owner.* ■

Conversion of Lost Property When a finder of lost property knows the true owner and fails to return the property to that person, the finder is guilty of the tort of *conversion*. In *Example 48.10,* if Kayla knows that the gold bracelet she found belongs to Geneva and does not return the bracelet, Kayla is guilty of conversion. Many states require the finder to make a reasonably diligent search to locate the true owner of lost property.

Estray Statutes Many states have **estray statutes,** which encourage and facilitate the return of property to its true owner and reward the finder for honesty if the property remains unclaimed. These laws provide an incentive for finders to report their discoveries by enabling them, at the end of a specified time, to acquire legal title to the found property.

Generally, the item must be lost property, not merely mislaid property, for estray statutes to apply. Estray statutes usually require the finder or the county clerk to advertise the property in an attempt to help the owner recover what has been lost.

■ **CASE IN POINT 48.11** Drug smugglers often enter the United States illegally from Canada via a frozen river that flows through Van Buren, Maine. When two railroad employees in Van Buren found a duffel bag that contained $165,580 in cash, they reported their find to U.S. Customs agents, who took custody of it. A drug-sniffing dog gave a positive alert on the bag for the scent of drugs. The federal government filed a lawsuit claiming title to the property under criminal forfeiture laws (because the property was involved in illegal drug transactions).

The two employees argued that they were entitled to the $165,580 under Maine's estray statute. That statute required finders to (1) provide written notice to the town clerk within seven days after finding the property, (2) post a public notice, and (3) advertise in the town's newspaper. Because the employees had not fulfilled these requirements, the court ruled that they had not acquired title to the property. Thus, the U.S. government had a right to seize the cash.[6] ■

48–3c Abandoned Property

Property that has been *discarded* by the true owner, who has *no intention* of reclaiming title to it, is **abandoned property.** Someone who finds abandoned property acquires title to it, and that title is good against the whole world, *including the original owner.* If a person finds abandoned property while trespassing on another's property, however, the trespasser will not acquire title.

The owner of lost property who eventually gives up any further attempt to find it is frequently held to have abandoned the property. ■ **EXAMPLE 48.12** While Alekis is hiking in the redwoods, her expensive watch falls off. She retraces her route and searches for the watch but cannot find it. She finally gives up her search and returns home some five hundred miles away. When Frye later finds the watch, he acquires title to it that is good even against Alekis. By completely giving up her search, Alekis abandoned the watch just as effectively as if she had intentionally discarded it. ■

Exhibit 48–1 summarizes the distinctions among these types of property.

---

4. The finder of mislaid property is an *involuntary bailee* (as will be discussed later in this chapter).
5. For a landmark English case establishing finders' rights in property, see *Armory v. Delamirie*, 93 Eng.Rep. 664 (K.B. [King's Bench] 1722).

6. *United States v. One Hundred Sixty-Five Thousand Five Hundred Eighty Dollars ($165,580) in U.S. Currency*, 502 F.Supp.2d 114 (D.Me. 2007).

EXHIBIT 48–1 Mislaid, Lost, and Abandoned Property

TYPE OF PROPERTY	DESCRIPTION
Mislaid Property	Property that is placed somewhere voluntarily by the owner and then inadvertently forgotten. A finder of mislaid property will not acquire title to the goods, and the owner of the place where the property was mislaid becomes a caretaker of the mislaid property.
Lost Property	Property that is involuntarily left by the owner. A finder of lost property can claim title to the property against the whole world except the true owner.
Abandoned Property	Property that has been discarded by the true owner, who has no intention of reclaiming title to the property in the future. A finder of abandoned property can claim title to it against the whole world, including the original owner.

48–4 Bailments

Many routine personal and business transactions involve bailments. A **bailment** is formed by the delivery of personal property, without transfer of title, by one person (called a **bailor**) to another (called a **bailee**). What distinguishes a bailment from a sale or a gift is that possession is transferred without passage of title or intent to transfer title.

Bailment agreements usually are made for a particular purpose—for example, to loan, lease, store, repair, or transport the property. On completion of the purpose, the bailee is obligated to return the bailed property in the same or better condition to the bailor or a third person or to dispose of it as directed.

Although bailments typically arise by agreement, not all of the elements of a contract must necessarily be present for a bailment to be created. ■ **EXAMPLE 48.13** If Amy lends her bicycle to a friend, a bailment is created, but not by contract, because there is no consideration. Note, though, that many commercial bailments, such as the delivery of clothing to the cleaners for dry cleaning, are based on contract. ■

48–4a Elements of a Bailment

Not all transactions involving the delivery of property from one person to another create a bailment. For such a transfer to become a bailment, the following three elements must be present:

1. Personal property.
2. Delivery of possession (without title).
3. Agreement that the property will be returned to the bailor or otherwise disposed of according to its owner's directions.

Personal Property Requirement Only personal property, not real property or persons, can be the subject of a bailment. ■ **EXAMPLE 48.14** When you check your bags at the airport, a bailment of your luggage is created because it is personal property. When you board the plane as a passenger, no bailment is created. ■

Bailments commonly involve *tangible* items—jewelry, cattle, automobiles, and the like. Nevertheless, *intangible* personal property, such as promissory notes and shares of stock, may also be bailed.

Delivery of Possession *Delivery of possession* means transfer of possession of the property to the bailee. For delivery to occur, the bailee must be given *exclusive possession and control* over the property, and the bailee must *knowingly* accept the property.[7] In other words, the bailee must *intend* to exercise control over it.

If either delivery of possession or knowing acceptance is lacking, there is no bailment relationship. ■ **EXAMPLE 48.15** Delacroix goes to a five-star restaurant and checks her coat. She forgets that there is a $20,000 diamond necklace in the coat pocket. In accepting the coat, the bailee does not *knowingly* also accept the necklace. Thus, a bailment of the coat exists—because the restaurant has exclusive possession and control over the coat and knowingly accepted it—but not a bailment of the necklace. ■

Physical versus Constructive Delivery. Either *physical* or *constructive delivery* will result in the bailee's exclusive possession of and control over the property. As discussed earlier (in the context of gifts), constructive delivery is a substitute, or symbolic, delivery. What is delivered to the bailee is not the actual property bailed (such as a car) but something so related to the property (such as the car keys) that the requirement of delivery is satisfied.

---

7. This rule applies to *voluntary bailments*, not to *involuntary bailments*.

Involuntary Bailments. In certain situations, a court will find that a bailment exists despite the apparent lack of the requisite elements of control and knowledge. One situation in which this occurs is when the bailee acquires the property accidentally or by mistake—as in finding someone else's lost or mislaid property. A bailment is created even though the bailor did not voluntarily deliver the property to the bailee. Such bailments are referred to as *constructive* or *involuntary* bailments.

■ **EXAMPLE 48.16** Several corporate managers attend a meeting at the law firm of Jacobs & Matheson. One of the corporate officers, Kyle Gustafson, inadvertently leaves his briefcase behind at the conclusion of the meeting. In this situation, a court could find that an involuntary bailment was created even though Gustafson did not voluntarily deliver the briefcase and the law firm did not intentionally accept it. If an involuntary bailment exists, the firm is responsible for taking care of the briefcase and returning it to Gustafson. ■

48–4b The Bailment Agreement

A bailment agreement can be express or implied. Although a written contract is not required for bailments for less than one year, it is a good idea to have one, especially when valuable property is involved.

The bailment agreement expressly or impliedly provides for the return of the bailed property to the bailor or to a third person, or for disposal of the property by the bailee. It is assumed that the bailee will return the identical goods originally given by the bailor. In certain types of bailments, though, such as bailments of fungible goods,[8] the property returned need only be equivalent property.

■ **EXAMPLE 48.17** A bailment is created when Holman stores his grain (fungible goods) in Joe's Warehouse. At the end of the storage period, however, the warehouse is not obligated to return to Holman exactly the same grain that he stored. As long as the warehouse returns grain of the same *type, grade,* and *quantity,* the warehouse—the bailee—has performed its obligation. ■

48–5 Ordinary Bailments

Bailments are either *ordinary* or *special (extraordinary).* There are three types of ordinary bailments. They are distinguished according to *which party receives a benefit*

from the bailment. This factor will dictate the rights and liabilities of the parties. In addition, the courts may use it to determine the standard of care required of the bailee in possession of the personal property.

The three types of ordinary bailments are listed below and described in the following subsections:

1. Bailment for the sole benefit of the bailor.
2. Bailment for the sole benefit of the bailee.
3. Bailment for the mutual benefit of the bailee and the bailor.

48–5a Bailment for the Sole Benefit of the Bailor

A bailment for the sole benefit of the bailor is a type of *gratuitous bailment*—meaning that it involves no consideration. The bailment is for the convenience and benefit of the bailor. Basically, the bailee is caring for the bailor's property as a favor. Therefore, the bailee owes only a slight duty of care and will be liable only if she or he is grossly negligent in caring for the property.

■ **EXAMPLE 48.18** Allen asks Sumi to store his car in her garage while he is away. If Sumi agrees to do so, then a gratuitous bailment is created, because the bailment is for the sole benefit of the bailor (Allen). If the car is damaged while in Sumi's garage, Sumi will not be responsible for the damage unless it was caused by her gross negligence. ■

48–5b Bailment for the Sole Benefit of the Bailee

When one person lends an item to another person (the bailee) solely for that person's convenience and benefit, a bailment for the sole benefit of the bailee is created. Because the bailee is borrowing the item for her or his own benefit, the bailee owes a duty to exercise the utmost care and will be liable for even slight negligence.

■ **EXAMPLE 48.19** Jeremy asks to borrow Sumi's boat so that he can take his girlfriend sailing over the weekend. The bailment of the boat is for Jeremy's (the bailee's) sole benefit. If Jeremy fails to pay attention and runs the boat aground, damaging its hull, he is liable for the costs of repairing the boat. ■

48–5c Mutual-Benefit Bailments

The most common kind of bailment is for the mutual benefit of the bailee and the bailor, and involves some form of compensation for storing items or holding

---

8. As mentioned earlier, *fungible goods* are goods that consist of identical particles, such as wheat. Fungible goods are defined in UCC 1–201(17).

property. It is a contractual bailment and is often referred to as a *bailment for hire* or a *commercial bailment.*

In a commercial bailment, the bailee must exercise ordinary care, which is the care that a reasonably prudent person would use under the circumstances. If the bailee fails to exercise reasonable care, he or she will be liable for ordinary negligence.

■ **EXAMPLE 48.20** Allen leaves his car at Midas for an oil change. Because Midas will be paid to change Allen's oil, this is a mutual-benefit bailment. If Midas fails to put the correct amount of oil back into Allen's car and the engine is damaged as a result, Midas will be liable for failure to have exercised reasonable care. ■

48–5d Rights of the Bailee

Certain rights are implicit in the bailment agreement. Generally, the bailee has the right to take possession of the property and to utilize it for accomplishing the purpose of the bailment. The bailee also has a right to receive compensation (unless the bailment is intended to be gratuitous). In addition, the bailee may have the right to limit her or his liability for the bailed goods. These rights of the bailee are present (with some limitations) in varying degrees in all bailment transactions.

Right of Possession A hallmark of the bailment agreement is that the bailee acquires the *right to control and possess the property temporarily.* The duration of a bailment depends on the terms of the agreement. If the agreement specifies its duration, then the bailment continues for that time period, and an earlier termination by the bailor is a breach of contract. If no duration is stated, the bailment ends when either the bailor or the bailee requests its termination and the bailed property is returned to the bailor.

A bailee's right of possession, even though temporary, permits the bailee to recover damages from any third parties for damage or loss to the property. ■ **EXAMPLE 48.21** No-Spot Dry Cleaners sends all suede leather garments to Cleanall Company for special processing. If Cleanall loses or damages any leather goods, No-Spot has the right to recover from Cleanall. ■ If the bailed property is stolen, the bailee has a legal right to regain possession of it.

Right to Use Bailed Property In some bailments, a bailee may have a right to use the bailed property. When no express provision is made, the extent of use depends on how necessary it is for the goods to be at the bailee's disposal for the ordinary purpose of the bailment to be carried out.

■ **EXAMPLE 48.22** If Lauren borrows a car to drive a friend to the airport, she, as the bailee, will obviously be expected to use the car. In contrast, if Devin drives his own car to the airport and places it in long-term storage nearby, the storage company, as the bailee, will not be expected to use the car. The ordinary purpose of a storage bailment does not include use of the property. The bailee will, however, be expected to use or move the car if necessary in an emergency (such as a hurricane or flood) to protect it from harm. ■

Right of Compensation Except in a gratuitous bailment, a bailee has a right to be compensated as provided for in the bailment agreement. The bailee also has the right to be reimbursed for costs incurred and services rendered in keeping the bailed property (even in a gratuitous bailment).

To enforce the right of compensation, the bailee has a right to place a *possessory lien* on the specific bailed property until she or he has been fully compensated. Such a lien is sometimes referred to as a **bailee's lien,** or artisan's lien. If the bailor refuses to pay or cannot pay, in most states the bailee is entitled to foreclose on the lien and sell the property to recover the amount owed.

■ **EXAMPLE 48.23** Liam leaves his car at Dusty's Automotive for repairs. Dusty's informs Liam that the car needs a new transmission, and Liam authorizes Dusty's to perform the work. When Liam returns to pick up the car, he refuses to pay the amount due for the transmission work. Dusty's has a right to keep the car and place a lien on it until Liam pays for the repairs. If Liam continues to refuse to pay, Dusty's can follow the state's statutory process for foreclosing on the lien and selling the car to recover what is owed. ■

Right to Limit Liability In ordinary bailments, bailees have the right to limit their liability provided that both of the following are true:

1. *The limitations are called to the attention of the bailor.* It is essential that the bailor be informed of the limitation in some way. ■ **EXAMPLE 48.24** A sign in Nikolai's garage states that Nikolai will not be responsible "for loss due to theft, fire, or vandalism." Whether the sign will constitute notice will depend on the size of the sign, its location, and any other circumstances affecting the likelihood that customers will see it. ■

2. *The limitations are not against public policy.* Courts consider certain types of disclaimers of liability to be against public policy and therefore illegal, whether or not the bailor is aware of them. As previously discussed, the courts carefully scrutinize *exculpatory*

clauses, which limit a person's liability for her or his own wrongful acts. In bailments, especially mutual-benefit bailments, exculpatory clauses are often held to be illegal. ■ **EXAMPLE 48.25** A receipt from a parking garage expressly disclaims liability for any damage to parked cars, regardless of the cause. Because the bailee (the garage) has attempted to exclude liability for the bailee's own negligence, the clause will likely be deemed unenforceable because it is against public policy. ■

48–5e Duties of the Bailee

The bailee's duties are based on a mixture of tort law and contract law, and include the following two basic responsibilities:

1. To take appropriate care of the property.
2. To surrender the property to the bailor or dispose of it in accordance with the bailor's instructions at the end of the bailment.

The Duty of Care The bailee must exercise reasonable care in preserving the bailed property. What constitutes reasonable care in a bailment situation normally depends on the nature and specific circumstances of the bailment.

As already mentioned, the courts determine the appropriate standard of care on the basis of the type of bailment involved. In a bailment for the sole benefit of the bailor, the bailee need exercise only a slight degree of care, whereas in a bailment for the sole benefit of the bailee, the bailee must exercise great care.

Exhibit 48–2 illustrates the degree of care required of bailees in bailment relationships. Determining whether a bailee exercised an appropriate degree of care is usually a question of fact for the jury or for the judge (in a nonjury trial). A bailee's failure to exercise appropriate care in handling the bailor's property results in tort liability. ■ **CASE IN POINT 48.26** Bridge Tower Dental contracted with Meridian Computer Center to develop a computer system for its dental practice. Bridge Tower paid a computer consultant, Al Colson, to install the system and to provide maintenance and support. When Colson noticed that one of the server's two hard drives had stopped working, he informed Bridge Tower and took the server to Meridian Computer to be repaired. Meridian's owner, Jason Patten, agreed to replace the failing hard drive under the warranty. In attempting to copy data from the mirrored hard drive, however, Patten accidentally erased all the data, which he had not backed up. As a result, Bridge Tower lost all of its patients' records and contact information.

Bridge Tower sued Meridian for negligence. The Supreme Court of Idaho ruled in favor of Bridge Tower. Colson had entrusted Meridian with a server containing a failing hard drive (which was to be replaced) and a fully functional mirrored hard drive containing data. Meridian had a duty to protect and safeguard this bailed property in order to return it in the same condition it was in when delivered. Patten mistakenly erased the data on the mirrored hard drive, which constituted negligence.[9] ■

Duty to Return Bailed Property At the end of the bailment, the bailee normally must hand over the original property to either the bailor or someone the bailor designates, or must otherwise dispose of it as directed.[10] Failure to give up possession at the time the bailment ends is a breach of contract and could result in a tort lawsuit for conversion or negligence.

■ **CASE IN POINT 48.27** SANY America, Inc., loaned a crane to Turner Brothers, LLC, a construction contractor, for demonstration purposes. SANY wanted to sell the crane to Turner and continued to allow Turner to use it during their negotiations, but the parties never came to an agreement on a price. After the negotiations ended, SANY asked Turner for the crane's location to arrange retrieval. Before SANY retrieved the crane from Turner,

---

9. *Bridge Tower Dental, P.A. v. Meridian Computer Center, Inc.,* 272 P.3d 541 (Idaho Sup.Ct. 2012).
10. As mentioned earlier, if the bailment involves fungible goods, such as grain, then the bailee is not required to return exactly the same goods to the bailor. Instead, the bailee must return goods of the same type, grade, and quantity.

EXHIBIT 48–2   Degree of Care Required of a Bailee

Bailment for the Sole Benefit of the Bailor	Mutual-Benefit Bailment	Bailment for the Sole Benefit of the Bailee
DEGREE OF CARE →		
SLIGHT	REASONABLE	GREAT

however, it was severely damaged while being operated at Turner's construction site.

Turner removed the inoperable crane from the site at its own expense and then notified SANY that it expected compensation for the transportation expenses. In addition, Turner refused to return the crane to SANY and began billing SANY for daily storage costs. SANY sued for conversion, and Turner counterclaimed. A federal district court held that the parties' transaction was a bailment. Because Turner had wrongfully retained the crane after SANY demanded its return, SANY was entitled to summary judgment for conversion.[11] ■

A bailee may be liable for conversion or misdelivery if the goods are given to the wrong person. Hence, a bailee should verify that any person other than the bailor to whom the goods are given is authorized to take possession.

Lost or Damaged Property If the bailed property has been lost or is returned damaged, a court will presume that the bailee was negligent. The bailee's obligation is excused, however, if the property was destroyed, lost, or stolen through no fault of the bailee (or claimed by a third party with a superior claim). In other words, the bailee can rebut the presumption of negligence by showing that he or she exercised due care.

■ **CASE IN POINT 48.28** Hornbeck Offshore Service engaged R&R Marine, Inc., to repair the ship *Erie*

Servic*e* at R&R's shipyard on Lake Sabine in Port Arthur, Texas. While repairs were being made, a tropical storm warning was issued for Port Arthur. R&R's personnel left the shipyard without securing or preparing the *Erie Service* for the storm. During the night, rain and water from Lake Sabine swamped the vessel. R&R's insurer, National Liability & Fire Insurance Company, asked a federal district court to declare that it was not required to pay the salvage cost. Hornbeck filed a counterclaim with the court alleging that R&R had been negligent. The lower court issued a decision in Hornbeck's favor, and R&R appealed.

A federal appellate court affirmed the lower court's ruling. The ship had been delivered to R&R afloat, R&R had full custody of the vessel, and it sank while in R&R's care. This gave rise to a presumption of negligence. The severity of the weather conditions in Port Arthur had been foreseeable, and R&R showed no evidence that it had exercised ordinary care. The court held that R&R—not the insurer—was liable for the salvage cost because R&R had been negligent in failing to protect the ship from damage from the storm.[12] ■

In the following case, the court had to determine whether a constructive bailment existed over the personal property of tenants who were evicted. If so, was the landlord-bailor negligent for removing the tenants' personal property and leaving it outside?

11. *SANY America, Inc. v. Turner Brothers, LLC,* ___ F.Supp.3d ___, 2016 WL 1452341 (D.Mass. 2016).

12. *National Liability & Fire Insurance Co. v. R&R Marine, Inc.,* 756 F.3d 825 (5th Cir. 2014).

Case Analysis 48.3

Zissu v. IH2 Property Illinois, L.P.
United States District Court, Northern District of Illinois, Eastern Division, __ F.Supp.3d __, 2016 WL 212937 (2016).

In the Language of the Court
John Z. *LEE,* United States District Judge

Plaintiffs Pavel Zissu and Aise Zissu bring suit [in this federal district court] against the owner of the property where they resided, IH2 Property Illinois, L.P. The Zissus claim that after a Cook County [Illinois] Sheriff turned over possession of the premises to IH2 pursuant to an eviction order, the company removed all of their personal property from the premises and put it outside. In their complaint, the Zissus assert [that the company's actions

constituted] negligence [and a constructive] bailment.

FACTUAL BACKGROUND
* * * The Zissus resided at a property in the City of Chicago owned by IH2. * * * [An Illinois state court judge] issued an order for possession, allowing IH2 to evict the Zissus. The order was executed by a Cook County Sheriff.

Once IH2 was given possession of the premises, its agents took all of the Zissus' personal property that was in the apartment and placed it outside on the curb. The property, which included

jewelry, furniture, and personal documents, was then either stolen or damaged.

LEGAL STANDARD
A motion [to dismiss under the Federal Rules of Procedure] challenges the sufficiency of the complaint.

*A complaint * * * must * * * allege sufficient factual matter, accepted as true, to state a claim to relief that is plausible on its face. For a claim to have facial plausibility, a plaintiff must plead factual content that allows the court to draw the reasonable*

Case 48.3 Continued

inference that the defendant is liable for the misconduct alleged. [Emphasis added.]

ANALYSIS

This is a diversity suit. As such, we apply state substantive law and federal procedural law. Both parties cite Illinois law in their briefing, so the Court will apply Illinois law.

I. Negligence

The Zissus allege that IH2 negligently removed their personal property from the premises following the eviction, causing much of it to be damaged or stolen. * * * In its motion to dismiss, IH2 argues that the Zissus cannot state a claim for negligence because IH2, as the landlord, did not owe a duty to protect personal property left on the premises following the eviction.
* * * *

Because [the statutes of Illinois are silent on this issue and] the Illinois Supreme Court has not addressed this issue, this Court must attempt to divine [guess] how the [Illinois] Supreme Court would rule. In fact, only two courts have addressed the question of a landlord's duty under Illinois law. [In] *Centagon, Inc. v. Board of Directors of 1212 Lake Shore Drive Condominium Association*, __ F.Supp.2d __, 2001 WL 1491523 (N.D.Ill. 2001), a condo association had obtained a judgment granting exclusive possession of a unit that had belonged to the plaintiff. The sheriff's office executed the eviction and * * * removed the personal property onto the curb and sidewalk.

* * * The court held that the facts in that case were insufficient to impose an affirmative duty upon defendants to care for any personal property left in the Unit after eviction. The mere fact that the representatives of the condo association had been present and had observed the eviction and removal of the property was not enough to establish a duty of care.

* * * An Illinois appellate court applied a similar analytical framework in *Dargis v. Paradise Park, Inc.,* 354 Ill. App.3d 171, 819 N.E.2d 1220 (2004). There, the court concluded that, while a landlord has no duty in such situations as a general matter, an exception is created when the landlord chooses to care for the property. * * * This decision is helpful because state appellate court decisions, although not binding, constitute persuasive authority.

In the end, the Court agrees with the reasoning in these cases and finds that the Illinois Supreme Court would hold that, although a landlord does not have a general duty under common law to care for the personal property of a former tenant after a proper and legal eviction, a duty of care does arise when a landlord acts as an actual or constructive bailee with respect to the tenant's property. [If] the complaint states a claim for bailment as further discussed below, the Court finds that Plaintiffs have sufficiently alleged the existence of a duty and a breach of that duty to survive a motion to dismiss as to their negligence claim.

II. Bailment

* * * The Zissus allege that a constructive (or implied) bailment was created when IH2 took control over the personal property that had been left behind. In its motion to dismiss, IH2 argues that the Zissus have failed to state a claim because IH2 never took possession of the personal property.

A bailment occurs when goods, or other personal property, are delivered to another, *who under contract either express or implied has agreed to accept delivery and deal with the property in a particular way.* To recover under a bailment theory, the plaintiff must allege: (1) an express or implied agreement to create a bailment, (2) delivery of the property, (3) the bailee's acceptance of the property, and (4) the bailee's failure to return the property or the bailee's delivery of the property in a damaged condition. [Emphasis added.]

An implied bailment—also called a constructive bailment—may be found where the property of one person is voluntarily received by another for some purpose other than that of obtaining ownership. The implied bailment may be deduced from the circumstances surrounding the transaction, including the benefits received by the parties, their intentions, the kind of property involved, and the opportunities of each to exercise control over the property.

The Zissus contend that, by actively removing the property from the premises and putting it on the street, IH2 assumed control over the property. Unlike in *Centagon,* in which the defendants had watched the sheriff take out the property, IH2 itself took possession of the property and put it outside.
* * * It was IH2's alleged actions after the sheriff had turned over possession of the premises to IH2 that gave rise to the bailment relationship. * * * The allegations are sufficient [to establish this claim] at the pleading stage.
* * * *

CONCLUSION

For the reasons stated herein, the Court denies IH2's motion to dismiss.

Legal Reasoning Questions

1. How did related cases addressing the issue of a landlord's duty under Illinois law affect the court's reasoning in this case?

2. Besides negligence, are there other tort claims that the Zissus might have successfully alleged in their complaint? Discuss.

3. Suppose that instead of putting the Zissus' personal property outside, IH2 had taken it to a storage facility. Would the result have been different?

48–5f Duties of the Bailor

The duties of a bailor are essentially the same as the rights of a bailee. A bailor has a duty to compensate the bailee, as discussed earlier. A bailor also has an all-encompassing duty to provide the bailee with goods that are free from known defects that could cause injury to the bailee.

Bailor's Duty to Reveal Defects   The bailor's duty to reveal defects to the bailee translates into two rules:

1. In a *mutual-benefit bailment,* the bailor must notify the bailee of all known defects and any hidden defects that the bailor knows of or could have discovered with reasonable diligence and proper inspection.
2. In a *bailment for the sole benefit of the bailee,* the bailor must notify the bailee of any known defects.

The bailor's duty to reveal defects is based on a negligence theory of tort law. A bailor who fails to give the appropriate notice is liable to the bailee and to any other person who might reasonably be expected to come into contact with the defective article.

■ **EXAMPLE 48.29** Rentco (the bailor) rents a tractor to Hal Iverson. Unknown to Rentco (but *discoverable* by reasonable inspection), the brake mechanism on the tractor is defective at the time the bailment is made. Iverson uses the defective tractor without knowledge of the brake problem and is injured along with two other field workers when the tractor rolls out of control. In this situation, Rentco is liable for the injuries sustained by Iverson and the other workers because it negligently failed to discover the defect and notify Iverson. ■

Warranty Liability for Defective Goods   A bailor can also incur warranty liability under contract law for injuries resulting from the bailment of defective articles. Property that is leased from a bailor must be *fit for the intended purpose of the bailment.* The bailor's knowledge of or ability to discover any defects is immaterial.

Warranties of fitness arise by law in sales contracts, and courts have held that these warranties apply to bailments "for hire." Article 2A of the Uniform Commercial Code (UCC) extends the implied warranties of merchantability and fitness for a particular purpose to bailments that include rights to use the bailed goods.[13]

---

13. UCC 2A–212, 2A–213.

48–6 Special Types of Bailments

A business is likely to engage in some special types of bailment transactions. These include bailments in which the bailee's duty of care is *extraordinary* and the bailee's liability for loss or damage to the property is absolute. Such situations usually involve common carriers and hotel operators. Warehouse companies have the same duty of care as ordinary bailees, but like carriers, they are subject to extensive federal and state laws, including Article 7 of the UCC.

48–6a Common Carriers

Common carriers are publicly licensed to provide transportation services to the general public. They are legally bound to carry all passengers or freight as long as there is enough space, the fee is paid, and there are no reasonable grounds to refuse service. Common carriers differ from private carriers, which operate transportation facilities for only a select clientele. A private carrier is not required to provide service to every person or company making a request.

Strict Liability Applies   The delivery of goods to a common carrier creates a bailment relationship between the shipper (bailor) and the common carrier (bailee). Unlike ordinary bailees, the common carrier is held to a standard of care based on *strict liability,* rather than reasonable care, in protecting the bailed personal property. This means that the common carrier is absolutely liable, regardless of care, for all loss or damage to goods except when damage was caused by a natural disaster or war.

Limitations on Liability   Common carriers cannot contract away their liability for damaged goods. Subject to government regulations, however, they are permitted to limit their dollar liability to an amount stated on the shipment contract or rate filing. Carriers may also limit the value of property that they will transport.

■ **CASE IN POINT 48.30** Treiber & Straub, Inc., a jewelry store, used UPS to ship a diamond ring worth $105,000. The owner of the jewelry store arranged for the shipment on UPS's Web site, which required him to click on two on-screen boxes to agree to "My UPS Terms and Conditions." In these terms, UPS and its insurer limited their liability and the amount of insurance coverage on packages to $50,000, and refused to ship items worth more than $50,000. Both UPS and its insurer disclaimed liability *entirely* for such items. Nevertheless, the store owner purchased $50,000 in insurance for the package.

When the ring was lost, the jewelry store filed suit against UPS to recover $50,000 under the insurance policy. The court held that UPS's disclaimer of liability was enforceable. It also found that the jewelry store had breached the contract by indicating that the shipment was worth less than $50,000 when the ring was worth much more.[14] ■

48–6b Warehouse Companies

Warehousing is the business of providing storage of property for compensation. Like ordinary bailees, warehouse companies are liable for loss or damage to property resulting from *negligence*. But because a warehouse company is a professional bailee, it is expected to exercise a high degree of care to protect and preserve the goods.

Limitations on Liability A warehouse company can limit the dollar amount of its liability. Under the UCC, however, it must give the bailor the option of paying a higher storage rate for an increase in the liability limit.[15]

Warehouse Receipts Unlike ordinary bailees, a warehouse company can issue *documents of title*—in particular, *warehouse receipts*.[16] A warehouse receipt describes the bailed property and the terms of the bailment contract. It can be negotiable or nonnegotiable, depending on how it is written. It is negotiable if its terms provide that the warehouse company will deliver the goods "to the bearer" of the receipt or "to the order of" a person named on the receipt.[17]

The warehouse receipt represents the goods (that is, it indicates title) and hence has value and utility in financing commercial transactions. ■ **EXAMPLE 48.31** Ossip delivers 6,500 cases of canned corn to Chaney, the owner of a warehouse. Chaney issues a negotiable warehouse receipt payable "to bearer" and gives it to Ossip. Ossip sells and delivers the warehouse receipt to Better Foods, Inc. Better Foods is now the owner of the corn and can obtain the cases by simply presenting the warehouse receipt to Chaney. ■

48–6c Hotel Operators

At common law, hotel owners were strictly liable for the loss of any cash or property that guests brought into their rooms. Today, state statutes continue to apply strict liability to hotel operators for any loss or damage to their guests' personal property. In many states, however, hotel operators can avoid strict liability for loss of guests' cash and valuables by:

1. Providing a safe in which to keep guests' valuables.
2. Notifying guests that a safe is available.

In addition, statutes often limit the liability of innkeepers with regard to articles that are not kept in the safe and may limit the availability of damages in the absence of negligence. Most statutes require that the hotel post these limitations on the doors of the rooms or otherwise notify guests.

■ **EXAMPLE 48.32** A guest at Crown Place hotel is traveling with jewelry valued at $1 million. She puts the jewelry in the safe in her room, but someone comes into the room and removes the jewelry from the safe without the use of force. The woman sues the hotel, which claims that it is not liable under the state statute. If Crown Place did not comply with statutory requirements that it post the legal limitations in the guest rooms, however, it will not be protected from liability. Crown Place will be strictly liable for the loss of the woman's jewelry. ■

Concept Summary 48.2 reviews the rights and duties of bailees and bailors.

---

14. *Treiber & Straub, Inc. v. United Parcel Service, Inc.,* 474 F.3d 379 (7th Cir. 2007).
15. UCC 7–204(1), (2).
16. A *document of title* is defined in UCC 1–201(15) as any "document which in the regular course of business or financing is treated as adequately evidencing that the person in possession of it is entitled to receive, hold, and dispose of the document and the goods it covers." A *warehouse receipt* is a document of title issued by a person engaged for hire in the business of storing goods.
17. UCC 7–104.

Concept Summary 48.2

Rights and Duties of the Bailee and the Bailor

Rights of a Bailee (Duties of a Bailor)	• The right of possession allows a bailee to sue any third parties who damage, lose, or convert the bailed property.
	• The right to use the property to the extent it is necessary to carry out the purpose of the bailment.
	• The right to be compensated or reimbursed for keeping bailed property. In the event of nonpayment, the bailee has a right to place a possessory (bailee's) lien on the bailed property.
	• The right to limit liability. An ordinary bailee can limit the types of risk, monetary amount, or both, provided proper notice is given and the limitation is not against public policy. In special bailments, limitations on liability for negligence usually are not allowed, but limitations on the monetary amount of loss are permitted.
Duties of a Bailee (Rights of a Bailor)	• A bailee must exercise appropriate care over property entrusted to her or him. What constitutes appropriate care normally depends on the nature and circumstances of the bailment. A common carrier (special bailee) is held to a standard of care based on strict liability except when damage was caused by a natural disaster or war.
	• Bailed goods in a bailee's possession must be returned to the bailor or be disposed of according to the bailor's directions. Failure to return the property gives rise to a presumption of negligence.

Reviewing: Personal Property and Bailments

Vanessa Denai purchased forty acres of land in rural Louisiana. On the property were a 1,600-square-foot house and a metal barn. Denai later met Lance Finney, who had been seeking a small plot of rural property to rent. After several meetings, Denai invited Finney to live on a corner of her property in exchange for Finney's assistance in cutting wood and tending the property. Denai agreed to store Finney's sailboat in her barn.

With Denai's consent, Finney constructed a concrete and oak foundation on Denai's property. Finney then purchased a 190-square-foot dome from Dome Baja for $3,395. The dome was shipped by Doty Express, a transportation company licensed to serve the public. When it arrived, Finney installed the dome frame and fabric exterior so that the dome was detachable from the foundation. A year after Finney installed the dome, Denai wrote Finney a note stating, "I've decided to give you four acres of land surrounding your dome as drawn on this map." This gift violated no local land-use restrictions. Using the information presented in the chapter, answer the following questions.

1. Is the dome real property or personal property? Explain.
2. Is Denai's gift of land to Finney a testamentary gift, a gift *causa mortis,* or a gift *inter vivos?*
3. What type of bailment relationship was created when Denai agreed to store Finney's boat? What degree of care was Denai required to exercise in storing the boat?
4. What standard of care applied to the shipment of the dome by Doty Express?

Debate This . . .   *Common carriers should not be able to limit their liability.*

Terms and Concepts

Issue Spotters

1. Quintana Corporation sends important documents to Regal Nursery, Inc., via Speedy Messenger Service. While the documents are in Speedy's care, a third party causes an accident to Speedy's delivery vehicle that results in the loss of the documents. Does Speedy have a right to recover from the third party for the loss of the documents? Why or why not? (See *Ordinary Bailments*.)

2. Rosa de la Mar Corporation ships a load of goods via Southeast Delivery Company. The load of goods is lost in a hurricane in Florida. Who suffers the loss? Explain your answer. (See *Special Types of Bailments*.)

• **Check your answers to the Issue Spotters against the answers provided in Appendix D at the end of this text.**

Business Scenarios

48–1. Duties of the Bailee. Atka owns a valuable speedboat. She is going on vacation and asks her neighbor, Regina, to store the boat in one stall of Regina's double garage. Regina consents, and the boat is moved into the garage. Regina, in need of some grocery items for dinner, drives to the store. She leaves the garage door open, as is her custom. While she is at the store, the speedboat is stolen. What standard of care is required in this situation? Has Regina breached that duty? (See *Ordinary Bailments*.)

48–2. Duties of the Bailee. Orlando borrows a gasoline-driven lawn edger from his neighbor, Max. Max has not used the lawn edger for two years. Orlando has never owned a lawn edger and is not familiar with its use. Max previously used this edger often, and if he had made a reasonable inspection, he would have discovered that the blade was loose. Orlando is injured when the blade becomes detached while he is edging his yard. (See *Ordinary Bailments*.)

(a) Can Orlando hold Max liable for his injuries? Why or why not?

(b) Would your answer be different if Orlando had rented the edger from Max and paid a fee? Explain.

Business Case Problems

48–3. Gifts. John Wasniewski opened a brokerage account with Quick and Reilly, Inc., in his son James's name. Twelve years later, when the balance was $52,085, the account was closed, and the funds were transferred to a joint account in the names of John and James's brother. James did not learn of the existence of the account in his name until the transfer, when he received a tax form for the account's final year. He filed a suit in a Connecticut state court against Quick and Reilly, alleging breach of contract and seeking to recover the account's principal and interest. What are the elements of a valid gift? Did John's opening of the account with Quick and Reilly constitute a gift to James? What is the likely result in this case, and why? [*Wasniewski v. Quick and Reilly, Inc.,* 292 Conn. 98, 971 A.2d 8 (2009)] (See *Acquiring Ownership of Personal Property*.)

48–4. Business Case Problem with Sample Answer—Bailment Obligation. Bob Moreland left his plane at Don Gray's aircraft repair shop to be painted. When Moreland picked up the airplane, he was disappointed in the quality of the work and pointed out numerous defects. Moreland refused to pay Gray and flew the plane to another shop to have the work redone. Gray sued to collect, contending that Moreland had no right to take the plane to another shop without giving Gray a chance to fix any defects. Gray further argued that by taking the plane, Moreland had accepted Gray's work. Moreland counterclaimed for his expenses. Which party should be awarded damages, and why? [*Gray v. Moreland,* 2010 Ark. App. 207, 374 S.W.3d 178 (2010)] (See *Bailments*.)

• For a sample answer to Problem 48–4, go to Appendix E at the end of this text.

48–5. Gifts. Jennifer Koerner adopted a dog—called the Stig—from the Anti-Cruelty Society in Chicago, Illinois, for $95. Koerner wrote a poem and presented it to Kent Nielsen, her live-in boyfriend. In the poem, she expressed her intent to give the Stig to him as a gift. While Koerner and Nielsen lived together, they were both involved in the Stig's day-to-day care. They ended their relationship a year later, and Nielsen agreed to leave their shared residence. Can Nielsen take the Stig with him, or is Koerner the Stig's rightful owner? Explain. [*Koerner v. Nielsen,* 8 N.E.3d 161 (Ill.App. 1 Dist. 2014)] (See *Acquiring Ownership of Personal Property.*)

48–6. Lost Property. Sara Simon misplaced her Galaxy cell phone in Manhattan, Kansas. Days later, Shawn Vargo contacted her, claiming to have bought the phone from someone else. He promised to mail it to Simon if she would wire $100 to him through a third party, Mark Lawrence. When Simon spoke to Lawrence about the wire transfer, she referred to the phone as hers and asked, "Are you going to send my phone to me?" Simon paid, but she did not get the phone. Instead, Lawrence took it to a Best Buy store and traded it in for credit. Charged with the theft of lost property, Lawrence claimed that he did not know Simon was the owner of the phone. Was Simon's phone lost, mislaid, or abandoned? What is the finder's responsibility with respect to this type of property? Can Lawrence successfully argue that he did not know the phone was Simon's? Explain. [*State of Kansas v. Lawrence,* 347 P.3d 240 (Kan.App. 2015)] (See *Mislaid, Lost, and Abandoned Property.*)

48–7. Bailments. Christie's Fine Art Storage Services Inc. (CFASS) is in the business of storing fine works of art at its warehouse in Brooklyn, New York. The warehouse is next to the East River in a flood zone. Boyd Sullivan owns works of art by Alberto Vargas, including *Beauty and the Beast* and *Miss Universe.* Sullivan contracted to store the works at CFASS's facility under an agreement that limited the warehouser's liability for damage to the goods to $200,000. A few months later, as Hurricane Sandy approached, CFASS was warned, along with the other businesses in the flood zone, of the potential for damage from the storm. CFASS e-mailed its clients that extra precautions were being taken. Despite this assurance, Sullivan's works were left exposed on a ground floor and sustained severe damage in the storm. Who is most likely to suffer the loss? Why? [*Sullivan v. Christie's Fine Art Storage Services, Inc.,* __ Misc.3d __, 2016 Slip Op. __, 2016 WL 427615 (Sup. N.Y. County, Trial Order No. 160733/2014 2016)] (See *Bailments.*)

48–8. A Question of Ethics—Gifts. Jason Crippen and Catharyn Campbell of Knoxville, Tennessee, were involved in a romantic relationship for many months. Their relationship culminated in an engagement on December 25, 2005, when Crippen placed an engagement ring on Campbell's finger and simultaneously proposed marriage. Campbell accepted the proposal, and the parties were engaged to be married. The engagement did not last, however. The parties broke up, their romantic relationship ended, and neither had any intent to marry the other. Crippen asked Campbell to return the ring. She refused. Crippen filed a suit in a Tennessee state court against Campbell to recover the ring. Both parties filed motions for summary judgment. The court ruled in Campbell's favor. Crippen appealed to a state intermediate appellate court. [*Crippen v. Campbell,* 2007 WL 2768076 (Tenn. App. 2007)] (See *Acquiring Ownership of Personal Property.*)

(a) Under what reasoning could the court affirm the award of the ring to Campbell? On what basis could the court reverse the judgment and order Campbell to return the ring? (Hint: Is an engagement ring a completed gift immediately on its delivery?) Which principle do you support, and why?

(b) Should the court determine who was responsible for breaking off the engagement before awarding ownership of the ring? Why or why not?

(c) If, instead of Crippen, one of his creditors had sought the ring in satisfaction of one of his debts, how should the court have ruled? Why?

Legal Reasoning Group Activity

48–9. Bailments. On learning that Sébastien planned to travel abroad, Roslyn asked him to deliver $25,000 in cash to her family in Mexico. During a customs inspection at the border, Sébastien told the customs inspector that he carried less than $10,000. The officer discovered the actual amount of cash that Sébastien was carrying, seized it, and arrested Sébastien. Roslyn asked the government to return what she claimed were her funds, arguing that the arrangement with Sébastien was a bailment and that she still held title to the cash. (See *Bailments.*)

(a) The first group will argue that Roslyn is entitled to the cash.

(b) The second group will take the position of the government and develop an argument that Roslyn's agreement with Sébastien does not qualify as a bailment.

CHAPTER 49

Real Property and Landlord-Tenant Law

From the earliest times, property has provided a means for survival. Primitive peoples lived off the fruits of the land, eating the vegetation and wildlife. Later, as the wildlife was domesticated and the vegetation cultivated, property provided pastures and farmland. Throughout history, property has continued to be an indicator of family wealth and social position. In the Western world, the protection of an individual's right to his or her property has become one of our most important rights.

In this chapter, we look at the nature of real property and the ways in which it can be owned. We examine the legal requirements involved in the transfer of real property. We even consider, in this chapter's *Spotlight Case,* whether the buyer of a haunted house can rescind the sale.

Realize that real property rights are never absolute. There is a higher right—that of the government to take, for compensation, private land for public use. Later in the chapter, we discuss this right, as well as other restrictions on the ownership or use of property, including zoning laws. We conclude the chapter with a discussion of landlord-tenant relationships.

49–1 The Nature of Real Property

Real property (or realty) consists of land and everything permanently attached to it, including structures and other fixtures. Real property encompasses airspace and subsurface rights, as well as rights to plants and vegetation. In essence, real property is immovable.

49–1a Land and Structures

Land includes the soil on the surface of the earth and the natural products or artificial structures that are attached to it. Land further includes all the waters contained on or under its surface and much, but not necessarily all, of the airspace above it. The exterior boundaries of land extend down to the center of the earth and up to the farthest reaches of the atmosphere (subject to certain qualifications).

49–1b Airspace and Subsurface Rights

The owner of real property has rights to both the airspace above the land and the soil and minerals underneath it. Any limitations on either airspace rights or subsurface rights, called *encumbrances,* normally must be indicated on the document that transfers title at the time of purchase. The ways in which ownership rights in real property can be limited will be examined later in this chapter.

Airspace Rights Disputes concerning airspace rights may involve the right of commercial and private planes to fly over property and the right of individuals and governments to seed clouds and produce artificial rain. Flights over private land normally do not violate property rights unless the flights are so low and so frequent that they directly interfere with the owner's enjoyment and use of the land. Leaning walls or projecting eave spouts or roofs may also violate the airspace rights of an adjoining property owner.

Subsurface Rights In many states, ownership of land can be separated from ownership of its subsurface. In other words, the owner of the surface may sell subsurface rights to another person. When ownership is separated into surface and subsurface rights, each owner can pass title to what she or he owns without the consent of the other owner.

Subsurface rights can be extremely valuable, as these rights include the ownership of minerals, oil, or natural gas. But a subsurface owner's rights would be of little value if he or she could not use the surface to exercise those rights. Hence, a subsurface owner has a right (called a *profit,* discussed later in this chapter) to go onto the surface of the land to, for instance, find and remove minerals.

Of course, conflicts can arise between the surface owner's use of the property and the subsurface owner's need to extract minerals, oil, or natural gas. In that situation, one party's interest may become subservient (secondary) to the other party's interest either by statute or by case law. If the owners of the subsurface rights excavate, they are absolutely (strictly) liable if their excavation causes the surface to collapse. Many states have statutes that also make the excavators liable for any damage to structures on the land. Typically, these statutes set out precise requirements for excavations of various depths.

49–1c Plant Life and Vegetation

Plant life, both natural and cultivated, is also considered to be real property. In many instances, the natural vegetation, such as trees, adds greatly to the value of realty. When a parcel of land is sold and the land has growing crops on it, the sale includes the crops, unless otherwise specified in the sales contract. When crops are sold by themselves, however, they are considered to be personal property, or goods. Consequently, the sale of crops is a sale of goods and is governed by the Uniform Commercial Code (UCC) rather than by real property law.

49–1d Fixtures

Certain personal property can become so closely associated with the real property to which it is attached that the law views it as real property. Such property is known as a **fixture**—an item affixed to realty, meaning that it is attached to the real property in a permanent way. The item may be embedded in the land or permanently attached to the property or to another fixture on the property by means of cement, plaster, bolts, nails, or screws. An item, such as a statue, may even sit on the land without being attached, as long as the owner *intends* it to be a fixture.

Fixtures are included in the sale of land unless the sales contract specifies otherwise. The issue of whether an item is a fixture (and thus real estate) or not a fixture (and thus personal property) often arises with respect to land sales, real property taxation, insurance coverage, and divorces. How the issue is resolved can have important consequences for the parties involved.

Typical Fixtures Some items can only be attached to property permanently—such as tile floors, cabinets, and carpeting. Because such items are attached permanently, it is assumed that the owner intended them to be fixtures. Also, when an item of property is custom-made for installation on real property, as storm windows are, the item usually is classified as a fixture.

In addition, an item that is firmly attached to the land and integral to its use may be deemed a fixture. For instance, a mobile home or a complex irrigation system bolted to a cement slab on a farm can be a fixture. The courts assume that owners, in making such installations, intend the objects to become part of their real property.

The Role of Intent Generally, when the courts need to determine whether a certain item is a fixture, they examine the intention of the party who placed the object on the real property. When the intent of that party is in dispute, the courts will usually deem that the item is a fixture if either or both of the following are true:

- The property attached cannot be removed without causing substantial damage to the remaining realty.
- The property attached is so adapted to the rest of the realty as to have become a part of it.

■ **CASE IN POINT 49.1** Terminal 5, a facility owned by the Port of Seattle (Port), was used in loading and unloading the shipping containers used to transport goods by ship. APL Limited entered into a long-term lease with the Port for use of Terminal 5 and for use of Port-owned container cranes. Terminal 5 was substantially rebuilt, and steel cranes were constructed and installed. The cranes were 100 feet apart, 198 feet tall, and 85 feet wide, and were mounted on rails embedded in concrete. They were hard-wired to a dedicated high-voltage electrical system built specifically for Terminal 5 and were attached to the power substation by cables.

APL later filed a lawsuit against the state of Washington for a refund of sales tax it had paid on the lease of the cranes. The state argued that the cranes were personal property and, as such, subject to sales tax. The trial court ruled in favor of the state, but a Washington appellate court reversed. The reviewing court found that the trial court had not sufficiently taken the Port's intent into account in determining that the cranes were personal property, not fixtures. "When the owner and the person that [attaches property to realty] are one and the same, a rebuttable presumption arises that the owner's intention was for the [property] to become part of the realty." The reviewing court remanded the case so the lower court could examine evidence of the Port's intent.[1] ■

---

1. *APL Limited v. Washington State Department of Revenue,* 154 Wash.App. 1020 (2010).

Trade Fixtures Are Personal Property Trade fixtures are an exception to the rule that fixtures are a part of the real property to which they are attached. A **trade fixture** is personal property that is installed for a commercial purpose *by a tenant* (one who rents real property from the owner, or landlord).

Trade fixtures remain the property of the tenant unless removal would irreparably damage the building or realty. A walk-in cooler, for instance, purchased and installed by a tenant who uses the premises for a restaurant, is a trade fixture. The tenant can remove the cooler from the premises when the lease terminates but ordinarily must repair any damage that the removal causes or compensate the landlord for the damage.

49–2 Ownership and Other Interests in Real Property

Ownership of property is an abstract concept that cannot exist independently of the legal system. No one can actually possess, or *hold,* a piece of land, the air above it, the earth below it, and all the water contained on it. One can only possess *rights* in real property.

Numerous rights are involved in real property ownership, which is why property ownership is often viewed as a bundle of rights. One who possesses the entire bundle of rights is said to hold the property in *fee simple,* which is the most complete form of ownership. When only some of the rights in the bundle are transferred to another person, the effect is to limit the ownership rights of both the transferor of the rights and the recipient.

Ownership interests in real property have traditionally been referred to as *estates in land,* which include fee simple estates, life estates, and leasehold estates. We examine these types of estates in this section, and we also discuss several forms of concurrent ownership of property. Finally, we describe certain interests in real property that is owned by others.

49–2a Ownership in Fee Simple

In a **fee simple absolute,** the owner has the greatest aggregation of rights, privileges, and power possible. The owner can give the property away or dispose of the property by *deed* or by *will.* When there is no will, the fee simple passes to the owner's legal heirs on her or his death. A fee simple absolute is potentially infinite in duration and is assigned forever to a person and

her or his heirs without limitation or condition.[2] The owner has the rights of *exclusive* possession and use of the property.

The rights that accompany a fee simple absolute include the right to use the land for whatever purpose the owner sees fit. Of course, other laws, including applicable zoning, noise, and environmental laws, may limit the owner's ability to use the property in certain ways. A person who uses his or her property in a manner that unreasonably interferes with others' right to use or enjoy their own property can be liable for the tort of *nuisance.*

■ **CASE IN POINT 49.2** Nancy and James Biglane owned and lived in a building next door to the Under the Hill Saloon, a popular bar that featured live music. During the summer, the Saloon, which had no air-conditioning, opened its windows and doors, and live music echoed up and down the street. The Biglanes installed extra insulation, thicker windows, and air-conditioning units in their building. Nevertheless, the noise from the Saloon kept the Biglanes awake at night. Eventually, they sued the owners of the Saloon for nuisance. The court held that the noise from the bar unreasonably interfered with the Biglanes' right to enjoy their property and prohibited the Saloon from opening its windows and doors while playing music.[3] ■

49–2b Life Estates

A **life estate** is an estate that lasts for the life of some specified individual. A **conveyance,** or transfer of real property, "to A for his life" creates a life estate.[4] The life tenant's ownership rights cease to exist on the life tenant's death.

The life tenant has the right to use the land, provided that he or she commits no **waste** (injury to the land). In other words, the life tenant cannot use the land in a manner that would adversely affect its value. The life tenant can use the land to harvest crops or, if mines and oil wells are already on the land, can extract minerals and oil from it, but the life tenant cannot establish new wells or mines. The life tenant can also create liens, *easements* (discussed shortly), and leases, but none can extend beyond the life

---

2. In another type of estate, the *fee simple defeasible,* ownership in fee simple automatically terminates if a stated event occurs. For instance, property might be conveyed (transferred) to a school only as long as it is used for school purposes. In addition, the fee simple may be subject to a *condition subsequent.* This means that if a stated event occurs, the prior owner of the property can bring an action to regain possession of the property.
3. *Biglane v. Under the Hill Corp.,* 949 So.2d 9 (Miss.Sup. 2007).
4. A less common type of life estate is created by the conveyance "to A for the life of B." This is known as an estate *pur autre vie*—that is, an estate for the duration of the life of another.

of the tenant. In addition, with few exceptions, the life tenant has an exclusive right to possession during his or her lifetime.

Along with these rights, the life tenant also has some duties—to keep the property in repair and to pay property taxes. In short, the owner of the life estate has the same rights as a fee simple owner except that she or he must maintain the value of the property during her or his tenancy.

In the following case, the life tenant refused to pay the taxes and the premiums for the insurance on the property. Was this waste?

Case 49.1

Main Omni Realty Corp. v. Matus

New York Supreme Court, Appellate Division, Second Department, 124 A.D.3d 604, 1 N.Y.S.3d 319 (2015).

Background and Facts Craig Matus held a life estate in certain residential real property in Huntington, New York. On the termination of the life estate, title to the property was to transfer to Main Omni Realty Corporation, a wholly owned subsidiary of New York Community Bank. For a dozen years, Matus refused to pay premiums for insurance on the property. He also refused to pay the property taxes, resulting in tax liens.

To preserve its interest in the property, Main Omni paid the premiums and the liens, which avoided a foreclosure and sale of the property. Main Omni then filed a suit in a New York state court against Matus, seeking to recover the amount of the premiums and taxes on the ground of unjust enrichment. In addition, it sought to extinguish (end) the life estate on the ground of waste based on Matus's refusal to pay the taxes. The court denied Main Omni's motion for summary judgment. Main Omni appealed.

In the Language of the Court
Ruth C. *BALKIN*, J.P. [Judge Presiding], L. Priscilla *HALL*, Leonard B. *AUSTIN*, and Betsey *BARROS*, JJ. [Judges].
* * * *

The essential inquiry in any action for unjust enrichment or restitution is whether it is against equity and good conscience to permit the defendant to retain what is sought to be recovered. *A plaintiff must show that (1) the other party was enriched, (2) at the plaintiff's expense, and (3) that it is against equity and good conscience to permit the other party to retain what is sought to be recovered.* [Emphasis added.]

The plaintiffs established their *prima facie* entitlement to judgment as a matter of law on their first cause of action, which alleged unjust enrichment and sought restitution, and their second cause of action, which alleged waste and sought to extinguish the defendant's life estate. As life tenant, the defendant was obligated to pay the property taxes and * * * insurance on the subject property, and the intentional failure to do so constitutes waste. It is undisputed that the defendant intentionally failed to pay the property taxes and * * * insurance on the subject property, and he has clearly expressed his intention not to do so in the future. Under these circumstances, the remainder interest in the subject property is in constant danger of forfeiture in a tax lien sale, unless the plaintiffs continue paying the property taxes and * * * insurance premiums the defendant is otherwise obligated to pay. The plaintiffs therefore demonstrated, *prima facie,* that the defendant was unjustly enriched by the plaintiffs' payment of these expenses for the defendant, and that equity warrants extinguishing his life estate in the subject property.

Decision and Remedy *A state intermediate appellate court reversed the lower court's denial of Main Omni's motion and ordered a summary judgment in the plaintiff's favor. Because Matus continued to refuse to pay the taxes on the property, the court ended his life estate.*

Critical Thinking
• **Economic** *Why would the owner of a life estate refuse to pay the taxes and insurance premiums on the property of the estate? Should any reason for this refusal have influenced the court's decision in this case?*

49–2c Concurrent Ownership

Persons who share ownership rights simultaneously in particular property (including real property and personal property) are said to have **concurrent ownership.** There are two principal types of concurrent ownership: *tenancy in common* and *joint tenancy.* Concurrent ownership rights can also be held in a *tenancy by the entirety* or as *community property,* but these types of concurrent ownership are less common.

Tenancy in Common The term **tenancy in common** refers to a form of co-ownership in which each of two or more persons owns an undivided interest in the property. The interest is undivided because each tenant shares rights in the whole property. On the death of a tenant in common, that tenant's interest in the property passes to her or his heirs.

■ **EXAMPLE 49.3** Four friends purchase a condominium unit in Hawaii together as tenants in common. This means that each of them has a one-fourth ownership interest in the whole. If one of the four owners dies a year after the purchase, his ownership interest passes to his heirs (his wife and children, for example) rather than to the other tenants in common. ■

Unless the co-tenants have agreed otherwise, a tenant in common can transfer her or his interest in the property to another without the consent of the remaining co-owners. In most states, it is presumed that a co-tenancy is a tenancy in common unless there is specific language indicating the intent to establish a joint tenancy.

Joint Tenancy In a **joint tenancy,** each of two or more persons owns an undivided interest in the property, but a deceased joint tenant's interest passes to the surviving joint tenant or tenants.

Right of Survivorship. The right of a surviving joint tenant to inherit a deceased joint tenant's ownership interest—referred to as a *right of survivorship*—distinguishes a joint tenancy from a tenancy in common. ■ **EXAMPLE 49.4** Jerrold and Eva are married and purchase a house as joint tenants. The title to the house clearly expresses the intent to create a joint tenancy because it refers to Jerrold and Eva as "joint tenants with right of survivorship." Jerrold has three children from a prior marriage. If Jerrold dies, his interest in the house automatically passes to Eva rather than to his children from the prior marriage. ■

Termination of a Joint Tenancy. A joint tenant can transfer her or his rights by sale or gift to another without the consent of the other joint tenants. Doing so terminates the joint tenancy, however. The person who purchases the property or receives it as a gift becomes a tenant in common, not a joint tenant. ■ **EXAMPLE 49.5** Three brothers, Brody, Saul, and Jacob, own a parcel of land as joint tenants. Brody is experiencing financial difficulties and sells his interest in the real property to Beth. The sale terminates the joint tenancy, and now Beth, Saul, and Jacob hold the property as tenants in common. ■

A joint tenant's interest can also be levied against (seized by court order) to satisfy the tenant's judgment creditors. If this occurs, the joint tenancy terminates, and the remaining owners hold the property as tenants in common. (Judgment creditors can also seize the interests of tenants in a tenancy in common.)

Tenancy by the Entirety A less common form of shared ownership of real property by married persons is a **tenancy by the entirety.** It differs from a joint tenancy in that neither spouse may separately transfer his or her interest during his or her lifetime unless the other spouse consents. In some states in which statutes give the wife the right to convey her property, this form of concurrent ownership has effectively been abolished. A divorce, either spouse's death, or mutual agreement will terminate a tenancy by the entirety.

Community Property A limited number of states[5] allow married couples to own property as **community property.** If property is held as community property, each spouse technically owns an undivided one-half interest in the property. This type of ownership applies to most property acquired by the husband or the wife during the course of the marriage. It generally does *not* apply to property acquired prior to the marriage or to property acquired by gift or inheritance as separate property during the marriage. After a divorce, community property is divided equally in some states and according to the discretion of the court in other states.

49–2d Leasehold Estates

A **leasehold estate** is created when a real property owner or lessor (landlord) agrees to convey the right to possess and use the property to a lessee (tenant) for a certain period of time. The tenant's right to possession is

---

5. These states include Alaska, Arizona, California, Idaho, Louisiana, Nevada, New Mexico, Texas, Washington, and Wisconsin. Puerto Rico allows property to be owned as community property as well.

temporary, which is what distinguishes a tenant from a purchaser, who acquires title to the property.

In every leasehold estate, the tenant has a *qualified* right to exclusive possession. It is qualified because the landlord has a right to enter onto the premises to ensure that no waste is being committed. In addition, the tenant can use the land—for instance, by harvesting crops—but cannot injure it by such activities as cutting down timber to sell or extracting oil.

Fixed-Term Tenancy A **fixed-term tenancy,** also called a *tenancy for years,* is created by an express contract stating that the property is leased for a specified period of time, such as a month, a year, or a period of years. Signing a one-year lease to occupy an apartment, for instance, creates a fixed-term tenancy. Note that the term need not be specified by date and can be conditioned on the occurrence of an event, such as leasing a cabin for the summer or an apartment during Mardi Gras.

At the end of the period specified in the lease, the lease ends (without notice), and possession of the property returns to the lessor. If the tenant dies during the period of the lease, the lease interest passes to the tenant's heirs as personal property. Often, leases include renewal or extension provisions.

Periodic Tenancy A **periodic tenancy** is created by a lease that does not specify a term but does specify that rent is to be paid at certain intervals, such as weekly, monthly, or yearly. The tenancy is automatically renewed for another rental period unless properly terminated. **■ EXAMPLE 49.6** Jewel, LLC, enters into a lease with Capital Properties. The lease states, "Rent is due on the tenth day of every month." This provision creates a periodic tenancy from month to month. **■** A periodic tenancy sometimes arises after a fixed-term tenancy ends when the landlord allows the tenant to retain possession and continue paying monthly or weekly rent.

Under the common law, to terminate a periodic tenancy, the landlord or tenant must give at least one period's notice to the other party. If the tenancy is month to month, for instance, one month's notice must be given prior to the last month's rent payment. Today, however, state statutes often require a different period of notice before the termination of a tenancy.

Tenancy at Will With a **tenancy at will,** either party can terminate the tenancy without notice. This type of tenancy can arise if a landlord rents property to a tenant "for as long as both agree" or allows a person to live on the premises without paying rent. Tenancy at will is rare today because most state statutes require a landlord to provide some period of notice to terminate a tenancy. States may also require a landowner to have sufficient cause (a legitimate reason) to end a residential tenancy.

Tenancy at Sufferance The mere possession of land without right is called a **tenancy at sufferance.** A tenancy at sufferance is not a true tenancy because it is created when a tenant *wrongfully* retains possession of property. Whenever a tenancy for years or a periodic tenancy ends and the tenant continues to retain possession of the premises without the owner's permission, a tenancy at sufferance is created.

49–2e Nonpossessory Interests

In contrast to the types of property interests just described, some interests in land do not include any rights to possess the property. These interests are therefore known as **nonpossessory interests.** They include *easements, profits,* and *licenses.*

An **easement** is the right of a person to make limited use of another person's real property without taking anything from the property. The right to walk across another's property, for example, is an easement. In contrast, a **profit** is the right to go onto land owned by another and take away some part of the land itself or some product of the land. **■ EXAMPLE 49.7** Shawn owns real property known as the Dunes. Shawn gives Carmen the right to go there and remove all of the sand and gravel that she needs for her cement business. Carmen has a profit. **■**

Easements and profits can be classified as either *appurtenant* or *in gross.* Because easements and profits are similar and the same rules apply to both, we discuss them together.

Easement or Profit Appurtenant An easement (or profit) *appurtenant* arises when the owner of one piece of land has a right to go onto (or remove something from) an adjacent piece of land owned by another. The land that is benefited by the easement is called the *dominant estate,* and the land that is burdened is called the *servient estate.*

Because easements appurtenant are intended to *benefit the land,* they run (are conveyed) with the land when it is transferred. **■ EXAMPLE 49.8** Owen has a right to drive his car across Green's land, which is adjacent to Owen's property. This right-of-way over Green's property is an easement appurtenant to Owen's land. If Owen sells his land, the easement runs with the land to benefit the new owner. **■**

Easement or Profit in Gross In an easement or profit *in gross,* the right to use or take things from another's land is given to one who does not own an adjacent tract of land. These easements are intended to *benefit a particular person or business,* not a particular piece of land, and cannot be transferred.

■ **EXAMPLE 49.9** Avery owns a parcel of land with a marble quarry. Avery conveys to Classic Stone Corporation the right to come onto her land and remove up to five hundred pounds of marble per day. Classic Stone owns a profit in gross and cannot transfer this right to another. ■ Similarly, when a utility company is granted an easement to run its power lines across another's property, it obtains an easement in gross.

Creation of an Easement or Profit Most easements and profits are created by an express grant in a contract, deed, or will. This allows the parties to include terms defining the extent and length of time of use. In some situations, however, an easement or profit can be created without an express agreement.

An easement or profit may arise by **implication** when the circumstances surrounding the division of a parcel of property imply its creation. ■ **EXAMPLE 49.10** Barrow divides a parcel of land that has only one well for drinking water. If Barrow conveys the half without a well to Dean, a profit by implication arises because Dean needs drinking water. ■

An easement may also be created by **necessity.** An easement by necessity does not require division of property for its existence. A person who rents an apartment, for instance, has an easement by necessity in the private road leading up to it.

An easement arises by **prescription** when one person exercises an easement, such as a right-of-way, on another person's land without the landowner's consent. The use must be apparent and continue for the length of time required by the applicable statute of limitations. (In much the same way, title to property may be obtained by adverse possession, as will be discussed later in this chapter.)

■ **CASE IN POINT 49.11** Junior and Wilma Thompson sold twenty-one of their fifty acres of land in Missouri to Walnut Bowls, Inc. The deed expressly reserved an easement to the Thompsons' remaining twenty-nine acres, but it did not fix a precise location for the easement. James and Linda Baker subsequently bought the remaining acreage of the Thompsons' land.

Many years later—on learning of the easement to the Bakers' property—a potential buyer of Walnut Bowls' property refused to go through with the sale. Walnut

Bowls then put steel cables across its driveway entrances, installed a lock and chain on an access gate, and bolted a "No Trespassing" sign facing the Bakers' property. The Bakers filed a suit in a Missouri state court to determine the location of the easement. Citing the lack of an express location, the court held that there was no easement.

The Bakers appealed, and a state intermediate appellate court reversed that decision. The reviewing court held that an easement existed and instructed the trial court to determine its location. An easement can be created by deed even though its specific location is not identified. The location can later be fixed by agreement between the parties or inferred from use. If the easement is not identified in either of these ways, a court must determine the location.[6] ■

Termination of an Easement or Profit An easement or profit can be terminated or extinguished in several ways. The simplest way is to deed it back to the owner of the land that is burdened by it. Similarly, if the owner of an easement or profit acquires the property burdened by it, then it is merged into the property.

Another way to terminate an easement or profit is to abandon it and provide evidence of the intent to relinquish the right to use it. Mere nonuse will not extinguish an easement or profit, however, *unless the nonuse is accompanied by an overt act showing the intent to abandon.* An overt act might be, for instance, installing and using a different access road to one's property and discontinuing using an easement across the neighboring property. In any case, a court must be convinced that there was an intent to abandon the easement or profit.

License In the context of real property, a **license** is the revocable right of a person to come onto another person's land. It is a personal privilege that arises from the consent of the owner of the land and can be revoked by the owner. A ticket to attend a movie at a theater or a concert is an example of a license.

In essence, a license grants a person the authority to enter the land of another and perform a specified act or series of acts without obtaining any permanent interest in the land. When a person with a license exceeds the authority granted and undertakes some action on the property that is not permitted, the property owner can sue that person for the tort of trespass.

■ **CASE IN POINT 49.12** A Catholic church granted Prince Realty Management, LLC, a three-month license to use a three-foot strip of its property adjacent to

---

6. *Baker v. Walnut Bowls, Inc.,* 423 S.W.3d 293 (Mo.App. 2014).

Prince's property. The license authorized Prince to "put up plywood panels," creating a temporary fence to protect Prince's property during the construction of a new building. During the license's term, Prince installed steel piles and beams on the licensed property. When Prince ignored the church's demands that these structures be removed, the church sued Prince for trespass. The court concluded that the license allowed only temporary structures and that Prince had exceeded its authority by installing steel piles and beams. Therefore, the church was entitled to damages.[7] ■

Exhibit 49–1 illustrates the various interests in real property discussed in this chapter.

49–3 Transfer of Ownership

Ownership interests in real property are frequently transferred by sale, and the terms of the transfer are specified in a real estate sales contract. When real property is sold, the type of interest being transferred and the conditions of the transfer normally are set forth in a *deed* executed by the person who is conveying the property. Real property ownership can also be transferred by gift, by will or inheritance, by adverse possession, or by eminent domain.

---

7. *Roman Catholic Church of Our Lady of Sorrows v. Prince Realty Management, LLC*, 47 A.D.3d 909, 850 N.Y.S.2d 569 (2008).

49–3a Real Estate Sales Contracts

In some ways, a sale of real estate is similar to a sale of goods because it involves a transfer of ownership, often with specific warranties. A sale of real estate, however, is a more complicated transaction that involves certain formalities that are not required in a sale of goods. In part because of these complications, real estate brokers or agents who are licensed by the state assist the buyers and sellers during the sales transaction.

Usually, after substantial negotiation (offers, counteroffers, and responses), the parties enter into a detailed contract setting forth their agreement. A contract for a sale of land includes such terms as the purchase price, the type of deed the buyer will receive, the condition of the premises, and any items that will be included.

Unless the buyer pays cash for the property, the buyer must obtain financing through a mortgage loan. Real estate sales contracts are often contingent on the buyer's ability to obtain financing at or below a specified rate of interest. The contract may also be contingent on certain events, such as the completion of a land survey or the property's passing one or more inspections. Normally, the buyer is responsible for having the premises inspected for physical or mechanical defects and for insect infestation.

Closing Date and Escrow The contract usually fixes a date for performance, or **closing,** that frequently is four to twelve weeks after the contract is signed. On this day,

---

EXHIBIT 49–1 Interests in Real Property

TYPE OF INTEREST	DESCRIPTION

Ownership Interests	1. *Fee simple*—The most complete form of ownership.
	2. *Life estate*—An estate that lasts for the life of a specified individual.
	3. *Concurrent ownership*—When two or more persons hold title to property together, concurrent ownership exists.
	  a. Tenancy in common
	  b. Joint tenancy
	  c. Tenancy by the entirety
	  d. Community property

Leasehold Estates	1. Fixed-term tenancy (tenancy for years) 2. Periodic tenancy 3. Tenancy at will 4. Tenancy at sufferance
Nonpossessory Interests	1. Easements 2. Profits 3. Licenses

the seller conveys the property to the buyer by delivering the deed to the buyer in exchange for payment of the purchase price.

Deposits toward the purchase price normally are held in a special account, called an **escrow account,** until all of the conditions of sale have been met. Once the closing takes place, the funds in the escrow account are transferred to the seller.

Marketable Title The title to a particular parcel of property is especially important to the buyer. A grantor (seller) is obligated to transfer **marketable title,** or good title, to the grantee (buyer). Marketable title means that the grantor's ownership is free from encumbrances (except those disclosed by the grantor) and free of defects.

If the buyer signs a purchase contract and then discovers that the seller does not have a marketable title, the buyer can withdraw from the contract. ■ **EXAMPLE 49.13** Chan enters into an agreement to buy Fortuna Ranch from Hal. Chan then discovers that Hal has given Pearl an option to purchase the ranch and the option has not expired. In this situation, the title is not marketable, because Pearl could exercise the option and Hal would be compelled to sell the ranch to her. Therefore, Chan can withdraw from the contract to buy the property. ■

The most common way of ensuring title is through **title insurance,** which insures the buyer against loss from defects in title to real property. When financing the purchase of real property, almost all lenders require title insurance to protect their interests in the collateral for the loan.

Implied Warranties in the Sale of New Homes
The common law rule of *caveat emptor* ("let the buyer beware") held that the seller of a home made no warranty as to its soundness or fitness (unless the contract or deed stated otherwise). Today, however, most states imply a warranty—the **implied warranty of habitability**—in the sale of new homes.

Under this warranty, the seller of a new house warrants that it will be fit for human habitation even if the deed or contract of sale does not include such a warranty. Essentially, the seller is warranting that the house is in reasonable working order and is of reasonably sound construction. The seller can be liable if the home is defective. In some states, the warranty protects not only the first purchaser but any subsequent purchaser as well.

Seller's Duty to Disclose Hidden Defects In most jurisdictions, courts impose on sellers a duty to disclose any known defect that materially affects the value of the property and that the buyer could not reasonably discover. Failure to disclose such a defect gives the buyer a right to rescind the contract and to sue for damages based on fraud or misrepresentation.

There is normally a limit to the time within which the buyer can bring a suit against the seller based on the defect. Time limits run from either the date of the sale or the day that the buyer discovered (or should have discovered) the defect. ■ **EXAMPLE 49.14** Ian Newson partially renovates a house in Louisiana and sells it to Jerry and Tabitha Moreland for $87,000. Two months after the Morelands move in, they discover rotten wood behind the tile in the bathroom and experience problems with the plumbing. The state statute specifies that the Morelands have one year from the date of the sale or the discovery of the defect to file a lawsuit. Therefore, the Morelands must file suit within twelve months of discovering the defects (which would be fourteen months from the date of the sale). ■

In the following *Spotlight Case,* the court had to decide whether the buyer of a house had the right to rescind the sales contract because he was not told that the house was allegedly haunted.

Spotlight on Sales of Haunted Houses

Case 49.2 Stambovsky v. Ackley
Supreme Court, Appellate Division, New York, 572 N.Y.S.2d 672, 169 A.D.2d 254 (1991).

Background and Facts Jeffrey Stambovsky signed a contract to buy Helen Ackley's home in Nyack, New York. After the contract was signed, Stambovsky discovered that the house was widely reputed to be haunted. The Ackley family claimed to have seen poltergeists on numerous occasions over the prior nine years. The Ackleys had been interviewed and quoted in both a national publication (*Reader's Digest*) and the local newspaper. The house was described as "a riverfront Victorian (with ghost)" when it was part of a walking tour of Nyack, New York. When Stambovsky discovered the house's reputation, he sued to rescind the contract and recover his down payment. He alleged that Ackley and

Case 49.2 Continues

Case 49.2 Continued

her real estate agent made material misrepresentations when they failed to disclose Ackley's belief that the home was haunted. Ackley argued that, under the doctrine of *caveat emptor,* she was under no duty to disclose to the buyer the home's haunted reputation. The trial court dismissed Stambovsky's case. Stambovsky appealed.

In the Language of the Court

Justice *RUBIN* delivered the opinion of the court.

* * * *

While I agree with [the trial court] that the real estate broker, as agent for the seller, is under no duty to disclose to a potential buyer the phantasmal reputation of the premises and that, in his pursuit of a legal remedy for fraudulent misrepresentation against the seller, plaintiff hasn't a ghost of a chance, I am nevertheless moved by the spirit of equity to allow the buyer to seek rescission of the contract of sale and recovery of his down payment. New York law fails to recognize any remedy for damages incurred as a result of the seller's mere silence, applying instead the strict rule of *caveat emptor.* Therefore, the theoretical basis for granting relief, even under the extraordinary facts of this case, is elusive if not ephemeral [short-lived].

* * * *

The doctrine of caveat emptor *requires that a buyer act prudently to assess the fitness and value of his purchase and operates to bar the purchaser who fails to exercise due care from seeking the equitable remedy of rescission.* * * * Applying the strict rule of *caveat emptor* to a contract involving a house possessed by poltergeists conjures up visions of a psychic or medium routinely accompanying the structural engineer and Terminix man on an inspection of every home subject to a contract of sale. It portends [warns] that the prudent attorney will establish an escrow account lest the subject of the transaction come back to haunt him and his client—or pray that his malpractice insurance coverage extends to supernatural disasters. In the interest of avoiding such untenable consequences, the notion that a haunting is a condition which can and should be ascertained upon reasonable inspection of the premises is a hobgoblin which should be exorcised from the body of legal precedent and laid quietly to rest. [Emphasis added.]

* * * *

In the case at bar [under consideration], defendant seller deliberately fostered the public belief that her home was possessed. Having undertaken to inform the public at large, to whom she has no legal relationship, about the supernatural occurrences on her property, she may be said to owe no less a duty to her contract vendee. It has been remarked that the occasional modern cases, which permit a seller to take unfair advantage of a buyer's ignorance so long as he is not actively misled are "singularly unappetizing." Where, as here, the seller not only takes unfair advantage of the buyer's ignorance but has created and perpetuated a condition about which he is unlikely to even inquire, enforcement of the contract (in whole or in part) is offensive to the court's sense of equity. Application of the remedy of rescission, within the bounds of the narrow exception to the doctrine of *caveat emptor* set forth herein, is entirely appropriate to relieve the unwitting purchaser from the consequences of a most unnatural bargain.

Decision and Remedy   *The New York appellate court found that the doctrine of* caveat emptor *did not apply in this case. The court allowed Stambovsky to rescind the purchase contract and recover the down payment.*

Critical Thinking

- **Ethical**   *In not disclosing the house's reputation to Stambovsky, was Ackley's behavior unethical? If so, was it unethical because she knew something he did not, or was it unethical because of the nature of the information she omitted? What if Ackley had failed to mention that the roof leaked or that the well was dry—conditions that a buyer would normally investigate? Explain your answer.*
- **Legal Environment**   *Why did the court decide that applying the strict rule of* caveat emptor *was inappropriate in this case? How would applying this doctrine increase costs for the purchaser?*

49–3b Deeds

Possession and title to land are passed from person to person by means of a **deed**—the instrument used to transfer real property. Deeds must meet certain requirements, but unlike a contract, a deed does not have to be supported by legally sufficient consideration. Gifts of real property are common, and they require deeds even though there is no consideration for the gift.

To be valid, a deed must include the following:

1. The names of the grantor (the giver or seller) and the grantee (the donee or buyer).
2. Words evidencing the intent to convey (for instance, "I hereby bargain, sell, grant, or give"). No specific words are necessary. If the deed does not specify the type of estate being transferred, it presumptively transfers the property in fee simple absolute.
3. A legally sufficient description of the land. The description must include enough detail to distinguish the property being conveyed from every other parcel of land. The property can be identified by reference to an official survey or recorded plat map, or each boundary can be described by metes and bounds. **Metes and bounds** is a system of measuring boundary lines by the distance between two points, often using physical features of the local geography. A property description might say, for instance, "beginning at the southwesterly intersection of Court and Main Streets, then West 40 feet to the fence, then South 100 feet, then Northeast approximately 120 feet back to the beginning."
4. The grantor's (and usually his or her spouse's) signature.
5. Delivery of the deed.

Different types of deeds provide different degrees of protection against defects of title, as discussed next.

Warranty Deeds A **warranty deed** contains the greatest number of warranties and thus provides the most extensive protection against defects of title. In most states, special language is required to create a general warranty deed. Warranty deeds commonly include the following covenants:

1. A covenant that the grantor has the title to, and the power to convey, the property.
2. A covenant of quiet enjoyment (a warranty that the buyer will not be disturbed in her or his possession of the land).
3. A covenant that transfer of the property is made without knowledge of adverse claims of third parties.

Generally, the warranty deed makes the grantor liable for all defects of title during the time that the property was held by the grantor and previous titleholders. ■ **EXAMPLE 49.15** Sanchez sells a two-acre lot and office building by warranty deed to Fast Tech, LLC. Subsequently, Amy shows that she has better title than Sanchez had and evicts Fast Tech. Here, Fast Tech can sue Sanchez for breaching the covenant of quiet enjoyment. Fast Tech can recover the purchase price of the land, plus any other damages incurred as a result. ■

Special Warranty Deed A **special warranty deed,** or *limited warranty deed,* in contrast, warrants only that the grantor or seller held good title during his or her ownership of the property. In other words, the seller does not guarantee that there are no adverse claims by third parties against any previous owners of the property.

If the special warranty deed discloses all liens or other encumbrances, the seller will not be liable to the buyer if a third person subsequently interferes with the buyer's ownership. If the third person's claim arises out of, or is related to, some act of the seller, however, the seller will be liable to the buyer for damages.

Quitclaim Deed A **quitclaim deed** offers the least protection against defects in the title. Basically, a quitclaim deed conveys to the grantee whatever interest the grantor had. If the grantor had no interest, then the grantee receives no interest. (Naturally, if the grantor had a defective title or no title at all, a conveyance by warranty deed or special warranty deed would not cure the defect. Such a deed, however, would give the buyer a cause of action to sue the seller.)

Quitclaim deeds are often used when the seller, or grantor, is uncertain as to the extent of his or her rights in the property. They may also be used to release a party's interest in a particular parcel of property. This may be necessary, for instance, in divorce settlements or business dissolutions when the grantors are dividing up their interests in real property.

Grant Deed With a **grant deed,** the grantor simply states, "I grant the property to you" or "I convey, or bargain and sell, the property to you." By state statute, grant deeds carry with them an implied warranty that the grantor owns the property and has not previously transferred it to someone else or encumbered it, except as set out in the deed.

49–3c Recording Statutes

Once the seller delivers the deed to the buyer (at closing), legal title to the property is conveyed. Nevertheless, the buyer should promptly record the deed with the state records office. Every state has a **recording statute,** which allows deeds to be recorded in the public record for a fee. Deeds generally are recorded in the county in which the property is located. Many state statutes require that the grantor sign the deed in the presence of two witnesses before it can be recorded.

Recording a deed gives notice to the public that a certain person is now the owner of a particular parcel of real estate. By putting everyone on notice as to the true owner, recording a deed prevents the previous owners from fraudulently conveying the land to other purchasers.

49–3d Adverse Possession

A person who wrongfully possesses the real property of another (by occupying or using the property) may eventually acquire title to it through adverse possession. **Adverse possession** is a means of obtaining title to land without delivery of a deed and without the consent of—or payment to—the true owner. Thus, adverse possession is a method of *involuntarily* transferring title to the property from the true owner to the adverse possessor.

Essentially, when one person possesses the real property of another for a certain statutory period of time, that person acquires title to the land. The statutory period varies from three to thirty years, depending on the state, with ten years being most common.

Requirements for Adverse Possession For property to be held adversely, four elements must be satisfied:

1. *Possession must be actual and exclusive.* The possessor must physically occupy the property. This requirement is clearly met if the possessor lives on the property, but it may also be met if the possessor builds fences, erects structures, plants crops, or even grazes animals on the land.

2. *The possession must be open, visible, and notorious, not secret or clandestine.* The possessor must occupy the land for all the world to see. This requirement ensures that the true owner is on notice that someone is possessing the owner's property wrongfully.

3. *Possession must be continuous and peaceable for the required period of time.* This requirement means that the possessor must not be interrupted in the occupancy by the true owner or by the courts. Continuous does not mean constant. It simply means that the possessor has continuously occupied the property in some fashion for the statutory time. Peaceable means that no force was used to possess the land.

4. *Possession must be hostile and adverse.* In other words, the possessor cannot be living on the property with the owner's permission and must claim the property as against the whole world.

■ **CASE IN POINT 49.16** Charles Scarborough and Mildred Rollins were adjoining landowners, sharing one common boundary. Based on Rollins's survey of the property, Rollins believed that she owned a portion of a gravel road located to the south of the apartment buildings she owned. In contrast, Scarborough believed that the gravel road was located totally on his property and that he owned some property north of the gravel road toward Rollins's apartment buildings.

Scarborough filed a complaint seeking a court order stating that he had title to the property and was its sole owner. The court, however, ruled that Rollins owned a portion of the gravel road by adverse possession. She had used it openly for more than thirty-five years, it was generally thought to be part of her apartment complex, and she had paid taxes on it.[8] ■

The following case raises the question of whether a landowner next to a rail line can acquire a portion of the right-of-way by adverse possession.

---

8. *Scarborough v. Rollins,* 44 So.3d 381 (Miss.App. 2010).

Montgomery County v. Bhatt

Court of Appeals of Maryland, 446 Md. 79, 130 A.3d 424 (2016).

In the Language of the Court
Glenn T. HARRELL, Jr., J. [Judge]

Driving that train, high on cocaine,
Casey Jones you better watch your speed.
Trouble ahead, trouble behind,

And you know that notion just
crossed my mind.

—The Grateful Dead, *Casey Jones,* on
Workingman's Dead (Warner Bros.
Records 1970).

Although the record of the present case does not reflect a comparable level of drama as captured by the refrain of "Casey Jones," it hints at plenty of potential trouble, both ahead and behind, for a pair of public works projects (one in place and the other incipient [in development]) cherished by the government and some citizens of Montgomery County.

The Capital Crescent Trail is a well-known hiker/biker route that runs between Georgetown in the District of Columbia and Silver Spring, Maryland. Its path was used formerly as the Georgetown Branch of the Baltimore & Ohio (B&O) Railroad. After the trains stopped running in 1985, the property was transferred in 1988 to the government of Montgomery County, Maryland, via a quitclaim deed for a consideration of $10 million. It is planned that the Maryland portion of the former rail line (and current interim hiker/biker trail) will become the proposed Purple Line, a commuter light rail project.

BACKGROUND

* * * Ajay Bhatt owns 3313 Coquelin Terrace (a subdivided, single-family residential lot—"Lot 8"—improved by a dwelling) in Chevy Chase, Montgomery County, Maryland. He purchased this property in 2006 from his aunt, who owned the property since at least the 1970s. The lot abuts the Georgetown Branch of the B&O Railroad/Capital Crescent Trail. In 1890, the right-of-way that was the rail line (and is today the hiker/biker trail) was conveyed in a fee-simple deed from George Dunlop, grantor, to the Metropolitan Southern Railroad Company ("the Railroad"), grantee.

The right-of-way was obtained by the County * * * from the Railroad pursuant to the federal Rails-to-Trails Act. [Federal regulations] allow the County to preserve the land as a hiker/biker trail until the County chooses whether and when to restore a form of rail service within the right-of-way.

On 18 October 2013, Montgomery County issued to Bhatt a civil citation asserting a violation of Section 49-10(b) of the Montgomery County Code, which prohibits a property owner from

erecting or placing "any structure, fence, post, rock, or other object in a public right-of-way." The * * * claimed violation was the placement and maintenance by Bhatt's predecessors-in-interest of Lot 8 of a fence and shed within the former rail line (and current hiker/biker trail) right-of-way, without a permit. * * * The District Court of Maryland, sitting in Montgomery County, * * * found Bhatt guilty * * * and ordered him to remove the fence and shed encroaching upon the County's right-of-way.

The appeal was heard *de novo* by the [Maryland] Circuit Court. [When a court hears a case *de novo*, it decides the issues without reference to the legal conclusions or assumptions made by the previous court.]

* * * *

Bhatt's defense to the charged violation of Section 49–10(b) was that he owned the encroached-upon land by adverse possession.

Bhatt argued that, because the fence had been located beyond the property line of Lot 8 since at least 1963, the Railroad was obliged to take action to remove it prior to the maturation of the twenty-year period for adverse possession.

* * * The Circuit Court vacated the District Court's judgment and dismissed the violation citation. * * * The Circuit Court concluded ultimately that Bhatt had a creditable claim for adverse possession.

The County petitioned this Court for a writ of *certiorari*. * * * We granted the Petition.

* * * *

DISCUSSION
I. Contentions

* * * The County contends * * * that, because this Court has considered previously a railroad line to be analogous to a public highway for most purposes, the land in question is not subject to an adverse possession claim.

* * * Bhatt rejects the public highway-railroad line analogy because the land was in private, not public, use during its operation as a rail line.

II. Analysis

a. Railroads as Public Highways

A railroad is in many essential respects a public highway, and the rules of law applicable to one are generally applicable to the other. Railroads are owned frequently by private corporations, but this has never been considered a matter of any importance * * * because the function performed is that of the State. Railroad companies operate as a public use and are not viewed strictly as private corporations since they are publicly regulated common carriers. *Essentially, a railroad is a highway dedicated to the public use.* [Emphasis added.]

* * * *

b. May a public highway (or any portion of its right-of-way, no matter the type of real property interest by which it is held) be possessed adversely by an abutting private citizen?

* * * *Nothing is more solidly established than the rule that title to property held by a municipal corporation in its governmental capacity, for a public use, cannot be acquired by adverse possession.* [Emphasis added.]

* * * *

* * * Because time does not run against the state, or the public, * * * public highways are not subject to a claim for adverse possession, except in the limited circumstances of a clear abandonment by the State. By parity [equivalence] of reasoning applied to the present case, railway lines [are] also not * * * subject to a claim for adverse possession, without evidence of clear abandonment or a clear shift away from public use.

c. Use of the right-of-way

* * * We do not find in this record, however, that there is any evidence of abandonment by the rail line operator (or Montgomery County) or that the right-of-way was taken out of public use such that a claim for adverse possession could ripen within this right-of-way.

* * * *

The 1890 Dunlop Deed shows that the purchase made by the Railroad was

Case 49.3 Continued

from a private landowner. There was no evidence adduced [offered] by Bhatt supporting a conclusion that the right-of-way was abandoned and was not being used by the public, even during the period from 1985 when the freight service ended and 1988 when the property was conveyed to the County and became a hiker/biker trail as an interim public use.

* * * *

Because no evidence was presented by Bhatt to show that the current use of the right-of-way by Montgomery County is unreasonable or that the Railroad or the County abandoned the right-of-way, no claim for adverse possession will lie. Accordingly, we shall reverse the judgment of the Circuit Court. Bhatt's fence and shed encroached upon the right-of-way in violation of Montgomery

County Code Section 49–10(b). The District Court got it right.

JUDGMENT OF THE CIRCUIT COURT FOR MONTGOMERY COUNTY REVERSED. CASE REMANDED TO THAT COURT WITH INSTRUCTIONS TO AFFIRM THE JUDGMENT OF THE DISTRICT COURT OF MARYLAND, SITTING IN MONTGOMERY COUNTY.

Legal Reasoning Questions

1. Bhatt claimed to have met all of the requirements to acquire a strip of public land through adverse possession. Which element did the court find had *not* been met? Why?

2. What is the "potential trouble, both ahead and behind, for a pair of public works projects" hinted at in this case? In whose favor is that "trouble" likely to be resolved?

3. Should a private party, by encroaching on a public right-of-way, be able to acquire title adverse to the public rights? Discuss.

Purpose of the Doctrine   There are a number of public-policy reasons for the adverse possession doctrine. These include society's interest in resolving boundary disputes, in determining title when title to property is in question, and in assuring that real property remains in the stream of commerce. More fundamentally, the doctrine punishes owners who do not take action when they see adverse possession and rewards possessors for putting land to productive use.

49–4 Limitations on the Rights of Property Owners

No ownership rights in real property can ever really be absolute—that is, an owner of real property cannot always do whatever she or he wishes on or with the property. Nuisance and environmental laws, for instance, restrict certain types of activities. Property ownership is also conditional on the payment of property taxes. Zoning laws and building permits frequently restrict the use of realty. In addition, if a property owner fails to pay debts, the property may be seized to satisfy judgment creditors. In short, the rights of every property owner are subject to certain conditions and limitations.

49–4a Eminent Domain

Even ownership in fee simple absolute is limited by a superior ownership. Just as the king was the ultimate

landowner in medieval England, today the government has an ultimate ownership right in all land in the United States. This right, known as **eminent domain,** is sometimes referred to as the *condemnation power* of government to take land for public use. It gives the government the right to acquire possession of real property in the manner directed by the U.S. Constitution and the laws of the state whenever the public interest requires it.

The power of eminent domain generally is invoked through **condemnation** proceedings. ■ **EXAMPLE 49.17** When a new public highway is to be built, the government decides where to build it and how much land to condemn. After the government determines that a particular parcel of land is necessary for the highway, it will first offer to buy the property. If the owner refuses the offer, the government brings a judicial (*condemnation*) proceeding to obtain title to the land. ■

Condemnation proceedings usually involve two distinct phases. The first seeks to establish the government's right to take the property, and the second determines the fair value of the property.

The Taking   When the government takes land owned by a private party for public use, it is referred to as a **taking.** Under the *takings clause* of the Fifth Amendment to the U.S. Constitution, the government may take private property for public use, but it must pay "just compensation" to the owner. State constitutions contain similar provisions. In the first phase of condemnation proceedings, the government must prove that it needs to acquire privately owned property for a public use.

■ **EXAMPLE 49.18** Franklin County, Iowa, engages Bosque Systems to build a liquefied natural gas pipeline that crosses the property of more than two hundred landowners. Some property owners consent to this use and accept the Bosque's offer of compensation. Others refuse the offer. A court will likely deem the pipeline to be a public use. Therefore, the government can exert its eminent domain power to "take" the land, provided that it pays just compensation to the property owners. ■

The Compensation The U.S. Constitution and state constitutions require that the government pay just compensation to the landowner when invoking its condemnation power. Just compensation means fair value. In the second phase of the condemnation proceeding, the court determines the fair value of the land, which usually is approximately equal to its market value.

Property may be taken by the government only for public use, not for private benefit. But can eminent domain be used to promote private development when the development is deemed to be in the public interest? See this chapter's *Ethics Today* for a discussion of this issue.

49–4b Inverse Condemnation

Typically, a government agency exercises the power of eminent domain in the manner just discussed. **Inverse condemnation,** in contrast, occurs when a government simply takes private property from a landowner without paying any compensation, thereby forcing the landowner to sue the government for compensation.

The taking can be physical, as when a government agency uses or occupies the land, or it may be constructive, as when an agency regulation results in loss of property value. The United States Supreme Court has held that even temporary flooding of land by the government may result in liability under the takings clause.[9]

■ **CASE IN POINT 49.19** In Walton County, Florida, water flows through a ditch from Oyster Lake to the Gulf of Mexico. When Hurricane Opal caused the water to rise in Oyster Lake, Walton County reconfigured the drainage to divert the overflow onto the nearby property of William and Patricia Hemby. The flow was eventually

9. *Arkansas Game and Fish Commission v. United States*, ___ U.S. ___, 133 S.Ct. 511, 184 L.Ed.2d 417 (2012).

ETHICS TODAY

Should Eminent Domain Be Used to Promote Private Development?

Issues of fairness often arise when the government takes private property for public use. One issue is whether it is fair for a government to take property by eminent domain and then convey it to private developers.

For instance, suppose a city government decides that it is in the public interest to have a larger parking lot for a local, privately owned sports stadium. Or suppose it decides that its citizens would benefit from having a manufacturing plant locate in the city to create more jobs. The government may condemn certain tracts of existing housing or business property and then convey the land to the privately owned stadium or manufacturing plant.

Such actions may bring in private developers and businesses that provide jobs and increase tax revenues, thus revitalizing communities. But is the land really being taken for "public use," as required by the Fifth Amendment to the U.S. Constitution?

The Supreme Court's Ruling

In 2005, the United States Supreme Court ruled that the power of eminent domain may be used to further

economic development.[a] At the same time, the Court recognized that individual states have the right to pass laws that prohibit takings for economic development.

The States' Responses

Since then, the vast majority of the states have passed laws to curb the government's ability to take private property and subsequently give it to private developers. Nevertheless, loopholes in some state legislation still allow takings for redevelopment of slum areas. Thus, the debate over whether (and when) it is fair for the government to take citizens' property for economic development continues.

Critical Thinking *At what point might the predicted benefits of a new private commercial endeavor outweigh the constitutional requirement of a taking only for public use?*

a. *Kelo v. City of New London, Connecticut,* 545 U.S. 469, 125 S.Ct. 2655, 162 L.Ed.2d 439 (2005).

restored to pre-hurricane conditions, but during a later emergency, water was diverted onto the Hembys' property again. This diversion was not restored.

The Hembys filed a suit against the county. After their deaths, their daughter Cozette Drake pursued the claim. The court found that by allowing the water diversion to remain on Drake's property long after the emergency had passed, the county had engaged in a permanent or continuous physical invasion. This invasion rendered Drake's property useless and deprived her of its beneficial enjoyment. Drake was therefore entitled to receive compensation from the county.[10] ∎

49–4c Restrictive Covenants

A private restriction on the use of land is known as a **restrictive covenant.** If the restriction is binding on the party who initially purchases the property and on subsequent purchasers as well, it is said to "run with the land." A covenant running with the land must be in writing (usually it is in the deed), and subsequent purchasers must have reason to know about it.

∎ **EXAMPLE 49.20** In the course of developing a fifty-lot suburban subdivision, Levitt records a declaration of restrictions effectively limiting construction on each lot to one single-family house. Each lot's deed includes a reference to the declaration with a provision that the purchaser and her or his successors are bound to those restrictions. Thus, each purchaser assumes ownership with notice of the restrictions. If an owner attempts to build a duplex (or any noncompliant structure) on a lot, the other owners may obtain a court order to prevent the construction.

Alternatively, Levitt might simply have included the restrictions on the subdivision's map, filed the map in the appropriate public office, and included a reference to the map in each deed. Under these circumstances, each owner would still have been held to have constructive notice of the restrictions. ∎

49–5 Zoning and Government Regulations

The rules and regulations that collectively manage the development and use of land are known as **zoning laws.** Zoning laws were first used in the United States to segregate slaughterhouses, distilleries, kilns, and other businesses that might pose a nuisance to nearby residences.

The growth of modern urban areas led to an increased need to organize uses of land. Today, zoning laws enable municipalities to control the speed and type of development within their borders by creating different zones and regulating the use of property allowed in each zone.

The United States Supreme Court has held that zoning is a constitutional exercise of a government's police powers.[11] Therefore, as long as zoning ordinances are rationally related to the health, safety, or welfare of the community, a municipal government has broad discretion to carry out zoning as it sees fit.

49–5a Purpose and Scope of Zoning Laws

The purpose of zoning laws is to manage the land within a community in a way that encourages sustainable and organized development while controlling growth in a manner that serves the interests of the community. One of the basic elements of zoning is the classification of land by permissible use, but zoning extends to other aspects of land use as well.

Permissible Uses of Land Municipalities generally divide their available land into districts according to the land's present and potential future uses. Typically, land is classified into the following types of permissible uses:

1. *Residential.* In areas dedicated for **residential use,** landowners can construct buildings for human habitation.

2. *Commercial.* Land assigned for business activities is designated as being for **commercial use,** sometimes called business use. An area with a number of retail stores, offices, supermarkets, and hotels might be designated as a commercial or business district. Land used for entertainment purposes, such as movie theaters and sports stadiums, also falls into this category, as does land used for government activities.

3. *Industrial.* Areas designated for **industrial use** typically encompass light and heavy manufacturing, shipping, and heavy transportation. For instance, undeveloped land with easy access to highways and railroads might be classified as suitable for future use by industry. Although industrial uses can be profitable for a city seeking to raise tax revenue, such uses can also result in noise, smoke, or vibrations that interfere with others' enjoyment of their property. Consequently, areas zoned for industrial use generally are kept as far as possible from residential districts and some commercial districts.

---

10. *Drake v. Walton County,* 6 So.3d 717 (Fla.App. 2009).

11. *Village of Euclid v. Ambler Realty Co.,* 272 U.S. 365, 47 S.Ct. 114, 71 L.Ed. 303 (1926).

4. *Conservation districts.* Some municipalities also establish certain areas that are dedicated to carrying out local soil and water conservation efforts. For instance, wetlands might be designated as a conservation district.

A city's residential, commercial, and industrial districts may be divided, in turn, into subdistricts. For instance, zoning ordinances may regulate the type, density, size, and approved uses of structures within a given district. Thus, a residential district may be divided into low-density (single-family homes with large lots), high-density (single- and multiple-family homes with small lots), and planned-unit (condominiums or apartments) subdistricts.

Other Zoning Restrictions Zoning rules extend to much more than the permissible use of land. In residential districts, for instance, an ordinance may require a house or garage to be set back a specific number of feet from a neighbor's property line.

In commercial districts, zoning rules may attempt to maintain a certain visual aesthetic. Therefore, businesses may be required to construct buildings of a certain height and width so that they conform to the style of other commercial buildings in the area.

Businesses may also be required to provide parking for patrons or take other measures to manage traffic. Sometimes, municipalities limit construction of new businesses to prevent traffic congestion.

Zoning laws may even attempt to regulate the public morals of the community. For instance, cities commonly impose severe restrictions on the location and operation of adult businesses and medical (or recreational) marijuana dispensaries.

49–5b Exceptions to Zoning Laws

Zoning restrictions are not absolute. It is impossible for zoning laws to account for every contingency. The purpose of zoning is to control development, not to prevent it altogether or to limit the government's ability to adapt to changing circumstances or unforeseen needs. Hence, legal processes have been developed to allow for exceptions to zoning laws, such as *variances* and *special-use permits*.

Variances A property owner who wants to use his or her land in a manner not permitted by zoning rules can request a **variance,** which allows an exception to the rules. The property owner making the request must demonstrate that the requested variance:

1. Is necessary for reasonable development.
2. Is the least intrusive solution to the problem.
3. Will not alter the essential character of the neighborhood.

Hardship Situations. Property owners normally request variances in *hardship situations*—that is, when complying with the zoning rules would be too difficult or costly due to existing property conditions. ■ **EXAMPLE 49.21** Lin, a homeowner, wants to replace her single-car garage with a two-car garage. If she does so, however, the garage will be closer to her neighbor's property than is permitted by the zoning rules. In this situation, she may ask for a variance. She can claim that the configuration of her property would make it difficult and costly to comply with the zoning code, so compliance would create a hardship for her. ■

Similarly, a church might request a variance from height restrictions in order to erect a new steeple. Or a furniture store might ask for a variance from *footprint* limitations so that it can expand its showroom. (A building's footprint is the area of ground that it covers.)

Note that the hardship may not be self-created. In other words, a person who buys property with zoning restrictions in effect cannot usually then argue that he or she needs a variance in order to use the property as intended.

Public Hearing. In almost all instances, before a variance is granted, there must be a public hearing with adequate notice to neighbors who may object to the exception. After the public hearing, a hearing examiner appointed by the municipality (or the local zoning board or commission) determines whether to grant the exception. When a variance is granted, it applies only to the specific parcel of land for which it was requested and does not create a regulation-free zone.

Special-Use Permits Sometimes, zoning laws permit a certain use only if the property owner complies with specific requirements to ensure that the proposed use does not harm the immediate neighborhood. In such instances, the zoning board can issue **special-use permits,** also called conditional-use permits.

■ **EXAMPLE 49.22** An area is designated as a residential district, but small businesses are permitted to operate there so long as they do not affect the characteristics of the neighborhood. A bank asks the zoning board for a special-use permit to open a branch in the area. At the public hearing, the bank demonstrates that the branch will be housed in a building that conforms to the style of other structures in the area. The bank also shows that adequate parking will be available and that landscaping will shield the parking lot from public view. Unless there are strong objections from the branch's prospective neighbors, the board will likely grant the permit. ■

Special Incentives In addition to granting exceptions to zoning regulations, municipalities may also wish to encourage certain kinds of development. To do so, they offer incentives, often in the form of lower tax rates or tax credits. For instance, to attract new businesses that will provide jobs and increase the tax base, a city may offer lower property tax rates for a period of years. Similarly, homeowners may receive tax credits for historic preservation if they renovate and maintain older homes.

49-6 Landlord-Tenant Relationships

A landlord-tenant relationship is established by a lease contract. A **lease** contract arises when a property owner (landlord) agrees to give another party (the tenant) the exclusive right to possess the property for a limited time. In most states, statutes require leases for terms exceeding one year to be in writing. The lease should describe the property and indicate the length of the term, the amount of the rent, and how and when it is to be paid.

State or local law often dictates permissible lease terms. For instance, a statute or ordinance might prohibit the leasing of a structure that is in a certain physical condition or is not in compliance with local building codes. As in other areas of law, the National Conference of Commissioners on Uniform State Laws has issued a model act to create more uniformity in the law governing landlord-tenant relations. Twenty-one states have adopted variations of the Uniform Residential Landlord and Tenant Act (URLTA).

49-6a Rights and Duties

The rights and duties of landlords and tenants generally pertain to four broad areas of concern—the possession, use, maintenance, and, of course, rent of leased property.

Possession A landlord is obligated to give a tenant possession of the property that the tenant has agreed to lease. After obtaining possession, the tenant retains the property exclusively until the lease expires, unless the lease states otherwise.

Quiet Enjoyment. The covenant of quiet enjoyment mentioned previously also applies to leased premises. Under this covenant, the landlord promises that during the lease term, neither the landlord nor anyone having a superior title to the property will disturb the tenant's use and enjoyment of the property. This covenant forms the essence of the landlord-tenant relationship, and if it is breached, the tenant can terminate the lease and sue for damages.

Eviction. If the landlord deprives the tenant of possession of the leased property or interferes with the tenant's use or enjoyment of it, an **eviction** occurs. An eviction occurs, for instance, when the landlord changes the lock and refuses to give the tenant a new key.

A **constructive eviction** occurs when the landlord wrongfully performs or fails to perform any of the duties the lease requires, thereby making the tenant's further use and enjoyment of the property exceedingly difficult or impossible. Examples of constructive eviction include a landlord's failure to provide heat in the winter, light, or other essential utilities.

Use of the Premises The tenant normally may make any use of the leased property, provided the use is legal and does not injure the landlord's interest. The parties are free to limit by agreement the uses to which the property may be put. A tenant is not entitled to create a nuisance by substantially interfering with others' quiet enjoyment of their property rights.

Maintenance of the Premises The tenant is responsible for any damage to the premises that he or she causes, intentionally or negligently. The landlord can hold the tenant liable for the cost of returning the property to the physical condition it was in at the lease's inception. The tenant usually is not responsible for ordinary wear and tear, and the property's consequent depreciation in value.

In some jurisdictions, landlords of residential property are required by statute to maintain the premises in good repair. Landlords must also comply with applicable state statutes and city ordinances regarding maintenance and repair of commercial buildings.

In addition, the implied warranty of habitability discussed earlier may apply to *residential* leases. The warranty requires a landlord who leases residential property to ensure that the premises are habitable—that is, safe and suitable to live in. Also, the landlord must make repairs to maintain the premises in that condition for the lease's duration. Generally, this warranty applies to major, or *substantial,* physical defects that the landlord knows or should know about and has had a reasonable time to repair. A large hole in the roof, for instance, would be a substantial defect.

■ **EXAMPLE 49.23** Carol and Ken Galprin own a house within the city limits of Redmond. A city regulation states that a residence must be connected to the city sewer system before anyone, including tenants, can live in the residence. The Galprins' house is not connected to the city system. Thus, it is not legally habitable, and they cannot lease it to tenants. ■

Rent *Rent* is the tenant's payment to the landlord for the tenant's occupancy or use of the landlord's real property. Usually, the tenant must pay the rent even if she or he refuses to occupy the property or moves out for unjustified reasons while the lease is in force.

Under the common law, if the leased premises were destroyed by fire or flood, the tenant still had to pay rent. Today, however, if an apartment building burns down, most states' laws do not require tenants to continue to pay rent.

In some situations, such as when a landlord breaches the implied warranty of habitability, a tenant may be allowed to withhold rent as a remedy. When rent withholding is authorized under a statute, the tenant must usually put the amount withheld into an *escrow account.* The funds are held in the name of the tenant and are returned to the tenant if the landlord fails to make the premises habitable.

49–6b Transferring Rights to Leased Property

Either the landlord or the tenant may wish to transfer her or his rights to the leased property during the term of the lease. If the landlord sells the leased property, the tenant becomes the tenant of the new owner. The new owner may collect subsequent rent but must abide by the terms of the existing lease.

Assignment The tenant's transfer of his or her entire interest in the leased property to a third person is an *assignment of the lease.* Many leases require that an assignment have the landlord's written consent. The landlord can nullify (avoid) an assignment made without the required consent. State statutes may specify that the landlord may not unreasonably withhold consent, however. Also, a landlord who knowingly accepts rent from the assignee may be held to have waived the consent requirement.

When an assignment is valid, the assignee acquires all of the tenant's rights under the lease. An assignment, however,

does not release the original tenant (assignor) from the obligation to pay rent if the assignee defaults. Also, if the assignee exercises an option under the original lease to extend the term, the original tenant remains liable for the rent during the extension, unless the landlord agrees otherwise.

Sublease The tenant's transfer of all or part of the premises for a period shorter than the lease term is a **sublease.** The same restrictions that apply to an assignment of the tenant's interest in leased property apply to a sublease. If the landlord's consent is required, a sublease without such permission is ineffective. Also, like an assignment, a sublease does not release the tenant from her or his obligations under the lease.

■ **EXAMPLE 49.24** Derek, a student, leases an apartment for a two-year period. Although Derek had planned on attending summer school, he decides to accept a job offer in Europe for the summer months instead. Derek therefore obtains his landlord's consent to sublease the apartment to Ava. Ava is bound by the same terms of the lease as Derek, and the landlord can hold Derek liable if Ava violates the lease terms. ■

49–6c Termination of the Lease

Usually, a lease terminates when its term ends. The tenant surrenders the property to the landlord, who retakes possession. If the lease states the time it will end, the landlord is not required to give the tenant notice. The lease terminates automatically.

A lease can also be terminated in several other ways. If the tenant purchases the leased property from the landlord during the term of the lease, for instance, the lease will be terminated. The parties may also agree to end a tenancy before it would otherwise terminate. Finally, the tenant may *abandon* the premises—move out completely with no intention of returning before the lease term expires.

At common law, a tenant who abandoned leased property was still obligated to pay the rent for the full term of the lease. The landlord could let the property stand vacant and charge the tenant for the remainder of the term. This is still the rule in some states. In most states today, however, the landlord has a duty to *mitigate* his or her damages—that is, to make a reasonable attempt to lease the property to another party. Consequently, the tenant's liability for unpaid rent is restricted to the period of time that the landlord would reasonably need to lease the property to another tenant. Damages may also be allowed for the landlord's costs in leasing the property again.

Reviewing: Real Property and Landlord-Tenant Law

Vern Shoepke purchased a two-story home from Walter and Eliza Bruster in the town of Roche, Maine. The warranty deed did not specify what covenants would be included in the conveyance. The property was adjacent to a public park that included a popular Frisbee golf course. (Frisbee golf is a sport similar to golf but using Frisbees.) Wayakichi Creek ran along the north end of the park and along Shoepke's property. The deed allowed Roche citizens the right to walk across a five-foot-wide section of the lot beside Wayakichi Creek as part of a two-mile public trail system. Teenagers regularly threw Frisbee golf discs from the walking path behind Shoepke's property over his yard to the adjacent park. Shoepke habitually shouted and cursed at the teenagers, demanding that they not throw objects over his yard. Two months after moving into his Roche home, Shoepke leased the second floor to Lauren Slater for nine months. After three months of tenancy, Slater sublet the second floor to a local artist, Javier Indalecio. (The lease agreement did not specify that Shoepke's consent would be required to sublease the second floor.) Over the remaining six months, Indalecio's use of oil paints damaged the carpeting in Shoepke's home. Using the information presented in the chapter, answer the following questions.

1. What is the term for the right of Roche citizens to walk across Shoepke's land on the trail?
2. What covenants would most courts infer were included in the warranty deed that was used in the property transfer from the Brusters to Shoepke?
3. Suppose that Shoepke wants to file a trespass lawsuit against some teenagers who continually throw Frisbees over his land. Shoepke discovers, however, that when the city put in the Frisbee golf course, the neighborhood homeowners signed an agreement that limited their right to complain about errant Frisbees. What is this type of promise or agreement called in real property law?
4. Can Shoepke hold Slater financially responsible for the damage to the carpeting caused by Indalecio? Why or why not?

Debate This . . .   *Under no circumstances should a local government be able to condemn property in order to sell it later to real estate developers for private use.*

Terms and Concepts

adverse possession 950	implication 945	recording statute 950
closing 946	implied warranty of habitability 947	residential use 954
commercial use 954	industrial use 954	restrictive covenant 954
community property 943	inverse condemnation 953	special-use permit 955
concurrent ownership 943	joint tenancy 943	special warranty deed 949
condemnation 952	lease 956	sublease 957
constructive eviction 956	leasehold estate 943	taking 952
conveyance 941	license 945	tenancy at sufferance 944
deed 949	life estate 941	tenancy at will 944
easement 944	marketable title 947	tenancy by the entirety 943
eminent domain 952	metes and bounds 949	tenancy in common 943
escrow account 947	necessity 945	title insurance 947
eviction 956	nonpossessory interest 944	trade fixture 941
fee simple absolute 941	periodic tenancy 944	variance 955
fixed-term tenancy 944	prescription 945	warranty deed 949
fixture 940	profit 944	waste 941
grant deed 949	quitclaim deed 949	zoning laws 954

Issue Spotters

1. Bernie sells his house to Consuela under a warranty deed. Later, Delmira appears, holding a better title to the house than Consuela has. Delmira wants to have Consuela evicted from the property. What can Consuela do? (See *Transfer of Ownership*.)

2. Grey owns a commercial building in fee simple. Grey transfers temporary possession of the building to Haven Corporation. Can Haven transfer possession for even less time to Idyll Company? Explain. (See *Ownership and Other Interests in Real Property*.)

• **Check your answers to the Issue Spotters against the answers provided in Appendix D at the end of this text.**

Business Scenarios

49–1. Property Ownership. Madison owned a tract of land, but he was not sure that he had full title to the property. When Rafael expressed an interest in buying the land, Madison sold it to Rafael and executed a quitclaim deed. Rafael properly recorded the deed immediately. Several months later, Madison learned that he had had full title to the tract of land. He then sold the land to Linda by warranty deed. Linda knew of the earlier purchase by Rafael but took the deed anyway and later sued to have Rafael evicted from the land. Linda claimed that because she had a warranty deed, her title to the land was better than that conferred by Rafael's quitclaim deed. Will Linda succeed in claiming title to the land? Explain. (See *Transfer of Ownership*.)

49–2. Eviction. James owns a three-story building. He leases the ground floor to Juan's Mexican restaurant. The lease is to run for a five-year period and contains an express covenant of quiet enjoyment. One year later, James leases the top two stories to the Upbeat Club, a dance club for teens. The club's hours run from 5:00 P.M. to 11:00 P.M. The noise from the Upbeat Club is so loud that it is driving customers away from Juan's restaurant. Juan has notified James of the interference and has called the police on a number of occasions. James refuses to talk to the owners of the Upbeat Club or to do anything to remedy the situation. Juan abandons the premises. James files a suit for breach of the lease agreement and for the rental payments still due under the lease. Juan claims that he was constructively evicted and files a countersuit for damages. Discuss who will be held liable. (See *Landlord-Tenant Relationships*.)

Business Case Problems

49–3. Commercial Lease Terms. Gi Hwa Park entered into a lease with Landmark HHH, LLC, for retail space in the Plaza at Landmark, a shopping center in Virginia. The lease required the landlord to keep the roof "in good repair" and the tenant to obtain insurance on her inventory and absolve the landlord from any losses to the extent of the insurance proceeds. Park opened a store—The Four Seasons—in the space, specializing in imported men's suits and accessories. Within a month and continuing for nearly eight years, water intermittently leaked through the roof, causing damage. Landmark eventually had a new roof installed, but water continued to leak into The Four Seasons. On a night of record rainfall, the store suffered substantial water damage, and Park was forced to close. On what basis might Park seek to recover from Landmark? What might Landmark assert in response? Which party's argument is more likely to succeed, and why? [*Landmark HHH, LLC v. Gi Hwa Park*, 277 Va. 50, 671 S.E.2d 143 (2009)] (See *Landlord-Tenant Relationships*.)

49–4. Business Case Problem with Sample Answer— **Adverse Possession.** The McKeag family operated a marina on their lakefront property in Bolton, New York. For more than forty years, the McKeags used a section of property belonging to their neighbors, the Finleys, as a beach for the marina's customers. The McKeags also stored a large float on the beach during the winter months, built their own retaining wall, and planted bushes and flowers there. The McKeags prevented others from using the property, including the Finleys. Nevertheless, the families always had a friendly relationship, and one of the Finleys gave the McKeags permission to continue using the beach in 1992. He also reminded them of his ownership several times, to which they said nothing. The McKeags also asked for permission to mow grass on the property and once apologized for leaving a jet ski there. Can the McKeags establish adverse possession over the statutory period of ten years? Why or why not? [*McKeag v. Finley*, 939 N.Y.S.2d 644 (N.Y.App.Div. 2012)] (See *Transfer of Ownership*.)

• **For a sample answer to Problem 49–4, go to Appendix E at the end of this text.**

49–5. Rent. Flawlace, LLC, leased unfinished commercial real estate in Las Vegas, Nevada, from Francis Lin to operate a beauty salon. The lease required Flawlace to obtain a "certificate of occupancy" from the city to commence business. This required the installation of a fire protection system. The lease did not allocate responsibility for the installation to either party. Lin voluntarily undertook to install the system. After a month of delays, Flawlace moved out. Three months later, the installation was complete, and Lin leased the premises to a new tenant. Did Flawlace owe rent for the three months between the time that it moved out and the time that the new tenant moved in? Explain. [*Tri-Lin Holdings, LLC v. Flawlace, LLC,* 2014 WL 1101577 (Nev.Sup.Ct. 2014)] (See *Landlord-Tenant Relationships.*)

49–6. Landlord-Tenant Relationships. Bhanmattie Kumar was walking on a sidewalk in Flushing, New York, when she tripped over a chipped portion of the sidewalk and fell. The defective sidewalk was in front of a Pretty Girl store—one of a chain of apparel stores headquartered in Brooklyn—on premises leased from PI Associates, LLC. Kumar filed a claim in a New York state court against PI, seeking to recover damages for her injuries. PI filed a cross-claim against Pretty Girl. On what basis would the court impose liability on PI? In what situation would Pretty Girl be the liable party? Is there any circumstance in which Kumar could be at least partially responsible for her injury? Discuss. [*Bhanmattie Rajkumar Kumar v. PI Associates, LLC,* 125 A.D.3d 609, 3 N.Y.S.3d 372 (2 Dept. 2015)] (See *Landlord-Tenant Relationships.*)

49–7. Ownership and Other Interests in Real Property. Arthur and Diana Ebanks owned three properties in the Cayman Islands in joint tenancy. With respect to joint tenancies, Cayman law is the same as U.S. law. When the Ebanks divorced, the decree did not change the tenancy in which the properties were held. On the same day as the divorce filing, Arthur executed a will providing that "any property in my name and that of another as joint tenants . . . will pass to the survivor, and I instruct my Personal Representative to make no claim thereto." Four years later, Arthur died. His brother Curtis, the personal representative of his estate, asserted that Arthur's interest in the Cayman properties was part of the estate. Diana said that the sole interest in the properties was

hers. Who do the Cayman properties belong to? Why? [*Ebanks v. Ebanks,* 41 Fla. L. Weekly D291, __ So.3d __ (2 Dist. 2016)] (See *Ownership and Other Interests in Real Property.*)

49–8. Special Case Analysis—Adverse Possession. Go to Case Analysis 49.3, *Montgomery County v. Bhatt.* Read the excerpt, and answer the following questions.

(a) Issue: What conflict, and between which parties, did this case highlight?

(b) Rule of Law: On which specific requirement of what rule of law did the outcome in this case depend?

(c) Applying the Rule of Law: What exception to the applied rule of law might have resulted in a decision in the plaintiff's favor? Why did that exception not apply in this case?

(d) Conclusion: In light of the rule of law applied in this case, what was the judgment?

49–9. A Question of Ethics—Adverse Possession. Alana Mansell built a garage on her property that encroached on the property of her neighbor, Betty Hunter, by fourteen feet. Hunter knew of the encroachment and informally agreed to it, but she did not transfer ownership of the property to Mansell. A survey twenty-eight years later confirmed the encroachment, and Hunter sought the removal of the garage. Mansell asked a court to declare that she was the owner of the property by adverse possession. [Hunter v. Mansell, *240 P.3d 469 (Colo.App. 2010)]* (See *Transfer of Ownership.*)

(a) Did Mansell obtain title by adverse possession? Would the open occupation of the property for nearly thirty years be in Mansell's favor? Why or why not?

(b) Was Mansell's conduct in any way unethical? Discuss.

Legal Reasoning Group Activity

49–10. Adverse Possession. The Wallen family owned a cabin on Lummi Island in the state of Washington. A driveway ran from the cabin across their property to South Nugent Road. Floyd Massey bought the adjacent lot and built a cabin on it in 1980. To gain access to his property, Massey used a bulldozer to extend the driveway, without the Wallens' permission but also without their objection. In 2005, the Wallens sold their property to Wright Fish Company. Massey continued to use and maintain the driveway without permission or objection. In 2011, Massey sold his property to Robert Drake. Drake and his employees continued to use and maintain the driveway without permission or objection, although Drake knew it was located largely on Wright's property. In 2013, Wright sold its lot to Robert Smersh. The next year, Smersh told Drake to stop using the driveway. Drake filed a suit against Smersh, claiming an easement by prescription

(which is created by meeting the same requirements as adverse possession). (See *Transfer of Ownership.*)

(a) The first group will decide whether Drake's use of the driveway meets all of the requirements for adverse possession (easement by prescription).

(b) The second group will determine how the court should rule in this case and why. Does it matter that Drake knew the driveway was located largely on Wright's (and then Smersh's) property? Should it matter? Why or why not?

(c) A third group will evaluate the underlying policy and fairness of adverse possession laws. Should the law reward persons who take possession of someone else's land for their own use? Does it make sense to punish owners who allow someone else to use their land without complaint? Explain.

CHAPTER 50

Insurance

Protecting against loss is a foremost concern of all property owners. No one can predict whether an accident or a fire will occur, so individuals and businesses typically protect their personal and financial interests by obtaining insurance.

Insurance is a contract in which the insurance company (the insurer) promises to pay or otherwise compensate another (either the insured or the beneficiary) for a particular loss.

Insurance may provide for compensation in the event of (1) the injury or death of the insured or another, (2) damage to the insured's property, or (3) other types of losses, such as those resulting from lawsuits. Basically, insurance is an arrangement for *transferring and allocating risk.* In general, **risk** can be described as a prediction concerning potential loss based on known and unknown factors.

Risk management normally involves the transfer of certain risks from the individual to the insurance company by a contractual agreement. We examine the insurance contract and its provisions in this chapter. First, however, we look at some basic insurance terminology and concepts.

50–1 Insurance Terminology and Concepts

Like other legal areas, insurance has its own special concepts and terminology. An insurance contract is called a **policy.** The consideration paid to the insurer is called a **premium,** and the insurance company is sometimes called an **underwriter.** The parties to an insurance policy are the *insurer* (the insurance company) and the *insured* (the person covered by its provisions).

Insurance contracts usually are obtained through an *agent,* who normally works for the insurance company, or through a *broker,* who is ordinarily an *independent contractor.* When a broker deals with an applicant for insurance, the broker is, in effect, the applicant's agent (and not an agent of the insurance company).

In contrast, an insurance agent is an agent of the insurance company, not an agent of the applicant. Thus, the agent owes fiduciary duties to the insurer (the insurance company), but not to the person who is applying for insurance. As a general rule, the insurance company is bound by the acts of its agents when they act within the scope of the agency relationship. In most situations, state law determines the status of all parties writing or obtaining insurance.

50–1a Classifications of Insurance

Insurance is classified according to the nature of the risk involved. Fire insurance, casualty insurance, life insurance, and title insurance apply to different types of risk and protect different persons and interests. This is reasonable because the types of losses that are expected and the types that are foreseeable or unforeseeable vary with the nature of the activity. Exhibit 50–1 provides a list of common insurance classifications.

50–1b Insurable Interest

A person must have an **insurable interest** in something in order to insure it. Without an insurable interest, there is no enforceable contract, and a transaction to purchase insurance coverage would have to be treated as a wager. The existence of an insurable interest is a primary concern in determining liability under an insurance policy.

Life Insurance In regard to life insurance, a person must have a reasonable expectation of benefit from the continued life of another to have an insurable interest in that person's life. The insurable interest must exist *at the time the policy is obtained.*

961

EXHIBIT 50–1 Selected Insurance Classifications

TYPE OF INSURANCE	COVERAGE
Accident	Covers expenses, losses, and suffering incurred by the insured because of accidents causing physical injury and any consequent disability; sometimes includes a specified payment to heirs of the insured if death results from an accident.
All-Risk	Covers all losses that the insured may incur except those that are specifically excluded. Typical exclusions are losses due to war, pollution, earthquakes, and floods.
Automobile	May cover damage to automobiles resulting from specified hazards or occurrences (such as fire, vandalism, theft, or collision); normally provides protection against liability for personal injuries and property damage resulting from the operation of the vehicle.
Casualty	Protects against losses incurred by the insured as a result of being held liable for personal injuries or property damage sustained by others.
Disability	Replaces a portion of the insured's monthly income from employment in the event that illness or injury causes a short- or long-term disability. Some states require employers to provide short-term disability insurance. Benefits typically last a set period of time, such as six months for short-term coverage or five years for long-term coverage.
Fire	Covers losses to the insured caused by fire.
Floater	Covers movable property, as long as the property is within the territorial boundaries specified in the contract.
Homeowners'	Protects homeowners against some or all risks of loss to their residences and the residences' contents or liability arising from the use of the property.
Key-Person	Protects a business in the event of the death or disability of a key employee.
Liability	Protects against liability imposed on the insured as a result of injuries to the person or property of another.
Life	Covers the death of the policyholder. On the death of the insured, the insurer pays the amount specified in the policy to the insured's beneficiary.
Major Medical	Protects the insured against major hospital, medical, or surgical expenses.
Malpractice	A form of liability insurance that protects professionals (physicians, lawyers, and others) against malpractice claims brought against them by their patients or clients.
Term Life	Provides life insurance for a specified period of time (term) with no cash surrender value. It usually is renewable.

Life Insurance on Family Members. Close family relationships give a person an insurable interest in the life of another. For instance, a husband can take out an insurance policy on his wife and vice versa, or parents can take out life insurance policies on their children. A policy that a person takes out on his or her spouse remains valid even if they divorce, unless a specific provision in the policy calls for its termination on divorce.

Key-Person Life Insurance. *Key-person insurance* is insurance obtained by an organization on the life of a person who is important to that organization. Because the organization expects to experience financial gain from the continuation of the key person's life or financial loss from the key person's death, the organization has an insurable interest.

Typically, a small company will insure the lives of its important employees. Similarly, a corporation has an insurable interest in the life of a key executive (such as a talented CEO) whose death would result in financial loss to the company. If a firm insures a key person's life and that person leaves the firm and subsequently dies, the firm can collect on the insurance policy, provided that it has continued to pay the premiums.

Property Insurance For property insurance, an insurable interest exists when the insured derives a monetary benefit from the preservation and continued existence of the property. The insurable interest must exist at the time the loss occurs but need not exist when the policy is purchased.

■ **CASE IN POINT 50.1** ABM Industries, Inc., operated the heating, ventilation, and air-conditioning systems at the World Trade Center (WTC) in New York City in 2001. ABM also maintained all of the WTC's common areas. At the time, ABM employed more than eight hundred workers at the WTC. Zurich American Insurance Company insured ABM against losses resulting from "business interruption" caused by direct physical loss or damage "to property owned, controlled, used, leased or intended for use" by ABM.

After the terrorist attacks on September 11, ABM filed a claim to recover for the loss of all income derived from its WTC operations. Zurich argued that the recovery should be limited to the income lost as a result of the destruction of ABM's office and storage space and supplies. A federal appellate court, however, ruled that ABM was entitled to compensation for the loss of all of its WTC operations. The court reasoned that the "policy's scope expressly includes real or personal property that the insured 'used,' 'controlled,' or 'intended for use.'" Because ABM's income depended on "the common areas and leased premises in the WTC complex," it had an insurable interest in that property at the time of the loss.[1] ■

In the following case, the plaintiff sought to retain his insurable interest in a home he no longer owned.

---

1. *Zurich American Insurance Co. v. ABM Industries, Inc.*, 397 F.3d 158 (2d Cir. 2005).

Case 50.1

Breeden v. Buchanan
Court of Appeals of Mississippi, 164 So.3d 1057 (2015).

Background and Facts Donald Breeden and Willie Buchanan were married in Marion County, Mississippi. They lived in a home in Sandy Hook. Nationwide Property & Casualty Insurance Company insured the home under a policy bought by Breeden that named him as the insured. The policy provided that the spouse of the named insured was covered as an insured. After eight years of marriage, Breeden and Buchanan divorced. Breeden transferred his interest in the home to Buchanan as part of the couple's property settlement.

Less than a year later, a fire completely destroyed the home. An insurance claim was filed with Nationwide. Nationwide paid Buchanan. Breeden then filed a suit in a Mississippi state court against Buchanan and Nationwide. The plaintiff asserted claims for breach of contract and bad faith, and sought to recover the proceeds under the policy. The court dismissed the suit. Breeden appealed.

In the Language of the Court
GRIFFIS, P.J. [Presiding Judge], for the Court:
* * * *

Breeden's claims for breach of contract [and] bad-faith denial of insurance benefits * * * are based on the insurance policy. The [lower] court ruled that Breeden had no "insurable interest" in the Nationwide policy and had no right to the proceeds of the policy. Specifically, the * * * court ruled:

> The court finds that the pleadings reflect no insurable interest in Breeden in and to the policy or to the proceeds, as Breeden transferred and conveyed his right, title, and interest in and to the insured property to his former spouse, Buchanan, as part and parcel of their divorce proceeding and property settlement agreement, this transfer and conveyance having transpired several months before the occurrence of the loss, which is the subject matter of Breeden's complaint.
>
> Finding that Breeden had no insurable interest in and to the property—and thus no entitlement to any of the insurance proceeds—it follows that Nationwide did not breach the insurance contract by failing to pay Breeden any insurance proceeds from the loss, nor did it act in bad faith.

Case 50.1 Continues

Case 50.1 Continued   * * * *

Breeden argues that the [lower] court was in error to determine that he had no insurable interest in the home. The home, which was Breeden's and Buchanan's marital residence, was insured under a Nationwide homeowners' insurance policy. The policy was effective from May 27, 2010, to May 27, 2011. The policy insured the home and its contents. At the beginning of the policy period, May 27, 2010, both Breeden and Buchanan had an insurable interest in the home because they were married and lived together in the home. The policy provided that the spouse of the named insured who resides at the same premises is covered as an insured. Based on the allegations of the complaint, the documents attached to the complaint, and Nationwide's motion [to dismiss], the * * * judge determined that Breeden did not have an insurable interest in the home at the time of the fire loss.

The fire loss occurred in April 2011. *At that time, Breeden did not have an insurable interest in the home. * * * The factual allegations of the complaint indicated that he did not have any ownership interest in the home at the time of the loss.* [Emphasis added.]
* * * *

Based on the complaint and the accompanying documents, there was simply nothing further that Nationwide owed under the insurance policy.

Decision and Remedy *A state intermediate appellate court affirmed the lower court's dismissal of Breeden's suit. Buchanan, not Breeden, was entitled to the proceeds of the insurance claim filed with Nationwide. At the time of the fire, the insurable interest in the property existed solely with Buchanan.*

Critical Thinking
- **Economic** *Why is an insurable interest required for the enforcement of an insurance contract?*

50–2 The Insurance Contract

An insurance contract is governed by the general principles of contract law, although the insurance industry is heavily regulated by each state.[2] Thus, for the insurance contract to be binding, consideration (in the form of a premium) must be given. In addition, the parties forming the contract must have the required contractual capacity to do so.

50–2a Application for Insurance

Customarily, a party offers to purchase insurance by submitting an application to the insurance company. The company can either accept or reject the offer. Sometimes, the insurance company's acceptance is conditional—on the results of a life insurance applicant's medical examination, for instance.

The filled-in application form is usually attached to the policy and made a part of the insurance contract. Thus, an insurance applicant is bound by any false statements that appear in the application (subject to certain exceptions). Insurance companies evaluate their risk

based on the information included in the application. Therefore, an applicant's misstatements or misrepresentations can void a policy, especially if the insurance company can show that it would not have extended insurance if it had known the facts.

50–2b Effective Date

The effective date of an insurance contract—that is, the date on which the insurance coverage begins—is important. Any loss sustained before the effective date will not be covered by the policy.

In some situations, the insurance applicant is not protected until a formal written policy is issued. In other situations, the applicant is protected between the time an application is received and the time the insurance company either accepts or rejects it. In these situations, a *binder* may be written.

Binder Recall that a broker is an agent of the applicant, not an agent of the insurance company. Therefore, if a person hires a broker to obtain insurance, and the broker fails to procure a policy, the applicant normally is not insured.

In contrast, a person who is obtaining insurance from an insurance company's agent is usually protected from

---

2. The states were given authority to regulate the insurance industry by the McCarran-Ferguson Act of 1945, 15 U.S.C. Sections 1011–1015.

the moment the application is made, provided that some form of premium has been paid. Usually, the agent will write a memorandum, or **binder,** indicating that a policy is pending and stating its essential terms. The binder provides temporary coverage until a formal policy is accepted or denied.

Life Insurance Parties may agree that a life insurance policy will be binding at the time the insured pays the first premium. The policy may, however, be expressly contingent on the applicant's passing a physical examination. If the applicant pays the premium and passes the examination, then the policy coverage is continuously in effect. If the applicant pays the premium but dies before having the physical examination, the policy may still be effective. In order to collect, the applicant's estate normally must show that the applicant would have passed the examination had he or she not died.

50–2c Provisions and Clauses

Some of the important provisions and clauses contained in insurance contracts are discussed in the following subsections and listed in Exhibit 50–2.

Provisions Mandated by Statute If a statute mandates that a certain provision be included in insurance contracts, a court will interpret the insurance policy as containing that provision. If a statute requires that any limitations on coverage be stated in the contract, a court will not allow an insurer to avoid liability by relying on an unexpressed restriction.

Incontestability Clauses Statutes commonly require that a policy for life or health insurance include an **incontestability clause**. Such a clause provides that after the policy has been in force for a specified length of time—often two or three years—the insurer cannot contest statements made in the application.

Once a policy becomes incontestable, the insurer cannot later avoid a claim on the basis of, for instance, fraud on the part of the insured, unless the clause provides an exception for that circumstance. The clause does not prevent an insurer from asserting other defenses to a claim, such as the nonpayment of premiums, failure to file proof of death, or lack of an insurable interest.

Coinsurance Clauses Often, when taking out fire insurance policies, property owners insure their property

EXHIBIT 50–2 Insurance Contract Provisions and Clauses

TYPE OF CLAUSE	DEFINITION
Antilapse Clause	An antilapse clause provides that a life insurance policy will not automatically lapse if no payment is made on the date due. Ordinarily, under such a provision, the insured has a *grace period* of thirty or thirty-one days within which to pay an overdue premium before the policy is canceled.
Appraisal Clause	Insurance policies frequently provide that if the parties cannot agree on the amount of a loss covered under the policy or the value of the property lost, an appraisal, or estimate, by an impartial and qualified third party can be demanded.
Arbitration Clause	Many insurance policies include clauses that call for arbitration of any disputes that arise between the insurer and the insured concerning the settlement of claims.
Coinsurance Clause	Many property insurance policies include a coinsurance clause that applies in the event of a partial loss and determines what percentage of the value of the property must be insured for an owner to be fully reimbursed for a loss. If the owner insures the property up to a specified percentage (typically 80 percent) of its value, she or he will recover any loss up to the face amount of the policy.
Incontestability Clause	An incontestability clause provides that after a policy has been in force for a specified length of time—usually two or three years—the insurer cannot contest statements made in the application.
Multiple Insurance Clause	Many insurance policies include a clause providing that if the insured has multiple insurance policies that cover the same property and the amount of coverage exceeds the loss, the loss will be shared proportionately by the insurance companies.

for less than full value because most fires do not result in a total loss. To encourage owners to insure their property for an amount as close to full value as possible, fire insurance policies generally include a coinsurance clause.

Typically, a **coinsurance clause** provides that if the owner insures the property up to a specified percentage—usually 80 percent—of its value, she or he will recover any loss up to the face amount of the policy. If the insurance is for less than the specified percentage, the owner is responsible for a proportionate share of the loss. In effect, the owner becomes a coinsurer.

Coinsurance applies only in instances of partial loss. The amount of the recovery is calculated by using the following formula:

$$\text{Loss} \times \left(\frac{\text{Amount of Insurance Coverage}}{\text{Coinsurance Percentage} \times \text{Property Value}} \right) = \text{Amount of Recovery}$$

■ **EXAMPLE 50.2** Madison, who owns property valued at $200,000, takes out a policy in the amount of $100,000. If Madison then suffers a loss of $80,000, her recovery will be $50,000. Madison will be responsible for (coinsure) the balance of the loss, or $30,000, which is the amount of loss ($80,000) minus the amount of recovery ($50,000).

$$\$80,000 \times \left(\frac{\$100,000}{0.8 \times \$200,000} \right) = \$50,000$$

Suppose that, instead, Madison had taken out a policy in the amount of 80 percent of the value of the property, or $160,000. Then, according to the same formula, she would have recovered the full amount of the loss (the face amount of the policy). ■

Appraisal and Arbitration Clauses

Most fire insurance policies provide that if the parties cannot agree on the amount of a loss covered under the policy or on the value of the property lost, an *appraisal* can be demanded. An appraisal is an estimate of the property's value determined by a suitably qualified individual who has no interest in the property. Typically, two appraisers are used, with one appointed by each party. A third party, or umpire, may be called on to resolve differences. Other types of insurance policies also contain provisions for appraisal and arbitration when the insured and insurer disagree on the value of a loss.

Multiple Insurance Coverage

Sometimes, an insured has *multiple insurance coverage*—that is, policies

with several companies covering the same insurable interest. If the amount of coverage exceeds the loss, the insured can collect from each insurer only the company's proportionate share of the liability relative to the total amount of insurance.

Many fire insurance policies include a pro rata clause, which requires that all carriers proportionately share in any loss. ■ **EXAMPLE 50.3** Green insured $50,000 worth of property with two companies. Each policy had a liability limit of $40,000. If the property is totally destroyed, Green can collect only $25,000 from each insurer. ■

Antilapse Clauses

A life insurance policy may provide, or a statute may require a policy to provide, that it will not automatically lapse if no payment is made on the date due. Ordinarily, under an **antilapse provision,** the insured has a *grace period* of thirty or thirty-one days within which to pay an overdue premium.

If the insured fails to pay a premium altogether, there are alternatives to cancellation:

1. The insurer may be required to extend the insurance for a period of time.
2. The insurer may issue a policy with less coverage to reflect the amount of the payments made.
3. The insurer may pay to the insured the policy's **cash surrender value**—the amount the insurer has agreed to pay on the policy's cancellation before the insured's death. (This value depends on the type of policy. It also depends on the period that the policy has already run, the amount of the premium, the insured's age and life expectancy, and amounts to be repaid on any outstanding loans taken out against the policy.)

When the insurance contract states that the insurer cannot cancel the policy, these alternatives are important.

50–2d Interpreting Provisions of an Insurance Contract

The courts recognize that most people do not have the special training necessary to understand the intricate terminology used in insurance policies. Therefore, when disputes arise, the courts will interpret the words used in an insurance contract according to their ordinary meanings in light of the nature of the coverage involved.

When there is an ambiguity in the policy, the provision generally is interpreted *against the insurance company*. Also, when it is unclear whether an insurance contract actually exists because the written policy has not been delivered, the uncertainty normally is resolved against the insurance company. The court presumes that the policy is in effect unless the company can show otherwise. Similarly, an insurer must make sure that the insured is adequately notified of any change in coverage under an existing policy.

Disputes over insurance often focus on the application of exclusions in the policy. ■ **CASE IN POINT 50.4** Alberto and Karelli Mila were insured under a liability policy that contained a list of twelve exclusions. "Exclusion k" stated that coverage did not apply to "bodily injury arising out of sexual molestation, corporal punishment or physical or mental abuse." Verushka Valero, on behalf of her child, filed a suit against the Milas, charging them with negligent supervision of a perpetrator who sexually molested Valero's child.

The Milas filed a claim with their insurer to provide a defense against the charges. The insurer refused and sought a court order declaring that it had no obligation under the policy to provide such a defense. The court ruled in favor of the insurer, and the decision was affirmed on appeal. The language in the Milas' policy excluding coverage for "bodily injury arising out of sexual molestation" was clear and unambiguous. The exclusion applied to preclude coverage.[3] ■

50–2e Cancellation

The insured can cancel a policy at any time, and the insurer can cancel under certain circumstances. When an insurance company can cancel its insurance contract, the policy or a state statute usually requires that the insurer give advance written notice of the cancellation. The same requirement applies when only part of a policy is canceled. Any premium paid in advance and not yet earned may be refundable on the policy's cancellation. The insured may also be entitled to a life insurance policy's cash surrender value.

The insurer may cancel an insurance policy for various reasons, depending on the type of insurance. For example:

1. Automobile insurance can be canceled for nonpayment of premiums or suspension of the insured's driver's license.
2. Property insurance can be canceled for nonpayment of premiums or for other reasons, including the insured's fraud or misrepresentation, gross negligence, or conviction for a crime that increases the risk assumed by the insurer.

3. Life and health policies can be canceled because of false statements made by the insured in the application, but the cancellation must take place before the effective date of an incontestability clause.

An insurer cannot cancel—or refuse to renew—a policy for discriminatory reasons or other reasons that violate public policy. Also, an insurer cannot cancel a policy because the insured has appeared as a witness in a case brought against the company.

50–2f Duties and Obligations of the Parties

Both parties to an insurance contract are responsible for the obligations they assume under the contract. In addition, both the insured and the insurer have an implied duty to act in good faith.

Duties of the Insured Good faith requires the party who is applying for insurance to reveal everything necessary for the insurer to evaluate the risk of issuing the policy. In other words, the applicant must disclose all facts that an insurer would consider in determining whether to charge a higher premium or to refuse to issue a policy altogether. Many insurance companies require that an applicant give the company permission to access other information, such as private medical records and credit ratings, for the purpose of evaluating risk.

Once the insurance policy is issued, the insured has three basic duties under the contract:

1. To pay the premiums as stated in the contract.
2. To notify the insurer within a reasonable time if an event occurs that gives rise to a claim.
3. To cooperate with the insurer during any investigation or litigation.

Duties of the Insurer Once the insurer has accepted the risk, and some event occurs that gives rise to a claim, the insurer has a *duty to investigate* to determine the facts. When a policy provides insurance against third party claims, the insurer is obligated to make reasonable efforts to settle any such claim.

If a settlement cannot be reached, then regardless of the claim's merit, the insurer has a *duty to defend* any suit against the insured. Usually, a policy provides that in this situation the insured must *cooperate* in the defense and attend hearings and trials if necessary.

The insurer also owes a *duty to pay* any legitimate claims up to the face amount of the policy. An insurer has a duty to provide or pay an attorney to defend its insured when a complaint alleges facts that could, if

---

3. *Valero v. Florida Insurance Guaranty Association, Inc.,* 59 So.3d 1166 (Fla. App. 2011).

proved, impose liability on the insured within the policy's coverage.

■ **CASE IN POINT 50.5** Dentist Robert Woo installed implants for one of his employees, Tina Alberts, whose family raised potbellied pigs. As a joke, while Alberts was anesthetized, Woo installed a set of "flippers" (temporary partial bridges) shaped like boar tusks and took photos. A month later, Woo's staff showed the photos to Alberts at a party. Alberts refused to return to work. She filed a suit against Woo for battery.

Woo's insurance company refused to defend him in the suit, and he ended up paying Alberts $250,000 to settle her claim. Woo then sued the insurance company and won. The court held that the insurance company had a duty to defend Woo under the professional liability provision of his policy because Woo's practical joke took place during a routine dental procedure.[4] ■

Bad Faith Actions Although insurance law generally follows contract law, most states now recognize a "bad faith" tort action against insurers. Thus, if an insurer in bad faith denies coverage of a claim, the insured may sue. If successful, the insured can recover an amount exceeding the policy's coverage limits and may also recover punitive damages. Some courts have held insurers liable for a bad faith refusal to settle claims for reasonable amounts within the policy limits.

50–2g Defenses against Payment

An insurance company can raise any of the defenses that would be valid in an ordinary action on a contract, as well as the following defenses:

1. *Fraud or misrepresentation.* If the insurance company can show that the policy was procured through fraud or misrepresentation, it may have a valid defense for not paying on a claim. (The insurance company may also have the right to disaffirm or rescind the insurance contract.)
2. *Lack of insurable interest.* An absolute defense exists if the insurer can show that the insured lacked an insurable interest—thus rendering the policy void from the beginning.
3. *Illegal actions of the insured.* Improper actions, such as those that are against public policy or that are otherwise illegal, can also give the insurance company a defense against the payment of a claim or allow it to rescind the contract.

---

4. *Woo v. Fireman's Fund Insurance Co.,* 161 Wash.2d 43, 164 P.3d 454 (2007).

In some situations, the insurance company may be prevented, or estopped, from asserting defenses that normally are available. For instance, an insurance company ordinarily cannot escape payment on the death of an insured on the ground that the person's age was stated incorrectly on the application. Also, incontestability clauses prevent the insurer from asserting certain defenses.

50–3 Types of Insurance

There are four general types of insurance coverage: life insurance, fire and homeowners' insurance, automobile insurance, and business liability insurance. We now examine briefly the coverage available under each of these types of insurance.

50–3a Life Insurance

There are five basic types of life insurance:

1. **Whole life** provides protection with an accumulated cash surrender value that can be used as collateral for a loan. The insured pays premiums during his or her entire lifetime, and the beneficiary receives a fixed payment on the death of the insured. (It is also sometimes referred to as straight life, ordinary life, or cash-value insurance.)
2. **Limited-payment life** is a type of policy under which premiums are paid for a stated number of years. After that time, the policy is paid up and fully effective during the insured's lifetime. For instance, a policy might call for twenty payments. Naturally, premiums are higher than for whole life. Like whole life, this insurance also has a cash surrender value.
3. **Term insurance** is a type of policy for which premiums are paid for a specified term. Payment on the policy is due only if death occurs within the term period. Premiums are lower than for whole life or limited-payment life, and there usually is no cash surrender value. Frequently, this type of insurance can be converted to another type of life insurance.
4. **Endowment insurance** involves fixed premium payments that are made for a definite term. At the end of the term, a fixed amount is paid to the insured or, if the insured dies during the specified term, to a beneficiary. Endowment insurance has a rapidly increasing cash surrender value, but premiums are high because a payment must be made at the end of the term even if the insured is still living.

5. **Universal life** combines aspects of both term insurance and whole life insurance. From every payment, usually called a "contribution," the issuing life insurance company makes two deductions. The first is a charge for term insurance protection. The second is for company expenses and profit. The funds that remain after these deductions earn interest for the policyholder at a rate determined by the company. The interest-earning amount is called the policy's *cash value,* but that term does not mean the same thing as it does for a traditional whole life insurance policy. With a universal life policy, the cash value grows at a variable interest rate rather than at a predetermined rate.

The rights and liabilities of the parties to life insurance contracts are basically dependent on the specific contract. A few features deserve special attention.

Insurer's Liability The life insurance contract determines not only the extent of the insurer's liability but also, generally, whether the insurer is liable on the death of the insured. Many life insurance contracts exclude liability for death caused by suicide, and some contain other exclusions, such as liability for death caused by military action during war. In the absence of contractual exclusion, most courts today construe any cause of death to be one of the insurer's risks.

Adjustment Due to Misstatement of Age The insurance policy constitutes the agreement between the parties. As noted earlier, the application for insurance is part of the policy and is usually attached to the policy. When the insured misstates his or her age on the application, an error is introduced, particularly as to the amount of premiums paid. As mentioned, misstatement of age is not a material error sufficient to allow the insurer to void the policy. Instead, on discovery of the error, the insurer will adjust the premium payments and/or benefits accordingly.

Assignment Most life insurance policies allow the insured to change beneficiaries. When this is permitted, in the absence of any prohibition or notice requirement, the insured can assign the rights to the policy without the consent of the insurer or the beneficiary. The insured may, for instance, wish to assign the rights to the policy as security for a loan.

If the beneficiary's right is *vested*—that is, has become absolute, entitling the beneficiary to payment of the proceeds—the policy cannot be assigned without the beneficiary's consent. For the most part, life insurance contracts permit assignment and require notice only to the insurer to be effective.

Creditors' Rights Unless insurance proceeds are exempt under state law, the insured's interest in life insurance is an asset that is subject to the rights of judgment creditors. These creditors generally can reach all of the following:

1. Insurance proceeds payable to the insured's estate.
2. Insurance proceeds payable to anyone if the payment of premiums constituted a fraud on creditors.
3. Insurance proceeds payable to a named beneficiary unless the beneficiary's rights have vested.

Creditors, however, cannot compel the insured to make available the cash surrender value of the policy or to change the named beneficiary to that of the creditor. Almost all states exempt at least a part of the proceeds of life insurance from creditors' claims.

Termination Although the insured can cancel and terminate the policy, the insurer generally cannot do so. Therefore, termination usually takes place only if one of the following occurs:

1. Default in premium payments, which causes the policy to lapse.
2. Death and payment of benefits.
3. Expiration of the term of the policy.
4. Cancellation by the insured.

50–3b Fire and Homeowners' Insurance

There are basically two types of insurance policies for a home: standard fire insurance policies and homeowners' policies.

Standard Fire Insurance Policies The standard fire insurance policy protects the homeowner against fire and lightning, as well as damage from smoke and water caused by the fire or the fire department. Most fire insurance policies are classified according to the type of property covered and the extent of the issuer's liability. Exhibit 50–3 lists typical fire insurance policies.

Liability. The insurer's liability is determined from the terms of the policy. Most policies limit recovery to losses resulting from *hostile* fires—basically, those that break out or begin in places where no fire was intended to burn. A *friendly* fire—one burning in a place where it was intended to burn—is often not covered. Therefore, smoke from a fireplace is not covered, but smoke from a fire caused by a defective electrical outlet is covered. Sometimes, owners add "extended coverage" to the fire policy to cover losses from "friendly" fires.

EXHIBIT 50–3 Typical Fire Insurance Policies

TYPE OF POLICY	COVERAGE
Blanket	Covers a class of property rather than specific property, because the property is expected to shift or vary in nature. A policy covering the inventory of a business is an example.
Floater	Usually supplements a specific policy. It is intended to cover property that may change in either location or quantity. For instance, if a painting is to be exhibited during the year at numerous locations throughout the state, a floater policy would be desirable.
Open	A policy that does not state an agreed-on value for the property. The policy usually provides for a maximum liability of the insurer, but payment for loss is restricted to the fair market value of the property at the time of loss or to the insurer's limit, whichever is less.
Specific	Covers a specific item of property at a specific location. An example is a particular painting located in a residence or a piece of machinery located in a factory or business.
Valued	A policy that, by agreement, places a specific value on the subject to be insured to cover the eventuality of its total loss.

If the policy is a *valued* policy (see Exhibit 50–3) and the subject matter is completely destroyed, the insurer is liable for the amount specified in the policy. If it is an *open* policy, then the extent of the actual loss must be determined. The insurer is liable only for the amount of the loss or for the maximum amount specified in the policy, whichever is less. For partial losses, actual loss must always be determined, and the insurer's liability is limited to that amount. Most insurance policies permit the insurer either to restore or replace the property destroyed or to pay for the loss.

Proof of Loss. As a condition for recovery, fire insurance policies require the insured to file a proof of loss with the insurer within a specified period or immediately (within a reasonable time). Failure to comply *could* allow the insurance carrier to avoid liability. Courts vary somewhat on the enforcement of such clauses.

Occupancy Clause. Most standard policies include clauses that require that the premises be occupied at the time of the loss. If the premises are vacant or unoccupied for a given period and the insurer has not consented to the vacancy, then coverage is suspended until the premises are reoccupied. Persons going on extended vacations should check their policies regarding this point.

In the following case, the court had to consider how long a house must be left vacant before it can be considered "unoccupied." The court also addressed the question of whether the risk of hazard is always greater when a home is unoccupied.

Case Analysis 50.2

Estate of Luster v. Allstate Insurance Co.

United States Court of Appeals, Seventh Circuit, 598 F.3d 903 (2010).

In the Language of the Court
POSNER, Circuit Judge.
* * * *

This diversity suit for breach of an insurance contract was dismissed on summary judgment * * * , and the plaintiff's [Estate of Luster's] appeal presents issues of both contract interpretation and Indiana insurance law.

[Wavie] Luster was a widow living alone in her house in Merrillville, Indiana. She had a homeowner's insurance policy from Allstate [Insurance Company]. In October 2001, when she was eighty-three, she was injured in a fall, and after being released from the hospital moved into an extended-care facility. She executed a power of attorney to her

lawyer, Rick Gikas, who is the representative of her estate in this litigation. She never returned home and died in April 2006, some four and a half years after her fall. Gikas had notified Allstate of his power of attorney and had directed the company to bill the insurance premiums to his law

Case 50.2 Continued

office. No one lived in the house after she left it.

Three months after her death—her house still unoccupied—a fire caused extensive damage. Gikas submitted a claim on behalf of the estate. An investigation indicated that the fire may well have been started by burglars, but the plaintiff denies this and the district judge made no finding.

In the course of the investigation Allstate discovered that the house had been unoccupied for four and a half years before Mrs. Luster's death and denied the claim, precipitating this suit. Allstate continued billing Gikas for premiums, however, and he continued paying them until October 2008, more than two years after the fire, when Allstate—which claims not to have known that the policy was still in force until its lawyers read the estate's summary-judgment brief that month—purported to cancel the policy retroactively to November 2001, and returned the premiums for the subsequent period to the estate.

The appeal requires us to consider [certain] provisions of the insurance policy: [The policy required the insured to notify Allstate of any change in occupancy of the premises and excluded coverage for property loss caused by "any substantial change or increase in hazard" or by "vandalism or malicious mischief" if the insured's dwelling was unoccupied for more than thirty consecutive days immediately prior to the vandalism or malicious mischief.]
* * * *

Gikas argues that * * * the house was *not* unoccupied, because right up until her death Luster expressed the intention of returning to live there when her health permitted.

*Regardless of the owner's intentions, * * * four and a half years of continuous absence of human occupation constitutes a change in occupancy.* [Emphasis added.]

The duty-to-notify provision entitled Allstate to cancel the policy in the event the house became unoccupied.

Although the policy expressly authorizes the insurer to cancel it for a violation of any of its terms, it also requires the insurer to give thirty days' notice of intention to cancel, and Allstate failed to do that after discovering in the wake of the fire that the house had been unoccupied for years. *The requirement of notice of intent to cancel is important; it gives the insured an opportunity to prevent a lapse of coverage, by taking steps to reinstate the policy or obtain a substitute policy from another insurer. Retroactive termination is inconsistent with the requirement of advance notice.* [Emphasis added.]
* * * *

The district judge ruled that leaving the house unoccupied constituted a "substantial change or increase in hazard" within the meaning [of the policy]. The judge seems to have thought that to leave a house unoccupied for however short a time causes an "increase in hazard" as a matter of law. Allstate takes the more moderate position that any gap in occupation of more than thirty days increases hazard as a matter of law.

Neither position is correct. Houses are rarely occupied continuously. A homeowner might take a thirty-one-day trip; Allstate implies that if a fire occurred during that period the insured would be uncovered. That is not the law.

Allstate's argument thus implies that if you have a second home the homeowner's policy on your primary residence is illusory; you're away a lot

and so coverage lapses. That's nonsense. And even if the house is unoccupied in the relevant sense—the sense that triggers the duty to notify the insurance company of a change in occupancy—it doesn't follow that you have created a "substantial * * * increase in hazard." Maybe you fitted the house with an array of locks and alarms and hired a security company to check on the house daily and so made the house more secure than when you were living there—an especially plausible inference if you happen to be an elderly person who might if in residence damage it inadvertently by leaving appliances on or failing to remove combustibles [flammable items] like cans containing paint or oil-soaked rags or to attend to defects in the electrical wiring of the house. *There is no rule that moving out of a house per se [in itself] increases the hazards against which the insurance company has insured you.* [Emphasis added.]
* * * *

There may well have been vandalism, by burglars, and if so it occurred more than thirty days after the house became unoccupied, whenever precisely occupancy ceased—sometime during the four and a half years between Luster's fall and her death. But we do not know whether the vandalism caused the loss—there is no judicial finding that the fire that was the immediate cause of the loss was the result of vandalism. To decide whether it was will require an evidentiary hearing, as will Allstate's alternative ground that nonoccupancy substantially increased the risk of loss.
* * * *

REVERSED AND REMANDED.

Legal Reasoning Questions

1. Why did the court conclude that an unoccupied house did not necessarily create a substantial increase in hazard?

2. Why did the court hold that Allstate's cancellation of the policy, retroactive to November 2001 (when Luster moved to an extended-care facility), was ineffective?

3. Was Luster's intent to return to her home when her health permitted sufficient to constitute occupancy? Why or why not?

Assignment. Before a loss has occurred, a fire insurance policy is not assignable without the consent of the insurer. The theory is that the fire insurance policy is a personal contract between the insured and the insurer. The non-assignability of a policy is extremely important when a house is purchased. It means that the purchaser must procure his or her own insurance. If the purchaser wishes to assume the seller's remaining period of insurance coverage, the insurer's consent is essential.

■ **EXAMPLE 50.6** Kiana is selling her home and lot to Jayden. Kiana has a one-year fire policy with Ajax Insurance Company, with six months of coverage remaining at the date on which the sale is to close. Kiana agrees to assign the balance of her policy, but Ajax has not given its consent. One day after passage of the deed, a fire totally destroys the house. Can Jayden recover from Ajax?

The answer is no. The policy is actually voided on the closing of the transaction and the deeding of the property. The reason the policy is voided is that Kiana no longer has an insurable interest at the time of loss, and Jayden has no rights in a nonassignable policy. ■

Homeowners' Policies A homeowners' policy provides protection against a number of risks under a single policy, allowing the policyholder to avoid the cost of buying each protection separately. There are two basic types of homeowners' coverage: property coverage and liability coverage.

Property Coverage. *Property coverage* includes the house, garage, and other private buildings on the policyholder's lot. It also includes the personal possessions and property of the policyholder at home, at work, or while traveling. If the policyholder is forced to live away from home because of a fire or some other covered peril, the policy covers additional living expenses.

Perils insured under property coverage often include fire, lightning, wind, hail, vandalism, and theft (of personal property). Standard homeowners' insurance typically does not cover flood damage. In the absence of a specific provision, such items of personal property as motor vehicles, farm equipment, airplanes, and boats normally are not included under property coverage. Coverage for other property, such as jewelry and securities, usually is limited to a specified dollar amount.

Liability Coverage. *Liability coverage* under a homeowners' policy is for personal liability in the event that someone is injured on the insured's property because of an unsafe condition on the property. It also applies when the insured damages someone else's property or injures someone else (unless the injury involves an automobile, as noted below). In addition, it applies when the policyholder is negligent.

Similar to liability coverage is coverage for the medical payments of others who are injured on the policyholder's property and for the property of others that is damaged by a member of the policyholder's family.

Liability coverage normally does not apply to a liability that arises from business or professional activities or from the operation of a motor vehicle, which are subjects for separate policies. Also excluded is liability arising from intentional misconduct.

Renters' Policies. Renters also take out insurance policies to protect against losses to personal property. Renters' insurance covers personal possessions against various perils and includes coverage for additional living expenses and liability.

50–3c Automobile Insurance

There are two basic kinds of automobile insurance: liability insurance and collision and comprehensive insurance.

Liability Insurance Automobile liability insurance covers liability for bodily injury and property damage. Liability limits are usually described by a series of three numbers, such as 100/300/50. This means that, for one accident, the policy will pay a maximum of $100,000 for bodily injury to one person, a maximum of $300,000 for bodily injury to more than one person, and a maximum of $50,000 for property damage. Many insurance companies offer liability coverage in amounts up to $500,000 and sometimes higher.

Individuals who are dissatisfied with the maximum liability limits offered by regular automobile insurance coverage can purchase separate coverage under an *umbrella policy.* Umbrella limits sometimes go as high as $10 million. Umbrella policies also cover personal liability in excess of the liability limits of a homeowners' policy.

Collision and Comprehensive Insurance Collision insurance covers damage to the insured's car in any type of collision. Usually, it is not advisable to purchase full collision coverage (otherwise known as *zero deductible*). The price per year is relatively high because it is likely that some small repair jobs will be required each year. Most people prefer to take out policies with a deductible of $250, $500, or $1,000, which cost substantially less than zero-deductible coverage.

Comprehensive insurance covers loss, damage, and destruction due to fire, hurricane, hail, vandalism, and theft. It can be obtained separately from collision insurance.

Other Automobile Insurance Other types of automobile insurance coverage include the following:

1. *Uninsured motorist coverage.* Uninsured motorist coverage insures the driver and passengers against injury caused by any driver without insurance or by a hit-and-run driver. Some states require that it be included in all auto insurance policies sold.
2. *Accidental death benefits.* Sometimes referred to as *double indemnity,* accidental death benefits provide for a payment of twice the policy's face amount if the policyholder dies in an accident. This coverage generally costs very little, but it may not be necessary if the insured has a sufficient amount of life insurance.
3. *Medical payment coverage.* Medical payment coverage provided by an auto insurance policy pays hospital and other medical bills and sometimes funeral expenses. This type of insurance protects all the passengers in the insured's car when the insured is driving.
4. *Other-driver coverage.* An **omnibus clause,** or *other-driver clause,* protects the vehicle owner who has taken out the insurance and anyone who drives the vehicle with the owner's permission. This coverage may be held to extend to a third party who drives the vehicle with the permission of the person to whom the owner gave permission.

50–3d Business Liability Insurance

A business may be vulnerable to all sorts of risks. A key employee may die or become disabled, a customer may be injured when using a manufacturer's product, or a professional may overlook some important detail and be liable for malpractice. If a key employee (such as the company president) dies, the firm may have some protection under a key-person insurance policy, discussed earlier. In the other circumstances, other types of insurance may apply.

General Liability Comprehensive general liability insurance can encompass as many risks as the insurer agrees to cover. It can protect a business from liability for injuries arising from on-premises events held after work hours, such as company social functions. It can protect bars and liquor stores, which in many jurisdictions are liable when a buyer of liquor becomes intoxicated as a result of the sale and injures a third party. General liability insurance can protect a business not only from liability for physical injuries, but also from liability for the loss of financial support suffered by a family because of the injuries.

Product Liability Manufacturers and retailers may be subject to liability for injuries resulting from the products they sell, and product liability insurance can be written to match specific products' risks. Coverage can be procured under a comprehensive general liability policy or under a separate policy. The coverage may include payment for expenses incurred to recall and replace a product that has proved to be defective.

Professional Malpractice Attorneys, physicians, architects, engineers, and other professionals often become the targets of negligence suits. Professionals purchase malpractice insurance to protect themselves against such claims. The large judgments in some malpractice suits have contributed to a significant increase in malpractice insurance premiums.

Workers' Compensation Workers' compensation insurance covers payments to employees who are injured in accidents arising out of and in the course of employment (that is, on the job). State statutes govern workers' compensation.

Reviewing: Insurance

Provident Insurance, Inc., issued an insurance policy to a company providing an employee, Steve Matlin, with disability insurance. Soon thereafter, Matlin was diagnosed with "panic disorder and phobia of returning to work." He lost his job and sought disability coverage. Provident denied coverage, doubting the diagnosis of disability. Matlin and his employer sued Provident.

During pretrial discovery, the insurer learned that Matlin had stated on the policy application that he had never been treated for any "emotional, mental, nervous, urinary, or digestive disorder" or any kind of heart disease. In fact, before Matlin filled out the application, he had visited a physician for chest pains and general anxiety, and the physician had prescribed an antidepressant and recommended that Matlin stop smoking. Using the information presented in the chapter, answer the following questions.

Continues

1. Did Matlin commit a misrepresentation on his policy application? Explain.
2. If there was any ambiguity on the application, should it be resolved in favor of the insured or the insurer? Why?
3. Assuming that the policy is valid, does Matlin's situation fall within the terms of the disability policy? Why or why not?
4. If Matlin is covered by the policy but is also disqualified by his misrepresentation on the application for coverage, might the insurer still be liable for bad faith denial of coverage? Explain.

Debate This . . .   *Whenever an insurance company can prove that the applicant committed fraud during the application process, it should not have to pay on the policy.*

Terms and Concepts

antilapse provision 966	insurable interest 961	risk 961
binder 965	insurance 961	risk management 961
cash surrender value 966	limited-payment life 968	term insurance 968
coinsurance clause 966	omnibus clause 973	underwriter 961
endowment insurance 968	policy 961	universal life 969
incontestability clause 965	premium 961	whole life 968

Issue Spotters

1. Neal applies to Farm Insurance Company for a life insurance policy. On the application, Neal understates his age. Neal obtains the policy, but for a lower premium than he would have had to pay had he disclosed his actual age. The policy includes an incontestability clause. Six years later, Neal dies. Can the insurer refuse payment? Why or why not? (See *The Insurance Contract*.)
2. Al is divorced and owns a house. Al has no reasonable expectation of benefit from the life of Bea, his former spouse, but applies for insurance on her life anyway. Al obtains a fire insurance policy on the house and then sells the house. Al continues to pay the premiums on both the life insurance policy and the fire insurance policy. Ten years later, Bea dies and the house is destroyed by fire. Can Al obtain payment for these events? Explain your answers. (See *Insurance Terminology and Concepts*.)

• **Check your answers to the Issue Spotters against the answers provided in Appendix D at the end of this text.**

Business Scenarios

50–1. Insurable Interest. Adia owns a house and has an elderly third cousin living with her. Adia decides she needs fire insurance on the house and a life insurance policy on her third cousin to cover funeral and other expenses that will result from her cousin's death. Adia takes out a fire insurance policy from Ajax Insurance Co. and a $10,000 life insurance policy from Beta Insurance Co. on her third cousin. Six months later, Adia sells the house to John and transfers title to him. Adia and her cousin move into an apartment. With two months remaining on the Ajax policy, a fire totally destroys the house. At the same time, Adia's third cousin dies. Both insurance companies say that they have no liability under the insurance contracts because Adia did not have an insurable interest, and they return the premiums. Discuss the companies' claims. (See *Insurance Terminology and Concepts*.)

50–2. Insurer's Defenses. Patrick contracts with an Ajax Insurance Co. agent for a $50,000 ordinary life insurance policy. The application form is filled in to show Patrick's age as thirty-two. In addition, the application form asks whether Patrick has ever had any heart ailments or problems. Patrick answers no, forgetting that as a young child he was diagnosed as having a slight heart murmur. A policy is issued. Three years later, Patrick becomes seriously ill and dies. A review of the policy discloses that Patrick was actually thirty-three at the time of the application and the issuance of the policy and that he erred in answering the question about a history of heart ailments. Discuss whether Ajax can void the policy and escape liability on Patrick's death. (See *The Insurance Contract*.)

50–3. Assignment. Sapata has an ordinary life insurance policy on her life and a fire insurance policy on her house.

Both policies have been in force for a number of years. Sapata's life insurance names her son, Rory, as beneficiary. Sapata has specifically removed her right to change beneficiaries, and the life insurance policy is silent on the right of assignment. Sapata is going on a one-year European vacation and borrows money from Leonard to finance the trip. Leonard takes an assignment of the life insurance policy as security for the loan, as the policy has accumulated a substantial cash surrender value. Sapata also rents out her house to Leonard and assigns her fire insurance policy to him. Discuss fully whether Sapata's assignment of these policies is valid. (See *Types of Insurance*.)

Business Case Problems

50–4. Interpreting Provisions. Richard Vanderbrook's home in New Orleans, Louisiana, was insured through Unitrin Preferred Insurance Co. His policy excluded coverage for "flood, surface water, waves, tidal water, overflow of a body of water, or spray from any of these, whether or not driven by wind." The policy did not define the term *flood*. In 2005, Hurricane Katrina struck along the coast of the Gulf of Mexico, devastating portions of Louisiana. In New Orleans, some of the most significant damage occurred when the levees along three canals ruptured, and water submerged about 80 percent of the city, including Vanderbrook's home. He filed a claim for the loss, but Unitrin refused to pay.

Vanderbrook and others whose policies contained similar exclusions asked a federal district court to order their insurers to pay. They contended that their losses were due to the negligent design, construction, and maintenance of the levees. They argued that the policies did not clearly exclude coverage for an inundation of water induced by negligence. On what does a decision in this case hinge? What reasoning supports a ruling in the plaintiffs' favor? In the defendants' favor? [*In re Katrina Canal Breaches Litigation*, 495 F.3d 191 (5th Cir. 2007)] (See *The Insurance Contract*.)

50–5. Duty to Cooperate. James Bubenik, a dentist, had two patients die while under sedation within six months. Bubenik had medical malpractice insurance with Medical Protective Co. (MPC). The families of both patients sued Bubenik for malpractice. A clause in Bubenik's policy stated that the "Insured shall at all times fully cooperate with the Company in any claim hereunder and shall attend and assist in the preparation and trial of any such claim." During the litigation, however, Bubenik refused to submit to depositions, answer interrogatories, or testify at trial, invoking the privilege against self-incrimination. He also refused to communicate with MPC and instead agreed to assist the patients in obtaining payment. MPC filed suit. Under these circumstances, did MPC have a legal or ethical duty to defend against the claim? Could MPC refuse to pay it? Explain. [*Medical Protective Co. v. Bubenik*, 594 F.3d 1047 (8th Cir. 2010)] (See *The Insurance Contract*.)

50–6. Bad Faith Actions. Leo and Mary Deters owned Deters Tower Service, Inc., in Iowa. Deters Tower serviced television and radio towers and antennas in a multistate area. The firm obtained a commercial general liability policy issued by USF Insurance Co. to provide coverage for its officers, including Leo. One afternoon, Leo and two Deters Tower employees were working on a TV tower in Council Bluffs when they fell from the tower to their deaths. The workers' families filed a negligence suit against Leo's estate. USF refused to defend the Deters estate against the suit and pay any resulting claim but did not provide a reason for its refusal. Is USF liable to the Deters estate for this refusal? If so, on what basis might the Deters estate recover, and how much? [*Deters v. USF Insurance Co.*, 797 N.W.2d 621 (Iowa App. 2011)] (See *The Insurance Contract*.)

50–7. Business Case Problem with Sample Answer— Insurance Provisions and Clauses. Darling's Rent-a-Car carried property insurance on its cars under a policy issued by Philadelphia Indemnity Insurance Co. The policy listed Darling's as the "insured." Darling's rented a car to Joshuah Farrington. In the rental contract, Farrington agreed to be responsible for any damage to the car and declined the optional insurance. Later, Farrington collided with a moose. Philadelphia paid Darling's for the damage to the car and sought to collect this amount from Farrington. Farrington argued that he was an "insured" under Darling's policy. How should "insured" be interpreted in this case? Why? [*Philadelphia Indemnity Insurance Co. v. Farrington*, 37 A.3d 305 (Me. 2012)] (See *The Insurance Contract*.)

- For a sample answer to Problem 50–7, go to Appendix E at the end of this text.

50–8. Types of Insurance. American National Property and Casualty Co. issued an insurance policy to Robert Houston, insuring certain residential property and its contents against fire and other hazards. Twenty months later, Houston issued a quitclaim deed to the property to John and Judy Sykes, reserving a life estate for himself. The American policy was renewed continuously by John, even after Houston died. When a fire substantially damaged the property, John filed a claim with the insurer on behalf of Houston, whom John said was out of town and unavailable. On learning that Houston had died, American refused to pay, claiming that it had no liability. Who will suffer the loss under these circumstances? Why? How might this loss have been avoided? Explain. [*American National Property and Casualty Co. v. Sykes*, __ F.Supp.3d __, 2016 WL 390069 (S.D.Miss., E.Div. 2016)] (See *Types of Insurance*.)

50–9. A Question of Ethics—Insurance Coverage.

 Paul and Julie Leonard's two-story home in Pascagoula, Mississippi, is only twelve feet above sea level and fewer than two hundred yards from the Gulf of Mexico. In 1989, the Leonards bought a homeowners' insurance policy from Jay Fletcher, an agent for Nationwide Mutual Insurance Co. The policy covered any damage caused by wind. It excluded all damage caused by water, including flooding. With each annual renewal, Nationwide reminded the Leonards that their policy did not cover flood damage, but that such coverage was available. The policy also contained an anti-concurrent-causation (ACC) clause that excluded coverage for damage caused by the synergistic action of a covered peril such as wind and an excluded peril such as water. In August 2005, Hurricane Katrina battered Pascagoula with torrential rain and sustained winds in excess of one hundred miles per hour. Wind damage to the Leonards' home was modest, but the storm drove ashore a seventeen-foot storm surge that flooded the ground floor. When Nationwide refused to pay for the damage to the ground floor, the Leonards filed a suit in a federal district court against the insurer. [Leonard v. Nationwide Mutual Insurance Co., 499 F.3d 419 (5th Cir. 2007)] (See *The Insurance Contract.*)

(a) Nationwide argued that the storm surge was a concurrently caused peril—a wall of water pushed ashore by hurricane winds. Thus, according to Nationwide, its damage was excluded under the ACC clause. How would you rule on this point? Should a court "enlarge" an insurer's policy obligations? Why or why not?

(b) When the Leonards bought their policy in 1989, Fletcher told them that all hurricane damage was covered. Ten years later, Fletcher told Paul Leonard that they did not need additional flood coverage. Did these statements materially misrepresent or alter the policy? Were they unethical? Discuss.

Legal Reasoning Group Activity

50–10. Insurance Coverage.

PAJ, Inc., a jewelry company, had a commercial general liability (CGL) policy from Hanover Insurance Co. The policy required PAJ to notify Hanover of any claim or suit against PAJ "as soon as practicable." Yurman Designs sued PAJ for copyright infringement because of the design of a particular jewelry line. Because PAJ did not realize that the CGL policy had a clause that covered infringement claims, it did not notify Hanover of the suit until four to six months after litigation began. Hanover contended that the policy did not apply to this incident because the late notification had violated its terms. PAJ sued Hanover, seeking a declaration that it was obligated to defend and indemnify PAJ. (See *The Insurance Contract.*)

(a) The first group will decide whether Hanover had an obligation to provide PAJ with legal assistance.

(b) The second group will determine the effect that PAJ's late notice to the insurance company had on its ability to provide assistance and mount a defense. Should the court require the insurance company to indemnify PAJ in this situation? Why or why not?

CHAPTER 51

Wills and Trusts

As the adage says, "You can't take it with you." After you die, all of the real and personal property that you own will be transferred to others. A person can direct the passage of his or her property after death by *will*, subject to certain limitations imposed by the state.

Alternatively, a person can transfer property through a *trust*. When a trust is created, the owner (who may be called the *grantor* or the *settlor*) of the property transfers legal title to a trustee. The trustee has a duty imposed by law to hold the property for the use or benefit of another (the beneficiary).

Wills and trusts are two basic devices used in the process of **estate planning**—determining in advance how one's property and obligations should be transferred on death. Estate planning may also involve transferring property through life insurance and joint-tenancy arrangements, as well as executing powers of attorney and living wills.

51–1 Wills

A **will** is the final declaration of how a person desires to have her or his property disposed of after death. It is a formal instrument that must follow exactly the requirements of state law to be effective.

A will can serve other purposes besides the distribution of property. It can appoint a guardian for minor children or incapacitated adults. It can also appoint a personal representative to settle the affairs of the deceased.

Exhibit 51–1 presents excerpts from the will of Michael Jackson, the "King of Pop," who died from cardiac arrest at the age of fifty. Jackson held a substantial amount of tangible and intangible property, including the publishing rights to most of The Beatles' music catalogue. Jackson's will also appointed his mother, Katherine Jackson, as the guardian of his three minor children.

51–1a Terminology of Wills

A person who makes a will is known as a **testator** (from the Latin *testari,* "to make a will"). A will is referred to as a *testamentary disposition* of property, and one who dies after having made a valid will is said to have died **testate.** The court responsible for administering any legal problems surrounding a will is called a *probate court*. When a person dies, a personal representative administers the estate and settles all of the decedent's (deceased person's) affairs.

An **executor** is a personal representative named in a will, whereas an **administrator** is a personal representative appointed by the court for a decedent who dies without a will. The court will also appoint a representative if the will does not name an executor or if the named person lacks the capacity to serve as an executor.

A person who dies without having created a valid will is said to have died **intestate.** In this situation, state **intestacy laws** (sometimes referred to as *laws of descent*) prescribe the distribution of the property among heirs or next of kin. If no heirs or kin can be found, the property will **escheat**[1] (title will be transferred to the state).

A gift of real estate by will is generally called a **devise,** and a gift of personal property by will is called a **bequest,** or **legacy.** The recipient of a gift by will is a **devisee** or a **legatee,** depending on whether the gift was a devise or a legacy.

51–1b Laws Governing Wills

To **probate** a will means to establish its validity and to carry the administration of the estate through a court process. Probate laws vary from state to state. The National

---

1. Pronounced is-*cheet.*

EXHIBIT 51–1 Excerpts from Michael Jackson's Will

I, MICHAEL JOSEPH JACKSON, a resident of the State of California, declare this to be my last Will, and do hereby revoke all former wills and codicils made by me.

I. I declare that I am not married. My marriage to DEBORAH JEAN ROWE JACKSON has been dissolved. I have three children now living, PRINCE MICHAEL JACKSON, JR., PARIS MICHAEL KATHERINE JACKSON and PRINCE MICHAEL JOSEPH JACKSON, II. I have no other children, living or deceased.

II. It is my intention by this Will to dispose of all property which I am entitled to dispose of by will. I specifically refrain from exercising all powers of appointment that I may possess at the time of my death.

III. I give my entire estate to the Trustee or Trustees then acting under that certain Amended and Restated Declaration of Trust executed on March 22, 2002 by me as Trustee and Trustor which is called the MICHAEL JACKSON FAMILY TRUST, giving effect to any amendments thereto made prior to my death. All such assets shall be held, managed and distributed as a part of said Trust according to its terms and not as a separate testamentary trust.

If for any reason this gift is not operative or is invalid, or if the aforesaid Trust fails or has been revoked, I give my residuary estate to the Trustee or Trustees named to act in the MICHAEL JACKSON FAMILY TRUST, as Amended and Restated on March 22, 2002, and I direct said Trustee or Trustees to divide, administer, hold and distribute the trust estate pursuant to the provisions of said Trust * * * .

        * * * *

IV. I direct that all federal estate taxes and state inheritance or succession taxes payable upon or resulting from or by reason of my death (herein "Death Taxes") attributable to property which is part of the trust estate of the MICHAEL JACKSON FAMILY TRUST, including property which passes to said trust

from my probate estate shall be paid by the Trustee of said trust in accordance with its terms. Death Taxes attributable to property passing outside this Will, other than property constituting the trust estate of the trust mentioned in the preceding sentence, shall be charged against the taker of said property.

V. I appoint JOHN BRANCA, JOHN McCLAIN and BARRY SIEGEL as co-Executors of this Will. In the event of any of their deaths, resignations, inability, failure or refusal to serve or continue to serve as a co-Executor, the other shall serve and no replacement need be named. The co-Executors serving at any time after my death may name one or more replacements to serve in the event that none of the three named individuals is willing or able to serve at any time.

The term "my executors" as used in this Will shall include any duly acting personal representative or representatives of my estate. No individual acting as such need post a bond.

I hereby give to my Executors, full power and authority at any time or times to sell, lease, mortgage, pledge, exchange or otherwise dispose of the property, whether real or personal comprising my estate, upon such terms as my Executors shall deem best, to continue any business enterprises, to purchase assets from my estate, to continue in force and pay any insurance policy * * * .

VI. Except as otherwise provided in this Will or in the Trust referred to in Article III hereof, I have intentionally omitted to provide for my heirs. I have intentionally omitted to provide for my former wife, DEBORAH JEAN ROWE JACKSON.

        * * * *

VIII. If any of my children are minors at the time of my death, I nominate my mother, KATHERINE JACKSON as guardian of the persons and estates of such minor children. If KATHERINE JACKSON fails to survive me, or is unable or unwilling to act as guardian, I nominate DIANA ROSS as guardian of the persons and estates of such minor children.

        * * * *

Conference of Commissioners on Uniform State Laws issued the Uniform Probate Code (UPC) to promote more uniformity among the states. The UPC codifies general principles and procedures for the resolution of conflicts in settling estates. The UPC also relaxes some of the requirements for a valid will contained in earlier state laws.

Almost half of the states have enacted some part of the UPC and incorporated it into their own probate codes. Nonetheless, succession and inheritance laws still vary

widely among the states, and one should always check the particular laws of the state involved.[2]

51–1c Types of Gifts

Gifts by will can be specific, general, or residuary. If a decedent's assets are not sufficient to cover all the gifts identified in the will, an abatement is necessary.

---

2. For example, California law differs substantially from the UPC.

Specific and General Devises or Bequests A *specific* devise or bequest (legacy) describes particular property (such as "Eastwood Estate" or "my gold pocket watch") that can be distinguished from all the rest of the testator's property.

A *general* devise or bequest (legacy) does not single out any particular item of property to be transferred by will. For instance, "I devise all my lands" is a general devise. A general bequest may specify the property's value in monetary terms (such as "two diamonds worth $10,000") or simply state a dollar amount (such as "$30,000 to my nephew, Carleton").

Residuary Clause Sometimes, a will provides that any assets remaining after the estate's debts have been paid and specific gifts have been made are to be distributed in a specific way through a *residuary clause*. Residuary clauses are often used when the exact amount to be distributed cannot be determined until all of the other gifts and payouts have been made. If the testator has not indicated what party or parties should receive the residuary of the estate, the residuary passes according to state laws of intestacy.

■ **CASE IN POINT 51.1** Katherine Hagan executed a will in 1994 that left the residuary of her estate to various organizations, such as the Humane Society. In 2001, Hagan inherited $830,000 from a relative. At this time, Hagan did not have the mental capacity to revise or modify her will. When she died in 2005, her residuary estate was worth $1.48 million.

Hagan's relatives, including Janice Benjamin, tried to invalidate the will's provisions regarding the residuary estate so that the funds would pass to them by intestacy laws. The court, however, found that Hagan's intent controlled. She had not intended to give any portion of her estate to her relatives. Because the will specifically stated that the residuary estate should be distributed to the charities, the court enforced these provisions (and Hagan's relatives received nothing).[3] ■

Abatement If the assets of an estate are insufficient to pay in full all general bequests provided for in the will, an *abatement* takes place. An abatement means that the legatees receive reduced benefits. ■ **EXAMPLE 51.2** Julie's will leaves $15,000 to each of her children, Tamara and Lynn. On Julie's death, only $10,000 is available to honor these bequests. By abatement, each child will receive $5,000. ■ If bequests are more complicated, abatement may be

more complex. The testator's intent, as expressed in the will, controls.

Lapsed Legacies If a legatee dies before the death of the testator or before the legacy is payable, a *lapsed legacy* results. At common law, the legacy failed. Today, the legacy may not lapse if the legatee is in a certain blood relationship to the testator (such as a child, grandchild, brother, or sister) and has left a child or other surviving descendant.

51–1d Requirements for a Valid Will

A will must comply with statutory formalities designed to ensure that the testator understood his or her actions at the time the will was made. These formalities are intended to help prevent fraud. Unless they are followed, the will is declared void, and the decedent's property is distributed according to the laws of intestacy of that state.

Although the required formalities vary among jurisdictions, most states have certain basic requirements for executing a will. Most states require proof of (1) the testator's capacity, (2) testamentary intent, (3) a written document, (4) the testator's signature, and (5) the signatures of persons who witnessed the testator's signing of the will.

Testamentary Capacity and Intent For a will to be valid, the testator must have testamentary capacity—that is, the testator must be of legal age and sound mind *at the time the will is made*. The minimum legal age for executing a will in most states and under the UPC is eighteen years [UPC 2–501]. Thus, the will of a twenty-one-year-old decedent written when the person was sixteen is invalid if, under state law, the legal age for executing a will is eighteen.

The concept of "being of sound mind" refers to the testator's ability to formulate and to comprehend a personal plan for the disposition of property. Persons who have been declared incompetent in a legal proceeding do not meet the sound mind requirement.

■ **CASE IN POINT 51.3** Marjorie Sirgo, a Louisiana resident, executed a will in which she left her estate equally to her children, Susie and Rene. Soon after, Marjorie—suffering from Parkinson's disease—began living at a nursing home. She stayed there until August 2005, when she was evacuated due to Hurricane Katrina. Three months later, while Marjorie was a resident of Poplar Springs Nursing Center, Susie took her to execute another will. This will left Marjorie's entire estate to Susie. Marjorie died, and Susie filed a petition in a

---

3. *Benjamin v. JPMorgan Chase Bank, N.A.*, 305 S.W.3d 446 (Ky.App. 2010).

Louisiana state court to probate her mother's second will. Rene objected, claiming their mother had lacked testamentary capacity when she had executed the second will. The court declared the second will void and ordered the probate of Marjorie's first will. Susie appealed.

A state intermediate appellate court affirmed the order of the lower court. Nurses' notes in Marjorie's medical records at Poplar Springs indicated that she suffered from cognitive impairment and lacked the ability to make even small decisions. In the same month in which she executed the second will, it was noted that Marjorie suffered from "short-term and long-term memory problems." For instance, she was unable to recall the current season or the location of her room.[4] ■

Related to the requirement of capacity is the concept of intent. A valid will is one that represents the maker's intention to transfer and distribute her or his property. Generally, a testator must:

1. Know the nature of the act (intend to make a will).
2. Comprehend and remember the people to whom the testator would naturally leave his or her estate (such as family members and friends).
3. Know the nature and extent of her or his property.
4. Understand the distribution of assets called for by the will.

Undue Influence. When it can be shown that the decedent's plan of distribution was the result of fraud or undue influence, the will is declared invalid. A court may sometimes infer undue influence when the named beneficiary was in a position to influence the making of the will. A presumption of undue influence might arise, for instance, if the testator ignored blood relatives and named as a beneficiary a nonrelative who was in constant close contact with the testator.

■ **CASE IN POINT 51.4** Belton Johnson, whose family owned the famous King Ranch in Texas, was married three times. He had three children from his first marriage and eight grandchildren. While married to his second wife, he executed a will that provided for her during her lifetime and left the remainder of his estate in a trust for his children and grandchildren. When his second wife died, he changed the will to give $1 million to each grandchild and the remainder to five charities. His children were provided for in a separate trust. While married to his third wife, Laura, he executed a will that left $1 million to each grandchild and the rest to Laura. Later, another will left his entire estate in trust to Laura for her life and then to a foundation that she controlled.

After Johnson's death, a dispute arose over the validity of the latest will.

The court concluded that Johnson's last will was invalid due to Laura's undue influence. Johnson was an admitted alcoholic with permanent cognitive defects and memory problems that would have caused him to be more susceptible to undue influence. Evidence suggested that Laura had exerted substantial control over many aspects of Johnson's life. Other evidence established that Johnson wanted to provide for his descendants, as well as for the charities named in the earlier will.[5] ■

Disinheritance. Although a testator must be able to remember the persons who would naturally be heirs to the estate, there is no requirement that testators give their estates to the natural heirs. A testator may decide to disinherit, or leave nothing to, an individual for various reasons. Most states have laws that attempt to prevent accidental disinheritance, however. There are also laws that protect minor children from the loss of the family residence. Therefore, the testator's intent to disinherit needs to be clear.

■ **CASE IN POINT 51.5** In 1975, William Melton executed a will that, among other things, stated that his daughter, Vicki Palm, was to receive nothing. In 1979, he added a handwritten note to the will, saying that his friend, Alberta Kelleher, was to receive a small portion of his estate.

In 1995, Melton sent a signed, handwritten letter to Kelleher. The letter said that Melton wanted to put "something in writing" leaving Kelleher his "entire estate." Melton also said, "I *do not* want my brother Larry J. Melton or Vicki Palm or any of my other relatives to have one penny of my estate."

When Melton died in 2008, Kelleher had already passed away, and Melton's daughter, Vicki Palm, was his only natural heir. The state of Nevada argued that it should receive everything because Palm had been disinherited. Nevertheless, the trial court applied the state's intestacy laws and distributed the entire estate to Palm. The state appealed. The Nevada Supreme Court reversed the judgment of the lower court. It held that the disinheritance clause was clear and enforceable and that Melton's estate should therefore go to the state of Nevada.[6] ■

Writing Requirements Generally, a will must be in writing. The writing itself can be informal as long as it substantially complies with the statutory requirements. In some states, a will can be handwritten in crayon or ink.

---

4. *In re Succession of Sirgo*, 164 So.3d 832 (La. 2014).

5. *In re Estate of Johnson*, 340 S.W.3d 769 (Tex.App.—San Antonio 2011).
6. *In re Estate of Melton*, 272 P.3d 668 (Nev.Sup.Ct. 2012).

It can be written on a sheet or scrap of paper, on a paper bag, or on a piece of cloth. A will that is completely in the handwriting of the testator is called a **holographic will** (sometimes referred to as an *olographic will*).

A **nuncupative will** is an oral will made before witnesses. Oral wills are not permitted in most states. Where authorized by statute, such wills are generally valid only if made during the last illness of the testator and are therefore sometimes referred to as *deathbed wills*. Normally, only personal property can be transferred by a nuncupative will. Statutes may also permit members of the military to make nuncupative wills when on active duty.

Signature Requirements A fundamental requirement is that the testator's signature must appear on the will, generally at the end. Each jurisdiction dictates by statute and court decision what constitutes a signature. Initials, an X or other mark, and words such as "Mom" have all been upheld as valid when it was shown that the testators *intended* them to be signatures.

Witness Requirements A will usually must be *attested* (sworn to) by two, and sometimes three, witnesses. The number of witnesses, their qualifications, and the manner in which the witnessing must be done are generally set out in a statute. A witness may be required to be disinterested—that is, not a beneficiary under the will. The UPC, however, allows even interested witnesses to attest to a will [UPC 2–505]. There are no age requirements for witnesses, but they must be mentally competent.

The purpose of the witnesses is to verify that the testator actually executed (signed) the will and had the requisite intent and capacity at the time. A witness need not read the contents of the will. Usually, the testator and all witnesses sign in the sight or the presence of one another. The UPC does not require all parties to sign in one another's presence, however, and deems it sufficient if the testator acknowledges her or his signature to the witnesses [UPC 2–502].

51–1e Revocation of Wills

The testator can revoke a will at any time during her or his life, either by a physical act, such as tearing up the will, or by a subsequent writing. Wills can also be revoked by operation of law. Revocation can be partial or complete, and it must follow certain strict formalities.

Revocation by a Physical Act A testator can revoke a will by *intentionally* burning, tearing, canceling, obliterating, or otherwise destroying it.[7] A testator can also revoke a will by intentionally having someone else destroy it in the testator's presence and at the testator's direction. Note that when a state statute prescribes the specific methods for revoking a will by a physical act, only those methods can be used to revoke the will.

In some states, a testator can partially revoke a will by the physical act of crossing out some provisions in the will. The portions that are crossed out are dropped, and the remaining portions are valid. In no circumstances, however, can a provision be crossed out and an additional or substitute provision written in its place. Such altered provisions require that the will be reexecuted (signed again) and reattested (rewitnessed).

In the following case, the court had to decide whether the testator had intended to revoke part or all of her will by making certain changes to it after it was executed.

---

7. The destruction cannot be inadvertent. The testator must have intent to revoke the will.

Case Analysis 51.1

Peterson v. Harrell

Supreme Court of Georgia, 690 S.E.2d 151 (2010).

In the Language of the Court
THOMPSON, Justice.

Testator Marion E. Peterson died in 2008. She was survived by her two siblings [brother and sister], Arvin Peterson and Carolyn Peterson Basner (caveators[a]).

After testator's death, Vasta Lucas, testator's longtime companion and executor of testator's estate, filed a petition to probate testator's will in solemn form. Lucas died during the pendency of this appeal [while the appeal was pending], and appellee Richard Harrell was appointed as successor executor and trustee for the estate. Caveators filed a caveat to the petition to probate, alleging the will was not properly executed or had been revoked due to obliterations. The trial court admitted the will to probate and caveators appealed.

OCGA [the Official Code of Georgia Annotated] Section 53-4-20(b) of the

Case 51.1 Continues

---

a. In the context of wills, a *caveator* is one who files a *caveat* attacking the validity of an alleged will.

Case 51.1 Continued

Revised Probate Code of 1998 provides that "a will shall be attested and subscribed in the presence of the testator by two or more competent witnesses." The record evidence in this case establishes that testator executed a will on June 9, 1976. The will was witnessed by two subscribing witnesses, only one of whom was living at the time of trial. Having been provided a copy of testator's will, the surviving witness testified to its due execution by deposition testimony presented at trial and via written interrogatories filed with the court. Caveators presented no evidence challenging either the validity of the signatures on the will or testator's capacity at the time the will was executed. Accordingly, the evidence supports the trial court's finding that the will was duly executed.

The will contained a bequest to Lucas in the form of a trust and provided that upon Lucas's death the trustee shall distribute any remaining assets to four beneficiaries, including caveators. Some time after the will was executed, testator struck through with an ink pen the names of all successor beneficiaries of the trust estate, as well as language in the will nominating Richard Harrell as

successor executor and trustee. None of the strike-throughs were witnessed or attested to. Near the end of the will, testator wrote, "My executrix is Julie Peterson." Caveators contend these alterations constitute material cancellations that effect a revocation of the will.

To effect a revocation of a will by obliteration, caveators must show that testator made material obliterations to her will or directed another to do so and that testator intended for this act to revoke the will. *Joint operation of act and intention is necessary to revoke a will. The intent to revoke the will in its entirety shall be presumed from the obliteration or cancellation of a material portion of the will, but such presumption may be overcome by a preponderance of the evidence.* [Emphasis added.]

Even assuming, arguendo [for the sake of argument], that the alterations to testator's will constituted a material cancellation within the meaning of OCGA Section 53-4-44, we find no error in the trial court's conclusion that testator did not intend to revoke her entire will. The record supports the trial court's findings that caveators had no knowledge of the circumstances surrounding what they

allege to be the revocation of the will, that testator never discussed revoking her will with caveators, and that caveators were not present when testator made the alterations to the will. Caveators presented no evidence of testator's intent other than the alterations themselves, and they satisfied their initial burden only by proving that testator made alterations to the will.

The record also shows, however, that the will was found in good condition on testator's desk among her personal papers. It bore the signatures of both testator and her subscribing witnesses and set out a primary bequest to Lucas which remained intact. Handwritten alterations crossing out the names of the successor beneficiaries with a single line were initialed by testator and she added language to the will indicating her desire to substitute Julie Peterson as her executrix. As found by the trial court, this evidence clearly indicates testator's intent to cancel only certain provisions of the will, not an intent to revoke the will in its entirety as required for revocation under OCGA Section 53-4-44.

* * * *

Judgment affirmed.

Legal Reasoning Questions

1. Why would the caveators argue that the entire will should be revoked? How would the will's revocation benefit them?

2. What could the testator have done differently to clarify her intentions in her will?

3. How might the availability of a secure online repository for a person's will affect a challenge to the will?

Revocation by a Subsequent Writing A will may also be wholly or partially revoked by a **codicil,** a written instrument separate from the will that amends or revokes provisions in the will. A codicil eliminates the necessity of redrafting an entire will merely to add to it or amend it. A codicil can also be used to revoke an entire will. The codicil must be executed with the same formalities required for a will, and it must refer expressly to the will. In effect, it updates a will because the will is "incorporated by reference" into the codicil.

A new will (second will) can be executed that may or may not revoke the first or a prior will, depending on

the language used. To revoke a prior will, the second will must use language specifically revoking other wills, such as, "This will hereby revokes all prior wills." If the second will is otherwise valid and properly executed, it will revoke all prior wills. If the express *declaration of revocation* is missing, then both wills are read together. If there are any discrepancies between the wills, the second will controls.

Revocation by Operation of Law Revocation by operation of law occurs when marriage, divorce, annulment, or the birth of a child takes place after a will has been executed.

Marriage and Divorce. In most states, when a testator marries after executing a will and the will does not provide for the new spouse, the new spouse can still receive a share of the testator's estate. On the testator's death, the surviving spouse can receive the amount he or she would have taken had the testator died intestate (intestacy laws will be discussed shortly). The rest of the estate passes under the will [UPC 2–301, 2–508].

If, however, the new spouse is otherwise provided for in the will (or by transfer of property outside the will), he or she will not be given an intestate amount. Also, if the parties had a valid *prenuptial agreement*, its provisions dictate what the surviving spouse receives.

Divorce does not necessarily revoke the entire will. Rather, a divorce or an annulment occurring after a will has been executed revokes those dispositions of property made under the will to the former spouse [UPC 2–508].

Children. If a child is born after a will has been executed, that child may be entitled to a portion of the estate. Most state laws allow a child of the deceased to receive some portion of a parent's estate even if no provision is made in the parent's will. This is true *unless it is clear from the will's terms that the testator intended to disinherit the child* (see *Case in Point 51.5,* presented earlier). Under the UPC, the rule is the same.

51–1f Rights under a Will

The law imposes certain limitations on the way a person can dispose of property in a will. For instance, a married person who makes a will generally cannot avoid leaving a certain portion of the estate to the surviving spouse unless there is a valid prenuptial agreement. In most states, this is called an *elective share* or a *forced share,* and it is often one-third of the estate or an amount equal to a spouse's share under intestacy laws.

Beneficiaries under a will have rights as well. A beneficiary can renounce (disclaim) his or her share of the property given under a will. Further, a surviving spouse can renounce the amount given under a will and elect to take the forced share when the forced share is larger than the amount of the gift. State statutes provide the methods by which a surviving spouse accomplishes renunciation. The purpose of these statutes is to allow the spouse to obtain whichever distribution would be more advantageous. The UPC gives the surviving spouse an elective right to take a percentage of the total estate determined by the length of time that the spouse and the decedent were married to each other [UPC 2–201].

51–1g Probate Procedures

Recall that probate is the court process by which a will is proved valid or invalid. As mentioned, probate laws vary from state to state. Typically, the procedures used to probate a will depend on the size of the decedent's estate.

Informal Probate For smaller estates, most state statutes provide for the distribution of assets without formal probate proceedings. Faster and less expensive methods are then used. Property can be transferred by *affidavit* (a written statement taken in the presence of a person who has authority to affirm it). Problems or questions can be handled during an administrative hearing. Some states allow title to cars, savings and checking accounts, and certain other property to be transferred simply by filling out forms.

A majority of states also provide for *family settlement agreements,* which are private agreements among the beneficiaries. Once a will is admitted to probate, the family members can agree among themselves on how to distribute the decedent's assets. Although a family settlement agreement speeds the settlement process, a court order is still needed to protect the estate from future creditors and to clear title to the assets involved.

Formal Probate For larger estates, formal probate proceedings normally are undertaken, and the probate court supervises every aspect of the process. Additionally, in some situations—such as when a guardian for minor children must be appointed—more formal probate procedures cannot be avoided.

Formal probate proceedings may take several months or several years to complete, depending on the size and complexity of the estate and whether the will is contested. When the will is contested, or someone objects to the actions of the personal representative, the duration of probate is extended. As a result, a sizable portion of the decedent's assets (as much as 10 percent) may go to pay the fees charged by attorneys and personal representatives, as well as court costs.

51–1h Property Transfers outside the Probate Process

Often, people can avoid the cost of probate by employing various **will substitutes.** Examples include *living trusts* (discussed later in this chapter), life insurance policies, and individual retirement accounts (IRAs) with named beneficiaries.

One way to transfer property outside the probate process is to make gifts to one's children or others while one is still living. Another way is to own property in a joint tenancy. As previously discussed, in a joint tenancy, when one joint tenant dies, the other joint tenant or tenants automatically inherit the deceased tenant's share of the property. This is true even if the deceased tenant has provided otherwise in her or his will. Not all alternatives to formal probate administration are suitable to every estate, however.

See Concept Summary 51.1 for a review of basic information about wills.

Concept Summary 51.1

Wills

Terminology

- *Intestate*—Describes one who dies without a valid will.
- *Testator*—A person who makes a will.
- *Personal representative*—A person appointed in a will or by a court to settle the affairs of a decedent. A personal representative named in the will is an *executor*. A personal representative appointed by the court for an intestate decedent is an *administrator*.
- *Devise*—A gift of real estate by will, whether general or specific. The recipient of a devise is a *devisee*.
- *Bequest or legacy*—A gift of personal property by will, which can be general or specific. The recipient of a bequest (legacy) is a *legatee*.

Requirements for a Valid Will

- The testator must have *testamentary capacity*—that is, be of legal age and sound mind at the time the will is made.
- A will must be in writing (except for nuncupative wills).
- A will must be signed by the testator, and usually several people must witness the signing, depending on the state statute.

Revocation of Wills

- *By a physical act*—Intentionally tearing up, canceling, obliterating, or deliberately destroying part or all of a will revokes it.
- *By subsequent writing*—
  1. Codicil—A formal, separate document that amends or revokes an existing will.
  2. Second will or new will—A new, properly executed will expressly revoking the existing will.
- *By operation of law*—
  1. Marriage—Generally revokes a will written before the marriage to the extent of providing for the spouse.
  2. Divorce or annulment—Revokes dispositions of property made to the former spouse under a will made before the divorce or annulment.
  3. Subsequently born child—It is inferred that the child is entitled to receive the portion of the estate granted under intestacy distribution laws.

Probate Procedures

- To *probate* a will means to establish its validity and to carry out the administration of the estate through a court process. Probate laws vary from state to state. Probate procedures may be informal or formal, depending on the size of the estate and other factors, such as whether a guardian for minor children must be appointed.

51–2 Intestacy Laws

Each state regulates by statute how property will be distributed when a person dies intestate (without a valid will). Intestacy laws attempt to carry out the likely intent and wishes of the decedent.

These laws assume that deceased persons would have intended that their natural heirs (spouses, children, grandchildren, or other family members) inherit their property. Therefore, intestacy statutes set out rules and priorities under which these heirs inherit the property. If no heirs exist, the state will assume ownership of the property.

The rules of descent vary widely from state to state. It is thus important to refer to the exact language of the applicable state statutes when addressing any problem of intestacy distribution.

51–2a Surviving Spouse and Children

Usually, state statutes provide that first the debts of the decedent must be satisfied out of the estate. Then the remaining assets pass to the surviving spouse and to the children. A surviving spouse usually receives only a share of the estate—typically, one-half if there is also a surviving child and one-third if there are two or more children.[8] Only if no children or grandchildren survive the decedent will a surviving spouse receive the entire estate.

■ **EXAMPLE 51.6** Adrian dies intestate and is survived by his wife, Betty, and his children, Duane and Tara. Allen's property passes according to intestacy laws. After his outstanding debts are paid, Betty will receive the family home (either in fee simple or as a life estate) and ordinarily a one-third to one-half interest in all other property. The remaining real and personal property will pass to Duane and Tara in equal portions. ■

Under most state intestacy laws and under the UPC, in-laws do not share in an estate. Thus, if a child dies before his or her parents, the child's spouse will not receive an inheritance on the parents' death. In *Example 51.6,* if Duane died before his father (Adrian), Duane's widow would not inherit his share of Adrian's estate.

51–2b When There Is No Surviving Spouse or Child

When there is no surviving spouse or child, the order of inheritance is generally grandchildren, then parents

of the decedent. These relatives usually are called *lineal* relatives.

If there are no lineal heirs, then *collateral heirs*—brothers and sisters, nieces and nephews, and aunts and uncles of the decedent—are the next groups that share. If there are no survivors in any of these groups, most statutes provide for the property to be distributed among the next of kin of the collateral heirs.

51–2c Stepchildren, Adopted Children, and Illegitimate Children

Under intestacy laws, stepchildren are not considered kin. Legally adopted children, however, are recognized as lawful heirs of their adoptive parents. (This is also true of children who are in the process of being adopted at the time of a prospective parent's death.)

Statutes vary from state to state in regard to the inheritance rights of illegitimate children (children born out of wedlock). Although illegitimate children have inheritance rights in most states, their rights are not necessarily identical to those of legitimate children.

In some states, an illegitimate child has the right to inherit only from the mother and her relatives, unless the father's paternity has been established by a legal proceeding. In the majority of states, however, a child born of any union that has the characteristics of a formal marriage relationship (such as unmarried parents who cohabit) is considered to be legitimate.

Under the revised UPC, a child is generally considered the child of the natural (biological) parents, regardless of their marital status. The child cannot inherit from a natural parent, however, unless that natural parent has openly treated the child as his (or hers) and has not refused to support the child [UPC 2–114].

51–2d Grandchildren

Usually, a decedent's will provides for how the estate will be distributed to descendants of deceased children (grandchildren whose parents have died). If a will does not include such a provision—or if a person dies intestate—the question arises as to what share the grandchildren of the decedent will receive. Each state uses one of two methods of distributing the assets of intestate decedents—*per stirpes* or *per capita*.

Per Stirpes Distribution Under the **per stirpes**[9] method, within a class or group of distributees (such as

---

8. UPC 2–102(2) provides a formula for computing a surviving spouse's share that is contingent on the number of surviving children and parents. For instance, if the decedent has no surviving children and one surviving parent, the surviving spouse takes the first $200,000, plus three-fourths of any balance of the intestate estate.

9. *Per stirpes* is a Latin term meaning "by the roots" or "by stock." When used in estate law, it means proportionally divided between beneficiaries according to each beneficiary's deceased ancestor's share.

grandchildren), the children of a descendant take the share that their deceased parent *would have been* entitled to inherit. Thus, a grandchild with no siblings inherits all of his or her parent's share, while grandchildren with siblings divide their parent's share.

■ **EXAMPLE 51.7** Michael, a widower, has two children, Scott and Jillian. Scott has two children (Becky and Holly), and Jillian has one child (Paul). Scott and Jillian die before their father. When Michael dies, if his estate is distributed *per stirpes,* Becky and Holly each receive one-fourth of the estate (dividing Scott's one-half share). Paul receives one-half of the estate (taking Jillian's one-half share). Exhibit 51–2 illustrates the *per stirpes* method of distribution. ■

Per Capita Distribution An estate may also be distributed on a ***per capita***[10] basis, which means that each person in a class or group takes an equal share of the estate. ■ **EXAMPLE 51.8** If Michael's estate is distributed *per capita,* Becky, Holly, and Paul will each receive a one-third share. Exhibit 51–3 illustrates the *per capita* method of distribution. ■

51-3 Trusts

A **trust** is any arrangement by which property is transferred from one person to a trustee to be administered for the transferor's or another party's benefit. It can also

---

10. *Per capita* is a Latin term meaning "per person" or "for each head." When used in estate law, it means divided equally among beneficiaries within a class.

be defined as a right of property (real or personal) held by one party for the benefit of another. A trust can be created to become effective during a person's lifetime or after a person's death. Trusts may be established for any purpose that is not illegal or against public policy, and they may be express or implied.

The essential elements of a trust are as follows:

1. A designated beneficiary (except in charitable trusts, discussed shortly).
2. A designated trustee.
3. A fund sufficiently identified to enable title to pass to the trustee.
4. Actual delivery by the *settlor* or *grantor* (the person creating the trust) to the trustee with the intention of passing title.

51-3a Express Trusts

An express trust is created or declared in explicit terms, usually in writing. There are numerous types of express trusts, each with its own special characteristics.

Living Trusts A **living trust**—or *inter vivos* trust (*inter vivos* is Latin for "between or among the living")—is a trust created by a grantor during her or his lifetime. Living trusts have become a popular estate-planning option because at the grantor's death, assets held in a living trust can pass to the heirs without going through probate.

Note, however, that living trusts do not necessarily shelter assets from estate taxes. The grantor may also have to pay income taxes on trust earnings, depending on whether the trust is revocable or irrevocable.

EXHIBIT 51–2 *Per Stirpes* Distribution

Under this method of distribution, an heir takes the share that his or her deceased parent would have been entitled to inherit had the parent lived. This may mean that a class of distributees—the grandchildren in this example—will not inherit in equal portions. Note that Becky and Holly receive only one-fourth of Michael's estate while Paul inherits one-half.

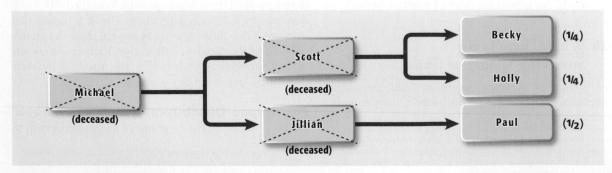

EXHIBIT 51–3 *Per Capita* Distribution

Under this method of distribution, all heirs in a certain class—in this example, the grandchildren—inherit equally. Note that Becky and Holly in this situation each inherit one-third, as does Paul.

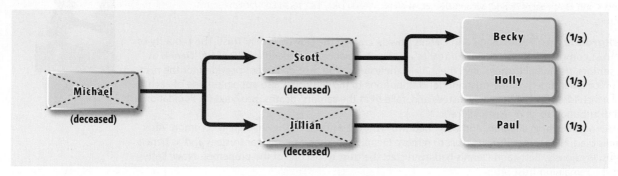

Revocable Living Trusts. In a revocable living trust, which is the most common type, the grantor retains control over the trust property during her or his lifetime. The grantor deeds the property to the trustee but retains the power to amend, alter, or revoke the trust during her or his lifetime.

The grantor may also serve as a trustee or co-trustee and can arrange to receive income earned by the trust assets during her or his lifetime. Because the grantor is in control of the funds, she or he is required to pay income taxes on the trust earnings. Unless the trust is revoked, the principal of the trust is transferred to the trust beneficiary on the grantor's death.

■ **EXAMPLE 51.9** James Cortez owns and operates a large farm. After his wife dies, James contacts his attorney to create a living trust for the benefit of his three children, Alicia, Emma, and Jacob. His attorney prepares the documents creating the trust. James executes a deed conveying the farm to the trust and transfers the farm's bank accounts into the name of the trust.

The trust designates James as the trustee and names his son Jacob as the *successor trustee,* who will take over the management of the trust when James dies or becomes incapacitated. Each of the children and James (as *income beneficiaries*) will receive an income from the trust while James is alive. When James dies, the farm will pass to them without having to go through probate. By holding the property in a revocable living trust, James retains control over the farm during his life (and can make changes to the trust at any time). This trust arrangement is illustrated in Exhibit 51–4. ■

The following case involved a revocable living trust that included the phrase "death of each." The resolution of the dispute turned on whether, in the context, "each" meant "either" or "both."

EXHIBIT 51–4 A Revocable Living Trust Arrangement

Grantor	Trust Property	Trustee	Income Beneficiaries	Remainder Beneficiaries
James Cortez	Farm and Accounts	James Cortez as Trustee of the James Cortez Living Trust	James Cortez during his lifetime and Alicia, Emma, and Jacob.	On the grantor's death, the trust property will be distributed to Alicia, Emma, and Jacob.

Dowdy v. Dowdy

District Court of Appeal of Florida, Second District, 41 Fla. L. Weekly D85, 182 So.3d 807 (2016).

Background and Facts   Betty and Dennis Dowdy created the Dowdy Family Trust. The property of the trust comprised of two parcels of real estate. The trust document identified Betty and Dennis as the settlors, the initial trustees, and the initial beneficiaries. The trust document provided for the revocation or amendment of the trust and for distributions to the settlors. It also appointed one of each settlor's children as co-successor trustees and, following the settlors' deaths, provided for liquidation and distribution to all of their children.

Dennis had three children, and Betty had two—they did not have any children in common. After Dennis died, Betty amended the trust to remove Dennis's children as successor trustees and as beneficiaries. Previously, Betty and Dennis had instructed the trust to sell one of the properties. Now, Betty sold the remaining trust property.

Dennis's son Michael, who was named as a co-successor trustee in the trust document, learned of the sale and filed a petition in a Florida state court against Betty. Michael maintained that Betty's amendment was invalid because it had been executed after Dennis's death. He argued that when Dennis died, the trust became irrevocable and he succeeded Dennis as co-trustee. The court ordered Betty to deposit the proceeds of the sale with the court pending its construction of the trust. Betty appealed.

In the Language of the Court

NORTHCUTT, Judge.

* * * *

* * * Article IV of the original trust document provided as follows:

> During the Settlors' lifetime, the Trustees, in the Trustees' sole discretion, may pay, invade, or apply the income or corpus [trust property], or so much as they may choose, to or for the benefit, support and maintenance of the initial primary beneficiaries * * * .

Thus, if Betty was the only trustee following the death of her husband, she had sole and unfettered authority to sell the trust property for her own benefit.

Michael claims to be a successor co-trustee under article III of the original trust:

> * * * In the event of the death of each of the Initial Trustees, * * * the Settlors nominate and appoint Settlors' son and stepson, Michael R. Dowdy * * * , and Settlors' daughter and stepdaughter, Deborah Ann Andrews [Betty's daughter], as Co-Successor Trustees.

In Michael's view, the phrase "death of each" meant the death of *either* initial trustee. Therefore, he asserts that he became a co-trustee with Betty upon his father's death.

* * * Our view [is] that the succession of trustees occurred only upon the death of *both* initial trustees. This view is confirmed by the use of the same phraseology elsewhere in the original trust document. Article V provides:

> After the death of each of the Settlors, the Co-Successor Trustees are directed to liquidate the Trust Estate and immediately pay and distribute the Trust Estate to the children and stepchildren of the Settlors * * * .

Clearly, in this instance the phrase "death of each" must mean the death of both. Otherwise, the article's direction to liquidate the trust estate and immediately distribute it to the settlors' children would nullify article IV's grant of authority to invade the income or corpus of the trust for the benefit of the initial primary beneficiaries "or the survivor." Indeed, upon the death of one settlor it would altogether nullify the survivor's status as beneficiary. This, of course, would be an absurd interpretation in complete contravention [contradiction] of a central purpose of the trust. [Emphasis added.]

There is nothing in the original trust document to suggest that the phrase "death of each" has a different meaning in article III. To the contrary, that article is otherwise consistent with this interpretation. We conclude, then, that Michael did not succeed Dennis as a trustee when Dennis died.

Case 51.2 Continued

Decision and Remedy *The state intermediate appellate court reversed the order of the lower court. Under the appellate court's interpretation of the terms of the trust, "at all times . . . , Betty has been the sole trustee and beneficiary of the trust . . . . As such, she had sole authority and discretion to sell the remaining trust property for her own benefit." The court concluded that Michael's petition had no likelihood of success.*

Critical Thinking
- **Legal Environment** *According to Michael's view of the phrase "death of each," how many co-trustees would have succeeded Dennis on his death? Explain.*
- **What If the Facts Were Different?** *Suppose that the Dowdy Family Trust had provided for a specific child to become co-trustee on the death of his or her parent—Deborah to succeed Betty, for example. How would the result have been different?*

Irrevocable Living Trusts. In an irrevocable living trust, the grantor permanently gives up control over the property to the trustee. The grantor executes a trust deed, and legal title to the trust property passes to the named trustee. The trustee has a duty to administer the property as directed by the grantor for the benefit and in the interest of the beneficiaries.

The trustee must preserve the trust property and make it productive. If required by the terms of the trust agreement, the trustee must pay income to the beneficiaries in accordance with the terms of the trust. Because the grantor has, in effect, given over the property for the benefit of the beneficiaries, he or she is no longer responsible for paying income taxes on the trust earnings.

Testamentary Trusts A **testamentary trust** is created by will and comes into existence on the grantor's death. Although a testamentary trust has a trustee who maintains legal title to the trust property, the trustee's actions are subject to judicial approval. The trustee can be named in the will or appointed by the court (if not named in the will). The legal responsibilities of the trustee are the same as in a living trust.

If a court finds that the will setting up a testamentary trust is invalid, then the trust will also be invalid. The property that was to be in the trust will then pass according to intestacy laws, not according to the terms of the trust.

If the court finds that a condition of the trust is invalid because it is illegal or against public policy, the court will invalidate that condition only and enforce the trust without it. ■ **EXAMPLE 51.10** Linzy Herman's will creates a testamentary trust. A condition of Herman's trust states, "to my son, if he never gets married." Because the condition is against public policy, the court will read the terms of the trust as not including the invalid restraint on marriage. ■

Charitable Trusts A **charitable trust** is an express trust designed for the benefit of a segment of the public or the public in general. It differs from other types of trusts in that the identities of the beneficiaries are uncertain and it can be established to last indefinitely. Usually, to be deemed a charitable trust, a trust must be created for charitable, educational, religious, or scientific purposes.

Spendthrift Trusts A **spendthrift trust** is created to provide for the maintenance of a beneficiary by preventing him or her from being careless with the bestowed funds. Unlike the beneficiaries of other trusts, the beneficiary in a spendthrift trust is not permitted to transfer or assign his or her rights to the trust's principal or future payments from the trust.

Essentially, the beneficiary can draw only a certain portion of the total amount to which he or she is entitled at any one time. The majority of states allow spendthrift trust provisions that prohibit creditors from attaching such trusts, with a few exceptions, such as for payment of a beneficiary's domestic-support obligations.

Totten Trusts A **Totten trust**[11] is created when a grantor deposits funds into an account in her or his own name with instructions that in the event of the grantor's death, whatever is in that account should go to a specific beneficiary. This type of trust is revocable at will until the depositor dies or completes the gift in her or his lifetime (by delivering the funds to the intended beneficiary, for instance). The beneficiary has no access to the funds until the depositor's death, when the beneficiary obtains property rights to the balance on hand.

---

11. This type of trust derives its unusual name from *In the Matter of Totten*, 179 N.Y. 112, 71 N.E. 748 (1904).

51–3b Implied Trusts

Sometimes, a trust will be imposed (implied) by law, even in the absence of an express trust. Implied trusts include constructive trusts and resulting trusts.

Constructive Trusts A **constructive trust** is imposed by a court in the interests of fairness and justice. In a constructive trust, the owner of the property is declared to be a trustee for the parties who are, in equity, actually entitled to the benefits that flow from the trust.

Courts often impose constructive trusts when someone who is in a confidential or fiduciary relationship with another person, such as a guardian to a ward, has breached a duty to that person. A court may also impose a constructive trust when someone wrongfully holds legal title to property. This may occur when the property was obtained through fraud or in breach of a legal duty, for instance.

■ **CASE IN POINT 51.11** Stella Jankowski added her niece Genevieve Viarengo as a joint owner on bank accounts and other financial assets valued at $500,000. Jankowski also executed a will that divided her estate equally among her ten nieces, nephews, and cousins. The will named Viarengo and Richard Golebiewski as coexecutors. She did not tell the attorney who drafted the will about the jointly held accounts.

When Jankowski died, Viarengo emptied Jankowski's safe and removed her financial records. Viarengo also claimed that the funds in the accounts were hers. Jankowski's other relatives filed a suit and asked the court to impose a constructive trust. The court found that Viarengo had committed fraud in obtaining the assets that she had held jointly with Jankowski and would be unjustly enriched if she were allowed to retain them. Therefore, the court imposed a constructive trust.[12] ■

Resulting Trusts A **resulting trust** arises from the conduct of the parties. Here, the trust results, or is created, when circumstances raise an inference that the party holding legal title to the property does so for the benefit of another. The trust will result unless the inference is refuted.

■ **EXAMPLE 51.12** Gabriela Fuentes wants to put one acre of land she owns on the market for sale. Because she is going out of the country for two years and will not be available to deed the property to a buyer during that period, she conveys the property to her good friend Raul Cruz. Cruz can then attempt to sell the property while Fuentes is gone.

The transaction in which Fuentes conveys the property to Cruz is intended to be neither a sale nor a gift. Consequently, Cruz will hold the property in a resulting trust for the benefit of Fuentes. When Fuentes returns, Cruz will be required either to deed the property back to her or, if the property has been sold, to turn over the proceeds (held in trust) to her. ■

Concept Summary 51.2 provides a synopsis of basic information about trusts.

51–3c The Trustee

The trustee is the person holding the trust property. Anyone legally capable of holding title to, and dealing in, property can be a trustee. If a trust fails to name a trustee, or if a named trustee cannot or will not serve, the trust does not fail. An appropriate court can appoint a trustee.

Trustee's Duties A trustee must act with honesty, good faith, and prudence in administering the trust and must exercise a high degree of loyalty toward the trust beneficiary. The general standard of care is the degree of care a prudent person would exercise in his or her own personal affairs.[13] The duty of loyalty requires that the trustee act in the exclusive interest of the beneficiary.

A trustee's specific duties include the following:

1. Maintain clear and accurate accounts of the trust's administration.
2. Furnish complete and correct information to the beneficiary.
3. Keep trust assets separate from her or his own assets.
4. Pay to an income beneficiary the net income of the trust assets at reasonable intervals.
5. Limit the risk of loss from investments by reasonable diversification and dispose of assets that do not represent prudent investments. (Prudent investment choices might include federal, state, or municipal bonds and some corporate bonds and stocks.)

Trustee's Powers When a grantor creates a trust, he or she may set forth the trustee's powers and performance. State law governs in the absence of specific terms in the trust, and the states often restrict the trustee's investment of trust funds.

Typically, statutes confine trustees to investments in conservative debt securities such as government, utility, and railroad bonds and certain real estate loans.

---

12. *Garrigus v. Viarengo,* 112 Conn.App. 655, 963 A.2d 1065 (2009).

13. Revised Uniform Principal and Income Act, Section 2(a)(3); and *Restatement (Third) of Trusts (Prudent Investor Rule),* Section 227. This rule is in force in a majority of the states by statute and a small number of states under common law.

Concept Summary 51.2

Trusts

Definition and Essential Elements	• A *trust* is any arrangement by which property is transferred from one person to a trustee to be administered for another's benefit. • The essential elements of a trust are a designated beneficiary, a designated trustee, a fund sufficiently identified to enable title to pass to the trustee, and actual delivery to the trustee with the intention of passing title.
Types of Trusts	• *Living* (inter vivos) *trust*—A trust executed by a grantor during his or her lifetime. A living trust may be revocable or irrevocable. • *Testamentary trust*—A trust created by will and coming into existence on the death of the grantor. • *Charitable trust*—A trust designed for the benefit of a segment of the public or the public in general. • *Spendthrift trust*—A trust created to provide for the maintenance of a beneficiary by allowing her or him to receive only a certain portion of the total amount at any one time. • *Totten trust*—A trust created when one person deposits funds in his or her own name with instructions that the funds should go to a beneficiary on the depositor's death.

Implied Trusts	• *Implied trusts*, which are imposed by law in the interests of fairness and justice, include the following:
	   1. *Constructive trust*—Arises by operation of law when a transaction occurs in which the person who takes title to property is, in equity, not entitled to enjoy the benefits from it.
	   2. *Resulting trust*—Arises from the conduct of the parties when an *apparent intention* to create a trust is present.

Frequently, though, a grantor gives a trustee discretionary investment power. In that circumstance, any statute may be considered only advisory, with the trustee's decisions subject in most states to the prudent person rule.

Of course, a trustee is responsible for carrying out the purposes of the trust. If the trustee fails to comply with the terms of the trust or the controlling statute, he or she is personally liable for any loss.

Allocations between Principal and Income

Often, a grantor will provide one beneficiary with a life estate and another beneficiary with the remainder interest in the trust. A farmer, for instance, may create a testamentary trust providing that the farm's income be paid to the surviving spouse and that, on the surviving spouse's death, the farm be given to their children. In this situation, the surviving spouse has a *life estate* in the farm's income, and the children have a *remainder interest* in the farm (the principal).

When a trust is set up in this manner, questions may arise as to how the receipts and expenses for the farm's management and the trust's administration should be allocated between income and principal. When a trust instrument does not provide instructions, a trustee must refer to applicable state law.

The general rule is that ordinary receipts and expenses are chargeable to the income beneficiary, whereas extraordinary receipts and expenses are allocated to the principal beneficiaries.[14] The receipt of rent from trust realty would be ordinary, as would the expense of paying the property's taxes. The cost of long-term improvements and proceeds from the property's sale, however, would be extraordinary.

51–3d Trust Termination

The terms of a trust should expressly state the event on which the grantor wishes it to terminate—for instance, the beneficiary's or the trustee's death. If the trust instrument does not provide for termination on the beneficiary's death, the beneficiary's death will not end the trust. Similarly, without an express provision, a trust will not terminate on the trustee's death.

Typically, a trust instrument specifies a termination date. For instance, a trust created to educate the grantor's child may provide that the trust ends when the beneficiary reaches the age of twenty-five. If the trust's purpose is fulfilled before that date, a court may order the trust's termination. If no date is specified, a trust will terminate when its purpose has been fulfilled. Of course, if a trust's purpose becomes impossible or illegal, the trust will terminate.

51–4 Other Estate-Planning Issues

Estate planning involves making difficult decisions about the future, such as who will inherit the family home and other assets and who will take care of minor children. Estate planning also involves preparing in advance for other contingencies, such as illness and incapacity. For instance, what happens if you become incapacitated and cannot make your own decisions? Who will take care of your finances and other affairs? Do you want to be kept alive by artificial means, and whom do you trust to make decisions about your health care in the event that you cannot? Powers of attorney and living wills are frequently executed in conjunction with a will or trust to help resolve these matters.

51–4a Power of Attorney

A power of attorney is often used in business situations to give a person (an agent) authority to act on another's behalf. The powers usually are limited to a specific context, such as negotiating a deal with a buyer or entering into various contracts necessary to achieve a particular

objective. Powers of attorney are also commonly used in estate planning.

Durable Power of Attorney One method of providing for future disability is to use a durable power of attorney. A **durable power of attorney** authorizes an individual to act on behalf of another when he or she becomes incapacitated. It can be drafted to take effect immediately or only after a physician certifies that the person is incapacitated. The person to whom the power is given can then write checks, collect insurance proceeds, and otherwise manage the incapacitated person's affairs, including health care.

Adult children may seek a durable power of attorney from their aging parents, particularly if the parents are becoming mentally incapacitated by Alzheimer's disease or some other condition. A husband and wife may give each other a power of attorney to make decisions in the event that one of them is hospitalized and unable to express her or his wishes. A person who is undergoing an operation may sign a durable power of attorney to a loved one who can take over his or her affairs in the event of incapacity.

If you become incapacitated without having executed a durable power of attorney, a court may need to appoint a conservator to handle your financial affairs. Although a spouse may have the ability to write checks on joint accounts, her or his power is often significantly limited. In most situations, it is better to have named a person you wish to handle your affairs in the event that you cannot.

Health-Care Power of Attorney A **health-care power of attorney** designates a person who will have the power to choose what type of and how much medical treatment a person who is unable to make such decisions will receive. The importance of appointing a person to make health-care decisions has grown as medical technology enables physicians and hospitals to keep people alive for ever-increasing periods of time.

■ **EXAMPLE 51.13** Terri Schiavo, a Florida woman, was kept alive in a vegetative state from 1990 to 2005. It took more than twenty court hearings for her husband to convince the court that he had a right to ask physicians to remove her feeding tube and let her die. If Schiavo had given her husband a health-care power of attorney, he would have had the right to make the decision to remove the feeding tube without going to court. ■

51–4b Living Will

A living will is not a will in the usual sense—that is, it does not appoint an estate representative, dispose of property, or establish a trust. Rather, a **living will** is an

---

14. Revised Uniform Principal and Income Act, Sections 3, 6, 8, and 13; and *Restatement (Third) of Trusts, (Prudent Investor Rule)*, Section 233.

advance health directive that allows a person to control what medical treatment may be used after a serious accident or illness. Through a living will, a person can indicate whether he or she wants certain lifesaving procedures to be undertaken in situations in which the treatment will not result in a reasonable quality of life.

Most states have enacted statutes permitting living wills, and it is important that the requirements of state law be followed exactly in creating such wills. Typically, state statutes require physicians to abide by the terms of living wills, and living wills are often included with a patient's medical records.

Reviewing: Wills and Trusts

In June 2016, Bernard Ramish set up a $48,000 trust fund through West Plains Credit Union to provide tuition for his nephew, Nathan Covacek, to attend Tri-State Polytechnic Institute. The trust was established under Ramish's control and went into effect that August. In December, Ramish suffered a brain aneurysm that caused frequent, severe headaches with no other symptoms. Shortly thereafter, Ramish met with an attorney to formalize in writing that he wanted no artificial life-support systems to be used should he suffer a serious illness. He also designated his cousin, Lizzie Johansen, to make decisions on his behalf should he become incapacitated.

In August 2017, Ramish developed heatstroke on the golf course at La Prima Country Club. After recuperating at the clubhouse, Ramish quickly wrote his will on the back of a wine list. It stated, "My last will and testament: Upon my death, I give all of my personal property to my friend Steve Eshom and my home to Lizzie Johansen." He signed the will at the bottom in the presence of five men in the La Prima clubhouse, and all five men signed as witnesses.

A week later, Ramish suffered a second aneurysm and died in his sleep. He was survived by his mother (Dorris Ramish), his nephew (Nathan Covacek), his son-in-law (Bruce Lupin), and his granddaughter (Tori Lupin). Using the information presented in the chapter, answer the following questions.

1. What type of trust did Ramish create for the benefit of Covacek? Was it revocable or irrevocable?
2. Does Ramish's testament on the back of the wine list meet the requirements for a valid will? Why or why not?
3. What would the order of inheritance have been if Ramish had died intestate?
4. Was Johansen granted a durable power of attorney or a health-care power of attorney for Ramish? Had Ramish created a living will? Explain.

Debate This . . .   *Any changes to existing, fully witnessed wills should also have to be witnessed.*

Terms and Concepts

administrator 977	health-care power of attorney 992	probate 977
bequest 977	holographic will 981	resulting trust 990
charitable trust 989	intestacy laws 977	spendthrift trust 989
codicil 982	intestate 977	testamentary trust 989
constructive trust 990	legacy 977	testate 977
devise 977	legatee 977	testator 977
devisee 977	living trust 986	Totten trust 989
durable power of attorney 992	living will 992	trust 986
escheat 977	nuncupative will 981	will 977
estate planning 977	*per capita* 986	will substitutes 983
executor 977	*per stirpes* 985	

Issue Spotters

1. Sheila makes a will leaving her property in equal thirds to Toby and Umeko, her children, and Velda, her niece. Two years later, Sheila is adjudged mentally incompetent, and that same year, she dies. Can Toby and Umeko have Sheila's will revoked on the ground that she did not have the capacity to make a will? Why or why not? (See *Wills*.)

2. Rafael dies without having made a will. He is survived by many relatives—a spouse, biological children, adopted children, sisters, brothers, uncles, aunts, cousins, nephews, and nieces. What determines who inherits what? (See *Intestacy Laws*.)

• **Check your answers to the Issue Spotters against the answers provided in Appendix D at the end of this text.**

Business Scenarios

51–1. Wills and Intestacy Laws. Benjamin is a widower who has two married children, Edward and Patricia. Patricia has two children, Perry and Paul. Edward has no children. Benjamin dies, and his typewritten will leaves all of his property equally to his children, Edward and Patricia, and provides that should a child predecease him, the grandchildren are to take *per stirpes*. The will was witnessed by Patricia and by Benjamin's lawyer, and it was signed by Benjamin in their presence. Patricia has predeceased Benjamin. Edward claims the will is invalid. (See *Intestacy Laws*.)

(a) Discuss whether the will is valid.

(b) Discuss the distribution of Benjamin's estate if the will is invalid.

(c) Discuss the distribution of Benjamin's estate if the will is valid.

51–2. Specific Bequests. Gary Mendel drew up a will in which he left his favorite car, a 1966 red Ferrari, to his daughter, Roberta. A year prior to his death, Mendel sold the 1966 Ferrari and purchased a 1969 Ferrari. Discuss whether Roberta will inherit the 1969 Ferrari under the terms of her father's will. (See *Wills*.)

51–3. Revocation of Wills. While single, James made out a will naming his mother, Carol, as sole beneficiary. Later, James married Lisa. (See *Wills*.)

(a) If James died while married to Lisa without changing his will, would the estate go to his mother, Carol? Explain.

(b) Assume that James made out a new will on his marriage to Lisa, leaving his entire estate to Lisa. Later, he divorced Lisa and married Mandis, but he did not change his will. Discuss the rights of Lisa and Mandis to James's estate after his death.

(c) Assume that James divorced Lisa, married Mandis, and changed his will, leaving his estate to Mandis. Later, a daughter, Claire, was born. James died without having included Claire in his will. Discuss fully whether Claire has any rights in the estate.

Business Case Problems

51–4. Intestacy Laws. A Florida statute provides that the right of election of a surviving spouse can be waived by written agreement: "A waiver of 'all rights,' or equivalent language, in the property or estate of a present or prospective spouse . . . is a waiver of all rights to elective share." The day before Mary Ann Taylor married Louis Taylor in Florida, they entered into a prenuptial agreement. The agreement stated that all property belonging to each spouse would "forever remain his or her personal estate, . . . forever free of claim by the other." The parties would retain "full rights and authority" over their property as they would have "if not married." After Louis died without a will, his only child, Joshua Taylor, filed a petition in a Florida state court for a determination of the beneficiaries of Louis's estate. How much of the estate can Mary Ann elect to receive? Explain. [*Taylor v. Taylor,* 1 So.3d 348 (Fla.App. 1 Dist. 2009)] (See *Intestacy Laws*.)

51–5. Wills. Elnora Maxey became the guardian of Sean Hall after his parents died. In 1996, Maxey died, and her will left the two houses in her estate to Hall. Julia Jordan became Hall's new guardian, and when she died, her husband, John Jordan, became Hall's guardian. In 1998, when Hall was eighteen years old, he died intestate, and Jordan was appointed as the administrator of Hall's estate. The two houses had remained in Maxey's estate, but Jordan paid the mortgage and tax payments on the houses for Hall's estate because Hall had inherited the houses. Anthony Cooper, a relative of Maxey, petitioned the probate court to be appointed executor of Maxey's estate, stating that there was now no heir. The court granted the request. Jordan was not aware of the proceedings. Cooper then sold both houses for the incredibly low price of $20,000 each to Quan Smith, without informing Jordan. The houses were then resold to JSD Properties, LLC, for a total of $190,000. Learning of the sale, Jordan sued, contending that Cooper had breached his fiduciary duty and had lied to the court, as Maxey's will had clearly left the houses to Hall. Does Jordan have the right to demand that JSD return the property? What factors would be considered in making this decision? [*Witcher v. JSD Properties, LLC,* 286 Ga. 717, 690 S.E.2d 855 (2010)] (See *Wills*.)

51–6. Business Case Problem with Sample Answer—Undue Influence.

Susie Walker executed a will that left her entire estate to her grandson. When her grandson died, Susie executed a new will that named her great-grandson as her sole beneficiary and specifically disinherited her son, Tommy. At the time, Tommy's ex-wife was living with Susie. After Susie died, Tommy filed a suit, claiming that her will was the product of undue influence on the part of his ex-wife. Several witnesses testified that Susie had been mentally competent when she executed her will. Does undue influence appear likely based on these facts? Why or why not? [*In re Estate of Walker,* 80 A.D.3d 865, 164 L.Ed.2d 480 (3 Dept. 2011)] (See *Wills.*)

• For a sample answer to Problem 51–6, go to Appendix E at the end of this text.

51–7. Requirements of a Will.
Sherman Hemsley was a well-known actor from the 1970s. Most notably, he played George Jefferson on the television shows *All in the Family* and *The Jeffersons.* He was born to Arsena Chisolm and William Thornton. Thornton was married to another woman, and Hemsley never had a relationship with his father or his father's side of the family. Hemsley never married and had no children. He lived with Flora Bernal, his business manager. Diagnosed with cancer, Hemsley executed a will naming Bernal the sole beneficiary of his estate. At the signing, Hemsley indicated that he knew he was executing his will and that he had deliberately chosen Bernal, but he did not discuss his relatives or the nature of his property with his attorney or the witnesses. After his death, the Thorntons challenged the will. Was Hemsley of sound mind? Discuss. [*In re Estate of Hemsley,* 460 S.W.3d 629 (Tex.App.—El Paso 2014)] (See *Wills.*)

51–8. Wills.
Andrew Walker executed a will giving a certain parcel of real estate in fee simple to his three children from a previous marriage, Mark Walker, Michelle Peters, and Andrea Knox. The will granted a "life use" in the property to Walker's current spouse, Nora Walker. A year later, Andrew, who suffered from asbestosis, was discharged from a hospital to spend his last days at home. He told Nora that he wished to execute a new will to change the disposition of the property to devise half of it to her. Nora recorded his wish and took her notes to the office of attorney Frederick Meagher to have the document drafted. Meagher did not see Nora's notes and did not talk to Walker..When Walker signed the document, he did not declare that it was his will, as required by state law, and no one from Meagher's office was present at the signing. Is the document a valid will? Explain. [*In re Estate of Walker,* 124 A.D.3d 970, 2 N.Y.S.3d 628 (3 Dept. 2015)] (See *Wills.*)

51–9. A Question of Ethics—Wills.

Vickie Lynn Smith, an actress and model also known as Anna Nicole Smith, met J. Howard Marshall II in 1991. During their courtship, J. Howard lavished gifts and large sums of money on Anna Nicole, and they married on June 27, 1994. J. Howard died on August 4, 1995. According to Anna Nicole, J. Howard had intended to provide for her financial security through a trust. Under the terms of his will, however, all of his assets were transferred to a trust for the benefit of E. Pierce Marshall, one of J. Howard's sons. While J. Howard's estate was subject to probate proceedings in a Texas state court, Anna Nicole filed for bankruptcy in a federal bankruptcy court. Pierce filed a claim in the bankruptcy proceeding, alleging that Anna Nicole had defamed him when her lawyers told the media that Pierce had engaged in forgery and fraud to gain control of his father's assets. Anna Nicole filed a counterclaim, alleging that Pierce had prevented the transfer of his father's assets to a trust for her. She claimed that, among other things, Pierce had imprisoned J. Howard against his wishes, surrounded him with security guards to prevent contact with her, and transferred property against his wishes. [Marshall v. Marshall, 547 U.S. 293, 126 S.Ct. 1735, 164 L.Ed.2d 480 (2006)] (See Wills.)

(a) What is the purpose underlying the requirements for a valid will? Which of these requirements might be at issue in this case? How should it apply here? Why?

(b) State courts generally have jurisdiction over the probate of a will and the administration of an estate. Does the Texas state court thus have the sole authority to adjudicate all of the claims in this case? Why or why not?

(c) How should Pierce's claim against Anna Nicole and her counterclaim be resolved?

(d) Anna Nicole executed her will in 2001. The beneficiary—Daniel, her son, who was not J. Howard's child—died in 2006, shortly after Anna Nicole gave birth to a daughter, Dannielynn. In 2007, before executing a new will, Anna Nicole died. What happens if a will's beneficiary dies before the testator? What happens if a child is born after a will is executed?

Legal Reasoning Group Activity

51–10. Intestacy Laws.
Three and a half years after Lauren and Warren Woodward were married, they were informed that Warren had leukemia. At the time, the couple had no children, and physicians told the Woodwards that the leukemia treatment might leave Warren sterile. The couple arranged for Warren's sperm to be collected and placed in a sperm bank for later use.

Two years after Warren died, Lauren gave birth to twin girls who had been conceived through artificial insemination using his sperm. The following year, Lauren applied for Social Security survivor benefits for the two children. Her application was rejected on the ground that she had not established that the twins were the husband's children within the meaning of the Social Security Act. Woodward then filed a paternity action in Massachusetts, and the probate court determined that Warren Woodward was the twins' father. She then filed an action in court to determine the inheritance rights of the twins. (See *Intestacy Laws.*)

(a) The first group will outline how a court should decide the inheritance rights of children conceived from the sperm of a deceased individual and his surviving spouse.

(b) The second group will decide if children conceived after a parent's death (by means of artificial insemination or *in vitro* fertilization) still inherit under intestate succession laws, and will explain why or why not.

(c) The third group will consider the inheritance rights of a child who was conceived by means of artificial insemination, *in vitro* fertilization, or a surrogate. Should they be different from the rights of a child conceived in the traditional manner? Assuming the biological parent is not part of the child's life, should the child still be able to inherit from the biological parent? Why or why not?

Application and Ethics

Business Planning for Divorce

Larry starts Auto Masters, an auto repair service. Through Larry's efforts, Auto Masters becomes successful. At the same time, however, Larry's marriage to Rachel falls apart. Unfortunately, Larry has not taken steps to make sure that his business will not break up along with his marriage.

The court orders a settlement that takes into consideration the value of all of the couple's assets, including the business. To pay the settlement, Larry is forced to sell Auto Masters for cash at a lower price than would otherwise have been possible.

As this example illustrates, planning for divorce is an important part of a business plan for the owners of the business.

Separate and Marital Property

A divorce formally dissolves a legal marriage. Following a divorce, if the spouses have not otherwise divided their property between them, a court can do it. For this purpose, there are two different types of property—separate and marital.

Separate Property Any property that only one spouse owns is *separate property*. This includes property owned by only one spouse before the marriage, as well as inheritances and gifts received by only one spouse during the marriage. Separate property commingled with marital assets may lose its separate status. In addition, in many states, *an increase in value* in separate property during a marriage may be considered a marital asset.[1]

Marital Property Any other property that the spouses acquired individually or jointly during the marriage is *marital property*. This can include professional licenses, such as an attorney's license, as well as shares of stock, interests in limited partnerships, and closely held businesses.

Dividing the Property In a few states—community property jurisdictions—spouses are held to be equal owners of the marital property.[2] Those assets are allocated in equal shares.

Most states provide instead for an equitable division of assets. An *equitable division* is an allocation consistent with fairness and justice, which may not call for equal shares. A court will consider a number of factors, including at least the following:

* The parties' respective contributions to the accumulation of marital property.
* The parties' respective liabilities.
* Whether only one spouse will receive income-producing property.
* The parties' respective earning capacity and employability.
* The value of each party's separate property.
* The tax consequences.[3]

---

1. See, for example, *St. Marie v. Roy*, 29 So.3d 708 (La.App. 3d Cir. 2010).
2. There are nine community property states—Arizona, California, Idaho, Louisiana, Nevada, New Mexico, Texas, Washington, and Wisconsin.
3. The Uniform Marriage and Divorce Act (UMDA), which has been adopted in eight states, lists these and other factors, including "the age, health, station, occupation, . . . and needs of each of the parties" [UMDA Section 307].

Continues

Is a Business Separate or Marital Property?

A business begun during marriage with joint funds is marital property. A business started before marriage or financed with separate funds during marriage is most likely separate property.

A business may be considered entirely or partially marital property, depending on the spouses' respective contributions to the business during the marriage. The contributions may be financial or operational.

Suppose, for instance, that Rita starts App Solutions, a software coding and development firm, with her own funds before marrying Hector. During the marriage, Hector markets the firm's services and contributes joint funds to its operation. The business grows and appreciates in value. If the spouses divorce, normally the business will be considered marital property.

Determining Value

To sell a business or to buy out one spouse's interest requires determining the value of the business and of each spouse's interest in it. This calculation usually requires the services of an accredited or certified professional business appraiser. The appraiser reviews the business's financial statements, tax returns, and other relevant data, and determines the value according to the appropriate method.[4]

Protecting Assets

A business owner can protect business assets from the claims of a spouse without concealing those assets or otherwise committing fraud. One way to obtain this protection is to avoid involving the spouse (or prospective spouse) in the business. If he or she does not contribute to the business, it is not likely to be construed as marital property. Other steps include prenuptial agreements, postnuptial agreements, and an agreement among the owners of the business to adhere to certain conditions.

Prenuptial Agreements As defined earlier, a *prenuptial agreement* is an agreement made before marriage that defines each party's ownership rights in the other's property. A court will normally enforce a prenuptial agreement in the following circumstances.

- Each future spouse was represented by an attorney.
- The agreement is in writing.
- Each party signed the agreement voluntarily.
- The assets covered by the agreement were fully disclosed.

If a business is subject to both parties' interests, the agreement should provide a projected split of the assets and a process or a method for determining the value. It should also identify how and when payment is to be made.

---

4. These methods include the *market approach*, which bases value on the price of a similar, recently sold business; the *income approach*, which converts expected profit or cash flow into current value; and the *asset approach*, which bases value on assets and liabilities.

Postnuptial Agreements A *postnuptial agreement* is an agreement made *after* marriage that defines each spouse's rights in the other spouse's property. Like a prenuptial agreement, a postnuptial agreement must involve each party's attorney, be in writing, be signed voluntarily, and be preceded by full disclosure. Unlike prenuptial agreements, postnuptial agreements are not recognized in all states. Even in states where these agreements are recognized, they may be more difficult to enforce than prenuptial agreements.[5]

Business Agreements For some types of businesses that could be subject to a spousal claim, an agreement among the owners can protect the owners' interests. This can be true whether the owners are partners, corporate shareholders, or members of limited liability companies.

Such an agreement can require an unmarried owner to provide the firm with a prenuptial agreement before marriage, including a waiver by the owner's prospective spouse of any future interest in the business. The agreement can also restrict the transfer of an owner's interest without the consent of the other owners. The other owners can be given the right to buy the interest to keep control of the enterprise. The method of valuation and means of payment should be included as well.

If both spouses are part of the firm, the agreement should provide that only persons actively involved in the business are entitled to own an interest in it. The agreement should add that if either spouse leaves the firm, his or her interest must be sold to the spouse who is still active. And it should be stipulated that in the event of a divorce, one spouse must quit (and agree not to compete, according to certain reasonable terms).

Ethical Connection

There is room for debate over the ethics of executing a plan to protect assets that might otherwise be considered the property of another. This is particularly true in the context of a marriage and a divorce.

Of course, everyone who creates a corporation, a partnership, or a limited liability company is taking a step to protect the business's assets from creditors and others. Most do not consider such actions unethical. Similarly, there is nothing unethical about asking a business's co-owner or a future spouse to consent to the terms of the agreements suggested here.

But it is not ethical to form a business organization to keep property out of the hands of an owner's spouse who might deserve better treatment. Perhaps it is the timing and the purpose of a plan that finally determine whether it should be considered ethical.

Ethics Question *With respect to the division of property on divorce, should the conduct of the spouses during the marriage be a factor? Why or why not?*

Critical Thinking *How might a spouse or ex-spouse overcome the business asset protection devices and techniques discussed in this feature? Explain.*

---

5. See, for example, *Bedrick v. Bedrick*, 17 A.3d 17, 300 Conn. 691 (2011).

How to Brief Cases and Analyze Case Problems

How to Brief Cases

To fully understand the law with respect to business, you need to be able to read and understand court decisions. To make this task easier, you can use a method of case analysis that is called *briefing*. There is a fairly standard procedure that you can follow when you "brief" any court case. You must first read the case opinion carefully. When you feel you understand the case, you can prepare a brief of it.

Although the format of the brief may vary, typically it will present the essentials of the case under headings such as the following:

1. **Citation.** Give the full citation for the case, including the name of the case, the date it was decided, and the court that decided it.
2. **Facts.** Briefly indicate (a) the reasons for the lawsuit; (b) the identity and arguments of the plaintiff(s) and defendant(s), respectively; and (c) the lower court's decision—if appropriate.
3. **Issue.** Concisely phrase, in the form of a question, the essential issue before the court. (If more than one issue is involved, you may have two—or even more—questions here.)
4. **Decision.** Indicate here—with a "yes" or "no," if possible—the court's answer to the question (or questions) in the *Issue* section above.
5. **Reason.** Summarize as briefly as possible the reasons given by the court for its decision (or decisions) and the case or statutory law relied on by the court in arriving at its decision.

An Example of a Briefed Sample Court Case

As an example of the format used in briefing cases, we present here a briefed version of the sample court case that was presented in Chapter 1 in Exhibit 1–6.

ROSA AND RAYMOND PARKS INSTITUTE FOR SELF DEVELOPMENT v. TARGET CORPORATION
United States Court of Appeals, Eleventh Circuit, 812 F.3d 824 (2016).

FACTS In December 1955, on a bus in Montgomery, Alabama, Rosa Parks refused to give up her seat to a white man in violation of the city's segregation law. This "courageous act" sparked the modern civil rights movement. Parks's role in "the most significant social movement in the history of the United States" has been chronicled in books and movies, and featured on mementoes, some of which are offered for sale by Target Corp. The Rosa and Raymond Parks Institute for Self Development is a Michigan firm that owns Parks's name and likeness. The Institute filed a suit in a federal district court against Target, alleging misappropriation in violation of the Institute's right of publicity. The court dismissed the complaint. The Institute appealed to the U.S. Court of Appeals for the Eleventh Circuit.

ISSUE Are Target's sales of books, movies, and other items that depict or discuss Rosa Parks and the modern civil rights movement protected by Michigan's common-law qualified privilege?

DECISION Yes. The U.S. Court of Appeals for the Eleventh Circuit affirmed the lower court's decision to dismiss the Institute's complaint. The items offered for sale by Target that feature or discuss Rosa Parks and her role in history are protected by Michigan's qualified privilege protecting matters of public interest.

REASON Michigan's common-law right of publicity prohibits the commercial use of a person's name or likeness without his or her consent. But this privacy right has limits. It "must yield to the qualified privilege to communicate on matters of public interest." The court recognized that "Rosa Parks is a figure of great historical significance and the civil rights movement a matter of legitimate and important public interest." The items identified by the Institute and sold by Target are "*bona fide* works" discussing Parks and her role in the modern civil rights movement. The items "communicate information, express opinions, recite grievances, and protest claimed abuses on behalf of a movement whose existence and objectives continue to be of the highest public interest and concern." Therefore, they fall within Michigan's qualified privilege.

A Review of the Briefed Sample Court Case

Here, we provide a review of the briefed case to indicate the kind of information that is contained in each section.

CITATION The name of the case is *Rosa and Raymond Parks Institute for Self Development v. Target Corporation*. The Rosa and Raymond Parks Institute for Self Development is the plaintiff. Target is the defendant. The U.S. Court of Appeals for the Eleventh Circuit decided this case in 2016. The citation states that this case can be found in Volume 812 of the *Federal Reporter, Third Series,* on page 824.

FACTS The *Facts* section identifies the plaintiff and the defendant. It also describes the events leading up to this suit and the allegations made by the plaintiff in the suit. Because this case is a decision of one of the U.S. courts of appeals, the lower court's ruling, the party appealing, and sometimes the appellant's contention on appeal are included here.

ISSUE The *Issue* section presents the central issue (or issues) decided by the court. In this case, the court considers whether the sales of books and other items that depict or discuss Rosa Parks and the modern civil rights movement are protected by Michigan's common-law qualified privilege.

DECISION The *Decision* section includes the court's decision on the issues before it. The decision reflects the opinion of the judge or justice hearing the case. In this case, the court decided that the items offered for sale focusing on or featuring Rosa Parks and her role in history fall within Michigan's qualified privilege, which protects depictions and discussions of matters of public interest. Decisions by appellate courts are frequently phrased in reference to the lower court's decision. That is, the appellate court may "affirm" the lower court's ruling or "reverse" it. A case may also be remanded, or sent back to the lower court, for further proceedings.

REASON The *Reason* section includes references to the relevant laws and legal principles that the court applied in coming to the conclusion arrived at in the case. The relevant law here includes Michigan's common-law qualified privilege protecting the use of others' names and likenesses in depictions and discussions of matters in the pubic interest. This section also explains the court's application of the law to the facts in this case.

Analyzing Case Problems

In addition to learning how to brief cases, students also find it helpful to know how to analyze case problems. Part of the study of business law and the legal environment usually involves analyzing case problems, such as those included in this text at the end of each chapter.

For each case problem in this book, we provide the relevant background and facts of the lawsuit and the issue before the court. When you are assigned one of these problems, your job will be to determine how the court should decide the issue, and why. In other words, you will need to engage in legal analysis and reasoning. Here, we offer some suggestions on how to make this task less daunting. We begin by presenting a SAMPLE PROBLEM:

> While Janet Lawson, a famous pianist, was shopping in Quality Market, she slipped and fell on a wet floor in one of the aisles. The floor had recently been mopped by one of the store's employees, but there were no signs

warning customers that the floor in that area was wet. As a result of the fall, Lawson injured her right arm and was unable to perform piano concerts for the next six months. Had she been able to perform the scheduled concerts, she would have earned approximately $60,000 over that period of time. Lawson sued Quality Market for this amount, plus another $10,000 in medical expenses. She claimed that the store's failure to warn customers of the wet floor constituted negligence and therefore the market was liable for her injuries. Will the court agree with Lawson? Discuss.

Understand the Facts

This may sound obvious, but before you can analyze or apply the relevant law to a specific set of facts, you must clearly understand those facts. In other words, you should read through the case problem carefully—more than once, if necessary—to make sure you understand the identity of the plaintiff(s) and defendant(s) in the case and the progression of events that led to the lawsuit.

In the sample case problem just given, the identity of the parties is fairly obvious. Janet Lawson is the one bringing the suit; therefore, she is the plaintiff. Quality Market, against whom she is bringing the suit, is the defendant. Some of the case problems you may work on have multiple plaintiffs or defendants. Often, it is helpful to use abbreviations for the parties. To indicate a reference to a plaintiff, for example, the *pi* symbol—π—is often used, and a defendant is denoted by a *delta*—Δ—a triangle.

The events leading to the lawsuit are also fairly straightforward. Lawson slipped and fell on a wet floor, and she contends that Quality Market should be liable for her injuries because it was negligent in not posting a sign warning customers of the wet floor.

When you are working on case problems, realize that the facts should be accepted as they are given. For example, in our sample problem, it should be accepted that the floor was wet and that there was no sign. In other words, avoid making conjectures, such as "Maybe the floor wasn't too wet," or "Maybe an employee was getting a sign to put up," or "Maybe someone stole the sign." Questioning the facts as they are presented only adds confusion to your analysis.

Legal Analysis and Reasoning

Once you understand the facts given in the case problem, you can begin to analyze the case. The IRAC method is a helpful tool to use in the legal analysis and reasoning process. IRAC is an acronym for Issue, Rule, Application, Conclusion. Applying this method to our sample problem would involve the following steps:

1. First, you need to decide what legal **issue** is involved in the case. In our sample case, the basic issue is whether Quality Market's failure to warn customers of the wet floor constituted negligence. As discussed in the text, negligence is a *tort*—a civil wrong. In a tort lawsuit, the plaintiff seeks to be compensated for another's wrongful act. A defendant will be deemed negligent if he or she breached a duty of care owed to the plaintiff and the breach of that duty caused the plaintiff to suffer harm.

2. Once you have identified the issue, the next step is to determine what **rule of law** applies to the issue. To make this determination, you will want to review carefully the text of the chapter in which the relevant rule of law for the problem appears. Our sample case problem involves the tort of negligence. The applicable rule of law is the tort law principle that business owners owe a duty to exercise reasonable care to protect their customers ("business invitees"). Reasonable care, in this context, includes either removing—or warning customers of—*foreseeable* risks about which the owner *knew* or *should have known*. Business owners need not warn customers of "open and obvious" risks, however. If a business owner breaches this duty of care (fails to exercise the appropriate degree of care toward customers), and the breach of duty causes a customer to be injured, the business owner will be liable to the customer for the customer's injuries.

3. The next—and usually the most difficult—step in analyzing case problems is the **application** of the relevant rule of law to the specific facts of the case you are studying. In the sample problem, applying the tort law principle just discussed presents few difficulties. An employee of the store had mopped the floor in the aisle where Lawson slipped and fell, but no sign was present indicating that the floor was wet. That a customer might fall on a wet floor is clearly a foreseeable risk. Therefore, the failure to warn customers about the wet floor was a breach of the duty of care owed by the business owner to the store's customers.

4. Once you have completed Step 3 in the IRAC method, you should be ready to draw your **conclusion.** In our sample problem, Quality Market is liable to Lawson for her injuries, because the market's breach of its duty of care caused Lawson's injuries.

The fact patterns in the business scenarios and case problems presented in this text are not always as simple as those presented in our sample problem. Often, for example, a case has more than one plaintiff or defendant. A case may also involve more than one issue and have more than one applicable rule of law. Furthermore, in some case problems the facts may indicate that the general rule of law should not apply.

For example, suppose that a store employee advised Lawson not to walk on the floor in the aisle because it was wet, but Lawson decided to walk on it anyway. This fact could alter the outcome of the case because the store could then raise the defense of assumption of risk. Nonetheless, a careful review of the chapter text should always provide you with the knowledge you need to analyze the problem thoroughly and arrive at accurate conclusions.

APPENDIX B

The Constitution of the United States

Preamble

We the People of the United States, in Order to form a more perfect Union, establish Justice, insure domestic Tranquility, provide for the common defence, promote the general Welfare, and secure the Blessings of Liberty to ourselves and our Posterity, do ordain and establish this Constitution for the United States of America.

Article I

Section 1. All legislative Powers herein granted shall be vested in a Congress of the United States, which shall consist of a Senate and House of Representatives.

Section 2. The House of Representatives shall be composed of Members chosen every second Year by the People of the several States, and the Electors in each State shall have the Qualifications requisite for Electors of the most numerous Branch of the State Legislature.

No Person shall be a Representative who shall not have attained to the Age of twenty five Years, and been seven Years a Citizen of the United States, and who shall not, when elected, be an Inhabitant of that State in which he shall be chosen.

Representatives and direct Taxes shall be apportioned among the several States which may be included within this Union, according to their respective Numbers, which shall be determined by adding to the whole Number of free Persons, including those bound to Service for a Term of Years, and excluding Indians not taxed, three fifths of all other Persons. The actual Enumeration shall be made within three Years after the first Meeting of the Congress of the United States, and within every subsequent Term of ten Years, in such Manner as they shall by Law direct. The Number of Representatives shall not exceed one for every thirty Thousand, but each State shall have at Least one Representative; and until such enumeration shall be made, the State of New Hampshire shall be entitled to chuse three, Massachusetts eight, Rhode Island and Providence Plantations one, Connecticut five, New York six, New Jersey four, Pennsylvania eight, Delaware one, Maryland six, Virginia ten, North Carolina five, South Carolina five, and Georgia three.

When vacancies happen in the Representation from any State, the Executive Authority thereof shall issue Writs of Election to fill such Vacancies.

The House of Representatives shall chuse their Speaker and other Officers; and shall have the sole Power of Impeachment.

Section 3. The Senate of the United States shall be composed of two Senators from each State, chosen by the Legislature thereof, for six Years; and each Senator shall have one Vote.

Immediately after they shall be assembled in Consequence of the first Election, they shall be divided as equally as may be into three Classes. The Seats of the Senators of the first Class shall be vacated at the Expiration of the second Year, of the second Class at the Expiration of the fourth Year, and of the third Class at the Expiration of the sixth Year, so that one third may be chosen every second Year; and if Vacancies happen by Resignation, or otherwise, during the Recess of the Legislature of any State, the Executive thereof may make temporary Appointments until the next Meeting of the Legislature, which shall then fill such Vacancies.

No Person shall be a Senator who shall not have attained to the Age of thirty Years, and been nine Years a Citizen of the United States, and who shall not, when elected, be an Inhabitant of that State for which he shall be chosen.

The Vice President of the United States shall be President of the Senate, but shall have no Vote, unless they be equally divided.

The Senate shall chuse their other Officers, and also a President pro tempore, in the Absence of the Vice President, or when he shall exercise the Office of President of the United States.

The Senate shall have the sole Power to try all Impeachments. When sitting for that Purpose, they shall be on Oath or Affirmation. When the President of the United States is tried, the Chief Justice shall preside: And no Person shall be convicted without the Concurrence of two thirds of the Members present.

Judgment in Cases of Impeachment shall not extend further than to removal from Office, and disqualification to hold and enjoy any Office of honor, Trust, or Profit under the United States: but the Party convicted shall nevertheless be liable and subject to Indictment, Trial, Judgment, and Punishment, according to Law.

Section 4. The Times, Places and Manner of holding Elections for Senators and Representatives, shall be prescribed in each State by the Legislature thereof; but the Congress may at any time by Law make or alter such Regulations, except as to the Places of chusing Senators.

The Congress shall assemble at least once in every Year, and such Meeting shall be on the first Monday in December, unless they shall by Law appoint a different Day.

Section 5. Each House shall be the Judge of the Elections, Returns, and Qualifications of its own Members, and a Majority of each shall constitute a Quorum to do Business; but a smaller Number may adjourn from day to day, and may be authorized to compel the Attendance of absent Members, in such Manner, and under such Penalties as each House may provide.

Each House may determine the Rules of its Proceedings, punish its Members for disorderly Behavior, and, with the Concurrence of two thirds, expel a Member.

Each House shall keep a Journal of its Proceedings, and from time to time publish the same, excepting such Parts as may in their Judgment require Secrecy; and the Yeas and Nays of the

Members of either House on any question shall, at the Desire of one fifth of those Present, be entered on the Journal.

Neither House, during the Session of Congress, shall, without the Consent of the other, adjourn for more than three days, nor to any other Place than that in which the two Houses shall be sitting.

Section 6. The Senators and Representatives shall receive a Compensation for their Services, to be ascertained by Law, and paid out of the Treasury of the United States. They shall in all Cases, except Treason, Felony and Breach of the Peace, be privileged from Arrest during their Attendance at the Session of their respective Houses, and in going to and returning from the same; and for any Speech or Debate in either House, they shall not be questioned in any other Place.

No Senator or Representative shall, during the Time for which he was elected, be appointed to any civil Office under the Authority of the United States, which shall have been created, or the Emoluments whereof shall have been increased during such time; and no Person holding any Office under the United States, shall be a Member of either House during his Continuance in Office.

Section 7. All Bills for raising Revenue shall originate in the House of Representatives; but the Senate may propose or concur with Amendments as on other Bills.

Every Bill which shall have passed the House of Representatives and the Senate, shall, before it become a Law, be presented to the President of the United States; If he approve he shall sign it, but if not he shall return it, with his Objections to the House in which it shall have originated, who shall enter the Objections at large on their Journal, and proceed to reconsider it. If after such Reconsideration two thirds of that House shall agree to pass the Bill, it shall be sent together with the Objections, to the other House, by which it shall likewise be reconsidered, and if approved by two thirds of that House, it shall become a Law. But in all such Cases the Votes of both Houses shall be determined by Yeas and Nays, and the Names of the Persons voting for and against the Bill shall be entered on the Journal of each House respectively. If any Bill shall not be returned by the President within ten Days (Sundays excepted) after it shall have been presented to him, the Same shall be a Law, in like Manner as if he had signed it, unless the Congress by their Adjournment prevent its Return in which Case it shall not be a Law.

Every Order, Resolution, or Vote, to which the Concurrence of the Senate and House of Representatives may be necessary (except on a question of Adjournment) shall be presented to the President of the United States; and before the Same shall take Effect, shall be approved by him, or being disapproved by him, shall be repassed by two thirds of the Senate and House of Representatives, according to the Rules and Limitations prescribed in the Case of a Bill.

Section 8. The Congress shall have Power To lay and collect Taxes, Duties, Imposts and Excises, to pay the Debts and provide for the common Defence and general Welfare of the United States; but all Duties, Imposts and Excises shall be uniform throughout the United States;

To borrow Money on the credit of the United States;

To regulate Commerce with foreign Nations, and among the several States, and with the Indian Tribes;

To establish an uniform Rule of Naturalization, and uniform Laws on the subject of Bankruptcies throughout the United States;

To coin Money, regulate the Value thereof, and of foreign Coin, and fix the Standard of Weights and Measures;

To provide for the Punishment of counterfeiting the Securities and current Coin of the United States;

To establish Post Offices and post Roads;

To promote the Progress of Science and useful Arts, by securing for limited Times to Authors and Inventors the exclusive Right to their respective Writings and Discoveries;

To constitute Tribunals inferior to the supreme Court;

To define and punish Piracies and Felonies committed on the high Seas, and Offenses against the Law of Nations;

To declare War, grant Letters of Marque and Reprisal, and make Rules concerning Captures on Land and Water;

To raise and support Armies, but no Appropriation of Money to that Use shall be for a longer Term than two Years;

To provide and maintain a Navy;

To make Rules for the Government and Regulation of the land and naval Forces;

To provide for calling forth the Militia to execute the Laws of the Union, suppress Insurrections and repel Invasions;

To provide for organizing, arming, and disciplining, the Militia, and for governing such Part of them as may be employed in the Service of the United States, reserving to the States respectively, the Appointment of the Officers, and the Authority of training the Militia according to the discipline prescribed by Congress;

To exercise exclusive Legislation in all Cases whatsoever, over such District (not exceeding ten Miles square) as may, by Cession of particular States, and the Acceptance of Congress, become the Seat of the Government of the United States, and to exercise like Authority over all Places purchased by the Consent of the Legislature of the State in which the Same shall be, for the Erection of Forts, Magazines, Arsenals, dock-Yards, and other needful Buildings;—And

To make all Laws which shall be necessary and proper for carrying into Execution the foregoing Powers, and all other Powers vested by this Constitution in the Government of the United States, or in any Department or Officer thereof.

Section 9. The Migration or Importation of such Persons as any of the States now existing shall think proper to admit, shall not be prohibited by the Congress prior to the Year one thousand eight hundred and eight, but a Tax or duty may be imposed on such Importation, not exceeding ten dollars for each Person.

The privilege of the Writ of Habeas Corpus shall not be suspended, unless when in Cases of Rebellion or Invasion the public Safety may require it.

No Bill of Attainder or ex post facto Law shall be passed.

No Capitation, or other direct, Tax shall be laid, unless in Proportion to the Census or Enumeration herein before directed to be taken.

No Tax or Duty shall be laid on Articles exported from any State.

No Preference shall be given by any Regulation of Commerce or Revenue to the Ports of one State over those of another: nor shall Vessels bound to, or from, one State be obliged to enter, clear, or pay Duties in another.

No Money shall be drawn from the Treasury, but in Consequence of Appropriations made by Law; and a regular Statement and Account of the Receipts and Expenditures of all public Money shall be published from time to time.

No Title of Nobility shall be granted by the United States: And no Person holding any Office of Profit or Trust under them, shall, without the Consent of the Congress, accept of any present, Emolument, Office, or Title, of any kind whatever, from any King, Prince, or foreign State.

Section 10. No State shall enter into any Treaty, Alliance, or Confederation; grant Letters of Marque and Reprisal; coin Money; emit Bills of Credit; make any Thing but gold and silver Coin a Tender in Payment of Debts; pass any Bill of Attainder, ex post facto Law, or Law impairing the Obligation of Contracts, or grant any Title of Nobility.

No State shall, without the Consent of the Congress, lay any Imposts or Duties on Imports or Exports, except what may be absolutely necessary for executing its inspection Laws: and the net Produce of all Duties and Imposts, laid by any State on Imports or Exports, shall be for the Use of the Treasury of the United States; and all such Laws shall be subject to the Revision and Controul of the Congress.

No State shall, without the Consent of Congress, lay any Duty of Tonnage, keep Troops, or Ships of War in time of Peace, enter into any Agreement or Compact with another State, or with a foreign Power, or engage in War, unless actually invaded, or in such imminent Danger as will not admit of delay.

Article II

Section 1. The executive Power shall be vested in a President of the United States of America. He shall hold his Office during the Term of four Years, and, together with the Vice President, chosen for the same Term, be elected, as follows:

Each State shall appoint, in such Manner as the Legislature thereof may direct, a Number of Electors, equal to the whole Number of Senators and Representatives to which the State may be entitled in the Congress; but no Senator or Representative, or Person holding an Office of Trust or Profit under the United States, shall be appointed an Elector.

The Electors shall meet in their respective States, and vote by Ballot for two Persons, of whom one at least shall not be an Inhabitant of the same State with themselves. And they shall make a List of all the Persons voted for, and of the Number of Votes for each; which List they shall sign and certify, and transmit sealed to the Seat of the Government of the United States, directed to the President of the Senate. The President of the Senate shall, in the Presence of the Senate and House of Representatives, open all the Certificates, and the Votes shall then be counted. The Person having the greatest Number of Votes shall be the President, if such Number be a Majority of the whole Number of Electors appointed; and if there be more than one who have such Majority, and have an equal Number of Votes, then the House of Representatives shall immediately chuse by Ballot one of them for President; and if no Person have a Majority, then from the five highest on the List the said House shall in like Manner chuse the President. But in chusing the President, the Votes shall be taken by States, the Representation from each State having one Vote; A quorum for this Purpose shall consist of a Member or Members from two thirds of the States, and a Majority of all the States shall be necessary to a Choice. In every Case, after the Choice of the President, the Person having the greater Number of Votes of the Electors shall be the Vice President. But if there should remain two or more who have equal Votes, the Senate shall chuse from them by Ballot the Vice President.

The Congress may determine the Time of chusing the Electors, and the Day on which they shall give their Votes; which Day shall be the same throughout the United States.

No person except a natural born Citizen, or a Citizen of the United States, at the time of the Adoption of this Constitution, shall be eligible to the Office of President; neither shall any Person be eligible to that Office who shall not have attained to the Age of thirty five Years, and been fourteen Years a Resident within the United States.

In Case of the Removal of the President from Office, or of his Death, Resignation or Inability to discharge the Powers and Duties of the said Office, the same shall devolve on the Vice President, and the Congress may by Law provide for the Case of Removal, Death, Resignation or Inability, both of the President and Vice President, declaring what Officer shall then act as President, and such Officer shall act accordingly, until the Disability be removed, or a President shall be elected.

The President shall, at stated Times, receive for his Services, a Compensation, which shall neither be increased nor diminished during the Period for which he shall have been elected, and he shall not receive within that Period any other Emolument from the United States, or any of them.

Before he enter on the Execution of his Office, he shall take the following Oath or Affirmation: "I do solemnly swear (or affirm) that I will faithfully execute the Office of President of the United States, and will to the best of my Ability, preserve, protect and defend the Constitution of the United States."

Section 2. The President shall be Commander in Chief of the Army and Navy of the United States, and of the Militia of the several States, when called into the actual Service of the United States; he may require the Opinion, in writing, of the principal Officer in each of the executive Departments, upon any Subject relating to the Duties of their respective Offices, and he shall have Power to grant Reprieves and Pardons for Offenses against the United States, except in Cases of Impeachment.

He shall have Power, by and with the Advice and Consent of the Senate to make Treaties, provided two thirds of the Senators present concur; and he shall nominate, and by and with the Advice and Consent of the Senate, shall appoint Ambassadors, other public Ministers and Consuls, Judges of the supreme

Court, and all other Officers of the United States, whose Appointments are not herein otherwise provided for, and which shall be established by Law; but the Congress may by Law vest the Appointment of such inferior Officers, as they think proper, in the President alone, in the Courts of Law, or in the Heads of Departments.

The President shall have Power to fill up all Vacancies that may happen during the Recess of the Senate, by granting Commissions which shall expire at the End of their next Session.

Section 3. He shall from time to time give to the Congress Information of the State of the Union, and recommend to their Consideration such Measures as he shall judge necessary and expedient; he may, on extraordinary Occasions, convene both Houses, or either of them, and in Case of Disagreement between them, with Respect to the Time of Adjournment, he may adjourn them to such Time as he shall think proper; he shall receive Ambassadors and other public Ministers; he shall take Care that the Laws be faithfully executed, and shall Commission all the Officers of the United States.

Section 4. The President, Vice President and all civil Officers of the United States, shall be removed from Office on Impeachment for, and Conviction of, Treason, Bribery, or other high Crimes and Misdemeanors.

Article III

Section 1. The judicial Power of the United States, shall be vested in one supreme Court, and in such inferior Courts as the Congress may from time to time ordain and establish. The Judges, both of the supreme and inferior Courts, shall hold their Offices during good Behaviour, and shall, at stated Times, receive for their Services a Compensation, which shall not be diminished during their Continuance in Office.

Section 2. The judicial Power shall extend to all Cases, in Law and Equity, arising under this Constitution, the Laws of the United States, and Treaties made, or which shall be made, under their Authority;—to all Cases affecting Ambassadors, other public Ministers and Consuls;—to all Cases of admiralty and maritime Jurisdiction;—to Controversies to which the United States shall be a Party;—to Controversies between two or more States;—between a State and Citizens of another State;—between Citizens of different States;—between Citizens of the same State claiming Lands under Grants of different States, and between a State, or the Citizens thereof, and foreign States, Citizens or Subjects.

In all Cases affecting Ambassadors, other public Ministers and Consuls, and those in which a State shall be a Party, the supreme Court shall have original Jurisdiction. In all the other Cases before mentioned, the supreme Court shall have appellate Jurisdiction, both as to Law and Fact, with such Exceptions, and under such Regulations as the Congress shall make.

The Trial of all Crimes, except in Cases of Impeachment, shall be by Jury; and such Trial shall be held in the State where the said Crimes shall have been committed; but when not committed within any State, the Trial shall be at such Place or Places as the Congress may by Law have directed.

Section 3. Treason against the United States, shall consist only in levying War against them, or, in adhering to their Enemies, giving them Aid and Comfort. No Person shall be convicted of Treason unless on the Testimony of two Witnesses to the same overt Act, or on Confession in open Court.

The Congress shall have Power to declare the Punishment of Treason, but no Attainder of Treason shall work Corruption of Blood, or Forfeiture except during the Life of the Person attainted.

Article IV

Section 1. Full Faith and Credit shall be given in each State to the public Acts, Records, and judicial Proceedings of every other State. And the Congress may by general Laws prescribe the Manner in which such Acts, Records and Proceedings shall be proved, and the Effect thereof.

Section 2. The Citizens of each State shall be entitled to all Privileges and Immunities of Citizens in the several States.

A Person charged in any State with Treason, Felony, or other Crime, who shall flee from Justice, and be found in another State, shall on Demand of the executive Authority of the State from which he fled, be delivered up, to be removed to the State having Jurisdiction of the Crime.

No Person held to Service or Labour in one State, under the Laws thereof, escaping into another, shall, in Consequence of any Law or Regulation therein, be discharged from such Service or Labour, but shall be delivered up on Claim of the Party to whom such Service or Labour may be due.

Section 3. New States may be admitted by the Congress into this Union; but no new State shall be formed or erected within the Jurisdiction of any other State; nor any State be formed by the Junction of two or more States, or Parts of States, without the Consent of the Legislatures of the States concerned as well as of the Congress.

The Congress shall have Power to dispose of and make all needful Rules and Regulations respecting the Territory or other Property belonging to the United States; and nothing in this Constitution shall be so construed as to Prejudice any Claims of the United States, or of any particular State.

Section 4. The United States shall guarantee to every State in this Union a Republican Form of Government, and shall protect each of them against Invasion; and on Application of the Legislature, or of the Executive (when the Legislature cannot be convened) against domestic Violence.

Article V

The Congress, whenever two thirds of both Houses shall deem it necessary, shall propose Amendments to this Constitution, or, on the Application of the Legislatures of two thirds of the several States, shall call a Convention for proposing Amendments, which, in either Case, shall be valid to all Intents and Purposes, as part of this Constitution, when ratified by the Legislatures of three fourths of the several States, or by Conventions in three fourths thereof, as the one or the other Mode of Ratification may be proposed by the Congress; Provided that no

Amendment which may be made prior to the Year One thousand eight hundred and eight shall in any Manner affect the first and fourth Clauses in the Ninth Section of the first Article; and that no State, without its Consent, shall be deprived of its equal Suffrage in the Senate.

Article VI

All Debts contracted and Engagements entered into, before the Adoption of this Constitution shall be as valid against the United States under this Constitution, as under the Confederation.

This Constitution, and the Laws of the United States which shall be made in Pursuance thereof; and all Treaties made, or which shall be made, under the Authority of the United States, shall be the supreme Law of the Land; and the Judges in every State shall be bound thereby, any Thing in the Constitution or Laws of any State to the Contrary notwithstanding.

The Senators and Representatives before mentioned, and the Members of the several State Legislatures, and all executive and judicial Officers, both of the United States and of the several States, shall be bound by Oath or Affirmation, to support this Constitution; but no religious Test shall ever be required as a Qualification to any Office or public Trust under the United States.

Article VII

The Ratification of the Conventions of nine States shall be sufficient for the Establishment of this Constitution between the States so ratifying the Same.

Amendment I [1791]

Congress shall make no law respecting an establishment of religion, or prohibiting the free exercise thereof; or abridging the freedom of speech, or of the press; or the right of the people peaceably to assembly, and to petition the Government for a redress of grievances.

Amendment II [1791]

A well regulated Militia, being necessary to the security of a free State, the right of the people to keep and bear Arms, shall not be infringed.

Amendment III [1791]

No Soldier shall, in time of peace be quartered in any house, without the consent of the Owner, nor in time of war, but in a manner to be prescribed by law.

Amendment IV [1791]

The right of the people to be secure in their persons, houses, papers, and effects, against unreasonable searches and seizures, shall not be violated, and no Warrants shall issue, but upon probable cause, supported by Oath or affirmation, and particularly describing the place to be searched, and the persons or things to be seized.

Amendment V [1791]

No person shall be held to answer for a capital, or otherwise infamous crime, unless on a presentment or indictment of a Grand Jury, except in cases arising in the land or naval forces, or in the Militia, when in actual service in time of War or public danger; nor shall any person be subject for the same offence to be twice put in jeopardy of life or limb; nor shall be compelled in any criminal case to be a witness against himself, nor be deprived of life, liberty, or property, without due process of law; nor shall private property be taken for public use, without just compensation.

Amendment VI [1791]

In all criminal prosecutions, the accused shall enjoy the right to a speedy and public trial, by an impartial jury of the State and district wherein the crime shall have been committed, which district shall have been previously ascertained by law, and to be informed of the nature and cause of the accusation; to be confronted with the witnesses against him; to have compulsory process for obtaining witnesses in his favor, and to have the Assistance of Counsel for his defence.

Amendment VII [1791]

In Suits at common law, where the value in controversy shall exceed twenty dollars, the right of trial by jury shall be preserved, and no fact tried by jury, shall be otherwise re-examined in any Court of the United States, than according to the rules of the common law.

Amendment VIII [1791]

Excessive bail shall not be required, nor excessive fines imposed, nor cruel and unusual punishments inflicted.

Amendment IX [1791]

The enumeration in the Constitution, of certain rights, shall not be construed to deny or disparage others retained by the people.

Amendment X [1791]

The powers not delegated to the United States by the Constitution, nor prohibited by it to the States, are reserved to the States respectively, or to the people.

Amendment XI [1795]

The Judicial power of the United States shall not be construed to extend to any suit in law or equity, commenced or prosecuted against one of the United States by Citizens of another State, or by Citizens or Subjects of any Foreign State.

Amendment XII [1804]

The Electors shall meet in their respective states, and vote by ballot for President and Vice-President, one of whom, at least, shall not be an inhabitant of the same state with themselves; they shall name in their ballots the person voted for as

President, and in distinct ballots the person voted for as Vice-President, and they shall make distinct lists of all persons voted for as President, and of all persons voted for as Vice-President, and of the number of votes for each, which lists they shall sign and certify, and transmit sealed to the seat of the government of the United States, directed to the President of the Senate;—The President of the Senate shall, in the presence of the Senate and House of Representatives, open all the certificates and the votes shall then be counted;—The person having the greatest number of votes for President, shall be the President, if such number be a majority of the whole number of Electors appointed; and if no person have such majority, then from the persons having the highest numbers not exceeding three on the list of those voted for as President, the House of Representatives shall choose immediately, by ballot, the President. But in choosing the President, the votes shall be taken by states, the representation from each state having one vote; a quorum for this purpose shall consist of a member or members from two-thirds of the states, and a majority of all states shall be necessary to a choice. And if the House of Representatives shall not choose a President whenever the right of choice shall devolve upon them, before the fourth day of March next following, then the Vice-President shall act as President, as in the case of the death or other constitutional disability of the President.—The person having the greatest number of votes as Vice-President, shall be the Vice-President, if such number be a majority of the whole number of Electors appointed, and if no person have a majority, then from the two highest numbers on the list, the Senate shall choose the Vice-President; a quorum for the purpose shall consist of two-thirds of the whole number of Senators, and a majority of the whole number shall be necessary to a choice. But no person constitutionally ineligible to the office of President shall be eligible to that of Vice-President of the United States.

Amendment XIII [1865]

Section 1. Neither slavery nor involuntary servitude, except as a punishment for crime whereof the party shall have been duly convicted, shall exist within the United States, or any place subject to their jurisdiction.

Section 2. Congress shall have power to enforce this article by appropriate legislation.

Amendment XIV [1868]

Section 1. All persons born or naturalized in the United States, and subject to the jurisdiction thereof, are citizens of the United States and of the State wherein they reside. No State shall make or enforce any law which shall abridge the privileges or immunities of citizens of the United States; nor shall any State deprive any person of life, liberty, or property, without due process of law; nor deny to any person within its jurisdiction the equal protection of the laws.

Section 2. Representatives shall be apportioned among the several States according to their respective numbers, counting the whole number of persons in each State, excluding Indians not taxed. But when the right to vote at any election for the choice of electors for President and Vice President of the United States, Representatives in Congress, the Executive and Judicial officers of a State, or the members of the Legislature thereof, is denied to any of the male inhabitants of such State, being twenty-one years of age, and citizens of the United States, or in any way abridged, except for participation in rebellion, or other crime, the basis of representation therein shall be reduced in the proportion which the number of such male citizens shall bear to the whole number of male citizens twenty-one years of age in such State.

Section 3. No person shall be a Senator or Representative in Congress, or elector of President and Vice President, or hold any office, civil or military, under the United States, or under any State, who having previously taken an oath, as a member of Congress, or as an officer of the United States, or as a member of any State legislature, or as an executive or judicial officer of any State, to support the Constitution of the United States, shall have engaged in insurrection or rebellion against the same, or given aid or comfort to the enemies thereof. But Congress may by a vote of two-thirds of each House, remove such disability.

Section 4. The validity of the public debt of the United States, authorized by law, including debts incurred for payment of pensions and bounties for services in suppressing insurrection or rebellion, shall not be questioned. But neither the United States nor any State shall assume or pay any debt or obligation incurred in aid of insurrection or rebellion against the United States, or any claim for the loss or emancipation of any slave; but all such debts, obligations and claims shall be held illegal and void.

Section 5. The Congress shall have power to enforce, by appropriate legislation, the provisions of this article.

Amendment XV [1870]

Section 1. The right of citizens of the United States to vote shall not be denied or abridged by the United States or by any State on account of race, color, or previous condition of servitude.

Section 2. The Congress shall have power to enforce this article by appropriate legislation.

Amendment XVI [1913]

The Congress shall have power to lay and collect taxes on incomes, from whatever source derived, without apportionment among the several States, and without regard to any census or enumeration.

Amendment XVII [1913]

Section 1. The Senate of the United States shall be composed of two Senators from each State, elected by the people thereof, for six years; and each Senator shall have one vote. The electors in each State shall have the qualifications requisite for electors of the most numerous branch of the State legislatures.

Section 2. When vacancies happen in the representation of any State in the Senate, the executive authority of such State shall issue writs of election to fill such vacancies: *Provided*, That the legislature of any State may empower the executive thereof to make temporary appointments until the people fill the vacancies by election as the legislature may direct.

Section 3. This amendment shall not be so construed as to affect the election or term of any Senator chosen before it becomes valid as part of the Constitution.

Amendment XVIII [1919]

Section 1. After one year from the ratification of this article the manufacture, sale, or transportation of intoxicating liquors within, the importation thereof into, or the exportation thereof from the United States and all territory subject to the jurisdiction thereof for beverage purposes is hereby prohibited.

Section 2. The Congress and the several States shall have concurrent power to enforce this article by appropriate legislation.

Section 3. This article shall be inoperative unless it shall have been ratified as an amendment to the Constitution by the legislatures of the several States, as provided in the Constitution, within seven years from the date of the submission hereof to the States by the Congress.

Amendment XIX [1920]

Section 1. The right of citizens of the United States to vote shall not be denied or abridged by the United States or by any State on account of sex.

Section 2. Congress shall have power to enforce this article by appropriate legislation.

Amendment XX [1933]

Section 1. The terms of the President and Vice President shall end at noon on the 20th day of January, and the terms of Senators and Representatives at noon on the 3d day of January, of the years in which such terms would have ended if this article had not been ratified; and the terms of their successors shall then begin.

Section 2. The Congress shall assemble at least once in every year, and such meeting shall begin at noon on the 3d day of January, unless they shall by law appoint a different day.

Section 3. If, at the time fixed for the beginning of the term of the President, the President elect shall have died, the Vice President elect shall become President. If the President shall not have been chosen before the time fixed for the beginning of his term, or if the President elect shall have failed to qualify, then the Vice President elect shall act as President until a President shall have qualified; and the Congress may by law provide for the case wherein neither a President elect nor a Vice President elect shall have qualified, declaring who shall then act as President, or the manner in which one who is to act shall be selected, and such person shall act accordingly until a President or Vice President shall have qualified.

Section 4. The Congress may by law provide for the case of the death of any of the persons from whom the House of Representatives may choose a President whenever the right of choice shall have devolved upon them, and for the case of the death of any of the persons from whom the Senate may choose a Vice President whenever the right of choice shall have devolved upon them.

Section 5. Sections 1 and 2 shall take effect on the 15th day of October following the ratification of this article.

Section 6. This article shall be inoperative unless it shall have been ratified as an amendment to the Constitution by the legislatures of three-fourths of the several States within seven years from the date of its submission.

Amendment XXI [1933]

Section 1. The eighteenth article of amendment to the Constitution of the United States is hereby repealed.

Section 2. The transportation or importation into any State, Territory, or possession of the United States for delivery or use therein of intoxicating liquors, in violation of the laws thereof, is hereby prohibited.

Section 3. This article shall be inoperative unless it shall have been ratified as an amendment to the Constitution by conventions in the several States, as provided in the Constitution, within seven years from the date of the submission hereof to the States by the Congress.

Amendment XXII [1951]

Section 1. No person shall be elected to the office of the President more than twice, and no person who has held the office of President, or acted as President, for more than two years of a term to which some other person was elected President shall be elected to the office of President more than once. But this Article shall not apply to any person holding the office of President when this Article was proposed by the Congress, and shall not prevent any person who may be holding the office of President, or acting as President, during the term within which this Article becomes operative from holding the office of President or acting as President during the remainder of such term.

Section 2. This article shall be inoperative unless it shall have been ratified as an amendment to the Constitution by the legislatures of three-fourths of the several States within seven years from the date of its submission to the States by the Congress.

Amendment XXIII [1961]

Section 1. The District constituting the seat of Government of the United States shall appoint in such manner as the Congress may direct:

A number of electors of President and Vice President equal to the whole number of Senators and Representatives in Congress to which the District would be entitled if it were a State, but in no event more than the least populous state; they shall be in addition to those appointed by the states, but they shall be considered, for the purposes of the election of President and Vice President, to be electors appointed by a state; and they shall meet in the District and perform such duties as provided by the twelfth article of amendment.

Section 2. The Congress shall have power to enforce this article by appropriate legislation.

Amendment XXIV [1964]

Section 1. The right of citizens of the United States to vote in any primary or other election for President or Vice President, for electors for President or Vice President, or for Senator or Representative in Congress, shall not be denied or abridged by the United States, or any State by reason of failure to pay any poll tax or other tax.

Section 2. The Congress shall have power to enforce this article by appropriate legislation.

Amendment XXV [1967]

Section 1. In case of the removal of the President from office or of his death or resignation, the Vice President shall become President.

Section 2. Whenever there is a vacancy in the office of the Vice President, the President shall nominate a Vice President who shall take office upon confirmation by a majority vote of both Houses of Congress.

Section 3. Whenever the President transmits to the President pro tempore of the Senate and the Speaker of the House of Representatives his written declaration that he is unable to discharge the powers and duties of his office, and until he transmits to them a written declaration to the contrary, such powers and duties shall be discharged by the Vice President as Acting President.

Section 4. Whenever the Vice President and a majority of either the principal officers of the executive departments or of such other body as Congress may by law provide, transmit to the President pro tempore of the Senate and the Speaker of the House of Representatives their written declaration that the President is unable to discharge the powers and duties of his office, the Vice President shall immediately assume the powers and duties of the office as Acting President.

Thereafter, when the President transmits to the President pro tempore of the Senate and the Speaker of the House of Representatives his written declaration that no inability exists, he shall resume the powers and duties of his office unless the Vice President and a majority of either the principal officers of the executive department or of such other body as Congress may by law provide, transmit within four days to the President pro tempore of the Senate and the Speaker of the House of Representatives their written declaration that the President is unable to discharge the powers and duties of his office. Thereupon Congress shall decide the issue, assembling within forty-eight hours for that purpose if not in session. If the Congress, within twenty-one days after receipt of the latter written declaration, or, if Congress is not in session, within twenty-one days after Congress is required to assemble, determines by two-thirds vote of both Houses that the President is unable to discharge the powers and duties of his office, the Vice President shall continue to discharge the same as Acting President; otherwise, the President shall resume the powers and duties of his office.

Amendment XXVI [1971]

Section 1. The right of citizens of the United States, who are eighteen years of age or older, to vote shall not be denied or abridged by the United States or by any State on account of age.

Section 2. The Congress shall have power to enforce this article by appropriate legislation.

Amendment XXVII [1992]

No law, varying the compensation for the services of the Senators and Representatives, shall take effect, until an election of Representatives shall have intervened.

APPENDIX C

The Uniform Commercial Code

(Adopted in fifty-two jurisdictions—all fifty States, although Louisiana has adopted only Articles 1, 3, 4, 7, 8, and 9; the District of Columbia; and the Virgin Islands.)

The Code consists of the following articles:

Article
1. General Provisions
2. Sales
2A. Leases
3. Negotiable Instruments
4. Bank Deposits and Collections
4A. Funds Transfers
5. Letters of Credit
6. Repealer of U.C.C.—Article 6: Bulk Transfers and [Revised] Article 6: Bulk Sales
7. Warehouse Receipts, Bills of Lading and Other Documents of Title
8. Investment Securities
9. Secured Transactions

ARTICLE 1: GENERAL PROVISIONS

Part 1—General Provisions

§ 1–101. Short Titles.
(a) This [Act] may be cited as Uniform Commercial Code.
(b) This article may be cited as Uniform Commercial Code—Uniform Provisions.

§ 1–102. Scope of Article.
This article applies to a transaction to the extent that it is governed by another article of [the Uniform Commercial Code].

§ 1–103. Construction of [Uniform Commercial Code] to Promote Its Purpose and Policies; Applicability of Supplemental Principles of Law.
(a) [The Uniform Commercial Code] must be liberally construed and applied to promote its underlying purposes and policies, which are:
　(1) to simplify, clarify, and modernize the law govern-ing commercial transactions;
　(2) to permit the continued expansion of commercial practices through custom, usage, and agreement of the parties; and
　(3) to make uniform the law among the various jurisdictions.
(b) Unless displaced by the particular provisions of [the Uniform Commercial Code], the principles of law and equity, including the law merchant and the law relative to capacity to contract, principal and agent, estoppel, fraud, misrepresentation, duress, coercion, mistake, bankruptcy, and other validating or invalidating cause, supplement its provisions.

§ 1–104. Construction Against Implicit Repeal.
This Act being a general act intended as a unified coverage of its subject matter, no part of it shall be deemed to be impliedly repealed by subsequent legislation if such construction can reasonably be avoided.

§ 1–105. Severability.
If any provision or clause of [the Uniform Commercial Code] or its application to any person or circumstance is held invalid, the invalidity does not affect other provisions or applications of [the Uniform Commercial Code] which can be given effect without the invalid provision or application, and to this end the provisions of [the Uniform Commercial Code] are severable.

§ 1–106. Use of Singular and Plural; Gender.
In [the Uniform Commercial Code], unless the statutory context otherwise requires:
(1) words in the singular number include the plural, and those in the plural include the singular; and
(2) words of any gender also refer to any other gender.

§ 1–107. Section Captions.
Section captions are part of [the Uniform Commercial Code].

§ 1–108. Relation to Electronic Signatures in Global and National Commerce Act.
This article modifies, limits, and supersedes the Federal Electronic Signatures in Global and National Commerce Act, 15 U.S.C. Sections 7001 *et seq.*, except that nothing in this article modifies, limits, or supersedes Section 7001(c) of that act or authorizes electronic delivery of any of the notices described in Section 7003(b) of that Act.

Part 2—General Definitions and Principles of Interpretation

§ 1–201. General Definitions.
Subject to additional definitions contained in the subsequent Articles of this Act which are applicable to specific Articles or Parts thereof, and unless the context otherwise requires, in this Act:
(1) "Action", in the sense of a judicial proceeding, includes recoupment, counterclaim, set-off, suit in equity, and any other proceedings in which rights are determined.
(2) "Aggrieved party" means a party entitled to resort to a remedy.
(3) "Agreement", as distinguished from "contract", means the bargain of the parties in fact, as found in their language or by implication from other circumstances, including course of performance, course of dealing, or usage of trade as provided in Section 1–303.
(4) "Bank" means a person engaged in the business of banking and includes a savings bank, savings and loan association, credit union, and trust company.
(5) "Bearer" means a person in control of a negotiable electronic document of title or a person in possession of a negotiable instrument,

negotiable tangible document of title, or certificated security that is payable to bearer or indorsed in blank.

(6) "Bill of lading" means a document of title evidencing the receipt of goods for shipment issued by a person engaged in the business of directly or indirectly transporting or forwarding goods. The term does not include a warehouse receipt.

(7) "Branch" includes a separately incorporated foreign branch of a bank.

(8) "Burden of establishing" a fact means the burden of persuading the trier of fact that the existence of the fact is more probable than its nonexistence.

(9) "Buyer in ordinary course of business" means a person that buys goods in good faith, without knowledge that the sale violates the rights of another person in the goods, and in the ordinary course from a person, other than a pawnbroker, in the business of selling goods of that kind. A person buys goods in the ordinary course if the sale to the person comports with the usual or customary practices in the kind of business in which the seller is engaged or with the seller's own usual or customary practices. A person that sells oil, gas, or other minerals at the wellhead or minehead is a person in the business of selling goods of that kind. A buyer in ordinary course of business may buy for cash, by exchange of other property, or on secured or unsecured credit, and may acquire goods or documents of title under a pre-existing contract for sale. Only a buyer that takes possession of the goods or has a right to recover the goods from the seller under Article 2 may be a buyer in ordinary course of business. A person that acquires goods in a transfer in bulk or as security for or in total or partial satisfaction of a money debt is not a buyer in ordinary course of business.

(10) "Conspicuous", with reference to a term, means so written, displayed, or presented that a reasonable person against which it is to operate ought to have noticed it. Whether a term is "conspicuous" or not is a decision for the court. Conspicuous terms include the following:

    (A) a heading in capitals equal to or greater in size than the surrounding text, or in contrasting type, font, or color to the surrounding text of the same or lesser size; and

    (B) language in the body of a record or display in larger type than the surrounding text, or in contrasting type, font, or color to the surrounding text of the same size, or set off from surrounding text of the same size by symbols or other marks that call attention to the language.

(11) "Consumer" means an individual who enters into a transaction primarily for personal, family, or household purposes.

(12) "Contract", as distinguished from "agreement", means the total legal obligation that results from the parties' agreement as determined by [the Uniform Commercial Code] as supplemented by any other laws.

(13) "Creditor" includes a general creditor, a secured creditor, a lien creditor and any representative of creditors, including an assignee for the benefit of creditors, a trustee in bankruptcy, a receiver in equity and an executor or administrator of an insolvent debtor's or assignor's estate.

(14) "Defendant" includes a person in the position of defendant in a counterclaim, cross-action, or third-party claim.

(15) "Delivery" with respect to an electronic document of title means voluntary transfer of control and with respect to an instrument, a tangible document of title, or chattel paper means voluntary transfer of possession.

(16) "Document of title" means a record (i) that in regular course of business or financing is treated as adequately evidencing that the person in possession or control of the record is entitled to receive, control, hold, and dispose of the record and the goods the record covers and (ii) that purports to be issued by or addressed to a bailee and to cover goods in the bailee's possession which are either identified or are fungible portions of an identified mass. The term includes a bill of lading, transport document, dock warrant, dock receipt, warehouse receipt, and order for delivery of goods. An electronic document of title means a document of title evidenced by a record consisting of information stored in an electronic medium. A tangible document of title means a document of title evidenced by a record consisting of information that is inscribed on a tangible medium.

(17) "Fault" means a default, breach, or wrongful act or omission.

(18) "Fungible goods" means:

    (A) goods of which any unit, by nature or usage of trade, is the equivalent of any other like unit; or

    (B) goods that by agreement are treated as equivalent.

(19) "Genuine" means free of forgery or counterfeiting.

(20) "Good faith," except as otherwise provided in Article 5, means honesty in fact and the observance of reasonable commercial standards of fair dealing.

(21) "Holder" means:

    (A) the person in possession of a negotiable instrument that is payable either to bearer or to an identified person that is the person in possession;

    (B) the person in possession of a negotiable tangible document of title if the goods are deliverable either to bearer or to the order of the person in possession; or

    (C) the person in control of a negotiable electronic document of title.

(22) "Insolvency proceeding" includes an assignment for the benefit of creditors or other proceeding intended to liquidate or rehabilitate the estate of the person involved.

(23) "Insolvent" means:

    (A) having generally ceased to pay debts in the ordinary course of business other than as a result of bona fide dispute;

    (B) being unable to pay debts as they become due; or

    (C) being insolvent within the meaning of federal bankruptcy law.

(24) "Money" means a medium of exchange currently authorized or adopted by a domestic or foreign government. The term includes a monetary unit of account established by an intergovernmental organization or by agreement between two or more countries.

(25) "Organization" means a person other than an individual.

(26) "Party", as distinguished from "third party", means a person that has engaged in a transaction or made an agreement subject to [the Uniform Commercial Code].

(27) "Person" means an individual, corporation, business trust, estate, trust, partnership, limited liability company, association, joint venture, government, governmental subdivision, agency, or instrumentality, public corporation, or any other legal or commercial entity.

(28) "Present value" means the amount as of a date certain of one or more sums payable in the future, discounted to the date certain by use of either an interest rate specified by the parties if that rate is not manifestly unreasonable at the time the transaction is entered into or, if an interest rate is not so specified, a commercially reasonable rate that takes into account the facts and circumstances at the time the transaction is entered into.

(29) "Purchase" means taking by sale, lease, discount, negotiation, mortgage, pledge, lien, security interest, issue or reissue, gift, or any other voluntary transaction creating an interest in property.

(30) "Purchaser" means a person that takes by purchase.

(31) "Record" means information that is inscribed on a tangible medium or that is stored in an electronic or other medium and is retrievable in perceivable form.

(32) "Remedy" means any remedial right to which an aggrieved party is entitled with or without resort to a tribunal.

(33) "Representative" means a person empowered to act for another, including an agent, an officer of a corporation or association, and a trustee, executor, or administrator of an estate.

(34) "Right" includes remedy.

(35) "Security interest" means an interest in personal property or fixtures which secures payment or performance of an obligation. "Security interest" includes any interest of a consignor and a buyer of accounts, chattel paper, a payment intangible, or a promissory note in a transaction that is subject to Article 9. "Security interest" does not include the special property interest of a buyer of goods on identification of those goods to a contract for sale under Section 2–401, but a buyer may also acquire a "security interest" by complying with Article 9. Except as otherwise provided in Section 2–505, the right of a seller or lessor of goods under Article 2 or 2A to retain or acquire possession of the goods is not a "security interest", but a seller or lessor may also acquire a "security interest" by complying with Article 9. The retention or reservation of title by a seller of goods notwithstanding shipment or delivery to the buyer under Section 2–401 is limited in effect to a reservation of a "security interest." Whether a transaction in the form of a lease creates a "security interest" is determined pursuant to Section 1–203.

(36) "Send" in connection with a writing, record, or notice means:

　(A) to deposit in the mail or deliver for transmission by any other usual means of communication with postage or cost of transmission provided for and properly addressed and, in the case of an instrument, to an address specified thereon or otherwise agreed, or if there be none to any address reasonable under the circumstances; or

　(B) in any other way to cause to be received any record or notice within the time it would have arrived if properly sent.

(37) "Signed" includes using any symbol executed or adopted with present intention to adopt or accept a writing.

(38) "State" means a State of the United States, the District of Columbia, Puerto Rico, the United States Virgin Islands, or any territory or insular possession subject to the jurisdiction of the United States.

(39) "Surety" includes a guarantor or other secondary obligor.

(40) "Term" means a portion of an agreement that relates to a particular matter.

(41) "Unauthorized signature" means a signature made without actual, implied, or apparent authority. The term includes a forgery.

(42) "Warehouse receipt" means a document of title issued by a person engaged in the business of storing goods for hire.

(43) "Writing" includes printing, typewriting, or any other intentional reduction to tangible form. "Written" has a corresponding meaning. As amended in 2003.

§ 1–202. Notice; Knowledge.

(a) Subject to subsection (f), a person has "notice" of a fact if the person:

　(1) has actual knowledge of it;

　(2) has received a notice or notification of it; or

　(3) from all the facts and circumstances known to the person at the time in question, has reason to know that it exists.

(b) "Knowledge" means actual knowledge. "Knows" has a corresponding meaning.

(c) "Discover", "learn", or words of similar import refer to knowledge rather than to reason to know.

(d) A person "notifies" or "gives" a notice or notification to another person by taking such steps as may be reasonably required to inform the other person in ordinary course, whether or not the other person actually comes to know of it.

(e) Subject to subsection (f), a person "receives" a notice or notification when:

　(1) it comes to that person's attention; or

　(2) it is duly delivered in a form reasonable under the circumstances at the place of business through which the contract was made or at another location held out by that person as the place for receipt of such communications.

(f) Notice, knowledge, or a notice or notification received by an organization is effective for a particular transaction from the time it is brought to the attention of the individual conducting that transaction and, in any event, from the time it would have been brought to the individual's attention if the organization had exercised due diligence. An organization exercises due diligence if it maintains reasonable routines for communicating significant information to the person conducting the transaction and there is reasonable compliance with the routines. Due diligence does not require an individual acting for the organization to communicate information unless the communication is part of the individual's regular duties or the individual has reason to know of the transaction and that the transaction would be materially affected by the information.

§ 1–203. Lease Distinguished from Security Interest.

(a) Whether a transaction in the form of a lease creates a lease or security interest is determined by the facts of each case.

(b) A transaction in the form of a lease creates a security interest if the consideration that the lessee is to pay the lessor for the right to possession and use of the goods is an obligation for the term of the lease and is not subject to termination by the lessee, and:

　(1) the original term of the lease is equal to or greater than the remaining economic life of the goods;

　(2) the lessee is bound to renew the lease for the remaining economic life of the goods or is bound to become the owner of the goods;

　(3) the lessee has an option to renew the lease for the remaining economic life of the goods for no additional consideration or for nominal additional consideration upon compliance with the lease agreement; or

　(4) the lessee has an option to become the owner of the goods for no additional consideration or for nominal additional consideration upon compliance with the lease agreement.

(c) A transaction in the form of a lease does not create a security interest merely because:

　(1) the present value of the consideration the lessee is obligated to pay the lessor for the right to possession and use of the goods is substantially equal to or is greater than the fair market value of the goods at the time the lease is entered into;

　(2) the lessee assumes risk of loss of the goods;

(3) the lessee agrees to pay, with respect to the goods, taxes, insurance, filing, recording, or registration fees, or service or maintenance costs;

(4) the lessee has an option to renew the lease or to become the owner of the goods;

(5) the lessee has an option to renew the lease for a fixed rent that is equal to or greater than the reasonably predictable fair market rent for the use of the goods for the term of the renewal at the time the option is to be performed; or

(6) the lessee has an option to become the owner of the goods for a fixed price that is equal to or greater than the reasonably predictable fair market value of the goods at the time the option is to be performed.

(d) Additional consideration is nominal if it is less than the lessee's reasonably predictable cost of performing under the lease agreement if the option is not exercised. Additional consideration is not nominal if:

(1) when the option to renew the lease is granted to the lessee, the rent is stated to be the fair market rent for the use of the goods for the term of the renewal determined at the time the option is to be performed; or

(2) when the option to become the owner of the goods is granted to the lessee, the price is stated to be the fair market value of the goods determined at the time the option is to be performed.

(e) The "remaining economic life of the goods" and "reasonably predictable" fair market rent, fair market value, or cost of performing under the lease agreement must be determined with reference to the facts and circumstances at the time the transaction is entered into.

§ 1–204. Value.

Except as otherwise provided in Articles 3, 4, [and] 5, [and 6], a person gives value for rights if the person acquires them:

(1) in return for a binding commitment to extend credit or for the extension of immediately available credit, whether or not drawn upon and whether or not a charge-back is provided for in the event of difficulties in collection;

(2) as security for, or in total or partial satisfaction of, a preexisting claim;

(3) by accepting delivery under a preexisting contract for purchase; or

(4) in return for any consideration sufficient to support a simple contract.

§ 1–205. Reasonable Time; Seasonableness.

(a) Whether a time for taking an action required by [the Uniform Commercial Code] is reasonable depends on the nature, purpose, and circumstances of the action.

(b) An action is taken seasonably if it is taken at or within the time agreed or, if no time is agreed, at or within a reasonable time.

§ 1–206. Presumptions.

Whenever [the Uniform Commercial Code] creates a "presumption" with respect to a fact, or provides that a fact is "presumed," the trier of fact must find the existence of the fact unless and until evidence is introduced that supports a finding of its nonexistence.

Part 3—Territorial Applicability and General Rules

§ 1–301. Territorial Applicability; Parties' Power to Choose Applicable Law.

(a) In this section:

(1) "Domestic transaction" means a transaction other than an international transaction.

(2) "International transaction" means a transaction that bears a reasonable relation to a country other than the United States.

(b) This section applies to a transaction to the extent that it is governed by another article of the [Uniform Commercial Code].

(c) Except as otherwise provided in this section:

(1) an agreement by parties to a domestic transaction that any or all of their rights and obligations are to be determined by the law of this State or of another State is effective, whether or not the transaction bears a relation to the State designated; and

(2) an agreement by parties to an international transaction that any or all of their rights and obligations are to be determined by the law of this State or of another State or country is effective, whether or not the transaction bears a relation to the State or country designated.

(d) In the absence of an agreement effective under subsection (c), and except as provided in subsections (e) and (g), the rights and obligations of the parties are determined by the law that would be selected by application of this State's conflict of laws principles.

(e) If one of the parties to a transaction is a consumer, the following rules apply:

(1) An agreement referred to in subsection (c) is not effective unless the transaction bears a reasonable relation to the State or country designated.

(2) Application of the law of the State or country determined pursuant to subsection (c) or (d) may not deprive the consumer of the protection of any rule of law governing a matter within the scope of this section, which both is protective of consumers and may not be varied by agreement: (A) of the State or country in which the consumer principally resides, unless subparagraph (B) applies; or (B) if the transaction is a sale of goods, of the State or country in which the consumer both makes the contract and take delivery of those goods, if such State or country is not the State or country in which the consumer principally resides.

(f) An agreement otherwise effective under subsection (c) is not effective to the extent that application of the law of the State or country designated would be contrary to a fundamental policy of the State or country whose law would govern in the absence of agreement under subsection (d).

(g) To the extent that [the Uniform Commercial Code] governs a transaction, if one of the following provisions of [the Uniform Commercial Code] specifies the applicable law, that provision governs and a contrary agreement is effective only to the extent permitted by the law so specified: (1) Section 2–402; (2) Sections 2A–105 and 2A–106; (3) Section 4–102; (4) Section 4A–507; (5) Section 5–116; [(6) Section 6–103;] (7) Section 8–110; (8) Sections 9–301 through 9–307.

§ 1–302. Variation by Agreement.

(a) Except as otherwise provided in subsection (b) or elsewhere in [the Uniform Commercial Code], the effect of provisions of [the Uniform Commercial Code] may be varied by agreement.

(b) The obligations of good faith, diligence, reasonableness, and care prescribed by [the Uniform Commercial Code] may not be disclaimed by agreement. The parties, by agreement, may determine the standards by which the performance of those obligations is to be measured if those standards are not manifestly unreasonable.

Whenever [the Uniform Commercial Code] requires an action to be taken within a reasonable time, a time that is not manifestly unreasonable may be fixed by agreement.

(c) The presence in certain provisions of [the Uniform Commercial Code] of the phrase "unless otherwise agreed", or words of similar import, does not imply that the effect of other provisions may not be varied by agreement under this section.

§ 1–303. Course of Performance, Course of Dealing, and Usage of Trade.

(a) A "course of performance" is a sequence of conduct between the parties to a particular transaction that exists if:

(1) the agreement of the parties with respect to the transaction involves repeated occasions for performance by a party; and

(2) the other party, with knowledge of the nature of the performance and opportunity for objection to it, accepts the performance or acquiesces in it without objection.

(b) A "course of dealing" is a sequence of conduct concerning previous transactions between the parties to a particular transaction that is fairly to be regarded as establishing a common basis of understanding for interpreting their expressions and other conduct.

(c) A "usage of trade" is any practice or method of dealing having such regularity of observance in a place, vocation, or trade as to justify an expectation that it will be observed with respect to the transaction in question. The existence and scope of such a usage must be proved as facts. If it is established that such a usage is embodied in a trade code or similar record, the interpretation of the record is a question of law.

(d) A course of performance or course of dealing between the parties or usage of trade in the vocation or trade in which they are engaged or of which they are or should be aware is relevant in ascertaining the meaning of the parties' agreement, may give particular meaning to specific terms of the agreement, and may supplement or qualify the terms of the agreement. A usage of trade applicable in the place in which part of the performance under the agreement is to occur may be so utilized as to that part of the performance.

(e) Except as otherwise provided in subsection (f), the express terms of an agreement and any applicable course of performance, course of dealing, or usage of trade must be construed whenever reasonable as consistent with each other. If such a construction is unreasonable:

(1) express terms prevail over course of performance, course of dealing, and usage of trade;

(2) course of performance prevails over course of dealing and usage of trade; and

(3) course of dealing prevails over usage of trade.

(f) Subject to Section 2–209 and Section 2A–208, a course of performance is relevant to show a waiver or modification of any term inconsistent with the course of performance.

(g) Evidence of a relevant usage of trade offered by one party is not admissible unless that party has given the other party notice that the court finds sufficient to prevent unfair surprise to the other party.

§ 1–304. Obligation of Good Faith.

Every contract or duty within [the Uniform Commercial Code] imposes an obligation of good faith in its performance and enforcement.

§ 1–305. Remedies to be Liberally Administered.

(a) The remedies provided by [the Uniform Commercial Code] must be liberally administered to the end that the aggrieved party may be put in as good a position as if the other party had fully performed but neither consequential or special damages nor penal damages may be had except as specifically provided in [the Uniform Commercial Code] or by other rule of law.

(b) Any right or obligation declared by [the Uniform Commercial Code] is enforceable by action unless the provision declaring it specifies a different and limited effect.

§ 1–306. Waiver or Renunciation of Claim or Right After Breach.

A claim or right arising out of an alleged breach may be discharged in whole or in part without consideration by agreement of the aggrieved party in an authenticated record.

§ 1–307. *Prima Facie* Evidence by Third-Party Documents.

A document in due form purporting to be a bill of lading, policy or certificate of insurance, official weigher's or inspector's certificate, consular invoice, or any other document authorized or required by the contract to be issued by a third party is *prima facie* evidence of its own authenticity and genuineness and of the facts stated in the document by the third party.

§ 1–308. Performance or Acceptance Under Reservation of Rights.

(a) A party that with explicit reservation of rights performs or promises performance or assents to performance in a manner demanded or offered by the other party does not thereby prejudice the rights reserved. Such words as "without prejudice," "under protest," or the like are sufficient.

(b) Subsection (a) does not apply to an accord and satisfaction.

§ 1–309. Option to Accelerate at Will.

A term providing that one party or that party's successor in interest may accelerate payment or performance or require collateral or additional collateral "at will" or when the party "deems itself insecure," or words of similar import, means that the party has power to do so only if that party in good faith believes that the prospect of payment or performance is impaired. The burden of establishing lack of good faith is on the party against which the power has been exercised.

§ 1–310. Subordinated Obligations.

An obligation may be issued as subordinated to performance of another obligation of the person obligated, or a creditor may subordinate its right to performance of an obligation by agreement with either the person obligated or another creditor of the person obligated. Subordination does not create a security interest as against either the common debtor or a subordinated creditor.

ARTICLE 2: SALES

Part 1—Short Title, General Construction and Subject Matter

§ 2–101. Short Title.

This Article shall be known and may be cited as Uniform Commercial Code—Sales.

§ 2–102. Scope; Certain Security and Other Transactions Excluded From This Article.

Unless the context otherwise requires, this Article applies to transactions in goods; it does not apply to any transaction which although in the form of an unconditional contract to sell or present sale is intended to operate only as a security transaction nor does this Article impair or repeal any statute regulating sales to consumers, farmers or other specified classes of buyers.

§ 2–103. Definitions and Index of Definitions.

(1) In this Article unless the context otherwise requires
    (a) "Buyer" means a person who buys or contracts to buy goods.
    (b) "Good faith" in the case of a merchant means honesty in fact and the observance of reasonable commercial standards of fair dealing in the trade.
    (c) "Receipt" of goods means taking physical possession of them.
    (d) "Seller" means a person who sells or contracts to sell goods.

(2) Other definitions applying to this Article or to specified Parts thereof, and the sections in which they appear are:
"Acceptance". Section 2–606.
"Banker's credit". Section 2–325.
"Between merchants". Section 2–104.
"Cancellation". Section 2–106(4).
"Commercial unit". Section 2–105.
"Confirmed credit". Section 2–325.
"Conforming to contract". Section 2–106.
"Contract for sale". Section 2–106.
"Cover". Section 2–712.
"Entrusting". Section 2–403.
"Financing agency". Section 2–104.
"Future goods". Section 2–105.
"Goods". Section 2–105.
"Identification". Section 2–501.
"Installment contract". Section 2–612.
"Letter of Credit". Section 2–325.
"Lot". Section 2–105.
"Merchant". Section 2–104.
"Overseas". Section 2–323.
"Person in position of seller". Section 2–707.
"Present sale". Section 2–106.
"Sale". Section 2–106.
"Sale on approval". Section 2–326.
"Sale or return". Section 2–326.
"Termination". Section 2–106.

(3) The following definitions in other Articles apply to this Article:
"Check". Section 3–104.
"Consignee". Section 7–102.
"Consignor". Section 7–102.
"Consumer goods". Section 9–109.
"Dishonor". Section 3–507.
"Draft". Section 3–104.

(4) In addition Article 1 contains general definitions and principles of construction and interpretation applicable throughout this Article.
As amended in 1994 and 1999.

§ 2–104. Definitions: "Merchant"; "Between Merchants"; "Financing Agency".

(1) "Merchant" means a person who deals in goods of the kind or otherwise by his occupation holds himself out as having knowledge or skill peculiar to the practices or goods involved in the transaction or to whom such knowledge or skill may be attributed by his employment of an agent or broker or other intermediary who by his occupation holds himself out as having such knowledge or skill.

(2) "Financing agency" means a bank, finance company or other person who in the ordinary course of business makes advances against goods or documents of title or who by arrangement with either the seller or the buyer intervenes in ordinary course to make or collect payment due or claimed under the contract for sale, as by purchasing or paying the seller's draft or making advances against it or by merely taking it for collection whether or not documents of title accompany the draft. "Financing agency" includes also a bank or other person who similarly intervenes between persons who are in the position of seller and buyer in respect to the goods (Section 2–707).

(3) "Between merchants" means in any transaction with respect to which both parties are chargeable with the knowledge or skill of merchants.

§ 2–105. Definitions: Transferability; "Goods"; "Future" Goods; "Lot"; "Commercial Unit".

(1) "Goods" means all things (including specially manufactured goods) which are movable at the time of identification to the contract for sale other than the money in which the price is to be paid, investment securities (Article 8) and things in action. "Goods" also includes the unborn young of animals and growing crops and other identified things attached to realty as described in the section on goods to be severed from realty (Section 2–107).

(2) Goods must be both existing and identified before any interest in them can pass. Goods which are not both existing and identified are "future" goods. A purported present sale of future goods or of any interest therein operates as a contract to sell.

(3) There may be a sale of a part interest in existing identified goods.

(4) An undivided share in an identified bulk of fungible goods is sufficiently identified to be sold although the quantity of the bulk is not determined. Any agreed proportion of such a bulk or any quantity thereof agreed upon by number, weight or other measure may to the extent of the seller's interest in the bulk be sold to the buyer who then becomes an owner in common.

(5) "Lot" means a parcel or a single article which is the subject matter of a separate sale or delivery, whether or not it is sufficient to perform the contract.

(6) "Commercial unit" means such a unit of goods as by commercial usage is a single whole for purposes of sale and division of which materially impairs its character or value on the market or in use. A commercial unit may be a single article (as a machine) or a set of articles (as a suite of furniture or an assortment of sizes) or a quantity (as a bale, gross, or carload) or any other unit treated in use or in the relevant market as a single whole.

§ 2–106. Definitions: "Contract"; "Agreement"; "Contract for Sale"; "Sale"; "Present Sale"; "Conforming" to Contract; "Termination"; "Cancellation".

(1) In this Article unless the context otherwise requires "contract" and "agreement" are limited to those relating to the present or future sale of goods. "Contract for sale" includes both a present sale of goods and a contract to sell goods at a future time. A "sale" consists in the passing of title from the seller to the buyer for a price (Section 2–401). A "present sale" means a sale which is accomplished by the making of the contract.

(2) Goods or conduct including any part of a performance are "conforming" or conform to the contract when they are in accordance with the obligations under the contract.

(3) "Termination" occurs when either party pursuant to a power created by agreement or law puts an end to the contract otherwise than for its breach. On "termination" all obligations which are still executory on both sides are discharged but any right based on prior breach or performance survives.

(4) "Cancellation" occurs when either party puts an end to the contract for breach by the other and its effect is the same as that of "termination" except that the cancelling party also retains any remedy for breach of the whole contract or any unperformed balance.

§ 2–107. Goods to Be Severed From Realty: Recording.

(1) A contract for the sale of minerals or the like (including oil and gas) or a structure or its materials to be removed from realty is a contract for the sale of goods within this Article if they are to be severed by the seller but until severance a purported present sale thereof which is not effective as a transfer of an interest in land is effective only as a contract to sell.

(2) A contract for the sale apart from the land of growing crops or other things attached to realty and capable of severance without material harm thereto but not described in subsection (1) or of timber to be cut is a contract for the sale of goods within this Article whether the subject matter is to be severed by the buyer or by the seller even though it forms part of the realty at the time of contracting, and the parties can by identification effect a present sale before severance.

(3) The provisions of this section are subject to any third party rights provided by the law relating to realty records, and the contract for sale may be executed and recorded as a document transferring an interest in land and shall then constitute notice to third parties of the buyer's rights under the contract for sale.
As amended in 1972.

Part 2—Form, Formation and Readjustment of Contract

§ 2–201. Formal Requirements; Statute of Frauds.

(1) Except as otherwise provided in this section a contract for the sale of goods for the price of $500 or more is not enforceable by way of action or defense unless there is some writing sufficient to indicate that a contract for sale has been made between the parties and signed by the party against whom enforcement is sought or by his authorized agent or broker. A writing is not insufficient because it omits or incorrectly states a term agreed upon but the contract is not enforceable under this paragraph beyond the quantity of goods shown in such writing.

(2) Between merchants if within a reasonable time a writing in confirmation of the contract and sufficient against the sender is received and the party receiving it has reason to know its contents, its satisfies the requirements of subsection (1) against such party unless written notice of objection to its contents is given within ten days after it is received.

(3) A contract which does not satisfy the requirements of subsection (1) but which is valid in other respects is enforceable

    (a) if the goods are to be specially manufactured for the buyer and are not suitable for sale to others in the ordinary course of the seller's business and the seller, before notice of repudiation is received and under circumstances which reasonably indicate that the goods are for the buyer, has made either a substantial beginning of their manufacture or commitments for their procurement; or

    (b) if the party against whom enforcement is sought admits in his pleading, testimony or otherwise in court that a contract for sale was made, but the contract is not enforceable under this provision beyond the quantity of goods admitted; or

    (c) with respect to goods for which payment has been made and accepted or which have been received and accepted (Sec. 2–606).

§ 2–202. Final Written Expression: Parol or Extrinsic Evidence.

Terms with respect to which the confirmatory memoranda of the parties agree or which are otherwise set forth in a writing intended by the parties as a final expression of their agreement with respect to such terms as are included therein may not be contradicted by evidence of any prior agreement or of a contemporaneous oral agreement but may be explained or supplemented

    (a) by course of dealing or usage of trade (Section 1–205) or by course of performance (Section 2–208); and

    (b) by evidence of consistent additional terms unless the court finds the writing to have been intended also as a complete and exclusive statement of the terms of the agreement.

§ 2–203. Seals Inoperative.

The affixing of a seal to a writing evidencing a contract for sale or an offer to buy or sell goods does not constitute the writing a sealed instrument and the law with respect to sealed instruments does not apply to such a contract or offer.

§ 2–204. Formation in General.

(1) A contract for sale of goods may be made in any manner sufficient to show agreement, including conduct by both parties which recognizes the existence of such a contract.

(2) An agreement sufficient to constitute a contract for sale may be found even though the moment of its making is undetermined.

(3) Even though one or more terms are left open a contract for sale does not fail for indefiniteness if the parties have intended to make a contract and there is a reasonably certain basis for giving an appropriate remedy.

§ 2–205. Firm Offers.

An offer by a merchant to buy or sell goods in a signed writing which by its terms gives assurance that it will be held open is not revocable, for lack of consideration, during the time stated or if no time is stated for a reasonable time, but in no event may such period of irrevocability exceed three months; but any such term of assurance on a form supplied by the offeree must be separately signed by the offeror.

§ 2–206. Offer and Acceptance in Formation of Contract.

(1) Unless other unambiguously indicated by the language or circumstances

    (a) an offer to make a contract shall be construed as inviting acceptance in any manner and by any medium reasonable in the circumstances;

    (b) an order or other offer to buy goods for prompt or current shipment shall be construed as inviting acceptance either by a prompt promise to ship or by the prompt or current shipment of conforming or nonconforming goods, but such a shipment of non-conforming goods does not constitute an acceptance if the seller seasonably notifies the buyer that the shipment is offered only as an accommodation to the buyer.

(2) Where the beginning of a requested performance is a reasonable mode of acceptance an offeror who is not notified of acceptance within a reasonable time may treat the offer as having lapsed before acceptance.

§ 2–207. Additional Terms in Acceptance or Confirmation.

(1) A definite and seasonable expression of acceptance or a written confirmation which is sent within a reasonable time operates as an acceptance even though it states terms additional to or different from those offered or agreed upon, unless acceptance is expressly made conditional on assent to the additional or different terms.

(2) The additional terms are to be construed as proposals for addition to the contract. Between merchants such terms become part of the contract unless:

    (a) the offer expressly limits acceptance to the terms of the offer;

    (b) they materially alter it; or

    (c) notification of objection to them has already been given or is given within a reasonable time after notice of them is received.

(3) Conduct by both parties which recognizes the existence of a contract is sufficient to establish a contract for sale although the writings of the parties do not otherwise establish a contract. In such case the terms of the particular contract consist of those terms on which the writings of the parties agree, together with any supplementary terms incorporated under any other provisions of this Act.

§ 2–208. Course of Performance or Practical Construction.

(1) Where the contract for sale involves repeated occasions for performance by either party with knowledge of the nature of the performance and opportunity for objection to it by the other, any course of performance accepted or acquiesced in without objection shall be relevant to determine the meaning of the agreement.

(2) The express terms of the agreement and any such course of performance, as well as any course of dealing and usage of trade, shall be construed whenever reasonable as consistent with each other; but when such construction is unreasonable, express terms shall control course of performance and course of performance shall control both course of dealing and usage of trade (Section 1–205).

(3) Subject to the provisions of the next section on modification and waiver, such course of performance shall be relevant to show a waiver or modification of any term inconsistent with such course of performance.

§ 2–209. Modification, Rescission and Waiver.

(1) An agreement modifying a contract within this Article needs no consideration to be binding.

(2) A signed agreement which excludes modification or rescission except by a signed writing cannot be otherwise modified or rescinded, but except as between merchants such a requirement on a form supplied by the merchant must be separately signed by the other party.

(3) The requirements of the statute of frauds section of this Article (Section 2–201) must be satisfied if the contract as modified is within its provisions.

(4) Although an attempt at modification or rescission does not satisfy the requirements of subsection (2) or (3) it can operate as a waiver.

(5) A party who has made a waiver affecting an executory portion of the contract may retract the waiver by reasonable notification received by the other party that strict performance will be required of any term waived, unless the retraction would be unjust in view of a material change of position in reliance on the waiver.

§ 2–210. Delegation of Performance; Assignment of Rights.

(1) A party may perform his duty through a delegate unless otherwise agreed or unless the other party has a substantial interest in having his original promisor perform or control the acts required by the contract. No delegation of performance relieves the party delegating of any duty to perform or any liability for breach.

(2) Except as otherwise provided in Section 9–406, unless otherwise agreed, all rights of either seller or buyer can be assigned except where the assignment would materially change the duty of the other party, or increase materially the burden or risk imposed on him by his contract, or impair materially his chance of obtaining return performance. A right to damages for breach of the whole contract or a right arising out of the assignor's due performance of his entire obligation can be assigned despite agreement otherwise.

(3) The creation, attachment, perfection, or enforcement of a security interest in the seller's interest under a contract is not a transfer that materially changes the duty of or increases materially the burden or risk imposed on the buyer or impairs materially the buyer's chance of obtaining return performance within the purview of subsection (2) unless, and then only to the extent that, enforcement actually results in a delegation of material performance of the seller. Even in that event, the creation, attachment, perfection, and enforcement of the security interest remain effective, but (i) the seller is liable to the buyer for damages caused by the delegation to the extent that the damages could not reasonably by prevented by the buyer, and (ii) a court having jurisdiction may grant other appropriate relief, including cancellation of the contract for sale or an injunction against enforcement of the security interest or consummation of the enforcement.

(4) Unless the circumstances indicate the contrary a prohibition of assignment of "the contract" is to be construed as barring only the delegation to the assignee of the assignor's performance.

(5) An assignment of "the contract" or of "all my rights under the contract" or an assignment in similar general terms is an assignment of rights and unless the language or the circumstances (as in an assignment for security) indicate the contrary, it is a delegation of performance of the duties of the assignor and its acceptance by the assignee constitutes a promise by him to perform those duties. This promise is enforceable by either the assignor or the other party to the original contract.

(6) The other party may treat any assignment which delegates performance as creating reasonable grounds for insecurity and may without prejudice to his rights against the assignor demand assurances from the assignee (Section 2–609).

As amended in 1999.

Part 3—General Obligation and Construction of Contract

§ 2–301. General Obligations of Parties.

The obligation of the seller is to transfer and deliver and that of the buyer is to accept and pay in accordance with the contract.

§ 2–302. Unconscionable Contract or Clause.

(1) If the court as a matter of law finds the contract or any clause of the contract to have been unconscionable at the time it was made the court may refuse to enforce the contract, or it may enforce the remainder of the contract without the unconscionable clause, or it may so limit the application of any unconscionable clause as to avoid any unconscionable result.

(2) When it is claimed or appears to the court that the contract or any clause thereof may be unconscionable the parties shall be afforded a reasonable opportunity to present evidence as to its commercial setting, purpose and effect to aid the court in making the determination.

§ 2–303. Allocations or Division of Risks.

Where this Article allocates a risk or a burden as between the parties "unless otherwise agreed", the agreement may not only shift the allocation but may also divide the risk or burden.

§ 2–304. Price Payable in Money, Goods, Realty, or Otherwise.

(1) The price can be made payable in money or otherwise. If it is payable in whole or in part in goods each party is a seller of the goods which he is to transfer.

(2) Even though all or part of the price is payable in an interest in realty the transfer of the goods and the seller's obligations with reference to them are subject to this Article, but not the transfer of the interest in realty or the transferor's obligations in connection therewith.

§ 2–305. Open Price Term.

(1) The parties if they so intend can conclude a contract for sale even though the price is not settled. In such a case the price is a reasonable price at the time for delivery if
   (a) nothing is said as to price; or
   (b) the price is left to be agreed by the parties and they fail to agree; or
   (c) the price is to be fixed in terms of some agreed market or other standard as set or recorded by a third person or agency and it is not so set or recorded.

(2) A price to be fixed by the seller or by the buyer means a price for him to fix in good faith.

(3) When a price left to be fixed otherwise than by agreement of the parties fails to be fixed through fault of one party the other may at his option treat the contract as cancelled or himself fix a reasonable price.

(4) Where, however, the parties intend not to be bound unless the price be fixed or agreed and it is not fixed or agreed there is no contract. In such a case the buyer must return any goods already received or if unable so to do must pay their reasonable value at the time of delivery and the seller must return any portion of the price paid on account.

§ 2–306. Output, Requirements and Exclusive Dealings.

(1) A term which measures the quantity by the output of the seller or the requirements of the buyer means such actual output or requirements as may occur in good faith, except that no quantity unreasonably disproportionate to any stated estimate or in the absence of a stated estimate to any normal or otherwise comparable prior output or requirements may be tendered or demanded.

(2) A lawful agreement by either the seller or the buyer for exclusive dealing in the kind of goods concerned imposes unless otherwise agreed an obligation by the seller to use best efforts to supply the goods and by the buyer to use best efforts to promote their sale.

§ 2–307. Delivery in Single Lot or Several Lots.

Unless otherwise agreed all goods called for by a contract for sale must be tendered in a single delivery and payment is due only on such tender but where the circumstances give either party the right to make or demand delivery in lots the price if it can be apportioned may be demanded for each lot.

§ 2–308. Absence of Specified Place for Delivery.

Unless otherwise agreed
   (a) the place for delivery of goods is the seller's place of business or if he has none his residence; but
   (b) in a contract for sale of identified goods which to the knowledge of the parties at the time of contracting are in some other place, that place is the place for their delivery; and
   (c) documents of title may be delivered through customary banking channels.

§ 2–309. Absence of Specific Time Provisions; Notice of Termination.

(1) The time for shipment or delivery or any other action under a contract if not provided in this Article or agreed upon shall be a reasonable time.

(2) Where the contract provides for successive performances but is indefinite in duration it is valid for a reasonable time but unless otherwise agreed may be terminated at any time by either party.

(3) Termination of a contract by one party except on the happening of an agreed event requires that reasonable notification be received by the other party and an agreement dispensing with notification is invalid if its operation would be unconscionable.

§ 2–310. Open Time for Payment or Running of Credit; Authority to Ship Under Reservation.

Unless otherwise agreed
   (a) payment is due at the time and place at which the buyer is to receive the goods even though the place of shipment is the place of delivery; and
   (b) if the seller is authorized to send the goods he may ship them under reservation, and may tender the documents of title, but the buyer may inspect the goods after their arrival before payment is due unless such inspection is inconsistent with the terms of the contract (Section 2–513); and
   (c) if delivery is authorized and made by way of documents of title otherwise than by subsection (b) then payment is due at the time and place at which the buyer is to receive the documents regardless of where the goods are to be received; and
   (d) where the seller is required or authorized to ship the goods on credit the credit period runs from the time of shipment but post-dating the invoice or delaying its dispatch will correspondingly delay the starting of the credit period.

§ 2–311. Options and Cooperation Respecting Performance.

(1) An agreement for sale which is otherwise sufficiently definite (subsection (3) of Section 2–204) to be a contract is not made invalid by the fact that it leaves particulars of performance to be specified by one of the parties. Any such specification must be made in good faith and within limits set by commercial reasonableness.

(2) Unless otherwise agreed specifications relating to assortment of the goods are at the buyer's option and except as otherwise provided in subsections (1)(c) and (3) of Section 2–319 specifications or arrangements relating to shipment are at the seller's option.

(3) Where such specification would materially affect the other party's performance but is not seasonably made or where one party's cooperation is necessary to the agreed performance of the other but is not seasonably forthcoming, the other party in addition to all other remedies

(a) is excused for any resulting delay in his own performance; and

(b) may also either proceed to perform in any reasonable manner or after the time for a material part of his own performance treat the failure to specify or to cooperate as a breach by failure to deliver or accept the goods.

§ 2–312. Warranty of Title and Against Infringement; Buyer's Obligation Against Infringement.

(1) Subject to subsection (2) there is in a contract for sale a warranty by the seller that

(a) the title conveyed shall be good, and its transfer rightful; and

(b) the goods shall be delivered free from any security interest or other lien or encumbrance of which the buyer at the time of contracting has no knowledge.

(2) A warranty under subsection (1) will be excluded or modified only by specific language or by circumstances which give the buyer reason to know that the person selling does not claim title in himself or that he is purporting to sell only such right or title as he or a third person may have.

(3) Unless otherwise agreed a seller who is a merchant regularly dealing in goods of the kind warrants that the goods shall be delivered free of the rightful claim of any third person by way of infringement or the like but a buyer who furnishes specifications to the seller must hold the seller harmless against any such claim which arises out of compliance with the specifications.

§ 2–313. Express Warranties by Affirmation, Promise, Description, Sample.

(1) Express warranties by the seller are created as follows:

(a) Any affirmation of fact or promise made by the seller to the buyer which relates to the goods and becomes part of the basis of the bargain creates an express warranty that the goods shall conform to the affirmation or promise.

(b) Any description of the goods which is made part of the basis of the bargain creates an express warranty that the goods shall conform to the description.

(c) Any sample or model which is made part of the basis of the bargain creates an express warranty that the whole of the goods shall conform to the sample or model.

(2) It is not necessary to the creation of an express warranty that the seller use formal words such as "warrant" or "guarantee" or that he have a specific intention to make a warranty, but an affirmation merely of the value of the goods or a statement purporting to be merely the seller's opinion or commendation of the goods does not create a warranty.

§ 2–314. Implied Warranty: Merchantability; Usage of Trade.

(1) Unless excluded or modified (Section 2–316), a warranty that the goods shall be merchantable is implied in a contract for their sale if the seller is a merchant with respect to goods of that kind. Under this section the serving for value of food or drink to be consumed either on the premises or elsewhere is a sale.

(2) Goods to be merchantable must be at least such as

(a) pass without objection in the trade under the contract description; and

(b) in the case of fungible goods, are of fair average quality within the description; and

(c) are fit for the ordinary purposes for which such goods are used; and

(d) run, within the variations permitted by the agreement, of even kind, quality and quantity within each unit and among all units involved; and

(e) are adequately contained, packaged, and labeled as the agreement may require; and

(f) conform to the promises or affirmations of fact made on the container or label if any.

(3) Unless excluded or modified (Section 2–316) other implied warranties may arise from course of dealing or usage of trade.

§ 2–315. Implied Warranty: Fitness for Particular Purpose.

Where the seller at the time of contracting has reason to know any particular purpose for which the goods are required and that the buyer is relying on the seller's skill or judgment to select or furnish suitable goods, there is unless excluded or modified under the next section an implied warranty that the goods shall be fit for such purpose.

§ 2–316. Exclusion or Modification of Warranties.

(1) Words or conduct relevant to the creation of an express warranty and words or conduct tending to negate or limit warranty shall be construed wherever reasonable as consistent with each other; but subject to the provisions of this Article on parol or extrinsic evidence (Section 2–202) negation or limitation is inoperative to the extent that such construction is unreasonable.

(2) Subject to subsection (3), to exclude or modify the implied warranty of merchantability or any part of it the language must mention merchantability and in case of a writing must be conspicuous, and to exclude or modify any implied warranty of fitness the exclusion must be by a writing and conspicuous. Language to exclude all implied warranties of fitness is sufficient if it states, for example, that "There are no warranties which extend beyond the description on the face hereof."

(3) Notwithstanding subsection (2)

(a) unless the circumstances indicate otherwise, all implied warranties are excluded by expressions like "as is", "with all faults" or other language which in common understanding calls the buyer's attention to the exclusion of warranties and makes plain that there is no implied warranty; and

(b) when the buyer before entering into the contract has examined the goods or the sample or model as fully as he desired or has refused to examine the goods there is no implied warranty with regard to defects which an examination ought in the circumstances to have revealed to him; and

(c) an implied warranty can also be excluded or modified by course of dealing or course of performance or usage of trade.

(4) Remedies for breach of warranty can be limited in accordance with the provisions of this Article on liquidation or limitation of damages and on contractual modification of remedy (Sections 2–718 and 2–719).

§ 2–317. Cumulation and Conflict of Warranties Express or Implied.

Warranties whether express or implied shall be construed as consistent with each other and as cumulative, but if such construction is unreasonable the intention of the parties shall determine which warranty is dominant. In ascertaining that intention the following rules apply:

(a) Exact or technical specifications displace an inconsistent sample or model or general language of description.

(b) A sample from an existing bulk displaces inconsistent general language of description.

(c) Express warranties displace inconsistent implied warranties other than an implied warranty of fitness for a particular purpose.

§ 2–318. Third Party Beneficiaries of Warranties Express or Implied.

Note: If this Act is introduced in the Congress of the United States this section should be omitted. (States to select one alternative.)

Alternative A

A seller's warranty whether express or implied extends to any natural person who is in the family or household of his buyer or who is a guest in his home if it is reasonable to expect that such person may use, consume or be affected by the goods and who is injured in person by breach of the warranty. A seller may not exclude or limit the operation of this section.

Alternative B

A seller's warranty whether express or implied extends to any natural person who may reasonably be expected to use, consume or be affected by the goods and who is injured in person by breach of the warranty. A seller may not exclude or limit the operation of this section.

Alternative C

A seller's warranty whether express or implied extends to any person who may reasonably be expected to use, consume or be affected by the goods and who is injured by breach of the warranty. A seller may not exclude or limit the operation of this section with respect to injury to the person of an individual to whom the warranty extends. As amended 1966.

§ 2–319. F.O.B. and F.A.S. Terms.

(1) Unless otherwise agreed the term F.O.B. (which means "free on board") at a named place, even though used only in connection with the stated price, is a delivery term under which

(a) when the term is F.O.B. the place of shipment, the seller must at that place ship the goods in the manner provided in this Article (Section 2–504) and bear the expense and risk of putting them into the possession of the carrier; or

(b) when the term is F.O.B. the place of destination, the seller must at his own expense and risk transport the goods to that place and there tender delivery of them in the manner provided in this Article (Section 2–503);

(c) when under either (a) or (b) the term is also F.O.B. vessel, car or other vehicle, the seller must in addition at his own expense and risk load the goods on board. If the term is F.O.B. vessel the buyer must name the vessel and in an appropriate case the seller must comply with the provisions of this Article on the form of bill of lading (Section 2–323).

(2) Unless otherwise agreed the term F.A.S. vessel (which means "free alongside") at a named port, even though used only in connection with the stated price, is a delivery term under which the seller must

(a) at his own expense and risk deliver the goods alongside the vessel in the manner usual in that port or on a dock designated and provided by the buyer; and

(b) obtain and tender a receipt for the goods in exchange for which the carrier is under a duty to issue a bill of lading.

(3) Unless otherwise agreed in any case falling within subsection (1)(a) or (c) or subsection (2) the buyer must seasonably give any needed instructions for making delivery, including when the term is F.A.S. or F.O.B. the loading berth of the vessel and in an appropriate case its name and sailing date. The seller may treat the failure of needed instructions as a failure of cooperation under this Article (Section 2–311). He may also at his option move the goods in any reasonable manner preparatory to delivery or shipment.

(4) Under the term F.O.B. vessel or F.A.S. unless otherwise agreed the buyer must make payment against tender of the required documents and the seller may not tender nor the buyer demand delivery of the goods in substitution for the documents.

§ 2–320. C.I.F. and C. & F. Terms.

(1) The term C.I.F. means that the price includes in a lump sum the cost of the goods and the insurance and freight to the named destination. The term C. & F. or C.F. means that the price so includes cost and freight to the named destination.

(2) Unless otherwise agreed and even though used only in connection with the stated price and destination, the term C.I.F. destination or its equivalent requires the seller at his own expense and risk to

(a) put the goods into the possession of a carrier at the port for shipment and obtain a negotiable bill or bills of lading covering the entire transportation to the named destination; and

(b) load the goods and obtain a receipt from the carrier (which may be contained in the bill of lading) showing that the freight has been paid or provided for; and

(c) obtain a policy or certificate of insurance, including any war risk insurance, of a kind and on terms then current at the port of shipment in the usual amount, in the currency of the contract, shown to cover the same goods covered by the bill of lading and providing for payment of loss to the order of the buyer or for the account of whom it may concern; but the seller may add to the price the amount of the premium for any such war risk insurance; and

(d) prepare an invoice of the goods and procure any other documents required to effect shipment or to comply with the contract; and

(e) forward and tender with commercial promptness all the documents in due form and with any indorsement necessary to perfect the buyer's rights.

(3) Unless otherwise agreed the term C. & F. or its equivalent has the same effect and imposes upon the seller the same obligations and risks as a C.I.F. term except the obligation as to insurance.

(4) Under the term C.I.F. or C. & F. unless otherwise agreed the buyer must make payment against tender of the required documents and the seller may not tender nor the buyer demand delivery of the goods in substitution for the documents.

§ 2–321. C.I.F. or C. & F.: "Net Landed Weights"; "Payment on Arrival"; Warranty of Condition on Arrival.

Under a contract containing a term C.I.F. or C. & F.

(1) Where the price is based on or is to be adjusted according to "net landed weights", "delivered weights", "out turn" quantity or quality or the like, unless otherwise agreed the seller must reasonably estimate the price. The payment due on tender of the documents called for by the contract is the amount so estimated, but after final adjustment of the price a settlement must be made with commercial promptness.

(2) An agreement described in subsection (1) or any warranty of quality or condition of the goods on arrival places upon the seller the risk of ordinary deterioration, shrinkage and the like in transportation but has no effect on the place or time of identification to the contract for sale or delivery or on the passing of the risk of loss.

(3) Unless otherwise agreed where the contract provides for payment on or after arrival of the goods the seller must before payment allow such preliminary inspection as is feasible; but if the goods are lost delivery of the documents and payment are due when the goods should have arrived.

§ 2–322. Delivery "Ex-Ship".

(1) Unless otherwise agreed a term for delivery of goods "ex-ship" (which means from the carrying vessel) or in equivalent language is not restricted to a particular ship and requires delivery from a ship which has reached a place at the named port of destination where goods of the kind are usually discharged.

(2) Under such a term unless otherwise agreed

    (a) the seller must discharge all liens arising out of the carriage and furnish the buyer with a direction which puts the carrier under a duty to deliver the goods; and

    (b) the risk of loss does not pass to the buyer until the goods leave the ship's tackle or are otherwise properly unloaded.

§ 2–323. Form of Bill of Lading Required in Overseas Shipment; "Overseas".

(1) Where the contract contemplates overseas shipment and contains a term C.I.F. or C. & F. or F.O.B. vessel, the seller unless otherwise agreed must obtain a negotiable bill of lading stating that the goods have been loaded on board or, in the case of a term C.I.F. or C. & F., received for shipment.

(2) Where in a case within subsection (1) a bill of lading has been issued in a set of parts, unless otherwise agreed if the documents are not to be sent from abroad the buyer may demand tender of the full set; otherwise only one part of the bill of lading need be tendered. Even if the agreement expressly requires a full set

    (a) due tender of a single part is acceptable within the provisions of this Article on cure of improper delivery (subsection (1) of Section 2–508); and

    (b) even though the full set is demanded, if the documents are sent from abroad the person tendering an incomplete set may nevertheless require payment upon furnishing an indemnity which the buyer in good faith deems adequate.

(3) A shipment by water or by air or a contract contemplating such shipment is "overseas" insofar as by usage of trade or agreement it is subject to the commercial, financing or shipping practices characteristic of international deep water commerce.

§ 2–324. "No Arrival, No Sale" Term.

Under a term "no arrival, no sale" or terms of like meaning, unless otherwise agreed,

    (a) the seller must properly ship conforming goods and if they arrive by any means he must tender them on arrival but he assumes no obligation that the goods will arrive unless he has caused the non-arrival; and

    (b) where without fault of the seller the goods are in part lost or have so deteriorated as no longer to conform to the contract or arrive after the contract time, the buyer may proceed as if there had been casualty to identified goods (Section 2–613).

§ 2–325. "Letter of Credit" Term; "Confirmed Credit".

(1) Failure of the buyer seasonably to furnish an agreed letter of credit is a breach of the contract for sale.

(2) The delivery to seller of a proper letter of credit suspends the buyer's obligation to pay. If the letter of credit is dishonored, the seller may on seasonable notification to the buyer require payment directly from him.

(3) Unless otherwise agreed the term "letter of credit" or "banker's credit" in a contract for sale means an irrevocable credit issued by a financing agency of good repute and, where the shipment is overseas, of good international repute. The term "confirmed credit" means that the credit must also carry the direct obligation of such an agency which does business in the seller's financial market.

§ 2–326. Sale on Approval and Sale or Return; Rights of Creditors.

(1) Unless otherwise agreed, if delivered goods may be returned by the buyer even though they conform to the contract, the transaction is

    (a) a "sale on approval" if the goods are delivered primarily for use, and

    (b) a "sale or return" if the goods are delivered primarily for resale.

(2) Goods held on approval are not subject to the claims of the buyer's creditors until acceptance; goods held on sale or return are subject to such claims while in the buyer's possession.

(3) Any "or return" term of a contract for sale is to be treated as a separate contract for sale within the statute of frauds section of this Article (Section 2–201) and as contradicting the sale aspect of the contract within the provisions of this Article or on parol or extrinsic evidence (Section 2–202).

As amended in 1999.

§ 2–327. Special Incidents of Sale on Approval and Sale or Return.

(1) Under a sale on approval unless otherwise agreed

    (a) although the goods are identified to the contract the risk of loss and the title do not pass to the buyer until acceptance; and

    (b) use of the goods consistent with the purpose of trial is not acceptance but failure seasonably to notify the seller of election to return the goods is acceptance, and if the goods conform to the contract acceptance of any part is acceptance of the whole; and

    (c) after due notification of election to return, the return is at the seller's risk and expense but a merchant buyer must follow any reasonable instructions.

(2) Under a sale or return unless otherwise agreed

    (a) the option to return extends to the whole or any commercial unit of the goods while in substantially their original condition, but must be exercised seasonably; and

    (b) the return is at the buyer's risk and expense.

§ 2–328. Sale by Auction.

(1) In a sale by auction if goods are put up in lots each lot is the subject of a separate sale.

(2) A sale by auction is complete when the auctioneer so announces by the fall of the hammer or in other customary manner. Where a bid is made while the hammer is falling in acceptance of a prior bid the auctioneer may in his discretion reopen the bidding or declare the goods sold under the bid on which the hammer was falling.

(3) Such a sale is with reserve unless the goods are in explicit terms put up without reserve. In an auction with reserve the auctioneer may withdraw the goods at any time until he announces completion of the sale. In an auction without reserve, after the auctioneer calls for bids on an article or lot, that article or lot cannot be withdrawn unless no bid is made within a reasonable time. In either case a bidder may retract his bid until the auctioneer's announcement of completion of the sale, but a bidder's retraction does not revive any previous bid.

(4) If the auctioneer knowingly receives a bid on the seller's behalf or the seller makes or procures such as bid, and notice has not been given that liberty for such bidding is reserved, the buyer may at his option avoid the sale or take the goods at the price of the last good faith bid prior to the completion of the sale. This subsection shall not apply to any bid at a forced sale.

Part 4—Title, Creditors and Good Faith Purchasers

§ 2–401. Passing of Title; Reservation for Security; Limited Application of This Section.

Each provision of this Article with regard to the rights, obligations and remedies of the seller, the buyer, purchasers or other third parties applies irrespective of title to the goods except where the provision refers to such title. Insofar as situations are not covered by the other provisions of this Article and matters concerning title became material the following rules apply:

(1) Title to goods cannot pass under a contract for sale prior to their identification to the contract (Section 2–501), and unless otherwise explicitly agreed the buyer acquires by their identification a special property as limited by this Act. Any retention or reservation by the seller of the title (property) in goods shipped or delivered to the buyer is limited in effect to a reservation of a security interest. Subject to these provisions and to the provisions of the Article on Secured Transactions (Article 9), title to goods passes from the seller to the buyer in any manner and on any conditions explicitly agreed on by the parties.

(2) Unless otherwise explicitly agreed title passes to the buyer at the time and place at which the seller completes his performance with reference to the physical delivery of the goods, despite any reservation of a security interest and even though a document of title is to be delivered at a different time or place; and in particular and despite any reservation of a security interest by the bill of lading

    (a) if the contract requires or authorizes the seller to send the goods to the buyer but does not require him to deliver them at destination, title passes to the buyer at the time and place of shipment; but

    (b) if the contract requires delivery at destination, title passes on tender there.

(3) Unless otherwise explicitly agreed where delivery is to be made without moving the goods,

    (a) if the seller is to deliver a document of title, title passes at the time when and the place where he delivers such documents; or

    (b) if the goods are at the time of contracting already identified and no documents are to be delivered, title passes at the time and place of contracting.

(4) A rejection or other refusal by the buyer to receive or retain the goods, whether or not justified, or a justified revocation of acceptance revests title to the goods in the seller. Such revesting occurs by operation of law and is not a "sale".

§ 2–402. Rights of Seller's Creditors Against Sold Goods.

(1) Except as provided in subsections (2) and (3), rights of unsecured creditors of the seller with respect to goods which have been identified to a contract for sale are subject to the buyer's rights to recover the goods under this Article (Sections 2–502 and 2–716).

(2) A creditor of the seller may treat a sale or an identification of goods to a contract for sale as void if as against him a retention of possession by the seller is fraudulent under any rule of law of the state where the goods are situated, except that retention of possession in good faith and current course of trade by a merchant-seller for a commercially reasonable time after a sale or identification is not fraudulent.

(3) Nothing in this Article shall be deemed to impair the rights of creditors of the seller

    (a) under the provisions of the Article on Secured Transactions (Article 9); or

    (b) where identification to the contract or delivery is made not in current course of trade but in satisfaction of or as security for a pre-existing claim for money, security or the like and is made under circumstances which under any rule of law of the state where the goods are situated would apart from this Article constitute the transaction a fraudulent transfer or voidable preference.

§ 2–403. Power to Transfer; Good Faith Purchase of Goods; "Entrusting".

(1) A purchaser of goods acquires all title which his transferor had or had power to transfer except that a purchaser of a limited interest acquires rights only to the extent of the interest purchased. A person with voidable title has power to transfer a good title to a good faith purchaser for value. When goods have been delivered under a transaction of purchase the purchaser has such power even though

    (a) the transferor was deceived as to the identity of the purchaser, or

    (b) the delivery was in exchange for a check which is later dishonored, or

    (c) it was agreed that the transaction was to be a "cash sale", or

    (d) the delivery was procured through fraud punishable as larcenous under the criminal law.

(2) Any entrusting of possession of goods to a merchant who deals in goods of that kind gives him power to transfer all rights of the entruster to a buyer in ordinary course of business.

(3) "Entrusting" includes any delivery and any acquiescence in retention of possession regardless of any condition expressed between the parties to the delivery or acquiescence and regardless of whether the procurement of the entrusting or the possessor's disposition of the goods have been such as to be larcenous under the criminal law.

(4) The rights of other purchasers of goods and of lien creditors are governed by the Articles on Secured Transactions (Article 9), Bulk Transfers (Article 6) and Documents of Title (Article 7).

As amended in 1988.

Part 5—Performance

§ 2–501. Insurable Interest in Goods; Manner of Identification of Goods.

(1) The buyer obtains a special property and an insurable interest in goods by identification of existing goods as goods to which the contract refers even though the goods so identified are non-conforming and he has an option to return or reject them. Such identification can be made at any time and in any manner explicitly agreed to by the parties. In the absence of explicit agreement identification occurs

(a) when the contract is made if it is for the sale of goods already existing and identified;

(b) if the contract is for the sale of future goods other than those described in paragraph (c), when goods are shipped, marked or otherwise designated by the seller as goods to which the contract refers;

(c) when the crops are planted or otherwise become growing crops or the young are conceived if the contract is for the sale of unborn young to be born within twelve months after contracting or for the sale of crops to be harvested within twelve months or the next normal harvest season after contracting whichever is longer.

(2) The seller retains an insurable interest in goods so long as title to or any security interest in the goods remains in him and where the identification is by the seller alone he may until default or insolvency or notification to the buyer that the identification is final substitute other goods for those identified.

(3) Nothing in this section impairs any insurable interest recognized under any other statute or rule of law.

§ 2–502. Buyer's Right to Goods on Seller's Insolvency.

(1) Subject to subsections (2) and (3) and even though the goods have not been shipped a buyer who has paid a part or all of the price of goods in which he has a special property under the provisions of the immediately preceding section may on making and keeping good a tender of any unpaid portion of their price recover them from the seller if:

(a) in the case of goods bought for personal, family, or household purposes, the seller repudiates or fails to deliver as required by the contract; or

(b) in all cases, the seller becomes insolvent within ten days after receipt of the first installment on their price.

(2) The buyer's right to recover the goods under subsection (1)(a) vests upon acquisition of a special property, even if the seller had not then repudiated or failed to deliver.

(3) If the identification creating his special property has been made by the buyer he acquires the right to recover the goods only if they conform to the contract for sale.

As amended in 1999.

§ 2–503. Manner of Seller's Tender of Delivery.

(1) Tender of delivery requires that the seller put and hold conforming goods at the buyer's disposition and give the buyer any notification reasonably necessary to enable him to take delivery. The manner, time and place for tender are determined by the agreement and this Article, and in particular

(a) tender must be at a reasonable hour, and if it is of goods they must be kept available for the period reasonably necessary to enable the buyer to take possession; but

(b) unless otherwise agreed the buyer must furnish facilities reasonably suited to the receipt of the goods.

(2) Where the case is within the next section respecting shipment tender requires that the seller comply with its provisions.

(3) Where the seller is required to deliver at a particular destination tender requires that he comply with subsection (1) and also in any appropriate case tender documents as described in subsections (4) and (5) of this section.

(4) Where goods are in the possession of a bailee and are to be delivered without being moved

(a) tender requires that the seller either tender a negotiable document of title covering such goods or procure acknowledgment by the bailee of the buyer's right to possession of the goods; but

(b) tender to the buyer of a non-negotiable document of title or of a written direction to the bailee to deliver is sufficient tender unless the buyer seasonably objects, and receipt by the bailee of notification of the buyer's rights fixes those rights as against the bailee and all third persons; but risk of loss of the goods and of any failure by the bailee to honor the non-negotiable document of title or to obey the direction remains on the seller until the buyer has had a reasonable time to present the document or direction, and a refusal by the bailee to honor the document or to obey the direction defeats the tender.

(5) Where the contract requires the seller to deliver documents

(a) he must tender all such documents in correct form, except as provided in this Article with respect to bills of lading in a set (subsection (2) of Section 2–323); and

(b) tender through customary banking channels is sufficient and dishonor of a draft accompanying the documents constitutes non-acceptance or rejection.

§ 2–504. Shipment by Seller.

Where the seller is required or authorized to send the goods to the buyer and the contract does not require him to deliver them at a particular destination, then unless otherwise agreed he must

(a) put the goods in the possession of such a carrier and make such a contract for their transportation as may be reasonable having regard to the nature of the goods and other circumstances of the case; and

(b) obtain and promptly deliver or tender in due form any document necessary to enable the buyer to obtain possession of the goods or otherwise required by the agreement or by usage of trade; and

(c) promptly notify the buyer of the shipment.

Failure to notify the buyer under paragraph (c) or to make a proper contract under paragraph (a) is a ground for rejection only if material delay or loss ensues.

§ 2–505. Seller's Shipment under Reservation.

(1) Where the seller has identified goods to the contract by or before shipment:

(a) his procurement of a negotiable bill of lading to his own order or otherwise reserves in him a security interest in the goods. His procurement of the bill to the order of a financing agency or of the buyer indicates in addition only the seller's expectation of transferring that interest to the person named.

(b) a non-negotiable bill of lading to himself or his nominee reserves possession of the goods as security but except in a case of conditional delivery (subsection (2) of Section 2–507) a non-negotiable bill of lading naming the buyer as consignee reserves no security interest even though the seller retains possession of the bill of lading.

(2) When shipment by the seller with reservation of a security interest is in violation of the contract for sale it constitutes an improper contract for transportation within the preceding section but impairs neither the rights given to the buyer by shipment and identification of the goods to the contract nor the seller's powers as a holder of a negotiable document.

§ 2–506. Rights of Financing Agency.

(1) A financing agency by paying or purchasing for value a draft which relates to a shipment of goods acquires to the extent of the payment or purchase and in addition to its own rights under the draft and any document of title securing it any rights of the shipper in the goods including the right to stop delivery and the shipper's right to have the draft honored by the buyer.

(2) The right to reimbursement of a financing agency which has in good faith honored or purchased the draft under commitment to or authority from the buyer is not impaired by subsequent discovery of defects with reference to any relevant document which was apparently regular on its face.

§ 2–507. Effect of Seller's Tender; Delivery on Condition.

(1) Tender of delivery is a condition to the buyer's duty to accept the goods and, unless otherwise agreed, to his duty to pay for them. Tender entitles the seller to acceptance of the goods and to payment according to the contract.

(2) Where payment is due and demanded on the delivery to the buyer of goods or documents of title, his right as against the seller to retain or dispose of them is conditional upon his making the payment due.

§ 2–508. Cure by Seller of Improper Tender or Delivery; Replacement.

(1) Where any tender or delivery by the seller is rejected because non-conforming and the time for performance has not yet expired, the seller may seasonably notify the buyer of his intention to cure and may then within the contract time make a conforming delivery.

(2) Where the buyer rejects a non-conforming tender which the seller had reasonable grounds to believe would be acceptable with or without money allowance the seller may if he seasonably notifies the buyer have a further reasonable time to substitute a conforming tender.

§ 2–509. Risk of Loss in the Absence of Breach.

(1) Where the contract requires or authorizes the seller to ship the goods by carrier

  (a) if it does not require him to deliver them at a particular destination, the risk of loss passes to the buyer when the goods are duly delivered to the carrier even though the shipment is under reservation (Section 2–505); but

  (b) if it does require him to deliver them at a particular destination and the goods are there duly tendered while in the possession of the carrier, the risk of loss passes to the buyer when the goods are there duly so tendered as to enable the buyer to take delivery.

(2) Where the goods are held by a bailee to be delivered without being moved, the risk of loss passes to the buyer

  (a) on his receipt of a negotiable document of title covering the goods; or

  (b) on acknowledgment by the bailee of the buyer's right to possession of the goods; or

  (c) after his receipt of a non-negotiable document of title or other written direction to deliver, as provided in subsection (4)(b) of Section 2–503.

(3) In any case not within subsection (1) or (2), the risk of loss passes to the buyer on his receipt of the goods if the seller is a merchant; otherwise the risk passes to the buyer on tender of delivery.

(4) The provisions of this section are subject to contrary agreement of the parties and to the provisions of this Article on sale on approval (Section 2–327) and on effect of breach on risk of loss (Section 2–510).

§ 2–510. Effect of Breach on Risk of Loss.

(1) Where a tender or delivery of goods so fails to conform to the contract as to give a right of rejection the risk of their loss remains on the seller until cure or acceptance.

(2) Where the buyer rightfully revokes acceptance he may to the extent of any deficiency in his effective insurance coverage treat the risk of loss as having rested on the seller from the beginning.

(3) Where the buyer as to conforming goods already identified to the contract for sale repudiates or is otherwise in breach before risk of their loss has passed to him, the seller may to the extent of any deficiency in his effective insurance coverage treat the risk of loss as resting on the buyer for a commercially reasonable time.

§ 2–511. Tender of Payment by Buyer; Payment by Check.

(1) Unless otherwise agreed tender of payment is a condition to the seller's duty to tender and complete any delivery.

(2) Tender of payment is sufficient when made by any means or in any manner current in the ordinary course of business unless the seller demands payment in legal tender and gives any extension of time reasonably necessary to procure it.

(3) Subject to the provisions of this Act on the effect of an instrument on an obligation (Section 3–310), payment by check is conditional and is defeated as between the parties by dishonor of the check on due presentment.

As amended in 1994.

§ 2–512. Payment by Buyer Before Inspection.

(1) Where the contract requires payment before inspection non-conformity of the goods does not excuse the buyer from so making payment unless

  (a) the non-conformity appears without inspection; or

  (b) despite tender of the required documents the circumstances would justify injunction against honor under this Act (Section 5–109(b)).

(2) Payment pursuant to subsection (1) does not constitute an acceptance of goods or impair the buyer's right to inspect or any of his remedies.

As amended in 1995.

§ 2–513. Buyer's Right to Inspection of Goods.

(1) Unless otherwise agreed and subject to subsection (3), where goods are tendered or delivered or identified to the contract for sale, the buyer has a right before payment or acceptance to inspect them at any reasonable place and time and in any reasonable manner. When the seller is required or authorized to send the goods to the buyer, the inspection may be after their arrival.

(2) Expenses of inspection must be borne by the buyer but may be recovered from the seller if the goods do not conform and are rejected.

(3) Unless otherwise agreed and subject to the provisions of this Article on C.I.F. contracts (subsection (3) of Section 2–321), the buyer is not entitled to inspect the goods before payment of the price when the contract provides

    (a) for delivery "C.O.D." or on other like terms; or

    (b) for payment against documents of title, except where such payment is due only after the goods are to become available for inspection.

(4) A place or method of inspection fixed by the parties is presumed to be exclusive but unless otherwise expressly agreed it does not postpone identification or shift the place for delivery or for passing the risk of loss. If compliance becomes impossible, inspection shall be as provided in this section unless the place or method fixed was clearly intended as an indispensable condition failure of which avoids the contract.

§ 2–514. When Documents Deliverable on Acceptance; When on Payment.

Unless otherwise agreed documents against which a draft is drawn are to be delivered to the drawee on acceptance of the draft if it is payable more than three days after presentment; otherwise, only on payment.

§ 2–515. Preserving Evidence of Goods in Dispute.

In furtherance of the adjustment of any claim or dispute

    (a) either party on reasonable notification to the other and for the purpose of ascertaining the facts and preserving evidence has the right to inspect, test and sample the goods including such of them as may be in the possession or control of the other; and

    (b) the parties may agree to a third party inspection or survey to determine the conformity or condition of the goods and may agree that the findings shall be binding upon them in any subsequent litigation or adjustment.

Part 6—Breach, Repudiation and Excuse

§ 2–601. Buyer's Rights on Improper Delivery.

Subject to the provisions of this Article on breach in installment contracts (Section 2–612) and unless otherwise agreed under the sections on contractual limitations of remedy (Sections 2–718 and 2–719), if the goods or the tender of delivery fail in any respect to conform to the contract, the buyer may

    (a) reject the whole; or

    (b) accept the whole; or

    (c) accept any commercial unit or units and reject the rest.

§ 2–602. Manner and Effect of Rightful Rejection.

(1) Rejection of goods must be within a reasonable time after their delivery or tender. It is ineffective unless the buyer seasonably notifies the seller.

(2) Subject to the provisions of the two following sections on rejected goods (Sections 2–603 and 2–604),

    (a) after rejection any exercise of ownership by the buyer with respect to any commercial unit is wrongful as against the seller; and

    (b) if the buyer has before rejection taken physical possession of goods in which he does not have a security interest under the provisions of this Article (subsection (3) of Section 2–711), he is under a duty after rejection to hold them with reasonable care at the seller's disposition for a time sufficient to permit the seller to remove them; but

    (c) the buyer has no further obligations with regard to goods rightfully rejected.

(3) The seller's rights with respect to goods wrongfully rejected are governed by the provisions of this Article on Seller's remedies in general (Section 2–703).

§ 2–603. Merchant Buyer's Duties as to Rightfully Rejected Goods.

(1) Subject to any security interest in the buyer (subsection (3) of Section 2–711), when the seller has no agent or place of business at the market of rejection a merchant buyer is under a duty after rejection of goods in his possession or control to follow any reasonable instructions received from the seller with respect to the goods and in the absence of such instructions to make reasonable efforts to sell them for the seller's account if they are perishable or threaten to decline in value speedily. Instructions are not reasonable if on demand indemnity for expenses is not forthcoming.

(2) When the buyer sells goods under subsection (1), he is entitled to reimbursement from the seller or out of the proceeds for reasonable expenses of caring for and selling them, and if the expenses include no selling commission then to such commission as is usual in the trade or if there is none to a reasonable sum not exceeding ten per cent on the gross proceeds.

(3) In complying with this section the buyer is held only to good faith and good faith conduct hereunder is neither acceptance nor conversion nor the basis of an action for damages.

§ 2–604. Buyer's Options as to Salvage of Rightfully Rejected Goods.

Subject to the provisions of the immediately preceding section on perishables if the seller gives no instructions within a reasonable time after notification of rejection the buyer may store the rejected goods for the seller's account or reship them to him or resell them for the seller's account with reimbursement as provided in the preceding section. Such action is not acceptance or conversion.

§ 2–605. Waiver of Buyer's Objections by Failure to Particularize.

(1) The buyer's failure to state in connection with rejection a particular defect which is ascertainable by reasonable inspection precludes him from relying on the unstated defect to justify rejection or to establish breach

    (a) where the seller could have cured it if stated seasonably; or

    (b) between merchants when the seller has after rejection made a request in writing for a full and final written statement of all defects on which the buyer proposes to rely.

(2) Payment against documents made without reservation of rights precludes recovery of the payment for defects apparent on the face of the documents.

§ 2–606. What Constitutes Acceptance of Goods.

(1) Acceptance of goods occurs when the buyer

(a) after a reasonable opportunity to inspect the goods signifies to the seller that the goods are conforming or that he will take or retain them in spite of their nonconformity; or

(b) fails to make an effective rejection (subsection (1) of Section 2–602), but such acceptance does not occur until the buyer has had a reasonable opportunity to inspect them; or

(c) does any act inconsistent with the seller's ownership; but if such act is wrongful as against the seller it is an acceptance only if ratified by him.

(2) Acceptance of a part of any commercial unit is acceptance of that entire unit.

§ 2–607. Effect of Acceptance; Notice of Breach; Burden of Establishing Breach After Acceptance; Notice of Claim or Litigation to Person Answerable Over.

(1) The buyer must pay at the contract rate for any goods accepted.

(2) Acceptance of goods by the buyer precludes rejection of the goods accepted and if made with knowledge of a non-conformity cannot be revoked because of it unless the acceptance was on the reasonable assumption that the non-conformity would be seasonably cured but acceptance does not of itself impair any other remedy provided by this Article for non-conformity.

(3) Where a tender has been accepted

(a) the buyer must within a reasonable time after he discovers or should have discovered any breach notify the seller of breach or be barred from any remedy; and

(b) if the claim is one for infringement or the like (subsection (3) of Section 2–312) and the buyer is sued as a result of such a breach he must so notify the seller within a reasonable time after he receives notice of the litigation or be barred from any remedy over for liability established by the litigation.

(4) The burden is on the buyer to establish any breach with respect to the goods accepted.

(5) Where the buyer is sued for breach of a warranty or other obligation for which his seller is answerable over

(a) he may give his seller written notice of the litigation. If the notice states that the seller may come in and defend and that if the seller does not do so he will be bound in any action against him by his buyer by any determination of fact common to the two litigations, then unless the seller after seasonable receipt of the notice does come in and defend he is so bound.

(b) if the claim is one for infringement or the like (subsection (3) of Section 2–312) the original seller may demand in writing that his buyer turn over to him control of the litigation including settlement or else be barred from any remedy over and if he also agrees to bear all expense and to satisfy any adverse judgment, then unless the buyer after seasonable receipt of the demand does turn over control the buyer is so barred.

(6) The provisions of subsections (3), (4) and (5) apply to any obligation of a buyer to hold the seller harmless against infringement or the like (subsection (3) of Section 2–312).

§ 2–608. Revocation of Acceptance in Whole or in Part.

(1) The buyer may revoke his acceptance of a lot or commercial unit whose non-conformity substantially impairs its value to him if he has accepted it

(a) on the reasonable assumption that its nonconformity would be cured and it has not been seasonably cured; or

(b) without discovery of such non-conformity if his acceptance was reasonably induced either by the difficulty of discovery before acceptance or by the seller's assurances.

(2) Revocation of acceptance must occur within a reasonable time after the buyer discovers or should have discovered the ground for it and before any substantial change in condition of the goods which is not caused by their own defects. It is not effective until the buyer notifies the seller of it.

(3) A buyer who so revokes has the same rights and duties with regard to the goods involved as if he had rejected them.

§ 2–609. Right to Adequate Assurance of Performance.

(1) A contract for sale imposes an obligation on each party that the other's expectation of receiving due performance will not be impaired. When reasonable grounds for insecurity arise with respect to the performance of either party the other may in writing demand adequate assurance of due performance and until he receives such assurance may if commercially reasonable suspend any performance for which he has not already received the agreed return.

(2) Between merchants the reasonableness of grounds for insecurity and the adequacy of any assurance offered shall be determined according to commercial standards.

(3) Acceptance of any improper delivery or payment does not prejudice the party's right to demand adequate assurance of future performance.

(4) After receipt of a justified demand failure to provide within a reasonable time not exceeding thirty days such assurance of due performance as is adequate under the circumstances of the particular case is a repudiation of the contract.

§ 2–610. Anticipatory Repudiation.

When either party repudiates the contract with respect to a performance not yet due the loss of which will substantially impair the value of the contract to the other, the aggrieved party may

(a) for a commercially reasonable time await performance by the repudiating party; or

(b) resort to any remedy for breach (Section 2–703 or Section 2–711), even though he has notified the repudiating party that he would await the latter's performance and has urged retraction; and

(c) in either case suspend his own performance or proceed in accordance with the provisions of this Article on the seller's right to identify goods to the contract notwithstanding breach or to salvage unfinished goods (Section 2–704).

§ 2–611. Retraction of Anticipatory Repudiation.

(1) Until the repudiating party's next performance is due he can retract his repudiation unless the aggrieved party has since the repudiation cancelled or materially changed his position or otherwise indicated that he considers the repudiation final.

(2) Retraction may be by any method which clearly indicates to the aggrieved party that the repudiating party intends to perform, but must include any assurance justifiably demanded under the provisions of this Article (Section 2–609).

(3) Retraction reinstates the repudiating party's rights under the contract with due excuse and allowance to the aggrieved party for any delay occasioned by the repudiation.

§ 2–612. "Installment Contract"; Breach.

(1) An "installment contract" is one which requires or authorizes the delivery of goods in separate lots to be separately accepted, even though the contract contains a clause "each delivery is a separate contract" or its equivalent.

(2) The buyer may reject any installment which is non-conforming if the non-conformity substantially impairs the value of that installment and cannot be cured or if the non-conformity is a defect in the required documents; but if the non-conformity does not fall within subsection (3) and the seller gives adequate assurance of its cure the buyer must accept that installment.

(3) Whenever non-conformity or default with respect to one or more installments substantially impairs the value of the whole contract there is a breach of the whole. But the aggrieved party reinstates the contract if he accepts a non-conforming installment without seasonably notifying of cancellation or if he brings an action with respect only to past installments or demands performance as to future installments.

§ 2–613. Casualty to Identified Goods.

Where the contract requires for its performance goods identified when the contract is made, and the goods suffer casualty without fault of either party before the risk of loss passes to the buyer, or in a proper case under a "no arrival, no sale" term (Section 2–324) then

(a) if the loss is total the contract is avoided; and

(b) if the loss is partial or the goods have so deteriorated as no longer to conform to the contract the buyer may nevertheless demand inspection and at his option either treat the contract as voided or accept the goods with due allowance from the contract price for the deterioration or the deficiency in quantity but without further right against the seller.

§ 2–614. Substituted Performance.

(1) Where without fault of either party the agreed berthing, loading, or unloading facilities fail or an agreed type of carrier becomes unavailable or the agreed manner of delivery otherwise becomes commercially impracticable but a commercially reasonable substitute is available, such substitute performance must be tendered and accepted.

(2) If the agreed means or manner of payment fails because of domestic or foreign governmental regulation, the seller may withhold or stop delivery unless the buyer provides a means or manner of payment which is commercially a substantial equivalent. If delivery has already been taken, payment by the means or in the manner provided by the regulation discharges the buyer's obligation unless the regulation is discriminatory, oppressive or predatory.

§ 2–615. Excuse by Failure of Presupposed Conditions.

Except so far as a seller may have assumed a greater obligation and subject to the preceding section on substituted performance:

(a) Delay in delivery or non-delivery in whole or in part by a seller who complies with paragraphs (b) and (c) is not a breach of his duty under a contract for sale if performance as agreed has been made impracticable by the occurrence of a contingency the nonoccurrence of which was a basic assumption on which the contract was made or by compliance in good faith with any applicable foreign or domestic governmental regulation or order whether or not it later proves to be invalid.

(b) Where the causes mentioned in paragraph (a) affect only a part of the seller's capacity to perform, he must allocate production and deliveries among his customers but may at his option include regular customers not then under contract as well as his own requirements for further manufacture. He may so allocate in any manner which is fair and reasonable.

(c) The seller must notify the buyer seasonably that there will be delay or non-delivery and, when allocation is required under paragraph (b), of the estimated quota thus made available for the buyer.

§ 2–616. Procedure on Notice Claiming Excuse.

(1) Where the buyer receives notification of a material or indefinite delay or an allocation justified under the preceding section he may by written notification to the seller as to any delivery concerned, and where the prospective deficiency substantially impairs the value of the whole contract under the provisions of this Article relating to breach of installment contracts (Section 2–612), then also as to the whole,

(a) terminate and thereby discharge any unexecuted portion of the contract; or

(b) modify the contract by agreeing to take his available quota in substitution.

(2) If after receipt of such notification from the seller the buyer fails so to modify the contract within a reasonable time not exceeding thirty days the contract lapses with respect to any deliveries affected.

(3) The provisions of this section may not be negated by agreement except in so far as the seller has assumed a greater obligation under the preceding section.

Part 7—Remedies

§ 2–701. Remedies for Breach of Collateral Contracts Not Impaired.

Remedies for breach of any obligation or promise collateral or ancillary to a contract for sale are not impaired by the provisions of this Article.

§ 2–702. Seller's Remedies on Discovery of Buyer's Insolvency.

(1) Where the seller discovers the buyer to be insolvent he may refuse delivery except for cash including payment for all goods theretofore delivered under the contract, and stop delivery under this Article (Section 2–705).

(2) Where the seller discovers that the buyer has received goods on credit while insolvent he may reclaim the goods upon demand made within ten days after the receipt, but if misrepresentation of solvency has been made to the particular seller in writing within three months before delivery the ten day limitation does not apply. Except as provided in this subsection the seller may not base a right to reclaim goods on the buyer's fraudulent or innocent misrepresentation of solvency or of intent to pay.

(3) The seller's right to reclaim under subsection (2) is subject to the rights of a buyer in ordinary course or other good faith purchaser under this Article (Section 2–403). Successful reclamation of goods excludes all other remedies with respect to them.

§ 2–703. Seller's Remedies in General.

Where the buyer wrongfully rejects or revokes acceptance of goods or fails to make a payment due on or before delivery or repudiates with respect to a part or the whole, then with respect to any goods directly affected and, if the breach is of the whole contract (Section 2–612), then also with respect to the whole undelivered balance, the aggrieved seller may

(a) withhold delivery of such goods;

(b) stop delivery by any bailee as hereafter provided (Section 2–705);

(c) proceed under the next section respecting goods still unidentified to the contract;

(d) resell and recover damages as hereafter provided (Section 2–706);

(e) recover damages for non-acceptance (Section 2–708) or in a proper case the price (Section 2–709);

(f) cancel.

§ 2–704. Seller's Right to Identify Goods to the Contract Notwithstanding Breach or to Salvage Unfinished Goods.

(1) An aggrieved seller under the preceding section may

(a) identify to the contract conforming goods not already identified if at the time he learned of the breach they are in his possession or control;

(b) treat as the subject of resale goods which have demonstrably been intended for the particular contract even though those goods are unfinished.

(2) Where the goods are unfinished an aggrieved seller may in the exercise of reasonable commercial judgment for the purposes of avoiding loss and of effective realization either complete the manufacture and wholly identify the goods to the contract or cease manufacture and resell for scrap or salvage value or proceed in any other reasonable manner.

§ 2–705. Seller's Stoppage of Delivery in Transit or Otherwise.

(1) The seller may stop delivery of goods in the possession of a carrier or other bailee when he discovers the buyer to be insolvent (Section 2–702) and may stop delivery of carload, truckload, planeload or larger shipments of express or freight when the buyer repudiates or fails to make a payment due before delivery or if for any other reason the seller has a right to withhold or reclaim the goods.

(2) As against such buyer the seller may stop delivery until

(a) receipt of the goods by the buyer; or

(b) acknowledgment to the buyer by any bailee of the goods except a carrier that the bailee holds the goods for the buyer; or

(c) such acknowledgment to the buyer by a carrier by reshipment or as warehouseman; or

(d) negotiation to the buyer of any negotiable document of title covering the goods.

(3) (a) To stop delivery the seller must so notify as to enable the bailee by reasonable diligence to prevent delivery of the goods.

(b) After such notification the bailee must hold and deliver the goods according to the directions of the seller but the seller is liable to the bailee for any ensuing charges or damages.

(c) If a negotiable document of title has been issued for goods the bailee is not obliged to obey a notification to stop until surrender of the document.

(d) A carrier who has issued a non-negotiable bill of lading is not obliged to obey a notification to stop received from a person other than the consignor.

§ 2–706. Seller's Resale Including Contract for Resale.

(1) Under the conditions stated in Section 2–703 on seller's remedies, the seller may resell the goods concerned or the undelivered balance thereof. Where the resale is made in good faith and in a commercially reasonable manner the seller may recover the difference between the resale price and the contract price together with any incidental damages allowed under the provisions of this Article (Section 2–710), but less expenses saved in consequence of the buyer's breach.

(2) Except as otherwise provided in subsection (3) or unless otherwise agreed resale may be at public or private sale including sale by way of one or more contracts to sell or of identification to an existing contract of the seller. Sale may be as a unit or in parcels and at any time and place and on any terms but every aspect of the sale including the method, manner, time, place and terms must be commercially reasonable. The resale must be reasonably identified as referring to the broken contract, but it is not necessary that the goods be in existence or that any or all of them have been identified to the contract before the breach.

(3) Where the resale is at private sale the seller must give the buyer reasonable notification of his intention to resell.

(4) Where the resale is at public sale

(a) only identified goods can be sold except where there is a recognized market for a public sale of futures in goods of the kind; and

(b) it must be made at a usual place or market for public sale if one is reasonably available and except in the case of goods which are perishable or threaten to decline in value speedily the seller must give the buyer reasonable notice of the time and place of the resale; and

(c) if the goods are not to be within the view of those attending the sale the notification of sale must state the place where the goods are located and provide for their reasonable inspection by prospective bidders; and

(d) the seller may buy.

(5) A purchaser who buys in good faith at a resale takes the goods free of any rights of the original buyer even though the seller fails to comply with one or more of the requirements of this section.

(6) The seller is not accountable to the buyer for any profit made on any resale. A person in the position of a seller (Section 2–707) or a buyer who has rightfully rejected or justifiably revoked acceptance must account for any excess over the amount of his security interest, as hereinafter defined (subsection (3) of Section 2–711).

§ 2–707. "Person in the Position of a Seller".

(1) A "person in the position of a seller" includes as against a principal an agent who has paid or become responsible for the price of goods on behalf of his principal or anyone who otherwise holds a security interest or other right in goods similar to that of a seller.

(2) A person in the position of a seller may as provided in this Article withhold or stop delivery (Section 2–705) and resell (Section 2–706) and recover incidental damages (Section 2–710).

§ 2–708. Seller's Damages for Non-Acceptance or Repudiation.

(1) Subject to subsection (2) and to the provisions of this Article with respect to proof of market price (Section 2–723), the measure of damages for non-acceptance or repudiation by the buyer is the difference between the market price at the time and place for tender and the unpaid contract price together with any incidental damages provided in this Article (Section 2–710), but less expenses saved in consequence of the buyer's breach.

(2) If the measure of damages provided in subsection (1) is inadequate to put the seller in as good a position as performance would have done then the measure of damages is the profit (including reasonable overhead) which the seller would have made from full performance by the buyer, together with any incidental damages provided in this Article (Section 2–710), due allowance for costs reasonably incurred and due credit for payments or proceeds of resale.

§ 2–709. Action for the Price.

(1) When the buyer fails to pay the price as it becomes due the seller may recover, together with any incidental damages under the next section, the price

    (a) of goods accepted or of conforming goods lost or damaged within a commercially reasonable time after risk of their loss has passed to the buyer; and

    (b) of goods identified to the contract if the seller is unable after reasonable effort to resell them at a reasonable price or the circumstances reasonably indicate that such effort will be unavailing.

(2) Where the seller sues for the price he must hold for the buyer any goods which have been identified to the contract and are still in his control except that if resale becomes possible he may resell them at any time prior to the collection of the judgment. The net proceeds of any such resale must be credited to the buyer and payment of the judgment entitles him to any goods not resold.

(3) After the buyer has wrongfully rejected or revoked acceptance of the goods or has failed to make a payment due or has repudiated (Section 2–610), a seller who is held not entitled to the price under this section shall nevertheless be awarded damages for non-acceptance under the preceding section.

§ 2–710. Seller's Incidental Damages.

Incidental damages to an aggrieved seller include any commercially reasonable charges, expenses or commissions incurred in stopping delivery, in the transportation, care and custody of goods after the buyer's breach, in connection with return or resale of the goods or otherwise resulting from the breach.

§ 2–711. Buyer's Remedies in General; Buyer's Security Interest in Rejected Goods.

(1) Where the seller fails to make delivery or repudiates or the buyer rightfully rejects or justifiably revokes acceptance then with respect to any goods involved, and with respect to the whole if the breach goes to the whole contract (Section 2–612), the buyer may cancel and whether or not he has done so may in addition to recovering so much of the price as has been paid

    (a) "cover" and have damages under the next section as to all the goods affected whether or not they have been identified to the contract; or

    (b) recover damages for non-delivery as pro-vided in this Article (Section 2–713).

(2) Where the seller fails to deliver or repudiates the buyer may also

    (a) if the goods have been identified recover them as provided in this Article (Section 2–502); or

    (b) in a proper case obtain specific performance or replevy the goods as provided in this Article (Section 2–716).

(3) On rightful rejection or justifiable revocation of acceptance a buyer has a security interest in goods in his possession or control for any payments made on their price and any expenses reasonably incurred in their inspection, receipt, transportation, care and custody and may hold such goods and resell them in like manner as an aggrieved seller (Section 2–706).

§ 2–712. "Cover"; Buyer's Procurement of Substitute Goods.

(1) After a breach within the preceding section the buyer may "cover" by making in good faith and without unreasonable delay any reasonable purchase of or contract to purchase goods in substitution for those due from the seller.

(2) The buyer may recover from the seller as damages the difference between the cost of cover and the contract price together with any incidental or consequential damages as hereinafter defined (Section 2–715), but less expenses saved in consequence of the seller's breach.

(3) Failure of the buyer to effect cover within this section does not bar him from any other remedy.

§ 2–713. Buyer's Damages for Non-Delivery or Repudiation.

(1) Subject to the provisions of this Article with respect to proof of market price (Section 2–723), the measure of damages for non-delivery or repudiation by the seller is the difference between the market price at the time when the buyer learned of the breach and the contract price together with any incidental and consequential damages provided in this Article (Section 2–715), but less expenses saved in consequence of the seller's breach.

(2) Market price is to be determined as of the place for tender or, in cases of rejection after arrival or revocation of acceptance, as of the place of arrival.

§ 2–714. Buyer's Damages for Breach in Regard to Accepted Goods.

(1) Where the buyer has accepted goods and given notification (subsection (3) of Section 2–607) he may recover as damages for any non-conformity of tender the loss resulting in the ordinary course of events from the seller's breach as determined in any manner which is reasonable.

(2) The measure of damages for breach of warranty is the difference at the time and place of acceptance between the value of the goods accepted and the value they would have had if they had been as warranted, unless special circumstances show proximate damages of a different amount.

(3) In a proper case any incidental and consequential damages under the next section may also be recovered.

§ 2–715. Buyer's Incidental and Consequential Damages.

(1) Incidental damages resulting from the seller's breach include expenses reasonably incurred in inspection, receipt, transportation and care and custody of goods rightfully rejected, any commercially reasonable charges, expenses or commissions in connection with effecting cover and any other reasonable expense incident to the delay or other breach.

(2) Consequential damages resulting from the seller's breach include

    (a) any loss resulting from general or particular requirements and needs of which the seller at the time of contracting had reason to know and which could not reasonably be prevented by cover or otherwise; and

(b) injury to person or property proximately resulting from any breach of warranty.

§ 2–716. Buyer's Right to Specific Performance or Replevin.

(1) Specific performance may be decreed where the goods are unique or in other proper circumstances.

(2) The decree for specific performance may include such terms and conditions as to payment of the price, damages, or other relief as the court may deem just.

(3) The buyer has a right of replevin for goods identified to the contract if after reasonable effort he is unable to effect cover for such goods or the circumstances reasonably indicate that such effort will be unavailing or if the goods have been shipped under reservation and satisfaction of the security interest in them has been made or tendered. In the case of goods bought for personal, family, or household purposes, the buyer's right of replevin vests upon acquisition of a special property, even if the seller had not then repudiated or failed to deliver.

As amended in 1999.

§ 2–717. Deduction of Damages From the Price.

The buyer on notifying the seller of his intention to do so may deduct all or any part of the damages resulting from any breach of the contract from any part of the price still due under the same contract.

§ 2–718. Liquidation or Limitation of Damages; Deposits.

(1) Damages for breach by either party may be liquidated in the agreement but only at an amount which is reasonable in the light of the anticipated or actual harm caused by the breach, the difficulties of proof of loss, and the inconvenience or nonfeasibility of otherwise obtaining an adequate remedy. A term fixing unreasonably large liquidated damages is void as a penalty.

(2) Where the seller justifiably withholds delivery of goods because of the buyer's breach, the buyer is entitled to restitution of any amount by which the sum of his payments exceeds

  (a) the amount to which the seller is entitled by virtue of terms liquidating the seller's damages in accordance with subsection (1), or

  (b) in the absence of such terms, twenty per cent of the value of the total performance for which the buyer is obligated under the contract or $500, whichever is smaller.

(3) The buyer's right to restitution under subsection (2) is subject to offset to the extent that the seller establishes

  (a) a right to recover damages under the provisions of this Article other than subsection (1), and

  (b) the amount or value of any benefits received by the buyer directly or indirectly by reason of the contract.

(4) Where a seller has received payment in goods their reasonable value or the proceeds of their resale shall be treated as payments for the purposes of subsection (2); but if the seller has notice of the buyer's breach before reselling goods received in part performance, his resale is subject to the conditions laid down in this Article on resale by an aggrieved seller (Section 2–706).

§ 2–719. Contractual Modification or Limitation of Remedy.

(1) Subject to the provisions of subsections (2) and (3) of this section and of the preceding section on liquidation and limitation of damages,

  (a) the agreement may provide for remedies in addition to or in substitution for those provided in this Article and may limit or alter the measure of damages recoverable under this Article, as by limiting the buyer's remedies to return of the goods and repayment of the price or to repair and replacement of nonconforming goods or parts; and

  (b) resort to a remedy as provided is optional unless the remedy is expressly agreed to be exclusive, in which case it is the sole remedy.

(2) Where circumstances cause an exclusive or limited remedy to fail of its essential purpose, remedy may be had as provided in this Act.

(3) Consequential damages may be limited or excluded unless the limitation or exclusion is unconscionable. Limitation of consequential damages for injury to the person in the case of consumer goods is *prima facie* unconscionable but limitation of damages where the loss is commercial is not.

§ 2–720. Effect of "Cancellation" or "Rescission" on Claims for Antecedent Breach.

Unless the contrary intention clearly appears, expressions of "cancellation" or "rescission" of the contract or the like shall not be construed as a renunciation or discharge of any claim in damages for an antecedent breach.

§ 2–721. Remedies for Fraud.

Remedies for material misrepresentation or fraud include all remedies available under this Article for non-fraudulent breach. Neither rescission or a claim for rescission of the contract for sale nor rejection or return of the goods shall bar or be deemed inconsistent with a claim for damages or other remedy.

§ 2–722. Who Can Sue Third Parties for Injury to Goods.

Where a third party so deals with goods which have been identified to a contract for sale as to cause actionable injury to a party to that contract

(a) a right of action against the third party is in either party to the contract for sale who has title to or a security interest or a special property or an insurable interest in the goods; and if the goods have been destroyed or converted a right of action is also in the party who either bore the risk of loss under the contract for sale or has since the injury assumed that risk as against the other;

(b) if at the time of the injury the party plaintiff did not bear the risk of loss as against the other party to the contract for sale and there is no arrangement between them for disposition of the recovery, his suit or settlement is, subject to his own interest, as a fiduciary for the other party to the contract;

(c) either party may with the consent of the other sue for the benefit of whom it may concern.

§ 2–723. Proof of Market Price: Time and Place.

(1) If an action based on anticipatory repudiation comes to trial before the time for performance with respect to some or all of the goods, any damages based on market price (Section 2–708 or Section 2–713) shall be determined according to the price of such goods prevailing at the time when the aggrieved party learned of the repudiation.

(2) If evidence of a price prevailing at the times or places described in this Article is not readily available the price prevailing within any reasonable time before or after the time described or at any other place which in commercial judgment or under usage of trade would serve as a reasonable substitute for the one described may be used, making any proper allowance for the cost of transporting the goods to or from such other place.

(3) Evidence of a relevant price prevailing at a time or place other than the one described in this Article offered by one party is not admissible unless and until he has given the other party such notice as the court finds sufficient to prevent unfair surprise.

§ 2–724. **Admissibility of Market Quotations.**

Whenever the prevailing price or value of any goods regularly bought and sold in any established commodity market is in issue, reports in official publications or trade journals or in newspapers or periodicals of general circulation published as the reports of such market shall be admissible in evidence. The circumstances of the preparation of such a report may be shown to affect its weight but not its admissibility.

§ 2–725. **Statute of Limitations in Contracts for Sale.**

(1) An action for breach of any contract for sale must be commenced within four years after the cause of action has accrued. By the original agreement the parties may reduce the period of limitation to not less than one year but may not extend it.

(2) A cause of action accrues when the breach occurs, regardless of the aggrieved party's lack of knowledge of the breach. A breach of warranty occurs when tender of delivery is made, except that where a warranty explicitly extends to future performance of the goods and discovery of the breach must await the time of such performance the cause of action accrues when the breach is or should have been discovered.

(3) Where an action commenced within the time limited by subsection (1) is so terminated as to leave available a remedy by another action for the same breach such other action may be commenced after the expiration of the time limited and within six months after the termination of the first action unless the termination resulted from voluntary discontinuance or from dismissal for failure or neglect to prosecute.

(4) This section does not alter the law on tolling of the statute of limitations nor does it apply to causes of action which have accrued before this Act becomes effective.

ARTICLE 2A: LEASES

Part 1—General Provisions

§ 2A–101. **Short Title.**

This Article shall be known and may be cited as the Uniform Commercial Code—Leases.

§ 2A–102. **Scope.**

This Article applies to any transaction, regardless of form, that creates a lease.

§ 2A–103. **Definitions and Index of Definitions.**

(1) In this Article unless the context otherwise requires:

(a) "Buyer in ordinary course of business" means a person who in good faith and without knowledge that the sale to him [or her] is in violation of the ownership rights or security interest or leasehold interest of a third party in the goods buys in ordinary course from a person in the business of selling goods of that kind but does not include a pawnbroker. "Buying" may be for cash or by exchange of other property or on secured or unsecured credit and includes receiving goods or documents of

title under a pre-existing contract for sale but does not include a transfer in bulk or as security for or in total or partial satisfaction of a money debt.

(b) "Cancellation" occurs when either party puts an end to the lease contract for default by the other party.

(c) "Commercial unit" means such a unit of goods as by commercial usage is a single whole for purposes of lease and division of which materially impairs its character or value on the market or in use. A commercial unit may be a single article, as a machine, or a set of articles, as a suite of furniture or a line of machinery, or a quantity, as a gross or carload, or any other unit treated in use or in the relevant market as a single whole.

(d) "Conforming" goods or performance under a lease contract means goods or performance that are in accordance with the obligations under the lease contract.

(e) "Consumer lease" means a lease that a lessor regularly engaged in the business of leasing or selling makes to a lessee who is an individual and who takes under the lease primarily for a personal, family, or household purpose [, if the total payments to be made under the lease contract, excluding payments for options to renew or buy, do not exceed $_____].

(f) "Fault" means wrongful act, omission, breach, or default.

(g) "Finance lease" means a lease with respect to which:

(i) the lessor does not select, manufacture or supply the goods;

(ii) the lessor acquires the goods or the right to possession and use of the goods in connection with the lease; and

(iii) one of the following occurs:

(A) the lessee receives a copy of the contract by which the lessor acquired the goods or the right to possession and use of the goods before signing the lease contract;

(B) the lessee's approval of the contract by which the lessor acquired the goods or the right to possession and use of the goods is a condition to effectiveness of the lease contract;

(C) the lessee, before signing the lease contract, receives an accurate and complete statement designating the promises and warranties, and any disclaimers of warranties, limitations or modifications of remedies, or liquidated damages, including those of a third party, such as the manufacturer of the goods, provided to the lessor by the person supplying the goods in connection with or as part of the contract by which the lessor acquired the goods or the right to possession and use of the goods; or

(D) if the lease is not a consumer lease, the lessor, before the lessee signs the lease contract, informs the lessee in writing (a) of the identity of the person supplying the goods to the lessor, unless the lessee has selected that person and directed the lessor to acquire the goods or the right to possession and use of the goods from that person, (b) that the lessee is entitled under this Article to any promises and warranties, including those of any third party, provided to the lessor by the person supplying the goods in connection with or as part of the contract by which the lessor acquired the goods or the right to possession and use of the goods, and (c) that the lessee may communicate with the person supplying the goods to the lessor and receive an accurate and complete statement of those promises and warranties, including any disclaimers and limitations of them or of remedies.

(h) "Goods" means all things that are movable at the time of identification to the lease contract, or are fixtures (Section 2A–309), but the term does not include money, documents, instruments, accounts, chattel paper, general intangibles, or minerals or the like, including oil and gas, before extraction. The term also includes the unborn young of animals.

(i) "Installment lease contract" means a lease contract that authorizes or requires the delivery of goods in separate lots to be separately accepted, even though the lease contract contains a clause "each delivery is a separate lease" or its equivalent.

(j) "Lease" means a transfer of the right to possession and use of goods for a term in return for consideration, but a sale, including a sale on approval or a sale or return, or retention or creation of a security interest is not a lease. Unless the context clearly indicates otherwise, the term includes a sublease.

(k) "Lease agreement" means the bargain, with respect to the lease, of the lessor and the lessee in fact as found in their language or by implication from other circumstances including course of dealing or usage of trade or course of performance as provided in this Article. Unless the context clearly indicates otherwise, the term includes a sublease agreement.

(l) "Lease contract" means the total legal obligation that results from the lease agreement as affected by this Article and any other applicable rules of law. Unless the context clearly indicates otherwise, the term includes a sublease contract.

(m) "Leasehold interest" means the interest of the lessor or the lessee under a lease contract.

(n) "Lessee" means a person who acquires the right to possession and use of goods under a lease. Unless the context clearly indicates otherwise, the term includes a sublessee.

(o) "Lessee in ordinary course of business" means a person who in good faith and without knowledge that the lease to him [or her] is in violation of the ownership rights or security interest or leasehold interest of a third party in the goods, leases in ordinary course from a person in the business of selling or leasing goods of that kind but does not include a pawnbroker. "Leasing" may be for cash or by exchange of other property or on secured or unsecured credit and includes receiving goods or documents of title under a pre-existing lease contract but does not include a transfer in bulk or as security for or in total or partial satisfaction of a money debt.

(p) "Lessor" means a person who transfers the right to possession and use of goods under a lease. Unless the context clearly indicates otherwise, the term includes a sublessor.

(q) "Lessor's residual interest" means the lessor's interest in the goods after expiration, termination, or cancellation of the lease contract.

(r) "Lien" means a charge against or interest in goods to secure payment of a debt or performance of an obligation, but the term does not include a security interest.

(s) "Lot" means a parcel or a single article that is the subject matter of a separate lease or delivery, whether or not it is sufficient to perform the lease contract.

(t) "Merchant lessee" means a lessee that is a merchant with respect to goods of the kind subject to the lease.

(u) "Present value" means the amount as of a date certain of one or more sums payable in the future, discounted to the date certain. The discount is determined by the interest rate specified by the parties if the rate was not manifestly unreasonable at the time the transaction

was entered into; otherwise, the discount is determined by a commercially reasonable rate that takes into account the facts and circumstances of each case at the time the transaction was entered into.

(v) "Purchase" includes taking by sale, lease, mortgage, security interest, pledge, gift, or any other voluntary transaction creating an interest in goods.

(w) "Sublease" means a lease of goods the right to possession and use of which was acquired by the lessor as a lessee under an existing lease.

(x) "Supplier" means a person from whom a lessor buys or leases goods to be leased under a finance lease.

(y) "Supply contract" means a contract under which a lessor buys or leases goods to be leased.

(z) "Termination" occurs when either party pursuant to a power created by agreement or law puts an end to the lease contract otherwise than for default.

(2) Other definitions applying to this Article and the sections in which they appear are:

"Accessions". Section 2A–310(1).

"Construction mortgage". Section 2A–309(1)(d).

"Encumbrance". Section 2A–309(1)(e).

"Fixtures". Section 2A–309(1)(a).

"Fixture filing". Section 2A–309(1)(b).

"Purchase money lease". Section 2A–309(1)(c).

(3) The following definitions in other Articles apply to this Article:

"Accounts". Section 9–106.

"Between merchants". Section 2–104(3).

"Buyer". Section 2–103(1)(a).

"Chattel paper". Section 9–105(1)(b).

"Consumer goods". Section 9–109(1).

"Document". Section 9–105(1)(f).

"Entrusting". Section 2–403(3).

"General intangibles". Section 9–106.

"Good faith". Section 2–103(1)(b).

"Instrument". Section 9–105(1)(i).

"Merchant". Section 2–104(1).

"Mortgage". Section 9–105(1)(j).

"Pursuant to commitment". Section 9–105(1)(k).

"Receipt". Section 2–103(1)(c).

"Sale". Section 2–106(1).

"Sale on approval". Section 2–326.

"Sale or return". Section 2–326.

"Seller". Section 2–103(1)(d).

(4) In addition Article 1 contains general definitions and principles of construction and interpretation applicable throughout this Article. As amended in 1990 and 1999.

§ 2A–104. Leases Subject to Other Law.

(1) A lease, although subject to this Article, is also subject to any applicable:

    (a) certificate of title statute of this State: (list any certificate of title statutes covering automobiles, trailers, mobile homes, boats, farm tractors, and the like);

    (b) certificate of title statute of another jurisdiction (Section 2A–105); or

    (c) consumer protection statute of this State, or final consumer protection decision of a court of this State existing on the effective date of this Article.

(2) In case of conflict between this Article, other than Sections 2A–105, 2A–304(3), and 2A–305(3), and a statute or decision referred to in subsection (1), the statute or decision controls.

(3) Failure to comply with an applicable law has only the effect specified therein.

As amended in 1990.

§ 2A–105. Territorial Application of Article to Goods Covered by Certificate of Title.

Subject to the provisions of Sections 2A–304(3) and 2A–305(3), with respect to goods covered by a certificate of title issued under a statute of this State or of another jurisdiction, compliance and the effect of compliance or noncompliance with a certificate of title statute are governed by the law (including the conflict of laws rules) of the jurisdiction issuing the certificate until the earlier of (a) surrender of the certificate, or (b) four months after the goods are removed from that jurisdiction and thereafter until a new certificate of title is issued by another jurisdiction.

§ 2A–106. Limitation on Power of Parties to Consumer Lease to Choose Applicable Law and Judicial Forum.

(1) If the law chosen by the parties to a consumer lease is that of a jurisdiction other than a jurisdiction in which the lessee resides at the time the lease agreement becomes enforceable or within 30 days thereafter or in which the goods are to be used, the choice is not enforceable.

(2) If the judicial forum chosen by the parties to a consumer lease is a forum that would not otherwise have jurisdiction over the lessee, the choice is not enforceable.

§ 2A–107. Waiver or Renunciation of Claim or Right After Default.

Any claim or right arising out of an alleged default or breach of warranty may be discharged in whole or in part without consideration by a written waiver or renunciation signed and delivered by the aggrieved party.

§ 2A–108. Unconscionability.

(1) If the court as a matter of law finds a lease contract or any clause of a lease contract to have been unconscionable at the time it was made the court may refuse to enforce the lease contract, or it may enforce the remainder of the lease contract without the unconscionable clause, or it may so limit the application of any unconscionable clause as to avoid any unconscionable result.

(2) With respect to a consumer lease, if the court as a matter of law finds that a lease contract or any clause of a lease contract has been induced by unconscionable conduct or that unconscionable conduct has occurred in the collection of a claim arising from a lease contract, the court may grant appropriate relief.

(3) Before making a finding of unconscionability under subsection (1) or (2), the court, on its own motion or that of a party, shall afford the parties a reasonable opportunity to present evidence as to the setting, purpose, and effect of the lease contract or clause thereof, or of the conduct.

(4) In an action in which the lessee claims unconscionability with respect to a consumer lease:

    (a) If the court finds unconscionability under subsection (1) or (2), the court shall award reasonable attorney's fees to the lessee.

    (b) If the court does not find unconscionability and the lessee claiming unconscionability has brought or maintained an action he [or she] knew to be groundless, the court shall award

reasonable attorney's fees to the party against whom the claim is made.

    (c) In determining attorney's fees, the amount of the recovery on behalf of the claimant under subsections (1) and (2) is not controlling.

§ 2A–109. Option to Accelerate at Will.

(1) A term providing that one party or his [or her] successor in interest may accelerate payment or performance or require collateral or additional collateral "at will" or "when he [or she] deems himself [or herself] insecure" or in words of similar import must be construed to mean that he [or she] has power to do so only if he [or she] in good faith believes that the prospect of payment or performance is impaired.

(2) With respect to a consumer lease, the burden of establishing good faith under subsection (1) is on the party who exercised the power; otherwise the burden of establishing lack of good faith is on the party against whom the power has been exercised.

Part 2—Formation and Construction of Lease Contract

§ 2A–201. Statute of Frauds.

(1) A lease contract is not enforceable by way of action or defense unless:

    (a) the total payments to be made under the lease contract, excluding payments for options to renew or buy, are less than $1,000; or

    (b) there is a writing, signed by the party against whom enforcement is sought or by that party's authorized agent, sufficient to indicate that a lease contract has been made between the parties and to describe the goods leased and the lease term.

(2) Any description of leased goods or of the lease term is sufficient and satisfies subsection (1)(b), whether or not it is specific, if it reasonably identifies what is described.

(3) A writing is not insufficient because it omits or incorrectly states a term agreed upon, but the lease contract is not enforceable under subsection (1)(b) beyond the lease term and the quantity of goods shown in the writing.

(4) A lease contract that does not satisfy the requirements of subsection (1), but which is valid in other respects, is enforceable:

    (a) if the goods are to be specially manufactured or obtained for the lessee and are not suitable for lease or sale to others in the ordinary course of the lessor's business, and the lessor, before notice of repudiation is received and under circumstances that reasonably indicate that the goods are for the lessee, has made either a substantial beginning of their manufacture or commitments for their procurement;

    (b) if the party against whom enforcement is sought admits in that party's pleading, testimony or otherwise in court that a lease contract was made, but the lease contract is not enforceable under this provision beyond the quantity of goods admitted; or

    (c) with respect to goods that have been received and accepted by the lessee.

(5) The lease term under a lease contract referred to in subsection (4) is:

    (a) if there is a writing signed by the party against whom enforcement is sought or by that party's authorized agent specifying the lease term, the term so specified;

(b) if the party against whom enforcement is sought admits in that party's pleading, testimony, or otherwise in court a lease term, the term so admitted; or

(c) a reasonable lease term.

§ 2A–202. Final Written Expression: Parol or Extrinsic Evidence.

Terms with respect to which the confirmatory memoranda of the parties agree or which are otherwise set forth in a writing intended by the parties as a final expression of their agreement with respect to such terms as are included therein may not be contradicted by evidence of any prior agreement or of a contemporaneous oral agreement but may be explained or supplemented:

(a) by course of dealing or usage of trade or by course of performance; and

(b) by evidence of consistent additional terms unless the court finds the writing to have been intended also as a complete and exclusive statement of the terms of the agreement.

§ 2A–203. Seals Inoperative.

The affixing of a seal to a writing evidencing a lease contract or an offer to enter into a lease contract does not render the writing a sealed instrument and the law with respect to sealed instruments does not apply to the lease contract or offer.

§ 2A–204. Formation in General.

(1) A lease contract may be made in any manner sufficient to show agreement, including conduct by both parties which recognizes the existence of a lease contract.

(2) An agreement sufficient to constitute a lease contract may be found although the moment of its making is undetermined.

(3) Although one or more terms are left open, a lease contract does not fail for indefiniteness if the parties have intended to make a lease contract and there is a reasonably certain basis for giving an appropriate remedy.

§ 2A–205. Firm Offers.

An offer by a merchant to lease goods to or from another person in a signed writing that by its terms gives assurance it will be held open is not revocable, for lack of consideration, during the time stated or, if no time is stated, for a reasonable time, but in no event may the period of irrevocability exceed 3 months. Any such term of assurance on a form supplied by the offeree must be separately signed by the offeror.

§ 2A–206. Offer and Acceptance in Formation of Lease Contract.

(1) Unless otherwise unambiguously indicated by the language or circumstances, an offer to make a lease contract must be construed as inviting acceptance in any manner and by any medium reasonable in the circumstances.

(2) If the beginning of a requested performance is a reasonable mode of acceptance, an offeror who is not notified of acceptance within a reasonable time may treat the offer as having lapsed before acceptance.

§ 2A–207. Course of Performance or Practical Construction.

(1) If a lease contract involves repeated occasions for performance by either party with knowledge of the nature of the performance and opportunity for objection to it by the other, any course of performance accepted or acquiesced in without objection is relevant to determine the meaning of the lease agreement.

(2) The express terms of a lease agreement and any course of performance, as well as any course of dealing and usage of trade, must be construed whenever reasonable as consistent with each other; but if that construction is unreasonable, express terms control course of performance, course of performance controls both course of dealing and usage of trade, and course of dealing controls usage of trade.

(3) Subject to the provisions of Section 2A–208 on modification and waiver, course of performance is relevant to show a waiver or modification of any term inconsistent with the course of performance.

§ 2A–208. Modification, Rescission and Waiver.

(1) An agreement modifying a lease contract needs no consideration to be binding.

(2) A signed lease agreement that excludes modification or rescission except by a signed writing may not be otherwise modified or rescinded, but, except as between merchants, such a requirement on a form supplied by a merchant must be separately signed by the other party.

(3) Although an attempt at modification or rescission does not satisfy the requirements of subsection (2), it may operate as a waiver.

(4) A party who has made a waiver affecting an executory portion of a lease contract may retract the waiver by reasonable notification received by the other party that strict performance will be required of any term waived, unless the retraction would be unjust in view of a material change of position in reliance on the waiver.

§ 2A–209. Lessee under Finance Lease as Beneficiary of Supply Contract.

(1) The benefit of the supplier's promises to the lessor under the supply contract and of all warranties, whether express or implied, including those of any third party provided in connection with or as part of the supply contract, extends to the lessee to the extent of the lessee's leasehold interest under a finance lease related to the supply contract, but is subject to the terms warranty and of the supply contract and all defenses or claims arising therefrom.

(2) The extension of the benefit of supplier's promises and of warranties to the lessee (Section 2A–209(1)) does not: (i) modify the rights and obligations of the parties to the supply contract, whether arising therefrom or otherwise, or (ii) impose any duty or liability under the supply contract on the lessee.

(3) Any modification or rescission of the supply contract by the supplier and the lessor is effective between the supplier and the lessee unless, before the modification or rescission, the supplier has received notice that the lessee has entered into a finance lease related to the supply contract. If the modification or rescission is effective between the supplier and the lessee, the lessor is deemed to have assumed, in addition to the obligations of the lessor to the lessee under the lease contract, promises of the supplier to the lessor and warranties that were so modified or rescinded as they existed and were available to the lessee before modification or rescission.

(4) In addition to the extension of the benefit of the supplier's promises and of warranties to the lessee under subsection (1), the lessee retains all rights that the lessee may have against the supplier which arise from an agreement between the lessee and the supplier or under other law.

As amended in 1990.

§ 2A–210. Express Warranties.

(1) Express warranties by the lessor are created as follows:

(a) Any affirmation of fact or promise made by the lessor to the lessee which relates to the goods and becomes part of the basis of the bargain creates an express warranty that the goods will conform to the affirmation or promise.

(b) Any description of the goods which is made part of the basis of the bargain creates an express warranty that the goods will conform to the description.

(c) Any sample or model that is made part of the basis of the bargain creates an express warranty that the whole of the goods will conform to the sample or model.

(2) It is not necessary to the creation of an express warranty that the lessor use formal words, such as "warrant" or "guarantee," or that the lessor have a specific intention to make a warranty, but an affirmation merely of the value of the goods or a statement purporting to be merely the lessor's opinion or commendation of the goods does not create a warranty.

§ 2A–211. Warranties Against Interference and Against Infringement; Lessee's Obligation Against Infringement.

(1) There is in a lease contract a warranty that for the lease term no person holds a claim to or interest in the goods that arose from an act or omission of the lessor, other than a claim by way of infringement or the like, which will interfere with the lessee's enjoyment of its leasehold interest.

(2) Except in a finance lease there is in a lease contract by a lessor who is a merchant regularly dealing in goods of the kind a warranty that the goods are delivered free of the rightful claim of any person by way of infringement or the like.

(3) A lessee who furnishes specifications to a lessor or a supplier shall hold the lessor and the supplier harmless against any claim by way of infringement or the like that arises out of compliance with the specifications.

§ 2A–212. Implied Warranty of Merchantability.

(1) Except in a finance lease, a warranty that the goods will be merchantable is implied in a lease contract if the lessor is a merchant with respect to goods of that kind.

(2) Goods to be merchantable must be at least such as

(a) pass without objection in the trade under the description in the lease agreement;

(b) in the case of fungible goods, are of fair average quality within the description;

(c) are fit for the ordinary purposes for which goods of that type are used;

(d) run, within the variation permitted by the lease agreement, of even kind, quality, and quantity within each unit and among all units involved;

(e) are adequately contained, packaged, and labeled as the lease agreement may require; and

(f) conform to any promises or affirmations of fact made on the container or label.

(3) Other implied warranties may arise from course of dealing or usage of trade.

§ 2A–213. Implied Warranty of Fitness for Particular Purpose.

Except in a finance of lease, if the lessor at the time the lease contract is made has reason to know of any particular purpose for which the goods are required and that the lessee is relying on the lessor's skill or judgment to select or furnish suitable goods, there is in the lease contract an implied warranty that the goods will be fit for that purpose.

§ 2A–214. Exclusion or Modification of Warranties.

(1) Words or conduct relevant to the creation of an express warranty and words or conduct tending to negate or limit a warranty must be construed wherever reasonable as consistent with each other; but, subject to the provisions of Section 2A–202 on parol or extrinsic evidence, negation or limitation is inoperative to the extent that the construction is unreasonable.

(2) Subject to subsection (3), to exclude or modify the implied warranty of merchantability or any part of it the language must mention "merchantability", be by a writing, and be conspicuous. Subject to subsection (3), to exclude or modify any implied warranty of fitness the exclusion must be by a writing and be conspicuous. Language to exclude all implied warranties of fitness is sufficient if it is in writing, is conspicuous and states, for example, "There is no warranty that the goods will be fit for a particular purpose".

(3) Notwithstanding subsection (2), but subject to subsection (4),

(a) unless the circumstances indicate otherwise, all implied warranties are excluded by expressions like "as is" or "with all faults" or by other language that in common understanding calls the lessee's attention to the exclusion of warranties and makes plain that there is no implied warranty, if in writing and conspicuous;

(b) if the lessee before entering into the lease contract has examined the goods or the sample or model as fully as desired or has refused to examine the goods, there is no implied warranty with regard to defects that an examination ought in the circumstances to have revealed; and

(c) an implied warranty may also be excluded or modified by course of dealing, course of performance, or usage of trade.

(4) To exclude or modify a warranty against interference or against infringement (Section 2A–211) or any part of it, the language must be specific, be by a writing, and be conspicuous, unless the circumstances, including course of performance, course of dealing, or usage of trade, give the lessee reason to know that the goods are being leased subject to a claim or interest of any person.

§ 2A–215. Cumulation and Conflict of Warranties Express or Implied.

Warranties, whether express or implied, must be construed as consistent with each other and as cumulative, but if that construction is unreasonable, the intention of the parties determines which warranty is dominant. In ascertaining that intention the following rules apply:

(a) Exact or technical specifications displace an inconsistent sample or model or general language of description.

(b) A sample from an existing bulk displaces inconsistent general language of description.

(c) Express warranties displace inconsistent implied warranties other than an implied warranty of fitness for a particular purpose.

§ 2A–216. Third-Party Beneficiaries of Express and Implied Warranties.

Alternative A

A warranty to or for the benefit of a lessee under this Article, whether express or implied, extends to any natural person who is in the family or household of the lessee or who is a guest in the lessee's home if it is reasonable to expect that such person may use, consume, or be affected by the goods and who is injured in person by breach of the warranty. This section does not displace principles of law and equity that extend a warranty to or for the benefit of a lessee to other persons. The operation of this section may not be excluded, modified, or limited, but an exclusion, modification, or limitation of the warranty, including any with respect to rights and remedies, effective against the lessee is also effective against any beneficiary designated under this section.

Alternative B

A warranty to or for the benefit of a lessee under this Article, whether express or implied, extends to any natural person who may reasonably be expected to use, consume, or be affected by the goods and who is injured in person by breach of the warranty. This section does not displace principles of law and equity that extend a warranty to or for the benefit of a lessee to other persons. The operation of this section may not be excluded, modified, or limited, but an exclusion, modification, or limitation of the warranty, including any with respect to rights and remedies, effective against the lessee is also effective against the beneficiary designated under this section.

Alternative C

A warranty to or for the benefit of a lessee under this Article, whether express or implied, extends to any person who may reasonably be expected to use, consume, or be affected by the goods and who is injured by breach of the warranty. The operation of this section may not be excluded, modified, or limited with respect to injury to the person of an individual to whom the warranty extends, but an exclusion, modification, or limitation of the warranty, including any with respect to rights and remedies, effective against the lessee is also effective against the beneficiary designated under this section.

§ 2A–217. Identification.

Identification of goods as goods to which a lease contract refers may be made at any time and in any manner explicitly agreed to by the parties. In the absence of explicit agreement, identification occurs:
(a) when the lease contract is made if the lease contract is for a lease of goods that are existing and identified;
(b) when the goods are shipped, marked, or otherwise designated by the lessor as goods to which the lease contract refers, if the lease contract is for a lease of goods that are not existing and identified; or
(c) when the young are conceived, if the lease contract is for a lease of unborn young of animals.

§ 2A–218. Insurance and Proceeds.

(1) A lessee obtains an insurable interest when existing goods are identified to the lease contract even though the goods identified are nonconforming and the lessee has an option to reject them.
(2) If a lessee has an insurable interest only by reason of the lessor's identification of the goods, the lessor, until default or insolvency or notification to the lessee that identification is final, may substitute other goods for those identified.
(3) Notwithstanding a lessee's insurable interest under subsections (1) and (2), the lessor retains an insurable interest until an option to buy has been exercised by the lessee and risk of loss has passed to the lessee.
(4) Nothing in this section impairs any insurable interest recognized under any other statute or rule of law.

(5) The parties by agreement may determine that one or more parties have an obligation to obtain and pay for insurance covering the goods and by agreement may determine the beneficiary of the proceeds of the insurance.

§ 2A–219. Risk of Loss.

(1) Except in the case of a finance lease, risk of loss is retained by the lessor and does not pass to the lessee. In the case of a finance lease, risk of loss passes to the lessee.
(2) Subject to the provisions of this Article on the effect of default on risk of loss (Section 2A–220), if risk of loss is to pass to the lessee and the time of passage is not stated, the following rules apply:
  (a) If the lease contract requires or authorizes the goods to be shipped by carrier
      (i) and it does not require delivery at a particular destination, the risk of loss passes to the lessee when the goods are duly delivered to the carrier; but
      (ii) if it does require delivery at a particular destination and the goods are there duly tendered while in the possession of the carrier, the risk of loss passes to the lessee when the goods are there duly so tendered as to enable the lessee to take delivery.
  (b) If the goods are held by a bailee to be delivered without being moved, the risk of loss passes to the lessee on acknowledgment by the bailee of the lessee's right to possession of the goods.
  (c) In any case not within subsection (a) or (b), the risk of loss passes to the lessee on the lessee's receipt of the goods if the lessor, or, in the case of a finance lease, the supplier, is a merchant; otherwise the risk passes to the lessee on tender of delivery.

§ 2A–220. Effect of Default on Risk of Loss.

(1) Where risk of loss is to pass to the lessee and the time of passage is not stated:
  (a) If a tender or delivery of goods so fails to conform to the lease contract as to give a right of rejection, the risk of their loss remains with the lessor, or, in the case of a finance lease, the supplier, until cure or acceptance.
  (b) If the lessee rightfully revokes acceptance, he [or she], to the extent of any deficiency in his [or her] effective insurance coverage, may treat the risk of loss as having remained with the lessor from the beginning.
(2) Whether or not risk of loss is to pass to the lessee, if the lessee as to conforming goods already identified to a lease contract repudiates or is otherwise in default under the lease contract, the lessor, or, in the case of a finance lease, the supplier, to the extent of any deficiency in his [or her] effective insurance coverage may treat the risk of loss as resting on the lessee for a commercially reasonable time.

§ 2A–221. Casualty to Identified Goods.

If a lease contract requires goods identified when the lease contract is made, and the goods suffer casualty without fault of the lessee, the lessor or the supplier before delivery, or the goods suffer casualty before risk of loss passes to the lessee pursuant to the lease agreement or Section 2A–219, then:
(a) if the loss is total, the lease contract is avoided; and
(b) if the loss is partial or the goods have so deteriorated as to no longer conform to the lease contract, the lessee may nevertheless demand inspection and at his [or her] option either treat the lease contract as avoided or, except in a finance lease that is not

a consumer lease, accept the goods with due allowance from the rent payable for the balance of the lease term for the deterioration or the deficiency in quantity but without further right against the lessor.

Part 3—Effect of Lease Contract

§ 2A–301. Enforceability of Lease Contract.
Except as otherwise provided in this Article, a lease contract is effective and enforceable according to its terms between the parties, against purchasers of the goods and against creditors of the parties.

§ 2A–302. Title to and Possession of Goods.
Except as otherwise provided in this Article, each provision of this Article applies whether the lessor or a third party has title to the goods, and whether the lessor, the lessee, or a third party has possession of the goods, notwithstanding any statute or rule of law that possession or the absence of possession is fraudulent.

§ 2A–303. Alienability of Party's Interest Under Lease Contract or of Lessor's Residual Interest in Goods; Delegation of Performance; Transfer of Rights.
(1) As used in this section, "creation of a security interest" includes the sale of a lease contract that is subject to Article 9, Secured Transactions, by reason of Section 9–109(a)(3).

(2) Except as provided in subsections (3) and Section 9–407, a provision in a lease agreement which (i) prohibits the voluntary or involuntary transfer, including a transfer by sale, sublease, creation or enforcement of a security interest, or attachment, levy, or other judicial process, of an interest of a party under the lease contract or of the lessor's residual interest in the goods, or (ii) makes such a transfer an event of default, gives rise to the rights and remedies provided in subsection (4), but a transfer that is prohibited or is an event of default under the lease agreement is otherwise effective.

(3) A provision in a lease agreement which (i) prohibits a transfer of a right to damages for default with respect to the whole lease contract or of a right to payment arising out of the transferor's due performance of the transferor's entire obligation, or (ii) makes such a transfer an event of default, is not enforceable, and such a transfer is not a transfer that materially impairs the prospect of obtaining return performance by, materially changes the duty of, or materially increases the burden or risk imposed on, the other party to the lease contract within the purview of subsection (4).

(4) Subject to subsection (3) and Section 9–407:

(a) if a transfer is made which is made an event of default under a lease agreement, the party to the lease contract not making the transfer, unless that party waives the default or otherwise agrees, has the rights and remedies described in Section 2A–501(2);

(b) if paragraph (a) is not applicable and if a transfer is made that (i) is prohibited under a lease agreement or (ii) materially impairs the prospect of obtaining return performance by, materially changes the duty of, or materially increases the burden or risk imposed on, the other party to the lease contract, unless the party not making the transfer agrees at any time to the transfer in the lease contract or otherwise, then, except as limited by contract, (i) the transferor is liable to the party not making the transfer for damages caused by the transfer to the extent that the damages could not reasonably be prevented by the party not making the transfer and (ii) a court having jurisdiction may

grant other appropriate relief, including cancellation of the lease contract or an injunction against the transfer.

(5) A transfer of "the lease" or of "all my rights under the lease", or a transfer in similar general terms, is a transfer of rights and, unless the language or the circumstances, as in a transfer for security, indicate the contrary, the transfer is a delegation of duties by the transferor to the transferee. Acceptance by the transferee constitutes a promise by the transferee to perform those duties. The promise is enforceable by either the transferor or the other party to the lease contract.

(6) Unless otherwise agreed by the lessor and the lessee, a delegation of performance does not relieve the transferor as against the other party of any duty to perform or of any liability for default.

(7) In a consumer lease, to prohibit the transfer of an interest of a party under the lease contract or to make a transfer an event of default, the language must be specific, by a writing, and conspicuous. As amended in 1990 and 1999.

§ 2A–304. Subsequent Lease of Goods by Lessor.
(1) Subject to Section 2A–303, a subsequent lessee from a lessor of goods under an existing lease contract obtains, to the extent of the leasehold interest transferred, the leasehold interest in the goods that the lessor had or had power to transfer, and except as provided in subsection (2) and Section 2A–527(4), takes subject to the existing lease contract. A lessor with voidable title has power to transfer a good leasehold interest to a good faith subsequent lessee for value, but only to the extent set forth in the preceding sentence. If goods have been delivered under a transaction of purchase the lessor has that power even though:

(a) the lessor's transferor was deceived as to the identity of the lessor;

(b) the delivery was in exchange for a check which is later dishonored;

(c) it was agreed that the transaction was to be a "cash sale"; or

(d) the delivery was procured through fraud punishable as larcenous under the criminal law.

(2) A subsequent lessee in the ordinary course of business from a lessor who is a merchant dealing in goods of that kind to whom the goods were entrusted by the existing lessee of that lessor before the interest of the subsequent lessee became enforceable against that lessor obtains, to the extent of the leasehold interest transferred, all of that lessor's and the existing lessee's rights to the goods, and takes free of the existing lease contract.

(3) A subsequent lessee from the lessor of goods that are subject to an existing lease contract and are covered by a certificate of title issued under a statute of this State or of another jurisdiction takes no greater rights than those provided both by this section and by the certificate of title statute.
As amended in 1990.

§ 2A–305. Sale or Sublease of Goods by Lessee.
(1) Subject to the provisions of Section 2A–303, a buyer or sublessee from the lessee of goods under an existing lease contract obtains, to the extent of the interest transferred, the leasehold interest in the goods that the lessee had or had power to transfer, and except as provided in subsection (2) and Section 2A–511(4), takes subject to the existing lease contract. A lessee with a voidable leasehold interest has power to transfer a good leasehold interest to a good faith buyer for value or a good faith sublessee for value, but only to the

extent set forth in the preceding sentence. When goods have been delivered under a transaction of lease the lessee has that power even though:

(a) the lessor was deceived as to the identity of the lessee;

(b) the delivery was in exchange for a check which is later dishonored;

(c) the delivery was procured through fraud punishable as larcenous under the criminal law.

(2) A buyer in the ordinary course of business or a sublessee in the ordinary course of business from a lessee who is a merchant dealing in goods of that kind to whom the goods were entrusted by the lessor obtains, to the extent of the interest transferred, all of the lessor's and lessee's rights to the goods, and takes free of the existing lease contract.

(3) A buyer or sublessee from the lessee of goods that are subject to an existing lease contract and are covered by a certificate of title issued under a statute of this State or of another jurisdiction takes no greater rights than those provided both by this section and by the certificate of title statute.

§ 2A–306. Priority of Certain Liens
Arising by Operation of Law.

If a person in the ordinary course of his [or her] business furnishes services or materials with respect to goods subject to a lease contract, a lien upon those goods in the possession of that person given by statute or rule of law for those materials or services takes priority over any interest of the lessor or lessee under the lease contract or this Article unless the lien is created by statute and the statute provides otherwise or unless the lien is created by rule of law and the rule of law provides otherwise.

§ 2A–307. Priority of Liens Arising by Attachment or Levy
on, Security Interests in, and Other Claims to Goods.

(1) Except as otherwise provided in Section 2A–306, a creditor of a lessee takes subject to the lease contract.

(2) Except as otherwise provided in subsection (3) and in Sections 2A–306 and 2A–308, a creditor of a lessor takes subject to the lease contract unless the creditor holds a lien that attached to the goods before the lease contract became enforceable.

(3) Except as otherwise provided in Sections 9–317, 9–321, and 9–323, a lessee takes a leasehold interest subject to a security interest held by a creditor of the lessor.

As amended in 1990 and 1999.

§ 2A–308. Special Rights of Creditors.

(1) A creditor of a lessor in possession of goods subject to a lease contract may treat the lease contract as void if as against the creditor retention of possession by the lessor is fraudulent under any statute or rule of law, but retention of possession in good faith and current course of trade by the lessor for a commercially reasonable time after the lease contract becomes enforceable is not fraudulent.

(2) Nothing in this Article impairs the rights of creditors of a lessor if the lease contract (a) becomes enforceable, not in current course of trade but in satisfaction of or as security for a pre-existing claim for money, security, or the like, and (b) is made under circumstances which under any statute or rule of law apart from this Article would constitute the transaction a fraudulent transfer or voidable preference.

(3) A creditor of a seller may treat a sale or an identification of goods to a contract for sale as void if as against the creditor retention of possession by the seller is fraudulent under any statute or rule of law, but retention of possession of the goods pursuant to a lease contract entered into by the seller as lessee and the buyer as lessor in connection with the sale or identification of the goods is not fraudulent if the buyer bought for value and in good faith.

§ 2A–309. Lessor's and Lessee's Rights When
Goods Become Fixtures.

(1) In this section:

(a) goods are "fixtures" when they become so related to particular real estate that an interest in them arises under real estate law;

(b) a "fixture filing" is the filing, in the office where a mortgage on the real estate would be filed or recorded, of a financing statement covering goods that are or are to become fixtures and conforming to the requirements of Section 9–502(a) and (b);

(c) a lease is a "purchase money lease" unless the lessee has possession or use of the goods or the right to possession or use of the goods before the lease agreement is enforceable;

(d) a mortgage is a "construction mortgage" to the extent it secures an obligation incurred for the construction of an improvement on land including the acquisition cost of the land, if the recorded writing so indicates; and

(e) "encumbrance" includes real estate mortgages and other liens on real estate and all other rights in real estate that are not ownership interests.

(2) Under this Article a lease may be of goods that are fixtures or may continue in goods that become fixtures, but no lease exists under this Article of ordinary building materials incorporated into an improvement on land.

(3) This Article does not prevent creation of a lease of fixtures pursuant to real estate law.

(4) The perfected interest of a lessor of fixtures has priority over a conflicting interest of an encumbrancer or owner of the real estate if:

(a) the lease is a purchase money lease, the conflicting interest of the encumbrancer or owner arises before the goods become fixtures, the interest of the lessor is perfected by a fixture filing before the goods become fixtures or within ten days thereafter, and the lessee has an interest of record in the real estate or is in possession of the real estate; or

(b) the interest of the lessor is perfected by a fixture filing before the interest of the encumbrancer or owner is of record, the lessor's interest has priority over any conflicting interest of a predecessor in title of the encumbrancer or owner, and the lessee has an interest of record in the real estate or is in possession of the real estate.

(5) The interest of a lessor of fixtures, whether or not perfected, has priority over the conflicting interest of an encumbrancer or owner of the real estate if:

(a) the fixtures are readily removable factory or office machines, readily removable equipment that is not primarily used or leased for use in the operation of the real estate, or readily removable replacements of domestic appliances that are goods subject to a consumer lease, and before the goods become fixtures the lease contract is enforceable; or

(b) the conflicting interest is a lien on the real estate obtained by legal or equitable proceedings after the lease contract is enforceable; or

(c) the encumbrancer or owner has consented in writing to the lease or has disclaimed an interest in the goods as fixtures; or

(d) the lessee has a right to remove the goods as against the encumbrancer or owner. If the lessee's right to remove terminates, the priority of the interest of the lessor continues for a reasonable time.

(6) Notwithstanding paragraph (4)(a) but otherwise subject to subsections (4) and (5), the interest of a lessor of fixtures, including the lessor's residual interest, is subordinate to the conflicting interest of an encumbrancer of the real estate under a construction mortgage recorded before the goods become fixtures if the goods become fixtures before the completion of the construction. To the extent given to refinance a construction mortgage, the conflicting interest of an encumbrancer of the real estate under a mortgage has this priority to the same extent as the encumbrancer of the real estate under the construction mortgage.

(7) In cases not within the preceding subsections, priority between the interest of a lessor of fixtures, including the lessor's residual interest, and the conflicting interest of an encumbrancer or owner of the real estate who is not the lessee is determined by the priority rules governing conflicting interests in real estate.

(8) If the interest of a lessor of fixtures, including the lessor's residual interest, has priority over all conflicting interests of all owners and encumbrancers of the real estate, the lessor or the lessee may (i) on default, expiration, termination, or cancellation of the lease agreement but subject to the agreement and this Article, or (ii) if necessary to enforce other rights and remedies of the lessor or lessee under this Article, remove the goods from the real estate, free and clear of all conflicting interests of all owners and encumbrancers of the real estate, but the lessor or lessee must reimburse any encumbrancer or owner of the real estate who is not the lessee and who has not otherwise agreed for the cost of repair of any physical injury, but not for any diminution in value of the real estate caused by the absence of the goods removed or by any necessity of replacing them. A person entitled to reimbursement may refuse permission to remove until the party seeking removal gives adequate security for the performance of this obligation.

(9) Even though the lease agreement does not create a security interest, the interest of a lessor of fixtures, including the lessor's residual interest, is perfected by filing a financing statement as a fixture filing for leased goods that are or are to become fixtures in accordance with the relevant provisions of the Article on Secured Transactions (Article 9).
As amended in 1990 and 1999.

§ 2A–310. Lessor's and Lessee's Rights When Goods Become Accessions.

(1) Goods are "accessions" when they are installed in or affixed to other goods.

(2) The interest of a lessor or a lessee under a lease contract entered into before the goods became accessions is superior to all interests in the whole except as stated in subsection (4).

(3) The interest of a lessor or a lessee under a lease contract entered into at the time or after the goods became accessions is superior to all subsequently acquired interests in the whole except as stated in subsection (4) but is subordinate to interests in the whole existing at the time the lease contract was made unless the holders of such interests in the whole have in writing consented to the lease or disclaimed an interest in the goods as part of the whole.

(4) The interest of a lessor or a lessee under a lease contract described in subsection (2) or (3) is subordinate to the interest of

(a) a buyer in the ordinary course of business or a lessee in the ordinary course of business of any interest in the whole acquired after the goods became accessions; or

(b) a creditor with a security interest in the whole perfected before the lease contract was made to the extent that the creditor makes subsequent advances without knowledge of the lease contract.

(5) When under subsections (2) or (3) and (4) a lessor or a lessee of accessions holds an interest that is superior to all interests in the whole, the lessor or the lessee may (a) on default, expiration, termination, or cancellation of the lease contract by the other party but subject to the provisions of the lease contract and this Article, or (b) if necessary to enforce his [or her] other rights and remedies under this Article, remove the goods from the whole, free and clear of all interests in the whole, but he [or she] must reimburse any holder of an interest in the whole who is not the lessee and who has not otherwise agreed for the cost of repair of any physical injury but not for any diminution in value of the whole caused by the absence of the goods removed or by any necessity for replacing them. A person entitled to reimbursement may refuse permission to remove until the party seeking removal gives adequate security for the performance of this obligation.

§ 2A–311. Priority Subject to Subordination.
Nothing in this Article prevents subordination by agreement by any person entitled to priority.
As added in 1990.

Part 4—Performance of Lease Contract: Repudiated, Substituted and Excused

§ 2A–401. Insecurity: Adequate Assurance of Performance.
(1) A lease contract imposes an obligation on each party that the other's expectation of receiving due performance will not be impaired.

(2) If reasonable grounds for insecurity arise with respect to the performance of either party, the insecure party may demand in writing adequate assurance of due performance. Until the insecure party receives that assurance, if commercially reasonable the insecure party may suspend any performance for which he [or she] has not already received the agreed return.

(3) A repudiation of the lease contract occurs if assurance of due performance adequate under the circumstances of the particular case is not provided to the insecure party within a reasonable time, not to exceed 30 days after receipt of a demand by the other party.

(4) Between merchants, the reasonableness of grounds for insecurity and the adequacy of any assurance offered must be determined according to commercial standards.

(5) Acceptance of any nonconforming delivery or payment does not prejudice the aggrieved party's right to demand adequate assurance of future performance.

§ 2A–402. Anticipatory Repudiation.
If either party repudiates a lease contract with respect to a performance not yet due under the lease contract, the loss of which performance will substantially impair the value of the lease contract to the other, the aggrieved party may:

(a) for a commercially reasonable time, await retraction of repudiation and performance by the repudiating party;

(b) make demand pursuant to Section 2A–401 and await assurance of future performance adequate under the circumstances of the particular case; or

(c) resort to any right or remedy upon default under the lease contract or this Article, even though the aggrieved party has notified the repudiating party that the aggrieved party would await the repudiating party's performance and assurance and has urged retraction. In addition, whether or not the aggrieved party is pursuing one of the foregoing remedies, the aggrieved party may suspend performance or, if the aggrieved party is the lessor, proceed in accordance with the provisions of this Article on the lessor's right to identify goods to the lease contract notwithstanding default or to salvage unfinished goods (Section 2A–524).

§ 2A–403. Retraction of Anticipatory Repudiation.

(1) Until the repudiating party's next performance is due, the repudiating party can retract the repudiation unless, since the repudiation, the aggrieved party has cancelled the lease contract or materially changed the aggrieved party's position or otherwise indicated that the aggrieved party considers the repudiation final.

(2) Retraction may be by any method that clearly indicates to the aggrieved party that the repudiating party intends to perform under the lease contract and includes any assurance demanded under Section 2A–401.

(3) Retraction reinstates a repudiating party's rights under a lease contract with due excuse and allowance to the aggrieved party for any delay occasioned by the repudiation.

§ 2A–404. Substituted Performance.

(1) If without fault of the lessee, the lessor and the supplier, the agreed berthing, loading, or unloading facilities fail or the agreed type of carrier becomes unavailable or the agreed manner of delivery otherwise becomes commercially impracticable, but a commercially reasonable substitute is available, the substitute performance must be tendered and accepted.

(2) If the agreed means or manner of payment fails because of domestic or foreign governmental regulation:

(a) the lessor may withhold or stop delivery or cause the supplier to withhold or stop delivery unless the lessee provides a means or manner of payment that is commercially a substantial equivalent; and

(b) if delivery has already been taken, payment by the means or in the manner provided by the regulation discharges the lessee's obligation unless the regulation is discriminatory, oppressive, or predatory.

§ 2A–405. Excused Performance.

Subject to Section 2A–404 on substituted performance, the following rules apply:

(a) Delay in delivery or nondelivery in whole or in part by a lessor or a supplier who complies with paragraphs (b) and (c) is not a default under the lease contract if performance as agreed has been made impracticable by the occurrence of a contingency the nonoccurrence of which was a basic assumption on which the lease contract was made or by compliance in good faith with any applicable foreign or domestic governmental regulation or order, whether or not the regulation or order later proves to be invalid.

(b) If the causes mentioned in paragraph (a) affect only part of the lessor's or the supplier's capacity to perform, he [or she] shall allocate production and deliveries among his [or her] customers but at his [or her] option may include regular customers not then under contract for sale or lease as well as his [or her] own requirements for further manufacture. He [or she] may so allocate in any manner that is fair and reasonable.

(c) The lessor seasonably shall notify the lessee and in the case of a finance lease the supplier seasonably shall notify the lessor and the lessee, if known, that there will be delay or nondelivery and, if allocation is required under paragraph (b), of the estimated quota thus made available for the lessee.

§ 2A–406. Procedure on Excused Performance.

(1) If the lessee receives notification of a material or indefinite delay or an allocation justified under Section 2A–405, the lessee may by written notification to the lessor as to any goods involved, and with respect to all of the goods if under an installment lease contract the value of the whole lease contract is substantially impaired (Section 2A–510):

(a) terminate the lease contract (Section 2A–505(2)); or

(b) except in a finance lease that is not a consumer lease, modify the lease contract by accepting the available quota in substitution, with due allowance from the rent payable for the balance of the lease term for the deficiency but without further right against the lessor.

(2) If, after receipt of a notification from the lessor under Section 2A–405, the lessee fails so to modify the lease agreement within a reasonable time not exceeding 30 days, the lease contract lapses with respect to any deliveries affected.

§ 2A–407. Irrevocable Promises: Finance Leases.

(1) In the case of a finance lease that is not a consumer lease the lessee's promises under the lease contract become irrevocable and independent upon the lessee's acceptance of the goods.

(2) A promise that has become irrevocable and independent under subsection (1):

(a) is effective and enforceable between the parties, and by or against third parties including assignees of the parties, and

(b) is not subject to cancellation, termination, modification, repudiation, excuse, or substitution without the consent of the party to whom the promise runs.

(3) This section does not affect the validity under any other law of a covenant in any lease contract making the lessee's promises irrevocable and independent upon the lessee's acceptance of the goods. As amended in 1990.

Part 5—Default

A. In General

§ 2A–501. Default: Procedure.

(1) Whether the lessor or the lessee is in default under a lease contract is determined by the lease agreement and this Article.

(2) If the lessor or the lessee is in default under the lease contract, the party seeking enforcement has rights and remedies as provided in this Article and, except as limited by this Article, as provided in the lease agreement.

(3) If the lessor or the lessee is in default under the lease contract, the party seeking enforcement may reduce the party's claim to judgment, or otherwise enforce the lease contract by self-help or any available judicial procedure or nonjudicial procedure, including administrative proceeding, arbitration, or the like, in accordance with this Article.

(4) Except as otherwise provided in Section 1–106(1) or this Article or the lease agreement, the rights and remedies referred to in subsections (2) and (3) are cumulative.

(5) If the lease agreement covers both real property and goods, the party seeking enforcement may proceed under this Part as to the goods, or under other applicable law as to both the real property and the goods in accordance with that party's rights and remedies in respect of the real property, in which case this Part does not apply. As amended in 1990.

§ 2A–502. Notice After Default.

Except as otherwise provided in this Article or the lease agreement, the lessor or lessee in default under the lease contract is not entitled to notice of default or notice of enforcement from the other party to the lease agreement.

§ 2A–503. Modification or Impairment of Rights and Remedies.

(1) Except as otherwise provided in this Article, the lease agreement may include rights and remedies for default in addition to or in substitution for those provided in this Article and may limit or alter the measure of damages recoverable under this Article.

(2) Resort to a remedy provided under this Article or in the lease agreement is optional unless the remedy is expressly agreed to be exclusive. If circumstances cause an exclusive or limited remedy to fail of its essential purpose, or provision for an exclusive remedy is unconscionable, remedy may be had as provided in this Article.

(3) Consequential damages may be liquidated under Section 2A–504, or may otherwise be limited, altered, or excluded unless the limitation, alteration, or exclusion is unconscionable. Limitation, alteration, or exclusion of consequential damages for injury to the person in the case of consumer goods is *prima facie* unconscionable but limitation, alteration, or exclusion of damages where the loss is commercial is not *prima facie* unconscionable.

(4) Rights and remedies on default by the lessor or the lessee with respect to any obligation or promise collateral or ancillary to the lease contract are not impaired by this Article. As amended in 1990.

§ 2A–504. Liquidation of Damages.

(1) Damages payable by either party for default, or any other act or omission, including indemnity for loss or diminution of anticipated tax benefits or loss or damage to lessor's residual interest, may be liquidated in the lease agreement but only at an amount or by a formula that is reasonable in light of the then anticipated harm caused by the default or other act or omission.

(2) If the lease agreement provides for liquidation of damages, and such provision does not comply with subsection (1), or such provision is an exclusive or limited remedy that circumstances cause to fail of its essential purpose, remedy may be had as provided in this Article.

(3) If the lessor justifiably withholds or stops delivery of goods because of the lessee's default or insolvency (Section 2A–525 or 2A–526), the lessee is entitled to restitution of any amount by which the sum of his [or her] payments exceeds:

> **(a)** the amount to which the lessor is entitled by virtue of terms liquidating the lessor's damages in accordance with subsection (1); or

> **(b)** in the absence of those terms, 20 percent of the then present value of the total rent the lessee was obligated to pay for the balance of the lease term, or, in the case of a consumer lease, the lesser of such amount or $500.

(4) A lessee's right to restitution under subsection (3) is subject to offset to the extent the lessor establishes:

> **(a)** a right to recover damages under the provisions of this Article other than subsection (1); and

> **(b)** the amount or value of any benefits received by the lessee directly or indirectly by reason of the lease contract.

§ 2A–505. Cancellation and Termination and Effect of Cancellation, Termination, Rescission, or Fraud on Rights and Remedies.

(1) On cancellation of the lease contract, all obligations that are still executory on both sides are discharged, but any right based on prior default or performance survives, and the cancelling party also retains any remedy for default of the whole lease contract or any unperformed balance.

(2) On termination of the lease contract, all obligations that are still executory on both sides are discharged but any right based on prior default or performance survives.

(3) Unless the contrary intention clearly appears, expressions of "cancellation," "rescission," or the like of the lease contract may not be construed as a renunciation or discharge of any claim in damages for an antecedent default.

(4) Rights and remedies for material misrepresentation or fraud include all rights and remedies available under this Article for default.

(5) Neither rescission nor a claim for rescission of the lease contract nor rejection or return of the goods may bar or be deemed inconsistent with a claim for damages or other right or remedy.

§ 2A–506. Statute of Limitations.

(1) An action for default under a lease contract, including breach of warranty or indemnity, must be commenced within 4 years after the cause of action accrued. By the original lease contract the parties may reduce the period of limitation to not less than one year.

(2) A cause of action for default accrues when the act or omission on which the default or breach of warranty is based is or should have been discovered by the aggrieved party, or when the default occurs, whichever is later. A cause of action for indemnity accrues when the act or omission on which the claim for indemnity is based is or should have been discovered by the indemnified party, whichever is later.

(3) If an action commenced within the time limited by subsection (1) is so terminated as to leave available a remedy by another action for the same default or breach of warranty or indemnity, the other action may be commenced after the expiration of the time limited and within 6 months after the termination of the first action unless the termination resulted from voluntary discontinuance or from dismissal for failure or neglect to prosecute.

(4) This section does not alter the law on tolling of the statute of limitations nor does it apply to causes of action that have accrued before this Article becomes effective.

§ 2A–507. Proof of Market Rent: Time and Place.

(1) Damages based on market rent (Section 2A–519 or 2A–528) are determined according to the rent for the use of the goods concerned for a lease term identical to the remaining lease term of the original lease agreement and prevailing at the times specified in Sections 2A–519 and 2A–528.

(2) If evidence of rent for the use of the goods concerned for a lease term identical to the remaining lease term of the original lease agreement and prevailing at the times or places described in this Article is not readily available, the rent prevailing within any reasonable time before or after the time described or at any other place or for a different lease term which in commercial judgment or under usage of trade would serve as a reasonable substitute for the one described may be used, making any proper allowance for the difference, including the cost of transporting the goods to or from the other place.

(3) Evidence of a relevant rent prevailing at a time or place or for a lease term other than the one described in this Article offered by one party is not admissible unless and until he [or she] has given the other party notice the court finds sufficient to prevent unfair surprise.

(4) If the prevailing rent or value of any goods regularly leased in any established market is in issue, reports in official publications or trade journals or in newspapers or periodicals of general circulation published as the reports of that market are admissible in evidence. The circumstances of the preparation of the report may be shown to affect its weight but not its admissibility.
As amended in 1990.

B. Default by Lessor

§ 2A–508.   Lessee's Remedies.

(1) If a lessor fails to deliver the goods in conformity to the lease contract (Section 2A–509) or repudiates the lease contract (Section 2A–402), or a lessee rightfully rejects the goods (Section 2A–509) or justifiably revokes acceptance of the goods (Section 2A–517), then with respect to any goods involved, and with respect to all of the goods if under an installment lease contract the value of the whole lease contract is substantially impaired (Section 2A–510), the lessor is in default under the lease contract and the lessee may:

  (a) cancel the lease contract (Section 2A–505(1));

  (b) recover so much of the rent and security as has been paid and is just under the circumstances;

  (c) cover and recover damages as to all goods affected whether or not they have been identified to the lease contract (Sections 2A–518 and 2A–520), or recover damages for nondelivery (Sections 2A–519 and 2A–520);

  (d) exercise any other rights or pursue any other remedies provided in the lease contract.

(2) If a lessor fails to deliver the goods in conformity to the lease contract or repudiates the lease contract, the lessee may also:

  (a) if the goods have been identified, recover them (Section 2A–522); or

  (b) in a proper case, obtain specific performance or replevy the goods (Section 2A–521).

(3) If a lessor is otherwise in default under a lease contract, the lessee may exercise the rights and pursue the remedies provided in the lease contract, which may include a right to cancel the lease, and in Section 2A–519(3).

(4) If a lessor has breached a warranty, whether express or implied, the lessee may recover damages (Section 2A–519(4)).

(5) On rightful rejection or justifiable revocation of acceptance, a lessee has a security interest in goods in the lessee's possession or control for any rent and security that has been paid and any expenses reasonably incurred in their inspection, receipt, transportation, and care and custody and may hold those goods and dispose of them in good faith and in a commercially reasonable manner, subject to Section 2A–527(5).

(6) Subject to the provisions of Section 2A–407, a lessee, on notifying the lessor of the lessee's intention to do so, may deduct all or any part of the damages resulting from any default under the lease contract from any part of the rent still due under the same lease contract. As amended in 1990.

§ 2A–509.   Lessee's Rights on Improper Delivery; Rightful Rejection.

(1) Subject to the provisions of Section 2A–510 on default in installment lease contracts, if the goods or the tender or delivery fail in any respect to conform to the lease contract, the lessee may reject or accept the goods or accept any commercial unit or units and reject the rest of the goods.

(2) Rejection of goods is ineffective unless it is within a reasonable time after tender or delivery of the goods and the lessee seasonably notifies the lessor.

§ 2A–510.   Installment Lease Contracts: Rejection and Default.

(1) Under an installment lease contract a lessee may reject any delivery that is nonconforming if the nonconformity substantially impairs the value of that delivery and cannot be cured or the nonconformity is a defect in the required documents; but if the nonconformity does not fall within subsection (2) and the lessor or the supplier gives adequate assurance of its cure, the lessee must accept that delivery.

(2) Whenever nonconformity or default with respect to one or more deliveries substantially impairs the value of the installment lease contract as a whole there is a default with respect to the whole. But, the aggrieved party reinstates the installment lease contract as a whole if the aggrieved party accepts a nonconforming delivery without seasonably notifying of cancellation or brings an action with respect only to past deliveries or demands performance as to future deliveries.

§ 2A–511.   Merchant Lessee's Duties as to Rightfully Rejected Goods.

(1) Subject to any security interest of a lessee (Section 2A–508(5)), if a lessor or a supplier has no agent or place of business at the market of rejection, a merchant lessee, after rejection of goods in his [or her] possession or control, shall follow any reasonable instructions received from the lessor or the supplier with respect to the goods. In the absence of those instructions, a merchant lessee shall make reasonable efforts to sell, lease, or otherwise dispose of the goods for the lessor's account if they threaten to decline in value speedily. Instructions are not reasonable if on demand indemnity for expenses is not forthcoming.

(2) If a merchant lessee (subsection (1)) or any other lessee (Section 2A–512) disposes of goods, he [or she] is entitled to reimbursement either from the lessor or the supplier or out of the proceeds for reasonable expenses of caring for and disposing of the goods and, if the expenses include no disposition commission, to such commission as is usual in the trade, or if there is none, to a reasonable sum not exceeding 10 percent of the gross proceeds.

(3) In complying with this section or Section 2A–512, the lessee is held only to good faith. Good faith conduct hereunder is neither acceptance or conversion nor the basis of an action for damages.

(4) A purchaser who purchases in good faith from a lessee pursuant to this section or Section 2A–512 takes the goods free of any rights of the lessor and the supplier even though the lessee fails to comply with one or more of the requirements of this Article.

§ 2A–512.   Lessee's Duties as to Rightfully Rejected Goods.

(1) Except as otherwise provided with respect to goods that threaten to decline in value speedily (Section 2A–511) and subject to any security interest of a lessee (Section 2A–508(5)):

  (a) the lessee, after rejection of goods in the lessee's possession, shall hold them with reasonable care at the lessor's or the supplier's disposition for a reasonable time after the lessee's seasonable notification of rejection;

  (b) if the lessor or the supplier gives no instructions within a reasonable time after notification of rejection, the lessee may store the rejected goods for the lessor's or the supplier's account or ship them to the lessor or the supplier or dispose of them for the lessor's or the supplier's account with reimbursement in the manner provided in Section 2A–511; but

  (c) the lessee has no further obligations with regard to goods rightfully rejected.

(2) Action by the lessee pursuant to subsection (1) is not acceptance or conversion.

§ 2A–513.   Cure by Lessor of Improper Tender or Delivery; Replacement.

(1) If any tender or delivery by the lessor or the supplier is rejected because nonconforming and the time for performance has not yet expired, the lessor or the supplier may seasonably notify the lessee of the lessor's or the supplier's intention to cure and may then make a conforming delivery within the time provided in the lease contract.

(2) If the lessee rejects a nonconforming tender that the lessor or the supplier had reasonable grounds to believe would be acceptable with or without money allowance, the lessor or the supplier may have a further reasonable time to substitute a conforming tender if he [or she] seasonably notifies the lessee.

§ 2A–514.   Waiver of Lessee's Objections.

(1) In rejecting goods, a lessee's failure to state a particular defect that is ascertainable by reasonable inspection precludes the lessee from relying on the defect to justify rejection or to establish default:

  (a) if, stated seasonably, the lessor or the supplier could have cured it (Section 2A–513); or

  (b) between merchants if the lessor or the supplier after rejection has made a request in writing for a full and final written statement of all defects on which the lessee proposes to rely.

(2) A lessee's failure to reserve rights when paying rent or other consideration against documents precludes recovery of the payment for defects apparent on the face of the documents.

§ 2A–515.   Acceptance of Goods.

(1) Acceptance of goods occurs after the lessee has had a reasonable opportunity to inspect the goods and

  (a) the lessee signifies or acts with respect to the goods in a manner that signifies to the lessor or the supplier that the goods are conforming or that the lessee will take or retain them in spite of their nonconformity; or

  (b) the lessee fails to make an effective rejection of the goods (Section 2A–509(2)).

(2) Acceptance of a part of any commercial unit is acceptance of that entire unit.

§ 2A–516.   Effect of Acceptance of Goods; Notice of Default; Burden of Establishing Default after Acceptance; Notice of Claim or Litigation to Person Answerable Over.

(1) A lessee must pay rent for any goods accepted in accordance with the lease contract, with due allowance for goods rightfully rejected or not delivered.

(2) A lessee's acceptance of goods precludes rejection of the goods accepted. In the case of a finance lease, if made with knowledge of a nonconformity, acceptance cannot be revoked because of it. In any other case, if made with knowledge of a nonconformity, acceptance cannot be revoked because of it unless the acceptance was on the reasonable assumption that the nonconformity would be seasonably cured. Acceptance does not of itself impair any other remedy provided by this Article or the lease agreement for nonconformity.

(3) If a tender has been accepted:

  (a) within a reasonable time after the lessee discovers or should have discovered any default, the lessee shall notify the lessor and the supplier, if any, or be barred from any remedy against the party notified;

  (b) except in the case of a consumer lease, within a reasonable time after the lessee receives notice of litigation for infringement or the like (Section 2A–211) the lessee shall notify the lessor or be barred from any remedy over for liability established by the litigation; and

  (c) the burden is on the lessee to establish any default.

(4) If a lessee is sued for breach of a warranty or other obligation for which a lessor or a supplier is answerable over the following apply:

  (a) The lessee may give the lessor or the supplier, or both, written notice of the litigation. If the notice states that the person notified may come in and defend and that if the person notified does not do so that person will be bound in any action against that person by the lessee by any determination of fact common to the two litigations, then unless the person notified after seasonable receipt of the notice does come in and defend that person is so bound.

  (b) The lessor or the supplier may demand in writing that the lessee turn over control of the litigation including settlement if the claim is one for infringement or the like (Section 2A–211) or else be barred from any remedy over. If the demand states that the lessor or the supplier agrees to bear all expense and to satisfy any adverse judgment, then unless the lessee after seasonable receipt of the demand does turn over control the lessee is so barred.

(5) Subsections (3) and (4) apply to any obligation of a lessee to hold the lessor or the supplier harmless against infringement or the like (Section 2A–211).

As amended in 1990.

§ 2A–517.   Revocation of Acceptance of Goods.

(1) A lessee may revoke acceptance of a lot or commercial unit whose nonconformity substantially impairs its value to the lessee if the lessee has accepted it:

  (a) except in the case of a finance lease, on the reasonable assumption that its nonconformity would be cured and it has not been seasonably cured; or

(b) without discovery of the nonconformity if the lessee's acceptance was reasonably induced either by the lessor's assurances or, except in the case of a finance lease, by the difficulty of discovery before acceptance.

(2) Except in the case of a finance lease that is not a consumer lease, a lessee may revoke acceptance of a lot or commercial unit if the lessor defaults under the lease contract and the default substantially impairs the value of that lot or commercial unit to the lessee.

(3) If the lease agreement so provides, the lessee may revoke acceptance of a lot or commercial unit because of other defaults by the lessor.

(4) Revocation of acceptance must occur within a reasonable time after the lessee discovers or should have discovered the ground for it and before any substantial change in condition of the goods which is not caused by the nonconformity. Revocation is not effective until the lessee notifies the lessor.

(5) A lessee who so revokes has the same rights and duties with regard to the goods involved as if the lessee had rejected them.
As amended in 1990.

§ 2A–518. Cover; Substitute Goods.

(1) After a default by a lessor under the lease contract of the type described in Section 2A–508(1), or, if agreed, after other default by the lessor, the lessee may cover by making any purchase or lease of or contract to purchase or lease goods in substitution for those due from the lessor.

(2) Except as otherwise provided with respect to damages liquidated in the lease agreement (Section 2A–504) or otherwise determined pursuant to agreement of the parties (Sections 1–102(3) and 2A–503), if a lessee's cover is by lease agreement substantially similar to the original lease agreement and the new lease agreement is made in good faith and in a commercially reasonable manner, the lessee may recover from the lessor as damages (i) the present value, as of the date of the commencement of the term of the new lease agreement, of the rent under the new lease agreement applicable to that period of the new lease term which is comparable to the then remaining term of the original lease agreement minus the present value as of the same date of the total rent for the then remaining lease term of the original lease agreement, and (ii) any incidental or consequential damages, less expenses saved in consequence of the lessor's default.

(3) If a lessee's cover is by lease agreement that for any reason does not qualify for treatment under subsection (2), or is by purchase or otherwise, the lessee may recover from the lessor as if the lessee had elected not to cover and Section 2A–519 governs.
As amended in 1990.

§ 2A–519. Lessee's Damages for Non-Delivery, Repudiation, Default, and Breach of Warranty in Regard to Accepted Goods.

(1) Except as otherwise provided with respect to damages liquidated in the lease agreement (Section 2A–504) or otherwise determined pursuant to agreement of the parties (Sections 1–102(3) and 2A–503), if a lessee elects not to cover or a lessee elects to cover and the cover is by lease agreement that for any reason does not qualify for treatment under Section 2A–518(2), or is by purchase or otherwise, the measure of damages for non-delivery or repudiation by the lessor or for rejection or revocation of acceptance by the lessee is the present value, as of the date of the default, of the then market rent minus the present value as of the same date of the original rent, computed for the remaining lease term of the original lease agreement, together with incidental and consequential damages, less expenses saved in consequence of the lessor's default.

(2) Market rent is to be determined as of the place for tender or, in cases of rejection after arrival or revocation of acceptance, as of the place of arrival.

(3) Except as otherwise agreed, if the lessee has accepted goods and given notification (Section 2A–516(3)), the measure of damages for non-conforming tender or delivery or other default by a lessor is the loss resulting in the ordinary course of events from the lessor's default as determined in any manner that is reasonable together with incidental and consequential damages, less expenses saved in consequence of the lessor's default.

(4) Except as otherwise agreed, the measure of damages for breach of warranty is the present value at the time and place of acceptance of the difference between the value of the use of the goods accepted and the value if they had been as warranted for the lease term, unless special circumstances show proximate damages of a different amount, together with incidental and consequential damages, less expenses saved in consequence of the lessor's default or breach of warranty.
As amended in 1990.

§ 2A–520. Lessee's Incidental and Consequential Damages.

(1) Incidental damages resulting from a lessor's default include expenses reasonably incurred in inspection, receipt, transportation, and care and custody of goods rightfully rejected or goods the acceptance of which is justifiably revoked, any commercially reasonable charges, expenses or commissions in connection with effecting cover, and any other reasonable expense incident to the default.

(2) Consequential damages resulting from a lessor's default include:

(a) any loss resulting from general or particular requirements and needs of which the lessor at the time of contracting had reason to know and which could not reasonably be prevented by cover or otherwise; and

(b) injury to person or property proximately resulting from any breach of warranty.

§ 2A–521. Lessee's Right to Specific Performance or Replevin.

(1) Specific performance may be decreed if the goods are unique or in other proper circumstances.

(2) A decree for specific performance may include any terms and conditions as to payment of the rent, damages, or other relief that the court deems just.

(3) A lessee has a right of replevin, detinue, sequestration, claim and delivery, or the like for goods identified to the lease contract if after reasonable effort the lessee is unable to effect cover for those goods or the circumstances reasonably indicate that the effort will be unavailing.

§ 2A–522. Lessee's Right to Goods on Lessor's Insolvency.

(1) Subject to subsection (2) and even though the goods have not been shipped, a lessee who has paid a part or all of the rent and security for goods identified to a lease contract (Section 2A–217) on making and keeping good a tender of any unpaid portion of the rent and security due under the lease contract may recover the goods identified from the lessor if the lessor becomes insolvent within 10 days after receipt of the first installment of rent and security.

(2) A lessee acquires the right to recover goods identified to a lease contract only if they conform to the lease contract.

C. Default by Lessee

§ 2A–523. Lessor's Remedies.

(1) If a lessee wrongfully rejects or revokes acceptance of goods or fails to make a payment when due or repudiates with respect to a part or the whole, then, with respect to any goods involved, and with respect to all of the goods if under an installment lease contract the value of the whole lease contract is substantially impaired (Section 2A–510), the lessee is in default under the lease contract and the lessor may:

(a) cancel the lease contract (Section 2A–505(1));

(b) proceed respecting goods not identified to the lease contract (Section 2A–524);

(c) withhold delivery of the goods and take possession of goods previously delivered (Section 2A–525);

(d) stop delivery of the goods by any bailee (Section 2A–526);

(e) dispose of the goods and recover damages (Section 2A–527), or retain the goods and recover damages (Section 2A–528), or in a proper case recover rent (Section 2A–529)

(f) exercise any other rights or pursue any other remedies provided in the lease contract.

(2) If a lessor does not fully exercise a right or obtain a remedy to which the lessor is entitled under subsection (1), the lessor may recover the loss resulting in the ordinary course of events from the lessee's default as determined in any reasonable manner, together with incidental damages, less expenses saved in consequence of the lessee's default.

(3) If a lessee is otherwise in default under a lease contract, the lessor may exercise the rights and pursue the remedies provided in the lease contract, which may include a right to cancel the lease. In addition, unless otherwise provided in the lease contract:

(a) if the default substantially impairs the value of the lease contract to the lessor, the lessor may exercise the rights and pursue the remedies provided in subsections (1) or (2); or

(b) if the default does not substantially impair the value of the lease contract to the lessor, the lessor may recover as provided in subsection (2).

As amended in 1990.

§ 2A–524. Lessor's Right to Identify Goods to Lease Contract.

(1) After default by the lessee under the lease contract of the type described in Section 2A–523(1) or 2A–523(3)(a) or, if agreed, after other default by the lessee, the lessor may:

(a) identify to the lease contract conforming goods not already identified if at the time the lessor learned of the default they were in the lessor's or the supplier's possession or control; and

(b) dispose of goods (Section 2A–527(1)) that demonstrably have been intended for the particular lease contract even though those goods are unfinished.

(2) If the goods are unfinished, in the exercise of reasonable commercial judgment for the purposes of avoiding loss and of effective realization, an aggrieved lessor or the supplier may either complete manufacture and wholly identify the goods to the lease contract or cease manufacture and lease, sell, or otherwise dispose of the goods for scrap or salvage value or proceed in any other reasonable manner. As amended in 1990.

§ 2A–525. Lessor's Right to Possession of Goods.

(1) If a lessor discovers the lessee to be insolvent, the lessor may refuse to deliver the goods.

(2) After a default by the lessee under the lease contract of the type described in Section 2A–523(1) or 2A–523(3)(a) or, if agreed, after other default by the lessee, the lessor has the right to take possession of the goods. If the lease contract so provides, the lessor may require the lessee to assemble the goods and make them available to the lessor at a place to be designated by the lessor which is reasonably convenient to both parties. Without removal, the lessor may render unusable any goods employed in trade or business, and may dispose of goods on the lessee's premises (Section 2A–527).

(3) The lessor may proceed under subsection (2) without judicial process if that can be done without breach of the peace or the lessor may proceed by action.

As amended in 1990.

§ 2A–526. Lessor's Stoppage of Delivery in Transit or Otherwise.

(1) A lessor may stop delivery of goods in the possession of a carrier or other bailee if the lessor discovers the lessee to be insolvent and may stop delivery of carload, truckload, planeload, or larger shipments of express or freight if the lessee repudiates or fails to make a payment due before delivery, whether for rent, security or otherwise under the lease contract, or for any other reason the lessor has a right to withhold or take possession of the goods.

(2) In pursuing its remedies under subsection (1), the lessor may stop delivery until

(a) receipt of the goods by the lessee;

(b) acknowledgment to the lessee by any bailee of the goods, except a carrier, that the bailee holds the goods for the lessee; or

(c) such an acknowledgment to the lessee by a carrier via reshipment or as warehouseman.

(3) (a) To stop delivery, a lessor shall so notify as to enable the bailee by reasonable diligence to prevent delivery of the goods.

(b) After notification, the bailee shall hold and deliver the goods according to the directions of the lessor, but the lessor is liable to the bailee for any ensuing charges or damages.

(c) A carrier who has issued a nonnegotiable bill of lading is not obliged to obey a notification to stop received from a person other than the consignor.

§ 2A–527. Lessor's Rights to Dispose of Goods.

(1) After a default by a lessee under the lease contract of the type described in Section 2A–523(1) or 2A–523(3)(a) or after the lessor refuses to deliver or takes possession of goods (Section 2A–525 or 2A–526), or, if agreed, after other default by a lessee, the lessor may dispose of the goods concerned or the undelivered balance thereof by lease, sale, or otherwise.

(2) Except as otherwise provided with respect to damages liquidated in the lease agreement (Section 2A–504) or otherwise determined pursuant to agreement of the parties (Sections 1–102(3) and 2A–503), if the disposition is by lease agreement substantially similar to the original lease agreement and the new lease agreement is made in good faith and in a commercially reasonable manner, the lessor may recover from the lessee as damages (i) accrued and unpaid rent as of the date of the commencement of the term of the new lease agreement, (ii) the present value, as of the same date, of the total rent for the then remaining lease term of the original lease agreement minus the present value, as of the same date, of the rent under the new lease agreement applicable to that period of the new lease term which is comparable to the then remaining term of the original lease agreement, and (iii) any incidental damages allowed under Section 2A–530, less expenses saved in consequence of the lessee's default.

(3) If the lessor's disposition is by lease agreement that for any reason does not qualify for treatment under subsection (2), or is by sale or otherwise, the lessor may recover from the lessee as if the lessor had elected not to dispose of the goods and Section 2A–528 governs.

(4) A subsequent buyer or lessee who buys or leases from the lessor in good faith for value as a result of a disposition under this section takes the goods free of the original lease contract and any rights of the original lessee even though the lessor fails to comply with one or more of the requirements of this Article.

(5) The lessor is not accountable to the lessee for any profit made on any disposition. A lessee who has rightfully rejected or justifiably revoked acceptance shall account to the lessor for any excess over the amount of the lessee's security interest (Section 2A–508(5)).
As amended in 1990.

§ 2A–528. Lessor's Damages for Non-acceptance, Failure to Pay, Repudiation, or Other Default.

(1) Except as otherwise provided with respect to damages liquidated in the lease agreement (Section 2A–504) or otherwise determined pursuant to agreement of the parties (Section 1–102(3) and 2A–503), if a lessor elects to retain the goods or a lessor elects to dispose of the goods and the disposition is by lease agreement that for any reason does not qualify for treatment under Section 2A–527(2), or is by sale or otherwise, the lessor may recover from the lessee as damages for a default of the type described in Section 2A–523(1) or 2A–523(3)(a), or if agreed, for other default of the lessee, (i) accrued and unpaid rent as of the date of the default if the lessee has never taken possession of the goods, or, if the lessee has taken possession of the goods, as of the date the lessor repossesses the goods or an earlier date on which the lessee makes a tender of the goods to the lessor, (ii) the present value as of the date determined under clause (i) of the total rent for the then remaining lease term of the original lease agreement minus the present value as of the same date of the market rent as the place where the goods are located computed for the same lease term, and (iii) any incidental damages allowed under Section 2A–530, less expenses saved in consequence of the lessee's default.

(2) If the measure of damages provided in subsection (1) is inadequate to put a lessor in as good a position as performance would have, the measure of damages is the present value of the profit, including reasonable overhead, the lessor would have made from full performance by the lessee, together with any incidental damages allowed under Section 2A–530, due allowance for costs reasonably incurred and due credit for payments or proceeds of disposition.
As amended in 1990.

§ 2A–529. Lessor's Action for the Rent.

(1) After default by the lessee under the lease contract of the type described in Section 2A–523(1) or 2A–523(3)(a) or, if agreed, after other default by the lessee, if the lessor complies with subsection (2), the lessor may recover from the lessee as damages:

> **(a)** for goods accepted by the lessee and not repossessed by or tendered to the lessor, and for conforming goods lost or damaged within a commercially reasonable time after risk of loss

passes to the lessee (Section 2A–219), (i) accrued and unpaid rent as of the date of entry of judgment in favor of the lessor (ii) the present value as of the same date of the rent for the then remaining lease term of the lease agreement, and (iii) any incidental damages allowed under Section 2A–530, less expenses saved in consequence of the lessee's default; and

> **(b)** for goods identified to the lease contract if the lessor is unable after reasonable effort to dispose of them at a reasonable price or the circumstances reasonably indicate that effort will be unavailing, (i) accrued and unpaid rent as of the date of entry of judgment in favor of the lessor, (ii) the present value as of the same date of the rent for the then remaining lease term of the lease agreement, and (iii) any incidental damages allowed under Section 2A–530, less expenses saved in consequence of the lessee's default.

(2) Except as provided in subsection (3), the lessor shall hold for the lessee for the remaining lease term of the lease agreement any goods that have been identified to the lease contract and are in the lessor's control.

(3) The lessor may dispose of the goods at any time before collection of the judgment for damages obtained pursuant to subsection (1). If the disposition is before the end of the remaining lease term of the lease agreement, the lessor's recovery against the lessee for damages is governed by Section 2A–527 or Section 2A–528, and the lessor will cause an appropriate credit to be provided against a judgment for damages to the extent that the amount of the judgment exceeds the recovery available pursuant to Section 2A–527 or 2A–528.

(4) Payment of the judgment for damages obtained pursuant to subsection (1) entitles the lessee to the use and possession of the goods not then disposed of for the remaining lease term of and in accordance with the lease agreement.

(5) After default by the lessee under the lease contract of the type described in Section 2A–523(1) or Section 2A–523(3)(a) or, if agreed, after other default by the lessee, a lessor who is held not entitled to rent under this section must nevertheless be awarded damages for non-acceptance under Sections 2A–527 and 2A–528.
As amended in 1990.

§ 2A–530. Lessor's Incidental Damages.

Incidental damages to an aggrieved lessor include any commercially reasonable charges, expenses, or commissions incurred in stopping delivery, in the transportation, care and custody of goods after the lessee's default, in connection with return or disposition of the goods, or otherwise resulting from the default.

§ 2A–531. Standing to Sue Third Parties for Injury to Goods.

(1) If a third party so deals with goods that have been identified to a lease contract as to cause actionable injury to a party to the lease contract (a) the lessor has a right of action against the third party, and (b) the lessee also has a right of action against the third party if the lessee:

> **(i)** has a security interest in the goods;
> **(ii)** has an insurable interest in the goods; or
> **(iii)** bears the risk of loss under the lease contract or has since the injury assumed that risk as against the lessor and the goods have been converted or destroyed.

(2) If at the time of the injury the party plaintiff did not bear the risk of loss as against the other party to the lease contract and there is no arrangement between them for disposition of the recovery, his [or her] suit or settlement, subject to his [or her] own interest, is as a fiduciary for the other party to the lease contract.

(3) Either party with the consent of the other may sue for the benefit of whom it may concern.

§ 2A–532. Lessor's Rights to Residual Interest.

In addition to any other recovery permitted by this Article or other law, the lessor may recover from the lessee an amount that will fully compensate the lessor for any loss of or damage to the lessor's residual interest in the goods caused by the default of the lessee.
As added in 1990.

REVISED ARTICLE 3: NEGOTIABLE INSTRUMENTS

Part 1—General Provisions and Definitions

§ 3–101. Short Title.

This Article may be cited as Uniform Commercial Code–Negotiable Instruments.

§ 3–102. Subject Matter.

(a) This Article applies to negotiable instruments. It does not apply to money, to payment orders governed by Article 4A, or to securities governed by Article 8.
(b) If there is conflict between this Article and Article 4 or 9, Articles 4 and 9 govern.
(c) Regulations of the Board of Governors of the Federal Reserve System and operating circulars of the Federal Reserve Banks supersede any inconsistent provision of this Article to the extent of the inconsistency.

§ 3–103. Definitions.

(a) In this Article:
 (1) "Acceptor" means a drawee who has accepted a draft.
 (2) "Drawee" means a person ordered in a draft to make payment.
 (3) "Drawer" means a person who signs or is identified in a draft as a person ordering payment.
 (4) "Good faith" means honesty in fact and the observance of reasonable commercial standards of fair dealing.
 (5) "Maker" means a person who signs or is identified in a note as a person undertaking to pay.
 (6) "Order" means a written instruction to pay money signed by the person giving the instruction. The instruction may be addressed to any person, including the person giving the instruction, or to one or more persons jointly or in the alternative but not in succession. An authorization to pay is not an order unless the person authorized to pay is also instructed to pay.
 (7) "Ordinary care" in the case of a person engaged in business means observance of reasonable commercial standards, prevailing in the area in which the person is located, with respect to the business in which the person is engaged. In the case of a bank that takes an instrument for processing for collection or payment by automated means, reasonable commercial standards do not require the bank to examine the instrument if the failure to examine does not violate the bank's prescribed procedures and the bank's procedures do not vary unreasonably from general banking usage not disapproved by this Article or Article 4.
 (8) "Party" means a party to an instrument.
 (9) "Promise" means a written undertaking to pay money signed by the person undertaking to pay. An acknowledgment of an obligation by the obligor is not a promise unless the obligor also undertakes to pay the obligation.
 (10) "Prove" with respect to a fact means to meet the burden of establishing the fact (Section 1–201(8)).
 (11) "Remitter" means a person who purchases an instrument from its issuer if the instrument is payable to an identified person other than the purchaser.
(b) [Other definitions' section references deleted.]
(c) [Other definitions' section references deleted.]
(d) In addition, Article 1 contains general definitions and principles of construction and interpretation applicable throughout this Article.

§ 3–104. Negotiable Instrument.

(a) Except as provided in subsections (c) and (d), "negotiable instrument" means an unconditional promise or order to pay a fixed amount of money, with or without interest or other charges described in the promise or order, if it:
 (1) is payable to bearer or to order at the time it is issued or first comes into possession of a holder;
 (2) is payable on demand or at a definite time; and
 (3) does not state any other undertaking or instruction by the person promising or ordering payment to do any act in addition to the payment of money, but the promise or order may contain (i) an undertaking or power to give, maintain, or protect collateral to secure payment, (ii) an authorization or power to the holder to confess judgment or realize on or dispose of collateral, or (iii) a waiver of the benefit of any law intended for the advantage or protection of an obligor.
(b) "Instrument" means a negotiable instrument.
(c) An order that meets all of the requirements of subsection (a), except paragraph (1), and otherwise falls within the definition of "check" in subsection (f) is a negotiable instrument and a check.
(d) A promise or order other than a check is not an instrument if, at the time it is issued or first comes into possession of a holder, it contains a conspicuous statement, however expressed, to the effect that the promise or order is not negotiable or is not an instrument governed by this Article.
(e) An instrument is a "note" if it is a promise and is a "draft" if it is an order. If an instrument falls within the definition of both "note" and "draft," a person entitled to enforce the instrument may treat it as either.
(f) "Check" means (i) a draft, other than a documentary draft, payable on demand and drawn on a bank or (ii) a cashier's check or teller's check. An instrument may be a check even though it is described on its face by another term, such as "money order."
(g) "Cashier's check" means a draft with respect to which the drawer and drawee are the same bank or branches of the same bank.
(h) "Teller's check" means a draft drawn by a bank (i) on another bank, or (ii) payable at or through a bank.
(i) "Traveler's check" means an instrument that (i) is payable on demand, (ii) is drawn on or payable at or through a bank, (iii) is designated by the term "traveler's check" or by a substantially similar term, and (iv) requires, as a condition to payment, a countersignature by a person whose specimen signature appears on the instrument.
(j) "Certificate of deposit" means an instrument containing an acknowledgment by a bank that a sum of money has been received by the bank and a promise by the bank to repay the sum of money. A certificate of deposit is a note of the bank.

§ 3–105. Issue of Instrument.

(a) "Issue" means the first delivery of an instrument by the maker or drawer, whether to a holder or nonholder, for the purpose of giving rights on the instrument to any person.

(b) An unissued instrument, or an unissued incomplete instrument that is completed, is binding on the maker or drawer, but nonissuance is a defense. An instrument that is conditionally issued or is issued for a special purpose is binding on the maker or drawer, but failure of the condition or special purpose to be fulfilled is a defense.

(c) "Issuer" applies to issued and unissued instruments and means a maker or drawer of an instrument.

§ 3–106. Unconditional Promise or Order.

(a) Except as provided in this section, for the purposes of Section 3–104(a), a promise or order is unconditional unless it states (i) an express condition to payment, (ii) that the promise or order is subject to or governed by another writing, or (iii) that rights or obligations with respect to the promise or order are stated in another writing. A reference to another writing does not of itself make the promise or order conditional.

(b) A promise or order is not made conditional (i) by a reference to another writing for a statement of rights with respect to collateral, prepayment, or acceleration, or (ii) because payment is limited to resort to a particular fund or source.

(c) If a promise or order requires, as a condition to payment, a countersignature by a person whose specimen signature appears on the promise or order, the condition does not make the promise or order conditional for the purposes of Section 3–104(a). If the person whose specimen signature appears on an instrument fails to countersign the instrument, the failure to countersign is a defense to the obligation of the issuer, but the failure does not prevent a transferee of the instrument from becoming a holder of the instrument.

(d) If a promise or order at the time it is issued or first comes into possession of a holder contains a statement, required by applicable statutory or administrative law, to the effect that the rights of a holder or transferee are subject to claims or defenses that the issuer could assert against the original payee, the promise or order is not thereby made conditional for the purposes of Section 3–104(a); but if the promise or order is an instrument, there cannot be a holder in due course of the instrument.

§ 3–107. Instrument Payable in Foreign Money.

Unless the instrument otherwise provides, an instrument that states the amount payable in foreign money may be paid in the foreign money or in an equivalent amount in dollars calculated by using the current bank-offered spot rate at the place of payment for the purchase of dollars on the day on which the instrument is paid.

§ 3–108. Payable on Demand or at Definite Time.

(a) A promise or order is "payable on demand" if it (i) states that it is payable on demand or at sight, or otherwise indicates that it is payable at the will of the holder, or (ii) does not state any time of payment.

(b) A promise or order is "payable at a definite time" if it is payable on elapse of a definite period of time after sight or acceptance or at a fixed date or dates or at a time or times readily ascertainable at the time the promise or order is issued, subject to rights of (i) prepayment, (ii) acceleration, (iii) extension at the option of the holder, or (iv) extension to a further definite time at the option of the maker or acceptor or automatically upon or after a specified act or event.

(c) If an instrument, payable at a fixed date, is also payable upon demand made before the fixed date, the instrument is payable on demand until the fixed date and, if demand for payment is not made before that date, becomes payable at a definite time on the fixed date.

§ 3–109. Payable to Bearer or to Order.

(a) A promise or order is payable to bearer if it:

(1) states that it is payable to bearer or to the order of bearer or otherwise indicates that the person in possession of the promise or order is entitled to payment;

(2) does not state a payee; or

(3) states that it is payable to or to the order of cash or otherwise indicates that it is not payable to an identified person.

(b) A promise or order that is not payable to bearer is payable to order if it is payable (i) to the order of an identified person or (ii) to an identified person or order. A promise or order that is payable to order is payable to the identified person.

(c) An instrument payable to bearer may become payable to an identified person if it is specially indorsed pursuant to Section 3–205(a). An instrument payable to an identified person may become payable to bearer if it is indorsed in blank pursuant to Section 3–205(b).

§ 3–110. Identification of Person to Whom Instrument Is Payable.

(a) The person to whom an instrument is initially payable is determined by the intent of the person, whether or not authorized, signing as, or in the name or behalf of, the issuer of the instrument. The instrument is payable to the person intended by the signer even if that person is identified in the instrument by a name or other identification that is not that of the intended person. If more than one person signs in the name or behalf of the issuer of an instrument and all the signers do not intend the same person as payee, the instrument is payable to any person intended by one or more of the signers.

(b) If the signature of the issuer of an instrument is made by automated means, such as a check-writing machine, the payee of the instrument is determined by the intent of the person who supplied the name or identification of the payee, whether or not authorized to do so.

(c) A person to whom an instrument is payable may be identified in any way, including by name, identifying number, office, or account number. For the purpose of determining the holder of an instrument, the following rules apply:

(1) If an instrument is payable to an account and the account is identified only by number, the instrument is payable to the person to whom the account is payable. If an instrument is payable to an account identified by number and by the name of a person, the instrument is payable to the named person, whether or not that person is the owner of the account identified by number.

(2) If an instrument is payable to:

(i) a trust, an estate, or a person described as trustee or representative of a trust or estate, the instrument is payable to the trustee, the representative, or a successor of either, whether or not the beneficiary or estate is also named;

(ii) a person described as agent or similar representative of a named or identified person, the instrument is payable to the represented person, the representative, or a successor of the representative;

(iii) a fund or organization that is not a legal entity, the instrument is payable to a representative of the members of the fund or organization; or

(iv) an office or to a person described as holding an office, the instrument is payable to the named person, the incumbent of the office, or a successor to the incumbent.

(d) If an instrument is payable to two or more persons alternatively, it is payable to any of them and may be negotiated, discharged, or enforced by any or all of them in possession of the instrument. If an instrument is payable to two or more persons not alternatively, it is payable to all of them and may be negotiated, discharged, or enforced only by all of them. If an instrument payable to two or more persons is ambiguous as to whether it is payable to the persons alternatively, the instrument is payable to the persons alternatively.

§ 3–111. Place of Payment.

Except as otherwise provided for items in Article 4, an instrument is payable at the place of payment stated in the instrument. If no place of payment is stated, an instrument is payable at the address of the drawee or maker stated in the instrument. If no address is stated, the place of payment is the place of business of the drawee or maker. If a drawee or maker has more than one place of business, the place of payment is any place of business of the drawee or maker chosen by the person entitled to enforce the instrument. If the drawee or maker has no place of business, the place of payment is the residence of the drawee or maker.

§ 3–112. Interest.

(a) Unless otherwise provided in the instrument, (i) an instrument is not payable with interest, and (ii) interest on an interest-bearing instrument is payable from the date of the instrument.

(b) Interest may be stated in an instrument as a fixed or variable amount of money or it may be expressed as a fixed or variable rate or rates. The amount or rate of interest may be stated or described in the instrument in any manner and may require reference to information not contained in the instrument. If an instrument provides for interest, but the amount of interest payable cannot be ascertained from the description, interest is payable at the judgment rate in effect at the place of payment of the instrument and at the time interest first accrues.

§ 3–113. Date of Instrument.

(a) An instrument may be antedated or postdated. The date stated determines the time of payment if the instrument is payable at a fixed period after date. Except as provided in Section 4–401(c), an instrument payable on demand is not payable before the date of the instrument.

(b) If an instrument is undated, its date is the date of its issue or, in the case of an unissued instrument, the date it first comes into possession of a holder.

§ 3–114. Contradictory Terms of Instrument.

If an instrument contains contradictory terms, typewritten terms prevail over printed terms, handwritten terms prevail over both, and words prevail over numbers.

§ 3–115. Incomplete Instrument.

(a) "Incomplete instrument" means a signed writing, whether or not issued by the signer, the contents of which show at the time of signing that it is incomplete but that the signer intended it to be completed by the addition of words or numbers.

(b) Subject to subsection (c), if an incomplete instrument is an instrument under Section 3–104, it may be enforced according to its terms if it is not completed, or according to its terms as augmented by completion. If an incomplete instrument is not an instrument under Section 3–104, but, after completion, the requirements of Section 3–104 are met, the instrument may be enforced according to its terms as augmented by completion.

(c) If words or numbers are added to an incomplete instrument without authority of the signer, there is an alteration of the incomplete instrument under Section 3–407.

(d) The burden of establishing that words or numbers were added to an incomplete instrument without authority of the signer is on the person asserting the lack of authority.

§ 3–116. Joint and Several Liability; Contribution.

(a) Except as otherwise provided in the instrument, two or more persons who have the same liability on an instrument as makers, drawers, acceptors, indorsers who indorse as joint payees, or anomalous indorsers are jointly and severally liable in the capacity in which they sign.

(b) Except as provided in Section 3–419(e) or by agreement of the affected parties, a party having joint and several liability who pays the instrument is entitled to receive from any party having the same joint and several liability contribution in accordance with applicable law.

(c) Discharge of one party having joint and several liability by a person entitled to enforce the instrument does not affect the right under subsection (b) of a party having the same joint and several liability to receive contribution from the party discharged.

§ 3–117. Other Agreements Affecting Instrument.

Subject to applicable law regarding exclusion of proof of contemporaneous or previous agreements, the obligation of a party to an instrument to pay the instrument may be modified, supplemented, or nullified by a separate agreement of the obligor and a person entitled to enforce the instrument, if the instrument is issued or the obligation is incurred in reliance on the agreement or as part of the same transaction giving rise to the agreement. To the extent an obligation is modified, supplemented, or nullified by an agreement under this section, the agreement is a defense to the obligation.

§ 3–118. Statute of Limitations.

(a) Except as provided in subsection (e), an action to enforce the obligation of a party to pay a note payable at a definite time must be commenced within six years after the due date or dates stated in the note or, if a due date is accelerated, within six years after the accelerated due date.

(b) Except as provided in subsection (d) or (e), if demand for payment is made to the maker of a note payable on demand, an action to enforce the obligation of a party to pay the note must be commenced within six years after the demand. If no demand for payment is made to the maker, an action to enforce the note is barred if neither principal nor interest on the note has been paid for a continuous period of 10 years.

(c) Except as provided in subsection (d), an action to enforce the obligation of a party to an unaccepted draft to pay the draft must be commenced within three years after dishonor of the draft or 10 years after the date of the draft, whichever period expires first.

(d) An action to enforce the obligation of the acceptor of a certified check or the issuer of a teller's check, cashier's check, or traveler's check must be commenced within three years after demand for payment is made to the acceptor or issuer, as the case may be.

(e) An action to enforce the obligation of a party to a certificate of deposit to pay the instrument must be commenced within six years after demand for payment is made to the maker, but if the instrument states a due date and the maker is not required to pay before that date, the six-year period begins when a demand for payment is in effect and the due date has passed.

(f) An action to enforce the obligation of a party to pay an accepted draft, other than a certified check, must be commenced (i) within six years after the due date or dates stated in the draft or acceptance if the obligation of the acceptor is payable at a definite time, or (ii) within six years after the date of the acceptance if the obligation of the acceptor is payable on demand.

(g) Unless governed by other law regarding claims for indemnity or contribution, an action (i) for conversion of an instrument, for money had and received, or like action based on conversion, (ii) for breach of warranty, or (iii) to enforce an obligation, duty, or right arising under this Article and not governed by this section must be commenced within three years after the [cause of action] accrues.

§ 3–119. Notice of Right to Defend Action.
In an action for breach of an obligation for which a third person is answerable over pursuant to this Article or Article 4, the defendant may give the third person written notice of the litigation, and the person notified may then give similar notice to any other person who is answerable over. If the notice states (i) that the person notified may come in and defend and (ii) that failure to do so will bind the person notified in an action later brought by the person giving the notice as to any determination of fact common to the two litigations, the person notified is so bound unless after seasonable receipt of the notice the person notified does come in and defend.

Part 2—Negotiation, Transfer, and Indorsement

§ 3–201. Negotiation.
(a) "Negotiation" means a transfer of possession, whether voluntary or involuntary, of an instrument by a person other than the issuer to a person who thereby becomes its holder.

(b) Except for negotiation by a remitter, if an instrument is payable to an identified person, negotiation requires transfer of possession of the instrument and its indorsement by the holder. If an instrument is payable to bearer, it may be negotiated by transfer of possession alone.

§ 3–202. Negotiation Subject to Rescission.
(a) Negotiation is effective even if obtained (i) from an infant, a corporation exceeding its powers, or a person without capacity, (ii) by fraud, duress, or mistake, or (iii) in breach of duty or as part of an illegal transaction.

(b) To the extent permitted by other law, negotiation may be rescinded or may be subject to other remedies, but those remedies may not be asserted against a subsequent holder in due course or a person paying the instrument in good faith and without knowledge of facts that are a basis for rescission or other remedy.

§ 3–203. Transfer of Instrument; Rights Acquired by Transfer.
(a) An instrument is transferred when it is delivered by a person other than its issuer for the purpose of giving to the person receiving delivery the right to enforce the instrument.

(b) Transfer of an instrument, whether or not the transfer is a negotiation, vests in the transferee any right of the transferor to enforce the instrument, including any right as a holder in due course, but the transferee cannot acquire rights of a holder in due course by a transfer, directly or indirectly, from a holder in due course if the transferee engaged in fraud or illegality affecting the instrument.

(c) Unless otherwise agreed, if an instrument is transferred for value and the transferee does not become a holder because of lack of indorsement by the transferor, the transferee has a specifically enforceable right to the unqualified indorsement of the transferor, but negotiation of the instrument does not occur until the indorsement is made.

(d) If a transferor purports to transfer less than the entire instrument, negotiation of the instrument does not occur. The transferee obtains no rights under this Article and has only the rights of a partial assignee.

§ 3–204. Indorsement.
(a) "Indorsement" means a signature, other than that of a signer as maker, drawer, or acceptor, that alone or accompanied by other words is made on an instrument for the purpose of (i) negotiating the instrument, (ii) restricting payment of the instrument, or (iii) incurring indorser's liability on the instrument, but regardless of the intent of the signer, a signature and its accompanying words is an indorsement unless the accompanying words, terms of the instrument, place of the signature, or other circumstances unambiguously indicate that the signature was made for a purpose other than indorsement. For the purpose of determining whether a signature is made on an instrument, a paper affixed to the instrument is a part of the instrument.

(b) "Indorser" means a person who makes an indorsement.

(c) For the purpose of determining whether the transferee of an instrument is a holder, an indorsement that transfers a security interest in the instrument is effective as an unqualified indorsement of the instrument.

(d) If an instrument is payable to a holder under a name that is not the name of the holder, indorsement may be made by the holder in the name stated in the instrument or in the holder's name or both, but signature in both names may be required by a person paying or taking the instrument for value or collection.

§ 3–205. Special Indorsement; Blank Indorsement; Anomalous Indorsement.
(a) If an indorsement is made by the holder of an instrument, whether payable to an identified person or payable to bearer, and the indorsement identifies a person to whom it makes the instrument payable, it is a "special indorsement." When specially indorsed, an instrument becomes payable to the identified person and may be negotiated only by the indorsement of that person. The principles stated in Section 3–110 apply to special indorsements.

(b) If an indorsement is made by the holder of an instrument and it is not a special indorsement, it is a "blank indorsement." When indorsed in blank, an instrument becomes payable to bearer and may be negotiated by transfer of possession alone until specially indorsed.

(c) The holder may convert a blank indorsement that consists only of a signature into a special indorsement by writing, above the signature of the indorser, words identifying the person to whom the instrument is made payable.

(d) "Anomalous indorsement" means an indorsement made by a person who is not the holder of the instrument. An anomalous indorsement does not affect the manner in which the instrument may be negotiated.

§ 3–206. Restrictive Indorsement.

(a) An indorsement limiting payment to a particular person or otherwise prohibiting further transfer or negotiation of the instrument is not effective to prevent further transfer or negotiation of the instrument.

(b) An indorsement stating a condition to the right of the indorsee to receive payment does not affect the right of the indorsee to enforce the instrument. A person paying the instrument or taking it for value or collection may disregard the condition, and the rights and liabilities of that person are not affected by whether the condition has been fulfilled.

(c) If an instrument bears an indorsement (i) described in Section 4–201(b), or (ii) in blank or to a particular bank using the words "for deposit," "for collection," or other words indicating a purpose of having the instrument collected by a bank for the indorser or for a particular account, the following rules apply:

> **(1)** A person, other than a bank, who purchases the instrument when so indorsed converts the instrument unless the amount paid for the instrument is received by the indorser or applied consistently with the indorsement.
>
> **(2)** A depositary bank that purchases the instrument or takes it for collection when so indorsed converts the instrument unless the amount paid by the bank with respect to the instrument is received by the indorser or applied consistently with the indorsement.
>
> **(3)** A payor bank that is also the depositary bank or that takes the instrument for immediate payment over the counter from a person other than a collecting bank converts the instrument unless the proceeds of the instrument are received by the indorser or applied consistently with the indorsement.
>
> **(4)** Except as otherwise provided in paragraph (3), a payor bank or intermediary bank may disregard the indorsement and is not liable if the proceeds of the instrument are not received by the indorser or applied consistently with the indorsement.

(d) Except for an indorsement covered by subsection (c), if an instrument bears an indorsement using words to the effect that payment is to be made to the indorsee as agent, trustee, or other fiduciary for the benefit of the indorser or another person, the following rules apply:

> **(1)** Unless there is notice of breach of fiduciary duty as provided in Section 3–307, a person who purchases the instrument from the indorsee or takes the instrument from the indorsee for collection or payment may pay the proceeds of payment or the value given for the instrument to the indorsee without regard to whether the indorsee violates a fiduciary duty to the indorser.
>
> **(2)** A subsequent transferee of the instrument or person who pays the instrument is neither given notice nor otherwise affected by the restriction in the indorsement unless the transferee or payor knows that the fiduciary dealt with the instrument or its proceeds in breach of fiduciary duty.

(e) The presence on an instrument of an indorsement to which this section applies does not prevent a purchaser of the instrument from becoming a holder in due course of the instrument unless the purchaser is a converter under subsection (c) or has notice or knowledge of breach of fiduciary duty as stated in subsection (d).

(f) In an action to enforce the obligation of a party to pay the instrument, the obligor has a defense if payment would violate an indorsement to which this section applies and the payment is not permitted by this section.

§ 3–207. Reacquisition.

Reacquisition of an instrument occurs if it is transferred to a former holder, by negotiation or otherwise. A former holder who reacquires the instrument may cancel indorsements made after the reacquirer first became a holder of the instrument. If the cancellation causes the instrument to be payable to the reacquirer or to bearer, the reacquirer may negotiate the instrument. An indorser whose indorsement is canceled is discharged, and the discharge is effective against any subsequent holder.

Part 3—Enforcement of Instruments

§ 3–301. Person Entitled to Enforce Instrument.

"Person entitled to enforce" an instrument means (i) the holder of the instrument, (ii) a nonholder in possession of the instrument who has the rights of a holder, or (iii) a person not in possession of the instrument who is entitled to enforce the instrument pursuant to Section 3–309 or 3–418(d). A person may be a person entitled to enforce the instrument even though the person is not the owner of the instrument or is in wrongful possession of the instrument.

§ 3–302. Holder in Due Course.

(a) Subject to subsection (c) and Section 3–106(d), "holder in due course" means the holder of an instrument if:

> **(1)** the instrument when issued or negotiated to the holder does not bear such apparent evidence of forgery or alteration or is not otherwise so irregular or incomplete as to call into question its authenticity; and
>
> **(2)** the holder took the instrument (i) for value, (ii) in good faith, (iii) without notice that the instrument is overdue or has been dishonored or that there is an uncured default with respect to payment of another instrument issued as part of the same series, (iv) without notice that the instrument contains an unauthorized signature or has been altered, (v) without notice of any claim to the instrument described in Section 3–306, and (vi) without notice that any party has a defense or claim in recoupment described in Section 3–305(a).

(b) Notice of discharge of a party, other than discharge in an insolvency proceeding, is not notice of a defense under subsection (a), but discharge is effective against a person who became a holder in due course with notice of the discharge. Public filing or recording of a document does not of itself constitute notice of a defense, claim in recoupment, or claim to the instrument.

(c) Except to the extent a transferor or predecessor in interest has rights as a holder in due course, a person does not acquire rights of a holder in due course of an instrument taken (i) by legal process or by purchase in an execution, bankruptcy, or creditor's sale or similar proceeding, (ii) by purchase as part of a bulk transaction not in ordinary course of business of the transferor, or (iii) as the successor in interest to an estate or other organization.

(d) If, under Section 3–303(a)(1), the promise of performance that is the consideration for an instrument has been partially performed, the holder may assert rights as a holder in due course of the instrument only to the fraction of the amount payable under the instrument equal to the value of the partial performance divided by the value of the promised performance.

(e) If (i) the person entitled to enforce an instrument has only a security interest in the instrument and (ii) the person obliged to pay the instrument has a defense, claim in recoupment, or claim to the instrument that may be asserted against the person who granted the security interest, the person entitled to enforce the instrument may assert rights as a holder in due course only to an amount payable under the instrument which, at the time of enforcement of the instrument, does not exceed the amount of the unpaid obligation secured.

(f) To be effective, notice must be received at a time and in a manner that gives a reasonable opportunity to act on it.

(g) This section is subject to any law limiting status as a holder in due course in particular classes of transactions.

§ 3–303. Value and Consideration.

(a) An instrument is issued or transferred for value if:

(1) the instrument is issued or transferred for a promise of performance, to the extent the promise has been performed;

(2) the transferee acquires a security interest or other lien in the instrument other than a lien obtained by judicial proceeding;

(3) the instrument is issued or transferred as payment of, or as security for, an antecedent claim against any person, whether or not the claim is due;

(4) the instrument is issued or transferred in exchange for a negotiable instrument; or

(5) the instrument is issued or transferred in exchange for the incurring of an irrevocable obligation to a third party by the person taking the instrument.

(b) "Consideration" means any consideration sufficient to support a simple contract. The drawer or maker of an instrument has a defense if the instrument is issued without consideration. If an instrument is issued for a promise of performance, the issuer has a defense to the extent performance of the promise is due and the promise has not been performed. If an instrument is issued for value as stated in subsection (a), the instrument is also issued for consideration.

§ 3–304. Overdue Instrument.

(a) An instrument payable on demand becomes overdue at the earliest of the following times:

(1) on the day after the day demand for payment is duly made;

(2) if the instrument is a check, 90 days after its date; or

(3) if the instrument is not a check, when the instrument has been outstanding for a period of time after its date which is unreasonably long under the circumstances of the particular case in light of the nature of the instrument and usage of the trade.

(b) With respect to an instrument payable at a definite time the following rules apply:

(1) If the principal is payable in installments and a due date has not been accelerated, the instrument becomes overdue upon default under the instrument for nonpayment of an installment, and the instrument remains overdue until the default is cured.

(2) If the principal is not payable in installments and the due date has not been accelerated, the instrument becomes overdue on the day after the due date.

(3) If a due date with respect to principal has been accelerated, the instrument becomes overdue on the day after the accelerated due date.

(c) Unless the due date of principal has been accelerated, an instrument does not become overdue if there is default in payment of interest but no default in payment of principal.

§ 3–305. Defenses and Claims in Recoupment.

(a) Except as stated in subsection (b), the right to enforce the obligation of a party to pay an instrument is subject to the following:

(1) a defense of the obligor based on (i) infancy of the obligor to the extent it is a defense to a simple contract, (ii) duress, lack of legal capacity, or illegality of the transaction which, under other law, nullifies the obligation of the obligor, (iii) fraud that induced the obligor to sign the instrument with neither knowledge nor reasonable opportunity to learn of its character or its essential terms, or (iv) discharge of the obligor in insolvency proceedings;

(2) a defense of the obligor stated in another section of this Article or a defense of the obligor that would be available if the person entitled to enforce the instrument were enforcing a right to payment under a simple contract; and

(3) a claim in recoupment of the obligor against the original payee of the instrument if the claim arose from the transaction that gave rise to the instrument; but the claim of the obligor may be asserted against a transferee of the instrument only to reduce the amount owing on the instrument at the time the action is brought.

(b) The right of a holder in due course to enforce the obligation of a party to pay the instrument is subject to defenses of the obligor stated in subsection (a)(1), but is not subject to defenses of the obligor stated in subsection (a)(2) or claims in recoupment stated in subsection (a)(3) against a person other than the holder.

(c) Except as stated in subsection (d), in an action to enforce the obligation of a party to pay the instrument, the obligor may not assert against the person entitled to enforce the instrument a defense, claim in recoupment, or claim to the instrument (Section 3–306) of another person, but the other person's claim to the instrument may be asserted by the obligor if the other person is joined in the action and personally asserts the claim against the person entitled to enforce the instrument. An obligor is not obliged to pay the instrument if the person seeking enforcement of the instrument does not have rights of a holder in due course and the obligor proves that the instrument is a lost or stolen instrument.

(d) In an action to enforce the obligation of an accommodation party to pay an instrument, the accommodation party may assert against the person entitled to enforce the instrument any defense or claim in recoupment under subsection (a) that the accommodated party could assert against the person entitled to enforce the instrument, except the defenses of discharge in insolvency proceedings, infancy, and lack of legal capacity.

§ 3–306. Claims to an Instrument.

A person taking an instrument, other than a person having rights of a holder in due course, is subject to a claim of a property or possessory right in the instrument or its proceeds, including a claim to rescind a negotiation and to recover the instrument or its proceeds. A person having rights of a holder in due course takes free of the claim to the instrument.

§ 3–307. Notice of Breach of Fiduciary Duty.

(a) In this section:

(1) "Fiduciary" means an agent, trustee, partner, corporate officer or director, or other representative owing a fiduciary duty with respect to an instrument.

(2) "Represented person" means the principal, beneficiary, partnership, corporation, or other person to whom the duty stated in paragraph (1) is owed.

(b) If (i) an instrument is taken from a fiduciary for payment or collection or for value, (ii) the taker has knowledge of the fiduciary status of the fiduciary, and (iii) the represented person makes a claim to the instrument or its proceeds on the basis that the transaction of the fiduciary is a breach of fiduciary duty, the following rules apply:

(1) Notice of breach of fiduciary duty by the fiduciary is notice of the claim of the represented person.

(2) In the case of an instrument payable to the represented person or the fiduciary as such, the taker has notice of the breach of fiduciary duty if the instrument is (i) taken in payment of or as security for a debt known by the taker to be the personal debt of the fiduciary, (ii) taken in a transaction known by the taker to be for the personal benefit of the fiduciary, or (iii) deposited to an account other than an account of the fiduciary, as such, or an account of the represented person.

(3) If an instrument is issued by the represented person or the fiduciary as such, and made payable to the fiduciary personally, the taker does not have notice of the breach of fiduciary duty unless the taker knows of the breach of fiduciary duty.

(4) If an instrument is issued by the represented person or the fiduciary as such, to the taker as payee, the taker has notice of the breach of fiduciary duty if the instrument is (i) taken in payment of or as security for a debt known by the taker to be the personal debt of the fiduciary, (ii) taken in a transaction known by the taker to be for the personal benefit of the fiduciary, or (iii) deposited to an account other than an account of the fiduciary, as such, or an account of the represented person.

§ 3–308. Proof of Signatures and Status as Holder in Due Course.

(a) In an action with respect to an instrument, the authenticity of, and authority to make, each signature on the instrument is admitted unless specifically denied in the pleadings. If the validity of a signature is denied in the pleadings, the burden of establishing validity is on the person claiming validity, but the signature is presumed to be authentic and authorized unless the action is to enforce the liability of the purported signer and the signer is dead or incompetent at the time of trial of the issue of validity of the signature. If an action to enforce the instrument is brought against a person as the undisclosed principal of a person who signed the instrument as a party to the instrument, the plaintiff has the burden of establishing that the defendant is liable on the instrument as a represented person under Section 3–402(a).

(b) If the validity of signatures is admitted or proved and there is compliance with subsection (a), a plaintiff producing the instrument is entitled to payment if the plaintiff proves entitlement to enforce the instrument under Section 3–301, unless the defendant proves a defense or claim in recoupment. If a defense or claim in recoupment is proved, the right to payment of the plaintiff is subject to the defense or claim, except to the extent the plaintiff proves that the plaintiff has rights of a holder in due course which are not subject to the defense or claim.

§ 3–309. Enforcement of Lost, Destroyed, or Stolen Instrument.

(a) A person not in possession of an instrument is entitled to enforce the instrument if (i) the person was in possession of the instrument and entitled to enforce it when loss of possession occurred, (ii) the loss of possession was not the result of a transfer by the person or a lawful seizure, and (iii) the person cannot reasonably obtain possession of the instrument because the instrument was destroyed, its whereabouts cannot be determined, or it is in the wrongful possession of an unknown person or a person that cannot be found or is not amenable to service of process.

(b) A person seeking enforcement of an instrument under subsection (a) must prove the terms of the instrument and the person's right to enforce the instrument. If that proof is made, Section 3–308 applies to the case as if the person seeking enforcement had produced the instrument. The court may not enter judgment in favor of the person seeking enforcement unless it finds that the person required to pay the instrument is adequately protected against loss that might occur by reason of a claim by another person to enforce the instrument. Adequate protection may be provided by any reasonable means.

§ 3–310. Effect of Instrument on Obligation for Which Taken.

(a) Unless otherwise agreed, if a certified check, cashier's check, or teller's check is taken for an obligation, the obligation is discharged to the same extent discharge would result if an amount of money equal to the amount of the instrument were taken in payment of the obligation. Discharge of the obligation does not affect any liability that the obligor may have as an indorser of the instrument.

(b) Unless otherwise agreed and except as provided in subsection (a), if a note or an uncertified check is taken for an obligation, the obligation is suspended to the same extent the obligation would be discharged if an amount of money equal to the amount of the instrument were taken, and the following rules apply:

(1) In the case of an uncertified check, suspension of the obligation continues until dishonor of the check or until it is paid or certified. Payment or certification of the check results in discharge of the obligation to the extent of the amount of the check.

(2) In the case of a note, suspension of the obligation continues until dishonor of the note or until it is paid. Payment of the note results in discharge of the obligation to the extent of the payment.

(3) Except as provided in paragraph (4), if the check or note is dishonored and the obligee of the obligation for which the instrument was taken is the person entitled to enforce the instrument, the obligee may enforce either the instrument or the obligation. In the case of an instrument of a third person which is negotiated to the obligee by the obligor, discharge of the obligor on the instrument also discharges the obligation.

(4) If the person entitled to enforce the instrument taken for an obligation is a person other than the obligee, the obligee may not enforce the obligation to the extent the obligation is suspended. If the obligee is the person entitled to enforce the instrument but no longer has possession of it because it was lost, stolen, or destroyed, the obligation may not be enforced to the extent of the amount payable on the instrument, and to that extent the obligee's rights against the obligor are limited to enforcement of the instrument.

(c) If an instrument other than one described in subsection (a) or (b) is taken for an obligation, the effect is (i) that stated in subsection (a) if the instrument is one on which a bank is liable as maker or acceptor, or (ii) that stated in subsection (b) in any other case.

§ 3–311. Accord and Satisfaction by Use of Instrument.

(a) If a person against whom a claim is asserted proves that (i) that person in good faith tendered an instrument to the claimant as full satisfaction of the claim, (ii) the amount of the claim was unliquidated or subject to a bona fide dispute, and (iii) the claimant obtained payment of the instrument, the following subsections apply.

(b) Unless subsection (c) applies, the claim is discharged if the person against whom the claim is asserted proves that the instrument or an accompanying written communication contained a conspicuous statement to the effect that the instrument was tendered as full satisfaction of the claim.

(c) Subject to subsection (d), a claim is not discharged under subsection (b) if either of the following applies:

(1) The claimant, if an organization, proves that (i) within a reasonable time before the tender, the claimant sent a conspicuous statement to the person against whom the claim is asserted that communications concerning disputed debts, including an instrument tendered as full satisfaction of a debt, are to be sent to a designated person, office, or place, and (ii) the instrument or accompanying communication was not received by that designated person, office, or place.

(2) The claimant, whether or not an organization, proves that within 90 days after payment of the instrument, the claimant tendered repayment of the amount of the instrument to the person against whom the claim is asserted. This paragraph does not apply if the claimant is an organization that sent a statement complying with paragraph (1)(i).

(d) A claim is discharged if the person against whom the claim is asserted proves that within a reasonable time before collection of the instrument was initiated, the claimant, or an agent of the claimant having direct responsibility with respect to the disputed obligation, knew that the instrument was tendered in full satisfaction of the claim.

§ 3–312. Lost, Destroyed, or Stolen Cashier's Check, Teller's Check, or Certified Check.*

(a) In this section:

(1) "Check" means a cashier's check, teller's check, or certified check.

(2) "Claimant" means a person who claims the right to receive the amount of a cashier's check, teller's check, or certified check that was lost, destroyed, or stolen.

(3) "Declaration of loss" means a written statement, made under penalty of perjury, to the effect that (i) the declarer lost possession of a check, (ii) the declarer is the drawer or payee of the check, in the case of a certified check, or the remitter or payee of the check, in the case of a cashier's check or teller's check, (iii) the loss of possession was not the result of a transfer by the declarer or a lawful seizure, and (iv) the declarer cannot reasonably obtain possession of the check because the check was destroyed, its whereabouts cannot be determined, or it is in the wrongful possession of an unknown person or a person that cannot be found or is not amenable to service of process.

(4) "Obligated bank" means the issuer of a cashier's check or teller's check or the acceptor of a certified check.

(b) A claimant may assert a claim to the amount of a check by a communication to the obligated bank describing the check with reasonable certainty and requesting payment of the amount of the check, if (i) the claimant is the drawer or payee of a certified check or the remitter or payee of a cashier's check or teller's check, (ii) the communication contains or is accompanied by a declaration of loss of the claimant with respect to the check, (iii) the communication is received at a time and in a manner affording the bank a reasonable

time to act on it before the check is paid, and (iv) the claimant provides reasonable identification if requested by the obligated bank. Delivery of a declaration of loss is a warranty of the truth of the statements made in the declaration. If a claim is asserted in compliance with this subsection, the following rules apply:

(1) The claim becomes enforceable at the later of (i) the time the claim is asserted, or (ii) the 90th day following the date of the check, in the case of a cashier's check or teller's check, or the 90th day following the date of the acceptance, in the case of a certified check.

(2) Until the claim becomes enforceable, it has no legal effect and the obligated bank may pay the check or, in the case of a teller's check, may permit the drawee to pay the check. Payment to a person entitled to enforce the check discharges all liability of the obligated bank with respect to the check.

(3) If the claim becomes enforceable before the check is presented for payment, the obligated bank is not obliged to pay the check.

(4) When the claim becomes enforceable, the obligated bank becomes obliged to pay the amount of the check to the claimant if payment of the check has not been made to a person entitled to enforce the check. Subject to Section 4–302(a)(1), payment to the claimant discharges all liability of the obligated bank with respect to the check.

(c) If the obligated bank pays the amount of a check to a claimant under subsection (b)(4) and the check is presented for payment by a person having rights of a holder in due course, the claimant is obliged to (i) refund the payment to the obligated bank if the check is paid, or (ii) pay the amount of the check to the person having rights of a holder in due course if the check is dishonored.

(d) If a claimant has the right to assert a claim under subsection (b) and is also a person entitled to enforce a cashier's check, teller's check, or certified check which is lost, destroyed, or stolen, the claimant may assert rights with respect to the check either under this section or Section 3–309.

Added in 1991.

Part 4—Liability of Parties

§ 3–401. Signature.

(a) A person is not liable on an instrument unless (i) the person signed the instrument, or (ii) the person is represented by an agent or representative who signed the instrument and the signature is binding on the represented person under Section 3–402.

(b) A signature may be made (i) manually or by means of a device or machine, and (ii) by the use of any name, including a trade or assumed name, or by a word, mark, or symbol executed or adopted by a person with present intention to authenticate a writing.

§ 3–402. Signature by Representative.

(a) If a person acting, or purporting to act, as a representative signs an instrument by signing either the name of the represented person or the name of the signer, the represented person is bound by the signature to the same extent the represented person would be bound if the signature were on a simple contract. If the represented person is bound, the signature of the representative is the "authorized signature of the represented person" and the represented person is liable on the instrument, whether or not identified in the instrument.

(b) If a representative signs the name of the representative to an instrument and the signature is an authorized signature of the represented person, the following rules apply:

(1) If the form of the signature shows unambiguously that the signature is made on behalf of the represented person who is identified in the instrument, the representative is not liable on the instrument.

(2) Subject to subsection (c), if (i) the form of the signature does not show unambiguously that the signature is made in a representative capacity or (ii) the represented person is not identified in the instrument, the representative is liable on the instrument to a holder in due course that took the instrument without notice that the representative was not intended to be liable on the instrument. With respect to any other person, the representative is liable on the instrument unless the representative proves that the original parties did not intend the representative to be liable on the instrument.

(c) If a representative signs the name of the representative as drawer of a check without indication of the representative status and the check is payable from an account of the represented person who is identified on the check, the signer is not liable on the check if the signature is an authorized signature of the represented person.

§ 3–403. Unauthorized Signature.

(a) Unless otherwise provided in this Article or Article 4, an unauthorized signature is ineffective except as the signature of the unauthorized signer in favor of a person who in good faith pays the instrument or takes it for value. An unauthorized signature may be ratified for all purposes of this Article.

(b) If the signature of more than one person is required to constitute the authorized signature of an organization, the signature of the organization is unauthorized if one of the required signatures is lacking.

(c) The civil or criminal liability of a person who makes an unauthorized signature is not affected by any provision of this Article which makes the unauthorized signature effective for the purposes of this Article.

§ 3–404. Impostors; Fictitious Payees.

(a) If an impostor, by use of the mails or otherwise, induces the issuer of an instrument to issue the instrument to the impostor, or to a person acting in concert with the impostor, by impersonating the payee of the instrument or a person authorized to act for the payee, an indorsement of the instrument by any person in the name of the payee is effective as the indorsement of the payee in favor of a person who, in good faith, pays the instrument or takes it for value or for collection.

(b) If (i) a person whose intent determines to whom an instrument is payable (Section 3–110(a) or (b)) does not intend the person identified as payee to have any interest in the instrument, or (ii) the person identified as payee of an instrument is a fictitious person, the following rules apply until the instrument is negotiated by special indorsement:

(1) Any person in possession of the instrument is its holder.

(2) An indorsement by any person in the name of the payee stated in the instrument is effective as the indorsement of the payee in favor of a person who, in good faith, pays the instrument or takes it for value or for collection.

(c) Under subsection (a) or (b), an indorsement is made in the name of a payee if (i) it is made in a name substantially similar to that of the payee or (ii) the instrument, whether or not indorsed, is deposited in a depositary bank to an account in a name substantially similar to that of the payee.

(d) With respect to an instrument to which subsection (a) or (b) applies, if a person paying the instrument or taking it for value or for collection fails to exercise ordinary care in paying or taking the instrument and that failure substantially contributes to loss resulting from payment of the instrument, the person bearing the loss may recover from the person failing to exercise ordinary care to the extent the failure to exercise ordinary care contributed to the loss.

§ 3–405. Employer's Responsibility for Fraudulent Indorsement by Employee.

(a) In this section:

(1) "Employee" includes an independent contractor and employee of an independent contractor retained by the employer.

(2) "Fraudulent indorsement" means (i) in the case of an instrument payable to the employer, a forged indorsement purporting to be that of the employer, or (ii) in the case of an instrument with respect to which the employer is the issuer, a forged indorsement purporting to be that of the person identified as payee.

(3) "Responsibility" with respect to instruments means authority (i) to sign or indorse instruments on behalf of the employer, (ii) to process instruments received by the employer for bookkeeping purposes, for deposit to an account, or for other disposition, (iii) to prepare or process instruments for issue in the name of the employer, (iv) to supply information determining the names or addresses of payees of instruments to be issued in the name of the employer, (v) to control the disposition of instruments to be issued in the name of the employer, or (vi) to act otherwise with respect to instruments in a responsible capacity. "Responsibility" does not include authority that merely allows an employee to have access to instruments or blank or incomplete instrument forms that are being stored or transported or are part of incoming or outgoing mail, or similar access.

(b) For the purpose of determining the rights and liabilities of a person who, in good faith, pays an instrument or takes it for value or for collection, if an employer entrusted an employee with responsibility with respect to the instrument and the employee or a person acting in concert with the employee makes a fraudulent indorsement of the instrument, the indorsement is effective as the indorsement of the person to whom the instrument is payable if it is made in the name of that person. If the person paying the instrument or taking it for value or for collection fails to exercise ordinary care in paying or taking the instrument and that failure substantially contributes to loss resulting from the fraud, the person bearing the loss may recover from the person failing to exercise ordinary care to the extent the failure to exercise ordinary care contributed to the loss.

(c) Under subsection (b), an indorsement is made in the name of the person to whom an instrument is payable if (i) it is made in a name substantially similar to the name of that person or (ii) the instrument, whether or not indorsed, is deposited in a depositary bank to an account in a name substantially similar to the name of that person.

§ 3–406. Negligence Contributing to Forged Signature or Alteration of Instrument.

(a) A person whose failure to exercise ordinary care substantially contributes to an alteration of an instrument or to the making of a forged signature on an instrument is precluded from asserting the alteration or the forgery against a person who, in good faith, pays the instrument or takes it for value or for collection.

(b) Under subsection (a), if the person asserting the preclusion fails to exercise ordinary care in paying or taking the instrument and that failure substantially contributes to loss, the loss is allocated between the person precluded and the person asserting the preclusion according to the extent to which the failure of each to exercise ordinary care contributed to the loss.

(c) Under subsection (a), the burden of proving failure to exercise ordinary care is on the person asserting the preclusion. Under subsection (b), the burden of proving failure to exercise ordinary care is on the person precluded.

§ 3–407.   Alteration.

(a) "Alteration" means (i) an unauthorized change in an instrument that purports to modify in any respect the obligation of a party, or (ii) an unauthorized addition of words or numbers or other change to an incomplete instrument relating to the obligation of a party.

(b) Except as provided in subsection (c), an alteration fraudulently made discharges a party whose obligation is affected by the alteration unless that party assents or is precluded from asserting the alteration. No other alteration discharges a party, and the instrument may be enforced according to its original terms.

(c) A payor bank or drawee paying a fraudulently altered instrument or a person taking it for value, in good faith and without notice of the alteration, may enforce rights with respect to the instrument (i) according to its original terms, or (ii) in the case of an incomplete instrument altered by unauthorized completion, according to its terms as completed.

§ 3–408.   Drawee Not Liable on Unaccepted Draft.

A check or other draft does not of itself operate as an assignment of funds in the hands of the drawee available for its payment, and the drawee is not liable on the instrument until the drawee accepts it.

§ 3–409.   Acceptance of Draft; Certified Check.

(a) "Acceptance" means the drawee's signed agreement to pay a draft as presented. It must be written on the draft and may consist of the drawee's signature alone. Acceptance may be made at any time and becomes effective when notification pursuant to instructions is given or the accepted draft is delivered for the purpose of giving rights on the acceptance to any person.

(b) A draft may be accepted although it has not been signed by the drawer, is otherwise incomplete, is overdue, or has been dishonored.

(c) If a draft is payable at a fixed period after sight and the acceptor fails to date the acceptance, the holder may complete the acceptance by supplying a date in good faith.

(d) "Certified check" means a check accepted by the bank on which it is drawn. Acceptance may be made as stated in subsection (a) or by a writing on the check which indicates that the check is certified. The drawee of a check has no obligation to certify the check, and refusal to certify is not dishonor of the check.

§ 3–410.   Acceptance Varying Draft.

(a) If the terms of a drawee's acceptance vary from the terms of the draft as presented, the holder may refuse the acceptance and treat the draft as dishonored. In that case, the drawee may cancel the acceptance.

(b) The terms of a draft are not varied by an acceptance to pay at a particular bank or place in the United States, unless the acceptance states that the draft is to be paid only at that bank or place.

(c) If the holder assents to an acceptance varying the terms of a draft, the obligation of each drawer and indorser that does not expressly assent to the acceptance is discharged.

§ 3–411.   Refusal to Pay Cashier's Checks, Teller's Checks, and Certified Checks.

(a) In this section, "obligated bank" means the acceptor of a certified check or the issuer of a cashier's check or teller's check bought from the issuer.

(b) If the obligated bank wrongfully (i) refuses to pay a cashier's check or certified check, (ii) stops payment of a teller's check, or (iii) refuses to pay a dishonored teller's check, the person asserting the right to enforce the check is entitled to compensation for expenses and loss of interest resulting from the nonpayment and may recover consequential damages if the obligated bank refuses to pay after receiving notice of particular circumstances giving rise to the damages.

(c) Expenses or consequential damages under subsection (b) are not recoverable if the refusal of the obligated bank to pay occurs because (i) the bank suspends payments, (ii) the obligated bank asserts a claim or defense of the bank that it has reasonable grounds to believe is available against the person entitled to enforce the instrument, (iii) the obligated bank has a reasonable doubt whether the person demanding payment is the person entitled to enforce the instrument, or (iv) payment is prohibited by law.

§ 3–412.   Obligation of Issuer of Note or Cashier's Check.

The issuer of a note or cashier's check or other draft drawn on the drawer is obliged to pay the instrument (i) according to its terms at the time it was issued or, if not issued, at the time it first came into possession of a holder, or (ii) if the issuer signed an incomplete instrument, according to its terms when completed, to the extent stated in Sections 3–115 and 3–407. The obligation is owed to a person entitled to enforce the instrument or to an indorser who paid the instrument under Section 3–415.

§ 3–413.   Obligation of Acceptor.

(a) The acceptor of a draft is obliged to pay the draft (i) according to its terms at the time it was accepted, even though the acceptance states that the draft is payable "as originally drawn" or equivalent terms, (ii) if the acceptance varies the terms of the draft, according to the terms of the draft as varied, or (iii) if the acceptance is of a draft that is an incomplete instrument, according to its terms when completed, to the extent stated in Sections 3–115 and 3–407. The obligation is owed to a person entitled to enforce the draft or to the drawer or an indorser who paid the draft under Section 3–414 or 3–415.

(b) If the certification of a check or other acceptance of a draft states the amount certified or accepted, the obligation of the acceptor is that amount. If (i) the certification or acceptance does not state an amount, (ii) the amount of the instrument is subsequently raised, and (iii) the instrument is then negotiated to a holder in due course, the obligation of the acceptor is the amount of the instrument at the time it was taken by the holder in due course.

§ 3–414. Obligation of Drawer.

(a) This section does not apply to cashier's checks or other drafts drawn on the drawer.

(b) If an unaccepted draft is dishonored, the drawer is obliged to pay the draft (i) according to its terms at the time it was issued or, if not issued, at the time it first came into possession of a holder, or (ii) if the drawer signed an incomplete instrument, according to its terms when completed, to the extent stated in Sections 3–115 and 3–407. The obligation is owed to a person entitled to enforce the draft or to an indorser who paid the draft under Section 3–415.

(c) If a draft is accepted by a bank, the drawer is discharged, regardless of when or by whom acceptance was obtained.

(d) If a draft is accepted and the acceptor is not a bank, the obligation of the drawer to pay the draft if the draft is dishonored by the acceptor is the same as the obligation of an indorser under Section 3–415(a) and (c).

(e) If a draft states that it is drawn "without recourse" or otherwise disclaims liability of the drawer to pay the draft, the drawer is not liable under subsection (b) to pay the draft if the draft is not a check. A disclaimer of the liability stated in subsection (b) is not effective if the draft is a check.

(f) If (i) a check is not presented for payment or given to a depositary bank for collection within 30 days after its date, (ii) the drawee suspends payments after expiration of the 30-day period without paying the check, and (iii) because of the suspension of payments, the drawer is deprived of funds maintained with the drawee to cover payment of the check, the drawer to the extent deprived of funds may discharge its obligation to pay the check by assigning to the person entitled to enforce the check the rights of the drawer against the drawee with respect to the funds.

§ 3–415. Obligation of Indorser.

(a) Subject to subsections (b), (c), and (d) and to Section 3–419(d), if an instrument is dishonored, an indorser is obliged to pay the amount due on the instrument (i) according to the terms of the instrument at the time it was indorsed, or (ii) if the indorser indorsed an incomplete instrument, according to its terms when completed, to the extent stated in Sections 3–115 and 3–407. The obligation of the indorser is owed to a person entitled to enforce the instrument or to a subsequent indorser who paid the instrument under this section.

(b) If an indorsement states that it is made "without recourse" or otherwise disclaims liability of the indorser, the indorser is not liable under subsection (a) to pay the instrument.

(c) If notice of dishonor of an instrument is required by Section 3–503 and notice of dishonor complying with that section is not given to an indorser, the liability of the indorser under subsection (a) is discharged.

(d) If a draft is accepted by a bank after an indorsement is made, the liability of the indorser under subsection (a) is discharged.

(e) If an indorser of a check is liable under subsection (a) and the check is not presented for payment, or given to a depositary bank for collection, within 30 days after the day the indorsement was made, the liability of the indorser under subsection (a) is discharged.
As amended in 1993.

§ 3–416. Transfer Warranties.

(a) A person who transfers an instrument for consideration warrants to the transferee and, if the transfer is by indorsement, to any subsequent transferee that:

(1) the warrantor is a person entitled to enforce the instrument;

(2) all signatures on the instrument are authentic and authorized;

(3) the instrument has not been altered;

(4) the instrument is not subject to a defense or claim in recoupment of any party which can be asserted against the warrantor; and

(5) the warrantor has no knowledge of any insolvency proceeding commenced with respect to the maker or acceptor or, in the case of an unaccepted draft, the drawer.

(b) A person to whom the warranties under subsection (a) are made and who took the instrument in good faith may recover from the warrantor as damages for breach of warranty an amount equal to the loss suffered as a result of the breach, but not more than the amount of the instrument plus expenses and loss of interest incurred as a result of the breach.

(c) The warranties stated in subsection (a) cannot be disclaimed with respect to checks. Unless notice of a claim for breach of warranty is given to the warrantor within 30 days after the claimant has reason to know of the breach and the identity of the warrantor, the liability of the warrantor under subsection (b) is discharged to the extent of any loss caused by the delay in giving notice of the claim.

(d) A [cause of action] for breach of warranty under this section accrues when the claimant has reason to know of the breach.

§ 3–417. Presentment Warranties.

(a) If an unaccepted draft is presented to the drawee for payment or acceptance and the drawee pays or accepts the draft, (i) the person obtaining payment or acceptance, at the time of presentment, and (ii) a previous transferor of the draft, at the time of transfer, warrant to the drawee making payment or accepting the draft in good faith that:

(1) the warrantor is, or was, at the time the warrantor transferred the draft, a person entitled to enforce the draft or authorized to obtain payment or acceptance of the draft on behalf of a person entitled to enforce the draft;

(2) the draft has not been altered; and

(3) the warrantor has no knowledge that the signature of the drawer of the draft is unauthorized.

(b) A drawee making payment may recover from any warrantor damages for breach of warranty equal to the amount paid by the drawee less the amount the drawee received or is entitled to receive from the drawer because of the payment. In addition, the drawee is entitled to compensation for expenses and loss of interest resulting from the breach. The right of the drawee to recover damages under this subsection is not affected by any failure of the drawee to exercise ordinary care in making payment. If the drawee accepts the draft, breach of warranty is a defense to the obligation of the acceptor. If the acceptor makes payment with respect to the draft, the acceptor is entitled to recover from any warrantor for breach of warranty the amounts stated in this subsection.

(c) If a drawee asserts a claim for breach of warranty under subsection (a) based on an unauthorized indorsement of the draft or an alteration of the draft, the warrantor may defend by proving that the indorsement is effective under Section 3–404 or 3–405 or the drawer is precluded under Section 3–406 or 4–406 from asserting against the drawee the unauthorized indorsement or alteration.

(d) If (i) a dishonored draft is presented for payment to the drawer or an indorser or (ii) any other instrument is presented for payment to a party obliged to pay the instrument, and (iii) payment is received, the following rules apply:

(1) The person obtaining payment and a prior transferor of the instrument warrant to the person making payment in good faith that the warrantor is, or was, at the time the warrantor transferred the instrument, a person entitled to enforce the instrument or authorized to obtain payment on behalf of a person entitled to enforce the instrument.

(2) The person making payment may recover from any warrantor for breach of warranty an amount equal to the amount paid plus expenses and loss of interest resulting from the breach.

(e) The warranties stated in subsections (a) and (d) cannot be disclaimed with respect to checks. Unless notice of a claim for breach of warranty is given to the warrantor within 30 days after the claimant has reason to know of the breach and the identity of the warrantor, the liability of the warrantor under subsection (b) or (d) is discharged to the extent of any loss caused by the delay in giving notice of the claim.

(f) A [cause of action] for breach of warranty under this section accrues when the claimant has reason to know of the breach.

§ 3–418. Payment or Acceptance by Mistake.

(a) Except as provided in subsection (c), if the drawee of a draft pays or accepts the draft and the drawee acted on the mistaken belief that (i) payment of the draft had not been stopped pursuant to Section 4–403 or (ii) the signature of the drawer of the draft was authorized, the drawee may recover the amount of the draft from the person to whom or for whose benefit payment was made or, in the case of acceptance, may revoke the acceptance. Rights of the drawee under this subsection are not affected by failure of the drawee to exercise ordinary care in paying or accepting the draft.

(b) Except as provided in subsection (c), if an instrument has been paid or accepted by mistake and the case is not covered by subsection (a), the person paying or accepting may, to the extent permitted by the law governing mistake and restitution, (i) recover the payment from the person to whom or for whose benefit payment was made or (ii) in the case of acceptance, may revoke the acceptance.

(c) The remedies provided by subsection (a) or (b) may not be asserted against a person who took the instrument in good faith and for value or who in good faith changed position in reliance on the payment or acceptance. This subsection does not limit remedies provided by Section 3–417 or 4–407.

(d) Notwithstanding Section 4–215, if an instrument is paid or accepted by mistake and the payor or acceptor recovers payment or revokes acceptance under subsection (a) or (b), the instrument is deemed not to have been paid or accepted and is treated as dishonored, and the person from whom payment is recovered has rights as a person entitled to enforce the dishonored instrument.

§ 3–419. Instruments Signed for Accommodation.

(a) If an instrument is issued for value given for the benefit of a party to the instrument ("accommodated party") and another party to the instrument ("accommodation party") signs the instrument for the purpose of incurring liability on the instrument without being a direct beneficiary of the value given for the instrument, the instrument is signed by the accommodation party "for accommodation."

(b) An accommodation party may sign the instrument as maker, drawer, acceptor, or indorser and, subject to subsection (d), is obliged to pay the instrument in the capacity in which the accommodation party signs. The obligation of an accommodation party may be enforced notwithstanding any statute of frauds and whether or not the accommodation party receives consideration for the accommodation.

(c) A person signing an instrument is presumed to be an accommodation party and there is notice that the instrument is signed for accommodation if the signature is an anomalous indorsement or is accompanied by words indicating that the signer is acting as surety or guarantor with respect to the obligation of another party to the instrument. Except as provided in Section 3–605, the obligation of an accommodation party to pay the instrument is not affected by the fact that the person enforcing the obligation had notice when the instrument was taken by that person that the accommodation party signed the instrument for accommodation.

(d) If the signature of a party to an instrument is accompanied by words indicating unambiguously that the party is guaranteeing collection rather than payment of the obligation of another party to the instrument, the signer is obliged to pay the amount due on the instrument to a person entitled to enforce the instrument only if (i) execution of judgment against the other party has been returned unsatisfied, (ii) the other party is insolvent or in an insolvency proceeding, (iii) the other party cannot be served with process, or (iv) it is otherwise apparent that payment cannot be obtained from the other party.

(e) An accommodation party who pays the instrument is entitled to reimbursement from the accommodated party and is entitled to enforce the instrument against the accommodated party. An accommodated party who pays the instrument has no right of recourse against, and is not entitled to contribution from, an accommodation party.

§ 3–420. Conversion of Instrument.

(a) The law applicable to conversion of personal property applies to instruments. An instrument is also converted if it is taken by transfer, other than a negotiation, from a person not entitled to enforce the instrument or a bank makes or obtains payment with respect to the instrument for a person not entitled to enforce the instrument or receive payment. An action for conversion of an instrument may not be brought by (i) the issuer or acceptor of the instrument or (ii) a payee or indorsee who did not receive delivery of the instrument either directly or through delivery to an agent or a co-payee.

(b) In an action under subsection (a), the measure of liability is presumed to be the amount payable on the instrument, but recovery may not exceed the amount of the plaintiff's interest in the instrument.

(c) A representative, other than a depositary bank, who has in good faith dealt with an instrument or its proceeds on behalf of one who was not the person entitled to enforce the instrument is not liable in conversion to that person beyond the amount of any proceeds that it has not paid out.

Part 5—Dishonor

§ 3–501. Presentment.

(a) "Presentment" means a demand made by or on behalf of a person entitled to enforce an instrument (i) to pay the instrument made to the drawee or a party obliged to pay the instrument or, in the case of a note or accepted draft payable at a bank, to the bank, or (ii) to accept a draft made to the drawee.

(b) The following rules are subject to Article 4, agreement of the parties, and clearing-house rules and the like:

(1) Presentment may be made at the place of payment of the instrument and must be made at the place of payment if the instrument is payable at a bank in the United States; may be made by any commercially reasonable means, including an oral, written, or electronic communication; is effective when the demand for payment or acceptance is received by the person to whom presentment is made; and is effective if made to any one of two or more makers, acceptors, drawees, or other payors.

(2) Upon demand of the person to whom presentment is made, the person making presentment must (i) exhibit the instrument, (ii) give reasonable identification and, if presentment is made on behalf of another person, reasonable evidence of authority to do so, and (. . .) sign a receipt on the instrument for any payment made or surrender the instrument if full payment is made.

(3) Without dishonoring the instrument, the party to whom presentment is made may (i) return the instrument for lack of a necessary indorsement, or (ii) refuse payment or acceptance for failure of the presentment to comply with the terms of the instrument, an agreement of the parties, or other applicable law or rule.

(4) The party to whom presentment is made may treat presentment as occurring on the next business day after the day of presentment if the party to whom presentment is made has established a cut-off hour not earlier than 2 p.m. for the receipt and processing of instruments presented for payment or acceptance and presentment is made after the cut-off hour.

§ 3–502. Dishonor.
(a) Dishonor of a note is governed by the following rules:

(1) If the note is payable on demand, the note is dishonored if presentment is duly made to the maker and the note is not paid on the day of presentment.

(2) If the note is not payable on demand and is payable at or through a bank or the terms of the note require presentment, the note is dishonored if presentment is duly made and the note is not paid on the day it becomes payable or the day of presentment, whichever is later.

(3) If the note is not payable on demand and paragraph (2) does not apply, the note is dishonored if it is not paid on the day it becomes payable.

(b) Dishonor of an unaccepted draft other than a documentary draft is governed by the following rules:

(1) If a check is duly presented for payment to the payor bank otherwise than for immediate payment over the counter, the check is dishonored if the payor bank makes timely return of the check or sends timely notice of dishonor or nonpayment under Section 4–301 or 4–302, or becomes accountable for the amount of the check under Section 4–302.

(2) If a draft is payable on demand and paragraph (1) does not apply, the draft is dishonored if presentment for payment is duly made to the drawee and the draft is not paid on the day of presentment.

(3) If a draft is payable on a date stated in the draft, the draft is dishonored if (i) presentment for payment is duly made to the drawee and payment is not made on the day the draft becomes payable or the day of presentment, whichever is later, or (ii) presentment for acceptance is duly made before the day the draft becomes payable and the draft is not accepted on the day of presentment.

(4) If a draft is payable on elapse of a period of time after sight or acceptance, the draft is dishonored if presentment for acceptance is duly made and the draft is not accepted on the day of presentment.

(c) Dishonor of an unaccepted documentary draft occurs according to the rules stated in subsection (b)(2), (3), and (4), except that payment or acceptance may be delayed without dishonor until no later than the close of the third business day of the drawee following the day on which payment or acceptance is required by those paragraphs.

(d) Dishonor of an accepted draft is governed by the following rules:

(1) If the draft is payable on demand, the draft is dishonored if presentment for payment is duly made to the acceptor and the draft is not paid on the day of presentment.

(2) If the draft is not payable on demand, the draft is dishonored if presentment for payment is duly made to the acceptor and payment is not made on the day it becomes payable or the day of presentment, whichever is later.

(e) In any case in which presentment is otherwise required for dishonor under this section and presentment is excused under Section 3–504, dishonor occurs without presentment if the instrument is not duly accepted or paid.

(f) If a draft is dishonored because timely acceptance of the draft was not made and the person entitled to demand acceptance consents to a late acceptance, from the time of acceptance the draft is treated as never having been dishonored.

§ 3–503. Notice of Dishonor.
(a) The obligation of an indorser stated in Section 3–415(a) and the obligation of a drawer stated in Section 3–414(d) may not be enforced unless (i) the indorser or drawer is given notice of dishonor of the instrument complying with this section or (ii) notice of dishonor is excused under Section 3–504(b).

(b) Notice of dishonor may be given by any person; may be given by any commercially reasonable means, including an oral, written, or electronic communication; and is sufficient if it reasonably identifies the instrument and indicates that the instrument has been dishonored or has not been paid or accepted. Return of an instrument given to a bank for collection is sufficient notice of dishonor.

(c) Subject to Section 3–504(c), with respect to an instrument taken for collection by a collecting bank, notice of dishonor must be given (i) by the bank before midnight of the next banking day following the banking day on which the bank receives notice of dishonor of the instrument, or (ii) by any other person within 30 days following the day on which the person receives notice of dishonor. With respect to any other instrument, notice of dishonor must be given within 30 days following the day on which dishonor occurs.

§ 3–504. Excused Presentment and Notice of Dishonor.
(a) Presentment for payment or acceptance of an instrument is excused if (i) the person entitled to present the instrument cannot with reasonable diligence make presentment, (ii) the maker or acceptor has repudiated an obligation to pay the instrument or is dead or in insolvency proceedings, (iii) by the terms of the instrument presentment is not necessary to enforce the obligation of indorsers or the drawer, (iv) the drawer or indorser whose obligation is being enforced has waived presentment or otherwise has no reason to expect or right to require that the instrument be paid or accepted, or (v) the drawer instructed the drawee not to pay or accept the draft or the drawee was not obligated to the drawer to pay the draft.

(b) Notice of dishonor is excused if (i) by the terms of the instrument notice of dishonor is not necessary to enforce the obligation of a party to pay the instrument, or (ii) the party whose obligation is being enforced waived notice of dishonor. A waiver of presentment is also a waiver of notice of dishonor.

(c) Delay in giving notice of dishonor is excused if the delay was caused by circumstances beyond the control of the person giving the notice and the person giving the notice exercised reasonable diligence after the cause of the delay ceased to operate.

§ 3–505. Evidence of Dishonor.

(a) The following are admissible as evidence and create a presumption of dishonor and of any notice of dishonor stated:

> **(1)** a document regular in form as provided in subsection (b) which purports to be a protest;
>
> **(2)** a purported stamp or writing of the drawee, payor bank, or presenting bank on or accompanying the instrument stating that acceptance or payment has been refused unless reasons for the refusal are stated and the reasons are not consistent with dishonor;
>
> **(3)** a book or record of the drawee, payor bank, or collecting bank, kept in the usual course of business which shows dishonor, even if there is no evidence of who made the entry.

(b) A protest is a certificate of dishonor made by a United States consul or vice consul, or a notary public or other person authorized to administer oaths by the law of the place where dishonor occurs. It may be made upon information satisfactory to that person. The protest must identify the instrument and certify either that presentment has been made or, if not made, the reason why it was not made, and that the instrument has been dishonored by nonacceptance or nonpayment. The protest may also certify that notice of dishonor has been given to some or all parties.

Part 6—Discharge and Payment

§ 3–601. Discharge and Effect of Discharge.

(a) The obligation of a party to pay the instrument is discharged as stated in this Article or by an act or agreement with the party which would discharge an obligation to pay money under a simple contract.

(b) Discharge of the obligation of a party is not effective against a person acquiring rights of a holder in due course of the instrument without notice of the discharge.

§ 3–602. Payment.

(a) Subject to subsection (b), an instrument is paid to the extent payment is made (i) by or on behalf of a party obliged to pay the instrument, and (ii) to a person entitled to enforce the instrument. To the extent of the payment, the obligation of the party obliged to pay the instrument is discharged even though payment is made with knowledge of a claim to the instrument under Section 3–306 by another person.

(b) The obligation of a party to pay the instrument is not discharged under subsection (a) if:

> **(1)** a claim to the instrument under Section 3–306 is enforceable against the party receiving payment and (i) payment is made with knowledge by the payor that payment is prohibited by injunction or similar process of a court of competent jurisdiction, or (ii) in the case of an instrument other than a cashier's check, teller's check, or certified check, the party making payment accepted, from the person having a claim to the instrument, indemnity against loss resulting from refusal to pay the person entitled to enforce the instrument; or
>
> **(2)** the person making payment knows that the instrument is a stolen instrument and pays a person it knows is in wrongful possession of the instrument.

§ 3–603. Tender of Payment.

(a) If tender of payment of an obligation to pay an instrument is made to a person entitled to enforce the instrument, the effect of tender is governed by principles of law applicable to tender of payment under a simple contract.

(b) If tender of payment of an obligation to pay an instrument is made to a person entitled to enforce the instrument and the tender is refused, there is discharge, to the extent of the amount of the tender, of the obligation of an indorser or accommodation party having a right of recourse with respect to the obligation to which the tender relates.

(c) If tender of payment of an amount due on an instrument is made to a person entitled to enforce the instrument, the obligation of the obligor to pay interest after the due date on the amount tendered is discharged. If presentment is required with respect to an instrument and the obligor is able and ready to pay on the due date at every place of payment stated in the instrument, the obligor is deemed to have made tender of payment on the due date to the person entitled to enforce the instrument.

§ 3–604. Discharge by Cancellation or Renunciation.

(a) A person entitled to enforce an instrument, with or without consideration, may discharge the obligation of a party to pay the instrument (i) by an intentional voluntary act, such as surrender of the instrument to the party, destruction, mutilation, or cancellation of the instrument, cancellation or striking out of the party's signature, or the addition of words to the instrument indicating discharge, or (ii) by agreeing not to sue or otherwise renouncing rights against the party by a signed writing.

(b) Cancellation or striking out of an indorsement pursuant to subsection (a) does not affect the status and rights of a party derived from the indorsement.

§ 3–605. Discharge of Indorsers and Accommodation Parties.

(a) In this section, the term "indorser" includes a drawer having the obligation described in Section 3–414(d).

(b) Discharge, under Section 3–604, of the obligation of a party to pay an instrument does not discharge the obligation of an indorser or accommodation party having a right of recourse against the discharged party.

(c) If a person entitled to enforce an instrument agrees, with or without consideration, to an extension of the due date of the obligation of a party to pay the instrument, the extension discharges an indorser or accommodation party having a right of recourse against the party whose obligation is extended to the extent the indorser or accommodation party proves that the extension caused loss to the indorser or accommodation party with respect to the right of recourse.

(d) If a person entitled to enforce an instrument agrees, with or without consideration, to a material modification of the obligation of a party other than an extension of the due date, the modification discharges the obligation of an indorser or accommodation party having a right of recourse against the person whose obligation is modified to the extent the modification causes loss to the indorser or accommodation party with respect to the right of recourse. The loss suffered by the indorser or accommodation party as a result of the modification is equal to the amount of the right of recourse unless the person enforcing the instrument proves that no loss was caused by the modification or that the loss caused by the modification was an amount less than the amount of the right of recourse.

(e) If the obligation of a party to pay an instrument is secured by an interest in collateral and a person entitled to enforce the instrument impairs the value of the interest in collateral, the obligation of an indorser or accommodation party having a right of recourse against the obligor is discharged to the extent of the impairment. The value of an interest in collateral is impaired to the extent (i) the value of the interest is reduced to an amount less than the amount of the right of recourse of the party asserting discharge, or (ii) the reduction in value of the interest causes an increase in the amount by which the amount of the right of recourse exceeds the value of the interest. The burden of proving impairment is on the party asserting discharge.

(f) If the obligation of a party is secured by an interest in collateral not provided by an accommodation party and a person entitled to enforce the instrument impairs the value of the interest in collateral, the obligation of any party who is jointly and severally liable with respect to the secured obligation is discharged to the extent the impairment causes the party asserting discharge to pay more than that party would have been obliged to pay, taking into account rights of contribution, if impairment had not occurred. If the party asserting discharge is an accommodation party not entitled to discharge under subsection (e), the party is deemed to have a right to contribution based on joint and several liability rather than a right to reimbursement. The burden of proving impairment is on the party asserting discharge.

(g) Under subsection (e) or (f), impairing value of an interest in collateral includes (i) failure to obtain or maintain perfection or recordation of the interest in collateral, (ii) release of collateral without substitution of collateral of equal value, (iii) failure to perform a duty to preserve the value of collateral owed, under Article 9 or other law, to a debtor or surety or other person secondarily liable, or (iv) failure to comply with applicable law in disposing of collateral.

(h) An accommodation party is not discharged under subsection (c), (d), or (e) unless the person entitled to enforce the instrument knows of the accommodation or has notice under Section 3–419(c) that the instrument was signed for accommodation.

(i) A party is not discharged under this section if (i) the party asserting discharge consents to the event or conduct that is the basis of the discharge, or (ii) the instrument or a separate agreement of the party provides for waiver of discharge under this section either specifically or by general language indicating that parties waive defenses based on suretyship or impairment of collateral.

ADDENDUM TO REVISED ARTICLE 3
Notes to Legislative Counsel

1. If revised Article 3 is adopted in your state, the reference in Section 2–511 to Section 3–802 should be changed to Section 3–310.

2. If revised Article 3 is adopted in your state and the Uniform Fiduciaries Act is also in effect in your state, you may want to consider amending Uniform Fiduciaries Act § 9 to conform to Section 3–307(b)(2)(iii) and (4)(iii). See Official Comment 3 to Section 3–307.

REVISED ARTICLE 4: BANK DEPOSITS AND COLLECTIONS

Part 1—General Provisions and Definitions

§ 4–101. Short Title.
This Article may be cited as Uniform Commercial Code—Bank Deposits and Collections.
As amended in 1990.

§ 4–102. Applicability.
(a) To the extent that items within this Article are also within Articles 3 and 8, they are subject to those Articles. If there is conflict, this Article governs Article 3, but Article 8 governs this Article.

(b) The liability of a bank for action or non-action with respect to an item handled by it for purposes of presentment, payment, or collection is governed by the law of the place where the bank is located. In the case of action or non-action by or at a branch or separate office of a bank, its liability is governed by the law of the place where the branch or separate office is located.

§ 4–103. Variation by Agreement; Measure of Damages; Action Constituting Ordinary Care.
(a) The effect of the provisions of this Article may be varied by agreement, but the parties to the agreement cannot disclaim a bank's responsibility for its lack of good faith or failure to exercise ordinary care or limit the measure of damages for the lack or failure. However, the parties may determine by agreement the standards by which the bank's responsibility is to be measured if those standards are not manifestly unreasonable.

(b) Federal Reserve regulations and operating circulars, clearing-house rules, and the like have the effect of agreements under subsection (a), whether or not specifically assented to by all parties interested in items handled.

(c) Action or non-action approved by this Article or pursuant to Federal Reserve regulations or operating circulars is the exercise of ordinary care and, in the absence of special instructions, action or non-action consistent with clearing-house rules and the like or with a general banking usage not disapproved by this Article, is *prima facie* the exercise of ordinary care.

(d) The specification or approval of certain procedures by this Article is not disapproval of other procedures that may be reasonable under the circumstances.

(e) The measure of damages for failure to exercise ordinary care in handling an item is the amount of the item reduced by an amount that could not have been realized by the exercise of ordinary care. If there is also bad faith it includes any other damages the party suffered as a proximate consequence.
As amended in 1990.

§ 4–104. Definitions and Index of Definitions.
(a) In this Article, unless the context otherwise requires:

    (1) "Account" means any deposit or credit account with a bank, including a demand, time, savings, passbook, share draft, or like account, other than an account evidenced by a certificate of deposit;

    (2) "Afternoon" means the period of a day between noon and midnight;

    (3) "Banking day" means the part of a day on which a bank is open to the public for carrying on substantially all of its banking functions;

    (4) "Clearing house" means an association of banks or other payors regularly clearing items;

    (5) "Customer" means a person having an account with a bank or for whom a bank has agreed to collect items, including a bank that maintains an account at another bank;

    (6) "Documentary draft" means a draft to be presented for acceptance or payment if specified documents, certificated securities (Section 8–102) or instructions for uncertificated securities (Section 8–102), or other certificates, statements, or the like are to be received by the drawee or other payor before acceptance or payment of the draft;

(7) "Draft" means a draft as defined in Section 3–104 or an item, other than an instrument, that is an order;

(8) "Drawee" means a person ordered in a draft to make payment;

(9) "Item" means an instrument or a promise or order to pay money handled by a bank for collection or payment. The term does not include a payment order governed by Article 4A or a credit or debit card slip;

(10) "Midnight deadline" with respect to a bank is midnight on its next banking day following the banking day on which it receives the relevant item or notice or from which the time for taking action commences to run, whichever is later;

(11) "Settle" means to pay in cash, by clearing-house settlement, in a charge or credit or by remittance, or otherwise as agreed. A settlement may be either provisional or final;

(12) "Suspends payments" with respect to a bank means that it has been closed by order of the supervisory authorities, that a public officer has been appointed to take it over, or that it ceases or refuses to make payments in the ordinary course of business.

(b) [Other definitions' section references deleted.]

(c) [Other definitions' section references deleted.]

(d) In addition, Article 1 contains general definitions and principles of construction and interpretation applicable throughout this Article.

§ 4–105. "Bank"; "Depository Bank"; "Payor Bank"; "Intermediary Bank"; "Collecting Bank"; "Presenting Bank".

In this Article:

(1) "Bank" means a person engaged in the business of banking, including a savings bank, savings and loan association, credit union, or trust company;

(2) "Depository bank" means the first bank to take an item even though it is also the payor bank, unless the item is presented for immediate payment over the counter;

(3) "Payor bank" means a bank that is the drawee of a draft;

(4) "Intermediary bank" means a bank to which an item is transferred in course of collection except the depository or payor bank;

(5) "Collecting bank" means a bank handling an item for collection except the payor bank;

(6) "Presenting bank" means a bank presenting an item except a payor bank.

§ 4–106. Payable Through or Payable at Bank: Collecting Bank.

(a) If an item states that it is "payable through" a bank identified in the item, (i) the item designates the bank as a collecting bank and does not by itself authorize the bank to pay the item, and (ii) the item may be presented for payment only by or through the bank.

Alternative A

(b) If an item states that it is "payable at" a bank identified in the item, the item is equivalent to a draft drawn on the bank.

Alternative B

(b) If an item states that it is "payable at" a bank identified in the item, (i) the item designates the bank as a collecting bank and does not by itself authorize the bank to pay the item, and (ii) the item may be presented for payment only by or through the bank.

(c) If a draft names a nonbank drawee and it is unclear whether a bank named in the draft is a co-drawee or a collecting bank, the bank is a collecting bank.

As added in 1990.

§ 4–107. Separate Office of Bank.

A branch or separate office of a bank is a separate bank for the purpose of computing the time within which and determining the place at or to which action may be taken or notices or orders shall be given under this Article and under Article 3.

As amended in 1962 and 1990.

§ 4–108. Time of Receipt of Items.

(a) For the purpose of allowing time to process items, prove balances, and make the necessary entries on its books to determine its position for the day, a bank may fix an afternoon hour of 2 p.m. or later as a cutoff hour for the handling of money and items and the making of entries on its books.

(b) An item or deposit of money received on any day after a cutoff hour so fixed or after the close of the banking day may be treated as being received at the opening of the next banking day.

As amended in 1990.

§ 4–109. Delays.

(a) Unless otherwise instructed, a collecting bank in a good faith effort to secure payment of a specific item drawn on a payor other than a bank, and with or without the approval of any person involved, may waive, modify, or extend time limits imposed or permitted by this [act] for a period not exceeding two additional banking days without discharge of drawers or indorsers or liability to its transferor or a prior party.

(b) Delay by a collecting bank or payor bank beyond time limits prescribed or permitted by this [act] or by instructions is excused if (i) the delay is caused by interruption of communication or computer facilities, suspension of payments by another bank, war, emergency conditions, failure of equipment, or other circumstances beyond the control of the bank, and (ii) the bank exercises such diligence as the circumstances require.

§ 4–110. Electronic Presentment.

(a) "Agreement for electronic presentment" means an agreement, clearing-house rule, or Federal Reserve regulation or operating circular, providing that presentment of an item may be made by transmission of an image of an item or information describing the item ("presentment notice") rather than delivery of the item itself. The agreement may provide for procedures governing retention, presentment, payment, dishonor, and other matters concerning items subject to the agreement.

(b) Presentment of an item pursuant to an agreement for presentment is made when the presentment notice is received.

(c) If presentment is made by presentment notice, a reference to "item" or "check" in this Article means the presentment notice unless the context otherwise indicates.

As added in 1990.

§ 4–111. Statute of Limitations.

An action to enforce an obligation, duty, or right arising under this Article must be commenced within three years after the [cause of action] accrues.

As added in 1990.

Part 2—Collection of Items: Depositary and Collecting Banks

§ 4–201. Status of Collecting Bank as Agent and Provisional Status of Credits; Applicability of Article; Item Indorsed "Pay Any Bank".

(a) Unless a contrary intent clearly appears and before the time that a settlement given by a collecting bank for an item is or becomes final, the bank, with respect to an item, is an agent or sub-agent of the owner of the item and any settlement given for the item is provisional. This provision applies regardless of the form of indorsement or lack of indorsement and even though credit given for the item is subject to immediate withdrawal as of right or is in fact withdrawn; but the continuance of ownership of an item by its owner and any rights of the owner to proceeds of the item are subject to rights of a collecting bank, such as those resulting from outstanding advances on the item and rights of recoupment or setoff. If an item is handled by banks for purposes of presentment, payment, collection, or return, the relevant provisions of this Article apply even though action of the parties clearly establishes that a particular bank has purchased the item and is the owner of it.

(b) After an item has been indorsed with the words "pay any bank" or the like, only a bank may acquire the rights of a holder until the item has been:

    (1) returned to the customer initiating collection; or

    (2) specially indorsed by a bank to a person who is not a bank.

As amended in 1990.

§ 4–202. Responsibility for Collection or Return; When Action Timely.

(a) A collecting bank must exercise ordinary care in:

    (1) presenting an item or sending it for presentment;

    (2) sending notice of dishonor or nonpayment or returning an item other than a documentary draft to the bank's transferor after learning that the item has not been paid or accepted, as the case may be;

    (3) settling for an item when the bank receives final settlement; and

    (4) notifying its transferor of any loss or delay in transit within a reasonable time after discovery thereof.

(b) A collecting bank exercises ordinary care under subsection (a) by taking proper action before its midnight deadline following receipt of an item, notice, or settlement. Taking proper action within a reasonably longer time may constitute the exercise of ordinary care, but the bank has the burden of establishing timeliness.

(c) Subject to subsection (a)(1), a bank is not liable for the insolvency, neglect, misconduct, mistake, or default of another bank or person or for loss or destruction of an item in the possession of others or in transit.

As amended in 1990.

§ 4–203. Effect of Instructions.

Subject to Article 3 concerning conversion of instruments (Section 3–420) and restrictive indorsements (Section 3–206), only a collecting bank's transferor can give instructions that affect the bank or constitute notice to it, and a collecting bank is not liable to prior parties for any action taken pursuant to the instructions or in accordance with any agreement with its transferor.

§ 4–204. Methods of Sending and Presenting; Sending Directly to Payor Bank.

(a) A collecting bank shall send items by a reasonably prompt method, taking into consideration relevant instructions, the nature of the item, the number of those items on hand, the cost of collection involved, and the method generally used by it or others to present those items.

(b) A collecting bank may send:

    (1) an item directly to the payor bank;

    (2) an item to a nonbank payor if authorized by its transferor; and

    (3) an item other than documentary drafts to a nonbank payor, if authorized by Federal Reserve regulation or operating circular, clearing-house rule, or the like.

(c) Presentment may be made by a presenting bank at a place where the payor bank or other payor has requested that presentment be made.

As amended in 1990.

§ 4–205. Depositary Bank Holder of Unindorsed Item.

If a customer delivers an item to a depositary bank for collection:

(1) the depositary bank becomes a holder of the item at the time it receives the item for collection if the customer at the time of delivery was a holder of the item, whether or not the customer indorses the item, and, if the bank satisfies the other requirements of Section 3–302, it is a holder in due course; and

(2) the depositary bank warrants to collecting banks, the payor bank or other payor, and the drawer that the amount of the item was paid to the customer or deposited to the customer's account.

As amended in 1990.

§ 4–206. Transfer Between Banks.

Any agreed method that identifies the transferor bank is sufficient for the item's further transfer to another bank.

As amended in 1990.

§ 4–207. Transfer Warranties.

(a) A customer or collecting bank that transfers an item and receives a settlement or other consideration warrants to the transferee and to any subsequent collecting bank that:

    (1) the warrantor is a person entitled to enforce the item;

    (2) all signatures on the item are authentic andauthorized;

    (3) the item has not been altered;

    (4) the item is not subject to a defense or claim in recoupment (Section 3–305(a)) of any party that can be asserted against the warrantor; and

    (5) the warrantor has no knowledge of any insolvency proceeding commenced with respect to the maker or acceptor or, in the case of an unaccepted draft, the drawer.

(b) If an item is dishonored, a customer or collecting bank transferring the item and receiving settlement or other consideration is obliged to pay the amount due on the item (i) according to the terms of the item at the time it was transferred, or (ii) if the transfer was of an incomplete item, according to its terms when completed as stated in Sections 3–115 and 3–407. The obligation of a transferor is owed to the transferee and to any subsequent collecting bank that takes the item in good faith. A transferor cannot disclaim its obligation under this subsection by an indorsement stating that it is made "without recourse" or otherwise disclaiming liability.

(c) A person to whom the warranties under subsection (a) are made and who took the item in good faith may recover from the warrantor as damages for breach of warranty an amount equal to the loss suffered as a result of the breach, but not more than the amount of the item plus expenses and loss of interest incurred as a result of the breach.

(d) The warranties stated in subsection (a) cannot be disclaimed with respect to checks. Unless notice of a claim for breach of warranty is given to the warrantor within 30 days after the claimant has reason to know of the breach and the identity of the warrantor, the warrantor is discharged to the extent of any loss caused by the delay in giving notice of the claim.

(e) A cause of action for breach of warranty under this section accrues when the claimant has reason to know of the breach.
As amended in 1990.

§ 4–208. Presentment Warranties.

(a) If an unaccepted draft is presented to the drawee for payment or acceptance and the drawee pays or accepts the draft, (i) the person obtaining payment or acceptance, at the time of presentment, and (ii) a previous transferor of the draft, at the time of transfer, warrant to the drawee that pays or accepts the draft in good faith that:

(1) the warrantor is, or was, at the time the warrantor transferred the draft, a person entitled to enforce the draft or authorized to obtain payment or acceptance of the draft on behalf of a person entitled to enforce the draft;

(2) the draft has not been altered; and

(3) the warrantor has no knowledge that the signature of the purported drawer of the draft is unauthorized.

(b) A drawee making payment may recover from a warrantor damages for breach of warranty equal to the amount paid by the drawee less the amount the drawee received or is entitled to receive from the drawer because of the payment. In addition, the drawee is entitled to compensation for expenses and loss of interest resulting from the breach. The right of the drawee to recover damages under this subsection is not affected by any failure of the drawee to exercise ordinary care in making payment. If the drawee accepts the draft (i) breach of warranty is a defense to the obligation of the acceptor, and (ii) if the acceptor makes payment with respect to the draft, the acceptor is entitled to recover from a warrantor for breach of warranty the amounts stated in this subsection.

(c) If a drawee asserts a claim for breach of warranty under subsection (a) based on an unauthorized indorsement of the draft or an alteration of the draft, the warrantor may defend by proving that the indorsement is effective under Section 3–404 or 3–405 or the drawer is precluded under Section 3–406 or 4–406 from asserting against the drawee the unauthorized indorsement or alteration.

(d) If (i) a dishonored draft is presented for payment to the drawer or an indorser or (ii) any other item is presented for payment to a party obliged to pay the item, and the item is paid, the person obtaining payment and a prior transferor of the item warrant to the person making payment in good faith that the warrantor is, or was, at the time the warrantor transferred the item, a person entitled to enforce the item or authorized to obtain payment on behalf of a person entitled to enforce the item. The person making payment may recover from any warrantor for breach of warranty an amount equal to the amount paid plus expenses and loss of interest resulting from the breach.

(e) The warranties stated in subsections (a) and (d) cannot be disclaimed with respect to checks. Unless notice of a claim for breach of

warranty is given to the warrantor within 30 days after the claimant has reason to know of the breach and the identity of the warrantor, the warrantor is discharged to the extent of any loss caused by the delay in giving notice of the claim.

(f) A cause of action for breach of warranty under this section accrues when the claimant has reason to know of the breach.
As amended in 1990.

§ 4–209. Encoding and Retention Warranties.

(a) A person who encodes information on or with respect to an item after issue warrants to any subsequent collecting bank and to the payor bank or other payor that the information is correctly encoded. If the customer of a depositary bank encodes, that bank also makes the warranty.

(b) A person who undertakes to retain an item pursuant to an agreement for electronic presentment warrants to any subsequent collecting bank and to the payor bank or other payor that retention and presentment of the item comply with the agreement. If a customer of a depositary bank undertakes to retain an item, that bank also makes this warranty.

(c) A person to whom warranties are made under this section and who took the item in good faith may recover from the warrantor as damages for breach of warranty an amount equal to the loss suffered as a result of the breach, plus expenses and loss of interest incurred as a result of the breach.
As added in 1990.

§ 4–210. Security Interest of Collecting Bank in Items, Accompanying Documents and Proceeds.

(a) A collecting bank has a security interest in an item and any accompanying documents or the proceeds of either:

(1) in case of an item deposited in an account, to the extent to which credit given for the item has been withdrawn or applied;

(2) in case of an item for which it has given credit available for withdrawal as of right, to the extent of the credit given, whether or not the credit is drawn upon or there is a right of charge-back; or

(3) if it makes an advance on or against the item.

(b) If credit given for several items received at one time or pursuant to a single agreement is withdrawn or applied in part, the security interest remains upon all the items, any accompanying documents or the proceeds of either. For the purpose of this section, credits first given are first withdrawn.

(c) Receipt by a collecting bank of a final settlement for an item is a realization on its security interest in the item, accompanying documents, and proceeds. So long as the bank does not receive final settlement for the item or give up possession of the item or accompanying documents for purposes other than collection, the security interest continues to that extent and is subject to Article 9, but:

(1) no security agreement is necessary to make the security interest enforceable (Section 9–203(1)(a));

(2) no filing is required to perfect the security interest; and

(3) the security interest has priority over conflicting perfected security interests in the item, accompanying documents, or proceeds.
As amended in 1990 and 1999.

§ 4–211. When Bank Gives Value for Purposes of Holder in Due Course.

For purposes of determining its status as a holder in due course, a bank has given value to the extent it has a security interest in an

item, if the bank otherwise complies with the requirements of Section 3–302 on what constitutes a holder in due course.
As amended in 1990.

§ 4–212. Presentment by Notice of Item Not Payable by, Through, or at Bank; Liability of Drawer or Indorser.

(a) Unless otherwise instructed, a collecting bank may present an item not payable by, through, or at a bank by sending to the party to accept or pay a written notice that the bank holds the item for acceptance or payment. The notice must be sent in time to be received on or before the day when presentment is due and the bank must meet any requirement of the party to accept or pay under Section 3–501 by the close of the bank's next banking day after it knows of the requirement.

(b) If presentment is made by notice and payment, acceptance, or request for compliance with a requirement under Section 3–501 is not received by the close of business on the day after maturity or, in the case of demand items, by the close of business on the third banking day after notice was sent, the presenting bank may treat the item as dishonored and charge any drawer or indorser by sending it notice of the facts.
As amended in 1990.

§ 4–213. Medium and Time of Settlement by Bank.

(a) With respect to settlement by a bank, the medium and time of settlement may be prescribed by Federal Reserve regulations or circulars, clearing-house rules, and the like, or agreement. In the absence of such prescription:

(1) the medium of settlement is cash or credit to an account in a Federal Reserve bank of or specified by the person to receive settlement; and

(2) the time of settlement is:

(i) with respect to tender of settlement by cash, a cashier's check, or teller's check, when the cash or check is sent or delivered;

(ii) with respect to tender of settlement by credit in an account in a Federal Reserve Bank, when the credit is made;

(iii) with respect to tender of settlement by a credit or debit to an account in a bank, when the credit or debit is made or, in the case of tender of settlement by authority to charge an account, when the authority is sent or delivered; or

(iv) with respect to tender of settlement by a funds transfer, when payment is made pursuant to Section 4A–406(a) to the person receiving settlement.

(b) If the tender of settlement is not by a medium authorized by subsection (a) or the time of settlement is not fixed by subsection (a), no settlement occurs until the tender of settlement is accepted by the person receiving settlement.

(c) If settlement for an item is made by cashier's check or teller's check and the person receiving settlement, before its midnight deadline:

(1) presents or forwards the check for collection, settlement is final when the check is finally paid; or

(2) fails to present or forward the check for collection, settlement is final at the midnight deadline of the person receiving settlement.

(d) If settlement for an item is made by giving authority to charge the account of the bank giving settlement in the bank receiving settlement, settlement is final when the charge is made by the bank receiving settlement if there are funds available in the account for the amount of the item.
As amended in 1990.

§ 4–214. Right of Charge-Back or Refund; Liability of Collecting Bank: Return of Item.

(a) If a collecting bank has made provisional settlement with its customer for an item and fails by reason of dishonor, suspension of payments by a bank, or otherwise to receive settlement for the item which is or becomes final, the bank may revoke the settlement given by it, charge back the amount of any credit given for the item to its customer's account, or obtain refund from its customer, whether or not it is able to return the item, if by its midnight deadline or within a longer reasonable time after it learns the facts it returns the item or sends notification of the facts. If the return or notice is delayed beyond the bank's midnight deadline or a longer reasonable time after it learns the facts, the bank may revoke the settlement, charge back the credit, or obtain refund from its customer, but it is liable for any loss resulting from the delay. These rights to revoke, charge back, and obtain refund terminate if and when a settlement for the item received by the bank is or becomes final.

(b) A collecting bank returns an item when it is sent or delivered to the bank's customer or transferor or pursuant to its instructions.

(c) A depositary bank that is also the payor may charge back the amount of an item to its customer's account or obtain refund in accordance with the section governing return of an item received by a payor bank for credit on its books (Section 4–301).

(d) The right to charge back is not affected by:

(1) previous use of a credit given for the item; or

(2) failure by any bank to exercise ordinary care with respect to the item, but a bank so failing remains liable.

(e) A failure to charge back or claim refund does not affect other rights of the bank against the customer or any other party.

(f) If credit is given in dollars as the equivalent of the value of an item payable in foreign money, the dollar amount of any charge-back or refund must be calculated on the basis of the bank-offered spot rate for the foreign money prevailing on the day when the person entitled to the charge-back or refund learns that it will not receive payment in ordinary course.
As amended in 1990.

§ 4–215. Final Payment of Item by Payor Bank; When Provisional Debits and Credits Become Final; When Certain Credits Become Available for Withdrawal.

(a) An item is finally paid by a payor bank when the bank has first done any of the following:

(1) paid the item in cash;

(2) settled for the item without having a right to revoke the settlement under statute, clearing-house rule, or agreement; or

(3) made a provisional settlement for the item and failed to revoke the settlement in the time and manner permitted by statute, clearing-house rule, or agreement.

(b) If provisional settlement for an item does not become final, the item is not finally paid.

(c) If provisional settlement for an item between the presenting and payor banks is made through a clearing house or by debits or credits in an account between them, then to the extent that provisional debits or credits for the item are entered in accounts between the presenting and payor banks or between the presenting and successive prior collecting banks seriatim, they become final upon final payment of the item by the payor bank.

(d) If a collecting bank receives a settlement for an item which is or becomes final, the bank is accountable to its customer for the amount of the item and any provisional credit given for the item in an account with its customer becomes final.

(e) Subject to (i) applicable law stating a time for availability of funds and (ii) any right of the bank to apply the credit to an obligation of the customer, credit given by a bank for an item in a customer's account becomes available for withdrawal as of right:

(1) if the bank has received a provisional settlement for the item, when the settlement becomes final and the bank has had a reasonable time to receive return of the item and the item has not been received within that time;

(2) if the bank is both the depositary bank and the payor bank, and the item is finally paid, at the opening of the bank's second banking day following receipt of the item.

(f) Subject to applicable law stating a time for availability of funds and any right of a bank to apply a deposit to an obligation of the depositor, a deposit of money becomes available for withdrawal as of right at the opening of the bank's next banking day after receipt of the deposit.

As amended in 1990.

§ 4– 216. Insolvency and Preference.

(a) If an item is in or comes into the possession of a payor or collecting bank that suspends payment and the item has not been finally paid, the item must be returned by the receiver, trustee, or agent in charge of the closed bank to the presenting bank or the closed bank's customer.

(b) If a payor bank finally pays an item and suspends payments without making a settlement for the item with its customer or the presenting bank which settlement is or becomes final, the owner of the item has a preferred claim against the payor bank.

(c) If a payor bank gives or a collecting bank gives or receives a provisional settlement for an item and thereafter suspends payments, the suspension does not prevent or interfere with the settlement's becoming final if the finality occurs automatically upon the lapse of certain time or the happening of certain events.

(d) If a collecting bank receives from subsequent parties settlement for an item, which settlement is or becomes final and the bank suspends payments without making a settlement for the item with its customer which settlement is or becomes final, the owner of the item has a preferred claim against the collecting bank.

As amended in 1990.

Part 3—Collection of Items: Payor Banks

§ 4–301. Deferred Posting; Recovery of Payment by Return of Items; Time of Dishonor; Return of Items by Payor Bank.

(a) If a payor bank settles for a demand item other than a documentary draft presented otherwise than for immediate payment over the counter before midnight of the banking day of receipt, the payor bank may revoke the settlement and recover the settlement if, before it has made final payment and before its midnight deadline, it

(1) returns the item; or

(2) sends written notice of dishonor or non-payment if the item is unavailable for return.

(b) If a demand item is received by a payor bank for credit on its books, it may return the item or send notice of dishonor and may revoke any credit given or recover the amount thereof withdrawn by its customer, if it acts within the time limit and in the manner specified in subsection (a).

(c) Unless previous notice of dishonor has been sent, an item is dishonored at the time when for purposes of dishonor it is returned or notice sent in accordance with this section.

(d) An item is returned:

(1) as to an item presented through a clearing house, when it is delivered to the presenting or last collecting bank or to the clearing house or is sent or delivered in accordance with clearing-house rules; or (2) in all other cases, when it is sent or delivered to the bank's customer or transferor or pursuant to instructions.

As amended in 1990.

§ 4–302. Payor Bank's Responsibility for Late Return of Item.

(a) If an item is presented to and received by a payor bank, the bank is accountable for the amount of:

(1) a demand item, other than a documentary draft, whether properly payable or not, if the bank, in any case in which it is not also the depositary bank, retains the item beyond midnight of the banking day of receipt without settling for it or, whether or not it is also the depositary bank, does not pay or return the item or send notice of dishonor until after its midnight deadline; or

(2) any other properly payable item unless, within the time allowed for acceptance or payment of that item, the bank either accepts or pays the item or returns it and accompanying documents.

(b) The liability of a payor bank to pay an item pursuant to subsection (a) is subject to defenses based on breach of a presentment warranty (Section 4–208) or proof that the person seeking enforcement of the liability presented or transferred the item for the purpose of defrauding the payor bank.

As amended in 1990.

§ 4–303. When Items Subject to Notice, Stop-Payment Order, Legal Process, or Setoff; Order in Which Items May Be Charged or Certified.

(a) Any knowledge, notice, or stop-payment order received by, legal process served upon, or setoff exercised by a payor bank comes too late to terminate, suspend, or modify the bank's right or duty to pay an item or to charge its customer's account for the item if the knowledge, notice, stop-payment order, or legal process is received or served and a reasonable time for the bank to act thereon expires or the setoff is exercised after the earliest of the following:

(1) the bank accepts or certifies the item;

(2) the bank pays the item in cash;

(3) the bank settles for the item without having a right to revoke the settlement under statute, clearing-house rule, or agreement;

(4) the bank becomes accountable for the amount of the item under Section 4–302 dealing with the payor bank's responsibility for late return of items; or

(5) with respect to checks, a cutoff hour no earlier than one hour after the opening of the next banking day after the banking day on which the bank received the check and no later than the close of that next banking day or, if no cutoff hour is fixed, the close of the next banking day after the banking day on which the bank received the check.

(b) Subject to subsection (a), items may be accepted, paid, certified, or charged to the indicated account of its customer in any order.

As amended in 1990.

Part 4—Relationship Between Payor Bank and Its Customer

§ 4–401. When Bank May Charge Customer's Account.

(a) A bank may charge against the account of a customer an item that is properly payable from the account even though the charge creates an overdraft. An item is properly payable if it is authorized by the customer and is in accordance with any agreement between the customer and bank.

(b) A customer is not liable for the amount of an overdraft if the customer neither signed the item nor benefited from the proceeds of the item.

(c) A bank may charge against the account of a customer a check that is otherwise properly payable from the account, even though payment was made before the date of the check, unless the customer has given notice to the bank of the postdating describing the check with reasonable certainty. The notice is effective for the period stated in Section 4–403(b) for stop-payment orders, and must be received at such time and in such manner as to afford the bank a reasonable opportunity to act on it before the bank takes any action with respect to the check described in Section 4–303. If a bank charges against the account of a customer a check before the date stated in the notice of postdating, the bank is liable for damages for the loss resulting from its act. The loss may include damages for dishonor of subsequent items under Section 4–402.

(d) A bank that in good faith makes payment to a holder may charge the indicated account of its customer according to:

    (1) the original terms of the altered item; or

    (2) the terms of the completed item, even though the bank knows the item has been completed unless the bank has notice that the completion was improper.

As amended in 1990.

§ 4–402. Bank's Liability to Customer for Wrongful Dishonor; Time of Determining Insufficiency of Account.

(a) Except as otherwise provided in this Article, a payor bank wrongfully dishonors an item if it dishonors an item that is properly payable, but a bank may dishonor an item that would create an overdraft unless it has agreed to pay the overdraft.

(b) A payor bank is liable to its customer for damages proximately caused by the wrongful dishonor of an item. Liability is limited to actual damages proved and may include damages for an arrest or prosecution of the customer or other consequential damages. Whether any consequential damages are proximately caused by the wrongful dishonor is a question of fact to be determined in each case.

(c) A payor bank's determination of the customer's account balance on which a decision to dishonor for insufficiency of available funds is based may be made at any time between the time the item is received by the payor bank and the time that the payor bank returns the item or gives notice in lieu of return, and no more than one determination need be made. If, at the election of the payor bank, a subsequent balance determination is made for the purpose of reevaluating the bank's decision to dishonor the item, the account balance at that time is determinative of whether a dishonor for insufficiency of available funds is wrongful.

As amended in 1990.

§ 4–403. Customer's Right to Stop Payment; Burden of Proof of Loss.

(a) A customer or any person authorized to draw on the account if there is more than one person may stop payment of any item drawn on the customer's account or close the account by an order to the bank describing the item or account with reasonable certainty received at a time and in a manner that affords the bank a reasonable opportunity to act on it before any action by the bank with respect to the item described in Section 4–303. If the signature of more than one person is required to draw on an account, any of these persons may stop payment or close the account.

(b) A stop-payment order is effective for six months, but it lapses after 14 calendar days if the original order was oral and was not confirmed in writing within that period. A stop-payment order may be renewed for additional six-month periods by a writing given to the bank within a period during which the stop-payment order is effective.

(c) The burden of establishing the fact and amount of loss resulting from the payment of an item contrary to a stop-payment order or order to close an account is on the customer. The loss from payment of an item contrary to a stop-payment order may include damages for dishonor of subsequent items under Section 4–402.

As amended in 1990.

§ 4–404. Bank Not Obliged to Pay Check More Than Six Months Old.

A bank is under no obligation to a customer having a checking account to pay a check, other than a certified check, which is presented more than six months after its date, but it may charge its customer's account for a payment made thereafter in good faith.

§ 4–405. Death or Incompetence of Customer.

(a) A payor or collecting bank's authority to accept, pay, or collect an item or to account for proceeds of its collection, if otherwise effective, is not rendered ineffective by incompetence of a customer of either bank existing at the time the item is issued or its collection is undertaken if the bank does not know of an adjudication of incompetence. Neither death nor incompetence of a customer revokes the authority to accept, pay, collect, or account until the bank knows of the fact of death or of an adjudication of incompetence and has reasonable opportunity to act on it.

(b) Even with knowledge, a bank may for 10 days after the date of death pay or certify checks drawn on or before the date unless ordered to stop payment by a person claiming an interest in the account.

As amended in 1990.

§ 4–406. Customer's Duty to Discover and Report Unauthorized Signature or Alteration.

(a) A bank that sends or makes available to a customer a statement of account showing payment of items for the account shall either return or make available to the customer the items paid or provide information in the statement of account sufficient to allow the customer reasonably to identify the items paid. The statement of account provides sufficient information if the item is described by item number, amount, and date of payment.

(b) If the items are not returned to the customer, the person retaining the items shall either retain the items or, if the items are destroyed, maintain the capacity to furnish legible copies of the items until the expiration of seven years after receipt of the items. A customer may request an item from the bank that paid the item, and that bank must provide in a reasonable time either the item or, if the item has been destroyed or is not otherwise obtainable, a legible copy of the item.

(c) If a bank sends or makes available a statement of account or items pursuant to subsection (a), the customer must exercise reasonable promptness in examining the statement or the items to determine whether any payment was not authorized because of an alteration of an item or because a purported signature by or on behalf of the customer was not authorized. If, based on the statement or items provided, the customer should reasonably have discovered the unauthorized payment, the customer must promptly notify the bank of the relevant facts.

(d) If the bank proves that the customer failed, with respect to an item, to comply with the duties imposed on the customer by subsection (c), the customer is precluded from asserting against the bank:

> (1) the customer's unauthorized signature or any alteration on the item, if the bank also proves that it suffered a loss by reason of the failure; and
>
> (2) the customer's unauthorized signature or alteration by the same wrongdoer on any other item paid in good faith by the bank if the payment was made before the bank received notice from the customer of the unauthorized signature or alteration and after the customer had been afforded a reasonable period of time, not exceeding 30 days, in which to examine the item or statement of account and notify the bank.

(e) If subsection (d) applies and the customer proves that the bank failed to exercise ordinary care in paying the item and that the failure substantially contributed to loss, the loss is allocated between the customer precluded and the bank asserting the preclusion according to the extent to which the failure of the customer to comply with subsection (c) and the failure of the bank to exercise ordinary care contributed to the loss. If the customer proves that the bank did not pay the item in good faith, the preclusion under subsection (d) does not apply.

(f) Without regard to care or lack of care of either the customer or the bank, a customer who does not within one year after the statement or items are made available to the customer (subsection (a)) discover and report the customer's unauthorized signature on or any alteration on the item is precluded from asserting against the bank the unauthorized signature or alteration. If there is a preclusion under this subsection, the payor bank may not recover for breach or warranty under Section 4–208 with respect to the unauthorized signature or alteration to which the preclusion applies.

As amended in 1990.

§ 4–407. **Payor Bank's Right to Subrogation on Improper Payment.**

If a payor has paid an item over the order of the drawer or maker to stop payment, or after an account has been closed, or otherwise under circumstances giving a basis for objection by the drawer or maker, to prevent unjust enrichment and only to the extent necessary to prevent loss to the bank by reason of its payment of the item, the payor bank is subrogated to the rights

> (1) of any holder in due course on the item against the drawer or maker;
>
> (2) of the payee or any other holder of the item against the drawer or maker either on the item or under the transaction out of which the item arose; and

> (3) of the drawer or maker against the payee or any other holder of the item with respect to the transaction out of which the item arose.

As amended in 1990.

Part 5—Collection of Documentary Drafts

§ 4–501. **Handling of Documentary Drafts; Duty to Send for Presentment and to Notify Customer of Dishonor.**

A bank that takes a documentary draft for collection shall present or send the draft and accompanying documents for presentment and, upon learning that the draft has not been paid or accepted in due course, shall seasonably notify its customer of the fact even though it may have discounted or bought the draft or extended credit available for withdrawal as of right.

As amended in 1990.

§ 4–502. **Presentment of "On Arrival" Drafts.**

If a draft or the relevant instructions require presentment "on arrival", "when goods arrive" or the like, the collecting bank need not present until in its judgment a reasonable time for arrival of the goods has expired. Refusal to pay or accept because the goods have not arrived is not dishonor; the bank must notify its transferor of the refusal but need not present the draft again until it is instructed to do so or learns of the arrival of the goods.

§ 4–503. **Responsibility of Presenting Bank for Documents and Goods; Report of Reasons for Dishonor; Referee in Case of Need.**

Unless otherwise instructed and except as provided in Article 5, a bank presenting a documentary draft:

> (1) must deliver the documents to the drawee on acceptance of the draft if it is payable more than three days after presentment, otherwise, only on payment; and
>
> (2) upon dishonor, either in the case of presentment for acceptance or presentment for payment, may seek and follow instructions from any referee in case of need designated in the draft or, if the presenting bank does not choose to utilize the referee's services, it must use diligence and good faith to ascertain the reason for dishonor, must notify its transferor of the dishonor and of the results of its effort to ascertain the reasons therefor, and must request instructions.

However, the presenting bank is under no obligation with respect to goods represented by the documents except to follow any reasonable instructions seasonably received; it has a right to reimbursement for any expense incurred in following instructions and to prepayment of or indemnity for those expenses.

As amended in 1990.

§ 4–504. **Privilege of Presenting Bank to Deal With Goods; Security Interest for Expenses.**

(a) A presenting bank that, following the dishonor of a documentary draft, has seasonably requested instructions but does not receive them within a reasonable time may store, sell, or otherwise deal with the goods in any reasonable manner.

(b) For its reasonable expenses incurred by action under subsection (a) the presenting bank has a lien upon the goods or their proceeds, which may be foreclosed in the same manner as an unpaid seller's lien.

As amended in 1990.

ARTICLE 4A: FUNDS TRANSFERS

Part 1—Subject Matter and Definitions

§ 4A–101. Short Title.
This Article may be cited as Uniform Commercial Code—Funds Transfers.

§ 4A–102. Subject Matter.
Except as otherwise provided in Section 4A–108, this Article applies to funds transfers defined in Section 4A–104.

§ 4A–103. Payment Order–Definitions.
(a) In this Article:

(1) "Payment order" means an instruction of a sender to a receiving bank, transmitted orally, electronically, or in writing, to pay, or to cause another bank to pay, a fixed or determinable amount of money to a beneficiary if:

(i) the instruction does not state a condition to payment to the beneficiary other than time of payment,

(ii) the receiving bank is to be reimbursed by debiting an account of, or otherwise receiving payment from, the sender, and

(iii) the instruction is transmitted by the sender directly to the receiving bank or to an agent, funds-transfer system, or communication system for transmittal to the receiving bank.

(2) "Beneficiary" means the person to be paid by the beneficiary's bank.

(3) "Beneficiary's bank" means the bank identified in a payment order in which an account of the beneficiary is to be credited pursuant to the order or which otherwise is to make payment to the beneficiary if the order does not provide for payment to an account.

(4) "Receiving bank" means the bank to which the sender's instruction is addressed.

(5) "Sender" means the person giving the instruction to the receiving bank.

(b) If an instruction complying with subsection (a)(1) is to make more than one payment to a beneficiary, the instruction is a separate payment order with respect to each payment.

(c) A payment order is issued when it is sent to the receiving bank.

§ 4A–104. Funds Transfer–Definitions.
In this Article:

(a) "Funds transfer" means the series of transactions, beginning with the originator's payment order, made for the purpose of making payment to the beneficiary of the order. The term includes any payment order issued by the originator's bank or an intermediary bank intended to carry out the originator's payment order. A funds transfer is completed by acceptance by the beneficiary's bank of a payment order for the benefit of the beneficiary of the originator's payment order.

(b) "Intermediary bank" means a receiving bank other than the originator's bank or the beneficiary's bank.

(c) "Originator" means the sender of the first payment order in a funds transfer.

(d) "Originator's bank" means (i) the receiving bank to which the payment order of the originator is issued if the originator is not a bank, or (ii) the originator if the originator is a bank.

§ 4A–105. Other Definitions.
(a) In this Article:

(1) "Authorized account" means a deposit account of a customer in a bank designated by the customer as a source of payment of payment orders issued by the customer to the bank. If a customer does not so designate an account, any account of the customer is an authorized account if payment of a payment order from that account is not inconsistent with a restriction on the use of that account.

(2) "Bank" means a person engaged in the business of banking and includes a savings bank, savings and loan association, credit union, and trust company. A branch or separate office of a bank is a separate bank for purposes of this Article.

(3) "Customer" means a person, including a bank, having an account with a bank or from whom a bank has agreed to receive payment orders.

(4) "Funds-transfer business day" of a receiving bank means the part of a day during which the receiving bank is open for the receipt, processing, and transmittal of payment orders and cancellations and amendments of payment orders.

(5) "Funds-transfer system" means a wire transfer network, automated clearing house, or other communication system of a clearing house or other association of banks through which a payment order by a bank may be transmitted to the bank to which the order is addressed.

(6) "Good faith" means honesty in fact and the observance of reasonable commercial standards of fair dealing.

(7) "Prove" with respect to a fact means to meet the burden of establishing the fact (Section 1–201(8)).

(b) Other definitions applying to this Article and the sections in which they appear are:

"Acceptance"	Section 4A–209
"Beneficiary"	Section 4A–103
"Beneficiary's bank"	Section 4A–103
"Executed"	Section 4A–301
"Execution date"	Section 4A–301
"Funds transfer"	Section 4A–104
"Funds-transfer system rule"	Section 4A–501
"Intermediary bank"	Section 4A–104
"Originator"	Section 4A–104
"Originator's bank"	Section 4A–104
"Payment by beneficiary's bank to beneficiary"	Section 4A–405
"Payment by originator to beneficiary"	Section 4A–406
"Payment by sender to receiving bank"	Section 4A–403
"Payment date"	Section 4A–401
"Payment order"	Section 4A–103
"Receiving bank"	Section 4A–103
"Security procedure"	Section 4A–201
"Sender"	Section 4A–103

(c) The following definitions in Article 4 apply to this Article:

"Clearing house"	Section 4–104
"Item"	Section 4–104
"Suspends payments"	Section 4–104

(d) In addition, Article 1 contains general definitions and principles of construction and interpretation applicable throughout this Article.

§ 4A–106. Time Payment Order Is Received.

(a) The time of receipt of a payment order or communication cancelling or amending a payment order is determined by the rules applicable to receipt of a notice stated in Section 1–201(27). A receiving bank may fix a cut-off time or times on a funds-transfer business day for the receipt and processing of payment orders and communications cancelling or amending payment orders. Different cut-off times may apply to payment orders, cancellations, or amendments, or to different categories of payment orders, cancellations, or amendments. A cut-off time may apply to senders generally or different cut-off times may apply to different senders or categories of payment orders. If a payment order or communication cancelling or amending a payment order is received after the close of a funds-transfer business day or after the appropriate cut-off time on a funds-transfer business day, the receiving bank may treat the payment order or communication as received at the opening of the next funds-transfer business day.

(b) If this Article refers to an execution date or payment date or states a day on which a receiving bank is required to take action, and the date or day does not fall on a funds-transfer business day, the next day that is a funds-transfer business day is treated as the date or day stated, unless the contrary is stated in this Article.

§ 4A–107. Federal Reserve Regulations and Operating Circulars.

Regulations of the Board of Governors of the Federal Reserve System and operating circulars of the Federal Reserve Banks supersede any inconsistent provision of this Article to the extent of the inconsistency.

§ 4A–108. Exclusion of Consumer Transactions Governed by Federal Law.

This Article does not apply to a funds transfer any part of which is governed by the Electronic Fund Transfer Act of 1978 (Title XX, Public Law 95–630, 92 Stat. 3728, 15 U.S.C. § 1693 *et seq.*) as amended from time to time.

Part 2—Issue and Acceptance of Payment Order

§ 4A–201. Security Procedure.

"Security procedure" means a procedure established by agreement of a customer and a receiving bank for the purpose of (i) verifying that a payment order or communication amending or cancelling a payment order is that of the customer, or (ii) detecting error in the transmission or the content of the payment order or communication. A security procedure may require the use of algorithms or other codes, identifying words or numbers, encryption, callback procedures, or similar security devices. Comparison of a signature on a payment order or communication with an authorized specimen signature of the customer is not by itself a security procedure.

§ 4A–202. Authorized and Verified Payment Orders.

(a) A payment order received by the receiving bank is the authorized order of the person identified as sender if that person authorized the order or is otherwise bound by it under the law of agency.

(b) If a bank and its customer have agreed that the authenticity of payment orders issued to the bank in the name of the customer as sender will be verified pursuant to a security procedure, a payment order received by the receiving bank is effective as the order of the customer, whether or not authorized, if (i) the security procedure is a commercially reasonable method of providing security against unauthorized payment orders, and (ii) the bank proves that it accepted the payment order in good faith and in compliance with the security procedure and any written agreement or instruction of the customer restricting acceptance of payment orders issued in the name of the customer. The bank is not required to follow an instruction that violates a written agreement with the customer or notice of which is not received at a time and in a manner affording the bank a reasonable opportunity to act on it before the payment order is accepted.

(c) Commercial reasonableness of a security procedure is a question of law to be determined by considering the wishes of the customer expressed to the bank, the circumstances of the customer known to the bank, including the size, type, and frequency of payment orders normally issued by the customer to the bank, alternative security procedures offered to the customer, and security procedures in general use by customers and receiving banks similarly situated. A security procedure is deemed to be commercially reasonable if (i) the security procedure was chosen by the customer after the bank offered, and the customer refused, a security procedure that was commercially reasonable for that customer, and (ii) the customer expressly agreed in writing to be bound by any payment order, whether or not authorized, issued in its name and accepted by the bank in compliance with the security procedure chosen by the customer.

(d) The term "sender" in this Article includes the customer in whose name a payment order is issued if the order is the authorized order of the customer under subsection (a), or it is effective as the order of the customer under subsection (b).

(e) This section applies to amendments and cancellations of payment orders to the same extent it applies to payment orders.

(f) Except as provided in this section and in Section 4A–203(a)(1), rights and obligations arising under this section or Section 4A–203 may not be varied by agreement.

§ 4A–203. Unenforceability of Certain Verified Payment Orders.

(a) If an accepted payment order is not, under Section 4A–202(a), an authorized order of a customer identified as sender, but is effective as an order of the customer pursuant to Section 4A–202(b), the following rules apply:

  (1) By express written agreement, the receiving bank may limit the extent to which it is entitled to enforce or retain payment of the payment order.

  (2) The receiving bank is not entitled to enforce or retain payment of the payment order if the customer proves that the order was not caused, directly or indirectly, by a person (i) entrusted at any time with duties to act for the customer with respect to payment orders or the security procedure, or (ii) who obtained access to transmitting facilities of the customer or who obtained, from a source controlled by the customer and without authority of the receiving bank, information facilitating breach of the security procedure, regardless of how the information was obtained or whether the customer was at fault. Information includes any access device, computer software, or the like.

(b) This section applies to amendments of payment orders to the same extent it applies to payment orders.

§ 4A–204. Refund of Payment and Duty of Customer to Report with Respect to Unauthorized Payment Order.

(a) If a receiving bank accepts a payment order issued in the name of its customer as sender which is (i) not authorized and not effective as the order of the customer under Section 4A–202, or (ii) not enforceable, in whole or in part, against the customer under Section 4A–203, the bank shall refund any payment of the payment order received from the customer to the extent the bank is not entitled to enforce payment and shall pay interest on the refundable amount calculated from the date the bank received payment to the date of the refund. However, the customer is not entitled to interest from the bank on the amount to be refunded if the customer fails to exercise ordinary care to determine that the order was not authorized by the customer and to notify the bank of the relevant facts within a reasonable time not exceeding 90 days after the date the customer received notification from the bank that the order was accepted or that the customer's account was debited with respect to the order. The bank is not entitled to any recovery from the customer on account of a failure by the customer to give notification as stated in this section.

(b) Reasonable time under subsection (a) may be fixed by agreement as stated in Section 1–204(1), but the obligation of a receiving bank to refund payment as stated in subsection (a) may not otherwise be varied by agreement.

§ 4A–205. Erroneous Payment Orders.

(a) If an accepted payment order was transmitted pursuant to a security procedure for the detection of error and the payment order (i) erroneously instructed payment to a beneficiary not intended by the sender, (ii) erroneously instructed payment in an amount greater than the amount intended by the sender, or (iii) was an erroneously transmitted duplicate of a payment order previously sent by the sender, the following rules apply:

> **(1)** If the sender proves that the sender or a person acting on behalf of the sender pursuant to Section 4A–206 complied with the security procedure and that the error would have been detected if the receiving bank had also complied, the sender is not obliged to pay the order to the extent stated in paragraphs (2) and (3).

> **(2)** If the funds transfer is completed on the basis of an erroneous payment order described in clause (i) or (iii) of subsection (a), the sender is not obliged to pay the order and the receiving bank is entitled to recover from the beneficiary any amount paid to the beneficiary to the extent allowed by the law governing mistake and restitution.

> **(3)** If the funds transfer is completed on the basis of a payment order described in clause (ii) of subsection (a), the sender is not obliged to pay the order to the extent the amount received by the beneficiary is greater than the amount intended by the sender. In that case, the receiving bank is entitled to recover from the beneficiary the excess amount received to the extent allowed by the law governing mistake and restitution.

(b) If (i) the sender of an erroneous payment order described in subsection (a) is not obliged to pay all or part of the order, and (ii) the sender receives notification from the receiving bank that the order was accepted by the bank or that the sender's account was debited with respect to the order, the sender has a duty to exercise ordinary care, on the basis of information available to the sender, to discover the error with respect to the order and to advise the bank of the relevant facts within a reasonable time, not exceeding 90 days, after the bank's notification was received by the sender. If the bank proves that the sender failed to perform that duty, the sender is liable to the bank for the loss the bank proves it incurred as a result of the failure, but the liability of the sender may not exceed the amount of the sender's order.

(c) This section applies to amendments to payment orders to the same extent it applies to payment orders.

§ 4A–206. Transmission of Payment Order through Funds-Transfer or Other Communication System.

(a) If a payment order addressed to a receiving bank is transmitted to a funds-transfer system or other third party communication system for transmittal to the bank, the system is deemed to be an agent of the sender for the purpose of transmitting the payment order to the bank. If there is a discrepancy between the terms of the payment order transmitted to the system and the terms of the payment order transmitted by the system to the bank, the terms of the payment order of the sender are those transmitted by the system. This section does not apply to a funds-transfer system of the Federal Reserve Banks.

(b) This section applies to cancellations and amendments to payment orders to the same extent it applies to payment orders.

§ 4A–207. Misdescription of Beneficiary.

(a) Subject to subsection (b), if, in a payment order received by the beneficiary's bank, the name, bank account number, or other identification of the beneficiary refers to a nonexistent or unidentifiable person or account, no person has rights as a beneficiary of the order and acceptance of the order cannot occur.

(b) If a payment order received by the beneficiary's bank identifies the beneficiary both by name and by an identifying or bank account number and the name and number identify different persons, the following rules apply:

> **(1)** Except as otherwise provided in subsection (c), if the beneficiary's bank does not know that the name and number refer to different persons, it may rely on the number as the proper identification of the beneficiary of the order. The beneficiary's bank need not determine whether the name and number refer to the same person.

> **(2)** If the beneficiary's bank pays the person identified by name or knows that the name and number identify different persons, no person has rights as beneficiary except the person paid by the beneficiary's bank if that person was entitled to receive payment from the originator of the funds transfer. If no person has rights as beneficiary, acceptance of the order cannot occur.

(c) If (i) a payment order described in subsection (b) is accepted, (ii) the originator's payment order described the beneficiary inconsistently by name and number, and (iii) the beneficiary's bank pays the person identified by number as permitted by subsection (b)(1), the following rules apply:

> **(1)** If the originator is a bank, the originator is obliged to pay its order.

> **(2)** If the originator is not a bank and proves that the person identified by number was not entitled to receive payment from the originator, the originator is not obliged to pay its order unless the originator's bank proves that the originator, before acceptance of the originator's order, had notice that payment of a payment order issued by the originator might be made by the beneficiary's bank on the basis of an identifying or bank account number even if it identifies a person different from the named beneficiary. Proof of notice may be made by any admissible evidence. The originator's bank satisfies the burden of proof if it proves that the originator, before the payment order was accepted, signed a writing stating the information to which the notice relates.

(d) In a case governed by subsection (b)(1), if the beneficiary's bank rightfully pays the person identified by number and that person was not entitled to receive payment from the originator, the amount paid may be recovered from that person to the extent allowed by the law governing mistake and restitution as follows:

(1) If the originator is obliged to pay its payment order as stated in subsection (c), the originator has the right to recover.

(2) If the originator is not a bank and is not obliged to pay its payment order, the originator's bank has the right to recover.

§ 4A–208. Misdescription of Intermediary Bank or Beneficiary's Bank.

(a) This subsection applies to a payment order identifying an intermediary bank or the beneficiary's bank only by an identifying number.

(1) The receiving bank may rely on the number as the proper identification of the intermediary or beneficiary's bank and need not determine whether the number identifies a bank.

(2) The sender is obliged to compensate the receiving bank for any loss and expenses incurred by the receiving bank as a result of its reliance on the number in executing or attempting to execute the order.

(b) This subsection applies to a payment order identifying an intermediary bank or the beneficiary's bank both by name and an identifying number if the name and number identify different persons.

(1) If the sender is a bank, the receiving bank may rely on the number as the proper identification of the intermediary or beneficiary's bank if the receiving bank, when it executes the sender's order, does not know that the name and number identify different persons. The receiving bank need not determine whether the name and number refer to the same person or whether the number refers to a bank. The sender is obliged to compensate the receiving bank for any loss and expenses incurred by the receiving bank as a result of its reliance on the number in executing or attempting to execute the order.

(2) If the sender is not a bank and the receiving bank proves that the sender, before the payment order was accepted, had notice that the receiving bank might rely on the number as the proper identification of the intermediary or beneficiary's bank even if it identifies a person different from the bank identified by name, the rights and obligations of the sender and the receiving bank are governed by subsection (b)(1), as though the sender were a bank. Proof of notice may be made by any admissible evidence. The receiving bank satisfies the burden of proof if it proves that the sender, before the payment order was accepted, signed a writing stating the information to which the notice relates.

(3) Regardless of whether the sender is a bank, the receiving bank may rely on the name as the proper identification of the intermediary or beneficiary's bank if the receiving bank, at the time it executes the sender's order, does not know that the name and number identify different persons. The receiving bank need not determine whether the name and number refer to the same person.

(4) If the receiving bank knows that the name and number identify different persons, reliance on either the name or the number in executing the sender's payment order is a breach of the obligation stated in Section 4A–302(a)(1).

§ 4A–209. Acceptance of Payment Order.

(a) Subject to subsection (d), a receiving bank other than the beneficiary's bank accepts a payment order when it executes the order.

(b) Subject to subsections (c) and (d), a beneficiary's bank accepts a payment order at the earliest of the following times:

(1) When the bank (i) pays the beneficiary as stated in Section 4A–405(a) or 4A–405(b), or (ii) notifies the beneficiary of receipt of the order or that the account of the beneficiary has been credited with respect to the order unless the notice indicates that the bank is rejecting the order or that funds with respect to the order may not be withdrawn or used until receipt of payment from the sender of the order;

(2) When the bank receives payment of the entire amount of the sender's order pursuant to Section 4A–403(a)(1) or 4A–403(a)(2); or

(3) The opening of the next funds-transfer business day of the bank following the payment date of the order if, at that time, the amount of the sender's order is fully covered by a withdrawable credit balance in an authorized account of the sender or the bank has otherwise received full payment from the sender, unless the order was rejected before that time or is rejected within (i) one hour after that time, or (ii) one hour after the opening of the next business day of the sender following the payment date if that time is later. If notice of rejection is received by the sender after the payment date and the authorized account of the sender does not bear interest, the bank is obliged to pay interest to the sender on the amount of the order for the number of days elapsing after the payment date to the day the sender receives notice or learns that the order was not accepted, counting that day as an elapsed day. If the withdrawable credit balance during that period falls below the amount of the order, the amount of interest payable is reduced accordingly.

(c) Acceptance of a payment order cannot occur before the order is received by the receiving bank. Acceptance does not occur under subsection (b)(2) or (b)(3) if the beneficiary of the payment order does not have an account with the receiving bank, the account has been closed, or the receiving bank is not permitted by law to receive credits for the beneficiary's account.

(d) A payment order issued to the originator's bank cannot be accepted until the payment date if the bank is the beneficiary's bank, or the execution date if the bank is not the beneficiary's bank. If the originator's bank executes the originator's payment order before the execution date or pays the beneficiary of the originator's payment order before the payment date and the payment order is subsequently cancelled pursuant to Section 4A–211(b), the bank may recover from the beneficiary any payment received to the extent allowed by the law governing mistake and restitution.

§ 4A–210. Rejection of Payment Order.

(a) A payment order is rejected by the receiving bank by a notice of rejection transmitted to the sender orally, electronically, or in writing. A notice of rejection need not use any particular words and is sufficient if it indicates that the receiving bank is rejecting the order or will not execute or pay the order. Rejection is effective when the notice is given if transmission is by a means that is reasonable in the circumstances. If notice of rejection is given by a means that is not reasonable, rejection is effective when the notice is received. If an agreement of the sender and receiving bank establishes the means to be used to reject a payment order, (i) any means complying with the agreement is reasonable and (ii) any means not complying is not reasonable unless no significant delay in receipt of the notice resulted from the use of the noncomplying means.

(b) This subsection applies if a receiving bank other than the beneficiary's bank fails to execute a payment order despite the existence on the execution date of a withdrawable credit balance in an authorized account of the sender sufficient to cover the order. If the sender does not receive notice of rejection of the order on the execution date and the authorized account of the sender does not bear interest, the bank is obliged to pay interest to the sender on the amount of the order for the number of days elapsing after the execution date to the earlier of the day the order is cancelled pursuant to Section 4A–211(d) or the day the sender receives notice or learns that the order was not executed, counting the final day of the period as an elapsed day. If the withdrawable credit balance during that period falls below the amount of the order, the amount of interest is reduced accordingly.

(c) If a receiving bank suspends payments, all unaccepted payment orders issued to it are are deemed rejected at the time the bank suspends payments.

(d) Acceptance of a payment order precludes a later rejection of the order. Rejection of a payment order precludes a later acceptance of the order.

§ 4A–211. Cancellation and Amendment of Payment Order.

(a) A communication of the sender of a payment order cancelling or amending the order may be transmitted to the receiving bank orally, electronically, or in writing. If a security procedure is in effect between the sender and the receiving bank, the communication is not effective to cancel or amend the order unless the communication is verified pursuant to the security procedure or the bank agrees to the cancellation or amendment.

(b) Subject to subsection (a), a communication by the sender cancelling or amending a payment order is effective to cancel or amend the order if notice of the communication is received at a time and in a manner affording the receiving bank a reasonable opportunity to act on the communication before the bank accepts the payment order.

(c) After a payment order has been accepted, cancellation or amendment of the order is not effective unless the receiving bank agrees or a funds-transfer system rule allows cancellation or amendment without agreement of the bank.

> **(1)** With respect to a payment order accepted by a receiving bank other than the beneficiary's bank, cancellation or amendment is not effective unless a conforming cancellation or amendment of the payment order issued by the receiving bank is also made.
>
> **(2)** With respect to a payment order accepted by the beneficiary's bank, cancellation or amendment is not effective unless the order was issued in execution of an unauthorized payment order, or because of a mistake by a sender in the funds transfer which resulted in the issuance of a payment order (i) that is a duplicate of a payment order previously issued by the sender, (ii) that orders payment to a beneficiary not entitled to receive payment from the originator, or (iii) that orders payment in an amount greater than the amount the beneficiary was entitled to receive from the originator. If the payment order is cancelled or amended, the beneficiary's bank is entitled to recover from the beneficiary any amount paid to the beneficiary to the extent allowed by the law governing mistake and restitution.

(d) An unaccepted payment order is cancelled by operation of law at the close of the fifth funds-transfer business day of the receiving bank after the execution date or payment date of the order.

(e) A cancelled payment order cannot be accepted. If an accepted payment order is cancelled, the acceptance is nullified and no person

has any right or obligation based on the acceptance. Amendment of a payment order is deemed to be cancellation of the original order at the time of amendment and issue of a new payment order in the amended form at the same time.

(f) Unless otherwise provided in an agreement of the parties or in a funds-transfer system rule, if the receiving bank, after accepting a payment order, agrees to cancellation or amendment of the order by the sender or is bound by a funds-transfer system rule allowing cancellation or amendment without the bank's agreement, the sender, whether or not cancellation or amendment is effective, is liable to the bank for any loss and expenses, including reasonable attorney's fees, incurred by the bank as a result of the cancellation or amendment or attempted cancellation or amendment.

(g) A payment order is not revoked by the death or legal incapacity of the sender unless the receiving bank knows of the death or of an adjudication of incapacity by a court of competent jurisdiction and has reasonable opportunity to act before acceptance of the order.

(h) A funds-transfer system rule is not effective to the extent it conflicts with subsection (c)(2).

§ 4A–212. Liability and Duty of Receiving Bank Regarding Unaccepted Payment Order.

If a receiving bank fails to accept a payment order that it is obliged by express agreement to accept, the bank is liable for breach of the agreement to the extent provided in the agreement or in this Article, but does not otherwise have any duty to accept a payment order or, before acceptance, to take any action, or refrain from taking action, with respect to the order except as provided in this Article or by express agreement. Liability based on acceptance arises only when acceptance occurs as stated in Section 4A–209, and liability is limited to that provided in this Article. A receiving bank is not the agent of the sender or beneficiary of the payment order it accepts, or of any other party to the funds transfer, and the bank owes no duty to any party to the funds transfer except as provided in this Article or by express agreement.

Part 3—Execution of Sender's Payment Order by Receiving Bank

§ 4A–301. Execution and Execution Date.

(a) A payment order is "executed" by the receiving bank when it issues a payment order intended to carry out the payment order received by the bank. A payment order received by the beneficiary's bank can be accepted but cannot be executed.

(b) "Execution date" of a payment order means the day on which the receiving bank may properly issue a payment order in execution of the sender's order. The execution date may be determined by instruction of the sender but cannot be earlier than the day the order is received and, unless otherwise determined, is the day the order is received. If the sender's instruction states a payment date, the execution date is the payment date or an earlier date on which execution is reasonably necessary to allow payment to the beneficiary on the payment date.

§ 4A–302. Obligations of Receiving Bank in Execution of Payment Order.

(a) Except as provided in subsections (b) through (d), if the receiving bank accepts a payment order pursuant to Section 4A–209(a), the bank has the following obligations in executing the order:

(1) The receiving bank is obliged to issue, on the execution date, a payment order complying with the sender's order and to follow the sender's instructions concerning (i) any intermediary bank or funds-transfer system to be used in carrying out the funds transfer, or (ii) the means by which payment orders are to be transmitted in the funds transfer. If the originator's bank issues a payment order to an intermediary bank, the originator's bank is obliged to instruct the intermediary bank according to the instruction of the originator. An intermediary bank in the funds transfer is similarly bound by an instruction given to it by the sender of the payment order it accepts.

(2) If the sender's instruction states that the funds transfer is to be carried out telephonically or by wire transfer or otherwise indicates that the funds transfer is to be carried out by the most expeditious means, the receiving bank is obliged to transmit its payment order by the most expeditious available means, and to instruct any intermediary bank accordingly. If a sender's instruction states a payment date, the receiving bank is obliged to transmit its payment order at a time and by means reasonably necessary to allow payment to the beneficiary on the payment date or as soon thereafter as is feasible.

(b) Unless otherwise instructed, a receiving bank executing a payment order may (i) use any funds-transfer system if use of that system is reasonable in the circumstances, and (ii) issue a payment order to the beneficiary's bank or to an intermediary bank through which a payment order conforming to the sender's order can expeditiously be issued to the beneficiary's bank if the receiving bank exercises ordinary care in the selection of the intermediary bank. A receiving bank is not required to follow an instruction of the sender designating a funds-transfer system to be used in carrying out the funds transfer if the receiving bank, in good faith, determines that it is not feasible to follow the instruction or that following the instruction would unduly delay completion of the funds transfer.

(c) Unless subsection (a)(2) applies or the receiving bank is otherwise instructed, the bank may execute a payment order by transmitting its payment order by first class mail or by any means reasonable in the circumstances. If the receiving bank is instructed to execute the sender's order by transmitting its payment order by a particular means, the receiving bank may issue its payment order by the means stated or by any means as expeditious as the means stated.

(d) Unless instructed by the sender, (i) the receiving bank may not obtain payment of its charges for services and expenses in connection with the execution of the sender's order by issuing a payment order in an amount equal to the amount of the sender's order less the amount of the charges, and (ii) may not instruct a subsequent receiving bank to obtain payment of its charges in the same manner.

§ 4A–303. Erroneous Execution of Payment Order.

(a) A receiving bank that (i) executes the payment order of the sender by issuing a payment order in an amount greater than the amount of the sender's order, or (ii) issues a payment order in execution of the sender's order and then issues a duplicate order, is entitled to payment of the amount of the sender's order under Section 4A–402(c) if that subsection is otherwise satisfied. The bank is entitled to recover from the beneficiary of the erroneous order the excess payment received to the extent allowed by the law governing mistake and restitution.

(b) A receiving bank that executes the payment order of the sender by issuing a payment order in an amount less than the amount of the sender's order is entitled to payment of the amount of the sender's order under Section 4A–402(c) if (i) that subsection is otherwise satisfied and (ii) the bank corrects its mistake by issuing an additional payment order for the benefit of the beneficiary of the sender's order. If the error is not corrected, the issuer of the erroneous order is entitled to receive or retain payment from the sender of the order it accepted only to the extent of the amount of the erroneous order. This subsection does not apply if the receiving bank executes the sender's payment order by issuing a payment order in an amount less than the amount of the sender's order for the purpose of obtaining payment of its charges for services and expenses pursuant to instruction of the sender.

(c) If a receiving bank executes the payment order of the sender by issuing a payment order to a beneficiary different from the beneficiary of the sender's order and the funds transfer is completed on the basis of that error, the sender of the payment order that was erroneously executed and all previous senders in the funds transfer are not obliged to pay the payment orders they issued. The issuer of the erroneous order is entitled to recover from the beneficiary of the order the payment received to the extent allowed by the law governing mistake and restitution.

§ 4A–304. Duty of Sender to Report Erroneously Executed Payment Order.

If the sender of a payment order that is erroneously executed as stated in Section 4A–303 receives notification from the receiving bank that the order was executed or that the sender's account was debited with respect to the order, the sender has a duty to exercise ordinary care to determine, on the basis of information available to the sender, that the order was erroneously executed and to notify the bank of the relevant facts within a reasonable time not exceeding 90 days after the notification from the bank was received by the sender. If the sender fails to perform that duty, the bank is not obliged to pay interest on any amount refundable to the sender under Section 4A–402(d) for the period before the bank learns of the execution error. The bank is not entitled to any recovery from the sender on account of a failure by the sender to perform the duty stated in this section.

§ 4A–305. Liability for Late or Improper Execution or Failure to Execute Payment Order.

(a) If a funds transfer is completed but execution of a payment order by the receiving bank in breach of Section 4A–302 results in delay in payment to the beneficiary, the bank is obliged to pay interest to either the originator or the beneficiary of the funds transfer for the period of delay caused by the improper execution. Except as provided in subsection (c), additional damages are not recoverable.

(b) If execution of a payment order by a receiving bank in breach of Section 4A–302 results in (i) noncompletion of the funds transfer, (ii) failure to use an intermediary bank designated by the originator, or (iii) issuance of a payment order that does not comply with the terms of the payment order of the originator, the bank is liable to the originator for its expenses in the funds transfer and for incidental expenses and interest losses, to the extent not covered by subsection (a), resulting from the improper execution. Except as provided in subsection (c), additional damages are not recoverable.

(c) In addition to the amounts payable under subsections (a) and (b), damages, including consequential damages, are recoverable to the extent provided in an express written agreement of the receiving bank.

(d) If a receiving bank fails to execute a payment order it was obliged by express agreement to execute, the receiving bank is liable to the sender for its expenses in the transaction and for incidental expenses and interest losses resulting from the failure to execute. Additional damages, including consequential damages, are recoverable to the extent provided in an express written agreement of the receiving bank, but are not otherwise recoverable.

(e) Reasonable attorney's fees are recoverable if demand for compensation under subsection (a) or (b) is made and refused before an action is brought on the claim. If a claim is made for breach of an agreement under subsection (d) and the agreement does not provide for damages, reasonable attorney's fees are recoverable if demand for compensation under subsection (d) is made and refused before an action is brought on the claim.

(f) Except as stated in this section, the liability of a receiving bank under subsections (a) and (b) may not be varied by agreement.

Part 4—Payment

§ 4A–401. Payment Date.

"Payment date" of a payment order means the day on which the amount of the order is payable to the beneficiary by the beneficiary's bank. The payment date may be determined by instruction of the sender but cannot be earlier than the day the order is received by the beneficiary's bank and, unless otherwise determined, is the day the order is received by the beneficiary's bank.

§ 4A–402. Obligation of Sender to Pay Receiving Bank.

(a) This section is subject to Sections 4A–205 and 4A–207.

(b) With respect to a payment order issued to the beneficiary's bank, acceptance of the order by the bank obliges the sender to pay the bank the amount of the order, but payment is not due until the payment date of the order.

(c) This subsection is subject to subsection (e) and to Section 4A–303. With respect to a payment order issued to a receiving bank other than the beneficiary's bank, acceptance of the order by the receiving bank obliges the sender to pay the bank the amount of the sender's order. Payment by the sender is not due until the execution date of the sender's order. The obligation of that sender to pay its payment order is excused if the funds transfer is not completed by acceptance by the beneficiary's bank of a payment order instructing payment to the beneficiary of that sender's payment order.

(d) If the sender of a payment order pays the order and was not obliged to pay all or part of the amount paid, the bank receiving payment is obliged to refund payment to the extent the sender was not obliged to pay. Except as provided in Sections 4A–204 and 4A–304, interest is payable on the refundable amount from the date of payment.

(e) If a funds transfer is not completed as stated in subsection (c) and an intermediary bank is obliged to refund payment as stated in subsection (d) but is unable to do so because not permitted by applicable law or because the bank suspends payments, a sender in the funds transfer that executed a payment order in compliance with an instruction, as stated in Section 4A–302(a)(1), to route the funds transfer through that intermediary bank is entitled to receive or retain payment from the sender of the payment order that it accepted. The first sender in

the funds transfer that issued an instruction requiring routing through that intermediary bank is subrogated to the right of the bank that paid the intermediary bank to refund as stated in subsection (d).

(f) The right of the sender of a payment order to be excused from the obligation to pay the order as stated in subsection (c) or to receive refund under subsection (d) may not be varied by agreement.

§ 4A–403. Payment by Sender to Receiving Bank.

(a) Payment of the sender's obligation under Section 4A–402 to pay the receiving bank occurs as follows:

    (1) If the sender is a bank, payment occurs when the receiving bank receives final settlement of the obligation through a Federal Reserve Bank or through a funds-transfer system.

    (2) If the sender is a bank and the sender (i) credited an account of the receiving bank with the sender, or (ii) caused an account of the receiving bank in another bank to be credited, payment occurs when the credit is withdrawn or, if not withdrawn, at midnight of the day on which the credit is withdrawable and the receiving bank learns of that fact.

    (3) If the receiving bank debits an account of the sender with the receiving bank, payment occurs when the debit is made to the extent the debit is covered by a withdrawable credit balance in the account.

(b) If the sender and receiving bank are members of a funds-transfer system that nets obligations multilaterally among participants, the receiving bank receives final settlement when settlement is complete in accordance with the rules of the system. The obligation of the sender to pay the amount of a payment order transmitted through the funds-transfer system may be satisfied, to the extent permitted by the rules of the system, by setting off and applying against the sender's obligation the right of the sender to receive payment from the receiving bank of the amount of any other payment order transmitted to the sender by the receiving bank through the funds-transfer system. The aggregate balance of obligations owed by each sender to each receiving bank in the funds-transfer system may be satisfied, to the extent permitted by the rules of the system, by setting off and applying against that balance the aggregate balance of obligations owed to the sender by other members of the system. The aggregate balance is determined after the right of setoff stated in the second sentence of this subsection has been exercised.

(c) If two banks transmit payment orders to each other under an agreement that settlement of the obligations of each bank to the other under Section 4A–402 will be made at the end of the day or other period, the total amount owed with respect to all orders transmitted by one bank shall be set off against the total amount owed with respect to all orders transmitted by the other bank. To the extent of the setoff, each bank has made payment to the other.

(d) In a case not covered by subsection (a), the time when payment of the sender's obligation under Section 4A–402(b) or 4A–402(c) occurs is governed by applicable principles of law that determine when an obligation is satisfied.

§ 4A–404. Obligation of Beneficiary's Bank to Pay and Give Notice to Beneficiary.

(a) Subject to Sections 4A–211(e), 4A–405(d), and 4A–405(e), if a beneficiary's bank accepts a payment order, the bank is obliged to pay the amount of the order to the beneficiary of the order. Payment is due on the payment date of the order, but if acceptance occurs on the payment date after the close of the funds-transfer business day of the bank, payment is due on the next funds-transfer business day. If the bank refuses to pay after demand by the beneficiary and receipt of notice of particular circumstances that will give rise to consequential damages as a result of nonpayment, the beneficiary may recover damages resulting from the refusal to pay to the extent the bank had notice of the damages, unless the bank proves that it did not pay because of a reasonable doubt concerning the right of the beneficiary to payment.

(b) If a payment order accepted by the beneficiary's bank instructs payment to an account of the beneficiary, the bank is obliged to notify the beneficiary of receipt of the order before midnight of the next funds-transfer business day following the payment date. If the payment order does not instruct payment to an account of the beneficiary, the bank is required to notify the beneficiary only if notice is required by the order. Notice may be given by first class mail or any other means reasonable in the circumstances. If the bank fails to give the required notice, the bank is obliged to pay interest to the beneficiary on the amount of the payment order from the day notice should have been given until the day the beneficiary learned of receipt of the payment order by the bank. No other damages are recoverable. Reasonable attorney's fees are also recoverable if demand for interest is made and refused before an action is brought on the claim.

(c) The right of a beneficiary to receive payment and damages as stated in subsection (a) may not be varied by agreement or a funds-transfer system rule. The right of a beneficiary to be notified as stated in subsection (b) may be varied by agreement of the beneficiary or by a funds-transfer system rule if the beneficiary is notified of the rule before initiation of the funds transfer.

§ 4A–405. Payment by Beneficiary's Bank to Beneficiary.

(a) If the beneficiary's bank credits an account of the beneficiary of a payment order, payment of the bank's obligation under Section 4A–404(a) occurs when and to the extent (i) the beneficiary is notified of the right to withdraw the credit, (ii) the bank lawfully applies the credit to a debt of the beneficiary, or (iii) funds with respect to the order are otherwise made available to the beneficiary by the bank.

(b) If the beneficiary's bank does not credit an account of the beneficiary of a payment order, the time when payment of the bank's obligation under Section 4A–404(a) occurs is governed by principles of law that determine when an obligation is satisfied.

(c) Except as stated in subsections (d) and (e), if the beneficiary's bank pays the beneficiary of a payment order under a condition to payment or agreement of the beneficiary giving the bank the right to recover payment from the beneficiary if the bank does not receive payment of the order, the condition to payment or agreement is not enforceable.

(d) A funds-transfer system rule may provide that payments made to beneficiaries of funds transfers made through the system are provisional until receipt of payment by the beneficiary's bank of the payment order it accepted. A beneficiary's bank that makes a payment that is provisional under the rule is entitled to refund from the beneficiary if (i) the rule requires that both the beneficiary and the originator be given notice of the provisional nature of the payment before the funds transfer is initiated, (ii) the beneficiary, the beneficiary's bank, and the originator's bank agreed to be bound by the rule, and (iii) the beneficiary's bank did not receive payment of the payment order that it accepted. If the beneficiary is obliged to refund payment to the beneficiary's bank, acceptance of the payment order by the beneficiary's bank is nullified and no payment by the originator of the funds transfer to the beneficiary occurs under Section 4A–406.

(e) This subsection applies to a funds transfer that includes a payment order transmitted over a funds-transfer system that (i) nets obligations multilaterally among participants, and (ii) has in effect a loss-sharing agreement among participants for the purpose of providing funds necessary to complete settlement of the obligations of one or more participants that do not meet their settlement obligations. If the beneficiary's bank in the funds transfer accepts a payment order and the system fails to complete settlement pursuant to its rules with respect to any payment order in the funds transfer, (i) the acceptance by the beneficiary's bank is nullified and no person has any right or obligation based on the acceptance, (ii) the beneficiary's bank is entitled to recover payment from the beneficiary, (iii) no payment by the originator to the beneficiary occurs under Section 4A–406, and (iv) subject to Section 4A–402(e), each sender in the funds transfer is excused from its obligation to pay its payment order under Section 4A–402(c) because the funds transfer has not been completed.

§ 4A–406. Payment by Originator to Beneficiary; Discharge of Underlying Obligation.

(a) Subject to Sections 4A–211(e), 4A–405(d), and 4A–405(e), the originator of a funds transfer pays the beneficiary of the originator's payment order (i) at the time a payment order for the benefit of the beneficiary is accepted by the beneficiary's bank in the funds transfer and (ii) in an amount equal to the amount of the order accepted by the beneficiary's bank, but not more than the amount of the originator's order.

(b) If payment under subsection (a) is made to satisfy an obligation, the obligation is discharged to the same extent discharge would result from payment to the beneficiary of the same amount in money, unless (i) the payment under subsection (a) was made by a means prohibited by the contract of the beneficiary with respect to the obligation, (ii) the beneficiary, within a reasonable time after receiving notice of receipt of the order by the beneficiary's bank, notified the originator of the beneficiary's refusal of the payment, (iii) funds with respect to the order were not withdrawn by the beneficiary or applied to a debt of the beneficiary, and (iv) the beneficiary would suffer a loss that could reasonably have been avoided if payment had been made by a means complying with the contract. If payment by the originator does not result in discharge under this section, the originator is subrogated to the rights of the beneficiary to receive payment from the beneficiary's bank under Section 4A–404(a).

(c) For the purpose of determining whether discharge of an obligation occurs under subsection (b), if the beneficiary's bank accepts a payment order in an amount equal to the amount of the originator's payment order less charges of one or more receiving banks in the funds transfer, payment to the beneficiary is deemed to be in the amount of the originator's order unless upon demand by the beneficiary the originator does not pay the beneficiary the amount of the deducted charges.

(d) Rights of the originator or of the beneficiary of a funds transfer under this section may be varied only by agreement of the originator and the beneficiary.

Part 5—Miscellaneous Provisions

§ 4A–501. Variation by Agreement and Effect of Funds-Transfer System Rule.

(a) Except as otherwise provided in this Article, the rights and obligations of a party to a funds transfer may be varied by agreement of the affected party.

(b) "Funds-transfer system rule" means a rule of an association of banks (i) governing transmission of payment orders by means of a funds-transfer system of the association or rights and obligations with respect to those orders, or (ii) to the extent the rule governs rights and obligations between banks that are parties to a funds transfer in which a Federal Reserve Bank, acting as an intermediary bank, sends a payment order to the beneficiary's bank. Except as otherwise provided in this Article, a funds-transfer system rule governing rights and obligations between participating banks using the system may be effective even if the rule conflicts with this Article and indirectly affects another party to the funds transfer who does not consent to the rule. A funds-transfer system rule may also govern rights and obligations of parties other than participating banks using the system to the extent stated in Sections 4A–404(c), 4A–405(d), and 4A–507(c).

§ 4A–502. Creditor Process Served on Receiving Bank; Setoff by Beneficiary's Bank.

(a) As used in this section, "creditor process" means levy, attachment, garnishment, notice of lien, sequestration, or similar process issued by or on behalf of a creditor or other claimant with respect to an account.

(b) This subsection applies to creditor process with respect to an authorized account of the sender of a payment order if the creditor process is served on the receiving bank. For the purpose of determining rights with respect to the creditor process, if the receiving bank accepts the payment order the balance in the authorized account is deemed to be reduced by the amount of the payment order to the extent the bank did not otherwise receive payment of the order, unless the creditor process is served at a time and in a manner affording the bank a reasonable opportunity to act on it before the bank accepts the payment order.

(c) If a beneficiary's bank has received a payment order for payment to the beneficiary's account in the bank, the following rules apply:

(1) The bank may credit the beneficiary's account. The amount credited may be set off against an obligation owed by the beneficiary to the bank or may be applied to satisfy creditor process served on the bank with respect to the account.

(2) The bank may credit the beneficiary's account and allow withdrawal of the amount credited unless creditor process with respect to the account is served at a time and in a manner affording the bank a reasonable opportunity to act to prevent withdrawal.

(3) If creditor process with respect to the beneficiary's account has been served and the bank has had a reasonable opportunity to act on it, the bank may not reject the payment order except for a reason unrelated to the service of process.

(d) Creditor process with respect to a payment by the originator to the beneficiary pursuant to a funds transfer may be served only on the beneficiary's bank with respect to the debt owed by that bank to the beneficiary. Any other bank served with the creditor process is not obliged to act with respect to the process.

§ 4A–503. Injunction or Restraining Order with Respect to Funds Transfer.

For proper cause and in compliance with applicable law, a court may restrain (i) a person from issuing a payment order to initiate a funds transfer, (ii) an originator's bank from executing the payment order of the originator, or (iii) the beneficiary's bank from releasing funds to the beneficiary or the beneficiary from withdrawing the funds. A court may not otherwise restrain a person from issuing a payment order, paying or receiving payment of a payment order, or otherwise acting with respect to a funds transfer.

§ 4A–504. Order in Which Items and Payment Orders May Be Charged to Account; Order of Withdrawals from Account.

(a) If a receiving bank has received more than one payment order of the sender or one or more payment orders and other items that are payable from the sender's account, the bank may charge the sender's account with respect to the various orders and items in any sequence.

(b) In determining whether a credit to an account has been withdrawn by the holder of the account or applied to a debt of the holder of the account, credits first made to the account are first withdrawn or applied.

§ 4A–505. Preclusion of Objection to Debit of Customer's Account.

If a receiving bank has received payment from its customer with respect to a payment order issued in the name of the customer as sender and accepted by the bank, and the customer received notification reasonably identifying the order, the customer is precluded from asserting that the bank is not entitled to retain the payment unless the customer notifies the bank of the customer's objection to the payment within one year after the notification was received by the customer.

§ 4A–506. Rate of Interest.

(a) If, under this Article, a receiving bank is obliged to pay interest with respect to a payment order issued to the bank, the amount payable may be determined (i) by agreement of the sender and receiving bank, or (ii) by a funds-transfer system rule if the payment order is transmitted through a funds-transfer system.

(b) If the amount of interest is not determined by an agreement or rule as stated in subsection (a), the amount is calculated by multiplying the applicable Federal Funds rate by the amount on which interest is payable, and then multiplying the product by the number of days for which interest is payable. The applicable Federal Funds rate is the average of the Federal Funds rates published by the Federal Reserve Bank of New York for each of the days for which interest is payable divided by 360. The Federal Funds rate for any day on which a published rate is not available is the same as the published rate for the next preceding day for which there is a published rate. If a receiving bank that accepted a payment order is required to refund payment to the sender of the order because the funds transfer was not completed, but the failure to complete was not due to any fault by the bank, the interest payable is reduced by a percentage equal to the reserve requirement on deposits of the receiving bank.

§ 4A–507. Choice of Law.

(a) The following rules apply unless the affected parties otherwise agree or subsection (c) applies:

(1) The rights and obligations between the sender of a payment order and the receiving bank are governed by the law of the jurisdiction in which the receiving bank is located.

(2) The rights and obligations between the beneficiary's bank and the beneficiary are governed by the law of the jurisdiction in which the beneficiary's bank is located.

(3) The issue of when payment is made pursuant to a funds transfer by the originator to the beneficiary is governed by the law of the jurisdiction in which the beneficiary's bank is located.

(b) If the parties described in each paragraph of subsection (a) have made an agreement selecting the law of a particular jurisdiction to govern rights and obligations between each other, the law of that jurisdiction governs those rights and obligations, whether or not the payment order or the funds transfer bears a reasonable relation to that jurisdiction.

(c) A funds-transfer system rule may select the law of a particular jurisdiction to govern (i) rights and obligations between participating banks with respect to payment orders transmitted or processed through the system, or (ii) the rights and obligations of some or all parties to a funds transfer any part of which is carried out by means of the system. A choice of law made pursuant to clause (i) is binding on participating banks. A choice of law made pursuant to clause (ii) is binding on the originator, other sender, or a receiving bank having notice that the funds-transfer system might be used in the funds transfer and of the choice of law by the system when the originator, other sender, or receiving bank issued or accepted a payment order. The beneficiary of a funds transfer is bound by the choice of law if, when the funds transfer is initiated, the beneficiary has notice that the funds-transfer system might be used in the funds transfer and of the choice of law by the system. The law of a jurisdiction selected pursuant to this subsection may govern, whether or not that law bears a reasonable relation to the matter in issue.

(d) In the event of inconsistency between an agreement under subsection (b) and a choice-of-law rule under subsection (c), the agreement under subsection (b) prevails.

(e) If a funds transfer is made by use of more than one funds-transfer system and there is inconsistency between choice-of-law rules of the systems, the matter in issue is governed by the law of the selected jurisdiction that has the most significant relationship to the matter in issue.

REVISED ARTICLE 5: LETTERS OF CREDIT

§ 5–101 Short Title.

This article may be cited as Uniform Commercial Code—Letters of Credit.

§ 5–102. Definitions.

(a) In this article:

(1) "Adviser" means a person who, at the request of the issuer, a confirmer, or another adviser, notifies or requests another adviser to notify the beneficiary that a letter of credit has been issued, confirmed, or amended.

(2) "Applicant" means a person at whose request or for whose account a letter of credit is issued. The term includes a person who requests an issuer to issue a letter of credit on behalf of another if the person making the request undertakes an obligation to reimburse the issuer.

(3) "Beneficiary" means a person who under the terms of a letter of credit is entitled to have its complying presentation honored. The term includes a person to whom drawing rights have been transferred under a transferable letter of credit.

(4) "Confirmer" means a nominated person who undertakes, at the request or with the consent of the issuer, to honor a presentation under a letter of credit issued by another.

(5) "Dishonor" of a letter of credit means failure timely to honor or to take an interim action, such as acceptance of a draft, that may be required by the letter of credit.

(6) "Document" means a draft or other demand, document of title, investment security, certificate, invoice, or other record, statement, or representation of fact, law, right, or opinion (i) which is presented in a written or other medium permitted by the letter of credit or, unless prohibited by the letter of credit, by the standard practice referred to in Section 5–108(e) and (ii) which is capable of being examined for compliance with the terms and conditions of the letter of credit. A document may not be oral.

(7) "Good faith" means honesty in fact in the conduct or transaction concerned.

(8) "Honor" of a letter of credit means performance of the issuer's undertaking in the letter of credit to pay or deliver an item of value. Unless the letter of credit otherwise provides, "honor" occurs

    (i) upon payment,

    (ii) if the letter of credit provides for acceptance, upon acceptance of a draft and, at maturity, its payment, or

    (iii) if the letter of credit provides for incurring a deferred obligation, upon incurring the obligation and, at maturity, its performance.

(9) "Issuer" means a bank or other person that issues a letter of credit, but does not include an individual who makes an engagement for personal, family, or household purposes.

(10) "Letter of credit" means a definite undertaking that satisfies the requirements of Section 5–104 by an issuer to a beneficiary at the request or for the account of an applicant or, in the case of a financial institution, to itself or for its own account, to honor a documentary presentation by payment or delivery of an item of value.

(11) "Nominated person" means a person whom the issuer (i) designates or authorizes to pay, accept, negotiate, or otherwise give value under a letter of credit and (ii) undertakes by agreement or custom and practice to reimburse.

(12) "Presentation" means delivery of a document to an issuer or nominated person for honor or giving of value under a letter of credit.

(13) "Presenter" means a person making a presentation as or on behalf of a beneficiary or nominated person.

(14) "Record" means information that is inscribed on a tangible medium, or that is stored in an electronic or other medium and is retrievable in perceivable form.

(15) "Successor of a beneficiary" means a person who succeeds to substantially all of the rights of a beneficiary by operation of law, including a corporation with or into which the beneficiary has been merged or consolidated, an administrator, executor, personal representative, trustee in bankruptcy, debtor in possession, liquidator, and receiver.

(b) Definitions in other Articles applying to this article and the sections in which they appear are:

"Accept" or "Acceptance" Section 3–409

"Value" Sections 3–303, 4–211

(c) Article 1 contains certain additional general definitions and principles of construction and interpretation applicable throughout this article.

§ 5–103. Scope.

(a) This article applies to letters of credit and to certain rights and obligations arising out of transactions involving letters of credit.

(b) The statement of a rule in this article does not by itself require, imply, or negate application of the same or a different rule to a situation not provided for, or to a person not specified, in this article.

(c) With the exception of this subsection, subsections (a) and (d), Sections 5–102(a)(9) and (10), 5–106(d), and 5–114(d), and except to the extent prohibited in Sections 1–102(3) and 5–117(d), the effect of this article may be varied by agreement or by a provision stated or incorporated by reference in an undertaking. A term in an agreement or undertaking generally excusing liability or generally limiting remedies for failure to perform obligations is not sufficient to vary obligations prescribed by this article.

(d) Rights and obligations of an issuer to a beneficiary or a nominated person under a letter of credit are independent of the existence, performance, or nonperformance of a contract or arrangement out of which the letter of credit arises or which underlies it, including contracts or arrangements between the issuer and the applicant and between the applicant and the beneficiary.

§ 5–104. Formal Requirements.

A letter of credit, confirmation, advice, transfer, amendment, or cancellation may be issued in any form that is a record and is authenticated (i) by a signature or (ii) in accordance with the agreement of the parties or the standard practice referred to in Section 5–108(e).

§ 5–105. Consideration.

Consideration is not required to issue, amend, transfer, or cancel a letter of credit, advice, or confirmation.

§ 5–106. Issuance, Amendment, Cancellation, and Duration.

(a) A letter of credit is issued and becomes enforceable according to its terms against the issuer when the issuer sends or otherwise transmits it to the person requested to advise or to the beneficiary. A letter of credit is revocable only if it so provides.

(b) After a letter of credit is issued, rights and obligations of a beneficiary, applicant, confirmer, and issuer are not affected by an amendment or cancellation to which that person has not consented except to the extent the letter of credit provides that it is revocable or that the issuer may amend or cancel the letter of credit without that consent.

(c) If there is no stated expiration date or other provision that determines its duration, a letter of credit expires one year after its stated date of issuance or, if none is stated, after the date on which it is issued.

(d) A letter of credit that states that it is perpetual expires five years after its stated date of issuance, or if none is stated, after the date on which it is issued.

§ 5–107. Confirmer, Nominated Person, and Adviser.

(a) A confirmer is directly obligated on a letter of credit and has the rights and obligations of an issuer to the extent of its confirmation. The confirmer also has rights against and obligations to the issuer as if the issuer were an applicant and the confirmer had issued the letter of credit at the request and for the account of the issuer.

(b) A nominated person who is not a confirmer is not obligated to honor or otherwise give value for a presentation.

(c) A person requested to advise may decline to act as an adviser. An adviser that is not a confirmer is not obligated to honor or give value for a presentation. An adviser undertakes to the issuer and to the beneficiary accurately to advise the terms of the letter of credit, confirmation, amendment, or advice received by that person and undertakes to the beneficiary to check the apparent authenticity of the request to advise. Even if the advice is inaccurate, the letter of credit, confirmation, or amendment is enforceable as issued.

(d) A person who notifies a transferee beneficiary of the terms of a letter of credit, confirmation, amendment, or advice has the rights and obligations of an adviser under subsection (c). The terms in the notice to the transferee beneficiary may differ from the terms in any notice to the transferor beneficiary to the extent permitted by the letter of credit, confirmation, amendment, or advice received by the person who so notifies.

§ 5–108. Issuer's Rights and Obligations.

(a) Except as otherwise provided in Section 5–109, an issuer shall honor a presentation that, as determined by the standard practice referred to in subsection (e), appears on its face strictly to comply with the terms and conditions of the letter of credit. Except as otherwise provided in Section 5–113 and unless otherwise agreed with the applicant, an issuer shall dishonor a presentation that does not appear so to comply.

(b) An issuer has a reasonable time after presentation, but not beyond the end of the seventh business day of the issuer after the day of its receipt of documents:

(1) to honor,

(2) if the letter of credit provides for honor to be completed more than seven business days after presentation, to accept a draft or incur a deferred obligation, or

(3) to give notice to the presenter of discrepancies in the presentation.

(c) Except as otherwise provided in subsection (d), an issuer is precluded from asserting as a basis for dishonor any discrepancy if timely notice is not given, or any discrepancy not stated in the notice if timely notice is given.

(d) Failure to give the notice specified in subsection (b) or to mention fraud, forgery, or expiration in the notice does not preclude the issuer from asserting as a basis for dishonor fraud or forgery as described in Section 5–109(a) or expiration of the letter of credit before presentation.

(e) An issuer shall observe standard practice of financial institutions that regularly issue letters of credit. Determination of the issuer's observance of the standard practice is a matter of interpretation for the court. The court shall offer the parties a reasonable opportunity to present evidence of the standard practice.

(f) An issuer is not responsible for:

(1) the performance or nonperformance of the underlying contract, arrangement, or transaction,

(2) an act or omission of others, or

(3) observance or knowledge of the usage of a particular trade other than the standard practice referred to in subsection (e).

(g) If an undertaking constituting a letter of credit under Section 5–102(a)(10) contains nondocumentary conditions, an issuer shall disregard the nondocumentary conditions and treat them as if they were not stated.

(h) An issuer that has dishonored a presentation shall return the documents or hold them at the disposal of, and send advice to that effect to, the presenter.

(i) An issuer that has honored a presentation as permitted or required by this article:

(1) is entitled to be reimbursed by the applicant in immediately available funds not later than the date of its payment of funds;

(2) takes the documents free of claims of the beneficiary or presenter;

(3) is precluded from asserting a right of recourse on a draft under Sections 3–414 and 3–415;

(4) except as otherwise provided in Sections 5–110 and 5–117, is precluded from restitution of money paid or other value given by mistake to the extent the mistake concerns discrepancies in the documents or tender which are apparent on the face of the presentation; and

(5) is discharged to the extent of its performance under the letter of credit unless the issuer honored a presentation in which a required signature of a beneficiary was forged.

§ 5–109. Fraud and Forgery.

(a) If a presentation is made that appears on its face strictly to comply with the terms and conditions of the letter of credit, but a required document is forged or materially fraudulent, or honor of the presentation would facilitate a material fraud by the beneficiary on the issuer or applicant:

(1) the issuer shall honor the presentation, if honor is demanded by (i) a nominated person who has given value in good faith and without notice of forgery or material fraud, (ii) a confirmer who has honored its confirmation in good faith, (iii) a holder in due course of a draft drawn under the letter of credit which was taken after acceptance by the issuer or nominated person, or (iv) an assignee of the issuer's or nominated person's deferred obligation that was taken for value and without notice of forgery or material fraud after the obligation was incurred by the issuer or nominated person; and

(2) the issuer, acting in good faith, may honor or dishonor the presentation in any other case.

(b) If an applicant claims that a required document is forged or materially fraudulent or that honor of the presentation would facilitate a material fraud by the beneficiary on the issuer or applicant, a court of competent jurisdiction may temporarily or permanently enjoin the issuer from honoring a presentation or grant similar relief against the issuer or other persons only if the court finds that:

(1) the relief is not prohibited under the law applicable to an accepted draft or deferred obligation incurred by the issuer;

(2) a beneficiary, issuer, or nominated person who may be adversely affected is adequately protected against loss that it may suffer because the relief is granted;

(3) all of the conditions to entitle a person to the relief under the law of this State have been met; and

(4) on the basis of the information submitted to the court, the applicant is more likely than not to succeed under its claim of forgery or material fraud and the person demanding honor does not qualify for protection under subsection (a)(1).

§ 5–110. Warranties.

(a) If its presentation is honored, the beneficiary warrants:

(1) to the issuer, any other person to whom presentation is made, and the applicant that there is no fraud or forgery of the kind described in Section 5–109(a); and

(2) to the applicant that the drawing does not violate any agreement between the applicant and beneficiary or any other agreement intended by them to be augmented by the letter of credit.

(b) The warranties in subsection (a) are in addition to warranties arising under Article 3, 4, 7, and 8 because of the presentation or transfer of documents covered by any of those articles.

§ 5–111. Remedies.

(a) If an issuer wrongfully dishonors or repudiates its obligation to pay money under a letter of credit before presentation, the beneficiary, successor, or nominated person presenting on its own behalf may recover from the issuer the amount that is the subject of the dishonor or repudiation. If the issuer's obligation under the letter of credit is not for the payment of money, the claimant may obtain specific performance or, at the claimant's election, recover an amount equal to the value of performance from the issuer. In either case, the claimant may also recover incidental but not consequential damages. The claimant is not obligated to take action to avoid damages that might be due from the issuer under this subsection. If, although not obligated to do so, the claimant avoids damages, the claimant's recovery from the issuer must be reduced by the amount of damages avoided. The issuer has the burden of proving the amount of damages avoided. In the case of repudiation the claimant need not present any document.

(b) If an issuer wrongfully dishonors a draft or demand presented under a letter of credit or honors a draft or demand in breach of its obligation to the applicant, the applicant may recover damages resulting from the breach, including incidental but not consequential damages, less any amount saved as a result of the breach.

(c) If an adviser or nominated person other than a confirmer breaches an obligation under this article or an issuer breaches an obligation not covered in subsection (a) or (b), a person to whom the obligation is owed may recover damages resulting from the breach, including incidental but not consequential damages, less any amount saved as a result of the breach. To the extent of the confirmation, a confirmer has the liability of an issuer specified in this subsection and subsections (a) and (b).

(d) An issuer, nominated person, or adviser who is found liable under subsection (a), (b), or (c) shall pay interest on the amount owed thereunder from the date of wrongful dishonor or other appropriate date.

(e) Reasonable attorney's fees and other expenses of litigation must be awarded to the prevailing party in an action in which a remedy is sought under this article.

(f) Damages that would otherwise be payable by a party for breach of an obligation under this article may be liquidated by agreement or undertaking, but only in an amount or by a formula that is reasonable in light of the harm anticipated.

§ 5–112. Transfer of Letter of Credit.

(a) Except as otherwise provided in Section 5–113, unless a letter of credit provides that it is transferable, the right of a beneficiary to draw or otherwise demand performance under a letter of credit may not be transferred.

(b) Even if a letter of credit provides that it is transferable, the issuer may refuse to recognize or carry out a transfer if:

(1) the transfer would violate applicable law; or

(2) the transferor or transferee has failed to comply with any requirement stated in the letter of credit or any other requirement relating to transfer imposed by the issuer which is within the standard practice referred to in Section 5–108(e) or is otherwise reasonable under the circumstances.

§ 5–113.   Transfer by Operation of Law.

(a) A successor of a beneficiary may consent to amendments, sign and present documents, and receive payment or other items of value in the name of the beneficiary without disclosing its status as a successor.

(b) A successor of a beneficiary may consent to amendments, sign and present documents, and receive payment or other items of value in its own name as the disclosed successor of the beneficiary. Except as otherwise provided in subsection (e), an issuer shall recognize a disclosed successor of a beneficiary as beneficiary in full substitution for its predecessor upon compliance with the requirements for recognition by the issuer of a transfer of drawing rights by operation of law under the standard practice referred to in Section 5–108(e) or, in the absence of such a practice, compliance with other reasonable procedures sufficient to protect the issuer.

(c) An issuer is not obliged to determine whether a purported successor is a successor of a beneficiary or whether the signature of a purported successor is genuine or authorized.

(d) Honor of a purported successor's apparently complying presentation under subsection (a) or (b) has the consequences specified in Section 5–108(i) even if the purported successor is not the successor of a beneficiary. Documents signed in the name of the beneficiary or of a disclosed successor by a person who is neither the beneficiary nor the successor of the beneficiary are forged documents for the purposes of Section 5–109.

(e) An issuer whose rights of reimbursement are not covered by subsection (d) or substantially similar law and any confirmer or nominated person may decline to recognize a presentation under subsection (b).

(f) A beneficiary whose name is changed after the issuance of a letter of credit has the same rights and obligations as a successor of a beneficiary under this section.

§ 5–114.   Assignment of Proceeds.

(a) In this section, "proceeds of a letter of credit" means the cash, check, accepted draft, or other item of value paid or delivered upon honor or giving of value by the issuer or any nominated person under the letter of credit. The term does not include a beneficiary's drawing rights or documents presented by the beneficiary.

(b) A beneficiary may assign its right to part or all of the proceeds of a letter of credit. The beneficiary may do so before presentation as a present assignment of its right to receive proceeds contingent upon its compliance with the terms and conditions of the letter of credit.

(c) An issuer or nominated person need not recognize an assignment of proceeds of a letter of credit until it consents to the assignment.

(d) An issuer or nominated person has no obligation to give or withhold its consent to an assignment of proceeds of a letter of credit, but consent may not be unreasonably withheld if the assignee possesses

and exhibits the letter of credit and presentation of the letter of credit is a condition to honor.

(e) Rights of a transferee beneficiary or nominated person are independent of the beneficiary's assignment of the proceeds of a letter of credit and are superior to the assignee's right to the proceeds.

(f) Neither the rights recognized by this section between an assignee and an issuer, transferee beneficiary, or nominated person nor the issuer's or nominated person's payment of proceeds to an assignee or a third person affect the rights between the assignee and any person other than the issuer, transferee beneficiary, or nominated person. The mode of creating and perfecting a security interest in or granting an assignment of a beneficiary's rights to proceeds is governed by Article 9 or other law. Against persons other than the issuer, transferee beneficiary, or nominated person, the rights and obligations arising upon the creation of a security interest or other assignment of a beneficiary's right to proceeds and its perfection are governed by Article 9 or other law.

§ 5–115.   Statute of Limitations.

An action to enforce a right or obligation arising under this article must be commenced within one year after the expiration date of the relevant letter of credit or one year after the [claim for relief] [cause of action] accrues, whichever occurs later. A [claim for relief] [cause of action] accrues when the breach occurs, regardless of the aggrieved party's lack of knowledge of the breach.

§ 5–116.   Choice of Law and Forum.

(a) The liability of an issuer, nominated person, or adviser for action or omission is governed by the law of the jurisdiction chosen by an agreement in the form of a record signed or otherwise authenticated by the affected parties in the manner provided in Section 5–104 or by a provision in the person's letter of credit, confirmation, or other undertaking. The jurisdiction whose law is chosen need not bear any relation to the transaction.

(b) Unless subsection (a) applies, the liability of an issuer, nominated person, or adviser for action or omission is governed by the law of the jurisdiction in which the person is located. The person is considered to be located at the address indicated in the person's undertaking. If more than one address is indicated, the person is considered to be located at the address from which the person's undertaking was issued. For the purpose of jurisdiction, choice of law, and recognition of interbranch letters of credit, but not enforcement of a judgment, all branches of a bank are considered separate juridical entities and a bank is considered to be located at the place where its relevant branch is considered to be located under this subsection.

(c) Except as otherwise provided in this subsection, the liability of an issuer, nominated person, or adviser is governed by any rules of custom or practice, such as the Uniform Customs and Practice for Documentary Credits, to which the letter of credit, confirmation, or other undertaking is expressly made subject. If (i) this article would govern the liability of an issuer, nominated person, or adviser under subsection (a) or (b), (ii) the relevant undertaking incorporates rules of custom or practice, and (iii) there is conflict between this article and those rules as applied to that undertaking, those rules govern except to the extent of any conflict with the nonvariable provisions specified in Section 5–103(c).

(d) If there is conflict between this article and Article 3, 4, 4A, or 9, this article governs.

(e) The forum for settling disputes arising out of an undertaking within this article may be chosen in the manner and with the binding effect that governing law may be chosen in accordance with subsection (a).

§ 5–117. Subrogation of Issuer, Applicant, and Nominated Person.

(a) An issuer that honors a beneficiary's presentation is subrogated to the rights of the beneficiary to the same extent as if the issuer were a secondary obligor of the underlying obligation owed to the beneficiary and of the applicant to the same extent as if the issuer were the secondary obligor of the underlying obligation owed to the applicant.

(b) An applicant that reimburses an issuer is subrogated to the rights of the issuer against any beneficiary, presenter, or nominated person to the same extent as if the applicant were the secondary obligor of the obligations owed to the issuer and has the rights of subrogation of the issuer to the rights of the beneficiary stated in subsection (a).

(c) A nominated person who pays or gives value against a draft or demand presented under a letter of credit is subrogated to the rights of:

(1) the issuer against the applicant to the same extent as if the nominated person were a secondary obligor of the obligation owed to the issuer by the applicant;

(2) the beneficiary to the same extent as if the nominated person were a secondary obligor of the underlying obligation owed to the beneficiary; and

(3) the applicant to same extent as if the nominated person were a secondary obligor of the underlying obligation owed to the applicant.

(d) Notwithstanding any agreement or term to the contrary, the rights of subrogation stated in subsections (a) and (b) do not arise until the issuer honors the letter of credit or otherwise pays and the rights in subsection (c) do not arise until the nominated person pays or otherwise gives value. Until then, the issuer, nominated person, and the applicant do not derive under this section present or prospective rights forming the basis of a claim, defense, or excuse.

§ 5–118. Security Interest of Issuer or Nominated Person.

(a) An issuer or nominated person has a security interest in a document presented under a letter of credit to the extent that the issuer or nominated person honors or gives value for the presentation.

(b) So long as and to the extent that an issuer or nominated person has not been reimbursed or has not otherwise recovered the value given with respect to a security interest in a document under subsection (a), the security interest continues and is subject to Article 9, but:

(1) a security agreement is not necessary to make the security interest enforceable under Section 9–203(b)(3);

(2) if the document is presented in a medium other than a written or other tangible medium, the security interest is perfected; and

(3) if the document is presented in a written or other tangible medium and is not a certificated security, chattel paper, a document of title, an instrument, or a letter of credit, the security interest is perfected and has priority over a conflicting security interest in the document so long as the debtor does not have possession of the document.

As added in 1999.

Transition Provisions

§ [ ]. Effective Date.
This [Act] shall become effective on _____, 20__.

§ [ ]. Repeal.
This [Act] [repeals] [amends] [insert citation to existing Article 5].

§ [ ]. Applicability.
This [Act] applies to a letter of credit that is issued on or after the effective date of this [Act]. This [Act] does not apply to a transaction, event, obligation, or duty arising out of or associated with a letter of credit that was issued before the effective date of this [Act].

§ [ ]. Savings Clause.
A transaction arising out of or associated with a letter of credit that was issued before the effective date of this [Act] and the rights, obligations, and interests flowing from that transaction are governed by any statute or other law amended or repealed by this [Act] as if repeal or amendment had not occurred and may be terminated, completed, consummated, or enforced under that statute or other law.

REPEALER OF U.C.C.—ARTICLE 6: BULK TRANSFERS AND [REVISED] ARTICLE 6: BULK SALES

(States to Select One Alternative)

Alternative A

§ 1. Repeal
Article 6 and Section 9–111 of the Uniform Commercial Code are hereby repealed, effective _____.

§ 2. Amendment
Section 1–105(2) of the Uniform Commercial Code is hereby amended to read as follows:

(2) Where one of the following provisions of this Act specifies the applicable law, that provision governs and a contrary agreement is effective only to the extent permitted by the law (including the conflict of laws rules) so specified:

Rights of creditors against sold goods. Section 2–402.
Applicability of the Article on Leases. Section 2A–105 and 2A–106.
Applicability of the Article on Bank Deposits and Collections. Section 4–102.
Applicability of the Article on Investment Securities. Section 8–106.
Perfection provisions of the Article on Secured Transactions. Section 9–103.

§ 3. Amendment.
Section 2–403(4) of the Uniform Commercial Code is hereby amended to read as follows:

(4) The rights of other purchasers of goods and of lien creditors are governed by the Articles on Secured Transactions (Article 9) and Documents of Title (Article 7).

§ 4. Savings Clause.
Rights and obligations that arose under Article 6 and Section 9–111 of the Uniform Commercial Code before their repeal remain valid and may be enforced as though those statutes had not been repealed.]

Alternative B

§ 6–101. Short Title.

This Article shall be known and may be cited as Uniform Commercial Code—Bulk Sales.

§ 6–102. Definitions and Index of Definitions.

(1) In this Article, unless the context otherwise requires:

(a) "Assets" means the inventory that is the subject of a bulk sale and any tangible and intangible personal property used or held for use primarily in, or arising from, the seller's business and sold in connection with that inventory, but the term does not include:

(i) fixtures (Section 9–102(a)(41)) other than readily removable factory and office machines;

(ii) the lessee's interest in a lease of real property; or

(iii) property to the extent it is generally exempt from creditor process under nonbankruptcy law.

(b) "Auctioneer" means a person whom the seller engages to direct, conduct, control, or be responsible for a sale by auction.

(c) "Bulk sale" means:

(i) in the case of a sale by auction or a sale or series of sales conducted by a liquidator on the seller's behalf, a sale or series of sales not in the ordinary course of the seller's business of more than half of the seller's inventory, as measured by value on the date of the bulk-sale agreement, if on that date the auctioneer or liquidator has notice, or after reasonable inquiry would have had notice, that the seller will not continue to operate the same or a similar kind of business after the sale or series of sales; and

(ii) in all other cases, a sale not in the ordinary course of the seller's business of more than half the seller's inventory, as measured by value on the date of the bulk-sale agreement, if on that date the buyer has notice, or after reasonable inquiry would have had notice, that the seller will not continue to operate the same or a similar kind of business after the sale.

(d) "Claim" means a right to payment from the seller, whether or not the right is reduced to judgment, liquidated, fixed, matured, disputed, secured, legal, or equitable. The term includes costs of collection and attorney's fees only to the extent that the laws of this state permit the holder of the claim to recover them in an action against the obligor.

(e) "Claimant" means a person holding a claim incurred in the seller's business other than:

(i) an unsecured and unmatured claim for employment compensation and benefits, including commissions and vacation, severance, and sick-leave pay;

(ii) a claim for injury to an individual or to property, or for breach of warranty, unless:

(A) a right of action for the claim has accrued;

(B) the claim has been asserted against the seller; and

(C) the seller knows the identity of the person asserting the claim and the basis upon which the person has asserted it; and

(States to Select One Alternative)

Alternative A

[**(iii)** a claim for taxes owing to a governmental unit.]

Alternative B

[**(iii)** a claim for taxes owing to a governmental unit, if:

(A) a statute governing the enforcement of the claim permits or requires notice of the bulk sale to be given to the governmental unit in a manner other than by compliance with the requirements of this Article; and

(B) notice is given in accordance with the statute.]

(f) "Creditor" means a claimant or other person holding a claim.

(g)(i) "Date of the bulk sale" means:

(A) if the sale is by auction or is conducted by a liquidator on the seller's behalf, the date on which more than ten percent of the net proceeds is paid to or for the benefit of the seller; and

(B) in all other cases, the later of the date on which:

(I) more than ten percent of the net contract price is paid to or for the benefit of the seller; or

(II) more than ten percent of the assets, as measured by value, are transferred to the buyer.

(ii) For purposes of this subsection:

(A) delivery of a negotiable instrument (Section 3–104(1)) to or for the benefit of the seller in exchange for assets constitutes payment of the contract price pro tanto;

(B) to the extent that the contract price is deposited in an escrow, the contract price is paid to or for the benefit of the seller when the seller acquires the unconditional right to receive the deposit or when the deposit is delivered to the seller or for the benefit of the seller, whichever is earlier; and

(C) an asset is transferred when a person holding an unsecured claim can no longer obtain through judicial proceedings rights to the asset that are superior to those of the buyer arising as a result of the bulk sale. A person holding an unsecured claim can obtain those superior rights to a tangible asset at least until the buyer has an unconditional right, under the bulk-sale agreement, to possess the asset, and a person holding an unsecured claim can obtain those superior rights to an intangible asset at least until the buyer has an unconditional right, under the bulk-sale agreement, to use the asset.

(h) "Date of the bulk-sale agreement" means:

(i) in the case of a sale by auction or conducted by a liquidator (subsection (c)(i)), the date on which the seller engages the auctioneer or liquidator; and

(ii) in all other cases, the date on which a bulk-sale agreement becomes enforceable between the buyer and the seller.

(i) "Debt" means liability on a claim.

(j) "Liquidator" means a person who is regularly engaged in the business of disposing of assets for businesses contemplating liquidation or dissolution.

(k) "Net contract price" means the new consideration the buyer is obligated to pay for the assets less:

(i) the amount of any proceeds of the sale of an asset, to the extent the proceeds are applied in partial or total satisfaction of a debt secured by the asset; and

(ii) the amount of any debt to the extent it is secured by a security interest or lien that is enforceable against the asset before and after it has been sold to a buyer. If a debt is secured by an asset and other property of the seller, the amount of the debt secured by a security interest or lien that is enforceable against the asset is determined by multiplying the debt by a fraction, the numerator of which is the value of the new consideration for the asset on the date of the bulk sale and the denominator of which is the value of all property securing the debt on the date of the bulk sale.

(l) "Net proceeds" means the new consideration received for assets sold at a sale by auction or a sale conducted by a liquidator on the seller's behalf less:

(i) commissions and reasonable expenses of the sale;

(ii) the amount of any proceeds of the sale of an asset, to the extent the proceeds are applied in partial or total satisfaction of a debt secured by the asset; and

(iii) the amount of any debt to the extent it is secured by a security interest or lien that is enforceable against the asset before and after it has been sold to a buyer. If a debt is secured by an asset and other property of the seller, the amount of the debt secured by a security interest or lien that is enforceable against the asset is determined by multiplying the debt by a fraction, the numerator of which is the value of the new consideration for the asset on the date of the bulk sale and the denominator of which is the value of all property securing the debt on the date of the bulk sale.

(m) A sale is "in the ordinary course of the seller's business" if the sale comports with usual or customary practices in the kind of business in which the seller is engaged or with the seller's own usual or customary practices.

(n) "United States" includes its territories and possessions and the Commonwealth of Puerto Rico.

(o) "Value" means fair market value.

(p) "Verified" means signed and sworn to or affirmed.

(2) The following definitions in other Articles apply to this Article:

(a) "Buyer."   Section 2–103(1)(a).
(b) "Equipment." Section 9–102(a)(33).
(c) "Inventory." Section 9–102(a)(48).
(d) "Sale."   Section 2–106(1).
(e) "Seller."   Section 2–103(1)(d).

(3) In addition, Article 1 contains general definitions and principles of construction and interpretation applicable throughout this Article.

As amended in 1999.

§ 6–103. Applicability of Article.

(1) Except as otherwise provided in subsection (3), this Article applies to a bulk sale if:

(a) the seller's principal business is the sale of inventory from stock; and

(b) on the date of the bulk-sale agreement the seller is located in this state or, if the seller is located in a jurisdiction that is not a part of the United States, the seller's major executive office in the United States is in this state.

(2) A seller is deemed to be located at his [or her] place of business. If a seller has more than one place of business, the seller is deemed located at his [or her] chief executive office.

(3) This Article does not apply to:

(a) a transfer made to secure payment or performance of an obligation;

(b) a transfer of collateral to a secured party pursuant to Section 9–503;

(c) a disposition of collateral pursuant to Section 9–610;

(d) retention of collateral pursuant to Section 9–620;

(e) a sale of an asset encumbered by a security interest or lien if (i) all the proceeds of the sale are applied in partial or total satisfaction of the debt secured by the security interest or lien or (ii) the security interest or lien is enforceable against the asset after it has been sold to the buyer and the net contract price is zero;

(f) a general assignment for the benefit of creditors or to a subsequent transfer by the assignee;

(g) a sale by an executor, administrator, receiver, trustee in bankruptcy, or any public officer under judicial process;

(h) a sale made in the course of judicial or administrative proceedings for the dissolution or reorganization of an organization;

(i) a sale to a buyer whose principal place of business is in the United States and who:

(i) not earlier than 21 days before the date of the bulk sale, (A) obtains from the seller a verified and dated list of claimants of whom the seller has notice three days before the seller sends or delivers the list to the buyer or (B) conducts a reasonable inquiry to discover the claimants;

(ii) assumes in full the debts owed to claimants of whom the buyer has knowledge on the date the buyer receives the list of claimants from the seller or on the date the buyer completes the reasonable inquiry, as the case may be;

(iii) is not insolvent after the assumption; and

(iv) gives written notice of the assumption not later than 30 days after the date of the bulk sale by sending or delivering a notice to the claimants identified in subparagraph (ii) or by filing a notice in the office of the [Secretary of State];

(j) a sale to a buyer whose principal place of business is in the United States and who:

(i) assumes in full the debts that were incurred in the seller's business before the date of the bulk sale;

(ii) is not insolvent after the assumption; and

(iii) gives written notice of the assumption not later than 30 days after the date of the bulk sale by sending or delivering a notice to each creditor whose debt is assumed or by filing a notice in the office of the [Secretary of State];

(k) a sale to a new organization that is organized to take over and continue the business of the seller and that has its principal place of business in the United States if:

(i) the buyer assumes in full the debts that were incurred in the seller's business before the date of the bulk sale;

(ii) the seller receives nothing from the sale except an interest in the new organization that is subordinate to the claims against the organization arising from the assumption; and

(iii) the buyer gives written notice of the assumption not later than 30 days after the date of the bulk sale by sending or delivering a notice to each creditor whose debt is assumed or by filing a notice in the office of the [Secretary of State];

(l) a sale of assets having:

    (i) a value, net of liens and security interests, of less than $10,000. If a debt is secured by assets and other property of the seller, the net value of the assets is determined by subtracting from their value an amount equal to the product of the debt multiplied by a fraction, the numerator of which is the value of the assets on the date of the bulk sale and the denominator of which is the value of all property securing the debt on the date of the bulk sale; or

    (ii) a value of more than $25,000,000 on the date of the bulk-sale agreement; or

(m) a sale required by, and made pursuant to, statute.

(4) The notice under subsection (3)(i)(iv) must state:(i) that a sale that may constitute a bulk sale has been or will be made; (ii) the date or prospective date of the bulk sale; (iii) the individual, partnership, or corporate names and the addresses of the seller and buyer; (iv) the address to which inquiries about the sale may be made, if different from the seller's address; and (v) that the buyer has assumed or will assume in full the debts owed to claimants of whom the buyer has knowledge on the date the buyer receives the list of claimants from the seller or completes a reasonable inquiry to discover the claimants.

(5) The notice under subsections (3)(j)(iii) and (3)(k)(iii) must state: (i) that a sale that may constitute a bulk sale has been or will be made; (ii) the date or prospective date of the bulk sale; (iii) the individual, partnership, or corporate names and the addresses of the seller and buyer; (iv) the address to which inquiries about the sale may be made, if different from the seller's address; and (v) that the buyer has assumed or will assume the debts that were incurred in the seller's business before the date of the bulk sale.

(6) For purposes of subsection (3)(l), the value of assets is presumed to be equal to the price the buyer agrees to pay for the assets. However, in a sale by auction or a sale conducted by a liquidator on the seller's behalf, the value of assets is presumed to be the amount the auctioneer or liquidator reasonably estimates the assets will bring at auction or upon liquidation.

As amended in 1999.

§ 6–104. Obligations of Buyer.

(1) In a bulk sale as defined in Section 6–102(1)(c)(ii) the buyer shall:

(a) obtain from the seller a list of all business names and addresses used by the seller within three years before the date the list is sent or delivered to the buyer;

(b) unless excused under subsection (2), obtain from the seller a verified and dated list of claimants of whom the seller has notice three days before the seller sends or delivers the list to the buyer and including, to the extent known by the seller, the address of and the amount claimed by each claimant;

(c) obtain from the seller or prepare a schedule of distribution (Section 6–106(1));

(d) give notice of the bulk sale in accordance with Section 6–105;

(e) unless excused under Section 6–106(4), distribute the net contract price in accordance with the undertakings of the buyer in the schedule of distribution; and

(f) unless excused under subsection (2), make available the list of claimants (subsection (1)(b)) by:

    (i) promptly sending or delivering a copy of the list without charge to any claimant whose written request is received by the buyer no later than six months after the date of the bulk sale;

    (ii) permitting any claimant to inspect and copy the list at any reasonable hour upon request received by the buyer no later than six months after the date of the bulk sale; or

    (iii) filing a copy of the list in the office of the [Secretary of State] no later than the time for giving a notice of the bulk sale (Section 6–105(5)). A list filed in accordance with this subparagraph must state the individual, partnership, or corporate name and a mailing address of the seller.

(2) A buyer who gives notice in accordance with Section 6–105(2) is excused from complying with the requirements of subsections (1)(b) and (1)(f).

§ 6–105. Notice to Claimants.

(1) Except as otherwise provided in subsection (2), to comply with Section 6–104(1)(d) the buyer shall send or deliver a written notice of the bulk sale to each claimant on the list of claimants (Section 6–104(1)(b)) and to any other claimant of which the buyer has knowledge at the time the notice of the bulk sale is sent or delivered.

(2) A buyer may comply with Section 6–104(1)(d) by filing a written notice of the bulk sale in the office of the [Secretary of State] if:

(a) on the date of the bulk-sale agreement the seller has 200 or more claimants, exclusive of claimants holding secured or matured claims for employment compensation and benefits, including commissions and vacation, severance, and sick-leave pay; or

(b) the buyer has received a verified statement from the seller stating that, as of the date of the bulk-sale agreement, the number of claimants, exclusive of claimants holding secured or matured claims for employment compensation and benefits, including commissions and vacation, severance, and sick-leave pay, is 200 or more.

(3) The written notice of the bulk sale must be accompanied by a copy of the schedule of distribution (Section 6–106(1)) and state at least:

(a) that the seller and buyer have entered into an agreement for a sale that may constitute a bulk sale under the laws of the State of _____ ;

(b) the date of the agreement;

(c) the date on or after which more than ten percent of the assets were or will be transferred;

(d) the date on or after which more than ten percent of the net contract price was or will be paid, if the date is not stated in the schedule of distribution;

(e) the name and a mailing address of the seller;

(f) any other business name and address listed by the seller pursuant to Section 6–104(1)(a);

(g) the name of the buyer and an address of the buyer from which information concerning the sale can be obtained;

(h) a statement indicating the type of assets or describing the assets item by item;

(i) the manner in which the buyer will make available the list of claimants (Section 6–104(1)(f)), if applicable; and

(j) if the sale is in total or partial satisfaction of an antecedent debt owed by the seller, the amount of the debt to be satisfied and the name of the person to whom it is owed.

(4) For purposes of subsections (3)(e) and (3)(g), the name of a person is the person's individual, partnership, or corporate name.

(5) The buyer shall give notice of the bulk sale not less than 45 days before the date of the bulk sale and, if the buyer gives notice in accordance with subsection (1), not more than 30 days after obtaining the list of claimants.

(6) A written notice substantially complying with the requirements of subsection (3) is effective even though it contains minor errors that are not seriously misleading.

(7) A form substantially as follows is sufficient to comply with subsection (3):

Notice of Sale

(1) _____, whose address is _____, is described in this notice as the "seller."

(2) _____, whose address is _____, is described in this notice as the "buyer."

(3) The seller has disclosed to the buyer that within the past three years the seller has used other business names, operated at other addresses, or both, as follows: _____

_____ .

(4) The seller and the buyer have entered into an agreement dated _____, for a sale that may constitute a bulk sale under the laws of the state of _____ .

(5) The date on or after which more than ten percent of the assets that are the subject of the sale were or will be transferred is _____, and [if not stated in the schedule of distribution] the date on or after which more than ten percent of the net contract price was or will be paid is _____ .

(6) The following assets are the subject of the sale: _____ .

(7) [If applicable] The buyer will make available to claimants of the seller a list of the seller's claimants in the following manner: _____ .

(8) [If applicable] The sale is to satisfy $ _____ of an antecedent debt owed by the seller to _____ .

(9) A copy of the schedule of distribution of the net contract price accompanies this notice.

[End of Notice]

§ 6–106. Schedule of Distribution.

(1) The seller and buyer shall agree on how the net contract price is to be distributed and set forth their agreement in a written schedule of distribution.

(2) The schedule of distribution may provide for distribution to any person at any time, including distribution of the entire net contract price to the seller.

(3) The buyer's undertakings in the schedule of distribution run only to the seller. However, a buyer who fails to distribute the net contract price in accordance with the buyer's undertakings in the schedule of distribution is liable to a creditor only as provided in Section 6–107(1).

(4) If the buyer undertakes in the schedule of distribution to distribute any part of the net contract price to a person other than the seller, and, after the buyer has given notice in accordance with Section 6–105, some or all of the anticipated net contract price is or becomes unavailable for distribution as a consequence of the buyer's or seller's having complied with an order of court, legal process, statute, or rule of law, the buyer is excused from any obligation arising under this Article or under any contract with the seller to distribute the net contract price in accordance with the buyer's undertakings in the schedule if the buyer:

(a) distributes the net contract price remaining available in accordance with any priorities for payment stated in the schedule of distribution and, to the extent that the price is insufficient to pay all the debts having a given priority, distributes the price pro rata among those debts shown in the schedule as having the same priority;

(b) distributes the net contract price remaining available in accordance with an order of court;

(c) commences a proceeding for interpleader in a court of competent jurisdiction and is discharged from the proceeding; or

(d) reaches a new agreement with the seller for the distribution of the net contract price remaining available, sets forth the new agreement in an amended schedule of distribution, gives notice of the amended schedule, and distributes the net contract price remaining available in accordance with the buyer's undertakings in the amended schedule.

(5) The notice under subsection (4)(d) must identify the buyer and the seller, state the filing number, if any, of the original notice, set forth the amended schedule, and be given in accordance with subsection (1) or (2) of Section 6–105, whichever is applicable, at least 14 days before the buyer distributes any part of the net contract price remaining available.

(6) If the seller undertakes in the schedule of distribution to distribute any part of the net contract price, and, after the buyer has given notice in accordance with Section 6–105, some or all of the anticipated net contract price is or becomes unavailable for distribution as a consequence of the buyer's or seller's having complied with an order of court, legal process, statute, or rule of law, the seller and any person in control of the seller are excused from any obligation arising under this Article or under any agreement with the buyer to distribute the net contract price in accordance with the seller's undertakings in the schedule if the seller:

(a) distributes the net contract price remaining available in accordance with any priorities for payment stated in the schedule of distribution and, to the extent that the price is insufficient to pay all the debts having a given priority, distributes the price pro rata among those debts shown in the schedule as having the same priority;

(b) distributes the net contract price remaining available in accordance with an order of court;

(c) commences a proceeding for interpleader in a court of competent jurisdiction and is discharged from the proceeding; or

(d) prepares a written amended schedule of distribution of the net contract price remaining available for distribution, gives notice of the amended schedule, and distributes the net contract price remaining available in accordance with the amended schedule.

(7) The notice under subsection (6)(d) must identify the buyer and the seller, state the filing number, if any, of the original notice, set forth the amended schedule, and be given in accordance with subsection (1) or (2) of Section 6–105, whichever is applicable, at least 14 days before the seller distributes any part of the net contract price remaining available.

§ 6–107. Liability for Noncompliance.

(1) Except as provided in subsection (3), and subject to the limitation in subsection (4):

(a) a buyer who fails to comply with the requirements of Section 6–104(1)(e) with respect to a creditor is liable to the creditor for damages in the amount of the claim, reduced by any amount that the creditor would not have realized if the buyer had complied; and

(b) a buyer who fails to comply with the requirements of any other subsection of Section 6–104 with respect to a claimant is liable to the claimant for damages in the amount of the claim, reduced by any amount that the claimant would not have realized if the buyer had complied.

(2) In an action under subsection (1), the creditor has the burden of establishing the validity and amount of the claim, and the buyer has the burden of establishing the amount that the creditor would not have realized if the buyer had complied.

(3) A buyer who:

(a) made a good faith and commercially reasonable effort to comply with the requirements of Section 6–104(1) or to exclude the sale from the application of this Article under Section 6–103(3); or

(b) on or after the date of the bulk-sale agreement, but before the date of the bulk sale, held a good faith and commercially reasonable belief that this Article does not apply to the particular sale is not liable to creditors for failure to comply with the requirements of Section 6–104. The buyer has the burden of establishing the good faith and commercial reasonableness of the effort or belief.

(4) In a single bulk sale the cumulative liability of the buyer for failure to comply with the requirements of Section 6–104(1) may not exceed an amount equal to:

(a) if the assets consist only of inventory and equipment, twice the net contract price, less the amount of any part of the net contract price paid to or applied for the benefit of the seller or a creditor; or

(b) if the assets include property other than inventory and equipment, twice the net value of the inventory and equipment less the amount of the portion of any part of the net contract price paid to or applied for the benefit of the seller or a creditor which is allocable to the inventory and equipment.

(5) For the purposes of subsection (4)(b), the "net value" of an asset is the value of the asset less (i) the amount of any proceeds of the sale of an asset, to the extent the proceeds are applied in partial or total satisfaction of a debt secured by the asset and (ii) the amount of any debt to the extent it is secured by a security interest or lien that is enforceable against the asset before and after it has been sold to a buyer. If a debt is secured by an asset and other property of the seller, the amount of the debt secured by a security interest or lien that is enforceable against the asset is determined by multiplying the debt by a fraction, the numerator of which is the value of the asset on the date of the bulk sale and the denominator of which is the value of all property securing the debt on the date of the bulk sale. The portion of a part of the net contract price paid to or applied for the benefit of the seller or a creditor that is "allocable to the inventory and equipment" is the portion that bears the same ratio to that part of the net contract price as the net value of the inventory and equipment bears to the net value of all of the assets.

(6) A payment made by the buyer to a person to whom the buyer is, or believes he [or she] is, liable under subsection (1) reduces pro tanto the buyer's cumulative liability under subsection (4).

(7) No action may be brought under subsection (1)(b) by or on behalf of a claimant whose claim is unliquidated or contingent.

(8) A buyer's failure to comply with the requirements of Section 6–104(1) does not (i) impair the buyer's rights in or title to the assets, (ii) render the sale ineffective, void, or voidable, (iii) entitle a creditor to more than a single satisfaction of his [or her] claim, or (iv) create liability other than as provided in this Article.

(9) Payment of the buyer's liability under subsection (1) discharges pro tanto the seller's debt to the creditor.

(10) Unless otherwise agreed, a buyer has an immediate right of reimbursement from the seller for any amount paid to a creditor in partial or total satisfaction of the buyer's liability under subsection (1).

(11) If the seller is an organization, a person who is in direct or indirect control of the seller, and who knowingly, intentionally, and without legal justification fails, or causes the seller to fail, to distribute the net contract price in accordance with the schedule of distribution is liable to any creditor to whom the seller undertook to make payment under the schedule for damages caused by the failure.

§ 6–108. Bulk Sales by Auction; Bulk Sales Conducted by Liquidator.

(1) Sections 6–104, 6–105, 6–106, and 6–107 apply to a bulk sale by auction and a bulk sale conducted by a liquidator on the seller's behalf with the following modifications:

(a) "buyer" refers to auctioneer or liquidator, as the case may be;

(b) "net contract price" refers to net proceeds of the auction or net proceeds of the sale, as the case may be;

(c) the written notice required under Section 6–105(3) must be accompanied by a copy of the schedule of distribution (Section 6–106(1)) and state at least:

(i) that the seller and the auctioneer or liquidator have entered into an agreement for auction or liquidation services that may constitute an agreement to make a bulk sale under the laws of the State of _____ ;

(ii) the date of the agreement;

(iii) the date on or after which the auction began or will begin or the date on or after which the liquidator began or will begin to sell assets on the seller's behalf;

(iv) the date on or after which more than ten percent of the net proceeds of the sale were or will be paid, if the date is not stated in the schedule of distribution;

(v) the name and a mailing address of the seller;

(vi) any other business name and address listed by the seller pursuant to Section 6–104(1)(a);

(vii) the name of the auctioneer or liquidator and an address of the auctioneer or liquidator from which information concerning the sale can be obtained;

(viii) a statement indicating the type of assets or describing the assets item by item;

(ix) the manner in which the auctioneer or liquidator will make available the list of claimants (Section 6–104(1)(f)), if applicable; and

(x) if the sale is in total or partial satisfaction of an antecedent debt owed by the seller, the amount of the debt to be satisfied and the name of the person to whom it is owed; and

(d) in a single bulk sale the cumulative liability of the auctioneer or liquidator for failure to comply with the requirements of this section may not exceed the amount of the net proceeds of the sale allocable to inventory and equipment sold less the amount of the portion of any part of the net proceeds paid to or applied for the benefit of a creditor which is allocable to the inventory and equipment.

(2) A payment made by the auctioneer or liquidator to a person to whom the auctioneer or liquidator is, or believes he [or she] is, liable under this section reduces pro tanto the auctioneer's or liquidator's cumulative liability under subsection (1)(d).

(3) A form substantially as follows is sufficient to comply with subsection (1)(c):

Notice of Sale

(1) _____, whose address is _____, is described in this notice as the "seller."

(2) _____, whose address is _____ , is described in this notice as the "auctioneer" or "liquidator."

(3) The seller has disclosed to the auctioneer or liquidator that within the past three years the seller has used other business names, operated at other addresses, or both, as follows: _____ .

(4) The seller and the auctioneer or liquidator have entered into an agreement dated _____ for auction or liquidation services that may constitute an agreement to make a bulk sale under the laws of the State of _____ .

(5) The date on or after which the auction began or will begin or the date on or after which the liquidator began or will begin to sell assets on the seller's behalf is _____, and [if not stated in the schedule of distribution] the date on or after which more than ten percent of the net proceeds of the sale were or will be paid is _____ .

(6) The following assets are the subject of the sale: _____ .

(7) [If applicable] The auctioneer or liquidator will make available to claimants of the seller a list of the seller's claimants in the following manner: _____ .

(8) [If applicable] The sale is to satisfy $ _____ of an antecedent debt owed by the seller to _____ .

(9) A copy of the schedule of distribution of the net proceeds accompanies this notice.

[End of Notice]

(4) A person who buys at a bulk sale by auction or conducted by a liquidator need not comply with the requirements of Section 6–104(1) and is not liable for the failure of an auctioneer or liquidator to comply with the requirements of this section.

§ 6–109. What Constitutes Filing; Duties of Filing Officer; Information from Filing Officer.

(1) Presentation of a notice or list of claimants for filing and tender of the filing fee or acceptance of the notice or list by the filing officer constitutes filing under this Article.

(2) The filing officer shall:

(a) mark each notice or list with a file number and with the date and hour of filing;

(b) hold the notice or list or a copy for public inspection;

(c) index the notice or list according to each name given for the seller and for the buyer; and

(d) note in the index the file number and the addresses of the seller and buyer given in the notice or list.

(3) If the person filing a notice or list furnishes the filing officer with a copy, the filing officer upon request shall note upon the copy the file number and date and hour of the filing of the original and send or deliver the copy to the person.

(4) The fee for filing and indexing and for stamping a copy furnished by the person filing to show the date and place of filing is $ _____ for the first page and $ _____ for each additional page. The fee for indexing each name beyond the first two is $ _____ .

(5) Upon request of any person, the filing officer shall issue a certificate showing whether any notice or list with respect to a particular seller or buyer is on file on the date and hour stated in the certificate. If a notice or list is on file, the certificate must give the date and hour of filing of each notice or list and the name and address of each seller, buyer, auctioneer, or liquidator. The fee for the certificate is $ _____ if the request for the certificate is in the standard form prescribed by the [Secretary of State] and otherwise is $ _____ . Upon request of any person, the filing officer shall furnish a copy of any filed notice or list for a fee of $ _____ .

(6) The filing officer shall keep each notice or list for two years after it is filed.

§ 6–110. Limitation of Actions.

(1) Except as provided in subsection (2), an action under this Article against a buyer, auctioneer, or liquidator must be commenced within one year after the date of the bulk sale.

(2) If the buyer, auctioneer, or liquidator conceals the fact that the sale has occurred, the limitation is tolled and an action under this Article may be commenced within the earlier of (i) one year after the person bringing the action discovers that the sale has occurred or (ii) one year after the person bringing the action should have discovered that the sale has occurred, but no later than two years after the date of the bulk sale. Complete noncompliance with the requirements of this Article does not of itself constitute concealment.

(3) An action under Section 6–107(11) must be commenced within one year after the alleged violation occurs.

Conforming Amendment to Section 2–403

States adopting Alternative B should amend Section 2–403(4) of the Uniform Commercial Code to read as follows:

(4) The rights of other purchasers of goods and of lien creditors are governed by the Articles on Secured Transactions (Article 9), Bulk Sales (Article 6) and Documents of Title (Article 7).

ARTICLE 7: WAREHOUSE RECEIPTS, BILLS OF LADING AND OTHER DOCUMENTS OF TITLE

Part 1—General

§ 7–101. Short Title.

This Article shall be known and may be cited as Uniform Commercial Code–Documents of Title.

§ 7–102. Definitions and Index of Definitions.

(1) In this Article, unless the context otherwise requires:

(a) "Bailee" means the person who by a warehouse receipt, bill of lading or other document of title acknowledges possession of goods and contracts to deliver them.

(b) "Consignee" means the person named in a bill to whom or to whose order the bill promises delivery.

(c) "Consignor" means the person named in a bill as the person from whom the goods have been received for shipment.

(d) "Delivery order" means a written order to deliver goods directed to a warehouseman, carrier or other person who in the ordinary course of business issues warehouse receipts or bills of lading.

(e) "Document" means document of title as defined in the general definitions in Article 1 (Section 1–201).

(f) "Goods" means all things which are treated as movable for the purposes of a contract of storage or transportation.

(g) "Issuer" means a bailee who issues a document except that in relation to an unaccepted delivery order it means the person who orders the possessor of goods to deliver. Issuer includes any person for whom an agent or employee purports to act in issuing a document if the agent or employee has real or apparent authority to issue documents, notwithstanding that the issuer received no goods or that the goods were misdescribed or that in any other respect the agent or employee violated his instructions.

(h) "Warehouseman" is a person engaged in the business of storing goods for hire.

(2) Other definitions applying to this Article or to specified Parts thereof, and the sections in which they appear are:

"Duly negotiate". Section 7–501.

"Person entitled under the document". Section 7–403(4).

(3) Definitions in other Articles applying to this Article and the sections in which they appear are:

"Contract for sale". Section 2–106.

"Overseas". Section 2–323.

"Receipt" of goods. Section 2–103.

(4) In addition Article 1 contains general definitions and principles of construction and interpretation applicable throughout this Article.

§ 7–103. Relation of Article to Treaty, Statute, Tariff, Classification or Regulation.

To the extent that any treaty or statute of the United States, regulatory statute of this State or tariff, classification or regulation filed or issued pursuant thereto is applicable, the provisions of this Article are subject thereto.

§ 7–104. Negotiable and Non-Negotiable Warehouse Receipt, Bill of Lading or Other Document of Title.

(1) A warehouse receipt, bill of lading or other document of title is negotiable

(a) if by its terms the goods are to be delivered to bearer or to the order of a named person; or

(b) where recognized in overseas trade, if it runs to a named person or assigns.

(2) Any other document is nonnegotiable. A bill of lading in which it is stated that the goods are consigned to a named person is not made negotiable by a provision that the goods are to be delivered only against a written order signed by the same or another named person.

§ 7–105. Construction Against Negative Implication.

The omission from either Part 2 or Part 3 of this Article of a provision corresponding to a provision made in the other Part does not imply that a corresponding rule of law is not applicable.

Part 2—Warehouse Receipts: Special Provisions

§ 7–201. Who May Issue a Warehouse Receipt; Storage Under Government Bond.

(1) A warehouse receipt may be issued by any warehouseman.

(2) Where goods including distilled spirits and agricultural commodities are stored under a statute requiring a bond against withdrawal or a license for the issuance of receipts in the nature of warehouse receipts, a receipt issued for the goods has like effect as a warehouse receipt even though issued by a person who is the owner of the goods and is not a warehouseman.

§ 7–202. Form of Warehouse Receipt; Essential Terms; Optional Terms.

(1) A warehouse receipt need not be in any particular form.

(2) Unless a warehouse receipt embodies within its written or printed terms each of the following, the warehouseman is liable for damages caused by the omission to a person injured thereby:

(a) the location of the warehouse where the goods are stored;

(b) the date of issue of the receipt;

(c) the consecutive number of the receipt;

(d) a statement whether the goods received will be delivered to the bearer, to a specified person, or to a specified person or his order;

(e) the rate of storage and handling charges, except that where goods are stored under a field warehousing arrangement a statement of that fact is sufficient on a non-negotiable receipt;

(f) a description of the goods or of the packages containing them;

(g) the signature of the warehouseman, which may be made by his authorized agent;

(h) if the receipt is issued for goods of which the warehouseman is owner, either solely or jointly or in common with others, the fact of such ownership; and

(i) a statement of the amount of advances made and of liabilities incurred for which the warehouseman claims a lien or security interest (Section 7–209). If the precise amount of such advances made or of such liabilities incurred is, at the time of the issue of the receipt, unknown to the warehouseman or to his agent who issues it, a statement of the fact that advances have been made or liabilities incurred and the purpose thereof is sufficient.

(3) A warehouseman may insert in his receipt any other terms which are not contrary to the provisions of this Act and do not impair his obligation of delivery (Section 7–403) or his duty of care (Section 7–204). Any contrary provisions shall be ineffective.

§ 7–203. Liability for Non-Receipt or Misdescription.

A party to or purchaser for value in good faith of a document of title other than a bill of lading relying in either case upon the description therein of the goods may recover from the issuer damages caused by the nonreceipt or misdescription of the goods, except to the extent that the document conspicuously indicates that the issuer does not know whether any part or all of the goods in fact were received or conform to the description, as where the description is in terms of marks or labels or kind, quantity or condition, or the receipt or description is qualified by "contents, condition and quality unknown", "said to contain" or the like, if such indication be true, or the party or purchaser otherwise has notice.

§ 7–204. Duty of Care; Contractual Limitation of Warehouseman's Liability.

(1) A warehouseman is liable for damages for loss of or injury to the goods caused by his failure to exercise such care in regard to them as a reasonably careful man would exercise under like circumstances but unless otherwise agreed he is not liable for damages which could not have been avoided by the exercise of such care.

(2) Damages may be limited by a term in the warehouse receipt or storage agreement limiting the amount of liability in case of loss or damage, and setting forth a specific liability per article or item, or value per unit of weight, beyond which the warehouseman shall not be liable; provided, however, that such liability may on written request of the bailor at the time of signing such storage agreement or within a reasonable time after receipt of the warehouse receipt be increased on part or all of the goods thereunder, in which event increased rates may be charged based on such increased valuation, but that no such increase shall be permitted contrary to a lawful limitation of liability contained in the warehouseman's tariff, if any. No such limitation is effective with respect to the warehouseman's liability for conversion to his own use.

(3) Reasonable provisions as to the time and manner of presenting claims and instituting actions based on the bailment may be included in the warehouse receipt or tariff.

(4) This section does not impair or repeal . . .

Note: *Insert in subsection (4) a reference to any statute which imposes a higher responsibility upon the warehouseman or invalidates contractual limitations which would be permissible under this Article.*

§ 7–205. Title Under Warehouse Receipt Defeated in Certain Cases.

A buyer in the ordinary course of business of fungible goods sold and delivered by a warehouseman who is also in the business of buying and selling such goods takes free of any claim under a warehouse receipt even though it has been duly negotiated.

§ 7–206. Termination of Storage at Warehouseman's Option.

(1) A warehouseman may on notifying the person on whose account the goods are held and any other person known to claim an interest in the goods require payment of any charges and removal of the goods from the warehouse at the termination of the period of storage fixed by the document, or, if no period is fixed, within a stated period not less than thirty days after the notification. If the goods are not removed before the date specified in the notification, the warehouseman may sell them in accordance with the provisions of the section on enforcement of a warehouseman's lien (Section 7–210).

(2) If a warehouseman in good faith believes that the goods are about to deteriorate or decline in value to less than the amount of his lien within the time prescribed in subsection (1) for notification, advertisement and sale, the warehouseman may specify in the notification any reasonable shorter time for removal of the goods and in case the goods are not removed, may sell them at public sale held not less than one week after a single advertisement or posting.

(3) If as a result of a quality or condition of the goods of which the warehouseman had no notice at the time of deposit the goods are a hazard to other property or to the warehouse or to persons, the warehouseman may sell the goods at public or private sale without advertisement on reasonable notification to all persons known to claim an interest in the goods. If the warehouseman after a reasonable effort is unable to sell the goods he may dispose of them in any lawful manner and shall incur no liability by reason of such disposition.

(4) The warehouseman must deliver the goods to any person entitled to them under this Article upon due demand made at any time prior to sale or other disposition under this section.

(5) The warehouseman may satisfy his lien from the proceeds of any sale or disposition under this section but must hold the balance for delivery on the demand of any person to whom he would have been bound to deliver the goods.

§ 7–207. Goods Must Be Kept Separate; Fungible Goods.

(1) Unless the warehouse receipt otherwise provides, a warehouseman must keep separate the goods covered by each receipt so as to permit at all times identification and delivery of those goods except that different lots of fungible goods may be commingled.

(2) Fungible goods so commingled are owned in common by the persons entitled thereto and the warehouseman is severally liable to

each owner for that owner's share. Where because of overissue a mass of fungible goods is insufficient to meet all the receipts which the warehouseman has issued against it, the persons entitled include all holders to whom overissued receipts have been duly negotiated.

§ 7–208. Altered Warehouse Receipts.

Where a blank in a negotiable warehouse receipt has been filled in without authority, a purchaser for value and without notice of the want of authority may treat the insertion as authorized. Any other unauthorized alteration leaves any receipt enforceable against the issuer according to its original tenor.

§ 7–209. Lien of Warehouseman.

(1) A warehouseman has a lien against the bailor on the goods covered by a warehouse receipt or on the proceeds thereof in his possession for charges for storage or transportation (including demurrage and terminal charges), insurance, labor, or charges present or future in relation to the goods, and for expenses necessary for preservation of the goods or reasonably incurred in their sale pursuant to law. If the person on whose account the goods are held is liable for like charges or expenses in relation to other goods whenever deposited and it is stated in the receipt that a lien is claimed for charges and expenses in relation to other goods, the warehouseman also has a lien against him for such charges and expenses whether or not the other goods have been delivered by the warehouseman. But against a person to whom a negotiable warehouse receipt is duly negotiated a warehouseman's lien is limited to charges in an amount or at a rate specified on the receipt or if no charges are so specified then to a reasonable charge for storage of the goods covered by the receipt subsequent to the date of the receipt.

(2) The warehouseman may also reserve a security interest against the bailor for a maximum amount specified on the receipt for charges other than those specified in subsection (1), such as for money advanced and interest. Such a security interest is governed by the Article on Secured Transactions (Article 9).

(3)(a) A warehouseman's lien for charges and expenses under subsection (1) or a security interest under subsection (2) is also effective against any person who so entrusted the bailor with possession of the goods that a pledge of them by him to a good faith purchaser for value would have been valid but is not effective against a person as to whom the document confers no right in the goods covered by it under Section 7–503.

(b) A warehouseman's lien on household goods for charges and expenses in relation to the goods under subsection (1) is also effective against all persons if the depositor was the legal possessor of the goods at the time of deposit. "Household goods" means furniture, furnishings and personal effects used by the depositor in a dwelling.

(4) A warehouseman loses his lien on any goods which he voluntarily delivers or which he unjustifiably refuses to deliver.

§ 7–210. Enforcement of Warehouseman's Lien.

(1) Except as provided in subsection (2), a warehouseman's lien may be enforced by public or private sale of the goods in bloc or in parcels, at any time or place and on any terms which are commercially reasonable, after notifying all persons known to claim an interest in the goods. Such notification must include a statement of the amount due, the nature of the proposed sale and the time and place of any public sale. The fact that a better price could have been obtained by a sale at a different time or in a different method from that selected by the warehouseman is not of itself sufficient to establish that the sale was not made in a commercially reasonable manner. If the warehouseman either sells the goods in the usual manner in any recognized market therefor, or if he sells at the price current in such market at the time of his sale, or if he has otherwise sold in conformity with commercially reasonable practices among dealers in the type of goods sold, he has sold in a commercially reasonable manner. A sale of more goods than apparently necessary to be offered to ensure satisfaction of the obligation is not commercially reasonable except in cases covered by the preceding sentence.

(2) A warehouseman's lien on goods other than goods stored by a merchant in the course of his business may be enforced only as follows:

(a) All persons known to claim an interest in the goods must be notified.

(b) The notification must be delivered in person or sent by registered or certified letter to the last known address of any person to be notified.

(c) The notification must include an itemized statement of the claim, a description of the goods subject to the lien, a demand for payment within a specified time not less than ten days after receipt of the notification, and a conspicuous statement that unless the claim is paid within the time the goods will be advertised for sale and sold by auction at a specified time and place.

(d) The sale must conform to the terms of the notification.

(e) The sale must be held at the nearest suitable place to that where the goods are held or stored.

(f) After the expiration of the time given in the notification, an advertisement of the sale must be published once a week for two weeks consecutively in a newspaper of general circulation where the sale is to be held. The advertisement must include a description of the goods, the name of the person on whose account they are being held, and the time and place of the sale. The sale must take place at least fifteen days after the first publication. If there is no newspaper of general circulation where the sale is to be held, the advertisement must be posted at least ten days before the sale in not less than six conspicuous places in the neighborhood of the proposed sale.

(3) Before any sale pursuant to this section any person claiming a right in the goods may pay the amount necessary to satisfy the lien and the reasonable expenses incurred under this section. In that event the goods must not be sold, but must be retained by the warehouseman subject to the terms of the receipt and this Article.

(4) The warehouseman may buy at any public sale pursuant to this section.

(5) A purchaser in good faith of goods sold to enforce a warehouseman's lien takes the goods free of any rights of persons against whom the lien was valid, despite noncompliance by the warehouseman with the requirements of this section.

(6) The warehouseman may satisfy his lien from the proceeds of any sale pursuant to this section but must hold the balance, if any, for delivery on demand to any person to whom he would have been bound to deliver the goods.

(7) The rights provided by this section shall be in addition to all other rights allowed by law to a creditor against his debtor.

(8) Where a lien is on goods stored by a merchant in the course of his business the lien may be enforced in accordance with either subsection (1) or (2).

(9) The warehouseman is liable for damages caused by failure to comply with the requirements for sale under this section and in case of willful violation is liable for conversion.
As amended in 1962.

Part 3—Bills of Lading: Special Provisions

§ 7–301.   Liability for Non-Receipt or Misdescription; "Said to Contain"; "Shipper's Load and Count"; Improper Handling.

(1) A consignee of a non-negotiable bill who has given value in good faith or a holder to whom a negotiable bill has been duly negotiated relying in either case upon the description therein of the goods, or upon the date therein shown, may recover from the issuer damages caused by the misdating of the bill or the nonreceipt or misdescription of the goods, except to the extent that the document indicates that the issuer does not know whether any part of all of the goods in fact were received or conform to the description, as where the description is in terms of marks or labels or kind, quantity, or condition or the receipt or description is qualified by "contents or condition of contents of packages unknown", "said to contain", "shipper's weight, load and count" or the like, if such indication be true.

(2) When goods are loaded by an issuer who is a common carrier, the issuer must count the packages of goods if package freight and ascertain the kind and quantity if bulk freight. In such cases "shipper's weight, load and count" or other words indicating that the description was made by the shipper are ineffective except as to freight concealed by packages.

(3) When bulk freight is loaded by a shipper who makes available to the issuer adequate facilities for weighing such freight, an issuer who is a common carrier must ascertain the kind and quantity within a reasonable time after receiving the written request of the shipper to do so. In such cases "shipper's weight" or other words of like purport are ineffective.

(4) The issuer may by inserting in the bill the words "shipper's weight, load and count" or other words of like purport indicate that the goods were loaded by the shipper; and if such statement be true the issuer shall not be liable for damages caused by the improper loading. But their omission does not imply liability for such damages.

(5) The shipper shall be deemed to have guaranteed to the issuer the accuracy at the time of shipment of the description, marks, labels, number, kind, quantity, condition and weight, as furnished by him; and the shipper shall indemnify the issuer against damage caused by inaccuracies in such particulars. The right of the issuer to such indemnity shall in no way limit his responsibility and liability under the contract of carriage to any person other than the shipper.

§ 7–302.   Through Bills of Lading and Similar Documents.

(1) The issuer of a through bill of lading or other document embodying an undertaking to be performed in part by persons acting as its agents or by connecting carriers is liable to anyone entitled to recover on the document for any breach by such other persons or by a connecting carrier of its obligation under the document but to the extent that the bill covers an undertaking to be performed overseas or in territory not contiguous to the continental United States or an undertaking including matters other than transportation this liability may be varied by agreement of the parties.

(2) Where goods covered by a through bill of lading or other document embodying an undertaking to be performed in part by persons other than the issuer are received by any such person, he is subject with respect to his own performance while the goods are in his possession to the obligation of the issuer. His obligation is discharged by delivery of the goods to another such person pursuant to the document, and does not include liability for breach by any other such persons or by the issuer.

(3) The issuer of such through bill of lading or other document shall be entitled to recover from the connecting carrier or such other person in possession of the goods when the breach of the obligation under the document occurred, the amount it may be required to pay to anyone entitled to recover on the document therefor, as may be evidenced by any receipt, judgment, or transcript thereof, and the amount of any expense reasonably incurred by it in defending any action brought by anyone entitled to recover on the document therefor.

§ 7–303. Diversion; Reconsignment; Change of Instructions.
(1) Unless the bill of lading otherwise provides, the carrier may deliver the goods to a person or destination other than that stated in the bill or may otherwise dispose of the goods on instructions from

(a) the holder of a negotiable bill; or

(b) the consignor on a non-negotiable bill not-withstanding contrary instructions from the consignee; or

(c) the consignee on a non-negotiable bill in the absence of contrary instructions from the consignor, if the goods have arrived at the billed destination or if the consignee is in possession of the bill; or

(d) the consignee on a non-negotiable bill if he is entitled as against the consignor to dispose of them.

(2) Unless such instructions are noted on a negotiable bill of lading, a person to whom the bill is duly negotiated can hold the bailee according to the original terms.

§ 7–304. Bills of Lading in a Set.
(1) Except where customary in overseas transportation, a bill of lading must not be issued in a set of parts. The issuer is liable for damages caused by violation of this subsection.

(2) Where a bill of lading is lawfully drawn in a set of parts, each of which is numbered and expressed to be valid only if the goods have not been delivered against any other part, the whole of the parts constitute one bill.

(3) Where a bill of lading is lawfully issued in a set of parts and different parts are negotiated to different persons, the title of the holder to whom the first due negotiation is made prevails as to both the document and the goods even though any later holder may have received the goods from the carrier in good faith and discharged the carrier's obligation by surrender of his part.

(4) Any person who negotiates or transfers a single part of a bill of lading drawn in a set is liable to holders of that part as if it were the whole set.

(5) The bailee is obliged to deliver in accordance with Part 4 of this Article against the first presented part of a bill of lading lawfully drawn in a set. Such delivery discharges the bailee's obligation on the whole bill.

§ 7–305. Destination Bills.
(1) Instead of issuing a bill of lading to the consignor at the place of shipment a carrier may at the request of the consignor procure the bill to be issued at destination or at any other place designated in the request.

(2) Upon request of anyone entitled as against the carrier to control the goods while in transit and on surrender of any outstanding bill of lading or other receipt covering such goods, the issuer may procure a substitute bill to be issued at any place designated in the request.

§ 7–306. Altered Bills of Lading.
An unauthorized alteration or filling in of a blank in a bill of lading leaves the bill enforceable according to its original tenor.

§ 7–307. Lien of Carrier.
(1) A carrier has a lien on the goods covered by a bill of lading for charges subsequent to the date of its receipt of the goods for storage or transportation (including demurrage and terminal charges) and for expenses necessary for preservation of the goods incident to their transportation or reasonably incurred in their sale pursuant to law. But against a purchaser for value of a negotiable bill of lading a carrier's lien is limited to charges stated in the bill or the applicable tariffs, or if no charges are stated then to a reasonable charge.

(2) A lien for charges and expenses under subsection (1) on goods which the carrier was required by law to receive for transportation is effective against the consignor or any person entitled to the goods unless the carrier had notice that the consignor lacked authority to subject the goods to such charges and expenses. Any other lien under subsection (1) is effective against the consignor and any person who permitted the bailor to have control or possession of the goods unless the carrier had notice that the bailor lacked such authority.

(3) A carrier loses his lien on any goods which he voluntarily delivers or which he unjustifiably refuses to deliver.

§ 7–308. Enforcement of Carrier's Lien.
(1) A carrier's lien may be enforced by public or private sale of the goods, in bloc or in parcels, at any time or place and on any terms which are commercially reasonable, after notifying all persons known to claim an interest in the goods. Such notification must include a statement of the amount due, the nature of the proposed sale and the time and place of any public sale. The fact that a better price could have been obtained by a sale at a different time or in a different method from that selected by the carrier is not of itself sufficient to establish that the sale was not made in a commercially reasonable manner. If the carrier either sells the goods in the usual manner in any recognized market therefor or if he sells at the price current in such market at the time of his sale or if he has otherwise sold in conformity with commercially reasonable practices among dealers in the type of goods sold he has sold in a commercially reasonable manner. A sale of more goods than apparently necessary to be offered to ensure satisfaction of the obligation is not commercially reasonable except in cases covered by the preceding sentence.

(2) Before any sale pursuant to this section any person claiming a right in the goods may pay the amount necessary to satisfy the lien and the reasonable expenses incurred under this section. In that event the goods must not be sold, but must be retained by the carrier subject to the terms of the bill and this Article.

(3) The carrier may buy at any public sale pursuant to this section.

(4) A purchaser in good faith of goods sold to enforce a carrier's lien takes the goods free of any rights of persons against whom the lien was valid, despite noncompliance by the carrier with the requirements of this section.

(5) The carrier may satisfy his lien from the proceeds of any sale pursuant to this section but must hold the balance, if any, for delivery on demand to any person to whom he would have been bound to deliver the goods.

(6) The rights provided by this section shall be in addition to all other rights allowed by law to a creditor against his debtor.

(7) A carrier's lien may be enforced in accordance with either subsection (1) or the procedure set forth in subsection (2) of Section 7–210.

(8) The carrier is liable for damages caused by failure to comply with the requirements for sale under this section and in case of willful violation is liable for conversion.

§ 7–309. Duty of Care; Contractual Limitation of Carrier's Liability.

(1) A carrier who issues a bill of lading whether negotiable or non-negotiable must exercise the degree of care in relation to the goods which a reasonably careful man would exercise under like circumstances. This subsection does not repeal or change any law or rule of law which imposes liability upon a common carrier for damages not caused by its negligence.

(2) Damages may be limited by a provision that the carrier's liability shall not exceed a value stated in the document if the carrier's rates are dependent upon value and the consignor by the carrier's tariff is afforded an opportunity to declare a higher value or a value as lawfully provided in the tariff, or where no tariff is filed he is otherwise advised of such opportunity; but no such limitation is effective with respect to the carrier's liability for conversion to its own use.

(3) Reasonable provisions as to the time and manner of presenting claims and instituting actions based on the shipment may be included in a bill of lading or tariff.

Part 4—Warehouse Receipts and Bills of Lading: General Obligations

§ 7–401. Irregularities in Issue of Receipt or Bill or Conduct of Issuer.

The obligations imposed by this Article on an issuer apply to a document of title regardless of the fact that

(a) the document may not comply with the requirements of this Article or of any other law or regulation regarding its issue, form or content; or

(b) the issuer may have violated laws regulating the conduct of his business; or

(c) the goods covered by the document were owned by the bailee at the time the document was issued; or

(d) the person issuing the document does not come within the definition of warehouseman if it purports to be a warehouse receipt.

§ 7–402. Duplicate Receipt or Bill; Overissue.

Neither a duplicate nor any other document of title purporting to cover goods already represented by an outstanding document of the same issuer confers any right in the goods, except as provided in the case of bills in a set, overissue of documents for fungible goods and substitutes for lost, stolen or destroyed documents. But the issuer is liable for damages caused by his overissue or failure to identify a duplicate document as such by conspicuous notation on its face.

§ 7–403. Obligation of Warehouseman or Carrier to Deliver; Excuse.

(1) The bailee must deliver the goods to a person entitled under the document who complies with subsections (2) and (3), unless and to the extent that the bailee establishes any of the following:

(a) delivery of the goods to a person whose receipt was rightful as against the claimant;

(b) damage to or delay, loss or destruction of the goods for which the bailee is not liable [, but the burden of establishing negligence in such cases is on the person entitled under the document];

Note: *The brackets in (1)(b) indicate that State enactments may differ on this point without serious damage to the principle of uniformity.*

(c) previous sale or other disposition of the goods in lawful enforcement of a lien or on warehouseman's lawful termination of storage;

(d) the exercise by a seller of his right to stop delivery pursuant to the provisions of the Article on Sales (Section 2–705);

(e) a diversion, reconsignment or other disposition pursuant to the provisions of this Article (Section 7–303) or tariff regulating such right;

(f) release, satisfaction or any other fact affording a personal defense against the claimant;

(g) any other lawful excuse.

(2) A person claiming goods covered by a document of title must satisfy the bailee's lien where the bailee so requests or where the bailee is prohibited by law from delivering the goods until the charges are paid.

(3) Unless the person claiming is one against whom the document confers no right under Sec. 7–503(1), he must surrender for cancellation or notation of partial deliveries any outstanding negotiable document covering the goods, and the bailee must cancel the document or conspicuously note the partial delivery thereon or be liable to any person to whom the document is duly negotiated.

(4) "Person entitled under the document" means holder in the case of a negotiable document, or the person to whom delivery is to be made by the terms of or pursuant to written instructions under a non-negotiable document.

§ 7–404. No Liability for Good Faith Delivery Pursuant to Receipt or Bill.

A bailee who in good faith including observance of reasonable commercial standards has received goods and delivered or otherwise disposed of them according to the terms of the document of title or pursuant to this Article is not liable therefor. This rule applies even though the person from whom he received the goods had no authority to procure the document or to dispose of the goods and even though the person to whom he delivered the goods had no authority to receive them.

Part 5—Warehouse Receipts and Bills of Lading: Negotiation and Transfer

§ 7–501. Form of Negotiation and Requirements of "Due Negotiation".

(1) A negotiable document of title running to the order of a named person is negotiated by his indorsement and delivery. After his indorsement in blank or to bearer any person can negotiate it by delivery alone.

(2) (a) A negotiable document of title is also negotiated by delivery alone when by its original terms it runs to bearer.

(b) When a document running to the order of a named person is delivered to him the effect is the same as if the document had been negotiated.

(3) Negotiation of a negotiable document of title after it has been indorsed to a specified person requires indorsement by the special indorsee as well as delivery.

(4) A negotiable document of title is "duly negotiated" when it is negotiated in the manner stated in this section to a holder who purchases it in good faith without notice of any defense against or claim to it on the part of any person and for value, unless it is established that the negotiation is not in the regular course of business or financing or involves receiving the document in settlement or payment of a money obligation.

(5) Indorsement of a nonnegotiable document neither makes it negotiable nor adds to the transferee's rights.

(6) The naming in a negotiable bill of a person to be notified of the arrival of the goods does not limit the negotiability of the bill nor constitute notice to a purchaser thereof of any interest of such person in the goods.

§ 7–502. Rights Acquired by Due Negotiation.

(1) Subject to the following section and to the provisions of Section 7–205 on fungible goods, a holder to whom a negotiable document of title has been duly negotiated acquires thereby:

(a) title to the document;

(b) title to the goods;

(c) all rights accruing under the law of agency or estoppel, including rights to goods delivered to the bailee after the document was issued; and

(d) the direct obligation of the issuer to hold or deliver the goods according to the terms of the document free of any defense or claim by him except those arising under the terms of the document or under this Article. In the case of a delivery order the bailee's obligation accrues only upon acceptance and the obligation acquired by the holder is that the issuer and any indorser will procure the acceptance of the bailee.

(2) Subject to the following section, title and rights so acquired are not defeated by any stoppage of the goods represented by the document or by surrender of such goods by the bailee, and are not impaired even though the negotiation or any prior negotiation constituted a breach of duty or even though any person has been deprived of possession of the document by misrepresentation, fraud, accident, mistake, duress, loss, theft or conversion, or even though a previous sale or other transfer of the goods or document has been made to a third person.

§ 7–503. Document of Title to Goods Defeated in Certain Cases.

(1) A document of title confers no right in goods against a person who before issuance of the document had a legal interest or a perfected security interest in them and who neither

(a) delivered or entrusted them or any document of title covering them to the bailor or his nominee with actual or apparent authority to ship, store or sell or with power to obtain delivery under this Article (Section 7–403) or with power of disposition under this Act (Sections 2–403 and 9–307) or other statute or rule of law; nor

(b) acquiesced in the procurement by the bailor or his nominee of any document of title.

(2) Title to goods based upon an unaccepted delivery order is subject to the rights of anyone to whom a negotiable warehouse receipt or bill of lading covering the goods has been duly negotiated. Such a title may be defeated under the next section to the same extent as the rights of the issuer or a transferee from the issuer.

(3) Title to goods based upon a bill of lading issued to a freight forwarder is subject to the rights of anyone to whom a bill issued by the freight forwarder is duly negotiated; but delivery by the carrier in accordance with Part 4 of this Article pursuant to its own bill of lading discharges the carrier's obligation to deliver.

As amended in 1999.

§ 7–504. Rights Acquired in the Absence of Due Negotiation; Effect of Diversion; Seller's Stoppage of Delivery.

(1) A transferee of a document, whether negotiable or nonnegotiable, to whom the document has been delivered but not duly negotiated, acquires the title and rights which his transferor had or had actual authority to convey.

(2) In the case of a nonnegotiable document, until but not after the bailee receives notification of the transfer, the rights of the transferee may be defeated

(a) by those creditors of the transferor who could treat the sale as void under Section 2–402; or

(b) by a buyer from the transferor in ordinary course of business if the bailee has delivered the goods to the buyer or received notification of his rights; or

(c) as against the bailee by good faith dealings of the bailee with the transferor.

(3) A diversion or other change of shipping instructions by the consignor in a nonnegotiable bill of lading which causes the bailee not to deliver to the consignee defeats the consignee's title to the goods if they have been delivered to a buyer in ordinary course of business and in any event defeats the consignee's rights against the bailee.

(4) Delivery pursuant to a nonnegotiable document may be stopped by a seller under Section 2–705, and subject to the requirement of due notification there provided. A bailee honoring the seller's instructions is entitled to be indemnified by the seller against any resulting loss or expense.

§ 7–505. Indorser Not a Guarantor for Other Parties.

The indorsement of a document of title issued by a bailee does not make the indorser liable for any default by the bailee or by previous indorsers.

§ 7–506. Delivery Without Indorsement: Right to Compel Indorsement.

The transferee of a negotiable document of title has a specifically enforceable right to have his transferor supply any necessary indorsement but the transfer becomes a negotiation only as of the time the indorsement is supplied.

§ 7–507. Warranties on Negotiation or Transfer of Receipt or Bill.

Where a person negotiates or transfers a document of title for value otherwise than as a mere intermediary under the next following section, then unless otherwise agreed he warrants to his immediate purchaser only in addition to any warranty made in selling the goods

(a) that the document is genuine; and

(b) that he has no knowledge of any fact which would impair its validity or worth; and

(c) that his negotiation or transfer is rightful and fully effective with respect to the title to the document and the goods it represents.

§ 7–508. Warranties of Collecting Bank as to Documents.

A collecting bank or other intermediary known to be entrusted with documents on behalf of another or with collection of a draft or other claim against delivery of documents warrants by such delivery of the documents only its own good faith and authority. This rule applies even though the intermediary has purchased or made advances against the claim or draft to be collected.

§ 7–509. Receipt or Bill: When Adequate Compliance With Commercial Contract.

The question whether a document is adequate to fulfill the obligations of a contract for sale or the conditions of a credit is governed by the Articles on Sales (Article 2) and on Letters of Credit (Article 5).

Part 6—Warehouse Receipts and Bills of Lading: Miscellaneous Provisions

§ 7–601. Lost and Missing Documents.

(1) If a document has been lost, stolen or destroyed, a court may order delivery of the goods or issuance of a substitute document and the bailee may without liability to any person comply with such order. If the document was negotiable the claimant must post security approved by the court to indemnify any person who may suffer loss as a result of non-surrender of the document. If the document was not negotiable, such security may be required at the discretion of the court. The court may also in its discretion order payment of the bailee's reasonable costs and counsel fees.

(2) A bailee who without court order delivers goods to a person claiming under a missing negotiable document is liable to any person injured thereby, and if the delivery is not in good faith becomes liable for conversion. Delivery in good faith is not conversion if made in accordance with a filed classification or tariff or, where no classification or tariff is filed, if the claimant posts security with the bailee in an amount at least double the value of the goods at the time of posting to indemnify any person injured by the delivery who files a notice of claim within one year after the delivery.

§ 7–602. Attachment of Goods Covered by a Negotiable Document.

Except where the document was originally issued upon delivery of the goods by a person who had no power to dispose of them, no lien attaches by virtue of any judicial process to goods in the possession of a bailee for which a negotiable document of title is outstanding unless the document be first surrendered to the bailee or its negotiation enjoined, and the bailee shall not be compelled to deliver the goods pursuant to process until the document is surrendered to him or impounded by the court. One who purchases the document for value without notice of the process or injunction takes free of the lien imposed by judicial process.

§ 7–603. Conflicting Claims; Interpleader.

If more than one person claims title or possession of the goods, the bailee is excused from delivery until he has had a reasonable time to ascertain the validity of the adverse claims or to bring an action to compel all claimants to interplead and may compel such interpleader, either in defending an action for nondelivery of the goods, or by original action, whichever is appropriate.

REVISED ARTICLE 8: INVESTMENT SECURITIES

Part 1—Short Title and General Matters

§ 8–101. Short Title.

This Article may be cited as Uniform Commercial Code—Investment Securities.

§ 8–102. Definitions.

(a) In this Article:

(1) "Adverse claim" means a claim that a claimant has a property interest in a financial asset and that it is a violation of the rights of the claimant for another person to hold, transfer, or deal with the financial asset.

(2) "Bearer form," as applied to a certificated security, means a form in which the security is payable to the bearer of the security certificate according to its terms but not by reason of an indorsement.

(3) "Broker" means a person defined as a broker or dealer under the federal securities laws, but without excluding a bank acting in that capacity.

(4) "Certificated security" means a security that is represented by a certificate.

(5) "Clearing corporation" means:

    (i) a person that is registered as a "clearing agency" under the federal securities laws;

    (ii) a federal reserve bank; or

    (iii) any other person that provides clearance or settlement services with respect to financial assets that would require it to register as a clearing agency under the federal securities laws but for an exclusion or exemption from the registration requirement, if its activities as a clearing corporation, including promulgation of rules, are subject to regulation by a federal or state governmental authority.

(6) "Communicate" means to:

    (i) send a signed writing; or

    (ii) transmit information by any mechanism agreed upon by the persons transmitting and receiving the information.

(7) "Entitlement holder" means a person identified in the records of a securities intermediary as the person having a security entitlement against the securities intermediary. If a person acquires a security entitlement by virtue of Section 8–501(b)(2) or (3), that person is the entitlement holder.

(8) "Entitlement order" means a notification communicated to a securities intermediary directing transfer or redemption of a financial asset to which the entitlement holder has a security entitlement.

(9) "Financial asset," except as otherwise provided in Section 8–103, means:

    (i) a security;

    (ii) an obligation of a person or a share, participation, or other interest in a person or in property or an enterprise of a person, which is, or is of a type, dealt in or traded on financial markets, or which is recognized in any area in which it is issued or dealt in as a medium for investment; or

(iii) any property that is held by a securities intermediary for another person in a securities account if the securities intermediary has expressly agreed with the other person that the property is to be treated as a financial asset under this Article. As context requires, the term means either the interest itself or the means by which a person's claim to it is evidenced, including a certificated or uncertificated security, a security certificate, or a security entitlement.

(10) "Good faith," for purposes of the obligation of good faith in the performance or enforcement of contracts or duties within this Article, means honesty in fact and the observance of reasonable commercial standards of fair dealing.

(11) "Indorsement" means a signature that alone or accompanied by other words is made on a security certificate in registered form or on a separate document for the purpose of assigning, transferring, or redeeming the security or granting a power to assign, transfer, or redeem it.

(12) "Instruction" means a notification communi-cated to the issuer of an uncertificated security which directs that the transfer of the security be registered or that the security be redeemed.

(13) "Registered form," as applied to a certificated security, means a form in which:

(i) the security certificate specifies a person entitled to the security; and

(ii) a transfer of the security may be registered upon books maintained for that purpose by or on behalf of the issuer, or the security certificate so states.

(14) "Securities intermediary" means:

(i) a clearing corporation; or

(ii) a person, including a bank or broker, that in the ordinary course of its business maintains securities accounts for others and is acting in that capacity.

(15) "Security," except as otherwise provided in Section 8–103, means an obligation of an issuer or a share, participation, or other interest in an issuer or in property or an enterprise of an issuer:

(i) which is represented by a security certificate in bearer or registered form, or the transfer of which may be registered upon books maintained for that purpose by or on behalf of the issuer;

(ii) which is one of a class or series or by its terms is divisible into a class or series of shares, participations, interests, or obligations; and

(iii) which:

(A) is, or is of a type, dealt in or traded on securities exchanges or securities markets; or

(B) is a medium for investment and by its terms expressly provides that it is a security governed by this Article.

(16) "Security certificate" means a certificate representing a security.

(17) "Security entitlement" means the rights and property interest of an entitlement holder with respect to a financial asset specified in Part 5.

(18) "Uncertificated security" means a security that is not represented by a certificate.

(b) Other definitions applying to this Article and the sections in which they appear are:

Appropriate person	Section 8–107
Control	Section 8–106
Delivery	Section 8–301
Investment company security	Section 8–103
Issuer	Section 8–201
Overissue	Section 8–210
Protected purchaser	Section 8–303
Securities account	Section 8–501

(c) In addition, Article 1 contains general definitions and principles of construction and interpretation applicable throughout this Article.

(d) The characterization of a person, business, or transaction for purposes of this Article does not determine the characterization of the person, business, or transaction for purposes of any other law, regulation, or rule.

§ 8–103. Rules for Determining Whether Certain Obligations and Interests Are Securities or Financial Assets.

(a) A share or similar equity interest issued by a corporation, business trust, joint stock company, or similar entity is a security.

(b) An "investment company security" is a security. "Investment company security" means a share or similar equity interest issued by an entity that is registered as an investment company under the federal investment company laws, an interest in a unit investment trust that is so registered, or a face-amount certificate issued by a face-amount certificate company that is so registered. Investment company security does not include an insurance policy or endowment policy or annuity contract issued by an insurance company.

(c) An interest in a partnership or limited liability company is not a security unless it is dealt in or traded on securities exchanges or in securities markets, its terms expressly provide that it is a security governed by this Article, or it is an investment company security. However, an interest in a partnership or limited liability company is a financial asset if it is held in a securities account.

(d) A writing that is a security certificate is governed by this Article and not by Article 3, even though it also meets the requirements of that Article. However, a negotiable instrument governed by Article 3 is a financial asset if it is held in a securities account.

(e) An option or similar obligation issued by a clearing corporation to its participants is not a security, but is a financial asset.

(f) A commodity contract, as defined in Section 9–102(a)(15), is not a security or a financial asset.

As amended in 1999.

§ 8–104. Acquisition of Security or Financial Asset or Interest Therein.

(a) A person acquires a security or an interest therein, under this Article, if:

(1) the person is a purchaser to whom a security is delivered pursuant to Section 8–301; or

(2) the person acquires a security entitlement to the security pursuant to Section 8–501.

(b) A person acquires a financial asset, other than a security, or an interest therein, under this Article, if the person acquires a security entitlement to the financial asset.

(c) A person who acquires a security entitlement to a security or other financial asset has the rights specified in Part 5, but is a purchaser of any security, security entitlement, or other financial asset held by the securities intermediary only to the extent provided in Section 8–503.

(d) Unless the context shows that a different meaning is intended, a person who is required by other law, regulation, rule, or agreement to transfer, deliver, present, surrender, exchange, or otherwise put in the possession of another person a security or financial asset satisfies that requirement by causing the other person to acquire an interest in the security or financial asset pursuant to subsection (a) or (b).

§ 8–105. Notice of Adverse Claim.

(a) A person has notice of an adverse claim if:

    (1) the person knows of the adverse claim;

    (2) the person is aware of facts sufficient to indicate that there is a significant probability that the adverse claim exists and deliberately avoids information that would establish the existence of the adverse claim; or

    (3) the person has a duty, imposed by statute or regulation, to investigate whether an adverse claim exists, and the investigation so required would establish the existence of the adverse claim.

(b) Having knowledge that a financial asset or interest therein is or has been transferred by a representative imposes no duty of inquiry into the rightfulness of a transaction and is not notice of an adverse claim. However, a person who knows that a representative has transferred a financial asset or interest therein in a transaction that is, or whose proceeds are being used, for the individual benefit of the representative or otherwise in breach of duty has notice of an adverse claim.

(c) An act or event that creates a right to immediate performance of the principal obligation represented by a security certificate or sets a date on or after which the certificate is to be presented or surrendered for redemption or exchange does not itself constitute notice of an adverse claim except in the case of a transfer more than:

    (1) one year after a date set for presentment or surrender for redemption or exchange; or

    (2) six months after a date set for payment of money against presentation or surrender of the certificate, if money was available for payment on that date.

(d) A purchaser of a certificated security has notice of an adverse claim if the security certificate:

    (1) whether in bearer or registered form, has been indorsed "for collection" or "for surrender" or for some other purpose not involving transfer; or

    (2) is in bearer form and has on it an unambiguous statement that it is the property of a person other than the transferor, but the mere writing of a name on the certificate is not such a statement.

(e) Filing of a financing statement under Article 9 is not notice of an adverse claim to a financial asset.

§ 8–106. Control.

(a) A purchaser has "control" of a certificated security in bearer form if the certificated security is delivered to the purchaser.

(b) A purchaser has "control" of a certificated security in registered form if the certificated security is delivered to the purchaser, and:

    (1) the certificate is indorsed to the purchaser or in blank by an effective indorsement; or

    (2) the certificate is registered in the name of the purchaser, upon original issue or registration of transfer by the issuer.

(c) A purchaser has "control" of an uncertificated security if:

    (1) the uncertificated security is delivered to the purchaser; or

    (2) the issuer has agreed that it will comply with instructions originated by the purchaser without further consent by the registered owner.

(d) A purchaser has "control" of a security entitlement if:

    (1) the purchaser becomes the entitlement holder;

    (2) the securities intermediary has agreed that it will comply with entitlement orders originated by the purchaser without further consent by the entitlement holder; or

    (3) another person has control of the security entitlement on behalf of the purchaser or, having previously acquired control of the security entitlement, acknowledges that it has control on behalf of the purchaser.

(e) If an interest in a security entitlement is granted by the entitlement holder to the entitlement holder's own securities intermediary, the securities intermediary has control.

(f) A purchaser who has satisfied the requirements of subsection (c) or (d) has control, even if the registered owner in the case of subsection (c) or the entitlement holder in the case of subsection (d) retains the right to make substitutions for the uncertificated security or security entitlement, to originate instructions or entitlement orders to the issuer or securities intermediary, or otherwise to deal with the uncertificated security or security entitlement.

(g) An issuer or a securities intermediary may not enter into an agreement of the kind described in subsection (c)(2) or (d)(2) without the consent of the registered owner or entitlement holder, but an issuer or a securities intermediary is not required to enter into such an agreement even though the registered owner or entitlement holder so directs. An issuer or securities intermediary that has entered into such an agreement is not required to confirm the existence of the agreement to another party unless requested to do so by the registered owner or entitlement holder. As amended in 1999.

§ 8–107. Whether Indorsement, Instruction, or Entitlement Order Is Effective.

(a) "Appropriate person" means:

    (1) with respect to an indorsement, the person specified by a security certificate or by an effective special indorsement to be entitled to the security;

    (2) with respect to an instruction, the registered owner of an uncertificated security;

    (3) with respect to an entitlement order, the entitlement holder;

    (4) if the person designated in paragraph (1), (2), or (3) is deceased, the designated person's successor taking under other law or the designated person's personal representative acting for the estate of the decedent; or

    (5) if the person designated in paragraph (1), (2), or (3) lacks capacity, the designated person's guardian, conservator, or other similar representative who has power under other law to transfer the security or financial asset.

(b) An indorsement, instruction, or entitlement order is effective if:

    (1) it is made by the appropriate person;

    (2) it is made by a person who has power under the law of agency to transfer the security or financial asset on behalf of the appropriate person, including, in the case of an instruction or entitlement order, a person who has control under Section 8–106(c)(2) or (d)(2); or

(3) the appropriate person has ratified it or is otherwise precluded from asserting its ineffectiveness.

(c) An indorsement, instruction, or entitlement order made by a representative is effective even if:

(1) the representative has failed to comply with a controlling instrument or with the law of the State having jurisdiction of the representative relationship, including any law requiring the representative to obtain court approval of the transaction; or

(2) the representative's action in making the indorsement, instruction, or entitlement order or using the proceeds of the transaction is otherwise a breach of duty.

(d) If a security is registered in the name of or specially indorsed to a person described as a representative, or if a securities account is maintained in the name of a person described as a representative, an indorsement, instruction, or entitlement order made by the person is effective even though the person is no longer serving in the described capacity.

(e) Effectiveness of an indorsement, instruction, or entitlement order is determined as of the date the indorsement, instruction, or entitlement order is made, and an indorsement, instruction, or entitlement order does not become ineffective by reason of any later change of circumstances.

§ 8–108. Warranties in Direct Holding.

(a) A person who transfers a certificated security to a purchaser for value warrants to the purchaser, and an indorser, if the transfer is by indorsement, warrants to any subsequent purchaser, that:

(1) the certificate is genuine and has not been materially altered;

(2) the transferor or indorser does not know of any fact that might impair the validity of the security;

(3) there is no adverse claim to the security;

(4) the transfer does not violate any restriction on transfer;

(5) if the transfer is by indorsement, the indorsement is made by an appropriate person, or if the indorsement is by an agent, the agent has actual authority to act on behalf of the appropriate person; and

(6) the transfer is otherwise effective and rightful.

(b) A person who originates an instruction for registration of transfer of an uncertificated security to a purchaser for value warrants to the purchaser that:

(1) the instruction is made by an appropriate person, or if the instruction is by an agent, the agent has actual authority to act on behalf of the appropriate person;

(2) the security is valid;

(3) there is no adverse claim to the security; and

(4) at the time the instruction is presented to the issuer:

(i) the purchaser will be entitled to the registration of transfer;

(ii) the transfer will be registered by the issuer free from all liens, security interests, restrictions, and claims other than those specified in the instruction;

(iii) the transfer will not violate any restriction on transfer; and

(iv) the requested transfer will otherwise be effective and rightful.

(c) A person who transfers an uncertificated security to a purchaser for value and does not originate an instruction in connection with the transfer warrants that:

(1) the uncertificated security is valid;

(2) there is no adverse claim to the security;

(3) the transfer does not violate any restriction on transfer; and

(4) the transfer is otherwise effective and rightful.

(d) A person who indorses a security certificate warrants to the issuer that:

(1) there is no adverse claim to the security; and

(2) the indorsement is effective.

(e) A person who originates an instruction for registration of transfer of an uncertificated security warrants to the issuer that:

(1) the instruction is effective; and

(2) at the time the instruction is presented to the issuer the purchaser will be entitled to the registration of transfer.

(f) A person who presents a certificated security for registration of transfer or for payment or exchange warrants to the issuer that the person is entitled to the registration, payment, or exchange, but a purchaser for value and without notice of adverse claims to whom transfer is registered warrants only that the person has no knowledge of any unauthorized signature in a necessary indorsement.

(g) If a person acts as agent of another in delivering a certificated security to a purchaser, the identity of the principal was known to the person to whom the certificate was delivered, and the certificate delivered by the agent was received by the agent from the principal or received by the agent from another person at the direction of the principal, the person delivering the security certificate warrants only that the delivering person has authority to act for the principal and does not know of any adverse claim to the certificated security.

(h) A secured party who redelivers a security certificate received, or after payment and on order of the debtor delivers the security certificate to another person, makes only the warranties of an agent under subsection (g).

(i) Except as otherwise provided in subsection (g), a broker acting for a customer makes to the issuer and a purchaser the warranties provided in subsections (a) through (f). A broker that delivers a security certificate to its customer, or causes its customer to be registered as the owner of an uncertificated security, makes to the customer the warranties provided in subsection (a) or (b), and has the rights and privileges of a purchaser under this section. The warranties of and in favor of the broker acting as an agent are in addition to applicable warranties given by and in favor of the customer.

§ 8–109. Warranties in Indirect Holding.

(a) A person who originates an entitlement order to a securities intermediary warrants to the securities intermediary that:

(1) the entitlement order is made by an appropriate person, or if the entitlement order is by an agent, the agent has actual authority to act on behalf of the appropriate person; and

(2) there is no adverse claim to the security entitlement.

(b) A person who delivers a security certificate to a securities intermediary for credit to a securities account or originates an instruction with respect to an uncertificated security directing that the uncertificated security be credited to a securities account makes to the securities intermediary the warranties specified in Section 8–108(a) or (b).

(c) If a securities intermediary delivers a security certificate to its entitlement holder or causes its entitlement holder to be registered as the owner of an uncertificated security, the securities intermediary makes to the entitlement holder the warranties specified in Section 8–108(a) or (b).

§ 8–110. Applicability; Choice of Law.

(a) The local law of the issuer's jurisdiction, as specified in subsection (d), governs:

(1) the validity of a security;

(2) the rights and duties of the issuer with respect to registration of transfer;

(3) the effectiveness of registration of transfer by the issuer;

(4) whether the issuer owes any duties to an adverse claimant to a security; and

(5) whether an adverse claim can be asserted against a person to whom transfer of a certificated or uncertificated security is registered or a person who obtains control of an uncertificated security.

(b) The local law of the securities intermediary's jurisdiction, as specified in subsection (e), governs:

(1) acquisition of a security entitlement from the securities intermediary;

(2) the rights and duties of the securities intermediary and entitlement holder arising out of a security entitlement;

(3) whether the securities intermediary owes any duties to an adverse claimant to a security entitlement; and

(4) whether an adverse claim can be asserted against a person who acquires a security entitlement from the securities intermediary or a person who purchases a security entitlement or interest therein from an entitlement holder.

(c) The local law of the jurisdiction in which a security certificate is located at the time of delivery governs whether an adverse claim can be asserted against a person to whom the security certificate is delivered.

(d) "Issuer's jurisdiction" means the jurisdiction under which the issuer of the security is organized or, if permitted by the law of that jurisdiction, the law of another jurisdiction specified by the issuer. An issuer organized under the law of this State may specify the law of another jurisdiction as the law governing the matters specified in subsection (a)(2) through (5).

(e) The following rules determine a "securities intermediary's jurisdiction" for purposes of this section:

(1) If an agreement between the securities intermediary and its entitlement holder specifies that it is governed by the law of a particular jurisdiction, that jurisdiction is the securities intermediary's jurisdiction.

(2) If an agreement between the securities intermediary and its entitlement holder does not specify the governing law as provided in paragraph (1), but expressly specifies that the securities account is maintained at an office in a particular jurisdiction, that jurisdiction is the securities intermediary's jurisdiction.

(3) If neither paragraph (1) nor paragraph (2) applies and an agreement between the securities intermediary and its entitlement holder governing the securities account expressly provides that the securities account is maintained at an office in a particular jurisdiction, that jurisdiction is the securities intermediary's jurisdiction.

(4) If none of the preceding paragraph applies, the securities intermediary's jurisdiction is the jurisdiction in which the office identified in an account statement as the office serving the entitlement holder's account is located.

(5) If none of the preceding paragraphs applies, the securities intermediary's jurisdiction is the jurisdiction in which the chief executive office of the securities intermediary is located.

(f) A securities intermediary's jurisdiction is not determined by the physical location of certificates representing financial assets, or by the jurisdiction in which is organized the issuer of the financial asset with respect to which an entitlement holder has a security entitlement, or by the location of facilities for data processing or other record keeping concerning the account.

As amended in 1999.

§ 8–111. Clearing Corporation Rules.

A rule adopted by a clearing corporation governing rights and obligations among the clearing corporation and its participants in the clearing corporation is effective even if the rule conflicts with this [Act] and affects another party who does not consent to the rule.

§ 8–112. Creditor's Legal Process.

(a) The interest of a debtor in a certificated security may be reached by a creditor only by actual seizure of the security certificate by the officer making the attachment or levy, except as otherwise provided in subsection (d). However, a certificated security for which the certificate has been surrendered to the issuer may be reached by a creditor by legal process upon the issuer.

(b) The interest of a debtor in an uncertificated security may be reached by a creditor only by legal process upon the issuer at its chief executive office in the United States, except as otherwise provided in subsection (d).

(c) The interest of a debtor in a security entitlement may be reached by a creditor only by legal process upon the securities intermediary with whom the debtor's securities account is maintained, except as otherwise provided in subsection (d).

(d) The interest of a debtor in a certificated security for which the certificate is in the possession of a secured party, or in an uncertificated security registered in the name of a secured party, or a security entitlement maintained in the name of a secured party, may be reached by a creditor by legal process upon the secured party.

(e) A creditor whose debtor is the owner of a certificated security, uncertificated security, or security entitlement is entitled to aid from a court of competent jurisdiction, by injunction or otherwise, in reaching the certificated security, uncertificated security, or security entitlement or in satisfying the claim by means allowed at law or in equity in regard to property that cannot readily be reached by other legal process.

§ 8–113. Statute of Frauds Inapplicable.

A contract or modification of a contract for the sale or purchase of a security is enforceable whether or not there is a writing signed or record authenticated by a party against whom enforcement is sought, even if the contract or modification is not capable of performance within one year of its making.

§ 8–114. Evidentiary Rules Concerning Certificated Securities.

The following rules apply in an action on a certificated security against the issuer:

(1) Unless specifically denied in the pleadings, each signature on a security certificate or in a necessary indorsement is admitted.

(2) If the effectiveness of a signature is put in issue, the burden of establishing effectiveness is on the party claiming under the signature, but the signature is presumed to be genuine or authorized.

(3) If signatures on a security certificate are admitted or established, production of the certificate entitles a holder to recover on it unless the defendant establishes a defense or a defect going to the validity of the security.

(4) If it is shown that a defense or defect exists, the plaintiff has the burden of establishing that the plaintiff or some person under whom the plaintiff claims is a person against whom the defense or defect cannot be asserted.

§ 8–115. Securities Intermediary and Others Not Liable to Adverse Claimant.

A securities intermediary that has transferred a financial asset pursuant to an effective entitlement order, or a broker or other agent or bailee that has dealt with a financial asset at the direction of its customer or principal, is not liable to a person having an adverse claim to the financial asset, unless the securities intermediary, or broker or other agent or bailee:

(1) took the action after it had been served with an injunction, restraining order, or other legal process enjoining it from doing so, issued by a court of competent jurisdiction, and had a reasonable opportunity to act on the injunction, restraining order, or other legal process; or

(2) acted in collusion with the wrongdoer in violating the rights of the adverse claimant; or

(3) in the case of a security certificate that has been stolen, acted with notice of the adverse claim.

§ 8–116. Securities Intermediary as Purchaser for Value.

A securities intermediary that receives a financial asset and establishes a security entitlement to the financial asset in favor of an entitlement holder is a purchaser for value of the financial asset. A securities intermediary that acquires a security entitlement to a financial asset from another securities intermediary acquires the security entitlement for value if the securities intermediary acquiring the security entitlement establishes a security entitlement to the financial asset in favor of an entitlement holder.

Part 2—Issue and Issuer

§ 8–201. Issuer.

(a) With respect to an obligation on or a defense to a security, an "issuer" includes a person that:

(1) places or authorizes the placing of its name on a security certificate, other than as authenticating trustee, registrar, transfer agent, or the like, to evidence a share, participation, or other interest in its property or in an enterprise, or to evidence its duty to perform an obligation represented by the certificate;

(2) creates a share, participation, or other interest in its property or in an enterprise, or undertakes an obligation, that is an uncertificated security;

(3) directly or indirectly creates a fractional interest in its rights or property, if the fractional interest is represented by a security certificate; or

(4) becomes responsible for, or in place of, another person described as an issuer in this section.

(b) With respect to an obligation on or defense to a security, a guarantor is an issuer to the extent of its guaranty, whether or not its obligation is noted on a security certificate.

(c) With respect to a registration of a transfer, issuer means a person on whose behalf transfer books are maintained.

§ 8–202. Issuer's Responsibility and Defenses; Notice of Defect or Defense.

(a) Even against a purchaser for value and without notice, the terms of a certificated security include terms stated on the certificate and terms made part of the security by reference on the certificate to another instrument, indenture, or document or to a constitution, statute, ordinance, rule, regulation, order, or the like, to the extent the terms referred to do not conflict with terms stated on the certificate. A reference under this subsection does not of itself charge a purchaser for value with notice of a defect going to the validity of the security, even if the certificate expressly states that a person accepting it admits notice. The terms of an uncertificated security include those stated in any instrument, indenture, or document or in a constitution, statute, ordinance, rule, regulation, order, or the like, pursuant to which the security is issued.

(b) The following rules apply if an issuer asserts that a security is not valid:

(1) A security other than one issued by a government or governmental subdivision, agency, or instrumentality, even though issued with a defect going to its validity, is valid in the hands of a purchaser for value and without notice of the particular defect unless the defect involves a violation of a constitutional provision. In that case, the security is valid in the hands of a purchaser for value and without notice of the defect, other than one who takes by original issue.

(2) Paragraph (1) applies to an issuer that is a government or governmental subdivision, agency, or instrumentality only if there has been substantial compliance with the legal requirements governing the issue or the issuer has received a substantial consideration for the issue as a whole or for the particular security and a stated purpose of the issue is one for which the issuer has power to borrow money or issue the security.

(c) Except as otherwise provided in Section 8–205, lack of genuineness of a certificated security is a complete defense, even against a purchaser for value and without notice.

(d) All other defenses of the issuer of a security, including nondelivery and conditional delivery of a certificated security, are ineffective against a purchaser for value who has taken the certificated security without notice of the particular defense.

(e) This section does not affect the right of a party to cancel a contract for a security "when, as and if issued" or "when distributed" in the event of a material change in the character of the security that is the subject of the contract or in the plan or arrangement pursuant to which the security is to be issued or distributed.

(f) If a security is held by a securities intermediary against whom an entitlement holder has a security entitlement with respect to the security, the issuer may not assert any defense that the issuer could not assert if the entitlement holder held the security directly.

§ 8–203. Staleness as Notice of Defect or Defense.

After an act or event, other than a call that has been revoked, creating a right to immediate performance of the principal obligation represented by a certificated security or setting a date on or after which the security is to be presented or surrendered for redemption or exchange, a purchaser is charged with notice of any defect in its issue or defense of the issuer, if the act or event:

(1) requires the payment of money, the delivery of a certificated security, the registration of transfer of an uncertificated security, or any of them on presentation or surrender of the security certificate, the money or security is available on the date set for payment or exchange, and the purchaser takes the security more than one year after that date; or

(2) is not covered by paragraph (1) and the purchaser takes the security more than two years after the date set for surrender or presentation or the date on which performance became due.

§ 8–204. Effect of Issuer's Restriction on Transfer.

A restriction on transfer of a security imposed by the issuer, even if otherwise lawful, is ineffective against a person without knowledge of the restriction unless:

(1) the security is certificated and the restriction is noted conspicuously on the security certificate; or

(2) the security is uncertificated and the registered owner has been notified of the restriction.

§ 8–205. Effect of Unauthorized Signature on Security Certificate.

An unauthorized signature placed on a security certificate before or in the course of issue is ineffective, but the signature is effective in favor of a purchaser for value of the certificated security if the purchaser is without notice of the lack of authority and the signing has been done by:

(1) an authenticating trustee, registrar, transfer agent, or other person entrusted by the issuer with the signing of the security certificate or of similar security certificates, or the immediate preparation for signing of any of them; or

(2) an employee of the issuer, or of any of the persons listed in paragraph (1), entrusted with responsible handling of the security certificate.

§ 8–206. Completion of Alteration of Security Certificate.

(a) If a security certificate contains the signatures necessary to its issue or transfer but is incomplete in any other respect:

(1) any person may complete it by filling in the blanks as authorized; and

(2) even if the blanks are incorrectly filled in, the security certificate as completed is enforceable by a purchaser who took it for value and without notice of the incorrectness.

(b) A complete security certificate that has been improperly altered, even if fraudulently, remains enforceable, but only according to its original terms.

§ 8–207. Rights and Duties of Issuer with Respect to Registered Owners.

(a) Before due presentment for registration of transfer of a certificated security in registered form or of an instruction requesting registration of transfer of an uncertificated security, the issuer or indenture trustee may treat the registered owner as the person exclusively entitled to vote, receive notifications, and otherwise exercise all the rights and powers of an owner.

(b) This Article does not affect the liability of the registered owner of a security for a call, assessment, or the like.

§ 8–208. Effect of Signature of Authenticating Trustee, Registrar, or Transfer Agent.

(a) A person signing a security certificate as authenticating trustee, registrar, transfer agent, or the like, warrants to a purchaser for value of the certificated security, if the purchaser is without notice of a particular defect, that:

(1) the certificate is genuine;

(2) the person's own participation in the issue of the security is within the person's capacity and within the scope of the authority received by the person from the issuer; and

(3) the person has reasonable grounds to believe that the certificated security is in the form and within the amount the issuer is authorized to issue.

(b) Unless otherwise agreed, a person signing under subsection (a) does not assume responsibility for the validity of the security in other respects.

§ 8–209. Issuer's Lien.

A lien in favor of an issuer upon a certificated security is valid against a purchaser only if the right of the issuer to the lien is noted conspicuously on the security certificate.

§ 8–210. Overissue.

(a) In this section, "overissue" means the issue of securities in excess of the amount the issuer has corporate power to issue, but an overissue does not occur if appropriate action has cured the overissue.

(b) Except as otherwise provided in subsections (c) and (d), the provisions of this Article which validate a security or compel its issue or reissue do not apply to the extent that validation, issue, or reissue would result in overissue.

(c) If an identical security not constituting an overissue is reasonably available for purchase, a person entitled to issue or validation may compel the issuer to purchase the security and deliver it if certificated or register its transfer if uncertificated, against surrender of any security certificate the person holds.

(d) If a security is not reasonably available for purchase, a person entitled to issue or validation may recover from the issuer the price the person or the last purchaser for value paid for it with interest from the date of the person's demand.

Part 3—Transfer of Certificated and Uncertificated Securities

§ 8–301. Delivery.

(a) Delivery of a certificated security to a purchaser occurs when:

(1) the purchaser acquires possession of the security certificate;

(2) another person, other than a securities intermediary, either acquires possession of the security certificate on behalf of the purchaser or, having previously acquired possession of the certificate, acknowledges that it holds for the purchaser; or

(3) a securities intermediary acting on behalf of the purchaser acquires possession of the security certificate, only if the certificate is in registered form and is (i) registered in the name of the purchaser, (ii) payable to the order of the purchaser, or (iii) specially indorsed to the purchaser by an effective indorsement and has not been indorsed to the securities intermediary or in blank.

(b) Delivery of an uncertificated security to a purchaser occurs when:

(1) the issuer registers the purchaser as the registered owner, upon original issue or registration of transfer; or

(2) another person, other than a securities intermediary, either becomes the registered owner of the uncertificated security on behalf of the purchaser or, having previously become the registered owner, acknowledges that it holds for the purchaser.

As amended in 1999.

§ 8–302. Rights of Purchaser.

(a) Except as otherwise provided in subsections (b) and (c), upon delivery of a certificated or uncertificated security to a purchaser, the purchaser acquires all rights in the security that the transferor had or had power to transfer.

(b) A purchaser of a limited interest acquires rights only to the extent of the interest purchased.

(c) A purchaser of a certificated security who as a previous holder had notice of an adverse claim does not improve its position by taking from a protected purchaser.
As amended in 1999.

§ 8–303. Protected Purchaser.

(a) "Protected purchaser" means a purchaser of a certificated or uncertificated security, or of an interest therein, who:

(1) gives value;

(2) does not have notice of any adverse claim to the security; and

(3) obtains control of the certificated or uncertificated security.

(b) In addition to acquiring the rights of a purchaser, a protected purchaser also acquires its interest in the security free of any adverse claim.

§ 8–304. Indorsement.

(a) An indorsement may be in blank or special. An indorsement in blank includes an indorsement to bearer. A special indorsement specifies to whom a security is to be transferred or who has power to transfer it. A holder may convert a blank indorsement to a special indorsement.

(b) An indorsement purporting to be only of part of a security certificate representing units intended by the issuer to be separately transferable is effective to the extent of the indorsement.

(c) An indorsement, whether special or in blank, does not constitute a transfer until delivery of the certificate on which it appears or, if the indorsement is on a separate document, until delivery of both the document and the certificate.

(d) If a security certificate in registered form has been delivered to a purchaser without a necessary indorsement, the purchaser may become a protected purchaser only when the indorsement is supplied. However, against a transferor, a transfer is complete upon delivery and the purchaser has a specifically enforceable right to have any necessary indorsement supplied.

(e) An indorsement of a security certificate in bearer form may give notice of an adverse claim to the certificate, but it does not otherwise affect a right to registration that the holder possesses.

(f) Unless otherwise agreed, a person making an indorsement assumes only the obligations provided in Section 8–108 and not an obligation that the security will be honored by the issuer.

§ 8–305. Instruction.

(a) If an instruction has been originated by an appropriate person but is incomplete in any other respect, any person may complete it as authorized and the issuer may rely on it as completed, even though it has been completed incorrectly.

(b) Unless otherwise agreed, a person initiating an instruction assumes only the obligations imposed by Section 8–108 and not an obligation that the security will be honored by the issuer.

§ 8–306. Effect of Guaranteeing Signature, Indorsement, or Instruction.

(a) A person who guarantees a signature of an indorser of a security certificate warrants that at the time of signing:

(1) the signature was genuine;

(2) the signer was an appropriate person to indorse, or if the signature is by an agent, the agent had actual authority to act on behalf of the appropriate person; and

(3) the signer had legal capacity to sign.

(b) A person who guarantees a signature of the originator of an instruction warrants that at the time of signing:

(1) the signature was genuine;

(2) the signer was an appropriate person to originate the instruction, or if the signature is by an agent, the agent had actual authority to act on behalf of the appropriate person, if the person specified in the instruction as the registered owner was, in fact, the registered owner, as to which fact the signature guarantor does not make a warranty; and

(3) the signer had legal capacity to sign.

(c) A person who specially guarantees the signature of an originator of an instruction makes the warranties of a signature guarantor under subsection (b) and also warrants that at the time the instruction is presented to the issuer:

(1) the person specified in the instruction as the registered owner of the uncertificated security will be the registered owner; and

(2) the transfer of the uncertificated security requested in the instruction will be registered by the issuer free from all liens, security interests, restrictions, and claims other than those specified in the instruction.

(d) A guarantor under subsections (a) and (b) or a special guarantor under subsection (c) does not otherwise warrant the rightfulness of the transfer.

(e) A person who guarantees an indorsement of a security certificate makes the warranties of a signature guarantor under subsection (a) and also warrants the rightfulness of the transfer in all respects.

(f) A person who guarantees an instruction requesting the transfer of an uncertificated security makes the warranties of a special signature guarantor under subsection (c) and also warrants the rightfulness of the transfer in all respects.

(g) An issuer may not require a special guaranty of signature, a guaranty of indorsement, or a guaranty of instruction as a condition to registration of transfer.

(h) The warranties under this section are made to a person taking or dealing with the security in reliance on the guaranty, and the guarantor is liable to the person for loss resulting from their breach. An indorser or originator of an instruction whose signature, indorsement, or instruction has been guaranteed is liable to a guarantor for any loss suffered by the guarantor as a result of breach of the warranties of the guarantor.

§ 8–307. Purchaser's Right to Requisites for Registration of Transfer.

Unless otherwise agreed, the transferor of a security on due demand shall supply the purchaser with proof of authority to transfer or with any other requisite necessary to obtain registration of the transfer of the security, but if the transfer is not for value, a transferor need not comply unless the purchaser pays the necessary expenses. If the transferor fails within a reasonable time to comply with the demand, the purchaser may reject or rescind the transfer.

Part 4—Registration

§ 8–401. Duty of Issuer to Register Transfer.

(a) If a certificated security in registered form is presented to an issuer with a request to register transfer or an instruction is presented to an issuer with a request to register transfer of an uncertificated security, the issuer shall register the transfer as requested if:

(1) under the terms of the security the person seeking registration of transfer is eligible to have the security registered in its name;

(2) the indorsement or instruction is made by the appropriate person or by an agent who has actual authority to act on behalf of the appropriate person;

(3) reasonable assurance is given that the indorsement or instruction is genuine and authorized (Section 8–402);

(4) any applicable law relating to the collection of taxes has been complied with;

(5) the transfer does not violate any restriction on transfer imposed by the issuer in accordance with Section 8–204;

(6) a demand that the issuer not register transfer has not become effective under Section 8–403, or the issuer has complied with Section 8–403(b) but no legal process or indemnity bond is obtained as provided in Section 8–403(d); and

(7) the transfer is in fact rightful or is to a protected purchaser.

(b) If an issuer is under a duty to register a transfer of a security, the issuer is liable to a person presenting a certificated security or an instruction for registration or to the person's principal for loss resulting from unreasonable delay in registration or failure or refusal to register the transfer.

§ 8–402. Assurance That Indorsement or Instruction Is Effective.

(a) An issuer may require the following assurance that each necessary indorsement or each instruction is genuine and authorized:

(1) in all cases, a guaranty of the signature of the person making an indorsement or originating an instruction including, in the case of an instruction, reasonable assurance of identity;

(2) if the indorsement is made or the instruction is originated by an agent, appropriate assurance of actual authority to sign;

(3) if the indorsement is made or the instruction is originated by a fiduciary pursuant to Section 8–107(a)(4) or (a)(5), appropriate evidence of appointment or incumbency;

(4) if there is more than one fiduciary, reasonable assurance that all who are required to sign have done so; and

(5) if the indorsement is made or the instruction is originated by a person not covered by another provision of this subsection, assurance appropriate to the case corresponding as nearly as may be to the provisions of this subsection.

(b) An issuer may elect to require reasonable assurance beyond that specified in this section.

(c) In this section:

(1) "Guaranty of the signature" means a guaranty signed by or on behalf of a person reasonably believed by the issuer to be responsible. An issuer may adopt standards with respect to responsibility if they are not manifestly unreasonable.

(2) "Appropriate evidence of appointment or incumbency" means:

(i) in the case of a fiduciary appointed or qualified by a court, a certificate issued by or under the direction or supervision of the court or an officer thereof and dated within 60 days before the date of presentation for transfer; or

(ii) in any other case, a copy of a document showing the appointment or a certificate issued by or on behalf of a person reasonably believed by an issuer to be responsible or, in the absence of that document or certificate, other evidence the issuer reasonably considers appropriate.

§ 8–403. Demand That Issuer Not Register Transfer.

(a) A person who is an appropriate person to make an indorsement or originate an instruction may demand that the issuer not register transfer of a security by communicating to the issuer a notification that identifies the registered owner and the issue of which the security is a part and provides an address for communications directed to the person making the demand. The demand is effective only if it is received by the issuer at a time and in a manner affording the issuer reasonable opportunity to act on it.

(b) If a certificated security in registered form is presented to an issuer with a request to register transfer or an instruction is presented to an issuer with a request to register transfer of an uncertificated security after a demand that the issuer not register transfer has become effective, the issuer shall promptly communicate to (i) the person who initiated the demand at the address provided in the demand and (ii) the person who presented the security for registration of transfer or initiated the instruction requesting registration of transfer a notification stating that:

(1) the certificated security has been presented for registration of transfer or the instruction for registration of transfer of the uncertificated security has been received;

(2) a demand that the issuer not register transfer had previously been received; and

(3) the issuer will withhold registration of transfer for a period of time stated in the notification in order to provide the person who initiated the demand an opportunity to obtain legal process or an indemnity bond.

(c) The period described in subsection (b)(3) may not exceed 30 days after the date of communication of the notification. A shorter period may be specified by the issuer if it is not manifestly unreasonable.

(d) An issuer is not liable to a person who initiated a demand that the issuer not register transfer for any loss the person suffers as a result of registration of a transfer pursuant to an effective indorsement or instruction if the person who initiated the demand does not, within the time stated in the issuer's communication, either:

(1) obtain an appropriate restraining order, injunction, or other process from a court of competent jurisdiction enjoining the issuer from registering the transfer; or

(2) file with the issuer an indemnity bond, sufficient in the issuer's judgment to protect the issuer and any transfer agent, registrar, or other agent of the issuer involved from any loss it or they may suffer by refusing to register the transfer.

(e) This section does not relieve an issuer from liability for registering transfer pursuant to an indorsement or instruction that was not effective.

§ 8–404. Wrongful Registration.

(a) Except as otherwise provided in Section 8–406, an issuer is liable for wrongful registration of transfer if the issuer has registered a transfer of a security to a person not entitled to it, and the transfer was registered:

(1) pursuant to an ineffective indorsement or instruction;

(2) after a demand that the issuer not register transfer became effective under Section 8–403(a) and the issuer did not comply with Section 8–403(b);

(3) after the issuer had been served with an injunction, restraining order, or other legal process enjoining it from registering the transfer, issued by a court of competent jurisdiction, and the issuer had a reasonable opportunity to act on the injunction, restraining order, or other legal process; or

(4) by an issuer acting in collusion with the wrongdoer.

(b) An issuer that is liable for wrongful registration of transfer under subsection (a) on demand shall provide the person entitled to the security with a like certificated or uncertificated security, and any payments or distributions that the person did not receive as a result of the wrongful registration. If an overissue would result, the issuer's liability to provide the person with a like security is governed by Section 8–210.

(c) Except as otherwise provided in subsection (a) or in a law relating to the collection of taxes, an issuer is not liable to an owner or other person suffering loss as a result of the registration of a transfer of a security if registration was made pursuant to an effective indorsement or instruction.

§ 8–405. Replacement of Lost, Destroyed, or Wrongfully Taken Security Certificate.

(a) If an owner of a certificated security, whether in registered or bearer form, claims that the certificate has been lost, destroyed, or wrongfully taken, the issuer shall issue a new certificate if the owner:

(1) so requests before the issuer has notice that the certificate has been acquired by a protected purchaser;

(2) files with the issuer a sufficient indemnity bond; and

(3) satisfies other reasonable requirements imposed by the issuer.

(b) If, after the issue of a new security certificate, a protected purchaser of the original certificate presents it for registration of transfer, the issuer shall register the transfer unless an overissue would result. In that case, the issuer's liability is governed by Section 8–210. In addition to any rights on the indemnity bond, an issuer may recover the new certificate from a person to whom it was issued or any person taking under that person, except a protected purchaser.

§ 8–406. Obligation to Notify Issuer of Lost, Destroyed, or Wrongfully Taken Security Certificate.

If a security certificate has been lost, apparently destroyed, or wrongfully taken, and the owner fails to notify the issuer of that fact within a reasonable time after the owner has notice of it and the issuer registers a transfer of the security before receiving notification, the owner may not assert against the issuer a claim for registering the transfer under Section 8–404 or a claim to a new security certificate under Section 8–405.

§ 8–407. Authenticating Trustee, Transfer Agent, and Registrar.

A person acting as authenticating trustee, transfer agent, registrar, or other agent for an issuer in the registration of a transfer of its securities, in the issue of new security certificates or uncertificated securities, or in the cancellation of surrendered security certificates has the same obligation to the holder or owner of a certificated or uncertificated security with regard to the particular functions performed as the issuer has in regard to those functions.

Part 5 Security Entitlements

§ 8–501. Securities Account; Acquisition of Security Entitlement from Securities Intermediary.

(a) "Securities account" means an account to which a financial asset is or may be credited in accordance with an agreement under which the person maintaining the account undertakes to treat the person for whom the account is maintained as entitled to exercise the rights that comprise the financial asset.

(b) Except as otherwise provided in subsections (d) and (e), a person acquires a security entitlement if a securities intermediary:

(1) indicates by book entry that a financial asset has been credited to the person's securities account;

(2) receives a financial asset from the person or acquires a financial asset for the person and, in either case, accepts it for credit to the person's securities account; or

(3) becomes obligated under other law, regulation, or rule to credit a financial asset to the person's securities account.

(c) If a condition of subsection (b) has been met, a person has a security entitlement even though the securities intermediary does not itself hold the financial asset.

(d) If a securities intermediary holds a financial asset for another person, and the financial asset is registered in the name of, payable to the order of, or specially indorsed to the other person, and has not been indorsed to the securities intermediary or in blank, the other person is treated as holding the financial asset directly rather than as having a security entitlement with respect to the financial asset.

(e) Issuance of a security is not establishment of a security entitlement.

§ 8–502. Assertion of Adverse Claim against Entitlement Holder.

An action based on an adverse claim to a financial asset, whether framed in conversion, replevin, constructive trust, equitable lien, or other theory, may not be asserted against a person who acquires a security entitlement under Section 8–501 for value and without notice of the adverse claim.

§ 8–503. Property Interest of Entitlement Holder in Financial Asset Held by Securities Intermediary.

(a) To the extent necessary for a securities intermediary to satisfy all security entitlements with respect to a particular financial asset, all interests in that financial asset held by the securities intermediary are held by the securities intermediary for the entitlement holders, are not property of the securities intermediary, and are not subject to claims of creditors of the securities intermediary, except as otherwise provided in Section 8–511.

(b) An entitlement holder's property interest with respect to a particular financial asset under subsection (a) is a pro rata property interest in all interests in that financial asset held by the securities intermediary, without regard to the time the entitlement holder acquired the security entitlement or the time the securities intermediary acquired the interest in that financial asset.

(c) An entitlement holder's property interest with respect to a particular financial asset under subsection (a) may be enforced against the securities intermediary only by exercise of the entitlement holder's rights under Sections 8–505 through 8–508.

(d) An entitlement holder's property interest with respect to a particular financial asset under subsection (a) may be enforced against a purchaser of the financial asset or interest therein only if:

(1) insolvency proceedings have been initiated by or against the securities intermediary;

(2) the securities intermediary does not have sufficient interests in the financial asset to satisfy the security entitlements of all of its entitlement holders to that financial asset;

(3) the securities intermediary violated its obligations under Section 8–504 by transferring the financial asset or interest therein to the purchaser; and

(4) the purchaser is not protected under sub-section (e).

The trustee or other liquidator, acting on behalf of all entitlement holders having security entitlements with respect to a particular financial asset, may recover the financial asset, or interest therein, from the purchaser. If the trustee or other liquidator elects not to pursue that right, an entitlement holder whose security entitlement remains unsatisfied has the right to recover its interest in the financial asset from the purchaser.

(e) An action based on the entitlement holder's property interest with respect to a particular financial asset under subsection (a), whether framed in conversion, replevin, constructive trust, equitable lien, or other theory, may not be asserted against any purchaser of a financial asset or interest therein who gives value, obtains control, and does not act in collusion with the securities intermediary in violating the securities intermediary's obligations under Section 8–504.

§ 8–504. Duty of Securities Intermediary to Maintain Financial Asset.

(a) A securities intermediary shall promptly obtain and thereafter maintain a financial asset in a quantity corresponding to the aggregate of all security entitlements it has established in favor of its entitlement holders with respect to that financial asset. The securities intermediary may maintain those financial assets directly or through one or more other securities intermediaries.

(b) Except to the extent otherwise agreed by its entitlement holder, a securities intermediary may not grant any security interests in a financial asset it is obligated to maintain pursuant to subsection (a).

(c) A securities intermediary satisfies the duty in subsection (a) if:

(1) the securities intermediary acts with respect to the duty as agreed upon by the entitlement holder and the securities intermediary; or

(2) in the absence of agreement, the securities intermediary exercises due care in accordance with reasonable commercial standards to obtain and maintain the financial asset.

(d) This section does not apply to a clearing corporation that is itself the obligor of an option or similar obligation to which its entitlement holders have security entitlements.

§ 8–505. Duty of Securities Intermediary with Respect to Payments and Distributions.

(a) A securities intermediary shall take action to obtain a payment or distribution made by the issuer of a financial asset. A securities intermediary satisfies the duty if:

(1) the securities intermediary acts with respect to the duty as agreed upon by the entitlement holder and the securities intermediary; or

(2) in the absence of agreement, the securities intermediary exercises due care in accordance with reasonable commercial standards to attempt to obtain the payment or distribution.

(b) A securities intermediary is obligated to its entitlement holder for a payment or distribution made by the issuer of a financial asset if the payment or distribution is received by the securities intermediary.

§ 8–506. Duty of Securities Intermediary to Exercise Rights as Directed by Entitlement Holder.

A securities intermediary shall exercise rights with respect to a financial asset if directed to do so by an entitlement holder. A securities intermediary satisfies the duty if:

(1) the securities intermediary acts with respect to the duty as agreed upon by the entitlement holder and the securities intermediary; or

(2) in the absence of agreement, the securities intermediary either places the entitlement holder in a position to exercise the rights directly or exercises due care in accordance with reasonable commercial standards to follow the direction of the entitlement holder.

§ 8–507. Duty of Securities Intermediary to Comply with Entitlement Order.

(a) A securities intermediary shall comply with an entitlement order if the entitlement order is originated by the appropriate person, the securities intermediary has had reasonable opportunity to assure itself that the entitlement order is genuine and authorized, and the securities intermediary has had reasonable opportunity to comply with the entitlement order. A securities intermediary satisfies the duty if:

(1) the securities intermediary acts with respect to the duty as agreed upon by the entitlement holder and the securities intermediary; or

(2) in the absence of agreement, the securities intermediary exercises due care in accordance with reasonable commercial standards to comply with the entitlement order.

(b) If a securities intermediary transfers a financial asset pursuant to an ineffective entitlement order, the securities intermediary shall reestablish a security entitlement in favor of the person entitled to it, and pay or credit any payments or distributions that the person did not receive as a result of the wrongful transfer. If the securities intermediary does not reestablish a security entitlement, the securities intermediary is liable to the entitlement holder for damages.

§ 8–508. Duty of Securities Intermediary to Change Entitlement Holder's Position to Other Form of Security Holding.

A securities intermediary shall act at the direction of an entitlement holder to change a security entitlement into another available form of holding for which the entitlement holder is eligible, or to cause the financial asset to be transferred to a securities account of the entitlement holder with another securities intermediary. A securities intermediary satisfies the duty if:

(1) the securities intermediary acts as agreed upon by the entitlement holder and the securities intermediary; or

(2) in the absence of agreement, the securities intermediary exercises due care in accordance with reasonable commercial standards to follow the direction of the entitlement holder.

§ 8–509. Specification of Duties of Securities Intermediary by Other Statute or Regulation; Manner of Performance of Duties of Securities Intermediary and Exercise of Rights of Entitlement Holder.

(a) If the substance of a duty imposed upon a securities intermediary by Sections 8–504 through 8–508 is the subject of other statute, regulation, or rule, compliance with that statute, regulation, or rule satisfies the duty.

(b) To the extent that specific standards for the performance of the duties of a securities intermediary or the exercise of the rights of an entitlement holder are not specified by other statute, regulation, or rule or by agreement between the securities intermediary and entitlement holder, the securities intermediary shall perform its duties and the entitlement holder shall exercise its rights in a commercially reasonable manner.

(c) The obligation of a securities intermediary to perform the duties imposed by Sections 8–504 through 8–508 is subject to:

(1) rights of the securities intermediary arising out of a security interest under a security agreement with the entitlement holder or otherwise; and

(2) rights of the securities intermediary under other law, regulation, rule, or agreement to withhold performance of its duties as a result of unfulfilled obligations of the entitlement holder to the securities intermediary.

(d) Sections 8–504 through 8–508 do not require a securities intermediary to take any action that is prohibited by other statute, regulation, or rule.

§ 8–510. Rights of Purchaser of Security Entitlement from Entitlement Holder.

(a) An action based on an adverse claim to a financial asset or security entitlement, whether framed in conversion, replevin, constructive trust, equitable lien, or other theory, may not be asserted against a person who purchases a security entitlement, or an interest therein, from an entitlement holder if the purchaser gives value, does not have notice of the adverse claim, and obtains control.

(b) If an adverse claim could not have been asserted against an entitlement holder under Section 8–502, the adverse claim cannot be asserted against a person who purchases a security entitlement, or an interest therein, from the entitlement holder.

(c) In a case not covered by the priority rules in Article 9, a purchaser for value of a security entitlement, or an interest therein, who obtains control has priority over a purchaser of a security entitlement, or an interest therein, who does not obtain control. Except as otherwise provided in subsection (d), purchasers who have control rank according to priority in time of:

(1) the purchaser's becoming the person for whom the securities account, in which the security entitlement is carried, is maintained, if the purchaser obtained control under Section 8–106(d)(1);

(2) the securities intermediary's agreement to comply with the purchaser's entitlement orders with respect to security entitlements carried or to be carried in the securities account in which the security entitlement is carried, if the purchaser obtained control under Section 8–106(d)(2); or

(3) if the purchaser obtained control through another person under Section 8–106(d)(3), the time on which priority would be based under this subsection if the other person were the secured party.

(d) A securities intermediary as purchaser has priority over a conflicting purchaser who has control unless otherwise agreed by the securities intermediary.
As amended in 1999.

§ 8–511. Priority among Security Interests and Entitlement Holders.

(a) Except as otherwise provided in subsections (b) and (c), if a securities intermediary does not have sufficient interests in a particular financial asset to satisfy both its obligations to entitlement holders who have security entitlements to that financial asset and its obligation to a creditor of the securities intermediary who has

a security interest in that financial asset, the claims of entitlement holders, other than the creditor, have priority over the claim of the creditor.

(b) A claim of a creditor of a securities intermediary who has a security interest in a financial asset held by a securities intermediary has priority over claims of the securities intermediary's entitlement holders who have security entitlements with respect to that financial asset if the creditor has control over the financial asset.

(c) If a clearing corporation does not have sufficient financial assets to satisfy both its obligations to entitlement holders who have security entitlements with respect to a financial asset and its obligation to a creditor of the clearing corporation who has a security interest in that financial asset, the claim of the creditor has priority over the claims of entitlement holders.

Part 6—Transition Provisions for Revised Article 8

§ 8–601. Effective Date.
This [Act] takes effect . . . .

§ 8–602. Repeals.
This [Act] repeals . . . .

§ 8–603. Savings Clause.

(a) This [Act] does not affect an action or proceeding commenced before this [Act] takes effect.

(b) If a security interest in a security is perfected at the date this [Act] takes effect, and the action by which the security interest was perfected would suffice to perfect a security interest under this [Act], no further action is required to continue perfection. If a security interest in a security is perfected at the date this [Act] takes effect but the action by which the security interest was perfected would not suffice to perfect a security interest under this [Act], the security interest remains perfected for a period of four months after the effective date and continues perfected thereafter if appropriate action to perfect under this [Act] is taken within that period. If a security interest is perfected at the date this [Act] takes effect and the security interest can be perfected by filing under this [Act], a financing statement signed by the secured party instead of the debtor may be filed within that period to continue perfection or thereafter to perfect.

REVISED ARTICLE 9: SECURED TRANSACTIONS

Part 1—General Provisions

[Subpart 1. Short Title, Definitions, and General Concepts]

§ 9–101. Short Title.
This article may be cited as Uniform Commercial Code—Secured Transactions.

§ 9–102. Definitions and Index of Definitions.

(a) In this article:

(1) "Accession" means goods that are physically united with other goods in such a manner that the identity of the original goods is not lost.

(2) "Account", except as used in "account for", means a right to payment of a monetary obligation, whether or not earned by performance, (i) for property that has been or is to be sold, leased, licensed, assigned, or otherwise disposed of, (ii) for services rendered or to be rendered, (iii) for a policy of insurance issued or to be issued, (iv) for a secondary obligation incurred or to be incurred, (v) for energy provided or to be pro-vided, (vi) for the use or hire of a vessel under a charter or other contract, (vii) arising out of the use of a credit or charge card or information contained on or for use with the card, or (viii) as winnings in a lottery or other game of chance operated or sponsored by a State, governmental unit of a State, or person licensed or authorized to operate the game by a State or governmental unit of a State. The term includes health-care insurance receivables. The term does not include (i) rights to payment evidenced by chattel paper or an instrument, (ii) commercial tort claims, (iii) deposit accounts, (iv) investment property, (v) letter-of-credit rights or letters of credit, or (vi) rights to payment for money or funds advanced or sold, other than rights arising out of the use of a credit or charge card or information contained on or for use with the card.

(3) "Account debtor" means a person obligated on an account, chattel paper, or general intangible. The term does not include persons obligated to pay a negotiable instrument, even if the instrument constitutes part of chattel paper.

(4) "Accounting", except as used in "accounting for", means a record:

    (A) authenticated by a secured party;

    (B) indicating the aggregate unpaid secured obligations as of a date not more than 35 days earlier or 35 days later than the date of the record; and

    (C) identifying the components of the obligations in reasonable detail.

(5) "Agricultural lien" means an interest, other than a security interest, in farm products:

    (A) which secures payment or performance of an obligation for:

        (i) goods or services furnished in connection with a debtor's farming operation; or

        (ii) rent on real property leased by a debtor in connection with its farming operation;

    (B) which is created by statute in favor of a person that:

        (i) in the ordinary course of its business furnished goods or services to a debtor in connection with a debtor's farming operation; or

        (ii) leased real property to a debtor in connection with the debtor's farming operation; and

    (C) whose effectiveness does not depend on the person's possession of the personal property.

(6) "As-extracted collateral" means:

    (A) oil, gas, or other minerals that are subject to a security interest that:

        (i) is created by a debtor having an interest in the minerals before extraction; and

        (ii) attaches to the minerals as extracted; or

    (B) accounts arising out of the sale at the wellhead or minehead of oil, gas, or other minerals in which the debtor had an interest before extraction.

(7) "Authenticate" means:

    (A) to sign; or

    (B) to execute or otherwise adopt a symbol, or encrypt or similarly process a record in whole or in part, with the present intent of the authenticating person to identify the person and adopt or accept a record.

(8) "Bank" means an organization that is engaged in the business of banking. The term includes savings banks, savings and loan associations, credit unions, and trust companies.

(9) "Cash proceeds" means proceeds that are money, checks, deposit accounts, or the like.

(10) "Certificate of title" means a certificate of title with respect to which a statute provides for the security interest in question to be indicated on the certificate as a condition or result of the security interest's obtaining priority over the rights of a lien creditor with respect to the collateral.

(11) "Chattel paper" means a record or records that evidence both a monetary obligation and a security interest in specific goods, a security interest in specific goods and software used in the goods, a security interest in specific goods and license of software used in the goods, a lease of specific goods, or a lease of specific goods and license of software used in the goods. In this paragraph, "monetary obligation" means a monetary obligation secured by the goods or owed under a lease of the goods and includes a monetary obligation with respect to software used in the goods. The term does not include (i) charters or other contracts involving the use or hire of a vessel or (ii) records that evidence a right to payment arising out of the use of a credit or charge card or information contained on or for use with the card. If a transaction is evidenced by records that include an instrument or series of instruments, the group of records taken together constitutes chattel paper.

(12) "Collateral" means the property subject to a security interest or agricultural lien. The term includes:

    (A) proceeds to which a security interest attaches;

    (B) accounts, chattel paper, payment intangibles, and promissory notes that have been sold; and

    (C) goods that are the subject of a consignment.

(13) "Commercial tort claim" means a claim arising in tort with respect to which:

    (A) the claimant is an organization; or

    (B) the claimant is an individual and the claim:

        (i) arose in the course of the claimant's business or profession; and

        (ii) does not include damages arising out of personal injury to or the death of an individual.

(14) "Commodity account" means an account maintained by a commodity intermediary in which a commodity contract is carried for a commodity customer.

(15) "Commodity contract" means a commodity futures contract, an option on a commodity futures contract, a commodity option, or another contract if the contract or option is:

    (A) traded on or subject to the rules of a board of trade that has been designated as a contract market for such a contract pursuant to federal commodities laws; or

    (B) traded on a foreign commodity board of trade, exchange, or market, and is carried on the books of a commodity intermediary for a commodity customer.

(16) "Commodity customer" means a person for which a commodity intermediary carries a commodity contract on its books.

(17) "Commodity intermediary" means a person that:

    (A) is registered as a futures commission merchant under federal commodities law; or

(B) in the ordinary course of its business provides clearance or settlement services for a board of trade that has been designated as a contract market pursuant to federal commodities law.

(18) "Communicate" means:

(A) to send a written or other tangible record;

(B) to transmit a record by any means agreed upon by the persons sending and receiving the record; or

(C) in the case of transmission of a record to or by a filing office, to transmit a record by any means prescribed by filing-office rule.

(19) "Consignee" means a merchant to which goods are delivered in a consignment.

(20) "Consignment" means a transaction, regardless of its form, in which a person delivers goods to a merchant for the purpose of sale and:

(A) the merchant:

(i) deals in goods of that kind under a name other than the name of the person making delivery;

(ii) is not an auctioneer; and

(iii) is not generally known by its creditors to be substantially engaged in selling the goods of others;

(B) with respect to each delivery, the aggregate value of the goods is $1,000 or more at the time of delivery;

(C) the goods are not consumer goods immediately before delivery; and

(D) the transaction does not create a security interest that secures an obligation.

(21) "Consignor" means a person that delivers goods to a consignee in a consignment.

(22) "Consumer debtor" means a debtor in a consumer transaction.

(23) "Consumer goods" means goods that are used or bought for use primarily for personal, family, or household purposes.

(24) "Consumer-goods transaction" means a consumer transaction in which:

(A) an individual incurs an obligation primarily for personal, family, or household purposes; and

(B) a security interest in consumer goods secures the obligation.

(25) "Consumer obligor" means an obligor who is an individual and who incurred the obligation as part of a transaction entered into primarily for personal, family, or household purposes.

(26) "Consumer transaction" means a transaction in which (i) an individual incurs an obligation primarily for personal, family, or household purposes, (ii) a security interest secures the obligation, and (iii) the collateral is held or acquired primarily for personal, family, or household purposes. The term includes consumer-goods transactions.

(27) "Continuation statement" means an amendment of a financing statement which:

(A) identifies, by its file number, the initial financing statement to which it relates; and

(B) indicates that it is a continuation statement for, or that it is filed to continue the effectiveness of, the identified financing statement.

(28) "Debtor" means:

(A) a person having an interest, other than a security interest or other lien, in the collateral, whether or not the person is an obligor;

(B) a seller of accounts, chattel paper, payment intangibles, or promissory notes; or

(C) a consignee.

(29) "Deposit account" means a demand, time, savings, passbook, or similar account maintained with a bank. The term does not include investment property or accounts evidenced by an instrument.

(30) "Document" means a document of title or a receipt of the type described in Section 7–201(2).

(31) "Electronic chattel paper" means chattel paper evidenced by a record or records consisting of information stored in an electronic medium.

(32) "Encumbrance" means a right, other than an ownership interest, in real property. The term includes mortgages and other liens on real property.

(33) "Equipment" means goods other than inventory, farm products, or consumer goods.

(34) "Farm products" means goods, other than standing timber, with respect to which the debtor is engaged in a farming operation and which are:

(A) crops grown, growing, or to be grown, including:

(i) crops produced on trees, vines, and bushes; and

(ii) aquatic goods produced in aquacultural operations;

(B) livestock, born or unborn, including aquatic goods produced in aquacultural operations;

(C) supplies used or produced in a farming operation; or

(D) products of crops or livestock in their unmanufactured states.

(35) "Farming operation" means raising, cultivating, propagating, fattening, grazing, or any other farming, livestock, or aquacultural operation.

(36) "File number" means the number assigned to an initial financing statement pursuant to Section 9–519(a).

(37) "Filing office" means an office designated in Section 9–501 as the place to file a financing statement.

(38) "Filing-office rule" means a rule adopted pursuant to Section 9–526.

(39) "Financing statement" means a record or records composed of an initial financing statement and any filed record relating to the initial financing statement.

(40) "Fixture filing" means the filing of a financing statement covering goods that are or are to become fixtures and satisfying Section 9–502(a) and (b). The term includes the filing of a financing statement covering goods of a transmitting utility which are or are to become fixtures.

(41) "Fixtures" means goods that have become so related to particular real property that an interest in them arises under real property law.

(42) "General intangible" means any personal property, including things in action, other than accounts, chattel paper, commercial tort claims, deposit accounts, documents, goods, instruments, investment property, letter-of-credit rights, letters of credit, money, and oil, gas, or other minerals before extraction. The term includes payment intangibles and software.

(43) "Good faith" means honesty in fact and the observance of reasonable commercial standards of fair dealing.

(44) "Goods" means all things that are movable when a security interest attaches. The term includes (i) fixtures, (ii) standing timber that is to be cut and removed under a conveyance or contract for sale, (iii) the unborn young of animals, (iv) crops grown, growing, or to be grown, even if the crops are produced on trees, vines, or bushes, and (v) manufactured homes. The term also includes a computer program embedded in goods and any supporting information provided in connection with a transaction relating to the program if (i) the program is associated with the goods in such a manner that it customarily is considered part of the goods, or (ii) by becoming the owner of the goods, a person acquires a right to use the program in connection with the goods. The term does not include a computer program embedded in goods that consist solely of the medium in which the program is embedded. The term also does not include accounts, chattel paper, commercial tort claims, deposit accounts, documents, general intangibles, instruments, investment property, letter-of-credit rights, letters of credit, money, or oil, gas, or other minerals before extraction.

(45) "Governmental unit" means a subdivision, agency, department, county, parish, municipality, or other unit of the government of the United States, a State, or a foreign country. The term includes an organization having a separate corporate existence if the organization is eligible to issue debt on which interest is exempt from income taxation under the laws of the United States.

(46) "Health-care-insurance receivable" means an interest in or claim under a policy of insurance which is a right to payment of a monetary obligation for health-care goods or services provided.

(47) "Instrument" means a negotiable instrument or any other writing that evidences a right to the payment of a monetary obligation, is not itself a security agreement or lease, and is of a type that in ordinary course of business is transferred by delivery with any necessary indorsement or assignment. The term does not include (i) investment property, (ii) letters of credit, or (iii) writings that evidence a right to payment arising out of the use of a credit or charge card or information contained on or for use with the card.

(48) "Inventory" means goods, other than farm products, which:

  (A) are leased by a person as lessor;

  (B) are held by a person for sale or lease or to be furnished under a contract of service;

  (C) are furnished by a person under a contract of service; or

  (D) consist of raw materials, work in process, or materials used or consumed in a business.

(49) "Investment property" means a security, whether certificated or uncertificated, security entitlement, securities account, commodity contract, or commodity account.

(50) "Jurisdiction of organization", with respect to a registered organization, means the jurisdiction under whose law the organization is organized.

(51) "Letter-of-credit right" means a right to payment or performance under a letter of credit, whether or not the beneficiary has demanded or is at the time entitled to demand payment or performance. The term does not include the right of a beneficiary to demand payment or performance under a letter of credit.

(52) "Lien creditor" means:

  (A) a creditor that has acquired a lien on the property involved by attachment, levy, or the like;

  (B) an assignee for benefit of creditors from the time of assignment;

  (C) a trustee in bankruptcy from the date of the filing of the petition; or

  (D) a receiver in equity from the time of appointment.

(53) "Manufactured home" means a structure, transportable in one or more sections, which, in the traveling mode, is eight body feet or more in width or 40 body feet or more in length, or, when erected on site, is 320 or more square feet, and which is built on a permanent chassis and designed to be used as a dwelling with or without a permanent foundation when connected to the required utilities, and includes the plumbing, heating, air-conditioning, and electrical systems contained therein. The term includes any structure that meets all of the requirements of this paragraph except the size requirements and with respect to which the manufacturer voluntarily files a certification required by the United States Secretary of Housing and Urban Development and complies with the standards established under Title 42 of the United States Code.

(54) "Manufactured-home transaction" means a secured transaction:

  (A) that creates a purchase-money security interest in a manufactured home, other than a manufactured home held as inventory; or

  (B) in which a manufactured home, other than a manufactured home held as inventory, is the primary collateral.

(55) "Mortgage" means a consensual interest in real property, including fixtures, which secures payment or performance of an obligation.

(56) "New debtor" means a person that becomes bound as debtor under Section 9–203(d) by a security agreement previously entered into by another person.

(57) "New value" means (i) money, (ii) money's worth in property, services, or new credit, or (iii) release by a transferee of an interest in property previously transferred to the transferee. The term does not include an obligation substituted for another obligation.

(58) "Noncash proceeds" means proceeds other than cash proceeds.

(59) "Obligor" means a person that, with respect to an obligation secured by a security interest in or an agricultural lien on the collateral, (i) owes payment or other performance of the obligation, (ii) has provided property other than the collateral to secure payment or other performance of the obligation, or (iii) is otherwise accountable in whole or in part for payment or other performance of the obligation. The term does not include issuers or nominated persons under a letter of credit.

(60) "Original debtor", except as used in Section 9–310(c), means a person that, as debtor, entered into a security agreement to which a new debtor has become bound under Section 9–203(d).

(61) "Payment intangible" means a general intangible under which the account debtor's principal obligation is a monetary obligation.

(62) "Person related to", with respect to an individual, means:

  (A) the spouse of the individual;

(B) a brother, brother-in-law, sister, or sister-in-law of the individual;

(C) an ancestor or lineal descendant of the individual or the individual's spouse; or

(D) any other relative, by blood or marriage, of the individual or the individual's spouse who shares the same home with the individual.

(63) "Person related to", with respect to an organization, means:

(A) a person directly or indirectly controlling, controlled by, or under common control with the organization;

(B) an officer or director of, or a person performing similar functions with respect to, the organization;

(C) an officer or director of, or a person performing similar functions with respect to, a person described in subparagraph (A);

(D) the spouse of an individual described in subparagraph (A), (B), or (C); or

(E) an individual who is related by blood or marriage to an individual described in subparagraph (A), (B), (C), or (D) and shares the same home with the individual.

(64) "Proceeds", except as used in Section 9–609(b), means the following property:

(A) whatever is acquired upon the sale, lease, license, exchange, or other disposition of collateral;

(B) whatever is collected on, or distributed on account of, collateral;

(C) rights arising out of collateral;

(D) to the extent of the value of collateral, claims arising out of the loss, nonconformity, or interference with the use of, defects or infringement of rights in, or damage to, the collateral; or

(E) to the extent of the value of collateral and to the extent payable to the debtor or the secured party, insurance payable by reason of the loss or nonconformity of, defects or infringement of rights in, or damage to, the collateral.

(65) "Promissory note" means an instrument that evidences a promise to pay a monetary obligation, does not evidence an order to pay, and does not contain an acknowledgment by a bank that the bank has received for deposit a sum of money or funds.

(66) "Proposal" means a record authenticated by a secured party which includes the terms on which the secured party is willing to accept collateral in full or partial satisfaction of the obligation it secures pursuant to Sections 9–620, 9–621, and 9–622.

(67) "Public-finance transaction" means a secured transaction in connection with which:

(A) debt securities are issued;

(B) all or a portion of the securities issued have an initial stated maturity of at least 20 years; and

(C) the debtor, obligor, secured party, account debtor or other person obligated on collateral, assignor or assignee of a secured obligation, or assignor or assignee of a security interest is a State or a governmental unit of a State.

(68) "Pursuant to commitment", with respect to an advance made or other value given by a secured party, means pursuant to the secured party's obligation, whether or not a subsequent event of default or other event not within the secured party's control has relieved or may relieve the secured party from its obligation.

(69) "Record", except as used in "for record", "of record", "record or legal title", and "record owner", means information that is inscribed on a tangible medium or which is stored in an electronic or other medium and is retrievable in perceivable form.

(70) "Registered organization" means an organization organized solely under the law of a single State or the United States and as to which the State or the United States must maintain a public record showing the organization to have been organized.

(71) "Secondary obligor" means an obligor to the extent that:

(A) the obligor's obligation is secondary; or

(B) the obligor has a right of recourse with respect to an obligation secured by collateral against the debtor, another obligor, or property of either.

(72) "Secured party" means:

(A) a person in whose favor a security interest is created or provided for under a security agreement, whether or not any obligation to be secured is outstanding;

(B) a person that holds an agricultural lien;

(C) a consignor;

(D) a person to which accounts, chattel paper, payment intangibles, or promissory notes have been sold;

(E) a trustee, indenture trustee, agent, collateral agent, or other representative in whose favor a security interest or agricultural lien is created or provided for; or

(F) a person that holds a security interest arising under Section 2–401, 2–505, 2–711(3), 2A–508(5), 4–210, or 5–118.

(73) "Security agreement" means an agreement that creates or provides for a security interest.

(74) "Send", in connection with a record or notification, means:

(A) to deposit in the mail, deliver for transmission, or transmit by any other usual means of communication, with postage or cost of transmission provided for, addressed to any address reasonable under the circumstances; or

(B) to cause the record or notification to be received within the time that it would have been received if properly sent under subparagraph (A).

(75) "Software" means a computer program and any supporting information provided in connection with a transaction relating to the program. The term does not include a computer program that is included in the definition of goods.

(76) "State" means a State of the United States, the District of Columbia, Puerto Rico, the United States Virgin Islands, or any territory or insular possession subject to the jurisdiction of the United States.

(77) "Supporting obligation" means a letter-of-credit right or secondary obligation that supports the payment or performance of an account, chattel paper, a document, a general intangible, an instrument, or investment property.

(78) "Tangible chattel paper" means chattel paper evidenced by a record or records consisting of information that is inscribed on a tangible medium.

(79) "Termination statement" means an amendment of a financing statement which:

(A) identifies, by its file number, the initial financing statement to which it relates; and

(B) indicates either that it is a termination statement or that the identified financing statement is no longer effective.

(80) "Transmitting utility" means a person primarily engaged in the business of:

(A) operating a railroad, subway, street railway, or trolley bus;

(B) transmitting communications electrically, electromagnetically, or by light;

(C) transmitting goods by pipeline or sewer; or

(D) transmitting or producing and transmitting electricity, steam, gas, or water.

(b) The following definitions in other articles apply to this article:

"Applicant."	Section 5–102
"Beneficiary."	Section 5–102
"Broker."	Section 8–102
"Certificated security."	Section 8–102
"Check."	Section 3–104
"Clearing corporation."	Section 8–102
"Contract for sale."	Section 2–106
"Customer."	Section 4–104
"Entitlement holder."	Section 8–102
"Financial asset."	Section 8–102
"Holder in due course."	Section 3–302
"Issuer" (with respect to a letter of credit or letter-of-credit right).	Section 5–102
"Issuer" (with respect to a security).	Section 8–201
"Lease."	Section 2A–103
"Lease agreement."	Section 2A–103
"Lease contract."	Section 2A–103
"Leasehold interest."	Section 2A–103
"Lessee."	Section 2A–103
"Lessee in ordinary course of business."	Section 2A–103
"Lessor."	Section 2A–103
"Lessor's residual interest."	Section 2A–103
"Letter of credit."	Section 5–102
"Merchant."	Section 2–104
"Negotiable instrument."	Section 3–104
"Nominated person."	Section 5–102
"Note."	Section 3–104
"Proceeds of a letter of credit."	Section 5–114
"Prove."	Section 3–103
"Sale."	Section 2–106
"Securities account."	Section 8–501
"Securities intermediary."	Section 8–102
"Security."	Section 8–102
"Security certificate."	Section 8–102
"Security entitlement."	Section 8–102
"Uncertificated security."	Section 8–102

(c) Article 1 contains general definitions and principles of construction and interpretation applicable throughout this article.
Amended in 1999 and 2000.

§ 9–103. Purchase-Money Security Interest; Application of Payments; Burden of Establishing.

(a) In this section:

(1) "purchase-money collateral" means goods or software that secures a purchase-money obligation incurred with respect to that collateral; and

(2) "purchase-money obligation" means an obligation of an obligor incurred as all or part of the price of the collateral or for value given to enable the debtor to acquire rights in or the use of the collateral if the value is in fact so used.

(b) A security interest in goods is a purchase-money security interest:

(1) to the extent that the goods are purchase-money collateral with respect to that security interest;

(2) if the security interest is in inventory that is or was purchase-money collateral, also to the extent that the security interest secures a purchase-money obligation incurred with respect to other inventory in which the secured party holds or held a purchase-money security interest; and

(3) also to the extent that the security interest secures a purchase-money obligation incurred with respect to software in which the secured party holds or held a purchase-money security interest.

(c) A security interest in software is a purchase-money security interest to the extent that the security interest also secures a purchase-money obligation incurred with respect to goods in which the secured party holds or held a purchase-money security interest if:

(1) the debtor acquired its interest in the software in an integrated transaction in which it acquired an interest in the goods; and

(2) the debtor acquired its interest in the software for the principal purpose of using the software in the goods.

(d) The security interest of a consignor in goods that are the subject of a consignment is a purchase-money security interest in inventory.

(e) In a transaction other than a consumer-goods transaction, if the extent to which a security interest is a purchase-money security interest depends on the application of a payment to a particular obligation, the payment must be applied:

(1) in accordance with any reasonable method of application to which the parties agree;

(2) in the absence of the parties' agreement to a reasonable method, in accordance with any intention of the obligor manifested at or before the time of payment; or

(3) in the absence of an agreement to a reasonable method and a timely manifestation of the obligor's intention, in the following order:

(A) to obligations that are not secured; and

(B) if more than one obligation is secured, to obligations secured by purchase-money security interests in the order in which those obligations were incurred.

(f) In a transaction other than a consumer-goods transaction, a purchase-money security interest does not lose its status as such, even if:

(1) the purchase-money collateral also secures an obligation that is not a purchase-money obligation;

(2) collateral that is not purchase-money collateral also secures the purchase-money obligation; or

(3) the purchase-money obligation has been renewed, refinanced, consolidated, or restructured.

(g) In a transaction other than a consumer-goods transaction, a secured party claiming a purchase-money security interest has the burden of establishing the extent to which the security interest is a purchase-money security interest.

(h) The limitation of the rules in subsections (e), (f), and (g) to transactions other than consumer-goods transactions is intended to leave to the court the determination of the proper rules in consumer-goods transactions. The court may not infer from that limitation the nature of the proper rule in consumer-goods transactions and may continue to apply established approaches.

§ 9–104. Control of Deposit Account.

(a) A secured party has control of a deposit account if:

(1) the secured party is the bank with which the deposit account is maintained;

(2) the debtor, secured party, and bank have agreed in an authenticated record that the bank will comply with instructions originated by the secured party directing disposition of the funds in the deposit account without further consent by the debtor; or

(3) the secured party becomes the bank's customer with respect to the deposit account.

(b) A secured party that has satisfied subsection (a) has control, even if the debtor retains the right to direct the disposition of funds from the deposit account.

§ 9–105. Control of Electronic Chattel Paper.

A secured party has control of electronic chattel paper if the record or records comprising the chattel paper are created, stored, and assigned in such a manner that:

(1) a single authoritative copy of the record or records exists which is unique, identifiable and, except as otherwise provided in paragraphs (4), (5), and (6), unalterable;

(2) the authoritative copy identifies the secured party as the assignee of the record or records;

(3) the authoritative copy is communicated to and maintained by the secured party or its designated custodian;

(4) copies or revisions that add or change an identified assignee of the authoritative copy can be made only with the participation of the secured party;

(5) each copy of the authoritative copy and any copy of a copy is readily identifiable as a copy that is not the authoritative copy; and

(6) any revision of the authoritative copy is readily identifiable as an authorized or unauthorized revision.

§ 9–106. Control of Investment Property.

(a) A person has control of a certificated security, uncertificated security, or security entitlement as provided in Section 8–106.

(b) A secured party has control of a commodity contract if:

(1) the secured party is the commodity intermediary with which the commodity contract is carried; or

(2) the commodity customer, secured party, and commodity intermediary have agreed that the commodity intermediary will apply any value distributed on account of the commodity contract as directed by the secured party without further consent by the commodity customer.

(c) A secured party having control of all security entitlements or commodity contracts carried in a securities account or commodity account has control over the securities account or commodity account.

§ 9–107. Control of Letter-of-Credit Right.

A secured party has control of a letter-of-credit right to the extent of any right to payment or performance by the issuer or any nominated person if the issuer or nominated person has consented to an assignment of proceeds of the letter of credit under Section 5–114(c) or otherwise applicable law or practice.

§ 9–108. Sufficiency of Description.

(a) Except as otherwise provided in subsections (c), (d), and (e), a description of personal or real property is sufficient, whether or not it is specific, if it reasonably identifies what is described.

(b) Except as otherwise provided in subsection (d), a description of collateral reasonably identifies the collateral if it identifies the collateral by:

(1) specific listing;

(2) category;

(3) except as otherwise provided in subsection (e), a type of collateral defined in [the Uniform Commercial Code];

(4) quantity;

(5) computational or allocational formula or procedure; or

(6) except as otherwise provided in subsection (c), any other method, if the identity of the collateral is objectively determinable.

(c) A description of collateral as "all the debtor's assets" or "all the debtor's personal property" or using words of similar import does not reasonably identify the collateral.

(d) Except as otherwise provided in subsection (e), a description of a security entitlement, securities account, or commodity account is sufficient if it describes:

(1) the collateral by those terms or as investment property; or

(2) the underlying financial asset or commodity contract.

(e) A description only by type of collateral defined in [the Uniform Commercial Code] is an insufficient description of:

(1) a commercial tort claim; or

(2) in a consumer transaction, consumer goods, a security entitlement, a securities account, or a commodity account.

[Subpart 2. Applicability of Article]

§ 9–109. Scope.

(a) Except as otherwise provided in subsections (c) and (d), this article applies to:

(1) a transaction, regardless of its form, that creates a security interest in personal property or fixtures by contract;

(2) an agricultural lien;

(3) a sale of accounts, chattel paper, payment intangibles, or promissory notes;

(4) a consignment;

(5) a security interest arising under Section 2–401, 2–505, 2–711(3), or 2A–508(5), as provided in Section 9–110; and

(6) a security interest arising under Section 4–210 or 5–118.

(b) The application of this article to a security interest in a secured obligation is not affected by the fact that the obligation is itself secured by a transaction or interest to which this article does not apply.

(c) This article does not apply to the extent that:

(1) a statute, regulation, or treaty of the United States preempts this article;

(2) another statute of this State expressly governs the creation, perfection, priority, or enforcement of a security interest created by this State or a governmental unit of this State;

(3) a statute of another State, a foreign country, or a governmental unit of another State or a foreign country, other than a statute generally applicable to security interests, expressly governs creation, perfection, priority, or enforcement of a security interest created by the State, country, or governmental unit; or

(4) the rights of a transferee beneficiary or nominated person under a letter of credit are independent and superior under Section 5–114.

(d) This article does not apply to:

(1) a landlord's lien, other than an agricultural lien;

(2) a lien, other than an agricultural lien, given by statute or other rule of law for services or materials, but Section 9–333 applies with respect to priority of the lien;

(3) an assignment of a claim for wages, salary, or other compensation of an employee;

(4) a sale of accounts, chattel paper, payment intangibles, or promissory notes as part of a sale of the business out of which they arose;

(5) an assignment of accounts, chattel paper, payment intangibles, or promissory notes which is for the purpose of collection only;

(6) an assignment of a right to payment under a contract to an assignee that is also obligated to perform under the contract;

(7) an assignment of a single account, payment intangible, or promissory note to an assignee in full or partial satisfaction of a preexisting indebtedness;

(8) a transfer of an interest in or an assignment of a claim under a policy of insurance, other than an assignment by or to a health-care provider of a health-care-insurance receivable and any subsequent assignment of the right to payment, but Sections 9–315 and 9–322 apply with respect to proceeds and priorities in proceeds;

(9) an assignment of a right represented by a judgment, other than a judgment taken on a right to payment that was collateral;

(10) a right of recoupment or set-off, but:

(A) Section 9–340 applies with respect to the effectiveness of rights of recoupment or set-off against deposit accounts; and

(B) Section 9–404 applies with respect to defenses or claims of an account debtor;

(11) the creation or transfer of an interest in or lien on real property, including a lease or rents thereunder, except to the extent that provision is made for:

(A) liens on real property in Sections 9 203 and 9–308;

(B) fixtures in Section 9–334;

(C) fixture filings in Sections 9–501, 9–502, 9–512, 9–516, and 9–519; and

(D) security agreements covering personal and real property in Section 9–604;

(12) an assignment of a claim arising in tort, other than a commercial tort claim, but Sections 9–315 and 9–322 apply with respect to proceeds and priorities in proceeds; or

(13) an assignment of a deposit account in a consumer transaction, but Sections 9–315 and 9–322 apply with respect to proceeds and priorities in proceeds.

§ 9–110. Security Interests Arising under Article 2 or 2A.
A security interest arising under Section 2–401, 2–505, 2–711(3), or 2A–508(5) is subject to this article. However, until the debtor obtains possession of the goods:

(1) the security interest is enforceable, even if Section 9–203(b)(3) has not been satisfied;

(2) filing is not required to perfect the security interest;

(3) the rights of the secured party after default by the debtor are governed by Article 2 or 2A; and

(4) the security interest has priority over a conflicting security interest created by the debtor.

Part 2—Effectiveness of Security Agreement; Attachment of Security Interest; Rights of Parties to Security Agreement

[Subpart 1. Effectiveness and Attachment]

§ 9–201. General Effectiveness of Security Agreement.
(a) Except as otherwise provided in [the Uniform Commercial Code], a security agreement is effective according to its terms between the parties, against purchasers of the collateral, and against creditors.

(b) A transaction subject to this article is subject to any applicable rule of law which establishes a different rule for consumers and [insert reference to (i) any other statute or regulation that regulates the rates, charges, agreements, and practices for loans, credit sales, or other extensions of credit and (ii) any consumer-protection statute or regulation].

(c) In case of conflict between this article and a rule of law, statute, or regulation described in subsection (b), the rule of law, statute, or regulation controls. Failure to comply with a statute or regulation described in subsection (b) has only the effect the statute or regulation specifies.

(d) This article does not:

(1) validate any rate, charge, agreement, or practice that violates a rule of law, statute, or regulation described in subsection (b); or

(2) extend the application of the rule of law, statute, or regulation to a transaction not otherwise subject to it.

§ 9–202. Title to Collateral Immaterial.
Except as otherwise provided with respect to consignments or sales of accounts, chattel paper, payment intangibles, or promissory notes, the provisions of this article with regard to rights and obligations apply whether title to collateral is in the secured party or the debtor.

§ 9–203. Attachment and Enforceability of Security Interest; Proceeds; Supporting Obligations; Formal Requisites.
(a) A security interest attaches to collateral when it becomes enforceable against the debtor with respect to the collateral, unless an agreement expressly postpones the time of attachment.

(b) Except as otherwise provided in subsections (c) through (i), a security interest is enforceable against the debtor and third parties with respect to the collateral only if:

(1) value has been given;

(2) the debtor has rights in the collateral or the power to transfer rights in the collateral to a secured party; and

(3) one of the following conditions is met:

(A) the debtor has authenticated a security agreement that provides a description of the collateral and, if the security interest covers timber to be cut, a description of the land concerned;

(B) the collateral is not a certificated security and is in the possession of the secured party under Section 9–313 pursuant to the debtor's security agreement;

(C) the collateral is a certificated security in registered form and the security certificate has been delivered to the secured party under Section 8–301 pursuant to the debtor's security agreement; or

(D) the collateral is deposit accounts, electronic chattel paper, investment property, or letter-of-credit rights, and the secured party has control under Section 9–104, 9–105, 9–106, or 9–107 pursuant to the debtor's security agreement.

(c) Subsection (b) is subject to Section 4–210 on the security interest of a collecting bank, Section 5–118 on the security interest of a letter-of-credit issuer or nominated person, Section 9–110 on a security interest arising under Article 2 or 2A, and Section 9–206 on security interests in investment property.

(d) A person becomes bound as debtor by a security agreement entered into by another person if, by operation of law other than this article or by contract:

(1) the security agreement becomes effective to create a security interest in the person's property; or

(2) the person becomes generally obligated for the obligations of the other person, including the obligation secured under the security agreement, and acquires or succeeds to all or substantially all of the assets of the other person.

(e) If a new debtor becomes bound as debtor by a security agreement entered into by another person:

(1) the agreement satisfies subsection (b)(3) with respect to existing or after-acquired property of the new debtor to the extent the property is described in the agreement; and

(2) another agreement is not necessary to make a security interest in the property enforceable.

(f) The attachment of a security interest in collateral gives the secured party the rights to proceeds provided by Section 9–315 and is also attachment of a security interest in a supporting obligation for the collateral.

(g) The attachment of a security interest in a right to payment or performance secured by a security interest or other lien on personal or real property is also attachment of a security interest in the security interest, mortgage, or other lien.

(h) The attachment of a security interest in a securities account is also attachment of a security interest in the security entitlements carried in the securities account.

(i) The attachment of a security interest in a commodity account is also attachment of a security interest in the commodity contracts carried in the commodity account.

§ 9–204. After-Acquired Property; Future Advances.

(a) Except as otherwise provided in subsection (b), a security agreement may create or provide for a security interest in after-acquired collateral.

(b) A security interest does not attach under a term constituting an after-acquired property clause to:

(1) consumer goods, other than an accession when given as additional security, unless the debtor acquires rights in them within 10 days after the secured party gives value; or

(2) a commercial tort claim.

(c) A security agreement may provide that collateral secures, or that accounts, chattel paper, payment intangibles, or promissory notes are sold in connection with, future advances or other value, whether or not the advances or value are given pursuant to commitment.

§ 9–205. Use or Disposition of Collateral Permissible.

(a) A security interest is not invalid or fraudulent against creditors solely because:

(1) the debtor has the right or ability to:

(A) use, commingle, or dispose of all or part of the collateral, including returned or repossessed goods;

(B) collect, compromise, enforce, or otherwise deal with collateral;

(C) accept the return of collateral or make repossessions; or

(D) use, commingle, or dispose of proceeds; or

(2) the secured party fails to require the debtor to account for proceeds or replace collateral.

(b) This section does not relax the requirements of possession if attachment, perfection, or enforcement of a security interest depends upon possession of the collateral by the secured party.

§ 9–206. Security Interest Arising in Purchase or Delivery of Financial Asset.

(a) A security interest in favor of a securities intermediary attaches to a person's security entitlement if:

(1) the person buys a financial asset through the securities intermediary in a transaction in which the person is obligated to pay the purchase price to the securities intermediary at the time of the purchase; and

(2) the securities intermediary credits the financial asset to the buyer's securities account before the buyer pays the securities intermediary.

(b) The security interest described in subsection (a) secures the person's obligation to pay for the financial asset.

(c) A security interest in favor of a person that delivers a certificated security or other financial asset represented by a writing attaches to the security or other financial asset if:

(1) the security or other financial asset:

(A) in the ordinary course of business is transferred by delivery with any necessary indorsement or assignment; and

(B) is delivered under an agreement between persons in the business of dealing with such securities or financial assets; and

(2) the agreement calls for delivery against payment.

(d) The security interest described in subsection (c) secures the obligation to make payment for the delivery.

[Subpart 2. Rights and Duties]

§ 9–207. Rights and Duties of Secured Party Having Possession or Control of Collateral.

(a) Except as otherwise provided in subsection (d), a secured party shall use reasonable care in the custody and preservation of collateral in the secured party's possession. In the case of chattel paper or an instrument, reasonable care includes taking necessary steps to preserve rights against prior parties unless otherwise agreed.

(b) Except as otherwise provided in subsection (d), if a secured party has possession of collateral:

(1) reasonable expenses, including the cost of insurance and payment of taxes or other charges, incurred in the custody, preservation, use, or operation of the collateral are chargeable to the debtor and are secured by the collateral;

(2) the risk of accidental loss or damage is on the debtor to the extent of a deficiency in any effective insurance coverage;

(3) the secured party shall keep the collateral identifiable, but fungible collateral may be commingled; and

(4) the secured party may use or operate the collateral:

  (A) for the purpose of preserving the collateral or its value;

  (B) as permitted by an order of a court having competent jurisdiction; or

  (C) except in the case of consumer goods, in the manner and to the extent agreed by the debtor.

(c) Except as otherwise provided in subsection (d), a secured party having possession of collateral or control of collateral under Section 9–104, 9–105, 9–106, or 9–107:

  (1) may hold as additional security any proceeds, except money or funds, received from the collateral;

  (2) shall apply money or funds received from the collateral to reduce the secured obligation, unless remitted to the debtor; and

  (3) may create a security interest in the collateral.

(d) If the secured party is a buyer of accounts, chattel paper, payment intangibles, or promissory notes or a consignor:

  (1) subsection (a) does not apply unless the secured party is entitled under an agreement:

    (A) to charge back uncollected collateral; or

    (B) otherwise to full or limited recourse against the debtor or a secondary obligor based on the nonpayment or other default of an account debtor or other obligor on the collateral; and

  (2) subsections (b) and (c) do not apply.

§ 9–208. Additional Duties of Secured Party Having Control of Collateral.

(a) This section applies to cases in which there is no outstanding secured obligation and the secured party is not committed to make advances, incur obligations, or otherwise give value.

(b) Within 10 days after receiving an authenticated demand by the debtor:

  (1) a secured party having control of a deposit account under Section 9–104(a)(2) shall send to the bank with which the deposit account is maintained an authenticated statement that releases the bank from any further obligation to comply with instructions originated by the secured party;

  (2) a secured party having control of a deposit account under Section 9–104(a)(3) shall:

    (A) pay the debtor the balance on deposit in the deposit account; or

    (B) transfer the balance on deposit into a deposit account in the debtor's name;

  (3) a secured party, other than a buyer, having control of electronic chattel paper under Section 9–105 shall:

    (A) communicate the authoritative copy of the electronic chattel paper to the debtor or its designated custodian;

    (B) if the debtor designates a custodian that is the designated custodian with which the authoritative copy of the electronic chattel paper is maintained for the secured party, communicate to the custodian an authenticated record releasing the designated custodian from any further obligation to comply with instructions originated by the secured party and instructing the custodian to comply with instructions originated by the debtor; and

    (C) take appropriate action to enable the debtor or its designated custodian to make copies of or revisions to the authoritative copy which add or change an identified assignee of the authoritative copy without the consent of the secured party;

  (4) a secured party having control of investment property under Section 8–106(d)(2) or 9–106(b) shall send to the securities intermediary or commodity intermediary with which the security entitlement or commodity contract is maintained an authenticated record that releases the securities intermediary or commodity intermediary from any further obligation to comply with entitlement orders or directions originated by the secured party; and

  (5) a secured party having control of a letter-of-credit right under Section 9–107 shall send to each person having an unfulfilled obligation to pay or deliver proceeds of the letter of credit to the secured party an authenticated release from any further obligation to pay or deliver proceeds of the letter of credit to the secured party.

§ 9–209. Duties of Secured Party If Account Debtor Has Been Notified of Assignment.

(a) Except as otherwise provided in subsection (c), this section applies if:

  (1) there is no outstanding secured obligation; and

  (2) the secured party is not committed to make advances, incur obligations, or otherwise give value.

(b) Within 10 days after receiving an authenticated demand by the debtor, a secured party shall send to an account debtor that has received notification of an assignment to the secured party as assignee under Section 9–406(a) an authenticated record that releases the account debtor from any further obligation to the secured party.

(c) This section does not apply to an assignment constituting the sale of an account, chattel paper, or payment intangible.

§ 9–210. Request for Accounting; Request Regarding List of Collateral or Statement of Account.

(a) In this section:

  (1) "Request" means a record of a type described in paragraph (2), (3), or (4).

  (2) "Request for an accounting" means a record authenticated by a debtor requesting that the recipient provide an accounting of the unpaid obligations secured by collateral and reasonably identifying the transaction or relationship that is the subject of the request.

  (3) "Request regarding a list of collateral" means a record authenticated by a debtor requesting that the recipient approve or correct a list of what the debtor believes to be the collateral securing an obligation and reasonably identifying the transaction or relationship that is the subject of the request.

  (4) "Request regarding a statement of account" means a record authenticated by a debtor requesting that the recipient approve or correct a statement indicating what the debtor believes to be the aggregate amount of unpaid obligations secured by collateral as of a specified date and reasonably identifying the transaction or relationship that is the subject of the request.

(b) Subject to subsections (c), (d), (e), and (f), a secured party, other than a buyer of accounts, chattel paper, payment intangibles, or promissory notes or a consignor, shall comply with a request within 14 days after receipt:

(1) in the case of a request for an accounting, by authenticating and sending to the debtor an accounting; and

(2) in the case of a request regarding a list of collateral or a request regarding a statement of account, by authenticating and sending to the debtor an approval or correction.

(c) A secured party that claims a security interest in all of a particular type of collateral owned by the debtor may comply with a request regarding a list of collateral by sending to the debtor an authenticated record including a statement to that effect within 14 days after receipt.

(d) A person that receives a request regarding a list of collateral, claims no interest in the collateral when it receives the request, and claimed an interest in the collateral at an earlier time shall comply with the request within 14 days after receipt by sending to the debtor an authenticated record:

(1) disclaiming any interest in the collateral; and

(2) if known to the recipient, providing the name and mailing address of any assignee of or successor to the recipient's interest in the collateral.

(e) A person that receives a request for an accounting or a request regarding a statement of account, claims no interest in the obligations when it receives the request, and claimed an interest in the obligations at an earlier time shall comply with the request within 14 days after receipt by sending to the debtor an authenticated record:

(1) disclaiming any interest in the obligations; and

(2) if known to the recipient, providing the name and mailing address of any assignee of or successor to the recipient's interest in the obligations.

(f) A debtor is entitled without charge to one response to a request under this section during any six-month period. The secured party may require payment of a charge not exceeding $25 for each additional response.

As amended in 1999.

Part 3—Perfection and Priority

[Subpart 1. Law Governing Perfection and Priority]

§ 9–301. Law Governing Perfection and Priority of Security Interests.

Except as otherwise provided in Sections 9–303 through 9–306, the following rules determine the law governing perfection, the effect of perfection or nonperfection, and the priority of a security interest in collateral:

(1) Except as otherwise provided in this section, while a debtor is located in a jurisdiction, the local law of that jurisdiction governs perfection, the effect of perfection or nonperfection, and the priority of a security interest in collateral.

(2) While collateral is located in a jurisdiction, the local law of that jurisdiction governs perfection, the effect of perfection or nonperfection, and the priority of a possessory security interest in that collateral.

(3) Except as otherwise provided in paragraph (4), while negotiable documents, goods, instruments, money, or tangible chattel paper is located in a jurisdiction, the local law of that jurisdiction governs:

(A) perfection of a security interest in the goods by filing a fixture filing;

(B) perfection of a security interest in timber to be cut; and

(C) the effect of perfection or nonperfection and the priority of a nonpossessory security interest in the collateral.

(4) The local law of the jurisdiction in which the wellhead or minehead is located governs perfection, the effect of perfection or nonperfection, and the priority of a security interest in as-extracted collateral.

§ 9–302. Law Governing Perfection and Priority of Agricultural Liens.

While farm products are located in a jurisdiction, the local law of that jurisdiction governs perfection, the effect of perfection or nonperfection, and the priority of an agricultural lien on the farm products.

§ 9–303. Law Governing Perfection and Priority of Security Interests in Goods Covered by a Certificate of Title.

(a) This section applies to goods covered by a certificate of title, even if there is no other relationship between the jurisdiction under whose certificate of title the goods are covered and the goods or the debtor.

(b) Goods become covered by a certificate of title when a valid application for the certificate of title and the applicable fee are delivered to the appropriate authority. Goods cease to be covered by a certificate of title at the earlier of the time the certificate of title ceases to be effective under the law of the issuing jurisdiction or the time the goods become covered subsequently by a certificate of title issued by another jurisdiction.

(c) The local law of the jurisdiction under whose certificate of title the goods are covered governs perfection, the effect of perfection or nonperfection, and the priority of a security interest in goods covered by a certificate of title from the time the goods become covered by the certificate of title until the goods cease to be covered by the certificate of title.

§ 9–304. Law Governing Perfection and Priority of Security Interests in Deposit Accounts.

(a) The local law of a bank's jurisdiction governs perfection, the effect of perfection or nonperfection, and the priority of a security interest in a deposit account maintained with that bank.

(b) The following rules determine a bank's jurisdiction for purposes of this part:

(1) If an agreement between the bank and the debtor governing the deposit account expressly provides that a particular jurisdiction is the bank's jurisdiction for purposes of this part, this article, or [the Uniform Commercial Code], that jurisdiction is the bank's jurisdiction.

(2) If paragraph (1) does not apply and an agreement between the bank and its customer governing the deposit account expressly provides that the agreement is governed by the law of a particular jurisdiction, that jurisdiction is the bank's jurisdiction.

(3) If neither paragraph (1) nor paragraph (2) applies and an agreement between the bank and its customer governing the deposit account expressly provides that the deposit account is maintained at an office in a particular jurisdiction, that jurisdiction is the bank's jurisdiction.

(4) If none of the preceding paragraphs applies, the bank's jurisdiction is the jurisdiction in which the office identified in an account statement as the office serving the customer's account is located.

(5) If none of the preceding paragraphs applies, the bank's jurisdiction is the jurisdiction in which the chief executive office of the bank is located.

§ 9–305. Law Governing Perfection and Priority of Security Interests in Investment Property.

(a) Except as otherwise provided in subsection (c), the following rules apply:

(1) While a security certificate is located in a jurisdiction, the local law of that jurisdiction governs perfection, the effect of perfection or nonperfection, and the priority of a security interest in the certificated security represented thereby.

(2) The local law of the issuer's jurisdiction as specified in Section 8–110(d) governs perfection, the effect of perfection or nonperfection, and the priority of a security interest in an uncertificated security.

(3) The local law of the securities intermediary's jurisdiction as specified in Section 8–110(e) governs perfection, the effect of perfection or nonperfection, and the priority of a security interest in a security entitlement or securities account.

(4) The local law of the commodity intermediary's jurisdiction governs perfection, the effect of perfection or nonperfection, and the priority of a security interest in a commodity contract or commodity account.

(b) The following rules determine a commodity intermediary's jurisdiction for purposes of this part:

(1) If an agreement between the commodity intermediary and commodity customer governing the commodity account expressly provides that a particular jurisdiction is the commodity intermediary's jurisdiction for purposes of this part, this article, or [the Uniform Commercial Code], that jurisdiction is the commodity intermediary's jurisdiction.

(2) If paragraph (1) does not apply and an agreement between the commodity intermediary and commodity customer governing the commodity account expressly provides that the agreement is governed by the law of a particular jurisdiction, that jurisdiction is the commodity intermediary's jurisdiction.

(3) If neither paragraph (1) nor paragraph (2) applies and an agreement between the commodity intermediary and commodity customer governing the commodity account expressly provides that the commodity account is maintained at an office in a particular jurisdiction, that jurisdiction is the commodity intermediary's jurisdiction.

(4) If none of the preceding paragraphs applies, the commodity intermediary's jurisdiction is the jurisdiction in which the office identified in an account statement as the office serving the commodity customer's account is located.

(5) If none of the preceding paragraphs applies, the commodity intermediary's jurisdiction is the jurisdiction in which the chief executive office of the commodity intermediary is located.

(c) The local law of the jurisdiction in which the debtor is located governs:

(1) perfection of a security interest in investment property by filing;

(2) automatic perfection of a security interest in investment property created by a broker or securities intermediary; and

(3) automatic perfection of a security interest in a commodity contract or commodity account created by a commodity intermediary.

§ 9–306. Law Governing Perfection and Priority of Security Interests in Letter-of-Credit Rights.

(a) Subject to subsection (c), the local law of the issuer's jurisdiction or a nominated person's jurisdiction governs perfection, the effect of perfection or nonperfection, and the priority of a security interest in a letter-of-credit right if the issuer's jurisdiction or nominated person's jurisdiction is a State.

(b) For purposes of this part, an issuer's jurisdiction or nominated person's jurisdiction is the jurisdiction whose law governs the liability of the issuer or nominated person with respect to the letter-of-credit right as provided in Section 5–116.

(c) This section does not apply to a security interest that is perfected only under Section 9–308(d).

§ 9–307. Location of Debtor.

(a) In this section, "place of business" means a place where a debtor conducts its affairs.

(b) Except as otherwise provided in this section, the following rules determine a debtor's location:

(1) A debtor who is an individual is located at the individual's principal residence.

(2) A debtor that is an organization and has only one place of business is located at its place of business.

(3) A debtor that is an organization and has more than one place of business is located at its chief executive office.

(c) Subsection (b) applies only if a debtor's residence, place of business, or chief executive office, as applicable, is located in a jurisdiction whose law generally requires information concerning the existence of a nonpossessory security interest to be made generally available in a filing, recording, or registration system as a condition or result of the security interest's obtaining priority over the rights of a lien creditor with respect to the collateral. If subsection (b) does not apply, the debtor is located in the District of Columbia.

(d) A person that ceases to exist, have a residence, or have a place of business continues to be located in the jurisdiction specified by subsections (b) and (c).

(e) A registered organization that is organized under the law of a State is located in that State.

(f) Except as otherwise provided in subsection (i), a registered organization that is organized under the law of the United States and a branch or agency of a bank that is not organized under the law of the United States or a State are located:

(1) in the State that the law of the United States designates, if the law designates a State of location;

(2) in the State that the registered organization, branch, or agency designates, if the law of the United States authorizes the registered organization, branch, or agency to designate its State of location; or

(3) in the District of Columbia, if neither paragraph (1) nor paragraph (2) applies.

(g) A registered organization continues to be located in the jurisdiction specified by subsection (e) or (f) notwithstanding:

(1) the suspension, revocation, forfeiture, or lapse of the registered organization's status as such in its jurisdiction of organization; or

(2) the dissolution, winding up, or cancellation of the existence of the registered organization.

(h) The United States is located in the District of Columbia.

(i) A branch or agency of a bank that is not organized under the law of the United States or a State is located in the State in which the branch or agency is licensed, if all branches and agencies of the bank are licensed in only one State.

(j) A foreign air carrier under the Federal Aviation Act of 1958, as amended, is located at the designated office of the agent upon which service of process may be made on behalf of the carrier.

(k) This section applies only for purposes of this part.

[Subpart 2. Perfection]

§ 9–308. When Security Interest or Agricultural Lien Is Perfected; Continuity of Perfection.

(a) Except as otherwise provided in this section and Section 9–309, a security interest is perfected if it has attached and all of the applicable requirements for perfection in Sections 9–310 through 9–316 have been satisfied. A security interest is perfected when it attaches if the applicable requirements are satisfied before the security interest attaches.

(b) An agricultural lien is perfected if it has become effective and all of the applicable requirements for perfection in Section 9–310 have been satisfied. An agricultural lien is perfected when it becomes effective if the applicable requirements are satisfied before the agricultural lien becomes effective.

(c) A security interest or agricultural lien is perfected continuously if it is originally perfected by one method under this article and is later perfected by another method under this article, without an intermediate period when it was unperfected.

(d) Perfection of a security interest in collateral also perfects a security interest in a supporting obligation for the collateral.

(e) Perfection of a security interest in a right to payment or performance also perfects a security interest in a security interest, mortgage, or other lien on personal or real property securing the right.

(f) Perfection of a security interest in a securities account also perfects a security interest in the security entitlements carried in the securities account.

(g) Perfection of a security interest in a commodity account also perfects a security interest in the commodity contracts carried in the commodity account.

Legislative Note: *Any statute conflicting with subsection (e) must be made expressly subject to that subsection.*

§ 9–309. Security Interest Perfected upon Attachment.

The following security interests are perfected when they attach:

(1) a purchase-money security interest in consumer goods, except as otherwise provided in Section 9–311(b) with respect to consumer goods that are subject to a statute or treaty described in Section 9–311(a);

(2) an assignment of accounts or payment intangibles which does not by itself or in conjunction with other assignments to the same assignee transfer a significant part of the assignor's outstanding accounts or payment intangibles;

(3) a sale of a payment intangible;

(4) a sale of a promissory note;

(5) a security interest created by the assignment of a health-care-insurance receivable to the provider of the health-care goods or services;

(6) a security interest arising under Section 2–401, 2–505, 2–711(3), or 2A–508(5), until the debtor obtains possession of the collateral;

(7) a security interest of a collecting bank arising under Section 4–210;

(8) a security interest of an issuer or nominated person arising under Section 5–118;

(9) a security interest arising in the delivery of a financial asset under Section 9–206(c);

(10) a security interest in investment property created by a broker or securities intermediary;

(11) a security interest in a commodity contract or a commodity account created by a commodity intermediary;

(12) an assignment for the benefit of all creditors of the transferor and subsequent transfers by the assignee thereunder; and

(13) a security interest created by an assignment of a beneficial interest in a decedent's estate; and

(14) a sale by an individual of an account that is a right to payment of winnings in a lottery or other game of chance.

§ 9–310. When Filing Required to Perfect Security Interest or Agricultural Lien; Security Interests and Agricultural Liens to Which Filing Provisions Do Not Apply.

(a) Except as otherwise provided in subsection (b) and Section 9–312(b), a financing statement must be filed to perfect all security interests and agricultural liens.

(b) The filing of a financing statement is not necessary to perfect a security interest:

(1) that is perfected under Section 9–308(d), (e), (f), or (g);

(2) that is perfected under Section 9–309 when it attaches;

(3) in property subject to a statute, regulation, or treaty described in Section 9–311(a);

(4) in goods in possession of a bailee which is perfected under Section 9–312(d)(1) or (2);

(5) in certificated securities, documents, goods, or instruments which is perfected without filing or possession under Section 9–312(e), (f), or (g);

(6) in collateral in the secured party's possession under Section 9–313;

(7) in a certificated security which is perfected by delivery of the security certificate to the secured party under Section 9–313;

(8) in deposit accounts, electronic chattel paper, investment property, or letter-of-credit rights which is perfected by control under Section 9–314;

(9) in proceeds which is perfected under Section 9–315; or

(10) that is perfected under Section 9–316.

(c) If a secured party assigns a perfected security interest or agricultural lien, a filing under this article is not required to continue the perfected status of the security interest against creditors of and transferees from the original debtor.

§ 9–311. Perfection of Security Interests in Property Subject to Certain Statutes, Regulations, and Treaties.

(a) Except as otherwise provided in subsection (d), the filing of a financing statement is not necessary or effective to perfect a security interest in property subject to:

(1) a statute, regulation, or treaty of the United States whose requirements for a security interest's obtaining priority over the rights of a lien creditor with respect to the property preempt Section 9–310(a);

(2) [list any certificate-of-title statute covering automobiles, trailers, mobile homes, boats, farm tractors, or the like, which provides for a security interest to be indicated on the certificate as a condition or result of perfection, and any non-Uniform Commercial Code central filing statute]; or

(3) a certificate-of-title statute of another jurisdiction which provides for a security interest to be indicated on the certificate as a condition or result of the security interest's obtaining priority over the rights of a lien creditor with respect to the property.

(b) Compliance with the requirements of a statute, regulation, or treaty described in subsection (a) for obtaining priority over the rights of a lien creditor is equivalent to the filing of a financing statement under this article. Except as otherwise provided in subsection (d) and Sections 9–313 and 9–316(d) and (e) for goods covered by a certificate of title, a security interest in property subject to a statute, regulation, or treaty described in subsection (a) may be perfected only by compliance with those requirements, and a security interest so perfected remains perfected notwithstanding a change in the use or transfer of possession of the collateral.

(c) Except as otherwise provided in subsection (d) and Section 9–316(d) and (e), duration and renewal of perfection of a security interest perfected by compliance with the requirements prescribed by a statute, regulation, or treaty described in subsection (a) are governed by the statute, regulation, or treaty. In other respects, the security interest is subject to this article.

(d) During any period in which collateral subject to a statute specified in subsection (a)(2) is inventory held for sale or lease by a person or leased by that person as lessor and that person is in the business of selling goods of that kind, this section does not apply to a security interest in that collateral created by that person.

Legislative Note: *This Article contemplates that perfection of a security interest in goods covered by a certificate of title occurs upon receipt by appropriate State officials of a properly tendered application for a certificate of title on which the security interest is to be indicated, without a relation back to an earlier time. States whose certificate-of-title statutes provide for perfection at a different time or contain a relation-back provision should amend the statutes accordingly.*

§ 9–312. Perfection of Security Interests in Chattel Paper, Deposit Accounts, Documents, Goods Covered by Documents, Instruments, Investment Property, Letter-of-Credit Rights, and Money; Perfection by Permissive Filing; Temporary Perfection without Filing or Transfer of Possession.

(a) A security interest in chattel paper, negotiable documents, instruments, or investment property may be perfected by filing.

(b) Except as otherwise provided in Section 9–315(c) and (d) for proceeds:

> **(1)** a security interest in a deposit account may be perfected only by control under Section 9–314;
>
> **(2)** and except as otherwise provided in Section 9–308(d), a security interest in a letter-of-credit right may be perfected only by control under Section 9–314; and
>
> **(3)** a security interest in money may be perfected only by the secured party's taking possession under Section 9–313.

(c) While goods are in the possession of a bailee that has issued a negotiable document covering the goods:

> **(1)** a security interest in the goods may be perfected by perfecting a security interest in the document; and
>
> **(2)** a security interest perfected in the document has priority over any security interest that becomes perfected in the goods by another method during that time.

(d) While goods are in the possession of a bailee that has issued a nonnegotiable document covering the goods, a security interest in the goods may be perfected by:

> **(1)** issuance of a document in the name of the secured party;
>
> **(2)** the bailee's receipt of notification of the secured party's interest; or
>
> **(3)** filing as to the goods.

(e) A security interest in certificated securities, negotiable documents, or instruments is perfected without filing or the taking of possession for a period of 20 days from the time it attaches to the extent that it arises for new value given under an authenticated security agreement.

(f) A perfected security interest in a negotiable document or goods in possession of a bailee, other than one that has issued a negotiable document for the goods, remains perfected for 20 days without filing if the secured party makes available to the debtor the goods or documents representing the goods for the purpose of:

> **(1)** ultimate sale or exchange; or
>
> **(2)** loading, unloading, storing, shipping, transshipping, manufacturing, processing, or otherwise dealing with them in a manner preliminary to their sale or exchange.

(g) A perfected security interest in a certificated security or instrument remains perfected for 20 days without filing if the secured party delivers the security certificate or instrument to the debtor for the purpose of:

> **(1)** ultimate sale or exchange; or
>
> **(2)** presentation, collection, enforcement, renewal, or registration of transfer.

(h) After the 20-day period specified in subsection (e), (f), or (g) expires, perfection depends upon compliance with this article.

§ 9–313. When Possession by or Delivery to Secured Party Perfects Security Interest without Filing.

(a) Except as otherwise provided in subsection (b), a secured party may perfect a security interest in negotiable documents, goods, instruments, money, or tangible chattel paper by taking possession of the collateral. A secured party may perfect a security interest in certificated securities by taking delivery of the certificated securities under Section 8–301.

(b) With respect to goods covered by a certificate of title issued by this State, a secured party may perfect a security interest in the goods by taking possession of the goods only in the circumstances described in Section 9–316(d).

(c) With respect to collateral other than certificated securities and goods covered by a document, a secured party takes possession of collateral in the possession of a person other than the debtor, the secured party, or a lessee of the collateral from the debtor in the ordinary course of the debtor's business, when:

> **(1)** the person in possession authenticates a record acknowledging that it holds possession of the collateral for the secured party's benefit; or
>
> **(2)** the person takes possession of the collateral after having authenticated a record acknowledging that it will hold possession of collateral for the secured party's benefit.

(d) If perfection of a security interest depends upon possession of the collateral by a secured party, perfection occurs no earlier than the time the secured party takes possession and continues only while the secured party retains possession.

(e) A security interest in a certificated security in registered form is perfected by delivery when delivery of the certificated security occurs under Section 8–301 and remains perfected by delivery until the debtor obtains possession of the security certificate.

(f) A person in possession of collateral is not required to acknowledge that it holds possession for a secured party's benefit.

(g) If a person acknowledges that it holds possession for the secured party's benefit:

> **(1)** the acknowledgment is effective under subsection (c) or Section 8–301(a), even if the acknowledgment violates the rights of a debtor; and
>
> **(2)** unless the person otherwise agrees or law other than this article otherwise provides, the person does not owe any duty to the secured party and is not required to confirm the acknowledgment to another person.

(h) A secured party having possession of collateral does not relinquish possession by delivering the collateral to a person other than the debtor or a lessee of the collateral from the debtor in the ordinary course of the debtor's business if the person was instructed before the delivery or is instructed contemporaneously with the delivery:

> **(1)** to hold possession of the collateral for the secured party's benefit; or
>
> **(2)** to redeliver the collateral to the secured party.

(i) A secured party does not relinquish possession, even if a delivery under subsection (h) violates the rights of a debtor. A person to which collateral is delivered under subsection (h) does not owe any duty to the secured party and is not required to confirm the delivery to another person unless the person otherwise agrees or law other than this article otherwise provides.

§ 9–314. Perfection by Control.

(a) A security interest in investment property, deposit accounts, letter-of-credit rights, or electronic chattel paper may be perfected by control of the collateral under Section 9–104, 9–105, 9–106, or 9–107.

(b) A security interest in deposit accounts, electronic chattel paper, or letter-of-credit rights is perfected by control under Section 9–104, 9–105, or 9–107 when the secured party obtains control and remains perfected by control only while the secured party retains control.

(c) A security interest in investment property is perfected by control under Section 9–106 from the time the secured party obtains control and remains perfected by control until:

> **(1)** the secured party does not have control; and
>
> **(2)** one of the following occurs:
>
>> **(A)** if the collateral is a certificated security, the debtor has or acquires possession of the security certificate;
>>
>> **(B)** if the collateral is an uncertificated security, the issuer has registered or registers the debtor as the registered owner; or
>>
>> **(C)** if the collateral is a security entitlement, the debtor is or becomes the entitlement holder.

§ 9–315. Secured Party's Rights on Disposition of Collateral and in Proceeds.

(a) Except as otherwise provided in this article and in Section 2–403(2):

> **(1)** a security interest or agricultural lien continues in collateral notwithstanding sale, lease, license, exchange, or other disposition thereof unless the secured party authorized the disposition free of the security interest or agricultural lien; and
>
> **(2)** a security interest attaches to any identifiable proceeds of collateral.

(b) Proceeds that are commingled with other property are identifiable proceeds:

> **(1)** if the proceeds are goods, to the extent provided by Section 9–336; and
>
> **(2)** if the proceeds are not goods, to the extent that the secured party identifies the proceeds by a method of tracing, including application of equitable principles, that is permitted under law other than this article with respect to commingled property of the type involved.

(c) A security interest in proceeds is a perfected security interest if the security interest in the original collateral was perfected.

(d) A perfected security interest in proceeds becomes unperfected on the 21st day after the security interest attaches to the proceeds unless:

> **(1)** the following conditions are satisfied:
>
>> **(A)** a filed financing statement covers the original collateral;
>>
>> **(B)** the proceeds are collateral in which a security interest may be perfected by filing in the office in which the financing statement has been filed; and
>>
>> **(C)** the proceeds are not acquired with cash proceeds;
>
> **(2)** the proceeds are identifiable cash proceeds; or
>
> **(3)** the security interest in the proceeds is perfected other than under subsection (c) when the security interest attaches to the proceeds or within 20 days thereafter.

(e) If a filed financing statement covers the original collateral, a security interest in proceeds which remains perfected under subsection (d)(1) becomes unperfected at the later of:

> **(1)** when the effectiveness of the filed financing statement lapses under Section 9–515 or is terminated under Section 9–513; or
>
> **(2)** the 21st day after the security interest attaches to the proceeds.

§ 9–316. Continued Perfection of Security Interest Following Change in Governing Law.

(a) A security interest perfected pursuant to the law of the jurisdiction designated in Section 9–301(1) or 9–305(c) remains perfected until the earliest of:

> **(1)** the time perfection would have ceased under the law of that jurisdiction;
>
> **(2)** the expiration of four months after a change of the debtor's location to another jurisdiction; or
>
> **(3)** the expiration of one year after a transfer of collateral to a person that thereby becomes a debtor and is located in another jurisdiction.

(b) If a security interest described in subsection (a) becomes perfected under the law of the other jurisdiction before the earliest time or event described in that subsection, it remains perfected thereafter. If the security interest does not become perfected under the law of the other jurisdiction before the earliest time or event, it becomes unperfected and is deemed never to have been perfected as against a purchaser of the collateral for value.

(c) A possessory security interest in collateral, other than goods covered by a certificate of title and as-extracted collateral consisting of goods, remains continuously perfected if:

(1) the collateral is located in one jurisdiction and subject to a security interest perfected under the law of that jurisdiction;

(2) thereafter the collateral is brought into another jurisdiction; and

(3) upon entry into the other jurisdiction, the security interest is perfected under the law of the other jurisdiction.

(d) Except as otherwise provided in subsection (e), a security interest in goods covered by a certificate of title which is perfected by any method under the law of another jurisdiction when the goods become covered by a certificate of title from this State remains perfected until the security interest would have become unperfected under the law of the other jurisdiction had the goods not become so covered.

(e) A security interest described in subsection (d) becomes unperfected as against a purchaser of the goods for value and is deemed never to have been perfected as against a purchaser of the goods for value if the applicable requirements for perfection under Section 9–311(b) or 9–313 are not satisfied before the earlier of:

(1) the time the security interest would have become unperfected under the law of the other jurisdiction had the goods not become covered by a certificate of title from this State; or

(2) the expiration of four months after the goods had become so covered.

(f) A security interest in deposit accounts, letter-of-credit rights, or investment property which is perfected under the law of the bank's jurisdiction, the issuer's jurisdiction, a nominated person's jurisdiction, the securities intermediary's jurisdiction, or the commodity intermediary's jurisdiction, as applicable, remains perfected until the earlier of:

(1) the time the security interest would have become unperfected under the law of that jurisdiction; or

(2) the expiration of four months after a change of the applicable jurisdiction to another jurisdiction.

(g) If a security interest described in subsection (f) becomes perfected under the law of the other jurisdiction before the earlier of the time or the end of the period described in that subsection, it remains perfected thereafter. If the security interest does not become perfected under the law of the other jurisdiction before the earlier of that time or the end of that period, it becomes unperfected and is deemed never to have been perfected as against a purchaser of the collateral for value.

[Subpart 3. Priority]

§ 9–317. Interests That Take Priority over or Take Free of Security Interest or Agricultural Lien.

(a) A security interest or agricultural lien is subordinate to the rights of:

(1) a person entitled to priority under Section 9–322; and

(2) except as otherwise provided in subsection (e), a person that becomes a lien creditor before the earlier of the time:

(A) the security interest or agricultural lien is perfected; or

(B) one of the conditions specified in Section 9–203(b)(3) is met and a financing statement covering the collateral is filed.

(b) Except as otherwise provided in subsection (e), a buyer, other than a secured party, of tangible chattel paper, documents, goods, instruments, or a security certificate takes free of a security interest or agricultural lien if the buyer gives value and receives delivery of the collateral without knowledge of the security interest or agricultural lien and before it is perfected.

(c) Except as otherwise provided in subsection (e), a lessee of goods takes free of a security interest or agricultural lien if the lessee gives value and receives delivery of the collateral without knowledge of the security interest or agricultural lien and before it is perfected.

(d) A licensee of a general intangible or a buyer, other than a secured party, of accounts, electronic chattel paper, general intangibles, or investment property other than a certificated security takes free of a security interest if the licensee or buyer gives value without knowledge of the security interest and before it is perfected.

(e) Except as otherwise provided in Sections 9–320 and 9–321, if a person files a financing statement with respect to a purchase-money security interest before or within 20 days after the debtor receives delivery of the collateral, the security interest takes priority over the rights of a buyer, lessee, or lien creditor which arise between the time the security interest attaches and the time of filing.

As amended in 2000.

§ 9–318. No Interest Retained in Right to Payment That Is Sold; Rights and Title of Seller of Account or Chattel Paper with Respect to Creditors and Purchasers.

(a) A debtor that has sold an account, chattel paper, payment intangible, or promissory note does not retain a legal or equitable interest in the collateral sold.

(b) For purposes of determining the rights of creditors of, and purchasers for value of an account or chattel paper from, a debtor that has sold an account or chattel paper, while the buyer's security interest is unperfected, the debtor is deemed to have rights and title to the account or chattel paper identical to those the debtor sold.

§ 9–319. Rights and Title of Consignee with Respect to Creditors and Purchasers.

(a) Except as otherwise provided in subsection (b), for purposes of determining the rights of creditors of, and purchasers for value of goods from, a consignee, while the goods are in the possession of the consignee, the consignee is deemed to have rights and title to the goods identical to those the consignor had or had power to transfer.

(b) For purposes of determining the rights of a creditor of a consignee, law other than this article determines the rights and title of a consignee while goods are in the consignee's possession if, under this part, a perfected security interest held by the consignor would have priority over the rights of the creditor.

§ 9–320. Buyer of Goods.

(a) Except as otherwise provided in subsection (e), a buyer in ordinary course of business, other than a person buying farm products from a person engaged in farming operations, takes free of a security interest created by the buyer's seller, even if the security interest is perfected and the buyer knows of its existence.

(b) Except as otherwise provided in subsection (e), a buyer of goods from a person who used or bought the goods for use primarily for personal, family, or household purposes takes free of a security interest, even if perfected, if the buyer buys:

(1) without knowledge of the security interest;

(2) for value;

(3) primarily for the buyer's personal, family, or household purposes; and

(4) before the filing of a financing statement covering the goods.

(c) To the extent that it affects the priority of a security interest over a buyer of goods under subsection (b), the period of effectiveness of a filing made in the jurisdiction in which the seller is located is governed by Section 9–316(a) and (b).

(d) A buyer in ordinary course of business buying oil, gas, or other minerals at the wellhead or minehead or after extraction takes free of an interest arising out of an encumbrance.

(e) Subsections (a) and (b) do not affect a security interest in goods in the possession of the secured party under Section 9–313.

§ 9–321. Licensee of General Intangible and Lessee of Goods in Ordinary Course of Business.

(a) In this section, "licensee in ordinary course of business" means a person that becomes a licensee of a general intangible in good faith, without knowledge that the license violates the rights of another person in the general intangible, and in the ordinary course from a person in the business of licensing general intangibles of that kind. A person becomes a licensee in the ordinary course if the license to the person comports with the usual or customary practices in the kind of business in which the licensor is engaged or with the licensor's own usual or customary practices.

(b) A licensee in ordinary course of business takes its rights under a nonexclusive license free of a security interest in the general intangible created by the licensor, even if the security interest is perfected and the licensee knows of its existence.

(c) A lessee in ordinary course of business takes its leasehold interest free of a security interest in the goods created by the lessor, even if the security interest is perfected and the lessee knows of its existence.

§ 9–322. Priorities among Conflicting Security Interests in and Agricultural Liens on Same Collateral.

(a) Except as otherwise provided in this section, priority among conflicting security interests and agricultural liens in the same collateral is determined according to the following rules:

(1) Conflicting perfected security interests and agricultural liens rank according to priority in time of filing or perfection. Priority dates from the earlier of the time a filing covering the collateral is first made or the security interest or agricultural lien is first perfected, if there is no period thereafter when there is neither filing nor perfection.

(2) A perfected security interest or agricultural lien has priority over a conflicting unperfected security interest or agricultural lien.

(3) The first security interest or agricultural lien to attach or become effective has priority if conflicting security interests and agricultural liens are unperfected.

(b) For the purposes of subsection (a)(1):

(1) the time of filing or perfection as to a security interest in collateral is also the time of filing or perfection as to a security interest in proceeds; and

(2) the time of filing or perfection as to a security interest in collateral supported by a supporting obligation is also the time of filing or perfection as to a security interest in the supporting obligation.

(c) Except as otherwise provided in subsection (f), a security interest in collateral which qualifies for priority over a conflicting security interest under Section 9–327, 9–328, 9–329, 9–330, or 9–331 also has priority over a conflicting security interest in:

(1) any supporting obligation for the collateral; and

(2) proceeds of the collateral if:

(A) the security interest in proceeds is perfected;

(B) the proceeds are cash proceeds or of the same type as the collateral; and

(C) in the case of proceeds that are proceeds of proceeds, all intervening proceeds are cash proceeds, proceeds of the same type as the collateral, or an account relating to the collateral.

(d) Subject to subsection (e) and except as otherwise provided in subsection (f), if a security interest in chattel paper, deposit accounts, negotiable documents, instruments, investment property, or letter-of-credit rights is perfected by a method other than filing, conflicting perfected security interests in proceeds of the collateral rank according to priority in time of filing.

(e) Subsection (d) applies only if the proceeds of the collateral are not cash proceeds, chattel paper, negotiable documents, instruments, investment property, or letter-of-credit rights.

(f) Subsections (a) through (e) are subject to:

(1) subsection (g) and the other provisions of this part;

(2) Section 4–210 with respect to a security interest of a collecting bank;

(3) Section 5–118 with respect to a security interest of an issuer or nominated person; and

(4) Section 9–110 with respect to a security interest arising under Article 2 or 2A.

(g) A perfected agricultural lien on collateral has priority over a conflicting security interest in or agricultural lien on the same collateral if the statute creating the agricultural lien so provides.

§ 9–323. Future Advances.

(a) Except as otherwise provided in subsection (c), for purposes of determining the priority of a perfected security interest under Section 9–322(a)(1), perfection of the security interest dates from the time an advance is made to the extent that the security interest secures an advance that:

(1) is made while the security interest is perfected only:

(A) under Section 9–309 when it attaches; or

(B) temporarily under Section 9–312(e), (f), or (g); and

(2) is not made pursuant to a commitment entered into before or while the security interest is perfected by a method other than under Section 9–309 or 9–312(e), (f), or (g).

(b) Except as otherwise provided in subsection (c), a security interest is subordinate to the rights of a person that becomes a lien creditor to the extent that the security interest secures an advance made more than 45 days after the person becomes a lien creditor unless the advance is made:

(1) without knowledge of the lien; or

(2) pursuant to a commitment entered into without knowledge of the lien.

(c) Subsections (a) and (b) do not apply to a security interest held by a secured party that is a buyer of accounts, chattel paper, payment intangibles, or promissory notes or a consignor.

(d) Except as otherwise provided in subsection (e), a buyer of goods other than a buyer in ordinary course of business takes free of a security interest to the extent that it secures advances made after the earlier of:

(1) the time the secured party acquires knowledge of the buyer's purchase; or

(2) 45 days after the purchase.

(e) Subsection (d) does not apply if the advance is made pursuant to a commitment entered into without knowledge of the buyer's purchase and before the expiration of the 45-day period.

(f) Except as otherwise provided in subsection (g), a lessee of goods, other than a lessee in ordinary course of business, takes the lease-hold interest free of a security interest to the extent that it secures advances made after the earlier of:

> **(1)** the time the secured party acquires knowledge of the lease; or
>
> **(2)** 45 days after the lease contract becomes enforceable.

(g) Subsection (f) does not apply if the advance is made pursuant to a commitment entered into without knowledge of the lease and before the expiration of the 45-day period.

As amended in 1999.

§ 9–324. Priority of Purchase-Money Security Interests.

(a) Except as otherwise provided in subsection (g), a perfected purchase-money security interest in goods other than inventory or livestock has priority over a conflicting security interest in the same goods, and, except as otherwise provided in Section 9–327, a perfected security interest in its identifiable proceeds also has priority, if the purchase-money security interest is perfected when the debtor receives possession of the collateral or within 20 days thereafter.

(b) Subject to subsection (c) and except as otherwise provided in subsection (g), a perfected purchase-money security interest in inventory has priority over a conflicting security interest in the same inventory, has priority over a conflicting security interest in chattel paper or an instrument constituting proceeds of the inventory and in proceeds of the chattel paper, if so provided in Section 9–330, and, except as otherwise provided in Section 9–327, also has priority in identifiable cash proceeds of the inventory to the extent the identifiable cash proceeds are received on or before the delivery of the inventory to a buyer, if:

> **(1)** the purchase-money security interest is perfected when the debtor receives possession of the inventory;
>
> **(2)** the purchase-money secured party sends an authenticated notification to the holder of the conflicting security interest;
>
> **(3)** the holder of the conflicting security interest receives the notification within five years before the debtor receives possession of the inventory; and
>
> **(4)** the notification states that the person sending the notification has or expects to acquire a purchase-money security interest in inventory of the debtor and describes the inventory.

(c) Subsections (b)(2) through (4) apply only if the holder of the conflicting security interest had filed a financing statement covering the same types of inventory:

> **(1)** if the purchase-money security interest is perfected by filing, before the date of the filing; or
>
> **(2)** if the purchase-money security interest is temporarily perfected without filing or possession under Section 9–312(f), before the beginning of the 20-day period thereunder.

(d) Subject to subsection (e) and except as otherwise provided in subsection (g), a perfected purchase-money security interest in livestock that are farm products has priority over a conflicting security interest in the same livestock, and, except as otherwise provided in Section 9–327, a perfected security interest in their identifiable proceeds and identifiable products in their unmanufactured states also has priority, if:

> **(1)** the purchase-money security interest is perfected when the debtor receives possession of the livestock;
>
> **(2)** the purchase-money secured party sends an authenticated notification to the holder of the conflicting security interest;
>
> **(3)** the holder of the conflicting security interest receives the notification within six months before the debtor receives possession of the livestock; and
>
> **(4)** the notification states that the person sending the notification has or expects to acquire a purchase-money security interest in livestock of the debtor and describes the livestock.

(e) Subsections (d)(2) through (4) apply only if the holder of the conflicting security interest had filed a financing statement covering the same types of livestock:

> **(1)** if the purchase-money security interest is perfected by filing, before the date of the filing; or
>
> **(2)** if the purchase-money security interest is temporarily perfected without filing or possession under Section 9–312(f), before the beginning of the 20-day period thereunder.

(f) Except as otherwise provided in subsection (g), a perfected purchase-money security interest in software has priority over a conflicting security interest in the same collateral, and, except as otherwise provided in Section 9–327, a perfected security interest in its identifiable proceeds also has priority, to the extent that the purchase-money security interest in the goods in which the software was acquired for use has priority in the goods and proceeds of the goods under this section.

(g) If more than one security interest qualifies for priority in the same collateral under subsection (a), (b), (d), or (f):

> **(1)** a security interest securing an obligation incurred as all or part of the price of the collateral has priority over a security interest securing an obligation incurred for value given to enable the debtor to acquire rights in or the use of collateral; and
>
> **(2)** in all other cases, Section 9–322(a) applies to the qualifying security interests.

§ 9–325. Priority of Security Interests in Transferred Collateral.

(a) Except as otherwise provided in subsection (b), a security interest created by a debtor is subordinate to a security interest in the same collateral created by another person if:

> **(1)** the debtor acquired the collateral subject to the security interest created by the other person;
>
> **(2)** the security interest created by the other person was perfected when the debtor acquired the collateral; and
>
> **(3)** there is no period thereafter when the security interest is unperfected.

(b) Subsection (a) subordinates a security interest only if the security interest:

> **(1)** otherwise would have priority solely under Section 9–322(a) or 9–324; or
>
> **(2)** arose solely under Section 2–711(3) or 2A–508(5).

§ 9–326. Priority of Security Interests Created by New Debtor.

(a) Subject to subsection (b), a security interest created by a new debtor which is perfected by a filed financing statement that is effective solely under Section 9–508 in collateral in which a new debtor has or acquires rights is subordinate to a security interest in the same collateral which is perfected other than by a filed financing statement that is effective solely under Section 9–508.

(b) The other provisions of this part determine the priority among conflicting security interests in the same collateral perfected by filed financing statements that are effective solely under Section 9–508. However, if the security agreements to which a new debtor became bound as debtor were not entered into by the same original debtor, the conflicting security interests rank according to priority in time of the new debtor's having become bound.

§ 9–327. Priority of Security Interests in Deposit Account.
The following rules govern priority among conflicting security interests in the same deposit account:

(1) A security interest held by a secured party having control of the deposit account under Section 9–104 has priority over a conflicting security interest held by a secured party that does not have control.

(2) Except as otherwise provided in paragraphs (3) and (4), security interests perfected by control under Section 9–314 rank according to priority in time of obtaining control.

(3) Except as otherwise provided in paragraph (4), a security interest held by the bank with which the deposit account is maintained has priority over a conflicting security interest held by another secured party.

(4) A security interest perfected by control under Section 9–104(a)(3) has priority over a security interest held by the bank with which the deposit account is maintained.

§ 9–328. Priority of Security Interests in Investment Property.
The following rules govern priority among conflicting security interests in the same investment property:

(1) A security interest held by a secured party having control of investment property under Section 9–106 has priority over a security interest held by a secured party that does not have control of the investment property.

(2) Except as otherwise provided in paragraphs (3) and (4), conflicting security interests held by secured parties each of which has control under Section 9–106 rank according to priority in time of:

(A) if the collateral is a security, obtaining control;

(B) if the collateral is a security entitlement carried in a securities account and:

(i) if the secured party obtained control under Section 8–106(d)(1), the secured party's becoming the person for which the securities account is maintained;

(ii) if the secured party obtained control under Section 8–106(d)(2), the securities intermediary's agreement to comply with the secured party's entitlement orders with respect to security entitlements carried or to be carried in the securities account; or

(iii) if the secured party obtained control through another person under Section 8–106(d)(3), the time on which priority would be based under this paragraph if the other person were the secured party; or

(C) if the collateral is a commodity contract carried with a commodity intermediary, the satisfaction of the requirement for control specified in Section 9–106(b)(2) with respect to commodity contracts carried or to be carried with the commodity intermediary.

(3) A security interest held by a securities intermediary in a security entitlement or a securities account maintained with the securities intermediary has priority over a conflicting security interest held by another secured party.

(4) A security interest held by a commodity intermediary in a commodity contract or a commodity account maintained with the commodity intermediary has priority over a conflicting security interest held by another secured party.

(5) A security interest in a certificated security in registered form which is perfected by taking delivery under Section 9–313(a) and not by control under Section 9–314 has priority over a conflicting security interest perfected by a method other than control.

(6) Conflicting security interests created by a broker, securities intermediary, or commodity intermediary which are perfected without control under Section 9–106 rank equally.

(7) In all other cases, priority among conflicting security interests in investment property is governed by Sections 9–322 and 9–323.

§ 9–329. Priority of Security Interests in Letter-of-Credit Right.
The following rules govern priority among conflicting security interests in the same letter-of-credit right:

(1) A security interest held by a secured party having control of the letter-of-credit right under Section 9–107 has priority to the extent of its control over a conflicting security interest held by a secured party that does not have control.

(2) Security interests perfected by control under Section 9–314 rank according to priority in time of obtaining control.

§ 9–330. Priority of Purchaser of Chattel Paper or Instrument.
(a) A purchaser of chattel paper has priority over a security interest in the chattel paper which is claimed merely as proceeds of inventory subject to a security interest if:

(1) in good faith and in the ordinary course of the purchaser's business, the purchaser gives new value and takes possession of the chattel paper or obtains control of the chattel paper under Section 9–105; and

(2) the chattel paper does not indicate that it has been assigned to an identified assignee other than the purchaser.

(b) A purchaser of chattel paper has priority over a security interest in the chattel paper which is claimed other than merely as proceeds of inventory subject to a security interest if the purchaser gives new value and takes possession of the chattel paper or obtains control of the chattel paper under Section 9–105 in good faith, in the ordinary course of the purchaser's business, and without knowledge that the purchase violates the rights of the secured party.

(c) Except as otherwise provided in Section 9–327, a purchaser having priority in chattel paper under subsection (a) or (b) also has priority in proceeds of the chattel paper to the extent that:

(1) Section 9–322 provides for priority in the proceeds; or

(2) the proceeds consist of the specific goods covered by the chattel paper or cash proceeds of the specific goods, even if the purchaser's security interest in the proceeds is unperfected.

(d) Except as otherwise provided in Section 9–331(a), a purchaser of an instrument has priority over a security interest in the instrument perfected by a method other than possession if the purchaser gives value and takes possession of the instrument in good faith and without knowledge that the purchase violates the rights of the secured party.

(e) For purposes of subsections (a) and (b), the holder of a purchase-money security interest in inventory gives new value for chattel paper constituting proceeds of the inventory.

(f) For purposes of subsections (b) and (d), if chattel paper or an instrument indicates that it has been assigned to an identified secured party other than the purchaser, a purchaser of the chattel paper or instrument has knowledge that the purchase violates the rights of the secured party.

§ 9–331. Priority of Rights of Purchasers of Instruments, Documents, and Securities under Other Articles; Priority of Interests in Financial Assets and Security Entitlements under Article 8.

(a) This article does not limit the rights of a holder in due course of a negotiable instrument, a holder to which a negotiable document of title has been duly negotiated, or a protected purchaser of a security. These holders or purchasers take priority over an earlier security interest, even if perfected, to the extent provided in Articles 3, 7, and 8.

(b) This article does not limit the rights of or impose liability on a person to the extent that the person is protected against the assertion of a claim under Article 8.

(c) Filing under this article does not constitute notice of a claim or defense to the holders, or purchasers, or persons described in subsections (a) and (b).

§ 9–332. Transfer of Money; Transfer of Funds from Deposit Account.

(a) A transferee of money takes the money free of a security interest unless the transferee acts in collusion with the debtor in violating the rights of the secured party.

(b) A transferee of funds from a deposit account takes the funds free of a security interest in the deposit account unless the transferee acts in collusion with the debtor in violating the rights of the secured party.

§ 9–333. Priority of Certain Liens Arising by Operation of Law.

(a) In this section, "possessory lien" means an interest, other than a security interest or an agricultural lien:

  (1) which secures payment or performance of an obligation for services or materials furnished with respect to goods by a person in the ordinary course of the person's business;

  (2) which is created by statute or rule of law in favor of the person; and

  (3) whose effectiveness depends on the person's possession of the goods.

(b) A possessory lien on goods has priority over a security interest in the goods unless the lien is created by a statute that expressly provides otherwise.

§ 9–334. Priority of Security Interests in Fixtures and Crops.

(a) A security interest under this article may be created in goods that are fixtures or may continue in goods that become fixtures. A security interest does not exist under this article in ordinary building materials incorporated into an improvement on land.

(b) This article does not prevent creation of an encumbrance upon fixtures under real property law.

(c) In cases not governed by subsections (d) through (h), a security interest in fixtures is subordinate to a conflicting interest of an encumbrancer or owner of the related real property other than the debtor.

(d) Except as otherwise provided in subsection (h), a perfected security interest in fixtures has priority over a conflicting interest of an encumbrancer or owner of the real property if the debtor has an interest of record in or is in possession of the real property and:

  (1) the security interest is a purchase-money security interest;

  (2) the interest of the encumbrancer or owner arises before the goods become fixtures; and

  (3) the security interest is perfected by a fixture filing before the goods become fixtures or within 20 days thereafter.

(e) A perfected security interest in fixtures has priority over a conflicting interest of an encumbrancer or owner of the real property if:

  (1) the debtor has an interest of record in the real property or is in possession of the real property and the security interest:

    (A) is perfected by a fixture filing before the interest of the encumbrancer or owner is of record; and

    (B) has priority over any conflicting interest of a predecessor in title of the encumbrancer or owner;

  (2) before the goods become fixtures, the security interest is perfected by any method permitted by this article and the fixtures are readily removable:

    (A) factory or office machines;

    (B) equipment that is not primarily used or leased for use in the operation of the real property; or

    (C) replacements of domestic appliances that are consumer goods;

  (3) the conflicting interest is a lien on the real property obtained by legal or equitable proceedings after the security interest was perfected by any method permitted by this article; or

  (4) the security interest is:

    (A) created in a manufactured home in a manufactured-home transaction; and

    (B) perfected pursuant to a statute described in Section 9–311(a)(2).

(f) A security interest in fixtures, whether or not perfected, has priority over a conflicting interest of an encumbrancer or owner of the real property if:

  (1) the encumbrancer or owner has, in an authenticated record, consented to the security interest or disclaimed an interest in the goods as fixtures; or

  (2) the debtor has a right to remove the goods as against the encumbrancer or owner.

(g) The priority of the security interest under paragraph (f)(2) continues for a reasonable time if the debtor's right to remove the goods as against the encumbrancer or owner terminates.

(h) A mortgage is a construction mortgage to the extent that it secures an obligation incurred for the construction of an improvement on land, including the acquisition cost of the land, if a recorded record of the mortgage so indicates. Except as otherwise provided in subsections (e) and (f), a security interest in fixtures is subordinate to a construction mortgage if a record of the mortgage is recorded before the goods become fixtures and the goods become fixtures before the completion of the construction. A mortgage has this priority to the same extent as a construction mortgage to the extent that it is given to refinance a construction mortgage.

(i) A perfected security interest in crops growing on real property has priority over a conflicting interest of an encumbrancer or owner of the real property if the debtor has an interest of record in or is in possession of the real property.

(j) Subsection (i) prevails over any inconsistent provisions of the following statutes:

[List here any statutes containing provisions inconsistent with subsection (i).]

Legislative Note: *States that amend statutes to remove provisions inconsistent with subsection (i) need not enact subsection (j).*

§ 9–335. Accessions.

(a) A security interest may be created in an accession and continues in collateral that becomes an accession.

(b) If a security interest is perfected when the collateral becomes an accession, the security interest remains perfected in the collateral.

(c) Except as otherwise provided in subsection (d), the other provisions of this part determine the priority of a security interest in an accession.

(d) A security interest in an accession is subordinate to a security interest in the whole which is perfected by compliance with the requirements of a certificate-of-title statute under Section 9–311(b).

(e) After default, subject to Part 6, a secured party may remove an accession from other goods if the security interest in the accession has priority over the claims of every person having an interest in the whole.

(f) A secured party that removes an accession from other goods under subsection (e) shall promptly reimburse any holder of a security interest or other lien on, or owner of, the whole or of the other goods, other than the debtor, for the cost of repair of any physical injury to the whole or the other goods. The secured party need not reimburse the holder or owner for any diminution in value of the whole or the other goods caused by the absence of the accession removed or by any necessity for replacing it. A person entitled to reimbursement may refuse permission to remove until the secured party gives adequate assurance for the performance of the obligation to reimburse.

§ 9–336. Commingled Goods.

(a) In this section, "commingled goods" means goods that are physically united with other goods in such a manner that their identity is lost in a product or mass.

(b) A security interest does not exist in commingled goods as such. However, a security interest may attach to a product or mass that results when goods become commingled goods.

(c) If collateral becomes commingled goods, a security interest attaches to the product or mass.

(d) If a security interest in collateral is perfected before the collateral becomes commingled goods, the security interest that attaches to the product or mass under subsection (c) is perfected.

(e) Except as otherwise provided in subsection (f), the other provisions of this part determine the priority of a security interest that attaches to the product or mass under subsection (c).

(f) If more than one security interest attaches to the product or mass under subsection (c), the following rules determine priority:

> **(1)** A security interest that is perfected under subsection (d) has priority over a security interest that is unperfected at the time the collateral becomes commingled goods.

> **(2)** If more than one security interest is perfected under subsection (d), the security interests rank equally in proportion to the value of the collateral at the time it became commingled goods.

§ 9–337. Priority of Security Interests in Goods Covered by Certificate of Title.

If, while a security interest in goods is perfected by any method under the law of another jurisdiction, this State issues a certificate of title that does not show that the goods are subject to the security interest or contain a statement that they may be subject to security interests not shown on the certificate:

> **(1)** a buyer of the goods, other than a person in the business of selling goods of that kind, takes free of the security interest if the buyer gives value and receives delivery of the goods after issuance of the certificate and without knowledge of the security interest; and

> **(2)** the security interest is subordinate to a conflicting security interest in the goods that attaches, and is perfected under Section 9–311(b), after issuance of the certificate and without the conflicting secured party's knowledge of the security interest.

§ 9–338. Priority of Security Interest or Agricultural Lien Perfected by Filed Financing Statement Providing Certain Incorrect Information.

If a security interest or agricultural lien is perfected by a filed financing statement providing information described in Section 9–516(b)(5) which is incorrect at the time the financing statement is filed:

> **(1)** the security interest or agricultural lien is subordinate to a conflicting perfected security interest in the collateral to the extent that the holder of the conflicting security interest gives value in reasonable reliance upon the incorrect information; and

> **(2)** a purchaser, other than a secured party, of the collateral takes free of the security interest or agricultural lien to the extent that, in reasonable reliance upon the incorrect information, the purchaser gives value and, in the case of chattel paper, documents, goods, instruments, or a security certificate, receives delivery of the collateral.

§ 9–339. Priority Subject to Subordination.

This article does not preclude subordination by agreement by a person entitled to priority.

[Subpart 4. Rights of Bank]

§ 9–340. Effectiveness of Right of Recoupment or Set-Off against Deposit Account.

(a) Except as otherwise provided in subsection (c), a bank with which a deposit account is maintained may exercise any right of recoupment or set-off against a secured party that holds a security interest in the deposit account.

(b) Except as otherwise provided in subsection (c), the application of this article to a security interest in a deposit account does not affect a right of recoupment or set-off of the secured party as to a deposit account maintained with the secured party.

(c) The exercise by a bank of a set-off against a deposit account is ineffective against a secured party that holds a security interest in the deposit account which is perfected by control under Section 9–104(a)(3), if the set-off is based on a claim against the debtor.

§ 9–341. Bank's Rights and Duties with Respect to Deposit Account.

Except as otherwise provided in Section 9–340(c), and unless the bank otherwise agrees in an authenticated record, a bank's rights and duties with respect to a deposit account maintained with the bank are not terminated, suspended, or modified by:

> **(1)** the creation, attachment, or perfection of a security interest in the deposit account;

> **(2)** the bank's knowledge of the security interest; or

> **(3)** the bank's receipt of instructions from the secured party.

§ 9–342. Bank's Right to Refuse to Enter into or Disclose Existence of Control Agreement.

This article does not require a bank to enter into an agreement of the kind described in Section 9–104(a)(2), even if its customer so requests or directs. A bank that has entered into such an agreement is not required to confirm the existence of the agreement to another person unless requested to do so by its customer.

Part 4—Rights of Third Parties

§ 9–401. Alienability of Debtor's Rights.

(a) Except as otherwise provided in subsection (b) and Sections 9–406, 9–407, 9–408, and 9–409, whether a debtor's rights in collateral may be voluntarily or involuntarily transferred is governed by law other than this article.

(b) An agreement between the debtor and secured party which prohibits a transfer of the debtor's rights in collateral or makes the transfer a default does not prevent the transfer from taking effect.

§ 9–402. Secured Party Not Obligated on Contract of Debtor or in Tort.

The existence of a security interest, agricultural lien, or authority given to a debtor to dispose of or use collateral, without more, does not subject a secured party to liability in contract or tort for the debtor's acts or omissions.

§ 9–403. Agreement Not to Assert Defenses against Assignee.

(a) In this section, "value" has the meaning provided in Section 3–303(a).

(b) Except as otherwise provided in this section, an agreement between an account debtor and an assignor not to assert against an assignee any claim or defense that the account debtor may have against the assignor is enforceable by an assignee that takes an assignment:

   (1) for value;

   (2) in good faith;

   (3) without notice of a claim of a property or possessory right to the property assigned; and

   (4) without notice of a defense or claim in recoupment of the type that may be asserted against a person entitled to enforce a negotiable instrument under Section 3–305(a).

(c) Subsection (b) does not apply to defenses of a type that may be asserted against a holder in due course of a negotiable instrument under Section 3–305(b).

(d) In a consumer transaction, if a record evidences the account debtor's obligation, law other than this article requires that the record include a statement to the effect that the rights of an assignee are subject to claims or defenses that the account debtor could assert against the original obligee, and the record does not include such a statement:

   (1) the record has the same effect as if the record included such a statement; and

   (2) the account debtor may assert against an assignee those claims and defenses that would have been available if the record included such a statement.

(e) This section is subject to law other than this article which establishes a different rule for an account debtor who is an individual and who incurred the obligation primarily for personal, family, or household purposes.

(f) Except as otherwise provided in subsection (d), this section does not displace law other than this article which gives effect to an agreement by an account debtor not to assert a claim or defense against an assignee.

§ 9–404. Rights Acquired by Assignee; Claims and Defenses against Assignee.

(a) Unless an account debtor has made an enforceable agreement not to assert defenses or claims, and subject to subsections (b) through (e), the rights of an assignee are subject to:

   (1) all terms of the agreement between the account debtor and assignor and any defense or claim in recoupment arising from the transaction that gave rise to the contract; and

   (2) any other defense or claim of the account debtor against the assignor which accrues before the account debtor receives a notification of the assignment authenticated by the assignor or the assignee.

(b) Subject to subsection (c) and except as otherwise provided in subsection (d), the claim of an account debtor against an assignor may be asserted against an assignee under subsection (a) only to reduce the amount the account debtor owes.

(c) This section is subject to law other than this article which establishes a different rule for an account debtor who is an individual and who incurred the obligation primarily for personal, family, or household purposes.

(d) In a consumer transaction, if a record evidences the account debtor's obligation, law other than this article requires that the record include a statement to the effect that the account debtor's recovery against an assignee with respect to claims and defenses against the assignor may not exceed amounts paid by the account debtor under the record, and the record does not include such a statement, the extent to which a claim of an account debtor against the assignor may be asserted against an assignee is determined as if the record included such a statement.

(e) This section does not apply to an assignment of a health-care-insurance receivable.

§ 9–405. Modification of Assigned Contract.

(a) A modification of or substitution for an assigned contract is effective against an assignee if made in good faith. The assignee acquires corresponding rights under the modified or substituted contract. The assignment may provide that the modification or substitution is a breach of contract by the assignor. This subsection is subject to subsections (b) through (d).

(b) Subsection (a) applies to the extent that:

   (1) the right to payment or a part thereof under an assigned contract has not been fully earned by performance; or

   (2) the right to payment or a part thereof has been fully earned by performance and the account debtor has not received notification of the assignment under Section 9–406(a).

(c) This section is subject to law other than this article which establishes a different rule for an account debtor who is an individual and who incurred the obligation primarily for personal, family, or household purposes.

(d) This section does not apply to an assignment of a health-care-insurance receivable.

§ 9–406. Discharge of Account Debtor; Notification of Assignment; Identification and Proof of Assignment; Restrictions on Assignment of Accounts, Chattel Paper, Payment Intangibles, and Promissory Notes Ineffective.

(a) Subject to subsections (b) through (i), an account debtor on an account, chattel paper, or a payment intangible may discharge its obligation by paying the assignor until, but not after, the account debtor receives a notification, authenticated by the assignor or the assignee, that the amount due or to become due has been assigned and that payment is to be made to the assignee. After receipt of the notification, the account debtor may discharge its obligation by paying the assignee and may not discharge the obligation by paying the assignor.

(b) Subject to subsection (h), notification is ineffective under subsection (a):

(1) if it does not reasonably identify the rights assigned;

(2) to the extent that an agreement between an account debtor and a seller of a payment intangible limits the account debtor's duty to pay a person other than the seller and the limitation is effective under law other than this article; or

(3) at the option of an account debtor, if the notification notifies the account debtor to make less than the full amount of any installment or other periodic payment to the assignee, even if:

(A) only a portion of the account, chattel paper, or payment intangible has been assigned to that assignee;

(B) a portion has been assigned to another assignee; or

(C) the account debtor knows that the assignment to that assignee is limited.

(c) Subject to subsection (h), if requested by the account debtor, an assignee shall seasonably furnish reasonable proof that the assignment has been made. Unless the assignee complies, the account debtor may discharge its obligation by paying the assignor, even if the account debtor has received a notification under subsection (a).

(d) Except as otherwise provided in subsection (e) and Sections 2A–303 and 9–407, and subject to subsection (h), a term in an agreement between an account debtor and an assignor or in a promissory note is ineffective to the extent that it:

(1) prohibits, restricts, or requires the consent of the account debtor or person obligated on the promissory note to the assignment or transfer of, or the creation, attachment, perfection, or enforcement of a security interest in, the account, chattel paper, payment intangible, or promissory note; or

(2) provides that the assignment or transfer or the creation, attachment, perfection, or enforcement of the security interest may give rise to a default, breach, right of recoupment, claim, defense, termination, right of termination, or remedy under the account, chattel paper, payment intangible, or promissory note.

(e) Subsection (d) does not apply to the sale of a payment intangible or promissory note.

(f) Except as otherwise provided in Sections 2A–303 and 9–407 and subject to subsections (h) and (i), a rule of law, statute, or regulation that prohibits, restricts, or requires the consent of a government, governmental body or official, or account debtor to the assignment or transfer of, or creation of a security interest in, an account or chattel paper is ineffective to the extent that the rule of law, statute, or regulation:

(1) prohibits, restricts, or requires the consent of the government, governmental body or official, or account debtor to the assignment or transfer of, or the creation, attachment, perfection, or enforcement of a security interest in the account or chattel paper; or

(2) provides that the assignment or transfer or the creation, attachment, perfection, or enforcement of the security interest may give rise to a default, breach, right of recoupment, claim, defense, termination, right of termination, or remedy under the account or chattel paper.

(g) Subject to subsection (h), an account debtor may not waive or vary its option under subsection (b)(3).

(h) This section is subject to law other than this article which establishes a different rule for an account debtor who is an individual and who incurred the obligation primarily for personal, family, or household purposes.

(i) This section does not apply to an assignment of a health-care-insurance receivable.

(j) This section prevails over any inconsistent provisions of the following statutes, rules, and regulations:

[List here any statutes, rules, and regulations containing provisions inconsistent with this section.]

Legislative Note: *States that amend statutes, rules, and regulations to remove provisions inconsistent with this section need not enact subsection (j).*

As amended in 1999 and 2000.

§ 9–407. Restrictions on Creation or Enforcement of Security Interest in Leasehold Interest or in Lessor's Residual Interest.

(a) Except as otherwise provided in subsection (b), a term in a lease agreement is ineffective to the extent that it:

(1) prohibits, restricts, or requires the consent of a party to the lease to the assignment or transfer of, or the creation, attachment, perfection, or enforcement of a security interest in an interest of a party under the lease contract or in the lessor's residual interest in the goods; or

(2) provides that the assignment or transfer or the creation, attachment, perfection, or enforcement of the security interest may give rise to a default, breach, right of recoupment, claim, defense, termination, right of termination, or remedy under the lease.

(b) Except as otherwise provided in Section 2A–303(7), a term described in subsection (a)(2) is effective to the extent that there is:

(1) a transfer by the lessee of the lessee's right of possession or use of the goods in violation of the term; or

(2) a delegation of a material performance of either party to the lease contract in violation of the term.

(c) The creation, attachment, perfection, or enforcement of a security interest in the lessor's interest under the lease contract or the lessor's residual interest in the goods is not a transfer that materially impairs the lessee's prospect of obtaining return performance or materially changes the duty of or materially increases the burden or risk imposed on the lessee within the purview of Section 2A–303(4) unless, and then only to the extent that, enforcement actually results in a delegation of material performance of the lessor.

As amended in 1999.

§ 9–408. Restrictions on Assignment of Promissory Notes, Health-Care-Insurance Receivables, and Certain General Intangibles Ineffective.

(a) Except as otherwise provided in subsection (b), a term in a promissory note or in an agreement between an account debtor and a debtor which relates to a health-care-insurance receivable or a general intangible, including a contract, permit, license, or franchise, and which term prohibits, restricts, or requires the consent of the person obligated on the promissory note or the account debtor to, the assignment or transfer of, or creation, attachment, or perfection of a security interest in, the promissory note, health-care-insurance receivable, or general intangible, is ineffective to the extent that the term:

(1) would impair the creation, attachment, or perfection of a security interest; or

(2) provides that the assignment or transfer or the creation, attachment, or perfection of the security interest may give rise to a default, breach, right of recoupment, claim, defense, termination, right of termination, or remedy under the promissory note, health-care-insurance receivable, or general intangible.

(b) Subsection (a) applies to a security interest in a payment intangible or promissory note only if the security interest arises out of a sale of the payment intangible or promissory note.

(c) A rule of law, statute, or regulation that prohibits, restricts, or requires the consent of a government, governmental body or official, person obligated on a promissory note, or account debtor to the assignment or transfer of, or creation of a security interest in, a promissory note, health-care-insurance receivable, or general intangible, including a contract, permit, license, or franchise between an account debtor and a debtor, is ineffective to the extent that the rule of law, statute, or regulation:

(1) would impair the creation, attachment, or perfection of a security interest; or

(2) provides that the assignment or transfer or the creation, attachment, or perfection of the security interest may give rise to a default, breach, right of recoupment, claim, defense, termination, right of termination, or remedy under the promissory note, health-care-insurance receivable, or general intangible.

(d) To the extent that a term in a promissory note or in an agreement between an account debtor and a debtor which relates to a health-care-insurance receivable or general intangible or a rule of law, statute, or regulation described in subsection (c) would be effective under law other than this article but is ineffective under subsection (a) or (c), the creation, attachment, or perfection of a security interest in the promissory note, health-care-insurance receivable, or general intangible:

(1) is not enforceable against the person obligated on the promissory note or the account debtor;

(2) does not impose a duty or obligation on the person obligated on the promissory note or the account debtor;

(3) does not require the person obligated on the promissory note or the account debtor to recognize the security interest, pay or render performance to the secured party, or accept payment or performance from the secured party;

(4) does not entitle the secured party to use or assign the debtor's rights under the promissory note, health-care-insurance receivable, or general intangible, including any related information or materials furnished to the debtor in the transaction giving rise to the promissory note, health-care-insurance receivable, or general intangible;

(5) does not entitle the secured party to use, assign, possess, or have access to any trade secrets or confidential information of the person obligated on the promissory note or the account debtor; and

(6) does not entitle the secured party to enforce the security interest in the promissory note, health-care-insurance receivable, or general intangible.

(e) This section prevails over any inconsistent provisions of the following statutes, rules, and regulations:

[List here any statutes, rules, and regulations containing provisions inconsistent with this section.]

Legislative Note: *States that amend statutes, rules, and regulations to remove provisions inconsistent with this section need not enact subsection (e).* As amended in 1999.

§ 9–409. Restrictions on Assignment of Letter-of-Credit Rights Ineffective.

(a) A term in a letter of credit or a rule of law, statute, regulation, custom, or practice applicable to the letter of credit which prohibits, restricts, or requires the consent of an applicant, issuer, or nominated person to a beneficiary's assignment of or creation of a security interest in a letter-of-credit right is ineffective to the extent that the term or rule of law, statute, regulation, custom, or practice:

(1) would impair the creation, attachment, or perfection of a security interest in the letter-of-credit right; or

(2) provides that the assignment or the creation, attachment, or perfection of the security interest may give rise to a default, breach, right of recoupment, claim, defense, termination, right of termination, or remedy under the letter-of-credit right.

(b) To the extent that a term in a letter of credit is ineffective under subsection (a) but would be effective under law other than this article or a custom or practice applicable to the letter of credit, to the transfer of a right to draw or otherwise demand performance under the letter of credit, or to the assignment of a right to proceeds of the letter of credit, the creation, attachment, or perfection of a security interest in the letter-of-credit right:

(1) is not enforceable against the applicant, issuer, nominated person, or transferee beneficiary;

(2) imposes no duties or obligations on the applicant, issuer, nominated person, or transferee beneficiary; and

(3) does not require the applicant, issuer, nominated person, or transferee beneficiary to recognize the security interest, pay or render performance to the secured party, or accept payment or other performance from the secured party.

As amended in 1999.

Part 5—Filing

[Subpart 1. Filing Office; Contents and Effectiveness of Financing Statement]

§ 9–501. Filing Office.

(a) Except as otherwise provided in subsection (b), if the local law of this State governs perfection of a security interest or agricultural lien, the office in which to file a financing statement to perfect the security interest or agricultural lien is:

(1) the office designated for the filing or recording of a record of a mortgage on the related real property, if:

(A) the collateral is as-extracted collateral or timber to be cut; or

(B) the financing statement is filed as a fixture filing and the collateral is goods that are or are to become fixtures; or

(2) the office of [ ] [or any office duly authorized by [ ]], in all other cases, including a case in which the collateral is goods that are or are to become fixtures and the financing statement is not filed as a fixture filing.

(b) The office in which to file a financing statement to perfect a security interest in collateral, including fixtures, of a transmitting utility is the office of [ ]. The financing statement also constitutes a fixture filing as to the collateral indicated in the financing statement which is or is to become fixtures.

Legislative Note: *The State should designate the filing office where the brackets appear. The filing office may be that of a governmental official (e.g., the Secretary of State) or a private party that maintains the State's filing system.*

§ 9–502. Contents of Financing Statement; Record of Mortgage as Financing Statement; Time of Filing Financing Statement.

(a) Subject to subsection (b), a financing statement is sufficient only if it:

(1) provides the name of the debtor;

(2) provides the name of the secured party or a representative of the secured party; and

(3) indicates the collateral covered by the financing statement.

(b) Except as otherwise provided in Section 9–501(b), to be sufficient, a financing statement that covers as-extracted collateral or timber to be cut, or which is filed as a fixture filing and covers goods that are or are to become fixtures, must satisfy subsection (a) and also:

(1) indicate that it covers this type of collateral;

(2) indicate that it is to be filed [for record] in the real property records;

(3) provide a description of the real property to which the collateral is related [sufficient to give constructive notice of a mortgage under the law of this State if the description were contained in a record of the mortgage of the real property]; and

(4) if the debtor does not have an interest of record in the real property, provide the name of a record owner.

(c) A record of a mortgage is effective, from the date of recording, as a financing statement filed as a fixture filing or as a financing statement covering as-extracted collateral or timber to be cut only if:

(1) the record indicates the goods or accounts that it covers;

(2) the goods are or are to become fixtures related to the real property described in the record or the collateral is related to the real property described in the record and is as-extracted collateral or timber to be cut;

(3) the record satisfies the requirements for a financing statement in this section other than an indication that it is to be filed in the real property records; and

(4) the record is [duly] recorded.

(d) A financing statement may be filed before a security agreement is made or a security interest otherwise attaches.

Legislative Note: *Language in brackets is optional. Where the State has any special recording system for real property other than the usual grantor-grantee index (as, for instance, a tract system or a title registration or Torrens system) local adaptations of subsection (b) and Section 9–519(d) and (e) may be necessary. See, e.g., Mass. Gen. Laws Chapter 106, Section 9–410.*

§ 9–503. Name of Debtor and Secured Party.

(a) A financing statement sufficiently provides the name of the debtor:

(1) if the debtor is a registered organization, only if the financing statement provides the name of the debtor indicated on the public record of the debtor's jurisdiction of organization which shows the debtor to have been organized;

(2) if the debtor is a decedent's estate, only if the financing statement provides the name of the decedent and indicates that the debtor is an estate;

(3) if the debtor is a trust or a trustee acting with respect to property held in trust, only if the financing statement:

(A) provides the name specified for the trust in its organic documents or, if no name is specified, provides the name of the settlor and additional information sufficient to distinguish the debtor from other trusts having one or more of the same settlors; and

(B) indicates, in the debtor's name or otherwise, that the debtor is a trust or is a trustee acting with respect to property held in trust; and

(4) in other cases:

(A) if the debtor has a name, only if it provides the individual or organizational name of the debtor; and

(B) if the debtor does not have a name, only if it provides the names of the partners, members, associates, or other persons comprising the debtor.

(b) A financing statement that provides the name of the debtor in accordance with subsection (a) is not rendered ineffective by the absence of:

(1) a trade name or other name of the debtor; or

(2) unless required under subsection (a)(4)(B), names of partners, members, associates, or other persons comprising the debtor.

(c) A financing statement that provides only the debtor's trade name does not sufficiently provide the name of the debtor.

(d) Failure to indicate the representative capacity of a secured party or representative of a secured party does not affect the sufficiency of a financing statement.

(e) A financing statement may provide the name of more than one debtor and the name of more than one secured party.

§ 9–504. Indication of Collateral.

A financing statement sufficiently indicates the collateral that it covers if the financing statement provides:

(1) a description of the collateral pursuant to Section 9–108; or

(2) an indication that the financing statement covers all assets or all personal property.

As amended in 1999.

§ 9–505. Filing and Compliance with Other Statutes and Treaties for Consignments, Leases, Other Bailments, and Other Transactions.

(a) A consignor, lessor, or other bailor of goods, a licensor, or a buyer of a payment intangible or promissory note may file a financing statement, or may comply with a statute or treaty described in Section 9–311(a), using the terms "consignor", "consignee", "lessor", "lessee", "bailor", "bailee", "licensor", "licensee", "owner", "registered owner", "buyer", "seller", or words of similar import, instead of the terms "secured party" and "debtor".

(b) This part applies to the filing of a financing statement under subsection (a) and, as appropriate, to compliance that is equivalent to filing a financing statement under Section 9–311(b), but the filing or compliance is not of itself a factor in determining whether the collateral secures an obligation. If it is determined for another reason that the collateral secures an obligation, a security interest held by the consignor, lessor, bailor, licensor, owner, or buyer which attaches to the collateral is perfected by the filing or compliance.

§ 9–506. Effect of Errors or Omissions.

(a) A financing statement substantially satisfying the requirements of this part is effective, even if it has minor errors or omissions, unless the errors or omissions make the financing statement seriously misleading.

(b) Except as otherwise provided in subsection (c), a financing statement that fails sufficiently to provide the name of the debtor in accordance with Section 9–503(a) is seriously misleading.

(c) If a search of the records of the filing office under the debtor's correct name, using the filing office's standard search logic, if any, would disclose a financing statement that fails sufficiently to provide the name of the debtor in accordance with Section 9–503(a), the name provided does not make the financing statement seriously misleading.

(d) For purposes of Section 9–508(b), the "debtor's correct name" in subsection (c) means the correct name of the new debtor.

§ 9–507. Effect of Certain Events on Effectiveness of Financing Statement.

(a) A filed financing statement remains effective with respect to collateral that is sold, exchanged, leased, licensed, or otherwise disposed of and in which a security interest or agricultural lien continues, even if the secured party knows of or consents to the disposition.

(b) Except as otherwise provided in subsection (c) and Section 9–508, a financing statement is not rendered ineffective if, after the financing statement is filed, the information provided in the financing statement becomes seriously misleading under Section 9–506.

(c) If a debtor so changes its name that a filed financing statement becomes seriously misleading under Section 9–506:

    (1) the financing statement is effective to perfect a security interest in collateral acquired by the debtor before, or within four months after, the change; and

    (2) the financing statement is not effective to perfect a security interest in collateral acquired by the debtor more than four months after the change, unless an amendment to the financing statement which renders the financing statement not seriously misleading is filed within four months after the change.

§ 9–508. Effectiveness of Financing Statement If New Debtor Becomes Bound by Security Agreement.

(a) Except as otherwise provided in this section, a filed financing statement naming an original debtor is effective to perfect a security interest in collateral in which a new debtor has or acquires rights to the extent that the financing statement would have been effective had the original debtor acquired rights in the collateral.

(b) If the difference between the name of the original debtor and that of the new debtor causes a filed financing statement that is effective under subsection (a) to be seriously misleading under Section 9–506:

    (1) the financing statement is effective to perfect a security interest in collateral acquired by the new debtor before, and within four months after, the new debtor becomes bound under Section 9B–203(d); and

    (2) the financing statement is not effective to perfect a security interest in collateral acquired by the new debtor more than four months after the new debtor becomes bound under Section 9–203(d) unless an initial financing statement providing the name of the new debtor is filed before the expiration of that time.

(c) This section does not apply to collateral as to which a filed financing statement remains effective against the new debtor under Section 9–507(a).

§ 9–509. Persons Entitled to File a Record.

(a) A person may file an initial financing statement, amendment that adds collateral covered by a financing statement, or amendment that adds a debtor to a financing statement only if:

    (1) the debtor authorizes the filing in an authenticated record or pursuant to subsection (b) or (c); or

    (2) the person holds an agricultural lien that has become effective at the time of filing and the financing statement covers only collateral in which the person holds an agricultural lien.

(b) By authenticating or becoming bound as debtor by a security agreement, a debtor or new debtor authorizes the filing of an initial financing statement, and an amendment, covering:

    (1) the collateral described in the security agreement; and

    (2) property that becomes collateral under Section 9–315(a)(2), whether or not the security agreement expressly covers proceeds.

(c) By acquiring collateral in which a security interest or agricultural lien continues under Section 9–315(a)(1), a debtor authorizes the filing of an initial financing statement, and an amendment, covering the collateral and property that becomes collateral under Section 9–315(a)(2).

(d) A person may file an amendment other than an amendment that adds collateral covered by a financing statement or an amendment that adds a debtor to a financing statement only if:

    (1) the secured party of record authorizes the filing; or

    (2) the amendment is a termination statement for a financing statement as to which the secured party of record has failed to file or send a termination statement as required by Section 9–513(a) or (c), the debtor authorizes the filing, and the termination statement indicates that the debtor authorized it to be filed.

(e) If there is more than one secured party of record for a financing statement, each secured party of record may authorize the filing of an amendment under subsection (d).

As amended in 2000.

§ 9–510. Effectiveness of Filed Record.

(a) A filed record is effective only to the extent that it was filed by a person that may file it under Section 9–509.

(b) A record authorized by one secured party of record does not affect the financing statement with respect to another secured party of record.

(c) A continuation statement that is not filed within the six-month period prescribed by Section 9–515(d) is ineffective.

§ 9–511. Secured Party of Record.

(a) A secured party of record with respect to a financing statement is a person whose name is provided as the name of the secured party or a representative of the secured party in an initial financing statement that has been filed. If an initial financing statement is filed under Section 9–514(a), the assignee named in the initial financing statement is the secured party of record with respect to the financing statement.

(b) If an amendment of a financing statement which provides the name of a person as a secured party or a representative of a secured party is filed, the person named in the amendment is a secured party of record. If an amendment is filed under Section 9–514(b), the assignee named in the amendment is a secured party of record.

(c) A person remains a secured party of record until the filing of an amendment of the financing statement which deletes the person.

§ 9–512. Amendment of Financing Statement.

[Alternative A]

(a) Subject to Section 9–509, a person may add or delete collateral covered by, continue or terminate the effectiveness of, or, subject to subsection (e), otherwise amend the information provided in, a financing statement by filing an amendment that:

(1) identifies, by its file number, the initial financing statement to which the amendment relates; and

(2) if the amendment relates to an initial financing statement filed [or recorded] in a filing office described in Section 9–501(a)(1), provides the information specified in Section 9–502(b).

[Alternative B]

(a) Subject to Section 9–509, a person may add or delete collateral covered by, continue or terminate the effectiveness of, or, subject to subsection (e), otherwise amend the information provided in, a financing statement by filing an amendment that:

(1) identifies, by its file number, the initial financing statement to which the amendment relates; and

(2) if the amendment relates to an initial financing statement filed [or recorded] in a filing office described in Section 9–501(a)(1), provides the date [and time] that the initial financing statement was filed [or recorded] and the information specified in Section 9–502(b).

[End of Alternatives]

(b) Except as otherwise provided in Section 9–515, the filing of an amendment does not extend the period of effectiveness of the financing statement.

(c) A financing statement that is amended by an amendment that adds collateral is effective as to the added collateral only from the date of the filing of the amendment.

(d) A financing statement that is amended by an amendment that adds a debtor is effective as to the added debtor only from the date of the filing of the amendment.

(e) An amendment is ineffective to the extent it:

(1) purports to delete all debtors and fails to provide the name of a debtor to be covered by the financing statement; or

(2) purports to delete all secured parties of record and fails to provide the name of a new secured party of record.

Legislative Note: *States whose real-estate filing offices require additional information in amendments and cannot search their records by both the name of the debtor and the file number should enact Alternative B to Sections 9–512(a), 9–518(b), 9–519(f), and 9–522(a).*

§ 9–513. Termination Statement.

(a) A secured party shall cause the secured party of record for a financing statement to file a termination statement for the financing statement if the financing statement covers consumer goods and:

(1) there is no obligation secured by the collateral covered by the financing statement and no commitment to make an advance, incur an obligation, or otherwise give value; or

(2) the debtor did not authorize the filing of the initial financing statement.

(b) To comply with subsection (a), a secured party shall cause the secured party of record to file the termination statement:

(1) within one month after there is no obligation secured by the collateral covered by the financing statement and no commitment to make an advance, incur an obligation, or otherwise give value; or

(2) if earlier, within 20 days after the secured party receives an authenticated demand from a debtor.

(c) In cases not governed by subsection (a), within 20 days after a secured party receives an authenticated demand from a debtor, the secured party shall cause the secured party of record for a financing statement to send to the debtor a termination statement for the financing statement or file the termination statement in the filing office if:

(1) except in the case of a financing statement covering accounts or chattel paper that has been sold or goods that are the subject of a consignment, there is no obligation secured by the collateral covered by the financing statement and no commitment to make an advance, incur an obligation, or otherwise give value;

(2) the financing statement covers accounts or chattel paper that has been sold but as to which the account debtor or other person obligated has discharged its obligation;

(3) the financing statement covers goods that were the subject of a consignment to the debtor but are not in the debtor's possession; or

(4) the debtor did not authorize the filing of the initial financing statement.

(d) Except as otherwise provided in Section 9–510, upon the filing of a termination statement with the filing office, the financing statement to which the termination statement relates ceases to be effective. Except as otherwise provided in Section 9–510, for purposes of Sections 9–519(g), 9–522(a), and 9–523(c), the filing with the filing office of a termination statement relating to a financing statement that indicates that the debtor is a transmitting utility also causes the effectiveness of the financing statement to lapse.

As amended in 2000.

§ 9–514. Assignment of Powers of Secured Party of Record.

(a) Except as otherwise provided in subsection (c), an initial financing statement may reflect an assignment of all of the secured party's power to authorize an amendment to the financing statement by providing the name and mailing address of the assignee as the name and address of the secured party.

(b) Except as otherwise provided in subsection (c), a secured party of record may assign of record all or part of its power to authorize an amendment to a financing statement by filing in the filing office an amendment of the financing statement which:

(1) identifies, by its file number, the initial financing statement to which it relates;

(2) provides the name of the assignor; and

(3) provides the name and mailing address of the assignee.

(c) An assignment of record of a security interest in a fixture covered by a record of a mortgage which is effective as a financing statement filed as a fixture filing under Section 9–502(c) may be made only by an assignment of record of the mortgage in the manner provided by law of this State other than [the Uniform Commercial Code].

§ 9–515. Duration and Effectiveness of Financing Statement; Effect of Lapsed Financing Statement.

(a) Except as otherwise provided in subsections (b), (e), (f), and (g), a filed financing statement is effective for a period of five years after the date of filing.

(b) Except as otherwise provided in subsections (e), (f), and (g), an initial financing statement filed in connection with a public-finance transaction or manufactured-home transaction is effective for a period of 30 years after the date of filing if it indicates that it is filed in connection with a public-finance transaction or manufactured-home transaction.

(c) The effectiveness of a filed financing statement lapses on the expiration of the period of its effectiveness unless before the lapse a continuation statement is filed pursuant to subsection (d). Upon lapse, a financing statement ceases to be effective and any security interest or agricultural lien that was perfected by the financing statement becomes unperfected, unless the security interest is perfected otherwise. If the security interest or agricultural lien becomes unperfected upon lapse, it is deemed never to have been perfected as against a purchaser of the collateral for value.

(d) A continuation statement may be filed only within six months before the expiration of the five-year period specified in subsection (a) or the 30-year period specified in subsection (b), whichever is applicable.

(e) Except as otherwise provided in Section 9–510, upon timely filing of a continuation statement, the effectiveness of the initial financing statement continues for a period of five years commencing on the day on which the financing statement would have become ineffective in the absence of the filing. Upon the expiration of the five-year period, the financing statement lapses in the same manner as provided in subsection (c), unless, before the lapse, another continuation statement is filed pursuant to subsection (d). Succeeding continuation statements may be filed in the same manner to continue the effectiveness of the initial financing statement.

(f) If a debtor is a transmitting utility and a filed financing statement so indicates, the financing statement is effective until a termination statement is filed.

(g) A record of a mortgage that is effective as a financing statement filed as a fixture filing under Section 9–502(c) remains effective as a financing statement filed as a fixture filing until the mortgage is released or satisfied of record or its effectiveness otherwise terminates as to the real property.

§ 9–516. What Constitutes Filing; Effectiveness of Filing.

(a) Except as otherwise provided in subsection (b), communication of a record to a filing office and tender of the filing fee or acceptance of the record by the filing office constitutes filing.

(b) Filing does not occur with respect to a record that a filing office refuses to accept because:

(1) the record is not communicated by a method or medium of communication authorized by the filing office;

(2) an amount equal to or greater than the applicable filing fee is not tendered;

(3) the filing office is unable to index the record because:

(A) in the case of an initial financing statement, the record does not provide a name for the debtor;

(B) in the case of an amendment or correction statement, the record:

(i) does not identify the initial financing statement as required by Section 9–512 or 9–518, as applicable; or

(ii) identifies an initial financing statement whose effectiveness has lapsed under Section 9–515;

(C) in the case of an initial financing statement that provides the name of a debtor identified as an individual or an amendment that provides a name of a debtor identified as an individual which was not previously provided in the financing statement to which the record relates, the record does not identify the debtor's last name; or

(D) in the case of a record filed [or recorded] in the filing office described in Section 9–501(a)(1), the record does not provide a sufficient description of the real property to which it relates;

(4) in the case of an initial financing statement or an amendment that adds a secured party of record, the record does not provide a name and mailing address for the secured party of record;

(5) in the case of an initial financing statement or an amendment that provides a name of a debtor which was not previously provided in the financing statement to which the amendment relates, the record does not:

(A) provide a mailing address for the debtor;

(B) indicate whether the debtor is an individual or an organization; or

(C) if the financing statement indicates that the debtor is an organization, provide:

(i) a type of organization for the debtor;

(ii) a jurisdiction of organization for the debtor; or

(iii) an organizational identification number for the debtor or indicate that the debtor has none;

(6) in the case of an assignment reflected in an initial financing statement under Section 9–514(a) or an amendment filed under Section 9–514(b), the record does not provide a name and mailing address for the assignee; or

(7) in the case of a continuation statement, the record is not filed within the six-month period prescribed by Section 9–515(d).

(c) For purposes of subsection (b):

(1) a record does not provide information if the filing office is unable to read or decipher the information; and

(2) a record that does not indicate that it is an amendment or identify an initial financing statement to which it relates, as required by Section 9–512, 9–514, or 9–518, is an initial financing statement.

(d) A record that is communicated to the filing office with tender of the filing fee, but which the filing office refuses to accept for a reason other than one set forth in subsection (b), is effective as a filed record except as against a purchaser of the collateral which gives value in reasonable reliance upon the absence of the record from the files.

§ 9–517. Effect of Indexing Errors.

The failure of the filing office to index a record correctly does not affect the effectiveness of the filed record.

§ 9–518. Claim Concerning Inaccurate or Wrongfully Filed Record.

(a) A person may file in the filing office a correction statement with respect to a record indexed there under the person's name if the person believes that the record is inaccurate or was wrongfully filed.

[Alternative A]

(b) A correction statement must:

(1) identify the record to which it relates by the file number assigned to the initial financing statement to which the record relates;

(2) indicate that it is a correction statement; and

(3) provide the basis for the person's belief that the record is inaccurate and indicate the manner in which the person believes the record should be amended to cure any inaccuracy or provide the basis for the person's belief that the record was wrongfully filed.

[Alternative B]

(b) A correction statement must:

(1) identify the record to which it relates by:

(A) the file number assigned to the initial financing statement to which the record relates; and

(B) if the correction statement relates to a record filed [or recorded] in a filing office described in Section 9–501(a)(1), the date [and time] that the initial financing statement was filed [or recorded] and the information specified in Section 9–502(b);

(2) indicate that it is a correction statement; and

(3) provide the basis for the person's belief that the record is inaccurate and indicate the manner in which the person believes the record should be amended to cure any inaccuracy or provide the basis for the person's belief that the record was wrongfully filed.

[End of Alternatives]

(c) The filing of a correction statement does not affect the effectiveness of an initial financing statement or other filed record.

Legislative Note: *States whose real-estate filing offices require additional information in amendments and cannot search their records by both the name of the debtor and the file number should enact Alternative B to Sections 9–512(a), 9–518(b), 9–519(f), and 9–522(a).*

[Subpart 2. Duties and Operation of Filing Office]

§ 9–519. Numbering, Maintaining, and Indexing Records; Communicating Information Provided in Records.

(a) For each record filed in a filing office, the filing office shall:

(1) assign a unique number to the filed record;

(2) create a record that bears the number assigned to the filed record and the date and time of filing;

(3) maintain the filed record for public inspection; and

(4) index the filed record in accordance with subsections (c), (d), and (e).

(b) A file number [assigned after January 1, 2002,] must include a digit that:

(1) is mathematically derived from or related to the other digits of the file number; and

(2) aids the filing office in determining whether a number communicated as the file number includes a single-digit or transpositional error.

(c) Except as otherwise provided in subsections (d) and (e), the filing office shall:

(1) index an initial financing statement according to the name of the debtor and index all filed records relating to the initial financing statement in a manner that associates with one another an initial financing statement and all filed records relating to the initial financing statement; and

(2) index a record that provides a name of a debtor which was not previously provided in the financing statement to which the record relates also according to the name that was not previously provided.

(d) If a financing statement is filed as a fixture filing or covers as-extracted collateral or timber to be cut, [it must be filed for record and] the filing office shall index it:

(1) under the names of the debtor and of each owner of record shown on the financing statement as if they were the mortgagors under a mortgage of the real property described; and

(2) to the extent that the law of this State provides for indexing of records of mortgages under the name of the mortgagee, under the name of the secured party as if the secured party were the mortgagee thereunder, or, if indexing is by description, as if the financing statement were a record of a mortgage of the real property described.

(e) If a financing statement is filed as a fixture filing or covers as-extracted collateral or timber to be cut, the filing office shall index an assignment filed under Section 9–514(a) or an amendment filed under Section 9–514(b):

(1) under the name of the assignor as grantor; and

(2) to the extent that the law of this State provides for indexing a record of the assignment of a mortgage under the name of the assignee, under the name of the assignee.

[Alternative A]

(f) The filing office shall maintain a capability:

(1) to retrieve a record by the name of the debtor and by the file number assigned to the initial financing statement to which the record relates; and

(2) to associate and retrieve with one another an initial financing statement and each filed record relating to the initial financing statement.

[Alternative B]

(f) The filing office shall maintain a capability:

(1) to retrieve a record by the name of the debtor and:

(A) if the filing office is described in Section 9–501(a)(1), by the file number assigned to the initial financing statement to which the record relates and the date [and time] that the record was filed [or recorded]; or

(B) if the filing office is described in Section 9–501(a)(2), by the file number assigned to the initial financing statement to which the record relates; and

(2) to associate and retrieve with one another an initial financing statement and each filed record relating to the initial financing statement.

[End of Alternatives]

(g) The filing office may not remove a debtor's name from the index until one year after the effectiveness of a financing statement naming the debtor lapses under Section 9–515 with respect to all secured parties of record.

(h) The filing office shall perform the acts required by subsections (a) through (e) at the time and in the manner prescribed by filing-office rule, but not later than two business days after the filing office receives the record in question.

[(i) Subsection[s] [(b)] [and] [(h)] do[es] not apply to a filing office described in Section 9–501(a)(1).]

Legislative Notes:

1. States whose filing offices currently assign file numbers that include a verification number, commonly known as a "check digit," or can implement this requirement before the effective date of this Article should omit the bracketed language in subsection (b).

2. In States in which writings will not appear in the real property records and indices unless actually recorded the bracketed language in subsection (d) should be used.

3. States whose real-estate filing offices require additional information in amendments and cannot search their records by both the name of the debtor and the file number should enact Alternative B to Sections 9–512(a), 9–518(b), 9–519(f), and 9–522(a).

4. A State that elects not to require real-estate filing offices to comply with either or both of subsections (b) and (h) may adopt an applicable variation of subsection (i) and add "Except as otherwise provided in subsection (i)," to the appropriate subsection or subsections.

§ 9–520.   Acceptance and Refusal to Accept Record.

(a) A filing office shall refuse to accept a record for filing for a reason set forth in Section 9–516(b) and may refuse to accept a record for filing only for a reason set forth in Section 9–516(b).

(b) If a filing office refuses to accept a record for filing, it shall communicate to the person that presented the record the fact of and reason for the refusal and the date and time the record would have been filed had the filing office accepted it. The communication must be made at the time and in the manner prescribed by filing-office rule but [, in the case of a filing office described in Section 9–501(a)(2),] in no event more than two business days after the filing office receives the record.

(c) A filed financing statement satisfying Section 9–502(a) and (b) is effective, even if the filing office is required to refuse to accept it for filing under subsection (a). However, Section 9–338 applies to a filed financing statement providing information described in Section 9–516(b)(5) which is incorrect at the time the financing statement is filed.

(d) If a record communicated to a filing office provides information that relates to more than one debtor, this part applies as to each debtor separately.

Legislative Note: *A State that elects not to require real-property filing offices to comply with subsection (b) should include the bracketed language.*

§ 9–521.   Uniform Form of Written Financing Statement and Amendment.

(a) A filing office that accepts written records may not refuse to accept a written initial financing statement in the following form and format except for a reason set forth in Section 9–516(b):

[NATIONAL UCC FINANCING STATEMENT (FORM UCC1) (REV. 7/29/98)]

[NATIONAL UCC FINANCING STATEMENT ADDENDUM (FORM UCC1Ad)(REV. 07/29/98)]

(b) A filing office that accepts written records may not refuse to accept a written record in the following form and format except for a reason set forth in Section 9–516(b):

[NATIONAL UCC FINANCING STATEMENT AMENDMENT (FORM UCC3)(REV. 07/29/98)]

[NATIONAL UCC FINANCING STATEMENT AMENDMENT ADDENDUM (FORM UCC3Ad)(REV. 07/29/98)]

§ 9–522.   Maintenance and Destruction of Records.

[Alternative A]

(a) The filing office shall maintain a record of the information provided in a filed financing statement for at least one year after the effectiveness of the financing statement has lapsed under Section 9–515 with respect to all secured parties of record. The record must be retrievable by using the name of the debtor and by using the file number assigned to the initial financing statement to which the record relates.

[Alternative B]

(a) The filing office shall maintain a record of the information provided in a filed financing statement for at least one year after the effectiveness of the financing statement has lapsed under Section 9–515 with respect to all secured parties of record. The record must be retrievable by using the name of the debtor and:

> **(1)** if the record was filed [or recorded] in the filing office described in Section 9–501(a)(1), by using the file number assigned to the initial financing statement to which the record relates and the date [and time] that the record was filed [or recorded]; or

> **(2)** if the record was filed in the filing office described in Section 9–501(a)(2), by using the file number assigned to the initial financing statement to which the record relates.

[End of Alternatives]

(b) Except to the extent that a statute governing disposition of public records provides otherwise, the filing office immediately may destroy any written record evidencing a financing statement. However, if the filing office destroys a written record, it shall maintain another record of the financing statement which complies with subsection (a).

Legislative Note: *States whose real-estate filing offices require additional information in amendments and cannot search their records by both the name of the debtor and the file number should enact Alternative B to Sections 9–512(a), 9–518(b), 9–519(f), and 9–522(a).*

§ 9–523.   Information from Filing Office; Sale or License of Records.

(a) If a person that files a written record requests an acknowledgment of the filing, the filing office shall send to the person an image of the record showing the number assigned to the record pursuant to Section 9–519(a)(1) and the date and time of the filing of the record. However, if the person furnishes a copy of the record to the filing office, the filing office may instead:

> **(1)** note upon the copy the number assigned to the record pursuant to Section 9–519(a)(1) and the date and time of the filing of the record; and

> **(2)** send the copy to the person.

(b) If a person files a record other than a written record, the filing office shall communicate to the person an acknowledgment that provides:

> **(1)** the information in the record;

> **(2)** the number assigned to the record pursuant to Section 9–519(a)(1); and

> **(3)** the date and time of the filing of the record.

(c) The filing office shall communicate or otherwise make available in a record the following information to any person that requests it:

(1) whether there is on file on a date and time specified by the filing office, but not a date earlier than three business days before the filing office receives the request, any financing statement that:

(A) designates a particular debtor [or, if the request so states, designates a particular debtor at the address specified in the request];

(B) has not lapsed under Section 9–515 with respect to all secured parties of record; and

(C) if the request so states, has lapsed under Section 9–515 and a record of which is maintained by the filing office under Section 9–522(a);

(2) the date and time of filing of each financing statement; and

(3) the information provided in each financing statement.

(d) In complying with its duty under subsection (c), the filing office may communicate information in any medium. However, if requested, the filing office shall communicate information by issuing [its written certificate] [a record that can be admitted into evidence in the courts of this State without extrinsic evidence of its authenticity].

(e) The filing office shall perform the acts required by subsections (a) through (d) at the time and in the manner prescribed by filing-office rule, but not later than two business days after the filing office receives the request.

(f) At least weekly, the [insert appropriate official or governmental agency] [filing office] shall offer to sell or license to the public on a nonexclusive basis, in bulk, copies of all records filed in it under this part, in every medium from time to time available to the filing office.

Legislative Notes:

1. States whose filing office does not offer the additional service of responding to search requests limited to a particular address should omit the bracketed language in subsection (c)(1)(A).

2. A State that elects not to require real-estate filing offices to comply with either or both of subsections (e) and (f) should specify in the appropriate subsection(s) only the filing office described in Section 9–501(a)(2).

§ 9–524. Delay by Filing Office.

Delay by the filing office beyond a time limit prescribed by this part is excused if:

(1) the delay is caused by interruption of communication or computer facilities, war, emergency conditions, failure of equipment, or other circumstances beyond control of the filing office; and

(2) the filing office exercises reasonable diligence under the circumstances.

§ 9–525. Fees.

(a) Except as otherwise provided in subsection (e), the fee for filing and indexing a record under this part, other than an initial financing statement of the kind described in subsection (b), is [the amount specified in subsection (c), if applicable, plus]:

(1) $[X] if the record is communicated in writing and consists of one or two pages;

(2) $[2X] if the record is communicated in writing and consists of more than two pages; and

(3) $[1/2X] if the record is communicated by another medium authorized by filing-office rule.

(b) Except as otherwise provided in subsection (e), the fee for filing and indexing an initial financing statement of the following kind is [the amount specified in subsection (c), if applicable, plus]:

(1) $_____ if the financing statement indicates that it is filed in connection with a public-finance transaction;

(2) $_____ if the financing statement indicates that it is filed in connection with a manufactured-home transaction.

[Alternative A]

(c) The number of names required to be indexed does not affect the amount of the fee in subsections (a) and (b).

[Alternative B]

(c) Except as otherwise provided in subsection (e), if a record is communicated in writing, the fee for each name more than two required to be indexed is $_____.

[End of Alternatives]

(d) The fee for responding to a request for information from the filing office, including for [issuing a certificate showing] [communicating] whether there is on file any financing statement naming a particular debtor, is:

(1) $_____ if the request is communicated in writing; and

(2) $_____ if the request is communicated by another medium authorized by filing-office rule.

(e) This section does not require a fee with respect to a record of a mortgage which is effective as a financing statement filed as a fixture filing or as a financing statement covering as-extracted collateral or timber to be cut under Section 9–502(c). However, the recording and satisfaction fees that otherwise would be applicable to the record of the mortgage apply.

Legislative Notes:

1. To preserve uniformity, a State that places the provisions of this section together with statutes setting fees for other services should do so without modification.

2. A State should enact subsection (c), Alternative A, and omit the bracketed language in subsections (a) and (b) unless its indexing system entails a substantial additional cost when indexing additional names. As amended in 2000.

§ 9–526. Filing-Office Rules.

(a) The [insert appropriate governmental official or agency] shall adopt and publish rules to implement this article. The filing-office rules must be[:

(1)] consistent with this article[; and

(2) adopted and published in accordance with the [insert any applicable state administrative procedure act]].

(b) To keep the filing-office rules and practices of the filing office in harmony with the rules and practices of filing offices in other jurisdictions that enact substantially this part, and to keep the technology used by the filing office compatible with the technology used by filing offices in other jurisdictions that enact substantially this part, the [insert appropriate governmental official or agency], so far as is consistent with the purposes, policies, and provisions of this article, in adopting, amending, and repealing filing-office rules, shall:

(1) consult with filing offices in other jurisdictions that enact substantially this part; and

(2) consult the most recent version of the Model Rules promulgated by the International Association of Corporate Administrators or any successor organization; and

(3) take into consideration the rules and practices of, and the technology used by, filing offices in other jurisdictions that enact substantially this part.

§ 9–527. Duty to Report.

The [insert appropriate governmental official or agency] shall report [annually on or before _____] to the [Governor and Legislature] on the operation of the filing office. The report must contain a statement of the extent to which:

(1) the filing-office rules are not in harmony with the rules of filing offices in other jurisdictions that enact substantially this part and the reasons for these variations; and

(2) the filing-office rules are not in harmony with the most recent version of the Model Rules promulgated by the International Association of Corporate Administrators, or any successor organization, and the reasons for these variations.

Part 6—Default

[Subpart 1. Default and Enforcement of Security Interest]

§ 9–601. Rights after Default; Judicial Enforcement; Consignor or Buyer of Accounts, Chattel Paper, Payment Intangibles, or Promissory Notes.

(a) After default, a secured party has the rights provided in this part and, except as otherwise provided in Section 9–602, those provided by agreement of the parties. A secured party:

(1) may reduce a claim to judgment, foreclose, or otherwise enforce the claim, security interest, or agricultural lien by any available judicial procedure; and

(2) if the collateral is documents, may proceed either as to the documents or as to the goods they cover.

(b) A secured party in possession of collateral or control of collateral under Section 9–104, 9–105, 9–106, or 9–107 has the rights and duties provided in Section 9–207.

(c) The rights under subsections (a) and (b) are cumulative and may be exercised simultaneously.

(d) Except as otherwise provided in subsection (g) and Section 9–605, after default, a debtor and an obligor have the rights provided in this part and by agreement of the parties.

(e) If a secured party has reduced its claim to judgment, the lien of any levy that may be made upon the collateral by virtue of an execution based upon the judgment relates back to the earliest of:

(1) the date of perfection of the security interest or agricultural lien in the collateral;

(2) the date of filing a financing statement covering the collateral; or

(3) any date specified in a statute under which the agricultural lien was created.

(f) A sale pursuant to an execution is a foreclosure of the security interest or agricultural lien by judicial procedure within the meaning of this section. A secured party may purchase at the sale and thereafter hold the collateral free of any other requirements of this article.

(g) Except as otherwise provided in Section 9–607(c), this part imposes no duties upon a secured party that is a consignor or is a buyer of accounts, chattel paper, payment intangibles, or promissory notes.

§ 9–602. Waiver and Variance of Rights and Duties.

Except as otherwise provided in Section 9–624, to the extent that they give rights to a debtor or obligor and impose duties on a secured party, the debtor or obligor may not waive or vary the rules stated in the following listed sections:

(1) Section 9–207(b)(4)(C), which deals with use and operation of the collateral by the secured party;

(2) Section 9–210, which deals with requests for an accounting and requests concerning a list of collateral and statement of account;

(3) Section 9–607(c), which deals with collection and enforcement of collateral;

(4) Sections 9–608(a) and 9–615(c) to the extent that they deal with application or payment of noncash proceeds of collection, enforcement, or disposition;

(5) Sections 9–608(a) and 9–615(d) to the extent that they require accounting for or payment of surplus proceeds of collateral;

(6) Section 9–609 to the extent that it imposes upon a secured party that takes possession of collateral without judicial process the duty to do so without breach of the peace;

(7) Sections 9–610(b), 9–611, 9–613, and 9–614, which deal with disposition of collateral;

(8) Section 9–615(f), which deals with calculation of a deficiency or surplus when a disposition is made to the secured party, a person related to the secured party, or a secondary obligor;

(9) Section 9–616, which deals with explanation of the calculation of a surplus or deficiency;

(10) Sections 9–620, 9–621, and 9–622, which deal with acceptance of collateral in satisfaction of obligation;

(11) Section 9–623, which deals with redemption of collateral;

(12) Section 9–624, which deals with permissible waivers; and

(13) Sections 9–625 and 9–626, which deal with the secured party's liability for failure to comply with this article.

§ 9–603. Agreement on Standards Concerning Rights and Duties.

(a) The parties may determine by agreement the standards measuring the fulfillment of the rights of a debtor or obligor and the duties of a secured party under a rule stated in Section 9–602 if the standards are not manifestly unreasonable.

(b) Subsection (a) does not apply to the duty under Section 9–609 to refrain from breaching the peace.

§ 9–604. Procedure If Security Agreement Covers Real Property or Fixtures.

(a) If a security agreement covers both personal and real property, a secured party may proceed:

(1) under this part as to the personal property without prejudicing any rights with respect to the real property; or

(2) as to both the personal property and the real property in accordance with the rights with respect to the real property, in which case the other provisions of this part do not apply.

(b) Subject to subsection (c), if a security agreement covers goods that are or become fixtures, a secured party may proceed:

(1) under this part; or

(2) in accordance with the rights with respect to real property, in which case the other provisions of this part do not apply.

(c) Subject to the other provisions of this part, if a secured party holding a security interest in fixtures has priority over all owners and encumbrancers of the real property, the secured party, after default, may remove the collateral from the real property.

(d) A secured party that removes collateral shall promptly reimburse any encumbrancer or owner of the real property, other than the debtor, for the cost of repair of any physical injury caused by the removal. The secured party need not reimburse the encumbrancer or owner for any diminution in value of the real property caused by the absence of the goods removed or by any necessity of replacing them. A person entitled to reimbursement may refuse permission to remove until the secured party gives adequate assurance for the performance of the obligation to reimburse.

§ 9–605. Unknown Debtor or Secondary Obligor.

A secured party does not owe a duty based on its status as secured party:

(1) to a person that is a debtor or obligor, unless the secured party knows:

(A) that the person is a debtor or obligor;

(B) the identity of the person; and

(C) how to communicate with the person; or

(2) to a secured party or lienholder that has filed a financing statement against a person, unless the secured party knows:

(A) that the person is a debtor; and

(B) the identity of the person.

§ 9–606. Time of Default for Agricultural Lien.

For purposes of this part, a default occurs in connection with an agricultural lien at the time the secured party becomes entitled to enforce the lien in accordance with the statute under which it was created.

§ 9–607. Collection and Enforcement by Secured Party.

(a) If so agreed, and in any event after default, a secured party:

(1) may notify an account debtor or other person obligated on collateral to make payment or otherwise render performance to or for the benefit of the secured party;

(2) may take any proceeds to which the secured party is entitled under Section 9–315;

(3) may enforce the obligations of an account debtor or other person obligated on collateral and exercise the rights of the debtor with respect to the obligation of the account debtor or other person obligated on collateral to make payment or otherwise render performance to the debtor, and with respect to any property that secures the obligations of the account debtor or other person obligated on the collateral;

(4) if it holds a security interest in a deposit account perfected by control under Section 9–104(a)(1), may apply the balance of the deposit account to the obligation secured by the deposit account; and

(5) if it holds a security interest in a deposit account perfected by control under Section 9–104(a)(2) or (3), may instruct the bank to pay the balance of the deposit account to or for the benefit of the secured party.

(b) If necessary to enable a secured party to exercise under subsection (a)(3) the right of a debtor to enforce a mortgage nonjudicially, the secured party may record in the office in which a record of the mortgage is recorded:

(1) a copy of the security agreement that creates or provides for a security interest in the obligation secured by the mortgage; and

(2) the secured party's sworn affidavit in recordable form stating that:

(A) a default has occurred; and

(B) the secured party is entitled to enforce the mortgage nonjudicially.

(c) A secured party shall proceed in a commercially reasonable manner if the secured party:

(1) undertakes to collect from or enforce an obligation of an account debtor or other person obligated on collateral; and

(2) is entitled to charge back uncollected collateral or otherwise to full or limited recourse against the debtor or a secondary obligor.

(d) A secured party may deduct from the collections made pursuant to subsection (c) reasonable expenses of collection and enforcement, including reasonable attorney's fees and legal expenses incurred by the secured party.

(e) This section does not determine whether an account debtor, bank, or other person obligated on collateral owes a duty to a secured party. As amended in 2000.

§ 9–608. Application of Proceeds of Collection or Enforcement; Liability for Deficiency and Right to Surplus.

(a) If a security interest or agricultural lien secures payment or performance of an obligation, the following rules apply:

(1) A secured party shall apply or pay over for application the cash proceeds of collection or enforcement under Section 9–607 in the following order to:

(A) the reasonable expenses of collection and enforcement and, to the extent provided for by agreement and not prohibited by law, reasonable attorney's fees and legal expenses incurred by the secured party;

(B) the satisfaction of obligations secured by the security interest or agricultural lien under which the collection or enforcement is made; and

(C) the satisfaction of obligations secured by any subordinate security interest in or other lien on the collateral subject to the security interest or agricultural lien under which the collection or enforcement is made if the secured party receives an authenticated demand for proceeds before distribution of the proceeds is completed.

(2) If requested by a secured party, a holder of a subordinate security interest or other lien shall furnish reasonable proof of the interest or lien within a reasonable time. Unless the holder complies, the secured party need not comply with the holder's demand under paragraph (1)(C).

(3) A secured party need not apply or pay over for application noncash proceeds of collection and enforcement under Section 9–607 unless the failure to do so would be commercially unreasonable. A secured party that applies or pays over for application noncash proceeds shall do so in a commercially reasonable manner.

(4) A secured party shall account to and pay a debtor for any surplus, and the obligor is liable for any deficiency.

(b) If the underlying transaction is a sale of accounts, chattel paper, payment intangibles, or promissory notes, the debtor is not entitled to any surplus, and the obligor is not liable for any deficiency. As amended in 2000.

§ 9–609. Secured Party's Right to Take Possession after Default.

(a) After default, a secured party:

(1) may take possession of the collateral; and

(2) without removal, may render equipment unusable and dispose of collateral on a debtor's premises under Section 9–610.

(b) A secured party may proceed under subsection (a):

(1) pursuant to judicial process; or

(2) without judicial process, if it proceeds without breach of the peace.

(c) If so agreed, and in any event after default, a secured party may require the debtor to assemble the collateral and make it available to the secured party at a place to be designated by the secured party which is reasonably convenient to both parties.

§ 9–610. Disposition of Collateral after Default.

(a) After default, a secured party may sell, lease, license, or otherwise dispose of any or all of the collateral in its present condition or following any commercially reasonable preparation or processing.

(b) Every aspect of a disposition of collateral, including the method, manner, time, place, and other terms, must be commercially reasonable. If commercially reasonable, a secured party may dispose of collateral by public or private proceedings, by one or more contracts, as a unit or in parcels, and at any time and place and on any terms.

(c) A secured party may purchase collateral:

(1) at a public disposition; or

(2) at a private disposition only if the collateral is of a kind that is customarily sold on a recognized market or the subject of widely distributed standard price quotations.

(d) A contract for sale, lease, license, or other disposition includes the warranties relating to title, possession, quiet enjoyment, and the like which by operation of law accompany a voluntary disposition of property of the kind subject to the contract.

(e) A secured party may disclaim or modify warranties under subsection (d):

(1) in a manner that would be effective to disclaim or modify the warranties in a voluntary disposition of property of the kind subject to the contract of disposition; or

(2) by communicating to the purchaser a record evidencing the contract for disposition and including an express disclaimer or modification of the warranties.

(f) A record is sufficient to disclaim warranties under subsection (e) if it indicates "There is no warranty relating to title, possession, quiet enjoyment, or the like in this disposition" or uses words of similar import.

§ 9–611. Notification before Disposition of Collateral.

(a) In this section, "notification date" means the earlier of the date on which:

(1) a secured party sends to the debtor and any secondary obligor an authenticated notification of disposition; or

(2) the debtor and any secondary obligor waive the right to notification.

(b) Except as otherwise provided in subsection (d), a secured party that disposes of collateral under Section 9–610 shall send to the persons specified in subsection (c) a reasonable authenticated notification of disposition.

(c) To comply with subsection (b), the secured party shall send an authenticated notification of disposition to:

(1) the debtor;

(2) any secondary obligor; and

(3) if the collateral is other than consumer goods:

(A) any other person from which the secured party has received, before the notification date, an authenticated notification of a claim of an interest in the collateral;

(B) any other secured party or lienholder that, 10 days before the notification date, held a security interest in or other lien on the collateral perfected by the filing of a financing statement that:

(i) identified the collateral;

(ii) was indexed under the debtor's name as of that date; and

(iii) was filed in the office in which to file a financing statement against the debtor covering the collateral as of that date; and

(C) any other secured party that, 10 days before the notification date, held a security interest in the collateral perfected by compliance with a statute, regulation, or treaty described in Section 9–311(a).

(d) Subsection (b) does not apply if the collateral is perishable or threatens to decline speedily in value or is of a type customarily sold on a recognized market.

(e) A secured party complies with the requirement for notification prescribed by subsection (c)(3)(B) if:

(1) not later than 20 days or earlier than 30 days before the notification date, the secured party requests, in a commercially reasonable manner, information concerning financing statements indexed under the debtor's name in the office indicated in subsection (c)(3)(B); and

(2) before the notification date, the secured party:

(A) did not receive a response to the request for information; or

(B) received a response to the request for information and sent an authenticated notification of disposition to each secured party or other lienholder named in that response whose financing statement covered the collateral.

§ 9–612. Timeliness of Notification before Disposition of Collateral.

(a) Except as otherwise provided in subsection (b), whether a notification is sent within a reasonable time is a question of fact.

(b) In a transaction other than a consumer transaction, a notification of disposition sent after default and 10 days or more before the earliest time of disposition set forth in the notification is sent within a reasonable time before the disposition.

§ 9–613. Contents and Form of Notification before Disposition of Collateral: General.

Except in a consumer-goods transaction, the following rules apply:

(1) The contents of a notification of disposition are sufficient if the notification:

(A) describes the debtor and the secured party;

(B) describes the collateral that is the subject of the intended disposition;

(C) states the method of intended disposition;

(D) states that the debtor is entitled to an accounting of the unpaid indebtedness and states the charge, if any, for an accounting; and

(E) states the time and place of a public disposition or the time after which any other disposition is to be made.

(2) Whether the contents of a notification that lacks any of the information specified in paragraph (1) are nevertheless sufficient is a question of fact.

(3) The contents of a notification providing substantially the information specified in paragraph (1) are sufficient, even if the notification includes:

(A) information not specified by that paragraph; or

(B) minor errors that are not seriously misleading.

(4) A particular phrasing of the notification is not required.

(5) The following form of notification and the form appearing in Section 9–614(3), when completed, each provides sufficient information:

NOTIFICATION OF DISPOSITION OF COLLATERAL

To: *[Name of debtor, obligor, or other person to which the notification is sent]*

From: *[Name, address, and telephone number of secured party]*

Name of Debtor(s): *[Include only if debtor(s) are not an addressee]*

[For a public disposition:]

We will sell [or lease or license, as applicable] the [describe collateral] [to the highest qualified bidder] in public as follows:

Day and Date: _____

Time: _____

Place: _____

[For a private disposition:]

We will sell [or lease or license, as *applicable*] the *[describe collateral]* privately sometime after *[day and date]*.

You are entitled to an accounting of the unpaid indebtedness secured by the property that we intend to sell [or lease or license, as applicable] [for a charge of $_____]. You may request an accounting by calling us at [telephone number].

[End of Form]

As amended in 2000.

§ 9–614. Contents and Form of Notification before Disposition of Collateral: Consumer-Goods Transaction.

In a consumer-goods transaction, the following rules apply:

(1) A notification of disposition must provide the following information:

(A) the information specified in Section 9–613(1);

(B) a description of any liability for a deficiency of the person to which the notification is sent;

(C) a telephone number from which the amount that must be paid to the secured party to redeem the collateral under Section 9–623 is available; and

(D) a telephone number or mailing address from which additional information concerning the disposition and the obligation secured is available.

(2) A particular phrasing of the notification is not required.

(3) The following form of notification, when completed, provides sufficient information:

[Name and address of secured party]

[Date]

NOTICE OF OUR PLAN TO SELL PROPERTY

[Name and address of any obligor who is also a debtor]

Subject: *[Identification of Transaction]*

We have your [describe collateral], because you broke promises in our agreement.

[For a public disposition:]

We will sell [describe collateral] at public sale. A sale could include a lease or license. The sale will be held as follows:

Date: _____

Time: _____

Place: _____

If you need more information about the sale call us at *[telephone number]* [or write us at *[secured party's address]*].

We are sending this notice to the following other people who have an interest in [describe collateral] or who owe money under your agreement:

[Names of all other debtors and obligors, if any]

[End of Form]

(4) A notification in the form of paragraph (3) is sufficient, even if additional information appears at the end of the form.

(5) A notification in the form of paragraph (3) is sufficient, even if it includes errors in information not required by paragraph (1), unless the error is misleading with respect to rights arising under this article.

(6) If a notification under this section is not in the form of paragraph (3), law other than this article determines the effect of including information not required by paragraph (1).

§ 9–615. Application of Proceeds of Disposition; Liability for Deficiency and Right to Surplus.

(a) A secured party shall apply or pay over for application the cash proceeds of disposition under Section 9–610 in the following order to:

(1) the reasonable expenses of retaking, holding, preparing for disposition, processing, and disposing, and, to the extent provided for by agreement and not prohibited by law, reasonable attorney's fees and legal expenses incurred by the secured party;

(2) the satisfaction of obligations secured by the security interest or agricultural lien under which the disposition is made;

(3) the satisfaction of obligations secured by any subordinate security interest in or other subordinate lien on the collateral if:

(A) the secured party receives from the holder of the subordinate security interest or other lien an authenticated demand for proceeds before distribution of the proceeds is completed; and

(B) in a case in which a consignor has an interest in the collateral, the subordinate security interest or other lien is senior to the interest of the consignor; and

(4) a secured party that is a consignor of the collateral if the secured party receives from the consignor an authenticated demand for proceeds before distribution of the proceeds is completed.

(b) If requested by a secured party, a holder of a subordinate security interest or other lien shall furnish reasonable proof of the interest or lien within a reasonable time. Unless the holder does so, the secured party need not comply with the holder's demand under subsection (a)(3).

(c) A secured party need not apply or pay over for application noncash proceeds of disposition under Section 9–610 unless the failure to do so would be commercially unreasonable. A secured party that applies or pays over for application noncash proceeds shall do so in a commercially reasonable manner.

(d) If the security interest under which a disposition is made secures payment or performance of an obligation, after making the payments and applications required by subsection (a) and permitted by subsection (c):

(1) unless subsection (a)(4) requires the secured party to apply or pay over cash proceeds to a consignor, the secured party shall account to and pay a debtor for any surplus; and

(2) the obligor is liable for any deficiency.

(e) If the underlying transaction is a sale of accounts, chattel paper, payment intangibles, or promissory notes:

(1) the debtor is not entitled to any surplus; and

(2) the obligor is not liable for any deficiency.

(f) The surplus or deficiency following a disposition is calculated based on the amount of proceeds that would have been realized in a disposition complying with this part to a transferee other than the secured party, a person related to the secured party, or a secondary obligor if:

(1) the transferee in the disposition is the secured party, a person related to the secured party, or a secondary obligor; and

(2) the amount of proceeds of the disposition is significantly below the range of proceeds that a complying disposition to a person other than the secured party, a person related to the secured party, or a secondary obligor would have brought.

(g) A secured party that receives cash proceeds of a disposition in good faith and without knowledge that the receipt violates the rights of the holder of a security interest or other lien that is not subordinate to the security interest or agricultural lien under which the disposition is made:

(1) takes the cash proceeds free of the security interest or other lien;

(2) is not obligated to apply the proceeds of the disposition to the satisfaction of obligations secured by the security interest or other lien; and

(3) is not obligated to account to or pay the holder of the security interest or other lien for any surplus.

As amended in 2000.

§ 9–616. Explanation of Calculation of Surplus or Deficiency.

(a) In this section:

(1) "Explanation" means a writing that:

(A) states the amount of the surplus or deficiency;

(B) provides an explanation in accordance with subsection (c) of how the secured party calculated the surplus or deficiency;

(C) states, if applicable, that future debits, credits, charges, including additional credit service charges or interest, rebates, and expenses may affect the amount of the surplus or deficiency; and

(D) provides a telephone number or mailing address from which additional information concerning the transaction is available.

(2) "Request" means a record:

(A) authenticated by a debtor or consumer obligor;

(B) requesting that the recipient provide an explanation; and

(C) sent after disposition of the collateral under Section 9–610.

(b) In a consumer-goods transaction in which the debtor is entitled to a surplus or a consumer obligor is liable for a deficiency under Section 9–615, the secured party shall:

(1) send an explanation to the debtor or consumer obligor, as applicable, after the disposition and:

(A) before or when the secured party accounts to the debtor and pays any surplus or first makes written demand

on the consumer obligor after the disposition for payment of the deficiency; and

(B) within 14 days after receipt of a request; or

(2) in the case of a consumer obligor who is liable for a deficiency, within 14 days after receipt of a request, send to the consumer obligor a record waiving the secured party's right to a deficiency.

(c) To comply with subsection (a)(1)(B), a writing must provide the following information in the following order:

(1) the aggregate amount of obligations secured by the security interest under which the disposition was made, and, if the amount reflects a rebate of unearned interest or credit service charge, an indication of that fact, calculated as of a specified date:

(A) if the secured party takes or receives possession of the collateral after default, not more than 35 days before the secured party takes or receives possession; or

(B) if the secured party takes or receives possession of the collateral before default or does not take possession of the collateral, not more than 35 days before the disposition;

(2) the amount of proceeds of the disposition;

(3) the aggregate amount of the obligations after deducting the amount of proceeds;

(4) the amount, in the aggregate or by type, and types of expenses, including expenses of retaking, holding, preparing for disposition, processing, and disposing of the collateral, and attorney's fees secured by the collateral which are known to the secured party and relate to the current disposition;

(5) the amount, in the aggregate or by type, and types of credits, including rebates of interest or credit service charges, to which the obligor is known to be entitled and which are not reflected in the amount in paragraph (1); and

(6) the amount of the surplus or deficiency.

(d) A particular phrasing of the explanation is not required. An explanation complying substantially with the requirements of subsection (a) is sufficient, even if it includes minor errors that are not seriously misleading.

(e) A debtor or consumer obligor is entitled without charge to one response to a request under this section during any six-month period in which the secured party did not send to the debtor or consumer obligor an explanation pursuant to subsection (b)(1). The secured party may require payment of a charge not exceeding $25 for each additional response.

§ 9–617. Rights of Transferee of Collateral.

(a) A secured party's disposition of collateral after default:

(1) transfers to a transferee for value all of the debtor's rights in the collateral;

(2) discharges the security interest under which the disposition is made; and

(3) discharges any subordinate security interest or other subordinate lien [other than liens created under [cite acts or statutes providing for liens, if any, that are not to be discharged]].

(b) A transferee that acts in good faith takes free of the rights and interests described in subsection (a), even if the secured party fails to comply with this article or the requirements of any judicial proceeding.

(c) If a transferee does not take free of the rights and interests described in subsection (a), the transferee takes the collateral subject to:

(1) the debtor's rights in the collateral;

(2) the security interest or agricultural lien under which the disposition is made; and

(3) any other security interest or other lien.

§ 9–618. Rights and Duties of Certain Secondary Obligors.

(a) A secondary obligor acquires the rights and becomes obligated to perform the duties of the secured party after the secondary obligor:

(1) receives an assignment of a secured obligation from the secured party;

(2) receives a transfer of collateral from the secured party and agrees to accept the rights and assume the duties of the secured party; or

(3) is subrogated to the rights of a secured party with respect to collateral.

(b) An assignment, transfer, or subrogation described in subsection (a):

(1) is not a disposition of collateral under Section 9–610; and

(2) relieves the secured party of further duties under this article.

§ 9–619. Transfer of Record or Legal Title.

(a) In this section, "transfer statement" means a record authenticated by a secured party stating:

(1) that the debtor has defaulted in connection with an obligation secured by specified collateral;

(2) that the secured party has exercised its post-default remedies with respect to the collateral;

(3) that, by reason of the exercise, a transferee has acquired the rights of the debtor in the collateral; and

(4) the name and mailing address of the secured party, debtor, and transferee.

(b) A transfer statement entitles the transferee to the transfer of record of all rights of the debtor in the collateral specified in the statement in any official filing, recording, registration, or certificate-of-title system covering the collateral. If a transfer statement is presented with the applicable fee and request form to the official or office responsible for maintaining the system, the official or office shall:

(1) accept the transfer statement;

(2) promptly amend its records to reflect the transfer; and

(3) if applicable, issue a new appropriate certificate of title in the name of the transferee.

(c) A transfer of the record or legal title to collateral to a secured party under subsection (b) or otherwise is not of itself a disposition of collateral under this article and does not of itself relieve the secured party of its duties under this article.

§ 9–620. Acceptance of Collateral in Full or Partial Satisfaction of Obligation; Compulsory Disposition of Collateral.

(a) Except as otherwise provided in subsection (g), a secured party may accept collateral in full or partial satisfaction of the obligation it secures only if:

(1) the debtor consents to the acceptance under subsection (c);

(2) the secured party does not receive, within the time set forth in subsection (d), a notification of objection to the proposal authenticated by:

(A) a person to which the secured party was required to send a proposal under Section 9–621; or

(B) any other person, other than the debtor, holding an interest in the collateral subordinate to the security interest that is the subject of the proposal;

(3) if the collateral is consumer goods, the collateral is not in the possession of the debtor when the debtor consents to the acceptance; and

(4) subsection (e) does not require the secured party to dispose of the collateral or the debtor waives the requirement pursuant to Section 9–624.

(b) A purported or apparent acceptance of collateral under this section is ineffective unless:

(1) the secured party consents to the acceptance in an authenticated record or sends a proposal to the debtor; and

(2) the conditions of subsection (a) are met.

(c) For purposes of this section:

(1) a debtor consents to an acceptance of collateral in partial satisfaction of the obligation it secures only if the debtor agrees to the terms of the acceptance in a record authenticated after default; and

(2) a debtor consents to an acceptance of collateral in full satisfaction of the obligation it secures only if the debtor agrees to the terms of the acceptance in a record authenticated after default or the secured party:

(A) sends to the debtor after default a proposal that is unconditional or subject only to a condition that collateral not in the possession of the secured party be preserved or maintained;

(B) in the proposal, proposes to accept collateral in full satisfaction of the obligation it secures; and

(C) does not receive a notification of objection authenticated by the debtor within 20 days after the proposal is sent.

(d) To be effective under subsection (a)(2), a notification of objection must be received by the secured party:

(1) in the case of a person to which the proposal was sent pursuant to Section 9–621, within 20 days after notification was sent to that person; and

(2) in other cases:

(A) within 20 days after the last notification was sent pursuant to Section 9–621; or

(B) if a notification was not sent, before the debtor consents to the acceptance under subsection (c).

(e) A secured party that has taken possession of collateral shall dispose of the collateral pursuant to Section 9–610 within the time specified in subsection (f) if:

(1) 60 percent of the cash price has been paid in the case of a purchase-money security interest in consumer goods; or

(2) 60 percent of the principal amount of the obligation secured has been paid in the case of a non-purchase-money security interest in consumer goods.

(f) To comply with subsection (e), the secured party shall dispose of the collateral:

(1) within 90 days after taking possession; or

(2) within any longer period to which the debtor and all secondary obligors have agreed in an agreement to that effect entered into and authenticated after default.

(g) In a consumer transaction, a secured party may not accept collateral in partial satisfaction of the obligation it secures.

§ 9–621.   Notification of Proposal to Accept Collateral.

(a) A secured party that desires to accept collateral in full or partial satisfaction of the obligation it secures shall send its proposal to:

(1) any person from which the secured party has received, before the debtor consented to the acceptance, an authenticated notification of a claim of an interest in the collateral;

(2) any other secured party or lienholder that, 10 days before the debtor consented to the acceptance, held a security interest in or other lien on the collateral perfected by the filing of a financing statement that:

(A) identified the collateral;

(B) was indexed under the debtor's name as of that date; and

(C) was filed in the office or offices in which to file a financing statement against the debtor covering the collateral as of that date; and

(3) any other secured party that, 10 days before the debtor consented to the acceptance, held a security interest in the collateral perfected by compliance with a statute, regulation, or treaty described in Section 9–311(a).

(b) A secured party that desires to accept collateral in partial satisfaction of the obligation it secures shall send its proposal to any secondary obligor in addition to the persons described in subsection (a).

§ 9–622.   Effect of Acceptance of Collateral.

(a) A secured party's acceptance of collateral in full or partial satisfaction of the obligation it secures:

(1) discharges the obligation to the extent consented to by the debtor;

(2) transfers to the secured party all of a debtor's rights in the collateral;

(3) discharges the security interest or agricultural lien that is the subject of the debtor's consent and any subordinate security interest or other subordinate lien; and

(4) terminates any other subordinate interest.

(b) A subordinate interest is discharged or terminated under subsection (a), even if the secured party fails to comply with this article.

§ 9–623.   Right to Redeem Collateral.

(a) A debtor, any secondary obligor, or any other secured party or lienholder may redeem collateral.

(b) To redeem collateral, a person shall tender:

(1) fulfillment of all obligations secured by the collateral; and

(2) the reasonable expenses and attorney's fees described in Section 9–615(a)(1).

(c) A redemption may occur at any time before a secured party:

(1) has collected collateral under Section 9–607;

(2) has disposed of collateral or entered into a contract for its disposition under Section 9–610; or

(3) has accepted collateral in full or partial satisfaction of the obligation it secures under Section 9–622.

§ 9–624.   Waiver.

(a) A debtor or secondary obligor may waive the right to notification of disposition of collateral under Section 9–611 only by an agreement to that effect entered into and authenticated after default.

(b) A debtor may waive the right to require disposition of collateral under Section 9–620(e) only by an agreement to that effect entered into and authenticated after default.

(c) Except in a consumer-goods transaction, a debtor or secondary obligor may waive the right to redeem collateral under Section 9–623 only by an agreement to that effect entered into and authenticated after default.

[Subpart 2.   Noncompliance with Article]

§ 9–625.   Remedies for Secured Party's Failure to Comply with Article.

(a) If it is established that a secured party is not proceeding in accordance with this article, a court may order or restrain collection, enforcement, or disposition of collateral on appropriate terms and conditions.

(b) Subject to subsections (c), (d), and (f), a person is liable for damages in the amount of any loss caused by a failure to comply with this article. Loss caused by a failure to comply may include loss resulting from the debtor's inability to obtain, or increased costs of, alternative financing.

(c) Except as otherwise provided in Section 9–628:

(1) a person that, at the time of the failure, was a debtor, was an obligor, or held a security interest in or other lien on the collateral may recover damages under subsection (b) for its loss; and

(2) if the collateral is consumer goods, a person that was a debtor or a secondary obligor at the time a secured party failed to comply with this part may recover for that failure in any event an amount not less than the credit service charge plus 10 percent of the principal amount of the obligation or the time-price differential plus 10 percent of the cash price.

(d) A debtor whose deficiency is eliminated under Section 9–626 may recover damages for the loss of any surplus. However, a debtor or secondary obligor whose deficiency is eliminated or reduced under Section 9–626 may not otherwise recover under subsection (b) for noncompliance with the provisions of this part relating to collection, enforcement, disposition, or acceptance.

(e) In addition to any damages recoverable under subsection (b), the debtor, consumer obligor, or person named as a debtor in a filed record, as applicable, may recover $500 in each case from a person that:

(1) fails to comply with Section 9–208;

(2) fails to comply with Section 9–209;

(3) files a record that the person is not entitled to file under Section 9–509(a);

(4) fails to cause the secured party of record to file or send a termination statement as required by Section 9–513(a) or (c);

(5) fails to comply with Section 9–616(b)(1) and whose failure is part of a pattern, or consistent with a practice, of noncompliance; or

(6) fails to comply with Section 9–616(b)(2).

(f) A debtor or consumer obligor may recover damages under subsection (b) and, in addition, $500 in each case from a person that, without reasonable cause, fails to comply with a request under Section 9–210. A recipient of a request under Section 9–210 which never claimed an interest in the collateral or obligations that are the subject of a request under that section has a reasonable excuse for failure to comply with the request within the meaning of this subsection.

(g) If a secured party fails to comply with a request regarding a list of collateral or a statement of account under Section 9–210, the secured party may claim a security interest only as shown in the list or statement included in the request as against a person that is reasonably misled by the failure.

As amended in 2000.

§ 9–626. Action in Which Deficiency or Surplus Is in Issue.

(a) In an action arising from a transaction, other than a consumer transaction, in which the amount of a deficiency or surplus is in issue, the following rules apply:

(1) A secured party need not prove compliance with the provisions of this part relating to collection, enforcement, disposition, or acceptance unless the debtor or a secondary obligor places the secured party's compliance in issue.

(2) If the secured party's compliance is placed in issue, the secured party has the burden of establishing that the collection, enforcement, disposition, or acceptance was conducted in accordance with this part.

(3) Except as otherwise provided in Section 9–628, if a secured party fails to prove that the collection, enforcement, disposition, or acceptance was conducted in accordance with the provisions of this part relating to collection, enforcement, disposition, or acceptance, the liability of a debtor or a secondary obligor for a deficiency is limited to an amount by which the sum of the secured obligation, expenses, and attorney's fees exceeds the greater of:

(A) the proceeds of the collection, enforcement, disposition, or acceptance; or

(B) the amount of proceeds that would have been realized had the noncomplying secured party proceeded in accordance with the provisions of this part relating to collection, enforcement, disposition, or acceptance.

(4) For purposes of paragraph (3)(B), the amount of proceeds that would have been realized is equal to the sum of the secured obligation, expenses, and attorney's fees unless the secured party proves that the amount is less than that sum.

(5) If a deficiency or surplus is calculated under Section 9–615(f), the debtor or obligor has the burden of establishing that the amount of proceeds of the disposition is significantly below the range of prices that a complying disposition to a person other than the secured party, a person related to the secured party, or a secondary obligor would have brought.

(b) The limitation of the rules in subsection (a) to transactions other than consumer transactions is intended to leave to the court the determination of the proper rules in consumer transactions. The court may not infer from that limitation the nature of the proper rule in consumer transactions and may continue to apply established approaches.

§ 9–627. Determination of Whether Conduct Was Commercially Reasonable.

(a) The fact that a greater amount could have been obtained by a collection, enforcement, disposition, or acceptance at a different time or in a different method from that selected by the secured party is not of itself sufficient to preclude the secured party from establishing that the collection, enforcement, disposition, or acceptance was made in a commercially reasonable manner.

(b) A disposition of collateral is made in a commercially reasonable manner if the disposition is made:

(1) in the usual manner on any recognized market;

(2) at the price current in any recognized market at the time of the disposition; or

(3) otherwise in conformity with reasonable commercial practices among dealers in the type of property that was the subject of the disposition.

(c) A collection, enforcement, disposition, or acceptance is commercially reasonable if it has been approved:

(1) in a judicial proceeding;

(2) by a bona fide creditors' committee;

(3) by a representative of creditors; or

(4) by an assignee for the benefit of creditors.

(d) Approval under subsection (c) need not be obtained, and lack of approval does not mean that the collection, enforcement, disposition, or acceptance is not commercially reasonable.

§ 9–628. Nonliability and Limitation on Liability of Secured Party; Liability of Secondary Obligor.

(a) Unless a secured party knows that a person is a debtor or obligor, knows the identity of the person, and knows how to communicate with the person:

(1) the secured party is not liable to the person, or to a secured party or lienholder that has filed a financing statement against the person, for failure to comply with this article; and

(2) the secured party's failure to comply with this article does not affect the liability of the person for a deficiency.

(b) A secured party is not liable because of its status as secured party:

(1) to a person that is a debtor or obligor, unless the secured party knows:

(A) that the person is a debtor or obligor;

(B) the identity of the person; and

(C) how to communicate with the person; or

(2) to a secured party or lienholder that has filed a financing statement against a person, unless the secured party knows:

(A) that the person is a debtor; and

(B) the identity of the person.

(c) A secured party is not liable to any person, and a person's liability for a deficiency is not affected, because of any act or omission arising out of the secured party's reasonable belief that a transaction is not a consumer-goods transaction or a consumer transaction or that goods are not consumer goods, if the secured party's belief is based on its reasonable reliance on:

(1) a debtor's representation concerning the purpose for which collateral was to be used, acquired, or held; or

(2) an obligor's representation concerning the purpose for which a secured obligation was incurred.

(d) A secured party is not liable to any person under Section 9–625(c)(2) for its failure to comply with Section 9–616.

(e) A secured party is not liable under Section 9–625(c)(2) more than once with respect to any one secured obligation.

Part 7—Transition

§ 9–701. Effective Date.

This [Act] takes effect on July 1, 2001.

§ 9–702. Savings Clause.

(a) Except as otherwise provided in this part, this [Act] applies to a transaction or lien within its scope, even if the transaction or lien was entered into or created before this [Act] takes effect.

(b) Except as otherwise provided in subsection (c) and Sections 9–703 through 9–709:

(1) transactions and liens that were not governed by [former Article 9], were validly entered into or created before this [Act] takes effect, and would be subject to this [Act] if they had been entered into or created after this [Act] takes effect, and the rights, duties, and interests flowing from those transactions and liens remain valid after this [Act] takes effect; and

(2) the transactions and liens may be terminated, completed, consummated, and enforced as required or permitted by this [Act] or by the law that otherwise would apply if this [Act] had not taken effect.

(c) This [Act] does not affect an action, case, or proceeding commenced before this [Act] takes effect.

As amended in 2000.

§ 9–703. Security Interest Perfected before Effective Date.

(a) A security interest that is enforceable immediately before this [Act] takes effect and would have priority over the rights of a person that becomes a lien creditor at that time is a perfected security interest under this [Act] if, when this [Act] takes effect, the applicable requirements for enforceability and perfection under this [Act] are satisfied without further action.

(b) Except as otherwise provided in Section 9–705, if, immediately before this [Act] takes effect, a security interest is enforceable and would have priority over the rights of a person that becomes a lien creditor at that time, but the applicable requirements for enforceability or perfection under this [Act] are not satisfied when this [Act] takes effect, the security interest:

(1) is a perfected security interest for one year after this [Act] takes effect;

(2) remains enforceable thereafter only if the security interest becomes enforceable under Section 9–203 before the year expires; and

(3) remains perfected thereafter only if the applicable requirements for perfection under this [Act] are satisfied before the year expires.

§ 9–704. Security Interest
Unperfected before Effective Date.

A security interest that is enforceable immediately before this [Act] takes effect but which would be subordinate to the rights of a person that becomes a lien creditor at that time:

(1) remains an enforceable security interest for one year after this [Act] takes effect;

(2) remains enforceable thereafter if the security interest becomes enforceable under Section 9–203 when this [Act] takes effect or within one year thereafter; and

(3) becomes perfected:

(A) without further action, when this [Act] takes effect if the applicable requirements for perfection under this [Act] are satisfied before or at that time; or

(B) when the applicable requirements for perfection are satisfied if the requirements are satisfied after that time.

§ 9–705. Effectiveness of Action Taken before Effective Date.

(a) If action, other than the filing of a financing statement, is taken before this [Act] takes effect and the action would have resulted in priority of a security interest over the rights of a person that becomes a lien creditor had the security interest become enforceable before this [Act] takes effect, the action is effective to perfect a security interest that attaches under this [Act] within one year after this [Act] takes effect. An attached security interest becomes unperfected one year after this [Act] takes effect unless the security interest becomes a perfected security interest under this [Act] before the expiration of that period.

(b) The filing of a financing statement before this [Act] takes effect is effective to perfect a security interest to the extent the filing would satisfy the applicable requirements for perfection under this [Act].

(c) This [Act] does not render ineffective an effective financing statement that, before this [Act] takes effect, is filed and satisfies the applicable requirements for perfection under the law of the jurisdiction governing perfection as provided in [former Section 9–103]. However, except as otherwise provided in subsections (d) and (e) and Section 9–706, the financing statement ceases to be effective at the earlier of:

(1) the time the financing statement would have ceased to be effective under the law of the jurisdiction in which it is filed; or

(2) June 30, 2006.

(d) The filing of a continuation statement after this [Act] takes effect does not continue the effectiveness of the financing statement filed before this [Act] takes effect. However, upon the timely filing of a continuation statement after this [Act] takes effect and in accordance with the law of the jurisdiction governing perfection as provided in Part 3, the effectiveness of a financing statement filed in the same office in that jurisdiction before this [Act] takes effect continues for the period provided by the law of that jurisdiction.

(e) Subsection (c)(2) applies to a financing statement that, before this [Act] takes effect, is filed against a transmitting utility and satisfies the applicable requirements for perfection under the law of the jurisdiction governing perfection as provided in [former Section 9–103] only to the extent that Part 3 provides that the law of a jurisdiction other than the jurisdiction in which the financing statement is filed governs perfection of a security interest in collateral covered by the financing statement.

(f) A financing statement that includes a financing statement filed before this [Act] takes effect and a continuation statement filed after this [Act] takes effect is effective only to the extent that it satisfies the requirements of Part 5 for an initial financing statement.

§ 9–706. When Initial Financing Statement Suffices
to Continue Effectiveness of Financing Statement.

(a) The filing of an initial financing statement in the office specified in Section 9–501 continues the effectiveness of a financing statement filed before this [Act] takes effect if:

(1) the filing of an initial financing statement in that office would be effective to perfect a security interest under this [Act];

(2) the pre-effective-date financing statement was filed in an office in another State or another office in this State; and

(3) the initial financing statement satisfies subsection (c).

(b) The filing of an initial financing statement under subsection (a) continues the effectiveness of the pre-effective-date financing statement:

(1) if the initial financing statement is filed before this [Act] takes effect, for the period provided in [former Section 9–403] with respect to a financing statement; and

(2) if the initial financing statement is filed after this [Act] takes effect, for the period provided in Section 9–515 with respect to an initial financing statement.

(c) To be effective for purposes of subsection (a), an initial financing statement must:

(1) satisfy the requirements of Part 5 for an initial financing statement;

(2) identify the pre-effective-date financing statement by indicating the office in which the financing statement was filed and providing the dates of filing and file numbers, if any, of the financing statement and of the most recent continuation statement filed with respect to the financing statement; and

(3) indicate that the pre-effective-date financing statement remains effective.

§ 9–707. Amendment of Pre-Effective-Date Financing Statement.

(a) In this section, "Pre-effective-date financing statement" means a financing statement filed before this [Act] takes effect.

(b) After this [Act] takes effect, a person may add or delete collateral covered by, continue or terminate the effectiveness of, or otherwise amend the information provided in, a pre-effective-date financing statement only in accordance with the law of the jurisdiction governing perfection as provided in Part 3. However, the effectiveness of a pre-effective-date financing statement also may be terminated in accordance with the law of the jurisdiction in which the financing statement is filed.

(c) Except as otherwise provided in subsection (d), if the law of this State governs perfection of a security interest, the information in a pre-effective-date financing statement may be amended after this [Act] takes effect only if:

(1) the pre-effective-date financing statement and an amendment are filed in the office specified in Section 9–501;

(2) an amendment is filed in the office specified in Section 9–501 concurrently with, or after the filing in that office of, an initial financing statement that satisfies Section 9–706(c); or

(3) an initial financing statement that provides the information as amended and satisfies Section 9–706(c) is filed in the office specified in Section 9–501.

(d) If the law of this State governs perfection of a security interest, the effectiveness of a pre-effective-date financing statement may be continued only under Section 9–705(d) and (f) or 9–706.

(e) Whether or not the law of this State governs perfection of a security interest, the effectiveness of a pre-effective-date financing statement filed in this State may be terminated after this [Act] takes effect by filing a termination statement in the office in which the pre-effective-date financing statement is filed, unless an initial financing statement that satisfies Section 9–706(c) has been filed in the office specified by the law of the jurisdiction governing perfection as provided in Part 3 as the office in which to file a financing statement.
As amended in 2000.

§ 9–708. Persons Entitled to File Initial Financing Statement or Continuation Statement.

A person may file an initial financing statement or a continuation statement under this part if:

(1) the secured party of record authorizes the filing; and

(2) the filing is necessary under this part:

(A) to continue the effectiveness of a financing statement filed before this [Act] takes effect; or

(B) to perfect or continue the perfection of a security interest.

As amended in 2000.

§ 9–709. Priority.

(a) This [Act] determines the priority of conflicting claims to collateral. However, if the relative priorities of the claims were established before this [Act] takes effect, [former Article 9] determines priority.

(b) For purposes of Section 9–322(a), the priority of a security interest that becomes enforceable under Section 9–203 of this [Act] dates from the time this [Act] takes effect if the security interest is perfected under this [Act] by the filing of a financing statement before this [Act] takes effect which would not have been effective to perfect the security interest under [former Article 9]. This subsection does not apply to conflicting security interests each of which is perfected by the filing of such a financing statement.
As amended in 2000.

APPENDIX D
Answers to the *Issue Spotters*

CHAPTER 1

1. *Under what circumstances might a judge rely on case law to determine the intent and purpose of a statute?* Case law includes courts' interpretations of statutes, as well as constitutional provisions and administrative rules. Statutes often codify common law rules. For these reasons, a judge might rely on the common law as a guide to the intent and purpose of a statute.

2. *Assuming that these convicted war criminals had not disobeyed any law of their country and had merely been following their government's orders, what law had they violated? Explain.* At the time of the Nuremberg trials, "crimes against humanity" were new international crimes. The laws criminalized such acts as murder, extermination, enslavement, deportation, and other inhumane acts committed against any civilian population. These international laws derived their legitimacy from "natural law."

Natural law, which is the oldest and one of the most significant schools of jurisprudence, holds that governments and legal systems should reflect the moral and ethical ideals that are inherent in human nature. Because natural law is universal and discoverable by reason, its adherents believe that all other law is derived from natural law. Natural law therefore supersedes laws created by humans (national, or "positive," law), and in a conflict between the two, national or positive law loses its legitimacy.

The Nuremberg defendants asserted that they had been acting in accordance with German law. The judges dismissed these claims, reasoning that the defendants' acts were commonly regarded as crimes and that the accused must have known that the acts would be considered criminal. The judges clearly believed the tenets of natural law and expected that the defendants, too, should have been able to realize that their acts ran afoul of it. The fact that the "positivist law" of Germany at the time required them to commit these acts is irrelevant. Under natural law theory, the international court was justified in finding the defendants guilty of crimes against humanity.

CHAPTER 2

1. *Does the court in Sue's state have jurisdiction over Tipton? What factors will the court consider in determining jurisdiction?* Yes, the court in Sue's state has jurisdiction over Tipton on the basis of the company's minimum contacts with the state.

Courts look at the following factors in determining whether minimum contacts exist: the quantity of the contacts, the nature and quality of the contacts, the source and connection of the cause of action to the contacts, the interest of the forum state, and the convenience of the parties. Attempting to exercise jurisdiction without sufficient minimum contacts would violate the due process clause. Generally, courts have found that jurisdiction is proper when there is substantial business conducted online (with contracts, sales, and so on). Even when there is only some interactivity through a Web site, courts have sometimes held that jurisdiction is proper. Jurisdiction is not proper when there is merely passive advertising.

Here, all of these factors suggest that the defendant had sufficient minimum contacts with the state to justify the exercise of jurisdiction over the defendant. Two especially important factors were that the plaintiff sold the security system to a resident of the state and that litigating in the defendant's state would be relatively inconvenient for the plaintiff.

2. *If the dispute is not resolved, or if either party disagrees with the decision of the mediator or arbitrator, will a court hear the case? Explain.* Yes, if the dispute is not resolved, or if either party disagrees with the decision of the mediator or arbitrator, a court will hear the case. It is required that the dispute be submitted to mediation or arbitration, but this outcome is not binding.

CHAPTER 3

1. *Tom can call his first witness. What else might he do?* Tom could file a motion for a directed verdict. This motion asks the judge to direct a verdict for Tom on the ground that Sue presented no evidence that would justify granting Sue relief. The judge grants the motion if there is insufficient evidence to raise an issue of fact.

2. *Who can appeal to a higher court?* Either a plaintiff or a defendant, or both, can appeal a judgment to a higher court. An appellate court can affirm, reverse, or remand a case, or take any of these actions in combination. To appeal successfully, it is best to appeal on the basis of an error of law, because appellate courts do not usually reverse on findings of fact.

CHAPTER 4

1. *Can a state, in the interest of energy conservation, ban all advertising by power utilities if conservation could be accomplished by less restrictive means? Why or why not?* No. Even if commercial speech is neither related to illegal activities nor misleading, it may be restricted if a state has a substantial interest that cannot be achieved by less restrictive means. In this case, the interest in energy conservation is substantial, but it could be achieved by less restrictive means. That would be the utilities' defense against the enforcement of this state law.

2. *Is this a violation of equal protection if the only reason for the tax is to protect the local firms from out-of-state competition? Explain.* Yes. The tax would limit the liberty of some persons (out-of-state businesses), so it is subject to a review under the equal protection clause. Protecting local businesses from out-of-state competition is not a legitimate government objective. Thus, such a tax would violate the equal protection clause.

CHAPTER 5

1. *Does this raise an ethical conflict between Acme's employees? Between Acme and its employees? Between Acme and its shareholders? Explain your answers.* When a corporation decides to respond to what it sees as a moral obligation to correct for past discrimination by adjusting pay differences among its employees, an ethical conflict is raised between the firm and its employees and between the firm and its shareholders. This dilemma arises directly out of the effect such a decision has on the firm's profits. If satisfying this obligation increases profitability, then the dilemma is easily resolved in favor of "doing the right thing."

2. *Does Delta have an ethical duty to remove this product from the market, even if the injuries result only from misuse? Why or why not?* Maybe. On the one hand, it is not the company's "fault" when a product is misused. Also, keeping the product on the market is not a violation of the law, and stopping sales would hurt profits. On the other hand, suspending sales could reduce suffering and could stop potential negative publicity.

CHAPTER 6

1. *Can Lou recover from Jana? Why or why not?* Probably. To recover on the basis of negligence, the injured party as a plaintiff must show that the truck's owner owed the plaintiff a duty of care, that the owner breached that duty, that the plaintiff was injured, and that the breach caused the injury.

In this situation, the owner's actions breached the duty of reasonable care. The billboard falling on the plaintiff was the direct cause of the injury, not the plaintiff's own negligence. Thus, liability turns on whether the plaintiff can connect the breach of duty to the injury. This involves the test of proximate cause—the question of foreseeability. The consequences to the injured party must have been a foreseeable result of the owner's carelessness.

2. *What might the firm successfully claim in defense?* The company might defend against this electrician's claim by asserting that the electrician should have known of the risk and, therefore, the company had no duty to warn. According to the problem, the danger is common knowledge in the electrician's field and should have been apparent to this electrician, given his years of training and experience. In other words, the company most likely had no need to warn the electrician of the risk.

The firm could also raise comparative negligence. Both parties' negligence, if any, could be weighed and the liability distributed proportionately. The defendant could also assert assumption of risk, claiming that the electrician voluntarily entered into a dangerous situation, knowing the risk involved.

CHAPTER 7

1. *Is Superior Vehicles liable? Explain your answer.* Yes. The manufacturer is liable for the injuries to the user of the product. A manufacturer is liable for its failure to exercise due care to any person who sustains an injury proximately caused by a negligently made (defective) product.

2. *What defense might Bensing assert to avoid liability under state law?* Bensing can assert the defense of preemption. An injured party may not be able to sue the manufacturer of defective products that are subject to comprehensive federal regulatory schemes. If the federal government has a comprehensive regulatory scheme (such as it does with medical devices and vaccines), then it is assumed that the rules were designed to ensure a product's safety, and the federal rules will preempt any state regulations. Therefore, Bensing could not be held liable under state law if it complied with the federal drug-labeling requirements.

CHAPTER 8

1. *Has Roslyn violated any of the intellectual property rights discussed in this chapter? Explain.* Yes, Roslyn has committed theft of trade secrets. Lists of suppliers and customers cannot be patented, copyrighted, or trademarked, but the information they contain is protected against appropriation by others as trade secrets. And most likely, Roslyn signed a contract agreeing not to use this information outside her employment by Organic. But even without this contract, Organic could make a convincing case against its ex-employee for a theft of trade secrets.

2. *Is this patent infringement? If so, how might Global save the cost of suing World for infringement and at the same time profit from World's sales?* This is patent infringement. A software maker in this situation might best protect its product, save litigation costs, and profit from its patent by the use of a license. In the context of this problem, a license would grant permission to sell a patented item. (A license can be limited to certain purposes and to the licensee only.)

CHAPTER 9

1. *Has Karl done anything wrong? Explain.* Karl may have committed trademark infringement. A site that appropriates the key words of other sites with more frequent hits will appear in the same search engine results as the more popular sites. But using another's trademark as a key word without the owner's permission normally constitutes trademark infringement. Of course, some uses of another's trademark as a meta tag may be permissible if the use is reasonably necessary and does not suggest that the owner authorized or sponsored the use.

2. *Can Eagle Corporation stop this use of eagle? If so, what must the company show? Explain.* Yes. This may be an instance of trademark dilution. Dilution occurs when a trademark is used, without permission, in a way that diminishes the distinctive quality of the mark. Dilution does not require proof that consumers are likely to be confused by the use of the unauthorized mark. The products involved do not have to be similar. Dilution does require, however, that a mark be famous when the dilution occurs.

CHAPTER 10

1. With respect to the gas station, has she committed a crime? If so, what is it? Yes. With respect to the gas station, she has obtained goods by false pretenses. She might also be charged with larceny and forgery, and most states have special statutes covering illegal use of credit cards.

2. Has Ben committed a crime? If so, what is it? Yes. The Counterfeit Access Device and Computer Fraud and Abuse Act provides that a person who accesses a computer online, without permission, to obtain classified data—such as consumer credit files in a credit agency's database—is subject to criminal prosecution. The crime has two elements: accessing the computer without permission and taking data. It is a felony if done for private financial gain. Penalties include fines and imprisonment for up to twenty years. The victim of the theft can also bring a civil suit against the criminal to obtain damages and other relief.

CHAPTER 11

1. Can Ed recover? Why or why not? No. This contract, although not fully executed, is for an illegal purpose and therefore is void. A void contract gives rise to no legal obligation on the part of any party. A contract that is void is no contract. There is nothing to enforce.

2. Can Alison recover from Jerry the amount that she paid? Why or why not? Yes, because a person who is unjustly enriched at the expense of another can be required to account for the benefit under the theory of quasi contract. The parties here did not have a contract, but the law will impose one to avoid the unjust enrichment.

CHAPTER 12

1. Do Fidelity and Ron have a contract? Why or why not? No. Revocation of an offer may be implied by conduct inconsistent with the offer. When the corporation hired someone else, and the offeree learned of the hiring, the offer was revoked. The acceptance was too late.

2. Under the Uniform Electronic Transactions Act, what determines the effect of the electronic documents evidencing the parties' deal? Is a party's "signature" necessary? Explain. First, it might be noted that the UETA does not apply unless the parties to a contract agree to use e-commerce in their transaction. In this deal, of course, the parties used e-commerce. The UETA removes barriers to e-commerce by giving the same legal effect to e-records and e-signatures as to paper documents and signatures. The UETA does not include rules for those transactions, however.

CHAPTER 13

1. Is the new contract binding? Explain. Yes. The original contract was executory. The parties rescinded it and agreed to a new contract. If Sharyn had broken the contract to accept a contract with another employer, she might have been held liable for damages for the breach.

2. Is Fred's promise binding? Explain. Yes. Under the doctrine of detrimental reliance, or promissory estoppel, the promisee is entitled to payment of $5,000 from the promisor on graduation. There was a promise, on which the promisee relied, the reliance was substantial and definite (the promisee went to college for the full term, incurring considerable expenses, and will likely graduate), and it would only be fair to enforce the promise.

CHAPTER 14

1. Can Kenwood enforce the lease against Joan? Why or why not? No. Joan is a minor and may disaffirm this contract. Because the apartment was a necessary, however, she remains liable for the reasonable value of her occupancy of the apartment.

2. If the cause of an accident is found to be the airline's negligence, can it use the clause as a defense to liability? Why or why not? No. Generally, an exculpatory clause (a clause attempting to absolve parties of negligence or other wrongs) is not enforced if the party seeking its enforcement is involved in a business that is important to the public as a matter of practical necessity, such as an airline. Because of the essential nature of such services, this party has an advantage in bargaining strength and could insist that anyone contracting for its services agree not to hold it liable.

CHAPTER 15

1. Can she rescind the deal? Why or why not? Yes. Rescission may be granted on the basis of fraudulent misrepresentation. The elements of fraudulent misrepresentation include intent to deceive, or *scienter*. *Scienter* exists if a party makes a statement recklessly, without regard to whether it is true or false, or if a party says or implies that a statement is made on some basis such as personal knowledge or personal investigation when it is not.

2. Can Elle be held liable to GCC? Why or why not? Yes. The accountant may be liable on the ground of negligent misrepresentation. A misrepresentation is negligent if a person fails to exercise reasonable care in disclosing material facts or does not use the skill and competence required by his or her business or profession.

CHAPTER 16

1. Can Midstate enforce a deal for the full $800? Explain your answer. No. Under the UCC, a contract for a sale of goods priced at $500 or more must be in writing to be enforceable. In this case, the contract is not enforceable beyond the quantity already delivered and paid for.

2. *Next Corporation argues that there is no written contract between them. What will the court say?* The court might conclude that under the doctrine of promissory estoppel, the employer is estopped from claiming the lack of a written contract as a defense. The oral contract may be enforced because the employer made a promise on which the employee justifiably relied in moving to New York, the reliance was foreseeable, and injustice can be avoided only by enforcing the promise. If the court strictly enforces the Statute of Frauds, however, the employee may be without a remedy.

CHAPTER 17

1. *Can Jeff successfully sue Ed for the $100? Why or why not?* Yes. When one person makes a promise with the intention of benefiting a third person, the third person can sue to enforce it. This is a third party beneficiary contract. The third party in this problem is an intended beneficiary.

2. *Can Good Credit enforce the contract against Frank? Why or why not?* Yes. Generally, if a contract clearly states that a right is not assignable, no assignment will be effective, but there are exceptions. Assignment of the right to receive monetary payment cannot be prohibited.

CHAPTER 18

1. *Before Ready or Stealth starts performing, can the parties call off the deal? What if Stealth has already shipped the pizzas? Explain your answers.* Contracts that are executory on both sides—contracts on which neither party has performed—can be rescinded solely by agreement. Contracts that are executed on one side—contracts on which one party has performed—can be rescinded only if the party who has performed receives consideration for the promise to call off the deal.

2. *What type of agreement is this? Are Ace's obligations discharged? Why or why not?* This is a novation because it substitutes a new party for an original party, by agreement of all the parties. The requirements are a previous valid obligation, an agreement of all the parties to a new contract, extinguishment of the old obligation, and a new, valid contract. Ace's obligations are discharged.

CHAPTER 19

1. *If Haney sues Greg, what will be the measure of recovery?* A nonbreaching party is entitled to his or her benefit of the bargain under the contract. Here, the innocent party is entitled to be put in the position she would have been in if the contract had been fully performed. The measure of the benefit is the cost to complete the work ($500). These are compensatory damages.

2. *Is Lyle liable for Marley's expenses in providing for the cattle? Why or why not?* No. To recover damages that flow from the consequences of a breach but that are caused by circumstances beyond the contract (consequential damages), the breaching party must know, or have reason to know, that special circumstances will cause the nonbreaching party to suffer the additional loss. That was not the circumstance in this problem.

CHAPTER 20

1. *Is this an acceptance of the offer or a counteroffer? If it is an acceptance, is it a breach of the contract? Why or why not? What if Fav-O-Rite told E-Design it was sending the printer stands as "an accommodation"?* A shipment of nonconforming goods constitutes an acceptance of the offer and a breach, unless the seller seasonably notifies the buyer that the nonconforming shipment does not constitute an acceptance and is offered only as an accommodation. Thus, since there was no notification here, the shipment was both an acceptance and a breach. If, however, Fav-O-Rite had notified E-Design that it was sending the printer stands as an accommodation, the shipment would not constitute an acceptance, and Fav-O-Rite would not be in breach.

2. *Is there an enforceable contract between them? Why or why not?* Yes. In a transaction between merchants, the requirement of a writing is satisfied if one of them sends to the other a signed written confirmation that indicates the terms of the agreement, and the merchant receiving it has reason to know of its contents. If the merchant who receives the confirmation does not object in writing within ten days after receipt, the writing will be enforceable against him or her even though he or she has not signed anything.

CHAPTER 21

1. *What are the consequences if Silk bore the risk? If Adams bore the risk?* Buyers and sellers can have an insurable interest in identical goods at the same time. If the buyer (Silk & Satin) bore the risk, it must pay and seek reimbursement from its insurance company. If the seller (Adams Textiles) bore the risk, it must seek reimbursement from its insurance company and may still have an obligation to deliver the identified goods (the fabric) to Silk & Satin.

2. *If Karlin files a lawsuit, will she prevail? Why or why not?* When a person "entrusts" goods to a merchant (a person who deals in goods of that kind), the merchant has the power to transfer a good title to any purchaser who acquires the goods in the *ordinary course of business.* Karlin entrusted her set to merchant Orken. Orken deals in goods of that kind. Therefore, Orken could pass good title to the set to a customer (Grady) who purchased the goods in the ordinary course of business. Consequently, Karlin cannot get the set back from Grady. (But the merchant is liable to the true owner, Karlin, for the equivalent value of the set.)

CHAPTER 22

1. *Does Country have the right to reject the shipment? Explain.* Yes. A seller is obligated to deliver goods in conformity with a contract in every detail. This is the perfect tender rule. The exception of the seller's right to cure does not apply here, because the seller delivered too little too late to take advantage of this exception.

2. Can Poster Planet sue Brite without waiting until May 1? Why or why not? Yes. When anticipatory repudiation occurs, a buyer (or lessee) can resort to any remedy for breach even if the buyer tells the seller (the repudiating party in this problem) that the buyer will wait for the seller's performance.

CHAPTER 23

1. When it does not perform to GCC's specifications, GCC sues Industrial, which claims, "We didn't expressly promise anything." What should GCC argue? The buyer should argue that the seller breached an implied warranty of fitness for a particular purpose. An implied warranty of fitness for a particular purpose arises when a seller knows a particular purpose for which a buyer will use goods and that the buyer is relying on the seller's skill and judgment to select suitable goods.

2. Can Stella recover for breach of the implied warranty of merchantability? Why or why not? Yes, Stella can recover from Roasted Bean for breach of the implied warranty of merchantability. An implied warranty of merchantability arises in every sale of goods sold by a merchant who deals in goods of the kind. Goods that are merchantable are fit for the ordinary purposes for which such goods are used. A sale of food or drink is a sale of goods. Merchantable food is food that is fit to eat or drink on the basis of consumer expectations. A consumer should reasonably expect hot coffee to be hot, but not to be so scalding that it causes third-degree burns.

CHAPTER 24

1. Under what circumstances would a U.S. court enforce the judgment of the Ecuadoran court? Under the principle of comity, a U.S. court would defer and give effect to foreign laws and judicial decrees that are consistent with U.S. law and public policy.

2. How can this attempt to undersell U.S. businesses be defeated? The practice described in this problem is known as dumping, which is regarded as an unfair international trade practice. Dumping is the sale of imported goods at "less than fair value." Based on the price of those goods in the exporting country, an extra tariff—known as an antidumping duty—can be imposed on the imports.

CHAPTER 25

1. Which of these phrases would prevent the instrument's negotiability? A statement that "I.O.U." money (or anything else) or an instruction to a bank stating, "I wish you would pay," would render any instrument nonnegotiable. To be negotiable, an instrument must contain an express promise to pay. An I.O.U. is only an acknowledgment of indebtedness. An order stating, "I wish you would pay," is not sufficiently precise.

2. Is Marit's note a demand note? Explain. Yes. Instruments that are payable on demand may state "Payable on demand." The nature of an instrument may indicate that it is payable on demand. If no time for payment is specified, then the instrument is also payable on demand. Here, the note required installments but did not state a date for their payment. That Donald did not make a demand for payment did not affect this characteristic of the note.

CHAPTER 26

1. What type of indorsement is this? What effect does this indorsement have on whether the check is considered an order instrument or a bearer instrument? Explain. This is a special indorsement, which names the indorsee (Kurt). No special words are needed. A special indorsement makes an instrument order paper. Thus, further negotiation requires Kurt's indorsement.

2. Can Carl become an HDC? Why or why not? No. One of the requirements for HDC status is that the holder must have performed the promise for which the instrument was issued. A holder takes the instrument for value only to the extent that the promise has been performed. Because Ben did not perform his promise to repair Amy's roof, he is not an HDC. Thus, Carl—who took the instrument from Ben—cannot trace his title back to an HDC, so he is not be protected as an HDC under the shelter principle.

CHAPTER 27

1. Does Suchin have any recourse against the bank for the payment? Why or why not? No. When a drawer's employee provides the drawer with the name of a fictitious payee (a payee whom the drawer does not actually intend to have any interest in an instrument), a forgery of the payee's name is effective to pass good title to subsequent transferees.

2. Was the bookstore a holder in due course on Skye's check? Yes. One of the requirements for HDC status is a lack of notice that an instrument is defective. A party will not attain this status if he or she knows, or has reason to know, that an incomplete instrument was later completed in an unauthorized manner. Notice of a defective instrument is given when a holder has reason to know that a defect exists, given all of the facts known at the time. Here, the bookstore did not have notice that Skye's check was incomplete when it was issued. The bookstore saw only a properly completed instrument.

CHAPTER 28

1. Is Lyn liable to Nan? Could Lyn be subject to criminal prosecution? Why or why not? Yes, to both questions. In a civil suit, a drawer (Lyn) is liable to a payee (Nan) or to a holder of a check that is not honored. If intent to defraud can be proved, the drawer (Lyn) can also be subject to criminal prosecution for writing a bad check.

2. Can the bank refuse to recredit Kay's account? If not, can the bank recover the amount paid to Will? Why or why not?

The general rule is that the bank must recredit a customer's account when it pays on a forged signature. The bank has no right to recover from a holder who, without knowledge, cashes a check bearing a forged drawer's signature. Thus, the bank in this problem can collect from neither its customer nor the party who cashed the check. The bank's recourse is to look for the thief.

CHAPTER 29

1. *What can Larry and Midwest do?* Each of the parties can place a mechanic's lien on the debtor's property. If the debtor does not pay what is owed, the property can be sold to satisfy the debt. The only requirements are that the lien be filed within a specific time from the time of the work, depending on the state statute, and that notice of the foreclosure and sale be given to the debtor in advance.

2. *If the employer complies with the order and Alyssa stays on the job, is one order enough to garnish all of Alyssa's wages for each pay period until the debt is paid? Explain.* No. In some states, a creditor must go back to court for a separate order of garnishment for each pay period. Also, federal and state laws limit the amount of money that can be garnished from a debtor's pay.

CHAPTER 30

1. *How can Olivia let other creditors know of her interest in the computer?* A creditor can put other creditors on notice by perfecting its interest: by filing a financing statement in the appropriate public office, or by taking possession of the collateral until the debtor repays the loan.

2. *Liberty could repossess and keep the car, but the bank does not want it. What are the alternatives?* When collateral is consumer goods with a PMSI, and the debtor has paid less than 60 percent of the debt or the purchase price, the creditor can dispose of the collateral in a commercially reasonable manner, which generally requires notice to the debtor of the place, time, and manner of sale. A debtor can waive the right to notice, but only after default. Before the disposal, a debtor can redeem the collateral by tendering performance of all of the obligations secured by it and by paying the creditor's reasonable expenses in retaking and maintaining it.

CHAPTER 31

1. *Are these debts dischargeable in bankruptcy? Explain.* No. Besides the claims listed in this problem, the debts that cannot be discharged in bankruptcy include amounts borrowed to pay back taxes, goods obtained by fraud, debts that were not listed in the petition, domestic support obligations, certain cash advances, and others.

2. *Can Quentin recover the $10,000 paid to Ogden on June 1? Why or why not?* Yes. A debtor's payment to a creditor made for a preexisting debt, within ninety days (one year in the case of an insider or fraud) of a bankruptcy filing, can be recovered if it gives a creditor more than he or she would have received in the

bankruptcy proceedings. A trustee can recover this preference using his or her specific avoidance powers.

CHAPTER 32

1. *Was Winona an independent contractor?* Yes. An independent contractor is a person who contracts with another—the principal—to do something but who is neither controlled by the other nor subject to the other's right to control with respect to the performance. Independent contractors are not employees, because those who hire them have no control over the details of their performance.

2. *When Nadine learns of this, she wants to buy the land and sell it to Dimka herself. Can she do this? Discuss.* No. Nadine, as an agent, is prohibited from taking advantage of the agency relationship to obtain property that the principal (Dimka Corporation) wants to purchase. This is the duty of loyalty that arises with every agency relationship.

CHAPTER 33

1. *Can Davis hold Estee liable for whatever damages he has to pay? Why or why not?* Yes. A principal has a duty to indemnify an agent for liabilities incurred because of authorized and lawful acts and transactions and for losses suffered because of the principal's failure to perform his or her duties.

2. *In what circumstance is Vivian liable on the note?* When a person enters into a contract on another's behalf without the authority to do so, the other may be liable on the contract if he or she approves or affirms that contract. In other words, the employer-principal would be liable for the note in this problem on ratifying it. Whether the employer-principal ratifies the note or not, the unauthorized agent is most likely also liable for it.

CHAPTER 34

1. *For Erin to obtain workers' compensation, must her injury have been caused by Fine Print's negligence? Does it matter whether the action causing the injury was intentional? Explain.* Workers' compensation laws establish a procedure for compensating workers who are injured on the job. Instead of suing to collect benefits, an injured worker notifies the employer of an injury and files a claim with the appropriate state agency.

The right to recover is normally determined without regard to negligence or fault, but intentionally inflicted injuries are not covered. Unlike the potential for recovery in a lawsuit based on negligence or fault, recovery under a workers' compensation statute is limited to the specific amount designated in the statute for the employee's injury.

2. *Are these conditions legal? Why or why not?* No. A closed shop (a company that requires union membership as a condition of employment) is illegal. A union shop (a company that does not require union membership as a condition of employment but requires workers to join the union after a certain time on the job) is illegal in a state with a right-to-work law, which makes it illegal to require union membership for continued employment.

CHAPTER 35

1. *Is this sexual harassment? Why or why not?* Yes. One type of sexual harassment occurs when a request for sexual favors is a condition of employment, and the person making the request is a supervisor or acts with the authority of the employer. A tangible employment action, such as continued employment, may also lead to the employer's liability for the supervisor's conduct. That the injured employee is a male and the supervisor a female, instead of the other way around, would not affect the outcome. Same-gender harassment is also actionable.

2. *Could Koko succeed in a suit against Lively for discrimination? Explain.* Yes, if she can show that Lively failed to hire her solely because of her disability. The other elements for a discrimination suit based on a disability are that the plaintiff (1) has a disability and (2) is otherwise qualified for the job. Both of these elements appear to be satisfied in this problem.

CHAPTER 36

1. *Would a sole proprietorship be an appropriate form for Frank's business? Why or why not?* Yes. When a business is relatively small and is not diversified, employs relatively few people, has modest profits, and is not likely to expand significantly or require extensive financing in the immediate future, the most appropriate form for doing business may be a sole proprietorship.

2. *Does this constitute "cause" for termination? Why or why not?* Yes. Failing to meet a specified sales quota can constitute a breach of a franchise agreement. If the franchisor is acting in good faith, "cause" may also include the death or disability of the franchisee, the insolvency of the franchisee, and a breach of another term of the franchise agreement.

CHAPTER 37

1. *When Darnell dies, his widow claims that as Darnell's heir, she is entitled to take his place as Eliana's partner or to receive a share of the firm's assets. Is she right? Why or why not?* No. A widow (or widower) has no right to take a dead partner's place. A partner's death causes dissociation, after which the partnership must purchase the dissociated partner's partnership interest. Therefore, the surviving partners must pay the decedent's estate (for his widow) the value of the deceased partner's interest in the partnership.

2. *Because the vehicles would otherwise be sitting idle in a parking lot, can Finian keep the income that results from leasing the delivery vehicles? Explain your answer.* No. Under the partners' fiduciary duty, a partner must account to the partnership for any personal profits or benefits derived without the consent of all the partners in connection with the use of any partnership property. Here, the leasing partner may not keep the money.

CHAPTER 38

1. *What are their options with respect to the management of their firm?* The members of a limited liability company (LLC) may designate a group to run their firm, in which situation the firm would be considered a manager-managed LLC. The group may include only members, only nonmembers, or members and nonmembers. If, instead, all members participate in management, the firm would be a member-managed LLC. In fact, unless the members agree otherwise, all members are considered to participate in the management of the firm.

2. *What do these forms of business organization have in common?* Although there are differences, all of these forms of business organizations resemble corporations. A joint stock company, for example, features ownership by shares of stock, is managed by directors and officers, and has perpetual existence. A business trust, like a corporation, distributes profits to persons who are not personally responsible for the debts of the organization. Management of a business trust is in the hands of trustees, just as the management of a corporation is in the hands of directors and officers. An incorporated cooperative, which is subject to state laws covering nonprofit corporations, distributes profits to its owners.

CHAPTER 39

1. *Is there a way for Northwest Brands to avoid this double taxation? Explain your answer.* Yes. Small businesses that meet certain requirements can qualify as S corporations, created specifically to permit small businesses to avoid double taxation. The six requirements of an S corporation are (1) the firm must be a domestic corporation, (2) the firm must not be a member of an affiliated group of corporations, (3) the firm must have less than a certain number of shareholders, (4) the shareholders must be individuals, estates, or qualified trusts (or corporations in some cases), (5) there can be only one class of stock, and (6) no shareholder can be a nonresident alien.

2. *Can they grant this authority to their firm? If so, how? If not, why not?* Broad authority to conduct business can be granted in a corporation's articles of incorporation. For example, the term "any lawful purpose" is often used. This can be important because acts of a corporation that are beyond the authority given to it in its articles or charter (or state statutes) are considered illegal, *ultra vires* acts.

CHAPTER 40

1. *Yvon, a Wonder shareholder, learns of the purchase and wants to sue the directors on Wonder's behalf. Can she do it? Explain.* Yes. A shareholder can bring a derivative suit on behalf of a corporation, if some wrong is done to the corporation. Normally, any damages recovered go into the corporate treasury.

2. *Discuss whether Nico owes a duty to Omega or the minority shareholders in selling his shares.* Yes. A single shareholder—or a few shareholders acting together—who owns enough stock to exercise *de facto* control over a corporation owes the corporation and minority shareholders a fiduciary duty when transferring those shares.

CHAPTER 41

1. *What is the term for this type of combination? What happens to the assets, property, and liabilities of Micro?* This combination is a consolidation (a new entity takes the place of the consolidating, disappearing firms). In a merger, in contrast, one of the merging entities continues to exist. In this consolidation, the new corporation, MM, Inc., inherits all of Micro's assets, property, and liabilities.

2. *Can McClellan hold Peppertree's shareholders personally liable for the debt? Why or why not?* Maybe. If a corporation organizes another corporation with practically the same shareholders and directors and transfers all the assets but does not pay all the first corporation's debts, a court can hold the new corporation liable. Here, the new corporation continued to carry on the same business as Peppertree with all of Peppertree's assets, so it would be fair for a court to hold the new corporation liable for Peppertree's obligations.

CHAPTER 42

1. *What sort of information would an investor consider material?* The average investor is not concerned with minor inaccuracies but with facts that if disclosed would tend to deter him or her from buying the securities. This would include facts that have an important bearing on the condition of the issuer and its business—liabilities, loans to officers and directors, customer delinquencies, and pending lawsuits.

2. *Can Lee take advantage of this information to buy and sell Magma stock? Why or why not?* No. The Securities Exchange Act of 1934 extends liability to officers and directors in their personal transactions for taking advantage of inside information when they know it is unavailable to the persons with whom they are dealing.

CHAPTER 43

1. *What safeguards promote the ALJ's fairness?* Under the Administrative Procedure Act (APA), the administrative law judge (ALJ) must be separate from the agency's investigative and prosecutorial staff. *Ex parte* communications between the ALJ and a party to a proceeding are prohibited. Under the APA, an ALJ is exempt from agency discipline except on a showing of good cause.

2. *Does the firm have any opportunity to express its opinion about the pending rule? Explain.* Yes. Administrative rulemaking starts with the publication of a notice of the rulemaking in the *Federal Register*. A public hearing is held at which proponents and opponents can offer evidence and question witnesses. After the hearing, the agency considers what was presented at the hearing and drafts the final rule.

CHAPTER 44

1. *To market the drug, what must United prove to the U.S. Food and Drug Administration?* Under an extensive set of procedures established by the U.S. Food and Drug Administration, which administers the federal Food, Drug, and Cosmetic Act, drugs must be shown to be effective as well as safe before they may be marketed to the public. In general, manufacturers are responsible for ensuring that the drugs they offer for sale are free of any substances that could injure consumers.

2. *What can Gert do?* Under the Truth-in-Lending Act, a buyer who wishes to withhold payment for a faulty product purchased with a credit card must follow specific procedures to settle the dispute. The credit card issuer then must intervene and attempt to settle the dispute.

CHAPTER 45

1. *Are there any reasons that the court might refuse to issue an injunction against Resource's operation? Explain.* Yes. On the ground that the hardships that would be imposed on the polluter and on the community are greater than the hardships suffered by the residents, the court might deny an injunction. If the plant is the core of the local economy, for instance, the residents may be awarded only damages.

2. *If the Environmental Protection Agency cleans up the site, from whom can it recover the cost?* The Comprehensive Environmental Response, Compensation, and Liability Act of 1980 regulates the clean-up of hazardous waste disposal sites. Any potentially responsible party can be charged with the entire cost of cleaning up a site. Potentially responsible parties include the person that generated the waste (ChemCorp) the person that transported the waste to the site (Disposal), the person that owned or operated the site at the time of the disposal (Eliminators), and the current owner or operator of the site (Fluid). A party held responsible for the entire cost may be able to recoup some of it in a lawsuit against other potentially responsible parties.

CHAPTER 46

1. *Under what circumstances would Pop's Market, a small store in a small, isolated town, be considered a monopolist? If Pop's is a monopolist, is it in violation of Section 2 of the Sherman Act? Why or why not?* Size alone does not determine whether a firm is a monopoly—size in relation to the market is what matters. A small store in a small, isolated town is a monopolist if it is the only store serving that market. Monopoly involves the power to affect prices and output. If a firm has sufficient market power to control prices and exclude competition, that firm has monopoly power. Monopoly power in itself is not a violation of Section 2 of the Sherman Act. The offense also requires that the defendant intended to acquire or maintain that power through anticompetitive means.

2. *What factors would a court consider to decide whether this arrangement violates the Clayton Act?* This agreement is a tying arrangement. The legality of a tying arrangement depends on the purpose of the agreement, the agreement's likely effect on competition in the relevant markets (the market for the tying product and the market for the tied product), and other factors. Tying arrangements for commodities are subject to Section 3 of the Clayton Act. Tying arrangements for services can be agreements in restraint of trade in violation of Section 1 of the Sherman Act.

CHAPTER 47

1. *Can the bank successfully sue Dave? Why or why not?* Yes. In these circumstances, when the accountant knows that the bank will use the statement, the bank is a foreseeable user. A foreseeable user is a third party within the class of parties to whom an accountant may be liable for negligence.

2. *Can Nora be held liable to Pat? Explain.* No. In the circumstances described, the accountant will not be held liable to a purchaser of the securities. Although an accountant may be liable under securities laws for including untrue statements or omitting material facts from financial statements, due diligence is a defense to liability.

Due diligence requires an accountant to conduct a reasonable investigation and have reason to believe that the financial statements were true at the time. The facts say that the misstatement of material fact in Omega's financial statement was not attributable to any fraud or negligence on Nora's part. Therefore, Nora can show that she used due diligence and will not be held liable to Pat.

CHAPTER 48

1. *Does Speedy have a right to recover from the third party for the loss of the documents? Why or why not?* Yes. A bailee's right of possession, even though temporary, permits the bailee to recover damages from any third persons for damage or loss to the property.

2. *Who suffers the loss? Explain your answer.* Rosa de la Mar Corporation, the shipper, suffers the loss. A common carrier is liable for damage caused by the willful acts of third persons or by an accident. Other losses must be borne by the shipper (or the recipient, depending on the terms of their contract). This shipment was lost due to an act of God.

CHAPTER 49

1. *Delmira wants to have Consuela evicted from the property. What can Consuela do?* This is a breach of the warranty deed's covenant of quiet enjoyment. The buyer can sue the seller and recover the purchase price of the house, plus any damages.

2. *Can Haven transfer possession for even less time to Idyll Company? Explain.* Yes. An owner of a fee simple has the most rights possible—he or she can give the property away, sell it, transfer it by will, use it for almost any purpose, possess it to the exclusion of all the world, or as in this case, transfer possession for any period of time. The party to whom possession is transferred can also transfer his or her interest (usually only with the owner's permission) for any lesser period of time.

CHAPTER 50

1. *Can the insurer refuse payment? Why or why not?* No. An incorrect statement as to the age of an insured is a misrepresentation. Under an incontestability clause, however, after a policy has been in force for a certain time (usually two or three years), the insurer cannot cancel the policy or avoid a claim on the basis of statements made in the application.

2. *Can Al obtain payment for these events? Explain your answers.* No. To obtain insurance, one must have a sufficiently substantial interest in whatever is to be insured. One has an insurable interest in property if one would suffer a pecuniary loss from its destruction. This interest must exist *when the loss occurs.*

To obtain insurance on another's life, one must have a reasonable expectation of benefit from the continued life of the other. The benefit may be founded on a relationship, but "ex-spouse" alone is not such a relationship. An interest in someone's life must exist *when the policy is obtained.*

CHAPTER 51

1. *Can Toby and Umeko have Sheila's will revoked on the ground that she did not have the capacity to make a will? Why or why not?* No. To have testamentary capacity, a testator must be of legal age and sound mind *at the time the will is made.* Generally, the testator must (1) know the nature of the act, (2) comprehend and remember the "natural objects of his or her bounty," (3) know the nature and extent of her or his property, and (4) understand the distribution of assets called for by the will. In this situation, Sheila had testamentary capacity at the time she made the will. The fact that she was ruled mentally incompetent two years after making the will does not provide sufficient grounds to revoke it.

2. *What determines who inherits what?* The estate will pass according to the state's intestacy laws. Intestacy laws set out how property is distributed when a person dies without a will. Their purpose is to carry out the likely intent of the decedent. The laws determine which of the deceased's natural heirs (including the surviving spouse, lineal descendants, parents, and collateral heirs) inherit his or her property.

APPENDIX E

Sample Answers for *Business Case Problems with Sample Answer*

Problem 1–5. *Reading Citations.* The court's opinion in this case—*Equal Employment Opportunity Commission v. Autozone, Inc.,* 809 F.3d 916 (7th Cir. 2016)—can be found in Volume 809 of *Federal Reporter, Third Series* on page 916. The U.S. Court of Appeals for the Seventh Circuit issued this opinion in 2016.

Problem 2–7. *Corporate Contacts.* No, the defendants' motion to dismiss the suit for lack of personal jurisdiction should not be granted. A corporation normally is subject to jurisdiction in a state in which it is doing business. A court applies the minimum-contacts test to determine whether it can exercise jurisdiction over an out-of-state corporation. This requirement is met if the corporation sells its products within the state or places its goods in the "stream of commerce" with the intent that the goods be sold in the state.

In this problem, the state of Washington filed a suit in a Washington state court against LG Electronics, Inc., and nineteen other foreign companies that participated in the global market for cathode ray tube (CRT) products. The state alleged a conspiracy to raise prices and set production levels in the market for CRTs in violation of a state consumer protection statute. The defendants filed a motion to dismiss the suit for lack of personal jurisdiction. These goods were sold for many years in high volume in the United States, including the state of Washington. In other words, the corporations purposefully established minimum contacts in the state of Washington. This is a sufficient basis for a Washington state court to assert personal jurisdiction over the defendants.

In the actual case on which this problem is based, the court dismissed the suit for lack of personal jurisdiction. On appeal, a state intermediate appellate court reversed on the reasoning stated above.

Problem 3–7. *Discovery.* Yes. The items that were deleted from a Facebook page can be recovered. Normally, a party must hire an expert to recover material in an electronic format, and this can be time consuming and expensive.

Electronic evidence, or e-evidence, consists of all computer-generated or electronically recorded information, such as posts on Facebook and other social media sites. The effect that e-evidence can have in a case depends on its relevance and what it reveals. In the facts presented in this problem, Isaiah should be sanctioned—he should be required to cover Allied's cost to hire the recovery expert and attorney's fees to confront the misconduct. In a jury trial, the court might also instruct the jury to presume that any missing items are harmful to Isaiah's case. If all of the material is retrieved and presented at the trial, any

prejudice to Allied's case might thereby be mitigated. If not, the court might go so far as to order a new trial.

In the actual case on which this problem is based, Allied hired an expert, who determined that Isaiah had in fact removed some photos and other items from his Facebook page. After the expert testified about the missing material, Isaiah provided Allied with all of it, including the photos that he had deleted. Allied sought a retrial, but the court instead reduced the amount of Isaiah's damages by the amount that it cost Allied to address his "misconduct."

Problem 4–4. *The Dormant Commerce Clause.* The court ruled that, like a state, Puerto Rico generally may not enact policies that discriminate against out-of-state commerce. The law requiring companies that sell cement in Puerto Rico to place certain labels on their products is clearly an attempt to regulate the cement market. The law imposed labeling regulations that affect transactions between the citizens of Puerto Rico and private companies. State laws that on their face discriminate against foreign commerce are almost always invalid, and this Puerto Rican law is such a law. The discriminatory labeling requirement placed sellers of cement manufactured outside Puerto Rico at a competitive disadvantage. This law therefore contravenes the dormant commerce clause.

Problem 5–3. *Online Privacy.* Facebook created a program that makes decisions for users. Using duty-based ethics, many believe that privacy is an extremely important right that should be fiercely protected. Accordingly, any program that has a default of giving out information is unethical. Facebook should create the program as an opt-in program. In addition, under the Kantian categorical imperative, if every company created opt-out programs that disclosed potentially personal information, the concept of privacy may be reduced to a theoretical concept only. One could argue that this reduction or elimination of privacy would not make the world a better place. From a utilitarian or outcome-based approach, the benefits of an opt-out program might be in ease of creation and start up, as well as ease of recruiting partner programs. The detriment is the elimination of choice on the part of users to disclose information about themselves. An opt-in program maintains that user control but may be harder to start, as it requires more marketing up front in order to convince users to opt in.

Problem 6–5. *Negligence.* Negligence requires proof that (1) the defendant owed a duty of care to the plaintiff, (2) the defendant breached that duty, (3) the defendant's breach caused the plaintiff's injury, and (4) the plaintiff suffered a legally recognizable injury. With respect to the duty of care, a business owner has a duty to use reasonable care to protect business invitees. This duty includes an obligation to discover and correct or warn of unreasonably dangerous conditions that the owner of the premises should reasonably foresee might endanger an invitee. Some risks are so obvious that an owner need not warn of them. But even if a risk is obvious, a business owner may not be excused from the duty to protect its customers from foreseeable harm.

Because Lucario was the Weatherford's business invitee, the hotel owed her a duty of reasonable care to make its premises safe for her use. The balcony ran nearly the entire width of the window in Lucario's room. She could have reasonably believed that the window was a means of access to the balcony. The window/balcony configuration was dangerous, however, because the window opened wide enough for an adult to climb out, but the twelve-inch gap between one side of the window and the balcony was unprotected. This unprotected gap opened to a drop of more than three stories to a concrete surface below.

Should the hotel have anticipated the potential harm to a guest who opened the window in Room 59 and attempted to access the balcony? The hotel encouraged guests to "step out onto the balcony" to smoke. The dangerous condition of the window/balcony configuration could have been remedied at a minimal cost. These circumstances could be perceived as creating an "unreasonably dangerous" condition. And it could be concluded that the hotel created or knew of the condition and failed to take reasonable steps to warn of it or correct it. Of course, the Weatherford might argue that the window/ balcony configuration was so obvious that the hotel was not liable for Lucario's fall.

In the actual case on which this problem is based, the court concluded that the Weatherford did not breach its duty of care to Lucario. On McMurtry's appeal, a state intermediate appellate court held that this conclusion was in error, vacated the lower court's judgment in favor of the hotel on this issue, and remanded the case.

Problem 7–6. *Product Liability.* Here, the accident was caused by Jett's inattention, not by the texting device in the cab of his truck. In a product liability case based on a design defect, the plaintiff has to prove that the product was defective at the time it left the hands of the seller or lessor. The plaintiff must also show that this defective condition made it "unreasonably dangerous" to the user or consumer. If the product was delivered in a safe condition and subsequent mishandling made it harmful to the user, the seller or lessor normally is not liable. To successfully assert a design defect, a plaintiff has to show that a reasonable alternative design was available and that the defendant failed to use it.

The plaintiffs could contend that the defendant manufacturer of the texting device owed them a duty of care because injuries to vehicle drivers and passengers, and others on the roads, were reasonably foreseeable due to the product's design, which (1) required the driver to divert his eyes from the road to view an incoming text from the dispatcher, and (2) permitted the

receipt of texts while the vehicle was moving. But manufacturers are not required to design a product incapable of distracting a driver. The duty owed by a manufacturer to the user or consumer of a product does not require guarding against hazards that are commonly known or obvious or protecting against injuries that result from a user's careless conduct. That is what happened here.

In the actual case on which this problem is based, the court reached the same conclusion, based on the reasoning stated above, and an intermediate appellate court affirmed the judgment.

Problem 8–6. *Patents.* One ground on which the denial of the patent application in this problem could be reversed on appeal is that the design of Raymond Gianelli's "Rowing Machine" is *not obvious* in light of the design of the "Chest Press Apparatus for Exercising Regions of the Upper Body."

To obtain a patent, an applicant must demonstrate to the satisfaction of the U.S. Patent and Trademark Office (PTO) that the invention, discovery, process, or design is novel, useful, and not obvious in light of current technology. In this problem, the PTO denied Gianelli's application for a patent for his "Rowing Machine"—an exercise machine on which a user *pulls* on handles to perform a rowing motion against a selected resistance to strengthen the back muscles. The PTO considered the device obvious in light of a patented "Chest Press Apparatus for Exercising Regions of the Upper Body"—a chest press exercise machine on which a user *pushes* on handles to overcome a selected resistance. But it can be easily argued that it is *not* obvious to modify a machine with handles designed to be *pushed* into one with handles designed to be *pulled*. In fact, anyone who has used exercise machines knows that a way to cause injury is to use a machine in a manner not intended by the manufacturer.

In the actual case on which this problem is based, the U.S. Court of Appeals for the Federal Circuit reversed the PTO's denial of Gianelli's application for a patent, based on the reasoning stated above.

Problem 9–3. *Privacy.* No, Rolfe did not have a privacy interest in the information obtained by the subpoenas issued to Midcontinent Communications. The right to privacy is guaranteed by at least one interpretation of the U.S. Constitution's Bill of Rights and by some state constitutions. A person must have a reasonable expectation of privacy, though, to maintain a suit or to assert a successful defense for an invasion of privacy. People clearly have a reasonable expectation of privacy when they enter their personal banking or credit card information online. They also have a reasonable expectation that online companies will follow their own privacy policies. But people do not have a reasonable expectation of privacy in statements made on Twitter and other data that they publicly disseminate. In other words, there is no violation of a subscriber's right to privacy when a third-party Internet provider receives a subpoena and discloses the subscriber's information.

Here, Rolfe supplied his e-mail address and other personal information, including his Internet protocol address, to

Midcontinent. In other words, Rolfe publicly disseminated this information. Law enforcement officers obtained this information from Midcontinent through the subpoenas issued by the South Dakota state court. Rolfe provided his information to Midcontinent—he had no legitimate expectation of privacy in that information.

In the actual case on which this problem is based, Rolfe was charged with, and convicted of, possessing, manufacturing, and distributing child pornography, as well as other crimes. As part of the proceedings, the court found that Rolfe had no expectation of privacy in the information that he made available to Midcontinent. On appeal, the South Dakota Supreme Court upheld the conviction.

Problem 10–4. *Criminal Liability.* Yes, Green exhibited the required mental state to establish criminal liability. A wrongful mental state (*mens rea*) is one of the elements typically required to establish criminal liability. The required mental state, or intent, is indicated in an applicable statute or law. For example, for murder, the required mental state is the intent to take another's life. A court can also find that the required mental state is present when a defendant's acts are reckless or criminally negligent. A defendant is criminally reckless if he or she consciously disregards a substantial and unjustifiable risk.

In this problem, Green was clearly aware of the danger to which he was exposing people on the street below. Although he did not indicate that he specifically intended to harm anyone, the risk of death created by his conduct was obvious. He must have known what was likely to happen if a bottle or plate thrown from the height of twenty-six stories hit a pedestrian or the windshield of an occupied motor vehicle on the street below. Despite his claim that he was intoxicated, he was sufficiently aware to stop throwing things from the balcony when he saw police in the area, and he later recalled what he had done and what had happened.

In the actual case on which this problem is based, after a jury trial, Green was convicted of reckless endangerment. On appeal, a state intermediate appellate court affirmed the conviction, based in part on the reasoning stated above.

Problem 11–4. *Quasi Contract.* Gutkowski does not have a valid claim for payment, nor should he recover on the basis of a quasi contract. Quasi contracts are imposed by courts on parties in the interest of fairness and justice. Usually, a quasi contract is imposed to avoid the unjust enrichment of one party at the expense of another. Gutkowski was compensated as a consultant. For him to establish a claim that he is due more compensation based on unjust enrichment, he must have proof. As it is, he has only his claim that there were discussions about his being a part owner of YES. Discussions and negotiations are not a basis for recovery on a quasi contract. In the actual case on which this problem is based, the court dismissed Gutkowski's claim for payment.

Problem 12–4. *Online Acceptances.* No. A shrink-wrap agreement is an agreement whose terms are expressed inside the box in which the goods are packaged. The party who opens the box may be informed that he or she agrees to the terms by keeping whatever is in the box. In many cases, the courts have enforced the terms of shrink-wrap agreements just as they enforce the terms of other contracts. But not all of the terms presented in shrink-wrap agreements have been enforced by the courts. One important consideration is whether the buyer had adequate notice of the terms.

A click-on agreement is formed when a buyer, completing a transaction on a computer, is required to indicate his or her assent to be bound by the terms of an offer by clicking on a button that says, for example, "I agree." In Reasonover's situation, no such agreement was formed with respect to Clearwire's "Terms of Service" (TOS). The e-mail did not give adequate notice of the TOS. It did not contain a direct link to the terms—accessing them required clicks on further links through the firm's homepage. The written, shrink-wrap materials accompanying the modem did not provide adequate notice of the TOS. There was only a reference to Clearwire's Web site in small print at the bottom of one page. Similarly, Reasonover's access to an "I accept terms" box did not establish notice of the terms. She did not click on the box but quit the page. Even if any of these references was sufficient notice, Reasonover kept the modem only because Clearwire told her that she could not return it.

In the actual case on which this problem is based, the court refused to compel arbitration on the basis of the clause in Clearwire's TOS.

Problem 13–7. *Consideration.* Citynet's employee incentive plan was an offer for a unilateral contract. A Citynet employee who stayed on the job when he or she was under no obligation to do so could be considered to have accepted Citynet's offer and to have provided sufficient consideration to make the offer a binding and enforceable promise. Consideration has two elements—it must consist of something of legal value and must provide the basis for the bargain between the parties. A unilateral contract involves a promise in return for performance. The promisor becomes bound to the contract when the promisee performs—or, in many cases, begins to perform—the act. Both the promise and the performance have legal value.

Here, Citynet set up an employee incentive plan "to attract and retain experienced individuals." The plan provided that a participant who left Citynet's employ could "cash out" his or her entire vested balance. When Ray Toney terminated his employment and asked to redeem his vested balance, however, Citynet refused. But Toney had long stayed on the job when he did not have to. This was sufficient consideration to make Citynet's offer under the incentive plan a binding and enforceable contract with Toney.

In the actual case on which this problem is based, a West Virginia state court issued a judgment in Toney's favor. The West Virginia Supreme Court of Appeals affirmed, on the reasoning and principles stated above.

Problem 14–3. *Unconscionable Contracts or Clauses.* In this case, the agreement that restricted the buyer's options for resolution of a dispute to arbitration and limited the amount of damages was both procedurally and substantively unconscionable. Procedural unconscionability concerns the manner in which the parties enter into a contract. Substantive unconscionability can occur when a contract leaves one party to the agreement without a remedy for the nonperformance of the other.

Here, GeoEx told customers that the arbitration terms in its release form were nonnegotiable and that climbers would encounter the same requirements with any other travel company. This amounted to procedural unconscionability, underscoring the customers' lack of bargaining power. The imbalance resulted in oppressive terms, with no real negotiation and an absence of meaningful choice. Furthermore, the restriction on forum (San Francisco) and the limitation on damages (the cost of the trip)—with no limitation on GeoEx's damages—amounted to substantive unconscionability. In the actual case on which this problem is based, the court ruled that the agreement was unconscionable.

Problem 15–7. *Fraudulent Misrepresentation.* Yes, the facts in this problem evidence fraud. There are three elements to fraud: (1) the misrepresentation of a material fact, (2) an intent to deceive, and (3) an innocent party's justifiable reliance on the misrepresentation. To collect damages, the innocent party must suffer an injury.

Here, Pervis represented to Pauley that no further commission would be paid by Osbrink. This representation was false—despite Pervis's statement to the contrary, Osbrink continued to send payments to Pervis. Pervis knew the representation was false, as shown by the fact that she made it more than once during the time that she was continuing to receive payments from Osbrink. Each time Pauley asked about commissions, Pervis replied that she was not receiving any. Pauley's reliance on her business associate's statements was justified and reasonable. And for the purpose of recovering damages, Pauley suffered an injury in the amount of her share of the commissions that Pervis received as a result of the fraud.

In the actual case on which this problem is based, Pauley filed a suit in a Georgia state court against Pervis, who filed for bankruptcy in a federal bankruptcy court to stay the state action. The federal court held Pervis liable on the ground of fraud for the amount of the commissions that were not paid to Pauley and denied Pervis a discharge of the debt.

Problem 16–5. *The Parol Evidence Rule.* Vaks and Mangano may not recover for breach of an oral contract. Under the parol evidence rule, if there is a written contract representing the complete and final statement of the parties' agreement, a party may not introduce any evidence of past agreements. Here, the written agreement was an integrated contract because the parties intended it to be a complete and final statement of the terms of their agreement. Vaks and Mangano therefore may not introduce evidence of any inconsistent oral representations made before the contract was executed.

Problem 17–7. *Third Party Beneficiary.* Yes, the Kincaids can bring an action against the Desses for breach of their contract with Sirva. A third person becomes an intended third party beneficiary of a contract when the original parties to the contract expressly agree that the performance should be rendered to or directly benefit a third person. As the intended beneficiary of a contract, a third party has legal rights and can sue the promisor directly for breach of the contract.

Here, the Desses agreed in their contract with Sirva to disclose all information about their property. They further agreed that Sirva and "other prospective buyers" could rely on the Desses' disclosure in deciding "whether and on what terms to purchase the Property." The Kincaids were not direct parties to the contract between Sirva and the Desses, but the Kincaids were "other prospective buyers." Thus, the language of the contract indicated that the Kincaids were intended by Sirva and the Desses to be third party beneficiaries of it. As intended beneficiaries of the contract, the Kincaids could sue the Desses directly for its breach.

In the actual case on which this problem is based, the Kincaids filed a suit in a Kansas state court against the Desses. From a judgment in the Desses' favor (for lack of privity), the Kincaids appealed. A state intermediate appellate court reversed on the basis of the reasoning stated above and remanded the case for trial.

Problem 18–4. *Material Breach.* Yes, STR breached the contract with NTI. A breach of contract is the nonperformance of a contractual duty. A breach is *material* when performance is not at least substantial. On a material breach, the nonbreaching party is excused from performance. If a breach is *minor*, the nonbreaching party's duty to perform can sometimes be suspended until the breach has been remedied, but the duty to perform is not entirely excused. Once a minor breach has been cured, the nonbreaching party must resume performance. Any breach—material or minor—entitles the nonbreaching party to sue for damages.

In this problem, NTI had to redo its work constantly because STR permitted its employees and the employees of other subcontractors to walk over and damage the newly installed tile. Furthermore, despite NTI's requests for payment, STR remitted only half the amount due under their contract. Thus, NTI was deprived of at least half of the money it was owed under the contract. And STR terminated the contract, apparently wrongfully and without cause—the tile work would have been completed satisfactorily if STR had not allowed other workers to trample on the newly installed tile before it had cured.

In the actual case on which this problem is based, when STR refused to pay NTI and then terminated their contract, the subcontractor filed a suit in a Texas state court to recover. From a jury verdict in NTI's favor, STR appealed. A state intermediate appellate court affirmed. "The evidence presented was legally sufficient for the jury to conclude that STR materially breached the contract."

Problem 19–5. *Consequential Damages.* Simard is liable only for the losses and expenses related to the first resale. Simard could reasonably have anticipated that his breach would require another sale and that the sales price might be less than what he had agreed to pay. Therefore, he should be liable for the difference between his sales price and the first resale price ($29,000), plus any expenses arising from the first resale. Simard is not liable, however, for any expenses and losses related to the second resale. After all, Simard did not cause the second purchaser's default, and he could not reasonably have foreseen that default as a probable result of his breach.

Problem 20–4. *Additional Terms.* No. Under the common law, variations in terms between the offer and the offeree's acceptance violate the mirror image rule, which requires that the terms of an acceptance exactly mirror the terms of the offer. The UCC dispenses with this rule. Under the UCC, a contract is formed if the offeree makes a definite expression of acceptance even though the terms of the acceptance modify or add to the terms of the offer. When both parties to the contract are merchants, the additional terms become part of their contract unless (1) the original offer expressly required acceptance of its terms, (2) the new or changed terms materially alter the contract, or (3) the offeror rejects the new or changed terms within a reasonable time.

In this problem, the UCC applies because the transactions involve sales of goods. The original offer stated, "By signing below, you agree to the terms." This statement could be construed to expressly require acceptance of the terms to make the offer a binding contract (Exception 1 above). The contract stated that JMAM was to receive credit for any rejected merchandise. Nothing indicated that the merchandise would be returned to BSI. Baracsi, BSI's owner (the offeree), signed JMAM's (the offeror's) letter in the appropriate location. This indicated BSI's agreement to the terms. Thus, BSI made a definite expression of acceptance. The practice of the parties—for six years rejected items were not returned—further supports the conclusion that their contract did not contemplate the return of those items. The "PS" could be interpreted as materially altering the contract (Exception 2 above).

In the actual case on which this problem is based, the court dismissed BSI's complaint.

Problem 21–5. *Passage of Title.* Altieri held title to the car that she was driving at the time of the accident in which Godfrey was injured. Once goods exist and are identified, title can be determined. Under the UCC, any explicit understanding between the buyer and the seller determines when title passes. If there is no such agreement, title passes to the buyer at the time and place that the seller physically delivers the goods. In lease contracts, title to the goods is retained by the lessor-owner of the goods. The UCC's provisions relating to passage to title do not apply to leased goods.

Here, Altieri originally leased the car from G.E. Capital Auto Lease, Inc., but by the time of the accident she had bought it. Even though she had not fully paid for the car or completed the transfer-of-title paperwork, she owned it. Title to the car passed to Altieri when she bought it and took delivery of it. Thus, Altieri, not G.E., was the owner of the car at the time of the accident. In the actual case on which this problem is based,

the court concluded that G.E. was not the owner of the vehicle when Godfrey was injured.

Problem 22–5. *Nonconforming Goods.* Padma notified Universal Exports about its breach, so Padma has two ways to recover even though it accepted the goods. Padma's first option is to argue that it revoked its acceptance, giving it the right to reject the goods. To revoke acceptance, Padma would have to show that (1) the nonconformity substantially impaired the value of the shipment, (2) it predicated its acceptance on a reasonable assumption that Universal Exports would cure the nonconformity, and (3) Universal Exports did not cure the nonconformity within a reasonable time. Padma's second option is to keep the goods and recover for the damages caused by Universal Exports' breach. Under this option, Padma could recover at least the difference between the value of the goods as promised and their value as accepted.

Problem 23–6. *Implied Warranties.* Yes, Absolute breached the implied warranties of merchantability and fitness for a particular purpose. Under the UCC, merchants impliedly warrant that the goods they sell or lease are merchantable and, in certain circumstances, fit for a particular purpose. To be merchantable, goods must be "reasonably fit for the ordinary purposes for which such goods are used." They must be at least average, fair, or medium-grade quality—quality that will pass without objection in the trade or market for the goods. For example, merchantable food is food that is fit to eat. To be fit for a particular purpose, the seller must know (or have reason to know) the purpose for which the buyer will use the goods and that the buyer is relying on the judgment of the seller to select suitable goods.

In this problem, Bariven agreed to buy 26,000 metric tons of powdered milk for $123.5 million from Absolute Trading Corp. to be delivered in shipments from China to Venezuela. Absolute assured Bariven that its milk was safe, but tests of samples of the milk revealed that it contained dangerous levels of melamine. This is not quality that will pass without objection in the market for the goods. Nor is milk contaminated with melamine "reasonably fit for the ordinary purposes for which such goods are used." The value of the milk as food was impaired because it was potentially lethal and thus not fit to be consumed. Absolute had reason to know the purpose for which Bariven bought the milk and that the buyer was relying on Absolute to select safe milk. In view of the potential hazards and liabilities of the contaminated milk, Absolute was in breach of the implied warranties of merchantability and fitness for a particular purpose.

In the actual case on which this problem is based, Bariven revoked its acceptance of the first nineteen shipments of the milk and canceled the twentieth. From a decision against Absolute in its suit against Bariven, the seller appealed. The U.S. Court of Appeals for the Eleventh Circuit affirmed. Bariven's revocation was not invalid because "the value of the milk was impaired."

Problem 24–6. *Import Controls.* Yes, an antidumping duty can be assessed retrospectively (retroactively). But it does not seem likely that such a duty should be assessed here.

In this problem, the Wind Tower Trade Coalition (an association of domestic manufacturers of utility-scale wind towers) filed a suit in the U.S. Court of International Trade against the U.S. Department of Commerce, challenging its decision to impose only *prospective* antidumping duties on imports of utility-scale wind towers from China and Vietnam. The Commerce Department had found that the domestic industry had not suffered any "material injury" or "threat of material injury," and that it would be protected by a prospective assessment. Without a previously cognizable injury—and given the fact that any retrospective duties collected would not be payable to the members of the domestic industry in any event—it does not seem likely that retroactive duties should be imposed.

In the actual case on which this problem is based, the court denied the plaintiff's request for an injunction. On appeal, the U.S. Court of Appeals for the Federal Circuit affirmed the denial, holding that the lower court acted within its discretion in determining that retrospective duties were not appropriate.

Problem 25–6. *Payable on Demand or at a Definite Time.*

No. Novel is not correct. The instrument is a note, and Novel is bound to pay it. For an instrument to be negotiable under UCC 3–104, it must meet the following requirements: (1) be in writing, (2) be signed by the maker or the drawer, (3) be an unconditional promise or order to pay, (4) state a fixed amount of money, (5) be payable on demand or at a definite time, and (6) be payable to order or to bearer unless it is a check. When no time for payment is stated on an instrument, the instrument is payable on demand.

Applying these principles to the facts in this problem, all of the requirements to establish the instrument as negotiable are met: (1) the instrument is in writing; (2) it is signed by Novel; (3) there are no conditions or promises other than the unconditional promise to pay; (4) the instrument states a fixed amount—$10,000; (5) the instrument does not include a definite repayment date, which means that it is payable on demand; and (6) the instrument is payable to Gallwitz. In the actual case on which this problem is based, the court ruled in favor of Gallwitz for payment of the note.

Problem 26–5. *Negotiation.*

A negotiable instrument can be transferred by assignment or by negotiation. An assignment is a transfer of rights by contract. A transfer by assignment to an assignee gives the assignee only those rights that the assignor possessed. Any defenses that can be raised against the assignor can be raised against the assignee. When an instrument is transferred by negotiation, the transferee becomes a holder. A holder receives at least the rights of the previous possessor. Unlike an assignment, a transfer by negotiation can make it possible for the holder to receive more rights in the instrument than the prior possessor had. A holder who receives greater rights is a holder in due course (HDC) and takes the instrument free of any claims to it and defenses against its payment. Negotiating order instruments requires delivery and indorsement. If a party to whom a negotiable note is made payable signs it and delivers it to a bank, the transfer is a negotiation, and the bank becomes a holder. If

the party does not sign the note, however, the transfer is treated as an assignment, and the bank becomes an assignee instead of a holder.

In this problem, Argent was the payee of the note and its holder. Argent transferred the note to Wells Fargo without an indorsement. Thus, the transfer was not a negotiation but an assignment. Wells Fargo did not then become a holder of the note but an assignee. As an assignee, the bank acquired only those rights that the lender possessed before the assignment. And any defenses—including fraud in connection with the note—that Ford could assert against the lender could also be asserted by the borrower against the bank. If Argent indorsed the note to Wells Fargo after the defendant's response to the complaint, the bank could become a holder of the note, but it could not become an HDC. One of the requirements for HDC status is that a holder must take an instrument without notice of defenses against payment. The bank could not do this, because it would now be aware of the borrower's defenses.

In the actual case on which this problem is based, the court issued a judgment in Wells Fargo's favor, and Ford appealed. A state intermediate appellate court reversed the judgment and remanded the case for trial, finding that the bank had failed to prove that it was a holder, an assignee, or even a transferee of the note.

Problem 27–4. *Defenses.*

When an instrument is transferred by negotiation, the transferee becomes a holder. A holder can become an HDC if the holder takes the instrument for value, in good faith, and without notice of any defects. An HDC takes an instrument free of most defenses against payment that could be asserted against the transferor. Defenses against payment fall into two categories. Universal defenses are good against all holders, including HDCs. Personal defenses are used to avoid payment to an ordinary holder, but not an HDC. Personal defenses include breach of contract, ordinary fraud, and any other defenses that can be asserted to avoid payment on a contract. Between the maker and the payee, a promissory note is a contract to pay money. Defenses that may be asserted by the maker against payment on a note include the personal defenses.

In this problem, Klutz does not qualify as an HDC. Thorbecke signed a note as the maker for most of the price for the purchase of the restaurant. Klutz may have taken Thorbecke's note for value—at least to the extent that he performed the part of the contract for the sale of the restaurant—but he did not take it in good faith or without notice. He misrepresented his authority to sell the franchise. In other words, under the facts as presented, Klutz appears to have committed fraud in the inducement and to have breached the contract of sale. Thorbecke appears to have reasonably relied on the misrepresentation and to be entitled to damages as a result. Thorbecke may also be justified in asserting these defenses against payment on the note.

In the actual case on which this problem is based, the court issued a decision in Thorbecke's favor to allow the suit to go to trial to determine whether Klutz misrepresented his authority to transfer the franchise, whether Thorbecke reasonably relied on the misrepresentation, the extent of any damages, and the amount due on the note.

Problem 28–5. *Honoring Checks.* A bank that pays a customer's check bearing a forged indorsement must recredit the customer's account or be liable to the customer-drawer for breach of contract. The bank must recredit the account because it failed to carry out the drawer's order to pay to the order of the named party. Eventually, the loss falls on the first party to take the instrument bearing the forged indorsement because a forged indorsement does not transfer title. Thus, whoever takes an instrument with a forged indorsement cannot become a holder.

Under these rules, Wells Fargo is liable to W Financial for the amount of the check. The bank had an obligation to ensure that the check was properly indorsed. The bank did not pay the check to the order of Lateef, the named payee, but accepted the check for deposit into the account of CA Houston without Lateef's indorsement. The bank did not obtain title to the instrument and could not become a holder, nor was it entitled to enforce the instrument on behalf of any other party who was entitled to enforce it. In the actual case on which this problem is based, the court held the bank liable to pay the amount of the check to W Financial.

Problem 29–5. *Liens.* Among the liens discussed in this chapter, a mechanic's lien would likely be most effective to Jirak in its attempt to collect the unpaid cost of its work for the Balks. A creditor can place a mechanic's lien on the real property of a debtor who has contracted for improvements to the property and has not paid the price. When a creditor obtains a mechanic's lien, the debtor's real estate becomes security for the debt. If the debtor does not pay, the creditor can foreclose on the property and sell it to collect the amount due.

In this problem, the Balks contracted with Jirak for the remodel of their farmhouse. Due to the Balks' changes to the project during the course of the work, the costs exceeded the amount of Jirak's original estimate. Although Jirak regularly advised the Balks about the increasing costs and provided an itemized breakdown at their request, they refused to pay the price. The use of a mechanic's lien is likely the best way for Jirak to collect the unpaid amount.

In the actual case on which this problem is based, Jirak filed a suit in an Iowa state court against the Balks to foreclose on their property by way of a mechanic's lien and collect the unpaid amount. The court entered a judgment in Jirak's favor and enforced the lien. A state intermediate appellate court affirmed the judgment.

Problem 30–7. *Perfecting a Security Interest.* Yes, these financing statements were sufficient to perfect the bank's security interests in Tille's equipment. In most situations, perfection is accomplished by filing a financing statement with the appropriate official. To effectively perfect a security interest, a financing statement must contain (1) the debtor's signature, (2) the debtor's and creditor's addresses, and (3) a description of the collateral by type or item.

In this case, all of Union's financing statements were sufficient to perfect security interests. Each of them provided the name and address of the debtor (Tille), the name and address

of the secured party (Union Bank), and a description of the collateral covered by the financing statement—for one loan, all of Tille's equipment, including after-acquired property; for another, the truck crane; and for the third, a Bobcat mini-excavator. These descriptions were clearly sufficient to put a prospective creditor on notice that the collateral was the subject of a security interest.

In the actual case on which this problem is based, the court concluded that all of the statements created perfected security interests.

Problem 31–5. *Discharge in Bankruptcy.* No, ECMC cannot now resume its effort to collect on Hann's loans. After the debtor has completed all payments, the court grants a discharge of all debts provided for by the repayment plan. All debts generally are dischargeable, especially those for which the court either declared that there was no obligation or disallowed on the ground that the underlying debt was satisfied.

In this problem, Hann financed her education partially through loans. When she filed a Chapter 13 petition, Educational Credit Management Corp. (ECMC) filed an unsecured proof of claim based on the loans. Hann believed that she had repaid the loans in full and objected. The court held a hearing at which ECMC failed to appear, and Hann submitted correspondence from the lender indicating the loans had been paid. The court then entered an order sustaining Hann's objection to ECMC's claim, in effect declaring that there was no obligation and the underlying debt was satisfied. By later attempting to renew efforts to collect on the loans, ECMC would violate the court's order.

In the actual case on which this problem is based, ECMC resumed collection efforts after the bankruptcy. Hann reopened her case and filed a complaint against ECMC, alleging that it had violated the order sustaining her objection. The court ruled in Hann's favor and sanctioned ECMC for attempting to collect on the debt. On ECMC's appeal, the U.S. Court of Appeals for the First Circuit affirmed.

Problem 32–7. *Determining Employee Status.* No, Cox is not liable to Cayer for any injuries or damage that she sustained in the accident with Ovalles. Generally, an employer is not liable for physical harm caused to a third person by the negligent act of an independent contractor in the performance of a contract. This is because the employer does not have the right to control the details of the performance. In determining whether a worker has the status of an independent contractor, how much control the employer can exercise over the details of the work is the most important factor weighed by the courts.

In this problem, Ovalles worked as a cable installer for Cox under an agreement with M&M. The agreement disavowed any employer-employee relationship between Cox and M&M's installers. Ovalles was required to designate his affiliation with Cox on his van, clothing, and an ID badge. But Cox had minimal contact with Ovalles and limited power to control the manner in which he performed his work. Cox supplied cable wire and other equipment, but these items were delivered to M&M, not Ovalles. These facts indicate that Ovalles was an independent contractor, not an employee. Thus, Cox was not liable to Cayer for the harm caused to her by Ovalles when his van rear-ended Cayer's car.

In the actual case on which this problem is based, the court issued a judgment in Cox's favor. The Rhode Island Supreme Court affirmed, applying the principles stated above to arrive at the same conclusion.

Problem 33–6. *Agent's Authority.* No, Rainbow cannot recoup the unpaid amounts from Basic. Express authority is authority declared in clear, direct, and definite terms. Express authority can be given orally or in writing. In most states, if the contract being executed is or must be in writing, then the agent's authority must also be in writing. Otherwise, the contract may be avoided (or ratified) by the principal. If it is ratified, the ratification must be in writing. An agent has the implied authority to do what is reasonably necessary to carry out express authority. For example, authority to manage a business implies authority to do what is reasonably required to operate the business. But an agent's implied authority cannot contradict his or her express authority. Thus, if a principal has limited an agent's express authority, then the fact that the agent customarily would have such authority is irrelevant.

In this problem, Basic Research advertised its products on television networks owned by Rainbow Media Holdings through an ad agency, Icebox Advertising. Basic paid Icebox for the ads, but Icebox did not make all of the payments to Rainbow. Icebox filed for bankruptcy. Rainbow cannot recover what it was owed from Basic. As Basic's agent, Icebox had the express authority to buy ads from Rainbow on Basic's behalf, but that authority was limited to purchasing ads with cash in advance. Thus, Icebox did not have the authority—express or implied—to buy ads on Basic's credit. And Basic did not ratify the contracts that represented purchases on credit.

In the actual case on which this problem is based, on Basic's appeal from a judgment in Rainbow's favor, the U.S. Court of Appeals for the Tenth Circuit reversed that judgment and ruled in Basic's favor.

Problem 34–6. *Unemployment Compensation.* Yes, Ramirez qualifies for unemployment compensation. Generally, to be eligible for unemployment compensation, a worker must be willing and able to work. Workers who have been fired for misconduct or who have voluntarily left their jobs are not eligible for benefits. In the facts of this problem, the applicable state statute disqualifies an employee from receiving benefits if he or she voluntarily leaves work without "good cause."

The issue is whether Ramirez left her job for "good cause." When her father in the Dominican Republic had a stroke, she asked her employer for time off to be with him. Her employer refused the request. But Ramirez left to be with her father and called to inform her employer. It seems likely that this family emergency would constitute "good cause," and Ramirez's call and return to work after her father's death indicated that she did not disregard her employer's interests.

In the actual case on which this problem is based, the state of Florida denied Ramirez unemployment compensation. On

Ramirez's appeal, a state intermediate appellate court reversed, on the reasoning stated above.

Problem 35–5. *Age Discrimination.* No, sanofi-aventis U.S. LLC (S-A) does not appear to have engaged in age discrimination. The Age Discrimination in Employment Act (ADEA) prohibits employment discrimination on the basis of age against individuals forty years of age or older. For the act to apply, an employer must have twenty or more employees, and the employer's business activities must affect interstate commerce. To establish a *prima facie* case, a plaintiff must show that he or she was (1) a member of the protected age group, (2) qualified for the position from which he or she was discharged, and (3) discharged because of age discrimination. If the employer offers a legitimate reason for its action, the plaintiff must show that the stated reason is only a pretext.

In this problem, Rangel was over forty years old. But he also had negative sales performance reviews for more than two years before he was terminated as part of S-A's nationwide reduction in force of all sales professionals who had not met the "Expectations" guidelines, including younger workers. The facts do not indicate that a person younger than Rangel replaced him or that S-A intended to discriminate against him on the basis of age. Based on these facts, Rangel could not establish a *prima facie* case of age discrimination on the part of S-A.

In the actual case on which this problem is based, in Rangel's suit against S-A alleging age discrimination, a federal district court issued a judgment in S-A's favor. On Rangel's appeal, the U.S. Court of Appeals for the Tenth Circuit affirmed, according to the reasoning stated above.

Problem 36–6. *Franchise Termination.* Oshana and GTO have stated a claim for wrongful termination of their franchise. A franchisor must act in good faith when terminating a franchise agreement. If the termination is arbitrary or unfair, a franchisee may have a claim for wrongful termination. In this case, Oshana and GTO have alleged that Buchanan acted in bad faith. Their failure to pay rent would ordinarily be a valid basis for termination, but not if it was entirely precipitated by Buchanan. Thus, Oshana and GTO may recover if they can prove that their allegations are true.

Problem 37–6. *Partnerships.* Yes, Sacco is entitled to 50 percent of the profits of Pierce Paxton Collections. The requirements for establishing a partnership are (1) a sharing of profits and losses, (2) a joint ownership of the business, and (3) an equal right to be involved in the management of the business.

The effort and time that Sacco expended in the business constituted a sharing of losses, and his proprietary interest in the assets of the partnership consisted of his share of the profits, which he had expressly left in the business to "grow the company" and "build sweat equity" for the future. He was involved in every aspect of the business. Although he was not paid a salary, he was reimbursed for business expenses charged to his personal credit card, which Paxton also used. These facts arguably meet the requirements for establishing a partnership.

In the actual case on which this problem is based, Sacco filed a suit in a Louisiana state court against Paxton, and the court awarded Sacco 50 percent of the profits. A state intermediate appellate court affirmed, based generally on the reasoning stated above.

Problem 38–6. *LLC Operation.* Part of the attractiveness of an LLC as a form of business enterprise is its flexibility. The members can decide how to operate the business through an operating agreement. For example, the agreement can set forth procedures for choosing or removing members or managers.

Here, the Bluewater operating agreement provided for a "super majority" vote to remove a member under circumstances that would jeopardize the firm's contractor status. Thus, one Bluewater member could not unilaterally "fire" another member without providing a reason. In fact, a majority of the members could not terminate the other's interest in the firm without providing a reason. Moreover, the only acceptable reason would be a circumstance that undercut the firm's status as a contractor.

The flexibility of the LLC business form relates to its framework, not to its members' capacity to violate its operating agreement. In the actual case on which this problem is based, Smith attempted to "fire" Williford without providing a reason. In Williford's suit, the court issued a judgment in his favor.

Problem 39–7. *Piercing the Corporate Veil.* Yes, there are sufficient grounds in the facts of this problem to support piercing the corporate veil and holding Kappeler personally liable to Snapp. First, in a case in which a plaintiff seeks to pierce a corporate veil, there must be a fraud or other injustice to be remedied. In that situation, the factors that a court will consider in determining whether to pierce the corporate veil include (1) a party is tricked or misled into dealing with the corporation rather than the individual, (2) the corporation has insufficient capital to meet its prospective debts or other potential liabilities, (3) corporate formalities, such as holding required corporate meetings, are not followed, and (4) personal and corporate interests are commingled.

In this problem, the amount that Snapp ultimately paid the builder exceeded the original estimate by nearly $1 million—and the project was still unfinished. Kappeler could not provide an accounting for the Snapp project—he could not explain double and triple charges nor whether the amount that Snapp paid had actually been spent on the project. These facts support a conclusion of fraud. And they also indicate that Kappeler may have tricked or misled Snapp into dealing with the corporation rather than with Kappeler as an individual. Castlebrook had issued no shares of stock, which indicates insufficient capitalization. The minutes of the corporate meetings "all looked exactly the same," indicating that in fact the required corporate meetings had not been held. And Kappeler had commingled personal and corporate funds.

In the actual case on which this problem is based, in Snapp's suit against the builder, the court pierced the corporate veil and held Kappeler personally liable. A state intermediate appellate court affirmed.

Problem 40–4. *Rights of Shareholders.* Yes. Woods has a right to inspect Biolustré's books and records. Every shareholder is entitled to examine corporate records. A shareholder can inspect the books in person or through an agent such as an attorney, accountant, or other authorized assistant.

The right of inspection is limited to the inspection and copying of corporate books and records for a proper purpose. This is because the power of inspection is fraught with potential for abuse—for example, it can involve the disclosure of trade secrets and other confidential information. Thus, a corporation is allowed to protect itself. Here, Woods, through Hair Ventures, has the right to inspect Biolustré's books and records. She has a proper purpose for the inspection—to obtain information about Biolustré's financial situation. She, along with other shareholders, had not received notice of shareholders' meetings or corporate financial reports for years, or notice of Biolustré's plan to issue additional stock. Hair Ventures had a substantial investment in the company. In the actual case on which this problem is based, the court ordered Biolustré to produce its books and records for Hair Ventures' inspection.

Problem 41–5. *Purchase of Assets.* Yes. Interline is most likely liable for the unpaid amount on the GATT contract with Call Center. An acquiring corporation will be held to have assumed the liabilities of the selling corporation in the following situations:

1. The purchasing corporation expressly or impliedly assumes the seller's liabilities.
2. The sale transaction is in effect a merger or consolidation of the two companies.
3. The purchaser continues the seller's business and retains the same personnel (shareholders, directors, and officers).
4. The sale is entered into fraudulently for the purpose of escaping liability.

In this problem, Interline acquired GATT's assets at a public sale. There is no indication that Interline agreed to assume GATT's liabilities, there was no merger or other combination of the two companies, and it does not appear that the sale was fraudulently entered into to escape liability.

Thus, the focus is on the third item listed above—whether Interline was liable for GATT's debts because it continued GATT's business with the same personnel. Boyd was not a GATT employee, but he was a former GATT director. Other members of Interline's staff were former GATT employees. GATT and Interline operated out of the same office building. Both companies were in the business of providing travel services to many of the same customers. These factors indicate that Interline is responsible for GATT's liabilities, including its debt to Call Center. In the actual case on which this problem is based, the court focused on the same principles discussed here to issue a judgment in Call Center's favor.

Problem 42–4. *Violations of the 1934 Act.* An omission or misrepresentation of a material fact in connection with the purchase or sale of a security may violate Section 10(b) of the Securities Exchange Act of 1934 and SEC Rule 10b-5. The key question is whether the omitted or misrepresented information

APPENDIX E   Sample Answers for *Business Case Problems with Sample Answer*   **A-167**

is material. A fact, by itself, is not automatically material. A fact will be regarded as material only if it is significant enough that it would likely affect an investor's decision as to whether to buy or sell the company's securities. For example, a company's potential liability in a product liability suit and the financial consequences to the firm are material facts that must be disclosed because they are significant enough to affect an investor's decision as to whether to buy stock in the company.

In this case, the plaintiffs' claim should not be dismissed. To prevail on their claim that the defendants made material omissions in violation of Section 10(b) and SEC Rule 10b-5, the plaintiffs must prove that the omission was material. Their complaint alleged the omission of information linking Zicam and anosmia (a loss of the sense of smell) and plausibly suggested that reasonable investors would have viewed this information as material. Zicam products account for 70 percent of Matrixx's sales. Matrixx received reports of consumers who suffered anosmia after using Zicam Cold Remedy.

In public statements discussing revenues and product safety, Matrixx did not disclose this information. But the information was significant enough to likely affect a consumer's decision to use the product, and this would affect revenue and ultimately the commercial viability of the product. The information was therefore significant enough to likely affect an investor's decision whether to buy or sell Matrixx's stock, and this would affect the stock price. Thus, the plaintiffs' allegations were sufficient. Contrary to the defendants' assertion, statistical sampling is not required to show materiality—reasonable investors could view reports of adverse events as material even if the reports did not provide statistically significant evidence.

Problem 43–4. *Agency Powers.* The United States Supreme Court held that greenhouse gases fit within the Clean Air Act's (CAA's) definition of "air pollutant." Thus, the Environmental Protection Agency (EPA) has the authority under that statute to regulate the emission of such gases from new motor vehicles. According to the Court, the definition, which includes "any" air pollutant, embraces all airborne compounds "of whatever stripe." The EPA's focus on Congress's 1990 amendments (or their lack) indicates nothing about the original intent behind the statute (and its amendments before 1990). Nothing in the statute suggests that Congress meant to curtail the agency's power to treat greenhouse gases as air pollutants. In other words, the agency has a preexisting mandate to regulate "any air pollutant" that may endanger the public welfare.

The EPA also argued that, even if it had the authority to regulate greenhouse gases, the agency would not exercise that authority because any regulation would conflict with other administration priorities. The Court acknowledged that the CAA conditions EPA action on the agency's formation of a "judgment," but explained that judgment must relate to whether a pollutant "cause[s], or contribute[s] to, air pollution which may reasonably be anticipated to endanger public health or welfare." Thus, the EPA can avoid issuing regulations only if the agency determines that greenhouse gases do not contribute to climate change (or if the agency reasonably explains why it cannot or will not determine whether they do). The EPA's refusal

to regulate was thus "arbitrary, capricious, or otherwise not in accordance with law," The Court remanded the case for the EPA to "ground its reasons for action or inaction in the statute."

Problem 44–5. *Fair Debt-Collection Practices.* Engler may recover under the Fair Debt Collection Practices Act (FDCPA). Atlantic is subject to the FDCPA because it is a debt-collection agency and was attempting to collect a debt on behalf of Bank of America. Atlantic used offensive tactics to collect from Engler. After all, Atlantic gave Engler's employer the false impression that Engler was a criminal, had a pending case, and was about to be arrested. Finally, Engler suffered harm because he experienced discomfort, embarrassment, and distress as a result of Atlantic's abusive conduct. Engler may recover actual damages, statutory damages, and attorneys' fees from Atlantic.

Problem 45–5. *Environmental Impact Statements.* Yes, an environmental impact statement (EIS) is required before the U.S. Forest Service (USFS) implements its proposed travel management plan (TMP). An EIS must be prepared for every major federal action that significantly affects the quality of the environment. An action is "major" if it involves a substantial commitment of resources. An action is "federal" if a federal agency has the power to control it. An EIS must analyze (1) the impact on the environment that the action will have, (2) any adverse effects on the environment and alternative actions that might be taken, and (3) irreversible effects that the action might generate.

Here, the resources committed to the implementation of the USFS's TMP could include the resources within the wilderness and the time and effort dedicated by the agency. The wilderness resources would include the soil, the vegetation, the wildlife, the wildlife habitat, any threatened or endangered species, and other natural assets impacted by the TMP. The agency's resources would include its funds and its staff—to design, map, maintain, and enforce the TMP. These resources seem substantial. Of course, the implementation of the TMP is federal because the USFS has the power to control it.

As for the aspects of the environment that the agency might consider in preparing the EIS, some of the important factors are listed above—the soil, vegetation, wildlife, wildlife habitat, and threatened or endangered species. Other aspects of the environment impacted by the TMP might include cultural resources, historical resources, wilderness suitability, and other authorized uses of the wilderness. There is a potential for impact by every route that is designed to be part of the system, as well as the "dispersed vehicle camping" to be permitted on the terrain.

In the actual case on which this problem is based, the USFS considered all of the factors listed above. The agency then issued an EIS and a decision implementing the TMP. On a challenge to the EIS, a federal district court issued a judgment in the USFS's favor. The U.S. Court of Appeals for the Ninth Circuit affirmed. "The Forest Service took the requisite hard look at the environmental impacts."

Problem 46–5. *Price Discrimination.* Spa Steel satisfies most of the requirements for a price discrimination claim under

Section 2 of the Clayton Act. Dayton Superior is engaged in interstate commerce, and it sells goods of like grade and quality to at least three purchasers. Moreover, Spa Steel can show that, because it sells Dayton Superior's products at a higher price, it lost business and thus suffered an injury. To recover, however, Spa Steel will also need to prove that Dayton Superior charged Spa Steel's competitors a lower price for the same product. Spa Steel cannot recover if its prices were higher for reasons related to its own business, such as having higher overhead expenses or seeking a larger profit.

Problem 47–7. *Potential Liability to Third Parties.* KPMG is potentially liable to the hedge funds' partners under the *Restatement (Second) of Torts*. Under Section 552 of the *Restatement*, an auditor owes a duty to "persons for whose benefit and guidance the accountant intends to supply . . . information." In this case, KPMG prepared annual reports on the hedge funds and addressed them to the funds' "Partners." Additionally, KPMG knew who the partners were because it prepared individual tax forms for them each year. Thus, KPMG's annual reports were for the partners' benefit and guidance. The partners relied on the reports, including their representations that they complied with generally accepted accounting principles. As a result, they lost millions of dollars, which exposes KPMG to possible liability under Section 552.

Problem 48–4. *Bailment Obligation.* Moreland should be awarded damages, and Gray should take nothing. The bailee must exercise reasonable care in preserving the bailed property. What constitutes reasonable care in a bailment situation normally depends on the nature and specific circumstances of the bailment. If the bailed property has been lost or is returned damaged, a court will presume that the bailee was negligent.

In the circumstances of this problem, when the bailor (Moreland, the owner of the aircraft) entrusted the plane to the bailee's (Gray's) repair shop for painting, the work was not properly performed. This violated the bailee's duty to exercise reasonable care and breached the bailment contract. Because the plane was returned damaged, this may also constitute negligence. In the event of a breach, the bailor may sue for damages. The measure of damages is the difference between the value of the bailed property in its present condition and what it would have been worth if the work had been properly performed.

Thus, Gray is liable to Moreland for failing to properly paint the plane. In the actual case on which this problem is based, the court upheld a jury award to Moreland of damages and attorneys' fees.

Problem 49–4. *Adverse Possession.* The McKeags satisfied the first three requirements for adverse possession:

1. Their possession was actual and exclusive because they used the beach and prevented others from doing so, including the Finleys.
2. Their possession was open, visible, and notorious because they made improvements to the beach and regularly kept their belongings there.

3. Their possession was continuous and peaceable for the required ten years. They possessed the property for more than four decades, and they even kept a large float there during the winter months.

Nevertheless, the McKeags' possession was *not* hostile and adverse, which is the fourth requirement. The Finleys had substantial evidence that they gave the McKeags permission to use the beach. Rather than reject the Finleys' permission as unnecessary, the McKeags sometimes said nothing and other times seemingly affirmed that the property belonged to the Finleys. Thus, because the McKeags did not satisfy all four requirements, they cannot establish adverse possession.

Problem 50–7. *Insurance Provisions and Clauses.* Farrington should not be included as an insured within the meaning of the property insurance policy between Darling's and Philadelphia. The existence of an insurable interest is a primary concern when determining liability under an insurance policy. In the case of personal property, an insurable interest exists when the insured derives a pecuniary benefit from the preservation and continued existence of the property. One has an insurable interest in property when one would sustain a financial loss from its destruction. As for an insurance policy's language, courts interpret the words according to their ordinary meanings and in light of the nature of the coverage involved.

Darling's is entitled to recover the value of the loss to covered vehicles by virtue of its ownership of those vehicles and the fact that it is the owner that suffers the loss when one of its vehicles is damaged. In other words, under the Philadelphia policy, Darling's had an insurable interest in the car when Farrington smashed into the moose. Farrington might have had an insurable interest as well when he agreed to be responsible for any damage to the car, but he declined the insurance coverage offered in the rental contract.

In the actual case on which this problem is based, in Philadelphia's suit against Farrington, the court entered a judgment in the insurer's favor.

Problem 51–6. *Undue Influence.* No, undue influence does not appear to have occurred in this problem. To invalidate a will on the basis of undue influence, a plaintiff must show that the decedent's plan of distribution was the result of improper pressure brought by another person. Undue influence may be inferred if the testator ignores blood relatives and names as a beneficiary a nonrelative who is in constant close contact and in a position to influence the making of the will.

In this problem, although Tommy's ex-wife lived with Susie and was thus in a position to influence Susie's will, she was not a beneficiary under it, so there is no inference of undue influence. Moreover, neither of the wills that Walker executed left any property to her son, so there was no indication that she had been influenced to change her mind regarding the distribution of her estate. Additionally, she expressly disinherited her son, and several witnesses testified that she was mentally competent at the time she made the will.

In the actual case on which this problem is based, the court presumed that the will was valid.

Glossary

A

abandoned property Property that has been discarded by the owner, who has no intention of reclaiming it.

acceleration clause (1) A clause in an installment contract that provides for all future payments to become due immediately on the failure to tender timely payments or on the occurrence of a specified event. (2) A clause in a mortgage loan contract that makes the entire loan balance become due if the borrower misses or is late making monthly mortgage payments.

acceptance (1) In contract law, the offeree's notification to the offeror that the offeree agrees to be bound by the terms of the offeror's proposal. (2) In negotiable instruments law, the drawee's signed agreement to pay a draft when presented.

acceptor The person (the drawee) who accepts a draft and who agrees to be primarily responsible for its payment.

accession The addition of value to personal property by the use of labor or materials.

accommodation party A person who signs an instrument for the purpose of lending his or her name as credit to another party on the instrument.

accord and satisfaction An agreement for payment (or other performance) between two parties, one of whom has a right of action against the other. After the payment has been accepted or other performance has been made, the "accord and satisfaction" is complete, and the obligation is discharged.

accredited investor In the context of securities offerings, sophisticated investors, such as banks, insurance companies, investment companies, the issuer's executive officers and directors, and persons whose income or net worth exceeds certain limits.

act of state doctrine A doctrine that provides that the judicial branch of one country will not examine the validity of public acts committed by a recognized foreign government within its own territory.

actionable Capable of serving as the basis of a lawsuit.

actual malice A condition that exists when a person makes a statement with either knowledge of its falsity or reckless disregard for the truth. In a defamation suit, a statement made about a public figure normally must be made with actual malice for liability to be incurred.

actus reus (pronounced *ak*-tus *ray*-uhs) A guilty (prohibited) act. The commission of a prohibited act and the intent to commit a crime are the two essential elements required for criminal liability.

adequate protection doctrine In bankruptcy law, a doctrine that protects secured creditors from losing their security as a result of an automatic stay. In certain circumstances, the bankruptcy court may provide adequate protection by requiring the debtor or trustee to pay the creditor or provide additional guaranties to protect the creditor against the losses suffered by the creditor as a result of the stay.

adhesion contract A "standard-form" contract, such as that between a large retailer and a consumer, in which the stronger party dictates the terms.

adjudication The process of resolving a dispute by presenting evidence and arguments before a neutral third party decision maker in a court or an administrative law proceeding.

administrative agency A federal or state government agency created by the legislature to perform a specific function, such as to make and enforce rules pertaining to the environment.

administrative law The body of law created by administrative agencies in order to carry out their duties and responsibilities.

administrative law judge (ALJ) One who presides over an administrative agency hearing and has the power to administer oaths, take testimony, rule on questions of evidence, and make determinations of fact.

administrative process The procedure used by administrative agencies in fulfilling their three basic functions: rulemaking, enforcement, and adjudication.

administrator One who is appointed by a court to administer an estate if the decedent died without a valid will or if the executor named in the will cannot serve.

adverse possession The acquisition of title to real property through open occupation, without the consent of the owner, for a period of time specified by a state statute. The occupation must be actual, exclusive, open, continuous, and in opposition to all others, including the owner.

affidavit A written voluntary statement of facts, confirmed by the oath or affirmation of the party making it and made before a person having the authority to administer the oath or affirmation.

affirmative action Job-hiring policies that give special consideration to members of protected classes in an effort to overcome present effects of past discrimination.

affirmative defense A response to a plaintiff's claim that does not deny the plaintiff's facts but attacks the plaintiff's legal right to bring an action. An example is the running of the statute of limitations.

after-acquired property Property of the debtor that is acquired after the execution of a security agreement.

age of majority The age at which an individual is considered legally capable of conducting himself or herself responsibly. A person of this age is entitled to the full rights of citizenship, including the right to vote. In contract law, the age at which one is no longer an infant and can no longer disaffirm a contract.

agency A relationship between two parties in which one party (the agent) agrees to represent or act for the other (the principal).

agency coupled with an interest An agency, created for the benefit of the agent, in which the agent has some legal right (interest) in the property that is the subject of the agency.

agent A person who agrees to represent or act for another, called the principal.

agreement A meeting of two or more minds in regard to the terms of a contract; usually broken down into two events—an offer by one party to form a contract, and an acceptance of the offer by the person to whom the offer is made.

alien corporation A corporation formed in another country but doing business in the United States.

alienation In real property law, the voluntary transfer of property from one person to another (as opposed to a transfer by operation of law).

allege To state, recite, assert, or charge.

alternative dispute resolution (ADR) The resolution of disputes in ways other than those involved in the traditional judicial process. Negotiation, mediation, and arbitration are forms of ADR.

answer Procedurally, a defendant's response to the plaintiff's complaint.

antecedent claim A preexisting claim. In negotiable instruments law, taking an instrument in satisfaction of an antecedent claim is taking the instrument for value.

anticipatory repudiation An assertion or action by a party indicating that he or she will not perform an obligation that he or she is contractually obligated to perform at a future time.

antilapse provision A clause in an insurance contract that gives the insured a grace period (usually thirty days) within which to pay an overdue premium.

antitrust law Laws protecting commerce from unlawful restraints and anticompetitive practices.

apparent authority Authority that is only apparent, not real. An agent's apparent authority arises when the principal causes a third party to believe that the agent has authority, even though she or he does not.

appellant The party who takes an appeal from one court to another.

appellee The party against whom an appeal is taken—that is, the party who opposes setting aside or reversing the judgment.

appraisal right The right of a dissenting shareholder, if he or she objects to an extraordinary transaction of the corporation (such as a merger or consolidation), to have his or her shares appraised and to be paid the fair value of the shares by the corporation.

arbitration The settling of a dispute by submitting it to a disinterested third party (other than a court), who renders a decision. The decision may or may not be legally binding.

arbitration clause A clause in a contract that provides that, in the event of a dispute, the parties will submit the dispute to arbitration rather than litigate the dispute in court.

arson The malicious burning of another's dwelling. Some statutes have expanded arson to include any real property, regardless of ownership, and the destruction of property by other means—for example, by explosion.

articles of incorporation The document that is filed with the appropriate state official, usually the secretary of state, when a business is incorporated and that contains basic information about the corporation.

articles of merger A document, filed with the secretary of state, that sets forth the terms and conditions of a merger.

articles of partnership A written agreement that sets forth each partner's rights and obligations with respect to the partnership.

artisan's lien A possessory lien given to a person who has made improvements and added value to another person's personal property as security for payment for services performed.

assault Any word or action intended to make another person fearful of immediate physical harm; a reasonably believable threat.

assignee The person to whom contract rights are assigned.

assignment The act of transferring to another all or part of one's rights arising under a contract.

assignor The person who assigns contract rights.

assumption of risk A defense against negligence that can be used when the plaintiff was aware of a danger and voluntarily assumed the risk of injury from that danger.

attachment (1) In the context of secured transactions, the process by which a security interest in the property of another becomes enforceable. (2) In the context of judicial liens, a court-ordered seizure and taking into custody of property prior to the securing of a judgment for a past-due debt.

attempted monopolization An action by a firm that involves anticompetitive conduct, the intent to gain monopoly power, and a "dangerous probability" of success in achieving monopoly power.

auditor An accountant qualified to perform audits (systematic inspections) of a business's financial records.

authenticate To sign or, on an electronic record, to adopt any symbol that verifies the intent to adopt or accept the record.

authorization card A card signed by an employee that gives a union permission to act on his or her behalf in negotiations with management.

automatic stay In bankruptcy proceedings, the suspension of almost all litigation and other action by creditors against the debtor or the debtor's property. The stay is effective the moment the debtor files a petition in bankruptcy.

award In the context of litigation, the amount of money awarded to a plaintiff in a civil lawsuit as damages. In the context of arbitration, the arbitrator's decision.

B

bailee One to whom goods are entrusted by a bailor.

bailee's lien A possessory (artisan's) lien that a bailee entitled to compensation can place on the bailed property to ensure that he or she will be paid for the services provided.

bailment A situation in which the personal property of one person (a bailor) is entrusted to another (a bailee), who is obligated to return the bailed property to the bailor or dispose of it as directed.

bailor One who entrusts goods to a bailee.

bait-and-switch advertising Advertising a product at an attractive price and then telling the consumer that the advertised product is not available or is of poor quality and encouraging her or him to purchase a more expensive item.

banker's acceptance A banker's acceptance is a promised future payment, or time draft, which is accepted and guaranteed by a bank and drawn on a deposit at the bank. The banker's acceptance specifies the amount of money, the date, and the person to which the payment is due, and is commonly used in international trade.

bankruptcy court A federal court of limited jurisdiction that handles only bankruptcy proceedings.

bankruptcy trustee A person appointed by the court to manage the debtor's funds in a bankruptcy proceeding.

battery The unprivileged, intentional touching of another.

bearer A person in the possession of an instrument payable to bearer or indorsed in blank.

bearer instrument Any instrument that is not payable to a specific person, including instruments payable to the bearer or to "cash."

benefit corporation A type of for-profit corporation, available by statute in a number of states, that seeks to have a material positive impact on society and the environment.

bequest A gift of personal property by will (from the verb *to bequeath*).

beyond a reasonable doubt The standard used to determine the guilt or innocence of a person criminally charged. To be guilty of a crime, one must be proved guilty "beyond and to the exclusion of every reasonable doubt." A reasonable doubt is one that would cause a prudent person to hesitate before acting in matters important to him or her.

bilateral contract A type of contract that arises when a promise is given in exchange for a promise.

bilateral mistake A mistake that occurs when both parties to a contract are mistaken about the same material fact.

Bill of Rights The first ten amendments to the U.S. Constitution.

binder A written, temporary insurance policy.

binding authority Any source of law that a court must follow when deciding a case.

blank indorsement An indorsement that specifies no particular indorsee and can consist of a mere signature. An order instrument that is indorsed in blank becomes a bearer instrument.

blue sky laws State laws that regulate the offer and sale of securities.

bona fide occupational qualification (BFOQ) An identifiable characteristic reasonably necessary to the normal operation of a particular business. Such characteristics can include gender, national origin, and religion, but not race.

bond A security that evidences a corporate (or government) debt.

botnet Short for robot network—a group of computers that run an application controlled and manipulated only by the software source. Usually, the term is reserved for computers that have been infected by malicious robot software.

breach To violate a law, by an act or an omission, or to break a legal obligation that one owes to another person or to society.

breach of contract The failure, without legal excuse, of a promisor to perform the obligations of a contract.

brief A formal legal document submitted by the attorney for the appellant—or the appellee (in answer to the appellant's brief)—to an appellate court when a case is appealed. The appellant's brief outlines the facts and issues of the case, the judge's rulings or jury's findings that should be reversed or modified, the applicable law, and the arguments on the client's behalf.

browse-wrap terms Terms and conditions of use that are presented to an Internet user at the time a product, such as software, is downloaded but that need not be agreed to before the product is installed or used.

bureaucracy A large organization that is structured hierarchically to carry out specific functions.

burglary The unlawful entry into a building with the intent to commit a felony. Some state statutes have expanded burglary to include the intent to commit any crime.

business ethics Ethics in a business context; a consensus of what constitutes right or wrong behavior in the world of business and the application of moral principles to situations that arise in a business setting.

business invitees Those people, such as customers or clients, who are invited onto business premises by the owner of those premises for business purposes.

business judgment rule A rule under which courts will not hold corporate officers and directors liable for honest mistakes of judgment and bad business decisions that were made in good faith.

business necessity A defense to an allegation of employment discrimination in which the employer demonstrates that an employment practice that discriminates against members of a protected class is related to job performance.

business trust A form of business organization, created by a written trust agreement, that resembles a corporation. Legal ownership and management of the trust's property stay with the trustees, and the profits are distributed to the beneficiaries, who have limited liability.

buy-sell agreement In the context of partnerships, an express agreement made at the time of partnership formation for one or more of the partners to buy out the other or others should the situation warrant.

buyer in the ordinary course of business A buyer who, in good faith and without knowledge that the sale violates the ownership rights or security interest of a third party in the goods, purchases goods in the ordinary course of business from a person in the business of selling goods of that kind.

buyout price The amount payable to a partner on his or her dissociation from a partnership, based on the amount distributable to that partner if the firm were wound up on that date, and offset by any damages for wrongful dissociation.

bylaws The internal rules of management adopted by a corporation at its first organizational meeting.

C

case law The rules of law announced in court decisions. Case law interprets statutes, regulations, constitutional provisions, and other case law.

case on point A previous case involving factual circumstances and issues that are similar to those in the case before the court.

cash surrender value The amount that the insurer has agreed to pay to the insured if a life insurance policy is canceled before the insured's death.

cashier's check A check drawn by a bank on itself.

categorical imperative A concept developed by the philosopher Immanuel Kant as an ethical guideline for behavior. In deciding whether an action is right or wrong, or desirable or undesirable, a person should evaluate the action in terms of what would happen if everybody else in the same situation, or category, acted the same way.

causation in fact An act or omission without ("but for") which an event would not have occurred.

cease-and-desist order An administrative or judicial order prohibiting a person or business firm from conducting activities that an agency or court has deemed illegal.

certificate of deposit (CD) A note of a bank in which the bank acknowledges a receipt of money from a party and promises to repay the money, with interest, to the party on a specified date.

certificate of limited partnership The document that must be filed with a designated state official to form a limited partnership.

certification mark A mark used by one or more persons, other than the owner, to certify the region, materials, mode of manufacture, quality, or accuracy of the owner's goods or services. Examples of certification marks include the "Good Housekeeping Seal of Approval" and "UL Tested."

certified check A check that has been accepted by the bank on which it is drawn. Essentially, the bank, by certifying (accepting) the check, promises to pay the check at the time the check is presented.

charging order In partnership law, an order granted by a court to a judgment creditor that entitles the creditor to attach a partner's interest in the partnership.

charitable trust A trust in which the property held by the trustee must be used for a charitable purpose, such as the advancement of health, education, or religion.

chattel Personal property.

check A draft drawn by a drawer ordering the drawee bank or financial institution to pay a certain amount of money to the holder on demand.

check A special type of draft that is drawn on a bank, ordering the bank to pay a fixed amount of money on demand.

checks and balances The system by which each of the three branches of the national government (executive, legislative, and judicial) exercises checks on the powers of the other branches.

choice-of-language clause A clause in a contract designating the official language by which the contract will be interpreted in the event of a future disagreement over the contract's terms.

choice-of-law clause A clause in a contract designating the law (such as the law of a particular state or nation) that will govern the contract.

citation A reference to a publication in which a legal authority—such as a statute or a court decision—or other source can be found.

civil law The branch of law dealing with the definition and enforcement of all private or public rights, as opposed to criminal matters.

civil law system A system of law derived from that of the Roman Empire and based on a code rather than case law; the predominant system of law in the nations of continental Europe and the nations that were once their colonies. In the United States, Louisiana is the only state that has a civil law system.

clearinghouse A system or place where banks exchange checks and drafts drawn on each other and settle daily balances.

click-on agreement An agreement that arises when a buyer, engaging in a transaction on a computer, indicates his or her assent to be bound by the terms of an offer by clicking on a button that says, for example, "I agree"; sometimes referred to as a *click-on license* or a *click-wrap agreement*.

close corporation A corporation whose shareholders are limited to a small group of persons, often family members.

closed shop A firm that requires union membership on the part of its workers as a condition of employment.

closing The final step in the sale of real estate, in which ownership is transferred to the buyer in exchange for payment of the purchase price.

closing argument An argument made at a trial after the plaintiff and defendant have rested their cases. Closing arguments are made prior to the jury charges.

cloud computing The delivery to users of on-demand services from third-party servers over a network.

co-surety A joint surety; one who assumes liability jointly with another surety for the payment of an obligation.

codicil A written supplement or modification to a will. A codicil must be executed with the same formalities as a will.

coinsurance clause A clause in an insurance contract that encourages property owners to insure their property for an amount as close to full value as possible. If the owner insures the property up to a specified percentage—usually 80 percent—of its value, she or he will recover any loss up to the face amount of the policy.

collateral Under Article 9 of the Uniform Commercial Code, the property subject to a security interest.

collateral promise A secondary promise that is ancillary (subsidiary) to a principal transaction or primary contractual relationship, such as a promise made by one person to pay the debts of another if the latter fails to perform. A collateral promise normally must be in writing to be enforceable.

collecting bank Any bank handling an item for collection, except the payor bank.

collective bargaining The process by which labor and management negotiate the terms and conditions of employment, including working hours and workplace conditions.

collective mark A mark used by members of a cooperative, association, or other organization to certify the region, materials, mode of manufacture, quality, or accuracy of the specific goods or services. Examples of collective marks include the labor union marks found on tags of certain products and the credits of movies, which indicate the various associations and organizations that participated in the making of the movies.

comity A deference by which one nation gives effect to the laws and judicial decrees of another nation.

commerce clause The provision in Article I, Section 8, of the U.S. Constitution that gives Congress the power to regulate interstate commerce.

commercial impracticability A doctrine under which a seller may be excused from performing a contract when (1) a contingency occurs, (2) the contingency's occurrence makes performance impracticable, and (3) the nonoccurrence of the contingency was a basic assumption on which the contract was made.

commercial use Use of land for business activities only; sometimes called *business use*.

commingle To put funds or goods together into one mass so that they are mixed to such a degree that they no longer have separate identities.

common law The body of law developed from custom or judicial decisions in English and U.S. courts, not attributable to a legislature.

common stock A security that evidences ownership in a corporation. A share of common stock gives the owner a proportionate interest in the corporation with regard to control, earnings, and net assets. Common stock is lowest in priority with respect to payment of dividends and distribution of the corporation's assets on dissolution.

community property A form of concurrent property ownership in which each spouse owns an undivided one-half interest in property acquired during the marriage.

comparative negligence A theory in tort law under which the liability for injuries resulting from negligent acts is shared by all parties who were negligent (including the injured party) on the basis of each person's proportionate negligence.

compelling government interest A test of constitutionality that requires the government to have compelling reasons for passing any law that restricts fundamental rights, such as free speech, or distinguishes between people based on a suspect trait.

compensatory damages A money award equivalent to the actual value of injuries or damages sustained by the aggrieved party.

complaint The pleading made by a plaintiff alleging wrongdoing on the part of the defendant; the document that, when filed with a court, initiates a lawsuit.

computer crime Any violation of criminal law that involves knowledge of computer technology for its perpetration, investigation, or prosecution.

concentrated industry An industry in which a single firm or a small number of firms control a large percentage of market sales.

concurrent conditions Conditions in a contract that must occur or be performed at the same time; they are mutually dependent. No obligations arise until these conditions are simultaneously performed.

concurrent jurisdiction Jurisdiction that exists when two different courts have the power to hear a case. For example, some cases can be heard in either a federal or a state court.

concurrent ownership Joint ownership.

concurring opinion A court opinion by one or more judges or justices who agree with the majority but want to make or emphasize a point that was not made or emphasized in the majority's opinion.

condemnation The judicial procedure by which the government exercises its power of eminent domain. It generally involves two phases: a taking and a determination of fair value.

condition A possible future event, the occurrence or nonoccurrence of which will trigger the performance of a legal obligation or terminate an existing obligation under a contract.

condition precedent A condition in a contract that must be met before a party's promise becomes absolute.

condition subsequent A condition in a contract that operates to terminate a party's absolute promise to perform.

confiscation A government's taking of privately owned business or personal property without a proper public purpose or an award of just compensation.

conforming goods Goods that conform to contract specifications.

confusion The mixing together of goods belonging to two or more owners to such an extent that the separately owned goods cannot be identified.

consequential damages Special damages that compensate for a loss that is not direct or immediate (for example, lost profits). The special damages must have been reasonably foreseeable at the time the breach or injury occurred in order for the plaintiff to collect them.

consideration Generally, the value given in return for a promise or a performance. The consideration, which must be present to make the contract legally binding, must be something of legally sufficient value and must be bargained for.

consolidation A contractual and statutory process in which two or more corporations join to become a completely new corporation.

constitutional law Law that is based on the U.S. Constitution and the constitutions of the various states.

constructive delivery A symbolic delivery of property that cannot be physically delivered.

constructive discharge A termination of employment brought about by making the employee's working conditions so intolerable that the employee reasonably feels compelled to leave.

constructive eviction A form of eviction that occurs when a landlord fails to perform adequately any of the duties required by the lease, thereby making the tenant's further use and enjoyment of the property exceedingly difficult or impossible.

constructive fraud Conduct that is treated as fraud under the law even when there is no proof of intent to defraud, usually because of the existence of a special relationship or fiduciary duty.

constructive trust An equitable trust that is imposed in the interests of fairness and justice when someone wrongfully holds legal title to property.

consumer-debtor One whose debts result primarily from the purchase of goods for personal, family, or household use.

consumer law The body of statutes, agency rules, and judicial decisions protecting consumers of goods and services from dangerous manufacturing techniques, mislabeling, unfair credit practices, deceptive advertising, and other such practices.

continuation statement A statement that, if filed within six months prior to the expiration date of the original financing statement, continues the perfection of the original security interest for another five years. The perfection of a security interest can be continued in the same manner indefinitely.

contract An agreement that can be enforced in court; formed by two or more parties, each of whom agrees to perform or to refrain from performing some act now or in the future.

contractual capacity The legal ability to enter into contracts; the threshold mental capacity required by law for a party who enters into a contract to be bound by that contract.

contributory negligence A theory in tort law under which a complaining party's own negligence contributed to or caused his or her injuries. Contributory negligence is an absolute bar to recovery in a minority of jurisdictions.

conversion The wrongful taking, using, or retaining possession of personal property that belongs to another.

conveyance The transfer of title to real property from one person to another by deed or other document.

cookie A small file sent from a Web site and stored in a user's Web browser to track the user's Web browsing activities.

"cooling-off" laws Laws that allow buyers of goods sold in certain transactions to cancel their contracts within three business days.

cooperative An association, which may or may not be incorporated, that is organized to provide an economic service to its members. Unincorporated cooperatives are often treated like partnerships for tax and other legal purposes.

copyright The exclusive right of authors to publish, print, or sell an intellectual production for a statutory period of time. A copyright has the same monopolistic nature as a patent or trademark, but it differs in that it applies exclusively to works of art, literature, and other works of authorship, including computer programs.

corporate governance A set of policies specifying the rights and responsibilities of the various participants in a corporation and spelling out the rules and procedures for making corporate decisions.

corporate social responsibility The concept that corporations can and should act ethically, and be accountable to society for their actions.

cost-benefit analysis A decision-making technique that involves weighing the costs of a given action against the benefits of the action.

counteradvertising New advertising that is undertaken to correct earlier false claims that were made about a product.

counterclaim A claim made by a defendant in a civil lawsuit that in effect sues the plaintiff.

counteroffer An offeree's response to an offer in which the offeree rejects the original offer and at the same time makes a new offer.

course of dealing Prior conduct between parties to a contract that establishes a common basis for their understanding.

course of performance The conduct that occurs under the terms of a particular agreement. Such conduct indicates what the parties to an agreement intended it to mean.

court of equity A court that decides controversies and administers justice according to the rules, principles, and precedents of equity.

court of law A court in which the only remedies that could be granted were things of value, such as money damages. In the early English king's courts, courts of law were distinct from courts of equity.

covenant not to compete A contractual promise to refrain from competing with another party for a certain period of time and within a certain geographic area. Although covenants not to compete restrain trade, they are commonly found in partnership agreements, business sale agreements, and employment contracts. If they are ancillary to such agreements, covenants not to compete will normally be enforced by the courts unless the time period or geographic area is deemed unreasonable.

covenant not to sue An agreement to substitute a contractual obligation for some other type of legal action based on a valid claim.

cover A buyer's or lessee's purchase on the open market of goods to substitute for those promised but never delivered by the seller or lessor. Under the Uniform Commercial Code, if the cost of cover exceeds the cost of the contract goods, the buyer or lessee can recover the difference, plus incidental and consequential damages.

cram-down provision A provision of the Bankruptcy Code that allows a court to confirm a debtor's Chapter 11 reorganization plan even though only one class of creditors has accepted it.

creditors' composition agreement An agreement formed between a debtor and his or her creditors in which the creditors agree to accept a lesser sum than that owed by the debtor in full satisfaction of the debt.

crime A wrong against society proclaimed in a statute and punishable by society through fines and/or imprisonment—or, in some cases, death.

criminal law The branch of law that defines and punishes wrongful actions committed against the public.

cross-collateralization The use of an asset that is not the subject of a loan to collateralize that loan.

cross-examination The questioning of an opposing witness during a trial.

crowdfunding A cooperative activity in which people network and pool funds and other resources via the Internet to assist a cause (such as disaster relief) or invest in a business venture (such as a startup).

cure Under the Uniform Commercial Code, the right of a party who tenders nonconforming performance to correct his or her performance within the contract period.

cyber crime A crime that occurs online, in the virtual community of the Internet, as opposed to the physical world.

cyber fraud Fraud that involves the online theft of credit-card information, banking details, and other information for criminal use.

cyber tort A tort committed via the Internet.

cyberlaw An informal term used to refer to all laws governing electronic communications and transactions, particularly those conducted via the Internet.

cybersquatting Registering a domain name that is the same as, or confusingly similar to, the trademark of another and then offering to sell that domain name back to the trademark owner.

D

damages A monetary award sought as a remedy for a breach of contract or a tortious act.

debtor Under Article 9 of the Uniform Commercial Code, any party who owes payment or performance of a secured obligation, whether or not the party actually owns or has rights in the collateral.

debtor in possession (DIP) In Chapter 11 bankruptcy proceedings, a debtor who is allowed to continue in possession of the estate in property (the business) and to continue business operations.

deceptive advertising Advertising that misleads consumers, either by making unjustified claims about a product's performance or by omitting a material fact concerning the product's composition or performance.

deed A document by which title to real property is passed.

defalcation Embezzlement or misappropriation of funds.

defamation Any published or publicly spoken false statement that causes injury to another's good name, reputation, or character.

default Failure to pay a debt when it is due.

default judgment A judgment entered by a court against a defendant who has failed to appear in court to answer or defend against the plaintiff's claim.

defendant One against whom a lawsuit is brought, or the accused person in a criminal proceeding.

defense Reasons that a defendant offers in an action or suit as to why the plaintiff should not obtain what he or she is seeking.

deficiency judgment A judgment against a debtor for the amount of a debt remaining unpaid after collateral has been repossessed and sold.

delegatee One to whom contract duties are delegated by another, called the delegator.

delegation The transfer of a contractual duty to a third party. The party delegating the duty (the delegator) to the third party (the delegatee) is still obliged to perform on the contract should the delegatee fail to perform.

delegation doctrine A doctrine based on Article I, Section 8, of the U.S. Constitution, which has been construed to allow Congress to delegate some of its power to make and implement laws to administrative agencies. The delegation is considered to be proper as long as Congress sets standards outlining the scope of the agency's authority.

delegator One who delegates his or her duties under a contract to another, called the delegatee.

depositary bank The first bank to receive a check for payment.

deposition The testimony of a party to a lawsuit or of a witness taken under oath before a trial.

destination contract A contract in which the seller is required to ship the goods by carrier and deliver them at a particular destination. The seller assumes liability for any losses or damage to the goods until they are tendered at the destination specified in the contract.

devise A gift of real property by will, or the act of giving real property by will.

devisee One designated in a will to receive a gift of real property.

digital cash Funds contained on computer software, in the form of secure programs stored on microchips and other computer devices.

dilution With respect to trademarks, a doctrine under which distinctive or famous trademarks are protected from certain unauthorized uses of the marks regardless of a showing of competition or a likelihood of confusion. Congress created a federal cause of action for dilution in 1995 with the passage of the Federal Trademark Dilution Act.

direct examination The examination of a witness by the attorney who calls the witness to the stand at trial to testify on behalf of the attorney's client.

disaffirmance The legal avoidance, or setting aside, of a contractual obligation.

discharge (1) The termination of an obligation, such as occurs when the parties to a contract have fully performed their contractual obligations. (2) The termination of a bankruptcy debtor's obligation to pay debts.

discharge in bankruptcy The release of a debtor from all debts that are provable, except those specifically excepted from discharge by statute.

disclosed principal A principal whose identity is known to a third party at the time the agent makes a contract with the third party.

discovery A phase in the litigation process during which the opposing parties may obtain information from each other and from third parties prior to trial.

dishonor To refuse to accept or pay a draft or a promissory note when it is properly presented. An instrument is dishonored when presentment is properly made and acceptance or payment is refused or cannot be obtained within the prescribed time.

disparagement of property An economically injurious false statement made about another's product or property. A general term for torts that are more specifically referred to as *slander of quality* or *slander of title*.

disparate-impact discrimination Discrimination that results from certain employer practices or procedures that, although not discriminatory on their face, have a discriminatory effect.

disparate-treatment discrimination A form of employment discrimination that results when an employer intentionally discriminates against employees who are members of protected classes.

dissenting opinion A court opinion that presents the views of one or more judges or justices who disagree with the majority's decision.

dissociation The severance of the relationship between a partner and a partnership.

dissolution The formal disbanding of a partnership, corporation, or other business entity. For instance, partnerships can be dissolved by acts of the partners, by operation of law, or by judicial decree.

distributed network A network that can be used by persons located (distributed) around the country or the globe to share computer files.

distribution agreement A contract between a seller and a distributor of the seller's products setting out the terms and conditions of the distributorship.

diversity of citizenship Under Article III, Section 2, of the Constitution, a basis for federal court jurisdiction over a lawsuit between (1) citizens of different states, (2) a foreign country and citizens of a state or of different states, or (3) citizens of a state and citizens or subjects of a foreign country. The amount in controversy must be more than $75,000 before a federal court can take jurisdiction in such cases.

divestiture A company's sale of one or more of its divisions' operating functions under court order as part of the enforcement of the antitrust laws.

dividend A distribution of corporate profits to the corporation's shareholders in proportion to the number of shares held.

document of title A writing exchanged in the regular course of business that evidences the right to possession of goods (for example, a bill of lading or a warehouse receipt).

domain name The series of letters and symbols used to identify a site operator on the Internet; an Internet "address."

domestic corporation In a given state, a corporation that is organized under the law of that state.

dominion Ownership rights in property, including the right to possess and control the property.

double jeopardy A situation occurring when a person is tried twice for the same criminal offense; prohibited by the Fifth Amendment to the Constitution.

down payment The part of the purchase price of real property that is paid in cash up front, reducing the amount of the loan or mortgage.

draft Any instrument (such as a check) drawn on a drawee (such as a bank) that orders the drawee to pay a certain sum of money, usually to a third party (the payee), on demand or at a definite future time.

dram shop act A state statute that imposes liability on the owners of bars and taverns, as well as those who serve alcoholic drinks to the public, for injuries resulting from accidents caused by intoxicated persons when the sellers or servers of alcoholic drinks contributed to the intoxication.

drawee The party that is ordered to pay a draft or check. With a check, a financial institution is always the drawee.

drawer The party that initiates a draft (writes a check, for example), thereby ordering the drawee to pay.

due diligence A required standard of care that certain professionals, such as accountants, must meet to avoid liability for securities violations.

due process clause The provisions of the Fifth and Fourteenth Amendments to the U.S. Constitution that guarantee that no person shall be deprived of life, liberty, or property without due process of law. Similar clauses are found in most state constitutions.

dumping The selling of goods in a foreign country at a price below the price charged for the same goods in the domestic market.

durable power of attorney A document that authorizes a person to act on behalf of another person—write checks, collect insurance proceeds, and otherwise manage the disabled person's affairs, including health care—when that person becomes incapacitated.

duress Unlawful pressure brought to bear on a person, causing the person to perform an act that he or she would not otherwise perform (or refrain from doing something the person would otherwise have done).

duty of care The duty of all persons, as established by tort law, to exercise a reasonable amount of care in their dealings with others. Failure to exercise due care, which is normally determined by the "reasonable person standard," constitutes the tort of negligence.

duty-based ethics An ethical philosophy rooted in the idea that every person has certain duties to others, including both humans and the planet. Those duties may be derived from religious principles or from other philosophical reasoning.

E

e-agent A semiautonomous computer program that is capable of executing specific tasks.

e-contract A contract that is entered into in cyberspace and is evidenced only by electronic impulses (such as those that make up a computer's memory), rather than, for example, a typewritten form.

e-evidence A type of evidence that consists of computer-generated or electronically recorded information, including e-mail, voice mail, spreadsheets, word-processing documents, and other data.

e-money Prepaid funds recorded on a computer or a card (such as a *smart card*).

e-signature As defined by the Uniform Electronic Transactions Act, "an electronic sound, symbol, or process attached to or logically associated with a record and executed or adopted by a person with the intent to sign the record."

early neutral case evaluation A form of alternative dispute resolution in which a neutral third party evaluates the strengths and weakness of the disputing parties' positions. The evaluator's opinion forms the basis for negotiating a settlement.

easement A nonpossessory right, established by express or implied agreement, to make limited use of another's property without removing anything from the property.

electronic fund transfer (EFT) A transfer of funds through the use of an electronic terminal, a telephone, a computer, or magnetic tape.

emancipation In regard to minors, the act of being freed from parental control; occurs when a child's parent or legal guardian relinquishes the legal right to exercise control over the child. Normally, a minor who leaves home to support himself or herself is considered emancipated.

embezzlement The fraudulent appropriation of money or other property by a person to whom the money or property has been entrusted.

eminent domain The power of a government to take land from private citizens for public use on the payment of just compensation.

employment at will A common law doctrine under which either party may terminate an employment relationship at any time for any reason, unless a contract specifies otherwise.

employment discrimination Unequal treatment of employees or job applicants on the basis of race, color, national origin, religion, gender, age, or disability; prohibited by federal statutes.

enabling legislation A statute enacted by Congress that authorizes the creation of an administrative agency and specifies the name, composition, purpose, and powers of the agency being created.

endowment insurance A type of life insurance in which the policyholder pays fixed premiums for a definite term, after which a fixed amount is paid to the policyholder or, if the policyholder has died, to a beneficiary.

entrapment In criminal law, a defense in which the defendant claims that he or she was induced by a public official—usually an undercover agent or police officer—to commit a crime that he or she would otherwise not have committed.

entrepreneur One who initiates and assumes the financial risk of a new business enterprise and undertakes to provide or control its management.

entrustment rule A rule under which entrusting goods to a merchant who deals in goods of that kind gives the merchant the power to transfer all rights to a buyer in the ordinary course of business.

environmental impact statement (EIS) A formal analysis required for any major federal action that will significantly affect the quality of the environment to determine the action's impact and explore alternatives.

equal dignity rule A rule requiring that an agent's authority be in writing if the contract to be made on behalf of the principal must be in writing.

equal protection clause The provision in the Fourteenth Amendment to the U.S. Constitution that guarantees that no state will "deny to any person within its jurisdiction the equal protection of the laws." This clause mandates that state governments treat similarly situated individuals in a similar manner.

equitable maxims General propositions or principles of law that have to do with fairness (equity).

equitable right of redemption The right of a defaulting borrower to redeem property before a foreclosure sale by paying the full amount of the debt, plus any interest and costs that have accrued.

escheat The transfer of property to the state when the owner of the property dies without heirs.

escrow account An account generally held in the name of the depositor and escrow agent. The funds in the account are paid to a third person on fulfillment of the escrow condition.

establishment clause The provision in the First Amendment to the U.S. Constitution that prohibits Congress from creating any law "respecting an establishment of religion."

estate planning Planning in advance how one's property and obligations should be transferred on one's death. Wills and trusts are two basic devices used in estate planning.

estopped Barred, impeded, or precluded.

estray statute A statute defining finders' rights in property when the true owners are unknown.

ethical reasoning A reasoning process in which an individual links his or her moral convictions or ethical standards to the particular situation at hand.

ethics Moral principles and values applied to social behavior.

eviction A landlord's act of depriving a tenant of possession of the leased premises.

exclusionary rule In criminal procedure, a rule under which any evidence that is obtained in violation of the accused's constitutional rights guaranteed by the Fourth, Fifth, and Sixth Amendments, as well as any evidence derived from illegally obtained evidence, will not be admissible in court.

exclusive agency An agency in which a principal grants an agent an exclusive territory and does not allow another agent to compete in that territory.

exclusive-dealing contract An agreement under which a seller forbids a buyer to purchase products from the seller's competitors.

exclusive jurisdiction Jurisdiction that exists when a case can be heard only in a particular court or type of court, such as a federal court or a state court.

exculpatory clause A clause that releases a contractual party from liability in the event of monetary or physical injury, no matter who is at fault.

executed contract A contract that has been completely performed by both parties.

execution An action to carry into effect the directions in a court decree or judgment.

executive agency An administrative agency within the executive branch of government. At the federal level, executive agencies are those within the cabinet departments.

executor A person appointed by a testator in a will to administer the testator's estate.

executory contract A contract that has not yet been fully performed.

exhaustion doctrine In administrative law, the principle that a complaining party normally must have exhausted all available administrative remedies before seeking judicial review.

export To sell products to buyers located in other countries.

express authority Authority expressly given by one party to another. In agency law, an agent has express authority to act for a principal if both parties agree, orally or in writing, that an agency relationship exists in which the agent has the power (authority) to act in the place of, and on behalf of, the principal.

express contract A contract in which the terms of the agreement are fully and explicitly stated in words, oral or written.

express warranty A seller's or lessor's oral or written promise, ancillary to an underlying sales or lease agreement, as to the quality, description, or performance of the goods being sold or leased.

expropriation The seizure by a government of privately owned business or personal property for a proper public purpose and with just compensation.

extension clause A clause in a time instrument that allows the instrument's date of maturity to be extended into the future.

extrinsic evidence Evidence that relates to a contract but is not contained within the document itself, including the testimony of the parties, the testimony of witnesses, and additional agreements and communications. A court may consider extrinsic evidence only when a contract term is ambiguous and the evidence does not contradict the express terms of the contract.

F

family limited liability partnership (FLLP) A limited liability partnership (LLP) in which the majority of the partners are members of a family.

federal form of government A system of government in which the states form a union and the sovereign power is divided between a central government and the member states.

federal question A question that pertains to the U.S. Constitution, acts of Congress, or treaties. A federal question provides a basis for federal jurisdiction.

Federal Reserve System A network of twelve central banks, located throughout the United States and headed by the Federal Reserve Board of Governors. Most banks in the United States have Federal Reserve accounts.

Federal Rules of Civil Procedure (FRCP) The rules controlling procedural matters in civil trials brought before the federal district courts.

fee simple absolute An ownership interest in land in which the owner has the greatest possible aggregation of rights, privileges, and power. The owner can use, possess, or dispose of the property as he or she chooses during his or her lifetime. On death, the interest in the property passes to the owner's heirs.

felony A crime—such as arson, murder, rape, or robbery—that carries the most severe sanctions, usually ranging from one year in a state or federal prison to the forfeiture of one's life.

fictitious payee A payee on a negotiable instrument whom the maker or drawer does not intend to have an interest in the instrument. Indorsements by fictitious payees are not treated as unauthorized under Article 3 of the Uniform Commercial Code.

fiduciary As a noun, a person having a duty created by his or her undertaking to act primarily for another's benefit in matters connected with the undertaking; as an adjective, a relationship founded on trust and confidence.

filtering software A computer program that screens incoming data according to rules built into the software and blocks access to Web sites with content not consistent with these rules.

final order The final decision of an administrative agency on an issue. If no appeal is taken, or if the case is not reviewed or considered anew by the agency commission, the administrative law judge's initial order becomes the final order of the agency.

financing statement A document prepared by a secured creditor and filed with the appropriate government official to give notice to the public that the creditor claims an interest in collateral belonging to the debtor named in the statement. The financing statement must contain the names and addresses of both the debtor and the creditor, and describe the collateral by type or item.

firm offer An offer (by a merchant) that is irrevocable without consideration for a period of time (not longer than three months). A firm offer by a merchant must be in writing and must be signed by the offeror.

fixed-term tenancy A type of tenancy under which property is leased for a specified period of time, such as a month, a year, or a period of years; also called a *tenancy for years*.

fixture An item of personal property that has become so closely associated with real property that it is legally regarded as part of that real property.

floating lien A security interest in proceeds, after-acquired property, or property purchased under a line of credit (or all three); a security interest in collateral that is retained even when the collateral changes in character, classification, or location.

forbearance The act of refraining from exercising a legal right; an agreement between a lender and a borrower in which the lender agrees to temporarily cease requiring mortgage payments, to delay foreclosure, or to accept smaller payments than previously scheduled.

force majeure (pronounced mah-*zhure*) **clause** A provision in a contract stipulating that certain unforeseen events—such as war, political upheavals, acts of God, and the like—will excuse a party from liability for nonperformance of contractual obligations.

foreclosure A proceeding in which a mortgagee either takes title to or forces the sale of the mortgagor's property in satisfaction of a debt.

foreign corporation In a given state, a corporation that does business in that state but is not incorporated there.

forgery The fraudulent making or altering of any writing in a way that changes the legal rights and liabilities of another.

formal contract A contract that by law requires a specific form, such as being executed under seal, to be valid.

forum-selection clause A provision in a contract designating the court, jurisdiction, or tribunal that will decide any disputes arising under the contract.

franchise Any arrangement in which the owner of a trademark, trade name, or copyright licenses another to use that trademark, trade name, or copyright in the selling of goods or services.

franchisee One receiving a license to use another's (the franchisor's) trademark, trade name, or copyright in the sale of goods and services.

franchisor One licensing another (the franchisee) to use the owner's trademark, trade name, or copyright in the selling of goods or services.

fraudulent misrepresentation (fraud) Any misrepresentation, either by misstatement or omission of a material fact, knowingly made with the intention of deceiving another and on which a reasonable person would and does rely to his or her detriment.

free exercise clause The provision in the First Amendment to the U.S. Constitution that prohibits Congress from making any law "prohibiting the free exercise" of religion.

free-writing prospectus A written, electronic, or graphic communication associated with the offer to sell a security and used during the waiting period to supplement other information about the security.

frustration of purpose A court-created doctrine under which a party to a contract will be relieved of his or her duty to perform when the objective purpose for performance no longer exists (due to reasons beyond that party's control).

full faith and credit clause A clause in Article IV, Section 1, of the U.S. Constitution that provides that "Full Faith and Credit shall be given in each State to the public Acts, Records, and Judicial Proceedings of every other State." The clause ensures that rights established under deeds, wills, contracts, and the like in one state will be honored by the other states and that any judicial decision with respect to such property rights will be honored and enforced in all states.

fully integrated contract A contract that completely sets forth all the terms and conditions agreed to by the parties and is intended as a final statement of their agreement.

fungible goods Goods that are alike by physical nature, by agreement, or by trade usage. Examples are wheat, oil, and wine that are identical in type and quality.

G

garnishment A legal process used by a creditor to collect a debt by seizing property of the debtor (such as wages) that is being held by a third party (such as the debtor's employer).

general damages In a tort case, an amount awarded to compensate individuals for the nonmonetary aspects of the harm suffered, such as pain and suffering; not available to companies.

general partner In a limited partnership, a partner who assumes responsibility for the management of the partnership and has full liability for all partnership debts.

generally accepted accounting principles (GAAP) The conventions, rules, and procedures developed by the Financial Accounting Standards Board to define accepted accounting practices at a particular time.

generally accepted auditing standards (GAAS) Standards established by the American Institute of Certified Public Accountants to define the professional qualities and judgment that should be exercised by an auditor in performing an audit.

gift A voluntary transfer of property made without consideration, past or present.

gift *causa mortis* A gift made in contemplation of imminent death. The gift is revoked if the donor does not die as contemplated.

gift *inter vivos* A gift made during one's lifetime and not in contemplation of imminent death, in contrast to a gift *causa mortis*.

good faith purchaser A purchaser who buys without notice of any circumstance that would put a person of ordinary prudence on inquiry as to whether the seller has valid title to the goods being sold.

Good Samaritan statute A state statute that provides that persons who rescue or provide emergency services to others in peril—unless they do so recklessly, thus causing further harm—cannot be sued for negligence.

goodwill In the business context, the valuable reputation of a business viewed as an intangible asset.

grand jury A group of citizens called to decide, after hearing the state's evidence, whether a reasonable basis (probable cause) exists for believing that a crime has been committed and whether a trial ought to be held.

grant deed A deed that simply states that property is being conveyed from the grantor to another. Under statute, a grant deed may impliedly warrant that the grantor has at least not conveyed the property's title to someone else.

group boycott An agreement by two or more sellers to refuse to deal with a particular person or firm.

guarantor A person who agrees to satisfy the debt of another (the debtor) only after the principal debtor defaults. A guarantor's liability is thus secondary.

H

hacker A person who uses one computer to break into another.

health-care power of attorney A document that designates a person who will have the power to choose what type of and how much medical treatment a person who is unable to make such a choice will receive.

hearsay An oral or written statement made out of court that is later offered in court by a witness (not the person who made the statement) to prove the truth of the matter asserted in the statement. Hearsay is generally inadmissible as evidence.

historical school A school of legal thought that looks to the past to determine what the principles of contemporary law should be.

holder Any person in the possession of an instrument drawn, issued, or indorsed to him or her, to his or her order, to bearer, or in blank.

holder in due course (HDC) A holder who acquires a negotiable instrument for value; in good faith; and without notice that the instrument is overdue, that it has been dishonored, that any person has a defense against it or a claim to it, or that the instrument contains unauthorized signatures, alterations, or is so irregular or incomplete as to call into question its authenticity.

holding company A company whose business activity is holding shares in another company.

holographic will A will written entirely in the testator's handwriting.

homeowner's insurance A form of property insurance that protects the home of the insured person and its contents against losses.

homestead exemption A law permitting a debtor to retain the family home, either in its entirety or up to a specified dollar amount, free from the claims of unsecured creditors or trustees in bankruptcy.

horizontal merger A merger between two firms that are competing in the same market.

horizontal restraint Any agreement that restrains competition between rival firms competing in the same market.

hot-cargo agreement An illegal agreement in which employers voluntarily agree with unions not to handle, use, or deal in the non-union-produced goods of other employers.

I

I-551 Alien Registration Receipt A document known as a "green card" that shows that a foreign-born individual can legally work in the United States.

I-9 verification The process of verifying the employment eligibility and identity of a new immigrant worker. It must be completed within three days after the worker commences employment.

identification In a sale of goods, the express designation of the specific goods provided for in the contract.

identity theft The act of stealing another's identifying information—such as a name, date of birth, or Social Security number—and using that information to access the victim's financial resources.

impeach To challenge the credibility of a person's testimony or attempt to discredit a party or witness.

implication A way of creating an easement or profit in real property when it is reasonable to imply its existence from the circumstances surrounding the division of the property.

implied authority Authority that is created not by an explicit oral or written agreement but by implication. In agency law, implied authority (of the agent) can be conferred by custom, inferred from the position the agent occupies, or implied by virtue of being reasonably necessary to carry out express authority.

implied contract A contract formed in whole or in part from the conduct of the parties (as opposed to an express contract).

implied warranty A warranty that the law derives by implication or inference from the nature of the transaction or the relative situation or circumstances of the parties.

implied warranty of fitness for a particular purpose A warranty that goods sold or leased are fit for a particular purpose. The warranty arises when any seller or lessor knows the particular purpose for which a buyer or lessee will use the goods and knows that the buyer or lessee is relying on the skill and judgment of the seller or lessor to select suitable goods.

implied warranty of habitability An implied promise by a seller of a new house that the house is fit for human habitation. Also, the implied promise by a landlord that rented residential premises are habitable.

implied warranty of merchantability A warranty that goods being sold or leased are reasonably fit for the ordinary purpose for which they are sold or leased, are properly packaged and labeled, and are of fair quality. The warranty automatically arises in every sale or lease of goods made by a merchant who deals in goods of the kind sold or leased.

impossibility of performance A doctrine under which a party to a contract is relieved of his or her duty to perform when performance becomes impossible or totally impracticable (through no fault of either party).

imposter One who, by use of the mail, telephone, or personal appearance, induces a maker or drawer to issue an instrument in the name of an impersonated payee. Indorsements by imposters are not treated as unauthorized under Article 3 of the Uniform Commercial Code.

in personam **jurisdiction** Court jurisdiction over the "person" involved in a legal action; personal jurisdiction.

in rem **jurisdiction** Court jurisdiction over a defendant's property.

incidental beneficiary A third party who incidentally benefits from a contract but whose benefit was not the reason the contract was formed. An incidental beneficiary has no rights in a contract and cannot sue to have the contract enforced.

incidental damages Damages that compensate for expenses directly incurred because of a breach of contract, such as those incurred to obtain performance from another source.

incontestability clause A clause in a policy for life or health insurance stating that after the policy has been in force for a specified length of time (usually two or three years), the insurer cannot contest statements made in the policyholder's application.

independent contractor One who works for, and receives payment from, an employer but whose working conditions and methods are not controlled by the employer. An independent contractor is not an employee but may be an agent.

independent regulatory agency An administrative agency that is not considered part of the government's executive branch and is not subject to the authority of the president. Independent agency officials cannot be removed without cause.

indictment (pronounced in-*dyte*-ment) A charge by a grand jury that a reasonable basis (probable cause) exists for believing that a crime has been committed and that a trial should be held.

indorsee A person to whom a negotiable instrument is transferred by indorsement.

indorsement A signature placed on an instrument for the purpose of transferring ownership rights in the instrument.

indorser A person who transfers an instrument by signing (indorsing) it and delivering it to another person.

industrial use Land use for light or heavy manufacturing, shipping, or heavy transportation.

informal contract A contract that does not require a specified form or formality in order to be valid.

information A formal accusation or complaint (without an indictment) issued in certain types of actions (usually criminal actions involving lesser crimes) by a law officer, such as a magistrate.

information return A tax return submitted by a partnership that reports the business's income and losses. The partnership itself does not pay taxes on the income, but each partner's share of the profit (whether distributed or not) is taxed as individual income to that partner.

initial order In the context of administrative law, an agency's disposition in a matter other than a rulemaking. An administrative law judge's initial order becomes final unless it is appealed.

innocent misrepresentation A false statement of fact or an act made in good faith that deceives and causes harm or injury to another.

inside director A person on a corporation's board of directors who is also an officer of the corporation.

insider (1) A corporate director or officer, or other employee or agent, with access to confidential information and a duty not to disclose that information in violation of insider-trading laws. (2) In bankruptcy proceedings, an individual, partner, partnership, corporation, or officer or director of a corporation (or a relative of one of these) who has a close relationship with the debtor.

insider trading The purchase or sale of securities on the basis of information that has not been made available to the public.

insolvent Under the Uniform Commercial Code, a term describing a person who ceases to pay "his debts in the ordinary course of business or cannot pay his debts as they become due or is insolvent within the meaning of federal bankruptcy law" [UCC 1–201(23)].

installment contract Under the Uniform Commercial Code, a contract that requires or authorizes delivery in two or more separate lots to be accepted and paid for separately.

insurable interest (1) A property interest in goods being sold or leased that is sufficiently substantial to permit a party to insure against damage to the goods. (2) An interest either in a person's life or well-being that is sufficiently substantial that insuring against injury to (or the death of) the person does not amount to a mere wagering (betting) contract.

insurance A contract by which the insurer promises to reimburse the insured or a beneficiary in the event that the insured is injured, dies, or sustains damage to property as a result of particular, stated contingencies.

intangible property Property that is incapable of being apprehended by the senses (such as by sight or touch). Intellectual property is an example of intangible property.

integrated contract A written contract that constitutes the final expression of the parties' agreement. If a contract is integrated, evidence extraneous to the contract that contradicts or alters the meaning of the contract in any way is inadmissible.

intellectual property Property resulting from intellectual, creative processes. Patents, trademarks, and copyrights are examples of intellectual property.

intended beneficiary A third party for whose benefit a contract is formed; an intended beneficiary can sue the promisor if such a contract is breached.

intentional tort A wrongful act knowingly committed.

intermediary bank Any bank to which an item is transferred in the course of collection, except the depositary or payor bank.

International Financial Reporting Standards (IFRS) A set of global accounting standards that are being phased in by companies in the United States.

international law The law that governs relations among nations. International customs and treaties are generally considered to be two of the most important sources of international law.

international organization In international law, a term that generally refers to an organization composed mainly of nations and usually established by treaty. The United States is a member of more than one hundred multilateral and bilateral organizations, including at least twenty through the United Nations.

Internet service provider (ISP) A business or organization that offers users access to the Internet and related services.

interpretive rule A nonbinding rule or policy statement issued by an administrative agency that explains how it interprets and intends to apply the statutes it enforces.

interrogatories A series of written questions for which written answers are prepared and then signed under oath by a party to a lawsuit, usually with the assistance of the party's attorney.

intestacy laws State statutes that specify how property will be distributed when a person dies intestate (without a valid will).

intestate As a noun, one who has died without having created a valid will. As an adjective, the state of having died without a will.

inverse condemnation The taking of private property by the government without payment of just compensation as required by the U.S. Constitution. The owner must sue the government to recover just compensation.

investment company A company that acts on the behalf of many smaller shareholders-owners by buying a large portfolio of securities and professionally managing that portfolio.

investment contract In securities law, a transaction in which a person invests in a common enterprise reasonably expecting profits that are derived primarily from the efforts of others.

issue In negotiable instruments law, the first transfer, or delivery, of an instrument to a holder.

J

joint and several liability In partnership law, a doctrine under which a plaintiff may sue, and collect a judgment from, all of the partners together (jointly) or one or more of the partners separately (severally, or individually). A partner can be held liable even if she or he did not participate in, ratify, or know about the conduct that gave rise to the lawsuit.

joint liability In partnership law, the partners' shared liability for partnership obligations and debts. A third party must sue all of the partners as a group, but each partner can be held liable for the full amount.

joint stock company A hybrid form of business organization that combines characteristics of a corporation and a partnership. Usually, a joint stock company is regarded as a partnership for tax and other legal purposes.

joint tenancy Joint ownership of property by two or more co-owners in which each co-owner owns an undivided portion of the property. On the death of one of the joint tenants, his or her interest automatically passes to the surviving joint tenant(s).

joint venture A joint undertaking by two or more persons or business entities to combine their efforts or their property for a single transaction or project, or for a related series of transactions or projects. A joint venture is generally treated like a partnership for tax and other legal purposes.

judicial review The process by which courts decide on the constitutionality of legislative enactments and actions of the executive branch.

junior lienholder A person or business that holds a lien that is subordinate to one or more other liens on the same property.

jurisdiction The authority of a court to hear a case and decide a specific action.

jurisprudence The science or philosophy of law.

L

laches The equitable doctrine that bars a party's right to legal action if the party has neglected for an unreasonable length of time to act on his or her rights.

larceny The wrongful taking and carrying away of another person's personal property with the intent to permanently deprive the owner of the property. Some states classify larceny as either grand or petit, depending on the property's value.

latent defect A defect that is not obvious or cannot readily be ascertained.

law A body of enforceable rules governing relationships among individuals and between individuals and their society.

lease Under Article 2A of the UCC, a transfer of the right to possess and use goods for a period of time in exchange for payment. In the context of real property, an agreement by which a property owner (landlord) agrees to give another party (the tenant) the exclusive right to possess the property for a limited time.

lease agreement In regard to the lease of goods, an agreement in which one person (the lessor) agrees to transfer the right to the possession and use of property to another person (the lessee) in exchange for rental payments.

leasehold estate An interest in real property that gives a tenant a qualified right to possess and/or use the property for a limited time under a lease.

legacy A gift of personal property under a will.

legal positivism A school of legal thought centered on the assumption that there is no law higher than the laws created by a national government. Laws must be obeyed, even if they are unjust, to prevent anarchy.

legal realism A school of legal thought that holds that the law is only one factor to be considered when deciding cases and that social and economic circumstances should also be taken into account.

legal reasoning The process of reasoning by which a judge harmonizes his or her opinion with the judicial decisions in previous cases.

legatee One designated in a will to receive a gift of personal property.

legislative rule An administrative agency rule that carries the same weight as a congressionally enacted statute.

lessee A person who pays for the use or possession of another's property.

lessor A property owner who allows others to use his or her property in exchange for the payment of rent.

letter of credit A written instrument, usually issued by a bank on behalf of a customer or other party, in which the issuer promises to honor drafts or other demands for payment by third parties in accordance with the terms of the instrument.

levy The obtaining of money by legal process through the seizure and sale of property, usually done after a writ of execution has been issued.

liability The state of being legally responsible (liable) for something, such as a debt or obligation.

libel Defamation in writing or in some other form (such as in a digital recording) having the quality of permanence.

license In the context of intellectual property, a contract permitting the use of a trademark, copyright, patent, or trade secret of certain purposes. In the context of real property, a revocable right or privilege of a person to come on another person's land.

licensee One who receives a license to use, or enter onto, another's property.

lien (pronounced *leen*) A claim against specific property to satisfy a debt.

life estate An interest in land that exists only for the duration of the life of a specified individual, usually the holder of the estate.

limited liability company (LLC) A hybrid form of business enterprise that offers the limited liability of a corporation and the tax advantages of a partnership.

limited liability limited partnership (LLLP) A type of limited partnership in which the liability of the general partner is the same as the liability of the limited partners—that is, the liability of all partners is limited to the amount of their investments in the firm.

limited liability partnership (LLP) A hybrid form of business organization that is used mainly by professionals who normally do business in a partnership. An LLP is a pass-through entity for tax purposes, but a partner's personal liability for the malpractice of other partners is limited.

limited partner In a limited partnership, a partner who contributes capital to the partnership but has no right to participate in its management and has no liability for partnership debts beyond the amount of her or his investment.

limited partnership (LP) A partnership consisting of one or more general partners and one or more limited partners.

limited-payment life A type of life insurance for which premiums are payable for a definite period, after which the policy is fully paid.

liquidated damages An amount, stipulated in the contract, that the parties to a contract believe to be a reasonable estimation of the damages that will occur in the event of a breach.

liquidated debt A debt that is due and certain in amount.

liquidation The sale of the nonexempt assets of a debtor and the distribution of the funds received to creditors.

litigation The process of resolving a dispute through the court system.

living trust A trust created by the grantor (settlor) and effective during his or her lifetime.

living will A document that allows a person to control the methods of medical treatment that may be used after a serious accident or illness.

lockout An action in which an employer shuts down to prevent employees from working, typically because it cannot reach a collective bargaining agreement with the employees' union.

long arm statute A state statute that permits a state to obtain personal jurisdiction over nonresident defendants. A defendant must have "minimum contacts" with that state for the statute to apply.

lost property Property that the owner has involuntarily parted with and then cannot find or recover.

M

mailbox rule A rule providing that an acceptance of an offer becomes effective on dispatch.

majority opinion A court opinion that represents the views of the majority (more than half) of the judges or justices deciding the case.

maker One who promises to pay a certain sum to the holder of a promissory note or certificate of deposit (CD).

malpractice Professional misconduct or the failure to exercise the requisite degree of skill as a professional. Negligence—the failure to exercise due care—on the part of a professional, such as a physician or an attorney, is commonly referred to as malpractice.

malware Malicious software programs designed to disrupt or harm a computer, network, smartphone, or other device.

market concentration The degree to which a small number of firms control a large percentage of a relevant market.

market power The power of a firm to control the market price of its product. A monopoly has the greatest degree of market power.

market-share liability A theory under which liability is shared among all firms that manufactured and distributed a particular product during a certain period of time. This theory of liability is used only when the specific source of the harmful product is unidentifiable.

marketable title Title to real estate that is reasonably free from encumbrances, defects in the chain of title, and other matters that affect title, such as adverse possession.

mechanic's lien A statutory lien on the real property of another, created to ensure payment for work performed and materials furnished in the repair or improvement of real property, such as a building.

mediation A method of settling disputes outside of court by using the services of a neutral third party, called a mediator. The mediator acts as a communicating agent between the parties and suggests ways in which the parties can resolve their dispute.

member A person who has an ownership interest in a limited liability company.

mens rea (pronounced *mehns ray*-uh) Criminal intent. The commission of a prohibited act and the intent to commit a crime are the two essential elements required for criminal liability.

merchant A person who is engaged in the purchase and sale of goods. Under the Uniform Commercial Code, a person who deals in goods of the kind involved in the sales contract; for further definitions, see UCC 2–104.

merger A contractual and statutory process in which one corporation (the surviving corporation) acquires all of the assets and liabilities of another corporation.

meta tag Word inserted into a Web site's key-words field to increase the site's appearance in search engine results.

metadata Data that are automatically recorded by electronic devices on their hard drives and that provide information about who created a file and when, and who accessed, modified, or transmitted it. Metadata can be described as "data about data."

metes and bounds A way of describing the boundary lines of land according to the distance between two points, often using physical features of the local geography.

mini-trial A private proceeding in which each party to a dispute argues its position before the other side. A neutral third party may be present and act as an adviser if the parties fail to reach an agreement.

minimum wage The lowest wage, either by government regulation or by union contract, that an employer may pay an hourly worker.

mirror image rule A common law rule that requires, for a valid contractual agreement, that the terms of the offeree's acceptance adhere exactly to the terms of the offeror's offer.

misdemeanor A lesser crime than a felony, punishable by a fine or imprisonment for up to one year in other than a state or federal penitentiary.

mislaid property Property that the owner has voluntarily parted with and then has inadvertently forgotten.

mitigation of damages A rule requiring a plaintiff to have done whatever was reasonable to minimize the damages caused by the defendant.

money laundering Falsely reporting income that has been obtained through criminal activity as income obtained through a legitimate business enterprise—in effect, "laundering" the "dirty money."

monopolization The possession of monopoly power in the relevant market and the willful acquisition or maintenance of that power, as distinguished from growth or development as a consequence of a superior product, business acumen, or historic accident.

monopoly A market in which there is a single seller or a very limited number of sellers.

monopoly power The ability of a monopoly to dictate what takes place in a given market.

moral minimum The minimum degree of ethical behavior expected of a business firm, which is usually defined as compliance with the law.

mortgage A written instrument that gives a creditor (the mortgagee) an interest in, or lien on, the debtor's (mortgagor's) real property as security for a debt. If the debt is not paid, the property can be sold by the creditor and the proceeds used to pay the debt.

mortgage insurance Insurance that compensates a lender for losses due to a borrower's default on a mortgage loan.

motion A procedural request or application presented by an attorney to the court on behalf of a client.

motion for a directed verdict In a state court, a party's request that the judge enter a judgment in her or his favor before the case is submitted to a jury because the other party has not presented sufficient evidence to support the claim. The federal courts refer to this request as a *motion for judgment as a matter of law*.

motion for a judgment as a matter of law In a federal court, a party's request that the judge enter a judgment in her or his favor before the case is submitted to a jury because the other party has not presented sufficient evidence to support the claim. The state courts refer to this request as a *motion for a directed verdict*.

motion for a new trial A motion asserting that the trial was so fundamentally flawed (because of error, newly discovered evidence, prejudice, or other reason) that a new trial is necessary to prevent a miscarriage of justice.

motion for judgment n.o.v. A motion requesting the court to grant judgment in favor of the party making the motion on the ground that the jury verdict against him or her was unreasonable and erroneous.

motion for judgment on the pleadings A motion by either party to a lawsuit at the close of the pleadings requesting the court to decide the issue solely on the pleadings without proceeding to trial. The motion will be granted only if no facts are in dispute.

motion for summary judgment A motion requesting the court to enter a judgment without proceeding to trial. The motion can be based on evidence outside the pleadings and will be granted only if no facts are in dispute.

motion to dismiss A pleading in which a defendant asserts that the plaintiff's claim fails to state a cause of action (that is, has no basis in law) or that there are other grounds on which a suit should be dismissed.

multiple product order An order requiring a firm that has engaged in deceptive advertising to cease and desist from false advertising in regard to all the firm's products.

mutual fund A specific type of investment company that continually buys or sells to investors shares of ownership in a portfolio.

mutual rescission An agreement between the parties to cancel their contract, releasing the parties from further obligations under the contract. The object of the agreement is to restore the parties to the positions they would have occupied had no contract ever been formed.

N

national law Law that pertains to a particular nation (as opposed to international law).

natural law The oldest school of legal thought, based on the belief that the legal system should reflect universal ("higher") moral and ethical principles that are inherent in human nature.

necessaries Necessities required for life, such as food, shelter, clothing, and medical attention; may include whatever is believed to be necessary to maintain a person's standard of living or financial and social status.

necessity In criminal law, a defense against liability. Under Section 3.02 of the Model Penal Code, this defense is justifiable if "the harm or evil sought to be avoided" by a given action "is greater than that sought to be prevented by the law defining the offense charged." In real property law, a way of creating an easement when one party must have the easement in order to have access to his or her property.

negligence The failure to exercise the standard of care that a reasonable person would exercise in similar circumstances.

negligent misrepresentation Any manifestation through words or conduct that amounts to an untrue statement of fact made in circumstances in which a reasonable and prudent person would not have done that which led to the misrepresentation. A representation made with an honest belief in its truth may still be negligent due to (1) a lack of reasonable care in ascertaining the facts, (2) the manner of expression, or (3) the absence of the skill or competence required by a particular business or profession.

negotiable instrument A signed writing that contains an unconditional promise or order to pay an exact sum of money, on demand or at an exact future time, to a specific person or order, or to bearer.

negotiation In regard to dispute settlement, a process in which parties attempt to settle their dispute without going to court, with or without attorneys to represent them. In regard to negotiable instruments, the transfer of an instrument in such a way that the transferee (the person to whom the instrument is transferred) becomes a holder.

nominal damages A small monetary award (often one dollar) granted to a plaintiff when no actual damage was suffered or when the plaintiff is unable to show such loss with sufficient certainty.

nonpossessory interest In the context of real property, an interest that involves the right to use land but not the right to possess it.

normal trade relations (NTR) status A status granted through an international treaty by which each member nation must treat other members at least as well as it treats the country that receives its most favorable treatment. This status was formerly known as most-favored-nation status.

notary public A public official authorized to attest to the authenticity of signatures.

notice-and-comment rulemaking An administrative rule-making procedure that involves the publication of a notice of a proposed rulemaking in the *Federal Register,* a comment period for interested parties to express their views on the proposed rule, and the publication of the agency's final rule in the *Federal Register.*

novation The substitution, by agreement, of a new contract for an old one, with the rights under the old one being terminated. Typically, there is a substitution of a new person who is responsible for the contract and the removal of an original party's rights and duties under the contract.

nuisance A common law doctrine under which persons may be held liable for using their property in a manner that unreasonably interferes with others' rights to use or enjoy their own property.

nuncupative will An oral will (often called a *deathbed will*) made before witnesses. Usually, such wills are limited to transfers of personal property.

O

objective theory of contracts A theory under which the intent to form a contract will be judged by outward, objective facts as interpreted by a reasonable person, rather than by the party's own secret, subjective intentions. Objective facts might include what a party said when entering into the contract, how a party acted or appeared, and the circumstances surrounding the transaction.

obligee One to whom an obligation is owed.

obligor One who owes an obligation to another.

offer A promise or commitment to perform or refrain from performing some specified act in the future.

offeree A person to whom an offer is made.

offeror A person who makes an offer.

omnibus clause A provision in an automobile insurance policy that protects the vehicle owner who has taken out the policy and anyone who drives the vehicle with the owner's permission.

online dispute resolution (ODR) The resolution of disputes with the assistance of organizations that offer dispute-resolution services via the Internet.

opening statement A statement made to the jury at the beginning of a trial by a party's attorney, prior to the presentation of evidence. The attorney briefly outlines the evidence that will be offered and the legal theory that will be pursued.

operating agreement An agreement in which the members of a limited liability company set forth the details of how the business will be managed and operated.

opinion A statement by a court expressing the reasons for its decision in a case.

option contract A contract under which the offeror cannot revoke his or her offer for a stipulated time period and the offeree can accept or reject the offer at any time during this period. The offeree must give consideration for the option to be enforceable.

order for relief A court's grant of assistance to a complainant. In bankruptcy proceedings, the order relieves the debtor of the immediate obligation to pay the debts listed in the bankruptcy petition.

order instrument A negotiable instrument that is payable "to the order of an identified person" or "to an identified person or order."

ordinance A law passed by a local governing unit, such as a city or a county.

outcome-based ethics An ethical philosophy that focuses on the impacts of a decision on society or on key stakeholders.

output contract An agreement in which a seller agrees to sell and a buyer agrees to buy all or up to a stated amount of what the seller produces.

outside director A person on a corporation's board of directors who does not hold a management position at the corporation.

overdraft A check written on a checking account in which there are insufficient funds to cover the amount of the check.

P

parent corporation A corporation that owns all of the shares of another corporation (known as its subsidiary).

parol evidence rule A substantive rule of contracts under which a court will not receive into evidence the parties' prior negotiations, prior agreements, or contemporaneous oral agreements if that evidence contradicts or varies the terms of the parties' written contract.

partially disclosed principal A principal whose identity is unknown by a third party, but the third party knows that the agent is or may be acting for a principal at the time the agent and the third party form a contract.

partnering agreement An agreement between a seller and a buyer who frequently do business with each other on the terms and conditions that will apply to all subsequently formed electronic contracts.

partnership An agreement by two or more persons to carry on, as co-owners, a business for profit.

partnership by estoppel A partnership imposed by a court when nonpartners have held themselves out to be partners, or have allowed themselves to be held out as partners, and others have detrimentally relied on their misrepresentations.

pass-through entity A business entity that has no tax liability. The entity's income is passed through to the owners, and they pay taxes on the income.

past consideration Something given or some act done in the past, which cannot ordinarily be consideration for a later bargain.

patent A government grant that gives an inventor the exclusive right or privilege to make, use, or sell his or her invention for a limited time period.

payee A person to whom an instrument is made payable.

payor bank The bank on which a check is drawn (the drawee bank).

peer-to-peer (P2P) networking The sharing of resources (such as files, hard drives, and processing styles) among multiple computers without the requirement of a central network server.

penalty A sum inserted into a contract not as a measure of compensation for its breach but rather as punishment for a default. The agreement as to the amount will not be enforced, and recovery will be limited to actual damages.

per capita A method of distributing an intestate's estate so that each heir in a certain class (such as grandchildren) receives an equal share.

per curiam **opinion** By the whole court; a court opinion written by the court as a whole instead of being authored by a judge or justice.

per se **violation** A restraint of trade that is so anticompetitive that it is deemed inherently (*per se*) illegal.

per stirpes A method of distributing an intestate's estate so that each heir in a certain class (such as grandchildren) takes the share to which her or his deceased ancestor (such as a mother or father) would have been entitled.

perfect tender rule A common law rule under which a seller was required to deliver to the buyer goods that conformed perfectly to the requirements stipulated in the sales contract. A tender of nonconforming goods would automatically constitute a breach of contract. Under the Uniform Commercial Code, the rule has been greatly modified.

perfection The legal process by which secured parties protect themselves against the claims of third parties who may wish to have their debts satisfied out of the same collateral; usually accomplished by the filing of a financing statement with the appropriate government official.

performance In contract law, the fulfillment of one's duties arising under a contract with another; the normal way of discharging one's contractual obligations.

periodic tenancy A lease interest in land for an indefinite period involving payment of rent at fixed intervals, such as week to week, month to month, or year to year.

personal defense A defense that can be used to avoid payment to an ordinary holder of a negotiable instrument but not a holder in due course (HDC) or a holder with the rights of an HDC. Personal defenses are also called *limited defenses*.

personal property Property that is movable; any property that is not real property.

persuasive authority Any legal authority or source of law that a court may look to for guidance but need not follow when making its decision.

petition in bankruptcy The document that is filed with a bankruptcy court to initiate bankruptcy proceedings.

petitioner In equity practice, a party that initiates a lawsuit.

petty offense In criminal law, the least serious kind of criminal offense, such as a traffic or building-code violation.

phishing Online fraud in which criminals pretend to be legitimate companies by using e-mails or malicious Web sites that trick individuals and companies into providing useful information, such as bank account numbers, Social Security numbers, and credit-card numbers.

piercing the corporate veil The action of a court to disregard the corporate entity and hold the shareholders personally liable for corporate debts and obligations.

plaintiff A party that initiates a lawsuit.

plea bargaining The process by which a criminal defendant and the prosecutor in a criminal case work out a mutually satisfactory disposition of the case, subject to court approval; usually involves the defendant's pleading guilty to a lesser offense in return for a lighter sentence.

pleadings Formal statements made by the plaintiff and the defendant in a lawsuit that detail the facts, allegations, and defenses involved in the litigation; the complaint and answer are part of the pleadings.

pledge A common law security device (retained in Article 9 of the Uniform Commercial Code) in which personal property is turned over to a creditor as security for the payment of a debt and retained by the creditor until the debt is paid.

plurality opinion A court opinion that is joined by the largest number of the judges or justices hearing the case, but fewer than half of the total number.

police powers Powers possessed by states as part of their inherent sovereignty. These powers may be exercised to protect or promote the public order, health, safety, morals, and general welfare.

policy In insurance law, the contract between the insurer and the insured.

potentially responsible party (PRP) A party liable for the costs of cleaning up a hazardous waste disposal site under the Comprehensive Environmental Response, Compensation, and Liability Act.

power of attorney Authorization for another to act as one's agent or attorney either in specified circumstances (special) or in all situations (general).

precedent A court decision that furnishes an example or authority for deciding subsequent cases involving identical or similar facts.

predatory pricing The pricing of a product below cost with the intent to drive competitors out of the market.

predominant-factor test A test courts use to determine whether a contract is primarily for the sale of goods or for the sale of services.

preemption A doctrine under which certain federal laws preempt, or take precedence over, conflicting state or local laws.

preemptive rights The right of a shareholder in a corporation to have the first opportunity to purchase a new issue of that corporation's stock in proportion to the amount of stock already owned by the shareholder.

preference In bankruptcy proceedings, a property transfer or payment made by the debtor that favors one creditor over others.

preferred creditor In the context of bankruptcy, a creditor who has received a preferential transfer from a debtor.

preferred stock A security that entitles the holder to payment of fixed dividends and that has priority over common stock in the distribution of assets on the corporation's dissolution.

premium In insurance law, the price paid by the insured for insurance protection for a specified period of time.

prenuptial agreement An agreement made before marriage that defines each partner's ownership rights in the other partner's property. Prenuptial agreements must be in writing to be enforceable.

prepayment penalty clause A provision in a mortgage loan contract that requires the borrower to pay a penalty if the mortgage is repaid in full within a certain period.

prescription A way of creating an easement or profit in real property by openly using the property, without the owner's consent, for the required period of time (similar to adverse possession).

presentment The act of presenting an instrument to the party liable on the instrument to collect payment; the act of presenting an instrument to a drawee for acceptance.

presentment warranty Implied warranty made by any person who presents an instrument for payment or acceptance that (1) he or she is entitled to enforce the instrument or authorized to obtain payment or acceptance on behalf of a person who is entitled, (2) the instrument has not been altered, and (3) he or she has no knowledge that the signature of the drawer is unauthorized.

pretrial conference A conference, scheduled before the trial begins, between the judge and the attorneys litigating the suit. The parties may settle the dispute, clarify the issues, schedule discovery, and so on during the conference.

pretrial motion A written or oral application to a court for a ruling or order, made before trial.

price discrimination A seller's act of charging competing buyers different prices for identical products or services.

price-fixing agreement An agreement between competitors to fix the prices of products or services at a certain level.

prima facie **case** A case in which the plaintiff has produced sufficient evidence of his or her claim that the case will be decided for the plaintiff unless the defendant produces evidence to rebut it.

principal In agency law, a person who agrees to have another, called the agent, act on his or her behalf.

principle of rights The principle that human beings have certain fundamental rights (to life, freedom, and the pursuit of happiness, for example). A key factor in determining whether a business decision is ethical under this theory is how that decision affects the rights of others, such as employees, consumers, suppliers, and the community.

private equity Capital funds invested by a private equity firm in an existing corporation, usually to purchase and reorganize it.

privilege In tort law, the ability to act contrary to another person's right without that person's having legal redress for such acts. Privilege may be raised as a defense to defamation.

privileges and immunities clause Article IV, Section 2, of the U.S. Constitution requires states not to discriminate against one another's citizens. A resident of one state cannot be treated as an alien when in another state; he or she may not be denied such privileges and immunities as legal protection, access to courts, travel rights, and property rights.

privity of contract The relationship that exists between the promisor and the promisee of a contract.

probable cause Reasonable grounds for believing that a search should be conducted or that a person should be arrested.

probate The process of proving and validating a will, and settling all matters pertaining to an estate.

probate court A state court of limited jurisdiction that conducts proceedings relating to the settlement of a deceased person's estate.

procedural law Law that establishes the methods of enforcing the rights established by substantive law.

proceeds Under Article 9 of the Uniform Commercial Code, whatever is received when collateral is sold or otherwise disposed of.

product liability The legal liability of manufacturers, sellers, and lessors of goods to consumers, users, and bystanders for injuries or damages that are caused by the goods.

product misuse A defense against product liability that may be raised when the plaintiff used a product in a manner not intended by the manufacturer. If the misuse is reasonably foreseeable, the seller will not escape liability unless measures were taken to guard against the harm that could result from the misuse.

profit In the context of real property, the right to enter onto another's property and remove something of value from that property.

promise A person's assurance that he or she will or will not do something.

promisee A person to whom a promise is made.

promisor A person who makes a promise.

promissory estoppel A doctrine that applies when a promisor makes a clear and definite promise on which the promisee justifiably relies. Such a promise is binding if justice will be better served by the enforcement of the promise.

promissory note A written promise made by one person (the maker) to pay a fixed sum of money to another person (the payee or a subsequent holder) on demand or on a specified date.

property Legally protected rights and interests in anything with an ascertainable value that is subject to ownership.

prospectus A written document required by securities laws when a security is being sold. The prospectus describes the security, the financial operations of the issuing corporation, and the risk attaching to the security.

protected class A group of persons protected by specific laws because of the group's defining characteristics, including race, color, religion, national origin, gender, age, and disability.

proximate cause Legal cause; exists when the connection between an act and an injury is strong enough to justify imposing liability.

proxy Authorization to represent a corporate shareholder to serve as his or her agent and vote his or her shares in a certain manner.

public corporation A corporation owned by a federal, state, or municipal government—not to be confused with a publicly held corporation.

public figure An individual in the public limelight. Public figures include government officials and politicians, movie stars, well-known businesspersons, and generally anybody who becomes known to the public because of his or her position or activities.

publicly held corporation A corporation whose shares are publicly traded in securities markets, such as the New York Stock Exchange or the NASDAQ.

puffery A salesperson's exaggerated claims concerning the quality of goods offered for sale. Such claims involve opinions rather than facts and are not considered to be legally binding promises or warranties.

punitive damages Money damages that may be awarded to a plaintiff to punish the defendant and deter future similar conduct.

purchase-money security interest (PMSI) A security interest that arises when a seller or lender extends credit for part or all of the purchase price of goods purchased by a buyer.

Q

qualified indorsement An indorsement on a negotiable instrument in which the indorser disclaims any contract liability on the instrument; the notation "without recourse" is commonly used to create a qualified indorsement.

quantum meruit A Latin phrase, meaning "as much as he deserves," that describes the extent of compensation owed under a quasi contract.

quasi contract A fictional contract imposed on parties by a court in the interests of fairness and justice; usually, quasi contracts are imposed to avoid the unjust enrichment of one party at the expense of another.

question of fact In a lawsuit, an issue involving a factual dispute. A question of fact can be decided by a judge or a jury.

question of law In a lawsuit, an issue involving the application or interpretation of a law. Only a judge, and not a jury, can decide a question of law.

quitclaim deed A deed that conveys only whatever interest the grantor had in the property and therefore offers the least amount of protection against defects of title.

quorum The number of members of a decision-making body that must be present before business may be transacted.

quota A quota is a government-imposed trade restriction that limits the number, or sometimes the value, of goods and services that can be imported or exported during a particular time period.

R

ratification The act of accepting and giving legal force to an obligation that previously was not enforceable.

reaffirmation agreement An agreement between a debtor and a creditor in which the debtor voluntarily agrees to pay a debt dischargeable in bankruptcy.

real property Land and everything attached to it, such as trees and buildings.

reasonable person standard The standard of behavior expected of a hypothetical "reasonable person." The standard against which negligence is measured and that must be observed to avoid liability for negligence.

rebuttal The refutation of evidence introduced by an adverse party's attorney.

receiver In a corporate dissolution, a court-appointed person who winds up corporate affairs and liquidates corporate assets.

record According to the Uniform Electronic Transactions Act, information that is either inscribed on a tangible medium or stored in an electronic or other medium, and that is retrievable.

recording statute A statute that allow deeds, mortgages, and other real property transactions to be recorded so as to provide notice to future purchasers or creditors of an existing claim on the property.

reformation A court-ordered correction of a written contract so that it reflects the true intentions of the parties.

Regulation E A set of rules issued by the Federal Reserve System's Board of Governors under the authority of the Electronic Fund Transfer Act to protect users of electronic fund transfer systems.

Regulation Z A set of rules issued by the Federal Reserve Board of Governors to implement the provisions of the Truth-in-Lending Act.

rejoinder The defendant's answer to the plaintiff's rebuttal.

release A contract in which one party forfeits the right to pursue a legal claim against the other party.

relevant evidence Evidence tending to make a fact at issue in the case more or less probable than it would be without the evidence. Only relevant evidence is admissible in court.

remedy The relief given to an innocent party to enforce a right or compensate for the violation of a right.

remedy at law A remedy available in a court of law. Money damages are awarded as a remedy at law.

remedy in equity A remedy allowed by courts in situations where remedies at law are not appropriate. Remedies in equity include injunction, specific performance, rescission and restitution, and reformation.

replevin (pronounced rih-*pleh*-vin) An action to recover specific goods in the hands of a party who is wrongfully withholding them from the other party.

reporter A publication in which court cases are published, or reported.

requirements contract An agreement in which a buyer agrees to purchase and the seller agrees to sell all or up to a stated amount of what the buyer needs or requires.

resale price maintenance agreement An agreement between a manufacturer and a retailer in which the manufacturer specifies what the retail prices of its products must be.

rescission (pronounced rih-*sih*-zhen) A remedy whereby a contract is canceled and the parties are returned to the positions they occupied before the contract was made; may be effected through the mutual consent of the parties, by their conduct, or by court decree.

residential use Use of land for construction of buildings for human habitation only.

respondeat superior A doctrine under which a principal-employer is liable for any harm caused to a third party by an agent-employee in the course or scope of employment.

respondent In equity practice, the party who answers a complaint or other proceeding.

restitution An equitable remedy under which a person is restored to his or her original position prior to loss or injury, or placed in the position he or she would have been in had the breach not occurred.

restraint of trade Any contract or combination that tends to eliminate or reduce competition, effect a monopoly, artificially maintain prices, or otherwise hamper the course of trade and commerce as it would be carried on if left to the control of natural economic forces.

restrictive covenant A private restriction on the use of land. If its benefit or obligation passes with the land's ownership, it is said to "run with the land."

restrictive indorsement Any indorsement on a negotiable instrument that requires the indorsee to comply with certain instructions regarding the funds involved. A restrictive indorsement does not prohibit the further negotiation of the instrument.

resulting trust An implied trust that arises when one party holds the legal title to another's property only for that other's benefit.

retained earnings The portion of a corporation's profits that has not been paid out as dividends to shareholders.

revocation In contract law, the withdrawal of an offer by an offeror. Unless an offer is irrevocable, it can be revoked at any time prior to acceptance without liability.

right of contribution The right of a co-surety who pays more than his or her proportionate share on a debtor's default to recover the excess paid from other co-sureties.

right of reimbursement The legal right of a person to be restored, repaid, or indemnified for costs, expenses, or losses incurred or expended on behalf of another.

right of subrogation The right of a person to stand in the place of (be substituted for) another, giving the substituted party the same legal rights that the original party had.

right-to-work law A state law providing that employees may not be required to join a union as a condition of retaining employment.

risk A prediction concerning potential loss based on known and unknown factors.

risk management In the context of insurance, the transfer of certain risks from the insured to the insurance company by contractual agreement.

robbery The act of forcefully and unlawfully taking personal property of any value from another; force or intimidation is usually necessary for an act of theft to be considered a robbery.

rule of four A rule of the United States Supreme Court under which the Court will not issue a writ of *certiorari* unless at least four justices agree to do so.

rule of reason A test used to determine whether an anticompetitive agreement constitutes a reasonable restraint on trade. Courts consider such factors as the purpose of the agreement, its effect on competition, and whether less restrictive means could have been used.

rulemaking The process by which an administrative agency formally adopts a new regulation or amends an old one.

rules of evidence Rules governing the admissibility of evidence in trial courts.

S

S corporation A close business corporation that has most of the attributes of a corporation, including limited liability, but qualifies under the Internal Revenue Code to be taxed as a partnership.

sale The passing of title (evidence of ownership rights) from a seller to a buyer for a price.

sale on approval A type of conditional sale in which the buyer may take the goods on a trial basis. The sale becomes absolute only when the buyer approves of (or is satisfied with) the goods being sold.

sale or return A type of conditional sale in which title and possession pass from the seller to the buyer; however, the buyer retains the option to return the goods during a specified period, even though the goods conform to the contract.

sales contract A contract for the sale of goods under which the ownership of goods is transferred from a seller to a buyer for a price.

scienter (pronounced sy-*en*-ter) Knowledge by the misrepresenting party that material facts have been falsely represented or omitted with an intent to deceive.

search warrant An order granted by a public authority, such as a judge, that authorizes law enforcement personnel to search particular premises or property.

seasonably Within a specified time period. If no period is specified, within a reasonable time.

SEC Rule 10b-5 A rule of the Securities and Exchange Commission that prohibits the commission of fraud in connection with the purchase or sale of any security.

secondary boycott A union's refusal to work for, purchase from, or handle the products of a secondary employer, with whom the union has no dispute, for the purpose of forcing that employer to stop doing business with the primary employer, with whom the union has a labor dispute.

secured party A lender, seller, or any other person in whose favor there is a security interest, including a person to whom accounts or chattel paper has been sold.

secured transaction Any transaction in which the payment of a debt is guaranteed, or secured, by personal property owned by the debtor or in which the debtor has a legal interest.

securities Generally, stocks, bonds, or other items that represent an ownership interest in a corporation or a promise of repayment of debt by a corporation.

security agreement An agreement that creates or provides for a security interest between the debtor and a secured party.

security interest Any interest "in personal property or fixtures which secures payment or performance of an obligation" [UCC 1–201(37)].

self-defense The legally recognized privilege to protect one's self or property against injury by another. The privilege of self-defense protects only acts that are reasonably necessary to protect one's self or property.

self-incrimination Giving testimony in a trial or other legal proceeding that could expose the person testifying to criminal prosecution.

seniority system A system in which those who have worked longest for an employer are first in line for promotions, salary increases, and other benefits, and are last to be laid off if the workforce must be reduced.

service mark A mark used in the sale or the advertising of services, such as to distinguish the services of one person from the services of others. Titles, character names, and other distinctive features of radio and television programs may be registered as service marks.

service of process The delivery of the complaint and summons to a defendant.

sexual harassment The demanding of sexual favors in return for job promotions or other benefits, or language or conduct that is so sexually offensive that it creates a hostile working environment.

share exchange A process in which some or all of the shares of one corporation are exchanged for some or all of the shares of another corporation, and both corporations continue to exist.

shareholder agreement An agreement between shareholders that restricts the transferability of shares, often entered into for the purpose of maintaining proportionate control of a close corporation.

shareholder's derivative suit A suit brought by a shareholder to enforce a corporate cause of action against a third person.

shelter principle The principle that the holder of a negotiable instrument who cannot qualify as a holder in due course (HDC), but who derives his or her title through an HDC, acquires the rights of an HDC.

shipment contract A contract in which the seller is required to ship the goods by carrier. The buyer assumes liability for any losses or damage to the goods after they are delivered to the carrier. Generally, a contract is assumed to be a shipment contract if nothing to the contrary is stated in the contract.

short-form merger A merger between a subsidiary corporation and a parent corporation that owns at least 90 percent of the outstanding shares of each class of stock issued by the subsidiary corporation.

short sale A sale of real property for an amount that is less than the balance owed on the mortgage loan, usually due to financial hardship.

short-swing profits Profits earned by a purchase and sale, or sale and purchase, of the same security within a six-month period.

shrink-wrap agreement An agreement whose terms are expressed in a document located inside a box in which goods (usually software) are packaged; sometimes called a *shrink-wrap license.*

signature Under the Uniform Commercial Code, "any symbol executed or adopted by a party with a present intention to authenticate a writing."

slander Defamation in oral form.

slander of quality The publication of false information about another's product, alleging that it is not what its seller claims.

slander of title The publication of a statement that denies or casts doubt on another's legal ownership of any property causing financial loss to that property's owner; also called *trade libel.*

small claims court Special courts in which parties may litigate small claims (usually, claims involving $2,500 or less). Attorneys are not required in small claims courts and in many states are not allowed to represent the parties.

smart card Prepaid funds recorded on a microprocessor chip embedded on a card; one type of *e-money.*

social media Forms of communication through which users create and share information, ideas, messages, and other content via the Internet.

sociological school A school of legal thought that views the law as a tool for promoting justice in society.

sole proprietorship The simplest form of business organization, in which the owner is the business. The owner reports business income on his or her personal income tax return and is legally responsible for all debts and obligations incurred by the business.

sovereign immunity A doctrine that immunizes foreign nations from the jurisdiction of U.S. courts when certain conditions are satisfied.

sovereignty The quality of having independent authority over a geographic area. For instance, state governments have the authority to regulate affairs within their borders.

space law Law consisting of the international and national laws that govern activities in outer space.

spam Bulk, unsolicited (junk) e-mail.

special damages In a tort case, an amount awarded to compensate the plaintiff for quantifiable monetary losses, such as medical expenses, property damage, and lost wages and benefits (now and in the future).

special indorsement An indorsement on an instrument that indicates the specific person to whom the indorser intends to make the instrument payable—that is, it names the indorsee.

special-use permit A permit granted by local zoning authorities that allows for a specific exemption to zoning regulations for a particular piece of land.

special warranty deed A deed that warrants only that the grantor held good title during his or her ownership of the property and does not warrant that there were no defects of title when the property was held by previous owners.

specific performance An equitable remedy requiring the breaching party to perform as promised under the contract; usually granted only when money damages would be an inadequate remedy and the subject matter of the contract is unique (for example, real property).

spendthrift trust A trust created to protect the beneficiary from spending all the funds to which she or he is entitled. Only a certain portion of the total amount is given to the beneficiary at any one time, and most states prohibit creditors from attaching assets of the trust.

stakeholders Groups, other than the company's shareholders, that are affected by corporate decisions. Stakeholders include employees, customers, creditors, suppliers, and the community in which the corporation operates.

stale check A check, other than a certified check, that is presented for payment more than six months after its date.

standing to sue The requirement that an individual must have a sufficient stake in a controversy before he or she can bring a lawsuit. The plaintiff must demonstrate that he or she has been either injured or threatened with injury.

stare decisis A common law doctrine under which judges are obligated to follow the precedents established in prior decisions.

Statute of Frauds A state statute under which certain types of contracts must be in writing to be enforceable.

statute of limitations A federal or state statute setting the maximum time period during which a certain action can be brought or certain rights enforced.

statute of repose Basically, a statute of limitations that is not dependent on the happening of a cause of action. Statutes of repose generally begin to run at an earlier date and run for a longer period of time than statutes of limitations.

statutory law The body of law enacted by legislative bodies (as opposed to constitutional law, administrative law, or case law).

stock An ownership (equity) interest in a corporation, measured in units of shares.

stock certificate A certificate issued by a corporation evidencing the ownership of a specified number of shares in the corporation.

stock option A right to buy a given number of shares of stock at a set price, usually within a specified time period.

stock warrant A certificate that grants the owner the option to buy a given number of shares of stock, usually within a set time period.

stop-payment order An order by a bank customer to his or her bank not to pay or certify a certain check.

strict liability Liability regardless of fault. In tort law, strict liability may be imposed on defendants in cases involving abnormally dangerous activities, dangerous animals, or defective products.

strike An action undertaken by unionized workers when collective bargaining fails. The workers leave their jobs, refuse to work, and (typically) picket the employer's workplace.

sublease A tenant's transfer of all or part of the leased premises to a third person for a period shorter than the lease term.

subsidiary corporation A corporation wholly owned by another corporation (the parent corporation).

substantive law Law that defines, describes, regulates, and creates legal rights and obligations.

substitute check A negotiable instrument that is a paper reproduction of the front and back of an original check and contains all of the same information required on checks for automated processing.

summary jury trial A method of settling disputes in which a trial is held, but the jury's verdict is not binding. The verdict acts only as a guide to both sides in reaching an agreement during the mandatory negotiations that immediately follow the summary jury trial.

summons A document informing a defendant that a legal action has been commenced against him or her and that the defendant must appear in court on a certain date to answer the plaintiff's complaint. The document is delivered by a sheriff or any other person so authorized.

superseding cause An intervening force or event that breaks the connection between a wrongful act and an injury to another; in negligence law, a defense to liability.

supremacy clause The provision in Article VI of the U.S. Constitution that provides that the Constitution, laws, and treaties of the United States are "the supreme Law of the Land." Under this clause, state and local laws that directly conflict with federal law will be rendered invalid.

surety A person, such as a cosigner on a note, who agrees to be primarily responsible for the debt of another.

suretyship An express contract in which a third party to a debtor-creditor relationship (the surety) promises to be primarily responsible for the debtor's obligation.

surviving corporation The remaining, or continuing, corporation following a merger.

symbolic speech Nonverbal conduct that expresses opinions or thoughts about a subject. Symbolic speech is protected under the First Amendment's guarantee of freedom of speech.

syndicate A group of individuals or firms that join together to finance a project; also called an *investment group*.

T

takeover The acquisition of control over a corporation through the purchase of a substantial number of the voting shares of the corporation.

taking The government's taking of private property for public use through the power of eminent domain.

tangible employment action A significant change in employment status or benefits, such as occurs when an employee is fired, refused a promotion, or reassigned to a lesser position.

tangible property Property that has physical existence and can be distinguished by the senses of touch, sight, and so on. A car is tangible property.

target corporation The corporation to be acquired in a corporate takeover; a corporation to whose shareholders a tender offer is submitted.

tariff A tax on imported goods.

tenancy at sufferance A tenancy that arises when a tenant wrongfully continues to occupy leased property after the lease has terminated.

tenancy at will A type of tenancy that either the landlord or the tenant can terminate without notice.

tenancy by the entirety Joint ownership of property by a married couple in which neither spouse can transfer his or her interest in the property without the consent of the other.

tenancy in common Joint ownership of property in which each party owns an undivided interest that passes to his or her heirs at death.

tender An unconditional offer to perform an obligation by a person who is ready, willing, and able to do so.

tender of delivery Under the Uniform Commercial Code, a seller's or lessor's act of placing conforming goods at the disposal of the buyer or lessee and giving the buyer or lessee whatever notification is reasonably necessary to enable the buyer or lessee to take delivery.

tender offer An offer to purchase made by one company directly to the shareholders of another (target) company; often referred to as a "takeover bid."

term insurance A type of life insurance policy for which premiums are paid for a specified term and payment is made by the insurer only if the insured dies within the term period.

testamentary trust A trust that is created by will and therefore does not take effect until the death of the testator.

testate Having left a will at death.

testator One who makes and executes a will.

third party beneficiary One for whose benefit a promise is made in a contract but who is not a party to the contract.

tippee A person who receives inside information.

title insurance Insurance commonly purchased by a purchaser of real property to protect against loss in the event that the title to the property is not free from liens or superior ownership claims.

tolling Temporary suspension of the running of a prescribed period (such as a statute of limitations). For instance, a statute of limitations may be tolled until the party suffering an injury has discovered it or should have discovered it.

tort A civil wrong not arising from a breach of contract. A breach of a legal duty that proximately causes harm or injury to another.

tortfeasor One who commits a tort.

Totten trust A trust created when a person deposits funds in his or her own name for a specific beneficiary, who will receive the funds on the depositor's death. The trust is revocable at will until the depositor dies or completes the gift.

toxic tort A civil wrong arising from exposure to a toxic substance, such as asbestos, radiation, or hazardous waste.

trade acceptance A draft that is drawn by a seller of goods ordering the buyer to pay a specified sum of money to the seller, usually at a stated time in the future. The buyer accepts the draft by signing the face of the draft, thus creating an enforceable obligation to pay the draft when it comes due. On a trade acceptance, the seller is both the drawer and the payee.

trade dress The image and overall appearance of a product—for example, the distinctive decor, menu, layout, and style of service of a particular restaurant. Basically, trade dress is subject to the same protection as trademarks.

trade fixture The personal property of a commercial tenant that has been installed or affixed to real property for a business purpose. When the lease ends, the tenant can remove the fixture but must repair any damage to the real property caused by the fixture's removal.

trade libel The publication of false information about another's product, alleging that it is not what its seller claims; also referred to as *slander of quality*.

trade name A term that is used to indicate part or all of a business's name and that is directly related to the business's reputation and goodwill. Trade names are protected under the common law (and under trademark law, if the name is the same as the firm's trademark).

trade secret Information or a process that gives a business an advantage over competitors who do not know the information or process.

trademark A distinctive mark, motto, device, or implement that a manufacturer stamps, prints, or otherwise affixes to the goods it produces so that they may be identified on the market and their origins made known. Once a trademark is established (under the common law or through registration), the owner is entitled to its exclusive use.

transfer warranty Implied warranty made by any person who transfers an instrument for consideration to subsequent transferees and holders who take the instrument in good faith that (1) the transferor is entitled to enforce the instrument, (2) all signatures are authentic and authorized, (3) the instrument has not been altered, (4) the instrument is not subject to a defense or claim of any party that can be asserted against the transferor, and (5) the transferor has no knowledge of any insolvency proceedings against the maker, the acceptor, or the drawer of the instrument.

transferred intent A legal principle under which a person who intends to harm one individual, but unintentionally harms a different individual, can be liable to the second victim for an intentional tort.

traveler's check A check that is payable on demand, drawn on or payable through a bank, and designated as a traveler's check.

treaty An agreement formed between two or more independent nations.

treble damages Damages that, by statute, are three times the amount of actual damages suffered.

trespass to land The entry onto, above, or below the surface of land owned by another without the owner's permission or legal authorization.

trespass to personal property The unlawful taking or harming of another's personal property; interference with another's right to the exclusive possession of his or her personal property.

triple bottom line The idea that investors and others should consider not only corporate profits, but also the corporation's impact on people and on the planet in assessing the firm. (The bottom line is people, planet, and profits.)

trust An arrangement in which title to property is held by one person (a trustee) for the benefit of another (a beneficiary).

trust indorsement An indorsement for the benefit of the indorser or a third person; also known as an *agency indorsement*. The indorsement results in legal title vesting in the original indorsee.

tying arrangement A seller's act of conditioning the sale of a product or service on the buyer's agreement to purchase another product or service from the seller.

typosquatting A form of cybersquatting that relies on mistakes, such as typographical errors, made by Internet users when inputting information into a Web browser.

U

U.S. trustee A government official who performs certain administrative tasks that a bankruptcy judge would otherwise have to perform.

ultra vires acts Acts of a corporation that are beyond its express and implied powers to undertake (the Latin phrase means "beyond the powers").

unconscionable (pronounced un-*kon*-shun-uh-bul) **contract or clause** A contract or clause that is void on the basis of public policy because one party, as a result of his or her disproportionate bargaining power, is forced to accept terms that are unfairly burdensome and that unfairly benefit the dominating party.

underwriter In insurance law, the insurer, or the one assuming a risk in return for the payment of a premium.

undisclosed principal A principal whose identity is unknown by a third party, and that person has no knowledge that the agent is acting for a principal at the time the agent and the third party form a contract.

undue influence Persuasion that is less than actual force but more than advice and that induces a person to act according to the will or purposes of the dominating party.

unenforceable contract A valid contract rendered unenforceable by some statute or law.

uniform law A model law created by the National Conference of Commissioners on Uniform State Laws and/or the American Law Institute for the states to consider adopting. If the state adopts the law, it becomes statutory law in that state. Each state has the option of adopting or rejecting all or part of a uniform law.

unilateral contract A contract that results when an offer can be accepted only by the offeree's performance.

unilateral mistake A mistake that occurs when one party to a contract is mistaken as to a material fact.

union shop A firm that requires all workers, once employed, to become union members within a specified period of time as a condition of their continued employment.

universal defense A defense that is valid against all holders of a negotiable instrument, including holders in due course (HDCs) and holders with the rights of HDCs. Universal defenses are also called *real defenses*.

universal life A type of insurance that combines some aspects of term insurance with some aspects of whole life insurance.

unliquidated debt A debt that is uncertain in amount.

unreasonably dangerous product In product liability, a product that is defective to the point of threatening a consumer's health and safety. A product will be considered unreasonably dangerous if it is dangerous beyond the expectation of the ordinary consumer or if a less dangerous alternative was economically feasible for the manufacturer, but the manufacturer failed to produce it.

usage of trade Any practice or method of dealing having such regularity of observance in a place, vocation, or trade as to justify an expectation that it will be observed with respect to the transaction in question.

usury Charging an illegal rate of interest.

utilitarianism An approach to ethical reasoning in which ethically correct behavior is related to an evaluation of the consequences of a given action on those who will be affected by it. In utilitarian reasoning, a "good" decision is one that results in the greatest good for the greatest number of people affected by the decision.

V

valid contract A contract that results when the elements necessary for contract formation (agreement, consideration, contractual capacity, and legality) are present.

validation notice An initial notice to a debtor from a collection agency informing the debtor that he or she has thirty days to challenge the debt and request verification.

variance An exception from zoning rules granted to a property owner by local zoning authorities.

venture capital Financing provided by professional, outside investors—that is, *venture capitalists,* usually groups of wealthy investors and securities firms—to new business ventures.

venue (pronounced *ven*-yoo) The geographical district in which an action is tried and from which the jury is selected.

verdict A formal decision made by a jury.

vertical merger   The acquisition by a company at one stage of production of a company at a higher or lower stage of production (as when a company merges with one of its suppliers or retailers).

vertical restraint   A restraint of trade created by an agreement between firms at different levels in the manufacturing and distribution process.

vertically integrated firm   A firm that carries out two or more functional phases (manufacturing, distribution, and retailing, for example) of the chain of production.

vesting   The creation of an absolute or unconditional right or power.

vicarious liability   Indirect liability imposed on a supervisory party (such as an employer) for the actions of a subordinate (such as an employee) because of the relationship between the two parties.

virus   A type of malware that is transmitted between computers and attempts to do deliberate damage to systems and data.

void contract   A contract having no legal force or binding effect.

voidable contract   A contract that may be legally avoided (canceled) at the option of one of the parties.

voir dire   A French phrase meaning, literally, "to see, to speak" that refers to the jury-selection process. In *voir dire*, the attorneys question prospective jurors to determine whether they are biased or have any connection with a party to the action or with a prospective witness.

voluntary consent   Knowing and voluntary agreement to the terms of a contract. If voluntary consent is lacking, the contract will be voidable.

voting trust   An agreement (trust contract) under which legal title to shares of corporate stock is transferred to a trustee who is authorized by the shareholders to vote the shares on their behalf.

W

waiver   An intentional, knowing relinquishment of a legal right.

warranty deed   A deed in which the grantor promises that she or he has title to the property conveyed in the deed, that there are no undisclosed encumbrances on the property, and that the grantee will enjoy quiet possession of the property; provides the greatest amount of protection for the grantee.

waste   The use of real property in a manner that damages or destroys its value.

watered stock   Shares of stock issued by a corporation for which the corporation receives, as payment, less than the fair market value of the shares.

wetlands   Areas of land designated by government agencies as protected areas that support wildlife and that therefore cannot be filled in or dredged by private parties.

whistleblowing   An employee's disclosure to government authorities, upper-level managers, or the media that the employer is engaged in unsafe or illegal activities.

white-collar crime   Nonviolent crime committed by individuals or corporations to obtain a personal or business advantage.

whole life   A type of life insurance in which the insured pays a level premium for his or her entire life and in which there is a constantly accumulating cash value that can be withdrawn or borrowed against by the borrower; sometimes referred to as *straight life insurance*.

will   An instrument made by a testator directing what is to be done with her or his property after death.

will substitutes   Various instruments, such as living trusts and life insurance plans, that may be used to avoid the formal probate process.

winding up   The second of two stages in the termination of a partnership or corporation, in which the firm's assets are collected, liquidated, and distributed, and liabilities are discharged.

workers' compensation law   A state statute establishing an administrative procedure for compensating workers for injuries that arise out of, or in the course of, their employment, regardless of fault. Instead of suing the employer, an injured worker files a claim with the state agency or board that administers local workers' compensation claims.

working papers   The documents used and developed by an accountant during an audit, such as notes, computations, and memoranda.

workout agreement   A formal contract between a debtor and his or her creditors in which the parties agree to negotiate a payment plan for the amount due on the loan instead of proceeding to foreclosure.

worm   A type of malware that is designed to copy itself from one computer to another without human interaction. A worm can copy itself automatically and can replicate in great volume and with great speed.

writ of attachment   A court's order, prior to a trial to collect a debt, directing the sheriff or other officer to seize nonexempt property of the debtor. If the creditor prevails at trial, the seized property can be sold to satisfy the judgment.

writ of *certiorari* (pronounced sur-shee-uh-*rah*-ree) A writ from a higher court asking the lower court for the record of a case.

writ of execution A court's order, after a judgment has been entered against the debtor, directing the sheriff to seize (levy) and sell any of the debtor's nonexempt real or personal property. The proceeds of the sale are used to pay off the judgment, accrued interest, and costs of the sale. Any surplus is paid to the debtor.

wrongful discharge An employer's termination of an employee's employment in violation of the law or an employment contract.

Z

zoning laws Rules and regulations that collectively manage the development and use of land.

Table of Cases

Following is a list of all the cases mentioned in this text, including those within the footnotes, features, and case problems. Any case that was an excerpted case for a chapter is given special emphasis by having its title **boldfaced**.

Index

A

Abandoned property, 927, 928
Abatement, 979
Abnormally dangerous activities, 134–135
Absolute privilege, 117–118
Absolute promises, 323
Abuse of process, 122
Abusive litigation, 122
Acceleration clause, 472
Acceptance, 925. *See also* Contract(s);
  Lease contract; Sales contract
  authorized means of, 241
  banker's, 463
  of bankruptcy reorganization plan,
    593–594
  of bribe, 197
  by buyer or lessee, 411–412
  communication of, 239–240
  of contract, 217, 231
  of drawee, 463
  of gift, 925
  mode and timeliness of, 241
  for mutual rescission, 329–330
  of offer, 231, 238–241
  online, 242–244
  partial, 412
  revocation of, 416–417
  silence as, 239
  substitute method of, 241
  trade, 463
  UCC on, 367–370, 371
  unequivocal, 239
Accepted goods, right to recover damages
    for, 418–419
Acceptor
  defined, 471
  liability of, 497–498
Accession, acquisition of personal
    property by, 925, 926
Accidental contracts, via e-mail, 238
Accidental death benefits, in automobile
    insurance, 973
Accident insurance, 962
Accommodation, 367. *See also* Reasonable
    accommodation
Accommodation parties, 499–500
Accord and satisfaction
  discharge by, 330
  settlement of claims through, 256–257
Accountability
  of administrative agencies, 838–839
  of benefit corporation shareholders,
    748
  corporate governance and, 814–815
  professional liability and, 896–913
  promotion of, 814

Accountant. *See also* Professional
  common law liability of, 910
  duty of care of, 896–899
  potential liability to clients, 896–900
  potential liability under securities laws,
    905–909
    criminal liability, 909
Accountant-client relationships, 912
Accounting
  agent's demand for, 618
  agent's duty of, 615
  debtor request for, 570
  GAAP and, 897–898
  global rules for, 103, 898
  of partnership assets/profits, 709
Accounting fraud, 896
Account party, 421
Accredited investors, 802–803
ACPA. *See* Anticybersquatting Consumer
    Protection Act
Acquisition of property, 922
  real property, 922–926
Action, tangible employment, 674
Actionable, 114
Action of the parties, termination by,
    236–237, 635–636
Act of commission, 189
Act of state doctrine, 442
Actual authority, of agent, 622, 624, 635
Actual fraud, 900
Actual knowledge
  of particular purpose, 433
  of security interest, 425
Actual malice, 116, 118
Actus reus (guilty act), 189, 191
ADA. *See* Americans with Disabilities Act
ADEA. *See* Age Discrimination in
    Employment Act
Adequacy of consideration, 253–254
Adequate protection doctrine, 583–584
Adhesion contract, 289–290
Adjudication, by administrative agencies,
    826, 833–834
Adjustable-rate mortgage (ARM), 544
Administrative agency, 824–830. *See also*
    Regulation(s)
  adjudication by, 826, 833–834
  creation of, 825
  defined, 4–5, 824
  enforcement by, 832
  executive agencies, 825
  hearing procedures for adjudication,
    833, 834
  implementation of legislation by, 824
  independent regulatory agencies, 825
  informal actions by, 832

  investigations, social media posts and,
    176–177
  judicial deference to decisions of,
    835–838
  limits on demands by, 832
  orders by, 832
  powers of, 825–829
  public accountability of, 838–839
  tests by, 832
  types of, 825
Administrative law. *See also*
    Administrative agency
  defined, 4–5
  finding, 14–15
  practical significance of, 824–825
Administrative law judge (ALJ), 833
Administrative Procedure Act (APA,
    1946), 827, 829–830, 832
Administrative process, 830–834
Administrator, 977
Admissible evidence, 56
Admissions
  for oral contracts, 301, 372
  requests for, 59
Adopted children, intestacy laws
    and, 985
ADR. *See* Alternative dispute resolution
    (ADR)
Ad testificandum subpoena, 832
Advance fee fraud, 204
Adversarial framework, of justice, 48
Adverse possession, 950
Advertisement, advertising, as invitation
    to negotiate, 233
Advertising, advertisement
  deceptive, 829, 843–849
  "native ads" and, 847
  of online business, 821
Advice of counsel. *See* Attorney
Advising bank, 421
Affidavit, 56, 543, 581
Affirmation, of fact or promise, 426
Affirmative action, 681
Affirmative defense, 52, 129
Affordable Care Act (ACA, Obamacare,
    2010), 70, 649, 650, 850
  small businesses and, 685–687
After-acquired evidence, of employee
    misconduct, 681
After-acquired property, 567
Age. *See also* Minor; Seniors
  discrimination based on, 675–676
  of majority, 263
  misstatement of, 969
Age Discrimination in Employment Act
    (ADEA, 1967), 664, 675–676